Lecture Notes in Computer Science 962

Edited by G. Goos, J. Hartmanis and J. van Leeuwen

Springer
Berlin
Heidelberg
New York
Barcelona
Budapest
Hong Kong
London
Milan
Paris
Tokyo

Insup Lee Scott A. Smolka (Eds.)

CONCUR '95: Concurrency Theory

6th International Conference
Philadelphia, PA, USA, August 21-24, 1995
Proceedings

Springer

Series Editors

Gerhard Goos, Karlsruhe University, Germany

Juris Hartmanis, Cornell University, NY, USA

Jan van Leeuwen, Utrecht University, The Netherlands

Volume Editors

Insup Lee
Department of Computer and Information Science
University of Pennsylvania
Philadelphia, PA 19104-6389, USA

Scott Smolka
Department of Computer Science, SUNY at Stony Brook
Stony Brook, NY 11794-4400, USA

Cataloging-in-Publication data applied for

Die Deutsche Bibliothek - CIP-Einheitsaufnahme

CONCUR <6, 1995, Philadelphia, Pa.>:
Proceedings / CONCUR '95 : concurrency theory ; 6th international conference, Philadelphia, PA, USA, August 1995 / Insup Lee ; Scott Smolka (ed.). - Berlin ; Heidelberg ; New York ; Barcelona ; Budapest ; Hong Kong ; London ; Milan ; Paris ; Tokyo : Springer, 1995
(Lecture notes in computer science ; Vol. 962)
ISBN 3-540-60218-6
NE: Lee, Insup [Hrsg.]; GT

CR Subject Classification (1991): F.3, F.1, D.3

ISBN 3-540-60218-6 Springer-Verlag Berlin Heidelberg New York

Typesetting: Camera-ready by author
SPIN 10486591 06/3142 – 5 4 3 2 1 0 Printed on acid-free paper

Preface

This volume contains the proceedings of the Sixth International Conference on Concurrency Theory (CONCUR '95), held in Philadelphia, Pennsylvania, August 21-24. The purpose of the CONCUR conference is to bring together researchers and practitioners who are interested in concurrency theory and its application. The conference's steering committee comprises Jos Baeten, Chair (T.U. Eindhoven), Eike Best (U. Hildesheim), Kim Larsen (U. Aalborg), Ugo Montanari (U. Pisa), Scott Smolka (Stony Brook), and Pierre Wolper (U. Liège).

This proceedings contains 33 papers that were culled from 91 submissions, 88 of which were received electronically; seven invited papers are also included. The program committee meeting was also held electronically, over a period of about one week in mid-April.

The papers selected for publication span a wide range of topics, including proof techniques for and applications of the π-calculus; model checking infinite-state systems, with an emphasis on compositionality; semantics and analysis of real-time systems; axioms and proof systems for various process algebras; decidability results for lossy channel systems, timed automata, and Petri nets; refinement theory for nondeterministic and concurrent processes; extensions of linear-time logic with causal independence and least fixed point; and abstract semantics for probabilistic processes.

We would like to thank the members of the program committee, and their subreferees, for their hard and superlative work in assembling this collection of papers. The program committee consists of Bard Bloom (Cornell), Rance Cleaveland (N.C. State), Pierpaolo Degano (U. Pisa), Rob van Glabbeek (Stanford), Rob Gerth (T.U. Eindhoven), Susanne Graf (VERIMAG), Jan Friso Groote (U. Utrecht), Connie Hietmeyer (NRL), Tom Henzinger (Cornell), Hardi Hungar (U. Oldenburg), Lalita Jategaonkar Jagadeesan (AT&T, Bell Labs), Alan Jeffrey (Sussex), Joachim Parrow (SICS), Alex Rabinovitch (Tel Aviv), Davide Sangiorgi (INRIA Sophia Antipolis), Steve Schneider (U. London), Arne Skou (U. Aalborg), Gene Stark (SUNY Stony Brook), Bent Thomsen (ECRC), and Michal Young (Purdue).

We would also like to thank Rich Gerber (U. Maryland) for serving as the Publicity Chair; Dale Miller (Penn) for serving as the Tutorials Chair; and Hanêne Ben-Abdallah (Penn), Karen Bernstein (Stony Brook), Jin-Young Choi (Penn), Duncan Clarke (Penn), Vijay Gehlot (Penn), Inhye Kang (Penn), Oleg Sokolsky (Stony Brook), and Hong-Liang Xie (Penn) for their much-valued help in organizing the conference.

Support for CONCUR '95 has generously been provided by the IRCS (Institute for Research in Cognitive Science) and SEAS (School of Engineering and Applied Science) of the University of Pennsylvania, AT&T, and Computer Command and Control Company.

Philadelphia
Stony Brook
June 1995

Insup Lee
Scott Smolka

Reviewers

P.A. Abdulla
S. Abramsky
L. Aceto
R. Alur
R. Amadio
T. Amtoft
E. Badouel
G. Bhat
F. de Boer
J. Bohn
M. Boreale
A. Bouajjani
H. Bowman
C. Brown
G. Bruns
O. Burkart
N. Busi
P. Ciancarini
D. Cohen
A. Corradini
F. Corradini
M. Dam
D. Dams
P. Darondeau
J. Davies
Z. Dayar
R. De Nicola
A. van Deursen
B. Dutertre
J. Engelfriet
K. Engelhardt
L. Feijs
G. Ferrari
W. Ferreira
M. Fiore
W. Fokkink
L. Fredlund
F. Gadducci
H. Garavel
R. Giacobazzi
A. Girault
S. Gnesi
J.C. Godskesen
E. Goubault
W. Griffioen
P. Habermehl
N. Halbachs
E. Harcourt
C. Hermida
J. Hillebrand
Y. Hirshfeld
P.H. Ho
M. Hollenberg
C. Huizing
M. van Hulst
H. Hüttel
A. Ingolfsdottir
P. Iyer
R. Jagadeesan
W. Janssen
R. Jeffords
B. Josko
B. von Karger
J.P. Katoen
P. Kelb
P. Kopke
F. Korf
H. Korver
R. Koymans
R. Kuiper
R. Kurshan
A. Labella
Y. Lakhnech
F. Laroussinie
K.G. Larsen
M. Lenisa
L. Leth
F. Liu
X. Liu
H. Loevengreen
C. Loiseaux
A M.-Schettini
O. Maler
F. Maraninchi
G. McCusker
K. McMillan
F. Moller
U. Montanari
L. Mounier
P. Mukherjee
D. Murphy
R. Nagarajan
V. Natarajan
X. Nicollin
M. Nielsen
G. Overgaard
P. Paczkowski
P. Panangaden
A. Patterson
D. Pavlovic
J. Pearson
T. Peikenkamp
W. Penczek
B. Pierce
J. van de Pol
A. Ponse
K.V.S. Prasad
V. Pratt
C. Priami
Y. Ramakrishna
J. Rathke
G. Reggio
M. Reniers
A. Rensink
H. Rischel
V. Sassone
M. Schenke
R. Schlör
A. Sellink
P. Sewell
W. Shen
M. Siegel
G. Siliprandi
S. Sims
J. Springintveld
J. Stark
K. Sunesen
C. Talcott
D. Turi
D.N. Turner
J.J. Vereijken
C. Verhoef
B. Victor
J.W. Riely
I. Walukiewicz
M. Weichert
H. Wong-Toi
W. Yi
S. Yovine
G. Zavattaro

Table of Contents

Session: Real-Time Systems II

Local Model Checking Games (Extended Abstract)

Colin Stirling*
Department of Computer Science
University of Edinburgh
Edinburgh EH9 3JZ, UK
email: cps@uk.ac.ed.dcs

1 Introduction

Model checking is a very successful technique for verifying temporal properties of finite state concurrent systems. It is standard to view this method as essentially algorithmic, and consequently a very fruitful relationship between temporal logics and automata has been developed. In the case of branching time logics the connection has not been quite so tight as tree automata are not naturally the correct semantics of programs. Hence the introduction of amorphous automata with varying branching degrees, and the use of alternating automata.

Local model checking was proposed as a proof system approach to verification which also applies to infinite-state concurrent systems. In part this was because it predominantly uses the process algebra model of concurrency (such as CCS) where a concurrent system is presented as an expression of the calculus. The question of verification is then whether a particular expression has a temporal property (rather than all the states of a transition system which have a property). In local model checking the proof system is developed in a goal directed fashion, that is a top down approach. When a property holds, there is a proof tree which witnesses this truth. It also allows there to be proofs for infinite-state systems. Moreover local model checking permits compositional reasoning, when a proof tree may be guided by the algebraic structure of the system as well as the logical structure of the formula expressing the property.

In this talk we show that in the finite-state case these two approaches, model checking as essentially algorithmic and model checking as a proof system, can be combined using *games* as an underlying conceptual framework that can enjoy the best of both worlds. The automata theoretic approach is captured via the resulting game graph (which is an alternating automaton), and on the other hand a witness for non-emptiness of a game graph is just a proof tree. Alternatively a game graph can be translated into a formula of boolean fixed point logic, which has provided a variant framework for model checking. Game playing also provides a very perspicuous basis for understanding branching time temporal logics and model checking of finite and infinite-state systems.

An important question is whether finite-state model checking of modal mu-calculus properties can be done in polynomial time. Emerson showed that this

* Research in part supported by ESPRIT BRA project Concur2.

problem belongs to NP $\cap$ co-NP. Games provide a very direct proof of this result. It appears that finer structure needs to be exposed to improve upon this. We believe that new insights may come from the relationship between these games and other graph games. For example model checking games can be reduced to simple stochastic games, an observation due to Mark Jerrum, whose decision procedure also belongs to NP $\cap$ co-NP.

2 Modal Mu-Calculus

Modal mu-calculus, modal logic with extremal fixed points, was introduced by Kozen [13]. Formulas of the logic given in positive form are defined by

$$\Phi ::= Z \mid \Phi_1 \wedge \Phi_2 \mid \Phi_1 \vee \Phi_2 \mid [K]\Phi \mid \langle K \rangle \Phi \mid \nu Z.\Phi \mid \mu Z.\Phi$$

where Z ranges over a family of propositional variables, and K over subsets[2] of an action set $\mathcal{A}$. The binder νZ is the greatest whereas μZ is the least fixed point operator.

Modal mu-calculus with action labels drawn from $\mathcal{A}$ is interpreted on labelled transition systems $(\mathcal{P}, \{\stackrel{a}{\longrightarrow} : a \in \mathcal{A}\})$ where $\mathcal{P}$ is a countable but non-empty set of processes (or states), and each $\stackrel{a}{\longrightarrow}$ is a binary transition relation on $\mathcal{P}$. Labelled transition systems are popular structures for modelling concurrent systems especially process calculi such as CCS [17]: $\mathcal{P}$ is then a transition closed set[3] of process expressions and $E \stackrel{a}{\longrightarrow} F$ means that E may evolve to F by performing the action a.

Assume a fixed transition system $(\mathcal{P}, \{\stackrel{a}{\longrightarrow} : a \in \mathcal{A}\})$, and let $\mathcal{V}$ be a valuation which assigns to each variable Z a subset $\mathcal{V}(Z)$ of processes in $\mathcal{P}$. Let $\mathcal{V}[\mathcal{E}/Z]$ be the valuation $\mathcal{V}'$ which agrees with $\mathcal{V}$ everywhere except possibly Z when $\mathcal{V}'(Z) = \mathcal{E}$. The subset of processes in $\mathcal{P}$ satisfying an arbitrary formula Ψ under the valuation $\mathcal{V}$ is inductively defined as the set $\| \Psi \|^{\mathcal{P}}_{\mathcal{V}}$ where for ease of notation we drop the superscript $\mathcal{P}$ which is assumed fixed throughout:

$$\begin{array}{ll}
\| Z \|_{\mathcal{V}} = \mathcal{V}(Z) \qquad \| \Phi \wedge \Psi \|_{\mathcal{V}} = \| \Phi \|_{\mathcal{V}} \cap \| \Psi \|_{\mathcal{V}} \qquad \| \Phi \vee \Psi \|_{\mathcal{V}} = \| \Phi \|_{\mathcal{V}} \cup \| \Psi \|_{\mathcal{V}} \\
\| [K]\Phi \|_{\mathcal{V}} = \{E \in \mathcal{P} : \text{if } a \in K \text{ and } E \stackrel{a}{\longrightarrow} F \text{ then } F \in \| \Phi \|_{\mathcal{V}}\} \\
\| \langle K \rangle \Phi \|_{\mathcal{V}} = \{E \in \mathcal{P} : E \stackrel{a}{\longrightarrow} F \text{ for some } a \in K \text{ and } F \in \| \Phi \|_{\mathcal{V}}\} \\
\| \nu Z.\Phi \|_{\mathcal{V}} = \bigcup \{\mathcal{E} \subseteq \mathcal{P} : \mathcal{E} \subseteq \| \Phi \|_{\mathcal{V}[\mathcal{E}/Z]}\} \\
\| \mu Z.\Phi \|_{\mathcal{V}} = \bigcap \{\mathcal{E} \subseteq \mathcal{P} : \| \Phi \|_{\mathcal{V}[\mathcal{E}/Z]} \subseteq \mathcal{E}\}
\end{array}$$

Any formula Φ determines the monotonic function $\lambda \mathcal{E} \subseteq \mathcal{P}.\ \| \Phi \|^{\mathcal{P}}_{\mathcal{V}[\mathcal{E}/Z]}$ with respect to the variable Z, the valuation $\mathcal{V}$, and the set $\mathcal{P}$. Hence the meaning of the greatest fixed point is the union of all postfixed points, and it is the intersection of all prefixed points in the case of the least fixed point. One consequence is that the meaning of $\sigma Z.\Phi$ is the same as its ***unfolding*** $\Phi\{\sigma Z.\Phi/Z\}$ (where

[2] It is very convenient to allow sets of labels to appear in modalities instead of the usual single labels.

[3] If $E \in \mathcal{P}$ and $E \stackrel{a}{\longrightarrow} F$ then $F \in P$.

$\Phi\{\Psi/Z\}$ is the substitution of Ψ for free occurrences of Z in Φ). Assume that $\mathtt{tt}$ (true) abbreviates $\nu Z.Z$, and $\mathtt{ff}$ (false) is $\mu Z.Z$. We use $E \models_{\mathcal{V}} \Phi$ as an abbreviation for $E \in \| \Phi \|^{\mathcal{P}}_{\mathcal{V}}$ when $\mathcal{P}$ contains E.

An alternative but equivalent interpretation of extremal fixed points is in terms of approximants. When $\sigma \in \{\nu, \mu\}$, and α is an ordinal let $\sigma Z^{\alpha}.\Phi$ be the α-unfolding with the following interpretation, where λ is a limit ordinal:

$$\begin{array}{llll} \| \nu Z^0.\Phi \|_{\mathcal{V}} & = \mathcal{P} & \| \mu Z^0.\Phi \|_{\mathcal{V}} & = \emptyset \\ \| \nu Z^{\alpha+1}.\Phi \|_{\mathcal{V}} & = \| \Phi \|_{\mathcal{V}[\| \nu Z^{\alpha}.\Phi \|_{\mathcal{V}}/Z]} & \| \mu Z^{\alpha+1}.\Phi \|_{\mathcal{V}} & = \| \Phi \|_{\mathcal{V}[\| \mu Z^{\alpha}.\Phi \|_{\mathcal{V}}/Z]} \\ \| \nu Z^{\lambda}.\Phi \|_{\mathcal{V}} & = \bigcap\{\| \nu Z^{\alpha}.\Phi \|_{\mathcal{V}} : \alpha < \lambda\} & \| \mu Z^{\lambda}.\Phi \|_{\mathcal{V}} & = \bigcup\{\| \mu Z^{\alpha}.\Phi \|_{\mathcal{V}} : \alpha < \lambda\} \end{array}$$

The set $\| \nu Z.\Phi \|_{\mathcal{V}}$ equals $\bigcap\{\| \nu Z^{\alpha}.\Phi \|_{\mathcal{V}} : \alpha \text{ is an ordinal}\}$ and $\| \mu Z.\Phi \|_{\mathcal{V}}$ is the same as $\bigcup\{\| \mu Z^{\alpha}.\Phi \|_{\mathcal{V}} : \alpha \text{ is an ordinal}\}$.

Modal mu-calculus is a very expressive propositional temporal logic with the ability to describe liveness, safety, fairness, and cyclic properties. It has been shown that it is as expressive as finite-state automata on infinite trees, and hence is as powerful as the monadic second-order theory of n successors [10]. This is a very general and fundamental decidable theory to which many other decidability results in logic can be reduced. Most propositional temporal and modal logics used in computer science are sublogics of mu-calculus. Consequently various subcalculi can be defined which contain other well known program logics. An important example is CTL which is contained within the *alternation free* fragment. This is the sublogic when the following pair of conditions are imposed on fixed point formulas:

if $\mu Z.\Phi$ ($\nu Z.\Phi$) is a subformula of $\nu Y.\Psi$ ($\mu Y.\Psi$) then Y is not free in Φ

This fragment of modal mu-calculus turns out to be very natural, for it is precisely the sublogic which is equi-expressive to *weak* monadic second-order theory of n successors[4]. This result follows from [3] where it is proved for Niwinski's tree mu-calculus. Other fragments of modal mu-calculus studied include those of k–alternation depth for any k, and those presented in [12].

3 Verification and model checking

Modal mu-calculus is a very rich temporal logic for describing properties of systems. Here are two examples presented purely for illustration:

Example 1 A finite-state CCS description of a level crossing from [5] consists of three components in parallel, the road, rail, and signal where the first two are simple cyclers.

$$\begin{array}{lll} \mathit{Road} & \stackrel{\text{def}}{=} & \mathtt{car}.\mathtt{up}.\overline{\mathtt{ccross}}.\overline{\mathtt{down}}.\mathit{Road} \\ \mathit{Rail} & \stackrel{\text{def}}{=} & \mathtt{train}.\mathtt{green}.\overline{\mathtt{tcross}}.\overline{\mathtt{red}}.\mathit{Rail} \\ \mathit{Signal} & \stackrel{\text{def}}{=} & \overline{\mathtt{green}}.\mathtt{red}.\mathit{Signal} + \overline{\mathtt{up}}.\mathtt{down}.\mathit{Signal} \\ \mathit{Crossing} & \stackrel{\text{def}}{=} & (\mathit{Road} \mid \mathit{Rail} \mid \mathit{Signal})\backslash\{\mathtt{green}, \mathtt{red}, \mathtt{up}, \mathtt{down}\} \end{array}$$

[4] when the second-order quantifiers range over finite sets.

The actions **car** and **train** represent the approach of a car and a train, **up** is the gates opening for the car, and $\overline{\texttt{ccross}}$ is the car crossing, and **down** closes the gates, and **green** is the receipt of a green signal by the train, $\overline{\texttt{tcross}}$ is the train crossing, and **red** automatically sets the light red. A safety property for the crossing is that it is never possible to reach a state where a train and a car are both able to cross, $\nu Z.([\texttt{tcross}]\texttt{ff} \vee [\texttt{ccross}]\texttt{ff}) \wedge [-]Z$[5]. The desirable liveness property for the crossing is that whenever a car approaches then eventually it crosses $\nu Z.\,[\texttt{car}](\mu Y.\,\langle - \rangle \texttt{tt} \wedge [-\overline{\texttt{ccross}}]Y) \wedge [-]Z$ (and similarly for a train). But this only holds if we assume that the signal is fair, which is also expressible in the logic.

Example 2 A second (somewhat artificial) example is a description of an arbitrary new clock. Let Cl_i be a clock that ticks i times before terminating, and let *Clock* be $\sum\{Cl_i \,:\, i \geq 1\}$. Like all new clocks, *Clock* will eventually break down, so has the property $\mu Z.\,[\texttt{tick}]Z$. However it fails to have $\mu Z^n.\,[\texttt{tick}]Z$ for all $n \geq 0$.

A process expression determines a (unique) transition graph according to the rules for transitions. The graph associated with *Crossing* is finite-state whereas it is infinite-state in the case of *Clock*. The verification problem in this framework is to find techniques for determining whether or not a process description E has the property Φ (relative to stipulations as to what the free variables say as summarized by a valuation $\mathcal{V}$). One technique for checking whether process E has Φ is to first *construct* the transition graph for E (or even a larger graph), and then second to calculate $\|\,\Phi\,\|_{\mathcal{V}}$ with respect to this structure, possibly using approximants, and then finally check whether E belongs to it. This seems reasonable for determining whether a process such as the crossing has a property, as its transition graph is small. As a general method it is very cumbersome and clearly not directly applicable to infinite-state processes such as the clock. These were grounds for introducing local model checking as in [20, 6]. It was not intended as an algorithmic method, but as a proof system, and this is why it was developed using tableaux, for which in the finite-state one might be able to extract a reasonable algorithm. In fact this is one consequence of using games as an alternative logical basis for local model checking.

4 Simple games

We now present an alternative account of the satisfaction relation between a process and a temporal formula using games which underpins the local model checking proof systems in [20, 6]. A property checking game is a pair (E, Φ) relative to $\mathcal{V}$ for which there are two players, player I and player II. It is the role of player I to try to show that E *fails* to have the property Φ whereas player II attempts to frustrate this. Unlike more standard games, players here do not

[5] To cut down on brackets we write $[a_1, \dots a_n]$ instead of $[\{a_1, \dots a_n\}]$, and the same within a diamond operator, and $-K$ abbreviates $\mathcal{A} - K$ (and so $[-]$ is $[\mathcal{A}]$).

necessarily take turns[6].

A play of the *property checking game* (E_0, Φ_0) relative to $\mathcal{V}$ is a finite or infinite sequence of the form, $(E_0, \Phi_0) \ldots (E_n, \Phi_n) \ldots$. The next move in a play, the step from (E_j, Φ_j) to (E_{j+1}, Φ_{j+1}), and which player makes it is determined by the main connective of Φ_j. An essential ingredient is the use of auxiliary propositional constants, ranged over by U, which are introduced as fixed point formulas are met and can be thought of as colours. Suppose an initial part of a play is $(E_0, \Phi_0) \ldots (E_j, \Phi_j)$. The next step (E_{j+1}, Φ_{j+1}) is as below:

- if $\Phi_j = \Psi_1 \wedge \Psi_2$ $(\Psi_1 \vee \Psi_2)$ then player I (player II) chooses one of the conjuncts (disjuncts) Ψ_i: the process E_{j+1} is E_j and Φ_{j+1} is Ψ_i.
- if $\Phi_j = [K]\Psi$ $(\langle K \rangle \Psi)$ then player I (player II) chooses a transition $E_j \xrightarrow{a} E_{j+1}$ with $a \in K$ and Φ_{j+1} is Ψ.
- if $\Phi_j = \nu Z.\Psi$ $(\mu Z.\Psi)$ then player I (player II) chooses a *new* constant U and sets $U \stackrel{\text{def}}{=} \nu Z.\Psi$ $(U \stackrel{\text{def}}{=} \mu Z.\Psi)$: the process E_{j+1} is E_j and Φ_{j+1} is U.
- if $\Phi_j = U$ and $U \stackrel{\text{def}}{=} \nu Z.\Psi$ $(U \stackrel{\text{def}}{=} \mu Z.\Psi)$ then player I (player II) unfolds the fixed point so Φ_{j+1} is $\Psi\{U/Z\}$ and E_{j+1} is E_j.

There is a strong duality between the rules for $\wedge$ and $\vee$, $[K]$ and $\langle K \rangle$, $\nu Z.\Psi$ and $\mu Z.\Psi$. In the case of the last pair new constants are introduced as abbreviations for those fixed points. Rules also govern occurrences of constants as the formula of the next step is the body of the defined fixed point when all the occurrences of the fixed point variable are replaced with the constant.

The rules for the next move in a play are backwards sound with respect to the intentions of the players. If player I makes the move (E_{j+1}, Φ_{j+1}) from (E_j, Φ_j) and E_{j+1} fails to satisfy Φ_{j+1} relative to $\mathcal{V}$ then also E_j fails to have Φ_j. In contrast when player II makes this move and $E_{j+1} \models_{\mathcal{V}} \Phi_{j+1}$ then also $E_j \models_{\mathcal{V}} \Phi_j$. In the case of a fixed point formula this is clear provided we understand the presence of a constant to be its defined equivalent. Formulas are no longer "pure" as they may contain constants. However we can recover a pure formula from an impure formula by replacing constants with their defined fixed points in reverse order of introduction: assuming that $U_1 \stackrel{\text{def}}{=} \Psi_1 \ldots U_n \stackrel{\text{def}}{=} \Psi_n$ is the sequence of declarations in order of introduction, the meaning of Ψ is just $\Psi\{\Psi_n/U_n\} \ldots \{\Psi_1/U_1\}$. Consequently the fixed point unfolding principle justifies the backwards soundness of the moves determined by the constants.

A player *wins* a play of a game in the circumstances depicted in figure 1. If the configuration $(E, \langle K \rangle \Phi)$ is reached and there is no available transition then player II can not establish that E has $\langle K \rangle \Phi$. Similarly if the configuration is $(E, [K]\Phi)$ and there is no available transition then player I cannot refute that E has $[K]\Phi$. Similar comments apply to the case when the configuration is (E, Z). The other circumstances when a player is said to win a play concern repetition. If the configuration reached is (E, U) when U abbreviates a maximal fixed point formula, and this same configuration occurs earlier in the game play then player II wins. Dually if U abbreviates a least fixed point it is player I

[6] It is straightforward to reformulate the definition so that players must take turns.

Player II wins	**Player I wins**
1. The play is $(E_0, \Phi_0) \ldots (E_n, \Phi_n)$ and $\Phi_n = Z$ and $E \in \mathcal{V}(Z)$.	1′. The play is $(E_0, \Phi_0) \ldots (E_n, \Phi_n)$ and $\Phi_n = Z$ and $E \notin \mathcal{V}(Z)$.
2. The play is $(E_0, \Phi_0) \ldots (E_n, \Phi_n)$ and $\Phi_n = [K]\Psi$ and the set $\{F : E_n \xrightarrow{a} F \text{ and } a \in K\} = \emptyset$.	2′. The play is $(E_0, \Phi_0) \ldots (E_n, \Phi_n)$ and $\Phi_n = \langle K \rangle \Psi$ and the set $\{F : E_n \xrightarrow{a} F \text{ and } a \in K\} = \emptyset$.
3. The play is $(E_0, \Phi_0) \ldots (E_n, \Phi_n)$ and $\Phi_n = U$ and $U \stackrel{\mathrm{def}}{=} \nu Z.\Phi$ and $E_i = E_n$ and $\Phi_i = \Phi_n$ for $i < n$.	3′. The play is $(E_0, \Phi_0) \ldots (E_n, \Phi_n)$ and $\Phi_n = U$ and $U \stackrel{\mathrm{def}}{=} \mu Z.\Phi$ and $E_i = E_n$ and $\Phi_i = \Phi_n$ for $i < n$.
4. The play $(E_0, \Phi_0) \ldots (E_i, \Phi_i) \ldots$ is infinite length and there is a constant $U \stackrel{\mathrm{def}}{=} \nu Z.\Phi$ such that for infinitely many j, $\Phi_j = U$.	4′. The play $(E_0, \Phi_0) \ldots (E_i, \Phi_i) \ldots$ is infinite length and there is a constant $U \stackrel{\mathrm{def}}{=} \mu Z.\Phi$ such that for infinitely many j, $\Phi_j = U$.

Fig. 1. Winning conditions

that wins[7]. More generally as a play can have infinite length (but only when the initial process is infinite state) this repeat condition for winning is generalized for these plays. Player I wins if there is a least fixed point constant U which is traversed infinitely often, and player II wins if instead there is a greatest fixed point constant U which occurs infinitely often. In any infinite length play there is only one constant that occurs infinitely often, and therefore just one of the players wins the play.

Lemma 1 *If* $(E_0, \Phi_0) \ldots (E_n, \Phi_n) \ldots$ *is an infinite length game play then there is exactly one constant* U *such that for infinitely many* j, $\Phi_j = U$.

A player is said to have a *winning strategy* for a game if she is able to win any play of it. This means that she can always respond effectively to the moves her opponent makes.

Theorem 1 $E \models_{\mathcal{V}} \Phi$ *iff player II has a winning strategy for* (E, Φ) *under* $\mathcal{V}$.

This provides an alternative characterization of the satisfaction relation between processes and formulas. Game playing does not depend upon explicit calculation of fixed points. It is also open-ended as to knowing only part or all of the transition graph of a process. There is another feature, the possibility of more sophisticated game playing where moves may also be guided by the algebraic structure of a process expression (the raw material in [2] provides a basis for this).

Player II has a winning strategy for the game $(Clock, \mu Z.[\mathtt{tick}]Z)$. Any play has finite length as player I must choose a transition $Clock \xrightarrow{\mathtt{tick}} Cl_i$ and so

[7] These two conditions are redundant, but are included because then any finite-state process can only have finite length game plays.

must end being stuck in a configuration $(Cl_0, [\texttt{tick}]U)$ when $U \stackrel{\text{def}}{=} \mu Z.[\texttt{tick}]Z$. Similarly the safety and liveness (under fairness) properties of the crossing can be established using games.

Game playing justifies the tableaux proof systems for verifying temporal properties of finite and infinite-state processes as developed in [6, 20]. A successful tableau for a process E and a property Φ turns out to be a *witness* for player II's successful strategy for (E, Φ). In the case that E is a finite-state process each branch in the tableau is a winning play for player II, and all choices available to player I are contained within it. In the case of an infinite-state system the idea is essentially the same.

Game playing provides a very transparent methodology for property proving. However in the case of a finite-state process it is not very time efficient: the length of a play may be exponential in the number of fixed point subformulas. By refining the definition of game we can dramatically improve efficiency, and yet retain transparency.

5 Refinement of games

In this section we refine the definition of game play to provide a more efficient characterization of the satisfaction relation. Constants are reintroduced when the same fixed point formula is met again. This means that the previous rule for introducing constants for fixed points is divided it into two cases. Recall that we are defining the next pair in the play $(E_0, \Phi_0) \ldots (E_j, \Phi_j)$:

- if $\Phi_j = \nu Z.\Psi$ $(\mu Z.\Psi)$ and player I (player II) has not previously introduced a constant $V \stackrel{\text{def}}{=} \nu Z.\Psi$ $(V \stackrel{\text{def}}{=} \mu Z.\Psi)$ then player I (player II) chooses a *new* constant U and sets $U \stackrel{\text{def}}{=} \nu Z.\Psi$ $(U \stackrel{\text{def}}{=} \mu Z.\Psi)$: the process E_{j+1} is E_j and Φ_{j+1} is U.
- if $\Phi_j = \nu Z.\Psi$ $(\mu Z.\Psi)$ and player I (player II) has previously introduced a constant $V \stackrel{\text{def}}{=} \nu Z.\Psi$ $(V \stackrel{\text{def}}{=} \mu Z.\Psi)$ then E_{j+1} is E_j and Φ_{j+1} is V.

The other rules are as before. As before a player wins a play in the circumstances 1, 1′, 2 and 2′ of figure 1. The other conditions for winning, when there is a repeat configuration and those for infinite length plays, need to be redefined because constants are reintroduced: an infinite length play may now contain more than one constant that recurs infinitely often. A little notation:

Definition 1 The constant U is *active* in Φ iff either U occurs in Φ, or some constant V occurs in Φ with $V \stackrel{\text{def}}{=} \sigma Z.\Psi$ and U is active in $\sigma Z.\Psi$.

The constraints on how constants are introduced ensure that being active is well defined. Activity of a constant can be extended to finite or infinite length sequences of formulas, U is *active* throughout $\Phi_0, \ldots, \Phi_n \ldots$ if it is active in each Φ_i.

Lemma 2 i. *If* $(E_0, \Phi_0), \ldots, (E_n, \Phi_n)$ *is an initial part of a game play and* $\Phi_i = \Phi_n$ *when* $i < n$ *then there is a unique constant* U *which is active throughout* $\Phi_i, \ldots, \Phi_n$ *and occurs there,* $\Phi_j = U$ *for some* $j : i \leq j \leq n$.

ii. *If* $(E_0, \Phi_0), \ldots, (E_n, \Phi_n) \ldots$ *is an infinite length game play then there is a unique constant* U *which occurs infinitely often and is active throughout* $\Phi_j, \ldots, \Phi_n \ldots$ *for some* $j \geq 0$.

Lemma 2 governs the remaining winning conditions for game playing, the replacements for 3, 3′, 4 and 4′ of figure 1. A repeat configuration (E, Ψ) when Ψ is *any formula*, and not just a constant, terminates play. Who wins depends on the sequence of formulas between (and including) the identical configurations. There is exactly one constant U which is active in this cycle and which occurs within it: if it abbreviates a maximal fixed point formula then player II wins and otherwise it must abbreviate a least fixed point formula and player I wins. In any infinite length play there is a unique constant which is traversed infinitely often and which is active for all but a finite prefix: if this constant abbreviates a maximal fixed point formula player II wins and otherwise player I wins.

As before a player is said to have a winning strategy for a game if she is able to win any play of it.

Theorem 2 $E \models_{\mathcal{V}} \Phi$ *iff player II has a winning strategy for* (E, Φ) *under* $\mathcal{V}$.

It is straightforward to present tableaux proof systems for verifying temporal properties of finite and infinite-state processes, which are underpinned by these more refined games and where again a successful tableau is a witness for player II's successful strategy.

Theorem 2 offers a different perspective on similar results for the finite-state case presented in [12] whose basis is tree automata, and [4] which is grounded in alternating automata. The proof in the general case, when processes may be infinite-state, is similar to the model construction in [19]. It also follows from Theorem 2 (which utilizes approximants) that a winning strategy for a game is stationary or history free. Hence for a player it is a function from configurations she is able to move from to unique successors.

Assume that E is finite-state. The *game graph* for (E, Φ) relative to $\mathcal{V}$ is the graph representing all possible plays of (E, Φ) modulo a canonical means of choosing constants. The vertices are pairs (F, Ψ), configurations of a possible game play, and there is a directed edge between two vertices $v_1 \longrightarrow v_2$ if a player can make as her next move v_2 from v_1. Let $\mathcal{G}(E, \Phi)$ be the game graph for (E, Φ), and let $|\mathcal{G}(E, \Phi)|$ be its vertex size. It follows that $|\mathcal{G}(E, \Phi)| \leq |E| * |\Phi|$ where $|E|$ is the number of processes in the transition graph for E, and $|\Phi|$ is the size of this formula. This means that any play of (E, Φ) has length at most $1 + (|E| * |\Phi|)$. The proof that model checking belongs to NP $\cap$ co-NP follows from the observation that given a strategy for player II or player I it is straightforward to check in polynomial time whether or not it is successful. (See [10] for a proof which has its roots in [9] using tree automata.) For the alternation free fragment game graphs obey the weak alternating automaton condition for partitioning vertices [18], and hence model checking can be determined in polynomial time.

(See [4] which directly uses alternating automata.)

We can easily ensure that game playing must proceed to infinity by adding extra moves when a player is stuck (and removing the redundant repeat termination condition). The resulting game graph is then an alternating automaton: the and-vertices are the configurations from which player I must proceed and the or-vertices are those from which player II moves, and the acceptance condition is given in terms of active constants.

Alternatively a game graph can be directly translated into a formula of boolean fixed point logic, defined as follows:

$$\Phi ::= Z \mid \mathtt{tt} \mid \mathtt{ff} \mid \Phi_1 \wedge \Phi_2 \mid \Phi_1 \vee \Phi_2 \mid \nu Z.\Phi \mid \mu Z.\Phi$$

Satisfiability (or really truth) checking of closed formulas of this logic is therefore also in NP $\cap$ co-NP. Various authors have, in effect, translated finite-state model checking into this logic, with a preference for a syntax utilizing equations [1, 14, 7]. One can also model check directly using approximants, where a careful utilization of monotonicity provides reasonable exponential algorithms [11, 15].

An important open question is whether model checking modal mu-calculus formulas can be done in polynomial time (with respect to the size of a game graph). One direction for research is to provide a finer analysis of successful strategies, and to be able to describe optimizations of them. New insights may come from the relationship between the games developed here and other graph games where there are such descriptions.

6 Graph games

The model checking game of the previous section can be abstracted into the following graph game. A game is a graph with vertices $\{1, \ldots, n\}$ where each vertex i has two directed edges $i \longrightarrow j_1$ and $i \longrightarrow j_2$, and which obeys the following condition: if $i \longrightarrow j$ and $j \leq i$ then there is a path $j \longrightarrow j_1 \longrightarrow \ldots \longrightarrow j_n = i$ where $j \leq j_1 \leq \ldots \leq j_n$. Each vertex is labelled I or II. A play is an infinite path through the graph starting at vertex 1, and player I moves from vertices labelled I and player II from vertices labelled II. The winner of a play is determined by the label of the *least* vertex i which is traversed infinitely often: if i is labelled I then player I wins, and if II then player II wins. A player wins the game if she is able to win any play. A winning strategy is again stationary.

Simple stochastic games [8] are graph games where the vertices are labelled I, II or A (average), and where there are two special vertices I-sink and II-sink (which have no outgoing edges). As above each I, II (and A) vertex has two outgoing edges. At an average vertex during a game play a coin is tossed to determine which of the two edges is traversed each having probability $\frac{1}{2}$. More generally one can assume that the two edges are labelled with probabilities of the form $\frac{p}{q}$ where $0 \leq p \leq q \leq 2^m$ for some m, as long as their sum is 1. A game play ends when a sink vertex is reached: player II wins if it is the II-sink, and player I otherwise. The decision question is whether the probability that player II wins is greater than $\frac{1}{2}$. It is not known whether this problem can be solved in polynomial time. In [16] a "subexponential" ($2^{O(\sqrt{n})}$) algorithm is presented, which works by refining optimal strategies. A polynomial time algorithm for simple stochastic games would imply that extending space bounded alternating Turing machines with randomness does not increase the class of languages that they accept.

Mark Jerrum noted that there is a reduction from the graph game to the simple stochastic game. The idea is to add the two sink vertices, and an average vertex $i1$ for each vertex i for which there is an edge $j \longrightarrow i$ with $j \geq i$. Each such edge $j \longrightarrow i$ when $j \geq i$ is changed to $j \longrightarrow i1$. And the vertex $i1$ has an edge to i, and to I-sink if i is labelled I or to II-sink otherwise. With suitable rational probabilities on the edges, player II has a winning strategy for the graph game iff she has one for the simple stochastic game. Another relevant graph game is the mean payoff game for which there is also a reduction from the model checking game.

Acknowledgement: I would like to thank Mark Jerrum for numerous discussions about model checking and games.

References

1. Andersen, H. (1994). Model checking and boolean graphs. *Theoretical Comp. Science*, **126**, 3-30.
2. Andersen, H., Stirling, C., and Winskel, G. (1994) A compositional proof system for the modal mu-calculus. *Procs LICS.*
3. Arnold, A., and Niwinski, D. (1992). Fixed point characterization of weak monadic logic definable sets of trees. In *Tree Automata and Languages*, ed. M. Nivat and A. Podelski, Elsevier, 159-188.
4. Bernholtz, O., Vardi, M. and Wolper, P. (1994). An automata-theoretic approach to branching-time model checking. *Procs. CAV 94.*
5. Bradfield, J. and Stirling, C. (1990). Verifying temporal properties of processes. *Lect. Notes in Comput. Science*, **458**, 115-125.
6. Bradfield, J. and Stirling, C. (1992). Local model checking for infinite state spaces. *Theoret. Comput. Science*, **96**, 157-174.
7. Cleaveland, R. and Steffen, B. (1992). A linear-time model checking algorithm for the alternation-free modal mu-calculus. *Lect. Notes in Comp Science*, **575**.
8. Condon, A. (1992). The complexity of stochastic games. *Inf. and Comp.*, **96**, 203-224.
9. Emerson, E. (1985). Automata, tableaux, and temporal logics. *Lect. Notes in Comput. Science*, **193**, 79-87.
10. Emerson, E., and Jutla, C. (1988). The complexity of tree automata and logics of programs. Extended version from FOCS '88.
11. Emerson, E, and Lei, C. (1986). Efficient model checking in fragments of the propositional mu-calculus. In *Proc. 1st IEEE Symp. on Logic in Comput. Science*, 267-278.
12. Emerson, E., Jutla, C., and Sistla, A. (1993). On model checking for fragments of μ-calculus. *Lect. Notes in Comput. Sci.*, **697**, 385-396.
13. Kozen, D. (1983). Results on the propositional mu-calculus. *Theoret. Comput. Sci* **27**, 333-354.

14. Larsen, K. (1992). Efficient local correctness checking. *Lect. Notes in Comput. Sci.*, **663**, 385-396.
15. Long, D., Browne, A., Clarke, E., Jha, S., and Marrero, W. (1994) An improved algorithm for the evaluation of fixpoint expressions. *Procs. CAV 94.*
16. Ludwig, W. (1995). A subexponential randomized algorithm for the simple stochastic game problem. *Inf. and Comp*, **117**, 151-155.
17. Milner, R. (1989). *Communication and Concurrency.* Prentice Hall.
18. Muller, D., Saoudi, A. and Schupp, P. (1986). Alternating automata, the weak monadic theory of the tree and its complexity. *Lect. Notes in Comput. Sci.*, **225**, 275-283.
19. Streett, R. and Emerson, E. (1989). An automata theoretic decision procedure for the propositional mu-calculus. *Inf. and Comp.*, **81**, 249-264.
20. Stirling, C. and Walker, D. (1991). Local model checking in the modal mu-calculus. *Theoret. Comput. Science*, **89**, 161-177.

Compositional Proof Systems for Model Checking Infinite State Processes

Mads Dam*

SICS, Box 1263, S-164 28 Kista, Sweden, e-mail: mfd@sics.se

Abstract. *We present the first compositional proof system for checking processes against formulas in the modal μ-calculus which is capable of handling general infinite-state processes. The proof system is obtained in a systematic way from the operational semantics of the underlying process algebra. A non-trivial proof example is given, and the proof system is shown to be sound in general, and complete for finite-state processes.*

1 Introduction

In this paper we address the problem of verifying modal μ-calculus properties of general infinite-state processes, and we present what we believe to be the first genuinely compositional solution to this problem.

The value of compositionality in program logics is well established. Compositionality allows better structuring and decomposition of the verification task, it allows proof reuse, and it allows reasoning about partially instantiated programs, thus supporting program synthesis. Even more fundamentally it allows, at least in principle, verification exercises to be undertaken which are beyond the scope of more global approaches because the set of reachable global states grows in an unbounded manner. The problem of how to build compositional proof systems for concurrent systems, however, has long been recognised as a very difficult one. Many techniques have been suggested in the literature, such as rely-guarantee pairs, history variables, quotienting, reduction, phantom moves, simulations, edge propositions, quiescent traces, to name but a few. These techniques, however, give only partial and ad-hoc solutions in that they work only for particular concurrency primitives, static process networks and, most often, linear time logic only.

Much recent research in the area has focused on process algebra and the modal μ-calculus. A large number of algorithms, tableau systems, and proof systems for verifying processes against modal μ-calculus specifications by some form of global state space exploration have been given (c.f. [3, 4, 6, 9, 13] and many others). Compositional accounts have been developed based on some form of quotienting, or reduction (c.f. [10, 2]). These approaches, however, are only applicable for finite-state processes, or at least when the holding of a property depends only on a finite portion of a potentially infinite-state process.

* Partially supported by ESPRIT BRA project 8130 LOMAPS.

Finite-state processes, however, are inadequate as modelling tools in many practical situations. Value- or channel passing, for instance, can cause even the simplest processes to become infinite state. While some decidability results can be obtained in the absence of process spawning (c.f. [5]), in general the model checking problem becomes undecidable, even in very sparse fragments of, e.g., CCS [7]. Process spawning, however, is needed in many applications: Unbounded buffers, dynamic resource or process creation/forking, data types and higher order features. In fact it is hard to conceive of useful program logics for modern concurrent functional languages such as CML, Facile, Erlang, or PICT that can not deal with process spawning, and indeed the development of such logics is one long-term aim of the research reported here.

Because of undecidability, and because the modal μ-calculus is closed under negation, finitary proof systems for model checking general infinite state processes will necessarily be incomplete. This, however, does not make the model checking problem go away! The currently prevailing finite-state approaches (iterative or local) provide little assistance: They are inadequate for even rather simple infinite state problems such as the "counter" example considered below. Here we explore instead a compositional approach. Our aim is to obtain a compositional proof system which is (1) sound, (2) practically useful, (3) powerful enough to prove the kinds of infinite state problems we would hope to be able to address, and (4) complete for the finite state fragment. For (1) and (4) we have positive answers, while more work is needed to answer (2) and (3).

Compositionality is addressed by taking a more general view of model checking. Instead of focusing on closed assertions like $\models P : \phi$ we look at sequents of the form $x_1 : \phi_1, ..., x_n : \phi_n \models P(x_1, ..., x_n) : \phi$. That is, properties of the open process term $P(x_1, ..., x_n)$ are relativised to properties of its free variables $x_1, ..., x_n$. This provides a more general proof-theoretical setting which can be used to give a structural account of recursive properties. This is a fairly easy task for those connectives like $\wedge$, $\vee$, or the modal operators, that depend only on "local" behaviour. For the fixed point operators the problem is much more difficult. Here we offer an approach based on loop detection. To guide us towards a general solution we offer in this paper a formal proof to show that the CCS process $Counter = up.(Counter \mid down.\mathbf{0})$ after any sequence of consecutive *up* transitions can only perform a finite sequence of consecutive *down* transitions.

An important feature of our approach is that, in contrast to other existing compositional accounts, the sequent style proof system we obtain is constructed from the operational semantics in quite a general and systematic manner. The proof system contains four separate elements: Structural rules, including a cut-rule, to account for sequent structure; logical rules that deal with boolean connectives and recursive formulas; dynamical rules that deal with the modal operators; and finally a single rule of discharge that is responsible for detecting "safe" recurrences of sequents. Only the dynamical rules are dependent upon the specific process algebra under consideration. Moreover the dynamical rules are constructed in a way that one can easily foresee being automated for a range of process algebras.

2 CCS and the Modal μ-Calculus

Our use of CCS follows [11] closely. An *action*, α, is either the invisible action τ or a label l. A *label* is either a (port- or channel-) *name* a, b, say, or a *co-name* $\overline{a}$, $\overline{b}$. Generally $\overline{\overline{a}}$ and a are identified. We assume that the set of labels is finite and ranged over by $l_0, \ldots, l_m$. Sets of labels are ranged over by L, K. *Agent expressions*, E, F, are given as follows:

$$E ::= 0 \,\Big|\, \alpha.E \,\Big|\, E + E \,\Big|\, E \mid E \,\Big|\, E \setminus L \,\Big|\, x \,\Big|\, \mathsf{fix}x.E$$

where x (and y) range over agent variables. An agent expression is an *agent* if it contains no free agent variables. Agents are ranged over by P, Q. The CCS renaming operator is omitted since it adds little of interest to the present account. We refer to [11] for the operational semantics rules.

The following syntax of the modal μ-calculus is augmented by equality and inequality of actions which are useful (though not required), primarily to give a reasonable account of the τ-indexed box operator.

$$\phi ::= \alpha = \beta \,\Big|\, \neg\phi \,\Big|\, \phi \wedge \phi \,\Big|\, [\alpha]\phi \,\Big|\, X \,\Big|\, \nu X.\phi$$

where X (Y, Z) ranges over propositional variables. To form fixed point formulas $\nu X.\phi$ the formal monotonicity condition that all occurrences of X in ϕ are within the scope of a even number of negation symbols is required. Other connectives are introduced by standard abbreviations, e.g. $\alpha \neq \beta = \neg(\alpha = \beta)$, $\mathit{ff} = \alpha \neq \alpha$, $\phi \vee \psi = \neg(\neg\phi \wedge \neg\psi)$, $\phi \supset \psi = \neg\phi \vee \psi$, $\langle\alpha\rangle\phi = \neg[\alpha]\neg\phi$, $\mu X.\phi = \neg\nu X.\neg\phi[\neg X/X]$. In particular $\forall\alpha.\phi = \bigwedge\{\phi(\alpha) \mid \alpha \text{ an action}\}$ where $\phi(\alpha) = \phi[\alpha/a]$ substitutes α for a name a in ϕ, and it is required that ϕ does not have free occurrences of the action $\overline{a}$ so that action terms like $\overline{\tau}$ are avoided.

The semantics of formulas, $||\phi||\mathcal{V} \subseteq \mathcal{A}$, where $\mathcal{V}$ is a valuation assigning sets of agents to propositional variables is standard and omitted. Instead of $P \in ||\phi||\mathcal{V}$ we sometimes write $\models_{\mathcal{V}} P : \phi$, or $\models P : \phi$ if ϕ is closed. Any closed formula can be rewritten, while preserving semantics, into *positive form*, using negation only as needed by use of the derived operators. The proof system below uses positive forms extensively.

3 Sequents

The basic judgment of the proof system is the sequent.

Definition 1. (Sequents, declarations, basic assertions) A *sequent* is an expression of the form $\Gamma \vdash t$ where Γ is a sequence of *declarations* of one of the forms $x : \phi$ or $X = \phi$, and t is a *basic assertion* of one of the forms $X = \phi$ or $E : \phi$.

Sequents are ranged over by s. Declarations of the form $X = \phi$ are called *namings*, and if s contains the naming $X = \phi$ then X is said to *name* ϕ in s. An occurrence of a variable X to the left of the equality sign in a naming $X = \phi$

is regarded as binding. Namings are used as constants in [13], and serve to keep track of the unfoldings of fixed point formula occurrences in the proof system. We use σ as a meta-variable over $\{\nu, \mu\}$. If X names a formula of the form $\sigma Y.\psi$ in s then X is called a *σ-variable.*

Declaration sequences and sequents are subject to an inductively defined *well-formedness constraint*, in order to ensure that (proposition and process) variables are properly declared. This condition states that variables can be declared at most once, and that for a sequent $\Gamma \vdash E : \phi$, if a variable occurs freely in E or in ϕ then it is declared in Γ, and, for a sequent $\Gamma_1, x : \phi_i, \Gamma_2 \vdash E : \phi$, if a variable occurs freely in ϕ_i then it is declared in Γ_1.

Definition 2. (Sequent semantics)

1. The sequent $\vdash P : \phi$ is $\mathcal{V}$-true if and only if $P \in \|\phi\|\mathcal{V}$
2. The sequent $\vdash X = \phi$ is $\mathcal{V}$-true if and only if $\mathcal{V}(X) = \|\phi\|\mathcal{V}$
3. The sequent $\Gamma, x : \phi \vdash t$ is $\mathcal{V}$-true if and only if for all agent expressions E, if $\Gamma \vdash E : \phi$ is $\mathcal{V}$-true then so is $\Gamma \vdash t[E/x]$.
4. The sequent $\Gamma, X = \phi \vdash t$ is $\mathcal{V}$-true if and only if $\Gamma \vdash t$ is $\mathcal{V}[X \mapsto \|\phi\|\mathcal{V}]$-true.

If the sequent s is well-formed then the $\mathcal{V}$-truthhood of s is well-defined and independent of $\mathcal{V}$. Notice that the quantification over agent expressions in def. 2.3 could equivalently be replaced by a quantification over agents.

4 Local Rules

We are now in a position to present the proof system. It consists of two subsystems, a *local* and a *global* one. We first introduce the local subsystem. The local subsystem is subdivided into three groups: *Structural rules* governing the use of declarations, *logical rules* responsible for the left and right introduction of logical operators, and finally *dynamical rules* for the modal operators which depend on process structure.

Structural rules:

$$\textsc{Declaration}\ \frac{\cdot}{\Gamma_1, t, \Gamma_2 \vdash t} \qquad \textsc{Cut}\ \frac{\Gamma_1, \Gamma_2 \vdash E : \phi \quad \Gamma_1, x : \phi, \Gamma_2 \vdash F : \psi}{\Gamma_1, \Gamma_2 \vdash F[E/x] : \psi}$$

Logical rules:

$$\neg\neg\text{-}\textsc{Right}\ \frac{\Gamma \vdash E : \phi}{\Gamma \vdash E : \neg\neg\phi} \qquad \neg\neg\text{-}\textsc{Left}\ \frac{\Gamma_1, x : \phi, \Gamma_2 \vdash E : \psi}{\Gamma_1, x : \neg\neg\phi, \Gamma_2 \vdash E : \psi}$$

$$=\text{-}\textsc{Right}\ \frac{\cdot}{\Gamma \vdash E : \alpha = \alpha} \qquad =\text{-}\textsc{Left}\ \frac{\cdot}{\Gamma_1, x : \alpha = \beta, \Gamma_2 \vdash E : \psi}\ (\alpha \neq \beta)$$

$$\neq\text{-}\textsc{Right}\ \frac{\cdot}{\Gamma \vdash E : \alpha \neq \beta}\ (\alpha \neq \beta) \qquad \neq\text{-}\textsc{Left}\ \frac{\cdot}{\Gamma_1, x : \alpha \neq \alpha, \Gamma_2 \vdash E : \psi}$$

$$\wedge\text{-}\textsc{Right}\ \frac{\Gamma \vdash E : \phi \quad \Gamma \vdash E : \psi}{\Gamma \vdash E : \phi \wedge \psi} \qquad \wedge\text{-}\textsc{Left}\ \frac{\Gamma_1, x : \phi, \Gamma_2 \vdash E : \gamma}{\Gamma_1, x : \phi \wedge \psi, \Gamma_2 \vdash E : \gamma}$$

$$\vee\text{-RIGHT}\ \frac{\Gamma \vdash E : \phi}{\Gamma \vdash E : \phi \vee \psi} \qquad \vee\text{-LEFT}\ \frac{\Gamma_1, x : \phi, \Gamma_2 \vdash E : \gamma \quad \Gamma_1, x : \psi, \Gamma_2 \vdash E : \gamma}{\Gamma_1, x : \phi \vee \psi, \Gamma_2 \vdash E : \gamma}$$

$$\sigma\text{-RIGHT}\ \frac{\Gamma, Y = \sigma X.\phi \vdash E : Y}{\Gamma \vdash E : \sigma X.\phi} \qquad \sigma\text{-LEFT}\ \frac{\Gamma_1, Y = \sigma X.\phi, x : Y, \Gamma_2 \vdash E : \psi}{\Gamma_1, x : \sigma X.\phi, \Gamma_2 \vdash E : \psi}$$

$$Y\text{-RIGHT}\ \frac{\Gamma \vdash Y = \sigma X.\phi \quad \Gamma \vdash E : \phi[Y/X]}{\Gamma \vdash E : Y}$$

$$Y\text{-LEFT}\ \frac{\Gamma_1 \vdash Y = \sigma X.\phi \quad \Gamma_1, x : \phi[Y/X], \Gamma_2 \vdash E : \psi}{\Gamma_1, x : Y, \Gamma_2 \vdash E : \psi}$$

Dynamical rules:

$$\mathbf{0}\text{-}\Box\ \frac{}{\Gamma \vdash \mathbf{0} : [\alpha]\phi} \qquad \alpha.\text{-}\Diamond\ \frac{\Gamma \vdash x : \psi}{\Gamma \vdash \alpha.x : \langle\alpha\rangle\psi}$$

$$\alpha.\text{-}\Box\text{-}1\ \frac{\Gamma \vdash x : \psi}{\Gamma \vdash \alpha.x : [\alpha]\psi} \qquad \alpha.\text{-}\Box\text{-}2\ \frac{}{\Gamma \vdash \alpha.E : [\beta]\phi}\ (\alpha \neq \beta)$$

$$+\text{-}\Diamond\ \frac{\Gamma_1, x : \phi, \Gamma_2 \vdash x : \psi}{\Gamma_1, x : \langle\alpha\rangle\phi, \Gamma_2 \vdash x + F : \langle\alpha\rangle\psi} \qquad +\text{-}\Box\ \frac{\Gamma_1, x : \phi_1, \Gamma_2, \Gamma_3 \vdash x : \psi \quad \Gamma_1, \Gamma_2, y : \phi_2, \Gamma_3 \vdash y : \psi}{\Gamma_1, x : [\alpha]\phi_1, \Gamma_2, y : [\alpha]\phi_2, \Gamma_3 \vdash x + y : [\alpha]\psi}$$

$$|\text{-}\langle\alpha\rangle\ \frac{\Gamma_1, x : \phi, \Gamma_2, y : \psi, \Gamma_3 \vdash x \mid y : \gamma}{\Gamma_1, x : \langle\alpha\rangle\phi, \Gamma_2, y : \psi, \Gamma_3 \vdash x \mid y : \langle\alpha\rangle\gamma} \qquad |\text{-}\langle\tau\rangle\ \frac{\Gamma_1, x : \phi, \Gamma_2, y : \psi, \Gamma_3 \vdash x \mid y : \gamma}{\Gamma_1, x : \langle l\rangle\phi, \Gamma_2, y : \langle\bar{l}\rangle\psi, \Gamma_3 \vdash x \mid y : \langle\tau\rangle\gamma}$$

$$|\text{-}[\alpha]\ \frac{\Gamma_1, x : \phi_1, \Gamma_2, y : \psi_2, \Gamma_3 \vdash x \mid y : \gamma \quad \Gamma_1, x : \phi_2, \Gamma_2, y : \psi_1, \Gamma_3 \vdash x \mid y : \gamma}{\Gamma_1, x : \phi_1 \wedge [\alpha]\phi_2, \Gamma_2, y : \psi_1 \wedge [\alpha]\psi_2, \Gamma_3 \vdash x \mid y : [\alpha]\gamma}\ (\alpha \neq \tau)$$

$$|\text{-}[\tau]\ \frac{\begin{array}{c}\Gamma_1, x : \phi_2(\tau), \Gamma_2, y : \psi_1, \Gamma_3 \vdash x \mid y : \gamma \\ \Gamma_1, x : \phi_1, \Gamma_2, y : \psi_2(\tau), \Gamma_3 \vdash x \mid y : \gamma \\ \Gamma_1, x : \phi_2(l_0), \Gamma_2, y : \psi_2(\overline{l_0}), \Gamma_3 \vdash x \mid y : \gamma \\ \vdots \\ \Gamma_1, x : \phi_2(l_m), \Gamma_2, y : \psi_2(\overline{l_m}), \Gamma_3 \vdash x \mid y : \gamma\end{array}}{\Gamma_1, x : \phi_1 \wedge \forall\alpha.[\alpha]\phi_2(\alpha), \Gamma_2, y : \psi_1 \wedge \forall\beta.[\beta]\psi_2(\beta), \Gamma_3 \vdash x \mid y : [\tau]\gamma}$$

$$\backslash\text{-}\Box\text{-}1\ \frac{\cdot}{\Gamma \vdash E \backslash K : [\alpha]\psi}\ (\alpha \in K) \qquad \backslash\text{-}\Box\text{-}2\ \frac{\Gamma_1, x : \phi, \Gamma_2 \vdash x \backslash K : \psi}{\Gamma_1, x : [\alpha]\phi, \Gamma_2 \vdash x \backslash K : [\alpha]\psi}$$

$$\backslash\text{-}\Diamond\ \frac{\Gamma_1, x : \phi, \Gamma_2 \vdash x \backslash K : \psi}{\Gamma_1, x : \langle\alpha\rangle\phi, \Gamma_2 \vdash x \backslash K : \langle\alpha\rangle\psi}\ (\alpha \notin K) \qquad \text{FIX}\ \frac{\Gamma \vdash E[\text{fix}x.E/x] : \phi}{\Gamma \vdash \text{fix}x.E : \phi}$$

The first two sets of rules require little comment, coming, as they do, straight from proof theory. Only noteworthy points are the use of variables to name fixed point formulas, and that symmetric versions of the $\wedge$-LEFT and $\vee$-RIGHT rules have been omitted. Similarly, symmetric versions of the $+$-$\Diamond$, $|$-$\Diamond$, and rules derived from $+$-$\Box$ and the rules for parallel composition, obtained by systematically exchanging the declarations for x and for y, have been omitted.

The rationale behind the dynamical rules is best explained through a little example. Suppose we wish to prove $\vdash P \mid Q : \langle\alpha\rangle\phi$, because we suspect that (1) $P \xrightarrow{\alpha} P'$ and (2) $\models P' \mid Q : \phi$. Our task is to

1. guess a property ϕ_1 of P' and a property ϕ_2 of Q,
2. prove $\vdash P : \langle\alpha\rangle\phi_1$ and $\vdash Q : \phi_2$,

3. prove $x_1 : \phi_1, x_2 : \phi_2 \vdash x_1 \mid x_2 : \phi$, and finally,
4. put (2) and (3) together using two cuts and $|\text{-}\langle\alpha\rangle$ to conclude $\vdash P \mid Q : \langle\alpha\rangle\phi$.

Comparing with local model checking systems such as Stirling and Walker's [13] this account has sacrificed a subformula property ($\vdash P \mid Q : \langle\alpha\rangle\phi$ is proved in terms of processes having the property ϕ) in favour of a subprocess property ($\vdash P \mid Q : \langle\alpha\rangle\phi$ is proved in terms of properties holding of the processes P and Q). We regard this as quite natural and reflecting closely the *compositional* nature of the proof system. We do not expect that any of the tasks (1)–(3) can be automated, although this is possible in special cases, in particular for the case of finite state processes considered later.

5 An Example Proof

In this section we give an example proof to (1) show the local rules at work, and to (2) serve as a setting for discussing termination conditions. The example proves that the infinite state process $Counter = \text{fix}x.up.(x \mid down.\mathbf{0})$ satisfies the property $\phi = \nu X.(\mu Y.[down]Y) \wedge [up]X$, i.e. after any finite consecutive sequence of *up*'s only a finite number of consecutive *down*'s is possible. We use a goal-directed approach. Thus the initial goal is $\vdash Counter : \phi$. We first name ϕ, obtaining the sequent

$$U{=}\phi \vdash Counter : U. \tag{1}$$

We then unfold *Counter* and U, apply CUT and $\wedge$-RIGHT, and arrive at the two subgoals

$$U{=}\phi \vdash up.(Counter \mid down.\mathbf{0}) : (\mu Y.[down]Y) \tag{2}$$
$$U{=}\phi \vdash up.(Counter \mid down.\mathbf{0}) : [up]U. \tag{3}$$

Subgoal (2) is easily handled by naming the μ-formula, unfolding, and then applying $\alpha.$-$\Box$-2, so we proceed refining subgoal (3). First using $\alpha.$-$\Box$-1 we obtain

$$U{=}\phi \vdash Counter \mid down.\mathbf{0} : U$$

Now let $\psi = [down][down]ff \wedge [up]ff$, and by two applications of CUT refine to the subgoals

$$U{=}\phi \vdash Counter : U \tag{4}$$
$$U{=}\phi \vdash down.\mathbf{0} : \psi \tag{5}$$
$$U{=}\phi, x : U, y : \psi \vdash x \mid y : U. \tag{6}$$

Of these, (5) is eliminated by $\wedge$-RIGHT, $\alpha.$-$\Box$-1 and $\alpha.$-$\Box$-2. For (4) our intention is to terminate because (4) has previously been expanded as (1), and U is a ν-variable so termination is safe. Indeed the termination conditions allow this. Thus, (6) is all that remains. Now, by unfolding and $\wedge$-RIGHT we obtain the subgoals

$$U{=}\phi, x : U, y : \psi \vdash x \mid y : \mu Y.[down]Y \tag{7}$$
$$U{=}\phi, x : U, y : \psi \vdash x \mid y : [up]U. \tag{8}$$

We delay consideration of (7) and concentrate on (8). First unfold the left hand occurrence of U to obtain

$$U{=}\phi, x : \mu Y.[down]Y \wedge [up]U, y : \psi \vdash x \mid y : [up]U. \tag{9}$$

Now the rule |-[α] applies to reduce to the four subgoals

$$U{=}\phi, x : \mu Y.[down]Y \wedge [up]U, y : \psi \vdash x : [up]U \tag{10}$$

$$U{=}\phi, x : \mu Y.[down]Y \wedge [up]U, y : \psi \vdash y : [up]ff \tag{11}$$

$$U{=}\phi, x : U, y : \psi \vdash x \mid y : U \tag{12}$$

$$U{=}\phi, x : \mu Y.[down]Y \wedge [up]U, y : ff \vdash x \mid y : U \tag{13}$$

Of these, (10) and (11) are easily proved using $\wedge$-L and some simple boolean reasoning. (13) is proved using $\neq$-LEFT. Finally, (12) is discharged using (6) since U is a ν-variable (!). We then need to consider (7). First name the right hand μ-formula, letting $\gamma = \mu Y.[down]Y$, then unfold the left-hand occurrence of U, and after an application of $\wedge$-LEFT we obtain

$$U{=}\phi, x : \gamma, y : \psi, V{=}\gamma \vdash x \mid y : V.$$

Now the left hand μ-formula is named too:

$$U{=}\phi, W{=}\gamma, x : W, y : \psi, V{=}\gamma \vdash x \mid y : V \tag{14}$$

and V is unfolded:

$$U{=}\phi, W{=}\gamma, x : W, y : \psi, V{=}\gamma \vdash x \mid y : [down]V. \tag{15}$$

Unfolding W to the left gives

$$U{=}\phi, W{=}\gamma, x : [down]W, y : \psi, V{=}\gamma \vdash x \mid y : [down]V. \tag{16}$$

which reduces through CUT, |-[α], and some logical reasoning to the two subgoals

$$U{=}\phi, W{=}\gamma, x : W, y : \psi, V{=}\gamma \vdash x \mid y : V \tag{17}$$

$$U{=}\phi, W{=}\gamma, x : [down]W, y : [down]ff, V{=}\gamma \vdash x \mid y : V. \tag{18}$$

We now arrive at a key point in the proof where we discharge (17) with reference to subgoal (14), because even though the μ-variable V to the right of the turnstyle has been unfolded from (14) to (17) so has another μ-variable, W, to the left of the turnstyle. Thus, intuitively, if we assume the left hand side to be true this will ensure that in fact W, and hence V, will only be unfolded a finite number of times, and hence termination at the point (17) is safe. Finally the proof is completed, refining (18) by first unfolding V and then using |-[α] in a very similar way to the way (15) was dealt with. This is left as an exercise for the reader.

6 Side-conditions and Global Rules

We proceed to explain the global rules justifying the discharge of hypotheses at steps (4), (12), and (17) in the previous section.

A *basic proof structure* (b.p.s.) $\mathcal{B}$ is a proof tree constructed according to the local proof rules. Basic proof structures may contain occurrence of *hypotheses*. The global subsystem consists of a single *rule of discharge* that determines which occurrences of hypotheses can be discharged, along the lines suggested in section 5. A *proof*, then, is a basic proof structure for which all occurrences of hypotheses have been discharged.

To arrive at a sound rule of discharge it is necessary to

1. consider the ways formulas are "regenerated" along paths through a basic proof structure, and
2. count the number of unfoldings of ν-variables.

The first problem is familiar from most accounts of local fixed point unfolding in the modal μ-calculus such as Strett and Emerson [14] where it is handled using a subformula condition, and Stirling and Walker [13] where it is handled using propositional constants. Here the problem is more delicate, due, principally, to the CUT rule which admits a branching of the regeneration relation which is not otherwise possible. The second problem is due to the fact that we are working with left- and right-handed sequents. Let us anticipate the soundness proof a little. We prove soundness by assuming a proof to be given and a sequent in the proof to be false. Let the sequent concerned be of the form $\Gamma \vdash E : X$, X a ν-variable. We can then find a substitution σ validating Γ and making $\sigma(X)$ false when X is annotated by some suitable ordinal. By applications of CUT this annotation may cause occurrences of X to the left of the turnstyle in some "later" sequent $\Gamma' \vdash E' : \phi'$ to be annotated too. Unfolding specific occurrences of X may cause the annotation of that occurrence to be decreased. We need to arrive at a contradiction even when $\Gamma' \vdash E' : \phi'$ is the conclusion of a nullary rule, say DECLARATION. But if the annotation of a X to the left is *less than* the annotation of X to the right then there is no guarantee of a contradiction, and soundness may fail.

6.1 Colouring, Generation, Activity

The basic device we use for handling regeneration is the concept of *colouring.*

Definition 3. (Colouring) A *colouring* of a sequent $\Gamma \vdash t$ is an assignment of distinct colours to formula occurrences either as ψ in a declaration $x : \psi$ or as ϕ when t has the form $E : \phi$.

Given a colouring of the conclusion of a local proof rule colourings for the antecedents are derived. A few examples suffice to illustrate the general pattern. Consider e.g. the rule $\land$-RIGHT as stated above, and assume a colouring of $\Gamma \vdash E : \phi \land \psi$. The antecedent $\Gamma \vdash E : \phi$ is coloured by keeping the colouring of Γ unchanged and colouring ϕ as $\phi \wedge \psi$. The other antecedent $\Gamma \vdash E : \psi$ is coloured similarly. All other rules except the rule CUT are coloured in a similar fashion. For CUT let a colouring of the conclusion $\Gamma_1, \Gamma_2 \vdash F[E/x] : \psi$ be given. The antecedent $\Gamma_1, \Gamma_2 \vdash E : \phi$ is coloured by keeping the colouring of Γ_1 and Γ_2 unchanged and colouring ϕ as ψ. The antecedent $\Gamma_1, x : \phi, \Gamma_2 \vdash F : \psi$, finally, is coloured by keeping the colourings of Γ_1, Γ_2, and ψ unchanged and choosing a new colour for ϕ. Now, a *coloured basic proof structure* is a b.p.s. $\mathcal{B}$ which is coloured according to the above rules.

Definition 4. (Generation) Let a coloured basic proof structure $\mathcal{B}$ and a sequent s_1 in $\mathcal{B}$ be given. Let $\Pi = s_1, \ldots, s_k$ be a path downwards from s_1 to some other sequent s_k in $\mathcal{B}$. Whenever formula occurrences ϕ_1 in s_1 and ϕ_k in s_k exists that are coloured with the same colour then ϕ_k is said to *generate* ϕ_1 *along* Π.

The term "generates" is chosen since we envisage proofs to be constructed in a bottom up fashion from goal to subgoals. Note that the generation relation is independent of choice of colouring. The notion of generation is important since it respects activity of variables in a sense which we go on to explain.

Definition 5. (Activity) Let $s = \Gamma \vdash t$ be a well-formed sequent and let ϕ be any formula. Then a variable X is said to be *active in* ϕ (with respect to s) if either X is free in ϕ or else some Y is free in ϕ, Y names some ψ in s, and X is active in ψ.

Note that well-formedness ensures that the "active-in" relation on variables is a preorder. We impose the following side condition on CUT:

Proviso 6 Applications of CUT are subject to the condition: For any ν-variable X, if X is active in ϕ then X is also active in ψ.

The following property concerning "preservation of activity" is crucial for soundness:

Proposition 7. *In a b.p.s.* $\mathcal{B}$ *let a path downwards from* s *to* s' *be given. Let* ϕ *(*ϕ'*) be an occurrence of a formula in* s *(*s'*). If* ϕ' *generates* ϕ*,* X *is declared in* s'*, and* X *is active in* ϕ *then* X *is active in* ϕ'*.* □

6.2 Indexing

We now turn to the counting of unfoldings. An *indexing* is a partial assignment of indices $n \in \omega$ to occurrences of names such that for any sequent $\Gamma \vdash t$, if two occurrences of X in the same formula in Γ or t is given then one is indexed n iff the other one is. Only the rules σ-LEFT, σ-RIGHT, Y-RIGHT, Y-LEFT, DECLARATION, and CUT are affected by indexing. The modifications needed are the following:

1. σ-LEFT and σ-RIGHT: Y is indexed by 0 in both rules.

2. Y-RIGHT and Y-LEFT: The occurrence of Y in the conclusion is indexed by n and occurrences of Y in the antecedent by $n+1$.
3. DECLARATION: If t has the form $X = \phi$ then there is no change. If t has the form $x : \phi$ then if X is an n-indexed ν-variable in ϕ to the right of the turnstyle then the corresponding occurrence of X in ϕ to the left of the turnstyle is indexed by some $n' \leq n$.
4. CUT: For any ν-variable X, if X is active in ϕ then all occurrences of X in ϕ or ψ are indexed by the same index.

6.3 Regeneration and the Rule of Discharge

We can now state the property of regeneration and the rule of discharge.

Definition 8. (Regeneration) In a b.p.s. $\mathcal{B}$ let a path Π downwards from s to s' be given. Suppose that (1) ϕ' generates ϕ along Π, that (2) ϕ and ϕ' are identical up to indexing of variables, that (3) a variable Y is active in ϕ, that (4) Y names the fixed point formula $\sigma X.\psi$ at s', and that (5) ϕ' generates Y along some strict suffix of Π such that Y results from the application of one of the rules Y-RIGHT or Y-LEFT. Then ϕ is *σ-regenerated along Π (through Y).*

Definition 9. (Rule of Discharge) Let $\mathrm{FV}(E) = \{x_1, \ldots, x_k\}$ and let

$$s = \Gamma(x_1 : \phi_1, \ldots, x_k : \phi_k) \vdash E : \phi$$

be an occurrence of a hypothesis in a given basic proof structure $\mathcal{B}$. Then s can be discharged provided there below s is, up to indexing, an occurrence of a sequent

$$s' = \Gamma'(x_1 : \phi_1, \ldots, x_k : \phi_k) \vdash E : \phi$$

such that condition (1) below holds along with one of conditions (2) or (3):

1. For all ν-variables X with respect to s', if X is active in ϕ with index n and if X is active in ϕ_i, $1 \leq i \leq k$, with index n' then $n' \leq n$.
2. ϕ is ν-regenerated along the path from s' to s through some X, say. Then it has to be the case that for all $i : 1 \leq i \leq k$, if ϕ_i is ν-regenerated along the path from s' to s through some Y which is active in X then $Y = X$, and if n (n') is the index of X in ϕ in s (s') and if m (m') is the index of Y in ϕ_i in s (s') then $m - m' \leq n - n'$.
3. ϕ is μ-regenerated along the path from s' to s. Then it has to be the case for some $i : 1 \leq i \leq k$, that ϕ_i is μ-regenerated along the path from s' to s too. Moreover, for all $i : 1 \leq i \leq k$, if ϕ_i is ν-regenerated along the path from s' to s through some Y then Y is not active in ϕ.

7 Soundness

We prove that if $\Gamma \vdash E : \phi$ is provable then it is true. The proof uses approximation ordinals. A *partial σ-approximation* ι of a sequent $s = \Gamma \vdash P : \phi$ is a partial annotation of ordinals to names X in s such that if X occurs in ϕ then X is a ν-variable. It is important to keep apart approximation ordinals and indexing. The latter is a pure book-keeping device designed to keep track of the number of times ν-variables are unfolded as one passes upwards in a proof structure. The semantics of formulas is extended slightly to take variable declarations and approximations into account by the clause

$$\|X\|\Gamma\mathcal{V} = \|\sigma^{(\kappa)}Y.\phi\|\Gamma\mathcal{V}$$

when Γ contains the declaration $X = \sigma Y.\phi$ and X is annotated by κ.

Definition 10. (Truth for substitution and partial approximation) The sequent $\Gamma \vdash P : \phi$ is *true for a substitution* σ of agent variables to agents, *and a partial approximation* ι if $P\sigma \in \|\phi\|\Gamma$ provided for all x which are free in P, if $x : \phi_x$ is the declaration of x in Γ then $\sigma(x) \in \|\phi_x\|\Gamma$.

We now embark on the soundness proof proper. Assume that the sequent $s_0 = \Gamma_0 \vdash E_0 : \phi_0$ is false for a substitution σ_0 and partial approximation ι_0. For simplicity we assume that ϕ_0 has no free occurrences of variables. Assume also we have given a proof of $\Gamma_0 \vdash E_0 : \phi_0$. We trace an infinite sequence of the form $\Pi = (s_0, \sigma_0, \iota_0), (s_1, \sigma_1, \iota_1), \ldots$ such that for all i, s_i is false for σ_i and ι_i, and s_i is the conclusion of a proof rule instance for which s_{i+1} is an antecedent. By use of approximation ordinals, and using the fact that infinitely many points along Π must correspond to hypotheses that have been discharged we can then arrive at a contradiction.

Suppose the construction has arrived at the sequent $s_i = \Gamma_i \vdash E_i : \phi_i$. The following properties are maintained invariant:

Property 11 *1. Let any two occurrences of a free variable X in ϕ_i be given. If one occurrence is annotated by ι_i they both are, and then the annotations are identical. The same holds for any ψ occurring as part of a declaration $x : \psi$ in Γ_i.*

2. We assume for all ν-variables X that if X is active in both ϕ_i and Γ_i such that X is active in a declaration in Γ_i of a variable which is free in E_i, the active occurrence of X in ϕ_i is indexed by n and approximated by κ, and the active occurrence of X in Γ_i is indexed by n' and approximated by κ', then $\kappa' + n' \geq \kappa + n$.

To motivate the condition 11.2 note that $n - n'$ counts how many more times X to the right of the turnstyle has been unfolded than the corresponding occurrence to the left. In some cases, however, unfolding to the left may temporarily outpace unfoldings to the right, violating the invariant temporarily. We postpone discussion of this case until we see it arising.

We show how we can identify $(s_{i+1}, \sigma_{i+1}, \iota_{i+1})$ such that s_{i+1} is false for σ_{i+1} and ι_{i+1} by considering each potential rule in turn.

Structural rules. The only circumstance in which DECLARATION could apply is where some ν-variable occurrence to the left of the turnstyle is annotated by a smaller approximation ordinal than its corresponding occurrence to the right. However, the invariant condition gives $\kappa' + n' \geq \kappa + n$ and $n' \leq n$ (where κ, κ', n and n' are determined as in 11.2), hence $\kappa' \geq \kappa$. Suppose then that s_i results from an application of the rule CUT. Consider the instance

$$\text{CUT}\ \frac{\Gamma_1', \Gamma_2' \vdash E' : \phi' \quad \Gamma_1', x' : \phi', \Gamma_2' \vdash F' : \psi'}{\Gamma_1', \Gamma_2' \vdash F'[E'/x'] : \psi'}$$

so that $s_i = \Gamma_1', \Gamma_2' \vdash F'[E'/x'] : \psi'$. Assume that

(i) $\Gamma_1', \Gamma_2' \vdash E' : \phi'$ is truc for σ_i and ι_i' where ι_i' annotates variables in Γ_1' or Γ_2' as ι_i, and variables in ϕ' as the corresponding variables in ψ' in s_i.

(ii) $\Gamma_1', x' : \phi', \Gamma_2' \vdash F' : \psi'$ is true for the substitution σ_i' and ι_i' where
- σ_i' is the substitution for which $\sigma_i'(y) = \sigma_i(y)$ whenever $y \neq x'$ and for which $\sigma_i'(x') = E'\sigma_i$.
- ι_i' annotates variable occurrences in Γ_1', Γ_2', and ψ' as the corresponding occurrences in s_i, it annotates no occurrences of μ-variables in ϕ', and it annotates ν-variables in ϕ' as they are annotated in ψ by ι_i.

From (i) and (ii) it follows that s_i must be true for σ_i and ι_i, hence one of them must fail, and we pick as $(s_{i+1}, \sigma_{i+1}, \iota_{i+1})$ whichever combination that does fail. Note that, due to the side-condition concerning activity for CUT, we ensure that if all ν-variables are annotated in ψ' then the same is true for ϕ'. Note also that the invariants are maintained true by this construction. Note thirdly that it is this step in the construction that requires ν-variables to be approximated (hence also indexed) both to the right and to the left of the turnstyle. This situation does not arise for μ-variables.

Logical rules. The delicate case concerns the rule Y-LEFT, for Y a ν-variable. Let κ' be the annotation of Y. If κ' is a successor ordinal κ' can decremented by 1 without affecting the invariant. However, if κ' is a limit ordinal the invariant may have to be broken. This is the situation, in particular, when $n' \geq n$ — i.e. when the left hand side, due to the application of Y-LEFT is (temporarily) overtaking the right hand side when counting numbers of unfoldings of Y. In this situation we need in obtaining ι_{i+1} to replace κ' by some $\kappa'' < \kappa'$. *Any* such choice of κ'' is in principle possible. Choose some such κ'' at random, and we argue that by using a little backtracking we can eventually reinstate the invariant. The strategy is the following: In the context of any subsequent choice of s_j with $j \geq i+1$ let n refer to the index of Y to the right of the turnstyle, and n' refer to the index of Y in that particular declaration which is generated by the occurrence of Y which is currently being unfolded. Whenever $n \geq n'$ then we can inspect the invariant to see if it is still broken, and if it is then we can backtrack and increment our choice of κ'' to reinstate the invariant at that particular point. We cannot reach a leaf which is not a discharged occurrence of a hypothesis without this situation having arisen. For the same reason neither can we reach a loop sequent — i.e. a sequent which serves as justification for the discharge of a hypothesis. If we reach a discharged occurrence of a hypothesis then, because of conditions 9.1–3, we would know that $n \geq n'$ so the invariant will have been reinstated. But then the backtracking argument is completed since we can bound how far into the future we will have to go before we can guarantee that the invariant will have been reinstated. This argument is what motivates condition 9.1.

Dynamical rules. These cause no real complications and are left to the reader.

Global rules. Finally we need to consider the case where s_i is a discharged occurrence of a hypothesis. We then find a sequent s_j, $j \leq i$, which is the loop sequent justifying the discharge of s_i. s_i will have the form $s_i = \Gamma_i(x_1 : \phi_{i,1}, \ldots, x_k : \phi_{i,k}) \vdash E_i : \phi_i$ and s_j will have the form $s_j = \Gamma_j(x_1 : \phi_{i,1}, \ldots, x_k : \phi_{i,k}) \vdash E_i : \phi_i$ where $\mathrm{FV}(E) = \{x_1, \ldots, x_k\}$. We know that the invariant holds for s_j (and that no subsequent backtracking will modify the annotations of s_j). In identifying $(s_{i+1}, \sigma_{i+1}, \iota_{i+1})$ we wish to replace s_i by s_j keeping σ_i and ι_i unchanged. We need to check that the invariant is maintained. Let X be any ν-variable which is active in ϕ_i, indexed n_j in s_j, n_i in s_i, and annotated by, say, κ in s_i. Further, let X also be active in one of the $\phi_{i,j}$, indexed n'_j in s_j, n'_i in s_i, and annotated by κ' in s_i. Since the invariant holds for s_i we know that $\kappa' + n'_i \geq \kappa + n_i$. There are two cases: Either X is the ν-variable through which ϕ_i is regenerated, and then $\kappa' + n'_j \geq \kappa' + n'_i - n_i + n_j \geq \kappa + n_j$ as desired. Otherwise ϕ_i is regenerated through some other ν- or μ-variable. In this case we know that, since X is active in ϕ_i that $n_i = n_j$. Moreover by conditions 9.2 and 3 we know that, since X is also active in $\phi_{i,j}$, that $n'_i = n'_j$ too. Hence also here $\kappa' + n'_j \geq \kappa + n_j$ and we have shown the invariant to be maintained. Now $(s_{i+1}, \sigma_{i+1}, \iota_{i+1})$ can be derived since one of the local rules apply.

Completing the proof. Having built the infinite sequence Π we find a σ-variable X which is infinitely often regenerated to the right of the turnstyle along Π. If $\sigma = \nu$ a contradiction is obtained since the initial annotation of X is infinitely often decreased along Π. If $\sigma = \mu$ we find a μ-variable which is infinitely often unfolded to the left of the turnstyle along Π and a similar argument applies, completing the soundness proof.

8 Completeness for Finite-state Processes

While we view soundness for general processes as the main contribution of the paper, completeness for finite-state processes is important as a check that no proof power has accidentally been sacrificed.

Theorem 12. *If P is a well-guarded finite-state process and $\models P : \phi$ then $\vdash P : \phi$ is provable.*

Proof. (Outline) Theorem 12 can be proved by embedding the tableau based model checker of Stirling and Walker [13] into the present setting. Consider the proof system obtained by restricting attention to sequents $\Gamma \vdash P : \phi$ where only namings are allowed in Γ, and where the dynamical rules are replaced by the following two global rules:

$$\langle\alpha\rangle\text{-RIGHT}\ \frac{\Gamma \vdash P' : \phi}{\Gamma \vdash P : \langle\alpha\rangle\phi}\ (P \xrightarrow{\alpha} P)$$

$$[\alpha]\text{-RIGHT}\ \frac{\{\Gamma \vdash P' : \phi \mid P \xrightarrow{\alpha} P'\}}{\Gamma \vdash P : [\alpha]\phi}$$

The rule of discharge is modified by allowing a sequent $s = \Gamma \vdash P : X$ to be discharged whenever X is a ν-variable and there strictly below s is another sequent of the form $\Gamma' \vdash P : X$. Call the proof system ensuing from these changes the *Stirling-Walker system*, and write $\Gamma \vdash_{sw} P : \phi$ for provability in this system. By soundness and completeness [13] we know that $\models P : \phi$ iff $\vdash_{sw} P : \phi$. So assume that P is finite-state and that a proof π of $\vdash_{sw} P : \phi$ is given. Assume for simplicity that $P = P_1 \mid P_2$. We derive by induction in the size of π formulas ϕ_1 and ϕ_2 such that $\vdash_{sw} P_1 : \phi_1$ and $\vdash_{sw} P_2 : \phi_2$ by proofs of size not greater than the size of π, and $x_1 : \phi_1, x_2 : \phi_2 \vdash x_1 \mid x_2 : \phi$ is provable in the compositional system. The details (which are not very difficult) are left out. Once a similar result has been proved for restriction (which is quite simple), it is an easy induction in the size of proof of $\vdash_{sw} P : \phi$ to show that then $\vdash P : \phi$ is provable in the compositional proof system too, establishing the result. □

In fact — since model checking in the Stirling-Walker system is decidable for finite-state processes — the proof of Theorem 12 gives an effective strategy for building proofs. Other strategies can be devised, based on e.g. characteristic formulas. Notice also that the proof makes only limited use of the global rules. Termination is needed for greatest fixed points only, and the side-conditions concerning activity and indexing can be eliminated altogether in favour of the much simpler side-condition for CUT that ϕ is a closed formula.

9 Conclusion

A precursor of the present work is [1] where a proof system for a process passing calculus is presented, though recursive specifications are not addressed.

The main issues left for future work are analyses of the proof power of the general proof system, and of its practical usefulness. The latter is best evaluated through experimentation. Constructed, as they are, in a systematic way, the local rules may turn out to be quite natural once practice is built up. Moreover, being compositional the proof system is well suited to support macros and derived rules. The quite complicated side-conditions, on the other hand, may seem disconcerting. The hope is that in most practical situations the technicalities concerning indexing and activity can in fact be hidden.

The only completeness criterion we have considered here is weak completeness for finite-state processes. Stronger completeness results are needed, maybe along the lines of the so-called well-described formulas explored in [1]. In this case rules which are not needed for weak completeness such as $\wedge$-$\vee$ distribution ($x : \phi \wedge (\psi \vee \gamma) \vdash x : (\phi \wedge \psi) \vee (\phi \wedge \gamma)$) and monotonicity under the modal operators (e.g. $x : \phi \vdash x : \psi$ implies $x : \langle\alpha\rangle\phi \vdash x : \langle\alpha\rangle\psi$) must be added. For unguarded recursive process terms our proof system is in most cases ineffective. It should be possible to remedy this by adding further reasoning principles along the lines of Hungar's "box recurrences" [8].

Another issue is to investigate the power of our approach for general, say, GSOS definable languages (c.f. Simpson's recent work on Hennessy-Milner logic [12]). For instance it is quite easy based on the present ideas to develop a sound proof system for context-free processes. Is this proof system complete?

Acknowledgements. Thanks are due to Roberto Amadio for numerous discussions on related topics.

References

1. R. Amadio and M. Dam. Reasoning about higher-order processes. SICS Research report RR:94–18, 1994. To appear in Proc. CAAP'95.
2. H. Andersen, C. Stirling, and G. Winskel. A compositional proof system for the modal μ-calculus. In Proc. LICS'94, 1994.
3. J. Bradfield and C. Stirling. Local model checking for infinite state spaces. *Theoretical Computer Science*, 96:157–174, 1992.
4. R. Cleaveland, M. Dreimüller, and B. Steffen. Faster model checking for the modal mu-calculus. In Proc. CAV'92, *Lecture Notes in Computer Science*, 663:383–394, 1992.
5. M. Dam. Model checking mobile processes (full version). SICS report RR 94:1, 1994. Prel. version appeared in Proc. Concur'93, LNCS 715, pp. 22–36.
6. E. A. Emerson and C. Lei. Efficient model checking in fragments of the propositional mu-calculus. In Proc. LICS'86, pages 267–278, 1986.
7. J. Esparza. Decidability of model checking for infinite-state concurrent systems. Manuscript, 1995.
8. H. Hungar. Model checking of macro processes. In Proc. CAV'94, *Lecture Notes in Computer Science*, 818:169–181, 1994.
9. K. G. Larsen. Efficient local correctness checking. In Proc. CAV'92, *Lecture Notes in Computer Science*, 663, 1992.
10. K. G. Larsen and L. Xinxin. Compositionality through an operational semantics of contexts. *Journal of Logic and Computation*, 1:761–795, 1991.
11. R. Milner. *Communication and Concurrency.* Prentice Hall International, 1989.
12. A. Simpson. Compositionality via cut-elimination: Hennessy-Milner logic for an arbitrary GSOS. Manuscript. To appear in Proc. LICS'95, 1995.
13. C. Stirling and D. Walker. Local model checking in the modal mu-calculus. *Theoretical Computer Science*, 89:161–177, 1991.
14. R. S. Streett and E. A. Emerson. An automata theoretic decision procedure for the propositional mu-calculus. *Information and Computation*, **81**:249–264, 1989.

Compositional Model Checking of Real Time Systems *

François Laroussinie, Kim G. Larsen

BRICS** , Aalborg Univ., Denmark ***

Abstract. We present a compositional model checking technique for networks of timed automata. This method is based on the same idea as the recent method proposed by Andersen [4] for untimed case. We present a quotient construction, which allows timed automata components to be gradually moved from the network expression into the specification. The intermediate specifications are kept small using minimization heuristics suggested by Andersen. The potential of the combined technique is demonstrated using a prototype implemented in CAML.

1 Introduction

Within the last decade model checking has turned out to be a useful technique for verifying temporal properties of finite state systems. Efficient model checking algorithms for finite state systems have been obtained with respect to a number of logics, and in the last few years, model checking techniques have been extended to real–time systems and logics using the region technique of Alur, Courcoubetis and Dill [1]. However, the major problem in applying model checking even to moderate–size systems is the potential combinatorial explosion of the state space arising from parallel composition. For real–time systems an additional explosion is induced in the number of regions. In order to avoid this problem algorithms have been sought that avoid exhaustive state (region) space exploration, either by *symbolic* representation of the states space such as in [13] and in the use of Binary Decision Diagrams [8], by application of *partial order* methods [12, 23] which suppresses unnecesarry interleavings of transitions, or by application of *abstractions* and *symmetries* [9, 10, 11].

So far the most successful results for larger systems have been obtained using the heuristics of Binary Decision Diagrams. However, recent work by Andersen [4] introduces a new very promising heuristic model checking technique for finite state systems, for which experimental results on specific examples shows an improvement compared with Binary Decision Diagrams. The technique is based on compositional proof rules for parallel composition.

* This work has been supported by the European Communities under CONCUR2, BRA 7166

** Basic Research in Computer Science, Centre of the Danish National Research Foundation.

*** Dept. of Computer Science, Aalborg University, Fredrik Bajers Vej 7-E, DK-9220 Aalborg, Denmark, (email: {fl,kgl}@iesd.auc.dk) fax: (45) 98.15.81.29

The aim of this paper is to make this new successful (compositional) model checking technique by Andersen [4] applicable to real–time systems. For example, consider the following typical model checking problem $(\mathcal{S}_1 \mid \ldots \mid \mathcal{S}_n) \models \varphi$ where the $\mathcal{S}_i$'s are real–time systems (described as timed automata [2]). We want to verify that the parallel composition of these timed automata satisfies the formula φ without having to construct the complete state (region) space of the process $(\mathcal{S}_1 \mid \ldots \mid \mathcal{S}_n)$. We will avoid this complete construction by removing the components $\mathcal{S}_i$ one by one while simultaneously transforming the formula accordingly. Thus, when removing the component $\mathcal{S}_n$ we will transform the formula φ into the *quotient* formula $\varphi \,/\, \mathcal{S}_n$ such that

$$\Big(\mathcal{S}_1 \mid \ldots \mid \mathcal{S}_n\Big) \models \varphi \quad \text{if and only if} \quad \Big(\mathcal{S}_1 \mid \ldots \mid \mathcal{S}_{n-1}\Big) \models \varphi \,/\, \mathcal{S}_n \tag{1}$$

Now clearly, if the quotient is not much larger than the original formula we have succeeded in simplifying the problem. Repeated application of quotienting yields

$$\Big(\mathcal{S}_1 \mid \ldots \mid \mathcal{S}_n\Big) \models \varphi \quad \text{if and only if} \quad \mathbf{1} \models \varphi \,/\, \mathcal{S}_n \,/ \mathcal{S}_{n-1} \,/\, \ldots \,/\, \mathcal{S}_1 \tag{2}$$

where $\mathbf{1}$ is the unit with respect to parallel composition.

For finite state systems the quotient with respect to parallel composition is an immediate application of work on compositional reasoning due to Andersen, Larsen, Stirling, Winskel and Xinxin [17, 18, 6, 5]. However, based on these ideas alone, (2) provides no solution to the problem as the explosion will now occur in the size of the final quotient formula instead. The crucial and experimentally "verified" observation by Andersen was that each quotienting should be followed by a *minimization* of the formula based on a collection of few, efficiently implementable strategies.

In this paper we provide the basis for and make an initial experimental investigation of the application of Andersen's compositional model checking technique for real–time systems (timed automata). In particular,

– We give an effective construction of the quotient formula $\varphi \,/\, \mathcal{S}$ satisfying the requirement of (1) for φ a formula of the timed logic L_ν introduced in [16] and $\mathcal{S}$ a real–time system given in terms of a timed automaton;
– Based on a prototype implemented in CAML we make an experimental investigation of the above quotient construction combined with (some of) the minimization heuristics of Andersen. In the examples we consider the minimized quotient formulas have been subject to dramatic reductions and are comparable in size to the original formulas. Thus, we may expect compositional model checking to be successful also for real–time systems.

The remainder of this paper is organized as follows: in the next section we give a short presentation of the notion of timed automata and composition used in this paper; in section 3, the logic L_ν is shortly presented, and in section 4 we review the region technique by Alur, Courcoubetis and Dill [1]. Section 5 presents the quotient construction, whereas section 6 presents and investigates the consequences of minimization.

2 Timed Transition Systems and Automata

Let $\mathcal{A}$ be a finite set of actions ranged over by $a, b, c, \ldots$. We denote by $\mathbf{N}$ the set of natural numbers and by $\mathbf{R}$ the set of non–negative real numbers. $\mathcal{D}$ denotes the set of delay actions $\{\epsilon(d) \mid d \in \mathbf{R}\}$, and $\mathcal{L}$ denotes the union $\mathcal{A} \cup \mathcal{D}$.

Definition 1. *A timed transition system over $\mathcal{A}$ is a tuple $\mathcal{S} = \langle S, s_0, \longrightarrow\rangle$, where S is a set of states, s_0 is the initial state and $\longrightarrow \subseteq S \times \mathcal{L} \times S$ is a transition relation. We require that for any $s \in S$ and $d \in \mathbf{R}$, there exists a (unique) state s^d such that $s \xrightarrow{\epsilon(d)} s^d$. Moreover $(s^d)^e = s^{d+e}$* [4].

Obviously, we may apply the standard notion of bisimulation [21, 19] to timed transition systems. For $\mathcal{S} = \langle S, s_0, \longrightarrow\rangle$ a timed transition system, strong (timed) bisimulation $\sim$ is defined as the largest symmetric relation over S such that whenever $s_1 \sim s_2$, $\ell \in \mathcal{A} \cup \mathcal{D}$ and $s_1 \xrightarrow{\ell} s_1'$ then there exists s_2' such that $s_2 \xrightarrow{\ell} s_2'$ and $s_1' \sim s_2'$. We may compare states from different timed transition systems by considering their disjoint union. Two timed transition systems $\mathcal{S}_1$ and $\mathcal{S}_2$ are said to be strong (timed) bisimilar, written $\mathcal{S}_1 \sim \mathcal{S}_2$, in case their initial states are strong bisimilar.

In order to study compositionality problems we introduce a parallel composition between timed transition systems. Following [14] we suggest a composition parameterized with a synchronization function generalizing a large range of existing notions of parallel compositions. A *synchronization function* f is a partial function $(\mathcal{A} \cup \{0\}) \times (\mathcal{A} \cup \{0\}) \hookrightarrow \mathcal{A}$, where 0 denotes a distinguished no–action symbol [5]. Now, let $\mathcal{S}_i = \langle S_i, s_{i,0}, \longrightarrow_i\rangle$, $i = 1, 2$, be two timed transition systems and let f be a synchronization function. Then the *parallel composition* $\mathcal{S}_1 \mid_f \mathcal{S}_2$ is the timed transition system $\langle S, s_0, \longrightarrow\rangle$, where $s_1 \mid_f s_2 \in S$ whenever $s_1 \in S_1$ and $s_2 \in S_2$, $s_0 = s_{1,0} \mid_f s_{2,0}$, and $\longrightarrow$ is given by the rule [6]:

$$\frac{s_1 \xrightarrow{a}_1 s_1' \qquad s_2 \xrightarrow{b}_2 s_2'}{s_1 \mid_f s_2 \xrightarrow{c} s_1' \mid_f s_2'} \; f(a,b) \simeq c$$

and the requirement that for any $d \in \mathbf{R}$, $(s_1 \mid_f s_2)^d = ({s_1}^d \mid_f {s_2}^d)$.

Syntactically, timed transition systems are described by timed automata [2], which are finite automata extended with a finite collection of real–valued clocks [7]. If C is a set of clocks, $\mathcal{B}(C)$ denotes the set of formulas built using boolean connectives over atomic formulas of the form $x \leq m$, $m \leq x$, $x \leq y + m$ and $y + m \leq x$ with $x, y \in C$ and $m \in \mathbf{N}$. Moreover $\mathcal{B}_M(C)$ denotes the subset of $\mathcal{B}(C)$ with no constant greater than M.

4 The existence of s^d corresponds to transition liveness, its unicity corresponds to time-determinism and the property $(s^d)^e = s(d + e)$ corresponds to time-continuity (or time-additivity) in [24].

5 We extend the transition relation of a timed transition system such that $s \xrightarrow{0} s'$ iff $s = s'$.

6 $f(a, b) \simeq c$ holds if f is defined for the pair (a, b) and the result is c.

7 Timed transition systems may alternatively be described using timed process calculi.

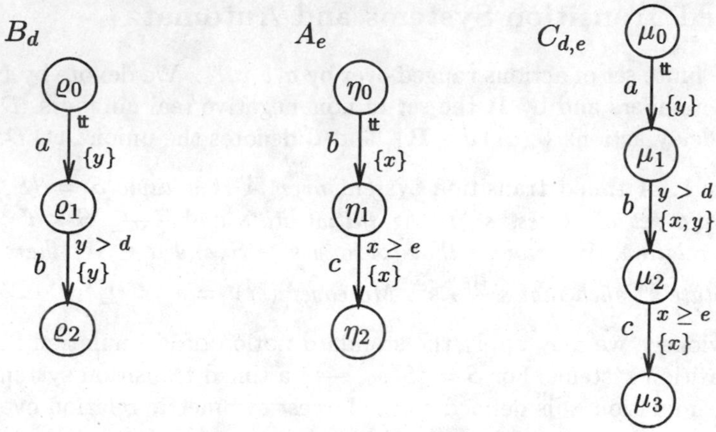

Fig. 1. Three timed automata

Definition 2. *A timed automaton A over $\mathcal{A}$ is a tuple $\langle N, \eta_0, C, E\rangle$ where N is a finite set of nodes, η_0 is the initial node, C is a finite set of clocks, and $E \subseteq N \times N \times \mathcal{A} \times 2^C \times \mathcal{B}(C)$ corresponds to the set of edges. $e = \langle \eta, \eta', a, r, b\rangle \in E$ represents an edge from the node η to the node η' with action a, r denoting the set of clocks to be reset and b is the enabling condition over the clocks of A.*

Example 1. Consider the automata A_e, B_d and $C_{d,e}$ in Figure 1 ($d, e \in \mathbf{N}$). The automaton $C_{d,e}$ has four nodes, μ_0, μ_1, μ_2 and μ_3, two clocks x and y, and three edges. The edge between μ_1 and μ_2 has b as action, $\{x, y\}$ as reset set and the enabling condition for the edge is $y > d$. □

Informally, the system starts at node η_0 with all its clocks initialized to 0. The values of the clocks increase synchronously with time. At any time, the automaton whose current node is η can change node by following an edge $\langle \eta, \eta', a, r, b\rangle \in E$ provided the current values of the clocks satisfy b. With this transition the clocks in r get reset to 0.

Formally a time assignment v for C is a function from C to $\mathbf{R}$. We denote by $\mathbf{R}^C$ the set of time assignments for C. For $v \in \mathbf{R}^C$, $x \in C$ and $d \in \mathbf{R}$, $v + d$ denotes the time assignment which maps each clock x in C to the value $v(x) + d$. For $C' \subseteq C$, $[C' \mapsto 0]v$ denotes the assignment for C which maps each clock in C' to the value 0 and agrees with v over $C \backslash C'$. Whenever $v \in \mathbf{R}^C$, $u \in \mathbf{R}^K$ and C and K are disjoint vu denotes the time assignment over $C \cup K$ such that $(vu)(x) = v(x)$ if $x \in C$ and $(vu)(x) = u(x)$ if $x \in K$. Given a condition $b \in \mathcal{B}(C)$ and a time assignment $v \in \mathbf{R}^C$, $b(v)$ is a boolean value describing whether b is satisfied by v or not. Finally a k–clock automata is a timed automata $\langle N, \eta_0, C, E\rangle$ such that $|C| = k$.

A *state* of an automaton A is a pair (η, v) where η is a node of A and v a time assignment for C. The initial state of A is (η_0, v_0) where v_0 is the time assignment mapping all clocks in C to 0.

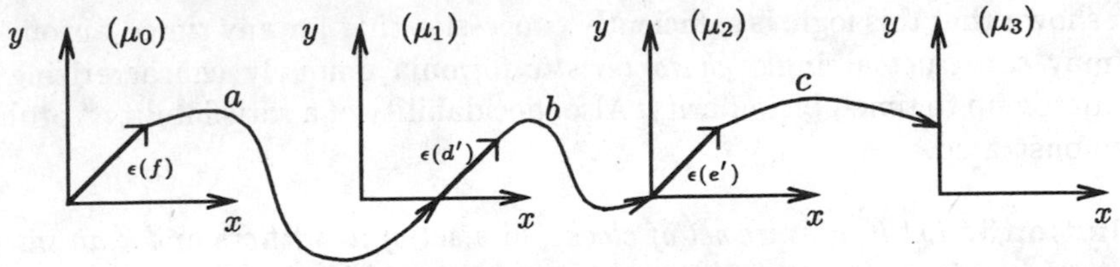

Fig. 2. Partial Behaviour of $C_{d,e}$.

The semantics of A is given by the timed transition system $\mathcal{S}_A = \langle S_A, \sigma_0, \longrightarrow_A \rangle$, where S_A is the set of states of A, σ_0 is the initial state (η_0, v_0), and $\longrightarrow_A$ is the transition relation defined as follows:

$$(\eta, v) \xrightarrow{a} (\eta', v') \text{ iff } \exists r, b.\ \langle \eta, \eta', a, r, b \rangle \in E \wedge b(v) \wedge v' = [r \mapsto 0]v$$
$$(\eta, v) \xrightarrow{\epsilon(d)} (\eta', v') \text{ iff } \eta = \eta' \text{ and } v' = v + d$$

Example 2. Reconsider the automaton $C_{d,e}$ of Figure 1. The coordinate systems in Figure 2 indicates (some of) the states of $C_{d,e}$. Each point of the coordinate systems represents a unique time assignment, with the coordinate systems representing states involving the nodes μ_0, μ_1, μ_2 and μ_3 respectively. We have indicated the following typical transition sequence (where $f \geq 0$, $d' > d$ and $e' \geq e$):

$$(\mu_0, (0,0)) \xrightarrow{\epsilon(f)} (\mu_0, (f, f)) \xrightarrow{a} (\mu_1, (f, 0)) \xrightarrow{\epsilon(d')} (\mu_1, (f + d', d'))$$
$$(\mu_1, (f + d', d')) \xrightarrow{b} (\mu_2, (0, 0)) \xrightarrow{\epsilon(e')} (\mu_2, (e', e')) \xrightarrow{c}$$

□

Parallel composition may now be extended to timed automata in the obvious way: for two timed automata A and B and a synchronization function f, the parallel composition $A \,|_f\, B$ denotes the timed transition system $\mathcal{S}_A \,|_f\, \mathcal{S}_b$. For two automata A and B and a synchronization function f one may effectively construct an automaton $A \otimes_f B$ such that $\mathcal{S}_{A \otimes_f B}$ is strong bisimilar to $\mathcal{S}_A \,|_f\, \mathcal{S}_B$. The nodes of $A \otimes_f B$ is simply the product of A's and B's nodes, the set of clocks is the (disjoint) union of A's and B's clocks, and the edges are based on synchronizable A and B edges with enabling conditions conjuncted and reset–sets unioned.

Example 3. Let f be the synchronization function completely specified by $f(a, 0) = a$, $f(b, b) = b$ and $f(0, c) = c$. Then the automaton $C_{d,e}$ in Figure 1 is isomorphic to the part of $B_d \otimes_f A_e$ which is reachable from (ρ_0, η_0). □

3 Timed Logic

We consider a dense–time logic L_ν with clocks and recursion. This logic may be seen as a certain fragment [8] of the μ–calculus T_μ presented in [13]. In [16] it has

[8] allowing only maximal recursion and using a slightly different notion of model

been shown that this logic is sufficiently expressive that for any timed automaton one may construct a single *characteristic* formula uniquely characterizing the automaton up to timed bisimilarity. Also, decidability of a satisfiability [9] problem is demonstrated.

Definition 3. *Let K a finite set of clocks,* Id *a set of identifiers and k an integer. The set L_ν of formulae over K,* Id *and k is generated by the abstract syntax with φ and ψ ranging over L_ν:*

$$\varphi ::= \mathtt{tt} \mid \mathtt{ff} \mid \varphi \wedge \psi \mid \varphi \vee \psi \mid \exists\, \varphi \mid \forall\, \varphi \mid \langle a \rangle\, \varphi \mid [a]\, \varphi$$
$$\mid x \,\mathsf{in}\, \varphi \mid x + n \bowtie y + m \mid\mid x \bowtie m \mid Z$$

where $a \in \mathcal{A}$; $x, y \in K$; $n, m \in \{0, 1, \ldots, k\}$; $\bowtie \in \{=, <, \leq, >, \geq\}$ and $Z \in$ Id.

The meaning of the identifiers is specified by a declaration $\mathcal{D}$ assigning a formula of L_ν to each identifier. When $\mathcal{D}$ is understood we write $Z \stackrel{\text{def}}{=} \varphi$ for $\mathcal{D}(Z) = \varphi$. The K clocks are called *formula clocks* and a formula φ is said to be *closed* if every formula clock x occurring in φ is in the scope of an "x in ..." operator.

Given a timed transition system $\mathcal{S}$ we interpret the L_ν formulas over an *extended state* $\langle s, u \rangle$, where s is a state of $\mathcal{S}$ and u is a time assignment for K. Informally, $\exists\, \varphi$ holds in an extended state if there is a delay transition leading to an extended state satisfying φ. Thus $\exists$ denotes existential quantification over (arbitrary) delay transitions. Similarly, $\forall$ denotes universal quantification over delay transitions, and $\langle a \rangle$ (resp. $[a]$) denotes existential (resp. universal) quantification over a–transitions. The formula ($x$inφ) initializes the formula clock x to 0; i.e. an extended state satisfies the formula in case the modified state with x being reset to 0 satisfies φ. Introduced formula clocks are used by formulas of the type $(x + n \bowtie y + m)$, which is satisfied by an extended state provided the values of the named formula clocks satisfies the required relationship. Finally, an extended state satisfies an identifier Z if it satisfies the corresponding declaration (or definition) $\mathcal{D}(Z)$. Formally, the satisfaction relation $\models_{\mathcal{D}}$ between extended states and formulas is defined as the largest relation satisfying the implications of Table 1. We have left out the cases for $\vee$, $[a]$ and $\forall$ as they are immediate duals.

Any relation satisfying the implications in Table 1 is called a *satisfiability* relation. It follows from standard fixpoint theory [22] that $\models_{\mathcal{D}}$ is the union of all satisfiability relations and that the implications in Table 1 in fact are bi-implications for $\models_{\mathcal{D}}$. We say that $\mathcal{S}$ satisfies a closed L_ν formula φ and write $\mathcal{S} \models \varphi$ when $\langle s_0, u \rangle \models_{\mathcal{D}} \varphi$ for any u. Note that if φ is closed, then $\langle s, u \rangle \models_{\mathcal{D}} \varphi$ iff $\langle s, u' \rangle \models_{\mathcal{D}} \varphi$ for any $u, u' \in \mathbf{R}^K$. Similarly, we say that a timed automaton A satisfies a closed L_ν formula φ in case $\mathcal{S}_A \models_{\mathcal{D}} \varphi$. We write $A \models_{\mathcal{D}} \varphi$ in this case.

[9] Bounded in the number of clocks and maximal constant allowed in the satisfying automata.

$$
\begin{aligned}
\langle s,u\rangle \models_{\mathcal{D}} \mathtt{tt} &\Rightarrow \text{true}\\
\langle s,u\rangle \models_{\mathcal{D}} \mathtt{ff} &\Rightarrow \text{false}\\
\langle s,u\rangle \models_{\mathcal{D}} \varphi \wedge \psi &\Rightarrow \langle s,u\rangle \models_{\mathcal{D}} \varphi \text{ and } \langle s,u\rangle \models_{\mathcal{D}} \psi\\
\langle s,u\rangle \models_{\mathcal{D}} \exists \varphi &\Rightarrow \exists d \in \mathbf{R}.\ \langle s^d, u+d\rangle \models_{\mathcal{D}} \varphi\\
\langle s,u\rangle \models_{\mathcal{D}} \langle a\rangle \varphi &\Rightarrow \exists s'.\ s \xrightarrow{a} s' \text{ and } \langle s',u\rangle \models_{\mathcal{D}} \varphi\\
\langle s,u\rangle \models_{\mathcal{D}} x+m \bowtie y+n &\Rightarrow u(x)+m \bowtie u(y)+n\\
\langle s,u\rangle \models_{\mathcal{D}} x \,\mathsf{in}\, \varphi &\Rightarrow \langle s,u'\rangle \models_{\mathcal{D}} \varphi \text{ where } u' = [\{x\} \mapsto 0]u\\
\langle s,u\rangle \models_{\mathcal{D}} Z &\Rightarrow \langle s,u\rangle \models_{\mathcal{D}} \mathcal{D}(Z)
\end{aligned}
$$

Table 1. Definition of satisfiability.

Example 4. Consider the following declaration $\mathcal{F}$ of the identifiers X_g and Z_g where $g \in \mathbf{N}$.

$$\mathcal{F} = \left\{ X_g \overset{\text{def}}{=} [a]\Big(y \,\mathsf{in}\, Z_g\Big), \quad Z_g \overset{\text{def}}{=} (y > g) \vee \Big([c]\mathtt{ff} \wedge [a]Z_g \wedge [b]Z_g \wedge \forall Z_g\Big) \right\}$$

That is X_g expresses the property that the accumulated time between an initial a– and a following c–transition must exceed g. Thus for any transition sequence of the form (where $\alpha_i \in \{a,b\}$): $s_0 \xrightarrow{a} t_0 \xrightarrow{\epsilon(d_1)} s_1 \xrightarrow{\alpha_1} t_2 \xrightarrow{\epsilon(d_2)} s_2 \xrightarrow{\alpha_2} \cdots t_n \xrightarrow{\epsilon(d_n)} s_n \xrightarrow{c}$ With $\sum d_i > g$. Now, reconsider the automata A_e, B_d and $C_{d,e}$ of Figure 1 and Examples 1 and 2. Then it may be argued that $C_{d,e} \models_{\mathcal{F}} X_{d+e}$ and (consequently), that $B_d \,|_f\, A_e \models_{\mathcal{F}} X_{d+e}$. □

Combining the parameterized parallel composition with L_ν we are able to express timed bisimilarity between timed transition systems as a single formula. This provides a timed extension of a similar characterization of strong bisimilarity for finite state systems [3]: First we close the action set $\mathcal{A}$ under tagging; i.e. $\mathcal{A}^t = \mathcal{A} \cup \mathcal{A} \times \{l\} \cup \mathcal{A} \times \{r\}$. Now consider the 'interleaving' synchronization function h over $\mathcal{A}^t$ completely defined by $h(a,0) = a_l$ and $h(0,a) = a_r$ where $a \in \mathcal{A}$ (i.e. h is undefined for all other pairs). Consider the following declaration $\mathcal{E}$ of the identifier $\mathcal{Z}$:

$$\mathcal{Z} \overset{\text{def}}{=} \bigwedge_{a \in \mathcal{A}} \Big([a_l]\langle a_r\rangle \mathcal{Z} \wedge [a_r]\langle a_l\rangle \mathcal{Z}\Big) \wedge \forall \mathcal{Z}$$

Then timed bisimilarity between timed transition systems is characterized as follows [10]:

Theorem 4. Let $\mathcal{S}$ be a timed transition system over $\mathcal{A}$, and let s_1, s_2 be states of $\mathcal{S}$. Then $s_1 \sim s_2$ if and only if $s_1 \,|_h\, s_2 \models_{\mathcal{E}} \mathcal{Z}$.

[10] It may be shown that the speed relation of [20] is characterized in a similar manner by Y defined recursively by $Y \overset{\text{def}}{=} \bigwedge_{a \in \mathcal{A}} ([a_1]\exists\langle a_2\rangle Y \wedge [a_2]\langle a_1\rangle Y) \wedge \forall Y$.

4 Regions

The model-checking problem for L_ν consists in deciding if a given timed automata A satisfies a given specification φ in L_ν. In [16] this problem has been shown decidable using the region technique of Alur and Dill [2, 1]. The region technique provides an abstract interpretation of timed automata sufficiently complete that all information necessary for model–checking with respect to L_ν is maintained, yet finitary and thus enabling standard algorithmic model–checking techniques to be applied.

The basic idea is that, given a timed automaton A, two states (η, v_1) and (η, v_2) which are close enough with respect to their clocks values (we will say that v_1 and v_2 are in the same *region*) can perform the same actions, and two extended states $\langle(\eta, v_1), u_1\rangle$ and $\langle(\eta, v_2), u_2\rangle$ where $v_1\, u_1$ and $v_2\, u_2$ are in the same region, satisfy the same L_ν formulas [11].

In fact the regions are defined as equivalence classes of a relation $\doteq$ over time assignments [13]. Formally, given C a set of clocks and k an integer, we say $u \doteq v$ if and only if u and v satisfy the same conditions of $\mathcal{B}_k(C)$. $[u]$ denotes the region which contains the time assignment u. $\mathcal{R}_k^C$ denotes the set of all regions for a set C of clocks and the maximal constant k. From a decision point of view it is important to note that $\mathcal{R}_k^C$ is finite.

For a region $\gamma \in \mathcal{R}_k^C$, we can define $b(\gamma)$ as the truth value of $b(u)$ for any u in γ. Conversely given a region γ, we can easily build a formula of $\mathcal{B}(C)$, called $\beta(\gamma)$, such that $\beta(\gamma)(u) = \mathtt{tt}$ iff $u \in \gamma$. Thus, given a region γ', $\beta(\gamma)(\gamma')$ is mapped to the value $\mathtt{tt}$ precisely when $\gamma = \gamma'$. Finally, note that $\beta(\gamma)$ itself can be viewed as a L_ν formula.

Given a region $[u]$ in $\mathcal{R}_k^C$ and $C' \subseteq C$ we define the following reset operator: $[C' \mapsto 0][u] = [[C' \mapsto 0]u]$. Moreover given a region γ, we can define the successor region of γ (denoted by $succ(\gamma)$): Informally the change from γ to $succ(\gamma)$ correspond to the minimal elapse of time which can modify the enabled actions of the current state(a formal definition is given in [16]).

We denote by γ^l the lth successor region of γ (i.e. $\gamma^l = succ^l(\gamma)$). From each region γ, it is possible to reach a region γ' s.t. $succ(\gamma') = \gamma'$, and we denote by l_γ the required number of step s.t. $\gamma^{l_\gamma} = succ(\gamma^{l_\gamma})$.

Example 5. Figure 3 gives an overview of the set of regions defined by two clocks x and y, and the maximal constant 1. In this case there are 32 different regions, of which only 17 are numbered in the figure. Corresponding $\mathcal{B}(C)$–formulas as well as successor regions are indicated for some of the regions. In general successor regions are determined by following 45° lines upwards to the right. □

Given a timed automata $A = \langle \mathcal{A}, N, \eta_0, C, E\rangle$, let k_A be the maximal constant occurring in the enabling condition of the edges E. Then for any $k \geq k_A$ we can define a symbolic semantics of A over symbolic states $[\eta, \gamma]_A$ where $\eta \in N$ and $\gamma \in \mathcal{R}_k^C$ as follows: for any $[\eta, \gamma]$ we have $[\eta, \gamma]_A \xrightarrow{a} [\eta', \gamma']_A$ iff $\exists\, u \in \gamma,\ \langle \eta, u\rangle_A \xrightarrow{a} \langle \eta', u'\rangle_A$ and $u' \in \gamma'$.

[11] W.l.o.g. we will in all the following assume that K and C are disjoint.

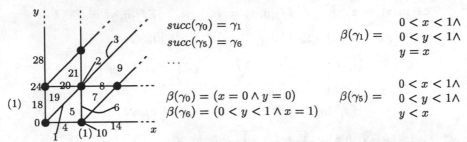

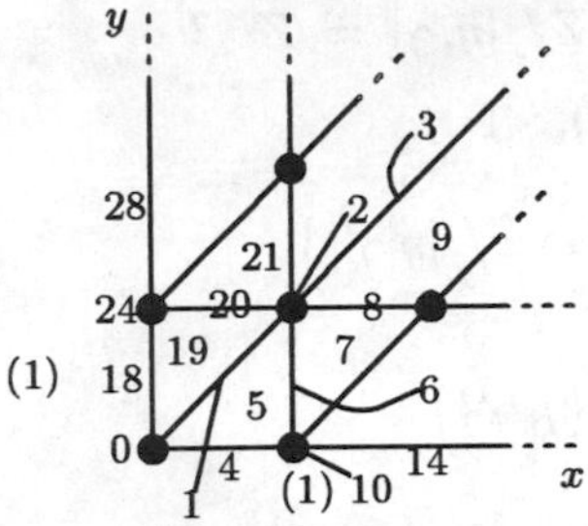

$$succ(\gamma_0) = \gamma_1$$
$$succ(\gamma_5) = \gamma_6$$
$$\ldots$$

$$\beta(\gamma_0) = (x = 0 \wedge y = 0)$$
$$\beta(\gamma_6) = (0 < y < 1 \wedge x = 1)$$

$$\beta(\gamma_1) = \begin{array}{l} 0 < x < 1 \wedge \\ 0 < y < 1 \wedge \\ y = x \end{array}$$

$$\beta(\gamma_5) = \begin{array}{l} 0 < x < 1 \wedge \\ 0 < y < 1 \wedge \\ y < x \end{array}$$

Fig. 3. $\mathcal{R}_k^C$ with $C = \{x, y\}$ and $k = 1$

Consider now L_ν with respect to formula clock set K and maximal constant k_L. Also consider a given timed automata $A = \langle N, \eta_0, C, E \rangle$ (s.t. K and C are disjoint). Then an *extended symbolic state* is a pair $[\eta, \gamma]_{A^+}$ where $\eta \in N$ and $\gamma \in \mathcal{R}_k^{C \cup K}$ with $k = max(k_A, k_L)$. Using the finitary symbolic semantics of timed automata a symbolic interpretation of L_ν formulas over extended symbolic states is defined in [16] faithfully reflecting the standard interpretation in Table 1. This symbolic interpretation provides the basis for decidability of model–checking for L_ν, and consequently (due to Theorem 4) for decidability of timed bisimilarity between timed automata.

5 Quotienting

Given an L_ν formula φ, and two timed transition systems $\mathcal{S}_1$ and $\mathcal{S}_2$ we aim at constructing a formula (called the *quotient*) $\varphi/_f\, \mathcal{S}_2$ such that

$$\mathcal{S}_1 \,|_f\, \mathcal{S}_2 \models \varphi \quad \text{if and only if} \quad \mathcal{S}_1 \models \varphi/_f\, \mathcal{S}_2 \tag{3}$$

The bi–implication indicates that we are moving parts of the parallel system into the formula. Clearly, if the quotient is not much larger than the original formula, we have simplified the task of model checking, as the (symbolic) semantics of $\mathcal{S}_1$ is significantly smaller than that of $\mathcal{S}_1 \,|_f\, \mathcal{S}_2$.

In general it will not be possible to express within L_ν such a quotienting formula. However, whenever $\mathcal{S}_2$ is described using a timed automata we are able to express the quotient using the (extended) symbolic semantics of automata. More precisely, whenever φ is a formula over K and A is a timed automaton over C, we define quotient formulas $\varphi/_f\, [\eta, \gamma]$ over $C \cup K$, where $[\eta, \gamma]$ is an extended symbolic state. For η_0 the initial node of A and γ_0 the initial region, $\varphi/_f\, [\eta_0, \gamma_0]$ will express the sufficient and necessary requirement to a timed transition system $\mathcal{S}$ in order that $\mathcal{S} \,|_f\, \mathcal{S}_A$ satisfies φ — see also Corollary 6 below. The quotient construction is defined structurally in Table 2. We have left out the cases for $[a]$, $\vee$, and $\forall$ as they are immediate duals. The Table uses the following notation [12]:

[12] $\gamma_{|C}$ (resp. $\gamma_{|K}$) denotes the set of time-assignments in γ restricted to the automata (resp. formula) clocks.

$$\mathtt{tt}/_f\,[\eta,\gamma] = \mathtt{tt} \qquad \mathtt{ff}/_f\,[\eta,\gamma] = \mathtt{ff} \qquad Z/_f\,[\eta,\gamma] = Z^{[\eta,\gamma]}$$
$$(\varphi_1 \wedge \varphi_2)/_f\,[\eta,\gamma] = (\varphi_1/_f\,[\eta,\gamma]) \wedge (\varphi_2/_f\,[\eta,\gamma])$$
$$\langle a\rangle\varphi/_f\,[\eta,\gamma] = \bigvee_{b,[\eta',\gamma']\in E(\eta,\gamma,a)} \langle b\rangle \left(r_{\gamma'} \text{ in } \varphi/_f\,[\eta'\gamma']\right)$$
$$\exists\varphi/_f\,[\eta,\gamma] = \exists\Big(\bigvee_{l=0\ldots l_\gamma} \beta(\gamma^l) \wedge \varphi/_f\,[\eta,\gamma^l]\Big)$$
$$(x + c \bowtie y + d)/_f\,[\eta,\gamma] = (x + c \bowtie y + d)(\gamma)$$
$$(x \text{ in } \varphi)/_f\,[\eta,\gamma] = x \text{ in } \left(\varphi/_f\,[\eta,\gamma']\right) \text{ where } \gamma' = [\{x\} \to 0]\gamma$$

Table 2. Structural definition of quotient, $\varphi/_f\,[\eta,\gamma]$.

$b,[\eta'\gamma'] \in E(\eta,\gamma,a)$ iff $[\eta,\gamma_{|C}] \xrightarrow{c} [\eta',\gamma'_{|C}]$, $\gamma'_{|K} = \gamma_{|K}$ and $f(b,c) \simeq a$ for some c. We denote by r_γ the set of C clocks which has the value 0 in γ. Moreover $(r \,\mathsf{in}\, \varphi)$ is an abbreviation for $(x_1 \,\mathsf{in}\, (x_2 \,\mathsf{in} \ldots (x_n \,\mathsf{in}\, \varphi)))$ whenever r is $\{x_1, \ldots, x_n\}$. Finally, $\langle 0\rangle\varphi = [0]\varphi = \varphi$.

Note that the quotient construction for identifiers introduces new identifiers of the form $Z^{[\eta,\gamma]}$, where $Z \in \mathsf{Id}$. The definition of these are collected in the (quotient) declaration $\mathcal{D}_A$ given by: $Z^{[\eta,\gamma]} \stackrel{\text{def}}{=} \mathcal{D}(Z)/_f\,[\eta,\gamma]$

The following Theorem and Corollary shows that the quotient construction of Table 2 satisfies the requirements of (3). A proof of Theorem 5 is sketched in [15].

Theorem 5. Let $\mathcal{S} = \langle S, s_0, \longrightarrow\rangle$ be a timed transition system, let $A = \langle N, \eta_0, C, E\rangle$ be a timed automaton, and let φ be an L_ν formula over clock set K, all over an action set $\mathcal{A}$. Then for any $s \in S$, $\eta \in N$, $v \in \mathbf{R}^C$, and $u \in \mathbf{R}^K$:

$$\Big\langle\, s\,|_f\,(\eta, v)\,,\, u \,\Big\rangle \models_{\mathcal{D}} \varphi \quad \textit{if and only if} \quad \langle\, s, v\, u\,\rangle \models_{\mathcal{D}_A} \varphi/_f\,\Big[\eta, [v\,u]\Big]$$

Corollary 6. Let $\mathcal{S}$ be a timed transition system, let A be a timed automaton with clock set C, and let φ be a closed L_ν formula over clock set K, all over an action set $\mathcal{A}$. Then: $\mathcal{S}\,|_f\,\mathcal{S}_A \models_{\mathcal{D}} \varphi$ *if and only if* $\mathcal{S} \models_{\mathcal{D}_A} \varphi/_f\,A$
where $\varphi/_f\,A$ abbreviates $\varphi/_f\,[\eta_0, \gamma_0]$ with η_0 being the initial node of A and γ_0 the initial region over $C \cup K$.

Example 6. Recall the timed automata and declaration from Examples 1 and 4. The quotient $X_1/_f\,A_1$ describes the sufficient and necessary requirement to a timed transition system $\mathcal{S}$ in order that $\mathcal{S}\,|_f\,\mathcal{S}_{A_1}$ satisfies X_1. Clearly, we expect the timed automata B_0 to satisfy this property. Now using a CAML prototype implementation of the quotient construction $X_1/_f\,A_1$ is computed. The definition of $X_1/_f\,A_1$ is found in the quotient declaration $\mathcal{F}_{A_1}$ part of which is given below:

$$X_1/_f\,A_1 \stackrel{\text{def}}{=} [a]\,y \text{ in } Z_1^{[\eta_0,\gamma_0]}$$

$$Z_1^{[\eta_0,\gamma_0]} \stackrel{\text{def}}{=} \mathrm{ff} \vee \Big[\mathrm{tt} \wedge ([b]x \text{ in } Z_1^{[\eta_1,\gamma_0]}) \wedge ([a]Z_1^{[\eta_0,\gamma_0]}) \wedge \mathbf{\forall}\Big(\beta(\gamma_0) \Rightarrow Z_1^{[\eta_0,\gamma_0]} \wedge \beta(\gamma_1) \Rightarrow Z_1^{[\eta_0,\gamma_1]} \wedge \beta(\gamma_2) \Rightarrow Z_1^{[\eta_0,\gamma_2]} \wedge \beta(\gamma_3) \Rightarrow Z_1^{[\eta_0,\gamma_3]} \Big) \Big]$$

$$Z_1^{[\eta_1,\gamma_0]} \stackrel{\text{def}}{=} \mathrm{ff} \vee \Big[\mathrm{tt} \wedge \mathrm{tt} \wedge ([a]Z_1^{[\eta_1,\gamma_0]}) \wedge \mathbf{\forall}\Big(\beta(\gamma_0) \Rightarrow Z_1^{[\eta_1,\gamma_0]} \wedge \beta(\gamma_1) \Rightarrow Z_1^{[\eta_1,\gamma_1]} \wedge \beta(\gamma_2) \Rightarrow Z_1^{[\eta_1,\gamma_2]} \wedge \beta(\gamma_3) \Rightarrow Z_1^{[\eta_1,\gamma_3]} \Big) \Big]$$

The quotient declaration $\mathcal{F}_{A_1}$ contains in total definitions of 96 identifiers. We expect $X_1/_f\, A_1$ to express that the accumulated time between an initial a–action and a following b–action must be strictly greater than 0 as described by the following property U_0:

$$U_0 \stackrel{\text{def}}{=} [a]\Big(y \text{ in } V_0 \Big) \qquad V_0 \stackrel{\text{def}}{=} (y > 0) \vee \Big([b]\mathrm{ff} \wedge [a]V_0 \wedge \mathbf{\forall} V_0 \Big)$$

In the next section we will present effective minimization strategies, which essentially transforms the large quotient declaration $\mathcal{F}_{A_1}$ into the small yet equivalent declaration above. □

Now, let π be the synchronization function completely specified by $\pi(0, a) = a$ for all $a \in \mathcal{A}$ (i.e. the left argument to π is completely ignored). Then it is easy to see that for any timed transition system $\mathcal{S}$, $\mathcal{S}_A$ and $\mathcal{S} \,|_\pi\, \mathcal{S}_A$ satisfy the same formulas. In particular $\mathcal{S}_A$ and $\mathcal{S}_{\mathbf{1}} \,|_\pi\, \mathcal{S}_A$ satisfy the same formula, where $\mathbf{1}$ is the 0–clock timed automaton with just one (initial) node and no edges. Using this observation, the quotient construction can be used to obtain alternative model–checking algorithms for L_ν as follows:

Corollary 7. Let A be a timed automaton with clock set C, and let φ be a closed L_ν formula over clock set K, all over an action set $\mathcal{A}$. Then:

$$A \models_{\mathcal{D}} \varphi \quad \textit{if and only if} \quad \mathbf{1} \models_{\mathcal{D}_A} \varphi/_\pi\, A \quad \textit{if and only if} \quad \varphi/_\pi\, A \Leftrightarrow \mathrm{tt}$$

Due to the projective nature of π it is clear that $\varphi/_\pi\, A$ contains no action modalities, and it is easy to build a special purpose model checker for the simple automata $\mathbf{1}$.

Example 7. Recall once more the timed automata and declaration from Examples 1 and 4. From these Examples we expect that $C_{0,1}$ satisfies the property X_1. Now, using the Corollary 7 we may verify this by showing that the quotient formula $X_1/_\pi\, C_{0,1}$ is either valid or satisfied by $\mathbf{1}$. The quotient declaration associated to $X_1/_\pi\, C_{0,1}$ computed by the CAML prototype (with subsequent application of boolean simplifications) contains 8 identifiers without any $\langle a \rangle$ or $[a]$ operator.

□

Finally, combining the characterization of timed bisimulation in Theorem 4 with the quotient construct of Table 2, we can for any timed automaton A construct a *characteristic* L_ν formula uniquely characterizing the automaton up to timed bisimilarity in the following manner: Let $\mathcal{E}$, $\mathcal{Z}$ and h be as in Theorem 4. Then for any timed transition system $\mathcal{S}$ the following holds:

$$\mathcal{S} \sim \mathcal{S}_A \quad \text{if and only if} \quad \mathcal{S} \models_{\mathcal{E}} \mathcal{Z}/_h [\eta_0, \gamma_0]$$

where η_0 is the initial node of A and γ_0 is the initial region over the clocks of A (note that Z is an L_ν formula over the empty set of clocks). This provides an alternative characteristic formula construction compared with [16].

6 Minimizations

It is evident from the examples in the previous section that repeated quotienting leads to an explosion in the formula. A similar phenomena was observed by Andersen for the quotient construction of modal μ–calculus formulas with respect to finite–state systems. The crucial observation by Andersen is that simple and cost effective transformations of the formulas in practice often lead to significant reductions.

We have implemented in CAML the quotient construction of the previous section as well as (simplified versions of some of) Andersen's minimization strategies. In the investigated examples the minimization strategies lead to dramatic reductions. Below we describe the transformations considered in terms of transformations on formulas and declarations (defining equations).

Reachability: When considering an initial quotient formula $\varphi/_f [\eta_0, \gamma_0]$ not all identifiers of $\mathcal{D}_A$ may be relevant or reachable. In our CAML implementation an "on–the–fly" technique insures that only the reachable part of $\mathcal{D}_A$ is generated.

Boolean Simplification: Formulas may be simplified using the following simple boolean equations and their duals: $\mathtt{ff} \wedge \varphi \equiv \mathtt{ff}$, $\mathtt{tt} \wedge \varphi \equiv \varphi$, $\langle a \rangle \mathtt{ff} \equiv \mathtt{ff}$, $\exists \mathtt{ff} \equiv \mathtt{ff}$, $x \text{ in } \mathtt{ff} \equiv \mathtt{ff}$, $\langle a \rangle \varphi \wedge [a] \mathtt{ff} \equiv \mathtt{ff}$.

Constant Propagation: Identifiers which are declared to either $\mathtt{tt}$ or $\mathtt{ff}$ may be removed while substituting their definitions in the declaration of all other identifiers.

Trivial Equation Elimination: Equations of the form $X \stackrel{\text{def}}{=} [a]X$ are easily seen to have $X = \mathtt{tt}$ as solution. More generally, whenever $X \stackrel{\text{def}}{=} \varphi$ where $\varphi[\mathtt{tt}/X]$ [13] can be simplified to $\mathtt{tt}$, we can perform a removal of the identifier X provided the value $\mathtt{tt}$ is propagated to all uses of X (as under Constant Propagation).

Equivalence Reduction: If two identifiers X and Y are equivalent (i.e. are satisfied by the same timed transition systems) we may collapse them into a single

[13] $\varphi[\mathtt{tt}/X]$ is the formula obtained by substituting all occurrences of X in φ with the formula $\mathtt{tt}$.

identifier. To obtain a cost effective strategy we approximate equivalence of identifiers with the following check: whenever $X \stackrel{\text{def}}{=} \varphi$ and $Y \stackrel{\text{def}}{=} \vartheta$ such that $\varphi[Y/X]$ is syntactically identical to $\vartheta[Y/X]$ we conclude that X and Y are equivalent and may be identified.

We apply the above transformation strategies repeatedly on quotient formulas and declarations. As can be seen in Table 2, quotienting transforms atomic propositions of the form $x + c \bowtie y + d$ into either tt or ff, thus yielding high applicability of Boolean Simplification and Constant Propagation. Also, quotient versions of the same original formula tend to have same structure thus making applicability of Equivalence Reduction high.

In our CAML prototype implementation we have implemented the above reported very simple strategies for Trivial Equation Elimination and Equivalence Reduction. Generalized and more sophisticated (yet still efficient) strategies can or course easily be given. However, even with the implemented simple versions we obtain a very high degree of reduction as observed in the following examples.

Example 8. Recall Example 6. Applying the minimization strategies of the CAML prototype we find that $X_1 /_f A_1$ is equivalent to Y_0 with the following definition:

$$Y_0 \stackrel{\text{def}}{=} [a]y \text{ in } Y_1$$

$$Y_1 \stackrel{\text{def}}{=} [b]\mathrm{ff} \wedge [a]Y_1 \wedge \forall\Big(\beta(\gamma_0) \Rightarrow Y_1 \wedge (\beta(\gamma_1) \vee \beta(\gamma_2)) \Rightarrow Y_2\Big)$$

$$Y_2 \stackrel{\text{def}}{=} [a]Y_2 \wedge \forall\Big(\beta(\gamma_0) \Rightarrow Y_1 \wedge (\beta(\gamma_1) \vee \beta(\gamma_2)) \Rightarrow Y_2\Big)$$

During minimization only 23 identifiers of $\mathcal{F}_{A_1}$ were found to be reachable from $X_1 /_f A_1$, 14 respectively 3 of which were found to be equivalent to tt respectively ff. The remaining 6 identifiers were finally partitioned into 3 classes. Though dramatically reduced, the declaration leaves room for *one* additional simplification as it may be observed that $(\beta(\gamma_1) \vee \beta(\gamma_2)) \Rightarrow Y_2$ is equivalent to tt. With this observation we finally obtain:

$$Y_0' \stackrel{\text{def}}{=} [a]y \text{ in } Y_1' \qquad\qquad Y_1' \stackrel{\text{def}}{=} [b]\mathrm{ff} \wedge [a]Y_1' \wedge \forall\Big(\beta(\gamma_0) \Rightarrow Y_1'\Big)$$

which clearly meets the expectations of 6. Minimization of the quotient formula $X_7 /_f A_{10}$ leads directly to the formula tt indicating that for any timed transition system $\mathcal{S}$ the composition $\mathcal{S} |_f \mathcal{S}_{A_{10}}$ satisfies X_7. Intuitively this is clear as the component A_{10} by itself ensures the delay required by X_7. The corresponding quotient declaration contains 3498 identifiers 617 of which were found to be reachable. Subsequently all these were simplified to tt. □

Example 9. Recall Example 7. Using the minimization strategies of the CAML prototype we find directly that $X_1 /_\pi C_{0,1}$ simplifies to tt thus implying that $C_{0,1}$ satisfies the property X_1. Similarly, minimization of the quotient formula $X_2 /_\pi C_{0,1}$ yields ff confirming that $C_{0,1}$ does not satisfy X_2! □

Example 10. Now we want to confirm that B_0 does indeed satisfy the requirement $X_1/_f A_1$ and hence that $B_0 |_f A_1$ satisfies X_1. Using the equivalent, minimized formula Y_0 from Example 8 it suffices according to Corollary 7 to verify validity of the quotient formula $Y_0/_\pi B_0$. The CAML prototype confirms this through immediate minimization to $\mathtt{tt}$. □

7 Conclusion

This paper has presented the basis for a compositional model checking technique for real–time systems. Based on initial experiments with the CAML prototype we conjecture that compositional model checking will prove not only a feasible but also an efficient technique for real–time systems. However, it is clear that many more experiments must be performed before the conjecture can be finally settled, and in this process we will need to extend our prototype with more sophisticated minimization strategies as the success of compositional model checking is completely determined by these.

Our work on quotient formulas extends that of [7], where a quotient construction for 1-clock automata has been given. Moreover it can be generalized trivially to logics with minimal fixpoint constructs (such as T_μ in [13]) as quotienting is easily seen to distribute over negation.

Acknowledgement

The authors would like to thank Henrik Reif Andersen for interesting and enlightening discussions on the topic of compositional (partial) model–checking.

References

1. R. Alur, C. Courcoubetis, and D. Dill. Model–checking for Real–Time Systems. In *Proceedings of Logic in Computer Science*, pages 414–425. IEEE Computer Society Press, 1990.
2. R. Alur and D. Dill. Automata for Modelling Real–Time Systems. *Theoretical Computer Science*, 126(2):183–236, April 1994.
3. H. R. Andersen. A Polyadic Modal μ–calculus. Id–tr: 1994–145, Department of Computer Science, Technical University of Denmark, 1994.
4. H. R. Andersen. Partial Model Checking. *To appear in Proceedings of LICS'95*, 1995.
5. H. R. Andersen, C. Stirling, and G. Winskel. A Compositional Proof System for the Modal Mu–Calculus. *Logic in Computer Science*, 1994.
6. H. R. Andersen and G. Winskel. Compositional checking of satisfaction. *Formal Methods in Systems Design*, 1992. To appear.
7. J. H. Andersen, K. J. Kristoffersen, K. G. Larsen, and J. Niedermann. Automatic Synthesis of Real Time Systems. *Lecture Notes in Computer Science*, 1995. To appear in Proceedings of ICALP'95.
8. J. R. Burch, E. M. Clarke, K. L. McMillan, D. L. Dill, and L. J. Hwang. Symbolic Model Checking: 10^{20} states and beyond. *Logic in Computer Science*, 1990.

9. E. M. Clarke, T. Filkorn, and S. Jha. Exploiting Symmetry in Temporal Logic Model Checking. *Lecture Notes in Computer Science*, 697, 1993.
10. E. M. Clarke, O. Grümberg, and D. E. Long. Model Checking and Abstraction. *Principles of Programming Languages*, 1992.
11. E. A. Emerson and C. S. Jutla. Symmetry and Model Checking. *Lecture Notes in Computer Science*, 697, 1993.
12. P. Godefroid and P. Wolper. A Partial Approach to Model Checking. *Logic in Computer Science*, 1991.
13. T. A. Henzinger, X. Nicollin, J. Sifakis, and S. Yovine. Symbolic model checking for real-time systems. In *Logic in Computer Science*, 1992.
14. H. Hüttel and K. G. Larsen. The use of static constructs in a modal process logic. *Lecture Notes in Computer Science, Springer Verlag*, 363, 1989.
15. F. Laroussinie and K. G. Larsen. Compositional Model Checking of Real Time Systems. Technical Report RS–95–19, BRICS, 1995. Accessible through WWW: http://www.brics.aau.dk/BRICS.
16. F. Laroussinie, K. G. Larsen, and C. Weise. From Timed Automata to Logic — and Back. 1995. To appear in Proceedings of MFCS'95.
17. K.G. Larsen. *Context–Dependent Bisimulation Between Processes*. PhD thesis, University of Edinburgh, Mayfield Road, Edinburgh, Scotland, 1986.
18. K.G. Larsen and L. Xinxin. Compositionality through an operational semantics of contexts. *Journal of Logic and Computation*, 1(6):761–795, 1991.
19. R. Milner. *Communication and Concurrency*. prentice, Englewood Cliffs, 1989.
20. F. Moller and C. Tofts. Relating Processes with Respect to Speed. Technical Report ECS–LFCS–91–143, Department of Computer Science, University of Edinburgh, 1991.
21. D. Park. Concurrency and automata on infinite sequences. In *Proceedings of 5th GI Conference*, volume 104 of *Lecture Notes in Computer Science, Springer Verlag*, Berlin, 1981. Springer.
22. A. Tarski. A lattice–theoretical fixpoint theorem and its applications. *Pacific Journal of Math.*, 5, 1955.
23. A. Valmari. A Stubborn Attack on State Explosion. *Theoretical Computer Science*, 3, 1990.
24. W. Yi. A Calculus of Real Time Systems. *Lecture Notes in Computer Science*, 458, 1990. In Proceedings of CONCUR.

Checking Bisimilarity for Finitary π-calculus*

Ugo Montanari and Marco Pistore

Computer Science Department, University of Pisa
Corso Italia 40, 56100 Pisa, Italy
{ugo,pistore}@di.unipi.it

Abstract. In this paper we associate to every π-calculus agent an *irredundant unfolding*, i.e., a labeled transition system equipped with the ordinary notion of strong bisimilarity, so that agents are mapped into strongly bisimilar unfoldings if and only if they are early strongly bisimilar. For a class of finitary agents (that strictly contains the finite control agents) without matching, the corresponding unfoldings are finite and can be built efficiently. The main consequence of the results presented in the paper is that the irredundant unfolding can be constructed also for a single agent, and then a minimal realization can be derived from it employing the ordinary partition refinement algorithm. Instead, according to previous results only *pairs* of π-calculus agents could be unfolded and tested for bisimilarity, and no minimization of a single agent was possible. Another consequence is the improvement of the complexity bound for checking bisimilarity of finitary agents without matching.

1 Introduction

Process description languages (the most studied of them is Milner CCS [11]) are useful for specifying and studying concurrent distributed systems. They are equipped with well-developed operational and abstract semantics, and program verification has been an issue in their design from the very beginning. In the *finite state* case, efficient and practical techniques and tools for verification have been developed [7, 10], and they are actually used in several application fields, e.g. in protocol and hardware design. Finite state verification is successful here, differently than in ordinary programming, since the control part and the data part of protocols and hardware components can be often cleanly separated, and the control part is usually both quite complex and finite state.

One of the most important checks in finite state verification is for bisimilarity. The most used algorithm for this check is a variant of Paige and Tarjan partition refinement algorithm [9, 15]. As for language equivalence of finite state automata, the algorithm checking for bisimilarity can produce at the end a *minimal realization*, which is often dramatically smaller than the state space of the given agent. Theoretical results make sure that the minimal realization can replace

* Work supported in part by Esprit Basic Research project CONFER and by Progetto Speciale CNR "Specifica ad Alto Livello e Verifica Formale di Sistemi Digitali".

the original agent in all subsequent checks, at least for properties expressible in the associated Hennessy-Milner logic.

While very convenient in practice, partition refinement algorithms are not presently available for all process description languages. In fact in some cases the observations labeling the transitions of agents are ***history dependent***, i.e., they may refer to observations occurring in previous transitions of the same agent. This is the case for instance for CCS with causality [4], where a visible transition exhibits, in addition to an action, also pointers to the transitions in the past it is caused from. A similar case is CCS with localities [1]. For history dependent agents, bisimilarity can presently be checked at two prices. The first is that the agents must remember the names of the past transitions they can possibly refer to in the future. This extra information tends to make the number of states infinite (if all the past transitions are remembered) but if the sizes of the agents involved in all the computations are bounded, it is possible to see that only a bounded number of past transitions must be stored. The second price is that the algorithm checking for bisimilarity, called ***on the fly*** [5, 2], requires the contemporary generation of the state spaces of both agents to be checked, and consequently it does not produce a minimal realization.

Another, quite interesting case of history dependent process description language is the π-calculus [13, 12]. It has the ability of sending channel names as messages and thus to dynamically reconfigurate agent acquaintances. More importantly, π-calculus names can model objects (in the sense of object oriented programming) and name sending thus models higher order communication. New names can be created at run time and referred to in subsequent input or output operations. It is thus evident the history dependent character of π-calculus.

Owing to the nature of input and bound output π-calculus transitions, also very simple agents do not exhibit a finite state behaviour; other finiteness requirements are more significant in this context. Particularly interesting is the class of ***finitary*** agents: an agent is finitary if there is a bound to the number of parallel components of all the agents derivable from it. This is a very liberal notion, but it does not correspond to a syntactical class of agents. A syntactical but more restrictive notion is that of ***finite control*** agents, i.e., the agents without parallel composition inside recursion.

Three kinds of bisimulation equivalences are relevant for π-calculus: early and late bisimilarity (introduced by Milner, Parrow and Walker in the first π-calculus paper [13]), and open bisimilarity (introduced by Sangiorgi [16]). An algorithm for checking open bisimilarity of finitary agents that follows the on the fly style has been included in the Mobility Workbench [19].

For early and late bisimilarity, decidability of equivalence is proved in [3], where it is shown that for every pair of finite control agents only a finite number of names is sufficient. Once the number of names is guessed, the state spaces of both agents can be built, and the efficient partition refinement algorithm can be applied. However, the number of names which is needed depends on both agents, and thus no state space of a single agent can be build, let alone reduced to a minimal realization. In fact, if the matching agent is left unspecified, the only possibility is to take an infinite number of names, and an infinite branching (and thus infinite) transition system is obtained. Moreover the guess of the number of names works only for the finite control agents and is not extendible to all the finitary agents.

In this paper we show another approach for checking (early strongly) bisimilarity. We show that, by suitably choosing the object name, it is possible to consider only one bound output transition. Similarly, by using as object names the names already in the agent plus one new name, only a finite number of input transitions is needed. The interesting point is how to choose these object names so that bisimilar agents will do the same choices of names: for a bound output, for instance, it is not possible to simply choose the first fresh name (i.e., the first name which does not occur free in the agent), since there are bisimilar agents with different sets of free names.

Our proposal is based on the following notion of *active* names[2]: a name x is active for P if $(\nu x)P$ is not bisimilar to P (with $(\nu x)P$ we represent agent P where name x has been restricted). Two bisimilar agents have the same sets of active names; moreover, if we restrict an agent P with respect to all its nonactive names we obtain a bisimilar agent $\Downarrow P$, whose free names are all active. After this restriction, the first fresh name can be safely chosen for a bound output.

Given an agent P we define its *irredundant unfolding* as the following labeled transition system: consider all the transitions of $\Downarrow P$ in the ordinary early transition system and discard *i)* all the bound output transitions that extrude a name different from the first fresh (nonactive) name in $\Downarrow P$ and *ii)* all the input transitions that receive a value not already active in $\Downarrow P$, except for the first nonactive one; for each remaining transition $\Downarrow P \xrightarrow{\mu} P'$, the transition $\Downarrow P \overset{\mu}{\longmapsto} \Downarrow P'$ is added to the irredundant unfolding and the construction continues from $\Downarrow P'$.

The first result we obtain holds for all the agents: two π-calculus agents are early bisimilar iff their irredundant unfoldings are bisimilar. Moreover, if an agent is finitary, the corresponding irredundant unfolding is finite: to decide whether two finitary agents are bisimilar we could build the corresponding unfoldings and then use the standard partition refinement algorithm for checking their bisimilarity.

To construct the irredundant unfoldings, however, the active names of the agents reached in the construction have to be computed. In the fragment of π-calculus without matching an efficient algorithm can be used to this purpose: in this case the active names of an agent can be computed by considering the names appearing in the labels of the computations of the agent. We also introduce a very compact structure (called *π-automaton*) that represents all the possible computations of an agent and that contains all the information for computing the active names and for generating the irredundant unfolding.

With this algorithm the bisimilarity of two finite control agents can be checked with a worst-case running time of $2^{\mathcal{O}(k^2 \log k)}$, where k is the syntac-

[2] The idea of active names used here is strongly related to the idea of *used* names introduced in [8] for constructing finite state transition systems for agents of a CCS with value passing.

tical size of the agents. This improves the time complexity mentioned in [3] for the same purpose, which is $2^{\mathcal{O}(k^3 \log k)}$. Moreover, our approach should improve over [3] even more in the average case than in the worst case.

2 Background

2.1 Labeled Transition Systems (lts)

A *labeled transition system* (lts) is a tuple $\langle \mathcal{Q}, q^0, \mathcal{L}, \longmapsto \rangle$, where:

- $\mathcal{Q}$ is a set of *states*;
- $q^0 \in \mathcal{Q}$ is the *initial state*;
- $\mathcal{L}$ is a set of *labels*;
- $\longmapsto\ \subset \mathcal{Q} \times \mathcal{L} \times \mathcal{Q}$ is a set of *transitions.*

If $\langle a, l, a' \rangle \in\ \longmapsto$ we write in brief $a \overset{l}{\longmapsto} a'$. We use different arrow symbols to distinguish between different lts.

Given two lts $A = \langle \mathcal{Q}_A, q_A^0, \mathcal{L}, \longrightarrow \rangle$ and $B = \langle \mathcal{Q}_B, q_B^0, \mathcal{L}, \longmapsto \rangle$, a relation $\mathcal{R} \subset \mathcal{Q}_A \times \mathcal{Q}_B$ is a *simulation* iff:

- whenever $a\mathcal{R}b$ and $a \overset{l}{\longrightarrow} a'$, there exists some $b \overset{l}{\longmapsto} b'$ such that $a'\mathcal{R}b'$.

A relation $\mathcal{R} \subset \mathcal{Q}_A \times \mathcal{Q}_B$ is a *bisimulation* iff both $\mathcal{R}$ and $\mathcal{R}^{-1}$ are simulations. The two lts are *bisimilar* ($A \sim B$) iff $q_A^0 \mathcal{R} q_B^0$ for some bisimulation $\mathcal{R}$.

2.2 π-calculus

The π-calculus we present here is *early* and *monadic*; it was first introduced in [14], but we present a slightly simplified version, following in part the style proposed in [18] for the polyadic π-calculus.

Given a countable infinite set of *names* $\mathcal{N}$ (denoted by $a, \ldots, z$), the π-calculus *agents* over $\mathcal{N}$ are defined by the syntax:

$$P ::= 0 \mid \alpha.P \mid P_1|P_2 \mid P_1 + P_2 \mid (\nu x)P \mid [x = y]P \mid A(x_1, \ldots, x_{r(A)})$$

where the *prefixes* α are defined by the syntax:

$$\alpha ::= \tau \mid \bar{x}y \mid x(y),$$

and $r(A)$ is the range of the *agent identifier* A. The occurrences of y in $x(y).P$ and $(\nu y)P$ are bound; *free names* are defined as usual and we indicate them with $fn(P)$. For each identifier A there is a definition $A(y_1, \ldots, y_{r(A)}) \overset{\text{def}}{=} P$ (with y_i all distinct and $fn(P) \subseteq \{y_1 \ldots y_{r(A)}\}$) and we assume that each agent identifier in P is in the scope of a prefix (guarded recursion).

If $\sigma : \mathcal{N} \to \mathcal{N}$, we denote with $P\sigma$ the agent P whose free names have been replaced according to substitution σ (possibly with changes in the bound names); we denote with $\{y_1/x_1 \cdots y_n/x_n\}$ the substitution that maps x_i into y_i for $i = 1, \ldots, n$ and which is the identity on the other names.

We define π-calculus agents up to a *structural congruence* $\equiv$ defined as follows:

- agents which differ by α-conversion are identified;
- $+$ is associative and commutative and 0 is its identity;
- $|$ is associative and commutative and 0 is its identity;
- $[x = x]P \equiv P$ and $[x = y]0 \equiv 0$;
- $(\nu x)0 \equiv 0$ and $(\nu x)(\nu y)P \equiv (\nu y)(\nu x)P$;
- if $x \notin fn(P)$ then $(\nu x)(P|Q) \equiv P|(\nu x)Q$.

The *actions* an agent can perform are defined by the following syntax:

$$\mu ::= \tau \mid \bar{x}y \mid \bar{x}(z) \mid xy;$$

x and y are free names of μ ($fn(\mu)$), whereas z is a bound name ($bn(\mu)$); $n(\mu) = fn(\mu) \cup bn(\mu)$.

The transitions for the *early operational semantics* are defined by the axiom schemata and the inference rules of Table 1.

Table 1. Early operational semantics.

TAU $\tau.P \xrightarrow{\tau} P$	OUT $\bar{x}y.P \xrightarrow{\bar{x}y} P$	IN $x(y).P \xrightarrow{xz} P\{z/y\}$
SUM $\dfrac{P_1 \xrightarrow{\mu} P'}{P_1 + P_2 \xrightarrow{\mu} P'}$	PAR $\dfrac{P_1 \xrightarrow{\mu} P_1'}{P_1\|P_2 \xrightarrow{\mu} P_1'\|P_2}$ if $bn(\mu) \cap fn(P_2) = \emptyset$	
COM $\dfrac{P_1 \xrightarrow{\bar{x}y} P_1' \quad P_2 \xrightarrow{xy} P_2'}{P_1\|P_2 \xrightarrow{\tau} P_1'\|P_2'}$	CLOSE $\dfrac{P_1 \xrightarrow{\bar{x}(y)} P_1' \quad P_2 \xrightarrow{xy} P_2'}{P_1\|P_2 \xrightarrow{\tau} (\nu y)(P_1'\|P_2')}$ if $y \notin fn(P_2)$	
RES $\dfrac{P \xrightarrow{\mu} P'}{(\nu x)P \xrightarrow{\mu} (\nu x)P'}$ if $x \notin n(\mu)$	OPEN $\dfrac{P \xrightarrow{\bar{x}y} P'}{(\nu y)P \xrightarrow{\bar{x}(z)} P'\{z/y\}}$ if $x \neq y, z \notin fn((\nu y)P')$	
IDE $\dfrac{P\{y_1/x_1, \ldots, y_{r(A)}/x_{r(A)}\} \xrightarrow{\mu} P'}{A(y_1, \ldots, y_{r(A)}) \xrightarrow{\mu} P'}$ if $A(x_1, \ldots, x_{r(A)}) \stackrel{\text{def}}{=} P$		

A relation $\mathcal{R}$ over agents is an *early simulation* iff, given $P\mathcal{R}Q$:

- whenever $P \xrightarrow{\mu} P'$ with $bn(\mu) \cap fn(P, Q) = \emptyset$, then $Q \xrightarrow{\mu} Q'$ and $P'\mathcal{R}Q'$.

A relation $\mathcal{R}$ is an *early bisimulation* iff both $\mathcal{R}$ and $\mathcal{R}^{-1}$ are early simulations. Two agents P and Q are *early bisimilar* ($P \sim Q$) iff $P\mathcal{R}Q$ for some early bisimulation $\mathcal{R}$.

3 From Agents to Unfoldings

It is easy to notice that, when checking the early bisimilarity of two agents, not all the names have to be considered as values of input transitions: only the names free in the agents plus one fresh name are required. Similarly, just one fresh name is required in the bound outputs.

This observation can lead to a naive construction that eliminates the infinite branching: let us consider the free names of the agent P (we call them *syntactically active names*). In constructing the state space of an agent, we then introduce at any time only one bound output transition, employing as object the first name not syntactically active, and as many input transitions as there are syntactically active names, plus again the first name not syntactically active. We call this transition system the *syntactical unfolding* of P.

The conjecture that two agents are early bisimilar iff their syntactical unfoldings are bisimilar (according to the usual notion of bisimulation on ordinary labeled transition systems) is clearly false. Let us consider for instance the following agents: $P = x(y).0$ and $Q = P + (\nu w)\bar{w}z$. Agents P and Q are bisimilar (the extra summand in Q is deadlocked), but their syntactical unfoldings are not: agent Q has z as a syntactically active name, and thus it is able to execute a transition labeled by xz, while P cannot.

From the above example it is clear that considering syntactically active names is inadequate, since bisimilar agents can have different sets of free names. We propose the following notion of *semantically active* or simply *active* name in P, based on the idea that if $(\nu x)P$ is bisimilar to P then x does not play any active role in P.

Definition 1. A name a is *active* for an agent P iff $P \not\sim (\nu a)P$; $an(P) = \{a \mid P \not\sim (\nu a)P\}$ is the set of *active names* for the agent P.

Proposition 2. *If* $P \sim P'$ *then* $an(P) = an(P')$.

In addition, we define the *irredundant closure* $\Downarrow P$ of P as the restriction of P with respect to all its nonactive names.

Definition 3. Given an agent P, its *irredundant closure* is the agent $\Downarrow P = (\nu a_1) \cdots (\nu a_n)P$, where $\{a_1, \ldots, a_n\} = fn(P) - an(P)$. An agent P is *irredundant* if $P = \Downarrow P$ (i.e., if $fn(P) = an(P)$).

Proposition 4. $P \sim \Downarrow P$ *for each agent* P.

Given an agent P, we define its *irredundant unfolding* in a similar fashion as the syntactical unfolding described above, getting however as states the irredundant closures of the agents instead of just the agents themselves. Since an agent and its irredundant closure are bisimilar, there is no problem if we apply a closure operation at each step of the construction of the state space of the agent. Moreover, in this way we are sure that bisimilar agents will agree in the choice of names for the input and extrusion transitions.

Definition 5. The *irredundant unfolding* of an agent P_0 is the lts *irr-unf*(P_0) with $\Downarrow P_0$ as initial state ($\Downarrow P_0 = q^0 \in \mathcal{Q}$) and such that whenever $P \in \mathcal{Q}$ then:

- if $P \xrightarrow{\tau} P'$ then $\Downarrow P' \in \mathcal{Q}$ and $P \xmapsto{\tau} \Downarrow P'$;
- if $P \xrightarrow{\bar{x}y} P'$ then $\Downarrow P' \in \mathcal{Q}$ and $P \xmapsto{\bar{x}y} \Downarrow P'$;

– if $P \xrightarrow{\bar{x}(y)} P'$ and $y = \min\{\mathcal{N} - fn(P)\}$ then $\Downarrow P' \in \mathcal{Q}$ and $P \overset{\bar{x}(y)}{\longmapsto} \Downarrow P'$;
– if $P \xrightarrow{xy} P'$ and $y \in fn(P)$ then $\Downarrow P' \in \mathcal{Q}$ and $P \overset{xy}{\longmapsto} \Downarrow P'$;
– if $P \xrightarrow{xy} P'$ and $y = \min\{\mathcal{N} - fn(P)\}$ then $\Downarrow P' \in \mathcal{Q}$ and $P \overset{x(y)}{\longmapsto} \Downarrow P'$.

If in the previous definition we do not apply the irredundant closure operator $\Downarrow$ to the initial state and to the targets of the transitions (i.e., if we replace $\Downarrow P'$ simply with P') we obtain a different lts, called the *syntactical unfolding* of the agent P_0 and denoted *syn-unf*(P_0) (its transitions are represented by $\longmapsto\!\!\!\!\rightarrow$).

In the unfoldings the input of name y from channel x is represented with $x(y)$ if y is new for the agent, with xy otherwise; this expedient, needed in the proof of the following theorem, makes the input labels more similar to the output labels, where we distinguish in a similar way the bound outputs from the free outputs.

Theorem 6. *Let* P_0 *and* Q_0 *be* π*-calculus agents; then* $P_0 \sim Q_0$ *iff* *irr-unf*(P_0) $\sim$ *irr-unf*(Q_0).

Proof (Sketch). For $\Longrightarrow$: the restriction of the π-calculus bisimilarity relation $\sim$ to the states of *irr-unf*(P_0) and *irr-unf*(Q_0) yields a bisimulation relation for the two lts. For $\Longleftarrow$: a bisimulation $\mathcal{R}$ for *irr-unf*(P_0) and *irr-unf*(Q_0) yields an early bisimulation up to $\sim$ and up to injective substitution on agents, i.e. if $P\mathcal{R}Q$ and $P \xrightarrow{\mu} P'$ ($bn(\mu) \cap fn(P,Q) = \emptyset$) then $Q \xrightarrow{\mu} Q'$ and $P'\sigma \sim \mathcal{R} \sim Q'\sigma$ for some injective substitution σ. By the results in [17], $P\mathcal{R}Q$ implies $P \sim Q$; since $\Downarrow P_0 \mathcal{R} \Downarrow Q_0$, we can conclude that $P_0 \sim \Downarrow P_0 \sim \Downarrow Q_0 \sim Q_0$. □

The previous theorem shows the full correspondence between bisimulations over agents and over their irredundant unfoldings. Therefore the latter can be used to check for the bisimilarity of the starting agents (using the standard partition refinement algorithms); however, the construction of the irredundant unfolding requires to identify the active names of agents and the definition of active names is given in terms of bisimilarity of agents.

To break this circle, we give now a different characterization of the active names, that is correct only for π-calculus without matching.

Assume that an agent P can perform the transition $P \xrightarrow{\mu} P'$; if x appears in μ as the channel of the communication or as the object of a free output, it is necessarily active for P; these names can also be seen as those playing an active role in the transition.

Definition 7. The *active names* $an(\mu)$ and the *inactive names* $\overline{an}(\mu)$ of a transition labeled by μ are defined in Table 2.

Let us consider again the transition $P \xrightarrow{\mu} P'$. If a name is active in P' then either it was active also in P or the transition has done it active; in the latter case the name must be the object of an extrusion or of an input; so, if a name is active in P' and does not appear in μ as inactive name, it is active in P too.

Summarizing, if $P \xrightarrow{\mu} P'$ and $x \in an(\mu)$ or $x \in an(P') - \overline{an}(\mu)$, then $x \in an(P)$. The inverse is not true in general, as the following example shows. Name

Table 2. Active names of transitions.

μ	an	$\overline{an}$
τ	$\emptyset$	$\emptyset$
$\bar{a}b$	$\{a,b\}$	$\emptyset$
$\bar{a}(b)$	$\{a\}$	$\{b\}$
ab	$\{a\}$	$\{b\}$
$a(b)$	$\{a\}$	$\{b\}$

z is active for $P = x(y).[y = z]\bar{x}x$, since $P \not\sim (\nu z)P$ (agent $(\nu z)P$ cannot do the computation $\xrightarrow{xz}\xrightarrow{\bar{x}x}$); however, if we consider all the possible transitions $P \xrightarrow{xv} [v = z]\bar{x}x$, we see that $z \notin an([v = z]\bar{x}x)$ and $z \notin an(xv)$ for all $v \in \mathcal{N}$.

The two rules described before, however, are sufficient to capture all the active names of an agent without matching.

Proposition 8. *A name x is active for an agent P without matching iff there is some transition $P \xrightarrow{\mu} P'$ such that $x \in an(\mu)$ or $x \in an(P') - \overline{an}(\mu)$.*

This proposition still holds if we consider the transitions $\longmapsto\!\!\!\!\!\rightarrow$ of the syntactical unfolding or the transitions $\longmapsto$ of the irredundant unfolding of P instead of the π-calculus transitions $\longrightarrow$.

In spite of the alternative characterization presented above, in the π-calculus (with or without matching) it is not decidable what names are active for an agent.

Proposition 9. *It is undecidable whether $P \sim (\nu x)P$.*

Proof (Sketch). If we could effectively decide whether $P \sim (\nu x)P$, we could effectively decide the halting problem for Turing machines, too. In fact, for every Turing machine (and starting tape) we can build a π-calculus agent T that simulates this machine: every step in the machine corresponds to a fixed number of τ actions and the agent can perform the action $\bar{o}o$ iff the machine is in a halting state. So the machine can halt iff the action $\bar{o}o$ can appear in some computation of T; if this happens then $T \not\sim (\nu o)T$, whereas $T \sim (\nu o)T$ if the output cannot be reached. □

We conclude this section noticing that the idea of active names is not original: in [8] an algorithm is presented for checking bisimilarity in the context of CCS with value passing, i.e., a version of CCS where values can be received and sent during the communications, but where no operations can be done on these values. In this case the transition system is kept finite branching by considering the input of just a symbolic name instead of all the (possibly infinite) values. The chosen name is the first *unused* one, where a name is unused for an agent if it is not possible for the agent to send it out before receiving it in an input: this is very similar to the alternative characterization of the active names of

Proposition 8. Also in this case the standard partition refinement algorithm can be used and a minimal realization can be obtained.

The richer context of π-calculus forces to deal also with bound outputs and to consider not only a fresh name for the inputs, but also the active ones. A difference of our approach is that in Definition 1 we give a characterization of active names, which seems to be rather interesting and more general than the one based on the names appearing in the transitions. In the next section, moreover, we present an efficient algorithm for computing the active names and constructing the unfolding, based on the π-automata, which is not present in [8] (although it can also be applied in that context).

4 Effective Construction of the Irredundant Unfolding

In this section we show how to construct effectively and efficiently the irredundant unfolding of a finitary agent without matching. We begin with the formal definition of the finitary agents.

Definition 10. The *degree of parallelism* of the agent P, $par(P)$, is defined as follows:

$$\begin{aligned} par(0) &= 0 \\ par(\alpha.P) &= 1 \\ par(P_1|P_2) &= par(P_1) + par(P_2) \\ par(P_1 + P_2) &= \max(par(P_1), par(P_2)) \\ par((\nu x)P) &= par(P) \\ par([x=y]P) &= par(P) \\ par(A(x_1, \ldots, x_{r(A)})) &= par(P\{x_1/y_1, \ldots, x_{r(A)}/y_{r(A)}\}) \\ &\qquad \text{if } A(y_1, \ldots y_{r(A)}) \stackrel{\text{def}}{=} P. \end{aligned}$$

An agent is *finitary* if the degree of parallelism of all the agents reachable from it is bound.

Function *par* describes the number of parallel components that are present in the agent; if the degree of parallelism can grow with no limits in some computation of an agent, it is obvious that we cannot hope to represent such an agent with a finite lts[3]. The following theorem shows that (when quotienting with respect to the structural axioms of π-calculus) the unfolding of a finitary agent (with or without matching) is finite.

Theorem 11. *Given an agent P, its syntactical unfolding syn-unf(P) and its irredundant unfolding irr-unf(P) are finite iff P is finitary.*

[3] It might be possible to give slightly more comprehensive definitions capturing agents with an unbound number of deadlocked parallel components, like $P = \bar{x}x.P|(\nu y)\bar{y}x$. However we cannot see how to do it in a systematic way.

Proof (Sketch). It is obvious that if P is not finitary the unfolding cannot be finite. For the other implication: each parallel component of an agent reachable from P has to appear, up to name substitutions and restrictions, in P or in a definition used by P, so the number of "types" of parallel components is finite; since the number of components is bound by hypothesis, also the reachable agents are finite, up to the usage of names. Finally, since in each of these there is only a bound number of name occurrences, only a finite subset of $\mathcal{N}$ is used in the unfolding. Also the possibility that the recursive definitions generate an unbound number of new restrictions is not a problem, since $(\nu x)P \equiv P$ if $x \notin fn(P)$ and so all but a bound number of restrictions can be erased using structural axioms. This assures that the unfolding is finite. □

Notice that in general it is not decidable whether an agent is finitary: otherwise it would be decidable whether an agent is finite (i.e., when the agent is finitary and the corresponding unfolding has no cycles), which is instead undecidable. However, there is an important class of finitary agents which can be characterized syntactically: the agents with *finite control*, i.e., the agents without recursive definitions containing parallel composition. In this case, after an initialization phase during which a finite set of processes acting in parallel is created, no new processes can be generated. To have an algorithm that works for all the finitary agents is important, because possibly there are less restrictive syntactical conditions that, while permitting the creation of new processes also after the initialization phase, still assure a bounded degree of parallelism in all the reachable agents. Further work has to be done in this sense.

We can now sketch a first algorithm for constructing the irredundant unfolding of a finitary agent without matching. It first builds the syntactical unfolding corresponding to the agent (which is finite according to Theorem 11) and then determines the active names of all its states, using Proposition 8. The irredundant unfolding can then be built using these informations. In fact, the states of the irredundant unfolding have the form $\Downarrow(Q\sigma)$, where Q is a state of the syntactical unfolding and σ is an injective substitution. The following proposition shows that the active names of $Q\sigma$ can be deduced from the active names of Q and so the irredundant closure $\Downarrow(Q\sigma)$ can be effectively built.

Proposition 12. *If $\sigma : fn(P) \to \mathcal{N}$ is an injective substitution, then $an(P\sigma) = \sigma(an(P))$.*

The role of the syntactical unfolding is now only of discovering the active names. However building the syntactical unfolding would be the bottleneck of the whole construction, since its size is usually significantly bigger than the irredundant unfolding. Exploiting the previous proposition, we can construct a more compact structure (we call it *π-automaton*) that merges all the states of the syntactical unfolding which differ only for an injective substitution. To this purpose, we assume to have a *normalization* function *norm* over agents, so that if $norm(P) = \langle \bar{P}, \sigma \rangle$ then $\bar{P}$ is the representative of the class of agents differing from P only by an injective substitution (it is called *normalized agent*) and $\sigma : fn(\bar{P}) \rightarrow fn(P)$ is the injective substitution such that $P = \bar{P}\sigma$ (it is called the *normalizing renaming*)[4]. During the construction of the unfolding, then, we still use the free names to approximate the active names, but the target of a transition is now normalized. Of course, each transition of the π-automaton must then store this normalizing renaming, so that the names of the target can be bounded to the corresponding names of the source.

Definition 13. The *π-automaton* corresponding to the agent P_0 is the lts $\pi\text{-}aut(P_0)$ with $P_0 \in \mathcal{Q}$ as initial state and such that whenever $P \in \mathcal{Q}$ then:

– if $P \xrightarrow{\tau} P'$ and $\langle P'', \sigma \rangle = norm(P')$ then $P'' \in \mathcal{Q}$ and $P \overset{\tau,\sigma}{\Longmapsto} P''$;

– if $P \xrightarrow{\bar{x}y} P'$ and $\langle P'', \sigma \rangle = norm(P')$ then $P'' \in \mathcal{Q}$ and $P \overset{\bar{x}y,\sigma}{\Longmapsto} P''$;

– if $P \xrightarrow{\bar{x}(y)} P'$, $y = \min\{\mathcal{N} - fn(P)\}$ and $\langle P'', \sigma \rangle = norm(P')$ then $P'' \in \mathcal{Q}$ and $P \overset{\bar{x}(y),\sigma}{\Longmapsto} P''$;

– if $P \xrightarrow{xy} P'$, $y \in fn(P)$ and $\langle P'', \sigma \rangle = norm(P')$ then $P'' \in \mathcal{Q}$ and $P \overset{xy,\sigma}{\Longmapsto} P''$;

– if $P \xrightarrow{xy} P'$, $y = \min\{\mathcal{N} - fn(P)\}$ and $\langle P'', \sigma \rangle = norm(P')$ then $P'' \in \mathcal{Q}$ and $P \overset{x(y),\sigma}{\Longmapsto} P''$.

Note that the normalization function does not act on the initial state, so that its free names are exactly the free names of agent P_0.

The sets of active names are now determined on the π-automaton essentially in the same way as in the syntactical unfolding.

Proposition 14. *If P is a state of the π-automaton A, corresponding to an agent without matching, then $an(P)$ is the smallest set such that $x \in an(P)$ iff for some transition $P \overset{\mu,\sigma}{\Longmapsto} P'$ in A we have $x \in an(\mu) \cup (\sigma(an(P')) - \overline{an}(\mu))$, where $an(\mu)$ and $\overline{an}(\mu)$ are defined as in Table 2.*

We can define an efficient algorithm for finding the active names of all the states of a π-automaton: suppose that a name x of a state P is represented with the pair $\langle P, x \rangle$ and that $\mathcal{G}$ is the direct graph with all these pairs as nodes and with an arc from $\langle P', x \rangle$ to $\langle P, \sigma(x) \rangle$ if $P \overset{\mu,\sigma}{\Longmapsto} P'$ and $\sigma(x) \notin \overline{an}(\mu)$. To find the active names we can use an algorithm that identifies the nodes of $\mathcal{G}$ reachable from the nodes in

$$I = \{\langle P, x \rangle \mid P \in \mathcal{Q}, P \overset{\mu,\sigma}{\Longmapsto} P' \text{ and } x \in an(\mu)\}.$$

From $\pi\text{-}aut(P)$ and from the information on the active names of its states we can build directly $irr\text{-}unf(P)$; we have *i)* to make irredundant the states of $\pi\text{-}aut(P)$ by restricting them (thus erasing some input transitions), and *ii)* to replace each

[4] Such a function can be obtained by defining a total ordering of the free names in an agent which depends only on the positions of the names in the syntactical tree of the agent and then by bijectively mapping these names in the initial segment of $\mathcal{N}$.

state of π-*aut*(P) with all its versions, differing by injective substitution, that are reachable from the initial state.

Definition 15. Given a π-automaton A, the lts $unw(A)$ corresponding to the *unwinding* of A is defined as follows. Its initial state is $\Downarrow P_0$, where P_0 is the initial state of A, and whenever $P \in \mathcal{Q}_A$ and $\Downarrow(P\sigma) \in \mathcal{Q}_{unw(A)}$ for some injective substitution σ, then:

- if $P \overset{\tau,\sigma'}{\Longmapsto} P'$, then $\Downarrow(P'\bar{\sigma}) \in \mathcal{Q}_{unw(A)}$ and $\Downarrow(P\sigma) \overset{\tau}{\longmapsto} \Downarrow(P'\bar{\sigma})$, where $\bar{\sigma} = \sigma \circ \sigma'$;
- if $P \overset{\bar{x}y,\sigma'}{\Longmapsto} P'$, then $\Downarrow(P'\bar{\sigma}) \in \mathcal{Q}_{unw(A)}$ and $\Downarrow(P\sigma) \overset{\bar{x}_\sigma y_\sigma}{\longmapsto} \Downarrow(P'\bar{\sigma})$, where $\bar{\sigma} = \sigma \circ \sigma'$;
- if $P \overset{\bar{x}(y),\sigma'}{\Longmapsto} P'$, then $\Downarrow(P'\bar{\sigma}) \in \mathcal{Q}_{unw(A)}$ and $\Downarrow(P\sigma) \overset{\bar{x}_\sigma(z)}{\longmapsto} \Downarrow(P'\bar{\sigma})$, where $z = \min\{\mathcal{N} - \sigma(an(P))\}$ and $\bar{\sigma} = \{z/y_\sigma\} \circ \sigma \circ \sigma'$;
- if $P \overset{xy,\sigma'}{\Longmapsto} P'$ and $y \in an(P)$, then $\Downarrow(P'\bar{\sigma}) \in \mathcal{Q}_{unw(A)}$ and $\Downarrow(P\sigma) \overset{x_\sigma y_\sigma}{\longmapsto} \Downarrow(P'\bar{\sigma})$, where $\bar{\sigma} = \sigma \circ \sigma'$;
- if $P \overset{x(y),\sigma'}{\Longmapsto} P'$, then $\Downarrow(P'\bar{\sigma}) \in \mathcal{Q}_{unw(A)}$ and $\Downarrow(P\sigma) \overset{x_\sigma(z)}{\longmapsto} \Downarrow(P'\bar{\sigma})$, where $z = \min\{\mathcal{N} - \sigma(an(P))\}$ and $\bar{\sigma} = \{z/y_\sigma\} \circ \sigma \circ \sigma'$;

where v_σ stays for $\sigma(v)$.

Proposition 16. *Given an agent P, irr-unf$(P) = unw(\pi\text{-}aut(P))$.*

Corollary 17. *Given two agents P and Q, then $P \sim Q$ iff $unw(\pi\text{-}aut(P)) \sim unw(\pi\text{-}aut(Q))$.*

Thus we have shown that finite irredundant unfoldings can be effectively constructed for finitary π-calculus agents without matching. For these agents we have an algorithm for checking bisimilarity: it first builds the irredundant unfoldings and then checks ordinary bisimilarity on these transition systems.

5 Complexity

In this section we consider the time complexity of the proposed algorithm. First we describe the time complexity of the bisimilarity test for two π-automata A and B as a function of the number s of their states, the number t of their transitions and the maximal number n of free names present in their states.

Proposition 18. *Let P and Q be two finitary agents without matching and suppose that A and B are the π-automata corresponding to them. If $|\mathcal{Q}_A|, |\mathcal{Q}_B| \leq s$, $|\longmapsto_A|, |\longmapsto_B| \leq t$ and $\max_{P \in \mathcal{Q}_A} |fn(P)|, \max_{P \in \mathcal{Q}_B} |fn(P)| \leq n$, the bisimilarity of P and Q can be tested, starting from the automata, in $2^{\mathcal{O}(\log t + \log s + n \log n)}$ steps.*

Proof (Sketch). The proof follows from the following considerations.

- The active names of each π-automaton can be computed in $\mathcal{O}(tn + (sn)^2)$: the construction of the initial set of active names is in $\mathcal{O}(t)$ (we have to consider the active names deriving from each transition, and there are at most two names in each of them), the construction of the graph is $\mathcal{O}(tn)$ (we have to consider all the transitions and, for each transition, the names of the target state), and the search of the reachable nodes is $\mathcal{O}((sn)^2)$ (sn is the maximal number of pairs state-name).
- Each unwinding generates a lts with at most $\mathcal{O}(sn!)$ states and $\mathcal{O}(tn!)$ transitions (and can be constructed in $\mathcal{O}(n!(s+t))$).
- If the states and the transitions of two lts are respectively $\leq s'$ and $\leq t'$, the Paige-Tarjan algorithm [15] can test bisimilarity in $\mathcal{O}(t' \log s' + s')$. □

Now we try to determine the values s, t and n for a π-automaton as a function of the syntactical size k of the corresponding π-calculus agent: the syntactical size of an agent P is defined as the sum of the lengths of P and of all the recursive definitions used by the agent.

The following proposition states that, in the general case, it is not possible for finitary agents to effectively bound the number of states of a π-automaton in function of the syntactical size of the corresponding agent.

Proposition 19. *There is no total computable function s such that, for each finitary agent P with syntactical size k, $|\mathcal{Q}_{\pi\text{-}aut(P)}| \leq s(k)$.*

Proof (Sketch). It such a function existed, it would be decidable whether an agent P is finitary (which we already noticed is clearly undecidable): one begins to construct π-*aut*(P) and stops when the construction is finished (P is finitary) or when more than $s(k)$ states have been generated (P is not finitary). □

However, for finite control agents it is possible to bound s, t and n as a function of the syntactical length: it can be shown that, in this case, $s, t \in 2^{\mathcal{O}(k^2 \log k)}$ and $n \in \mathcal{O}(k^2)$. If we assume that we can produce the transitions of an agent in a time polynomial in its syntactical size, the time complexity of the construction of the π-automaton of a finite control agent is in $2^{\mathcal{O}(k^2 \log k)}$.

Theorem 20. *The bisimilarity of two finite control agents can be checked with a worst-case running time of $2^{\mathcal{O}(k^2 \log k)}$, where k is the syntactical size of the agents.*

Proof (Sketch). There are at most k parallel components in all the reachable agents and, up to name substitution and restriction, for each component there are at most k possible types, since these must be subterms of the starting agent. Each reachable agent has at most k^2 name occurrences ($n \in \mathcal{O}(k^2)$), so, considering all the possible partitions of the name occurrences and all the possible restrictions, the number of states of the π-automata is at most $s = k^k k^{2k^2} \in 2^{\mathcal{O}(k^2 \log k)}$. From each state there are $\mathcal{O}(k^2 n)$ outgoing transitions, so $t \in 2^{\mathcal{O}(k^2 \log k)}$. The theorem follows by Proposition 18. □

The time complexity mentioned in [3] for the same purpose is $2^{\mathcal{O}(k^3 \log k)}$. In addition, notice that for every input here we consider only the names which are strictly necessary and just a name for every extrusion. In [3], instead, after having guessed the number of names, all of them are used for each input and similarly all of the non-free names are used for each extrusion; this is particularly unpleasant since the proposed guess is very rough and in many cases a much smaller number of names suffices. Thus our approach should improve over [3] even more in the average case than in the worst case.

6 Conclusions

In the paper we define a semantic notion of active names in π-calculus agents, and we show that, when limiting the infinite branching of the input moves and of the bound output moves accordingly, we obtain a labeled transition system, called irredundant unfolding, which ordinary bisimulation can handle. Active names are in general undecidable, but when there is a bound to the degree of parallelism of all the agents derivable from P, and P contains no occurrence of the matching operator, the irredundant unfolding of P can be effectively built. The main consequence of the results presented in the paper is that the irredundant unfolding can be constructed also for a single agent, and then a minimal realization can be derived from it employing the ordinary partition refinement algorithm. Instead, according to previous results only *pairs* of π-calculus agents could be unfolded and tested for bisimilarity, and no minimization of a single agent was possible. Also the upper bound of the complexity has been improved for the class of finite control agents (without matching). Our results could be a significant step for improving the effectiveness and applicability of finite state verification techniques for the π-calculus.

In the paper we presented our approach in the early, strong case. However it is immediate to extend it to the late semantics (it is enough to split every input move into two, as in [6]) and to the weak case (using the same irredundant unfolding and the weak variant of the partition refinement algorithm). Also branching bisimilarity should pose no problem.

It seems also possible, although not straightforward, to apply our approach to open bisimilarity. It is more difficult, instead, to find a way of handling matching: further work has to be done on this problem, although some preliminary results are encouraging.

As mentioned in the introduction, π-calculus is an instance of a larger class of calculi called history dependent, where partition refinement minimization was not previously possible. We think that the approach we presented here can be applied without difficulties also to other history dependent calculi, like CCS with locality or causality.

In the paper we introduced a notion of π-automaton. Its role was ancillary, since its purpose was only to improve the average behaviour of our procedure. However, we think that π-automata are potentially quite interesting, since they describe in a syntax-independent way the structure of a history-dependent transition system. For instance, π-calculus bisimilarity could be defined directly on them, and acyclic π-automata (defined up to bisimilarity) could be useful for defining the denotational semantics of π-calculus.

Acknowledgement. We would like to thank Gianluigi Ferrari and Davide Sangiorgi for the interesting discussions.

References

1. G. Boudol, I. Castellani, M. Hennessy and A. Kiehn. Observing localities. *Theoretical Computer Science*, 114:31–61, 1993.
2. F. Corradini and R. De Nicola. Distribution and locality of concurrent systems. In *Proc. ICALP'94*, LNCS 820. Springer Verlag, 1994.
3. M. Dam. On the decidability of process equivalences for the π-calculus. SICS Research Report RR:94-20, 1994.
4. Ph. Darondeau and P. Degano. Causal trees. In *Proc. ICALP'89*, LNCS 372. Springer Verlag, 1989.
5. J.-C. Fernandez and L. Mounier. "On the fly" verification of behavioural equivalences and preorders. In *Proc. CAV'91*, LNCS 575. Springer Verlag, 1991.
6. G. Ferrari, U. Montanari and P. Quaglia. The weak late π-calculus semantics as observation equivalence. To appear in *Proc. CONCUR'95*.
7. P. Inverardi and C. Priami. Evaluation of tools for the analysis of communicating systems. *Bulletin of the EATCS*, 45:158–185, 1991.
8. B. Jonsson and J. Parrow. Deciding bisimulation equivalences for a class of non-finite-state programs. *Information and Computation*, 107:272–302, 1993.
9. P. C. Kanellakis and S. A. Smolka. CCS expressions, finite state processes, and three problems of equivalence. *Information and Computation*, 86:43–68, 1990.
10. E. Madelaine. Verification tools for the CONCUR project. *Bulletin of the EATCS*, 47:110–126, 1992.
11. R. Milner. *Communication and Concurrency*. Prentice Hall, 1989.
12. R. Milner. The polyadic π-calculus: a tutorial. In *Logic and Algebra of Specification*, NATO ASI Series F, Vol. 94. Springer Verlag, 1993.
13. R. Milner, J. Parrow and D. Walker. A calculus of mobile processes (parts I and II). *Information and Computation*, 100:1–77, 1992.
14. R. Milner, J. Parrow and D. Walker. Modal logic for mobile processes. In *Proc. CONCUR'91*, LNCS 527. Springer Verlag, 1992.
15. R. Paige and R. E. Tarjan. Three partition refinement algorithms. *SIAM Journal on Computing*, 16(6):973–989, 1987.
16. D. Sangiorgi. A theory of bisimulation for the π-calculus. In *Proc. CONCUR'93*, LNCS 715. Springer Verlag, 1993.
17. D. Sangiorgi. On the bisimulation proof method. Tech. Rep. ECS–LFCS–94–299, LFCS, Dept. of Comp. Sci., Edinburgh Univ., 1994. An extended abstract will appear in *Proc. MFCS'95*.
18. D. Sangiorgi. *Expressing mobility in process algebras: first-order and higher-order paradigms*. PhD Thesis CST-99-93, University of Edinburgh, 1992.
19. B. Victor and F. Moller. The Mobility Workbench — A tool for the π-calculus. In *Proc. CAV'94*, LNCS 818. Springer Verlag, 1994.

The Weak Late π-calculus Semantics as Observation Equivalence*

Gian-Luigi Ferrari   Ugo Montanari   Paola Quaglia

Dipartimento di Informatica, Università di Pisa
{giangi,ugo,quaglia}@di.unipi.it

Abstract. We show that the Weak Late π-calculus semantics can be characterized as ordinary Observation congruence over a specialized transition system where both the instantiation of input placeholders and the name substitutions, due *e.g.* to communication, are explicitly handled via suitable constructors. The approach presented here allows to axiomatize the Weak Late π-calculus semantics by simply adding Milner's τ-laws to the proof system for the Strong equivalence. Resorting to Observation equivalence provides a framework which is general enough to allow to recover, in straightforward ways, other bisimulation semantics (*e.g.* Early, both Strong and Weak, and Dynamic and Branching, both Early and Late).

0 Introduction

This paper aims at contributing to the understanding of the Weak π-calculus bisimulation semantics [Mil90]. The π-calculus [MPW92] is an instance of value-passing process algebra where values are names, and then communication causes substitution of names for names.

In [FMQ94] we proposed an alternative formulation of the Strong π-calculus semantics. There, contrary to the original definition of the calculus, name substitutions were explicitly handled via the introduction of a suitable state operator. That approach allowed the characterization of the π-calculus transitional semantics as ordinary (*i.e.* CCS-like [Mil80]) labelled transition system, where the usual notion of Strong bisimulation applies.

We claim that reasoning about the π-calculus semantics in terms of ordinary bisimulation may be of both theoretical and pragmatic interest: General theorems of the format-based theory may be applied (*e.g.* those proved in [DS85, ABV94]), and algorithms for CCS automated verification tools may be re-used (*e.g.* [CPS93]). This paper provides a further step towards accomplishing the task of interpreting the π-calculus semantics as ordinary bisimulation. We generalize the techniques adopted in [FMQ94] in order to fairly deal with the

* Work partially supported by ESPRIT BRA Project 6454 CONFER, and by *Progetto Coordinato CNR 'Strumenti per la Specifica e la Verifica di Proprietà Critiche di Sistemi Concorrenti e Distribuiti'*.

π-calculus Weak bisimulation equivalences which, ignoring the silent actions representing internal communications, have surely more practical interest than their Strong duals. We discuss in full detail the Weak Late bisimulation semantics, and show how to retrieve other semantics by minor changes.

According to the Late π-calculus semantics, the fact that names can be transmitted in interactions shows up in a 'functional' operational intuition about input actions. Precisely, the transition $P_1 \xrightarrow{x(y)} P_1'$ means that the process P_1 evolves into P_1' by inputting any name, formally called y, over the channel named x. The name y is only a placeholder. It stands for any name w whose input would force P_1 to proceed as $P_1'\{^w/y\}$, namely as P_1' where all the free occurrences of y are replaced by w, with suitable α-conversions to avoid name clashes. For instance, when P_1 runs in parallel with the process $P_2 = \overline{x}w.P_2'$, which can output w on x and then behave like P_2', the communication is expressed by the transition $P_1|P_2 \xrightarrow{\tau} P_1'\{^w/y\}|P_2'$.

The functional intuition about input actions has an impact on behavioural equivalences, and particularly on the Weak bisimulation. Letting $\Longrightarrow$ be the reflexive and transitive closure of $\xrightarrow{\tau}$, and $\stackrel{\alpha}{\Longrightarrow}$ be $\Longrightarrow\xrightarrow{\alpha}\Longrightarrow$, and $\stackrel{\widehat{\alpha}}{\Longrightarrow}$ be $\Longrightarrow$ if $\alpha = \tau$, and $\stackrel{\alpha}{\Longrightarrow}$ otherwise, the ordinary Weak bisimulation clause is as follows [Mil89]:

(W) if $P \xrightarrow{\alpha} P'$ then for some Q', $Q \stackrel{\widehat{\alpha}}{\Longrightarrow} Q'$ and P' is Weak bisimilar to Q'.

The Late interpretation of input actions breaks the above double arrow in two, and the bisimulation clause becomes [Mil90]:

(WL) if $P \xrightarrow{x(y)} P'$ then for some Q', $Q \Longrightarrow \xrightarrow{x(y)} Q'$ and for all w there exists Q'' such that $Q'\{^w/y\} \Longrightarrow Q''$ and $P'\{^w/y\}$ is Weak Late bisimilar to Q''.

The universal quantification on w, and the claim that the instantiation of y takes place just after the input move, make **(WL)** dramatically different than **(W)**, and suggests that the actual instantiation of the input placeholder can be assigned an operational meaning.

In this paper we show that the Weak Late π-calculus semantics can be characterized as ordinary Weak equivalence (also called Observation equivalence) over a specialized transition system where the placeholder instantiation becomes a distinguished move. Intuitively, the input move '$\bullet \xrightarrow{x(y)} \bullet$' is rendered as something like the following

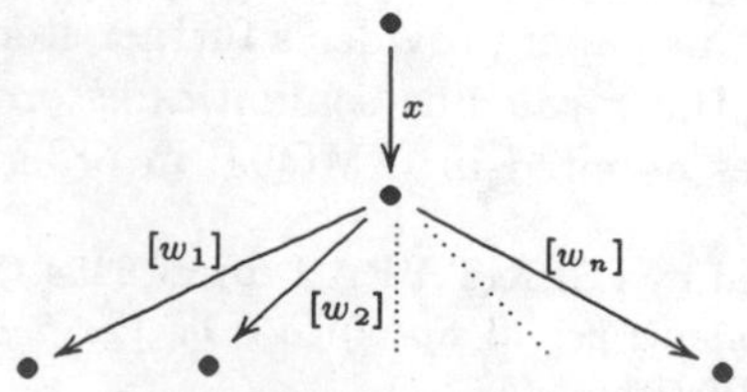

where $w_1, \ldots, w_n$ correspond to the possible instantiations of the name y. Thinking of the placeholder instantiation as an observable event strengthens the opportunity of the quite unusual requirement of breaking the double arrow down in **(WL)**. Whenever an input move is compulsorily followed by observable instantiation steps, the input move itself is obviously not allowed to absorb silent actions after it.

More generally, the transition system we propose handles explicitly name instantiation of any kind (*e.g.* name substitution due to communication). An explanation of our approach follows. Assume that ξ represents some association between names. The pair $\xi :: P$, where P is (essentially) a π-calculus process, is an agent of a new calculus we call $\pi\xi$-calculus. The process $\xi :: P$ describes an intermediate state of a π-calculus computation: P gives the part of the program which has still to be executed, while ξ keeps track of the associations among names carried out in the past of the ongoing computation. Hence ξ can be viewed as an environment giving the actual associations of names.

Since name instantiation has a syntactic counterpart in the $\pi\xi$-calculus, the transition system we define is actually a two levels one. The idea is that a step in the execution of a π-calculus process has a side effect on name associations, and then on the $\pi\xi$-calculus process. So, the top level transition system is defined by inference rules like the following one:

$$\frac{P \xrightarrow{\omega} P'}{\xi :: P \overset{\delta(\xi',\omega)}{\longrightarrow\!\!\!\!\triangleright} \xi' :: P'} \quad \xi' \in \eta(\xi, \omega)$$

The possibly many-valued function η takes care of extending the environment ξ with the name associations activated by the low level transition $P \xrightarrow{\omega} P'$, while the function δ yields the observable result of the move.

In [FMQ95b] we characterized both the Early and the Late Strong bisimulations [MPW93] in terms of the ordinary Strong bisimulation [Par81, Mil83] over specialized transition systems which made use of suitable definitions of the pair (η,δ). That approach, where the instantiation of the input placeholder is not assigned a distinguished operational meaning, is not general enough to allow to retrieve the Weak Late semantics by simply adding Milner's τ-laws [Mil89] to the axiom system for the Strong equivalence.

In this paper we put forward a transition system for the $\pi\xi$-calculus which, to some extent, can be considered *initial* w.r.t. those presented in [FMQ95b]. We show that the $\pi\xi$-calculus directly captures the Strong Late π-calculus semantics and it comes equipped with a complete axiom system which, when augmented with the τ-laws, characterizes the Weak Late semantics. Also, both the Strong and the Weak Early semantics can be retrieved straightforwardly.

The main contributions of our paper are the characterization and the axiomatization of the Weak Late bisimulation in terms of Observation equivalence. This exports to the π-calculus setting existing algorithms and tools for checking process equivalences (*e.g.* [CPS93]). Also, by virtue of standard results, the axiomatizations of other τ-forgetting equivalences can be straightforwardly got (*e.g.* Dynamic [MS92], and Branching [vGW89], both Early and Late).

Up-to-date, the Weak Late π-calculus bisimulation was only axiomatized relying on the notion of Symbolic bisimulation [Lin95], whose relationship with Branching and Dynamic equivalence is still not investigated.

Finally, as during the execution of finite processes only finitely many names are considered, our approach allows π-calculus processes to be modelled by *finitely branching* labelled trees. This peculiarity, together with the use of a behavioural equivalence which abstracts away from τ moves, can be of practical interest in the implementation of automated verification tools [FMQ95a].

1 The $\pi\xi$-calculus

A $\pi\xi$-calculus process is written $\xi :: P$, where ξ is an environment keeping track of the associations among names, and P is a process built up by the π-calculus syntax plus a new kind of prefix. As the main features of the $\pi\xi$-calculus can be expressed without recursion or replication, here we consider only finite processes. However the approach can be extended to deal with infinite processes.

Let $\mathcal{N}$ be a denumerably infinite set of names (ranged over by x, y, z, ...). The syntax of the P-component of the $\pi\xi$-calculus process $\xi :: P$ is defined as follows.

$$P ::= \mathbf{0} \mid \tau.P \mid x(y).P \mid \lambda y.P \mid \overline{x}y.P \mid [x=y]P \mid P+P \mid P|P \mid (y)P$$

The prefix λy, which is a formal binder resembling the abstraction operator of [Mil91], is the only novelty w.r.t. the π-calculus syntax: It calls for an actual instantiation of the name y. In spite of the new prefix, we refer to the right component of any $\pi\xi$-calculus process as π-calculus process (ranged over by P, Q, ...). As usual, the sets of the free and of the bound names of a process P (of an action α) are written $fn(P)$ $(fn(\alpha))$, and $bn(P)$ $(bn(\alpha))$ respectively, while $fn(P,Q)$ is used as a shorthand for $fn(P) \cup fn(Q)$.

1.0 The symbolic operational semantics

We first define, in the style of [Plo81], the low level transition relation between π-calculus processes. The operational semantics is called 'symbolic' in that name instantiation is not applied to processes, but rather recorded by transition labels (ranged over by ω, ω', ...). Transition labels are pairs of the form $\langle \alpha, C \rangle$. The first component is essentially an action in the same sense of the π-calculus. The second component, called *obligation*, is a logical formula which symbolically codes requirements on names. Transition labels are equipped with some operations, so they form an 'observation algebra' [FGM91]. The symbolic operational semantics is reported in Tab. 1.

Notice that the execution of the new prefix λy results in the action $[y]$ which, although resembling the concretions of [Mil91], has no counterpart in the π-calculus dynamics. Also, communication is characterized by a single inference rule. More precisely, we avoided to use the Close rule which describes the communication of a private name and causes a restriction to appear on top of synchronizing processes. In the $\pi\xi$-calculus the information about the privacy of

$$\tau.P \xrightarrow{\langle \tau, true \rangle} P \qquad \overline{x}y.P \xrightarrow{\langle \overline{x}y,\, x\downarrow \rangle} P \qquad x(y).P \xrightarrow{\langle x(y),\, x\downarrow \rangle} P$$

$$\lambda y.P \xrightarrow{\langle [y], true \rangle} P \qquad \frac{P \xrightarrow{\omega} P'}{P+Q \xrightarrow{\omega} P'} \qquad \frac{Q \xrightarrow{\omega} Q'}{P+Q \xrightarrow{\omega} Q'}$$

$$\frac{P \xrightarrow{\omega} P'}{[x=y]P \xrightarrow{\mu_y^x(\omega)} P'} \qquad \frac{P \xrightarrow{\omega} P'}{(y)P \xrightarrow{o_y\omega} P'} \qquad \frac{P \xrightarrow{\omega} P'}{(y)P \xrightarrow{\nu_y\omega} (y)P'}$$

$$\frac{P \xrightarrow{\omega} P'}{P \mid Q \xrightarrow{\omega} P' \mid Q} \qquad \frac{Q \xrightarrow{\omega} Q'}{P \mid Q \xrightarrow{\omega} P \mid Q'} \qquad \frac{P \xrightarrow{\omega} P',\ Q \xrightarrow{\omega'} Q'}{P \mid Q \xrightarrow{\omega \| \omega'} P' \mid Q'}$$

$$\mu_y^x(\langle \alpha, C \rangle) = \langle \alpha, C \wedge x = y \rangle$$

$$\langle \alpha_1, C_1' \rangle \parallel \langle \alpha_2, C_2' \rangle = \begin{cases} \langle \tau[y/w], C_1 \wedge C_2 \wedge x = z \rangle & \text{if } \alpha_1 \in \{\overline{x}y, \overline{x}(y)\}\ ,\ C_1' = x\downarrow \wedge C_1 \\ & \text{and } \alpha_2 = z(w)\ ,\ C_2' = z\downarrow \wedge C_2 \\ & \text{or symmetrically} \\ \langle \tau, false \rangle & \text{otherwise} \end{cases}$$

$$\nu_y\langle \alpha, C \rangle = \begin{cases} \langle \alpha, C \wedge y \neq z \rangle & \text{if } \alpha = \overline{x}z \\ \langle \alpha, C \rangle & \text{otherwise} \end{cases} \qquad o_y\langle \alpha, C \rangle = \begin{cases} \langle \overline{x}(z), C \wedge y = z \rangle & \text{if } \alpha = \overline{x}z \\ \langle \alpha, false \rangle & \text{otherwise} \end{cases}$$

Table 1. Symbolic operational semantics and accompanying observation algebra.

names is completely captured by environments. Before plunging processes into environments, we impose a consistency requirement: No process must be allowed to commit on a link which is not known outside. That is why the input and the output transition labels include the obligation $x\downarrow$. It actually demands for an *a posteriori* check on the fact that the communication channel is globally known.

The other requirements on names encapsulated by the operators of the observation algebra are immediate. For instance, the operator $\parallel$ includes the requirement that processes communicate on the same port. Notice that the label of the synchronization transition records the name substitution activated by the communication.

1.1 Environments

Let $\mathcal{D}$ be a denumerably infinite set of constants (ranged over by $c, c_1, c_2, \ldots$) disjoint from the set $\mathcal{N}$ of names. The intuition about constants is that they give names semantic meaning. In fact, environments represent, via constants, associations between names.

In order to make our model fully concrete we assume to be working with π-calculus processes where there is no homonymy either among bound names or among free and bound names. That assumption, which takes completely away the issue of α-conversion, could be fulfilled, for instance, by indexing names with the access path in the process leading to their declarations. We assume that the free and the bound names of any process P are taken from two disjoint, infinite, subsets of $\mathcal{N}$, called $\mathcal{N}_I$ and $\mathcal{N}_{RT}$, respectively. Similarly, we assume that the set of constants $\mathcal{D}$ is partitioned into two disjoint sets $\mathcal{D}_I$ and $\mathcal{D}_{RT}$.

Environments are equivalence relations over names and constants. Given the $\pi\xi$-calculus process $\xi :: P$, the association $x\xi y$ says that the names x and y are semantically the same even if they are syntactically different. If there is no pair $x\xi c$, then the name x is not known in the environment, *i.e.* it is in every respect a private name of P.

Definition 1 (Environments) An *environment* ξ (the family of all the environments is denoted by $\mathcal{E}$) is an equivalence relation over $\mathcal{N} \cup \mathcal{D}$ which is: *(i) consistent*, *i.e.* $c_i \xi c_j$ implies $c_i = c_j$; *(ii) finitely active*, *i.e.* the set $\{(a, b) \mid a\xi b, a \neq b\}$ is finite. A constant c is *active* in ξ iff there exists x with $x\xi c$. □

In view of the consistency requirement, we shall let ξ sometimes assume the reading of a partial function. Precisely, whenever $x\xi c$, we shall denote c as $\xi(x)$. Furthermore, the partial function $\xi(\_)$ is defined on y (denoted by $\xi(y)\downarrow$) iff for some c it holds that $y\xi c$. If $\xi(\_)$ is not defined on y, then we write $\xi(y)\uparrow$.

Definition 2 (Initial environments) Letting $N \subseteq \mathcal{N}_I$, the *initial environment* ξ^N is defined as $\xi^N = \{(a, a) \mid a \in \mathcal{N} \cup \mathcal{D}\} + \{(x, \imath(x)) \mid x \in \mathcal{N}\}$ where, letting R be any relation over $\mathcal{N} \cup \mathcal{D}$, $\xi + R$ is defined as the smallest equivalence relation including $(\xi \cup R)$, and $\imath : \mathcal{N}_I \rightarrow \mathcal{D}_I$ is bijective, with $\mathcal{N}_I \cap \mathcal{N}_{RT} = \emptyset$ and $\mathcal{N}_I \cup \mathcal{N}_{RT} = \mathcal{N}$, and $\mathcal{D}_I \cap \mathcal{D}_{RT} = \emptyset$ and $\mathcal{D}_I \cup \mathcal{D}_{RT} = \mathcal{D}$. □

We start running any $\pi\xi$-calculus process into an initial environment, then, during its execution, we need to generate fresh constants. As it is the case for store allocation and deallocation in the denotational semantics of block programming languages, we assume the existence of suitable functions on environments. The function $\underline{All\mathcal{D}} : \mathcal{E} \rightarrow 2^{\mathcal{D}}_f$ takes an environment ξ and returns the finite set of all the constants which are active in it. The function $\underline{New\mathcal{D}} : \mathcal{E} \rightarrow \mathcal{D}_{RT}$ takes an environment ξ and returns a constant which is inactive in ξ.

1.2 Name instantiation

The operational behaviour of $\pi\xi$-calculus processes is described by the inference rules of Tab. 2. They make use of the functions η and δ, called the update and the result function respectively. Both $R0$ and $R1$ allow to infer the behaviour of $\xi :: P$ starting from a symbolic transition of P. The possibly many-valued function η takes care of extending the environment ξ with the name associations activated by the transition. The function δ yields the observable result out of the transition (ranged over by ρ, $\rho_1, \ldots$).

The rule $R1$, which has no counterpart in the transition system of [FMQ94], shows the first-class role of instantiation in the $\pi\xi$-calculus. Correspondingly to

$$R0 \; \frac{P \xrightarrow{\omega} P' \quad , \quad \omega \neq \langle x(y), C \rangle}{\xi :: P \overset{\delta(\xi',\omega)}{\longrightarrow\!\!\triangleright} \xi' :: P'} \quad \xi' \in \eta(\xi, \omega)$$

$$R1 \; \frac{P \overset{\langle x(y), C\rangle}{\longrightarrow} P'}{\xi :: P \overset{\delta(\xi',\langle x(y),C\rangle)}{\longrightarrow\!\!\triangleright} \xi' :: \lambda y.P'} \quad \xi' \in \eta(\xi, \langle x(y), C\rangle)$$

Table 2. Definition of $\longrightarrow\!\!\triangleright$.

the symbolic execution of the input action $x(y)$, the process $\xi :: P$ evolves to a process whose π-calculus component is explicitly a function of the placeholder y, the process $\xi' :: \lambda y.P'$. The next move of the process $\xi' :: \lambda y.P'$ shall be the instantiation of the inputted name y.

As a final remark, notice that the inference rules of Tab. 1 and of Tab. 2 fit with a mild generalization of the De Simone format [DS85].

The update and the result functions (η,δ) are reported in Tab. 3 in McCarthy style [McC60]. In the definition of η, we coerce elements to be singleton sets. The first step in computing the update function η consists in checking the satisfability of the obligation. If the obligation evaluates to false in the environment (*i.e.* $\neg[\![C]\!]\xi$), then the function η results in the empty set. Otherwise, depending on the structure of the action α, a pair is possibly added to ξ.

As the information about the privacy of names is consistently captured only at the semantic level (*i.e.* by environments), outputting the (syntactically) free name y may be the same as outputting a private name. Precisely, if $\xi(y)\uparrow$, then $\eta\xi\overline{x}yC$ is exactly the same as $\eta\xi\overline{x}(y)C$: It results into an environment where the name y is associated with a new constant.

Finally observe that, when the action is a placeholder instantiation (*i.e.* $\alpha = [y]$), the function η yields as many environments as the possible choices of c in $\underline{AllD}\ \xi$, plus a new constant. As constants are to be thought of as semantic meanings of names, this intuitively corresponds to instantiate y with all the free names plus a new, fresh, one.

Consider now the result function δ. It yields either τ or the constant(s) associated with the relevant name(s). The parameter of the action $x(y)$ is not relevant: When inputting, the process becomes a function of the actual instantiation of y. The parameter will become observable at the next step.

The result function δ computes *concrete* labels which do not include obligations anymore. As an example, letting $N = \{x, z\}$, the tree associated with the process $\xi^N :: x(y).[y = z]\tau.\mathbf{0}$ is depicted in Fig. 1. The tree shows the deterministic nature of the input move and, by contrast, the non-deterministic nature of the actual instantiation of the input parameter y. As expected, associating the name y with constants distinct from $\xi^N(z)$ results in deadlocked processes.

Since $\pi\xi$-calculus processes (ranged over by S, $S_1, \ldots$) are modelled by a

$$\eta\xi\alpha C = \neg[\![C]\!]\xi \longrightarrow \emptyset \text{ , } \mathbf{case}\ \alpha\ \mathbf{in}$$

$$\begin{array}{rl}
\tau : & \xi \\
\tau[x/y] : & \xi + (y,x) \\
\overline{x}(y), \overline{x}y : & \xi(y)\downarrow \longrightarrow \xi, \quad \xi + (y, \underline{New\mathcal{D}}\ \xi) \\
x(y) : & \xi \\
[y] : & \bigcup_{c \in (\underline{All\mathcal{D}}\ \xi\ \cup\ \underline{New\mathcal{D}}\ \xi)} \xi + (y,c)
\end{array}$$

$$\mathbf{end\_case}$$

$$\text{where } [\![C]\!]\xi = \mathbf{case}\ C\ \mathbf{in}$$

$$\begin{array}{rl}
true : & \mathbf{true} \\
false : & \mathbf{false} \\
x\downarrow : & \xi(x)\downarrow \longrightarrow \mathbf{true}, \quad \mathbf{false} \\
x = y : & x\xi y \longrightarrow \mathbf{true}, \quad \mathbf{false} \\
x \neq y : & x\xi y \longrightarrow \mathbf{false}, \quad \mathbf{true} \\
C_1 \wedge C_2 : & [\![C_1]\!]\xi \text{ and } [\![C_2]\!]\xi
\end{array}$$

$$\mathbf{end\_case}$$

$$\delta\xi\alpha C = \mathbf{case}\ \alpha\ \mathbf{in}$$

$$\begin{array}{rl}
\tau, \tau[x/y] : & \tau \\
\overline{x}(y), \overline{x}y : & \overline{\langle \xi(x), \xi(y) \rangle} \\
x(y) : & \xi(x) \\
[y] : & [\xi(y)]
\end{array}$$

$$\mathbf{end\_case}$$

Table 3. Definition of (η, δ).

standard labelled transition system, the ordinary notions of Strong bisimulation [Par81, Mil83] and of Weak (also called Observation) bisimulation and congruence [Mil89] apply.

Definition 3 (Ordinary equivalences) Let $\Longrightarrow$ be the reflexive and transitive closure of $\xrightarrow{\tau}$, and $\xRightarrow{\rho}$ be $\Longrightarrow \xrightarrow{\rho} \Longrightarrow$, and $\xRightarrow{\widehat{\rho}}$ be $\Longrightarrow$ if $\rho = \tau$, and $\xRightarrow{\rho}$ if $\rho \neq \tau$. Also, let $\mathcal{S}$ be a binary symmetric relation on $\pi\xi$-calculus processes. Then $\mathcal{S}$ is

- a *Strong bisimulation* if $S_1 \mathcal{S} S_2$ implies that if $S_1 \xrightarrow{\rho} S_1'$ then for some S_2', $S_2 \xrightarrow{\rho} S_2'$ and $S_1' \mathcal{S} S_2'$. Process S_1 is *Strong bisimilar* to S_2, written $S_1 \sim S_2$, if $S_1 \mathcal{S} S_2$ for some Strong bisimulation $\mathcal{S}$.
- a *Weak bisimulation* if $S_1 \mathcal{S} S_2$ implies that if $S_1 \xrightarrow{\rho} S_1'$ then for some S_2', $S_2 \xRightarrow{\widehat{\rho}} S_2'$ and $S_1' \mathcal{S} S_2'$. Process S_1 is *Weak bisimilar* to S_2, written $S_1 \approx S_2$, if $S_1 \mathcal{S} S_2$ for some Weak bisimulation $\mathcal{S}$.

S_1 is *Weak congruent* to S_2, written $S_1 \approx^c S_2$, iff whenever $S_1 \xrightarrow{\rho} S_1'$ then for some S_2', $S_2 \xRightarrow{\rho} S_2'$ and $S_1' \approx S_2'$, and symmetrically. □

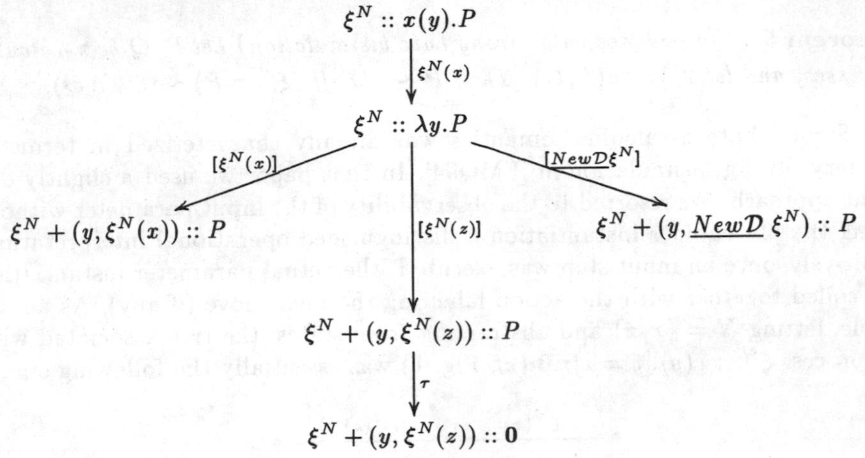

Fig. 1. The tree for $\xi^N :: x(y).P$ with $N = \{x, z\}$ and $P = [y = z]\tau.\mathbf{0}$.

2 Main characterization: the Late semantics

This section is devoted to present our main results. We first review the actual definitions of the Strong Late bisimulation, the Weak Late bisimulation, and the Weak Late ground-equality [Mil90]. Analogously to the Observation semantics of CCS, the last equivalence, in order to guarantee substitutivity in choice contexts, requires a silent action to be matched by at least one silent move.

Definition 4 (Late equivalences) Let $\Longrightarrow$ be the reflexive and transitive closure of $\stackrel{\tau}{\longrightarrow}$, and $\stackrel{\alpha}{\Longrightarrow}$ be $\Longrightarrow\stackrel{\alpha}{\longrightarrow}\Longrightarrow$, and $\stackrel{\widehat{\alpha}}{\Longrightarrow}$ be $\Longrightarrow$ if $\alpha = \tau$, and $\stackrel{\alpha}{\Longrightarrow}$ if $\alpha \neq \tau$. Also, let $\mathcal{S}$ be a binary symmetric relation on π-calculus processes. Then $\mathcal{S}$ is

- a *Strong Late bisimulation* if $P\mathcal{S}Q$ implies that if $P\stackrel{\alpha}{\longrightarrow}P'$ with $\alpha \neq x(y)$ and $bn(\alpha)$ fresh, then for some Q', $Q\stackrel{\alpha}{\longrightarrow}Q'$ and $P'\mathcal{S}Q'$; **(SL)** if $P\stackrel{x(y)}{\longrightarrow}P'$ with y fresh, then for some Q', $Q\stackrel{x(y)}{\longrightarrow}Q'$ and, for all w, $P'\{^w/y\}\mathcal{S}Q'\{^w/y\}$. Process P is *Strong Late bisimilar* to Q, written $P \sim_L Q$, if $P\mathcal{S}Q$ for some Strong Late bisimulation $\mathcal{S}$.
- a *Weak Late bisimulation* if $P\mathcal{S}Q$ implies that if $P\stackrel{\alpha}{\longrightarrow}P'$ with $\alpha \neq x(y)$ and $bn(\alpha)$ fresh, then for some Q', $Q\stackrel{\widehat{\alpha}}{\Longrightarrow}Q'$ and $P'\mathcal{S}Q'$; **(WL)** if $P\stackrel{x(y)}{\longrightarrow}P'$ with y fresh, then for some Q', $Q\Longrightarrow\stackrel{x(y)}{\longrightarrow}Q'$ and for all w there exists Q'' such that $Q'\{^w/y\}\Longrightarrow Q''$ and $P'\{^w/y\}\mathcal{S}Q''$. Process P is *Weak Late bisimilar* to Q, written $P \approx_L Q$, if $P\mathcal{S}Q$ for some Weak Late bisimulation $\mathcal{S}$.

P is *Weak Late ground-equal* to Q, written $P \dot{\simeq}_L Q$, iff $P \approx_L Q$, and whenever $P\stackrel{\tau}{\longrightarrow}P'$ then for some Q', $Q\stackrel{\tau}{\Longrightarrow}Q'$ with $P' \approx_L Q'$, and symmetrically. □

The first result we present is relative to the Late Strong bisimulation.

Theorem 5 *(Coincidence with Strong Late bisimulation) Let P, Q be π-calculus processes, and let $N = fn(P,Q)$. Then $P \dot{\sim}_L Q$ iff $(\xi^N :: P) \sim (\xi^N :: Q)$.* □

The Strong Late π-calculus semantics was already characterized in terms of ordinary Strong bisimulation in [FMQ94]. In that paper we used a slightly different approach: We resorted to the observability of the input parameter without giving the placeholder instantiation a distinguished operational interpretation. Intuitively, once an input step was executed, the actual parameter instantiation was coded together with the action labelling the next move (if any). As an example, letting $N = \{x, z\}$ and abstracting from states, the tree associated with the process $\xi^N :: x(y).[y = z]\tau.\mathbf{0}$ (*cf.* Fig. 1) was essentially the following one:

$$\bullet \xrightarrow{\xi^N(x)} \bullet \xrightarrow{\langle \xi^N(z), \tau\rangle} \bullet$$

There, the pair $\langle \xi^N(z), \tau\rangle$ could be considered unobservable: For instance the above process $\xi^N :: x(y).[y = z]\tau.\mathbf{0}$ is expected to be Observation equivalent to $\xi^N :: x(y).\mathbf{0}$. However, in $\langle \xi^N(z), \tau\rangle$, τ is invisible, $\xi^N(z)$ is not. As an example, the pair $\langle \xi^N(z), \tau\rangle$ could not safely be viewed as invisible when comparing, for $\alpha \neq \tau$, the behaviours of the two processes $\xi^N :: x(y).[y = z]\tau.\alpha.\mathbf{0}$ and $\xi^N :: x(y).\alpha.\mathbf{0}$, which are not expected to be Observation equivalent.

As a τ-step can convey extra information, for the transition system presented in [FMQ94], the axiomatization of the Weak bisimulation needs more efforts than simply augmenting the proof system for the Strong equivalence with Milner's τ-laws. By contrast, assigning to the parameter instantiation a distinguished operational meaning allows us to uniformly deal with both the Strong and the Weak cases. To that extent, although a slightly different statement was already proved in [FMQ94], Theorem 5 can be considered a contribution of this paper.

Commenting on Theorem 5, notice that the observability of the placeholder instantiation is a *must* when one tries to characterize the Late universal quantification on w of **(SL)** in a Strong bisimulation setting. As the only universal quantification in the ordinary Strong bisimulation clause is that on moves, instantiation must become a move. Thinking of the placeholder instantiation as an observable event compulsorily following the actual input step also strengthens the opportunity of breaking the double arrow down in **(WL)**. As no silent action can be performed after an input move, any double arrow $\stackrel{x(y)}{\Longrightarrow}$ for sure corresponds to $\Longrightarrow\xrightarrow{x(y)}$ rather than to $\Longrightarrow\xrightarrow{x(y)}\stackrel{\tau}{\Longrightarrow}$.

Theorem 6 *(Coincidence with Weak Late bisimulation and ground-equality) Let P, Q be π-calculus processes, and let $N = fn(P,Q)$. Then $P \dot{\approx}_L Q$ iff $(\xi^N :: P) \approx (\xi^N :: Q)$, and $P \simeq_L Q$ iff $(\xi^N :: P) \approx^c (\xi^N :: Q)$.* □

We now provide an equational characterization of the Strong bisimulation semantics over finite $\pi\xi$-calculus processes. Then the axiom system for the Observation congruence is obtained by adding Milner's τ-laws. The terms of the axiom systems are given by the grammar $S ::= \xi :: P \mid \rho \triangleright S \mid S \oplus S$ where '$\triangleright$' is a prefix operator, '$\oplus$' is a choice operator, and P is an expression having the following syntax:

$$P ::= \mathbf{0} \mid \omega.P \mid [x=y]P \mid P+P \mid P|P \mid P \parallel P \mid P \rfloor\!\rfloor P \mid (y)P \mid (\nu_y)P \mid (o_y)P$$

The equational theory of the $\pi\xi$-calculus processes is based on the axiomatic characterization of the low level π-calculus processes. This last axiomatization is gotten by exploiting the procedure presented in [ABV94]. The idea of [ABV94] is to reduce processes to head normal forms (finite labelled trees) by introducing suitable auxiliary operators. Thus, proving completeness is reduced to proving equalities of labelled finite trees. This problem was already solved in [HM85].

The first step of the procedure consists in breaking down, by means of auxiliary operators, each process constructors f whose operational behaviour is described by more than one inference rule. One auxiliary operator f_j per rule is introduced, and the equation $f(v) = \sum_j f_j(v)$ is imposed. For instance, in the case of the restriction operator the expansion law $(y)P = (\nu_y)P + (o_y)P$ is obtained. The next step of the procedure is to impose distributive and action laws. Distributive laws describe the interplay between the non-deterministic choice operator and the other (smooth) operators (*e.g.* $(\nu_y)(P+Q) = (\nu_y)P + (\nu_y)Q$). Action laws describe the interactions of the operators with prefixing. Here, we need to extend the action laws to the case of the generalized prefixing $\omega.P$ (*e.g.* $(\nu_y)(\omega.P) = \nu_y(\omega).(y)P$). Finally, the so called inaction laws are stated. They identify as the deadlocked process any expression having no outgoing transition (*e.g.* $(\nu_y)\mathbf{0} = \mathbf{0}$).

The axiom systems $\mathcal{A}_s$ and $\mathcal{A}_w$ are reported in Tab. 4. We use $\mathcal{A}\_ \vdash S_1 = S_2$ to indicate that the equality is proved using the system $\mathcal{A}\_$. As usual we assume that $\bigoplus_\emptyset$ denotes the identity of $\oplus$, *i.e.* $\xi :: \mathbf{0}$. Notice that, while U and V are of course axiom schemata with an infinite number of instantiations, in every instantiation the sum $\oplus_{\xi'}$ is extended to a *finite* number of summands. Also, observe that auxiliary operators are only used for the axiomatization of the low level π-calculus processes. This avoids the problems discussed in [Ace94].

Theorem 7 *(Axiomatic characterizations of the Late semantics) Let P, Q be finite π-calculus processes, and let $N = fn(P,Q)$. Then $P \dot{\sim}_L Q$ iff $\mathcal{A}_s \vdash (\xi^N :: P) = (\xi^N :: Q)$, and $P \dot{\simeq}_L Q$ iff $\mathcal{A}_s, \mathcal{A}_w \vdash (\xi^N :: P) = (\xi^N :: Q)$.* □

3 Further results

In this section we sketch some results induced by the previous characterization of the Late semantics.

The fact that names can be transmitted in interactions makes the π-calculus semantics naturally proliferate in two distinct families depending on the operational intuition about input actions [MPW93]. The act of inputting and the

$\mathcal{A}_s$:	$(HM1)$	$P_1 + P_2 = P_2 + P_1$
	$(HM2)$	$(P_1 + P_2) + P_3 = P_1 + (P_2 + P_3)$
	$(HM3)$	$P + P = P$
	$(HM4)$	$P + \mathbf{0} = P$
	(EX)	$P_1 \mid P_2 = P_1 \,⌊\!⌊\, P_2 + P_2 \,⌊\!⌊\, P_1 + P_1 \parallel P_2$
	(R)	$(x)P = (\nu_x)P + (o_x)P$
	$(A1)$	$[x = y]\, \omega.P = \mu_y^x(\omega).P$
	$(A2)$	$\omega.P_1 \,⌊\!⌊\, P_2 = \omega.(P_1 \mid P_2)$
	$(A3)$	$\omega_1.P_1 \parallel \omega_2.P_2 = (\omega_1 \parallel \omega_2).(P_1 \mid P_2)$
	$(A4)$	$(\nu_x)(\omega.P) = \nu_x(\omega).(x)P$
	$(A5)$	$(o_x)(\omega.P) = o_x(\omega).P$
	$(D1)$	$[x = y](P_1 + P_2) = [x = y]P_1 + [x = y]P_2$
	$(D2)$	$(P_1 + P_2) \,⌊\!⌊\, P = P_1 \,⌊\!⌊\, P + P_2 \,⌊\!⌊\, P$
	$(D3)$	$(P_1 + P_2) \parallel P = P_1 \parallel P + P_2 \parallel P$
	$(D4)$	$P \parallel (P_1 + P_2) = P \parallel P_1 + P \parallel P_2$
	$(D5)$	$(\nu_x)(P_1 + P_2) = (\nu_x)P_1 + (\nu_x)P_2$
	$(D6)$	$(o_x)(P_1 + P_2) = (o_x)P_1 + (o_x)P_2$
	(IN)	$[x = y]\mathbf{0} = (\nu_x)\mathbf{0} = (o_x)\mathbf{0} = \mathbf{0} \,⌊\!⌊\, P = P \parallel \mathbf{0} = \mathbf{0} \parallel P = \mathbf{0}$
	$(S1)$	$S_1 \oplus S_2 = S_2 \oplus S_1$
	$(S2)$	$(S_1 \oplus S_2) \oplus S_3 = S_1 \oplus (S_2 \oplus S_3)$
	$(S3)$	$S \oplus S = S$
	$(S4)$	$S \oplus \xi :: \mathbf{0} = S$
	(U)	$\xi :: \omega.P = \bigoplus_{\xi' \in \eta(\xi,\omega)} \delta(\xi', \omega) \triangleright (\xi' :: P) \quad \text{if } \omega \neq \langle x(y), C\rangle$
	(V)	$\xi :: \langle x(y), C\rangle.P = \bigoplus_{\xi' \in \eta(\xi,\langle x(y),C\rangle)} \delta(\xi', \langle x(y), C\rangle) \triangleright (\xi' :: \langle [y], \mathit{true}\rangle.P)$
	(D)	$\xi :: (P_1 + P_2) = \xi :: P_1 \oplus \xi :: P_2$
$\mathcal{A}_w$:	$(T1)$	$\rho \triangleright \tau \triangleright S = \rho \triangleright S$
	$(T2)$	$S \oplus \tau \triangleright S = \tau \triangleright S$
	$(T3)$	$\rho \triangleright (S_1 \oplus \tau \triangleright S_2) \oplus \rho \triangleright S_2 = \rho \triangleright (S_1 \oplus \tau \triangleright S_2)$

Table 4. Axiom systems $\mathcal{A}_s$ and $\mathcal{A}_w$.

choice of the received name can be considered either as one single atomic event (Early view) or as two conceptually different events (Late view). We already commented on the Late view; the Early view is exactly that adopted when translating value passing CCS into infinitary pure CCS. The above discussion should suffice to convince the reader that the Early π-calculus semantics (both Strong and Weak) can be easily retrieved by imposing the atomicity of the input and of the subsequent instantiation move (this is indeed an easy consequence of a result proved in [FMQ95b]). For instance, letting $N = \{x, z\}$, the Early tree for the process $\xi^N :: x(y).[y = z]\tau.\mathbf{0}$ (*cf.* Fig. 1) is displayed in Fig. 2.

The $\pi\xi$-calculus also allows to characterize the Branching [vGW89] and the Dynamic [MS92] equivalence, which obviously proliferate into Early and Late

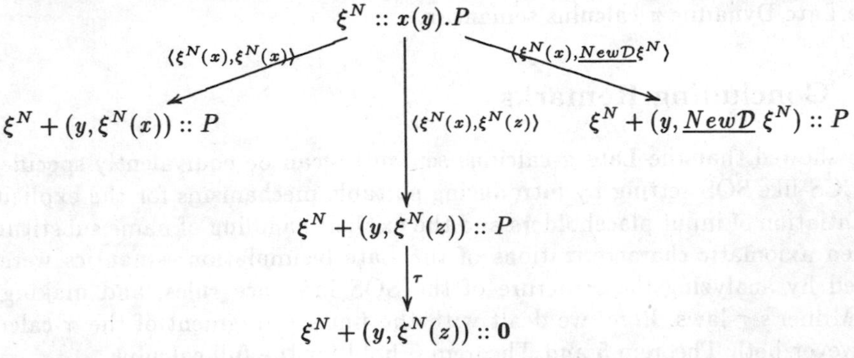

Fig. 2. The Early tree for $\xi^N :: x(y).P$ with $N = \{x, z\}$ and $P = [y = z]\tau.\mathbf{0}$.

versions. We consider here only their Late views, the Early ones could be dealt with as well. Both Branching and Dynamic equivalences refine Observation equivalence. The first one aims to equate processes with as close as possible branching capabilities. As the execution of arbitrarily many τ-moves potentially results in disregarding external choices, when matching a single arrow move with a double arrow step, the Branching bisimulation clause asks for intermediate bisimulation checks. Precisely, **(W)** is refined as follows:

(B) if $P \xrightarrow{\alpha} P'$ then either $\alpha = \tau$ and P' is Branching bisimilar to Q, or for some Q_1, Q_2, Q', $Q \Longrightarrow Q_1 \xrightarrow{\alpha} Q_2 \Longrightarrow Q'$ and the pairs of processes (P, Q_1), (P', Q_2), (P', Q') are all Branching bisimilar.

For instance, the Branching bisimulation breaks the Observational equivalence of the two CCS-like processes $a + \tau.(b+c) + c$ and $a + \tau.(b+c)$. In fact no Branching bisimulation game can match the c-labelled transition of the first process. By a standard result [vGW89], we got the following statement.

Proposition 8 *(Axiomatic characterizations of the Branching semantics) Let P, Q be finite π-calculus processes, and let $N = fn(P, Q)$. Then $\xi^N :: P$ is Branching equivalent to $\xi^N :: Q$ iff $\mathcal{A}_s, T1, T2 \vdash (\xi^N :: P) = (\xi^N :: Q)$.* □

Proposition 8 induces the characterization of the Late Branching π-calculus semantics which could be formally defined in the obvious way.

We now sketch an analogous result on Dynamic equivalence, the largest Weak bisimulation which is also a Weak congruence. The axiomatization of the Dynamic equivalence differs from that of the Observational equivalence only for disregarding the first τ-law [MS92]. *E.g.*, as $\tau.b \approx b$ but $\tau.b \not\approx^c b$, the Weak congruent CCS-like processes $a.\tau.b$ and $a.b$ are not Dynamic equivalent. For the Dynamic equivalence, we get the following result.

Proposition 9 *(Axiomatic characterizations of the Dynamic semantics) Let P, Q be finite π-calculus processes, and let $N = fn(P, Q)$. Then $\xi^N :: P$ is Dynamic equivalent to $\xi^N :: Q$ iff $\mathcal{A}_s, T2, T3 \vdash (\xi^N :: P) = (\xi^N :: Q)$.* □

A straightforward corollary of Proposition 9 would state the characterization of the Late Dynamic π-calculus semantics.

4 Concluding Remarks

We showed that the Late π-calculus semantics can be equivalently specified in a CCS-like SOS setting by introducing suitable mechanisms for the explicit instantiation of input placeholders and the explicit handling of name substitution. Then axiomatic characterizations of the Late bisimulation semantics were derived by analyzing the structure of the SOS inference rules, and making use of Milner's τ-laws. Here, we dealt with the finitary fragment of the π-calculus, however both Theorem 5 and Theorem 6 hold for the full calculus.

The characterization and the axiomatization of the Weak Late semantics as Observation equivalence is an original contribution. A previous definition of the Strong Late semantics in terms of ordinary bisimulation already appeared in [FMQ94], where the actual instantiation of the input placeholder was not assigned a distinguished operational interpretation. The present framework generalizes the approach exploited in [FMQ94] which is not flexible enough to allow to retrieve the Weak Late semantics in the expected way, *i.e.* by simply adding the τ-laws to the axiom system for the Strong equivalence.

Our approach is general enough to allow to recover, in straightforward ways, other bisimulation semantics. The Early semantics can be retrieved by imposing the atomicity of the input and of the subsequent instantiation move. Also, by virtue of well-known results, complete axiomatizations of the Branching and of the Dynamic bisimulations can be gotten by simply removing from the axiom system $\mathcal{A}_w$ the equation $(T3)$ and the equation $(T1)$ respectively.

Up-to-date, the Weak Late π-calculus bisimulation was only axiomatized relying on the notion of Symbolic bisimulation [Lin95]. The Symbolic bisimulation is usually got as closure on top of a family of indexed bisimulation relations [HL93]. To our knowledge, no result is available in that setting about the Branching and the Dynamic equivalence.

References

[ABV94] L. Aceto, B. Bloom, and F. Vaandrager. Turning SOS Rules into Equations. *Information and Computation*, 111(1):1–52, 1994.

[Ace94] L. Aceto. On "axiomatising finite concurrent processes". *SIAM Journal of Computing*, 23(4):852–863, 1994.

[CPS93] R. Cleaveland, J. Parrow, and B. Steffen. The Concurrency Workbench: A Semantics-Based Tool for the Verification of Concurrent Systems. *ACM Trans. on Programming Languages and Systems*, 15(1):36–72, 1993.

[DS85] R. De Simone. Higher level synchronizing devices in MEIJE-SCCS. *Theoretical Computer Science*, 37(3):245–267, 1985.

[FGM91] G.-L. Ferrari, R. Gorrieri, and U. Montanari. An Extended Expansion Theorem. In S. Abramsky and T.S.E. Maibaum, editors, *Proc. 3rd TAPSOFT*, volume 494 of *LNCS*. Springer-Verlag, 1991.

[FMQ94] G.-L. Ferrari, U. Montanari, and P. Quaglia. A π-calculus with Explicit Substitutions: the Late Semantics. In I. Prívara, B. Rovan, and P. Ružička, editors, *Proc. 19th MFCS*, volume 841 of *Lecture Notes in Computer Science*. Springer-Verlag, 1994.

[FMQ95a] G.-L. Ferrari, G. Modoni, and P. Quaglia. Towards a Semantic-Based Verification Environment for the π-calculus. Submitted for publication, 1995.

[FMQ95b] G.-L. Ferrari, U. Montanari, and P. Quaglia. A π-calculus with Explicit Substitutions. Full version of [FMQ94], to appear in *Theoretical Computer Science*, 1995.

[HL93] M. Hennessy and H. Lin. Proof Systems for Message-Passing Process Algebras. In E. Best, editor, *Proc. 4th CONCUR*, volume 715 of *LNCS*. Springer-Verlag, 1993.

[HM85] M. Hennessy and R. Milner. Algebraic Laws for Nondeterminism and Concurrency. *Journal of the ACM*, 32(1):137–161, 1985.

[Lin95] H. Lin. Complete Inference Systems for Weak Bisimulation Equivalences in the π-Calculus. To appear in the Proc. of TAPSOFT '95, 1995.

[McC60] J. McCarthy. Recursive Functions of Symbolic Expressions and Their Computation by Machine, Part 1. *Communications of the ACM*, 3, 1960.

[Mil80] R. Milner. *A Calculus of Communicating Systems*, volume 92 of *LNCS*. Springer-Verlag, 1980.

[Mil83] R. Milner. Calculi for synchrony and asynchrony. *Theoretical Computer Science*, 25:267–310, 1983.

[Mil89] R. Milner. *Communication and Concurrency*. International Series in Computer Science. Prentice Hall, 1989.

[Mil90] R. Milner. Weak bisimilarity: congruences and equivalences. Unpublished notes, 1990.

[Mil91] R. Milner. The Polyadic π-Calculus: a Tutorial. Report ECS-LFCS-91-180, Comp. Science Dep., Edinburgh University, 1991.

[MPW92] R. Milner, J. Parrow, and D. Walker. A Calculus of Mobile Processes, Part I and II. *Information and Computation*, 100(1):1–77, 1992.

[MPW93] R. Milner, J. Parrow, and D. Walker. Modal logics for mobile processes. *Theoretical Computer Science*, 114(1):149–171, 1993.

[MS92] U. Montanari and V. Sassone. Dynamic congruence vs. progressing bisimulation for CCS. *Fundamenta Informaticae*, XVI:171–199, 1992.

[Par81] D. Park. Concurrency and automata on infinite sequences. In *Proc. 5th GI-Conference*, volume 104 of *LNCS*. Springer-Verlag, 1981.

[Plo81] G. D. Plotkin. A Structural Approach to Operational Semantics. Technical Report DAIMI-FN-19, Comp. Science Dep., Aarhus University, 1981.

[vGW89] R.J. van Glabbeek and W.P. Weijland. Branching time and abstraction in bisimulation semantics (extended abstract). In *Information Processing, Proc. IFIP 11th World Computer Congress*, pages 613–618, 1989.

The Fixpoint-Analysis Machine

Bernhard Steffen*

Andreas Claßen Marion Klein Jens Knoop Tiziana Margaria

Universität Passau
Germany

Abstract. We present a fixpoint-analysis machine, for the efficient computation of *homogeneous*, *hierarchical*, and *alternating* fixpoints over *regular*, *context-free/push-down* and *macro* models. Applications of such fixpoint computations include intra- and interprocedural data flow analysis, model checking for various temporal logics, and the verification of behavioural relations between distributed systems. The fixpoint-analysis machine identifies an adequate (parameterized) level for a uniform treatment of all those problems, which, despite its uniformity, outperforms the 'standard iteration based' special purpose tools usually by factors around 10, even if the additional compilation time is taken into account.

1 Introduction and Motivation

A great number of analysis and verification problems such as abstract interpretation, data flow analysis, model checking, determination of behavioural relations between distributed systems, hardware verification and synthesis, etc., boil down to the computation of a specific kind of fixpoint. In fact, in all these areas of application, specific fixpoint solving tools have been independently constructed and tuned for their special purposes.

The idea behind the fixpoint-analysis machine is to define a uniform platform for fixpoint computations, which, despite its uniformity, outperforms the 'iteration based' special purpose tools. This goal is approached by translating the specific fixpoint problems into very fine-grained but computationally advantageous representations, which allow us to eliminate as much redundancy as possible. Our design stems from the observation that almost all fixpoint problems considered in practice can be formulated as a model checking problem of a certain kind. Currently we are uniformly covering the kinds of fixpoint computations summarized in Table 1, which depend on the structure of the underlying model and formula. The structure of the analysis machine is a consequence of the observation that, although each of the different kinds of fixpoint computations requires special care, there is a large common core as soon as one breaks down

* Lehrstuhl für Programmiersysteme, Universität Passau, Innstraße 33, D-94032 Passau (Germany), tel: +49 851 509.3090, fax: +49 851 509.3092, steffen@fmi.uni-passau.de

the problem to the appropriate kind of granularity and allows a limited form of parameterization. In fact, the machine architecture we are going to present allows us to uniformly cover all the kinds of fixpoint problems mentioned without performance penalty, as our choice of granularity is tailored for runtime optimization. In fact, the differences between these kinds of problems and their corresponding fixpoint computations only require a change in the data domain the fixpoint is computed over and in the program controlling the order of the fixpoint computation. Thus the architecture and the remaining data structures of the machine coincide in all these applications.

Fixpoint class	Model class		
	regular	CFR/PDA	macro
homogeneous	(chaotic, $\mathbb{B}$)	(chaotic, $\mathcal{F}_{\mathbb{B}}$)	(chaotic, high.ord. $\mathcal{F}_{\mathbb{B}}$)
hierarchical	(layered, $\mathbb{B}$)	(layered, $\mathcal{F}_{\mathbb{B}}$)	(layered, high.ord. $\mathcal{F}_{\mathbb{B}}$)
alternated nesting	(backtrack, $\mathbb{B}$)	(backtrack, $\mathcal{F}_{\mathbb{B}}$)	(backtrack, high.ord. $\mathcal{F}_{\mathbb{B}}$)

Table 1. Classification of the Fixpoint Computations as (strategy, domain)

Our practical experience with the analysis machine confirms the well-known fact that compilation is better than interpretation. In fact, even taking the additional translation effort into account, the analysis machine outperforms the computations on standard data structures by factors usually around 10. Details are reported in Section 6.

The uniform and general structure of our machine also leads to excellent experimental features. On the practical side, it supports the investigation of heuristics, which are important when dealing with complex kinds of fixpoint problems. On the theoretical side, it supports the study e.g. of the essence of alternated nesting, which is still a matter of research.

It should be noted that we focus on global iterative fixpoint computations here. Therefore very specific heuristics (like e.g. the Binary Decision Diagram-based techniques for model checking) which are extremely efficient in 'good' cases, but much worse than the standard iteration techniques in 'bad' cases, are not covered.

The fixpoint machine constitutes a central component of the computational core of the META-Frame [StMC95, SFCM94, MaCS95], which is a uniform environment for high-level construction, verification and analysis of hardware and software systems.

The next section summarizes the domain of application, while Section 3 presents our analysis machine. Subsequently, Section 4 discusses the optimizing compilation, Section 5 describes the fixpoint computation mechanism, Section 6 reports on the performance of the machine, and Section 7 draws our conclusions.

2 The Application Domains: The Present Scenario

Figure 1 summarizes the scenario discussed in this paper. The upper two rows of the figure address the currently considered application areas, ranging from several kinds of dataflow analyses [Hech77] and the verification of behavioural relations (top row) to various classes of model checking (second upper row). As each of the top row applications can be reduced to model checking via logical characterization without runtime penalty, the second upper row, showing a hierarchy of model checking problems, represents both an application level and a common platform for the top row applications.

We will first explain the upper two rows of the figure, and subsequently sketch the lower part discussing the implementation of the various kinds of model checkers.

- *Intraprocedural dataflow analysis*: algorithms of this kind can be realized efficiently and at almost no implementation cost on our analysis machine via a data flow analysis generator which automatically produces fixpoint machine code from high level specifications [Stef91, Stef93, Stef94]. We will discuss this implementation and its performance in Section 6.

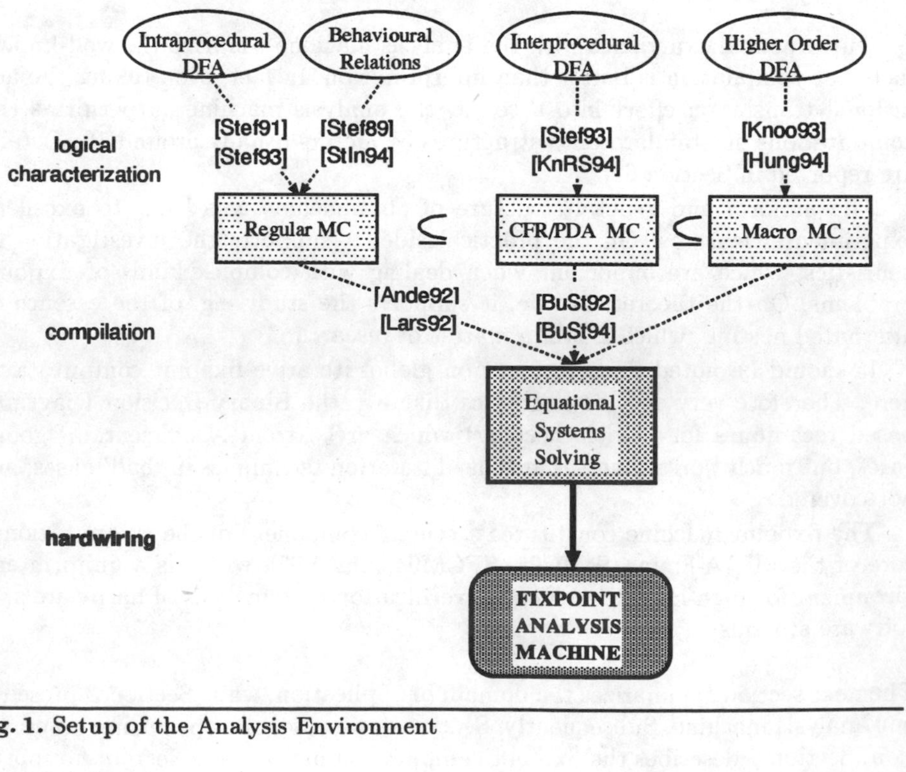

Fig. 1. Setup of the Analysis Environment

- *Interprocedural data flow analysis*: in this setting we are able to cover a wide class of programs that contain recursive procedures with value parameters. The corresponding data flow analysis generator, which uses the same high level specifications as the intraprocedural version, is under implementation. It requires the combination of the methods presented in [Stef93, BuSt94, KnSt92a, KnRS94].
- *Higher order data flow analysis*: this setting allows us to deal with further types of parameters, like reference and procedure parameters. Whereas the case of reference parameters is still rather efficient, the optimal treatment of arbitrary (finite mode) procedures requires an unacceptable effort and should therefore be handled approximatively. For details the reader is referred to [Knoo93], where a method is presented that is safe, efficient, and optimal for programs of mode two without global formal procedure parameters. Essentially, all these methods boil down to adding a specific preprocess to an interprocedural analysis, which can efficiently be realized on the analysis machine. The corresponding extension of the interprocedural data flow analysis generator to this case is rather simple, as the preprocess is independent of the specific analysis.
- *Behavioural relation checking*: the verification of behavioural relations between distributed systems can also be transformed into a particular model checking problem via logical characterization [Stef89, StIn94].

The second row of Figure 1 presents a hierarchy of model checking problems that are classified according to the structure of the underlying model [Stef94]. Beside this structure, the possibility and the extent of interference between minimal and maximal fixpoints – generating homogeneous, hierarchical or alternating fixpoints [EmLe86] – is an important classification criterion.

Whereas all the top row applications require at most hierarchical fixpoints, alternating fixpoints are necessary when dealing with properties like fairness. Altogether we face a potential of nine structurally different model checking problems, two of which (the alternating case for context-free/push-down and macro models), see Table 1, even though decidable, do not have a fixpoint characterization yet. The other seven cases can be uniformly represented by means of a finite equational system together with a parity vector specifying the particular solution (minimal, maximal) of interest. This leads to the third row. Actually, we proposed such transformations also for the two exceptional cases, but their correctness is still a conjecture. While standard model checkers work on the representation level of equational systems, our computation takes place on the level of the fixpoint-analysis machine. Moreover, as most of the translation into the equational representation, which can be regarded as a common intermediate level, is more or less standard, we will concentrate on the analysis machine in the sequel.

Besides presenting the architecture of the analysis machine, the next sections will show how to translate an equational description of the third level into machine code. In fact, the point of this paper lies in the impact of this optimizing translation on the performances, which will be discussed in detail for the hierarchical regular setting. The extensions to other settings are more complicated, not yet fully implemented, and will therefore only be sketched.

3 The Fixpoint-Analysis Machine

The structure of the machine reflects the observation that, although each of the different kinds of fixpoint computations of Table 1 requires special care, there is a large common core as soon as one breaks down the problem to the appropriate kind of granularity and allows a limited form of parameterization. In fact, the machine architecture we are going to present allows us to uniformly cover all the mentioned kinds of fixpoint problems without performance penalty, as our choice of granularity is tailored for runtime optimization.

The machine architecture is illustrated in Figure 2. Here, the white parts are common to all analyses. Only the value array and the control unit (shaded in the figure) are parameterized in the kind of problem. The parameter for the value array is the type of values considered (the second component in Table 1), which depends on the kind of model under investigation, and the control unit steers the order (chaotic, layered or with backtrack) of the fixpoint computation accordingly. Instruction array, parity vector, block graph, and worklist are completely problem-independent. The following paragraphs sketch the 'abstract data type' of each functional unit.

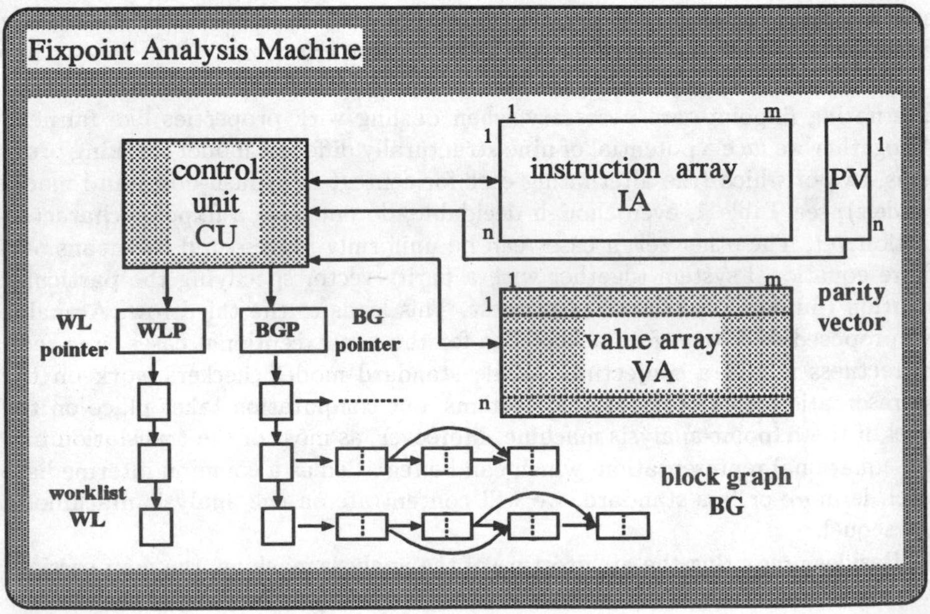

Fig. 2. The Architecture of the Fixpoint-Analysis Machine.

3.1 The Instruction and Value Arrays

The fixpoint computation proceeds by successively updating the components of the *value array* (encoding the information of n equations for m states of the model) by means of component-specific operations that are stored in the *instruction array*. Our choice of granularity leads to a very simple structure that must be modeled by the instruction array: *AND/OR/COMP graphs*. They represent (i) the kind of *operation* to perform (conjunction, disjunction, or functional composition), (ii) the *list of operands* for this operation, in form of a list of components of the value array, and (iii) the *influence list*, i.e. those components that are influenced by the value of the considered component. All this can easily and automatically be determined by means of a simple compiler (see section 4).

Whereas the structure of the instruction array is completely independent of the considered fixpoint problem, the component type of the value array depends on the kind of model we are considering (see Table 1, second component):

- In the *regular* case single bits are sufficient. They indicate whether a specific node of the model satisfies a particular formula.
- In the *CFR/PDA* case the elements correspond to property (predicate) transformers, and are therefore Boolean functions $\mathcal{F}_{\mathbb{B}} : \mathbb{B}^n \to \mathbb{B}$ of an arity determined by the size of the considered system and formula. For reasons of efficiency, they are represented as Binary Decision Diagrams (BDDs) [Brya86].
- In the *macro* case, elements correspond to mappings between property transformers. Thus we are dealing with higher order Boolean functions here.

The instruction array is completely constructed at compile-time. Thus there is only read-access at runtime. In contrast, the value array must be read and written at runtime, and only its space allocation is a matter of compilation.

3.2 The Parity Vector

A fixpoint problem is completely specified by a system of mutually recursive equations, where each equation is classified as maximal or minimal according to the kind of fixpoint of interest.

The instruction array does not contain this classification: it merely stands for a set of fixpoint problems. The classification is specified separately in a vector that stores for each row of the instruction array the desired kind (min, max) of fixpoint, called its *parity*. Note that it would be technically simple, but algorithmically unpleasant, to allow changes of the parity component-wise, but there is currently no demand in this direction.

Like the instruction array, the parity vector is created at compile-time and only read-accessed at runtime.

3.3 The Block Graph

Homogeneous fixpoint problems can be solved by means of a totally *chaotic* iteration [GKLR94] over the value array. But whenever both kinds of fixpoints are involved, the order of the fixpoint computation becomes essential. For hierarchical systems, a layered approach is sufficient, while alternating fixpoint formulas require a very strict discipline involving backtracking. This observation motivates the structure of our block graphs, which are ***lists of DAGs***[2] (directed acyclic graphs). The basic underlying idea is that edges represent ordering constraints and nodes collect ***blocks***, i.e., collections of equations whose fixpoints can be computed in an arbitrary order. In fact, we will see that this graph structure is already sufficient to uniformly capture even the strongly optimized organization of the fixpoint computation for the alternating case.

Technically, the need for blocks arises as soon as there are depending minimal and maximal fixpoints. This dependency requires a strict organization of the order in which these fixpoints are computed. In the hierarchical case, a simple sequentialization (layered computation) is sufficient, and in the more complicated alternating case a backtracking procedure must be organized following the strucure of the underlying block graph. It is convenient to additionally split blocks according to their parity, which leads to the notions of ***min-blocks*** and ***max-blocks***. This additional separation is uncritical as a single block could anyhow only comprise completely independent minimal and maximal equations.

Blocks are important, as they allow an efficient fixpoint computation. The switching between different blocks according to ordering constraints is more expensive than the worklist-oriented chaotic iteration allowed within a block. Thus efficient fixpoint algorithms will completely determine the fixpoint of a block before taking a switch. This approach is only guaranteed to be optimal when using counters (cf. Section 5).

- For ***homogeneous fixpoints***, a one component list containing a single node DAG is sufficient, as we are here dealing with a single block where no ordering constraints need to be taken care of.
- *Hierarchical fixpoint* computations postpone the evaluation of an equation until all equations of different parity which may influence it have reached their fixpoints. In terms of model checking, this corresponds to an 'innermost' strategy for the evaluation of the formula. This requirement can be expressed sufficiently by means of a list of sets of formulas, i.e. by a list of one node DAGs.
- *Alternating fixpoint* computations require backtracking, which leads to an exponential complexity in the alternation depth ([EmLe86]) of the considered formula. Thus the most important source of optimization is the reduction of backtracking steps. Block graphs support such a reduction by structuring the global dependence graph between the fixpoint equations in the following fashion:
  - The list structure reflects the dependence (ordering constraints) between the strongly connected components of the dependence graph. Of course, these constraints form in general a DAG structure. However, as in the hierarchical case, we can simply collapse this DAG to a list without runtime penalty.

[2] This choice is an elaboration of the block graphs presented in [ClSt91b, ClKS92].

- The DAG structure reflects part of the ordering constraints within a strongly connected component: a constraint between two equations e_1 and e_2 is only kept if the row of e_1 precedes the row of e_2 in the value array. This DAG of equations is then collapsed by combining all equations that have a 'similar' dependence relation into a node. We will here omit the exact definition of this rather complicated collapse.

Block graphs are constructed at compile-time, and there is only read-access at runtime. In fact, we only need the operations **NEXT_BL** to access the next set of equations, whose evaluation can be performed in an arbitrary order in case no backtracking is required, and **RESET_BL**, to provide a similar set in case backtracking is needed.

3.4 The Worklist

Whereas the block graph is a mean to steer the fixpoint computation globally, i.e. between blocks, the worklist organizes the fixpoint computation inside a block. It contains the addresses of the value array components of the current block whose values must be updated as a consequence of earlier changes in the value array. The list is dynamically initialized when entering a new block, and it is updated during the computation by appending the addresses of all the influenced value array components.

The worklist is a pure runtime entity, initialized, updated, and read at runtime.

4 Optimizing Compilation

The organization of the impact of the interference between minimal and maximal fixpoints on the fixpoint computation by means of the block graph is an essential part of the compilation. As this has been discussed already, and as the corresponding programs of the control unit are rather straightforward, we concentrate here on the treatment of the different kinds of models (regular, CFR/PDA, macro). As mentioned already, this only concerns the value array, even though the instruction array is indirectly affected too, since simple data domains support more optimizations. In particular, we will see that the partial evaluation feature of our compiler completely evaluates all function compositions in the regular case.

A central feature of the translation is *partial evaluation*. Whereas certain basic techniques are always applied, more specific techiques are used depending on the analysis context. We explain this in the context of a model checking problem starting with the standard case.

1. The knowledge of the *logic formula* alone suffices to determine the kind of fixpoint to be computed, the involved AND/OR/COMP subformulas, their parity, and part of their organization in blocks. This instantiation provides a tool for checking the considered formula for arbitrary models. Knowing the kind of models to be considered allows us to determine the domain of the

fixpoint computation. Machines of this kind correspond to the usual intra- or interprocedural data flow analysis algorithms ([Stef91, Stef93]).
Beside this straightforward partial evaluation, our compilers also contain a rewriting machine, which aims at a minimal equational characterization of the considered formula. This rewriting machine is rather complex, thus it should only be applied if the formula will be used for the investigation of several models, as it is the case in data flow analysis.

2. The knowledge of the *model* under investigation determines the domain of the fixpoint computation and preliminary versions of the influence and dependence sets are fixed.
Beside this partial evaluation, we also provide minimization procedures that e.g. collapse the model up to bisimulation ([Miln89]). This step only makes sense if a single model is going to be investigated with respect to several formulas. Typically, this arises during the development of a system, when designers want to verify certain safety and liveness properties for their design.

The results of the separate compilation steps above are then merged to a single combined representation, which is the basis for the instantiation of the instruction array. Of course, if both the model and the formula are known already at the beginning, the instruction array is directly instantiated.

Finally, we discuss how the AND/OR/COMP functions constituting the components of the instruction array can be further optimized:

1. Functional composition is necessary to describe the effect of a transition step in the model. If the effect of this step is known at compile-time, which is e.g. the case when modelling intraprocedural (i.e. regular) analyses, all the functional compositions can be immediately evaluated. In the more complicated case of interprocedural (i.e. CFR/PDA) analyses, some of the transitions denote procedure calls. Thus their effect is not known at compile-time. However, the functional compositions associated with all the other transitions can still be evaluated. The runtime gain of this partial evaluation is usually much higher than the partial evaluation time itself.
2. Several entries of the instruction array will be constant functions. Thus we can perform constant propagation and folding on the instruction array.
3. A particularly strong optimization is possible for regular model structures, i.e. in cases where the components of the value array store bits. From the first step we know already that we only need to consider conjunction and disjunction in this case. This observation leads to the introduction of counters, which intuitively measure the distance to a change in the value array. We will explain this idea, a modified version of which can already be found in [ClSt91], in the case of a homogeneous system of maximal equations. Homogeneous systems of minimal equations behave dually.
Maximal fixpoints are computed by successively updating a maximally initialized value array, where (essentially) all components are assumed to be *true* [Tars55]. Thus for monotonicity reasons, an update can only switch from *true* to *false*. For a conjunction, this happens as soon as one operand switches

to *false*. Thus the counter is initialized to 1. In contrast, for disjunction all the operands must switch before the value changes. Thus the counter is initialized with the number of operands. Working on counters avoids to evaluate any of the instructions of the instruction array, as the only operation we need is a decrement of the corresponding counter whenever one of the operands changes its value. Only when the counter of an array component reaches zero (indicating a switch of its corresponding boolean value) all influenced components need to be informed to decrement their counters via insertion in the worklist.
This optimization is also applicable to the fixpoint computation for single blocks in the hierarchical and alternating case.

5 Computing Fixpoints

In this section we sketch the computation mechanism for the various kinds of fixpoint problems. We start by considering the three regular problems, which only require a fixpoint computation for bitvectors. Subsequently we discuss the extension to context-free structures. Even though the decidability of the model checking problem is implied by decidability results about monadic second order logic [MuSc85], the known efficient algorithms cover alternation free, i.e. hierarchical formulas, only. The best known algorithm for the general case is non-elementary. The further extension to push-down structures, which in contrast to classical automata theory do not coincide with context-free structures when the branching structure of the models is essential, is rather straightforward and still in the range of tractability. This is no longer the case for macro structures [Hung94], which require a very expensive higher-order treatment and will not be discussed here.

5.1 First-Order Fixpoints

Homogeneous Fixpoints: The case of homogeneous regular problems can be regarded as the common core of all the regular fixpoint computations. It consists of the determination of the fixpoint over a single block. As indicated in the previous section, this computation is performed on a counter array, by successively decrementing counters until the fixpoint is reached. This process is steered by a worklist that contains references to all the components whose counters are currently known to require decrement. The worklist is updated by adding references to all influenced components, whenever one counter became zero, which indicates a change of its corresponding boolean value [ClSt91, ClSt91b].

Hierarchical Fixpoints: Here, blocks are sequentially computed in the order indicated by the block graph. The fixpoint computation within the blocks is identical to the one in the homogeneous case. It should be noted that the counters for a block must be initialized immediately before its fixpoint computation. This is necessary in order to capture the effects of the earlier fixpoint computations [ClSt91b].

Alternating Fixpoints: Again blocks are treated exactly as in the homogeneous case. However, in contrast to the previous two cases, this computation must be repeated according to changes in blocks of different parity that are higher in the hierarchy but still in the same strongly connected component. A detailed description of this procedure is rather complicated (cf. [ClSt91b, ClKS92]), and omitted here.

5.2 Second-Order (and Higher Order) Fixpoints

Structurally, these fixpoint computations follow exactly the same lines as the first order case. Only the domain of the value array components is now *second order*, i.e., instead of determining properties for states of the considered systems, we must determine property transformers for certain classes of states, with the consequence that the 'counter optimization' is not applicable. Moreover, in the alternating case it is still an open problem whether the straightforward extension to the second order domains computes the intended values. We hope that experimenting with our machine will help us clarifying this point.

The essence of our algorithm deciding the alternation-free modal mu-calculus for *context-free* processes, i.e. for processes that are given in terms of a context-free grammar, becomes apparent when viewing these processes as mutually recursive systems of regular processes. In this case, the regular component processes contain ***call transitions*** that are labelled with the name of the called component process.[3] Our algorithm works directly on this 'procedural' process representation. Its heart is the computation of ***property transformers*** telling which properties (formulas) are valid at the nodes of a component process depending on the properties considered to be valid after the 'termination' of this component process. The subsequent decision step completing the model checking procedure is straightforward. See [BuSt92, BuSt94] for details.

The complexity of the resulting algorithm is linear in the size of the system's representation and exponential in the size of the property. This is quite promising, as many practically relevant problems can be composed of very small properties: e.g. bitvector analyses, which are common in data flow analysis, have exponent one ([KnSt93a])!

6 Implementation and Performances

A prototype of the fixpoint-analysis machine has been implemented in C++ as part of the META-Frame([StMC95, SFCM94, MaCS95]), our environment for the development of heterogeneous analysis and verification tools, which currently runs on a SUN SparcStation 20 under UNIX. In order to give an impression of the performance gain, we report on two series of examples.

The first series deals with the verification of hierarchical properties of increasing size for versions of Milner's scheduler with growing numbers of agents

[3] Considering the labels of these call transitions as nonterminals and the other labels as terminals establishes the formal match to context-free processes.

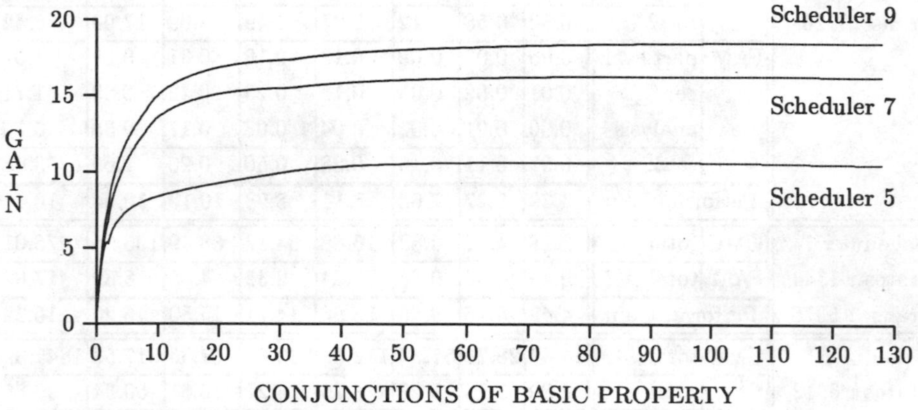

Fig. 3. Scheduler Performance Gain.

[Miln89]. The schedulers are represented by regular models and the investigated properties are checked by a hierarchical fixpoint analysis. To get an indication to the impact of the property size we checked an increasing number of conjunctions of a basic property expressing aspects of the alternating behaviour of the cells. Figure 3 graphically demonstrates the performance gain when comparing the runtime results of our FAM analysis machine with the 'conventional' model checker CMC presented in [ClKS92]. Initially the gain rises very quickly for properties of increasing size before it asymptotically approximates constant factors between 10 and 18 for the schedulers with 5, 7, and 9 agents.

Figure 2 shows the individual runtime results for the various properties and schedulers. For the scheduler with 5 agents we detail the total time as the sum of the time for the partial evaluation and configuration (config.), and the analysis. One observes that the higher the analysis share of the total runtime, the higher the performance gain of the analysis machine, i.e. the initial partial evaluation and configuration of the machine are better exploited if the considered problems are hard in the sense of requiring a high computation effort compared with the initialization phase. Furthermore, the higher branching factors of the larger schedulers also favour the analysis machine that determines the models' successor information only once in the partial evaluation step prior to the actual fixpoint analysis.

The second series of examples checks a property of alternation depth 2 with different parameters of the modal operators for a sequence of regular models M_k of increasing size (cf. Figure 4). The modal property expresses that the atomic proposition A holds infinitely often along all $(\{a,b,c\})$ paths. Assuming that all transitions are labeled with $(\{a,b,c\})$, this is only true for state v as all other states reach the loop at s which does not satisfy A. For model M_k with k states

N. of Property Conjuncts			1	2	4	8	16	32	64	128
Scheduler 5	CMC	config.	0.03	0.04	0.07	0.12	0.21	0.41	0.80	1.62
states : 240		analysis	0.27	0.54	1.05	2.15	4.28	8.68	17.19	34.80
trans : 720		total	0.30	0.58	1.12	2.27	4.49	9.09	17.99	36.42
	FAM	part.eval.	0.06	0.08	0.09	0.12	0.19	0.31	0.56	1.07
		config.	0.01	0.02	0.05	0.12	0.23	0.42	0.80	1.71
		analysis	0.00	0.01	0.02	0.04	0.08	0.17	0.33	0.70
		total	0.07	0.11	0.16	0.28	0.50	0.90	1.69	3.48
	Perform. Gain		4.29	5.27	7.00	8.11	8.98	10.10	10.64	10.47
Scheduler 7	CMC	total	2.18	4.26	8.62	16.88	34.12	68.49	135.95	276.01
states : 1344	FAM	total	0.49	0.63	0.88	1.34	2.32	4.42	8.39	17.02
trans : 5376	Perform. Gain		4.45	6.76	9.80	12.60	14.71	15.50	16.20	16.22
Scheduler 9	CMC	total	14.47	28.76	57.34	114.82	233.38	461.56	917.53	1845.39
states : 6912	FAM	total	2.90	3.75	5.20	8.26	14.27	26.61	50.34	99.85
trans : 34560	Perform. Gain		4.99	7.67	11.03	13.90	16.35	17.35	18.23	18.48

Table 2. Runtime Results.

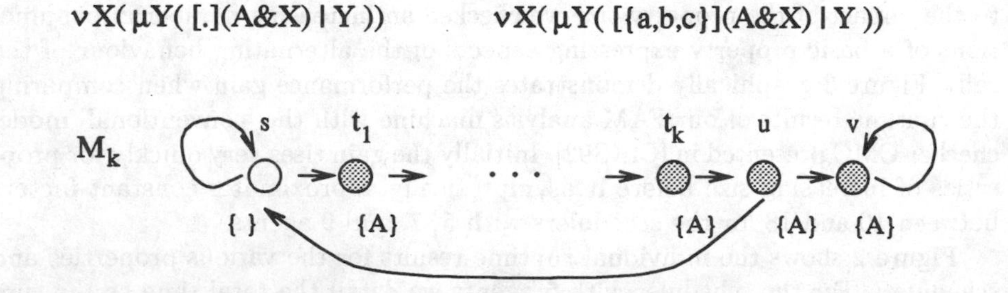

Fig. 4. Model and Property for Alternating-Fixpoint Analysis.

t_i we need $k+1$ resettings and recomputations of the inner minimal fixpoint until we reach the solution.

Figure 3 shows the runtime results for the analysis machine FAM and the conventional model checker CMC. The analysis time increases with larger models but the performance gain is constant for a fixed property. This is due to the fact that the initialization phase is almost neglectable here from the very beginning. In fact, the partial evaluation and configuration takes less than 2% of the overall time here.

If we only use 'unparameterized' modalities, which concern all possible transitions, the analysis machine outperforms the conventional model checker by a factor of 11. However, as soon as we use modality parameterization explicitly, the analysis machine outperforms the conventional model checker even by a factor around 30. This is due to the fact that alternating fixpoint analysis requires backtracking with resetting and recomputation of several intermediate results. As the costly selection of the successors of interest is only made once by the analysis machine in the partial evaluation step prior to fixpoint computation, the fixpoint analysis itself nearly takes all the runtime also in this case.

Index of Modal Operator		any	$\{a, b, c\}$
M_{500}	CMC	33.84	90.44
states : 503	FAM	2.88	2.90
trans : 505	Performance Gain	11.75	31.19
M_{1000}	CMC	138.51	364.30
states : 1003	FAM	11.64	11.38
trans : 1005	Performance Gain	11.90	32.01
M_{1500}	CMC	312.10	808.08
states : 1503	FAM	26.61	26.52
trans : 1505	Performance Gain	11.73	30.47

Table 3. Runtime Results for Alternating Fixpoints.

Beside these two series of examples we also compared the analysis machine and the conventional model checker on a variety of other applications. The performance gains differ with the complexity of the fixpoint problem. For data flow analysis for example we only achieve factors between 2 and 4 as the problems only require very simple hierarchical or homogeneous fixpoint computations (cf. [KnRS92]). Thus the partial evaluation and specific machine configuration was hardly exploited. But even in these 'worst cases', we still managed to half the computation time. On the other hand, performance gains were very high for computation intensive problems requiring an alternating fixpoint analysis.

7 Conclusions

We have presented a fixpoint-analysis machine, which allows the efficient computation of *homogeneous*, *hierarchical*, and *alternating* fixpoints over *regular*, *context-free/push-down* and *macro* models covering applications that reach from intra- and interprocedural data flow analysis, over model checking for various temporal logics to the verification of behavioural relations between distributed systems. It has turned out that the fixpoint-analysis machine identifies an adequate (parameterized) level for a uniform treatment of all those problems, as it, despite its uniformity, outperforms the 'iteration based' special purpose tools by factors around 10 even if the additional compilation time is taken into account.

We hope that beside its performance, the conceptual structure of the fixpoint-analysis machine will also help to improve the understanding of complex fixpoint problems, like e.g. the second order model checking for alternating formulas.

Acknowledgement

The work presented in this paper was strongly influenced by collaboration and intensive discussion with Olaf Burkart, Gerald Lüttgen and Oliver Rüthing. Moreover, the implementation and the embedding in the overall system META-Frame was strongly supported by Carsten Friedrich and Dirk Koschützki.

References

[Ande92] H. Andersen: *"Model Checking and Boolean Graphs"*, Proc. of ESOP '92, LNCS 582, Springer Verlag, 1992.

[Brya86] R. Bryant: *"Graph-Based Algorithm for Boolean Function Manipulation"*, IEEE Trans. on Computers, Vol. C-35, No. 8, pp. 677-691, 1986.

[BuSt92] O. Burkart, B. Steffen: *"Model Checking for Context-Free Processes"*, Proc. of CONCUR '92, Stony Brook (NJ), August 1992, LNCS 630, pp. 123-137, Springer Verlag.

[BuSt94] O. Burkart, B. Steffen: *"Pushdown Processes: Parallel Composition and Model Checking"*, Proc. of CONCUR '94, Stockholm (Sweden), August 1994, LNCS 836, pp. 98-113, Springer Verlag.

[ClKS92] R. Cleaveland, M. Klein, B. Steffen: *"Faster Model Checking for the Modal Mu-Calculus"*, Proc. of CAV '92, Montreal (Canada) LNCS 663, pp. 410-422, Springer V., 1992.

[ClSt91] R. Cleaveland, B. Steffen: *"A Linear-Time Model-Checking Algorithm for the Alternation-Free Modal Mu-Calculus"*, Proc. CAV '91, Aalborg (Denmark), July 1991, LNCS 575, pp.48-58, Springer V.

[ClSt91b] R. Cleaveland, B. Steffen: *"Computing Behavioural Relations, Logically"*, Proc. ICALP'91, Segovia (Spain), Aug. 1991, LNCS 510, Springer V.

[EmLe86] A. Emerson, C.-L. Lei: *"Efficient Model Checking in Fragments of the Propositional Mu-Calculus"*, Proc. of LICS'86, IEEE Computer Society Press, pp. 267–278, 1986.

[GKLR94] Geser, A., J. Knoop, G. Lüttgen, O. Rüthing, B. Steffen: *"Chaotic Fixed Point Iterations"*, Tech. Rep. N. MIP-9403, University of Passau (Germany), 1994.

[Hech77] M. Hecht: *"Flow Analysis of Computer Programs"*, Elsevier, North-Holland, 1977.

[Hung94] H. Hungar: *"Model Checking of Macro Processes"*, Proc. of CAV'94, Palo Alto (CA), June 1994, LNCS 818, Springer V., pp.169-181.

[Knoo93] J. Knoop: *"Optimal Interprocedural Program Optimization: A new Framework and its Application"*, PhD thesis, Dep. of Computer Science, Univ. of Kiel, Germany, 1993. To appear as LNCS monograph, Springer V.

[KnRS92] J. Knoop, O. Rüthing, B. Steffen: *"Lazy Code Motion"*, Proc. PLDI Conference'92, San Francisco, CA, June 1992, ACM SIGPLAN Notices, Vol.27, pp. 224-234.

[KnRS94] J. Knoop, O. Rüthing, B. Steffen: *"A Tool Kit for Constructing Optimal Interprocedural Data Flow Analyses"*, Fakultät für Mathematik und Informatik, Univ. Passau, Germany, MIP-Bericht Nr. 9413 (1994).

[KnSt92a] J. Knoop, B. Steffen: *"The Interprocedural Coincidence Theorem"*, Proc. CC'92, Paderborn (Germany), LNCS N.641, pp. 125-140, Springer V., 1992.

[KnSt93a] J. Knoop, B. Steffen: *"Efficient and Optimal Bit-vector Data Flow Analyses: A Uniform Interprocedural Framework"*, Inst. für Informatik und Praktische Mathematik, Universität Kiel (Germany), Bericht Nr. 9309 (1993).

[Lars92] K.G. Larsen: *"Efficient Local Correctness Checking"*, Proc. of CAV'92, Montreal (CAN), LNCS N.663, pp. 410-422, Springer V.

[MaCS95] T. Margaria, A. Claßen, B. Steffen: *"Computer Aided Tool Synthesis in the* META-Frame ", 3. GI/ITG Workshop on "Anwendung formaler Methoden beim Entwurf von Hardwaresystemen", Passau (Germany), March 1995, pp. 11-20, Shaker Verlag.

[Miln89] R. Milner: *"Communication and Concurrency"*, Prentice Hall, 1989.

[MuSc85] D. Muller, P. Schupp: *"The Theory of Ends, Pushdown Automata, and Second-Order Logic"*, TCS N. 37, pp. 51-75, 1985.

[SFCM94] B. Steffen, B. Freitag, A. Claßen, T. Margaria, U. Zukowski: *"Intelligent Software Synthesis in the* DaCapo *Environment"*, Proc. 6th Nordic Workshop on Programming Theory, Aarhus (Denmark), October 1994, BRICS Report N. 94/6, December 1994, pp.466-481.

[StMC95] B. Steffen, T. Margaria, A. Claßen: *"The META-Frame: An Environment for Flexible Tool Management"*, Proc. TAPSOFT'95, Aarhus, Denmark, May 1995, LNCS N. 915.

[Stef89] B. Steffen: *"Characteristic Formulae"*, Proc. of ICALP'89, Stresa (Italy), LNCS N. 372, Springer Verlag, 1989.

[Stef91] B. Steffen: *"Data Flow Analysis as Model Checking"*, Proc. TACS'91, Sendai (Japan), LNCS N. 526, pp. 346-364, Springer V., 1991.

[Stef93] B. Steffen: *"Generating Data Flow Analysis Algorithms from Modal Specifications"*, Science of Computer Programming N.21, 1993, pp.115-139.

[Stef94] B. Steffen: *"Finite Model Checking and Beyond"*, (invited talk) Proc. 6th Nordic Workshop on Programming Theory, Aarhus (Denmark), October 1994, BRICS Report N. 94/6, December 1994, pp. 2-17.

[StIn94] B. Steffen, A. Ingólfsdóttir: *"Characteristic Formulae for Finite State Processes"*, Information and Computation, Vol. 110, No. 1, 1994.

[Tars55] A. Tarski: *"A Lattice-Theoretical Fixpoint Theorem and its Applications"*, *Pacific Journal of Mathematics*, v. 5, 1955.

Unique Fixpoint Induction for Mobile Processes

H. Lin*
Laboratory for Computer Science
Institute of Software, Chinese Academy of Sciences
P.O Box 8718, Beijing 100080
E-mail: lhm@ios.ac.cn

Abstract

Complete proof systems for bisimulation equivalences in the π-calculus *with recursion* are presented. The key inference rule dealing with recursion is *unique fixpoint induction* which generalises that used in [Mil84] for regular pure-CCS. It is shown that the proof systems are sound, and also complete when restricted to the subset of π-calculus where recursions are guarded and the parallel composition is disallowed. These results on the one hand extend the proof systems for recursion-free π-calculus in [Lin94, Lin95] to infinite processes, on the other hand extend the inference system for guarded regular pure-CCS of [Mil84] to π-calculus.

1 Introduction

There has been growing interest in providing sound and complete proof systems for the π-calculus. Various notions of equivalences have been axiomatised: late and early strong bisimulation congruence [PS93, BD94, Lin94], open bisimulation [San93], late and early weak bisimulation equivalences [Lin95], and testing equivalences [Hen91, BD92]; Different styles of proof systems have been used: equational axiomatisation [PS93, San93] and *symbolic* inference systems [BD94, Lin94, Lin95].

All these proof systems are only for *recursion-free* π-calculus in which processes can perform only a finite number of actions. The same is also true for message-passing calculi in general ([HL93]).

Unique fixpoint induction was proposed in [Mil84] as the key inference rule to reason about recursion in pure-CCS (i.e. CCS without value-passing):

$$\frac{P = Q[P/X]}{P = \mathbf{fix} X Q} \qquad X \text{ guarded in } Q \tag{1}$$

***Supported by the President Fund of the Chinese Academy of Sciences, the National Science Foundation of China, and the EU KIT project SYMSEM.**

where P, Q are process expressions. Milner showed that the inference system consisting of the usual axioms for strong bisimulation for finite *CCS* together with this rule and a rule for folding/unfolding recursive definitions are complete for strong bisimulations equivalence in guarded regular *CCS*.

It is not immediately clear whether this result can be generalised to π-calculus, because the completeness proof in [Mil84] relies on the finite-state property of regular *CCS*, while in π-calculus even trivial processes can exhibit infinite state behaviour. There are two constructions in π-calculus that can entail such infinity: the behaviour after an input action depends on the received name, and there are infinite many possible names to receive; a recursively defined process identifier is usually parameterised on names, so each identifier definition can give rise to infinite number of instantiations, one for each vector of name parameters ([MPW92]).

The symbolic theories for the π-calculus, as advocated in [BD94, Lin94, Lin95], overcome the first source of infinity by working symbolically, without instantiating input names in either operational semantics or bisimulation definition. The current paper will show how this "symbolic" technique can also be exploited to eliminate the second source of infinity, the infinity resulted from instantiating name parameters of recursively defined processes.

The language we will work with is the π-calculus analogue of regular pure-*CCS*, in which the parallel operator does not occur in recursion bodies. Unlike pure-*CCS*, in the π-calculus process variables and recursions may take name parameters. To avoid the complexity caused by the interplay between free names and process variables, we use ***abstraction*** to form recursive expressions. So typical recursion has the form

$$\mathbf{fix}X(\tilde{x})T$$

where $(\tilde{x})T$ is an abstraction with free names of T in $\tilde{x}$, *i.e.* $(\tilde{x})T$ is name-closed. Such a term is itself an abstraction, and to form a recursive expression name parameters must be supplied. Analogous to lambda calculus we use ***application*** to realise parameter-passing: to pass name parameter $\tilde{w}$ to recursive abstraction $\mathbf{fix}X(\tilde{x})T$ we write

$$(\mathbf{fix}X(\tilde{x})T)\tilde{w}.$$

One may call $\tilde{x}$ and $\tilde{w}$ the "formal" and "actual" parameters, respectively, of the recursive expression.

By introducing abstraction and application into π-calculus, the concern of parameter-passing is separated from that of recursion. As a consequence the rules dealing with recursion appear simple. In fact they are syntactically identical to their pure-*CCS* counterparts. Here is the unique fixpoint induction rule:

$$\frac{F = G[F/X]}{F = \mathbf{fix}XG} \qquad X \text{ guarded in } G \tag{2}$$

where both F and G are abstractions. Since in pure-*CCS* process variables and recursions do not take parameters and as such can be regarded as nullary abstraction, rule (1) is a special case of (2).

The main result of this paper is that the proof systems obtained by adding (2) and a rule for unfolding recursion to those for the finite π-calculus of [Lin94] are sound, and also complete for strong bisimulation equivalences in the subset of π-calculus without parallel composition.

The proof structure of the completeness theorem follows the beautiful proof of [Mil84]: we first show that any process provably satisfies a finite set of standard equations. As mentioned before recursive processes may have infinite states. However, with symbolic transitional semantics, modulo renaming of free names there are only a finite number of abstract states a recursively defined process can reach, and this set of equations represent all such states. The second step is to establish that if two process are symbolically bisimular then an equation set can be constructed which is provably satisfied by both. Finally we show that two processes can be proved equal if they satisfy the same set of equations. Compared with [Mil84] extra complexities are caused by the presence of free names, the restriction operator, and the conditional construction.

The rest of the paper is organised as follows: The calculus and its semantics are introduced in the next section. The inference system is presented in Section 3. Section 4 is devoted to the completeness proof of the inference system. Section 5 demonstrates how the theory developed for late equivalence can be carried over to the early case. The paper is concluded with Section 6.

2 π-Calculus And Bisimulations

2.1 The Language And Operational Semantics

To give the syntax for the π-calculus we first presuppose an infinite set $\mathcal{N}$ of *names*, ranging over by a, b, x, y, w, ..., and a countably infinite set of *process abstraction variables* (or just *process variables* for short), *Var*, ranged over by $X, Y, Z, W, \ldots$. Each process abstraction variable is associated with an *arity* indicating the number of names it should take to form a process expression. The language of π-calculus can then be given by the following BNF grammar

$$\begin{array}{lcl} T & ::= & \mathbf{0} \mid \alpha.T \mid T+T \mid T|T \mid \phi T \mid \nu x T \mid F\tilde{x} \\ F & ::= & X \mid (\tilde{x})T \mid \mathbf{fix}XF \\ \alpha & ::= & \tau \mid a(x) \mid \bar{a}x \\ \phi & ::= & [x=y] \mid \phi \wedge \phi \mid \neg\phi \end{array}$$

We refer to [MPW92] for the intended meaning of these operators. The precedences are listed below (in decreasing order):

$$. \quad \nu x \quad \text{conditional} \quad | \quad + \quad \mathbf{fix}X$$

In $a(x).T$ and $\nu x T$ x is a bound name with scope T. In $(\tilde{x})T$ $\tilde{x}$ are also bound in T. We use $bn(T)$ and $fn(T)$ for the set of bound and free names in T, respectively. For any expression e $n(e)$ denotes the set of names appearing in e.

An *abstraction* is either a process variable, a process abstraction $(\tilde{x})T$ (where $\tilde{x}$ is a vector of distinct names), or a recursive abstraction $\mathbf{fix}XF$. We shall only use name-closed abstractions, so in $(\tilde{x})T$ it is always required that $fn(T) \subseteq \tilde{x}$. Abstractions are ranged over by F, G. A recursive abstraction $\mathbf{fix}XF$ binds X in F, and we use $FV(T)$ to denote the set of free process variables of T. The *degree* of an abstraction is defined inductively by: the degree of X is the arity of X; the degree of $(\tilde{x})T$ is the length of $\tilde{x}$; the degree of $\mathbf{fix}XF$ is the degree of F. For a recursion $\mathbf{fix}XF$ to be well-formed the degree of F must be equal to the arity of X. For an application $F\tilde{x}$ to be well-formed the degree of F must be equal to the length of $\tilde{x}$. We shall assume that all the expressions we write are syntactically well-formed. The notation $(\tilde{x})^{\phi}T$, read "abstraction over ϕ", will be used as a shorthand for $(\tilde{x})(\phi T)$. In this paper we shall only be interested in *guarded* recursion $\mathbf{fix}XF$ where each occurrence of X in F is within the scope of some prefix operator $\alpha.-$. In Section 4 concerning the completeness result it is further required that parallel composition $|$ does not appear in recursion bodies. This sub-language, as termed *finite control* in [Dam94], is the π-calculus analogue of the regular subset of pure-CCS. Processes are terms without free occurrences of process variables and will be ranged over by P, Q, ...

Bound names and bound variables induce the notion of α-equivalence as usual. In the sequel we will not distinguish between α-equivalent terms and will use $\equiv$ for both syntactical equality and α-equivalence.

Name substitutions, ranged over by σ and δ, are mappings from $\mathcal{N}$ to $\mathcal{N}$ that are identity almost everywhere. $[\tilde{y}/\tilde{x}]$ is the name substitution sending $\tilde{x}$ to $\tilde{y}$ and is identity otherwise. If $\sigma = [\tilde{y}/\tilde{x}]$ then $n(\sigma) = \{\tilde{y}\} \cup \{\tilde{x}\}$. If S is a set of expressions then $S\sigma = \{\, e\sigma \mid e \in S \,\}$. Name substitutions on actions are defined as usual. We will take the liberty to identify $((\tilde{x})T)\tilde{w}$ with $T[\tilde{w}/\tilde{x}]$, the term resulted by substituting $\tilde{w}$ for $\tilde{x}$ in T.

A *process substitution* is a partial function from process variables to abstractions. $[F_i/X_i|1 \leq i \leq m]$ is a process substitution that sends X_i to F_i for $1 \leq i \leq m$. We will often simply write $T[F_i/X_i|i]$ when the range of i is clear from the context. Substitutions are postfix operators, and have higher precedence than the operators in the language. In name and process substitutions bound names and bound variables will be renamed when necessary to avoid capture. We will not go to technical details of defining these syntactical substitutions, and only list below some properties that substitutions ought to satisfy:

> Let $\{\, X_i \mid 1 \leq i \leq m \,\}$ and $\{\, Y_j \mid 1 \leq j \leq n \,\}$ be different process variables. Then
>
> $$T[F_i/X_i|i][G_j/Y_j|j] \equiv T[F_i[G_j/Y_j|j], G_j/X_i, Y_j|i,j]$$
>
> In particular, if $\{\, Y_j \mid 1 \leq j \leq n \,\} \cap FV(T) = \emptyset$ then
>
> $$T[F_i/X_i|i][G_j/Y_j|j] \equiv T[F_i[G_j/Y_j|j]/X_i|i]$$
>
> As abstractions are name-closed, process substitution communicates with parameter passing:
>
> $$(F[G/X])\tilde{x} = (F\tilde{x})[G/X]$$

For the bulk of this paper we will concentrate on *late* bisimulation, and we will sketch in a later section how these results can be carried over to *early* bisimulation in a systematic manner. We refer to [MPW92] for the definitions of transitional semantics, ground bisimulation ($\dot\sim$) and bisimulation congruence ($\sim$). Here we only give the definitions for symbolic transitional semantics and symbolic bisimulation.

We write $\sigma \models \phi$ if σ satisfies ϕ in the usual sense. $\phi \Rightarrow \psi$ means $\sigma \models \phi$ implies $\sigma \models \psi$ for any substitution σ.

Proposition 2.1 *The relation $\phi \Rightarrow \psi$ is decidable.*

A condition ϕ is consistent if there are no $x,\ y \in \mathcal{N}$ such that $\phi \Rightarrow x = y$ and $\phi \Rightarrow x \neq y$. ϕ is *maximally consistent* on $V \subset \mathcal{N}$ if ϕ is consistent and for any $x,\ y \in V$ either $\phi \Rightarrow x = y$ or $\phi \Rightarrow x \neq y$.

ψ is a *maximally consistent extension* of ϕ on V, written $\psi \in MCE_V(\phi)$, if $\psi \models \phi$ and ψ is maximally consistent on V. The set of maximally consistent extensions of a given condition on a finite set of names V is finite. We will abbreviate $MCE_V(true)$ as MC_V.

Lemma 2.2 $\bigvee MCE_V(\phi) = \phi$

Proposition 2.3 *Suppose ϕ is maximally consistent on V. If σ and σ' both satisfy ϕ, then $\sigma =^V \sigma'\delta$ for some injective substitution δ.*

Lemma 2.4

1. *If $\phi \Rightarrow \psi$ and σ is injective on $fn(\phi, \psi)$, then $\phi\sigma \Rightarrow \psi\sigma$.*
2. *If $\psi \in MCE_V(\phi)$ and σ is injective on $V \cup n(\phi, \psi)$, then $\psi\sigma \in MCE_{V\sigma}(\phi\sigma)$.*
3. *If σ is injective on V then $(MC_V)\sigma = MC_{V\sigma}$.*

The symbolic transitional semantics of the π-calculus is given in Figure 1, where the symmetric rules of Sum and Par have been omitted. ν_x is an operation on conditions defined thus ([BD94]):

$$\begin{array}{ll} \nu_x true = true & \nu_x[x = x] = true \\ \nu_x[x = y] = false & \nu_x[y = z] = [y = z] \\ \nu_x \neg\phi = \neg\nu_x\phi & \nu_x(\phi \wedge \psi) = \nu_x\phi \wedge \nu_x\psi \end{array}$$

Clearly $x \notin n(\nu_x\phi)$.

Lemma 2.5 $\nu_x\phi \wedge (\bigwedge_{y \in n(\phi)} x \neq y) \Rightarrow \phi$.

In the following definition of symbolic bisimulation we use $\alpha =^\phi \beta$ to mean

$$\begin{array}{l} \text{if } \alpha \equiv \tau \text{ then } \beta \equiv \tau \\ \text{if } \alpha \equiv \overline{a}x \text{ then } \beta \equiv \overline{b}y \text{ and } \phi \Rightarrow a = b,\ \phi \Rightarrow x = y \\ \text{if } \alpha \equiv \overline{a}(x) \text{ then } \beta \equiv \overline{b}(x) \text{ and } \phi \Rightarrow a = b \\ \text{if } \alpha \equiv a(x) \text{ then } \beta \equiv b(x) \text{ and } \phi \Rightarrow a = b \end{array}$$

$$\text{Pre} \quad \frac{}{\alpha.P \xrightarrow{true,\alpha} P} \qquad\qquad \text{Cond} \quad \frac{P \xrightarrow{\phi,\alpha} P'}{\psi P \xrightarrow{\phi\wedge\psi,\alpha} P'}$$

$$\text{Sum} \quad \frac{P \xrightarrow{\phi,\alpha} P'}{P+Q \xrightarrow{\phi,\alpha} P'} \qquad\qquad \text{Par} \quad \frac{P \xrightarrow{\phi,\alpha} P'}{P \mid Q \xrightarrow{\phi,\alpha} P' \mid Q} \quad bn(\alpha) \cap fn(Q) = \emptyset$$

$$\text{Res} \quad \frac{P \xrightarrow{\phi,\alpha} P'}{\nu x P \xrightarrow{\nu_x\phi,\alpha} \nu x P'} \quad x \notin n(\alpha) \qquad \text{Com} \quad \frac{P \xrightarrow{\phi,a(x)} P' \quad Q \xrightarrow{\psi,\bar{b}y} Q'}{P \mid Q \xrightarrow{\phi\wedge\psi\wedge a=b,\tau} P'[y/x] \mid Q'}$$

$$\text{Open} \quad \frac{P \xrightarrow{\phi,\bar{a}x} P'}{\nu x P \xrightarrow{\nu_x\phi,\bar{a}(x)} P'} \quad x \neq a \qquad \text{Close} \quad \frac{P \xrightarrow{\phi,a(x)} P' \quad Q \xrightarrow{\psi,\bar{b}(x)} Q'}{P \mid Q \xrightarrow{\phi\wedge\psi\wedge a=b,\tau} \nu x(P' \mid Q')}$$

$$\text{Rec} \quad \frac{F\tilde{v}[\mathbf{fix}XF/X] \xrightarrow{\phi,\alpha} P'}{(\mathbf{fix}XF)\tilde{v} \xrightarrow{\phi,\alpha} P'}$$

Figure 1: π-Calculus Symbolic Transitional Semantics

Definition 2.6 A condition indexed family of symmetric relations $\mathcal{S} = \{S^\phi\}$ is a late symbolic bisimulation if $(P,Q) \in S^\phi$ implies for each $\psi \in MCE_{fn(P,Q)}(\phi)$ whenever $P \xrightarrow{\phi',\alpha} P'$ with $bn(\alpha) \cap fn(P,Q) = \emptyset$ and $\psi \Rightarrow \phi'$, then there is a $Q \xrightarrow{\psi',\beta} Q'$ such that $\psi \Rightarrow \psi'$, and $(P',Q') \in S^{\psi''}$ where

$$\psi'' = \begin{cases} \psi \cup \{\, x \neq y \mid y \in fn(\alpha.P', \beta.Q') \,\} & \textit{if } \alpha \equiv \bar{a}(x) \\ \psi & \textit{otherwise} \end{cases}$$

Let $\sim_L$ be the largest late symbolic bisimulation.
For abstractions, $F \sim_L^{true} G$ iff $F\tilde{x} \sim_L^{true} G\tilde{x}$ for any $\tilde{x}$.
For process expressions T, U with free process variables in $\tilde{X}$, $T \sim_L^\phi U$ iff $T[\tilde{F}/\tilde{X}] \sim_L^\phi U[\tilde{F}/\tilde{X}]$ for any vector $\tilde{F}$ of variable-free abstractions. □

Symbolic bisimulation is preserved by injective substitutions:

Proposition 2.7 *If $T \sim_L^\phi U$ and σ is injective then $T\sigma \sim_L^{\phi\sigma} U\sigma$*

The soundness and completeness of $\sim_L$ with respect to $\sim$ is stated by the following theorem:

Theorem 2.8 $T \sim_L^\phi U$ *iff* $T\sigma \sim U\sigma$ *for any* $\sigma \models \phi$.

3 The Inference System

The inference system for late symbolic bisimulation consists of a set of inference rules (Figure 3), together with the standard equations for choice (S1 – S4) and

$$\text{ALPHA} \quad \frac{}{true \rhd T = U} \quad T \equiv U$$

$$\text{AXIOM} \quad \frac{}{true \rhd T = U} \quad T = U \text{ is an axiom instance}$$

$$\text{CHOICE} \quad \frac{\phi \rhd T_i = U_i}{\phi \rhd T_1 + T_2 = U_1 + U_2}$$

$$\text{TAU} \quad \frac{\phi \rhd T = U}{\phi \rhd \tau.T = \tau.U}$$

$$\text{L-INPUT} \quad \frac{\phi \rhd T = U}{\phi \rhd a(x).T = b(x).U} \quad \phi \Rightarrow a = b, \quad x \notin n(\phi)$$

$$\text{OUTPUT} \quad \frac{\phi \rhd T = U}{\phi \rhd \overline{a}x.T = \overline{b}y.U} \quad \phi \Rightarrow a = b, \ \phi \Rightarrow x = y$$

$$\text{COND} \quad \frac{\phi \wedge \psi \rhd T = U \qquad \phi \wedge \neg\psi \rhd \mathbf{0} = U}{\phi \rhd \psi T = U}$$

$$\text{RES} \quad \frac{\phi \wedge \{\, x \neq y \mid y \in fn(\nu x T, \nu x U) \,\} \rhd T = U}{\phi \rhd \nu x T = \nu x U} \quad x \notin n(\phi)$$

$$\text{ABS} \quad \frac{true \rhd T = U}{true \rhd (\tilde{x})T = (\tilde{x})U}$$

$$\text{APP} \quad \frac{true \rhd F = G}{true \rhd F\tilde{w} = G\tilde{w}}$$

$$\text{CONGR-}\mathbf{fix} \quad \frac{true \rhd F = G}{true \rhd \mathbf{fix}XF = \mathbf{fix}XG}$$

$$\text{REC} \quad \frac{}{true \rhd \mathbf{fix}XF = F[\mathbf{fix}XF/X]}$$

$$\text{UFI} \quad \frac{true \rhd F = G[F/X]}{true \rhd F = \mathbf{fix}XG}$$

$$\text{CUT} \quad \frac{\phi_1 \rhd T = U \qquad \phi_2 \rhd T = U}{\phi \rhd T = U} \quad \phi \Rightarrow \phi_1 \vee \phi_2$$

$$\text{ABSURD} \quad \frac{}{false \rhd T = U}$$

Figure 2: The Inference Rules for Late Symbolic Bisimulation

restriction (R1 – R6) (Figure 3). To deal with parallel composition we also need the expansion law which can be found in [PS93, Lin94]. There are two kinds of judgments: conditional behaviour equations of the form

$$\phi \rhd T = U$$

S1	$X + 0 = X$	S2	$X + X = X$
S3	$X + Y = Y + X$	S4	$(X + Y) + Z = X + (Y + Z)$
R1	$\nu x \mathbf{0} = \mathbf{0}$	R2	$\nu x \alpha.X = \alpha.\nu x X \quad x \notin n(\alpha)$
R3	$\nu x \alpha.X = \mathbf{0} \quad x$ is the port of α	R4	$\nu x \nu y X = \nu y \nu x X$
R5	$\nu x(X + Y) = \nu x X + \nu x Y$	R6	$\nu x X(\tilde{w}) = X(\tilde{w}) \quad x \notin \{\tilde{w}\}$

Figure 3: The Axioms for Choice And Restriction

and unconditional abstraction equations of the form

$$true \rhd F = G$$

Rules ABS and APP are employed to switch between these two kinds of judgments.

We shall write $\vdash \phi \rhd T = U$ if $\phi \rhd T = U$ can be derived from this inference system.

Lemma 3.1 *Suppose $n(\psi) \subseteq fn(T, U)$.*

1. *If $\phi \Rightarrow \psi$ and $\vdash \phi \rhd T = U$ then $\vdash \phi \rhd \psi T = U$.*
2. *If $\phi \wedge \psi \Rightarrow false$ then $\vdash \phi \rhd \psi T = \mathbf{0}$.*
3. *$\vdash \psi(T + U) = \psi T + \psi U$.*
4. *$\vdash \nu x(\psi T) = (\nu_x \psi)\nu x T$.*

Proposition 3.2 *Suppose $n(\psi, \phi) \cup fn(T, U) \subseteq V$. If $\vdash \psi \rhd T = U$ for each $\psi \in MCE_V(\phi)$ then $\vdash \phi \rhd T = U$.*

If $a \neq x$ then we abbreviate $\nu x \overline{a} x.T$ as $\overline{a}(x).T$. $\overline{a}(x)$ is a derived action and is called *bound output*.

Proposition 3.3 *Suppose $\phi \Rightarrow a = b$, $x \notin n(\phi)$. If $\vdash \phi \cup \{ x \neq y \mid y \in fn(\overline{a}(x).T, \overline{b}(x).U) \} \rhd T = U$ then $\vdash \phi \rhd \overline{a}(x).T = \overline{b}(x).U$.*

Lemma 3.4 *Suppose $fn(T, \phi) \subseteq \{\tilde{x}\}$. Then $\vdash (\mathbf{fix} X(\tilde{x})^{\phi} T)\tilde{x} = \phi(\mathbf{fix} X(\tilde{x})^{\phi} T)\tilde{x}$*

Proposition 3.5 *Suppose $fn(T, U, \phi) \subseteq \{\tilde{x}\}$ and X is guarded in T. Then from*

$$\vdash \phi \rhd U = T[(\tilde{x})^{\phi} U/X]$$

infer

$$\vdash \phi \rhd U = (\mathbf{fix} X(\tilde{x})^{\phi} T)\tilde{x}$$

Proposition 3.6 *If $\vdash \phi \rhd T = U$ then $\vdash \phi\sigma \rhd T\sigma = U\sigma$ for any injective name substitution σ.*

All except ABS, APP, CONGR-**fix**, REC and UFI of the inference rules have already appeared in [Lin94], and their soundness was shown there. The soundness of ABS, APP and REC is not difficult to see. The following proposition can be used to show UFI is sound. Its proof uses the "bisimulation upto" technique ([MPW92]). Recently Sangiorgi gave a simpler proof which employs a technique based on *respectful functions* on relations ([San94]). The soundness of CONGR-**fix** can be established in a similar way.

Proposition 3.7 *Suppose X is guarded in G. If $F_1 \sim_L^{true} G[F_1/X]$ and $F_2 \sim_L^{true} G[F_2/X]$ then $F_1 \sim_L^{true} F_2$.*

Theorem 3.8 *(Soundness of $\vdash$) If $\vdash \phi \rhd T = U$ then $T \sim_L^{\phi} U$.*

4 Completeness of $\vdash$

This section is devoted to establish the completeness result for $\vdash$. As mentioned in Section 2, the completeness result holds only for a subset of the π-calculus and we will confine ourselves with the fragment without the parallel operator $|$.

The proof of the completeness result consists of three steps: First, Proposition 4.1 shows that any process expression can be proved to satisfy a standard set of equations. Next, Proposition 4.2 demonstrates if two process expressions are symbolically bisimilar than an equation set can be constructed which is provably satisfied by both. Finally, Proposition 4.3 shows that two process expressions satisfying the same set of equations can be proved equal.

For technical convenience we shall assume that in an application $F\tilde{x}$ the name parameters in $\tilde{x}$ are distinct. This does not present any restriction to our result because an application with duplicate name parameters can always be replaced by one with fewer but distinct parameters.

4.1 Standard Equations

Let $\tilde{X} = \{X_1, X_2, ..., X_m\}$ and $\tilde{W} = \{W_1, W_2, ..., W_n\}$ be disjoint sets of process variables. Then

$$E : X_i(\tilde{x}_i) = H_i \qquad 1 \le i \le m,$$

where $fn(H_i) \subseteq \{\tilde{x}_i\}$ and $FV(H_i) \subseteq \tilde{X} \cup \tilde{W}$, is a set of equations with formal process variables in $\tilde{X}$ and free process variables in $\tilde{W}$. E is *standard* if each H_i has the form

$$\sum_{\psi_{ik} \in MC_{\{\tilde{x}\}}} \psi_{ik}\left(\sum_{p \in P_{ik}} \alpha_{ikp}.X_{f(i,k,p)}(\tilde{x}_{ikp}) + \sum_{p' \in P'_{ik}} \nu\tilde{w}'_{ikp'} W_{f'(i,k,p')}(\tilde{w}_{ikp'})\right)$$

where $\tilde{w}'_{ikp'} \subseteq \tilde{w}_{ikp'}$, $\alpha_{ikp} \in \{\tau, a(x), \overline{a}x, \overline{a}(x)\}$. A process expression T provably $\tilde{\phi}$-satisfies an equation set E if there exist T_i with $fn(T_i) \subseteq \{\tilde{x}_i\}$, $1 \le i \le m$ and $T_1 \equiv T$ s.t.

$$\vdash \phi_i \rhd T_i = H_i[(\tilde{x}_k)^{\phi_k} T_k / X_k | 1 \le k \le m] \qquad 1 \le i \le m$$

We will call T_1 the *leading equation* of E. We will simply say "T provably satisfies E" when $\phi_i \equiv true$ for all i.

Proposition 4.1 *Any guarded process expression T with free process variables in $\tilde{W}$ provably satisfies a standard equation set E with free process variables in $\tilde{W}$.*

Proof: (Sketch) Given any term, using axioms R1 – R6 and Lemma 3.1.4 we can push restrictions inwards, until they either give rise to bound outputs, or disappear, or get in front of process variables with the restricted names occuring in their actual argument lists. We assume T is already in such form.

We first show, by structural induction, that T provably satisfies a set of pre-standard equations of the form

$$X_i(\tilde{x}_i) = \sum_j \phi_{ij}\alpha_{ij}.X_{f(i,j)}(\tilde{x}_{ij}) + \sum_k \phi'_{ik}\nu\tilde{w}'_{ik}W_{f'(i,k)}(\tilde{w}_{ik})$$

where $\tilde{w}'_{ij} \subseteq \tilde{w}_{ij}$.

Next we show that each pre-standard equation set can be transformed into a standard one. Take a typical pre-standard equation

$$X(\tilde{x}) = \sum_{i\in I} \phi_i\alpha_i.(\tilde{x}'_i)X_{f(i)}(\tilde{x}_i) + \sum_{j\in J} \phi'_j\nu\tilde{w}'_jW_{f'(j)}(\tilde{w}'_j)$$

For each $\psi_k \in MC_{\{\tilde{x}\}}$ let $P_k = \{\, p \mid p \in I,\ \psi_k \Rightarrow \phi_p \,\}$ and $P'_k = \{\, p' \mid p' \in J,\ \psi_k \Rightarrow \phi'_{p'} \,\}$. It is straightforward to verify

$$\vdash X(\tilde{x}) = \sum_{\psi_k\in MC_{\{\tilde{x}\}}} \psi_k(\sum_{p\in P_k} \alpha_p. \sum_{p'\in P'_k} \nu\tilde{w}'_{p'}W_{f'(p')}(\tilde{w}_{p'}))$$

□

Proposition 4.2 *Suppose T, U are guarded process expressions with free process variables in $\{\tilde{W}\}$. If $T \sim^{\phi}_{L} U$ then there exist a set of standard equations E with free process variables in $\{\tilde{W}\}$ and a vector of booleans $\tilde{\phi}$ with $\phi_1 \equiv \phi$ such that both T and U provably $\tilde{\phi}$-satisfy E.*

Proof: (Sketch) For simplicity we only consider the case $\{\tilde{W}\} = \emptyset$ here.

Let E_1, E_2 be the standard equation sets provably satisfied by T, U, respectively:

$$\begin{array}{lll} E_1: & X_i(\tilde{x}_i) = G_i & 1 \le i \le m \\ E_2: & Y_j(\tilde{y}_j) = H_j & 1 \le j \le n \end{array}$$

where

$$\begin{array}{ll} G_i \equiv \sum_{k\in K_i} \phi'_{ik}G_{ik} & G_{ik} \equiv \sum_{p\in P_{ik}} \alpha'_{ikp}.X_{f(i,k,p)}(\tilde{x}_{ikp}) \\ H_j \equiv \sum_{l\in L_j} \psi'_{jl}H_{jl} & H_{jl} \equiv \sum_{q\in Q_{jl}} \beta'_{jlq}.Y_{g(j,l,q)}(\tilde{y}_{jlq}) \end{array}$$

We assume in E_1, E_2 all input prefixes use the same name z which is different from any other names used so far.

So there exist T'_i with $fn(T_i) \subseteq \tilde{x}_i$, $T'_1 \equiv T$, and U'_j with $fn(U_j) \subseteq \tilde{y}_j$, $U'_1 \equiv U$, such that

$$\begin{aligned} \vdash T'_i &= G_i[(\tilde{x}_k)T'_k/X_k|1 \leq k \leq m] && (3)\\ \vdash U'_j &= H_j[(\tilde{y}_l)U'_l/Y_l|1 \leq l \leq n] && (4)\end{aligned}$$

For each i, j, let $\tilde{z}_{ij}$ be a vector of new names with $\tilde{z}_{11} = \tilde{x}_1 = \tilde{y}_1$. Let also

$T_{ij} = T'_i[\tilde{z}_{ij}/\tilde{x}_i]$ $\quad$ $U_{ij} = U'_j[\tilde{z}_{ij}/\tilde{y}_j]$
$T_{(ikpj)} = T'_{f(i,k,p)}[\tilde{x}_{ikp}[\tilde{z}_{ij}/\tilde{x}_i]/\tilde{x}_{f(i,k,p)}]$ $\quad$ $U_{(jlqi)} = U'_{g(j,l,q)}[\tilde{y}_{jlq}[\tilde{z}_{ij}/\tilde{y}_j]/\tilde{y}_{g(j,l,q)}]$
$\phi_{ik} = \phi'_{ik}[\tilde{z}_{ij}/\tilde{x}_i]$ $\quad$ $\psi_{jl} = \psi'_{jl}[\tilde{z}_{ij}/\tilde{y}_j]$
$\alpha_{ikp} = \alpha'_{ikp}[\tilde{z}_{ij}/\tilde{x}_i]$ $\quad$ $\beta_{jlq} = \beta'_{jlq}[\tilde{z}_{ij}/\tilde{y}_j]$

From (3) and (4) we have

$$\begin{aligned} \vdash T_{ij} &= \sum_{k \in K_i} \phi_{ik} T_{ijk} && (5)\\ \vdash U_{ij} &= \sum_{l \in L_j} \psi_{jl} U_{ijl} && (6)\end{aligned}$$

where

$$T_{ijk} \equiv G_{ik}[(\tilde{x}_k)T'_k/X_k|k][\tilde{z}_{ij}/\tilde{x}_i] \equiv \textstyle\sum_{p \in P_{ik}} \alpha_{ikp}.T_{(ikpj)}$$
$$U_{ijl} \equiv H_{jl}[(\tilde{y}_l)U'_l/Y_l|l][\tilde{z}_{ij}/\tilde{y}_j] \equiv \textstyle\sum_{q \in Q_{jl}} \beta_{jlq}.U_{(jlqi)}$$

Since $\{\, \phi'_{ik} \mid k \in K_i \,\} = MC_{\{\tilde{x}_i\}}$, $\{\, \psi'_{jl} \mid l \in L_j \,\} = MC_{\{\tilde{y}_i\}}$, and $[\tilde{z}_{ij}/\tilde{x}_i]$, $[\tilde{z}_{ij}/\tilde{y}_j]$ are injective on $\tilde{x}_i$, $\tilde{y}_j$, respectively, by Lemma 2.4 $\{\, \phi_{ik} \mid k \in K_i \,\} = MC_{\{\tilde{z}_{ij}\}} = \{\, \psi_{jl} \mid l \in L_j \,\}$.

Set $\Phi_{ij} = \{\, \psi \in MC_{\tilde{z}_{ij}} \mid T_{ij} \sim_L^{\psi} U_{ij} \,\}$ and $\phi_{ij} = \bigvee \Phi_{ij}$. Then $T_{ij} \sim_L^{\phi_{ij}} U_{ij}$ and $\phi' \Rightarrow \phi_{ij}$ for any ϕ' s.t. $T_{ij} \sim_L^{\phi'} U_{ij}$.

Note that $\Phi_{ij} \subseteq MC_{\{\tilde{z}_{ij}\}}$, so for each $\psi \in \Phi_{ij}$ there is a unique $k \in K_i$ and unique $l \in L_j$ s.t. $\psi = \phi_{ik} = \psi_{jl}$. For easy reference we write such ψ as ψ_{ijkl}.

From (5) and (6) it follows

$$\begin{aligned} \vdash \phi_{ij} \rhd T_{ij} &= \sum_{\psi_{ijkl} \in \Phi_{ij}} \psi_{ijkl} T_{ijk} && (7)\\ \vdash \phi_{ij} \rhd U_{ij} &= \sum_{\psi_{ijkl} \in \Phi_{ij}} \psi_{ijkl} U_{ijl} && (8)\end{aligned}$$

Also for each $\psi_{ijkl} \in \Phi_{ij}$, $T_{ijk} \sim_L^{\psi_{ijkl}} U_{ijl}$ because $T_{ij} \sim_L^{\psi_{ijkl}} U_{ij}$.

Now we group the summands of T_{ijk} into T^{τ}, $T^{FO_{[d]}}$, $T^{BO_{[d]}}$ and $T^{IN_{[d]}}$, where $[d]$ ranges over the equivalence classes on $\{\tilde{z}_{ij}\}$ determined by ψ_{ijkl}:

$$T^{\tau} = \sum_{\alpha_{ikp} \equiv \tau} \tau.T_{(ikpj)} \qquad T^{FO_{[d]}} = \sum_{\alpha_{ikp} \equiv \overline{a}w,\ a \in [d]} \overline{a}w.T_{(ikpj)}$$
$$T^{BO_{[d]}} = \sum_{\alpha_{ikp} \equiv \overline{a}(z),\ a \in [d]} \overline{a}(z).T_{(ikpj)} \qquad T^{IN_{[d]}} = \sum_{\alpha_{ikp} \equiv a(z),\ a \in [d]} a(z).T_{(ikpj)}$$

Similarly define U^{τ}, $U^{FO_{[d]}}$, $U^{BO_{[d]}}$ and $U^{IN_{[d]}}$. Then

$$\vdash T_{ijk} = T^{\tau} + \textstyle\sum_{[d]} T^{FO_{[d]}} + \sum_{[d]} T^{BO_{[d]}} + \sum_{[d]} T^{IN_{[d]}}$$
$$\vdash U_{ijl} = U^{\tau} + \textstyle\sum_{[d]} U^{FO_{[d]}} + \sum_{[d]} U^{BO_{[d]}} + \sum_{[d]} U^{IN_{[d]}}$$

We have $T^{\tau} \sim_L^{\psi_{ijkl}} U^{\tau}$, $T^{FO_{[d]}} \sim_L^{\psi_{ijkl}} U^{FO_{[d]}}$, $T^{BO_{[d]}} \sim_L^{\psi_{ijkl}} U^{BO_{[d]}}$ and $T^{IN_{[d]}} \sim_L^{\psi_{ijkl}} U^{IN_{[d]}}$, for each $[d]$.

Define

$$I^{\tau}_{ijkl} = \{\, (p,q) \mid \alpha_{ikp} \equiv \tau,\ \beta_{jlq} \equiv \tau,\ T_{(ikpj)} \sim_L^{\psi_{ijkl}} U_{(jlqi)} \,\}$$

$$I^{FO_{[d]}}_{ijkl} = \{\, (p,q) \mid \begin{array}{l} \alpha_{ikp} \equiv \overline{a}w,\ a,b \in [d], \\ \beta_{jlq} \equiv \overline{b}v,\ \psi_{ijkl} \Rightarrow w = v, \end{array} \ T_{(ikpj)} \sim_L^{\psi_{ijkl}} U_{(jlqi)} \,\}$$

$$I^{BO_{[d]}}_{ijkl} = \{\, (p,q) \mid \begin{array}{l} \alpha_{ikp} \equiv \overline{a}(z) \\ \beta_{jlq} \equiv \overline{b}(z) \end{array} \ a,b \in [d], T_{(ikpj)} \sim_L^{\psi_{ijkl} \cup \{\, z' \neq z \mid z' \in \{\tilde{z}_{ij}\}\,\}} U_{(jlqi)} \,\}$$

$$I^{IN_{[d]}}_{ijkl} = \{\, (p,q) \mid \alpha_{ikp} \equiv a(z),\ \beta_{jlq} \equiv b(z),\ a,b \in [d],\ T_{(ikpj)} \sim_L^{\psi_{ijkl}} U_{(jlqi)} \,\}$$

We may assume $\tilde{x}_{ikp}[\tilde{z}_{ij}/\tilde{x}_i] = \tilde{y}_{jlq}[\tilde{z}_{ij}/\tilde{y}_j]$. Note that each of the four relations defined above is surjective in both the first and the second components.

Let $\{\, Z_{ij} \mid 1 \le i \le m,\ 1 \le j \le n \,\}$ be a set of new process variables. Let also $\tilde{z}_{ikpjlq} = \tilde{x}_{ikp}[\tilde{z}_{ij}/\tilde{x}_i] = \tilde{y}_{jlq}[\tilde{z}_{ij}/\tilde{y}_j]$ so that

$$\tilde{z}_{ikpjlq}[\tilde{x}_i/\tilde{z}_{ij}] = \tilde{x}_{ikp} \qquad \tilde{z}_{ikpjlq}[\tilde{y}_j/\tilde{z}_{ij}] = \tilde{y}_{jlq} \tag{9}$$

Consider the equation set

$$E:\ Z_{ij}(\tilde{z}_{ij}) = \sum_{\psi_{ijkl} \in \Phi_{ij}} \psi_{ijkl}(V^{\tau} + \sum_{[d]} V^{FO_{[d]}} + \sum_{[d]} V^{BO_{[d]}} + \sum_{[d]} V^{IN_{[d]}})$$

where

$$V^{\tau} \equiv \sum_{(p,q) \in I^{\tau}_{ijkl}} \tau . Z_{f(i,k,p)g(j,l,q)}(\tilde{z}_{ikpjlq})$$
$$V^{FO_{[d]}} \equiv \sum_{(p,q) \in I^{FO_{[d]}}_{ijkl}} \alpha_{ikp} . Z_{f(i,k,p)g(j,l,q)}(\tilde{z}_{ikpjlq})$$
$$V^{BO_{[d]}} \equiv \sum_{(p,q) \in I^{BO_{[d]}}_{ijkl}} \alpha_{ikp} . Z_{f(i,k,p)g(j,l,q)}(\tilde{z}_{ikpjlq})$$
$$V^{IN_{[d]}} \equiv \sum_{(p,q) \in I^{IN_{[d]}}_{ijkl}} \alpha_{ikp} . Z_{f(i,k,p)g(j,l,q)}(\tilde{z}_{ikpjlq})$$

Then it can be shown that$E$ is provably $\{\, \phi_{ij} \mid i,j \,\}$-satisfied by T when each Z_{ij} is instantiated with $(\tilde{z}_{ij})T_{ij}$ over ϕ_{ij}, and provably $\{\, \phi_{ij} \mid i,j \,\}$-satisfied by U when each Z_{ij} is instantiated with $(\tilde{z}_{ij})U_{ij}$ over ϕ_{ij}. □

Proposition 4.3 *Let $E : X_i(\tilde{x}_i) = H_i$, $1 \leq i \leq m$, be a guarded equation set with free process variables in $\tilde{W}$. If T, U both provably $\tilde{\phi}$-satisfy E then $\vdash \phi_1 \rhd T = U$.*

Proof: (Sketch) By induction on m. The base case $m = 1$ can be settled easily by Proposition 3.5.

Assume the result for m and let E contain $m+1$ equations. Since T provably $\tilde{\phi}$-satisfies E, there exist T_i, $1 \leq i \leq m+1$, with free variables in $\tilde{W}$ and $T_1 \equiv T$ s.t.

$$\vdash \phi_i \rhd T_i = H_i[(\tilde{x}_i)^{\phi_i} T_i / X_i | 1 \leq i \leq m+1]$$

Since X_j:s do not appear in any T_i, we have

$$\begin{array}{rcl} \vdash \phi_{m+1} \rhd T_{m+1} & = & H_{m+1}[(\tilde{x}_i)^{\phi_i} T_i / X_i | 1 \leq i \leq m+1] \\ & = & H_{m+1}[(\tilde{x}_i)^{\phi_i} T_i / X_i | 1 \leq i \leq m][(\tilde{x}_{m+1})^{\phi_{m+1}} T_{m+1} / X_{m+1}] \end{array}$$

By Proposition 3.5

$$\vdash \phi_{m+1} \rhd T_{m+1} = (\mathbf{fix} X_{m+1}(\tilde{x}_{m+1})^{\phi_{m+1}} H_{m+1}[(\tilde{x}_i^{\phi_i} T_i / X_i | 1 \leq i \leq m])\tilde{x}_{m+1}$$

Now let $G_{m+1} \equiv (\mathbf{fix} X_{m+1}(\tilde{x}_{m+1})^{\phi_{m+1}} H_{m+1})\tilde{x}_{m+1}$ and define

$$G_i \equiv H_i[(\tilde{x}_{m+1})^{\phi_{m+1}} G_{m+1} / X_{m+1}],\ 1 \leq i \leq m$$

Then T provably $\{\phi_1, ..., \phi_m\}$-satisfies the m equation

$$E' : X_i(\tilde{x}_i) = G_i \qquad 1 \leq i \leq m$$

Similarly U provably $\{\phi_1, ..., \phi_m\}$-satisfies E'. By the induction hypothesis, $\vdash \phi_1 \rhd T = U$. □

Combining Propositions 4.1, 4.2 and 4.3 gives the main theorem of the paper:

Theorem 4.4 *(Completeness of $\vdash$) Let T, U be guarded process expressions. Then $T \sim_L^{\phi} U$ implies $\vdash \phi \rhd T = U$.*

5 The Early Case

Early symbolic bisimulation is obtained by changing the clause for input transition in Definition 2.6:

> whenever $T \xrightarrow{\phi', a(x)}_L T'$ with $x \notin fn(T, U)$, then for each $\psi \in MCE_{fn(T,U) \cup \{x\}}(\phi \cup \phi')$ there is a $U \xrightarrow{\psi', b(x)}_L U'$ such that $\phi' \Rightarrow \psi'$, $\psi \models a = b$, and $(T', U') \in S^{\psi}$

Let $\sim_E$ be the largest early symbolic bisimulation.

With these definitions the early version of Proposition 2.8 still holds.

The proof system for early bisimulation can be obtained by replacing the L-INPUT rule in Figure 3 with the following one

$$\text{E-INPUT} \quad \frac{\phi \rhd \sum_{i\in I} \tau.T_i = \sum_{j\in J} \tau.U_j}{\phi \rhd \sum_{i\in I} a_i(x).T = \sum_{j\in J} b_j(x).U} \quad \begin{array}{l} \phi \Rightarrow a_i = b_j,\ i \in I,\ j \in J \\ x \notin n(\phi) \end{array}$$

Let us write $\vdash_E \phi \rhd T = U$ to mean $\phi \rhd T = U$ can be derived from the new proof system. The soundness of E-INPUT is not difficult to see. For the completeness proof, Lemma 4.1 and Proposition 4.3 still hold. For Proposition 4.2, only the input case of the proof needs modifying. We omit the details.

Theorem 5.1 *(Completeness of $\vdash_E$) Let T, U be guarded process expressions. Then $T \sim_E^\phi U$ implies $\vdash_E \phi \rhd T = U$.*

6 Conclusions

We have presented sound proof systems for both early and late bisimulation equivalences in the π-calculus with recursion. These systems are also complete when restricted to the sublanguage where the parallel composition does not appear under recursion. These results on the one hand extend the proof systems proposed in [Lin94] for recursion-free π-calculus to infinite processes, and on the other hand extend the inference system of [Mil84] for regular pure-*CCS* to π-calculus. The key rule to deal with recursion is unique fixpoint induction which generalises that for pure-*CCS* to the setting of π-calculus. Syntactical simplicity has been achieved by introducing abstraction to form recursive expressions and application to realise parameter passing.

The version of the π-calculus we work with in this paper includes the *mismatch* construction. Mismatch has been used in [Hen91, BD92, PS93, BD94] for the purpose of complete axiomatisation for testing and bisimulation equivalences. In [Lin94, Lin95] we managed to exclude mismatch from the calculus by using it *only in the meta-language*: in any statement $C \rhd T = U$ only the condition C may contain mismatch. We failed to keep such separation of matches (which consist of only name equalities and can appear in process expressions) and conditions (which may contain name inequalities and can only be used in the judgments of the proof system or as indexes in symbolic bisimulations) in the present work, because in the completeness proof we need to *internalise* boolean conditions of judgments as conditions in process expressions.

The inference system of [Mil84] includes an equation $\mathbf{fix}X(X+T) = \mathbf{fix}XT$ to transform unguarded recursions into guarded ones. We believe that similar result can be obtained for the π-calculus by formulating an appropriate version of this equation. It is also interesting to see if the techniques used in this paper can be exploited to obtain complete axiomatisations for other equivalences such as *open bisimulation* [San93].

Acknowledgment Thanks to the anonymous referees for detailed comments.

References

[BD92] M. Boreale and R. DeNicola. Testing equivalence for mobile processes. In *CONCUR'92*, number 630 in Lecture Notes in Computer Science, pages 2 – 16. Springer–Verlag, 1992.

[BD94] M. Boreale and R. DeNicola. A symbolic semantics for the π-calculus. In *CONCUR'94*, Lecture Notes in Computer Science. Springer–Verlag, 1994.

[Dam94] M. Dam. On the decidability of process equivalences for the π-calculus. *Submitted*, 1994. Swedish institute of Computer Science.

[Hen91] M. Hennessy. A proof system for communicating processes with value-passing. *Formal Aspects of Computing*, 3:346–366, 1991.

[HL93] M. Hennessy and H. Lin. Proof systems for message-passing process algebras. In *CONCUR'93*, number 715 in Lecture Notes in Computer Science, pages 202–216, 1993.

[Lin94] H. Lin. Symbolic bisimulations and proof systems for the π-calculus. Report 7/94, Computer Science, University of Sussex, 1994.

[Lin95] H. Lin. Complete inference systems for weak bisimulation equivalences in the π-calculus. In *Proceedings of Sixth International Joint Conference on the Theory and Practice of Software Development*, Lecture Notes in Computer Science. Springer–Verlag, 1995.

[Mil84] R. Milner. A complete inference system for a class of regular behaviours. *J. Computer and System Science*, 28:439–466, 1984.

[MPW92] R. Milner, J. Parrow, and D. Walker. A calculus of mobile proceses, part I,II. *Information and Computation*, 100:1–77, 1992.

[PS93] J. Parrow and D. Sangiorgi. Algebraic theories for name-passing calculi. Report ECS-LFCS-93-262, LFCS, University of Edinburgh, 1993.

[San93] D. Sangiorgi. A theory of bisimulation for the π-calculus. In *CONCUR'93*, number 715 in Lecture Notes in Computer Science, 1993.

[San94] D. Sangiorgi. On the bisimulation proof method. Technical Report ECS-LFCS-94-299, LFCS, Edinburgh University, 1994. Extended abstract to appear in MFCS'95.

A Polymorphic Type System for the Polyadic π-calculus

Xinxin Liu* and David Walker

Department of Computer Science, University of Warwick
Coventry CV4 7AL, U.K.

Abstract. A type system for the polyadic π-calculus is introduced. Within this system every process possesses a type. A class of consistent types is isolated which is such that if a process can be assigned a consistent type then it is free from type errors under reduction. Further, for each type which is not consistent there is a process with that type which is not free from type errors. It is decidable whether or not a given process can be assigned a consistent type. Algorithms for type checking and type inference are given.

1 Introduction

The π-calculus is a process calculus whose terms describe systems whose communication structure may evolve during computation. Its primitive notion is naming. Terms (processes) use names to interact with one another; and by passing names in interactions, processes may pass to one another the ability to interact with other processes. The theory of the π-calculus is now quite well developed; see e.g. [7, 6]. Its relationship with λ-calculus remains an active area of study [5, 11]. The calculus has been used to good effect as a semantic basis for parallel object-based programming languages [15, 2, 3]. Moreover it has been shown [10] that higher-order processes may be faithfully encoded in the π-calculus, and interesting connections with non-interleaving semantics of concurrency have been investigated [12]. The development of the π-calculus led to the introduction of action structures [4] an important new class of computational models. Moreover the calculus has been used as the basis for an interesting experiment in programming language design [8].

In the monadic π-calculus no distinctions of type are made among names: an interaction between two processes via a name a consists in one process using a to send a name while the other uses a to receive it; the recipient may subsequently use the received name for sending or receiving other names or may send it to other processes by mentioning it in interactions. In the polyadic π-calculus processes interact by passing tuples of names. In this setting it is natural to impose a type or sort discipline under which names are distinguished according to the ways in which they may be used. A sorting system in the sense of [6] consists of a

* Supported by a grant from the U.K. Engineering and Physical Sciences Research Council

partial function from names to a set Σ of sorts and a sorting $ob : \Sigma \longrightarrow \Sigma^*$ which stipulates that a name of sort $s \in \mathsf{dom}(ob)$ may be used only to send and to receive tuples of names whose sort is the tuple $ob(s)$. The associated notion of well-sortedness provides a criterion for eliminating processes whose reduction may lead to a 'run-time type error' (see below). In addition, by exploiting sorting information subtler analyses of processes become possible; see e.g. [3, 9].

The papers [1, 14] address the problem of inferring most general sorts in the system of [6]. It is shown that a process has a most general sort and that it may be computed. In [9] another kind of sorting system is introduced. It uses structural matching of sorts instead of name matching as in [6], and in addition it incorporates a notion of subtyping derived from information about whether names may be used for input only, for output only or for both input and output. Sorting in the π-calculus is also addressed, we understand, in [13] although this work is not yet published.

Returning to 'run-time type errors', let us say that a process *contains a communication mismatch* if an intraaction between components of it is possible in which the sender and the receiver have different expectations as to the length of the tuple to be passed. For example

$$R \equiv \nu a\,(\overline{a}\langle b, c, d\rangle.\, P \mid a(x, y).\, Q)$$

contains a communication mismatch. Let us say also that a process is *free from mismatches* if none of its derivatives under reduction contains a communication mismatch. Then, for example, the process

$$R' \equiv (\nu a\,\overline{e}\langle a\rangle.\,\overline{a}\langle b, c, d\rangle.\, P) \mid e(z).\, z(x, y).\, Q$$

is not free from mismatches since $R' \longrightarrow R$.

If a process is well-sorted with respect to a sorting of the kind introduced in [6] then it is free from mismatches. This follows from the nature of the sorting regime: each name is assigned a sort and the sorting associates with each sort on which it is defined a unique tuple of sorts, and for a process to be well-sorted all prefixes in it must be consonant with the sorting. Well-sortedness in the system of [9] also guarantees freedom from mismatches, and in addition no derivative under reduction of a well-sorted process may attempt to use a name in violation of the sending/receiving constraints imposed by the sorting. These results are established via an analysis involving the use of a tagged reduction semantics.

One would wish a sorting system to decree ill-sorted only those processes which may violate the intended discipline in the use of names which the system attempts to capture. But one may argue that the systems introduced hitherto do not attain this ideal. The main aim of this paper is to explore an approach to typing of processes which while employing only syntactic analysis appears initially more liberal than that introduced in [6]. It addresses issues somewhat different from those of [9]: we use name matching of sorts and do not consider subtyping. We introduce a new kind of sorting signature $\mathcal{S} = (\Sigma, ob^+, ob^-)$ which associates with a sort $s \in \Sigma$ an *input sort* $ob^+(s)$ and an *output sort* $ob^-(s)$, each of which is a set of tuples of sorts. The intention is that if $s_1 \ldots s_n \in ob^+(s)$

then a name of sort s may be used to input a tuple of names of sort $s_1 \ldots s_n$, and if $t_1 \ldots t_m \in ob^-(s)$ then a name of sort s may be used to output a tuple of names of sort $t_1 \ldots t_m$. We give a system of rules for deriving typing judgments of the form $P : (\mathcal{S}, \phi)$ where P is a process, $\mathcal{S}$ is a sorting signature and ϕ is a partial function from names to sorts of $\mathcal{S}$. In contrast to many type inference systems, this system is such that every process may be assigned a type. Indeed we define a notion of *most general type*, show that every process has a most general type, and show how to compute the most general type of a process. We also introduce a notion of *consistent type* and show that a process which possesses such a type is free from mismatches. Moreover we show that for each type which is not consistent there is a process which possesses this type and which is not free from mismatches. Further we give an algorithm for determining whether or not a type is consistent. Finally we show that a process has a consistent type iff its most general type is consistent.

From the algorithm for determining consistency of types it can be seen that the class of processes which possess a consistent type in the apparently more liberal regime but do not respect a sorting as in [6] is rather small. Moreover the fact that each type which is not consistent may be assigned to a process which is not free from mismatches suggests a definite limit to what can be achieved with this kind of approach: a more liberal regime of this kind must take some account of the structure and behaviour of processes. We hope that the kind of sorting discipline introduced here may be a useful step towards such typing systems. We consider that the sort inference and consistency checking algorithms presented here give more insight into typing of processes than do the methods of [1, 14].

The following section gives a brief account of the π-calculus. The technical development is contained in sections 3 and 4. The paper ends with some concluding remarks.

Acknowledgment. We are indebted to the (anonymous) referee who discovered an error in an earlier version of this paper and to Davide Sangiorgi.

2 Processes and reduction semantics

We consider the fragment of the polyadic π-calculus with processes given as follows:

$$P ::= \mathbf{0} \mid P_1|P_2 \mid \nu a P \mid a(a_1,\ldots,a_n).P \mid \overline{a}\langle a_1,\ldots,a_n\rangle.P \mid !P$$

where a and the a_i's are from an infinite set $\mathcal{N}$ of names. $\mathbf{0}$ is the inactive process, $P_1|P_2$ is the composition of P_1 and P_2, and in $\nu a P$ the scope of a is restricted to P. Further, $a(a_1,\ldots,a_n).P$ and $\overline{a}\langle a_1,\ldots,a_n\rangle.P$ are input-prefixed and output-prefixed processes respectively, with n being the arity of the input (output) prefix. Finally, $!P$ is the replication of P. Like [9, 14] we exclude the summation operator: it contributes no particular difficulties to typing in the π-calculus and its incorporation into the present system is straightforward.

Restriction νa and input prefix $a(a_1, \ldots, a_n)$ are the two operators which bind names. We assume the usual definitions of free and bound names and of α-conversion. Assuming $a_1, \ldots, a_n$ are pairwise distinct we write $P\{b_1/a_1, \ldots, b_n/a_n\}$ for the usual capture-avoiding simultaneous substitution of the b_i for the free occurrences of the a_i in P.

Definition 1. *The structural congruence relation* $\equiv$ *is the least congruence which includes* α*-conversion and is closed under the following rules:* $P|Q \equiv Q|P$, $(P|Q)|R \equiv P|(Q|R)$, $P|\mathbf{0} \equiv P$, $!P \equiv P|!P$, $(\nu aP)|Q \equiv \nu a(P|Q)$ *if* a *is not free in* Q, $\nu a \nu b P \equiv \nu b \nu a P$, *and* $\nu a \mathbf{0} \equiv \mathbf{0}$.

Definition 2. *The reduction relation is the least relation* $\longrightarrow$ *on processes closed under the following rules:*

$$\text{R-com}\ \frac{}{a(b_1, \ldots, b_n).P|\overline{a}\langle c_1, \ldots, c_n\rangle.Q \longrightarrow P\{c_1/b_1, \ldots, c_n/b_n\}|Q}$$

$$\text{R-par}\ \frac{P \longrightarrow P'}{P|Q \longrightarrow P'|Q}$$

$$\text{R-res}\ \frac{P \longrightarrow P'}{\nu a P \longrightarrow \nu a P'}$$

$$\text{R-eqv}\ \frac{P \equiv P' \quad P' \longrightarrow Q' \quad Q' \equiv Q}{P \longrightarrow Q}$$

In rule R-com it is required that the arities of the input prefix and the output prefix be equal. If a process R contains unguarded prefixes $a(b_1, \ldots, b_n).P$ and $\overline{a}\langle c_1, \ldots, c_m\rangle.Q$ where $m \neq n$ and the two occurrences of a in subject position are bound in R, if at all, by the same binding occurrence, then we say that R *contains a communication mismatch*. We say that R is *free from mismatches* if whenever $R \longrightarrow^* R'$ then R' does not contain a communication mismatch.

3 Sorting and process typing

Definition 3. *A sorting signature is a structure* $\mathcal{S} = (\Sigma_\mathcal{S}, ob^+_\mathcal{S}, ob^-_\mathcal{S})$*, where* $\Sigma_\mathcal{S}$ *is a finite set, the set of subject sorts of* $\mathcal{S}$*, and* $ob^+_\mathcal{S}, ob^-_\mathcal{S} : \Sigma_\mathcal{S} \rightarrow \wp(\Sigma^*_\mathcal{S})$ *are functions called the input sorting and the output sorting of* $\mathcal{S}$ *respectively, where* $\wp(\Sigma^*_\mathcal{S})$ *is the set of finite subsets of* $\Sigma^*_\mathcal{S}$.

We call the elements of $\Sigma^*_\mathcal{S}$ the *object sorts* of $\mathcal{S}$. If $s_1 \ldots s_n \in ob^+_\mathcal{S}(s)$ (resp. $ob^-_\mathcal{S}(s)$) we say that the subject sort s *allows input* (resp. *allows output*) of the object sort $s_1 \ldots s_n$. Note that if we require that for every $s \in \Sigma_\mathcal{S}$, $ob^+_\mathcal{S}(s) = ob^-_\mathcal{S}(s)$ and is either a singleton or $\emptyset$, we obtain Milner's original sorting structure [6] (with $\emptyset$ corresponding to undefined).

Definition 4. *A type is a pair $(\mathcal{S}, \phi)$ where $\mathcal{S}$ is a sorting signature and ϕ is a partial function $\phi : \mathcal{N} \rightharpoonup \Sigma_{\mathcal{S}}$. A process P has type $(\mathcal{S}, \phi)$, written $P : (\mathcal{S}, \phi)$, if this can be inferred from the following rules (where $\phi\{s_1/b_1, \ldots, s_n/b_n\}$ is the partial function which agrees with ϕ except that it maps each b_i to s_i):*

nil $\quad \mathbf{0} : (\mathcal{S}, \phi)$ $\qquad$ par $\quad \dfrac{P : (\mathcal{S}, \phi) \quad Q : (\mathcal{S}, \phi)}{P|Q : (\mathcal{S}, \phi)}$

rep $\quad \dfrac{P : (\mathcal{S}, \phi)}{!P : (\mathcal{S}, \phi)}$ $\qquad$ res $\quad \dfrac{P : (\mathcal{S}, \phi\{s/a\})}{\nu a P : (\mathcal{S}, \phi)}$

$$\text{in} \quad \frac{P\{b_1/a_1, \ldots, b_n/a_n\} : (\mathcal{S}, \phi\{s_1/b_1, \ldots, s_n/b_n\})}{a(a_1, \ldots, a_n).P : (\mathcal{S}, \phi)} \qquad s_1 \ldots s_n \in ob^+_{\mathcal{S}}(\phi(a))$$

$b_1, \ldots, b_n$ *are pairwise distinct and do not occur free in* $a(a_1, \ldots, a_n).P$

$$\text{out} \quad \frac{P : (\mathcal{S}, \phi)}{\overline{a}\langle a_1, \ldots, a_n \rangle.P : (\mathcal{S}, \phi)} \qquad \phi(a_1) \ldots \phi(a_n) \in ob^-_{\mathcal{S}}(\phi(a))$$

The change of names in the side condition of rule in is to ensure that a process such as $a(a).\overline{a}\langle b \rangle.\mathbf{0}$ is typed correctly. We first note that structurally-congruent processes have the same types.

Lemma 5. *If $P : (\mathcal{S}, \phi)$ and $P \equiv Q$ then $Q : (\mathcal{S}, \phi)$.* □

Soundness is the first consideration of any type system: a well-typed process should be free from mismatches. However, under Definition 4 every process possesses a type.

Example 1. The process $P \equiv \overline{a}\langle b \rangle.\mathbf{0} \mid a(x, y).\overline{y}\langle x \rangle.\mathbf{0}$ contains a communication mismatch but $P : (\mathcal{S}, \phi)$ can be inferred by the rules in Definition 4 where $\Sigma_{\mathcal{S}} = \{s\}$, $ob^+_{\mathcal{S}}, ob^-_{\mathcal{S}} : \Sigma_{\mathcal{S}} \to \wp(\Sigma^*_{\mathcal{S}})$ are such that $ob^+_{\mathcal{S}}(s) = \{s, ss\}, ob^-_{\mathcal{S}}(s) = \{s, ss\}$, and ϕ is such that $\phi(a) = s, \phi(b) = s$ and $\phi(c)$ is undefined for $c \neq a, b$. □

Thus, a general sorting signature is too loose to guarantee soundness. To attain it we identify a class of *consistent* sorting signatures and show that any process typed by such a signature is free from mismatches. An important idea in achieving this is the notion of *map* between signatures introduced below.

In general, for two (partial) functions f, g we write gf for the composed (partial) function such that $gf(x) = g(f(x))$ if $f(x)$ and $g(f(x))$ are defined, and otherwise $gf(x)$ is undefined. For two partial functions $\phi, \psi : \mathcal{N} \rightharpoonup \Sigma$, we write $\phi \sqsubseteq \psi$ if for all a, if $\phi(a)$ is defined then $\psi(a)$ is also defined and $\phi(a) = \psi(a)$.

Definition 6. *Let $\mathcal{S}_1, \mathcal{S}_2$ be sorting signatures. A map from $\mathcal{S}_1$ to $\mathcal{S}_2$ is a partial function $\theta : \Sigma_{\mathcal{S}_1} \rightharpoonup \Sigma_{\mathcal{S}_2}$ such that if $s \in \Sigma_{\mathcal{S}_1}$, $* \in \{+, -\}$ and $s_1 \ldots s_n \in ob^*_{\mathcal{S}_1}(s)$ then $\theta(s_1) \ldots \theta(s_n) \in ob^*_{\mathcal{S}_2}(\theta(s))$. In this case we write $\mathcal{S}_1 \xrightarrow{\theta} \mathcal{S}_2$.*

Let $(\mathcal{S}_1, \phi_1), (\mathcal{S}_2, \phi_2)$ be types and θ a map from $\mathcal{S}_1$ to $\mathcal{S}_2$. θ is a specialization from $(\mathcal{S}_1, \phi_1)$ to $(\mathcal{S}_2, \phi_2)$ if $\theta\phi_1 \sqsubseteq \phi_2$. In this case we write $(\mathcal{S}_1, \phi_1) \sqsubseteq_\theta (\mathcal{S}_2, \phi_2)$. We write $(\mathcal{S}_1, \phi_1) \sqsubseteq (\mathcal{S}_2, \phi_2)$ if there exists a specialization from $(\mathcal{S}_1, \phi_1)$ to $(\mathcal{S}_2, \phi_2)$.

The following three results are quite straightforward.

Lemma 7. *If $\mathcal{S}_1, \mathcal{S}_2, \mathcal{S}_3$ are sorting signatures and θ_1, θ_2 are maps such that $\mathcal{S}_1 \xrightarrow{\theta_1} \mathcal{S}_2, \mathcal{S}_2 \xrightarrow{\theta_2} \mathcal{S}_3$, then $\theta_2\theta_1$ is a map from $\mathcal{S}_1$ to $\mathcal{S}_3$.*

Moreover if $(\mathcal{S}_1, \phi_1), (\mathcal{S}_2, \phi_2), (\mathcal{S}_3, \phi_3)$ are types and θ_1, θ_2 are maps such that $(\mathcal{S}_1, \phi_1) \sqsubseteq_{\theta_1} (\mathcal{S}_2, \phi_2)$, $(\mathcal{S}_2, \phi_2) \sqsubseteq_{\theta_2} (\mathcal{S}_3, \phi_3)$, then $(\mathcal{S}_1, \phi_1) \sqsubseteq_{\theta_2\theta_1} (\mathcal{S}_3, \phi_3)$. □

Lemma 8. *If $(\mathcal{S}_1, \phi_1) \sqsubseteq (\mathcal{S}_2, \phi_2)$ and $P : (\mathcal{S}_1, \phi_1)$ then $P : (\mathcal{S}_2, \phi_2)$.* □

Lemma 9. *If $P : (\mathcal{S}, \phi\{s_1/a_1, \ldots, s_n/a_n\})$ and $\phi(b_1) = s_1, \ldots, \phi(b_n) = s_n$, then $P\{b_1/a_1, \ldots, b_n/a_n\} : (\mathcal{S}, \phi)$.* □

This last lemma simply says that if a, b are assigned the same subject sort by ϕ, then substituting one for the other in a process does not change its type.

We are now prepared for the first main result of the paper.

Definition 10. *A sorting signature $\mathcal{S}$ is self-consistent if for every $s \in \Sigma_\mathcal{S}$, whenever $s_1 \ldots s_n \in ob^+_\mathcal{S}(s)$ and $t_1 \ldots t_m \in ob^-_\mathcal{S}(s)$ then $m = n$ and there exists a map θ from $\mathcal{S}$ to $\mathcal{S}$ such that $\theta(s_i) = \theta(t_i)$ for $1 \leq i \leq n$.*

A type $(\mathcal{S}, \phi)$ is consistent if there exists a type $(\mathcal{S}_0, \psi)$ such that $\mathcal{S}_0$ is self-consistent and $(\mathcal{S}, \phi) \sqsubseteq (\mathcal{S}_0, \psi)$.

Theorem 11. *If $P : (\mathcal{S}, \phi)$, $\mathcal{S}$ is self-consistent and $P \longrightarrow Q$, then $Q : (\mathcal{S}, \psi)$ for some ψ.*

PROOF: By induction on the reduction relation $\longrightarrow$. We already have Lemma 5. Here we look at the main case: when $P \equiv a(a_1, \ldots, a_n).P_1 | \overline{a}\langle c_1, \ldots, c_n\rangle.P_2$ and $Q \equiv P_1\{c_1/a_1, \ldots, c_n/a_n\}|P_2$. As $P : (\mathcal{S}, \phi)$, by rule par it must be that $a(a_1, \ldots, a_n).P_1 : (\mathcal{S}, \phi)$. Then by rule in it must be that $P_1\{b_1/a_1, \ldots, b_n/a_n\} : (\mathcal{S}, \phi\{s_1/b_1, \ldots, s_n/b_n\})$ for some $s_1 \ldots s_n \in ob^+_\mathcal{S}(\phi(a))$ and $b_1, \ldots, b_n$ which are pairwise distinct and do not occur free in $a(a_1, \ldots, a_n).P_1$. On the other hand, because $P : (\mathcal{S}, \phi)$, by rule par it must be that $\overline{a}\langle c_1, \ldots, c_n\rangle.P_2 : (\mathcal{S}, \phi)$, and by rule out it must be that $P_2 : (\mathcal{S}, \phi)$ with $\phi(c_1) \ldots \phi(c_n) \in ob^-_\mathcal{S}(\phi(a))$. Now since $\mathcal{S}$ is self-consistent there exists a map θ from $\mathcal{S}$ to $\mathcal{S}$ such that $\theta(s_i) = \theta(\phi(c_i))$ for $1 \leq i \leq n$. By Lemma 8, $P_2 : (\mathcal{S}, \theta\phi)$ and $P_1\{b_1/a_1, \ldots, b_n/a_n\} : (\mathcal{S}, \theta(\phi\{s_1/b_1, \ldots, s_n/b_n\}))$. Thus $P_1\{b_1/a_1, \ldots, b_n/a_n\} : (\mathcal{S}, (\theta\phi)\{\theta(s_1)/b_1, \ldots, \theta(s_n)/b_n\})$, and applying Lemma 9, $P_1\{c_1/a_1, \ldots, c_n/a_n\} : (\mathcal{S}, \theta\phi)$. Then by rule par we obtain $Q : (\mathcal{S}, \theta\phi)$. □

Corollary 12. *If $P : (\mathcal{S}, \phi)$ and $(\mathcal{S}, \phi)$ is consistent then P is free from mismatches.*

PROOF: Because $(\mathcal{S}, \phi)$ is consistent there exists a type $(\mathcal{S}_0, \psi)$ such that $\mathcal{S}_0$ is self-consistent and $(\mathcal{S}, \phi) \sqsubseteq (\mathcal{S}_0, \psi)$. By Lemma 8, $P : (\mathcal{S}_0, \psi)$. The self-consistency of $\mathcal{S}_0$ ensures that P is free from communication mismatches. The theorem guarantees that this property is preserved by reduction. □

Now we can say that a process P is *well-typed* by $(\mathcal{S}, \phi)$ if $P : (\mathcal{S}, \phi)$ and $(\mathcal{S}, \phi)$ is a consistent type. As the next result we present an algorithm to decide whether or not a given type is consistent.

Let Π be a partition of some set Σ. For $s \in \Sigma$ we write $[s]_\Pi$ for the set $S \in \Pi$ such that $s \in S$.

Definition 13. *Let $\mathcal{S}$ be a sorting signature. A consistent partition of $\mathcal{S}$ is a partition Π of $\Sigma_\mathcal{S}$ such that for every $S \in \Pi$, whenever $s, t \in S$, $s_1 \dots s_n \in ob^+_\mathcal{S}(s)$ and $t_1 \dots t_m \in ob^-_\mathcal{S}(t)$ then $m = n$ and moreover $[s_i]_\Pi = [t_i]_\Pi$ for $1 \le i \le n$.*

For a sorting signature $\mathcal{S}$ we say a partition Π of $\Sigma_\mathcal{S}$ is *arity consistent* if for every $S \in \Pi$, whenever $s, t \in S$, $s_1 \dots s_n \in ob^+_\mathcal{S}(s)$ and $t_1 \dots t_m \in ob^-_\mathcal{S}(t)$ then $m = n$. Thus a consistent partition is arity consistent.

For $\theta : \Sigma \to \Sigma', t \in \Sigma'$, we write $\theta^{-1}(t)$ for $\{s \in \Sigma \mid \theta(s) = t\}$.

Theorem 14. *A type $(\mathcal{S}, \phi)$ is consistent if and only if $\mathcal{S}$ has a consistent partition.*

PROOF: (If) Assume that Π is a consistent partition of $\mathcal{S}$. Construct a sorting signature $\mathcal{S}_\mathsf{C} = (\Sigma_\mathsf{C}, ob^+_\mathsf{C}, ob^-_\mathsf{C})$ where $\Sigma_\mathsf{C} = \Pi$ and $ob^+_\mathsf{C}, ob^-_\mathsf{C}$ are defined by setting for $S \in \Sigma_\mathsf{C}$, $* \in \{+, -\}$, $ob^*_\mathsf{C}(S) = \{[s_1]_\Pi \dots [s_n]_\Pi \mid \exists s \in S. s_1 \dots s_n \in ob^*_\mathcal{S}(s)\}$. We show that $\mathcal{S}_\mathsf{C}$ is self-consistent. For that suppose $S \in \Sigma_\mathsf{C}$, $[s_1]_\Pi \dots [s_n]_\Pi \in ob^+_\mathsf{C}(S)$ and $[t_1]_\Pi \dots [t_m]_\Pi \in ob^-_\mathsf{C}(S)$. Since Π is a consistent partition of $\mathcal{S}$, $m = n$ and $[s_i]_\Pi = [t_i]_\Pi$ for $1 \le i \le n$. Thus $\mathcal{S}_\mathsf{C}$ is self-consistent as the identity is a map from $\mathcal{S}_\mathsf{C}$ to $\mathcal{S}_\mathsf{C}$. Finally, let $\iota : \Sigma_\mathcal{S} \to \Sigma_\mathsf{C}$ be defined by setting for $s \in \Sigma_\mathcal{S}, \iota(s) = [s]_\Pi$. It is easy to see that ι is a map from $\mathcal{S}$ to $\mathcal{S}_\mathsf{C}$ and $(\mathcal{S}, \phi) \sqsubseteq_\iota (\mathcal{S}_\mathsf{C}, \iota\phi)$. Thus $(\mathcal{S}, \phi)$ is consistent.

(Only if) Suppose that $(\mathcal{S}, \phi) \sqsubseteq_{\eta_0} (\mathcal{S}_0, \psi)$ where $\mathcal{S}_0$ is self-consistent. First note that if there exists a map η from $\mathcal{S}$ to $\mathcal{S}_0$ such that for all $s, t \in \Sigma_\mathcal{S}$ with $\eta(s) = \eta(t)$ it holds that whenever $s_1 \dots s_n \in ob^+_\mathcal{S}(s), t_1 \dots t_m \in ob^-_\mathcal{S}(t)$ then $n = m$ and $\eta(s_i) = \eta(t_i)$ for $1 \le i \le n$, then $\mathcal{S}$ has a consistent partition which is $\{\eta^{-1}(u) \mid u \in \Sigma_{\mathcal{S}_0}\} \cup \{\{s\} \mid s \in \Sigma_\mathcal{S}, \eta(s) \text{ is not defined}\}$. To see that such an η exists we start from $\mathcal{S} \xrightarrow{\eta_0} \mathcal{S}_0$. Since $\mathcal{S}_0$ is self-consistent, for all $s, t \in \Sigma_\mathcal{S}$ with $\eta_0(s) = \eta_0(t)$ it holds that whenever $s_1 \dots s_n \in ob^+_\mathcal{S}(s), t_1 \dots t_m \in ob^-_\mathcal{S}(t)$ then $n = m$. Now suppose there is a pair $s, t \in \Sigma_\mathcal{S}$ with $\eta_0(s) = \eta_0(t)$ and $s_1 \dots s_n \in ob^+_\mathcal{S}(s), t_1 \dots t_n \in ob^-_\mathcal{S}(t)$ such that $\eta_0(s_i) \ne \eta_0(t_i)$ for some $1 \le i \le n$. Then since $\mathcal{S}_0$ is self-consistent there exists a map $\mathcal{S}_0 \xrightarrow{\theta} \mathcal{S}_0$ such that $\theta(\eta_0(s_i)) = \theta(\eta_0(t_i))$ for $1 \le i \le n$. Then let $\eta_1 = \theta\eta_0$. Then $\mathcal{S} \xrightarrow{\eta_1} \mathcal{S}_0$. We may apply the same argument to η_1. Since $ob^*_\mathcal{S}(s)$ is a finite set for $s \in \Sigma_\mathcal{S}$, repeating the argument yields a map η_k from $\mathcal{S}$ to $\mathcal{S}_0$ such that for all $s, t \in \Sigma_\mathcal{S}$ with $\eta_k(s) = \eta_k(t)$ it holds that whenever $s_1 \dots s_n \in ob^+_\mathcal{S}(s), t_1 \dots t_m \in ob^-_\mathcal{S}(t)$ then $n = m$ and $\eta_k(s_i) = \eta_k(t_i)$ for $1 \le i \le n$. □

In the following we present an algorithm which, for a given sorting signature $\mathcal{S}$, either constructs a consistent partition of $\mathcal{S}$ if one exists or terminates with failure. It begins from the discrete partition $\{\{s\} \mid s \in \Sigma_{\mathcal{S}}\}$ of $\Sigma_{\mathcal{S}}$.

Algorithm 15 Set $\Pi := \{\{s\} \mid s \in \Sigma_{\mathcal{S}}\}$. While Π is arity consistent and Π is not a consistent partition of $\mathcal{S}$ do the following:

Let $s, t \in \Sigma_{\mathcal{S}}$, $s_1 \ldots s_n \in ob^{+}_{\mathcal{S}}(s), t_1 \ldots t_n \in ob^{-}_{\mathcal{S}}(t)$ such that $[s]_\Pi = [t]_\Pi$ and $[s_i]_\Pi \neq [t_i]_\Pi$ where $1 \leq i \leq n$. Update $\Pi := \Pi - \{[s_i]_\Pi, [t_i]_\Pi\} \cup \{[s_i]_\Pi \cup [t_i]_\Pi\}$.

Theorem 16. *Algorithm 15 terminates for every input sorting signature $\mathcal{S}$. If it terminates with an arity-inconsistent partition then $\mathcal{S}$ does not have a consistent partition. Otherwise on termination Π is a consistent partition of $\mathcal{S}$.* □

By Corollary 12 possession of a consistent type guarantees freedom from mismatches. But many processes to which no consistent type may be assigned are free from mismatches. A simple example is

$$P \equiv !\,\overline{a}\langle b\rangle.\mathbf{0} \mid a(c).\overline{c}\langle c\rangle.a(d).\overline{d}\langle\,\rangle.\mathbf{0} \mid a(c).c(e).a(d).d(\,).\mathbf{0}\,.$$

That P can not be assigned a consistent type follows from the fact that the most general type of P is not consistent: see section 4. Up to isomorphism that type is $(\mathcal{S}, \phi)$ where $\Sigma_{\mathcal{S}} = \{s, t, u, v, w\}$, $\mathsf{dom}(\phi) = \{a, b\}$ and $\phi(a) = s$, $\phi(b) = t$, and

$$\begin{array}{l} ob^{+}_{\mathcal{S}}(s) = \{u, v\},\ ob^{+}_{\mathcal{S}}(t) = \emptyset,\ ob^{+}_{\mathcal{S}}(u) = \{w\},\ ob^{+}_{\mathcal{S}}(v) = \{(\,)\},\ ob^{+}_{\mathcal{S}}(w) = \emptyset, \\ ob^{-}_{\mathcal{S}}(s) = \{t\},\quad ob^{-}_{\mathcal{S}}(t) = \emptyset,\ ob^{-}_{\mathcal{S}}(u) = \{u\},\ ob^{-}_{\mathcal{S}}(v) = \{(\,)\},\ ob^{-}_{\mathcal{S}}(w) = \emptyset. \end{array}$$

By examining the execution of algorithm 15 on $\mathcal{S}$ we can isolate the following process which has type $(\mathcal{S}, \phi)$ but is not free from mismatches:

$$Q \equiv \overline{a}\langle b\rangle.\mathbf{0} \mid \overline{a}\langle b\rangle.\mathbf{0} \mid a(d).\overline{d}\langle\,\rangle.\mathbf{0} \mid a(c).c(e).\mathbf{0}\,.$$

Indeed we can extend the algorithm so that given a sorting signature $\mathcal{S}$ which has no consistent partition, a process R containing only $\mathbf{0}$, prefixing and composition is constructed so that $R : (\mathcal{S}, \phi)$ for some ϕ and R is not free from mismatches.

Theorem 17. *If $(\mathcal{S}, \phi)$ is not consistent then there exists P such that $P : (\mathcal{S}, \phi)$ and P is not free from mismatches.* □

Thus a more liberal typing discipline of the kind considered here must take some account of the structure and behaviour of processes.

Rather than giving the proof of the theorem, which is notationally heavy, we illustrate the main ideas in it by considering $\mathcal{S}$ and Q above. We now write $\mathcal{S}_0$ for $\mathcal{S}$ and ob_0 for $ob_{\mathcal{S}}$. Applying the algorithm to the discrete partition Π_0 of $\mathcal{S}_0$ yields the partitions $\Pi_1 = \{\{s\}, \{t, u\}, \{v\}, \{w\}\}$ and $\Pi_2 = \{\{s\}, \{t, u, v\}, \{w\}\}$ and thus the sorting signatures Σ_1 and Σ_2 where $\Sigma_{\mathcal{S}_1} = \{s, tu, v, w\}$ and

$$\begin{array}{l} ob^{+}_{1}(s) = \{tu, v\},\ ob^{+}_{1}(tu) = \{w\},\quad ob^{+}_{1}(v) = \{(\,)\},\ ob^{+}_{1}(w) = \emptyset, \\ ob^{-}_{1}(s) = \{tu\},\quad ob^{-}_{1}(tu) = \{tu\},\quad ob^{-}_{1}(v) = \{(\,)\},\ ob^{-}_{1}(w) = \emptyset, \end{array}$$

and $\Sigma_{\mathcal{S}_2} = \{s, tuv, w\}$ and

$$ob_2^+(s) = \{tuv\},\ ob_2^+(tuv) = \{w, ()\},\ \ ob_2^+(w) = \emptyset,$$
$$ob_2^-(s) = \{tuv\},\ ob_2^-(tuv) = \{tuv, ()\},\ ob_2^-(w) = \emptyset.$$

Here we abbreviate $[s]_1$ and $[s]_2$ to s etc. and write tu for $[t]_1$ which equals $[u]_1$, and tuv for $[t]_2$ which equals $[u]_2$ and also $[v]_2$.

Π_2 is arity inconsistent and we can construct the process

$$P_2 \equiv \overline{b}\langle\rangle.\mathbf{0} \mid b(e).\mathbf{0}$$

which contains a communication mismatch and is such that $P_2 : (\mathcal{S}_2, \phi_2)$ where $\phi_2(b) = tuv$. Now $() \in ob_2^-(tuv)$ as $() \in ob_1^-(v)$, and $w \in ob_2^+(tuv)$ as $w \in ob_1^+(tu)$. Moreover $v \in ob_1^+(s)$ and $tu \in ob_1^-(s)$. Hence $P_1 : (\mathcal{S}_1, \phi_1)$ where

$$P_1 \equiv \overline{a}\langle b\rangle.\mathbf{0} \mid a(d).\overline{d}\langle\rangle.\mathbf{0} \mid b(e).\mathbf{0}$$

and $\phi_1(a) = s$, $\phi_1(b) = tu$. Similarly, $tu \in ob_1^-(s)$ as $t \in ob_0^-(s)$, and $w \in ob_1^+(tu)$ as $w \in ob_0^+(u)$. Moreover $u \in ob_0^+(s)$ and $t \in ob_0^-(s)$. Hence $P_0 : (\mathcal{S}_0, \phi_0)$ where

$$P_0 \equiv \overline{a}\langle b\rangle.\mathbf{0} \mid \overline{a}\langle b\rangle.\mathbf{0} \mid a(d).\overline{d}\langle\rangle.\mathbf{0} \mid a(c).c(e).\mathbf{0}$$

and $\phi_0(a) = s$, $\phi_0(b) = t$. That is, $Q : (\mathcal{S}, \phi)$ above.

4 Type inference

In the last section we addressed the soundness of our type system and showed that if $P : (\mathcal{S}, \phi)$ for some consistent type $(\mathcal{S}, \phi)$ then P is free from mismatches. Besides soundness another major concern is type inference. In the present case the problem is to determine for a given process P whether there exists a consistent type $(\mathcal{S}, \phi)$ such that $P : (\mathcal{S}, \phi)$ and, if so, how to construct such a type.

In this section we solve this problem by constructing, for each given process P, a *most general* type $\mathcal{T}(P)$ of P such that $P : \mathcal{T}(P)$ and moreover if $P : (\mathcal{S}, \phi)$ then $\mathcal{T}(P) \sqsubseteq (\mathcal{S}, \phi)$. From this it follows that P has a consistent type if and only if $\mathcal{T}(P)$ is consistent.

We first define some useful operators for constructing new sorting signatures and types from existing ones.

Definition 18. *Let $\mathcal{S}_1, \mathcal{S}_2$ be sorting signatures. A map θ from $\mathcal{S}_1$ to $\mathcal{S}_2$ is an isomorphism if $\theta : \Sigma_{\mathcal{S}_1} \to \Sigma_{\mathcal{S}_2}$ is a bijection and its inverse is also a map from $\mathcal{S}_2$ to $\mathcal{S}_1$. We say $\mathcal{S}_1$ and $\mathcal{S}_2$ are isomorphic if there exists an isomorphism between them. We say that two types $(\mathcal{S}_1, \phi_1)$ and $(\mathcal{S}_2, \phi_2)$ are isomorphic if there is an isomorphism θ from $\mathcal{S}_1$ to $\mathcal{S}_2$ and for $a \in \mathcal{N}$, either both $\phi_1(a), \phi_2(a)$ are undefined or they are both defined and $\theta(\phi_1(a)) = \phi_2(a)$.*

Lemma 19. *For given sorting signatures $\mathcal{S}_0, \mathcal{S}_1$, there exists a sorting signature $\mathcal{S}$ with two maps ι_0, ι_1 such that $\mathcal{S}_0 \xrightarrow{\iota_0} \mathcal{S}$ and $\mathcal{S}_1 \xrightarrow{\iota_1} \mathcal{S}$, and moreover for any sorting signature $\mathcal{S}'$ and pair of maps θ_0, θ_1 such that $\mathcal{S}_0 \xrightarrow{\theta_0} \mathcal{S}'$ and $\mathcal{S}_1 \xrightarrow{\theta_1} \mathcal{S}'$, there exists a unique map θ from $\mathcal{S}$ to $\mathcal{S}'$ such that $\theta_0 = \theta\iota_0$ and $\theta_1 = \theta\iota_1$.*

PROOF: First we construct a sorting signature $\mathcal{S}$ such that $\Sigma_{\mathcal{S}} = \{(0,s) \mid s \in \Sigma_{\mathcal{S}_0}\} \cup \{(1,t) \mid t \in \Sigma_{\mathcal{S}_1}\}$ and $ob^+_{\mathcal{S}}, ob^-_{\mathcal{S}}$ are defined by setting for $(i,s) \in \Sigma_{\mathcal{S}}, * \in \{+,-\}, ob^*_{\mathcal{S}}((i,s)) = \{(i,s_1)\dots(i,s_n) \mid s_1 \dots s_n \in ob^*_{\mathcal{S}_i}(s)\}$. Next we define $\iota_0 : \Sigma_{\mathcal{S}_0} \to \Sigma_{\mathcal{S}}$ and $\iota_1 : \Sigma_{\mathcal{S}_1} \to \Sigma_{\mathcal{S}}$ by setting for $s \in \Sigma_{\mathcal{S}_i}, \iota_i(s) = (i,s)$. It is easy to check that $\mathcal{S}_0 \xrightarrow{\iota_0} \mathcal{S}$ and $\mathcal{S}_1 \xrightarrow{\iota_1} \mathcal{S}$.

Suppose $\mathcal{S}'$ is a sorting signature with two maps θ_0, θ_1 such that $\mathcal{S}_0 \xrightarrow{\theta_0} \mathcal{S}', \mathcal{S}_1 \xrightarrow{\theta_1} \mathcal{S}'$. In this case we define $\theta : \Sigma_{\mathcal{S}} \to \Sigma_{\mathcal{S}'}$ by setting for $(i,s) \in \Sigma, \theta((i,s)) = \theta_i(s)$. It is easy to check that θ is a map from $\mathcal{S}$ to $\mathcal{S}'$, and $\theta_0 = \theta\iota_0, \theta_1 = \theta\iota_1$. Now we show that such θ is unique. Suppose θ' is a map from $\mathcal{S}$ to $\mathcal{S}'$ such that $\theta_0 = \theta'\iota_0, \theta_1 = \theta'\iota_1$. Take arbitrary $(i,s) \in \Sigma_{\mathcal{S}}$. By the construction of θ we have $\theta((i,s)) = \theta_i(s)$. On the other hand we have $\theta'((i,s)) = \theta'(\iota_i(s)) = \theta_i(s)$. Thus $\theta' = \theta$. □

We call $\mathcal{S}$ with ι_0, ι_1 in the lemma a *disjoint sum* of $\mathcal{S}_0, \mathcal{S}_1$. It is easy to show that the disjoint sum of $\mathcal{S}_0, \mathcal{S}_1$ is unique upto isomorphism.

For two partial functions $\phi, \psi : \mathcal{N} \rightharpoonup \Sigma$, we say that ϕ, ψ are *compatible* if for $a \in \mathcal{N}$, whenever $\phi(a), \psi(a)$ are both defined then $\phi(a) = \psi(a)$. It is a simple fact that if ϕ_0, ϕ_1 are compatible then there exists a unique ϕ such that $\phi_0 \sqsubseteq \phi, \phi_1 \sqsubseteq \phi$ and whenever $\phi_0 \sqsubseteq \psi, \phi_1 \sqsubseteq \psi$ then $\phi \sqsubseteq \psi$. We will write $\phi_0 + \phi_1$ for this ϕ.

Lemma 20. *For given types $(\mathcal{S}, \phi_0), (\mathcal{S}, \phi_1)$ with the same sorting signature, there exists a type $(\mathcal{S}_m, \phi_m)$ with a map η from $\mathcal{S}$ to $\mathcal{S}_m$ such that $(\mathcal{S}, \phi_0) \sqsubseteq_\eta (\mathcal{S}_m, \phi_m)$ and $(\mathcal{S}, \phi_1) \sqsubseteq_\eta (\mathcal{S}_m, \phi_m)$, and moreover if $(\mathcal{S}', \phi')$ is another type with a map η' from $\mathcal{S}$ to $\mathcal{S}'$ such that $(\mathcal{S}, \phi_0) \sqsubseteq_{\eta'} (\mathcal{S}', \phi')$ and $(\mathcal{S}, \phi_1) \sqsubseteq_{\eta'} (\mathcal{S}', \phi')$, then there exists a unique map θ from $\mathcal{S}_m$ to $\mathcal{S}'$ such that $\eta = \theta\eta'$ and $(\mathcal{S}_m, \phi_m) \sqsubseteq_\theta (\mathcal{S}', \phi')$.*

PROOF: Let Π be the finest partition of $\Sigma_{\mathcal{S}}$ such that whenever $a \in \mathcal{N}$ and both $\phi_0(a), \phi_1(a)$ are defined then there exists $S \in \Pi$ such that $\phi_0(a), \phi_1(a) \in S$. Let $\eta : \Sigma_{\mathcal{S}} \to \Pi$ be such that for $s \in \Sigma_{\mathcal{S}}, \eta(s) = S$ just when $s \in S$. Now construct $\mathcal{S}_m$ such that $\Sigma_{\mathcal{S}_m} = \Pi$, and $ob^+_{\mathcal{S}_m}, ob^-_{\mathcal{S}_m}$ are defined by setting for $S \in \Pi, * \in \{+,-\}, ob^*_{\mathcal{S}_m}(S) = \{S_1 \dots S_n \mid \exists s \in S, s_1 \in S_1, \dots s_n \in S_n . s_1 \dots s_n \in ob^*_{\mathcal{S}}(s)\}$. It is easy to check that η is a map from $\mathcal{S}$ to $\mathcal{S}_m$. It is also easy to see that $\eta\phi_0, \eta\phi_1$ are compatible. Thus setting $\phi_m = \eta\phi_0 + \eta\phi_1$ we have $(\mathcal{S}, \phi_0) \sqsubseteq_\eta (\mathcal{S}_m, \phi_m)$ and $(\mathcal{S}, \phi_1) \sqsubseteq_\eta (\mathcal{S}_m, \phi_m)$.

Now suppose that $(\mathcal{S}', \phi')$ is a type and η' a map from $\mathcal{S}$ to $\mathcal{S}'$ such that $(\mathcal{S}, \phi_0) \sqsubseteq_{\eta'} (\mathcal{S}', \phi')$ and $(\mathcal{S}, \phi_1) \sqsubseteq_{\eta'} (\mathcal{S}', \phi')$. Note that η' induces a partition Π' of $\Sigma_{\mathcal{S}}$ such that $s_1, s_2 \in S$ for some $S \in \Pi'$ just in case $\eta'(s_1) = \eta'(s_2)$. Because $\eta'\phi_0 \sqsubseteq \phi', \eta'\phi_1 \sqsubseteq \phi'$, Π' has the property that if $a \in \mathcal{N}$ and both $\phi_0(a), \phi_1(a)$ are defined then there exists $S \in \Pi'$ such that $\phi_0(a), \phi_1(a) \in \Pi'$. Thus Π is a refinement of Π'. Now we define $\theta : \Pi \to \Sigma_{\mathcal{S}'}$ by setting for $S \in \Pi, \theta(S) = \eta'(s)$ where $s \in S$. This θ is well defined because (by the above discussion) η' maps all the elements of S to the same value. It is also direct to check that θ is a map from $\mathcal{S}_m$ to $\mathcal{S}'$ and that $\eta' = \theta\eta$. Finally we show that such a θ is unique. Suppose θ' is a map from $\mathcal{S}_m$ to $\mathcal{S}'$ such that $\eta' = \theta'\eta$. Then for any $S \in \Pi$, $\theta(S) = \eta'(s)$

for some $s \in S$, so $\eta(s) = S$. On the other hand, $\theta'(S) = \theta'(\eta(s)) = \eta'(s)$. Thus $\theta' = \theta$. □

We call $(\mathcal{S}_m, \phi_m)$ with η as in the theorem a *merge* of $(\mathcal{S}, \phi_0)$ and $(\mathcal{S}, \phi_1)$. It is easy to show that the merge of $(\mathcal{S}, \phi_0)$ and $(\mathcal{S}, \phi_1)$ is unique upto isomorphism.

Theorem 21. *For given types $(\mathcal{S}_0, \phi_0), (\mathcal{S}_1, \phi_1)$, there exists a type $(\mathcal{S}_u, \phi_u)$ with two maps ξ_0, ξ_1 such that $(\mathcal{S}_0, \phi_0) \sqsubseteq_{\xi_0} (\mathcal{S}_u, \phi_u)$, $(\mathcal{S}_1, \phi_1) \sqsubseteq_{\xi_1} (\mathcal{S}_u, \phi_u)$, and moreover if $(\mathcal{S}', \phi')$ is another type with two maps θ_0, θ_1 such that $(\mathcal{S}_0, \phi_0) \sqsubseteq_{\theta_0} (\mathcal{S}', \phi'), (\mathcal{S}_1, \phi_1) \sqsubseteq_{\theta_1} (\mathcal{S}', \phi')$, there exists a unique map θ such that $(\mathcal{S}_u, \phi_u) \sqsubseteq_{\theta} (\mathcal{S}', \phi')$ with $\theta_0 = \theta\xi_0, \theta_1 = \theta\xi_1$.*

PROOF: Let $\mathcal{S}_2$ with ι_0, ι_1 be the disjoint sum of $\mathcal{S}_0$ and $\mathcal{S}_1$, so we have

$$(\mathcal{S}_0, \phi_0) \sqsubseteq_{\iota_0} (\mathcal{S}_2, \iota_0\phi_0), \quad (\mathcal{S}_1, \phi_1) \sqsubseteq_{\iota_1} (\mathcal{S}_2, \iota_1\phi_1).$$

Let $(\mathcal{S}_u, \phi_u)$ with η be the merge of $(\mathcal{S}_2, \iota_0\phi_0)$ and $(\mathcal{S}_2, \iota_1\phi_1)$, so

$$(\mathcal{S}_2, \iota_0\phi_0) \sqsubseteq_{\eta} (\mathcal{S}_u, \phi_u), \quad (\mathcal{S}_2, \iota_1\phi_1) \sqsubseteq_{\eta} (\mathcal{S}_u, \phi_u).$$

Letting $\xi_0 = \eta\iota_0, \xi_1 = \eta\iota_1$, we have $(\mathcal{S}_0, \phi_0) \sqsubseteq_{\xi_0} (\mathcal{S}_u, \phi_u), (\mathcal{S}_1, \phi_1) \sqsubseteq_{\xi_1} (\mathcal{S}_u, \phi_u)$.

Now suppose $(\mathcal{S}', \phi')$ is a type with two maps θ_0, θ_1 such that $(\mathcal{S}_0, \phi_0) \sqsubseteq_{\theta_0} (\mathcal{S}', \phi'), (\mathcal{S}_1, \phi_1) \sqsubseteq_{\theta_1} (\mathcal{S}', \phi')$. We show that there exists a unique map θ such that $(\mathcal{S}_u, \phi_u) \sqsubseteq_{\theta} (\mathcal{S}', \phi')$ with $\theta_0 = \theta\xi_0, \theta_1 = \theta\xi_1$. We first show the existence of such θ. Since in this case $\mathcal{S}_0 \xrightarrow{\theta_0} \mathcal{S}', \mathcal{S}_1 \xrightarrow{\theta_1} \mathcal{S}'$, and $\mathcal{S}_2$ with ι_0, ι_1 is a disjoint sum of $\mathcal{S}_0, \mathcal{S}_1$, there exists a unique map θ_2 from $\mathcal{S}_2$ to $\mathcal{S}'$ such that $\theta_0 = \theta_2\iota_0, \theta_1 = \theta_2\iota_1$. Since $\theta_0\phi_0 \sqsubseteq \phi', \theta_1\phi_1 \sqsubseteq \phi'$, we have

$$(\mathcal{S}_2, \iota_0\phi_0) \sqsubseteq_{\eta} (\mathcal{S}', \phi'), \quad (\mathcal{S}_2, \iota_1\phi_1) \sqsubseteq_{\eta} (\mathcal{S}', \phi').$$

Since $(\mathcal{S}_u, \phi_u)$ with η is a merge of $(\mathcal{S}_2, \iota_0\phi_0), (\mathcal{S}_2, \iota_1\phi_1)$, there exists a unique map θ from $\mathcal{S}_u$ to $\mathcal{S}'$ such that $\theta_2 = \theta\eta$. Calculation gives $\theta_0 = \theta\eta\iota_0 = \theta\xi_0, \theta_1 = \theta\eta\iota_1 = \theta\xi_1$. Finally we show the uniqueness of θ. Suppose θ' is map such that $(\mathcal{S}_u, \phi_u) \sqsubseteq_{\theta'} (\mathcal{S}', \phi')$ with $\theta_0 = \theta'\xi_0, \theta_1 = \theta'\xi_1$. For this θ' it holds that $\theta_0 = \theta'\xi_0 = \theta'\eta\iota_0, \theta_1 = \theta'\xi_1 = \theta'\eta\iota_1$. Since $\mathcal{S}_2$ with ι_0, ι_1 is the disjoint sum of $\mathcal{S}_0, \mathcal{S}_1$, $\theta'\eta = \theta_2$. Then since $(\mathcal{S}_u, \phi_u)$ with η is the merge of $(\mathcal{S}_2, \iota_0\phi_0)$ and $(\mathcal{S}_2, \iota_1\phi_1)$, thus $\theta' = \theta$. □

We call $(\mathcal{S}_u, \phi_u)$ with ξ_0, ξ_1 as in the theorem a *union* of $(\mathcal{S}_0, \phi_0)$ and $(\mathcal{S}_1, \phi_1)$. It is easy to show the union of $(\mathcal{S}_0, \phi_0)$ and $(\mathcal{S}_1, \phi_1)$ is unique upto isomorphism. In the following, we will write such $(\mathcal{S}_u, \phi_u)$ as $(\mathcal{S}_0, \phi_0) \uplus (\mathcal{S}_1, \phi_1)$.

Intuitively, the sorting signature of the union of two types is obtained by first taking the disjoint sum of the two sorting signatures of the given types, then identifying those subject sorts which are assigned to the same name in the two types.

Let $N \subseteq \mathcal{N}$ be a set of names. We write $\phi\backslash N$ for the partial function which agrees with ϕ outside N and is undefined otherwise. We abbreviate $\phi\backslash\{a\}$ as $\phi\backslash a$.

Definition 22. *The constructor $\mathcal{T}_0$ which takes an input or output prefix α and produces a type is defined as follows. If $\alpha = a_0(a_1, \ldots, a_n)$ (where $a_i \neq a_j$ for $0 \leq i < j \leq n$), then $\mathcal{T}_0(\alpha)$ is the type*

$$((\{s_0, \ldots, s_n\}, ob^+, ob^-), \phi)$$

where ob^+, ob^- are defined by $ob^-(s_i) = \emptyset$ for $0 \leq i \leq n$, and $ob^+(s_0) = \{s_1 \ldots s_n\}$ and $ob^+(s_i) = \emptyset$ for $1 \leq i \leq n$, and ϕ is such that for $a = a_i, 0 \leq i \leq n$ $\phi(a) = s_i$, otherwise $\phi(a)$ is not defined. If $\alpha = \overline{a}_0\langle a_1, \ldots, a_n\rangle$, then $\mathcal{T}_0(\alpha)$ is the type

$$((\Sigma, ob^+, ob^-), \phi)$$

where $\Sigma = \{s_b \mid b = a_i, 0 \leq i \leq n\}$ and ob^+, ob^- are defined by setting for $s \in \Sigma$, $ob^+(s) = \emptyset$ and $ob^-(s) = \{s_{a_1} \ldots s_{a_n}\}$ if $s = s_{a_0}$, otherwise $ob^-(s) = \emptyset$, and ϕ is such that for $a \in \{a_0, \ldots, a_n\}$ $\phi(a) = s_a$, otherwise $\phi(a)$ is not defined.

The constructor $\mathcal{T}$ which takes a process P and produces a type is defined inductively on the structure of P as follows:

1. *$\mathcal{T}(\mathbf{0}) = (\mathcal{S}_\emptyset, \phi_\emptyset)$, where $\mathcal{S}_\emptyset$ is the empty sorting signature with empty set of subject sorts, $\phi_\emptyset$ is the partial function that is undefined everywhere;*
2. *$\mathcal{T}(P|Q) = \mathcal{T}(P) \uplus \mathcal{T}(Q)$;*
3. *$\mathcal{T}(\nu a P) =$ let $(\mathcal{S}, \phi) = \mathcal{T}(P)$ in $(\mathcal{S}, \phi \backslash a)$;*
4. *$\mathcal{T}(\overline{a}\langle a_1, \ldots, a_n\rangle.P) = \mathcal{T}_0(\overline{a}\langle a_1, \ldots, a_n\rangle) \uplus \mathcal{T}(P)$;*
5. *$\mathcal{T}(a(a_1, \ldots, a_n).P) =$ let $(\mathcal{S}, \phi) = \mathcal{T}_0(a(b_1, \ldots, b_n)) \uplus \mathcal{T}(P\{b_1/a_1, \ldots, b_n/a_n\})$ in $(\mathcal{S}, \phi \backslash \{b_1, \ldots, b_n\})$, where $b_1, \ldots, b_n$ are pairwise distinct and do not occur free in $a(a_1, \ldots, a_n).P$;*
6. *$\mathcal{T}(!P) = \mathcal{T}(P)$.*

Note that clause 5 is well-defined since by Lemma 9 the choice of the b_i's does not affect the type.

Theorem 23. *Let P be a process, $(\mathcal{S}, \phi)$ a type. If $P : (\mathcal{S}, \phi)$ then $\mathcal{T}(P) \sqsubseteq (\mathcal{S}, \phi)$.*

PROOF: Induction on the structure of P.

The case $P \equiv \mathbf{0}$ is trivial because $(\mathcal{S}_\emptyset, \phi_\emptyset) \sqsubseteq (\mathcal{S}, \phi)$ for any $(\mathcal{S}, \phi)$.

Suppose $P \equiv P_1|P_2 : (\mathcal{S}, \phi)$. By rule par in this case it must be that $P_1 : (\mathcal{S}, \phi)$ and $P_2 : (\mathcal{S}, \phi)$. By the induction hypothesis $\mathcal{T}(P_1) \sqsubseteq (\mathcal{S}, \phi), \mathcal{T}(P_2) \sqsubseteq (\mathcal{S}, \phi)$. By Theorem 21, $\mathcal{T}(P_1) \uplus \mathcal{T}(P_2) \sqsubseteq (\mathcal{S}, \phi)$. Thus $\mathcal{T}(P_1|P_2) \sqsubseteq (\mathcal{S}, \phi)$.

Suppose $P \equiv \nu a\, Q : (\mathcal{S}, \phi)$. By rule res in this case it must be that $Q : (\mathcal{S}, \phi\{s/a\})$ for some $s \in \Sigma_\mathcal{S}$. Suppose $\mathcal{T}(Q) = (\mathcal{S}_0, \phi_0)$, by the induction hypothesis $(\mathcal{S}_0, \phi_0) \sqsubseteq (\mathcal{S}, \phi\{s/a\})$. Thus $\mathcal{T}(\nu a Q) = (\mathcal{S}_0, \phi_0 \backslash a) \sqsubseteq (\mathcal{S}, \phi)$.

Suppose $P \equiv \overline{a}_0\langle a_1, \ldots, a_n\rangle.Q : (\mathcal{S}, \phi)$. By rule out in this case it must be that 1) $Q : (\mathcal{S}, \phi)$ and 2) $\phi(a_1) \ldots \phi(a_n) \in ob^-_\mathcal{S}(\phi(a_0))$. By 1) and the induction hypothesis $\mathcal{T}(Q) \sqsubseteq (\mathcal{S}, \phi)$. Let $\mathcal{T}_0(\overline{a}_0\langle a_1, \ldots, a_n\rangle)$ be as defined in Definition 22, then by 2) it is easy to check that $\mathcal{T}_0(\overline{a}_0\langle a_1, \ldots, a_n\rangle) \sqsubseteq_\theta (\mathcal{S}, \phi)$, where $\theta : \{s_b \mid b = a_i, 0 \leq i \leq n\} \rightarrow \Sigma_\mathcal{S}$ is defined by setting for $0 \leq i \leq n, \theta(s_{a_i}) = \phi(a_i)$. By Theorem 21, $\mathcal{T}_0(\overline{a}_0\langle a_1, \ldots, a_n\rangle) \uplus \mathcal{T}(Q) \sqsubseteq (\mathcal{S}, \phi)$. Thus $\mathcal{T}(\overline{a}_0\langle a_1, \ldots, a_n\rangle.Q) \sqsubseteq (\mathcal{S}, \phi)$.

Suppose $P \equiv a_0(a_1, \ldots, a_n).Q : (\mathcal{S}, \phi)$. By rule in in this case it must be that 1) for some $b_1, \ldots, b_n$ which are pairwise distinct and do not occur free in P it holds that $Q\{b_1/a_1, \ldots, b_n/a_n\} : (\mathcal{S}, \phi\{t_1/b_1, \ldots, t_n/b_n\})$, and 2) $t_1 \ldots t_n \in ob^+_{\mathcal{S}}(\phi(a_0))$. By 1) and the induction hypothesis $\mathcal{T}(Q\{b_1/a_1, \ldots, b_n/a_n\}) \sqsubseteq (\mathcal{S}, \phi\{t_1/b_1, \ldots, t_n/b_n\})$. Letting $\mathcal{T}_0(a_0(b_1, \ldots, b_n))$ be as defined in Definition 22, by 2) it is easy to check that $\mathcal{T}_0(a_0(b_1, \ldots, b_n)) \sqsubseteq_\theta (\mathcal{S}, \phi\{t_1/b_1, \ldots, t_n/b_n\})$, where $\theta : \{s_0, \ldots, s_n\} \rightarrow \Sigma_{\mathcal{S}}$ is such that $\theta(s_0) = \phi(a_0)$ and for $1 \leq i \leq n, \theta(s_i) = t_i$. Let $(\mathcal{S}_0, \phi_0) = \mathcal{T}_0(a_0(b_1, \ldots, b_n)) \uplus \mathcal{T}(Q\{b_1/a_1, \ldots, b_n/a_n\})$. By Theorem 21, $(\mathcal{S}_0, \phi_0) \sqsubseteq (\mathcal{S}, \phi\{t_1/b_1, \ldots, t_n/b_n\})$. Thus $\mathcal{T}(a_0(a_1, \ldots, a_n).Q) = (\mathcal{S}_0, \phi_0 \backslash \{b_1, \ldots, b_n\}) \sqsubseteq (\mathcal{S}, \phi)$.

The last case is $P \equiv !Q : (\mathcal{S}, \phi)$. By rule rep in this case $Q : (\mathcal{S}, \phi)$, thus by the induction hypothesis $\mathcal{T}(Q) \sqsubseteq (\mathcal{S}, \phi)$. Thus $\mathcal{T}(!Q) \sqsubseteq (\mathcal{S}, \phi)$. □

By Definition 10 and Lemma 7, we immediately obtain the following.

Corollary 24. *Let P by a process. There exists a consistent type $(\mathcal{S}, \phi)$ such that $P : (\mathcal{S}, \phi)$ if and only if $\mathcal{T}(P)$ is consistent.* □

5 Conclusion

In this paper the following results have been presented:

1. A type system for the polyadic π-calculus is introduced. It is proved that if a process can be assigned a consistent type then it is free from mismatches. It is proved also that if a type is not consistent then there is a process which possesses that type and which is not free from mismatches.
2. An algorithm is presented for deciding whether or not a given type is consistent.
3. A systematic way of constructing a most general type for a process is established such that the process in question can be well-typed if and only if the most general type is consistent.

The results show that the type system is not only sound in the sense that a well-typed process is free from run-time type errors, but also complete in the sense that it is decidable whether or not a process can be well-typed. The ideas and techniques introduced shed new light on typing of π-calculus processes. The limitations of this kind of approach to typing are sharply drawn. We hope that ideas introduced here may be a useful step towards more liberal typing systems.

References

1. S. Gay. A sort inference algorithm for the polyadic π-calculus. In *Proceedings of 20th POPL*. ACM Press, 1993.
2. C. Jones. A pi-calculus semantics for an object-based design notation. In *Proceedings of CONCUR'93*, pages 158–172. Springer, 1993.
3. X. Liu and D. Walker. Confluence of processes and systems of objects. In *Proceedings of CAAP'95*. Springer, to appear.

4. R. Milner. Action structures. Technical report, University of Edinburgh, 1992.
5. R. Milner. Functions as processes. *Mathematical Structures in Computer Science*, 2:119–141, 1992.
6. R. Milner. The polyadic π-calculus: a tutorial. In *Logic and Algebra of Specification*. Springer, 1992.
7. R. Milner, J. Parrow, and D. Walker. A calculus of mobile processes, parts 1 and 2. *Information and Computation*, 100:1–77, 1992.
8. B. Pierce. Programming in the π-calculus. Technical report, University of Edinburgh, 1994.
9. B. Pierce and D. Sangiorgi. Typing and subtyping for mobile processes. In *Proceedings of LICS'93*, pages 376–385. Computer Society Press, 1993.
10. D. Sangiorgi. *Expressing mobility in process algebras: first-order and higher-order paradigms*. PhD thesis, University of Edinburgh, 1992.
11. D. Sangiorgi. The lazy lambda-calculus in a concurrency scenario. *Information and Computation*, 111:120–153, 1994.
12. D. Sangiorgi. Locality and true-concurrency in calculi for mobile processes. In *Proceedings of TACS'94*, pages 405–420. Springer, 1994.
13. D. Turner. PhD thesis, University of Edinburgh, forthcoming.
14. V. Vasconcelos and K. Honda. Principal typing schemes in the polyadic π-calculus. In *Proceedings of CONCUR'93*. Springer, 1993.
15. D. Walker. Objects in the π-calculus. *Information and Computation*, 116:253–271, 1995.

Fibrational control structures

*Claudio Hermida** *John Power***

Abstract

We provide a category theoretic reformulation of control structures, which avoids explicit reference to *names*. The basis of the formulation is what we call a *binding structure*, which accounts for *naming* and the associated operation of *binding* in isolation, *i.e.* without reference to extra features. Upon adding structure to such a binding structure we arrive at *fibrational control structures*, which (with a mild extra condition) we show equivalent to *locally finite* control structures, those in which every action has a finite surface.

1 Introduction

Over recent years, Robin Milner and various colleagues have been elaborating an algebraic framework in which to analyse calculi for interactive computation [Mil92, Mil93]. It is related to the work of Meseguer and Montanari [MM90], who used a monoidal category to account for the algebraic structure of processes associated to a Petri net. In Milner's setting, particular emphasis is placed on the manipulation of *names* within the abovementioned calculi, the π-calculus being the paradigmatic example.

The first kind of structure Milner introduced is that of *action structure*, which has *actions* as its primitive objects. These are endowed with *input* and *output* arities. The algebraic structure on actions is given by a *dataflow composition*, which sets up a category with arities $m, n, \ldots$ as objects and actions $a : m \longrightarrow n, \ldots$ as morphisms, with domain and codomain corresponding to input and output respectively. Furthermore, the category is *locally preordered*, *i.e.* is a $\mathcal{P}reord$-category; the preorder in the hom-sets is intended to capture the dynamic aspect of actions, expressing a *reaction relation* between them. The category is also symmetric monoidal (in the enriched sense); the tensor product corresponds to parallel composition of actions. Each action has (implicitly) associated a set of names, called its *surface*, through which it can interact with other actions. The remaining, crucial feature is a (functorial) *parameterisation* of actions on a 'name', for which a set of names X with specified arity, written $x : m$ is assumed as part of the structure. Such parameterisation corresponds to making the parameterised name an (implicitly, positionally named) additional input of the action; functoriality is achieved by making the name simultaneously available as an additional output.

Actions structures were further elaborated into *control structures* [MMP95], which have additional features. A primary new feature is an assigment of actions to names $(x : m) \mapsto (\langle x \rangle : 1 \longrightarrow m)$ (where 1 is the unit of the monoidal structure). There is also a 'forgetful' action $\omega_m : m \longrightarrow 1$. Finally, the structure is parametric on a set of control operators $\mathcal{K}$, which correspond to the particular features of the calculus being modelled. In this setting, the functorial parameterisation is expressible in terms of a more primitive 'binding' operation, which turns a free name in an action (a name in the surface of the action, in Milner's terminology) into an input parameter.

* Computer Science Department, Aarhus University, DK-8000 Denmark. e-mail:chermida@daimi.aau.dk. This author acknowledges funding from the CLICS II ESPRIT project.

** LFCS, University of Edinburgh, Edinburgh EH9 3JZ, UK. e-mail: ajp@dcs.ed.ac.uk. This author gratefully acknowledges the support of ESPRIT Basic Research Action 6453: Types for proofs and programs, and also the BRICS grant, which has funded two visits to Aarhus to work on this paper.

Thus, a fundamental structural difference between control structures and other category theoretic constructions used in the semantics of concurrency is that a control structure has, as part of its data, a set of names X. It is more common in category theoretic accounts of semantics to have names, or variables, implicit, but with the operation of *naming* explicit, as in categorical logic [LS86]. For instance, in a cartesian (closed) category, free variables in a term are accounted for positionally, in de Bruijn's-indices style. That is, a term $t : \tau$ with free variables of arity $\tau_1, \ldots, \tau_n$ is interpreted as an arrow $t : \tau_1 \times \ldots \times \tau_n \longrightarrow \tau$. In fact, in analogy with cartesian closed categories, as far as names are concerned, control structures play a role that is closer to that of the simply typed λ-calculus, which corresponds to the internal language of a cartesian closed category. So a natural question arises: is it possible to give an equivalent abstract category theoretic formulation of control structures in which the set of names is left implicit?

A positive answer to this question would provide further evidence of the adequacy of the definition of control structures, as such a result amounts to a syntax/semantics equivalence, validating the syntax. It would also bring control structures into line with the broader use of category theory in semantics, for instance allowing the likelihood of precise comparison with Abramsky's interaction categories [Abr95], for which names are implicit. Note though that the paradigm in *ibid.* is based on synchronisation (symmetric) rather than communication; dataflow is involved in the latter.

In this paper, we provide an equivalent formulation of control structures satisfying the additional condition that every action has only a finite surface. The *surface* of an action, developed in [MMP95], consists of the set of names through which that action may communicate with other actions. In general, any action that arises from the basic operations and data of a control structure necessarily has finite surface. That includes all control structures that arise from process calculi such as the π-calculus, and from factoring them under an arbitrary equivalence: see the action calculi and results of [MMP95]. So our restriction to control structures for which every action has finite surface is a mild one; we call such control structures *locally finite*. Upon making that restriction, we can indeed define a *fibrational control structure*. It accounts explicitly for the arity of the names (potentially) in the surface of an action, and the interaction between surface and input, given by binding. We finally introduce the related concept of *abstract control structure*, satisfying a condition which allows us to recover a control structure, and prove an equivalence between the category of abstract control structures and that of locally finite control structures. This paper is devoted to providing the definition and proof.

The definition of control structures involves quite a number of axioms (see Section 2), which look somewhat arbitrary. The formulation given here is more compact, and a good many of the axioms of control structures follow from the 'naturality' (or fibred) conditions imposed on the structure. For instance, the functoriality of the abstractor functors follows from the naturality condition on our definition of composition. In fact, it is possible to give a very concise presentation of a fibrational control structure as (essentially) a "monoidal category object in the 2-category of fibrations", with simple extra conditions. However, such formulation would demand more categorical knowledge by the reader than we are willing to assume.

The paper is organized as follows. In Section 2, we recall from [MMP95] the definition of control structure. In Section 3, we introduce the one abstract category theoretic construction we need to account for the interaction between inputs and free names. In Section 4, we outline the construction that will give us a fibrational control structure, starting from a control structure. This motivates the analysis in Section 5 of the basic new structure we introduce, namely a *binding structure*, which gives a name-free account of naming and the associated operation of *binding*. In Section 6, we start the construction of a control structure from an abstract one. We consider added structure in Section 7, define fibrational and abstract control structures in Section 8, and prove our main result (Corollary 9.13) in Section 9.

For a standard reference in category theory, see [Mac71]. We deliberately avoid subtle category theoretic definitions in order to make this paper more accessible, although we firmly believe that some abstract category theoretic definitions are insightful for this study. Furthermore, to understand the way we set up a binding structure, some familiarity with basic categorical logic as in [LS86] would be helpful.

Ackowledgements: We wish to thank Robin Milner and Vladimiro Sassone for discussions and comments on the paper.

2 Control structures

In this section, we recall from [MMP95] the definition of control structures. An *action structure* consists of a strict monoidal category A, locally preordered, whose objects $k, l, m, n, \cdots$ are called *arities* and whose morphisms $a, b, c, \cdots$ are called *actions*. The monoid of objects of A is denoted $(M, \otimes, 1)$, and we denote the composite of $a : l \longrightarrow m$ with $b : m \longrightarrow n$ by $a \cdot b$. The identity id_m is maximal in the preorder $A(m, m)$ for all m. An action structure is also equipped with a countable set X of *names*; each name x is assigned an arity k, denoted $x : k$, and a preorder-enriched functor $ab_x : A \longrightarrow A$ such that if $x : k$ and $a : m \longrightarrow n$, then $ab_x a : k \otimes m \longrightarrow k \otimes n$.

The name-set X is assumed to be fixed, as is the arity monoid M and the assignment of arities to names. Moreover, M is assumed to be the free monoid on a set P of *prime* arities, and the arity of each name is assumed to be prime, and infinitely many names are associated with each prime arity. Note that this implies that P is countable.

A *control* K is an operator that builds an action $K(\vec{a})$ from a sequence $\vec{a}$ of actions. It has an associated rule of arity, which specifies the arity of the input sequence $(a_i : m_i \longrightarrow n_i)$ of length r, and that of the result $K(\vec{a}) : m \longrightarrow n$. This rule is subject to a side-condition that may constrain the values of r, m_i, n_i, m and n.

A *symmetric action structure* is an action structure with a symmetry c on the underlying strict monoidal category, such that

- $ab_x c = id \otimes c$
- $ab_x(ab_x a) = id \otimes ab_x a$
- $ab_x(a \otimes id) = ab_x a \otimes id$
- $(c_{k,l} \otimes id_m) \cdot ab_y ab_x a = ab_x ab_y a \cdot (c_{k,l} \otimes id_{m'})$ if $x \neq y$.

A *control structure* consists of a signature $\mathcal{K}$ of controls and a symmetric action structure A equipped with

- a *datum* action $\langle x \rangle : 1 \longrightarrow p$ for each $x : p \in X$
- a *discard* action $\omega : p \longrightarrow 1$ for each prime p
- a *control* operation K for each $K \in \mathcal{K}$, obeying the arity rules for $\mathcal{K}$,

such that

- $ab_x \langle y \rangle = id \otimes \langle y \rangle$ if $x \neq y$
- $ab_x \omega = id \otimes \omega$

- $(x)\langle x\rangle = id$
- $[x/x]a = a$
- $[y/x](\langle x\rangle \otimes \langle x\rangle) = \langle y\rangle \otimes \langle y\rangle$
- $[y/x]K(a_1, \cdots, a_n) = K([y/x]a_1, \cdots, [y/x]a_n)$

where for all $a : m \longrightarrow n$ and $x, y : p \in X$, $(x)a$ is defined to be $(ab_x a).(\omega_p \otimes id_n)$ and $[y/x]a$ is defined to be $(\langle y\rangle \otimes id_m) \cdot (x)a$. The action $[y/x]a$ should be thought of as a renaming x to y in a.

We recall from [MMP95] the notion of *surface* of actions, *i.e.* those names through which an action can interact. For an action a, let $surf(a) = \{x : k \mid ab_x(a) \neq id_x \otimes a\}$. Informally, these are the names which occur freely in the action.

A morphism of control structures from $(A, \otimes, c, ab, \langle\ \rangle, \omega, \mathcal{K})$ to $(A', \otimes', c', ab', \langle\ \rangle', \omega', \mathcal{K})$ (with the same control signature, sets P and X) is a strict symmetric monoidal functor $f : A \longrightarrow A'$ which is the identity on objects and preserves the additional structure, *i.e.* ab, $\langle\ \rangle$, ω and the controls. It follows that for any action a in A, $surf(f(a)) \subseteq surf(a)$.

For a concrete example, the free control structure (= action calculus) for π-calculus (without replication) has actions generated by the following (constant) controls: $\tau : 1 \longrightarrow 1$ (silent action), $\nu : 1 \longrightarrow k$ (a new name of arity k), $\mathbf{out}_x : k \longrightarrow 1$ (output through port x) and $\mathbf{in}_x : 1 \longrightarrow k$ (read input through port x). There is one axiom which expresses communication through matching input/output ports, namely $\mathbf{out}_x \otimes \mathbf{in}_x \leq \tau \otimes id_k$. The remaining preorder structure is freely induced by this axiom and the preorder-enriched monoidal category structure.

3 The "swap" construction

In this section, we introduce one abstract category theoretic construction which we will use to organise the indexing of actions by both the arity of names (potentially) in their surface and their input arity. This construction has recently been used in semantics in the context of an account of indeterminates, see [HJ93]. Its role will be elucidated in Definition 5.1.

First, we give an explicit description of the free category with strictly associative finite products on a set P. The idea is that P will be the set of primes used in the definition of control structure, and our main constructions are based upon the free category with strictly associative finite products built from it.

3.1 Proposition Given a set P, the free category P with strictly associative finite products on P may be described as follows:

- an object of P is a finite sequence $(p_1, \cdots, p_m)$ of elements of P
- an arrow from $(p_1, \cdots, p_m)$ to $(q_1, \cdots, q_n)$ is a function $\phi : \{1, \cdots, n\} \longrightarrow \{1, \cdots, m\}$ such that for all i, $q_i = p_{\phi(i)}$
- composition is given by composition of functions.

3.2 Definition Given any category $\mathcal{M}$ with finite products, we define a category $s(\mathcal{M})$ as follows:

- an object is a pair (k, m) of objects of $\mathcal{M}$
- an arrow from (k, m) to (k', m') is a pair (f, g) of arrows in $\mathcal{M}$ with $f : k \longrightarrow k'$ and $g : k \times m \longrightarrow m'$
- The identity on (k, m) is $1_k, \pi'_{k,m} : (k, m) \longrightarrow (k, m)$. Given $(f, g) : (k, m) \longrightarrow (k', m')$ and $(h, l) : (k', m') \longrightarrow (k'', m'')$, their composite is $(hf, l\langle f\pi, g\rangle) : (k, m) \longrightarrow (k'', m'')$.

3.3 Proposition The category $s(\mathcal{M})$ has finite products. Moreover, if $\mathcal{M}$ has strictly associative finite products, so does $s(\mathcal{M})$.

Semantically, it is more common to have categories with finite products that need not be strictly associative, but any such category is equivalent to one with strictly associative finite products, so there is no loss of generality in assuming the latter structure.

3.4 Convention We write $\pi : k \times m \longrightarrow k$ and $\pi' : k \times m \longrightarrow m$ for the first and second projection out of a product. We use subscripts whenever convenient. We write $t : k \longrightarrow 1$ for the unique morphism into the terminal object 1.

3.5 Proposition In $s(\mathcal{M})$, every map $(f, g) : (k, m) \longrightarrow (k', m')$ factors uniquely as a map of the form (id, g) followed by one of the form (f, π').

3.6 Remark The above factorization results from the fact that there is a functor $\pi_{\mathcal{M}} : s(\mathcal{M}) \longrightarrow \mathcal{M}$, projecting onto the first component, which is a split fibration, *cf.*[HJ93].

4 The construction of a fibration from a control structure

We assume X, P, $ar : X \longrightarrow P$ and $\mathcal{K}$ are all fixed. Let $\mathcal{M}$ be the free category with strictly associative finite products on the set P. So $|\mathcal{M}|$, the underlying discrete category of $\mathcal{M}$, *i.e.* its set of objects, is the free monoid on P. Moreover, we extend the definition of arity so that a vector $\vec{x}$ of names has arity determined by the composite of the arities of its elements. Finally, to each arity k, we ascribe a vector $\vec{x}_k$ of distinct names, with $ar(\vec{x}_k) = k$, such that if $k \neq k'$, the two vectors are pairwise distinct.

Given a control structure $(A, \otimes, c, ab, \langle\ \rangle, \omega, \mathcal{K})$, we will define a functor

$$A_c : s(\mathcal{M})^{op} \times |\mathcal{M}| \longrightarrow Preord$$

where *Preord* is the category of preorders and monotone functions.

4.1 Notation Given a control structure $A = (A, \otimes, c, ab, \langle\ \rangle, \omega, \mathcal{K})$, let $A_c(k, m, n)$ denote the preorder of actions $a : m \longrightarrow n$ for which $surf(a) \subseteq |\vec{x}_k|$, where $|\vec{x}_k|$ denotes the set of elements of the vector $\vec{x}_k$, with preorder relation given by that of the control structure.

Note that an action a in $A_c(k, m, n)$ may have fewer names in its surface than indicated by the arity k. This fact becomes important as we make the converse construction (of a control structure from a fibrational one) in Section 6, particularly for $\otimes$ and $\cdot$.

We denote an arbitrary element of $A_c(k, m, n)$ by $\vec{x}_k : k \vdash a : m \longrightarrow n$, the idea being that the turnstile represents the fact that we are factoring out the specific choice of names and allowing weakening. This is in accord with standard type theoretic notation.

In order to complete our construction of a functor $A_c : s(\mathcal{M})^{op} \times |\mathcal{M}| \longrightarrow Preord$, we must define its behaviour on maps. To do so, we use Proposition 3.5: that every map in $s(\mathcal{M})$ is uniquely a composite of the form (id, g) followed by (f, π'). Since morphisms in $s(\mathcal{M})^{op} \times |\mathcal{M}|$ are determined by those of $s(\mathcal{M})$, we omit the third argument in specifying the action of A_c in morphisms, *i.e.* we write $A_c(f, g)$ for $A_c(f, g, n)$.

Recall that a map $f : (p_1, \cdots, p_m) \longrightarrow (q_1, \cdots, q_n)$ in $\mathcal{M}$ is a function $\phi : \{1, \cdots, n\} \longrightarrow \{1, \cdots, m\}$ such that $q_i = p_{\phi(i)}$. So if $k = p_1 \cdots p_m$ and $k' = q_1 \cdots q_n$, given $f : k \longrightarrow k'$, we denote by $f(\vec{x}_k)$ the sequence $(y_1, \cdots, y_n)$ where $y_i = x_{\phi(i)}$.

4.2 Proposition Given a control structure $A = (A, \otimes, c, ab, \langle\ \rangle, \omega, \mathcal{K})$, the graph morphism $A_c : s(\mathcal{M})^{op} \times |\mathcal{M}| \longrightarrow Preord$ determined by

- $A_c(k,m,n) = \{a \in A(m,n) | surf(a) \subseteq |\vec{x}_k|\}$ with the preorder induced by that on $A(m,n)$, with $\vec{x}_k$ the vector assigned to k
- $A_c(f,\pi')a = [f(\vec{x}_k)/\vec{x}_{k'}]a$, where $f(\vec{x}_k)$ is the sequence with j-th component $x_{\phi(j)}$ of $\vec{x}_k$
- $A_c(id,g)a = \langle g \rangle \cdot a$, where $\langle g \rangle = (\langle \vec{x}_k \rangle \otimes id_m) \cdot (\vec{x}_{k\times m})\langle g(\vec{x}_{k\times m})\rangle$.

is a functor ■

We end this section by observing the following fact about our construction A_c.

4.3 Definition Call a map in $s(\mathcal{M})$ of the form $(\pi,\pi') : (k_1 \times k_2 \times k_3, m) \longrightarrow (k_1 \times k_3, m)$ a *weakening*. Call a commutative square in $s(\mathcal{M}) \times |\mathcal{M}|$ with source and target vertex given by $(k_1 \times k_2 \times k_3 \times k_4 \times k_5, m, n)$ and $(k_1 \times k_3 \times k_5, m, n)$ respectively, a *weakening square*.

$$\begin{array}{ccc} k_1 \times k_2 \times k_3 \times k_4 \times k_5 & \xrightarrow{\pi_{1345}} & k_1 \times k_3 \times k_4 \times k_5 \\ \downarrow{\scriptstyle \pi_{1235}} & & \downarrow{\scriptstyle \pi_{135}} \\ k_1 \times k_2 \times k_3 \times k_5 & \xrightarrow[\pi_{135}]{} & k_1 \times k_3 \times k_5 \end{array}$$

Then we have

4.4 Proposition The functor $A_c : s(\mathcal{M})^{op} \times |\mathcal{M}| \longrightarrow$ *Preord* sends all weakening squares to pullbacks. ■

The above fact will be used in §6 to recover the actions of a control structure from the objects in the fibres of a fibrational control structure satisfying the above pullback condition. See Lemma 6.2 and the definition of the graph $F(h)$.

5 Naming and binding

In this section we analyse *binding* in terms of the functor $A_c : s(\mathcal{M})^{op} \times |\mathcal{M}| \longrightarrow$ *Preord*. First, let us elaborate on the meaning of this functor.

The fibres $A_c(k,m,n)$ represent actions with input arity m, output arity n, and (potentially) 'free names', *i.e.* names on the surface of the action, of arity k. Hence, such actions can receive input in two ways: by supplying data to its m 'input ports' (or wires, if one makes an analogy with circuits) and by substituting some names on its surface. The inputs we provide can in turn be themselves free names or be the result of the output of another action.

This two-way input-feeding into an action is what the above functor A_c intends to capture, by considering the "swap" construction $s(\mathcal{M})$. Recall that in $s(\mathcal{M})$ a morphism $(f,g) : (k,m) \longrightarrow (k',m')$ is given by two morphisms $f : k \longrightarrow k'$ and $g : k \times m \longrightarrow m'$. Here f allows the 'substitution of free names', *i.e.* renaming of names in the surface, while g supplies input to the action, coming from free names (those of arity k) or outputs (those of arity m).

Now, notice that the binding operation

$$(\vec{x}_k : k \vdash a : m \longrightarrow n) \longmapsto (* : 1 \vdash (\vec{x}_k)a : k \times m \longrightarrow n)$$

is inverse to the operation

$$(* : 1 \vdash b : k \times m \longrightarrow n) \longmapsto (\vec{x}_k : k \vdash (\langle \vec{x}_k \rangle \otimes id_m) \cdot a : m \longrightarrow n)$$

thus establishing an isomorphism $A_c(k,m,n) \cong A_c(1, k \times m, n)$. In terms of control structures, this establishes a bijection between the set of actions $a : m \longrightarrow n$ with surface contained in $|\vec{x}_k|$ and the set of actions $b : k \times m \longrightarrow n$ with empty surface.

Although we have not introduced identity actions yet, we have enough structure to account for the inverse operation of binding, namely provision of free names as inputs, thanks to the swap construction. In fact, only a limited form of composition is required, namely precomposition with datum actions. This is what we call *naming*; it amounts to the provision of names as inputs to actions. More precisely, consider the following morphism in $s(\mathcal{M})$: $(\pi_{j,k}, \pi'_{j,k\times m}) : (j \times k, m) \longrightarrow (j, k \times m)$. The inverse action of binding is given by the (preorder) morphism $h(\pi_{1,k}, \pi'_{1,k\times m}) : A_c(1, k \times m, n) \longrightarrow A_c(k, m, n)$. Of course, we further parameterise this operation by allowing the presence of extra free names, taking an arbitrary arity j instead of 1, *i.e.* we want to be able to bind only some of the names of the action. Hence, we arrive at the following

5.1 Definition

- A *naming structure* is a functor $h : s(\mathcal{M})^{op} \times |\mathcal{M}| \longrightarrow$ *Preord*, where $\mathcal{M}$ is a category with finite products.
- A *binding structure* is a naming structure, such that for all objects j, k, m, n of $\mathcal{M}$, the preorder morphism $h(\pi_{j,k}, \pi'_{1,k\times m}) : h(j, k \times m, n) \longrightarrow h(j \times k, m, n)$ is a preorder isomorphism (natural in all its arguments). We denote its inverse by $(\ )^{-}$.

We regard this structure as basic, in the sense that it expresses binding purely in the context of naming, without reference to *names* nor any other structure.

We single out a substructure of a naming structure which deals only with renaming. Let $s(\mathcal{M})_g$ be the full-on-objets subcategory of $s(\mathcal{M})$ with only those morphisms of the form (f, π'). Then, the structure obtained by restricting a naming structure h to a functor $h : s(\mathcal{M})_g^{op} \times |\mathcal{M}| \longrightarrow$ *Preord* allows us to talk about operations on actions (objects of the fibres of h) which are compatible with renaming, *e.g.* the controls in Definition 8.1.

A morphism $f : h \longrightarrow h'$ between naming structures is simply a natural transformation between the functors h and h'.

6 The construction of a control structure from a fibration with extra structure

Assume P is a fixed countable set and let $\mathcal{M}$ be the free category with strictly associative finite products on it, as in §2.

Now assume we are given a functor $h : s(\mathcal{M})^{op} \times |\mathcal{M}| \longrightarrow$ *Preord* that sends all weakening squares to pullbacks. We extend Definition 4.3 to

6.1 Definition An element a of $h(k_1 \times k_2 \times k_3, m, n)$ is called a *weakening* of an element $a' \in h(k_1 \times k_3, m, n)$ if $a = h(\pi, \pi')a'$, where $\pi : k_1 \times k_2 \times k_3 \longrightarrow k_1 \times k_3$ is the evident projection.

6.2 Lemma For all (k, m, n) and $a \in h(k, m, n)$, there exists a unique element b of some (k', m, n) such that a is a weakening of b, but b is not a weakening of anything else. ■

We will call such b as in the above statement a *strong* element.

Now, to each $p \in P$, assign a countable set X_p, and let X be the disjoint union of the X_p's. For simplicity of exposition, we will assume that X is well ordered: it is not essential to our constructions, but it allows us to speak of sequences rather than sets, which is convenient. Moreover, as in our definitions of P and $\mathcal{M}$, we will tacitly assume that this countable set X agrees with that in the definition of control structure, and that the vectors $\vec{x}_k$ we ascribed to each k agree with the order on X.

Now define a directed graph $F(h)$ as follows:

- objects are those of $\mathcal{M}$.
- an arrow $([x_1, \cdots, x_l], a) : m \longrightarrow n$ consists of a strong element a of some $h(k, m, n)$ together with a sequence $[x_1, \cdots, x_l]$ of distinct names of X, respecting the well order of X, such that $k = p_1 \cdots p_l$, where $x_i \in X_{p_i}$.

We define the function $F_{ar} : X \longrightarrow P$ by sending x to p if $x \in X_p$.

6.3 Definition We call a control structure *locally finite* if every action has finite surface.

We need to use two results about control structures in general.

6.4 Proposition For any action a with $y \notin surf(a)$, we have $[x/y][y/x]a = a$.

∎

6.5 Proposition If $x \in surf(a)$ and $y \notin surf(a)$, then $surf([y/x]a) = (surf(a) - \{x\}) \cup \{y\}$.

∎

Now we can show that if we start with a locally finite control structure, apply Construction 4.2, then apply F, we get the same graph and arity function as we had originally.

6.6 Proposition Let $A = (A, \otimes, c, ab, \langle\ \rangle, \omega, \mathcal{K})$ be a locally finite control structure. Then the underlying directed graph G of A together with the function $ar : X \longrightarrow P$ is isomorphic to $F(A_c)$ together with F_{ar}.

Proof The only non-trivial part is to show that for each m and n, the set of actions from m to n in A is in bijection with the set of edges from m to n in $F(A_c)$. Given $a : m \longrightarrow n$ in A, it has a surface, which is uniquely ordered to be consistent with the order on X, say $[y_1, \cdots, y_l]$, with corresponding arity $k = p_1 \cdots p_l$. If the vector $\vec{y}$ is disjoint from the specified vector $\vec{x}_k$, then $[\vec{x}_k/\vec{y}]a$ appears in $A_c(k, m, n)$, and is a strong element. So send a to $([y_1, \cdots, y_l], [\vec{x}_k/\vec{y}]a)$. If $\vec{y}$ and $\vec{x}_k$ are not disjoint, pass via a vector $\vec{z}$ that is disjoint from both of them.

That this function is a bijection follows from the fact that the strong elements of $A_c(k, m, n)$ are precisely those with surface of arity k, and Propositions 6.4 and 6.5.

∎

6.7 Remark In following sections, we will add further structure to $h : s(\mathcal{M})^{op} \times |\mathcal{M}| \longrightarrow Preord$ in order to enrich the construction $F(h)$ to a control structure. Then we will ensure that $surf([x_1, \cdots, x_l], a) = \{x_1, \cdots, x_l\}$. It will follow that $F(h)_c$ is isomorphic to h. This will give us a full inclusion of the category of "abstract" control structures (fibrational control structures sending weakening squares to pullbacks) into the category of control structures, with right adjoint given by $(\ )_c$, and with image the locally finite control structures. This will show that the category of abstract control structures is equivalent to the category of locally finite control structures.

7 Added structure: identities, symmetries, datum, discard

We could complete our definition of abstract control structure immediately here. But it has several parts. So in this section, we motivate part of the definition by showing what we gain by adding identities to our functor h: merely asserting their existence gives us name free accounts of the symmetries, datum and ω of control structures.

7.1 Lemma Given a locally finite control structure $A = (A, \otimes, ab, c, \langle\ \rangle, \omega, K)$

1. $(x : p \vdash \langle x \rangle : 1 \longrightarrow p) = A_c(t, id)id_p$ where $(t, id) : (p, 1) \longrightarrow (1, p)$ in $s(\mathcal{M})$
2. $(\vdash c : p \times q \longrightarrow q \times p) = A_c(id, c)id_{q \times p}$ with $(id, c) : (1, p \times q) \longrightarrow (1, q \times p)$
3. $(\vdash \omega_p : p \longrightarrow 1) = A_c(id, t)id_1$ with $(id, t) : (1, p) \longrightarrow (1, 1)$
4. $(\vdash (x)\langle xx \rangle : 1 \longrightarrow k) = A_c(id, \Delta)id_{k \times k} = \bar{\Delta}$ with $(id, \Delta) : (1, k) \longrightarrow (1, k \times k)$
5. $(x : p \vdash \langle xx \rangle : 1 \longrightarrow p \times p) = A_c(\Delta, \pi')\langle y_0, y_1 \rangle$ with $(\Delta, \pi') : (p, 1) \longrightarrow (p \times p, 1)$

■

The lemma motivates the construction of more of the data for a control structure $F(h)$ from $h : s(\mathcal{M})^{op} \times |\mathcal{M}| \longrightarrow$ *Preord* satisfying our pullback condition and having for each m, an id_m in $h(1, m, m)$.

7.2 Definition Given $h : s(\mathcal{M})^{op} \times |\mathcal{M}| \longrightarrow$ *Preord* with such id_m and satisfying our pullback condition,

1. for each $m \in M$, define $id_m : m \longrightarrow m$ in $F(h)$ to be $([\,], id_m)$
2. define $c : p \times q \longrightarrow q \times p$ in $F(h)$ to be $([\,], h(id, c)id_{q \times p})$
3. define $\omega_p : p \longrightarrow 1$ to be $([\,], h(id, t)id_1)$.

These are all well defined, since the second component of each ordered pair is necessarily strong, with surface arity 1.

Finally, we need a little delicacy in defining $\langle x \rangle$ in $F(h)$ because $h(t, id)id_p$ may not be strong, with $(t, id) : (p, 1) \longrightarrow (1, p)$. So we define

7.3 Definition In $F(h)$, we put $\langle x \rangle_{F(h)}$ equal to $([x], h(t, id)id_p)$ if $h(t, id)id_p$ is strong, and $([\,], a)$ where $h(t, id)id_p$ is a weakening of a, otherwise.

It follows immediately from Lemma 7.1 that the construction $F((\ )_c)$ respects identities, symmetry and ω; to see that it respects datum, we need the following lemma:

7.4 Lemma If $x : p$ and $y : p$ and $surf\langle x \rangle$ is empty, then $surf\langle y \rangle$ is also empty.

Proof Since $surf\langle x \rangle$ is empty, $x \notin surf\langle x \rangle$. So $\langle y \rangle = [y/x]\langle x \rangle = \langle x \rangle$, so $surf\langle y \rangle$ is empty. ■

It now follows immediately that $F((\ )_c)$ respects datum as any x will have empty surface if and only if the canonical one has empty surface. Our mapping from a control structure A to $F(A_c)$ takes $\langle x \rangle$ to $([x], \langle x' \rangle)$ if the surface of the canonical $\langle x' \rangle$ is non-empty, and to $([\,], \langle x' \rangle)$ otherwise; thus it respects the constructions $\langle\ \rangle : X \longrightarrow M$ and $\langle\ \rangle_{F((\ )_c)}$.

8 The definition of an abstract control structure

In this section, we finally give our definition of an abstract control structure, and in the following section, we will complete the proof of our main result Corollary 9.13.

8.1 Definition A *fibrational control structure* consists of

1. a binding structure $h : s(\mathcal{M})^{op} \times |\mathcal{M}| \longrightarrow$ *Preord*. The functor h determines a locally preordered graph G_h with vertex set M and with edge preorder from m to n given by the disjoint union over k of $h(k, m, n)$. We denote the underlying ordinary graph by G_{h0}.

2. a strict monoidal (locally preordered) category structure on G_h such that
   - composition restricts to a family of preorder maps $\cdot : h(k,m,n) \times h(k',n,p) \longrightarrow h(k \times k', m, p)$ natural in the first variable with respect to $s(\mathcal{M})$, meaning that for all $(f,g) : (k,m) \longrightarrow (k'', m'')$ in $s(\mathcal{M})$, the evident diagram commutes, and natural in the second variable with respect to maps of the form $(f', \pi') : (k', n) \longrightarrow (k'', n)$
   - the tensor product restricts to a family of maps $\otimes : h(k,m,n) \times h(k',m',n') \longrightarrow h(k \times k', m \times m', n \times n')$, natural in $s(\mathcal{M})$ in both variables, meaning that for all $(f,g) : (k,m) \longrightarrow (k'', m'')$ in $s(\mathcal{M})$, the evident diagram commutes, and dually *w.r.t.* (k', m').
   - id_m (which necessarily lies in $h(1,m,m)$) is maximal in the preorder, as are its weakenings

3. the family $c_{m,n} \in h(1, m \times n, n \times m)$ given by $h(id, c)id_{n \times m}$ provides a symmetry for this strict monoidal structure, modulo the evident composition with $h(c_{k,k'}, \pi')$, and $id_1 \in h(1,1,1)$ is a unit for the monoidal structure.

4. for each control K with arity information $((m_1,n_1), \cdots, (m_l,n_l)) \mapsto (m,n)$ and each $(k_1, \cdots, k_l)$, a function $G_{h0}(k_1,m_1,n_1) \times \cdots \times G_{h0}(k_l,m_l,n_l) \longrightarrow G_{h0}(k_1 \cdots k_l, m, n)$, natural in each variable with respect to maps of the form $(f_i, \pi') : (k_i, m_i) \longrightarrow (k'_i, m_i)$ (renamings).

A fibrational control structure for which the functor h sends weakening squares to pullbacks is called an *abstract control structure.*

Morphisms between fibrational control structures are morphisms between the corresponding naming structures which preserve the symmetric monoidal category structure and the controls. Notice that, since morphisms of control structures do not increase the surface of actions, it is adequate for morphisms between fibrational control structures to preserve the potential arity (the first component of an object of $s(\mathcal{M})^{op} \times |\mathcal{M}|$) of the surfaces of its elements.

8.2 Remark It is possible to give a defnition of fibrational control structures , with the added structure given in terms of fibred functors, which makes the naturality requirements in the above definition implicit and exhibits more neatly the algebraic flavour of the structure. For lack of space we include only the above definition which makes the transition to control structures smoother; for details see the expanded version of the paper [HP95].

Some corollaries of the definition are

8.3 Corollary

1. by 8.1(2), for any $g : k \times m \longrightarrow m'$, we have $h(t,g)id \cdot a = h(\pi_1, \pi \cdot g)a$

2. by 8.1(2), it also follows that the evident two maps from $h(1,k,k) \times h(1,k',k')$ to $h(k, k', k \times k')$ using $\otimes$ and $(t : k \longrightarrow 1, id)$ agree, so agree when composed with the map choosing the identities, *i.e.*, "$\langle x \rangle \otimes id_{k'} = h(t, id) id_{k \times k'}$"

3. also by 8.1(2), for all $g : m \longrightarrow n$ and $g' : m' \longrightarrow n'$, $h(t \times t', \pi' \cdot (g \times g'))id = h(t, \pi' \cdot g)id \otimes h(t', \pi' \cdot g')id$.

8.4 Remark Since all our structure respects weakening, it is equivalent to consider the graph given by the disjoint union over k of $h(k, m, n)$ factored by weakening. With mild abuse of our conventions, we will pass freely between these two formulations. So for instance, we may ask whether $a \otimes b \in h(k \times k', m \times m', n \times n')$ lies in $h(j, m \times m', n \times n')$ for some subsequence j of kk'.

9 Extending the constructions to obtain the equivalence

It is reasonably clear how to extend Construction 4.2 of $(\ )_c$ and the construction F of Section 6 to complete constructions on control structures and on abstract control structures respectively.

For the former, we need to describe $\otimes$, $\cdot$ and each control K on A_c. They are all defined similarly: for tensors, $(\vec{x}_k : k \vdash a : m \longrightarrow n) \otimes_c (\vec{x}_{k'} : k' \vdash a' : m' \longrightarrow n') = [\pi_1(\vec{x}_{k\times k'})/\vec{x}_k]a \otimes [\pi'(\vec{x}_{k\times k'})/\vec{x}_{k'}]a'$.

For the inverse, we define $\otimes$, $\cdot$, c, $\langle x \rangle$, ω, $(x)a$ and K, then define $ab_x a = (x)(\langle x \rangle \otimes a)$. For tensors, define $([\vec{x}], a) \otimes_{F(h)} ([\vec{y}], b)$ as follows:

- first juxtapose $\vec{x}$ and $\vec{y}$, then reorder the juxtaposed sequence and delete repetitions so that it is ordered consistently with the order on X, giving, say, $\vec{z}$ with corresponding sequence of arities $p_1 \cdots p_l$
- then take the strongest copy of $(\vec{x}_l : p_1 \cdots p_l \vdash h(f, \pi')a \otimes h(f', \pi')b : m \times m' \longrightarrow n \times n')$, where f and f' are determined by the construction of $\vec{z}$ from $\vec{x}$ and $\vec{y}$
- take the corresponding subsequence of $\vec{z}$ as first component, and the strongest copy as above for the second.

Composition and controls are done similarly, while c, $\langle x \rangle$ and ω are as we defined them in Section 7. The construction $(x)-$ is defined by two cases:

1. if $x = x_j$ lies in $\vec{x}$, then put $(x)([\vec{x}], a) = ([x_1 \cdots \hat{x_j} \cdots x_l], (\ )h(id \times c_{p_{j+1}\cdots p_l, p_j}, \pi')a)$
2. if not, $(x)([\vec{x}], a) = ([\vec{x}], \omega \otimes a)$.

It follows from the definition of $(\ )-$ in Definition 5.1 and from Corollary 8.3 that $(x)-$ is well defined, as the second component of each pair in the definition is strong. For the second case, we could have defined $(x)-$ by weakening a to account for x_j, then using the defining property of $(\ )-$; but it follows from a routine calculation that that agrees with the definition we have given. Moreover, it follows immediately from the definition, specifically by inspection of the first components, that once we have proved $F(h)$ is a control structure, $surf([\vec{x}], a) = |\vec{x}|$, as we promised in Remark 6.7.

9.1 Proposition $F(h)$ is a control structure.

Proof This follows from the evident series of lemmas, the main ones being as follows.

9.2 Lemma In $F(h)$, $[x/y]([y], a)$, which is *defined* to be $(\langle x \rangle \otimes id).(y)([y], a)$, is equal to $([x], a)$. ■

9.3 Notation In h, define $\langle\ \rangle_p$ to be $h(t, id)id_p$, *cf* Definition 7.3.

9.4 Lemma In $F(h)$, $[y/x](\langle x \rangle \otimes \langle x \rangle) = \langle y \rangle \otimes \langle y \rangle$.

Proof There are two cases, dependent upon whether $h(id, \Delta)(\langle\ \rangle \otimes \langle\ \rangle)$ is strong or not. If not, the result is trivial; if it is strong, the result follows from the definitions and Lemma 9.2. ■

9.5 Lemma In $F(h)$, $K([y/x]\vec{a}) = [y/x]K(\vec{a})$. ■

9.6 Proposition A_c is an abstract control structure. ■

9.7 Theorem For a locally finite control structure A, we have $F(A_c) \simeq A$.

Proof This follows from our development of the construction of F through the course of this paper. It makes heavy use of the fact that in a control structure, we have $[x/y](a \otimes b) = [x/y]a \otimes [x/y]b$ and the series of results corresponding to Lemma 7.4, which asserts that if there is some x for which $surf\langle x \rangle$ is empty, then for all x, $surf\langle x \rangle$ is empty. ■

Finally, we seek to prove the converse. That requires a little more effort.

9.8 Proposition For any h, x and y, we have $\langle x \rangle \otimes_{F(h)} \langle y \rangle = \langle xy \rangle$.

Proof This uses the first two parts of Corollary 8.3 and the definition of $\langle\ \rangle$, as $\langle x \rangle \otimes \langle y \rangle = \langle y \rangle \cdot (\langle x \rangle \otimes id)$. ■

9.9 Proposition Given strong $(\vec{x}_k : k \vdash a : m \longrightarrow n)$ and $f : k' \longrightarrow k$, then in $F(h)$, $([\vec{x}_{k'}], h(f, \pi')a) = (\langle f(\vec{x}_{k'}) \rangle \otimes id) \cdot (\vec{x}_k)([\vec{x}_k], a)$ if $h(f, \pi')a$ is strong.

Proof We defined composition in $F(h)$ by use of $h(f, \pi')$; similarly for $\otimes$, and hence for $\langle f(\vec{x}_{k'}) \rangle$: so to find $\langle f(\vec{x}_{k'}) \rangle$, first take $([f(\vec{x}_{k'})], \langle\ \rangle \otimes \cdots \otimes \langle\ \rangle)$, then reduce for order, etcetera, according to the sequence $f(\vec{x}_{k'})$, *i.e.*, according to f.

So, applying the naturality condition on composition in an abstract control structure, $((\langle f(\vec{x}_{k'}) \rangle \otimes id) \cdot (\vec{x}_k)([\vec{x}_k], a)$ is given by reorganizing the sequence in $([f(\vec{x}_{k'})], (\langle\rangle \otimes \cdots \otimes \langle\rangle \otimes id) \cdot (\ )a))$ and modifying the second component accordingly: but the second component equals a by definition of $(\ )-$, so the pair reduces to $([\vec{x}_{k'}], h(f, \pi')a)$ as desired. ■

It is clear from the proof of Proposition 9.9 that, with the evident amended statement, the result extends to the trivial case of $h(f, \pi')a$ not being strong.

9.10 Proposition In $F(h)$, $(\vec{x}_m)\langle g(\vec{x}_m) \rangle = ([\,], h(id, g)id_{m'})$ for all $g : m \longrightarrow m'$.

Proof We use the definition of $(\ )-$ as inverse to $h(t, id) : h(1, m, m') \longrightarrow h(m, 1, m')$. So it suffices to show that the second component of $\langle g(\vec{x}_m) \rangle$ is the strongest copy of $h(t, id)(h(id, g)id_{m'}))$, which by functoriality of h, is $h(t, g)id_{m'}$ which, again by functoriality of h, is $h(g, t)h(t, id)id_{m'}$. Now the result follows from Proposition 9.9 and another use of the definition of $(\ )-$. ■

9.11 Corollary Given any $g : k \times m \longrightarrow m'$ and strong $(\vec{x}_k \vdash a : m \longrightarrow n)$ in h, we have $([\vec{x}_k], h(id, g)a) = (\langle \vec{x}_k \rangle \otimes id) \cdot (\vec{z})\langle g(\vec{z}) \rangle \cdot ([\vec{x}_k], a)$ if $h(id, g)a$ is strong.

Proof Starting with the right hand side, use Propostion 9.10 and three applications of Corollary 8.3 and the definition of $\langle x \rangle$. ■

Again, it is evident from the earlier proofs how to extend the result to the trivial case in which $h(id, g)a$ is not strong. This finally allows us to deduce the second half of our main result: with the evident notion of isomorphism of abstract control structures,

9.12 Theorem For an abstract control structure h, we have $F(h)_c \simeq h$.

Proof This follows from Proposition 9.9 and Corollary 9.11. ■

Putting Theorems 9.7 and 9.12 together (the action on morphisms being evident), we conclude

9.13 Corollary The category of locally finite control structures is equivalent to that of abstract control structures.

10 Concluding remarks

We have provided an equivalent formulation of control structures, subject to the condition of finite surfaces, which eliminates the reference to a set of names, while keeping an account of naming and binding. This seems in line with the programme in [Abr95], which refers to the intentional nature of the set of labels in process calculi as one of the reasons which alienates such calculi from a denotational treatment.

In [Gar95], Gardner introduced closed action calculi to give a name-free account of action calculi, and she proved the two notions equivalent. Fibrational control structures give a name-free account of control structures, and the latter are the models of action calculi. However, closed action calculi and fibrational control structures are name-free in different ways: the former correspond to those actions with empty surface, whereas the latter abstract from the specific choice of names in the surface, but still allow non-empty surface. Gardner's contextual action calculi, which she introduced in the course of her proof, seem more closely related to fibrational control structures, and that relationship deserves further attention.

We expect that the analysis presented here could be further elaborated, with the aim of putting control structures, which arise from an analysis of communication and concurrency, in the realm of abstract denotational semantics. In this sense it is worth mentioning that there is a relationship between fibrational control structures and the reformulation of notions of computation (based on premonoidal categories) given in [PR95], which indicates that the above goal may well be achievable.

References

[Abr95] S. Abramsky. Interaction categories and the foundations of typed concurrent programming. In *Proc. '94 Marktoberdorf Summer School*. Springer-Verlag, 1995. to appear.

[Gar95] P. Gardner. A name-free account of action calculi. In *Proc. 11th Conf. on Mathematical Foundations of Program Semantics*, 1995.

[HJ93] C. Hermida and B. Jacobs. Fibrations with indeterminates: Contextual and functional completeness for polymorphic lambda calculi. In Book of Abstracts of *Category Theory in Computer Science 5*, september 1993. Extended version to appear in *Mathematical Structures in Computer Science*.

[HP95] C. Hermida and A.J. Power. Fibrational control structures (expanded version). available by ftp from `ftp.cl.cam.ac.uk` as `acpi/cs4.ps.Z`, May 1995.

[LS86] J. Lambek and P.J. Scott. *Introduction to Higher-Order Categorical Logic*, volume 7 of *Cambridge Studies in Advanced Mathematics*. Cambridge University Press, 1986.

[Mac71] S. MacLane. *Categories for the Working Mathematician*. Springer Verlag, 1971.

[Mil92] R. Milner. Action structures. Technical Report LFCS-92-249, Laboratory for Foundations of Computer Science, Dept. of Comp. Sci., Univ. of Edinburgh, 1992.

[Mil93] R. Milner. Action calculi, or syntactic action structures. In *Proc. MFCS '93*, volume 711 of *Lecture Notes in Computer Science*, pages 105–121. Springer Verlag, 1993.

[MM90] J. Meseguer and U. Montanari. Petri nets are monoids. *Information and Computation*, 88:105–155, 1990.

[MMP95] A. Mifsud, R. Milner, and J. Power. Control structures. In *Proc. 10th Conf. on Logic in Computer Science (LICS)*. IEEE, 1995.

[PR95] J. Power and E. Robinson. Premonoidal categories and notions of computation. unpublished draft, 1995.

Fully Abstract Models for Nondeterministic Regular Expressions

Flavio Corradini, Rocco De Nicola and Anna Labella

Università di Roma "La Sapienza"
Dipartimento di Scienze dell'Informazione
Via Salaria 113, I-00198 Roma, Italy

Abstract. Regular expressions and Kleene Algebras have been a direct inspiration for many constructs and axiomatizations for concurrency models. These, however, put a different stress on nondeterminism. With concurrent interpretations in mind, we study the effect of removing the idempotence law $X + X = X$ and distribution law $X \bullet (Y + Z) = X \bullet Y + X \bullet Z$ from Kleene Algebras. We propose an operational semantics that is sound and complete w.r.t. the new set of axioms and is fully abstract w.r.t. a denotational semantic based on trees. The operational semantics is based on labelled transition systems that keep track of the performed choices and on a preorder relation (we call it *resource simulation*) that takes also into account the number of states reachable via every action. An important property we exhibit is that *resource bisimulation equivalence* can be obtained as the kernel of *resource simulation*.

1 Introduction

The theory of regular languages over an alphabet A was first studied by Kleene [8] and then axiomatized by Salomaa [12] to obtain so called Kleene Algebras, see Table 1. These are algebraic structures with $+$, $\bullet$, *, 0 and 1 operators satisfying certain properties that have been used fruitfully also in a number of other settings.

Building on an alphabet A, regular expressions can be defined via the syntax below. In the sequel, we will refer to the set of terms generated by this BNF as **PL**, for process language.

$$P ::= 0 \;\Big|\; 1 \;\Big|\; a \;\Big|\; P + P \;\Big|\; P \bullet P \;\Big|\; P^* \qquad \text{where } a \text{ is in } A.$$

Recently a new axiomatization of Kleene Algebras has been proposed by Kozen [9], that relies on the original axiomatization of Table 1 proposed in [12] for finite (without *) terms, and on the laws of Table 2 for infinite expressions. There, $\leq$ stands for the partial order, preserved by $\bullet$ and $+$, and such that $P \leq P + Q$.

Regular Expressions and Kleene Algebras have also been a direct inspiration for many of the constructs and axiomatizations of concurrency models such as CCS, CSP and ACP (see, e.g., [10], [7] and [2]), generally referred to as *process algebras.* The main differences between the axiomatization of finite regular

Table 1. Complete set of axioms for finite regular expressions.

$X + Y = Y + X$	(C1)
$(X + Y) + Z = X + (Y + Z)$	(C2)
$X + 0 = X$	(C3)
$X + X = X$	(C4)
$(X \bullet Y) \bullet Z = X \bullet (Y \bullet Z)$	(S1)
$X \bullet 1 = X$	(S2)
$1 \bullet X = X$	(S3)
$X \bullet 0 = 0$	(S4)
$0 \bullet X = 0$	(S5)
$(X + Y) \bullet Z = (X \bullet Z) + (Y \bullet Z)$	(RD)
$X \bullet (Y + Z) = (X \bullet Y) + (X \bullet Z)$	(LD)

Table 2. Axioms for *.

$1 + P \bullet P^*$	$\leq$	P^*	(*1)
$1 + P^* \bullet P$	$\leq$	P^*	(*1d)
$R + P \bullet Q \leq Q$	implies	$P^* \bullet R \leq Q$	(*2)
$R + Q \bullet P \leq Q$	implies	$R \bullet P^* \leq Q$	(*2d)

expressions and those for process algebras are essentially due to the different stress that concurrency models put on nondeterminism. Indeed, due to the distributivity law, the possible structure induced by the + operators is ignored by the traditional interpretation of regular expressions as sets of strings. Process algebras, instead, consider nondeterminism as a direct outcome of interactions, and thus central to the concurrency theory.

If one considers **PL** as defined above, it is possible to interpret its operator symbols in terms of basic processes and operations for process composition. Thus 0 can be seen as the empty process [1], 1 as the successfully terminating one, a as the process that executes action a and then successfully terminates, + can be seen as a choice operator and $\bullet$ as a sequentialization operator.

In this paper, by following the interpretation suggested above, we study the effect of removing the two axioms of finite Kleene algebras that lead to ignoring nondeterministic behaviour. We will thus look for an operational semantics of **PL** that is sound and complete w.r.t. the set of axioms of Kleene Algebras once the idempotence law for + and distribution law of $\bullet$ over + are discarded from Table 1 (see Table 3). We will first look for the operational characterization of finite nondeterministic regular expression as determined by the reduced set of axioms, then we will move to considering the nondeterministic infinite behaviours induced by the * operator and their impact on the rules of Table 2 proposed by [9]. Here, we study also the relationships of our operational semantics with the denotational characterization of the same set of axioms, presented in a companion paper [5]. Before moving on to describe the content of the paper

Table 3. Unwanted Axioms.

$X + X = X$	(C4)
$X \bullet (Y + Z) = (X \bullet Y) + (X \bullet Z)$	(LD)

more precisely, we would like to provide motivations for the presence or absence of some laws from the axiomatization we consider.

The necessity of avoiding the distributivity axiom (LD) when describing deadlock sensitive systems is well known. Here we want only to suggest considering the following instance of (LD): $a \bullet (b + c) = a \bullet b + a \bullet c$ to see that while the left hand side can always perform an action b after action a, the right hand side has the possibility of refusing to do so, and it is thus more prone to deadlock.

Axiom $X + X = X$, instead, is present in all process algebras axiomatizations; nevertheless if one wants to be faithful to tree models, there are many good reasons for leaving it out. An independent, more semantic, motivation for eliminating idempotence of $+$ is the interest in formalizing fault tolerant systems. As a simple example consider process $a + a$ corresponding to the nondeterministic composition of two processes that can perform an a action and then successfully terminate. If a hardware fault leads to the shutdown of the system where one of the processes is located, while the other is unaffected, the global process $a + a$ still offers the expected behaviour. The same cannot be said for process a that can perform a single a action. In fact, a fault of the system where a is located would be noticed. Then, one would say that $a + a$ is more tolerant to faults then a. Our kind of fault tolerant systems relies on a form of the so called "cold redundancy", i.e. on the requirement that different inactive copies of the same process be kept. We do not assume any form of restart, as usual for cold redundancy, and whenever an alternative has been chosen the other ones are immediately discarded.

Another axiom, worth of note, is $X \bullet 0 = 0$ that reduces to 0 all those processes that eventually reach a deadlock state. This law is not present in the axiomatizations of process algebras (an exception is [1]), but it is used in formal languages and automata theory where the following point of view is assumed: a word is considered "accepted" by an automata if it allows a transition from the initial state to a final one; prefixes are not considered. This means that, if a deadlock state occurs before reaching the final state, the whole computation is ignored. If one wants to take into account the actions performed before reaching a deadlocked state, then he has the possibility of writing $P \bullet (1 + Q)$ instead of $P \bullet Q$ at specification time.

We are now ready to sketch the content of the paper. In Section 2, we will introduce an operational semantics for regular expressions; it is based on transition systems sufficiently detailed to permit determining the number of choices terms have in performing a given action. On the top of this operational semantics, we will introduce a preorder relation that we call *resource simulation* (*r-simulation*) and an equivalence relation that we call *resource bisimulation* (*r-bisimulation*). An important property of these relations (that will permit us to to restrict attention to the preorder) is that r-bisimulation can be obtained as the kernel of r-simulation. We study in full detail the preorder $\lhd_c$ induced by r-simulation and prove that over finite terms it is consistent and complete with respect to the set of axioms obtained from Table 1 by removing (C4) and (RD) and adding those of Table 4; of course, in Table 1, $T_1 = T_2$ should be read as $T_1 \leq T_2$ and $T_2 \leq T_1$. The complete axiomatization of the equivalence is obtained by

Table 4. Basic Preorder.

$X \leq X + Y$	(PR)
$X \leq Y$ and $X' \leq Y'$ imply $X{\bullet}X' \leq Y{\bullet}Y'$	(CP)
$X \leq Y$ and $X' \leq Y'$ imply $X + X' \leq Y + Y'$	(CS)

removing $X \leq X + Y$ from that of the preorder.

We end the section by studying the relationships between operational and denotational semantics. In [5], a family of trees described as sets of labelled runs (sets of traces) with additional information about their branching structure, are used as target model for the language of regular expressions. We prove that the two semantics coincide.

Section 3 is dedicated to enriching the language and to studying the impact of the extensions on the axiomatization. In the first part we include the *-operator and consider the induced infinite behaviours. In order to avoid considering infinite sequences of 1-actions we restrict attention to terms with no 1-transitions within *-contexts. This essentially amounts to saying that we permit inserting in $[\_]^*$ context only those terms that do not have the empty word property [12].

We have that not all theorems of [9] are sound for our interpretation and that we cannot use axiom (*1d) [1] and inference rule (*2d) of Table 2. We have also to replace (*2) with a more powerful $\omega-$induction rule (see Table 5) to naturally establish the equivalence of operational and denotational semantics also for infinite behaviour.

Table 5. $\omega-$induction rule.

$If\ \ \forall d \in FIN(P)\ d \leq Q\ then\ P \leq Q$	(ω–R)

We rely on the correspondence between finite approximants of terms and those terms that are built by unfolding terms via $P^* \longrightarrow 1 + P{\bullet}P^*$. In the

[1] Processes $1 + a^*{\bullet}a$ and a^* are trace equivalent but are not r-similar because the term on the l.h.s. can execute two initial a-actions while that on the r.h.s can execute only one.

denotational semantics, these terms allow us to build the interpretation of P^* as a colimit and to obtain a complete proof system for the enriched language.

In the final part of Section 3, we extend the language with a binary operator for parallel composition and provide a complete axiomatization also for this richer language. Section 4 is devoted to extending the theory to invisible actions (τ-actions) and to discuss further work.

2 Models for Finite Nondeterministic Regular Behaviours

2.1 Operational Semantics

Here we provide an observational account of finite (without *) nondeterministic regular expressions, by interpreting them as equivalence classes of labelled transition systems. The proposed equivalence relies on the same recursive pattern of bisimulation but takes into account also the number of equivalent states that are reachable from a given one.

Definition 1. A labelled transition system is a triple $< Z, L, T >$ where Z is a set of states, L is a set of labels and $T = \{\stackrel{l}{\longrightarrow} \subseteq Z \times Z \mid l \in L\}$ is a transition relation.

In our case, states are terms of **PL** (as defined in the Introduction), and labels are pairs $< \mu, u >$ with $\mu \in Act \cup \{1\}$ and u a term, called *choice sequence*, generated by:

$$u ::= \epsilon \mid lu \mid ru \qquad \text{with } l, r \text{ tags}$$

The transition relation relies on the predicate defined in Table 6 and is defined in Table 7; we write $z \stackrel{l}{\longrightarrow} z'$ instead of $< z, z' > \in \stackrel{l}{\longrightarrow}$. It is worth remarking that 1- actions do not play the same role of invisible τ- actions. They simply report successful terminated states. We have two kinds of transitions:

Table 6. Active predicate.

$active(1)$
$active(a)$
$active(P) \vee active(Q) \Longrightarrow active(P + Q)$
$active(P) \wedge active(Q) \Longrightarrow active(P \bullet Q)$

- $P \stackrel{<a,u>}{\longrightarrow} P'$: P performs an action a, possibly preceded by 1-actions with choice sequence u.
- $P \stackrel{<1,u>}{\longrightarrow} 1$: P performs 1-actions to reach process 1 with choice sequence u.

Table 7. Operational Semantics for **PL**.

Tic)	$\dfrac{}{1 \overset{<1,\epsilon>}{\longrightarrow} 1}$		
Atom)	$\dfrac{}{a \overset{<a,\epsilon>}{\longrightarrow} 1}$		
Sum$_1$)	$\dfrac{P \overset{<\mu,u>}{\longrightarrow} P'}{P+Q \overset{<\mu,lu>}{\longrightarrow} P'}$	Sum$_2$)	$\dfrac{Q \overset{<\mu,u>}{\longrightarrow} Q'}{P+Q \overset{<\mu,ru>}{\longrightarrow} Q'}$
Seq$_1$)	$\dfrac{P \overset{<a,u>}{\longrightarrow} P',\ active(Q)}{P\bullet Q \overset{<a,u>}{\longrightarrow} P'\bullet Q}$	Seq$_2$)	$\dfrac{P \overset{<1,u>}{\longrightarrow} 1,\ Q \overset{<\mu,u'>}{\longrightarrow} Q'}{P\bullet Q \overset{<\mu,uu'>}{\longrightarrow} Q'}$

These transitions are atomic; they cannot be interrupted and keep no track of intermediate states. In both cases, u is used to keep information about the possible nondeterministic structure of P, and will permit distinguishing those transitions of P whose action label and target state have the same name. Thus for $a + a$, it is possible to record that it can perform two different a actions: $a + a \overset{<a,l>}{\longrightarrow} 1$ and $a + a \overset{<a,r>}{\longrightarrow} 1$. Without l and r, we would have only the $a + a \overset{a}{\longrightarrow} 1$ transition.

The predicate *active* over **PL** processes is used to detect empty processes.

The rules of Table 7 should be self-explanatory. We want just comment on those for $+$ and $\bullet$. The rule for $P + Q$ says that if P can perform $< \mu, u >$ to become P' then $P+Q$ can perform $< \mu, lu >$ to become P' where l records that action μ has been performed by the left alternative. The right alternative is dealt with symmetrically. Seq$_1$) mimics sequential composition of P and Q; it states that if P can perform $< \mu, u >$ then $P\bullet Q$ can evolve with the same label to $P'\bullet Q$. The premise $active(Q)$ of the inference rule ensures that Q can successfully terminates. Note that $active(Q)$ in Seq$_1$) could be replaced by $\exists Q'\ Q \overset{<\mu,u'>}{\longrightarrow} Q'$ that is by requiring Q to perform any transition. This choice, however, would require a "look ahead" that would be heavy when mechanically checking successful termination of a process. We can, instead, statically check whether a process eventually reach a deadlock state.

In order to determine the alternatives a process has for performing a specific action, we introduce a new transition relation that associates to every pair $P \in$ **PL**, $\mu \in Act \cup \{1\}$, a multiset M, representing all processes that are target of (initial) $< \mu, u >$-transitions by P. It is defined as the least relation such that:

$$P \overset{\mu}{\longrightarrow} \{\!|\, P' \mid \exists \mu\, P \overset{<\mu,u>}{\longrightarrow} P' \,|\!\}$$

Thus, $a + a \overset{a}{\longrightarrow} \{\!| 1, 1 |\!\}$ because $a + a \overset{<a,l>}{\longrightarrow} 1$ and $a + a \overset{<a,r>}{\longrightarrow} 1$, $(1 + 1)\bullet(a + a) \overset{a}{\longrightarrow} \{\!| 1, 1, 1, 1 |\!\}$ because $(1 + 1)\bullet(a + a) \overset{<a,ll>}{\longrightarrow} 1$, $(1 + 1)\bullet(a + a) \overset{<a,lr>}{\longrightarrow} 1$, $(1 + 1)\bullet(a + a) \overset{<a,rl>}{\longrightarrow} 1$ and $(1 + 1)\bullet(a + a) \overset{<a,rr>}{\longrightarrow} 1$. We also have that $1 + 1 \overset{1}{\longrightarrow} \{\!| 1, 1 |\!\}$ while $1 \overset{1}{\longrightarrow} \{\!| 1 |\!\}$. We take the occasion to remark that we have to count also 1- transitions. Had we ignored them, we would have been forced to identify $X + X$ and X by $(1+1) \bullet X$ and $1 \bullet X$.

2.2 Resource Simulation and Resource Bisimulation

The Transition relation $\xrightarrow{\mu}$ is the basis for defining *resource simulation* and *resource equivalence.*

Definition 2 (Resource Simulation and Resource Equivalence).

1a. A relation $\Re \subseteq \mathbf{PL} \times \mathbf{PL}$ is a *r-simulation* if for each $< P, Q > \in \Re$ and for each $\mu \in A \cup \{1\}$:
- $P \xrightarrow{\mu} M$ implies $Q \xrightarrow{\mu} M'$ and $\exists f$ injective: $M \rightarrow M'$, s.t. $\forall P' \in M, < P', f(P') > \in \Re$;

1b. P and Q, are *r-similar* ($P \triangleleft_c Q$), if there exists a *r-simulation* $\Re$ containing $< P, Q >$.

2a. A relation $\Re \subseteq \mathbf{PL} \times \mathbf{PL}$ is a *r-bisimulation* if for each $< P, Q > \in \Re$, for each $\mu \in A \cup \{1\}$:
- $P \xrightarrow{\mu} M$ implies $Q \xrightarrow{\mu} M'$ and $\exists f$ injective: $M \rightarrow M'$, s.t. $\forall P' \in M, < P', f(P') > \in \Re$;
- $Q \xrightarrow{\mu} M'$ implies $P \xrightarrow{\mu} M$ and $\exists g$ injective: $M' \rightarrow M$, s.t. $\forall Q' \in M', < g(Q'), Q' > \in \Re$;

2b. P and Q are *r-equivalent* ($P \sim_c Q$), if there exists a *r-bisimulation* $\Re$ containing $< P, Q >$.

The above definitions should be self explanatory. We want simply to remark that the injection $f : M \rightarrow M'$ is used to ensure that different (indexed) processes in M are simulated by different (indexed) processes in M' [2]. Thus the cardinality of M is less or equal to the cardinality of M'.

It worth noting that this theory extends to every language that gives rise to image finite transition systems.

With standard techniques it is possible to show that $\sim_c$ is an equivalence relation and it is preserved by nondeterministic composition and sequential composition. It is not difficult to check that $a \triangleleft_c a + a$, $a \not\triangleright_c a + a$, $a + b \sim_c b + a$ and $(1+1) \bullet a \sim_c a + a$.

Proposition 3 (Completeness). *The laws of Table 1, without of those in Table 3, but with those of Table 4 soundly and completely axiomatize r-simulation over finite* **PL**.

Proof. (Sketch of) To prove completeness we show that the axioms suffice to reduce finite **PL** terms to normal forms that are either 0 or terms of the form

$$(\sum_{i \in I} a_i + \sum_{j \in J} a_j \bullet n_j) + \sum_{k \in K} P_k \text{ (where for all } k \ P_k = 1)$$

where every n_j is a normal form different from 0 and 1.

[2] Since a multiset can be seen as a set of indexed elements, an injection between multisets will be seen just as an ordinary injection between sets.

Proposition 4 (Completeness). *The laws of Table 1, without of those in Table 3, soundly and completely axiomatize r-bisimulation over finite* **PL**.

2.3 A Preorder whose Kernel is Resource Equivalence

In this section we show that the kernel of $\lhd_c$, coincide with resource equivalence. This result is new for simulation-like semantics; it does not hold for simulation and bisimulation [3] [11, 10].

Proposition 5. *For processes P and Q, $P \sim_c Q$ iff $P \lhd_c Q$ and $Q \lhd_c P$.*

Proof. (Sketch of) The case $P \sim_c Q$ implies $P \lhd_c Q$ and $Q \lhd_c P$ follows by definitions of $\sim_c$ and $\lhd_c$. To prove the vice versa we show that relation:

$$\Re = \{< P_1, Q_1 > \mid P_1 \lhd_c Q_1 \text{ and } Q_1 \lhd_c P_1\}$$

is a r-bisimulation. To do this we rely on the following two lemmas

1. Let $S = \{P_1, ..., P_n\}$ and $S' = \{Q_1, ..., Q_n\}$ two sets of **PL** processes and $f : S \to S'$, $g : S' \to S$ two injections such that $\forall P_i \in S$, $P_i \lhd_c f(P_i)$ and $\forall Q_i \in S'$, $Q_i \lhd_c g(Q_i)$. Then for each $P_{i_1} \in S$, $i_1 \in [1..n]$ there exists a chain $P_{i_1} \lhd_c Q_{i_1} \lhd_c P_{i_2} \lhd_c Q_{i_2} \lhd_c \ldots \lhd_c Q_{i_m} \lhd_c P_{i_1}$ for some $m \in [1..n]$, $\{i_1, ..., i_m\} \subseteq [1..n]$, $P_{i_j} \in S$, $Q_{i_j} \in S'$ and $P_{i_j} \neq P_{i_k}$, $Q_{i_j} \neq Q_{i_k}$ for each $j \neq k$.
2. Let $S = \{P_1, ..., P_n\}$ and $S' = \{Q_1, ..., Q_n\}$ two sets of **PL** processes and $f : S \to S'$, $g : S' \to S$ two injections such that $\forall P_i \in S$, $P_i \lhd_c f(P_i)$ and $\forall Q_i \in S'$, $Q_i \lhd_c g(Q_i)$. Then for each $P_i \in S$, $i \in [1..n]$, $P_i \lhd_c f(P_i)$ and $f(P_i) \lhd_c P_i$.

2.4 Denotational Semantics

Here we summarize the denotational semantics for finite **PL** presented in [5]; it interprets language **PL** over a category of labelled trees.

Each tree is modeled as a set of runs and by an agreement function between them. Thus, the tree that describes a choice between the two sequences of actions $a.b$ and $a.c$ (denoted by $a.b{+}a.c$) will be modeled by the set consisting of two runs, x and y, labelled by $a.b$ and $a.c$ respectively, and by the additional information that the agreement between x and y is ϵ. In contrast, the tree denoted by $a.(b{+}c)$ and representing the possibility of executing an a and then performing the choice between b and c will be modelled again by the set $\{x, y\}$ with the same labels but with agreement a.

Definition 6. Let $\mathcal{A} = (A^*, \leq, \wedge, \epsilon)$ be the meet semilattice where A^* is the set of words on A, $\leq$ is the prefix order of words, $\wedge$ is the largest common prefix operation on words and ϵ is the empty word.

Definition 7. An *$\mathcal{A}$-tree* $t = (X, \alpha, \beta)$ consists of:

[3] Consider terms $a{\bullet}b$ and $a + (a{\bullet}b)$, they are not bisimilar but can simulate each other.

i. a set X of *runs*;
ii. a map $\alpha : X \longrightarrow A^*$, the *extent map*, giving the computation $\alpha(x)$ performed on a run x;
iii. a map $\beta : X \times X \longrightarrow A^*$, saying to what extent two computations *agree*. It is required, that for all x, y, z in X, $\beta(x, x) = \alpha(x)$; $\beta(x, y) \leq \alpha(x) \wedge \alpha(y)$; $\beta(x, y) \wedge \beta(y, z) \leq \beta(x, z)$; $\beta(x, y) = \beta(y, x)$.

We will write t, t_1 and t_2 for typical trees, with components $t = (X, \alpha, \beta)$, $t_1 = (X_1, \alpha_1, \beta_1)$ and $t_2 = (X_2, \alpha_2, \beta_2)$. We now present an appropriate notion for comparing trees:

Definition 8. A *tree morphism* $f : t_1 \rightarrow t_2$ is a map $f : X_1 \rightarrow X_2$ satisfying $\alpha_2(f(x)) = \alpha_1(x)$ and $\beta_2(f(x), f(y)) \geq \beta_1(x, y)$. A tree morphism is called a *strict monomorphism* if f is injective and $\beta_2(f(x), f(y)) = \beta_1(x, y)$

The structure with *objects*, trees ($t = (X, \alpha, \beta)$); *arrows*, tree morphisms; *identities*, ($id_t = id_X$) defined in terms of identities over set of runs; and *composition*, ($g \circ f$), given by function composition is a category of $\mathcal{A}$-labelled trees. We write $\mathbf{T}$ for this category and $\mathbf{T}^{fin}$ for the subcategory of finite trees. Note that in $\mathbf{T}^{fin}$ if $f_1 : t_1 \rightarrow t_2$ and $f_2 : t_2 \rightarrow t_1$ are strict monomorphism then t_1 and t_2 are isomorphic.

For two trees t_1 and t_2, $t_1 \oplus t_2$ is defined as $(X_1 \uplus X_2,\ \alpha_1 \uplus \alpha_2,\ \beta_1 \uplus \beta_2)$ (where $\uplus$ denote disjoint set union and $\beta_1 \uplus \beta_2$ denotes the agreement function that behaves as β_1 on pairs from X_1, as β_2 on pairs from X_2, and is ϵ on mixed pairs). Canonical injections $i_1 : t_1 \longrightarrow t_1 \oplus t_2$ and $i_2 : t_2 \longrightarrow t_1 \oplus t_2$ are strict monomorphisms.

Proposition 9. $\mathbf{T}$ *has initial object given by the empty tree,* $\mathbf{0} = (\emptyset,\ \emptyset,\ \emptyset)$, *and coproducts* $\oplus$.

Definition 10. Given two trees, $t_1 = (X_1, \alpha_1, \beta_1)$ and $t_2 = (X_2, \alpha_2, \beta_2)$ sequential composition $\otimes$ is defined as follows (here . is used to denote string concatenation): $t_1 \otimes t_2 =< X, \alpha, \beta >$, where $X = X_1 \times X_2$; $\alpha(< x_1, x_2 >) = \alpha_1(x_1).\alpha_2(x_2)$; $\beta(< x_1, x_2 >, < y_1, y_2 >) = \beta_1(x_1, y_1).\beta_2(x_2, y_2)$ if $\alpha_1(x_1) = \alpha_1(y_1) = \beta_1(x_1, y_1)$ if not, it is instead equal to $\beta_1(x_1, y_1)$.

Proposition 11. *Tree* $\mathbf{1} = (\bullet,\ \alpha(\bullet) = \epsilon,\ \beta(\bullet, \bullet) = \epsilon)$ *is the object unit of sequential composition* $\otimes$.

Terms of **PL** are interpreted as trees in the category $\mathbf{T}$ by means of a function $\mathcal{T}$ defined by induction on the structure of terms.

Definition 12 (Denotational Semantics). An algebraic interpretation of finite **PL** terms is obtained by associating to them a tree in $\mathbf{T}$ via function $\mathcal{T}$:

- $\mathcal{T}[\![0]\!] = \mathbf{0}$,
- $\mathcal{T}[\![1]\!] = \mathbf{1}$,
- $\mathcal{T}[\![a]\!] = (x, \alpha(x) = a, \beta(x, x) = a)$,

- $\mathcal{T}[\![P+Q]\!] = \mathcal{T}[\![P]\!] \oplus \mathcal{T}[\![Q]\!]$,
- $\mathcal{T}[\![P \bullet Q]\!] = \mathcal{T}[\![P]\!] \otimes \mathcal{T}[\![Q]\!]$

Theorem 13 ($\mathbf{T}^{fin}$ is the free model of Nondet. Regular Expressions). *Let $Tree^{fin}$ be the set of $\mathbf{T}^{fin}$ objects. ($Tree^{fin}$, $\oplus$, $\otimes$, $\mathbf{0}$, $\mathbf{1}$) is equivalent to the free model induced by the laws of Table 1, without those of Table 3, but with those of Table 4.*

2.5 Observational and Denotational Semantics

In this section we compare observational and denotational semantics; to conclude that they coincide, it would be sufficient to observe that they are sound and complete with respect to the same set of axioms. We can, however, exhibit a more direct correspondence by showing that the tree obtained by unfolding the transition system associated to P, $LTS(P)$, is isomorphic to the tree obtained by interpreting process P via interpretation function $\mathcal{T}$.

Definition 14. Let P be a term:

- $LTS(P)$ denotes the transition system associated to P according to the transition rules in Table 7;
- $run(P)$ denotes the set of transition sequences, called runs or computations $P \stackrel{<\mu_1,u_1>}{\longrightarrow} P_1 \stackrel{<\mu_2,u_2>}{\longrightarrow} \ldots \stackrel{<\mu_{n-1},u_{n-1}>}{\longrightarrow} P_{n-1} \stackrel{<\mu_n,u_n>}{\longrightarrow} P'$ performed by P;
- $forget$ is a function from runs to sequences of actions; given a run x, $P \stackrel{<\mu_1,u_1>}{\longrightarrow} P_1 \stackrel{<\mu_2,u_2>}{\longrightarrow} \ldots \stackrel{<\mu_{n-1},u_{n-1}>}{\longrightarrow} P_{n-1} \stackrel{<\mu_n,u_n>}{\longrightarrow} P'$, $forget(x) = \mu_1\mu_2 \ldots \mu_{n-1}\mu_n$ extracts the sequence of performed actions.
- The tree associated to $LTS(P)$ is $Unf(P) =< X, \alpha, \beta >$, defined by $X = \{x \mid x \in run(P)\}$, $\alpha(x) = forget(x)$, $\beta(x,y) = forget(x \wedge y)$ where $x \wedge y$ denotes the largest common prefix of x and y.

Proposition 15. *$Unf(P)$ and $\mathcal{T}[\![P]\!]$ are isomorphic.*

Proposition 16. *$P \lhd_c Q$ if and only if there exists a strict monomorphism f : $Unf(P) \rightarrow Unf(Q)$.*

Proof. (Sketch of) Transitions with different choice sequences and equal action, fired from the same state of the transition system, do correspond to different branches of the same node of the associated tree and vice versa. Based on this strong correspondence, we show that given a simulation containing the pair $< P, Q >$, we can find a strict monomorphism from $Unf(P)$ to $Unf(Q)$. The vice versa follows by induction on the sum of the length of all runs of LTS(P).

Theorem 17. *$P \lhd_c Q$ if and only if there exists a strict monomorphism f : $\mathcal{T}[\![P]\!] \rightarrow \mathcal{T}[\![Q]\!]$.*

3 Infinity and Parallelism

3.1 Dealing with Infinite Terms

We consider now the full language with the star operator. To avoid considering infinite sequences of 1-actions we restrict attention to terms with no 1-transitions within *-contexts (that is, terms that do not have the empty word property [12]). This suffices to guarantee that the transition system associated to a term is image finite. The wanted property is defined by a guardedness predicate.

Definition 18 (Convergence and Guardedness Predicates).
Let $\Downarrow$ and *guarded* be the least predicates over **PL** terms that satisfy

- $a \Downarrow$; $0 \Downarrow$; if $P \Downarrow$ and $Q \Downarrow$ then $P + Q \Downarrow$; if $P \Downarrow$ or $Q \Downarrow$ then $P \bullet Q \Downarrow$.
- a, 0 and 1 are *guarded*; if P and Q are *guarded*, then $P + Q$ and $P \bullet Q$ are *guarded*; if P is *guarded* and $P \Downarrow$, then P^* is *guarded.*

The operational semantics for *guarded* infinite terms is described in Table 8. We extend predicate *active* of Table 6 to *-terms by asserting: *active*(P^*).

Table 8. Operational Semantics of *.

$$\text{Star}_1) \quad \frac{}{P^* \xrightarrow{<1,\epsilon>} 1}$$

$$\text{Star}_2) \quad \frac{P \xrightarrow{<\mu,u>} P'}{P^* \xrightarrow{<\mu,u>} P';P^*}$$

An arbitrary term Q with a * may be considered as a finite notation for an infinite tree. This tree is obtained by unwinding its P^* sub-terms via $P^* \rightarrow 1 + P \bullet P^*$. To make sense of the ω-induction rule,we need to define finite approximants of infinite trees.

Definition 19 (Finite Approximants).
$FIN(P) = \{d \mid d$ does not contain * and $d \leq P\}$

Proposition 20 (Completeness). *Axioms (C1)-(C3), (S1)-(S5) and (RD) of Table 1, the laws of Table 4, axiom (*1) of Table 2 and the ω-induction rule, soundly and completely axiomatize r-simulation over full* **PL**.

Proof. Soundness of (*1) is proved by exhibiting a simulation containing the pair $< 1 + P \bullet P^*, P^* >$. The soundness of the ω-induction rule, instead, is more involved. We proceed by contradiction and assume $P \not\lessapprox_c Q$ while the premises of the rule hold. Then we show that if $P \not\lessapprox_c Q$ we can find a finite sequence of moves of P that Q cannot successfully simulate. This, with the premises of the rule, leads to a contradiction. In fact, there exists a finite approximant d of P, that can perform exactly the same transitions of the critical sequence performed by P. But then Q can simulate P because $d \lhd_c Q$ and all moves of d can be successfully simulated by transitions of Q.

Completeness follows from that of the finite case, indeed, ω-induction allows us to use results for finite approximants. To prove $P \lhd_c Q$ it suffices to prove that for any d, $d \lhd_c Q$ implies $d \leq Q$, but this follows by induction on the depth of the finite approximant d.

In the denotational semantics, the interpretation of P^* is given as the colimit of the chain of its finite approximants [13]. Actually one can prove ([5]) that trees obtained as interpretations of unwindings of P^* are related by strict monomorphisms. It is easily seen that the ω-rule is sound also in the denotational framework. This guarantees that observational and denotational semantics coincide also for the extended language.

3.2 Dealing with Parallelism

We can further extend our language with a binary operator | that can be seen as parallel composition. The resulting language will be denoted by **PPL**.

In the rest of this section we give operational and denotational semantics for the new operator and show that the two semantics do coincide.

Table 9. Operational Semantics for **PPL**.

$$\mathrm{Par}_1)\ \frac{P \xrightarrow{<a,u>} P',\ Q \xrightarrow{<a,u'>} Q',\ active(P'|Q')}{P|Q \xrightarrow{<a,u|u'>} P'|Q'} \qquad \mathrm{Par}_2)\ \frac{P \xrightarrow{<1,u>} 1,\ Q \xrightarrow{<1,u'>} 1}{P|Q \xrightarrow{<1,u|u'>} 1}$$

Definition of $active(P|Q)$ is more involved than that for the other operators. To model a multiway communication as in [7] we need to ensure that P and Q can perform a common maximal trace before both of them reach successful terminating states. This is obtained by associating to P and Q, the set of sequences of actions they can perform ($Lang(P)$, $Lang(Q)$) and requiring that their intersection is non-empty. This ensure us that there exists a sequence $s = \mu_1\mu_2...\mu_n$ such that $P \xrightarrow{<\mu_1,u_1>} \ldots \xrightarrow{<\mu_n,u_n>} 1$ and $Q \xrightarrow{<\mu_1,u'_1>} \ldots \xrightarrow{<\mu_n,u'_n>} 1$. Hence also $P|Q \xrightarrow{<\mu_1,u_1 \bullet u'_1>} \ldots \xrightarrow{<\mu_n,u_n \bullet u'_n>} 1$ that is $P|Q$ can successfully terminate. Formally $Lang(P)$, is defined by extending the usual rules that permit to associate a regular language to a regular expression with the rule $Lang(P|Q) = Lang(P) \cap Lang(Q)$.

Thus **PPL** is a simple extension of the regular expression language. It is possible to show that for each **PPL** term, P, there exists a finite state automata that accepts $Lang(P)$. Moreover, as in the regular setting, the set of our languages is closed with respect complementation and union of languages and it is decidable whether $Lang(P) \cap Lang(Q)$ is empty or not. This permits us to define $active(P|Q)$ by: $Lang(P) \cap Lang(Q) \neq \emptyset \implies active(P|Q)$. We have a complete axiomatization of r-simulation also for the richer language.

Table 10. A complete set of axioms for Parallelism.

$X\|Y = Y\|X$		(Par1)
$(X\|Y)\|Z = X\|(Y\|Z)$		(Par2)
$X\|(Y+Z) = X\|Y + X\|Z$		(Par3)
$X\|0 = 0$		(Par4)
$\mu\bullet X\|\mu'\bullet Y = \mu\bullet(X\|Y)$	if $\mu = \mu'$	(Par5)
$\mu\bullet X\|\mu'\bullet Y = 0$	if $\mu \neq \mu'$	(Par6)
$1\|1 = 1$		(Par7)

Proposition 21 (Completeness). *The axioms for* **PL** *and those in Table 10 completely axiomatize r-simulation over* **PPL**.

3.3 A Denotational Interpretation of Parallelism

In order to interpret the parallel combinator, we take advantage of properties of $\mathbf{T}^{fin}$.

Proposition 22. $\mathbf{T}^{fin}$ *has products.*

Proof. Given $t_1 = (X_1, \alpha_1, \beta_1)$ and $t_2 = (X_2, \alpha_2, \beta_2)$, $t_1 \times t_2 \ = < X, \alpha, \beta >$ is defined by

- $X = \{< x_1, x_2 > \in X_1 \times X_2 \mid \alpha_1(x_1) = \alpha_2(x_2)\}$
- $\alpha(< x_1, x_2 >) = \alpha_1(x_1) = \alpha_2(x_2)$
- $\beta(< x_1, x_2 >, < y_1, y_2 >) = min(\beta_1(x_1, y_1), \beta_2(x_2, y_2))$

We can extend our algebraic interpretation by defining $\mathcal{T}[\![P|Q]\!] = \mathcal{T}[\![P]\!] \times \mathcal{T}[\![Q]\!]$, and again obtain a model for the full system of axioms.

4 Further Work: Invisible Actions

In this section we sketch how this work can be extended to languages with invisible (τ-) actions; i.e. we study the "weak" versions of resource simulation and resource bisimulation. To do this, **PL** language is extended with process τ which can perform action τ and successfully terminates. The operational semantics of **PL** of Table 7, has to be extended with axiom:

$$\text{Tau)} \qquad \frac{}{\tau \xrightarrow{<\tau,\epsilon>} 1}$$

Weak transitions can be defined from the $\xrightarrow{<\mu,u>}$, $\mu = a$ or $\mu = \tau$ arrow.

To observe the branching structure of terms by concentrating only on those states of a non deterministic system which are *real choice points* (in the sense that different alternatives can be taken) we introduce a new relation $\stackrel{\tau}{\longmapsto}$. It describes the execution of consecutive τ actions (possibly interleaved by 1's actions) with choice sequence ϵ (modulo axioms $\epsilon \bullet u = u \bullet \epsilon = u$). Relation $\stackrel{\tau}{\longmapsto}$ is defined by the axioms and inference rules in Table 11 where σ and σ' range over $\{\tau, 1\}$.

Table 11. Executing τ steps without choices.

Tic')	$\dfrac{}{1 \stackrel{1}{\longmapsto} 1}$		
Tau')	$\dfrac{}{\tau \stackrel{\tau}{\longmapsto} 1}$		
Sum'_1)	$\dfrac{P \stackrel{\sigma}{\longmapsto} P',\ \neg active(Q)}{P+Q \stackrel{\sigma}{\longmapsto} P'}$	Sum'_2)	$\dfrac{Q \stackrel{\sigma}{\longmapsto} Q',\ \neg active(P)}{P+Q \stackrel{\sigma}{\longmapsto} Q'}$
Seq'_1)	$\dfrac{P \stackrel{\tau}{\longmapsto} 1,\ Q \stackrel{\tau}{\longmapsto} Q'}{P \bullet Q \stackrel{\tau}{\longmapsto} Q'}$	Seq'_2)	$\dfrac{P \stackrel{1}{\longmapsto} 1,\ Q \stackrel{\sigma}{\longmapsto} Q'}{P \bullet Q \stackrel{\sigma}{\longmapsto} Q'}$
Seq'_3)	$\dfrac{P \stackrel{\sigma}{\longmapsto} 1,\ Q \stackrel{1}{\longmapsto} Q'}{P \bullet Q \stackrel{\sigma}{\longmapsto} Q'}$		
Seq'_4)	$\dfrac{P \stackrel{\sigma}{\longmapsto} P',\ P' \stackrel{\sigma'}{\not\longmapsto},\ active(Q)}{P \bullet Q \stackrel{\sigma}{\longmapsto} P' \bullet Q}$	Seq'_5)	$\dfrac{P \stackrel{\sigma}{\longmapsto} 1,\ Q \stackrel{\sigma'}{\not\longmapsto},\ active(Q)}{P \bullet Q \stackrel{\sigma}{\longmapsto} Q'}$

The only rules of the table above worth of note, are Sum'_1) and Sum'_2). They say that the non deterministic composition between two processes P and Q is a real choice point if both processes are active. It is easy to see that a transition $\stackrel{\tau}{\longmapsto}$ is such that if $P \stackrel{\tau}{\longmapsto} P'$ then $P' \stackrel{\tau}{\not\longmapsto}$ (that is $P' \stackrel{\tau}{\longmapsto} P''$ for no P'').

Now a weak silent transition $\stackrel{<\tau,u>}{\Longrightarrow}$ is either a $\stackrel{\tau}{\longmapsto}$ transition, or a sequence of $\stackrel{<\tau,u_i>}{\longrightarrow}$, with choice sequence u_i different from ϵ, preceded and followed by $\stackrel{\tau}{\longmapsto}$ transitions ($\stackrel{\tau}{\longmapsto} \stackrel{<\tau,u_i>}{\longrightarrow} \stackrel{\tau}{\longmapsto}$). In the latter case the choice sequence is obtained by concatenating those of the involved single step transitions.

As usual a visible weak transition $\stackrel{<a,u>}{\Longrightarrow}$ is a transition $\stackrel{<a,u'>}{\longrightarrow}$ eventually preceded and followed by invisible weak transitions. Thus $\stackrel{<a,u>}{\Longrightarrow} = \stackrel{<\tau,u_1>}{\Longrightarrow} \stackrel{<a,u_2>}{\longrightarrow} \stackrel{<\tau,u_3>}{\Longrightarrow}$ and $u = u_1 u_2 u_3$.

Weak resource simulation and bisimulation can be obtained by replacing $\stackrel{<\mu,u>}{\longrightarrow}$ with $\stackrel{<\mu,u>}{\Longrightarrow}$ in Definition 2. The resulting relations will equate $\tau \bullet \tau$ with τ, and differentiate process $\tau + \tau$ from τ. The reason for the latter differentiation is similar to that behind $1 + 1 \not\sim_c 1$. Indeed $(\tau + \tau) \bullet a$ is equal to $\tau \bullet a + \tau \bullet a$ (by axiom (RD)) which has to be different (in this new setting) by $\tau \bullet a$.

Also weak resource simulation and bisimulation are preserved by all operators of **PL**; noticeably they are preserved by $+$. This is another interesting property of our relations. Indeed, weak equivalences are usually not preserved by $+$ and additional work is needed isolate the coarsest congruence contained in them.

We have completely axiomatized weak resource bisimulation over **PL**. The set of axioms is the same as that for resource bisimulation (see Table 1, without of those Table 3) with the addition of the simple τ-law in Table 12 with $\alpha \in A \cup \{\tau\}$.

Table 12. Axiom for weak resource bisimulation.

$\alpha \bullet \tau \bullet X = \alpha \bullet X$

We would like to conclude by remarking that Proposition 5 holds also in this new setting; i.e. weak resource bisimulation is the kernel of weak resource simulation. We are still working on the complete axiomatization of weak resource simulation, this problem seems to be harder. This and the impact of parallel and hiding operators on the weak setting will be the subject of further investigation.

Acknowledgments

The paper has benefitted from discussions with Michele Boreale and from suggestions by Luca Aceto and Davide Sangiorgi.

References

1. Baeten,J.C.M., Bergstra,J.A.: Process Algebra with a Zero Object. In Proc. Concur'90, Springer-Verlag LNCS **458** (1990) 83-98.
2. Bergstra,J.A., Klop,J.W.: Process Theory based on Bisimulation Semantics. In LNCS **354** (1989) 50-122.
3. Baeten,J., Weijland, P.: *Process Algebras.* Cambridge University Press (1990).
4. De Nicola,R., Labella,A.: A Functorial Assessment of Bisimulation. Internal Report, Università di Roma "La Sapienza", SI-92-06 (1992).
5. De Nicola,R., Labella,A.: A Completeness Theorem for Nondeterministic Kleene Algebras. In Proc. MFCS'94, Springer-Verlag LNCS **841** (1994) 536-545.
6. Hennessy,M., Milner,R.: Algebraic Laws for Nondeterminism and Concurrency. Journal of ACM **32** (1985) 137-161.
7. Hoare, C.A.R.: *Communicating Sequential Processes.* Prentice Hall (1989).
8. Kleene,S.C.: Representation of Events in Nerve Nets and Finite Automata. Automata Studies (Shannon and McCarthy ed.) Princeton Univ. Pr. (1956) 3-41.
9. Kozen,D.: A Completeness Theorem for Kleene Algebras and the Algebra of Regular Events. Information and Computation **110** (1994) 366-390.
10. Milner,R.: *Communication and Concurrency.* Prentice Hall (1989).
11. Park,D.: Concurrency and Automata on Infinite sequences. In Proc. GI, LNCS **104** (1981) 167-183.
12. Salomaa,A.: Two Complete Axiom Systems for the Algebra of Regular Events. Journal of ACM **13** (1966) 158-169.
13. Smith,M.B., Plotkin,G.D.: The category-Theoretic Solution of Recursive Domain Equation. SIAM Journal on Computing **11** (1982) 762-783.

A Petri Net Semantics for π-Calculus *

Nadia Busi[1] and Roberto Gorrieri[2]

[1] Dipartimento di Matematica, Università di Siena,
Via del Capitano 15, I-53100 Siena, Italy
e-mail: busi@cs.unibo.it

[2] Dipartimento di Scienze dell'Informazione, Università di Bologna,
Piazza di Porta S. Donato 5, I-40127 Bologna, Italy
e-mail: gorrieri@cs.unibo.it

Abstract. A distributed semantics for π-calculus, based on P/T Petri nets with inhibitor arcs, is presented. This net semantics is sound w.r.t. the original early transition system semantics: the interleaving semantics of an agent p is retrievable from the net by considering the interleaving marking graph for the associated marking $dec(p)$. Furthermore, π-calculus is equipped with a multistep and a causal semantics. The latter is compared with recent proposals appeared in the literature.

1 Introduction

Distributed semantics for CCS and related languages based on (different classes of) Petri Nets have received a lot of attention in recent years (see, e.g., [5, 8, 10, 19], just to mention a few).

The Place/Transition net semantics proposed in the literature can be classified into two main groups. The first one, we call *location*-oriented, exploits the syntactical structure of the process terms (notably, the parallel operator) to define their associated sets of places [5, 19]. The second one, we call *label*-oriented, ignores the syntactical structure of the parallel operator and keeps only the information on the label of the transitions [9, 11]. While the former approach has the merit of being very general and successfully applied to several process algebras, the latter has the merit of producing small(er) net representations. Conversely, the former usually produces rather huge (1-safe P/T) nets, while the latter cannot be easily extended to cope with certain operators, e.g., restriction and alternative composition (see [12] for a discussion on this topic).

In a recent paper [3], we have shown how the label-oriented approach can be extended in a natural way to CCS by exploiting *inhibitor arcs*. This extension is conservative in the sense that, on the sublanguage without restriction and summation, inhibitor arcs are never used. The main features of our proposal were:

(i) For each action a, there is a place named (νa) which, when containing at least one token, inhibits the execution of all the transitions with label a or $\bar{a}$.

* Research partially supported by EC BRA n. 9102 COORDINATION.

(ii) Each agent of the form $p+q$ is first translated into the term $(\{k\}p|\{\bar{k}\}q)$, where k is called a *conflict* name and $\bar{k}$ is its contrasting conflict name. Hence, the two alternative agents are considered as parallel agents "decorated" by contrasting conflict names. The net semantics contains a place for any conflict name k, which, when holding at least one token, inhibits all the transitions starting from places/agents decorated by $\bar{k}$ (and symmetrically for $\bar{k}$, with the assumption that $\bar{\bar{k}} = k$).

(iii) Moreover, as we do not consider the syntactical structure of parallel composition, we always need fresh names for actions to rename the restriction binders.

Hence, this net semantics implements restriction and alternative composition by checking whether the transition is inhibited by any restrictions or conflicts it might be subject to.

In this paper we show that our approach can be extended to process algebras for mobile processes, by studying the prominent case of π-calculus [16]. The main new problems one has to face are the following:

(i) the explicit presence of values for messages (which are actually names), and the fact that

(ii) restriction is a *dynamic* operator which changes the scope of application as the computation proceeds.

Both aspects are easily accommodated in our approach, yielding the first – to the best of our knowledge – net-oriented semantics for full π-calculus. Note that the location oriented approach is not easily extensible to π-calculus because of extrusion: to perform a bound output of a channel y, all the sequential subprocesses inside the scope of (νy) need to be updated. This can be obtained by an explicit synchronisation of all these subprocesses, thus introducing possibly wrong causes.

We claim that our net semantics is simple because:

(i) Its definition is very concise if compared with the original one, based on transition systems. As a matter of fact, only five axiom schemata are needed to generate the whole set of net transitions. Moreover, they are very much in the style of the CHAM [1], where no induction on the syntactic structure needs to be performed.

(ii) The intuition behind the net semantics is immediate, once one has understood the role of inhibitors. Indeed, our semantics clearly reflects the "inhibiting role" played by restriction and the nature of distributed choice implemented through inhibiting conflict names.

(iii) It provides concise net descriptions of both distributed choice (*linear* in the size of the components, as discussed in [3]) and restriction (by not forcing to interpret parallel composition as *disjoint* union on places).

We prove a *retrievability* result: the interleaving marking graph associated to the net for π-calculus tightly corresponds to its *early* interleaving transition system.

As far as non-interleaving semantics are concerned, we observe that nets with inhibitor arcs have not been deeply studied: only some contrasting proposals are reported in the literature [14, 18]. We adapt one of these [18] to P/T nets which is suited for our aims, hence providing π-calculus with a multistep semantics (new – to the best of our knowledge). Finally, we present a causal semantics for P/T nets with inhibitor arcs; the induced causal semantics for π-calculus is compared with those recently appeared in the literature [2, 6].

1.1 Related Work

Net Semantics

The only paper we know dealing with a net semantics is [7]. There Engelfriet considers the small π-calculus (no alternative composition), for which he studies the reduction semantics (communications only). Because of these limited aims, the semantics is greatly simplified: the restriction operator can always be syntactically removed by simply renaming bound actions to fresh names. Hence, there is no need for inhibitors. It is easy to see that our net semantics conservatively extends his proposal.[3]

Causal Semantics

The first causal semantics was proposed in [2], where Boreale and Sangiorgi define a causal transition system in the style of [4]. They observe that there are two different sources of causality: the structural (or subject) dependencies due to the syntactical structure of terms (causes produced by the nesting of prefixing or inherited through communications) and the link (or object) dependencies due to extrusion, which enables transitions which were previously blocked by the presence of restriction. However, only the class of structural causes is explicitly described in the transition system. Our causal semantics, instead, joins together the causes originated by both classes of phenomena. Consider the two processes $p = (\nu y)(\bar{x}y.\mathbf{0} \mid \bar{y}z.\mathbf{0})$ and $q = (\nu y)(\bar{x}y.\bar{y}z.\mathbf{0})$. These processes are not causal bisimilar according to [2] (there is a link dependency in the former agent), whereas they are causal bisimilar for us.

Our approach to causality is also different from the one given in [6]. First of all, they follow the so-called *read-write* causality, according to which outputs can pass their causes to inputs but not viceversa (i.e., the cause-crossing in communication is not symmetric but directioned from outputs to inputs). The "symmetric" causes missing in communication are classified as structural priority. Similarly for link dependencies, they define object priority. We conjecture that the reflexive closure of our causal semantics coincides with the enabling relation of [6], which roughly corresponds to the transitive and reflexive closure of the union of the four relations above.

In [17] Montanari and Pistore propose a graph–rewriting system (based on the double pushout approach) as a semantic model for a subset of π-calculus,

[3] To be precise, this is true with the only exception of the bang operator, as we prefer to use guarded CCS-like recursion in order to avoid the problem of managing markings composed by infinite places and/or infinite tokens in a place (see the concluding section for more details).

where + is omitted and the bang operator is applied only to input prefixing. Apart from the technical differences, the basic intuition about restriction is similar to ours, even if "complemented": a "token" in a "place" for x means that x is free; hence they test for presence of a token in the "place" for x. However, this causes the debatable phenomenon of parallel extrusion. Consider the process $p = (\nu y)(\bar{x}y.0 \mid y(w).0 \mid \bar{z}y.0)$: the two actions $\bar{x}(y)$ and $\bar{z}(y)$ are considered independent and executable in parallel in [17], while in interleaving semantics only one of the two outputs is actually a bound output.

The last paper is [15], where a data-flow semantics for π-calculus, based on dI-domains, is proposed. As the notion of causality they use is classical, we claim that it coincides with our one.

2 The π-Calculus

We recall the syntax and the interleaving semantics of (our variant of) the π-calculus [16].

Let $\mathcal{N}$ be a denumerable set of names, ranged over by $a, b, \ldots, x, y, \ldots$, such that $\tau \notin \mathcal{N}$. Let $\mathcal{X}$ be a denumerable set of process variables, disjoint from $\mathcal{N} \cup \{\tau\}$, ranged over by $X, Y, Z, \ldots$. The terms are generated from names by the following grammar:

$$p ::= 0 \mid \mu.p \mid p + p \mid p|p \mid (\nu x)p \mid X \mid recX.p$$

where the prefix μ can be either an input $x(y)$, an output $\bar{x}y$ or a silent move τ.

The set $\mathcal{P}$ of *processes* contains those terms which are *closed* (w.r.t. process variables) and *guarded*. $\mathcal{P}$ will be ranged over by $p, q, \ldots$. A process of the form $\mu.p$ is called *sequential*. The sets of names, free names and bound names of a process p, called $n(p)$, $fn(p)$ and $bn(p)$ respectively, are defined as usual. The definitions of substitution and alpha conversion are standard, with the use of renaming to avoid name clashes.

The (early) operational semantics for the π-calculus is the labelled transition system generated by the rules listed in Table 1. The labels of the transitions are of four different kinds: the silent action τ, the input xy, the free and bound outputs $\bar{x}y$ and $\bar{x}(y)$. The set of labels is called $\mathcal{A}$ and is ranged over by α. The free and bound names of an action α, $fn(\alpha)$ and $bn(\alpha)$, are defined as follows: $fn(\tau) = bn(\tau) = \emptyset$, $fn(\bar{x}y) = fn(xy) = \{x, y\}$, $bn(\bar{x}y) = bn(xy) = \emptyset$, $fn(\bar{x}(y)) = \{x\}$, $bn(\bar{x}(y)) = \{y\}$.

The names of α are $n(\alpha) = fn(\alpha) \cup bn(\alpha)$.

Definition 1. A binary relation R over the set of terms is an *early bisimulation* if $(p, q) \in R$ implies:

- if $p \xrightarrow{\alpha} p'$ and $bn(\alpha) \cap fn(p, q) = \emptyset$ there exists then q' such that $q \xrightarrow{\alpha} q'$ and $(p', q') \in R$;
- symmetrically for q derivations.

Two terms p and q are *bisimilar*, written $p \sim q$, if there exists a bisimulation R such that $(p, q) \in R$. □

$$\text{(Tau)} \quad \tau.p \xrightarrow{\tau} p$$

$$\text{(In)} \quad x(z).p \xrightarrow{xy} p\{y/z\}$$

$$\text{(Out)} \quad \bar{x}y.p \xrightarrow{\bar{x}y} p$$

$$\text{(Sum)} \quad \frac{p \xrightarrow{\alpha} p'}{p + q \xrightarrow{\alpha} p'}$$

$$\text{(Par)} \quad \frac{p \xrightarrow{\alpha} p'}{p \,|\, q \xrightarrow{\alpha} p' \,|\, q} \quad bn(\alpha) \cap fn(q) = \emptyset$$

$$\text{(Com)} \quad \frac{p \xrightarrow{\bar{x}y} p' \quad q \xrightarrow{xy} q'}{p \,|\, q \xrightarrow{\tau} p' \,|\, q'}$$

$$\text{(Close)} \quad \frac{p \xrightarrow{\bar{x}(w)} p' \quad q \xrightarrow{xw} q'}{p \,|\, q \xrightarrow{\tau} (\nu w)(p' \,|\, q')} \quad w \notin fn(q)$$

$$\text{(Res)} \quad \frac{p \xrightarrow{\alpha} p'}{(\nu y)p \xrightarrow{\alpha} (\nu y)p'} \quad y \notin n(\alpha)$$

$$\text{(Open)} \quad \frac{p \xrightarrow{\bar{x}y} p'}{(\nu y)p \xrightarrow{\bar{x}(w)} p'\{w/y\}} \quad y \neq x \wedge w \notin fn((\nu y)p')$$

$$\text{(Rec)} \quad \frac{p\{\mathrm{rec}\, X.p/X\} \xrightarrow{\alpha} p'}{\mathrm{rec}\, X.p \xrightarrow{\alpha} p'}$$

Table 1. early semantics (symmetric rules omitted)

3 P/T Nets with Inhibitor Arcs

We recall simple Place/Transition nets without capacity constraints on places (see, e.g., [10]). Then, we extend them with the so-called inhibitor arcs (see, e.g., [13, 14, 18]). Here we provide a characterization of this model which is convenient for our aims.

Definition 2. Given a set S, a *finite multiset* over S is a function $m : S \to \omega$ such that the set $dom(m) = \{s \in S \,|\, m(s) \neq 0\}$ is finite. The *multiplicity* of an element s in m is given by the natural number $m(s)$. The set of all finite multisets over S, denoted by $\mathcal{M}_{fin}(S)$, is ranged over by m. A multiset m such that $dom(m) = \emptyset$ is called *empty* . The set of all finite sets over S is denoted by

$\wp_{fin}(S)$. If A is a finite subset of S, sometimes with abuse of notation we use A to denote the multiset m_A defined as follows: $m_A(s) =$ if $s \in A$ then 1 else 0.

We write $m \subseteq m'$ if $m(s) \leq m'(s)$ for all $s \in S$. The operator $\oplus$ denotes *multiset union*: $m \oplus m'(s) = m(s) + m'(s)$. The operator $\setminus$ denotes *multiset difference*: $m \setminus m'(s) = m(s) \dot{-} m'(s)$ where $i \dot{-} j = i - j$ if $i > j$, $i \dot{-} j = 0$ otherwise. Finally, the *scalar product*, $j \cdot m$, of a number j with a multiset m is $(j \cdot m)(s) = j \cdot (m(s))$. □

Let f be a function on S. The function is extended to multiset over S in the following way: if $m \in \mathcal{M}_{fin}(S)$ then $(f(m))(s) = \sum_{f(\bar{s})=s} m(\bar{s})$.

Definition 3. A P/T net is a tuple $N = (S, Act, T)$ where S is the set of *places*, Act is the set of *labels* and $T \subseteq \mathcal{M}_{fin}(S) \times Act \times \mathcal{M}_{fin}(S)$ is the set of *transitions*. A finite multiset over the set S of places is called a *marking*. Given a marking m and a place s, we say that the place s contains $m(s)$ *tokens*.

A transition $t = (c, a, p)$ is usually written in the form $c \xrightarrow{a} p$. The marking c, usually denoted with ${}^\bullet t$, is called the *preset* of t and represents the tokens to be "consumed"; the marking p, usually denoted with $t^\bullet$, is called the *postset* of t and represents the tokens to be "produced"; a is called the *label* of t, sometimes denoted by $l(t)$. A transition t is *enabled* at m if ${}^\bullet t \subseteq m$. The execution of a transition t enabled at m produces the marking $m' = (m \setminus {}^\bullet t) \oplus t^\bullet$. This is written as $m[t\rangle m'$.

A *marked* P/T net is a tuple $N(m_0) = (S, Act, T, m_0)$, where (S, Act, T) is a P/T net and m_0 is a nonempty finite multiset over S, called the *initial marking*. □

Definition 4. A P/T net *with inhibitor arcs* (NI net for short) is a tuple $N = (S, Act, T)$ where S is the set of places, Act the set of labels and $T \subseteq \mathcal{M}_{fin}(S) \times \wp_{fin}(S) \times Act \times \mathcal{M}_{fin}(S)$ is the set of transitions.

A transition $t = (c, i, a, p)$ is usually written in the form $(c, i) \xrightarrow{a} p$. The set i, denoted with ${}^\circ t$, is called the *inhibitor-set* of t and represents the tokens to be "tested for absence"; markings c and p are as above. This changes the definition of enabling: a transition t is enabled at m if ${}^\bullet t \subseteq m$ and $dom(m) \cap {}^\circ t = \emptyset$. Thus, any transition t for which ${}^\circ t \cap dom({}^\bullet t) \neq \emptyset$ is called *blocked*, *unblocked* otherwise.

The execution of a transition t enabled at m producing the marking m', written $m[t\rangle m'$, is defined as above. □

Definition 5. Let $N = (S, Act, T)$ be a net. The *interleaving marking graph* of N is $IMG_N = (\mathcal{M}_{fin}(S), \rightarrow, Act)$, where $\rightarrow \subseteq \mathcal{M}_{fin}(S) \times Act \times \mathcal{M}_{fin}(S)$ is defined by $m \xrightarrow{l(t)} m'$ iff there exists a transition $t \in T$ such that $m[t\rangle m'$. With $IMG_N(m)$ we denote the interleaving marking graph reachable from the initial marking m. □

4 Net Semantics

Let $\mathcal{C}$ be a denumerable set of symbols disjoint from $\mathcal{N} \cup \{\tau\}$ and from $\mathcal{X}$. Let $\bar{\mathcal{C}} = \{\bar{k} \mid k \in \mathcal{C}\}$ and $Con = \mathcal{C} \cup \bar{\mathcal{C}}$. Con is ranged over by $k, h, \ldots$, with the assumption that $\bar{\bar{k}} = k$. A *conflict set* is a finite subset of $Con = \mathcal{C} \cup \bar{\mathcal{C}}$, ranged over by $I, J, \ldots$; $\bar{I} = \{\bar{k} \mid k \in I\}$. When I is a singleton, we drop the set brackets for notational convenience. The set S_π of places is defined as follows:

$$S_\pi = \{I[\mu.p]_{\equiv_\alpha} \mid I \subseteq Con \wedge \mu.p \in \mathcal{P}\} \cup Con \cup \{(\nu x) \mid x \in \mathcal{N}\}$$

$I\mu.p$ represents a sequential process with conflict set I. This set, sometimes omitted when empty, is essential for the implementation of the distributed choice mechanism, as will be made clear in the following. Sequential processes which are alpha convertible are identified. This abstraction step is not necessary for the technical development, but it makes net description more concise. For instance, processes $x(y).(\nu z)\bar{y}z$ and $x(v).(\nu w)\bar{v}w$ are mapped to the same place $\emptyset[x(y).(\nu z)\bar{y}z]_{\equiv_\alpha}$. For notational convenience, we usually write $I\mu.p$ for $I[\mu.p]_{\equiv_\alpha}$.

Every conflict name k is a place (with the same name). k is used to prevent the execution of any transition from any sequential process $I\mu.p$ such that $\bar{k} \in I$. To better describe the implementation of the distributed choice, assume that p and q are sequential processes; $p+q$ is interpreted as the parallel composition of $\{k\}p$ and $\{\bar{k}\}q$; with the execution of an action from $\{k\}p$ we produce a token in place k, hence preventing a later execution of an action from $\{\bar{k}\}q$.

Finally, observe that for any name x there is a place (νx). A token in such a place prevents the execution of input, output and bound output actions along channel x, as well as to send x as a free value or to receive x; however, it has no influence on synchronizations.

In order to define the decomposition function dec which associates a finite multiset on S_π to each process, we need some auxiliary definitions.

The operator $I(\_)$ is defined on places as follows: $I(J\mu.p) = (I \cup J)\mu.p$, $I(k) = k$ and $I((\nu x)) = (\nu x)$.

The renaming is defined on places as follows: $(I\mu.p)\{y/x\} = I(\mu.p)\{y/x\}$, $k\{y/x\}$
$= k$, $(\nu x)\{y/x\} = (\nu y)$ and $(\nu z)\{y/x\} = (\nu z)$ if $z \neq x$.

The renaming of conflicts is defined on places as follows: $h\{k/h\} = k$, $\bar{h}\{k/h\} = \bar{k}$, $h'\{k/h\} = h'$ if $h' \neq h, \bar{h}$, $I\{k/h\} = \{h'\{k/h\} \mid h' \in I\}$, $(I\mu.p)\{k/h\} = I\{k/h\}\mu.p$ and $(\nu x)\{k/h\} = (\nu x)$.

The set $c(s)$ of *conflicts of place* s is defined as: $c(I\mu.p) = \{k \in \mathcal{C} \mid k \in I \cup \bar{I}\}$, $c(k) =$ if $k \in \mathcal{C}$ then $\{k\}$ else $\{\bar{k}\}$, $c((\nu x)) = \emptyset$ and extended to markings as: $c(m) = \bigcup_{s \in dom(m)} c(s)$.

The set $n(s)$ of *names of place* s is defined as: $n(I\mu.p) = n(\mu.p)$, $n(k) = \emptyset$ and $n((\nu x)) = \{x\}$ and extended to markings as: $n(m) = \bigcup_{s \in dom(m)} n(s)$.

The set $r(m)$ of *restricted* names in marking m is defined as follows: $r(m) = \{x \mid (\nu x) \in dom(m)\}$.

For the sake of simplicity, we often write the functions above with multiple arguments, meaning the union of the applications to each argument. E.g., $r(m, m')$ means $r(m) \cup r(m')$.

We define a notion of alpha conversion on markings, which states that the conflicts and restricted names actually used are inessential.

Definition 6. The binary relation $\equiv^1_\alpha$ on markings is defined as the least relation generated by the two rules below:

(i) If $k, \bar{k} \notin c(m)$, then $m\{k/h\} \equiv^1_\alpha m$.
(ii) Let $x \in r(m)$. If $w \notin n(m)$, then $m\{w/x\} \equiv^1_\alpha m$.

Alpha conversion on markings, denoted $\equiv_\alpha$ with abuse of notation, is the reflexive and transitive closure of $\equiv^1_\alpha$. I.e., $m \equiv_\alpha m'$ if $m(\equiv^1_\alpha)^* m'$. □

$dec(\mathbf{0}) = \emptyset$
$dec(\mu.p) = \{\emptyset\mu.p\}$
$dec(p+q) = k dec(p) \oplus \bar{k} dec(q)$ $\quad k$ new
$dec(p \mid q) = dec(p) \oplus dec(q)$
$dec((\nu x)p) = dec(p\{z/x\}) \oplus \{(\nu z)\}$ z new
$dec(\mathrm{rec}\, X.p) = dec(p\{\mathrm{rec}\, X.p/X\})$

Table 2. Decomposition function

The function $dec : \mathcal{P} \to \mathcal{M}_{fin}(S_\pi)$, which defines the decomposition of processes into markings, is reported in Table 2. Agent $\mathbf{0}$ generates no places. The decomposition of $\mu.p$ produces one place, where $\mu.p$ has an empty set of conflicts. The case of alternative composition is interesting, as it shows that $p+q$ is turned into the multiset union of the markings for p and q, where each place of $dec(p)$ is decorated by the singleton $\{k\}$ and, symmetrically, each place in $dec(q)$ is decorated by $\{\bar{k}\}$. Parallel composition is interpreted as multiset union. The decomposition of a restricted process $(\nu x)p$ generates a token in a restriction place (νz) (for a new name z) and the multiset obtained from the decomposition of p where the new name z is substituted for the bound name x. Finally, a recursive process is first unwounded once and then decomposed. Note that function dec is defined up to alpha conversion of markings, because the actual choice of the *new* conflict k and of the *new* name z is inessential.

The NI net for π-calculus is the triple $N_\pi = (S_\pi, \mathcal{A}, T_\pi)$, where the set T_π of net transitions is the least set generated by the axiom schemata reported in Table 3.

Axiom (tau) is trivial: if no token is present in the places of the contrasting conflict names, then the transition produces, besides the tokens of $dec(p)$, also one token in each place of the conflicts in I. In this way, any other sequential process decorated with a conflict in $\bar{I}$ is blocked forever. Axiom (in) is also very easy: besides the contrasting conflict names, there is to check the absence of tokens on the restriction place for the channel name x and for the received value y. Axiom (out) is very similar to the above. Axiom (open) clearly reveals the essence of the bound output: it differs from (out) because the token in the restriction place (νy) is now to be consumed. Indeed, the effect of the extrusion of the name y is the removal of the restriction on y. Finally, axiom (sync) describes the interaction: if the two sequential processes are *compatible* (i.e., there are no contrasting conflicts, as required by the side-condition $I \cap \bar{J} = \emptyset$), then the communication can take place. Note that axioms (tau) and (sync) are the only two which do not make any use of the restriction places. Note also that a *reduction* semantics for full π-calculus can be described via axiom (sync) only. Finally, observe that conflicts are never consumed by transitions.

(tau)	$(\{I\tau.p\}, \bar{I}) \xrightarrow{\tau} dec(p) \oplus I$
(in)	$(\{Ix(z).p\}, \bar{I} \cup \{(\nu x), (\nu y)\}) \xrightarrow{xy} dec(p\{y/z\}) \oplus I$
(out)	$(\{I\bar{x}y.p\}, \bar{I} \cup \{(\nu x), (\nu y)\}) \xrightarrow{\bar{x}y} dec(p) \oplus I$
(open)	$(\{I\bar{x}y.p, (\nu y)\}, \bar{I} \cup \{(\nu x)\}) \xrightarrow{\bar{x}(y)} dec(p) \oplus I$
(sync)	$(\{Ix(y).p, J\bar{x}z.q\}, \bar{I} \cup \bar{J}) \xrightarrow{\tau} dec(p\{z/y\}) \oplus dec(q) \oplus I \oplus J$ if $I \cap \bar{J} = \emptyset$

Table 3. Axiom schemata for (early) transitions

Example 1. Here we provide a few examples which may help in better understanding the net semantics.

- Transition $(\{\{k\}x(y).0, \{\bar{k}, (\nu x), (\nu z)\}\}) \xrightarrow{xz} \{k\}$ is one of the two transitions firable from the marking $dec(x(y).0 + v(w).0)$. If it is fired, there is no way to fire the other transition, because of the generated token in the place k.
- Consider process $(\nu y)(\bar{x}y.p|x(z).0)$, which is mapped to the marking $\{(\nu w), \bar{x}w.p, x(z).0\}$. There are three possible enabled transitions from this marking, one for the asynchronous execution of the bound output of the left subprocesses, one for the asynchronous execution of an input from the right subprocess, and one for the synchronisation. The bound output transition is $(\{\bar{x}w.p, (\nu w)\}, \{(\nu x)\}) \xrightarrow{\bar{x}(w)} dec(p)$. Instead the synchronisation is $(\{\bar{x}w.p,$

$x(z).0\}, \emptyset) \xrightarrow{\tau} dec(p)$. It is interesting to notice that for synchronisation the restriction places play no role.

– Transition $(\{\bar{x}x.0, (\nu x)\}, \{(\nu x)\}) \xrightarrow{\bar{x}(x)} \emptyset$ is derivable by axiom (open), but it is blocked, because it needs to consume a token from a place where the presence of a token inhibits the transition itself. In the interleaving semantics, instead, a transition from $(\nu z)\bar{z}z.0$ is not derivable, because of the side condition $x \neq y$ in rule (Open). □

Given a process p, the NI net associated to p is the subnet of N_π reachable from the initial marking $dec(p)$. We can extend the definition of bisimulation on markings, provided that we devote some care to the treatment of bound names in our net semantics.

Definition 7. A binary relation R over the set of markings is an *early bisimulation* if $(m_1, m_2) \in R$ implies:

- if $m_1 \xrightarrow{\bar{x}y} m_1'$, there exists then m_2' such that $m_2 \xrightarrow{\bar{x}y} m_2'$ and $(m_1', m_2') \in R$;
- if $m_1 \xrightarrow{xy} m_1'$ and $y \notin r(m_1, m_2)$, there exists then m_2' such that $m_2 \xrightarrow{xy} m_2'$ and $(m_1', m_2') \in R$;
- if $m_1 \xrightarrow{\bar{x}(y)} m_1'$, there exist then m_2' and z such that $m_2 \xrightarrow{\bar{x}(z)} m_2'$ and – for $w \notin n(m_1, m_2)$ – $(m_1'\{w/y\}, m_2'\{w/z\}) \in R$;
- if $m_1 \xrightarrow{\tau} m_1'$, there exists then m_2' such that $m_2 \xrightarrow{\tau} m_2'$ and $(m_1', m_2') \in R$;
- symmetrically for m_2 derivations.

Two markings m_1 and m_2 are *bisimilar*, written $m_1 \sim m_2$, if there exists a bisimulation R such that $(m_1, m_2) \in R$. □

Proposition 8. *Let m, m' be markings. If $m \equiv_\alpha m'$ then $m \sim m'$.* □

4.1 Retrievability

In this section, we briefly sketch the proof of retrievability of the early interleaving semantics for process p from the interleaving marking graph of the net N_π marked with the initial marking $dec(p)$. The explicit treatment of bound names makes the correspondence a bit complex. The next two theorems compare the transition system with the interleaving marking graph. Then, the final corollary states that our net translation is fully abstract w.r.t. early interleaving bisimulation equivalence.

Theorem 9. *Let p be a process.*

- *If $p \xrightarrow{\bar{x}y} p'$, then there exists m such that $dec(p) \xrightarrow{\bar{x}y} m$ and $m \sim dec(p')$.*
- *If $p \xrightarrow{xy} p'$ and $y \notin r(dec(p))$, then there exists m such that $dec(p) \xrightarrow{xy} m$ and $m \sim dec(p')$.*
- *If $p \xrightarrow{\bar{x}(y)} p'$, then there exists m and w such that $dec(p) \xrightarrow{\bar{x}(w)} m$ and $m \sim dec(p'\{w/y\})$.*

– *If* $p \xrightarrow{\tau} p'$, *then there exists* m *such that* $dec(p) \xrightarrow{\tau} m$ *and* $m \sim dec(p')$. □

Theorem 10. *Let* p *be a process.*

– *If* $dec(p) \xrightarrow{\alpha} m$ *and* α *is not a bound output, then there exists* p' *such that* $p \xrightarrow{\alpha} p'$ *and* $m \sim dec(p')$.
– *If* $dec(p) \xrightarrow{\bar{x}(w)} m$, *then for every* $y \notin fn(p)$ *there exists* p' *such that* $p \xrightarrow{\bar{x}(y)} p'$ *and* $m \sim dec(p'\{w/y\})$. □

Corollary 11. *Let* p *and* q *be processes. Then we have that* $p \sim q$ *if and only if* $dec(p) \sim dec(q)$. □

5 Non-interleaving Semantics

We study the multistep semantics and the causal semantics for P/T nets with inhibitor arcs, and the induced non-interleaving semantics on π-calculus, through some examples.

5.1 Multistep Semantics

For nets with inhibitor arcs, a transition may be considered to be *concurrent* to another only if the former neither produces nor consumes tokens inhibiting the latter and vice versa. In other words, if a marking enables both, they can be executed in either order. Formally, a subset T' of unblocked transitions is a *set of possibly concurrent transitions* (SPCT for short) if $\forall t_1, t_2 \in T'. t_1 \neq t_2$ we have that $dom(t_1{}^\bullet) \cap {}^\circ t_2 = \emptyset = dom({}^\bullet t_1) \cap {}^\circ t_2$. A transition t which produces some token in its inhibitor-set (i.e., $dom(t^\bullet) \cap {}^\circ t \neq \emptyset$) is called *not self-concurrent.*

It is easy to observe that the net N_π contains self-concurrent transitions only.

Definition 12. Given a NI $N = (S, Act, T)$, let $G \in \mathcal{M}_{fin}(T)$ be a finite multiset of transitions. G is *enabled* at *marking* m iff

(*i*) $dom(G)$ is a SPCT,
(*ii*) if $t \in dom(G)$ is not self-concurrent, then $G(t) = 1$,
(*iii*) $m_1 \subseteq m$, where $m_1 = \bigoplus_{t \in dom(G)} G(t) \cdot {}^\bullet t$, and
(*iv*) $m(s) = 0$ for all $s \in \bigcup_{t \in dom(G)} {}^\circ t$.

If G is enabled at m, G is called a *multistep* from m to m', where $m' = (m \setminus m_1) \oplus m_2$ with $m_2 = \bigoplus_{t \in dom(G)} G(t) \cdot t^\bullet$. This will be denoted by $m[G\rangle m'$. □

Definition 13. Let $N = (S, Act, T)$ be a net. Its *multistep marking graph* is $MMG_N \stackrel{\text{def}}{=} (\mathcal{M}_{fin}(S), \rightarrow, Act)$ where $\rightarrow \subseteq \mathcal{M}_{fin}(S) \times \mathcal{M}_{fin}(Act) \times \mathcal{M}_{fin}(S)$ is defined by $m \xrightarrow{L} m'$ iff $\exists G \in \mathcal{M}_{fin}(T). m[G\rangle m'$ and $L \in \mathcal{M}_{fin}(Act)$ is such that $\forall a \in Act. L(a) = \sum_{l(t)=a} G(t)$. With $MMG_N(m)$ we denote the multistep marking graph reachable from the initial marking m. □

Example 2. We present two examples, in order to clarify what cannot be performed in parallel.

- The process $\bar{a}x.0 + \bar{b}x.0$ is mapped on the marking $m = \{k\bar{a}x.0, k\bar{b}x.0\}$. In m two transitions are enabled: $t_1 = (\{k\bar{a}x.0\}, \{\bar{k}, (\nu a), (\nu x)\}) \xrightarrow{\bar{a}x} \{k\}$ and $t_2 = (\{\bar{k}\bar{b}x.0\}, \{k, (\nu b), (\nu x)\}) \xrightarrow{\bar{b}x} \{\bar{k}\}$. On the contrary, the step $\{t_1, t_2\}$ is not enabled at m, because it is not a SPTC: $dom(t_1^\bullet) \cap {}^\circ t_2 = \{k\} \neq \emptyset$.
- The process $(\nu y)(\bar{x}y.0 \,|\, y(v).nil \,|\, \bar{z}y.0)$ is mapped onto $m = \{(\nu w), \bar{x}w.0, y(v).0, \bar{z}w.0\}$. Two transitions are enabled: $t_1 = (\{\bar{x}w.0, (\nu w)\}, \{(\nu x)\}) \xrightarrow{\bar{x}(w)} \emptyset$ and $t_2 = (\{\bar{z}w.0, (\nu w)\}, \{(\nu z)\}) \xrightarrow{\bar{z}(w)} \emptyset$. The step $\{t_1, t_2\}$ is not enabled because ${}^\bullet t_1 \oplus {}^\bullet t_2 \not\subseteq m$. In [17] the concurrent execution of t_1 and t_2 is allowed. □

The step bisimulation between markings can be defined similarly to interleaving bisimulation, and it is finer than this.

5.2 Causal Semantics

Given a marked NI net, we show how to generate a causal tree [4] in a rather simple way. This gives us a means for talking about (strong) causal bisimulation for π-calculus.

The construction proceeds by first defining types of tokens: they are essentially a decoration to a token that records some information about the way it has been generated, namely the occurrence of the transition which produced it. A place does not contain simply a set of tokens, rather a multiset of token types, because each individual token remembers its origin. Then, we introduce a notion of configuration of a marked net which essentially defines three pieces of information. The first is the present marking of the net, where the tokens are decorated by their type/history. The second is a function which associates to each place the set of transitions which have consumed tokens from that place; it will be useful because we consider that if a transition t consumes a token from the inhibitor set of a transition t', then t causes t'. The third piece of information is a counter of occurrences of transitions.

Definition 14. Let $N = (S, Act, T, m_0)$ be a marked P/T net with inhibitor arcs. The set of *token types* is $\Theta = (T \times \omega^+) \cup \{*\}$, ranged over by θ, where (t, i) is the type of tokens produced by the i-th occurrence of transition t and $*$ is the type of tokens in the initial marking.

A *configuration* γ of a net is a triple (p, e, o), where

- $p : S \to \Theta \to \omega$ describes for each place the number of tokens of each type it contains.
- $e : S \to \wp(T \times \omega^+)$ describes for each place the set of (occurrences of) transitions which have consumed tokens from that place.
- $o : T \to \omega$ defines the number of occurrences of each transition.

The *initial configuration* of the net is $\gamma_0 = (p_0, e_0, o_0)$, where

$$p_0(s)(\theta) = \begin{cases} m_0(s) & \text{if } \theta = * \\ 0 & \text{otherwise} \end{cases} \qquad e_0(s) = 0 \qquad o_0(t) = 0 \qquad \Box$$

With $\gamma[t^i, C > \gamma'$ we denote the firing of transition t from configuration γ to configuration γ'. Actually, it is the i-th time that transition t is fired. Set C records the immediate causes for the firing of this occurrence; its elements are occurrences of transitions.

Definition 15. The rule for the i-causal firing rule is as follows: $(p, e, o)[t^i, C > (p', e', o')$ if and only if

- $\exists p_1 \subseteq p$ such that for all $s \in S$ $\;{}^\bullet t(s) = \sum_\theta p_1(s)(\theta)$
- $\forall s \in {}^\circ t \; \sum_\theta p(s)(\theta) = 0$
- $o(t) = i - 1$
- $C = C_1 \cup C_2$, where $C_1 = \{(t, i) \mid \exists s : p_1(s)(t, i) > 0\}$ and $C_2 = \bigcup_{s \in {}^\circ t} e(s)$
- $p' = (p \setminus p_1) \oplus p_2$, where $p_2(s)(\theta) = \begin{cases} t^\bullet(s) & \text{if } \theta = (t, i) \\ 0 & \text{otherwise} \end{cases}$
- $e'(s) = \begin{cases} e(s) \cup \{(t, i)\} & \text{if } s \in {}^\bullet t \setminus t^\bullet \\ e(s) & \text{otherwise} \end{cases}$
- $o'(u) = \begin{cases} i & \text{if } u = t \\ o(u) & \text{otherwise} \end{cases}$ $\Box$

As in C we have only the immediate causes, we want to define a causal firing sequence where the causal labelling contains all the causes via transitive closure of the immediate causes.

Definition 16. A causal firing sequence is defined inductively as follows:

- γ_0 is a causal firing sequence
- if $\gamma_0 \xrightarrow{t_1^{i_1}, D_1} \gamma_1 \cdots \xrightarrow{t_n, D_n} \gamma_n$ is a causal firing sequence and $\gamma_n[t_{n+1}^{i_{n+1}}, C > \gamma_{n+1}$ is a i-causal firing then $\gamma_0 \xrightarrow{t_1^{i_1}, D_1} \gamma_1 \cdots \xrightarrow{t_n, D_n} \gamma_n \xrightarrow{t_{n+1}^{i_{n+1}}, D_{n+1}} \gamma_{n+1}$, where $D_{n+1} = C \cup \bigcup_{t_j^{i_j} \in C} D_j$, is a causal firing sequence. $\Box$

Finally, we build a causal tree from the set of causal firing sequences, by ordering them by prefix.

Definition 17. The causal tree of a net $N = (S, Act, T, m_0)$ is $CT(N) = (V, A, f)$, where

- V is the set of causal firing sequences of N;
- $A \subseteq V \times V$, $A = \{(\sigma, \sigma \xrightarrow{t^i, D} \gamma) \mid \sigma \wedge \sigma \xrightarrow{t^i, D} \gamma$ are causal firing sequences$\}$
- $f : A \to Act \times \wp(\omega^+)$, $f(\sigma, \sigma \xrightarrow{t_n^{i_n}, D_n} \gamma_n) = (l(t), \{n - k \mid t_k^{i_k} \in D_n\})$

  for $\sigma = \gamma_0 \xrightarrow{t_1^{i_1}, D_1} \gamma_1 \cdots \xrightarrow{t_{n-1}^{i_{n-1}}, D_{n-1}} \gamma_{n-1}$ $\Box$

Example 3. The net for the process $(\nu y)(\bar{x}y.\mathbf{0}\,|\,\bar{y}z.\mathbf{0})$ is drawn in Figure 1. This net can perform a causal transition labelled $\xrightarrow{\bar{x}(w),\emptyset}$, followed by the transition labelled $\xrightarrow{\bar{w}z,\{1\}}$. According to our definition above, the second transition is caused by the first one, because the first removes the inhibiting token. Instead, in [2], the second transition is not caused by the first one, because they do not consider explicitly link dependencies. □

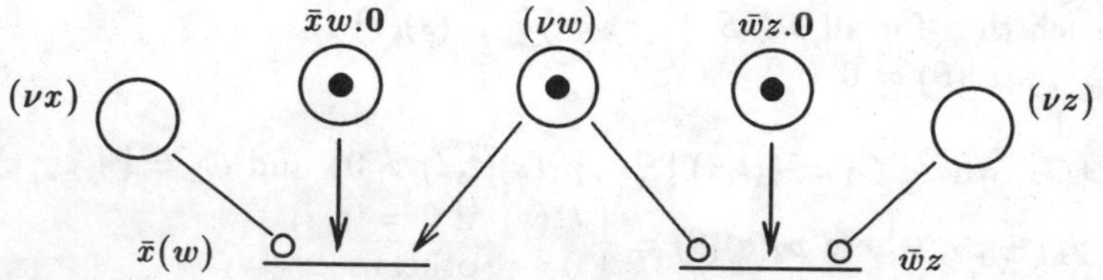

Fig. 1. The net for $(\nu y)(\bar{x}y.\mathbf{0}\,|\,\bar{y}z.\mathbf{0})$

The causal bisimulation between markings can be defined similarly to interleaving bisimulation, and it is finer than step bisimulation.

6 Conclusions

In [2, 6] it is considered important to distinguish the *structural* dependencies from the *link* dependencies. We want to stress that this kind of separation can be very naturally represented in our approach. Indeed, set C of immediate causes in Definition 15 is the union of two sets, C_1 and C_2. The first one considers all the causes due to the consumption of tokens produced by previously executed transitions. These are the causes due to flow arcs of the P/T net. Set C_2 contains, as causes of the present transition t, those transitions which have removed tokens from the inhibiting places of t. These are the causes due to the presence of inhibitor arcs. It is interesting to observe that the first set corresponds to the structural dependencies for π-calculus, while the second set expresses the link dependencies. So, a treatment of structural and link dependencies in our approach can be easily done by defining C as a pair (C_1, C_2).

References

1. G. Berry, G. Boudol, "The Chemical Abstract Machine", *Theoretical Computer Science* 96, 217-248, 1992.

2. M. Boreale, D. Sangiorgi, "A fully abstract semantics of causality in the π-calculus", Technical Report ECS-LFCS-94-297, 1994.
3. N. Busi, R. Gorrieri, "Distributed Conflicts in Communicating Systems", UBLCS-TR-94-08, April 1994. in Proc. *Workshop on Models and Languages for Coordination of Parallelism and Distribution*, LNCS 924, Springer, 1995.
4. Ph. Darondeau, P. Degano, "Causal Trees", in Proc. *ICALP'89*, LNCS 372, Springer, 234-248, 1989.
5. P. Degano, R. De Nicola, U. Montanari, "A Distributed Operational Semantics for CCS based on C/E Systems", *Acta Informatica* 26, 59-91, 1988.
6. P. Degano, C. Priami, "Causality for Mobile Processes", to appear in Proc. *ICALP'95*, LNCS, Springer, 1995.
7. J. Engelfriet, "A Multiset Semantics for the π-calculus with Replication", in Proc. *CONCUR'93*, LNCS 715, Springer, 7-21, 1993.
8. R. van Glabbeek, F. Vaandrager, "Petri Net Models for Algebraic Theories of Concurrency", in Proc. *PARLE'87*, LNCS 259, Springer, 224-242, 1987.
9. U. Goltz, "On Representing CCS Programs by Finite Petri Nets", in Proc. *MFCS'88*, LNCS 324, Springer, 339-350, 1988.
10. U. Goltz, "CCS and Petri Nets", LNCS 469, Springer, 334-357, 1990.
11. R. Gorrieri, U. Montanari, "SCONE: A Simple Calculus of Nets", in Proc. *CONCUR'90*, LNCS 458, Springer, 2-30, 1990.
12. R. Gorrieri, U. Montanari, "On the Implementation of Concurrent Calculi in Net Calculi: Two Case Studies", *Theoretical Computer Science* 141 (1-2), 195-252, 1995.
13. M. Hack, "Petri Net Languages", Technical Report 159, MIT, 1976.
14. R. Janicki, M. Koutny, "Invariant Semantics of Nets with Inhibitor Arcs", in Proc. *CONCUR'91*, LNCS 527, Springer, 317-331, 1991.
15. L. Jategaonkar Jagadeesan, R. Jagadeesan, "Causality and True Concurrency: A Data-flow Analysis of the Pi-Calculus", to appear in Proc. *AMAST'95*, 1995.
16. R. Milner, J. Parrow, D. Walker, "A Calculus of Mobile Processes", *Information and Computation* 100, 1-77, 1992.
17. U. Montanari, M. Pistore, "Concurrent Semantics for the π-calculus", in Proc. MFPS'95, ENCS 1, Elsevier, 1995.
18. U. Montanari, F. Rossi "Contextual Nets", *Acta Informatica*, to appear.
19. E. R. Olderog, *Nets, Terms and Formulas*, Cambridge Tracts in Theoretical Computer Science 23, CUP, 1991.

A Complete Theory of Deterministic Event Structures*

Arend Rensink

Institut für Informatik, University of Hildesheim

Abstract. We present an ω-complete algebra of a class of *deterministic event structures*, which are labelled prime event structures where the labelling function satisfies a certain distinctness condition. The operators of the algebra are summation, sequential composition and join. Each of these gives rise to a monoid; in addition a number of distributivity properties hold. Summation loosely corresponds to choice and join to parallel composition, with however some nonstandard aspects.
The space of models is a complete partial order (in fact a complete lattice) in which all operators are continuous; hence minimal fixpoints can be defined inductively. Moreover, the submodel relation can be captured within the algebra by summation ($x \sqsubseteq y$ iff $x + y = y$); therefore the effect of fixpoints can be captured by an infinitary proof rule, yielding a complete proof system for recursively defined deterministic event structures.

1 Introduction

It is generally recognised that *prime event structures* constitute a fundamental partial order model of behaviour, analogous to *synchronisation trees* in the field of interleaving models. In contrast to synchronisation trees however, there is no algebraic theory for prime event structures that (1) is complete for finite structures and (2) extends easily to infinite structures, especially those obtained through fixpoint constructions. In this paper we present such a theory, although not for the full class of event structures but rather for the subclass of *deterministic* ones (where the notion of determinism extends beyond that usually defined for transition systems).

1.1 Models

First we give some basic definitions. Throughout the paper we assume a universe of *events* $\mathbf{E}$, ranged over by d, e, f, and a set of *actions* $\mathbf{A}$, ranged over by a, b, c. The following is the standard prime event structure model with general conflict (see Winskel [22]), extended slightly to account for termination.

---

* The research reported in this paper was partially supported by the HCM Cooperation Network "EXPRESS" (Expressiveness of Languages for Concurrency) and the Esprit Basic Research Working Group 6067 CALIBAN (Causal Calculi Based on Nets).

Definition 1 event structures. An *event structure* is a tuple $\langle E, \checkmark, <, C, \ell \rangle$ where

- $E \subseteq \mathbf{E}$ is a set of *events*;
- $\checkmark \subseteq \mathbf{E}$ is a set of *termination events* such that $E \cap \checkmark = \varnothing$; we also denote $E^{\checkmark} = E \cup \checkmark$;
- $< \subseteq E \times E^{\checkmark}$ is an irreflexive and transitive *causal ordering relation* which is *finitary* (for all $e \in E^{\checkmark}$ the set $\{d \in E \mid d < e\}$ is finite);
- $C \subseteq Fin(E^{\checkmark})$ is a *consistency predicate* on finite sets of events, which is *subset closed* ($F \subseteq G \in C$ implies $F \in C$) and such that *all events are consistent* ($\{e\} \in C$ for all $e \in E^{\checkmark}$), *termination events are pairwise inconsistent* (for all $d, e \in \checkmark$, if $\{d, e\} \in C$ then $d = e$) and *consistency propagates backwards over causality* (for all $d, e \in E^{\checkmark}$, if $d < e \in F \in C$ then $\{d\} \cup F \in C$);
- $\ell: E \to \mathbf{A}$ is a *labelling function* (note that termination events are unlabelled).

A *configuration* is a consistent set $F \in C$ which is *causally closed* ($d < e \in F$ implies $d \in F$). An *lposet configuration* is a tuple $p = \langle E_p, \checkmark_p, <_p, \ell_p \rangle$ where $E_p \subseteq E$ and $\checkmark_p \subseteq \checkmark$ such that $E_p^{\checkmark}$ is a configuration (note that it follows that $|\checkmark_p| \leq 1$), and furthermore, $<_p = < \cap (E_p \times E_p^{\checkmark})$ and $\ell_p = \ell \upharpoonright E_p$.

Notation. The class of all event structures is denoted **ES** and ranged over by $\mathcal{E}$; the lposet configurations of $\mathcal{E}$ are collected in $\mathcal{P}(\mathcal{E})$. If $\mathcal{E}$ is a prime event structure then we use $E_{\mathcal{E}}$, $\checkmark_{\mathcal{E}}$, $<_{\mathcal{E}}$, $C_{\mathcal{E}}$ and $\ell_{\mathcal{E}}$ to denote the components of $\mathcal{E}$. If $F \notin C_{\mathcal{E}}$ we say that the events in F are in *conflict*.[2] Furthermore, for all $d \in E_{\mathcal{E}}^{\checkmark}$ we use $\Downarrow_{\mathcal{E}} d := \{e \in E_{\mathcal{E}} \mid e <_{\mathcal{E}} d\}$ to denote the set of proper predecessors of d.

Briefly, the intuition behind prime event structures is as follows: the causal ordering relation expresses which events are necessary for others to occur, the consistency predicate which events may occur together during a system run. This intuition is formalised by the standard notion of *configurations*, which represent partial runs. The *lposet configurations*, studied in Rensink [19], are basically configurations enriched with the ordering relation and labelling function of the event structure; one may regard these again as (so-called *elementary*) event structures where the consistency predicate is omitted; the intuition is that all events are consistent.

Two prime event structures $\mathcal{E}$, $\mathcal{F}$ are *isomorphic*, denoted $\mathcal{E} \cong \mathcal{F}$, when there exists a bijection $\varphi: E_{\mathcal{E}}^{\checkmark} \to E_{\mathcal{F}}^{\checkmark}$ which preserves and reflects causal ordering, consistency and labelling in the standard way. Event structures are always regarded *up to isomorphism*; another way of saying this is that we are actually dealing with *isomorphism classes*, although in practice we will use suitably chosen representatives. For more details see Winskel [22]. The isomorphism classes of the lposet configurations (regarded as elementary event structures) are in fact *pomsets* with termination information; we will call them *pomset configurations*.

[2] An important subclass of event structures are those with *binary conflict*, see e.g. Winskel [23], in which all sets of pairwise non-conflicting events are consistent. In this paper, however, we need the more general notion of conflict.

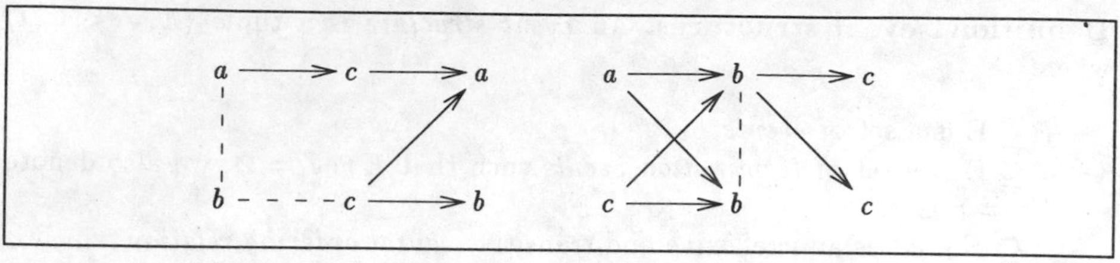

Fig. 1. Event structure examples

Definition 2. An event structure $\mathcal{E}$ is called *deterministic* if for all $d, e \in E$:

$$(\Downarrow_{\mathcal{E}} d = \Downarrow_{\mathcal{E}} e) \wedge (d, e \in \surd_{\mathcal{E}} \vee \ell_{\mathcal{E}}(d) = \ell_{\mathcal{E}}(e)) \Longrightarrow (d = e) \ .$$

Hence we call an event structure deterministic if distinct events either have different causal predecessors or distinct labels. This immediately extends to pomsets as well. The class of all deterministic event structures is denoted **DES**.[3]

It should be remarked that the above notion of determinism is less restrictive than one might think. In particular, the resulting models are more general than the deterministic behaviour models studied in [21]. If the ordering relation $<$ is in fact *sequential*, in the sense that all consistent events are ordered, then determinism in the above sense precisely coincides with the usual notion of determinism on trees. However, consider the left hand event structure in Fig. 1. (Event names are omitted from the picture; the causal ordering is represented by arrows and conflicting events are connected by dotted lines, where for the purpose of this example we assume that conflict is in fact binary.) The left hand structure is easily seen to be deterministic in the sense of Def. 2, but the transition system generated by the corresponding set of configurations is *not* deterministic in the usual sense: for instance, from the configuration consisting of the initial a-event, there are two different c-labelled events that are enabled.

On the other hand, the right hand event structure in Fig. 1 is in two places nondeterministic. Namely, the two conflicting b-events have the same set of predecessors; and indeed this is the traditional form of nondeterminism, where from a given state there are two conflicting ways to perform a certain action. Equationally, such a circumstance is ruled out by requiring $x;(y+z) = x;y+x;z$. But also, the two concurrent c-events have the same set of predecessors and hence also violate the condition in Def. 2; hence certain forms of *auto-concurrency* (concurrent occurrences of the same action) are also ruled out in deterministic event structures —albeit not all forms, as can be seen from the c-events on the left hand side. In our proof system below, such cases of nondeterminism are ruled out by the analogous axiom $x;(y \sqcup z) = x;y \sqcup x;z$ (where $\sqcup$ roughly corresponds with parallel composition).

Another characterisation of determinism is that the *partial runs* of a system completely determine the behaviour. This holds for deterministic event structures as well, if we take as partial runs *pomset configurations*: deterministic event

[3] Under an appropriate notion of morphism, **DES** is a reflective subcategory of **ES**. Details have to be omitted here; see [20] for a similar result on pomsets.

Table 2. Theory Ax over signature $\Sigma = \{\delta, \varepsilon, +, ;, \sqcup\}$

$\delta + x = x$	(1)
$(x+y)+z = x+(y+z)$	(2)
$x+y = y+x$	(3)
$x+x = x$	(4)
$\varepsilon; x = x$	(5)
$x; \varepsilon = x$	(6)
$(x;y);z = x;(y;z)$	(7)
$\varepsilon \sqcup x = x$	(8)
$(x \sqcup y) \sqcup z = x \sqcup (y \sqcup z)$	(9)
$x \sqcup y = y \sqcup x$	(10)
$\delta; x = \delta$	(11)
$x; \delta = x \sqcup \delta$	(12)
$(x+y);z = x;z+y;z$	(13)
$x;(y+z) = x;y+x;z$	(14)
$x \sqcup (y+z) = (x \sqcup y)+(x \sqcup z)$	(15)
$x;(y \sqcup z) = x;y \sqcup x;z$	(16)

structures are basically the same objects as prefix closed sets of deterministic pomsets. (Deterministic pomsets are studied in detail in Rensink [20].)

Proposition 3. *$\mathcal{P}$ is a bijection between (isomorphism classes of) deterministic event structures and prefix closed sets of deterministic pomsets.*

It should be noted that many event structure variations known from the literature can be regarded as deterministic event structures in which the labelling function maps not to actions but to an intermediate layer of *abstract events*, which are in turn labelled by actions. Alternatively, one may treat the labels of deterministic event structures as such abstract events, and add another layer of labels on top of them; this would allow one to get around the restriction of determinism, although at the price of adding a layer of complexity and almost certainly losing completeness.

1.2 Language and Theory

Consider the signature $\Sigma = \{\delta, \varepsilon, +, ;, \sqcup\}$, with approximately the following intuition: δ denotes *deadlock* and ε *successful termination*; $\mathcal{E} + \mathcal{F}$ expresses the *choice* between $\mathcal{E}$ and $\mathcal{F}$, although isomorphic initial parts are merged together (so determinism is preserved); $\mathcal{E}; \mathcal{F}$ is the *sequential composition* and $\mathcal{E} \sqcup \mathcal{F}$ the *join* of two event structures, where the latter is a kind of parallel composition except that isomorphic initial parts are again merged rather than put in parallel. Over this signature we consider the equational theory Ax presented in Table 2. It is seen that each of the operators of Σ gives rise to a monoid, which for summation and join is commutative and idempotent ($x \sqcup x = x$ is derivable); the neutral elements of sequential composition and join coincide on the constant for successful termination; the neutral element of summation is the deadlock constant, which is moreover left cancellative for sequential composition whereas its effect as a right operand of sequential composition equals its effect as an operand of join. Furthermore, there is a number of distributivity properties.

If one compares Ax with the standard axiom system of ACP (see Bergstra and Klop [4], Baeten and Weijland [3]) then the difference is that we have Axiom 12 and the distributivity properties in Axioms 14–16. As discussed above, the latter capture the notion of determinism. (It should be remarked, however, that these axioms are crucial to the completeness result of this paper; one cannot simply drop them and so obtain a complete theory of arbitrary event structures.)

1.3 Results

The main theorem of this paper, presented in Sect. 2, is that Ax is complete for isomorphism of finite structures in **DES**, and ω-complete if **A** is large enough. That is, not only can all finite deterministic event structures be denoted, but also all terms denoting isomorphic event structures are provably equal in Ax.

Furthermore, it is straightforward to generalise the theory to infinite structures. This is worked out in Sect. 3. **DES** is in fact a complete lattice under the submodel relation defined by $x \sqsubseteq y \;:\Leftrightarrow\; x + y = y$. The distributivity properties in Axioms 13–15 already imply that sequential composition and join are monotonic with respect to $\sqsubseteq$; the corresponding semantic operators are in fact continuous. It follows that all context-free equations in Σ have inductively defined least fixpoint solutions. This makes it feasible to add a least fixpoint constructor $\mu x.\, t$ to the language (with $x \in \mathbf{V}$ an arbitrary variable occurring free in the term t) and thereby allow the recursive definition of infinite behaviour.

A simple *guardedness* condition on terms characterises those recursive equations with a *unique* fixpoint solution. This provides us with an additional proof rule for such guarded terms t:

$$\frac{x = t[x/y]}{x = \mu y.\, t}$$

Finally, the fact that the submodel relation can be characterised within the language allows us some degree of inductive reasoning as well. In particular, for arbitrary t one may infer:

$$\frac{t_x^i \sqsubseteq y \quad \text{for all } i \in \mathbb{N}}{\mu x.\, t \sqsubseteq y}$$

(where the t_x^i denote inductive approximations of $\mu x.\, t$). The resulting proof system is then ω-complete for Σ with recursion.

2 Soundness and Completeness

In this section we discuss the first of our main claims: that the theory in Table 2 is complete for isomorphism of deterministic event structures. For this purpose, we first define a Σ-algebra on deterministic event structures. The constants δ and ε and actions $s \in \mathbf{A}$ are modelled by the following deterministic event structures:

$$\begin{aligned}\mathcal{E}_\delta &:= \langle \emptyset, \emptyset, \emptyset, \{\emptyset\}, \emptyset\rangle \\ \mathcal{E}_\varepsilon &:= \langle \emptyset, \{e\}, \emptyset, \{\emptyset, \{e\}\}, \emptyset\rangle \\ \mathcal{E}_a &:= \langle \{d\}, \{e\}, \{(d,e)\}, \{\emptyset, \{d\}, \{e\}, \{d,e\}\}, \{(d,a)\}\rangle \quad (a \in \mathbf{A}).\end{aligned}$$

To define the operators we need some additional notions. If $\rho \subseteq \mathbf{E}^2$ is a relation over events, then the *domain* of ρ is given by $\operatorname{dom}\rho = \{e \in \mathbf{E} \mid \exists d \in \mathbf{E}.\, (e,d) \in \rho\}$ and the *codomain* by $\operatorname{cod}\rho = \{e \in \mathbf{E} \mid \exists d \in \mathbf{E}.\, (d,e) \in \rho\}$. We denote $F\ \rho\ G$ whenever $F \subseteq \operatorname{dom}\rho$ and $G = \{e \mid \exists d \in F.\, (d,e) \in \rho\}$. A *prefix relation* between $\mathcal{E}$ and $\mathcal{F}$ is a relation $\rho \subseteq E_{\mathcal{E}}^{\checkmark} \times E_{\mathcal{F}}^{\checkmark}$ such that

$$\rho = \{(d,e) \mid ((d,e) \in (\checkmark_{\mathcal{E}} \times \checkmark_{\mathcal{F}}) \vee \ell_{\mathcal{E}}(d) = \ell_{\mathcal{F}}(e)) \wedge (\Downarrow_{\mathcal{E}} d)\ \rho\ (\Downarrow_{\mathcal{F}} e)\}\ .$$

By induction on the depth, it is straightforward to establish that between arbitrary $\mathcal{E}, \mathcal{F} \in \mathbf{DES}$ there is a unique prefix relation ρ, which is *one-to-one* ($(d,e),(d,e') \in \rho$ implies $e = e'$) and *injective* ($(d,e),(d',e) \in \rho$ implies $d = d'$). In the following, we use a special symbol $* \notin \mathbf{E}$, and we assume that $\mathbf{E}$ is closed under pairing, i.e., $(\mathbf{E} \cup \{*\})^2 \subseteq \mathbf{E}$. For arbitrary $E \subseteq \mathbf{E}$ and $i = 1,2$ we use $\pi_i(E) = \{e_i \mid (e_1, e_2) \in E\}$.

Definition 4 summation. Let $\mathcal{E}, \mathcal{F} \in \mathbf{DES}$ and let ρ be the prefix relation between them. The *sum* of $\mathcal{E}$ and $\mathcal{F}$ is given by $\mathcal{E} + \mathcal{F} = \langle E, \checkmark, <, C, \ell\rangle$ where

$$\begin{aligned}E &= ((E_{\mathcal{E}} \setminus \operatorname{dom}\rho) \times \{*\}) \cup (\{*\} \times (E_{\mathcal{F}} \setminus \operatorname{cod}\rho)) \cup (\rho \cap (E_{\mathcal{E}} \times E_{\mathcal{F}})) \\ \checkmark &= ((\checkmark_{\mathcal{E}} \setminus \operatorname{dom}\rho) \times \{*\}) \cup (\{*\} \times (\checkmark_{\mathcal{F}} \setminus \operatorname{cod}\rho)) \cup (\rho \cap (\checkmark_{\mathcal{E}} \times \checkmark_{\mathcal{F}})) \\ < &= \{((d,e),(d',e')) \in E \times E^{\checkmark} \mid (d <_{\mathcal{E}} d' \vee d' = *) \wedge (e <_{\mathcal{F}} e' \vee e' = *)\} \\ C &= \{F \subseteq E^{\checkmark} \mid \pi_1(F) \in C_{\mathcal{E}} \vee \pi_2(F) \in C_{\mathcal{F}}\} \\ \ell &= \{((d,e),a) \in E \times \mathbf{A} \mid a = \ell_{\mathcal{E}}(d) \vee a = \ell_{\mathcal{F}}(e)\}\ .\end{aligned}$$

This basically corresponds to the usual definition of choice on event structures, except that where usually one requires $E_{\mathcal{E}} \cap E_{\mathcal{F}} = \emptyset$, here we *merge* parts of the operands $\mathcal{E}$ and $\mathcal{F}$, viz. those parts that are related by ρ. If $\rho = \emptyset$ then the definition is in fact precisely that of choice. The following is the natural definition of sequential composition on event structures, where a copy of the second operand is created and appended at every exit point of the first operand.

Definition 5 sequential composition. Let $\mathcal{E}, \mathcal{F} \in \mathbf{DES}$. The *sequential composition* of $\mathcal{E}$ and $\mathcal{F}$ is given by $\mathcal{E}; \mathcal{F} = \langle E, \checkmark, <, C, \ell\rangle$ where

$$\begin{aligned}E &= (E_{\mathcal{E}} \times \{*\}) \cup (\checkmark_{\mathcal{E}} \times E_{\mathcal{F}}) \\ \checkmark &= \checkmark_{\mathcal{E}} \times \checkmark_{\mathcal{F}} \\ < &= \{((d,e),(d',e')) \in E \times E^{\checkmark} \mid d <_{\mathcal{E}} d' \vee (d = d' \wedge e <_{\mathcal{F}} e')\} \\ C &= \{F \subseteq E^{\checkmark} \mid \pi_1(F) \in C_{\mathcal{E}} \wedge \pi_2(F) \setminus \{*\} \in C_{\mathcal{F}}\} \\ \ell &= \{((d,e),a) \in E \times \mathbf{A} \mid a = \ell_{\mathcal{E}}(d) \vee a = \ell_{\mathcal{F}}(e)\}\ .\end{aligned}$$

Finally, we define the *join* of two event structures, which again merges the ρ-related parts. The difference with summation is twofold: in the join of two structures, two events are conflicting if its projection is conflicting in *either* of its operands rather than *both* its operands as for choice; and termination events are synchronised. If $\rho = \emptyset$ then join coincides with the standard definition of *parallel composition* (without synchronisation) of event structures.

Definition 6 join. Let $\mathcal{E}, \mathcal{F} \in \mathbf{DES}$ and let ρ be the unique prefix relation between them. The *join* of $\mathcal{E}$ and $\mathcal{F}$ is given by $\mathcal{E} \sqcup \mathcal{F} = \langle E, \checkmark, <, C, \ell \rangle$ where

$$E = ((E_{\mathcal{E}} \setminus \operatorname{dom} \rho) \times \{*\}) \cup (\{*\} \times (E_{\mathcal{F}} \setminus \operatorname{cod} \rho)) \cup (\rho \cap (E_{\mathcal{E}} \times E_{\mathcal{F}}))$$

$$\checkmark = \checkmark_{\mathcal{E}} \times \checkmark_{\mathcal{F}}$$

$$< = \{((d,e),(d',e')) \in E \times E^{\checkmark} \mid (d <_{\mathcal{E}} d' \vee d' = *) \wedge (e <_{\mathcal{F}} e' \vee e' = *)\}$$

$$C = \{F \cup G \cup H \mid F, G \subseteq E \wedge H \subseteq \checkmark \wedge \pi_1(F \cup H) \in C_{\mathcal{E}} \wedge \pi_2(G \cup H) \in C_{\mathcal{F}}\}$$

$$\ell = \{((d,e),a) \in E \times \mathbf{A} \mid a = \ell_{\mathcal{E}}(d) \vee a = \ell_{\mathcal{F}}(e)\} \ .$$

Note that these operations extend to lposets if we ignore the consistency predicate. The following properties may provide more insight into these operations, and will be important in the next section:

$$\mathcal{P}(\mathcal{E} + \mathcal{F}) = \mathcal{P}(\mathcal{E}) \cup \mathcal{P}(\mathcal{F}) \tag{17}$$

$$\mathcal{P}(\mathcal{E}; \mathcal{F}) = \{p; q \mid p \in \mathcal{P}(\mathcal{E}), q \in \mathcal{P}(\mathcal{F})\} \tag{18}$$

$$\mathcal{P}(\mathcal{E} \sqcup \mathcal{F}) = \{p \sqcup q \mid p \in \mathcal{P}(\mathcal{E}), q \in \mathcal{P}(\mathcal{F})\} \ . \tag{19}$$

In fact, due to Prop. 3, these equations in themselves completely characterise the operations. This establishes the interpretation of Σ. It is now important to distinguish carefully between objects (event structures) and their denotations (terms of Σ). $T_\Sigma(\mathbf{V})$, ranged over by s, t, will denote the set of Σ-terms on generators $\mathbf{A}$ and variables $\mathbf{V}$, and T_Σ the corresponding set of *ground terms*, i.e. terms without variables. A *substitution* is a function $\sigma: \mathbf{V} \to T_\Sigma(\mathbf{V})$, usually denoted by a list $s/x, t/y$ etc. of the non-identity substitutions. σ is called *ground* if its images are ground terms. Substitutions inductively give rise to functions $\sigma: T_\Sigma(\mathbf{V}) \to T_\Sigma(\mathbf{V})$ (note the overloading of the symbol σ); applications of the latter are postfix denoted, e.g. $t\sigma$. The *semantics* of Σ is expressed by a function $[\![\_]\!]: T_\Sigma \to \mathbf{DES}$ defined inductively on the structure of ground terms.

Example 1.

1. The left hand event structure in Fig. 1 is generated by $((c; b \sqcup (a; c \sqcup c); a) + b); \delta$;
2. The term $(a \sqcup b) + (b \sqcup c) + (a \sqcup c)$ yields an event structure $\mathcal{E}$ where conflict is not binary: if $\ell_{\mathcal{E}}(e_x) = x$ then $\{e_a, e_b\}, \{e_b, e_c\}, \{e_a, e_c\} \in C_{\mathcal{E}}$ but $\{e_a, e_b, e_c\} \notin C_{\mathcal{E}}$.

The following *soundness* theorem states that the semantics is well-behaved in that it maps to the intended class of models (deterministic event structures) and preserves provable equality as event structure isomorphism; in other words, that **DES** is indeed a model of Ax.

Theorem 7 soundness. *For arbitrary* $s, t \in T_\Sigma$, $[\![t]\!] \in \mathbf{DES}$ *and* $\mathrm{Ax} \vdash s = t$ *implies* $[\![s]\!] = [\![t]\!]$.

Next, we state that all the objects of our model can be denoted. For the proof, the following meta-notation is convenient: $\sum T$ for finite sets $T \subseteq T_\Sigma$ stands for the sum of all $t \in T$, where $\sum \varnothing = \delta$ and $\sum\{t\} = t$. This meta-notation is well-defined up to provable equality of terms, due to the fact that $+$ is commutative, associative and idempotent with identity δ (Axioms 1–4). Similarly, $\bigsqcup T$ for finite T stands for the *join* of all $t \in T$, where $\bigsqcup \varnothing = \varepsilon$. Now we inductively define functions $R, S\colon \mathbf{DES} \to T_\Sigma$ as follows:

$$R(\mathcal{E}) := \textstyle\sum_{p \in \mathcal{P}(\mathcal{E}), |\checkmark_p| = 0} S(p); \delta + \sum_{p \in \mathcal{P}(\mathcal{E}), |\checkmark_p| = 1} S(p)$$
$$S(\mathcal{E}) := \textstyle\bigsqcup_{e \in E_\mathcal{E}} S(\mathcal{E} \restriction \Downarrow_\mathcal{E} e); \ell_\mathcal{E}(e) \ .$$

$S\colon \mathbf{DES} \to T_\Sigma$ is only defined on elementary event structures (where $E_\mathcal{E} \in C_\mathcal{E}$) such that $[\![S(\mathcal{E}); \delta]\!] = \mathcal{E}$. Hence R decomposes $\mathcal{E}$ into the sum of all its lposet configurations, which in turn are constructed as the join of their elements. The following theorem states that this yields denotations for all finite structures.

Theorem 8 no junk. $\mathcal{E} = [\![R(\mathcal{E})]\!]$ *for all finite* $\mathcal{E} \in \mathbf{DES}$.

Finally, we state that Ax is strong enough to prove all equalities that hold in the model.

Theorem 9 no confusion. *For all* $s, t \in T_\Sigma$, *if* $[\![s]\!] = [\![t]\!]$ *then* $\mathrm{Ax} \vdash s = t$.

As usual, this theorem is proved by rewriting terms to *normal forms*.

Definition 10 normal forms. A term $t \in T_\Sigma$ is in *elementary normal form* if it is of the form $t = (\bigsqcup T); a$, where T is a *closed set of elementary normal form terms* in the sense that if $(\bigsqcup T'); a' \in T$ then $T' \subseteq T$. Furthermore, t is in *normal form* if it is of the form

$$t = \textstyle\sum_{m \in M} (\bigsqcup T_m); \delta + \sum_{n \in N} (\bigsqcup T_n) \ .$$

where $N \subseteq M$ and for all $m \in M$, T_m is a closed set of elementary form terms such that if $T \subseteq T_m$ is a closed set of elementary form terms then $T = T_k$ for some $k \in M$.

A brief explanation is called for. An elementary normal form $(\bigsqcup T); a$ correspond to *topped deterministic pomsets*, i.e., with a greatest element: in fact, the subterm $\bigsqcup T$ yields the pomset minus its greatest element, whereas a is the label of the top element. The closure of T is necessary to obtain uniqueness. It is a fact that every finite deterministic pomset can be obtained as the finite join of such "topped" ones; see Rensink [20]. Normal forms consist of a set of deterministic pomsets (first component), a subset of which is terminated (second component).

. The function R used in the proof of Th. 8 in fact yields normal forms; moreover, R is left inverse of the semantic mapping on normal forms. It follows that there is at most one normal form term describing a given event structure.

Lemma 11 normal forms are unique. *$R([\![t]\!]) = t$ for all normal forms t.*

It follows that syntactically different normal form terms yield different pomsets, which is one of the two crucial properties of normal forms. The second crucial property is that every term can be rewritten up to provable equality to a normal form term. To see that this holds, we define a function $norm: T_\Sigma \to T_\Sigma$ which constructs normal forms. Assume that $norm(t_i) = \sum_{m\in M_i}(\bigsqcup T_m);\delta + \sum_{n\in N_i}(\bigsqcup T_n)$ for $i = 1, 2$; then $norm$ is defined inductively as follows

$$\begin{aligned}
norm(\delta) &:= \textstyle\sum\{\varepsilon;\delta\} + \sum\varnothing \\
norm(\varepsilon) &:= \textstyle\sum\{\varepsilon;\delta\} + \sum\{\varepsilon\} \\
norm(a) &:= \textstyle\sum\{(\bigsqcup\{\varepsilon;a\});\delta\} + \sum\{\bigsqcup\{\varepsilon;a\}\} \\
norm(t_1+t_2) &:= \textstyle\sum_{m\in M_1\cup M_2}(\bigsqcup T_m);\delta + \sum_{n\in N_1\cup N_2}(\bigsqcup T_n) \\
norm(t_1;t_2) &:= \textstyle\sum_{m_1\in M_1, n_i\in N_i}(\bigsqcup T_{m_1}\cup\{norm'((\bigsqcup T_{n_1});s)\mid s\in T_{m_2}\});\delta \\
&\quad\ \textstyle+\sum_{n_i\in N_i}(\bigsqcup\{norm'((\bigsqcup T_{n_1});s)\mid s\in T_{n_2}\}) \\
norm(t_1\sqcup t_2) &:= \textstyle\sum_{m_i\in M_i}(\bigsqcup T_{m_1}\cup T_{m_2});\delta + \sum_{n_i\in N_i}(\bigsqcup T_{n_1}\cup T_{n_2})
\end{aligned}$$

Here, $norm': T_\Sigma \to T_\Sigma$ is an auxiliary function inductively defined on terms of the form $t;s$ where $t = \bigsqcup T_t$ (T_t a closed set of elementary normal forms) and $s = (\bigsqcup T_s);a$ is an elementary normal form:

$$norm'(t;s) = (\bigsqcup\{norm'(t;s')) \mid s' \in T_s\});a$$

It can be proved by induction on the term structure that for such t and s, $norm'$ always yields an elementary normal form term such that $\mathrm{Ax} \vdash t;s = norm'(t;s)$, and that for all $t \in T_\Sigma$, $norm(t)$ yields a normal form term provably equal to t.

Lemma 12 normal forms exist. *For all terms $t \in T_\Sigma$, $norm(t)$ is in normal form and $\mathrm{Ax} \vdash t = norm(t)$.*

Theorem 9 is then proved as follows: if $[\![s]\!] = [\![t]\!]$ for two terms $s, t \in T_\Sigma$ then Lemma 12 and Lemma 11 imply $\mathrm{Ax} \vdash s = norm(s) = R([\![s]\!]) = R([\![t]\!]) = norm(t) = t$.

If there are enough elements around (**A** is large enough) then not only the completeness property of Th. 9 holds, but one which is even stronger, viz. *completeness for open terms.* This is the property that if two open terms denote the same object *under arbitrary ground substitutions* then they are are provably equal *before substitution.* See e.g. [12, 13, 14] for a general discussion.

Theorem 13 Ax is ω-complete. *Assume $|\mathbf{A}| = \omega$. For all $s, t \in T_\Sigma(\mathbf{V})$, if $[\![s\sigma]\!] = [\![t\sigma]\!]$ for all ground substitutions $\sigma: \mathbf{V} \to T_\Sigma$ then $\mathrm{Ax} \vdash s = t$.*

The side condition $|\mathbf{A}| = \omega$ is needed to ensure that for any pair of terms $s, t \in T_\Sigma(\mathbf{V})$ there are enough "unused elements," i.e. not occurring in s or t, to "encode" the free variables of t. For instance, if $|\mathbf{A}| = 1$ then Ax is not ω-complete. The deterministic event structures over a one-element action set are in fact sequential, and hence for instance $x;y = y;x$ holds under all ground substitutions. However, this equations are not provable in Ax (and in fact does not hold in general), hence ω-completeness does not hold.

To prove ω-completeness one can apply the technique described by Heering in [13] and by Lazrek, Lescanne and Thiel in [14], which uses *open* normal forms with the following properties:

- for any open term there is an open normal form that is provably equal to it;
- for any pair of different open normal forms there is a "characteristic" ground substitution that maps them to (closed) terms denoting different objects.

In our case, open normal forms are a simple variation on Def. 10 in which variables x are treated in the exact same way as actions a. Since Ax does not distinguish between variables and actions, the first step of the ω-completeness proof is immediate. The characteristic substitution required in the second step is obtained by mapping every variable to a distinct new element.

3 Infinite and Recursive Behaviour

The signature Σ only allows to express finite behaviour. For the description of infinite behaviour there are basically two mechanisms known from the literature: a constructor for unbounded repetition (the *Kleene star*) and a constructor for (least or greatest) fixpoints with respect to some ordering. We investigate the latter. It should be noted that this section mostly relies on standard theory, the applicability of which follows from the developments above.

The ordering on which the fixpoints will be based is generated by summation:

$$x \sqsubseteq y :\Leftrightarrow x + y = y \ .$$

In terms of deterministic event structures, this implies that $\mathcal{E} \sqsubseteq \mathcal{F}$ iff the prefix relation ρ between $\mathcal{E}$ and $\mathcal{F}$ is total on $E_{\mathcal{E}}^{\checkmark}$. Taking (17) into account, it follows that for arbitrary deterministic event structures $\mathcal{E}, \mathcal{F}$

$$\mathcal{E} \sqsubseteq \mathcal{F} \iff \mathcal{P}(\mathcal{E}) \subseteq \mathcal{P}(\mathcal{F}) \ .$$

Standard order theory implies that the space of nonempty prefix closed sets of deterministic pomsets is a complete lattice under the subset relation, with unions as suprema, intersections as infima, and the singleton set consisting of the empty pomset as the bottom element. Due to Prop. 3 it follows that **DES**, too, is a complete lattice under $\sqsubseteq$ as defined above, with bottom element $\mathcal{E}_\delta$. The supremum of $\{\mathcal{E}_i\}_{i \in I}$ can be regarded as the infinite sum $\sum_{i \in I} \mathcal{E}_i$. The properties (17)–(19) then imply that all operators of Σ are continuous w.r.t. $\sqsubseteq$. As a consequence, arbitrary open terms, when regarded as functions over **DES**, are continuous in all variables and hence give rise to inductively definable least (and greatest) fixpoints. The *approximations of* t *in* x are defined as usual: $t_x^0 := \delta$ and $t_x^{i+1} := t[t_x^i/x]$ for all $i \in \mathbb{N}$.

Theorem 14 least fixpoints. *For all $t \in T_\Sigma(\{x\})$, $\mathcal{E} = \sum_{i\in\mathbb{N}}[\![t_x^i]\!]$ is the $\sqsubseteq$-smallest deterministic event structure such that $[\![t]\!](\mathcal{E}) = \mathcal{E}$ (where $[\![t]\!]$ is interpreted as a function in x).*

To be able to denote such behaviours (without having to introduce infinitary sums) one can use the extended signature $\Sigma_\mu = \Sigma \cup \{\mu x\}_{x\in\mathbf{V}}$ where the μx are second-order fixpoint constructors whose effect on event structures is defined by

$$[\![\mu x.\, t]\!] := \textstyle\sum_{i\in\mathbb{N}}[\![t_x^i]\!] \; . \tag{20}$$

To reason equationally about fixpoint terms, one may first of all add the axiom of unfolding:

$$\mu x.\, t = t[\mu x.\, t/x] \; . \tag{21}$$

The validity follows immediately from (20) in combination with the definition of the approximations t_x^i. However, the resulting proof system is not complete; for instance the (valid) equation

$$a; (\mu x.\, b; a; x) = \mu y.\, a; b; y \tag{22}$$

cannot be proved using unfolding. There are two (standard) ways in which the power of the proof system can be extended further. The first relies on *uniqueness of fixpoint solutions*; it has the advantage that reasoning remains finite, but it does not restore completeness.

Definition 15 guardedness. Let $t, u \in T_{\Sigma_\mu}(\mathbf{V})$ with $x \in \mathbf{V}$.

- δ and a are guarded in x ($a \in \mathbf{A}$ arbitrary);
- ε and y are not guarded in x ($y \in \mathbf{V}$ arbitrary);
- $t + u$ and $t \sqcup u$ are guarded in x iff both t and u are;
- $t; u$ is guarded in x iff t is;
- $\mu y.\, t$ is guarded in x iff t is guarded in x and y.

One can prove that if t is guarded in x, then $[\![t]\!](\mathcal{E})$ is completely determined up to depth n by the fragment of $\mathcal{E}$ up to depth $n-1$. But then the minimal fixpoint $\mu x.\, t$ and the *maximal* fixpoint $\nu x.\, t$ (which is defined in an analogous fashion by approximating from *above*, i.e., starting with the top element of **DES**) are identical up to arbitrary depth, hence identical; hence the fixpoint equation $x = t[x/y]$ has $x = \mu y.t$ as its unique solution. But then the following rule holds:

$$\frac{x = t[x/y] \quad (y \text{ guarded in } t)}{x = \mu y.\, t} \tag{23}$$

Indeed, this suffices to prove (22) above: (21) together with Axiom 7 implies $a; (\mu x.\, b; a; x) = a; b; (a; (\mu x.\, b; a; x)) = a; b; (a; (\mu x.\, b; a; x))$, and hence (23) is applicable for $t = a; b; y$. Unfortunately, the proof system continues to be incomplete. To obtain completeness for T_{Σ_μ} we have to allow infinitary reasoning. One way is to introduce infinitary *terms*, in particular the infinite sums shown above. This in fact gets us more than we wanted, since in principle *every* infinite deterministic event structure can then be denoted, rather than just the recursively defined ones we are considering. A more restricted idea is to express the fact that $\mu x.\, t$ is the $\sqsubseteq$-infimum of its approximations, in the form of the following infinitary proof rule:

$$\frac{s[t^i_x/y] \sqsubseteq z \quad \text{for all } i \in \mathbb{N}}{s[\mu x.\, t/y] \sqsubseteq z} \tag{24}$$

Here s and t are arbitrary, i.e., not necessarily guarded. The validity of (24) is immediate, since summation distributes over all other operands, and hence $s[\mu x.\, t/y] = s[\sum_{i\in\mathbb{N}} t^i_x/y] = \sum_{i\in\mathbb{N}} s[t^i_x/y]$. (Note: the dual statement $s[t^i_x/y] \sqsubseteq s[\mu x.t/y]$ can be derived from (21) by induction on i.) The resulting proof system Ax_μ, consisting of Ax and (24), is (ω)-complete for equality of terms in T_{Σ_μ}.

Theorem 16 Ax_μ **is sound and complete.** *For all* $s, t \in T_{\Sigma_\mu}$, $[\![s]\!] = [\![t]\!]$ *if and only if* $\mathrm{Ax}_\mu \vdash s = t$.

Proof sketch for completeness. To prove $s = t$, prove $s \sqsubseteq t$ and $t \sqsubseteq s$ separately by approximating the outermost fixpoint operators in respectively s and t, proving the inequalities for the resulting terms, and applying (24). To see that such inequality proofs $s \sqsubseteq t$ can always be carried through, bear in mind that for finite s, i.e. not containing fixpoints, $s \sqsubseteq t$ iff $s \sqsubseteq t'$ for some t' obtained by substituting high enough approximations for all the fixpoint subterms of t. By induction on the number of fixpoints in s it then follows that $s \sqsubseteq t$ is provable for arbitrary s. □

The next theorem states ω-completeness. This is independent of Th. 16 since it inherits the assumption in Th. 13 that there are enough labels in **A**; however, the proof strategy is identical.

Theorem 17 Ax_μ **is** ω**-complete.** *Assume* $|\mathbf{A}| = \omega$. *For all* $s, t \in T_{\Sigma_\mu}(\mathbf{V})$, *if* $[\![s\sigma]\!] = [\![t\sigma]\!]$ *for all ground substitutions* $\sigma\colon \mathbf{V} \to T_{\Sigma_\mu}$ *then* $\mathrm{Ax}_\mu \vdash s = t$.

4 Concluding Remarks

We briefly review the results we have achieved and try to put them into a somewhat wider context. In addition, we compare our work with several existing results.

4.1 Evaluation

The results we have achieved, consisting of an ω-complete theory for a particular class of event-based models including recursively defined ones, are rather strong but will be hard to extend or transfer to other classes of models. They are strong because they represent about the best one can expect in equational reasoning; in fact we do not know of other ω-completeness results for similar (event-based or causality-based) models. They will be hard to extend because the operators we have used are quite specific for the type of model we have studied. Especially the restriction to *deterministic* models is rather severe but also quite essential to our setup. In the introduction we have already suggested that by adding a layer of labelling one can in a sense get around this restriction, but probably only at the price of losing completeness. A similar remark can be made concerning the fact that our models have general, rather than binary, conflict: to restrict to binary conflict does not at all seem easy.

Because of the above, we regard the work presented in this paper in a sense as an "end point," presenting somehow the maximum that can be achieved using this particular approach. However, the algebra itself lends itself to further study. For instance, one may try to characterise other, weaker equivalences such as history preserving bisimulation (cf. Rabinovich and Trakhtenbrot [18], Van Glabbeek and Goltz [10]) by adding axioms to Ax_μ; or, regarding our labels **A** as abstract events rather than actions, one may study the differences between various types of event-based models such as (for example) flow or stable event structures (cf. [6, 22]) in terms of Ax_μ.

4.2 Comparison

Let us review a few comparable results in the literature. Quite close to this paper is the theory of *series-parallel pomsets*; cf. Grabowski [11], Pratt [17], Gischer [9], Aceto [2]. The syntactic difference with our theory is minimal: they do not have Axiom 16 and additionally have $x;\delta = \delta$. However, the resulting class of pomsets is quite different, and their theory deals with *augmentation* closed rather than *prefix* closed sets of pomsets. Indeed, outside the class of deterministic pomsets the prefix relation is not so well-behaved, as shown in Rensink [20], and consequently the connection to event structures expressed in Prop. 3 is lost immediately. With respect to infinite models, [9] and [17] consider regular expressions but not generally recursive ones.

Worth mentioning is also Boudol and Castellani [5], who present a theory of (nondeterministic) event structures inspired by the work on series-parallel pomsets. They omit all distributivity properties. The class of event structures that can then be denoted is restricted in quite a different sense than ours: certain order structures cannot be generated, a limitation which is inherited directly from the series-parallel pomsets. Infinite behaviour is not considered.

Another approach constitute the *Mazurkiewicz traces*, investigated e.g. by Mazurkiewicz in [15] and by Aaldersberg and Rozenberg in [1]. These in fact form a subclass of deterministic pomsets; however, the operation of *partially commutative concatenation* on traces is really incomparable with any of ours: it combines aspects of sequential composition and join. The relation of Mazurkiewicz traces to event structures is discussed exhaustively in Nielsen, Sassone and Winskel [16]. Infinite traces are considered especially in the form of *regular languages*.

Finally, consider the treatment of deadlock and successful termination. In [5], there is a single constant combining properties of both; in [9], deadlock is right cancellative for sequential composition. See also De Nicola and Labella [8] for a discussion of this point. Our theory was motivated by the wish to obtain monotonicity (in fact, continuity) of sequential composition – hence deadlock and successful termination are distinguished – and to remain, in some sense, operational – hence sequential composition is not right cancellative. This is compatible with the interleaving theory of ACP presented e.g. in Baeten and Weijland [3], albeit Axiom 12 is not a basic axiom there (but is inductively derivable).

References

1. I. J. Aalbersberg and G. Rozenberg. Theory of traces. *Theoretical Comput. Sci.*, 60:1–82, 1988.
2. L. Aceto. Full abstraction for series-parallel pomsets. In S. Abramsky and T. S. E. Maibaum, editors, *TAPSOFT '91, Volume 1*, vol. 493 of *Lecture Notes in Computer Science*, pp. 1–25. Springer-Verlag, 1991.
3. J. C. M. Baeten and W. P. Weijland. *Process Algebra.* Cambridge University Press, 1990.
4. J. A. Bergstra and J. W. Klop. Algebra of communicating processes with abstraction. *Theoretical Comput. Sci.*, 37(1):77–121, 1985.
5. G. Boudol and I. Castellani. A non-interleaving semantics for CCS based on proved transitions. *Fund. Informaticae*, XI(4):433–452, Dec. 1988.
6. G. Boudol and I. Castellani. Permutations of transitions: An event structure semantics for CCS and SCCS. In de Bakker et al. [7], pp. 411–427.
7. J. W. de Bakker, W.-P. de Roever, and G. Rozenberg, editors. *Linear Time, Branching Time and Partial Order in Logics and Models for Concurrency*, vol. 354 of *Lecture Notes in Computer Science*. Springer-Verlag, 1989.
8. R. De Nicola and A. Labella. A completeness theorem for nondeterministic Kleene algebras. In I. Prívara, B. Rovan, and P. Ružička, editors, *Mathematical Foundations of Computer Science 1994*, vol. 841 of *Lecture Notes in Computer Science*, pp. 536–545. Springer-Verlag, 1994.
9. J. L. Gischer. The equational theory of pomsets. *Theoretical Comput. Sci.*, 61:199–224, 1988.
10. R. van Glabbeek and U. Goltz. Equivalences and refinement. In I. Guessarian, editor, *Semantics of Systems of Concurrent Processes*, vol. 469 of *Lecture Notes in Computer Science*. Springer-Verlag, 1990.
11. J. Grabowski. On partial languages. *Fund. Informaticae*, IV(2):427–498, 1981.
12. J. F. Groote. *Process Algebra and Structured Operational Semantics.* PhD thesis, University of Amsterdam, 1991.
13. J. Heering. Partial evaulation and ω-completeness of algebraic specifications. *Theoretical Comput. Sci.*, 43:149–167, 1986.
14. A. Lazrek, P. Lescanne, and J.-J. Thiel. Tools for proving inductive equalities, relative completeness, and ω-completeness. *Information and Computation*, 84:47–70, 1990.
15. A. Mazurkiewicz. Basic notions of trace theory. In de Bakker et al. [7], pp. 285–363.
16. M. Nielsen, V. Sassone, and G. Winskel. Relationships between models for concurrency. In J. W. de Bakker, W.-P. de Roever, and G. Rozenberg, editors, *A Decade of Concurrency*, vol. 803 of *Lecture Notes in Computer Science*, pp. 425–476. Springer-Verlag, 1994.
17. V. R. Pratt. Modeling concurrency with partial orders. *International Journal of Parallel Programming*, 15(1):33–71, 1986.

18. A. Rabinovich and B. A. Trakhtenbrot. Behaviour structure and nets. *Fund. Informaticae*, XI(4):357–404, Dec. 1988.
19. A. Rensink. Posets for configurations! In W. R. Cleaveland, editor, *Concur '92*, vol. 630 of *Lecture Notes in Computer Science*, pp. 269–285. Springer-Verlag, 1992.
20. A. Rensink. Deterministic pomsets. Hildesheimer Informatik-Berichte 94/30, Institut für Informatik, Universität Hildesheim, Nov. 1994.
21. V. Sassone, M. Nielsen, and G. Winskel. Deterministic behavioural models for concurrency. In S. M. Borzyszkowski and S. Sokolowksi, editors, *Mathematical Foundations of Computer Science*, vol. 711 of *Lecture Notes in Computer Science*. Springer-Verlag, 1993.
22. G. Winskel. Event structures. In W. Brauer, W. Reisig, and G. Rozenberg, editors, *Petri Nets: Applications and Relationships to Other Models of Concurrency*, vol. 255 of *Lecture Notes in Computer Science*, pp. 325–392. Springer-Verlag, 1987.
23. G. Winskel. An introduction to event structures. In de Bakker et al. [7], pp. 364–397.

Characterizing Behavioural Congruences for Petri Nets

Mogens Nielsen,* *Lutz Priese*,** *Vladimiro Sassone*,*,◇
*BRICS – University of Aarhus, **University of Koblenz

Abstract. We exploit a notion of *interface* for Petri nets in order to design a set of net *combinators*. For such a calculus of nets, we focus on the *behavioural congruences* arising from four simple notions of behaviour, *viz.*, traces, maximal traces, step, and maximal step traces, and from the corresponding four notions of bisimulation, *viz.*, weak and weak step bisimulation and their maximal versions. We characterize such congruences via *universal contexts* and via *games*, providing in such a way an understanding of their discerning powers.

Introduction

In the early days of Petri net theory some important classes of Petri nets (**PN**) were introduced, such as Marked Graphs (**MG**), State Machines (**SM**), Free Choice nets (**FC**), Simple nets (**SN**), and inhibitory Petri nets (**iPN**). The 'expressive power' hierarchy among these classes is folklore, namely

$$\mathbf{MG}, \mathbf{SM} \prec \mathbf{FC} \prec \mathbf{SN} \prec \mathbf{PN} \prec \mathbf{iPN},$$

where, for instance, $\mathbf{SN} \prec \mathbf{PN}$ reads that simple nets do not possess the modelling power of arbitrary Petri nets. In proving this fact, Patil [18] shows that no simple net possesses the behaviour of the so-called '3-smoker-net', i.e., that for a certain notion $\approx$ of behavioural equivalence, '3-smoker-net' $\not\approx$ *SN*, for all simple nets *SN*. However, $\approx$ was not defined formally; the clever and convincing argument remained at a rather informal level. The same consideration applies to various decomposition results of that time. For instance, another folklore result at the Project MAC of the MIT was that every Petri net can be obtained as 'composition' of few, very simple components. Also in this case, the semantic and the composition operations were not defined formally. The proofs simply gave a decomposition technique preserving firing sequences and some 'concurrency properties'. Looking back to these and to related works (e.g. [6, 4, 24, 10, 19]), it is now clear that the intuition behind $\approx$ was the today-well-know idea of behavioural congruence, i.e., for a fixed notion of behaviour $\mathcal{B}$,

$$N_0 \approx N_1 \quad \Leftrightarrow \quad \mathcal{B}(\mathcal{C}[N_0]) = \mathcal{B}(\mathcal{C}[N_1]), \text{ for all 'net contexts' } \mathcal{C}.$$

Inspired by these ideas, in this paper we plan to formalize the notions of 'composition' and, consequently, of 'net context', drawing on the experience of developments in concurrency theory. Moreover, we focus on some simple notions of behaviours, namely four kinds of traces for labelled nets with (invisible) τ-transitions, and on the corresponding branching behavioural equivalences, namely four kinds of (weak) bisimulation, studying the behavioural congruences which arise from them, and providing characterizations of these congruences.

---

* Basic Research in Computer Science, Centre of the Danish National Research Foundation.
◇ Supported by EU Human Capital and Mobility grant ERBCHBGCT920005.

Our first aim, therefore, is to define a set **CM** of combinators of Petri nets. Several works have focused on algebraic aspects of Petri nets, e.g. [16, 23, 11, 5, 7, 3, 2, 14, 21]. Here we shall consider a minimal set of combinators, focusing on (versions of) parallel composition, relabelling, restriction, and recursion, and allowing a rather general form of interaction.

Similarly to [2], our approach is entirely based on a notion of *interface* for Petri nets, introduced in Section 1. In fact, although some of the operations of composition we have in mind could be safely described on ordinary nets, the most interesting ones, those entailing 'cooperation', give sensible results only when defined through a notion of interface. Informally, an interface for a net N is a selection of places and transitions of N which specifies what parts of N are *public*, i.e., accessible to the environment, and what parts are *private* to N. The private places and transitions cannot be accessed and, therefore, they cannot be used for connecting N with other nets. More precisely, net interfaces are built out of two components: an 'input' interface, consisting of places, and an 'output' interface, consisting of transitions. Intuitively, the input interface provides the buffers in which the tokens arriving from the environment are gathered, whilst the output interface sends tokens out to the environment. From a different viewpoint, interfaces can be viewed as a simple form of *typing* of nets on which the combinators in **CM** can be built.

The partition of interfaces in input and output parts is the actual key to the design of a significant, yet manageable, set of combinators for nets. In fact, the main way of combining nets provided by **CM** is directly suggested by such a notion: it consists of connecting the outputs of one net to the inputs of another net and, possibly, vice versa, as schematically shown by the following picture.

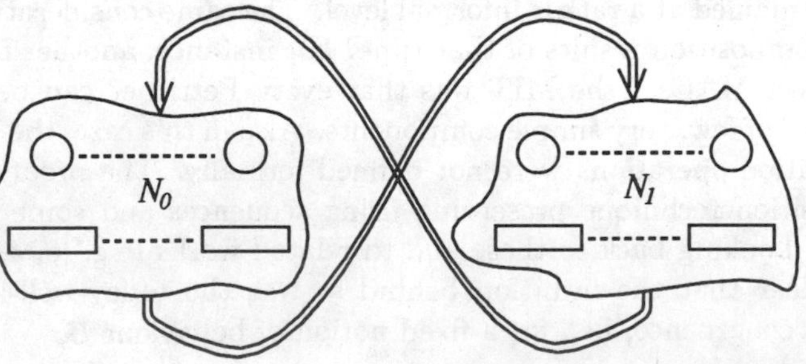

Following the principle of considering as simple operations as possible, we shall realize this by means of two more basic combinators: *par*, which simply puts its two arguments side by side, and *add*, which augments its argument by a new arc from an interface-transition to an interface-place. The operation illustrated above is then obtained by repeatedly applying *add* to $par(N_0, N_1)$. Clearly, *add* in isolation provides an interesting form of *recursion* consisting of feeding back outputs to inputs. We moreover introduce combinators dealing with *relabelling* and *hiding* intended to make easier the description of (large) modular systems. It is important to notice that, respecting our intuition about input and output parts of interfaces, it is *not* possible to connect inputs to outputs, i.e., to inspect other net's inputs or to feed other net's outputs. The only possible kind of cooperation is realized by *sending* and *receiving* tokens. Besides matching the current ideas in concurrency theory, our main observation is that this restriction makes **CM** manageable: it is difficult for us to imagine formal results along the lines of this paper without it. Notice that, enriching our setting with the operation of adding arcs from inputs to outputs, *every* finite net could be built in the calculus from the 'single-place' net and the 'single-transition' net. However, our choice of combinators still seems to provide a rather expressive 'calculus of nets'. We provide some evidence of this in Section 2, where we present a derived combinator *plus* modelling an interesting form of nondeterministic composition similar to the *internal choice* of process algebras [9, 8], and we express the *task scheduler* of [12, 13] in our calculus.

In Section 3, we focus on four simple notions of behaviour $\mathcal{B}$, namely traces and maximal traces (the *interleaving* case), and step traces and maximal step traces (the *noninterleaving* one). For each of these notions, we consider the corresponding behavioural equivalence $\approx_{\mathcal{B}}$ and the corresponding bisimulation $\leftrightarroweq_{\mathcal{B}}$. Then, we focus on the largest congruences for **CM** contained in $\approx_{\mathcal{B}}$ and $\leftrightarroweq_{\mathcal{B}}$, written, respectively, as $\approx^c_{\mathcal{B}}$ and $\leftrightarroweq^c_{\mathcal{B}}$.

Section 4 and Section 5 are devoted to simple characterizations of the behavioural congruences $\approx^c_{\mathcal{B}}$ and $\leftrightarroweq^c_{\mathcal{B}}$, which, from the technical viewpoint, are the main results of the paper. In Section 4, we identify a minimal set of contexts which is *universal* for $\approx^c_{\mathcal{B}}$. More precisely, for each pair N_0 and N_1 of nets with interface there exists a readily-identified context $\mathcal{C}$ such that N_0 and N_1 are $\approx_{\mathcal{B}}$-congruent if and only if $\mathcal{C}$ does not distinguish them. This result lifts to $\leftrightarroweq^c_{\mathcal{B}}$ provided a rather mild and reasonable condition is imposed on nets with interface, namely that interface-transitions must carry visible labels.

The nature of these results allows to transport results from the equivalences we considered to the corresponding congruences. For instance, we obtain fully abstract models for $\approx^c_{\mathcal{B}}$ in terms of formal languages; these results, reported in the full version of the paper [17], are omitted in this exposition. As a further example, following recent accounts of bisimulation in terms of games, e.g. [22, 15], we present in Section 5 game theoretic characterizations of $\approx^c_{\mathcal{B}}$ and $\leftrightarroweq^c_{\mathcal{B}}$. More precisely, we design for each of our $\mathcal{B}$'s a two-player game played on nets with interface N_0 and N_1 in such a way that a designated player has a winning strategy if and only if N_0 and N_1 are $\approx_{\mathcal{B}}$-congruent. A corresponding result, modulo the condition on labels mentioned above, is obtained for $\leftrightarroweq^c_{\mathcal{B}}$.

1 Petri Nets, Interfaces, and Combinators

In this section we recall the definition of Petri nets (see also [20]), we introduce a notion of interface for nets, and design a small set of combinators by means of which nets can be composed to and interact with each other via interfaces.

<u>Remark</u>. A *multiset* on a set P is a function $\mu\colon P \to \mathbb{N}$; the *union* of multisets μ_0 and μ_1 on P is the multiset $\mu_0 + \mu_1$ such that $(\mu_0 + \mu_1)(p) = \mu_0(p) + \mu_1(p)$. We shall use $\mu(P)$ to denote the set of multisets on P. We make the convention that, whenever we

consider words of multisets, we identify the empty word ϵ with the empty multiset, i.e., the function yielding 0 on all $p \in P$.

A *Petri net* can be regarded as an automaton whose states are represented by distributions of 'tokens' in a set of atomic state components called *places*. Similarly, the transition of state are determined by the concurrent 'firing' of multisets of atomic computational steps called *transitions*. Here we are interested in finite nets whose transitions are labelled by (possibly invisible) actions. To this aim, we shall use a *countable* set Act of *visible* actions $\alpha_1, \alpha_2, \alpha_3, \ldots$, and a distinguished *invisible* action τ.

DEFINITION 1.1 (*Labelled Petri Nets*)
A (finite) labelled Petri net is a tuple $N = (T_N, P_N, F_N, s_N, \lambda_N)$, where

- ▷ *T_N is a finite set of transitions, P_N is a finite set of places, and $T_N \cap P_N = \varnothing$,*
- ▷ *$F_N\colon (T_N \times P_N) \cup (P_N \times T_N) \to \mathbb{N}$ is the flow (multi)relation defining directed (multi)arcs between transitions and places,*
- ▷ *$s_N \in \mu(P_N)$ is the initial state (or marking),*
- ▷ *$\lambda_N\colon T_N \to Act \cup \{\tau\}$ is a labelling function.*

We shall use **PN** *to refer to the class of (finite) labelled Petri nets.*

The dynamic of nets is regulated by the notion of *fireable step*. Intuitively, a finite multiset of transitions, in the following called *step*, may fire at given state if the latter provides enough resources.

DEFINITION 1.2 (*Steps and Step Sequences*)
A step $X \in \mu(T_N)$ is fireable at state $s \in \mu(P_N)$, if $\sum_{t \in T_N} X(t) \cdot F_N(p,t) \leq s(p)$ for all $p \in P_N$; the firing of X at s leads to the state s', denoted as $s[X\rangle s'$, where $s'(p) = s(p) + \sum_{t \in T_N} X(t) \cdot (F_N(t,p) - F_N(p,t))$, for all $p \in P_N$.
A step sequence of N is a sequence $s[X_1\rangle s_1 \cdots s_{n-1}[X_n\rangle s_n$ of firings of steps. A step sequence $s[X_1 \cdots X_n\rangle s_n$ is maximal if no non-empty step is fireable at s_n. We shall write respectively $S(N)$ and $S_m(N)$ for the sets of step sequences and maximal step sequences of N fireable at the initial state s_N.

Considering the sequences of multisets of visible actions labelling the transitions occurring in step sequences and maximal step sequences, we obtain the following classical notions of languages (sets of *traces*) of Petri nets. When needed, we shall single out sequences corresponding to maximal step sequences by marking them with a distinguished symbol $\checkmark$. This allows to represent faithfully enough 'non-termination', yet avoiding to deal explicitly with infinite sequences.

DEFINITION 1.3 (*Step Languages*)
For X a step of N, let $\hat\lambda_N(X)$ be the multiset of non-τ actions of X, i.e., for all $\alpha \in Act$, $\hat\lambda_N(X)(\alpha) = \sum_{t \in \lambda_N^{-1}(\alpha)} X(t)$. For a step sequence $SX = s[X_1 \cdots X_n\rangle s_n$ of N, let $\hat\lambda_N(SX)$ be $\hat\lambda_N(X_1 \cdots X_n) = \hat\lambda_N(X_1) \cdots \hat\lambda_N(X_n)$. Then, the step language of N is the set $\mathcal{S}(N) = \{\hat\lambda_N(SX) \mid SX \in S(N)\} \subset \mu(Act)^*$, and, writing SL for $\{\hat\lambda_N(SX) \mid SX \in S_m(N)\}$, the maximal-step language of N is the set $\mathcal{S}_m(N) = \{\mu_1 \cdots \mu_n \checkmark \mid \mu_1 \cdots \mu_n \in SL\} \cup \mathcal{S}(N) \subset \mu(Act)^* \cdot \{\epsilon, \checkmark\}$.

The step sequences whose steps consist of *at most* one transition are called *firing sequences*. We denote respectively by $\mathcal{L}(N)$ and $\mathcal{L}_m(N)$ the subsets of $\mathcal{S}(N)$ and $\mathcal{S}_m(N)$ corresponding to firing sequences. The sets $\mathcal{L}(N)$ and $\mathcal{L}_m(N)$ are called, respectively, the *language* and the *maximal-trace language* of N.

We aim at defining a minimal set of net combinators which will be expressive enough to form a rudimentary calculus of nets. It should certainly include operations allowing (forms of) communication, parallel composition, relabelling, restriction, and recursion. Pondering the issue, it becomes soon evident that, to avoid a chaotic 'structural' calculus where everything is permitted, some restrictions on the allowed connections via places and transitions must be imposed. Our solution is interfaces and their input/output partitions. An interface is an ordered collection of places, the 'input', and an ordered collection of transitions, the 'output', which specifies the parts of the net that are public and can, therefore, be used by other nets to interact. Interfaces readily suggest a reasonable discipline of interaction: connections between nets should go from outputs to inputs, involving only public components. This formalizes the well-motivated and solid intuition that the only allowed interactions are achieved by *sending* and *receiving* along interfaces, to be thought of as communication channels.

DEFINITION 1.4 (*Labelled Nets with Interface*)
A net with interface is a structure $p_1, \ldots, p_n; t_1, \ldots, t_m \triangleright N$, where N is a net in **PN**, *and $p_1, \ldots, p_n \in P_N$, $t_1, \ldots, t_m \in T_N$ are all distinct.*
We shall use **IPN** *to denote the class of nets with interface.*

Stressing the intuition of interface places and transitions as bound variables, we consider net with interface up to renaming. More precisely,

$$(p_1, \ldots, p_n; t_1, \ldots, t_m \triangleright N) \equiv (p'_1, \ldots, p'_n; t'_1, \ldots, t'_m \triangleright N')$$

if there is an isomorphism between N and N' which maps p_i to p'_i and t_j to t'_j, for $1 \leq i \leq n$ and $1 \leq j \leq m$. We shall often use $\vec{p}$ as a shorthand for $p_1, \ldots, p_n$; in such a case, $|\vec{p}|$ stands for n. Analogously for $\vec{t}$.

DEFINITION 1.5 (*Combinators of Nets with Interface*)
The set **CM** *of combinators of nets with interface consists of the combinators defined by the following rules.*

$$\triangleright \quad \frac{\vec{p}_0; \vec{t}_0 \triangleright N_0 \quad \text{and} \quad \vec{p}_1; \vec{t}_1 \triangleright N_1 \quad \textit{disjoint}}{\mathit{par}(\vec{p}_0; \vec{t}_0 \triangleright N_0, \vec{p}_1; \vec{t}_1 \triangleright N_1) = \vec{p}_0, \vec{p}_1; \vec{t}_0, \vec{t}_1 \triangleright N_0 \| N_1}$$

where $N_0 \| N_1$ is the (componentwise) union of N_0 and N_1;

$$\triangleright \quad \frac{1 \leq i \leq |\vec{p}| \quad \text{and} \quad 1 \leq j \leq |\vec{t}|}{\mathit{add}(i, j, \vec{p}; \vec{t} \triangleright N) = \vec{p}; \vec{t} \triangleright N\langle p_i \leftarrow\!\!\dashv t_j \rangle}$$

where $N\langle p \leftarrow\!\!\dashv t \rangle$ is the net N augmented with an arc from t to p;

$\triangleright$ $\mathit{rel}(\phi, \vec{p}; \vec{t} \triangleright N) = \vec{p}; \vec{t} \triangleright N[\phi]$,

where ϕ: $Act \to Act \cup \{\tau\}$ is a 'relabelling' function, and $N[\phi]$ is obtained from N by relabelling via ϕ the transitions that carry non-τ actions;

$$\triangleright \frac{\max(P) \leq |\vec{p}| \quad and \quad \max(T) \leq |\vec{t}|}{hide(P, T, \vec{p}; \vec{t} \triangleright N) = \vec{p} \setminus P; \vec{t} \setminus T \triangleright N}$$

where P and T are finite sets of positive natural numbers ($\max(\varnothing) = 0$), and $\vec{x} \setminus X$ is the string obtained from $\vec{x}$ by removing x_i, for all $i \in X$.

Observe that, since the $par(\_,\_)$ combinator is defined explicitly only for disjoint nets, a renaming is generally needed before applying it to its arguments. This implies that no 'fusion' of nets is allowed by **CM**. Notice also that the operations dealing with interface places and transitions refer to them via the respective ordering, and they are not defined if the interfaces are not large enough. For instance, $add(i, j, \_)$ simply adds an arc from the ith place to the jth transitions of the interface. It provides both a form of recursion and, used in connection with $par(\_,\_)$, a form of 'asynchronous message passing' which feeds the inputs of a net with the outputs of another one. Finally, the self-explanatory $rel(\phi, \_)$ and $hide(P, T, \_)$ are intended to facilitate the description of modular systems.

Notation. For $\alpha(i)$ and $\beta(i)$ positive integer expressions in a positive integer variable i, we use $add_{i=1}^{k}(\alpha(i), \beta(i), \vec{p}; \vec{t} \triangleright N)$ for $add(\alpha(1), \beta(1), add(\cdots, add(\alpha(k), \beta(k), \vec{p}; \vec{t} \triangleright N) \cdots))$. Using the obvious associativity of $par(\_,\_)$, given $\vec{p}_1; \vec{t}_1 \triangleright N_1, \ldots, \vec{p}_k; \vec{t}_k \triangleright N_k$, we write $par(\vec{p}_1; \vec{t}_1 \triangleright N_1, \ldots, \vec{p}_k; \vec{t}_k \triangleright N_k)$, or also $par_{i=1}^{k}(\vec{p}_i; \vec{t}_i \triangleright N_i)$, for their parallel composition.

In the framework of computation theories, a context represents an environment in which a computing agent may operate. They are formalized as expressions with a hole $(\_)$ representing the place to be filled by the agent. In our case, **CM**-contexts are generated as follows, where i and j range over $\mathbb{N} \setminus \{0\}$, P and T over finite subsets of $\mathbb{N} \setminus \{0\}$, and ϕ over the functions $Act \to Act \cup \{\tau\}$.

$$\mathcal{C} ::= (\_) \mid \vec{p}; \vec{t} \triangleright N \mid par(\mathcal{C}, \mathcal{C}) \mid add(i, j, \mathcal{C}) \mid rel(\phi, \mathcal{C}) \mid hide(P, T, \mathcal{C}).$$

We shall write **CTX** to indicate the class of contexts $\mathcal{C}$.

The insertion of a net $\vec{p}; \vec{t} \triangleright N$ in a context $\mathcal{C}$ consists of replacing $(\_)$ by $\vec{p}; \vec{t} \triangleright N$ and evaluating the expression so obtained according to the rules in Definition 1.5. If the evaluation is not possible, because of the side conditions, we say that $\mathcal{C}[\vec{p}; \vec{t} \triangleright N]$ is undefined, in symbols $\mathcal{C}[\vec{p}; \vec{t} \triangleright N] = \perp$.

2 Two Examples: Nondeterministic Composition and Task Scheduler

In order to substantiate our claims on the expressiveness of our combinators, in this section we derive a combinator for a simple form of nondeterministic composition suitable for nets with interface; moreover, we consider Milner's example of a n-task scheduler, and we realize it using nets with interface and their combinators. As a byproduct, the section covers an interesting aspect of system composition, viz., nondeterminism, that we did not consider in **CM**. It may be observed that we allow ourselves to consider in our 'calculus' any net whatsoever. It is then noteworthy that the following constructions build on only two very simple nets, viz., *MCh* and *SCh*.

Driven by the notion of input interface, the following idea arises naturally: a sensible form of nondeterministic composition of nets $\vec{p}_0; \vec{t}_0 \triangleright N_0$ and $\vec{p}_1; \vec{t}_1 \triangleright N_1$

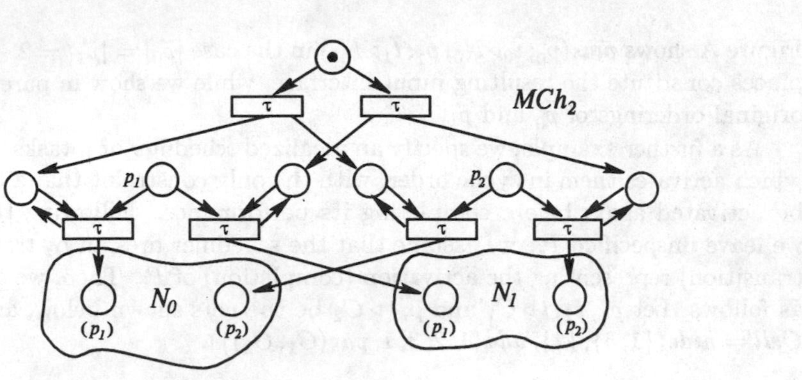

Figure A

with compatible input interfaces, i.e., $|\vec{p}_0| = n = |\vec{p}_1|$, is the net with n input channels which decides *nondeterministically*, once and for all, to forward the tokens it receives from the environment to N_0 or to N_1. The input interfaces of the component nets are private to the new net, while their outputs are still public. Of course, a symmetric combinator acting on the output interfaces can be conceived. For the time being, however, we limit ourselves to the inputs.

Let $\varnothing; t_1, t_2 \rhd MCh$ and $p_1, p_2, p_3; t_1, t_2 \rhd SCh$ be the nets shown below.

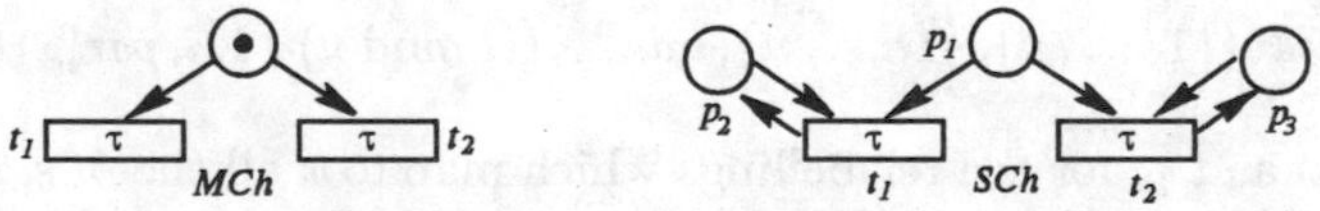

For $n \in \mathbb{N}$, let SCh_n be $par_{i=1}^{n}(p_1, p_2, p_3; t_1, t_2 \rhd SCh)$ and consider

$$MCh_n = hide\Big(\{3i{-}1, 3i \mid i = 1, \ldots, n\}, \{1, 2\},\\ add_{i=1}^{n}(3i{-}1, 1, add_{i=1}^{n}(3i, 2, par(MCh, SCh_n)))\Big).$$

The transitions of SCh_n are initially *disabled* by looping places (see Figure A). The MCh component *nondeterministically* enables all the 'left' or all the 'right' branches of the SCh's by feeding one token into the corresponding looping place. Since MCh cannot repeat its choice, this implements the 'once-and-for-all' strategy we wanted. Then, we can define $plus(\_, \_)$ in the following obvious way:

$$\frac{|\vec{p}_0| = n = |\vec{p}_1|}{plus(\vec{p}_0; \vec{t}_0 \rhd N_0, \vec{p}_1; \vec{t}_1 \rhd N_1) = \mathsf{A}_n(MCh_n, \vec{p}_0; \vec{t}_0 \rhd N_0, \vec{p}_1; \vec{t}_1 \rhd N_1)},$$

where A_n denotes the following parametric definition, in which X, Y, and Z stand for nets with interface and $n \in \mathbb{N}$.

$$\mathsf{A}_n(\mathsf{X}, \mathsf{Y}, \mathsf{Z}) = hide\Big(\{n{+}1, \ldots, 3n\}, \{1, \ldots, 2n\},\\ add_{i=1}^{n}(n{+}i, 2i{-}1, add_{i=1}^{n}(2n{+}i, 2i, par(\mathsf{X}, \mathsf{Y}, \mathsf{Z})))\Big).$$

Figure A shows $plus(\vec{p}_0;\vec{t}_0 \triangleright N_0, \vec{p}_1;\vec{t}_1 \triangleright N_1)$ in the case $|\vec{p}_0| = |\vec{p}_1| = 2$. The named places constitute the resulting input interface, while we show in parentheses the original orderings of $\vec{p}_0$ and $\vec{p}_1$.

As a further example, we specify an idealized scheduler of n tasks, $P_1, \ldots, P_n$, which activates them in cyclic order, with the only constraint that a task cannot be activated again before completing its performance. Following [12, pp. 37], we leave unspecified P_i: we assume that the scheduler fires an α_i-transition (β_i-transition) representing the activation (completion) of P_i. Then, we can proceed as follows. Let $p_1, p_2; t \triangleright C_1$ and $p; t \triangleright C_2$ be the nets shown below, and consider $Cell = hide\big(\{1,3\}, \{2\}, add\big(1,2;3,1, par(C_1, C_2)\big)\big)$.

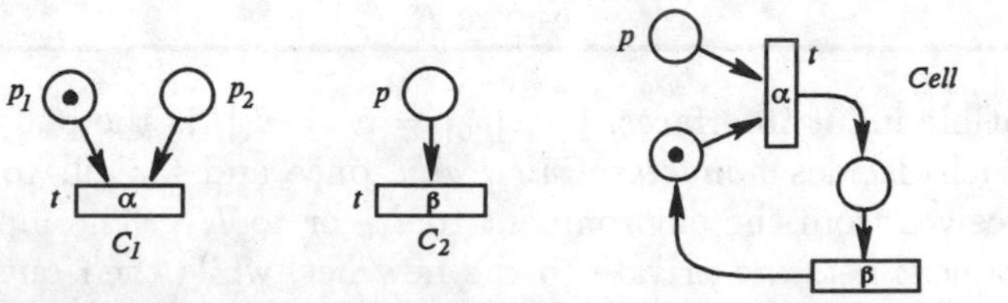

For $i = 1, \ldots, n$, let $Cell_i$ be $rel\big(\{^{\alpha_i}/_{\alpha}, ^{\beta_i}/_{\beta}\}, Cell\big)$, augment the initial marking of $Cell_1$ by adding one token to its (unique) interface-place, and define

$$Sched = hide\big(\{1, \ldots, n\}, \{1, \ldots, n\}, add_{i=1}^{n}\big((i \bmod n)+1, i, par_{i=1}^{n}(Cell_i)\big)\big).$$

Writing ϕ and ϕ_i for the relabellings which map to τ all the β_i's, and respectively every label except α_i and β_i, we have that the languages of $rel(\phi, Sched)$ and $rel(\phi_i, Sched)$ are, respectively, the prefix-closures of $\{\alpha_1 \cdots \alpha_n\}^*$ and of $\{\alpha_i\beta_i\}^*$, which is one way of saying that *Sched* satisfies its specification.

3 $\mathcal{B}$-Behavioural Congruences for Petri Nets

The semantic equivalence of concurrent systems can be described in terms of several kinds of models, e.g., languages, traces, pomsets, event structures, etc., which reflect different assumptions about how system behaviour is to be observed. For nets with interface we consider the following simple cases.

DEFINITION 3.1 (*$\mathcal{B}$-Behavioural Equivalences*)
Let $\mathcal{B}: \mathbf{PN} \to \mathbf{B}$ be a function which assigns behaviours to nets in a chosen domain of behaviours $\mathbf{B}$. We extend $\mathcal{B}$ to a function $\mathbf{IPN} \to \mathbf{B}$ by decreeing that $\mathcal{B}(\vec{p};\vec{t} \triangleright N) = \mathcal{B}(N)$. The $\mathcal{B}$-behavioural equivalence is the equivalence $\approx_{\mathcal{B}}$ induced by $\mathcal{B}$ on $\mathbf{IPN}$, viz., $\vec{p}_0;\vec{t}_0 \triangleright N_0 \approx_{\mathcal{B}} \vec{p}_0;\vec{t}_1 \triangleright N_1$ if $\mathcal{B}(\vec{p}_0;\vec{t}_0 \triangleright N_0) = \mathcal{B}(\vec{p}_1;\vec{t}_1 \triangleright N_1)$.

Following this pattern for the notions of language, step language, and their maximal versions given in Definition 1.3, in correspondence of the functions $\mathcal{L}: \mathbf{PN} \to \wp(Act^*)$, $\mathcal{L}_m: \mathbf{PN} \to \wp\big(Act^* \cdot \{\epsilon, \checkmark\}\big)$, $\mathcal{S}: \mathbf{PN} \to \wp\big(\mu(Act)^*\big)$, and $\mathcal{S}_m: \mathbf{PN} \to \wp\big(\mu(Act)^* \cdot \{\epsilon, \checkmark\}\big)$, we find the equivalences $\approx_{\mathcal{L}}$, $\approx_{\mathcal{L}_m}$, $\approx_{\mathcal{S}}$, and $\approx_{\mathcal{S}_m}$, called, respectively, *trace*, *maximal-trace*, *step*, and *maximal-step equivalence*.

Although Definition 3.1 accounts for a greater generality, in the following we shall let $\mathcal{B}$ range only on $\mathcal{L}$, $\mathcal{L}_m$, $\mathcal{S}$, and $\mathcal{S}_m$.

The equivalences $\approx_{\mathcal{B}}$ introduced above are the traditional non-branching equivalences for nets; branching versions can be obtained applying the idea of *bisimulation* [13] to the kinds of behaviour we are considering. We obtain four notions: *(trace) bisimulation* and *maximal-trace bisimulation*, corresponding to $\mathcal{L}$ and $\mathcal{L}_m$, for the interleaving case, and *step* and *maximal-step bisimulation*, corresponding to $\mathcal{S}$ and $\mathcal{S}_m$, for the noninterleaving one.

DEFINITION 3.2 (*$\mathcal{B}$-Bisimulations*)
A (step) bisimulation of N_0 and N_1 is a relation $\mathcal{R} \subseteq \mu(P_{N_0}) \times \mu(P_{N_1})$ such that $s_{N_0} \, \mathcal{R} \, s_{N_1}$, and whenever $s \, \mathcal{R} \, \bar{s}$, then (1) for each firing $s[X\rangle s'$ of a transition (respectively a step) in N_0, there exists a firing sequence (respectively a step sequence) $\bar{s}[Y_1 \cdots Y_n\rangle \bar{s}'$ in N_1 with $s' \, \mathcal{R} \, \bar{s}'$ and $\hat{\lambda}_{N_0}(X) = \hat{\lambda}_{N_1}(Y_1 \cdots Y_n)$, and (2) vice versa exchanging the roles of N_0 and N_1.
A (step) bisimulation $\mathcal{R}$ is a maximal-trace (maximal-step) bisimulation if, in (1) and (2) above, each maximal firing (step) $s[X\rangle s'$ can be matched by a maximal firing (step) sequence $\bar{s}[Y_1 \cdots Y_n\rangle \bar{s}'$.
Nets $\vec{p}_0; \vec{t}_0 \triangleright N_0$ and $\vec{p}_1; \vec{t}_1 \triangleright N_1$ are (trace), maximal-trace, step, maximal-step bisimilar, written $\vec{p}_0; \vec{t}_0 \triangleright N_0 \leftrightarrows_{\mathcal{B}} \vec{p}_1; \vec{t}_1 \triangleright N_1$, $\mathcal{B} \in \{\mathcal{L}, \mathcal{L}_m, \mathcal{S}, \mathcal{S}_m\}$, if there exists a (trace), a maximal-trace, a step, a maximal-step bisimulation of N_0 and N_1.

The relationships between the discriminating powers of the equivalences defined above is shown by the following diagram, where $\Rightarrow$, which stands for *strict* set inclusion, follows easily from the definitions.

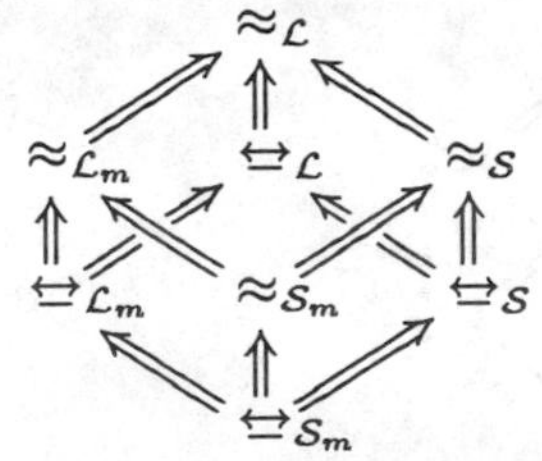

For engineering reasons, related to feasibility of correctness verification for complex systems, for mathematical reasons, related to the availability of equational reasoning, and for more conceptual reasons, related to common intuitions about system equivalence, it is important to consider equivalences which are congruences for a chosen set of system constructors. This guarantees that systems can be replaced by equivalent ones in any context. As shown by the following example, none of the equivalences described above is a congruence for **CM**.

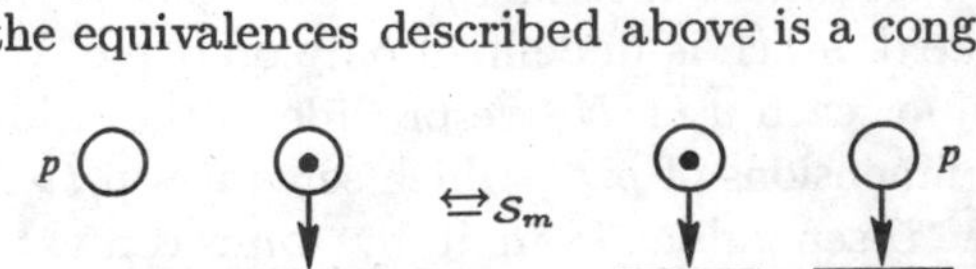

Assuming p in the interface and inserting these nets in the context which connects p with the output of a simple net which can only fire a τ-transitions once, we get different behaviours of the global systems. It should be immediately clear that the problematic combinator is $add(i, j, \_)$.

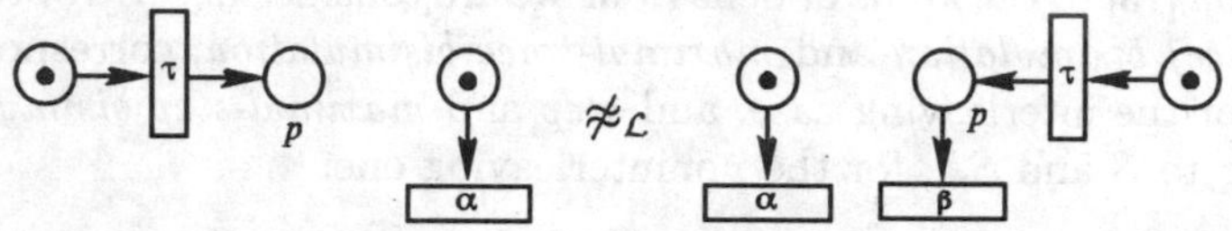

We are thus led to the largest congruences contained in these equivalences.

DEFINITION 3.3 (*$\mathcal{B}$-Behavioural Congruences*)
For $\approx$ an equivalence on **IPN**, *let $\approx^c$ denote the largest congruence for* **CM** *contained in $\approx$, i.e., $\vec{p}_0; \vec{t}_0 \triangleright N_0 \approx^c \vec{p}_1; \vec{t}_1 \triangleright N_1$ if and only if, for each $\mathcal{C} \in$* **CTX**, *either $\mathcal{C}[\vec{p}_0; \vec{t}_0 \triangleright N_0] = \bot = \mathcal{C}[\vec{p}_1; \vec{t}_1 \triangleright N_1]$ or $\mathcal{C}[\vec{p}_0; \vec{t}_0 \triangleright N_0] \approx \mathcal{C}[\vec{p}_1; \vec{t}_1 \triangleright N_1]$.*

Applying Definition 3.3 to the $\mathcal{B}$-behavioural equivalences we consider, we obtain $\approx^c_{\mathcal{L}}$, $\approx^c_{\mathcal{L}_m}$, $\approx^c_{\mathcal{S}}$, $\approx^c_{\mathcal{S}_m}$, $\leftrightarrows^c_{\mathcal{L}}$, $\leftrightarrows^c_{\mathcal{L}_m}$, $\leftrightarrows^c_{\mathcal{S}}$, and $\leftrightarrows^c_{\mathcal{S}}$, which may be called, respectively, *trace*, *maximal-trace*, *step*, *maximal-step*, *bisimulation*, *maximal-trace-bisimulation*, *step-bisimulation*, and *maximal-step-bisimulation congruence*. The relationships between $\approx^c_{\mathcal{B}}$ and $\leftrightarrows^c_{\mathcal{B}}$ are analogous to those between the corresponding equivalences, as can be seen by noticing that for subclass of nets with empty interfaces, i.e., for **PN**, $\approx_{\mathcal{B}}$ and $\approx^c_{\mathcal{B}}$, $\leftrightarrows_{\mathcal{B}}$ and $\leftrightarrows^c_{\mathcal{B}}$ coincide. Thus the global picture can be summarized by the diagram given for $\approx_{\mathcal{B}}$ and $\leftrightarrows_{\mathcal{B}}$ and the following diagrams.

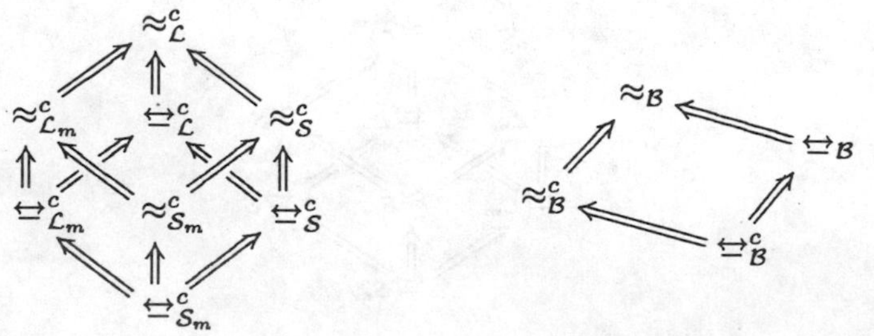

4 Universal Contexts for $\mathcal{B}$-Behavioural Congruences

In the rest of the paper we focus on characterizing the $\mathcal{B}$-behavioural congruences introduced above. In this section we shall identify a minimal set of contexts which is *universal* for $\approx^c_{\mathcal{B}}$. To make this statement precise, first observe that two nets with interface whose interfaces have different dimensions cannot be congruent, as a context which is undefined only on one of them is easily formulated. Furthermore, for each $\vec{p}; \vec{t} \triangleright N$, we provide in the following *one* context—determined by the dimensions of $\vec{p}; \vec{t}$—which separates $\vec{p}; \vec{t} \triangleright N$ from all and only the nets which are '$\mathcal{B}$-separable' from it by some context in **CTX**, i.e., the nets not $\approx_{\mathcal{B}}$-congruent to it, and which have interfaces of the same dimensions as $\vec{p};\vec{t}$. All this means that to determine whether two nets are $\approx_{\mathcal{B}}$-congruent, it is enough to verify that the numbers of places and transitions in the respective interfaces coincide and, in case, to compare their $\mathcal{B}$-behaviours into a single 'universal' context. This result can be extended to $\leftrightarrows^{c}_{\mathcal{B}}$, provided we restrict ourselves to *well-labelled* nets with interface, where $p_1, \ldots, p_n; t_1, \ldots, t_m \triangleright N$ is well-labelled if $\lambda_N(t_i) \neq \tau$, for $i = 1, \ldots, m$. Observe that, in view of the intuition of interface-transitions as public 'output' channels, this is a rather mild and reasonable condition to impose on nets with interface.

Recalling that *Act* is equipped with an enumeration $\alpha_1, \alpha_2, \ldots$, let ψ be the relabelling function $\alpha_i \mapsto \alpha_{3i}$, $i \in \mathbb{N}$. Let $\varnothing; t \triangleright U$ and $p; \varnothing \triangleright U'$ be the nets with interface shown in the figure below.

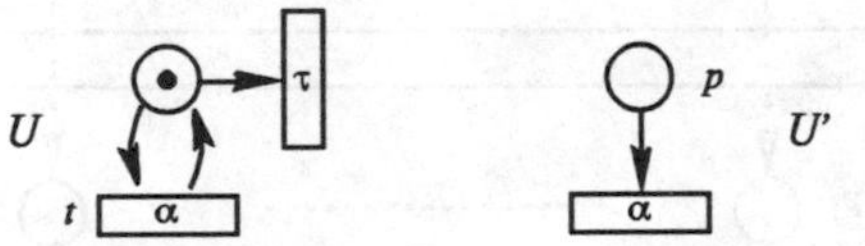

DEFINITION 4.1 (*Universal Contexts*)
Let $\mathcal{C}_{i,j}$ and $\mathcal{U}_{i,j}$, $i, j \in \mathbb{N}$, be the contexts defined below.

$$\mathcal{C}_{i,j} = par\Big(par^{i}_{k=1}(\varnothing; t \triangleright U[^{\alpha_{3k-2}}/_{\alpha}]),\, par^{j}_{k=1}(p; \varnothing \triangleright U'[^{\alpha_{3k-1}}/_{\alpha}])\Big),$$

$$\mathcal{U}_{i,j} = add^{j}_{k=1}\Big(k, i{+}k, add^{i}_{k=1}\Big(j{+}k, k, par\big(\mathcal{C}_{i,j}, rel(\psi, \_)\big)\Big)\Big).$$

Figure B presents $\mathcal{U}_{i,j}[\vec{p};\vec{t} \triangleright N]$ for a $\vec{p};\vec{t} \triangleright N$ with $|\vec{p}| = i$ and $|\vec{t}| = j$. The interface of $\mathcal{U}_{i,j}[\vec{p};\vec{t} \triangleright N]$ is shown by naming and numbering the places and transitions which belong to it. The information in parentheses concern the orderings in $\vec{p};\vec{t}$. Concerning the labels, we use ι_k for α_{3k-2}, $k = 1, \ldots, i$, o_k for α_{3k-1}, $k = 1, \ldots, j$, and $\alpha_{k_1}, \ldots \alpha_{k_j}$ for the labels of $\vec{t}$ in N. The dashed arrows are those inserted by *add*.

The contexts $\mathcal{U}_{i,j}$ are conceptually very simple. They provide a copy of $\varnothing; t \triangleright U$ for each place in $\vec{p}$, and a copy of $p; \varnothing \triangleright U'$ for each transition in $\vec{t}$. The cascade of $add(i, j, \_)$ combinators connects together the transition-place pairs so created. The role of the collection of $\varnothing; t \triangleright U$ is to test the 'reactivity' of the 'input' sites of $\vec{p};\vec{t} \triangleright N$ by sending in any number of tokens, at any relative speed, and independently for any place in $\vec{p}$. The collection of $p; \varnothing \triangleright U'$ tests the 'output'-behaviour by recording the occurrences of the transitions in $\vec{t}$.

In order for these contexts to form universal collections, we need to be able to distinguish in the behaviour of $\mathcal{U}_{i,j}[\vec{p};\vec{t} \triangleright N]$ the actions stemming from $\mathcal{U}_{i,j}$ from those stemming from N. This is achieved using the $rel(\psi, \_)$ combinator: since the actions of N are uniformly 'remapped' to $3k$-numbered actions, we are free to use differently numbered actions in the contexts. The soundness of this technique relies on the fact that ψ is injective and, therefore, no equivalences are enforced by the ψ-relabelling.

We can now make precise our statements about the universality of the contexts $\mathcal{U}_{i,j}$. We start by defining eight equivalences on **IPN**, viz., $\approx^{u}_{\mathcal{B}}$ and $\leftrightarrows^{u}_{\mathcal{B}}$

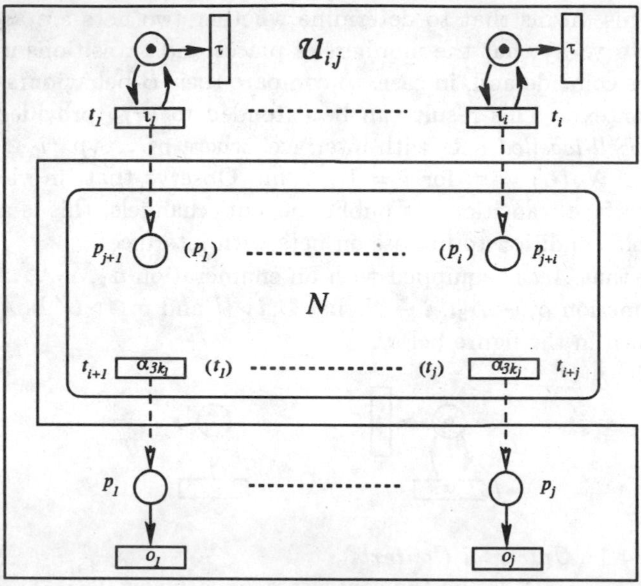

Figure B

---

for $\mathcal{B} \in \{\mathcal{L}, \mathcal{L}_m, \mathcal{S}, \mathcal{S}_m\}$, which take into account *only* the behaviour inside one universal context, chosen depending on the size of the interface of the involved nets. Theorem 4.3 will establish that such '$\approx_{\mathcal{B}}$-universal' equivalences coincide, respectively, with trace, maximal-trace, step, and maximal step congruences. Finally, Theorem 4.4 extends the result to the '$\leftrightarrows_{\mathcal{B}}$-universal' equivalences and bisimulation and step-bisimulation congruences in the case of well-labelled nets with interface.

Due to the extended abstract nature of this exposition and the space limitation, here and in the following section all the proofs will be omitted.

DEFINITION 4.2 (*$\mathcal{B}$-Universal Equivalences*)
For $\mathcal{B} \in \{\mathcal{L}, \mathcal{L}_m, \mathcal{S}, \mathcal{S}_m\}$, let $\approx^u_{\mathcal{B}}$ be the equivalence $\lesssim^u_{\mathcal{B}} \cap \gtrsim^u_{\mathcal{B}}$, where $\lesssim^u_{\mathcal{B}}$ denotes the following preorder on **IPN**.

$$\vec{p}_0;\vec{t}_0 \triangleright N_0 \lesssim^u_{\mathcal{B}} \vec{p}_1;\vec{t}_1 \triangleright N_1 \;\Leftrightarrow\; |\vec{p}_0| = |\vec{p}_1| = i,\; |\vec{t}_0| = |\vec{t}_1| = j, \text{ and } \mathcal{B}(\mathcal{U}_{i,j}[\vec{p}_0;\vec{t}_0 \triangleright N_0]) \subseteq \mathcal{B}(\mathcal{U}_{i,j}[\vec{p}_1;\vec{t}_1 \triangleright N_1]).$$

For $\mathcal{B} \in \{\mathcal{L}, \mathcal{L}_m, \mathcal{S}, \mathcal{S}_m\}$, let $\leftrightarrows^u_{\mathcal{B}}$ be the following equivalence on **IPN**.

$$\vec{p}_0;\vec{t}_0 \triangleright N_0 \leftrightarrows^u_{\mathcal{B}} \vec{p}_1;\vec{t}_1 \triangleright N_1 \;\Leftrightarrow\; |\vec{p}_0| = |\vec{p}_1| = i,\; |\vec{t}_0| = |\vec{t}_1| = j, \text{ and } \mathcal{U}_{i,j}[\vec{p}_0;\vec{t}_0 \triangleright N_0] \leftrightarrows_{\mathcal{B}} \mathcal{U}_{i,j}[\vec{p}_1;\vec{t}_1 \triangleright N_1].$$

THEOREM 4.3 (*The $\mathcal{U}_{i,j}$'s are Universal, I*)
$\approx^u_{\mathcal{L}} = \approx^c_{\mathcal{L}}$, $\approx^u_{\mathcal{L}_m} = \approx^c_{\mathcal{L}_m}$, $\approx^u_{\mathcal{S}} = \approx^c_{\mathcal{S}}$, and $\approx^u_{\mathcal{S}_m} = \approx^c_{\mathcal{S}_m}$.

THEOREM 4.4 (*The $\mathcal{U}_{i,j}$'s are Universal, II*)
For $\mathcal{B} \in \{\mathcal{L}, \mathcal{L}_m, \mathcal{S}, \mathcal{S}_m\}$, and $\vec{p}_0;\vec{t}_0 \triangleright N_0$ and $\vec{p}_1;\vec{t}_1 \triangleright N_1$ well-labelled nets with interface, $\vec{p}_0;\vec{t}_0 \triangleright N_0 \leftrightarrows^c_{\mathcal{B}} \vec{p}_1;\vec{t}_1 \triangleright N_1$ if and only if $\vec{p}_0;\vec{t}_0 \triangleright N_0 \leftrightarrows^u_{\mathcal{B}} \vec{p}_1;\vec{t}_1 \triangleright N_1$.

5 A Game Theoretic Approach to $\mathcal{B}$-Behavioural Congruences

In this section we sketch game theoretic characterizations of the $\mathcal{B}$-behavioural congruences introduced in the paper. The results here are simply 're-readings' in terms of games of Theorems 4.3 and 4.4. The exposition will be rather informal; the reader is referred to [1, 22] for a formal presentation of games.

Notation. For simplicity, in this section we shall assume that $Act \cap (Act \times \mathbb{N}) = \emptyset$. For $\vec{p}; \vec{t} \triangleright N$ a net with interface, let $\lambda_N^{\vec{t}}$ be the modification of λ_N which records explicitly the occurrences of interface-transitions by assigning the pair $\langle \lambda_N(t), k\rangle$ to $t = t_k \in \vec{t}$ and simply $\lambda_N(t)$ to $t \notin \vec{t}$. As in Definition 1.3, we use $\hat{\lambda}_N^{\vec{t}}$ for the obvious extension of $\lambda_N^{\vec{t}}$ to steps. Notice that $\hat{\lambda}_N^{\vec{t}}$ disregards the τ-transitions, but not the $\langle \tau, k\rangle$-transitions.

We start by describing the game $\mathsf{G}_{\mathcal{L}}$. The game is played on two nets with interface $\vec{p}_0; \vec{t}_0 \triangleright N_0$ and $\vec{p}_1; \vec{t}_1 \triangleright N_1$ such that $|\vec{p}_0| = |\vec{p}_1| = i$ and $|\vec{t}_0| = |\vec{t}_1| = j$. There are two players: Player, who plays with $\vec{p}_0; \vec{t}_0 \triangleright N_0$, and Opponent, who plays with $\vec{p}_1; \vec{t}_1 \triangleright N_1$. At any round $k \geq 1$ of the game, Player 0 starts from a state s_k of N_0, whilst Opponent maintains a finite set S_k of states of N_1; assume $s_0 = s_{N_0}$ and $S_0 = \{s_{N_1}\}$. Round k is played as follows.

- ▷ Player selects i natural numbers $\vec{n}_k$, updates s_{k-1} to s'_k by inserting $\vec{n}_k$ tokens in the places $\vec{p}_0$, fires a *transition* $s'_k[t\rangle s_k$ of N_0, and presents $\hat{\lambda}_{N_0}^{\vec{t}_0}(t)$ to Opponent. (I.e., Player shows only the visible actions, but *declares* the occurrence of transitions in $\vec{t}_0$.)
- ▷ Opponent answers by selecting $\bar{s} \in S_{k-1}$, updating it to $\bar{s}'$ with the insertion of $\vec{n}_k$ tokens in the places $\vec{p}_1$, and by producing a *firing sequence* $\bar{s}'[Y_1 \cdots Y_m\rangle \bar{s}''$ of N_1 such that $\hat{\lambda}_{N_1}^{\vec{t}_1}(Y_1 \cdots Y_m) = \hat{\lambda}_{N_0}^{\vec{t}_0}(t)$. Then, Opponent chooses S_k as a finite set of states reachable from a state in S_{k-1} in the way $\bar{s}''$ is reached from $\bar{s}$.
- ▷ If Opponent cannot answer, then Player *wins* the game. Otherwise, the players start round $k+1$.

Opponent *wins* if after round k Player reaches a state s_k in which no transitions are fireable, or if the game does not terminate. In the following we shall also consider three simple variations of $\mathsf{G}_{\mathcal{L}}$.

Var1: Instead of *transitions* and *firing sequences*, the players play, respectively, with *steps* and *step sequences*.

Var2: If at round k Player reaches a state s_k in which no transition of N_0 can fire, then Opponent wins the game *only* if there exists $\bar{s}_k \in S_k$ in which no transition of N_1 is fireable. Otherwise, Player wins.

Var3: Opponent plays with only *one* state, and at each round Player chooses whether to play the round on $\vec{p}_0; \vec{t}_0 \triangleright N_0$ or on $\vec{p}_1; \vec{t}_1 \triangleright N_1$.

We write $\mathsf{G}_{\mathcal{L}_m}$ for $\mathsf{G}_{\mathcal{L}}$ with Var2, $\mathsf{G}_{\mathcal{S}}$ for $\mathsf{G}_{\mathcal{L}}$ with Var1, and $\mathsf{G}_{\mathcal{S}_m}$ for $\mathsf{G}_{\mathcal{L}}$ with Var1 and Var2. Moreover, $\mathsf{GB}_{\mathcal{B}}$ stands for $\mathsf{G}_{\mathcal{B}}$ with Var3. For $\mathsf{G}_{\mathcal{B}}$ and $\mathsf{GB}_{\mathcal{B}}$ we have the following simple results.

THEOREM 5.1 (*Game Characterization of* $\approx^{c}_{\mathcal{B}}$)
For $\mathcal{B} \in \{\mathcal{L}, \mathcal{L}_m, \mathcal{S}, \mathcal{S}_m\}$, Opponent has a winning strategy for $\mathsf{G}_{\mathcal{B}}$ played on $\vec{p}_0; \vec{t}_0 \triangleright N_0$ and $\vec{p}_1; \vec{t}_1 \triangleright N_1$ if and only if $\vec{p}_0; \vec{t}_0 \triangleright N_0 \lesssim^{u}_{\mathcal{B}} \vec{p}_1; \vec{t}_1 \triangleright N_1$.

In other words, $\vec{p}_0;\vec{t}_0 \triangleright N_0 \approx^c_{\mathcal{B}} \vec{p}_1;\vec{t}_1 \triangleright N_1$ if and only if Opponent has a winning strategy for $\mathsf{G}_{\mathcal{B}}$, whether he plays with $\vec{p}_0;\vec{t}_0 \triangleright N_0$ or with $\vec{p}_1;\vec{t}_1 \triangleright N_1$

THEOREM 5.2 (*Game Characterization of* $\leftrightarrows^c_{\mathcal{B}}$)
For $\mathcal{B} \in \{\mathcal{L}, \mathcal{L}_m, \mathcal{S}, \mathcal{S}_m\}$, *Opponent has a winning strategy for* $\mathsf{GB}_{\mathcal{B}}$ *played on* $\vec{p}_0;\vec{t}_0 \triangleright N_0$ *and* $\vec{p}_1;\vec{t}_1 \triangleright N_1$ *if and only if* $\vec{p}_0;\vec{t}_0 \triangleright N_0 \leftrightarrows^u_{\mathcal{B}} \vec{p}_1;\vec{t}_1 \triangleright N_1$.

Therefore, for $\vec{p}_0;\vec{t}_0 \triangleright N_0$ and $\vec{p}_1;\vec{t}_1 \triangleright N_1$ *well-labelled* nets with interface, $\vec{p}_0;\vec{t}_0 \triangleright N_0 \leftrightarrows^c_{\mathcal{B}} \vec{p}_1;\vec{t}_1 \triangleright N_1$ if and only if Opponent has a winning strategy for $\mathsf{GB}_{\mathcal{B}}$ played on $\vec{p}_0;\vec{t}_0 \triangleright N_0$ and $\vec{p}_1;\vec{t}_1 \triangleright N_1$.

Conclusion and Future Work

We introduced a simple notion of interface for Petri nets and, based on this, a minimal set **CM** of combinators of nets with interface, which looks promising expressive while remaining very manageable. The key to the tractability of **CM** is the input/output partition of interfaces, which formalizes the intuition that interaction consists of communicating along channels. Moreover, we studied eight behavioural congruences derived from a choice of four simple behavioural notions, and we characterized them via universal contexts and games.

We believe that this work opens some interesting questions, which we must leave for future work. Among them we single out the following ones.

Bisimulations. Work finalized to characterize the **CM**-congruences based on weak bisimulation in the case of non-well-labelled nets is ongoing.

Expressiveness. Adding selected sets of 'constants' to our combinators gives rise to quite powerful *'syntactic' calculi of nets.* E.g., exploiting the results from MIT mentioned in the introduction, we know that such languages can be rich enough to express, *up to* $\approx^c_{\mathcal{B}}$, all finite Petri nets. The interesting question we plan to study is whether this can be achieved also for bisimulations.

Denotational Models. Theorems 4.3, 4.4, 5.1, and 5.2 seem to provide ground for defining semantic models for nets with interface *fully abstract* with respect to $\approx^c_{\mathcal{B}}$ and $\leftrightarrows^c_{\mathcal{B}}$. For $\approx^c_{\mathcal{B}}$ the issue is addressed in the full version of this paper [17].

Action Structures. In retrospect, the algebra presented here has strong analogies, but also non trivial differences, with Milner's (*reflexive*) *action calculus of nets* [14]. We plan to study such connections in further details.

Acknowledgements. We thank Eike Best, Egon Börger, Andrea Corradini, Pierpaolo Degano, and Ugo Montanari for valuable discussions on the argument of this paper. Many thanks to Edmund Robinson for his insightful comments on an earlier version of this paper.

References

[1] S. Abramsky, and R. Jagadeesan, *"Games and Full Completeness for Multiplicative Linear Logic"*, Technical Report DoC 92/24, Imperial College, 1992.

[2] E. Best, R. Devillers, and J. Hall, "The Petri Box Calculus: a New Causal Algebra with Multilabel Communication", in *Advances in Petri Nets*, G. Rozenberg, Ed., LNCS n. 609, pp. 21–69, Springer-Verlag, 1992.

[3] C. BROWN, D. GURR, AND V. DE PAIVA, *"A Linear Specification Language for Petri Nets"*, Report DAIMI PB-363, Computer Science Dept., University of Aarhus, 1991.

[4] J. BRUNO, AND S.M. ALTMAN, "A Theory of Asynchronous Control Networks", *IEEE Transactions on Computers*, Vol. C-20, pp. 629–638, 1971.

[5] P. DEGANO, J. MESEGUER, AND U. MONTANARI, "Axiomatizing Net Computations and Processes", in *Proceedings of the 4th LICS Symposium*, pp. 175–185, IEEE Press, 1989.

[6] J.B. DENNIS, "Modular, Asynchronous Control Structures for a High Performance Processor", in *Record of the Project MAC Conference on Concurrent Systems and Parallel Computation*, ACM Press, 1970.

[7] R. GORRIERI, AND U. MONTANARI, "Scone: A Simple Calculus of Nets", in *Proceedings of CONCUR '90*, LNCS n. 458, J. Baeten, J. Klop, Eds., pp. 2–31, Springer-Verlag, 1990.

[8] M. HENNESSY, *"Algebraic Theory of Processes"*. MIT Press, 1988.

[9] C.A.R. HOARE, *"Communicating Sequential Processes"*. Prentice Hall, 1985.

[10] R.M. KELLER, "Towards a Theory of Universal Speed-Independent Modules", *IEEE Transactions on Computers*, Vol. C-23, pp. 21–33, 1974.

[11] J. MESEGUER, AND U. MONTANARI, "Petri Nets are Monoids", *Information and Computation*, n. 88, Academic Press, pp. 105–154, 1990.

[12] R. MILNER, *"A Calculus of Communicating Systems"*. LNCS n. 92, Springer-Verlag, 1980.

[13] R. MILNER, *"Communication and Concurrency"*. Prentice Hall, 1989.

[14] R. MILNER, "Action Calculi or Syntactic Action Structures", in *Proceedings of MFCS '93*, LNCS n. 711, A. Borzyszkowski, S. Sokolowski, Eds., pp. 105–121, Springer-Verlag, 1993.

[15] M. NIELSEN, AND C. CLAUSEN, "Bisimulation for Models in Concurrency", in *Proceedings of CONCUR '94*, LNCS n. 836, B. Jonsson, J. Parrow, Eds., pp. 385–400, Springer-Verlag, 1994.

[16] M. NIELSEN, G. PLOTKIN, AND G. WINSKEL, "Petri Nets, Event Structures and Domains, Part 1", *Theoretical Computer Science*, n. 13, Elsevier, pp. 85–108, 1981.

[17] M. NIELSEN, L. PRIESE, AND V. SASSONE, *"An Algebra of Petri Nets"*, To appear as Technical Report BRICS, RS Series, 1995.

[18] S.S. PATIL, *"Limitations and Capabilities of Dijkstra's Semaphore Primitives for Coordination among Processes"*, Computation Structure Group Memo n. 57, Project MAC, MIT, 1971.

[19] L. PRIESE, "Automata and Concurrency", *Theoretical Computer Science*, n. 25, Elsevier, pp. 221–265, 1983.

[20] W. REISIG, *"Petri Nets"*. Springer-Verlag, 1985.

[21] V. SASSONE, "On the Category of Petri Net Computations", in *Proceedings of TAPSOFT '95*, P. Mosses, M. Nielsen, M.I. Schwartzbach, Eds., LNCS n. 915, pp. 334–348, Springer-Verlag, 1995.

[22] C. STIRLING, *"Modal and Temporal Logics for Processes"*, Notes for Summer School in Logic Methods in Concurrency, Computer Science Dept., University of Aarhus, 1993.

[23] G. WINSKEL, "Petri Nets, Algebras, Morphisms and Compositionality", *Information and Computation*, n. 72, Academic Press, pp. 197–238, 1987,

[24] M. YOELI, *"Petri Nets and Asynchronous Control Networks"*, Report CS–73–07, Dept. of Applied Mathematics and Computer Science, University of Waterloo, 1973.

Verification of a Distributed Summation Algorithm

Frits Vaandrager *

Department of Software Technology, CWI
P.O. Box 94079, 1090 GB Amsterdam, The Netherlands
fritsv@cwi.nl

Abstract. A correctness proof of a variant of Segall's Propagation of Information with Feedback protocol is outlined. The proof, which is carried out within the I/O automata model of Lynch and Tuttle, is standard except for the use of a prophecy variable. The aim of this paper is to show that, unlike what has been suggested in the literature, assertional methods based on invariant reasoning support an intuitive way to think about and understand this algorithm.

1 Introduction

Reasoning about distributed algorithms appears to be intrinsically difficult and will probably always require a great deal of ingenuity. Nevertheless, research on formal verification has provided a whole range of well-established concepts and techniques that may help us to tackle problems in this area. It seems that by now the basic principles for reasoning about distributed algorithms have been discovered and that the main issue that remains is the problem of scale: we know how to analyze small algorithms but are still lacking methods and tools to manage the complexity of the the bigger ones.

Not everybody agrees with this view, however, and frequently one can hear claims that existing approaches cannot deal in a 'natural' way with certain types of distributed algorithms. A new approach is then proposed to address this problem. A recent example of this is a paper by Chou [4], who offers a rather pessimistic view on the state-of-the-art in formal verification:

> At present, reasoning about distributed algorithms is still an *ad hoc*, trial-and-error process that needs a great deal of ingenuity. What is lacking is a practical method that supports, on the one hand, an *intuitive* way to think about and understand distributed algorithms and, on the other hand, a *formal* technique for reasoning about distributed algorithms using that intuitive understanding.

In his paper, Chou proposes an extension of the assertional methods of [2, 7, 8, 9, 10, 12, 15], and argues that this extension allows for a more direct formalization

* The author was supported by Esprit BRA 7166 CONCUR 2. This paper is dedicated to P.C. Baayen who, like the root node in Segall's algorithm, initiated a cascade of mathematical activity.

of intuitive, operational reasoning about distributed algorithms. To illustrate his method, Chou discusses a variant of Segall's PIF (Propagation of Information with Feedback) protocol [19]. A complex and messy proof of this algorithm using existing methods is contrasted with a slightly simpler but definitely more structured proof based on the new method.

Is the process of using assertional methods based on invariant reasoning ad hoc? Personally, I believe it is not. On the contrary, I find that these methods provide significant guidance and structure to verifications. After one has described both the algorithm and its specification as abstract programs, it is usually not so difficult to come up with a first guess of a simulation relation from the state space of the algorithm to the state space of the specification. In order to state this simulation, it is sometimes necessary to add auxiliary history and prophecy variables to the low-level program. By just starting to prove that the guessed simulation relation is indeed a simulation, i.e., that for each execution of the low-level program there exists a corresponding execution of the high-level program, one discovers the need for certain invariants, properties that are valid for all reachable states of the programs. To state these invariant properties it is sometimes convenient or even necessary to introduce auxiliary state variables. Frequently one also has to prove other auxiliary invariants first. The existence of a simulation relation guarantees that the algorithm is safe with respect to the specification: all the finite behaviors of the algorithm are allowed by the specification. The concepts of invariants, history and prophecy variables, and simulation relations are so powerful that in most cases they allow one to formalize the intuitive reasoning about safety properties of distributed algorithms. When a simulation (and thereby safety) has been established, this simulation often provides guidance in the subsequent proof that the algorithm satisfies the required liveness properties: typically one proves that the simulation relates each fair execution of the low-level program to a fair execution of the high-level program. Here modalities from temporal logic such as "eventually" and "leads to" often make it quite easy to formalize intuitions about the liveness properties of the algorithm.

As an illustration of the use of existing assertional methods, I outline in this paper a verification within the I/O automata model [12, 13] of the algorithm discussed by Chou [4]. Altogether, it took me about two hours to come up with a sketch of the proof (during a train ride from Leiden to Eindhoven), and about three weeks to work it out, polish it, and write this paper. The proof is routine, except for a few nice invariants and the use of a prophecy variable. Unlike history variables, which date back to the sixties [11], prophecy variables have been introduced only recently [1], and there are not that many examples of their use. My proof is not particularly short, but it does formalize in a direct way my own intuitions about the behavior of this algorithm. It might very well be the case that for more complex distributed algorithms new methods, such as the one of Chou [4], will pay off and lead to shorter proofs that are closer to intuition. This paper shows that invariant based assertional methods still work very well for a variant of Segall's PIF protocol.

The structure of this paper is as follows. Section 2 describes the algorithm formally as an I/O automaton. Section 3 presents the correctness criterion and the proof that the algorithm meets this criterion. Finally, Section 4 contains some concluding remarks. For reasons of space all the proofs of the lemmas and theorems have been omitted in this extended abstract. They can be found in the full version [21], which also contains a brief account of those parts of I/O automata theory [12, 13, 14] that we used in this paper.

2 Description of the Algorithm

We consider a graph $\mathbf{G} = (\mathbf{V}, \mathbf{E})$, where $\mathbf{V}$ is a nonempty, finite collection of nodes and $\mathbf{E} \subseteq \mathbf{V} \times \mathbf{V}$ is a collection of links. We assume that graph $\mathbf{G}$ is undirected in the sense that $(v, w) \in \mathbf{E} \Leftrightarrow (w, v) \in \mathbf{E}$, and connected. To each node v in the graph a value weight(v) is associated, taken from some set $\mathbf{M}$. We assume that $\mathbf{M}$ contains an element 0 and that there is a binary operator $+$ on $\mathbf{M}$, such that $(\mathbf{M}, +, 0)$ is an Abelian monoid.[2]

Nodes of $\mathbf{G}$ represent autonomous processors and links represent communication channels via which these processors can send messages to each other. We assume that the communication channels are reliable and that messages are received in the same order as they are sent. We discuss a simple distributed algorithm to compute the sum of the weights of all the nodes in the network. The algorithm is a minor[3] rephrasing of an algorithm described by Chou [4], which in turn is a variant of Segall's PIF (Propagation of Information with Feedback) protocol [19].

The only messages that are required by the algorithm are elements from $\mathbf{M}$. A node in the network enters the protocol when it receives a first message from one of its neighbors. Initially, the communication channels for all the links are empty, except the channel associated to the link e_0 from a fixed root node v_0 to itself, which contains a single message.[4] When an arbitrary node v receives a first message, it marks the node w from which this message was received. It then sends a 0 message to all its neighbors, except w. Upon receiving subsequent messages, the values of these messages are added to the weight of v. As soon as, for a non-root node, the total number of received messages equals the total number of neighbors, the value that has been computed is sent back to the node from which the first message was received. When, for root node v_0, the total number of received messages equals the total number of neighbors, the value that has been computed by v_0 is produced as the final outcome of the algorithm.

In Figure 1, the algorithm is specified as an I/O automaton *DSum* using the standard precondition/effect notation [12, 13, 6]. A minor subtlety is the occurrence of the variable v in the definition of the step relation, which is neither a state variable nor a formal parameter of the actions. Semantically, the meaning of v is determined by an implicit existential quantification: an action a is enabled in a state s if there exists a valuation ξ of all the variables (including v) that agrees with s on the state variables and with a on the parameters of the actions, such that the precondition of a holds under ξ. If action a is enabled in s under ξ then the effect part of a and ξ determine the resulting state s'.

---

[2] So, for all $m, m', m'' \in \mathbf{M}$, $m + m' = m' + m$, $m + (m' + m'') = (m + m') + m''$ and $m + 0 = 0 + m = m$.

[3] The unit element 0 of the monoid is used where Chou [4] uses a special Start message.

[4] The assumption that $\mathsf{e}_0 = (\mathsf{v}_0, \mathsf{v}_0) \in \mathbf{E}$ is not required, but allows for a more uniform description of the algorithm for each node.

Internal: *MSG*
REPORT
Output: *RESULT*

State Variables: $busy : \mathbf{V} \rightarrow \mathbf{Bool}$
$par : \mathbf{V} \rightarrow \mathbf{E}$
$total : \mathbf{V} \rightarrow \mathbf{M}$
$cnt : \mathbf{V} \rightarrow \mathbf{Int}$
$mq : \mathbf{E} \rightarrow \mathbf{M}^*$

Init: $\wedge\ \forall v : \neg busy[v]$
$\wedge\ \forall e : mq[e] = \textsf{if } e{=}\mathsf{e_0} \textsf{ then append}(0, \textsf{empty}) \textsf{ else empty}$

$MSG(e : \mathbf{E}, m : \mathbf{M})$
Precondition:
$v = \mathsf{target}(e) \wedge m = \mathsf{head}(mq[e])$
Effect:
$mq[e] := \mathsf{tail}(mq[e])$
if $\neg busy[v]$ **then** $busy[v] := \mathsf{true}$
$par[v] := e$
$total[v] := \mathsf{weight}(v)$
$cnt[v] := \mathsf{size}(\mathsf{to}(v)) - 1$
for $f \in \mathsf{from}(v)/\{e^{-1}\}$ **do** $mq[f] := \mathsf{append}(0, mq[f])$
else $total[v] := total[v] + m$
$cnt[v] := cnt[v] - 1$

$REPORT(e : \mathbf{E}, m : \mathbf{M})$
Precondition:
$v = \mathsf{source}(e) \neq \mathsf{v_0} \wedge busy[v] \wedge cnt[v] = 0 \wedge e^{-1} = par[v] \wedge m = total[v]$
Effect:
$busy[v] := \mathsf{false}$
$mq[e] := \mathsf{append}(m, mq[e])$

$RESULT(m : \mathbf{M})$
Precondition:
$busy[\mathsf{v_0}] \wedge cnt[\mathsf{v_0}] = 0 \wedge m = total[\mathsf{v_0}]$
Effect:
$busy[\mathsf{v_0}] := \mathsf{false}$

Fig. 1. I/O automaton *DSum*.

For each link $e{=}(v, w)$, the source v is denoted source(e), the target w is denoted target(e), and the reverse link (w, v) is denoted e^{-1}. For each node v, from(v) gives the set of links with source v and to(v) gives the set of links with target v, so $e \in \mathsf{from}(v) \Leftrightarrow \mathsf{source}(e){=}v$ and $e \in \mathsf{to}(v) \Leftrightarrow \mathsf{target}(e){=}v$. All the other data types and operation symbols used in the specification have the obvious meaning. The states of *DSum* are interpretations of five state variables in their domains. Four of these variables represent the values of program variables at each node:

- *busy* tells for each node whether or not it is currently participating in the protocol; initially $busy[v] = \mathsf{false}$ for each v;
- *par* is used to remember the link via which a node has been activated;
- *total* records the sum of the values seen by a node during a run of the protocol;
- *cnt* gives the number of values that a node still wants to see before it will terminate.

The fifth state variable *mq* represents the contents of the message queue for each link. Initially, $mq[e]$ is empty for each link e except $\mathsf{e_0}$.

I/O automaton *DSum* has three (parametrized) actions: (1) *MSG*, which describes the receipt and processing of a message, (2) *REPORT*, by which a non root node sends the final value that it has computed to its parent, and (3) *RESULT*, which is used by the root node to deliver the final result of the computation. The partition of *DSum* contains an equivalence class B_v for each node v, which gives all the actions in which node v participates:

$$B_{\mathsf{v_0}} \triangleq \{MSG(e, m) \mid e \in \mathsf{to}(\mathsf{v_0}),\ m \in \mathbf{M}\} \cup \{RESULT(m) \mid m \in \mathbf{M}\}$$

and, for $v \neq \mathsf{v_0}$,

$$B_v \triangleq \{MSG(e, m) \mid e \in \mathsf{to}(v),\ m \in \mathbf{M}\} \cup \{REPORT(e, m) \mid e \in \mathsf{from}(v),\ m \in \mathbf{M}\}$$

Actually, since it will turn out that *DSum* only has finite executions, it does not matter how we define the partition of *DSum*. The above definition seems to be the most natural, since it reflects the intuition that each node in the network represents an autonomous processor.

3 Correctness Proof

3.1 Correctness Criterion

The correctness property that we want to establish is that the fair traces of *DSum* are contained in those of the I/O automaton S of Figure 2. I/O automaton S is extremely simple. It has only two states: an initial state where *done*=false and a final state where *done*=true. There is one step, which starts in the initial state, has label $RESULT(\sum_{v \in \mathbf{V}} \mathsf{weight}(v))$, and ends in the final state. Finally, $part(S)$ contains a single equivalence class $\{RESULT(m) \mid m \in \mathbf{M}\}$.

We will prove $traces(DSum) \subseteq traces(S)$ using a standard recipe of Abadi and Lamport [1]: first we establish a history relation from *DSum* to an I/O automaton $DSum^h$, then a prophecy relation from $DSum^h$ to an I/O automaton $DSum^{hp}$, and finally a refinement from $DSum^{hp}$ to S. The fact that $traces(DSum) \subseteq traces(S)$ does not guarantee that $fairtraces(DSum) \subseteq fairtraces(S)$. In order to prove this, we will show that *DSum* has no infinite sequence of consecutive internal actions and cannot get into a state of deadlock before an output step has been performed.

Output: *RESULT*

State Variables: *done* : **Bool**

Init: $\neg done$

$RESULT(m : \mathbf{M})$
Precondition:
$\neg done \wedge m = \sum_{v \in \mathbf{V}} \mathsf{weight}(v)$
Effect:
$done := \mathsf{true}$

Fig. 2. I/O automaton S.

3.2 Adding a History Variable

As observed by Segall [19], a crucial property of the PIF protocol is that in each maximal execution exactly one message travels on each link. As a first step towards the proof of this property, we will establish that in each execution of *DSum* at most one message travels on each link. In order to state this formally as an invariant, we add a variable *rcvd* to automaton *DSum* that records for each link e how many messages have been received on e. This variable is similar to the variable N that Segall [19] uses in his presentation of PIF to mark the receipt of a message over a link. Figure 3 describes the automaton $DSum^h$ obtained in this way. Boxes highlight the places where $DSum^h$ differs from *DSum*. Variable *rcvd* is an auxiliary/history variable in the sense of Owicki and Gries [18] because it does not occur in conditions nor at the right-hand-side of assignments to other variables. Clearly, adding *rcvd* does not change the behavior of automaton *DSum*. This can be formalized via the following trivial result (Here a strong history relation is a relation on states whose inverse is a functional strong bisimulation, see [14].).

Theorem 1. *The inverse of the projection function that maps states from $DSum^h$ to states of DSum is a strong history relation from DSum to $DSum^h$.*

We will use a state function $Sent(e)$ to denote the number of messages sent over a link e, and a state function $Rcvd(v)$ to denote the number of messages received by a node v. Formally, these functions are defined by:

$$Sent(e) \triangleq rcvd[e] + \mathsf{len}(mq[e])$$
$$Rcvd(v) \triangleq \sum_{e \in \mathsf{to}(v)} rcvd[e]$$

Invariant I below gives some basic sanity properties involving $rcvd[e]$ and $Rcvd(v)$: at any time the number of messages received from a link is nonnegative, if a node is busy then it has received at least one message, and as soon as at least one message has been received by a node, a message has been received over the parent link, which points towards that node.

Internal: MSG
$REPORT$
Output: $RESULT$

State Variables: $busy : \mathbf{V} \to \mathbf{Bool}$
$par : \mathbf{V} \to \mathbf{E}$
$total : \mathbf{V} \to \mathbf{M}$
$cnt : \mathbf{V} \to \mathbf{Int}$
$mq : \mathbf{E} \to \mathbf{M}^*$
$\boxed{rcvd : \mathbf{E} \to \mathbf{Int}}$

Init: $\wedge\ \forall v : \neg busy[v]$
$\wedge\ \forall e : mq[e] = \text{if } e{=}e_0 \text{ then append}(0, \text{empty}) \text{ else empty}$
$\boxed{\wedge\ \forall e : rcvd[e] = 0}$

$MSG(e : \mathbf{E}, m : \mathbf{M})$
Precondition:
$v = \text{target}(e) \wedge m = \text{head}(mq[e])$
Effect:
$mq[e] := \text{tail}(mq[e])$
$\boxed{rcvd[e] := rcvd[e] + 1}$
if $\neg busy[v]$ **then** $busy[v] := \text{true}$
$par[v] := e$
$total[v] := \text{weight}(v)$
$cnt[v] := \text{size}(\text{to}(v)) - 1$
for $f \in \text{from}(v)/\{e^{-1}\}$ **do** $mq[f] := \text{append}(0, mq[f])$
else $total[v] := total[v] + m$
$cnt[v] := cnt[v] - 1$

$REPORT(e : \mathbf{E}, m : \mathbf{M})$
Precondition:
$v = \text{source}(e) \neq \text{v}_0 \wedge busy[v] \wedge cnt[v] = 0 \wedge e^{-1} = par[v] \wedge m = total[v]$
Effect:
$busy[v] := \text{false}$
$mq[e] := \text{append}(m, mq[e])$

$RESULT(m : \mathbf{M})$
Precondition:
$busy[\text{v}_0] \wedge cnt[\text{v}_0] = 0 \wedge m = total[\text{v}_0]$
Effect:
$busy[\text{v}_0] := \text{false}$

Fig. 3. I/O automaton $DSum^h$ obtained from $DSum$ by adding history variable *rcvd*.

Lemma 2. *Let I be the conjunction, for all v and e, of the following properties:*

$$I_1(e) \triangleq rcvd[e] \geq 0$$
$$I_2(v) \triangleq busy[v] \;\rightarrow\; Rcvd(v) > 0$$
$$I_3(v) \triangleq Rcvd(v) > 0 \;\rightarrow\; par[v] \in \mathsf{to}(v) \wedge rcvd[par[v]] > 0$$

Then I holds for all reachable states of $DSum^h$.

The real work starts with the proof of the next invariant I', which is the conjunction, for all v, of the following formulas:

$$\begin{aligned}
I_4(v) &\triangleq Init(v) \vee busy[v] \vee Done(v)\\
I_5 &\triangleq Init(\mathsf{v}_0) \;\rightarrow\; \mathbf{Init}(DSum^h)\\
I_6(v) &\triangleq v \neq \mathsf{v}_0 \wedge Init(v) \;\rightarrow\; \forall e \in \mathsf{from}(v) : Sent(e) = 0\\
I_7(v) &\triangleq \neg Init(v) \;\rightarrow\; \forall e \in \mathsf{from}(v)/\{par[v]^{-1}\} : Sent(e) = 1\\
I_8 &\triangleq \neg Init(\mathsf{v}_0) \;\rightarrow\; par(\mathsf{v}_0) = \mathsf{e}_0 \wedge Sent(\mathsf{e}_0) = 1\\
I_9(v) &\triangleq v \neq \mathsf{v}_0 \wedge busy[v] \;\rightarrow\; Sent(par[v]^{-1}) = 0\\
I_{10}(v) &\triangleq v \neq \mathsf{v}_0 \wedge Done(v) \;\rightarrow\; Sent(par[v]^{-1}) = 1\\
I_{11}(v) &\triangleq \neg Init(v) \;\rightarrow\; cnt[v] + Rcvd(v) = \mathsf{size}(\mathsf{to}(v))
\end{aligned}$$

in which the following state functions are used:

$$\begin{aligned}
Init(v) &\triangleq \forall e \in \mathsf{to}(v) : rcvd[e] = 0\\
Done(v) &\triangleq \neg busy[v] \wedge \forall e \in \mathsf{to}(v) : rcvd[e] = 1
\end{aligned}$$

Even though at first sight formula I' may look complicated, it is easy to give intuition for it. As long as a node v has not received any message, it does not participate is the protocol and is in state $Init(v)$. Upon arrival of a first message, the node changes status and moves to $busy[v]$. The node remains in this state until it has received a message from all its neighbors, then performs a *REPORT* or *RESULT* action, and moves to its final state $Done(v)$. The following "mutual exclusion" property is a logical consequence of invariant I_2 and the definition of state functions *Init* and *Done*, and therefore holds for all reachable states of $DSum^h$:

$$ME(v) \triangleq \neg(Init(v) \wedge busy[v]) \wedge \neg(Init(v) \wedge Done(v)) \wedge \neg(busy[v] \wedge Done(v))$$

Together with formula $I_4(v)$, $ME(v)$ says that in any reachable state each node is in exactly one of the three states $Init(v)$, $busy[v]$ or $Done(v)$. Formulas I_5-I_{10} specify, for each node v, for each of the three possible states of v, and for each outgoing link of v, how many messages have been sent over that link. And since this number is always either 0 or 1, this implies that during each execution at most one message can be sent over each link (formula C_1 below). In order to make the induction work, a final conjunct I_{11} is needed in I' that says that, except for the initial state of v, $cnt[v]$ gives the total number of links over which no message has yet been received by v. In the routine proof that I' is an invariant, it is convenient to use the logical consequences C_1-C_3 of $I \wedge I'$ that are stated in Lemma 3. Properties C_4-C_7 of Lemma 3 are also logical consequences of $I \wedge I'$, and will play a role later on in this paper.

Lemma 3. *For all v and e, the following formulas are logical consequences of $I \wedge I'$ and the definitions of the state functions:*

$$C_1(e) \triangleq Sent(e) \leq 1$$
$$C_2(v) \triangleq (\forall e \in \mathsf{to}(v) : rcvd[e] = 1) \leftrightarrow Rcvd(v) = \mathsf{size}(\mathsf{to}(v))$$
$$C_3(e) \triangleq mq[e] \neq \mathsf{empty} \wedge \neg busy[\mathsf{target}(e)] \rightarrow Init(\mathsf{target}(e))$$
$$C_4(e) \triangleq e \neq \mathsf{e}_0 \wedge mq[e] \neq \mathsf{empty} \rightarrow \neg Init(\mathsf{source}(e))$$
$$C_5(v) \triangleq \neg Init(v) \rightarrow \neg Init(\mathsf{source}(par[v]))$$
$$C_6(e) \triangleq Init(\mathsf{target}(e)) \wedge mq[e] = \mathsf{empty} \rightarrow Init(\mathsf{source}(e))$$
$$C_7(v) \triangleq v \neq \mathsf{v}_0 \wedge \neg Init(v) \wedge Sent(par[v]^{-1}) = 1 \rightarrow Done(v)$$

Lemma 4. *Property I' holds for all reachable states of $DSum^h$.*

3.3 Adding a Prophecy Variable

Intuitively, in the first phase of the algorithm a spanning tree is constructed with root v_0, and this spanning tree is used to accumulate values in the second phase. When the algorithm starts, it not clear how the spanning tree is going to look like and in fact any spanning tree is still possible. While the algorithm proceeds, the spanning tree is constructed step by step. The choice whether an arbitrary link will be part of the spanning tree depends on the relative speeds of the processors, and is entirely nondeterministic. Such unpredictable, nondeterministic behavior is typical for distributed computation but often complicates analysis.

Fortunately, the concept of a *prophecy variable* of Abadi and Lamport [1] allows us to reduce the nondeterminism of the algorithm or, more precisely, to push nondeterminism backwards to the initial state. We add to $DSum^h$ a new variable *tree*, which records an initial guess of the spanning tree and enforces (as a self-fulfilling prophecy) that the actual spanning tree that is constructed during execution is equal to this initial guess. Figure 4 describes the automaton $DSum^{hp}$ obtained in this way. Boxes highlight the places where $DSum^{hp}$ differs from $DSum^h$. In Figure 4, tree is a function that tells for each set of links whether or not it is a tree. More formally, for $E \subseteq \mathbf{E}$ and $V = \{\mathsf{source}(e), \mathsf{target}(e) \mid e \in E\}$, $\mathsf{tree}(E) = \mathsf{true}$ iff either $E = \emptyset$ or there exists a node $v \in V$ such that for all $v' \in V$ there is a unique path of links in E leading from v to v'.

In order to show that *tree* is a prophecy variable in the sense of [1, 14], i.e., a backrward simulation whose inverse is a refinement, we establish a prophecy relation from $DSum^h$ to $DSum^{hp}$ For this, we need two trivial invariants and two further lemmas.

Lemma 5. *For all reachable states of $DSum^{hp}$ and for all v:*

$$T_1(v) \triangleq \neg Init(v) \rightarrow par[v] = tree[v]$$

Lemma 6. *For all reachable states of $DSum^{hp}$:*

$$T_2 \triangleq tree[\mathsf{v}_0] = \mathsf{e}_0 \wedge (\forall v : v = \mathbf{target}(tree[v])) \wedge \mathbf{tree}(\{tree[v] \mid v \in \mathbf{V}/\{\mathsf{v}_0\}\})$$

Internal: *MSG*
REPORT
Output: *RESULT*

State Variables: $busy : \mathbf{V} \rightarrow \mathbf{Bool}$
$par : \mathbf{V} \rightarrow \mathbf{E}$
$total : \mathbf{V} \rightarrow \mathbf{M}$
$cnt : \mathbf{V} \rightarrow \mathbf{Int}$
$mq : \mathbf{E} \rightarrow \mathbf{M}^*$
$rcvd : \mathbf{E} \rightarrow \mathbf{Int}$
$\boxed{tree : \mathbf{V} \rightarrow \mathbf{E}}$

Init: $\wedge\ \forall v : \neg busy[v]$
$\wedge\ \forall e : mq[e] = \text{if } e{=}\mathsf{e}_0 \text{ then append}(0, \text{empty}) \text{ else empty}$
$\wedge\ \forall e : rcvd[e] = 0$
$\boxed{\wedge\ tree[\mathsf{v}_0] = \mathsf{e}_0 \wedge (\forall v : v = \text{target}(tree[v])) \wedge \text{tree}(\{tree[v] \mid v \in \mathbf{V}/\{\mathsf{v}_0\}\})}$

MSG$(e : \mathbf{E}, m : \mathbf{M})$
Precondition:
$v = \text{target}(e) \wedge m = \text{head}(mq[e])\ \boxed{\wedge\ (busy[v] \vee e = tree[v])}$
Effect:
$mq[e] := \text{tail}(mq[e])$
$rcvd[e] := rcvd[e] + 1$
if $\neg busy[v]$ **then** $busy[v] := \text{true}$
$par[v] := e$
$total[v] := \text{weight}(v)$
$cnt[v] := \text{size}(\text{to}(v)) - 1$
for $f \in \text{from}(v)/\{e^{-1}\}$ **do** $mq[f] := \text{append}(0, mq[f])$
else $total[v] := total[v] + m$
$cnt[v] := cnt[v] - 1$

REPORT$(e : \mathbf{E}, m : \mathbf{M})$
Precondition:
$v = \text{source}(e) \neq \mathsf{v}_0 \wedge busy[v] \wedge cnt[v] = 0 \wedge e^{-1} = par[v] \wedge m = total[v]$
Effect:
$busy[v] := \text{false}$
$mq[e] := \text{append}(m, mq[e])$

RESULT$(m : \mathbf{M})$
Precondition:
$busy[\mathsf{v}_0] \wedge cnt[\mathsf{v}_0] = 0 \wedge m = total[\mathsf{v}_0]$
Effect:
$busy[\mathsf{v}_0] := \text{false}$

Fig. 4. I/O automaton $DSum^{hp}$ obtained from $DSum^{h}$ by adding prophecy variable *tree*.

Lemma 7. *Define $T \triangleq \forall v : T_1(v) \wedge T_2$ and let π be the projection function that maps states of $DSum^{hp}$ to states of $DSum^h$. Suppose a is an action and u and u' are states of $DSum^{hp}$ such that*

1. *$u.tree = u'.tree$,*
2. *$u' \models T$,*
3. *$\pi(u) \xrightarrow{a} \pi(u')$ is a step of $DSum^h$,*
4. *$\pi(u)$ is reachable.*

Then $u \xrightarrow{a} u'$ is a step of $DSum^{hp}$ and $u \models T$.

Lemma 8. *Suppose u is a state of $DSum^{hp}$ such that $\pi(u)$ is reachable and $u \models T$. Then u is reachable.*

Theorem 9. *The inverse of projection function π is a strong image-finite prophecy relation from $DSum^h$ to $DSum^{hp}$.*

3.4 A Refinement

In this subsection we will prove the existence of a refinement from $DSum^{hp}$ to S. For this we need two final invariants, which state that non-unit messages can only travel on the reversed spanning tree, and that there is a conservation of weight in the network.

Lemma 10. *For all reachable states of $DSum^{hp}$ and for all e,*

$$\mathsf{head}(mq[e]) \neq 0 \rightarrow e = tree[\mathsf{source}(e)]^{-1}$$

Lemma 11. *For all reachable states of $DSum^{hp}$:*

$$\begin{aligned}\sum_{v \in \mathbf{V}} \mathsf{weight}(v) = & \sum_{\{v \in \mathbf{V} \mid Init(v)\}} \mathsf{weight}(v) \\ & + \sum_{\{v \in \mathbf{V} \mid busy[v]\}} total[v] \\ & + \sum_{\{e \in \mathbf{E} \mid mq[e] \neq \mathsf{empty}\}} \mathsf{head}(mq[e]) \\ & + \text{if } Done(\mathsf{v_0}) \text{ then } total[\mathsf{v_0}] \text{ else } 0\end{aligned}$$

Theorem 12. *The function r from states of $DSum^{hp}$ to states of S defined by*

$$r(s) \models done \Leftrightarrow s \models Done(\mathsf{v_0})$$

is a refinement from $DSum^{hp}$ to S.

3.5 Inclusion of Fair Traces

Note that *traces*(*DSum*) $\subseteq$ *traces*(*S*) does not imply *fairtraces*(*DSum*) $\subseteq$ *fairtraces*(*S*). It might be that *DSum* does not produce any output but instead performs an infinite sequence of consecutive internal actions or gets into a state of deadlock before an output step has been done. However, using Lemma 4, we can prove the absence of divergent computation:

Lemma 13. *I/O automaton* $DSum^h$ *has no infinite executions.*

The proof that $DSum^h$ has no premature deadlocks is slightly more involved.

Lemma 14. *If a reachable state of* $DSum^h$ *has no outgoing steps then* $Done(\mathsf{v}_0)$ *holds in that state.*

Theorem 15. *fairtraces*(*DSum*) $\subseteq$ *fairtraces*(*S*).

4 Concluding Remarks

History relations together with refinements form a complete proof method for trace inclusion if the abstract automaton is deterministic [14]. Since I/O automaton *S* is trivially deterministic, this means that at least in theory there is no need to use prophecy variables in the correctness proof of *DSum*. In fact, it is not so difficult to eliminate the prophecy variable construction from this paper. The key step is to establish as an additional invariant that for all reachable states of $DSum^h$ the set $\{par[v] \mid v \neq \mathsf{v}_0 \wedge \neg Init(v)\}$ forms a tree with root v_0. This alternative proof is even slightly shorter than the proof outlined in this paper. However, I do not think that this is an argument against the use of the prophecy variable *tree*. This auxiliary variable formalizes an important intuition about the algorithm, namely that in each execution a spanning tree is constructed. By fixing this tree, the prophecy variable makes it conceptually simpler to reason about the algorithm.

Since forward simulations form a complete proof method for trace inclusion if the abstract automaton is deterministic [14], the history variable *rcvd* can be eliminated from the proof of this paper in favor of a forward simulation relation. But again, even though this will probably lead to a small reduction in the size of the proof, there are good reasons to keep this auxiliary variable. In the intuitive reasoning about the protocol the number of messages received over the links plays an important role, and the history variable construction makes it possible to formalize this reasoning.

The verification of this paper has not yet been proof-checked by computer. I think that it will be worthwhile to do this, building on earlier work of [20, 6, 17, 3]. An interesting question here is whether the correctness of the history variable construction can be verified fully automatically by a theorem prover, by simply checking the (trivial) proof obligations of a history relation (This would eliminate the need to formalize the meta-theory of history variables.). Another question is whether the prophecy variable construction can be formalized easily, or whether it is simpler to formalize a proof that does not use this construction.

Although I have carried out the verification using the I/O automaton model, it is probably trivial to translate this story to other state based models, such as

Lamport's Temporal Logic of Actions [10]. Since liveness issues do not play a rôle, also a process algebraic verification in a calculus such as μCRL [5] should not be too difficult.

Acknowledgement

Ching-Tsun Chou outlined how the prophecy variable construction in my proof can be avoided and suggested many improvements. Thanks to David Griffioen for proofreading.

References

1. M. Abadi and L. Lamport. The existence of refinement mappings. *Theoretical Computer Science*, 82(2):253–284, 1991.
2. K.M. Chandy and J. Misra. *Parallel Program Design. A Foundation.* Addison-Wesley, 1988.
3. C.-T. Chou. Mechanical verification of distributed algorithms in higher-order logic. In T.F. Melham and J. Camilleri, editors, *Proceedings 7th International Workshop on Higher-Order Logic and its Applications*, volume 859 of *Lecture Notes in Computer Science*, pages 158–176. Springer-Verlag, 1994. A revised version will appear in *The Computer Journal*, 1995.
4. C.-T. Chou. Practical use of the notions of events and causality in reasoning about distributed algorithms. CS Report #940035, UCLA, October 1994. Available via anonymous ftp at the URL ftp://ftp.cs.ucla.edu/pub/chou/nil.ps.
5. J.F. Groote and A. Ponse. Proof theory for μCRL: A language for processes with data. In D.J. Andrews, J.F. Groote, and C.A. Middelburg, editors, *Proceedings of the International Workshop on Semantics of Specification Languages*, Workshops in Computer Science, pages 231–250. Springer-Verlag, 1993.
6. L. Helmink, M.P.A. Sellink, and F.W. Vaandrager. Proof-checking a data link protocol. In H. Barendregt and T. Nipkow, editors, *Proceedings International Workshop TYPES'93*, Nijmegen, The Netherlands, May 1993, volume 806 of *Lecture Notes in Computer Science*, pages 127–165. Springer-Verlag, 1994. Full version available as Report CS-R9420, CWI, Amsterdam, March 1994.
7. B. Jonsson. Compositional specification and verification of distributed systems. *ACM Transactions on Programming Languages and Systems*, 16(2):259–303, March 1994.
8. S.S. Lam and A.U. Shankar. Protocol verification via projections. *IEEE Transactions on Software Engineering*, 10(4):325–342, July 1984.
9. L. Lamport. Specifying concurrent program modules. *ACM Transactions on Programming Languages and Systems*, 5(2):190–222, 1983.
10. L. Lamport. The temporal logic of actions. *ACM Transactions on Programming Languages and Systems*, 16(3):872–923, March 1994.
11. P. Lucas. Two constructive realizations of the block concept and their equivalence. Technical Report 25.085, IBM Laboratory, Vienna, June 1968.
12. N.A. Lynch and M.R. Tuttle. Hierarchical correctness proofs for distributed algorithms. In *Proceedings of the 6th Annual ACM Symposium on Principles of Distributed Computing*, pages 137–151, August 1987. A full version is available as MIT Technical Report MIT/LCS/TR-387.
13. N.A. Lynch and M.R. Tuttle. An introduction to input/output automata. *CWI Quarterly*, 2(3):219–246, September 1989.

14. N.A. Lynch and F.W. Vaandrager. Forward and backward simulations – part I: Untimed systems. Technical Memo MIT/LCS/TM-486.b (new version of TM-486), Laboratory for Computer Science, Massachusetts Institute of Technolog, Cambridge, MA, August 1994. To appear in *Information and Computation.*
15. Z. Manna and A. Pnueli. *The Temporal Logic of Reactive and Concurrent Systems: Specification.* Springer-Verlag, 1992.
16. R. Milner. *Communication and Concurrency.* Prentice-Hall International, Englewood Cliffs, 1989.
17. T. Nipkow and K. Slind. I/O automata in Isabelle/HOL. In *Proceedings International Workshop TYPES'94*, Lecture Notes in Computer Science. Springer-Verlag, 1995. To appear.
18. S. Owicki and D. Gries. An axiomatic proof technique for parallel programs. *Acta Informatica*, 6(4):319–340, 1976.
19. A. Segall. Distributed network protocols. *IEEE Transactions on Information Theory*, IT-29(2):23–35, January 1983.
20. J. Søgaard-Andersen, S. Garland, J. Guttag, N.A. Lynch, and A. Pogosyants. Computer-assisted simulation proofs. In C. Courcoubetis, editor, *Proceedings of the 5th International Conference on Computer Aided Verification*, Elounda, Greece, volume 697 of *Lecture Notes in Computer Science*, pages 305–319. Springer-Verlag, 1993.
21. F.W. Vaandrager. Verification of a distributed summation algorithm. Report CS-R9505, CWI, Amsterdam, January 1995. A preliminary version appeared in K.R. Apt, A. Schrijver, N.M. Temme, editors, *From Universal Morphisms to Megabytes – a Baayen Space Odyssey*, pages 593–608, CWI, Amsterdam, 1994.

Confluence for Process Verification

J.F. Groote and M.P.A. Sellink

Department of Philosophy, Utrecht University,
P.O. Box 80.126, 3508 TC Utrecht, The Netherlands,
jfg@phil.ruu.nl, alex@phil.ruu.nl

Abstract. We provide several notions of confluence in processes and we show how these relate to τ-inertness, i.e. if $s \xrightarrow{\tau} s'$, then s and s' are equivalent. Using deterministic linear processes we show how these notions can conveniently be used to reduce the size of state spaces and simplify the structure of processes while preserving equivalence.

1 Introduction

In his seminal book [8] Milner devotes a chapter to the notions strong- and observation confluence in process theory. Many other authors have confirmed the importance of confluence. E.g. in [7, 9] the notion is used for on the fly reduction of finite state spaces and in [8] it has been used for the verification of protocols.

We felt that a more general treatment of the notion of confluence is in order. The first reason for this is that the treatment of confluence has always been somewhat ad hoc in the setting of process theory. This strongly contrasts with for instance term rewriting, where confluence is one of the major topics. In particular, we want to clarify the relation with *τ-inertness*, which says that if $s \xrightarrow{\tau} s'$, then s and s' are equivalent in some sense.

The second reason is that we want to develop systematic ways to prove distributed systems correct in a precise and formal fashion. In this way we want to provide techniques to construct fault free distributed systems. For this purpose the language μCRL is designed, being process algebra extended with data [6]. In [5] a proof theory has been developed and in [10] it has been shown how correctness proofs can be checked using proof checkers, giving us the means to deliver proofs with the highest thinkable level of precision. In order to show the applicability of the techniques several protocols have been verified (see [5] for an overview), both from theoretical and practical perspectives. Experience with these protocols gave rise to the development of new and the adaptation of existing techniques to make systematic verification possible [3, 4]. Employing confluence also belongs to these techniques. It appears to enable easier verification of distributed systems, which in essence boils down to the application of τ-inertness.

In the first part of the paper we address the relationship between confluence and τ-inertness. The comparable notions proposed in [8] all imply τ-inertness. We come up with a more general notion, namely weakly $\sim$-confluence where $\sim$ is finite trace equivalence or weak- or branching bisimulation. For several notions of equivalence we show that weakly $\sim$-confluence and τ-inertness with respect to $\sim$ coincide provided the process is τ-well founded (there are no infinite τ paths).

However, there are many protocols, with infinite τ paths, for instance communication protocols over unreliable channels. Therefore, we introduce the distinction between progressing and non-progressing τ's and show that weakly progressing confluence is enough to guarantee τ-inertness. Contrary to what one would expect, weakly progressing $\sim$-confluence does not imply τ-inertness.

In the second part of this paper we direct our attention to establishing confluence. It does hardly make sense to establish confluence directly on Transition Systems (TSs), because these are generally far too large to be represented. Therefore, we try to establish confluence on Linear Processes [4] which can represent large transition systems in a compact symbolic way.

In the third part we show how we can use τ-inertness to reduce state spaces both on TSs and on linear processes. We provide two examples illustrating that exploiting confluence often reduces the size of state spaces considerably and simplifies the structure of distributed systems, while preserving branching bisimulation. This is in general a very profitable preprocessing step before analysis, testing or simulation of a distributed system.

Acknowledgements. We thank Marc Bezem for discussion in an early phase of the project and Frits Vaandrager for demonstrating the importance of confluence in the verification of a leader election protocol. Furthermore we thank Jaco van de Pol and Wan Fokkink for comments on a draft version of this paper.

2 Preliminary Definitions

Throughout this paper we fix the set of actions ACT, which contains an internal action τ. From Section 4 onwards we assume that ACT contains $\tau_>$ and $\tau_<$.

Definition 2.1. *A Transition System (TS) is a pair* $(S, \longrightarrow\!\!\!\triangleright)$ *with* S *a set and* $\longrightarrow\!\!\!\triangleright \subseteq S \times \text{ACT} \times S$. *We write* $s \xrightarrow{a}\!\!\triangleright\, t$ *instead of* $\longrightarrow\!\!\!\triangleright(s, a, t)$.

Definition 2.2. *A TS* $(S, \longrightarrow\!\!\!\triangleright)$ *is called a-well-founded iff there is no infinite sequence of the form* $s_1 \xrightarrow{a}\!\!\triangleright\, s_2 \xrightarrow{a}\!\!\triangleright\, s_3 \xrightarrow{a}\!\!\triangleright \cdots$.

Convention 2.3. *We introduce the following notations* $(n \geq 1)$:

- $s \xrightarrow{a^*}\!\!\triangleright\, t$ *means* $s \equiv u_1 \xrightarrow{a}\!\!\triangleright \cdots \xrightarrow{a}\!\!\triangleright\, u_n \equiv t$ *for some* $u_1, \ldots, u_n$.
- $s \xrightarrow{ab}\!\!\triangleright\, t$ *means* $s \xrightarrow{a}\!\!\triangleright\, u \xrightarrow{b}\!\!\triangleright\, t$ *for some* u.
- $s \xRightarrow{a}\!\!\triangleright\, t$ *means* $s \xrightarrow{\tau^*}\!\!\triangleright\, u_1 \xrightarrow{a}\!\!\triangleright\, u_2 \xrightarrow{\tau^*}\!\!\triangleright\, t$ *for some* u_1, u_2.
- $s \underset{a}{\Longrightarrow}\!\!\triangleright\, t$ *means* $s \xRightarrow{a}\!\!\triangleright\, t \vee (a \equiv \tau \wedge s \xrightarrow{\tau^*}\!\!\triangleright\, t)$.

Definition 2.4. *A relation $R \subseteq S \times S'$ is called a branching bisimulation on $(S, \longrightarrow\!\!\!\rhd)$ and $(S', \longrightarrow\!\!\!\blacktriangleright)$ iff*

$$sRs' \Longrightarrow \begin{cases} s \overset{a}{\longrightarrow\!\!\!\rhd} t & \Longrightarrow \; [a \equiv \tau \wedge tRs'] \vee \\ & \; [\exists u, u' . s' \overset{\tau^*}{\longrightarrow\!\!\!\blacktriangleright} u \overset{a}{\longrightarrow\!\!\!\blacktriangleright} u' \wedge sRu \wedge tRu'] \\ s' \overset{a}{\longrightarrow\!\!\!\blacktriangleright} t' & \Longrightarrow \; [a \equiv \tau \wedge sRt'] \vee \\ & \; [\exists u, u' . s \overset{\tau^*}{\longrightarrow\!\!\!\rhd} u \overset{a}{\longrightarrow\!\!\!\rhd} u' \wedge uRs' \wedge u'Rt'] \end{cases}$$

for all $s \in S$ and $s' \in S'$. We say that R is a branching bisimulation on $(S, \longrightarrow\!\!\!\rhd)$ iff R is a branching bisimulation on $(S, \longrightarrow\!\!\!\rhd)$ and $(S, \longrightarrow\!\!\!\rhd)$. The union of all branching bisimulations is denoted as $\underline{\leftrightarrow}_b$.

In [8] weak bisimulation is introduced, which we denote here by $\underline{\leftrightarrow}_w$. Another well-known equivalence is finite trace equivalence with invisible τ's, which we denote by $\approx_{\mathrm{Tr}}$. As these notions are fairly standard we do not define them explicitly. But as $\underline{\leftrightarrow}_b \subseteq \underline{\leftrightarrow}_w \subseteq \approx_{\mathrm{Tr}}$, almost all results that we present for branching bisimulation carry immediately over to weak bisimulation and finite trace equivalence.

3 Confluence and τ-Inertness

In this section we present three different notions of *confluence*, namely strong confluence, weak confluence and weak $\sim$-confluence, where $\sim$ is an arbitrary equivalence relation. We investigate whether or not the different notions of confluence are strong enough to serve as a condition for

$$s \overset{\tau}{\longrightarrow\!\!\!\rhd} t \;\Longrightarrow\; s \sim t \tag{1}$$

to hold. TSs that satisfy (1) for all $s, t \in S$ are called *τ-inert with respect to $\sim$.*

3.1 Strong Confluence

Definition 3.1. *A TS $(S, \longrightarrow\!\!\!\rhd)$ is called strongly confluent iff for all pairs $s \overset{a}{\longrightarrow\!\!\!\rhd} t$ and $s \overset{\tau}{\longrightarrow\!\!\!\rhd} s'$ of different steps there exists a state t' such that $t \overset{\tau}{\longrightarrow\!\!\!\rhd} t'$ and $s' \overset{a}{\longrightarrow\!\!\!\rhd} t'$. In a diagram:*

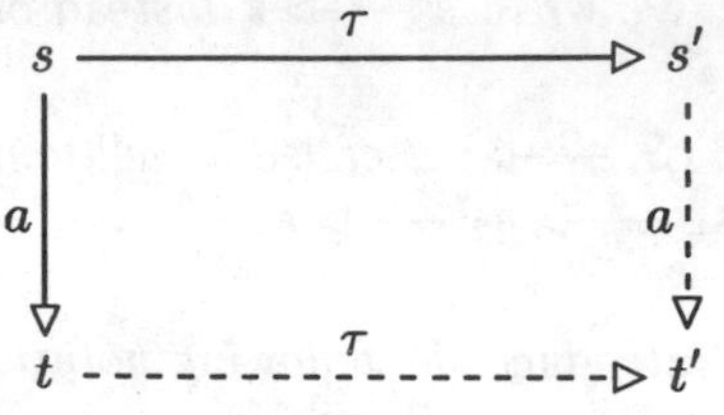

Omitting the word 'different' in Definition 3.1 would give a stronger notion.

$$s \overset{\tau}{\longrightarrow\!\!\!\rhd} t$$

is strongly confluent, but would not be strongly confluent if the word 'different' was omitted.

Theorem 3.2. *Strongly confluent TSs are τ-inert with respect to $\leftrightarrow_b$ ($\leftrightarrow_w$ and $\approx_{\mathrm{Tr}}$).*

The converse of Theorem 3.2 is obviously not valid. A TS that is τ-inert with respect to $\leftrightarrow_b$, is not necessarily strongly confluent. As a counter example one can take the process

$$t \xleftarrow{\tau} s \xrightarrow{\tau} s' \tag{2}$$

This counter example means that strong confluence is actually a stronger notion than we need since we are primarily interested in τ-inertness (wrt. $\leftrightarrow_b$). Hence we introduce a weaker notion of confluence, which differs from strong confluence in that we allow zero or more τ-steps in the paths from t to t' and from s' to t'.

3.2 Weak confluence

Definition 3.3. *A TS $(S, \longrightarrow)$ is called weakly confluent iff for each pair $s \xrightarrow{a} t$ and $s \xrightarrow{\tau} s'$ of different steps there exists a state t' such that $s' \stackrel{a}{\Longrightarrow} t'$ and $t \xrightarrow{\tau^*} t'$. In a diagram:*

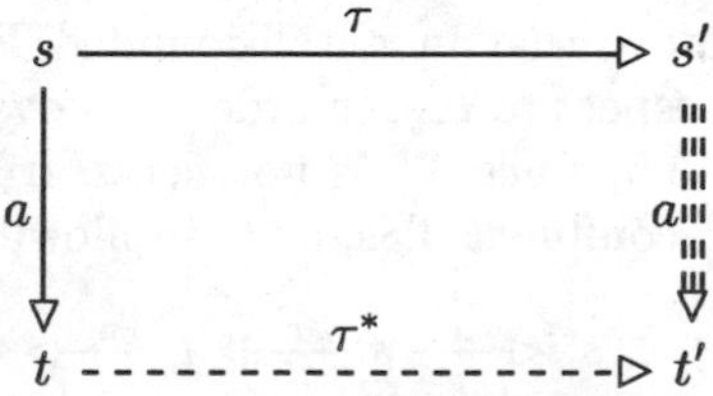

The following example (due to Roland Bol) shows that weak confluence is too weak to serve as a condition for (1) to hold, i.e. weakly confluent TSs are not necessarily τ-inert with respect to $\leftrightarrow_b$.

$$t \xleftarrow{a} s \underset{\tau}{\overset{\tau}{\rightleftarrows}} s' \xrightarrow{\tau} t' \tag{3}$$

This TS is weakly confluent but $s' \xrightarrow{\tau} t'$ does not connect bisimilar states if $a \not\equiv \tau$. Note that (3) is not τ-well-founded. In Theorem 3.5 we state that τ-well-founded, weakly confluent TSs are τ-inert with respect to $\leftrightarrow_b$.

The following lemma is frequently used in the proofs of the main theorems.

Lemma 3.4. *Let $(S, \longrightarrow)$ be τ-well-founded and weakly confluent. If $s \xrightarrow{\tau^*} s'$ and $s \xrightarrow{\tau^*} t$, then there exists a t' such that $s' \xrightarrow{\tau^*} t'$ and $t \xrightarrow{\tau^*} t'$.*

Theorem 3.5. *Let $(S, \longrightarrow)$ be τ-well-founded and weakly confluent, then $(S, \longrightarrow)$ is τ-inert with respect to $\leftrightarrow_b$ ($\leftrightarrow_w$ and $\approx_{\mathrm{Tr}}$).*

This theorem is proven by showing that $\mathcal{T}^* = \{(x, y) \mid x \xrightarrow{\tau^*} y\}$ is a branching bisimulation.

Note that the process depicted by (2) also shows that τ-inertness with respect to $\leftrightarrow_b$ does not imply weak confluence. So weak confluence and τ-inertness with respect to $\leftrightarrow_b$ are independent notions. If we restrict ourselves to the τ-well-founded TSs we have a strict inclusion of the weakly confluent TSs into the TSs that are τ-inert with respect to $\leftrightarrow_b$.

3.3 Weak $\sim$-Confluence

In the definition below we introduce weak $\sim$-confluence where $\sim$ is one of $\leftrightarrows_b$, $\leftrightarrows_w$ or $\approx_{\mathrm{Tr}}$. For branching and weak bisimulation, weak $\sim$-confluence is optimal in the sense that it is equivalent with τ-inertness with respect to $\sim$ for τ-well-founded systems. For $\approx_{\mathrm{Tr}}$ it is a sufficient condition.

Definition 3.6. *A TS $(S, \longrightarrow)$ is called weakly $\sim$-confluent iff for all $a \in$ Act and for each pair $s \xrightarrow{a} t$ and $s \xrightarrow{\tau} s'$ of different steps there exists states u and u' such that $u \sim u'$, $s' \overset{a}{\Longrightarrow} u'$ and $t \xrightarrow{\tau^*} u$. In a diagram:*

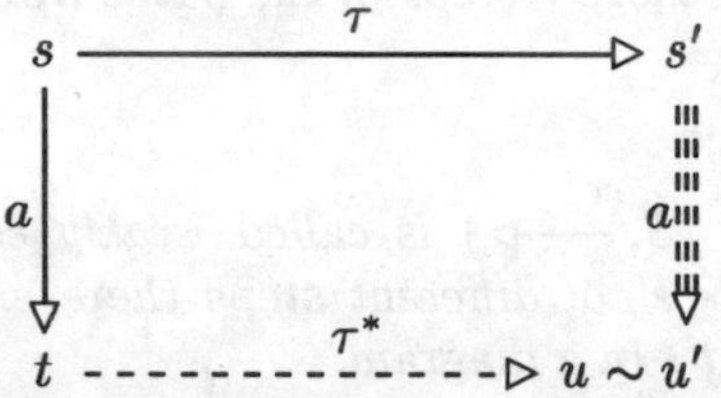

Suppose we want to prove that in τ-well-founded TSs weak $\leftrightarrows_b$-confluence implies τ-inertness with respect to $\leftrightarrows_b$. In order to prove this we cannot simply copy the proof of Theorem 3.5, since $\mathcal{T}^*$ is not necessarily a branching bisimulation relation on weakly $\leftrightarrows_b$-confluent TSs, as the following example shows:

$$s' \xleftarrow{a} s \xrightarrow{\tau} t \xrightarrow{a} t' \tag{4}$$

Here $\{(s,s),(s',s'),(s,t),(t,t),(t',t')\}$ is not a branching bisimulation relation although the TS is weakly $\leftrightarrows_b$-confluent. The diagram above is also an example of a TS that is weakly $\leftrightarrows_b$-confluent but not weakly confluent.

Theorem 3.7. *Let $(S, \longrightarrow)$ be τ-well-founded. Then $(S, \longrightarrow)$ is weakly $\leftrightarrows_b$-confluent iff $(S, \longrightarrow)$ is τ-inert with respect to $\leftrightarrows_b$.*

Theorem 3.8. *Let $(S, \longrightarrow)$ be τ-well-founded. Then $(S, \longrightarrow)$ is weakly $\leftrightarrows_w$-confluent iff $(S, \longrightarrow)$ is τ-inert with respect to $\leftrightarrows_w$.*

We need the τ-well-foundedness of $(S, \longrightarrow)$ in Theorems 3.7 and 3.8 only in the proof from left to right.

Theorem 3.9. *Let $(S, \longrightarrow)$ be τ-well-founded. If $(S, \longrightarrow)$ is weakly $\approx_{\mathrm{Tr}}$-confluent then $(S, \longrightarrow)$ is τ-inert with respect to $\approx_{\mathrm{Tr}}$.*

The converse of Theorem 3.9 does not hold.

We conclude this section with an overview of the results, which have been depicted in Figure 1. Below the horizontal line we have the τ-well-founded TSs. We see that strong confluence always implies τ-inertness with respect to $\leftrightarrows_b$. The other two notions of confluence do not imply τ-inertness with respect to $\leftrightarrows_b$. However, the counter examples are not τ-well-founded (above the horizontal line). Finally, we see that weak $\leftrightarrows_b$-confluence and τ-inertness with respect to $\leftrightarrows_b$ coincide for τ-well-founded TSs (below the horizontal line).

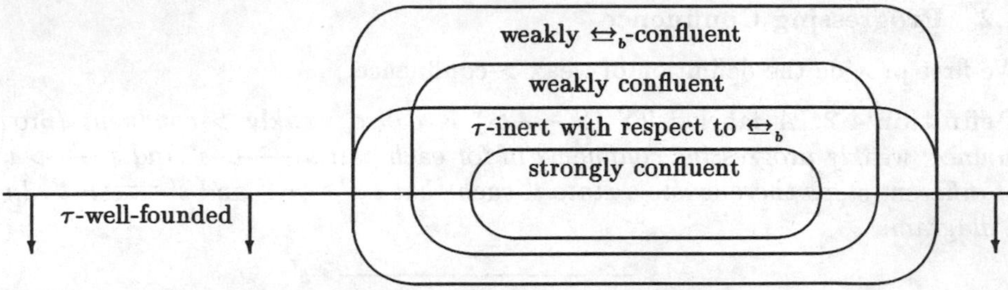

Fig. 1. The TSs in a diagram

4 Transition Systems that are not τ-Well-Founded

Most of the results in Section 3 rely on τ-well-foundedness of the TS in question. However, many realistic examples of protocol specifications correspond to TSs that are not τ-well-founded. As soon as a protocol internally consists in some kind of correction mechanism (e.g. retransmissions in a data link protocol) the specification of that protocol will contain a τ-loop. In Section 7.2 we see an example of this phenomenon.

Since we feel applicability to realistic examples is important, we considered the requirement that the TS has to be τ-well-founded a serious drawback. Therefore, we distinguish between what we call *progressing* τ-steps, denoted by $\tau_>$ and *non-progressing* τ-steps, denoted by $\tau_<$. This enables us to formulate a slightly more subtle notion of confluence, which is sufficiently strong for our purposes and only relies on well-foundedness of the *progressing* τ-steps.

4.1 Progressing and non-progressing τ-steps

Convention 4.1. *We use the following notations:*

- $s \xrightarrow{\tau_>} t$ *for a progressing* τ*-step from* s *to* t,
- $s \xrightarrow{\tau_<} t$ *for a non-progressing* τ*-step from* s *to* t,
- $s \xrightarrow{\tau} t$ *for* $s \xrightarrow{\tau_>} t$ *or* $s \xrightarrow{\tau_<} t$,
- $s \stackrel{a}{\Longrightarrow} t$ *for* $s \xrightarrow{\tau_>^*} s' \xrightarrow{a} t' \xrightarrow{\tau_>^*} t$.
- $s \stackrel{a}{\Longrightarrow} t$ *for* $s \stackrel{a}{\Longrightarrow} t \;\vee\; (a \equiv \tau \wedge s \xrightarrow{\tau_>^*} t)$.

From now on we try to prove $\tau_>$-inertness with respect to $\sim$, instead of τ-inertness with respect to $\sim$. In a formula:

$$s \xrightarrow{\tau_>} t \implies s \sim t \tag{5}$$

It should be noted that the definition of finite trace equivalence, and branching and weak bisimulation are not affected by the distinction of progressing and non-progressing τ-steps.

4.2 Progressing Confluence

We first provide the definition of weak $>$-confluence.

Definition 4.2. *A labeled TS $(S, \longrightarrow\!\!\triangleright)$ is called weakly $>$-confluent (pronounce: weakly progressing confluent) iff for each pair $s \xrightarrow{\tau_>}\!\!\triangleright\, s'$ and $s \xrightarrow{a}\!\!\triangleright\, t$ of different steps there exists a state t' such that $t \xrightarrow{\tau_>^*}\!\!\triangleright\, t'$ and $s' \stackrel{a}{\Longrightarrow}\!\!\triangleright\, t'$. In a diagram:*

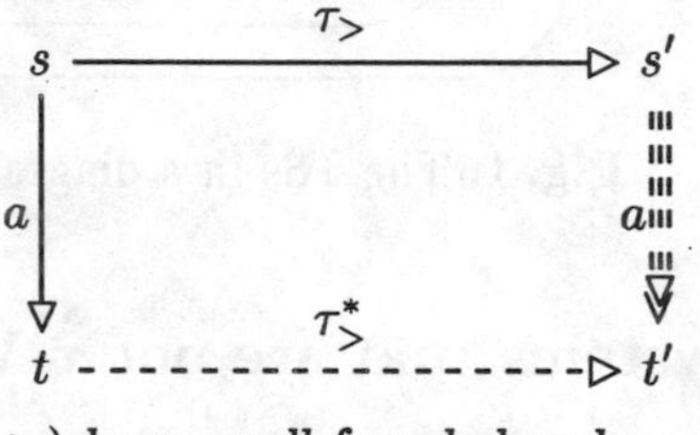

Theorem 4.3. *Let $(S, \longrightarrow\!\!\triangleright)$ be $\tau_>$-well-founded and weakly $>$-confluent, then $(S, \longrightarrow\!\!\triangleright)$ is $\tau_>$-inert with respect to $\leftrightarrow_b$ ($\leftrightarrow_w$ and $\approx_{\mathrm{Tr}}$).*

We could not weaken the notion of weak $>$-confluence to its progressing counterpart, maintaining $\tau_>$-inertness. Below we provide the obvious definition of weak $>$-$\sim$-confluence. In Proposition 4.5 we give a counter example.

Definition 4.4. *A labeled TS $(S, \longrightarrow\!\!\triangleright)$ is called weakly $>$-$\sim$-confluent iff for each pair $s \xrightarrow{\tau_>}\!\!\triangleright\, s'$ and $s \xrightarrow{a}\!\!\triangleright\, t$ of different steps there exist states u and u' such that $t \xrightarrow{\tau_>^*}\!\!\triangleright\, u$, $s' \stackrel{a}{\Longrightarrow}\!\!\triangleright\, u'$ and $u \sim u'$. In a diagram:*

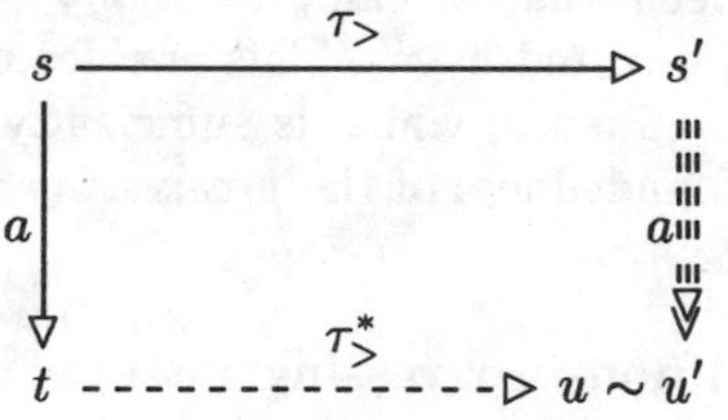

Proposition 4.5. *Let $\sim \in \{\leftrightarrow_b, \leftrightarrow_w, \approx_{\mathrm{Tr}}\}$ and suppose that $(S, \longrightarrow\!\!\triangleright)$ is weakly $>$-$\sim$-confluent and $\tau_>$-well-founded. Then $(S, \longrightarrow\!\!\triangleright)$ is not necessarily $\tau_>$-inert with respect to $\sim$.*

Proof. Let $a \not\equiv \tau$. The following TS is not $\tau_>$-inert with respect to $\sim$ since $s_4 \xrightarrow{\tau_>}\!\!\triangleright\, s_6$ and $s_4 \not\sim s_6$. However, weak $>$-$\sim$-confluence holds.

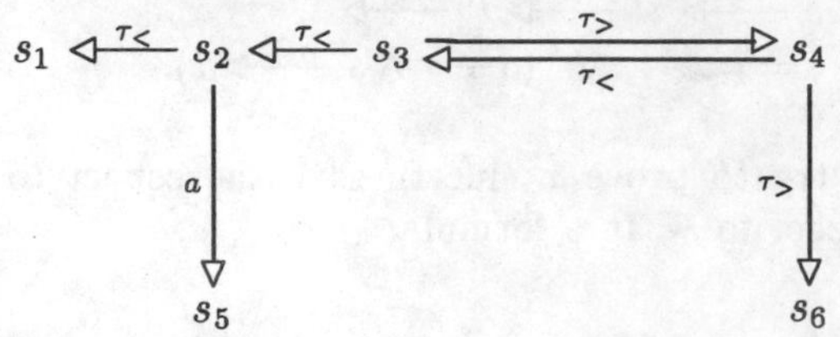

The non-trivial point to check is s_3. Weak $>$-$\sim$-confluence in this case is a direct consequence of the observation that $s_2 \sim s_4$. (Note that the τ-step from s_3 to s_2 can also be chosen progressing in this counter example.) □

5 Confluence of Linear Processes

We want to use the notion confluence to verify the correctness of processes. In order to do so, we must be able to determine whether a TS is confluent. This is in general not possible, because the TSs belonging to distributed systems are often too large to be handled as plain objects. In order to manipulate with large state spaces (*Deterministic*) *Linear Process* ((*D-*)*LPs*) [4] can be used as in these D-LPs the state space is compactly encoded using data parameters. Moreover, processes that are described using the common process algebra operators, including parallelism and recursion, can straightforwardly be transformed to a D-LP, maintaining strong bisimulation.

In this section we describe how a D-LP can be shown to be confluent. In the next section we show how confluence is used to reduce the size of state spaces.

5.1 Linear Processes

Definition 5.1. *Let* $Act \subseteq \textsc{Act}$ *be a finite set of actions. A deterministic linear process equation is an expression of the form*

$$p(d) = \sum_{a \in Act} \sum_{e_a : E_a} a(f_a(d, e_a)) \cdot p(g_a(d, e_a)) \triangleleft b_a(d, e_a) \triangleright \delta$$

for data sorts D, E_a *and* F_a *and functions* $f_a : D \times E_a \longrightarrow F_a$, $g_a : D \times E_a \longrightarrow D$ *and* $b_a : D \times E_a \longrightarrow \mathbb{B}$ *where* $\mathbb{B}$ *is the sort of booleans. We assume that the internal action* τ ($\tau_>$ *and* $\tau_<$ *if progressing and non-progressing* τ*'s are distinguished) has no data parameter.*

In [4] summands without a recursive call are also allowed in the definition of a linear process. We omit these summands here.

It is straightforward to see how a linear process equation determines a TS. The process $p(d)$ can perform an action $a(f_a(d, e_a))$ for every $a \in Act$ and every data element e_a of sort E_a, provided the condition $b_a(d, e_a)$ holds. The process then continues as $p(g_a(d, e_a))$. Hence, the notions defined in the previous sections carry over directly.

It is well-known that modulo strong bisimulation a deterministic linear process equation has a unique solution p which is called a *deterministic linear process* (*D-LP*).

A linear process is called *convergent* iff the corresponding TS is τ-well-founded. When we distinguish between progressing and non-progressing τ's, we use the notion convergence with respect to the progressing τ's (i.e. $\tau_>$).

Definition 5.2. *A linear process as defined in definition 5.1 is called* $>$*-convergent iff there is a well-founded ordering* $<$ *on* D *such that for all* $d{:}D$ *and* $e_{\tau_>}{:}D_{\tau_>}$ *if* $b_{\tau_>}(d, e_{\tau_>})$, *then* $g_{\tau_>}(d, e_{\tau_>}) < d$.

5.2 A Condition for Strong Confluence

We provide sufficient criteria for p to be strongly confluent. Let p be a deterministic linear process as defined in Definition 5.1. The criteria can best be understood via the following diagram.

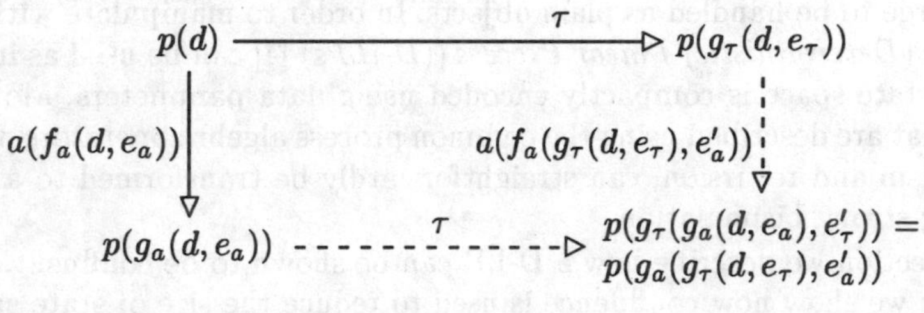

Note that in this diagram $p(g_a(d, e_a))$ and $p(g_\tau(d, e_\tau))$ are supposed to be different if $a = \tau$. We summarise the conditions in the following theorem.

Theorem 5.3. *The process p as defined in Definition 5.1 is strongly confluent if for all $a \in Act$, $e_1{:}E_a$, $e_2{:}E_\tau$ such that*

(i) $a = \tau \Rightarrow g_a(d, e_1) \neq g_\tau(d, e_2)$
(ii) $b_a(d, e_1) \wedge b_\tau(d, e_2)$

the following property holds:

$$\exists e_3{:}E_a, e_4{:}E_\tau \begin{cases} f_a(d, e_1) = f_a(g_\tau(d, e_2), e_3) \wedge \\ b_a(g_\tau(d, e_2), e_3) \wedge \\ b_\tau(g_a(d, e_1), e_4) \wedge \\ g_a(g_\tau(d, e_2), e_3) = g_\tau(g_a(d, e_1), e_4). \end{cases}$$

5.3 A Condition for Weak Progressing Confluence

In this section we derive a condition to establish that a D-LP is weakly confluent. This is more involved, because we must now speak about sequences of transitions.

In order to keep notation compact, we introduce some convenient abbreviations. Let $\sigma, \sigma', \ldots$ range over lists of pairs $\langle a, e_a \rangle$ with $a \in Act$ and $e_a{:}E_a$. We define $\mathcal{G}_d(\sigma)$ with $d \in D$ by induction over the length of σ:

$$\mathcal{G}_d(\lambda) = d \qquad \mathcal{G}_d(\sigma\langle a, e_a \rangle) = g_a(\mathcal{G}_d(\sigma), e_a)$$

Each σ determines an execution fragment:

$$\underbrace{p(d) \longrightarrow p(\mathcal{G}_d(\sigma))}_{\text{determined by } \sigma} \xrightarrow{a(f_a(\mathcal{G}_d(\sigma), e_a))} p(\mathcal{G}_d(\sigma\langle a, e_a \rangle))$$

is the execution fragment determined by $\sigma\langle a, e_a \rangle$. This execution fragment is allowed for $p(d)$ iff the conjunction $\mathcal{B}_d(\sigma)$ of all conditions associated to the actions in σ evaluates to *true*. The boolean $\mathcal{B}_d(\sigma)$ is also defined by induction to the length of σ:

$$\mathcal{B}_d(\lambda) = true \qquad\qquad \mathcal{B}_d(\sigma\langle a, e_a\rangle) = \mathcal{B}_d(\sigma) \wedge b_a(\mathcal{G}_d(\sigma), e_a)$$

We write $\pi_1(\sigma)$ for the sequence of actions that is obtained from σ by applying the first projection to all its elements. E.g. $\pi_1(\langle a, e_a\rangle\langle b, e_b\rangle) = ab$.

The diagram for weak >-confluence can be redrawn instantiated for D-LPs as shown below. The actions in the (possibly empty) sequences σ_1, σ_2 and σ_3 must all be progressing τ-steps, that is: $\pi_1(\sigma_i) = \tau_>^*$ for all $i = 1, 2, 3$.

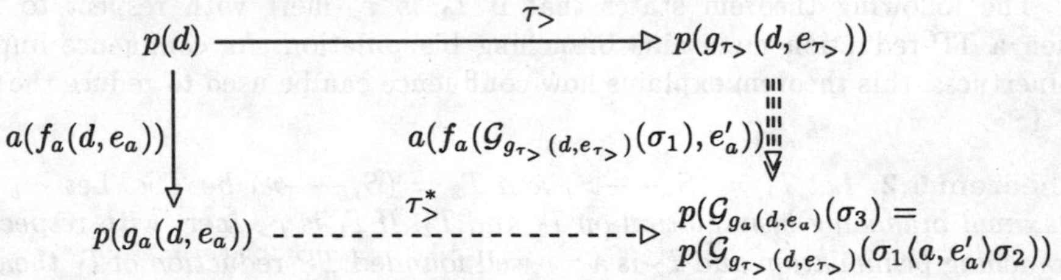

We summarise this diagram in the following theorem. Due to its generality the theorem looks rather complex. However, in those applications that we considered, the lists that are existentially quantified were mainly empty, which trivialises the main parts of the theorem.

Theorem 5.4. *The process p as defined in Definition 5.1 is weakly >-confluent if p is >-convergent and for all* $e_1{:}E_a$, $e_2{:}E_{\tau_>}$ *such that*

(i) $a = \tau_> \Rightarrow g_a(d, e_1) \neq g_{\tau_>}(d, e_2)$
(ii) $b_a(d, e_1) \wedge b_{\tau_>}(d, e_2)$

the following property holds:

$$\exists \sigma_1, e_3, \sigma_2, \sigma_3 \begin{cases} \pi_1(\sigma_i) = \tau_>^* \text{ for all } i = 1, 2, 3 \ \wedge \\ f_a(d, e_1) = f_a(\mathcal{G}_{g_{\tau_>}(d,e_2)}(\sigma_1), e_3) \ \wedge \\ \mathcal{B}_{g_a(d,e_1)}(\sigma_3) \ \wedge \\ \mathcal{B}_{g_{\tau_>}(d,e_2)}(\sigma) \ \wedge \\ \mathcal{G}_{g_a(d,e_1)}(\sigma_3) = \mathcal{G}_{g_{\tau_>}(d,e_2)}(\sigma) \end{cases}$$

where $\sigma = \sigma_1\langle a, e_3\rangle\sigma_2$, *or* $a = \tau$ *and* $\sigma = \sigma_1\sigma_2$.

6 State Space Reduction

Here we employ the results about confluence and τ-inertness that we have obtained thus far to achieve state space reductions and to simplify the behaviour of processes. In this section we work in the setting of branching bisimulation, but the results apply to weak bisimulation as well. First we present the results on TSs in general, and then on linear processes. This is done as for TSs the results are easy to understand. However, as argued in the previous section, the results can be applied more conveniently in the setting of linear processes.

Definition 6.1. *Let $T_1 = (S, \longrightarrow\!\!\triangleright)$ and $T_2 = (S, \longrightarrow\!\!\!\blacktriangleright)$ be TSs. We call T_2 a τ-Prioretised-reduction (TP-reduction) of T_1 iff*

(i) $\longrightarrow\!\!\!\blacktriangleright \subseteq \longrightarrow\!\!\triangleright$,
(ii) *for all $s, s' \in S$ if $s \xrightarrow{a}\!\!\triangleright s'$ then $s \xrightarrow{a}\!\!\!\blacktriangleright s'$ or $s \xrightarrow{\tau_>}\!\!\!\blacktriangleright s''$ for some s''.*

Clearly, T_2 can be obtained from T_1 by iteratively removing transitions from states as long as these keep at least one outgoing progressing τ-step. It does not need any comment that this may considerably reduce the state space of T_1, especially because large parts may become unreachable.

The following theorem states that if T_1 is $\tau_>$-inert with respect to $\leftrightarrow_b$, then a TP-reduction maintains branching bisimulation. As confluence implies τ-inertness, this theorem explains how confluence can be used to reduce the size of TSs.

Theorem 6.2. *Let $T_1 = (S, \longrightarrow\!\!\triangleright)$ and $T_2 = (S, \longrightarrow\!\!\!\blacktriangleright)$ be TSs. Let $\leftrightarrow_b$ the maximal branching bisimulation on T_1 and T_2. If T_1 is $\tau_>$-inert with respect to branching bisimulation and T_2 is a $\tau_>$-well founded TP-reduction of T_1 then for each state $s \in S$ $s \leftrightarrow_b s$.*

As has been shown in the previous section, weak $>$-confluence can relatively easy be determined on Linear Processes. We provide a way to reduce the complexity of a Linear Process. Below we reformulate the notion of a TP-reduction on linear processes. We assume that p is a linear process according to definition 5.1 and that the data sort E_τ is ordered by some total ordering $\prec$, which assigns priority among τ-actions in the TP-reduction.

Definition 6.3. *The TP-reduction of p is the linear process*

$$p_r(d) = \sum_{a \in Act} \sum_{e_a : E_a} a(f_a(d, e_a))\, p_r(g_a(d, e_a)) \lhd b_a(d, e_a) \wedge c_a(d, e_a) \rhd \delta$$

where

$$c_a(d, e_a) \equiv \begin{cases} \neg \exists e_{\tau_>} : E_{\tau_>}\ b(d, e_{\tau_>}) & \text{if } a \neq \tau_> \\ \neg \exists e_{\tau_>} : E_{\tau_>}\ e_a \prec e_{\tau_>} \wedge b(d, e_{\tau_>}) & \text{if } a = \tau_> \end{cases}$$

Note that for the sake of conciseness, we use $\exists$ in the condition $c_a(d, e_a)$, which does not adhere to the formal definition of μCRL.

Theorem 6.4. *If the linear process p is $>$-convergent and weakly $>$-confluent, then for all d:D*

$$\boxed{p(d) \leftrightarrow_b p_r(d)}$$

7 Two Examples

We illustrate how we apply the theory by means of two examples, where the structure of the processes is considerably simplified by a confluence argument.

7.1 Concatenation of Two Queues

Consider the following linear process $Q(\langle q_1, q_2\rangle)$ describing the concatenation of two queues q_1 and q_2. The boolean expression $ne(q)$ evaluates to *true* iff q is not empty. The function *in* is used to insert an element into a queue and the function *untoe* is used to remove that element of a queue which has been inserted first. The function *toe* returns this first element.

$$\begin{array}{rll} Q(\langle q_1,q_2\rangle) = \sum_{e_r:E_r} r(e_r)\cdot Q(\langle in(e_r,q_1),q_2\rangle) & \lhd\ true & \rhd\ \delta\ + \\ \tau\cdot Q(\langle untoe(q_1), in(toe(q_1),q_2)\rangle) & \lhd\ ne(q_1) & \rhd\ \delta\ + \\ s(toe(q_2))\cdot Q(\langle q_1, untoe(q_2)\rangle) & \lhd\ ne(q_2) & \rhd\ \delta \end{array}$$

As we can see, the process $Q(\langle q_1, q_2\rangle)$ can always read a datum and insert it in q_1. If q_2 is not empty then the 'toe' of q_2 can be sent. The internal action τ removes the first element of q_1 and inserts it in q_2.

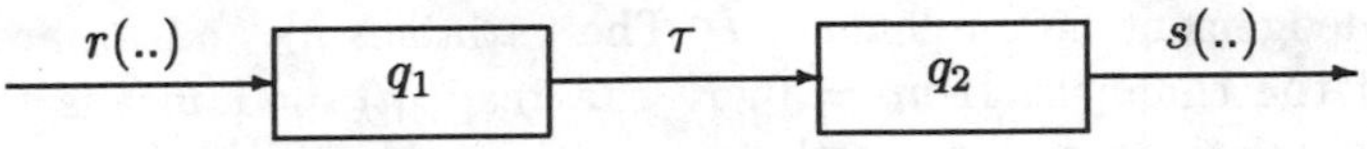

Using Theorem 5.3 we can straightforwardly prove that $Q(\langle q_1, q_2\rangle)$ is strongly confluent. For the read action r we find the condition that for all queues q_1, q_2 and $e_r{:}E_r$

$$\begin{array}{l} ne(q_1) \Rightarrow \exists e'_r{:}E_r\ e_r = e'_r \wedge ne(in(d,q_1)) \wedge \\ \langle in(e'_r, untoe(q_1)), in(toe(q_1),q_2)\rangle = \langle untoe(in(e_r,q_1)), in(toe(in(e_r,q_1)),q_2)\rangle. \end{array}$$

Similarly, we can formulate the following conditions for the action s. For all queues q_1, q_2

$$\begin{array}{l} (ne(q_2)\wedge ne(q_1)) \Rightarrow \\ \quad toe(q_2) = toe(in(toe(q_1),q_2)) \wedge \\ \quad ne(in(toe(q_1),q_2)) \wedge ne(q_1) \wedge \\ \quad \langle untoe(q_1), untoe(in(toe(q_1),q_2))\rangle = \langle untoe(q_1), in(toe(q_1), untoe(q_2))\rangle. \end{array}$$

With the appropriate axioms for queues, the validity of these facts is easily verified.

For the $a = \tau$ we find that the precondition $a = \tau\ \Rightarrow\ g_a(d,e_1) \neq g_\tau(d,e_2)$ is instantiated to $\tau = \tau \Rightarrow \langle untoe(q_1), in(toe(q_1),q_2)\rangle \neq \langle untoe(q_1), in(toe(q_1),q_2)\rangle$, which is a trivial contradiction.

Now, by Theorem 6.4, the following TP-reduced version (see Definition 6.3) of $Q(\langle q_1, q_2\rangle)$ is branching bisimilar to $Q(\langle q_1, q_2\rangle)$.

$$\begin{array}{lll} Q_r(\langle q_1,q_2\rangle) = & & \\ \sum_{e_r:E_r} r(e_r)\cdot\ Q_r(\langle in(e_r,q_1),q_2\rangle) & \lhd\ true\wedge empty(q_1) & \rhd\ \delta\ + \\ \quad\tau\cdot\ Q_r(\langle untoe(q_1), in(toe(q_1),q_2)\rangle) & \lhd\ ne(q_1) & \rhd\ \delta\ + \\ s(toe(q_2))\cdot\ Q_r(\langle q_1, untoe(q_2)\rangle) & \lhd\ ne(q_2)\wedge empty(q_1) & \rhd\ \delta \end{array}$$

Note that after the TP-reduction q_1 never contains more than one element!

7.2 The Alternating Bit Protocol

The alternating bit protocol (ABP) consists of a sender S, a receiver R and two unreliable channels K and L (See e.g. [2], page 108). Below we describe the ABP as the expanded parallel composition $S\|K\|L\|R$ where we leave the read action of the sender $r_1(x)$ and the send action of the receiver $s_4(d_r)$ visible. All other actions are renamed to progressing $\tau_>$'s, except those that correspond to the loss of data, which we renamed to $\tau_<$.

The variables d_s, b_s and n_s are the data parameter, the bit and the state of the sender; if $n_s = 0$, S can read a fresh datum ($r_1(x)$), if $n_s = 1$, it wants to send data to channel K and if $n_s = 2$, S is waiting for an acknowledgement. The variables d_r, b_r and n_r are respectively data, bit and state of the receiver; if $n_r = 0$, R is waiting for data to arrive via channel K, if $n_r = 1$, R wants to send an acknowledgement via L and if $n_r = 2$ R is ready to execute action $s_4(d_r)$, i.e. deliver a datum. d_k and b_k are data and bit in channel K and b_ℓ is the acknowledgement bit in channel L. The variables n_ℓ and n_k are the state variables of the channels. If $n_k = 0$, K can read; $n_k = 1$ means that K can choose to deliver the datum correctly ($n_k := 2$) or to loose the datum and report a checksum error *ce* ($n_k := 3$). After delivery of either message, K can read again. The meaning of the value of n_ℓ is similar.

$$
\begin{array}{l}
X(d_s,b_s,n_s,d_k,b_k,n_k,b_\ell,n_\ell,d_r,b_r,n_r) \; = \\
\sum_{x:\mathrm{D}} r_1(x)\cdot X[x/d_s][1/n_s] \lhd n_s = 0 \rhd \delta \; + \\
s_4(d_r)\cdot X[1/n_r] \lhd n_r = 2 \rhd \delta \; + \\
\sum_{n:\mathrm{N}} \tau_< \cdot X \left\{ \begin{array}{l} [3/n_k] \text{ if } n = 1 \\ [3/n_\ell] \text{ if } n = 2 \end{array} \right. \lhd \left\{ \begin{array}{l} (n_k = 1 \wedge n = 1) \vee \\ (n_\ell = 1 \wedge n = 2) \end{array} \right. \rhd \delta \; + \\
\sum_{n:\mathrm{N}} \tau_> \cdot X \left\{ \begin{array}{ll}
[2/n_s][d_s/d_k][b_s/b_k][1/n_k] & \text{if } n{=}1 \\
[0/n_s][0/n_\ell][\neg b_s/b_s] & \text{if } n{=}2 \\
[1/n_s][0/n_\ell] & \text{if } n{=}3 \\
[1/n_s][0/n_\ell] & \text{if } n{=}4 \\
[d_k/d_r][1/n_r][0/n_k] & \text{if } n{=}5 \\
[d_k/d_r][2/n_r][0/n_k][\neg b_r/b_r] & \text{if } n{=}6 \\
[1/n_r][0/n_k] & \text{if } n{=}7 \\
[0/n_r][b_r/b_\ell][1/n_\ell] & \text{if } n{=}8 \\
[2/n_k] & \text{if } n{=}9 \\
[2/n_\ell] & \text{if } n{=}10
\end{array} \right. \lhd \left\{ \begin{array}{l}
(n_s{=}1 \wedge n_k{=}0 \wedge n{=}1) \vee \\
(b_\ell{=}b_s \wedge n_s{=}2 \wedge n_\ell{=}2 \wedge n{=}2) \vee \\
(b_\ell{\neq}b_s \wedge n_s{=}2 \wedge n_\ell{=}2 \wedge n{=}3) \vee \\
(n_s{=}2 \wedge n_\ell{=}3 \wedge n{=}4) \vee \\
(b_k{=}b_r \wedge n_r{=}0 \wedge n_k{=}2 \wedge n{=}5) \vee \\
(b_k{\neq}b_r \wedge n_r{=}0 \wedge n_k{=}2 \wedge n{=}6) \vee \\
(n_k{=}3 \wedge n_r{=}0 \wedge n{=}7) \vee \\
(n_r{=}1 \wedge n_\ell{=}0 \wedge n{=}8) \vee \\
(n_k{=}1 \wedge n{=}9) \vee \\
(n_\ell{=}1 \wedge n{=}10)
\end{array} \right. \rhd \delta
\end{array}
$$

where $X[a/b]$ stands for the process, that is obtained from X by replacing b by a.

Lemma 7.1. *Let d:D and b:$\mathbb{B}$. The following (invariant) properties hold in every state of $X(d, b, 0, d, b, 0, \neg b, 0, d, \neg b, 0)$.*

(i) $n_k \neq 0 \Rightarrow (n_s = 2 \wedge d_s = d_k \wedge b_s = b_k)$
(ii) $n_\ell \neq 0 \Rightarrow (n_s = 2 \wedge n_r = 0 \wedge n_k = 0 \wedge b_r = b_\ell)$
(iii) $n_r \neq 0 \Rightarrow (n_k = 0 \wedge n_s = 2)$
(iv) $n_r = 0 \Rightarrow b_r = b_\ell$
(v) $b_s = b_r \Rightarrow (d_s = d_r \wedge n_s \neq 0)$

Lemma 7.2. *$X(d, b, 0, d, b, 0, \neg b, 0, d, \neg b, 0)$ is weakly $>$-confluent.*

Proof. Confluence must be checked for all $a \in Act$ and $e_a{:}E_a$, with respect to all $e_{\tau_>}{:}E_{\tau_>}$. We do this by a straightforward application of Theorem 5.4. We have distinguished 140 cases that have been listed in the table below. For 68 cases, marked with a $\times$ in the table the condition $b_a(d, e_a) \wedge b_{\tau_>}(d, e_{\tau_>})$ does not hold. In 10 cases, marked with a ■, the condition $a = \tau_> \Rightarrow g_a(d, e_a) \neq g_{\tau_>}(d, e_{\tau_>})$ is violated. In 60 of the remaining 62 confluence is immediately clear from the fact that the substitutions do not affect each other (i.e. they are commutative). These cases are marked with a $\circ$ in the table below.

	r_1	s_4	$\tau_<1$	$\tau_<2$	$\tau_>1$	$\tau_>2$	$\tau_>3$	$\tau_>4$	$\tau_>5$	$\tau_>6$	$\tau_>7$	$\tau_>8$	$\tau_>9$	$\tau_>10$
$\tau_>1$	×	○	×	○	■	×	×	×	×	×	×	○	×	○
$\tau_>2$	×	○	○	×	×	■	×	×	○	○	○	×	○	×
$\tau_>3$	×	○	○	×	×	×	■	×	○	○	○	×	○	×
$\tau_>4$	×	○	○	×	×	×	×	■	○	○	○	×	○	×
$\tau_>5$	○	×	×	○	×	○	○	○	■	×	×	×	×	○
$\tau_>6$	○	×	×	○	×	○	○	○	×	■	×	×	×	○
$\tau_>7$	○	×	×	○	×	○	○	○	×	×	■	×	×	○
$\tau_>8$	○	×	○	×	○	×	×	×	×	×	×	■	○	×
$\tau_>9$	○	○		○	×	○	○	○	×	×	×	○	■	○
$\tau_>10$	○	○	○		○	×	×	×	○	○	○	×	○	■

So, there are 2 cases left. Each case corresponds to the choice of a channel to corrupt the datum or not. We only treat the case $\tau_<1$ and $\tau_>9$.

We take σ_2 empty and $\sigma = \sigma_1$ using that $a = \tau_<$. So, e'_a is irrelevant. We distinguish the following two cases

- Assume $b_r = b_s$. We take for $\sigma_1 = \langle \tau_>, 5 \rangle$ and $\sigma_3 = \langle \tau_>, 7 \rangle$. We must now check the three requirements

  $$\mathcal{B}_{g_a(d,e_a)}(\sigma_3), \mathcal{B}_{g_{\tau_>}(d,e_{\tau_>})}(\sigma) \text{ and } \mathcal{G}_{g_a(d,e_a)}(\sigma_3) = \mathcal{G}_{g_{\tau_>}(d,e_{\tau_>})}(\sigma)$$

  These boil down to the following three proof obligations, where the trivial ones have been omitted. All obligations follow from the invariant in Lemma 7.1 in a straightforward fashion as we know that $n_k = 1$.

  $$n_r = 0, b_k = b_r \wedge n_r = 0 \text{ and } d_k = d_r.$$

- In the case that $b_r \neq b_s$, we take σ_1 empty and $\sigma_3 = \langle \tau_>, 7 \rangle \langle \tau_>, 8 \rangle \langle \tau_>, 10 \rangle \langle \tau_>, 3 \rangle \langle \tau_>, 1 \rangle \langle \tau_>, 9 \rangle$. The three requirements now become

  $$n_r = 0 \wedge n_\ell = 0 \wedge b_r \neq b_s \wedge n_s = 2, \mathit{true} \text{ and}$$
  $$n_s = 2 \wedge b_r = b_\ell \wedge n_\ell = 0 \wedge n_r = 0 \wedge d_s = d_k \wedge b_s = b_k.$$

  These also follow from the invariant and the fact that $n_k = 1$. □

The TP-reduction now prescribes that in all states where there is a progressing τ-step all other actions can be removed. In the cases where $n_k = 1$ or $n_\ell = 1$ this is applicable; we can remove the non-progressing τ-steps. By removing all transitions that have become unreachable in this way, we obtain the following simple process of which each state has only one outgoing transition. In particular, the channels have become reliable. By Theorem 6.4 this reduced process is branching bisimilar to the alternating bit protocol.

$$
\begin{array}{l}
Z(d_s, b_s, n_s, d_k, b_k, n_k, b_\ell, n_\ell, d_r, b_r, n_r) \; = \\
\sum_{x:\mathrm{D}} r_1(x) \cdot Z[x/d_s][1/n_s] \lhd n_s{=}0 \rhd \delta + \\
s_4(d_r) \cdot Z[1/n_r] \lhd n_r{=}2 \rhd \delta + \\
\sum_{n:\mathrm{N}} \tau_> \cdot Z \left\{ \begin{array}{ll}
[2/n_s][d_s/d_k][b_s/b_k][1/n_k] & \text{if } n{=}1 \\
[0/n_s][0/n_\ell][\neg b_s/b_s] & \text{if } n{=}2 \\
[d_k/d_r][2/n_r][0/n_k][\neg b_r/b_r] & \text{if } n{=}6 \\
[0/n_r][b_r/b_\ell][1/n_\ell] & \text{if } n{=}7 \\
[2/n_k] & \text{if } n{=}9 \\
[2/n_\ell] & \text{if } n{=}10
\end{array} \right. \lhd \left\{ \begin{array}{l}
(n_s{=}1 \wedge n_k{=}0 \wedge n{=}1) \vee \\
(b_\ell{=}b_s \wedge n_s{=}2 \wedge n_\ell{=}2 \wedge n{=}2) \vee \\
(b_k{\neq}b_r \wedge n_r{=}0 \wedge n_k{=}2 \wedge n{=}6) \vee \\
(n_r{=}1 \wedge n_\ell{=}0 \wedge n{=}7) \vee \\
(n_k{=}1 \wedge n{=}9) \vee \\
(n_\ell{=}1 \wedge n{=}10)
\end{array} \right. \rhd \delta
\end{array}
$$

References

1. D.J. Andrews, J.F. Groote, and C.A. Middelburg, editors. *Proceedings of the International Workshop on Semantics of Specification Languages*, Utrecht, The Netherlands. Workshops in Computing, Springer-Verlag, 1993.
2. J.C.M. Baeten and W.P. Weijland. *Process Algebra*, vol. 18 of *Cambridge Tracts in Theoretical Computer Science*. Cambridge University Press, Cambridge, 1990.
3. M.A. Bezem and J.F. Groote. A correctness proof of a one-bit sliding window protocol in μCRL. *The Computer Journal*, 37(4):289–307, 1994.
4. M.A. Bezem and J.F. Groote. Invariants in process algebra with data. In B. Jonsson and J. Parrow, editors, *Proceedings of the 5th Conference on Theories of Concurrency, CONCUR '94*, Uppsala, Sweden, August 1994, vol. 836 of *Lecture Notes in Computer Science*, pages 401–416. Springer-Verlag, 1994.
5. J.F. Groote and A. Ponse. Proof theory for μCRL: a language for processes with data. In Andrews et al. [1], pages 231–250.
6. J.F. Groote and A. Ponse. The syntax and semantics of μCRL. In A. Ponse, C. Verhoef, and S.F.M. van Vlijmen, editors, *Proceedings of the 1st Workshop in the Algebra of Communicating Processes, ACP '94*, Utrecht, the Netherlands, July 1994, pages 26–62. Springer-Verlag, July 1994.
7. G.J. Holzmann and D. Peled. An improvement in formal verification. In *Proceedings FORTE 1994 Conference, Bern, Switzerland*, 1994.
8. R. Milner. *A Calculus of Communicating Systems*, vol. 92 of *Lecture Notes in Computer Science*. Springer-Verlag, Berlin, 1980.
9. H. Qin. Efficient verification of determinate processes. In J.C.M. Baeten and J.F. Groote, editors, *Proceedings of the 2nd Conference on Theories of Concurrency, CONCUR '91*, Amsterdam, the Netherlands, August 1991, vol. 527 of *Lecture Notes in Computer Science*, pages 471–494. Springer-Verlag, 1991.
10. M.P.A. Sellink. Verifying process algebra proofs in type theory. In Andrews et al. [1], pages 315–339.

Axiomatisations of Weak Equivalences for De Simone Languages

Irek Ulidowski

Research Institute for Mathematical Sciences, Kyoto University, Japan.
Email: irek@kurims.kyoto-u.ac.jp.

Abstract. Aceto, Bloom and Vaandrager proposed in [ABV92] a procedure for generating a complete axiomatisation of strong bisimulation for process languages in the GSOS format. However, the choice operator +, which the procedure uses, as well as other auxiliary GSOS operators, which it introduces to obtain a finite axiomatisation, do not preserve many of weak equivalences. We propose a modification of this procedure, which works for a subclass of process languages in the De Simone format with a special treatment of silent actions. A choice of such a subclass of process languages guarantees that all the considered and auxiliary operators preserve many of weak equivalences. Our procedure generates a complete axiomatisation of refusal simulation preorder and it can be easily adapted to coarser preorders. The completeness result depends on the completeness result for the basic process language, which we prove. This language does not use prefixing with τ and the choice operator +. Instead, we employ the CSP external and internal choice operators as well as the third choice operator.

1 Introduction

In recent years there has been a considerable interest in *structural operational semantics* (SOS) as a mechanism to give operational meaning to classes of process languages. Main ingredients of such a semantics are SOS rules, which describe how the behaviour of a composite process depends on the behaviour of its component processes. Many general formats for SOS rules have been proposed (e.g. [dS85, BIM88, GV90, Gro90]), and a number of important results for process languages defined in these formats have been established. For example, various behavioural equivalences on processes were shown to be preserved by all process operators definable in these formats [dS85, BIM88, GV90, Gro90, Vaa91, Uli92, vG93, Blo93] and (completed) trace congruences with respect to these formats where discovered [BIM88, GV90, Gro90, Vaa91, Uli92, vG93]. In [ABV92, Ace94] Aceto, Bloom and Vaandrager showed how axiomatic characterisations can be derived for equivalences on processes. More recently, SOS was used as a specification language in [Blo95] and denotational models for classes of languages defined by certain formats were developed in [AI95].

Among the general research on formats of rules, there is a number of contributions concerning formats with a special treatment of silent actions [Blo90, Vaa91, Uli92, Blo93, Uli94]. In these formats, the traditional meaning of silent actions, as independent from the environment, invisible and spontaneous actions, is guaranteed by imposing certain restrictions on the form rules can take. In this paper, we are interested in process languages in such formats of rules.

We aim to build upon the work started by Aceto, Bloom and Vaandrager in [ABV92]. They proposed two procedures for generating finite complete axiomatisations, possibly with one infinitary induction rule, for any process language defined by rules in the GSOS format [BIM88]. Their procedures introduce auxiliary operators as they are needed. For example, for the axiomatisation of the parallel operator of ACP [BK84], the left-merge and communication merge operators are automatically introduced.

In this paper, our interest is in *weak* equivalences, where silent actions are treated as invisible, with *divergence*. Examples of these are *weak* bisimulation and *refusal simulation* equivalences [Uli92, Uli94]. The last has a natural characterisation in terms of local tests consisting of trace, refusal and copy tests [Uli92, Uli94]. Our aim is to adapt the procedure from [ABV92] to generate axiomatisations for refusal simulation equivalence and other coarser (weak) equivalences. However, it is well known that + and some other GSOS process operators, left-merge and communication merge among them, do *not* preserve these and many other weak equivalences. This is due to their interaction with silent actions. For example, consider the left-merge operator defined by the following single rule, where α is any (visible or silent) action:

$$\frac{X \xrightarrow{\alpha} X'}{X \mathbin{\|\!\lfloor} Y \xrightarrow{\alpha} X \parallel Y'.}$$

Although the processes $a\mathbf{0}$ and $\tau a\mathbf{0}$ are weakly trace equivalent, but $a\mathbf{0} \mathbin{\|\!\lfloor} b\mathbf{0}$ and $\tau a\mathbf{0} \mathbin{\|\!\lfloor} b\mathbf{0}$ are not: the second process can perform a sequence of action τba which cannot be matched by any equivalent trace of the first process. The implication is that the above mentioned operators and many other auxiliary operators, which are introduced by the procedure from [ABV92], cannot be easily used in verifications with respect to many weak equivalences. This problem is addressed in [vGV93], where it is postulated to use *module logic* instead of standard equational logic in reasoning about weak equivalences in the presence of operators like + and $\mathbin{\|\!\lfloor}$. Another solution is given by Bloom in [Blo93]. Instead of weak bisimulation, he considers a number of versions of *rooted* weak bisimulation and *rooted branching* bisimulation since they are preserved by operators like + and $\mathbin{\|\!\lfloor}$. Several classes of process languages, all subclasses of GSOS languages, are proposed such that they preserve the relevant versions of rooted bisimulations. The author describes how to adapt the methods of [ABV92] to produce sound axiomatisations of some of the rooted versions of bisimulations for the relevant process languages.

We propose an alternative solution to the above problem, together with a new procedure to derive complete axiom systems for refusal simulation preorder. The results are as follows. Firstly, we limit our attention to a subformat of the GSOS format which preserves weak bisimulation, refusal simulation and many other weak equivalences. This format is the De Simone format [dS85] with a special treatment of silent actions as described in [Uli92, Uli94]. We call this format the τDeS format. Secondly, instead of using $+$ and prefixing with silent action τ we use the CSP external and internal choice operators $\boxplus$ and $\oplus$ respectively [BHR84, Hoa85]. These operators were used, instead of $+$ and τ, in CCS [NH87, Hen88] and in ACP [Ace91]. We also use the third choice operator $\triangleright$, called *mixed* choice in [Uli94], which together with the null process, prefixing and the other two choice operators is needed to represent finite processes up to refusal simulation equivalence. We give a complete axiomatisation for refusal simulation preorder for the basic language augmented with the explicit divergent process. Thirdly, we present a new procedure, based on the procedure from [ABV92], for generating complete axiomatisations of refusal simulation preorder for well-founded τDeS languages. Our procedure introduces auxiliary operators too, as they are needed. However, all our auxiliary operators are τDeS, hence they preserve refusal simulation.

The paper is organised as follows. We define, in Sect. 2, τDeS process languages and refusal simulation preorder. In Sect. 3, we introduce our basic process language and give a complete characterisation of refusal simulation preorder for this language. In Sect. 4, we present a procedure for generating a sound axiomatisation for an arbitrary τDeS language. The completeness results for well-founded and for finitely branching τDeS languages are given in Sect. 5. The last section suggests a number of improvements to our procedure and outlines future work.

Due to the lack of space the proofs of our results are not included in this paper. These proofs as well as examples illustrating the applications of our axiomatisation procedure can be found in the full version of the paper [Uli95].

2 Preliminaries

This section defines notions of τDeS process languages, labelled transition systems with divergence and refusal simulation preorder. We assume a knowledge of basic ideas, definitions and results for process algebras as, for example, in [BHR84, Mil89, Hen88, BW90, BIM88, GV90].

Let Var be a countable set of variables ranged by $X, X_i, Y, Y_i, \ldots$. A signature Σ is a set process operators which are pairs (f, n), where $f \notin \mathsf{Var}$ and $n \in \mathbb{N}$ is an arity of f. Often, when the arity of the operator is clear from the context, the operator is simply abbreviated by its name, for example f. The set of open terms over Σ with variables in Var, denoted by $\mathbf{T}(\Sigma)$, is ranged by $P, Q, \ldots$. The set of closed terms, written as $\mathrm{T}(\Sigma)$, is ranged by $p, q, \ldots$. $var(T)$ denotes a set of variables appearing in a term T. Σ context with n holes $C[X_1, \ldots, X_n]$ is a member of $\mathrm{T}(\Sigma, \{X_1, \ldots, X_n\})$ in which X_i, $1 \leq i \leq n$, occurs only once. If $t_1, \ldots, t_n$ are Σ terms then $C[t_1, \ldots, t_n]$ is a term obtained by substituting X_i by t_i, $1 \leq i \leq n$. A preorder $\sqsubseteq$ on $\mathrm{T}(\Sigma)$ is a precongruence (or substitutive) if for all Σ contexts $C[\boldsymbol{X}]$ we have $\boldsymbol{t} \sqsubseteq \boldsymbol{t}'$ implies $C[\boldsymbol{t}] \sqsubseteq C[\boldsymbol{t}']$. A (closed) ***substitution*** ρ is a mapping from Var to $(\mathrm{T}(\Sigma))$ $\mathbf{T}(\Sigma)$. The substitution ρ extends to a mapping $\mathbf{T}(\Sigma) \to \mathbf{T}(\Sigma)$ in a standard way. We will write $P[P_1/X_1, \ldots, P_n/X_n]$ to denote the substitution which assigns each X_i to P_i. $\mathsf{Act} = \mathsf{Vis} \cup \{\tau\}$, ranged by $\alpha, \ldots$, is a countably infinite set of actions, where Vis is the set of visible actions, ranged by $a, b, \ldots$, and τ is a silent, internal action not in Vis.

Definition 1. A De Simone rule for (f, n) has the following form:

$$\frac{\{ X_i \xrightarrow{a_i} X_i' \}_{i \in I}}{f(X_1, \ldots, X_n) \xrightarrow{a} C[\mathbf{Y}],} \tag{1}$$

where X_i, X_i' are all different variables and $I \subseteq \{1, \ldots, n\}$. $C[\mathbf{Y}]$ contains at most the variables $Y_1, \ldots, Y_n$, where $Y_i = X_i'$ if $i \in I$ and $Y_i = X_i$ otherwise. We say that (f, n) *tests* its m-th argument and the m-th argument for (f, n) is *active* if there is a De Simone rule for (f, n) with $m \in I$. The notions of the *operator* of the rule, the *action, trigger, antecedents* and *consequent* are as usual.

A τ-rule for the above rule is any of the following rules for $i \in I$:

$$\frac{X_i \xrightarrow{\tau} X_i'}{f(X_1, \ldots, X_i, \ldots, X_n) \xrightarrow{\tau} f(X_1, \ldots, X_i', \ldots, X_n).}$$

A set of all τ-rules for the operator f is called its set of *associated* τ-rules. A set of rules is in the De Simone format (τDeS) if it consists of De Simone rules and their associated τ-rules. A process operator is τDeS if the set of its defining rules is in τDeS. A τDeS process language is a triple $(\Sigma, A \cup \{\tau\}, R)$, where Σ is a finite set of operators, $A \subset_{fin}$ Vis and R is a finite set of τDeS rules defining the operational meaning of the operators in Σ.

Most of the operators in process algebras are τDeS except, for example, for the CCS and ACP + and the ACP left-merge operators, which do not have the associated τ-rules. De Simone rules were introduced, in a slightly more general form (with no distinction between silent and visible actions), in [dS85]. The notion of τ-rules was introduced by Bloom in [Blo90] and it was used in [Vaa91] and [Uli92] in connection with the De Simone[1] and the ISOS formats respectively.

In order to represent divergent and underspecified processes in τDeS languages we will employ the operator $(\Omega, 0)$, which we will simply write as Ω.

Definition 2. Let $G = (\Sigma_G, A \cup \{\tau\}, R_G)$ be a τDeS language. A *labelled transition system with divergence* is a structure $(\mathrm{T}(\Sigma_G), A \cup \{\tau\}, \rightarrow_G, \uparrow_G)$, where $\mathrm{T}(\Sigma_G)$ is a set of *process terms* or *processes*, $\rightarrow_G \subseteq \mathrm{T}(\Sigma_G) \times A \cup \{\tau\} \times (\mathrm{T}(\Sigma_G)$ is the unique *transition relation* generated by G[2] and $\uparrow_G \subseteq \mathrm{T}(\Sigma_G)$ is the (postfix) *divergence predicate.* $\uparrow_G$ is defined as the least relation satisfying $\Omega \uparrow_G$ if $\Omega \in \Sigma_G$, and $f(p) \uparrow_G$, for any $f \in \Sigma_G$, if $p_i \uparrow_G$ for some active i-th argument of f.

[1] Our τDeS languages are somewhat different from De Simone languages in [Vaa91]. Vaandrager allows silent actions in the antecedents of De Simone rules, provides an extra "idling" axiom and, separately, provides recursion.

[2] Full details of the construction of transition relation from the language definition in a general format of rules can be found in, for example, [BIM88, GV90].

We will often call this transition system the basic transition system for G, and omit the subscript G when it is clear from the context. We will use some standard notation: for $(p, a, q) \in \rightarrow$ we write $p \xrightarrow{a} q$ and interpret it as process p performs a and in doing so becomes q. The convergence predicate is defined as $p\downarrow_G \equiv \neg\, p\uparrow_G$, and read as '$p$ converges'. The abbreviations we will use are: $p \xrightarrow{a}$ for $\exists q \in \mathrm{T}(\Sigma).\ p \xrightarrow{a} q$ and $p \stackrel{a}{\nrightarrow}$ for $\neg\exists q \in \mathrm{T}(\Sigma).\ p \xrightarrow{a} q$.

We are interested in weak equivalences which are usually defined over some form of a derived transition system. In the derived transition system, which we consider, we hide silent actions and internalise refusals of actions ($\tilde{a}$, for all $a \in A$). Thus, we label the derived transition relation with both actions and refusals of actions—the two basic elements of observable process behaviour.

Definition 3. [Uli94] Let $(\mathrm{T}(\Sigma), A\cup\{\tau\}, \rightarrow, \uparrow)$ be the basic transition system for a τDeS language G. A structure $(\mathrm{T}(\Sigma), A \cup \tilde{A} \cup \{\varepsilon\}, \Rightarrow, \Uparrow)$ is a *derived* transition system with divergence, where $p\Uparrow \equiv (\exists q.\ p \xrightarrow{\tau^*} q\ \&\ \ q\uparrow) \vee p \xrightarrow{\tau^\omega}$ and $\Rightarrow \subseteq \mathrm{T}(\Sigma) \times A \cup \tilde{A} \cup \{\varepsilon\} \times \mathrm{T}(\Sigma)$ is a *derived* transition relation defined as follows:

$$
\begin{aligned}
p \stackrel{a}{\Rightarrow} q &\equiv p \xrightarrow{\tau^*} \xrightarrow{a} q,\\
p \stackrel{\tilde{a}}{\Rightarrow} q &\equiv p \xrightarrow{\tau^*} q \stackrel{\tau}{\nrightarrow}\ \ \&\ \ q\downarrow\ \&\ q \stackrel{a}{\nrightarrow},\\
p \stackrel{\varepsilon}{\Rightarrow} q &\equiv p \xrightarrow{\tau^*} q.
\end{aligned}
$$

For simplicity we will call this transition system the derived transition system.

Finally, we introduce refusal simulation preorder [Uli92, Uli94].

Definition 4. Let $(\mathrm{T}(\Sigma), \Lambda, \Rightarrow, \Uparrow)$ be the derived transition system for a τDeS language G, where $\Lambda = A \cup \tilde{A} \cup \{\varepsilon\}$. Relations R and $S : \mathrm{T}(\Sigma) \times \mathrm{T}(\Sigma)$ are *L-simulation* and *U-simulation* relations respectively if for all p, q

$$pRq \text{ implies } \forall \mu \in \Lambda,\ \forall p'.\ p \stackrel{\mu}{\Rightarrow} p' \text{ implies } \exists q'.\ q \stackrel{\mu}{\Rightarrow} q'\ \&\ p'Rq',$$

$$pSq \text{ implies } \forall \mu \in \Lambda.\quad p\Downarrow \text{ implies } q\Downarrow\ \&\ (\forall q'.\ q \stackrel{\mu}{\Rightarrow} q' \text{ implies } \exists p'.\ p \stackrel{\mu}{\Rightarrow} p'\ \&\ p'Sq').$$

We define $\sqsubseteq_L$, $\sqsubseteq_U$ and *refusal simulation* relation, $\sqsubseteq_{RS}$, as a binary relation over $\mathrm{T}(\Sigma)$ as follows:

$$
\begin{aligned}
p \sqsubseteq_L q &\equiv \exists R.\ R \text{ is an } L\text{-simulation and } pRq,\\
p \sqsubseteq_U q &\equiv \exists S.\ S \text{ is a } U\text{-simulation and } pSq,\\
p \sqsubseteq_{RS} q &\equiv\ p \sqsubseteq_L q\ \&\ p \sqsubseteq_U q.
\end{aligned}
$$

It can be demonstrated that $\sqsubseteq_L, \sqsubseteq_U$ and $\sqsubseteq_{RS}$ are preorders. Refusal simulation equivalence, $\approx_{RS}$, is defined in a following way: $p \approx_{RS} q \equiv p \sqsubseteq_{RS} q\ \&\ q \sqsubseteq_{RS} p$. Moreover, $\sqsubseteq_{RS}$ and weak bisimulation preorder (a version which takes divergence into account [Uli94]) are precongruences for all τDeS process languages.

Lemma 5. [Uli92, Uli94] $\sqsubseteq_{RS}$ is a precongruence for all τDeS process languages.

Definition 6. [ABV92] A τDeS language H is a *disjoint extension* of a τDeS language G, written as $G \leq H$, if the signature and rules of H include those of G, and H introduces no new rule for the operators in G.

Following the notational agreements in [ABV92, Ace94], for a given τDeS language G we will use $\mathsf{RSim}(G)$ to denote the quotient algebra of elements of $\mathrm{T}(\Sigma)$ factored by $\lesssim_{RS}$. That is $\mathsf{RSim}(G) \models P \sqsubseteq Q$ iff $\rho(P) \lesssim_{RS} \rho(Q)$, for all $P, Q \in \mathrm{T}(\Sigma_G)$ and all closed Σ_G substitutions ρ. Moreover, since we will consider axioms which are preserved by taking disjoint extensions of τDeS languages we will need $\mathsf{RSIM}(G)$, a class of all algebras $\mathsf{RSim}(G')$ where G' is a disjoint extension of G. We have, for $P, Q \in \mathrm{T}(\Sigma_G)$,

$$\mathsf{RSIM}(G) \models P \sqsubseteq Q \ \text{ iff } \ (\forall G'.G \leq G' \text{ implies } \mathsf{RSim}(G') \models P \sqsubseteq Q).$$

3 Basic Language

The basic language, as we mentioned in the introduction, contains the external, internal and mixed choice operators instead of + and the prefixing with τ. The main reason for not using + is that it does not preserve many of weak equivalences. This is due to its interaction with τ. Another criticism of + is that it represents a mixture of different types of nondeterministic choice. Consider the following three terms:

$$ap + bq, \qquad \tau ap + \tau bq \qquad \text{and} \qquad ap + \tau bq.$$

The first term represents the external choice between ap and bq, the (external) user can choose to synchronise on either a or b. The second term represents the internal choice between ap and bq. The choice is made internally by the process (represented the two τ actions), and the user has no control over which of a and b is offered for synchronisation. The third term represent a mixture of both the external and internal choice. Here, the user is guaranteed to synchronise on b if she/he chooses to, but not on a—the process may internally evolve to bq, thus disabling a. Such choice can be interpreted as offering a synchronisation on a and b but with a *preference* to the one on b. These different types of nondeterministic choice between ap and bq are represented in our language as follows:

$$ap \boxplus bq, \qquad ap \oplus bq \qquad \text{and} \qquad ap \rhd bq.$$

When $a = b$ then the user has no control over which of the actions a is offered. Since we are considering weak equivalences, which are defined in terms of the observable behaviour of processes, we find prefixing with τ counterintuitive. We think that silent actions should be a result of interactions between process operators, like between the prefixing and parallel composition operators in CCS and ACP, prefixing and hiding operators in CSP, rather than an explicit method of process creation. Hence, in this paper we do not use prefixing with τ.

3.1 Operational Semantics

Our basic language is a finite version of the ISOS process language introduced in [Uli94] with an extra constant Ω to represent totally divergent processes.

Table 1. The operational semantics for B.

prefixing	$aX \xrightarrow{a} X$		
external choice	$\dfrac{X \xrightarrow{a} X'}{X \boxplus Y \xrightarrow{a} X'}$	$\dfrac{Y \xrightarrow{a} Y'}{X \boxplus Y \xrightarrow{a} Y'}$	
	$\dfrac{X \xrightarrow{\tau} X'}{X \boxplus Y \xrightarrow{\tau} X' \boxplus Y}$	$\dfrac{Y \xrightarrow{\tau} Y'}{X \boxplus Y \xrightarrow{\tau} X \boxplus Y'}$	
internal choice	$X \oplus Y \xrightarrow{\tau} X$	$X \oplus Y \xrightarrow{\tau} Y$	
mixed choice	$\dfrac{X \xrightarrow{a} X'}{X \rhd Y \xrightarrow{a} X'}$	$\dfrac{X \xrightarrow{\tau} X'}{X \rhd Y \xrightarrow{\tau} X' \rhd Y}$	$X \rhd Y \xrightarrow{\tau} Y$

Definition 7. The basic language, denoted by B, is a τDeS process language $(\Sigma, A \cup \{\tau\}, R)$, where $\Sigma = \Sigma_0 \cup \Sigma_1 \cup \Sigma_2$ is defined below, $A \subset_{fin}$ Vis and R is a set of τDeS rules in Table 1.

$$\Sigma_0 = \{(\mathbf{0}, 0), (\Omega, 0)\}$$
$$\Sigma_1 = \{(a, 1) \mid a \in A\}$$
$$\Sigma_2 = \{(\boxplus, 2), (\oplus, 2), (\rhd, 2)\}.$$

The precedence of operators is given by $a > \boxplus > \oplus > \rhd$.

B generates the basic transition system $B = (\mathrm{T}(\Sigma), A \cup \{\tau\}, \rightarrow, \uparrow)$ as in Definition 2. Note that all processes in $\mathrm{T}(\Sigma)$ are *finite*. Given B the derived transition system $(\mathrm{T}(\Sigma), A \cup \tilde{A} \cup \{\tau\}, \Rightarrow, \Uparrow)$ is defined as in Definition 3. One can check that divergence predicate $\Uparrow$ is the least relation satisfying the following: $\Omega\Uparrow$ and if $p\Uparrow$ then $(p \boxplus q)\Uparrow$, $(q \boxplus p)\Uparrow$, $(p \oplus q)\Uparrow$, $(q \oplus p)\Uparrow$, $(p \rhd q)\Uparrow$ and $(q \rhd p)\Uparrow$. Refusal simulation preorder, $\sqsubseteq_{RS}$, on D is defined as in Definition 4.

Example 1. We show why the operator $\rhd$ is needed in B. The operators $\boxplus$ and $\oplus$ are the only choice operators used in the language TCCS [NH87]. This is because they are sufficiently expressive for testing equivalence, but they are not for refusal simulation equivalence: testing equivalent processes $(a \boxplus b) \oplus b$ and $a \rhd b$ are not refusal simulation equivalent: $(a \boxplus b) \oplus b \overset{\tilde{c}}{\Rightarrow} a \boxplus b \overset{a}{\Rightarrow}$ but $a \rhd b \overset{\tilde{c}}{\Rightarrow} b \overset{a}{\not\Rightarrow}$.

3.2 Axiom System

In this section, we give a complete axiom system RS for $\sqsubseteq_{RS}$ on processes in the basic language B. The system RS consists of equations and inequations given in Table 2 as well as the usual properties of precongruences (e.g. substitutivity: if $p \sqsubseteq q$ then $f(p) \sqsubseteq f(q)$), as in [Hen88]. The inequations in Table 2 are new, but the equations are taken from the axiomatisation of copy+refusal preorder in [Uli94], where they are motivated and discussed. At this point, we only comment on $E2$, which does not hold without the side condition. A counterexample is

Table 2. Axioms for refusal simulation preorder.

$E1$	$X \boxplus \mathbf{0} = X$	
$E2$	$X \boxplus X = X$	if $X \stackrel{\tau}{\not\rightarrow}$
$E3$	$X \boxplus Y = Y \boxplus X$	
$E4$	$X \boxplus (Y \boxplus Z) = (X \boxplus Y) \boxplus Z$	
$I2$	$X \oplus X = X$	
$I3$	$X \oplus Y = Y \oplus X$	
$I4$	$X \oplus (Y \oplus Z) = (X \oplus Y) \oplus Z$	
$M1$	$\mathbf{0} \rhd X = X$	
$M2$	$X \rhd X = X$	
$M4$	$X \rhd (Y \rhd Z) = (X \rhd Y) \rhd Z$	
$D1$	$X \boxplus (Y \oplus Z) = (X \boxplus Y) \oplus (X \boxplus Z)$	
$D2$	$X \boxplus (Y \rhd Z) = Y \rhd (X \boxplus Z)$	
$D3$	$X \oplus (Y \rhd Z) = Y \rhd (X \oplus Z)$	
$D4$	$(X \rhd Y) \rhd Z = (X \boxplus Y) \rhd Z$	
$D5$	$(X \oplus Y) \rhd Z = (X \boxplus Y) \rhd Z$	
$C1$	$aX \boxplus aY = aX \boxplus aY \oplus aX$	
$C2$	$a(X \boxplus Y \rhd V \oplus Z) = a(X \boxplus Y \rhd V \oplus Z) \boxplus a(X \rhd V)$	
$\Omega 1$	$\Omega \sqsubseteq X$	
$\Omega 2$	$X \boxplus \Omega \sqsubseteq X \rhd \Omega$	
$\Omega 3$	$\Omega \rhd X \sqsubseteq \Omega \oplus X$	

$(a \oplus b) \boxplus (a \oplus b) \not\sqsubseteq_{RS} (a \oplus b)$: the left process can become stable and then do a and b, which cannot be matched by the right process. This property of $\boxplus$ will force us to use similar side conditions in the laws concerning $\boxplus$ in Sect. 4. Note that $E2$ can be replaced by a family of axioms $aX \boxplus aX = aX$, one for each a.

We will use the summation notation $\sum_{i \in I} X_i$ and $\bigoplus_{j \in J} Y_j$, for $J \neq \emptyset$, since $\boxplus$ and $\oplus$ are associative. We will write $\mathrm{T} \vdash p \sqsubseteq q$, $(p = q)$ to mean that $p \sqsubseteq q$, $(p = q)$ can be derived from the axiomatic theory T.

Theorem 8. $\mathsf{RS} \vdash p \sqsubseteq q$ if and only if $\mathsf{RSim(B)} \models p \sqsubseteq q$.

The completeness part is proved, as usual, by extracting *normal* and *head normal forms*. Their definitions and the details of the proof can be found in [Uli95].

4 Deriving Sound Axioms for τ-DeS Process Languages

In this section, we give a procedure for deriving sound axiomatisations of refusal simulation preorder for arbitrary τDeS process languages. The derived axiomatisations are head normalising, but they are infinite and conditional. We illustrate the application of our procedure by deriving axioms for the CSP hiding and the ACP merge operators.

We begin by noting that all τDeS operators are *smooth*, as in [ABV92]. We will need to distinguish two subclasses of τDeS operators, namely *distinctive*, after [ABV92], and *τ-introducing* operators.

Definition 9. A τ-DeS operator (f, n) is *distinctive* if for each argument i either all rules for f, which are not τ-rules, test i or none of them does, and also for each pair of different non-τ-rules for f there is an argument for which both rules have the same antecedents, but with a different action. A non-τ-rule is *τ-introducing* if it has action τ in the consequent. A τDeS operator (f, n) is *τ-introducing* if one of its rules is τ-introducing.

The following three lemmas introduce the action and inaction laws, adapted from [ABV92], and the new divergence laws.

Lemma 10. **(Action Laws).** Let (f, n) be a distinctive operator of a τDeS language G, a disjoint extension of B, with a rule of the form (1). Let $P_i \equiv a_i X_i'$ for $i \in I$ and $P_i \equiv X_i$ otherwise. If $\alpha \in \mathsf{Vis}$ then, for an appropriate $\boldsymbol{P}'$, we have

$$\mathsf{RSIM}(G) \models f(\boldsymbol{P}) = \alpha C[\boldsymbol{P}'] \tag{2}$$

else, for some $\boldsymbol{P}'$, we have

$$\mathsf{RSIM}(G) \models f(\boldsymbol{P}) = C[\boldsymbol{P}']. \tag{3}$$

Lemma 11. **(Inaction Laws).** Let (f, n) be an operator of a τDeS language G, a disjoint extension of B. Suppose that for each rule for f of the form (1) there is an index $i \in I$ such that either $P_i \equiv \mathbf{0}$ or $P_i \equiv aX_i'$, for some $a \neq a_i$. Then

$$\mathsf{RSIM}(G) \models f(\boldsymbol{P}) = \mathbf{0}. \tag{4}$$

Lemma 12. **(Divergence Laws).** Let (f, n) be an operator of a τDeS language G, a disjoint extension of B. Suppose that there is a rule for f of the form (1) such that for some $i \in I$ we have $P_i \equiv \Omega$, and, for all other rules for f of the form

$$\frac{\{\, X_i \xrightarrow{a_i} X_i' \,\}_{i \in I'}}{f(X_1, \ldots, X_n) \xrightarrow{\alpha} C'[\mathbf{Y}],}$$

there is an index $i \in I'$ such that $P_i \equiv \mathbf{0}$, $P_i \equiv \Omega$ or $P_i \equiv aX_i'$, for some $a \neq a_i$. Then

$$\mathsf{RSIM}(G) \models f(\boldsymbol{P}) \sqsubseteq \Omega. \tag{5}$$

Next, we present the distributivity laws, which together with the above laws are needed to transform terms to head normal form. We will need two predicates over process terms to describe their structural properties. The first predicate $\mathsf{sum}(f, \boldsymbol{p})$ is true if all elements of $\boldsymbol{p}$, which are active for f, have the form $\sum_I a_i p_i$ or $\sum_I a_i p_i \boxplus \Omega$, where $I \subset_{fin} \mathbb{N}$. The second predicate $\mathsf{tau}(f(\boldsymbol{p}))$ is true if $f(\boldsymbol{p})$ can perform τ as a result of applying a τ-introducing rule, possibly after a number of actions τ due to the application of τ-rules.

Lemma 13. Let (f, n) be an operator of a τDeS language G, the disjoint extension of B, and suppose that i is an argument of f such that each rule for f has an antecedent for i.
(Distributivity over $\boxplus$ laws). Let $X_i \equiv X \boxplus Y$. If f is non-τ-introducing then

$$\mathsf{RSIM}(G) \models f(\boldsymbol{X}) = f(\boldsymbol{X})[X/X_i] \;\boxplus\; f(\boldsymbol{X})[Y/X_i] \quad \text{if } \mathsf{sum}(f, \boldsymbol{X})), \tag{6}$$

else (f is τ-introducing) the following laws are valid in $\mathsf{RSIM}(G)$:

$$f(\boldsymbol{X}) = f(\boldsymbol{X})[X/X_i] \;\boxplus\; f(\boldsymbol{X})[Y/X_i]$$
$$\text{if } \mathsf{sum}(f, \boldsymbol{X})) \;\&\; \neg\mathsf{tau}(f(\boldsymbol{X})[X/X_i]) \;\&\; \neg\mathsf{tau}(f(\boldsymbol{X})[Y/X_i]) \tag{7}$$

$$f(\boldsymbol{X}) = f(\boldsymbol{X})[X/X_i] \;\triangleright\; f(\boldsymbol{X})[Y/X_i]$$
$$\text{if } \mathsf{sum}(f, \boldsymbol{X})) \;\&\; \neg\mathsf{tau}(f(\boldsymbol{X})[X/X_i]) \;\&\; \mathsf{tau}(f(\boldsymbol{X})[Y/X_i]) \tag{8}$$

$$f(\boldsymbol{X}) = f(\boldsymbol{X})[X/X_i] \;\oplus\; f(\boldsymbol{X})[Y/X_i]$$
$$\text{if } \mathsf{sum}(f, \boldsymbol{X})) \;\&\; \mathsf{tau}(f(\boldsymbol{X})[X/X_i]) \;\&\; \mathsf{tau}(f(\boldsymbol{X})[Y/X_i]). \tag{9}$$

(Distributivity over $\triangleright$ laws). Let $X_i \equiv X \triangleright Y$. If f is non-τ-introducing then

$$\mathsf{RSIM}(G) \models f(\boldsymbol{X}) = f(\boldsymbol{X})[X/X_i] \;\triangleright\; f(\boldsymbol{X})[Y/X_i], \tag{10}$$

else (f is τ-introducing) the following laws are valid in $\mathsf{RSIM}(G)$:

$$f(\boldsymbol{X}) = f(\boldsymbol{X})[X/X_i] \;\triangleright\; f(\boldsymbol{X})[Y/X_i] \quad \text{if } \neg\mathsf{tau}(f(\boldsymbol{X})[X/X_i]) \tag{11}$$

$$f(\boldsymbol{X}) = f(\boldsymbol{X})[X/X_i] \;\oplus\; f(\boldsymbol{X})[Y/X_i] \quad \text{if } \mathsf{tau}(f(\boldsymbol{X})[X/X_i]) \tag{12}$$

(Distributivity over $\oplus$ laws). Let $X_i \equiv X \oplus Y$. Then

$$\mathsf{RSIM}(G) \models f(\boldsymbol{X}) = f(\boldsymbol{X})[X/X_i] \;\oplus\; f(\boldsymbol{X})[Y/X_i]. \tag{13}$$

The presence of sum and tau predicates in the conditions of the above laws makes the resulting axiomatisations infinite. It is not clear whether or not there are finite axiomatisations of $\approx_{RS}$ for arbitrary τDeS languages (disjoint extensions of B). In practice tau predicates can be removed from the conditions: this is briefly described in the last section. However, we see no way to replace sum predicates: giving more structure to the subterms and using extra τDeS operators does not seem to remove the infinitary character of axiomatisations.

Theorem 14. Let G be a τDeS language such that $\mathsf{B} \leq G$. Let $\Sigma \subseteq \Sigma_G \setminus \Sigma_{\mathsf{B}}$ be a set of distinctive operators. Suppose that T is an equational theory that extends RS with the following (conditional) equations (inequations) for each f in Σ: an action law (2) or (3) for each rule for f; all the inaction laws (4); all the divergence laws (5); for each active argument of f the distributivity over the three choice operators laws. Then $\mathsf{RSIM}(G) \models \mathrm{T}$ and T is head normalising.

Next, consider the CSP hiding operator $\backslash a$ defined by the following rules:

$$\frac{X \xrightarrow{a} X'}{X\backslash a \xrightarrow{\tau} X'\backslash a} \qquad \frac{X \xrightarrow{b} X'}{X\backslash a \xrightarrow{b} X'\backslash a}\; b \neq a \qquad \frac{X \xrightarrow{\tau} X'}{X\backslash a \xrightarrow{\tau} X'\backslash a.}$$

Below, we present a set of conditional axioms for $\backslash a$ as an example of the application of Theorem 14. In the following $\mathsf{sum}(\cdot)$ denotes $\mathsf{sum}(\boxplus, X, Y)$.

$$\begin{aligned}
(X \boxplus Y)\backslash a &= X\backslash a \boxplus Y\backslash a && \text{if } \mathsf{sum}(\cdot),\ \neg\mathsf{tau}(X\backslash a),\ \neg\mathsf{tau}(Y\backslash a) && (14)\\
(X \boxplus Y)\backslash a &= X\backslash a \rhd Y\backslash a && \text{if } \mathsf{sum}(\cdot),\ \neg\mathsf{tau}(X\backslash a),\ \mathsf{tau}(Y\backslash a) && (15)\\
(X \boxplus Y)\backslash a &= X\backslash a \oplus Y\backslash a && \text{if } \mathsf{sum}(\cdot),\ \mathsf{tau}(X\backslash a),\ \mathsf{tau}(Y\backslash a) && (16)\\
(X \rhd Y)\backslash a &= X\backslash a \rhd Y\backslash a && \text{if } \neg\mathsf{tau}(X\backslash a) && (17)\\
(X \rhd Y)\backslash a &= X\backslash A \oplus Y\backslash a && \text{if } \mathsf{tau}(X\backslash a) && (18)\\
(X \oplus Y)\backslash a &= X\backslash a \oplus Y\backslash a && &&\\
(bX)\backslash a &= a(X\backslash a) && \text{if } b \neq a &&\\
(aX)\backslash a &= X\backslash a && &&\\
\mathbf{0}\backslash a &= \mathbf{0} && &&\\
\Omega\backslash a &\sqsubseteq \Omega && &&
\end{aligned}$$

Note that due to the presence of **sum** and **tau** this axiomatisation is infinite.

The next two lemmas show how to axiomatise non-distinctive operators.

Lemma 15. Let (f, n) be a non-distinctive non-τ-introducing operator of a τDeS language G, the disjoint extension of B. Then there exists a disjoint extension G' of G with n-ary distinctive operators $f_1, \ldots, f_k$ such that G' is a τDeS language and the following (conditional) equations hold in $\mathsf{RSIM}(G)$:

$$f(\boldsymbol{X}) = f_1(\boldsymbol{X}) \boxplus \ldots \boxplus f_k(\boldsymbol{X}) \quad \text{if } \mathsf{sum}(f, \boldsymbol{X})), \tag{19}$$

for each active argument i of f and for $X_i \equiv X \rhd Y$

$$f(\boldsymbol{X}) = f_1(\boldsymbol{X}) \boxplus \ldots \boxplus f_k(\boldsymbol{X}) \rhd f(\boldsymbol{X})[Y/X_i], \tag{20}$$

for each active argument i of f and for $X_i \equiv X \oplus Y$

$$f(\boldsymbol{X}) = f_1(\boldsymbol{X}) \boxplus \ldots \boxplus f_k(\boldsymbol{X}) \rhd f(\boldsymbol{X})[X/X_i] \oplus f(\boldsymbol{X})[Y/X_i]. \tag{21}$$

Lemma 16. Let (f, n) be a non-distinctive τ-introducing operator of a τDeS language G, the disjoint extension of B. Then there exists a disjoint extension G' of G with n-ary distinctive non-τ-introducing operators f_k, $k \in K \subset_{fin} \mathbb{N}$, and n-ary distinctive τ-introducing operators g_l, $l \in L \subset_{fin} \mathbb{N}$, such that G' is a τDeS language and the following (conditional) equations hold in $\mathsf{RSIM}(G)$:

$$f(\boldsymbol{X}) = \sum_K f_k(\boldsymbol{X}) \boxplus \sum_L g_l(\boldsymbol{X})$$
$$\text{if } \mathsf{sum}(f, \boldsymbol{X}))\ \&\ \forall l.\ \neg\mathsf{tau}(g_l(\boldsymbol{X})), \tag{22}$$

$$f(\boldsymbol{X}) = \sum_K f_k(\boldsymbol{X}) \boxplus \sum_{m \in L \setminus N} g_m(\boldsymbol{X}) \rhd \bigoplus_{N \neq \emptyset} g_n(\boldsymbol{X})$$
$$\& \text{ if } \mathsf{sum}(f, \boldsymbol{X})) \;\&\; \forall m.\, \neg\mathsf{tau}(g_m(\boldsymbol{X})) \;\&\; \forall n.\, \mathsf{tau}(g_n(\boldsymbol{X})), \quad (23)$$

for each active argument i of f and for $X_i \equiv X \rhd Y$

$$f(\boldsymbol{X}) = \sum_K f_k(\boldsymbol{X}) \boxplus \sum_L g_l(\boldsymbol{X})[X/X_i] \;\rhd\; f(\boldsymbol{X})[Y/X_i]$$
$$\text{if } \forall l.\, \neg\mathsf{tau}(g_l(\boldsymbol{X})[X/X_i]), \quad (24)$$

$$f(\boldsymbol{X}) = \sum_K f_k(\boldsymbol{X}) \boxplus \sum_{m \in L \setminus N} g_m(\boldsymbol{X})[X/X_i] \rhd \bigoplus_{N \neq \emptyset} g_n(\boldsymbol{X})[X/X_i] \oplus f(\boldsymbol{X})[Y/X_i]$$
$$\text{if } \forall m.\, \neg\mathsf{tau}(g_m(\boldsymbol{X})[X/X_i]) \;\&\; \forall n.\, \mathsf{tau}(g_n(\boldsymbol{X})[X/X_i]), \quad (25)$$

for each active argument i of f and for $X_i \equiv X \oplus Y$

$$f(\boldsymbol{X}) = \sum_K f_k(\boldsymbol{X}) \boxplus \sum_L g_l(\boldsymbol{X}) \;\rhd\; f(\boldsymbol{X})[X/X_i] \;\oplus\; f(\boldsymbol{X})[Y/X_i]. \quad (26)$$

Below, we give algorithm A, based on the algorithm form [ABV92], for generating a sound and head normalising axiom system for $\sqsubseteq_{RS}$ for any τDeS language.

1. If G is not a disjoint extension of B then add to G a disjoint copy of B. Call the resulting language G'''.
2. For each non-distinctive and non-τ-introducing operator $f \notin \Sigma_{\mathsf{B}}$ in G''' apply the construction of Lemma 15 in order to obtain distinctive non-τ-introducing operators $f_1, \ldots, f_k$. Call the resulting language G''. Add to RS all the resulting instances of axioms (19)–(21) and call the resulting system T″.
3. For each non-distinctive τ-introducing operator $f \notin \Sigma_{\mathsf{B}}$ in G'' apply the construction of Lemma 16 in order to obtain distinctive non-τ-introducing operators $f_1, \ldots, f_k$ and distinctive τ-introducing operators $g_1, \ldots, g_l$. Call the resulting language G'. Add to T″ all the resulting instances of axioms (22)–(26) and call thus obtained system T′.
4. Add to T′ the axioms produced by applying Theorem 14 to all distinctive operators in $\Sigma_{G'} \setminus \Sigma_{\mathsf{B}}$. Call the resulting system T.

Theorem 17. Let G be a τDeS process language and G' be a disjoint extension of G produced by algorithm A. Moreover, let T be the axiom system produced by algorithm A. Then $\mathsf{RSIM}(G) \models$ T and T is head normalising.

As an example of the application of Theorem 17, we present below a set of conditional axioms for the merge operator $\|$ [BW90], which is defined by the following rules:

$$\frac{X \xrightarrow{\alpha} X'}{X \| Y \xrightarrow{\alpha} X' \| Y} \qquad \frac{Y \xrightarrow{\alpha} Y'}{X \| Y \xrightarrow{\alpha} X \| Y'}.$$

The axiomatisation uses the auxiliary operators left-merge $\lfloor\!\lfloor$, defined in the introduction, and the right-merge which, due to the lack of space, is replaced below by $\lfloor\!\lfloor$. For the precedence of $\|$ and $\lfloor\!\lfloor$ we assume $a > \| > \lfloor\!\lfloor > \boxplus$.

$$
\begin{aligned}
X \parallel Y &= X \lfloor\!\lfloor Y \boxplus Y \lfloor\!\lfloor X && \text{if } \mathsf{sum}(\|, X, Y)\\
X \parallel (Y \oplus Z) &= X \lfloor\!\lfloor (Y \oplus Z) \boxplus (Y \oplus Z) \lfloor\!\lfloor X && \rhd\ X \parallel Y \oplus X \parallel Z\\
(Y \oplus Z) \parallel X &= Y \oplus Z) \lfloor\!\lfloor X \boxplus X \lfloor\!\lfloor (Y \oplus Z) && \rhd\ Y \parallel X \oplus Z \parallel X\\
X \parallel (Y \rhd Z) &= X \lfloor\!\lfloor (Y \rhd Z) \boxplus (Y \rhd Z) \lfloor\!\lfloor X && \rhd\ X \parallel Z\\
(Y \rhd Z) \parallel X &= (Y \rhd Z) \lfloor\!\lfloor X \boxplus X \lfloor\!\lfloor (Y \rhd Z) && \rhd\ Z \parallel X\\
(X \boxplus Y) \lfloor\!\lfloor Z &= X \lfloor\!\lfloor Z \boxplus Y \lfloor\!\lfloor Z\\
(X \oplus Y) \lfloor\!\lfloor Z &= X \lfloor\!\lfloor Z \oplus Y \lfloor\!\lfloor Z\\
(X \rhd Y) \lfloor\!\lfloor Z &= X \lfloor\!\lfloor Z \rhd Y \lfloor\!\lfloor Z\\
aX \lfloor\!\lfloor Y &= a(X \parallel Y)\\
\mathbf{0} \lfloor\!\lfloor X &= \mathbf{0}\\
\Omega \lfloor\!\lfloor X &\sqsubseteq \Omega
\end{aligned}
$$

5 Completeness

Algorithm A produces, for any τDeS process language G, a disjoint extension G' with the axiom system T, which allows conversion of process terms into head normal form. If G is *well-founded* (defined below) then we can eliminate all the operators not in B from any term over G. It is done by applying the reduction to head normal form a finite number of times. In all such languages, those with a finite alphabet and no recursion, the problem of the completeness of their axiom systems reduces to the problem of head normalisation in the basic language B, which we addressed in Sect. 3.2. The following definition is from [ABV92]:

Definition 18. Let G be a τDeS process language. A term $p \in \mathrm{T}(\Sigma_G)$ is *well-founded* iff there exists no infinite sequence $p_0, a_0, p_1, a_1, \ldots$ with $p \equiv p_0$ and $p_i \xrightarrow{a_i} p_{i+1}$ for all $i \geq 1$. G is well-founded iff all terms in $\mathrm{T}(\Sigma_G)$ are well-founded.

It is easy to show that, given any well-founded τDeS process language G with $\mathsf{B} \leq G$, the disjoint extension G' produced by algorithm A is also well-founded. Thus, similarly as in [ABV92], we obtain the completeness result.

Theorem 19. Let G be a well-founded τDeS process language such that $\mathsf{B} \leq G$. Let G' and T denote the disjoint extension and the axiom system produced by algorithm A respectively. Then for all $p, q \in \mathrm{T}(\Sigma_{G'})$ if $\mathsf{RSim}(G') \models p \sqsubseteq q$ then $\mathrm{T} \vdash p \sqsubseteq q$.

The second completeness result is for τDeS languages which generate finitely branching derived transition systems. The axiom system is augmented with the following rule, based on AIP$^-$ [BW90] and similar to the rule in [ABV92],

$$\frac{X/b^n\Omega \ \sqsubseteq\ Y/b^n\Omega \qquad \text{(for all } n)}{X \sqsubseteq Y,}$$

together with the axioms for the extra operator $\cdot/\cdot$, which is defined in [ABV92]. The details concerning this completeness result can be found in [Uli95].

6 Conclusion

We have described how to derive complete axiomatisations of refusal simulation preorder for well-founded and for finitely branching τDeS languages. Our procedure can be easily adapted to coarser preorders such as refusal preorder [Phi87] or testing preorder [Hen88]. As our axioms are valid for any such preorder, we only need to augment the axioms for B with the extra axioms for that preorder.

For many τ-introducing operators, it is possible to remove tau conditions in favour of using extra operators and more structure in the subterms. Consider $\not\downarrow A$, the 'initial' restriction of actions in A operator, from [ABV92]. Axioms (14)-(16) can be rewritten, with a changed but obvious meaning of sum, as follows:

$$(X\not\downarrow\{a\} \boxplus Y\not\downarrow\{a\})\backslash a = X\not\downarrow\{a\}\backslash a \boxplus Y\not\downarrow\{a\}\backslash a \qquad \text{if } \mathsf{sum}(X,Y) \quad (27)$$
$$(X\not\downarrow\{a\} \boxplus aY \boxplus Z)\backslash a = X\not\downarrow\{a\}\backslash a \rhd (aY \boxplus Z)\backslash a \qquad \text{if } \mathsf{sum}(X,Z) \quad (28)$$
$$(aX \boxplus aY \boxplus Z)\backslash a = aX\backslash a \oplus (aY \boxplus Z)\backslash a. \qquad \text{if } \mathsf{sum}(Z) \quad (29)$$

The axioms (17) and (18) can be similarly rewritten. However, for the operators like the CCS parallel the above trick will work provided that extra conditions concerning the initial actions of the subterms are used.

Finally, it would be interesting to find out if there are finite axiomatisations of $\approx_{RS}$ for arbitrary τDeS languages (possibly with auxiliary τDeS operators).

Acknowledgements

I would like to thank the referees for their comments and suggestions. Thanks are also due to Paul Taylor for his Proof Trees macros.

References

[ABV92] L. Aceto, B. Bloom, and F.W. Vaandrager. Turning SOS rules into equations. In *Proceedings of 7th Annual IEEE Symposium on Logic in Computer Science*, Santa Cruz, California, 1992.

[Ace91] L. Aceto. A theory of testing for ACP. In *Proceedings of 2nd International Conference* CONCUR'91, Amsterdam, The Netherlands, 1991. LNCS 527.

[Ace94] L. Aceto. Deriving complete inteference systems fo a class of GSOS languages generating regular behaviours. In *Proceedings of 5th International Conference* CONCUR'94, Uppsala, Sweden, 1994. LNCS 789.

[AI95] L. Aceto and A. Ingólfdóttir. CPO models for a class of GSOS languages. In *TAPSOFT'95*, Aarhus, Denmark, 1995.

[BHR84] S.D. Brookes, C.A.R. Hoare, and W. Roscoe. A theory of communicating sequential processes. *Journal of ACM*, Vol. 31, pp. 560–599, 1984.

[BIM88] B. Bloom, S. Istrail, and A.R. Meyer. Bisimulation can't be traced: preliminary report. In *Conference Record of the 15th ACM Symposium on Principles of Programming Languages*, San Diego, California, 1988.

[BK84] J.A. Bergstra and J.W. Klop. Process algebra for synchronous communication. *Information and Computation*, Vol. 60, pp. 109–137, 1984.

[Blo90] B. Bloom. Strong process equivalence in the presence of hidden moves. Preliminary report, MIT, 1990.

[Blo93] B. Bloom. Structural operational semantics for weak bisimulations. Technical Report TR 93-1373, Cornell, 1993. To appear in *Theoretical Computer Science*.

[Blo95] B. Bloom. Stuctured operational semantics as a specification language. In *Conference Record of the 22nd ACM Symposium on Principles of Programming Languages*, San Francisco, California, 1995.

[BW90] J.C.M Baeten and W.P Weijland. *Process Algebra*. Cambridge Tracts in Theoretical Computer Science, 1990.

[dS85] R. de Simone. Higher-level synchronising devices in MEIJE-SCCS. *Theoretical Computer Science*, Vol. 37, pp. 245–267, 1985.

[Gro90] J.F. Groote. Transition system specifications with negative premises. In J.C.M. Baeten and J.W. Klop, editors, *Proceedings of* CONCUR'90, Berlin, 1990. Springer-Verlag. LNCS 458.

[GV90] J.F. Groote and F. Vaandrager. Structured operational semantics and bisimulation as a congruence. *Information and Computation*, Vol. 100, pp. 202–260, 1990.

[Hen88] M. Hennessy. *An Algebraic Theory of Processes*. The MIT Press, 1988.

[Hoa85] C.A.R. Hoare. *Communicating Sequential Processes*. Prentice Hall, 1985.

[Mil89] R. Milner. *Communication and Concurrency*. Prentice Hall, 1989.

[NH87] R. De Nicola and M. Hennessy. CCS without τ's. In H. Ehrig, R. Kowalski, G. Levi, and U. Montanari, editors, *TAPSOFT'87*, Berlin, 1987. Springer-Verlag. LNCS 250.

[Phi87] I.C.C. Phillips. Refusal testing. *Theoretical Computer Science*, Vol. 50, 1987.

[Uli92] I. Ulidowski. Equivalences on observable processes. In *Proceedings of 7th Annual IEEE Symposium on Logic in Computer Science*, Santa Cruz, California, 1992.

[Uli94] I. Ulidowski. *Local Testing and Implementable Concurrent Processes*. PhD thesis, University of London, 1994.

[Uli95] I. Ulidowski. Axiomatisations of weak equivalences for de Simone languages. Technical report, RIMS, Kyoto University, 1995.

[Vaa91] F.W. Vaandrager. On the relationship between process algebra and input/output automata. In *Proceedings of 6th Annual IEEE Symposium on Logic in Computer Science*, Amsterdam, 1991.

[vG93] R.J. van Glabbeek. Full abstraction in structured operational semantics. In M. Nivat, C. Rattray, T. Rus, and G. Scollo, editors, *Proceedings of the 3rd AMAST Conference*. Workshops in Computing, Springer-Verlag, 1993.

[vGV93] R.J. van Glabbeek and F. Vaandrager. Modular specifications of process algebras. *Theoretical Computer Science*, Vol. 113, pp. 293–348, 1993.

A Compositional Trace-Based Semantics for Probabilistic Automata *

Roberto Segala

MIT Laboratory for Computer Science
Cambridge, MA 02139

Abstract. We extend the trace semantics for labeled transition systems to a randomized model of concurrent computation. The main objective is to obtain a compositional semantics. The role of a trace in the randomized model is played by a probability distribution over traces, called a *trace distribution*. We show that the preorder based on trace distribution inclusion is not a precongruence, and we build an elementary context, called the *principal context*, that is sufficiently powerful to characterize the coarsest precongruence that is contained in the trace distribution preorder. Finally, we introduce a notion of a *probabilistic forward simulation* and we prove that it is sound for the trace distribution precongruence. An important characteristic of probabilistic forward simulations is that they relate states to probability distributions over states.

1 Introduction

The growing interest in randomized algorithms for the solutions of problems in distributed computation [2, 3] has created a need for formal models where randomized distributed systems can be analyzed. The formal models should be able to deal at least with randomization, which is used to describe the choices of a system that are due to some random draws, and nondeterminism, which is the basic mathematical tool to express the unpredictable behavior of an external environment and the unpredictable relative speeds of two or more systems. Several formal models for randomized concurrent systems were studied in the past [5, 7, 8, 10, 13, 19–23], and among those, the models of [8, 19, 20, 22] distinguish between probability and nondeterminism.

Our long term goal is to build a model that extends Labeled Transition Systems [16], that has a strong mathematical foundation, and that can be used for the actual verification of systems. The choice of labeled transition systems is due to their successful application to model concurrency. In [20] we have extended the labeled transition systems model to account for randomization and we have extended the classical simulation and bisimulation relations to it; in [14, 17] we have shown how the model of [20] can be used for the actual analysis of randomized distributed systems. The main objects of [20] are called *probabilistic automata*, and they differ from ordinary labeled transition systems in that a transition leads to a probability distribution over states rather than to a single state. Probabilistic automata are an extension of the probabilistic automata of Rabin [18] where the occurrence of an action can lead to several probability distributions over states. Choosing a transition represents the nondeterministic behavior of a probabilistic automaton; choosing a state to reach within a transition represents the probabilistic behavior of a probabilistic automaton.

* Supported by NSF grant CCR-92-25124, by DARPA contract N00014-92-J-4033, and by AFOSR-ONR contract F49620-94-1-0199.

In this paper we show how it is possible to define a compositional semantics for probabilistic automata that relies on some form of traces rather than simulation relations; then, we show how the simulation method of [15] extends to the new framework. The problem is not simple since trace-based semantics are known to be linear, i.e., to be independent of the branching structure of a system, while in the probabilistic framework the branching structure of a system can be used to create dependencies between events in the context of a parallel composition. In other words, a trace semantics that is sufficiently expressive to capture part of the probabilistic behavior of a system must be sensitive to part of the branching structure of a system in order to be compositional. The problem, then, is to see how sensitive such a relation should be.

We define a simple and natural trace-based semantics for probabilistic automata, where the main objects to be observed are probability distributions over traces, called ***trace distributions***. Then, we define a preorder on probabilistic automata, called ***trace distribution preorder***, which is based on trace distribution inclusion. Our trace distributions are a conservative extension of the traces of ordinary labeled transition systems (called automata), and the trace distribution preorder is a conservative extension of the trace inclusion preorder of ordinary automata. We observe that the trace distribution preorder is not a precongruence, and thus, following standard arguments, we define the trace distribution precongruence as the coarsest precongruence that is contained in the trace distribution preorder.

Our first main theorem is that the trace distribution precongruence can be characterized in an alternative and more intuitive way. Namely, we show that there is a context, which we call the ***principal context***, that is sufficient to distinguish every pair of probabilistic automata that are not in the trace distribution precongruence relation. As a consequence, the trace distribution precongruence can be characterized as inclusion of principal trace distributions, where a principal trace distribution of a probabilistic automaton is a trace distribution of the probabilistic automaton in parallel with the principal context.

We extend the simulation method of [15] by studying a new relation for probabilistic automata in the style of the forward simulations of [15]. The new relation, which is called ***probabilistic forward simulation***, is coarser than the relations of [20] and relates states to probability distributions over states. Probabilistic forward simulations allow us to simulate a probabilistic transition like rolling a dice with eight faces by flipping three fair coins one after the other; this is not possible with the simulation relations of [20]. Our second main theorem is that probabilistic forward simulations are sound for the trace distribution precongruence.

We believe that our methodology can be applied to the study of other semantics based on abstract observations. In particular, in further work we plan to extend the failure semantics of [4] to the probabilistic framework, and possibly to study a related theory of testing.

The rest of the paper is organized as follows. Section 2 gives some background on measure theory; Section 3 introduces the probabilistic automata of [19, 20]; Section 4 introduces the trace distributions and the trace distribution precongruence; Section 5 introduces the principal context and the alternative characterization of the trace distribution precongruence; Section 6 introduces our new simulation relations and shows their soundness for the trace distribution precongruence; Section 7 gives some concluding remarks.

2 Preliminaries

A ***probability space*** is a triple $(\Omega, \mathcal{F}, P)$ where Ω is a set, $\mathcal{F}$ is a collection of subsets of Ω that is closed under complement and countable union and such that $\Omega \in \mathcal{F}$, and P is a function from $\mathcal{F}$ to $[0,1]$ such that $P[\Omega] = 1$ and such that for any collection $\{C_i\}_i$ of at most countably many pairwise disjoint elements of $\mathcal{F}$, $P[\cup_i C_i] = \sum_i P[C_i]$. The set Ω is called the *sample space*, $\mathcal{F}$ is called the *σ-field*, and P is called the *probability measure*.

A probability space $(\Omega, \mathcal{F}, P)$ is *discrete* if $\mathcal{F} = 2^{\Omega}$ and for each $C \subseteq \Omega$, $P[C] = \sum_{x \in C} P[\{x\}]$. Given a set X, denote by $Probs(X)$ the set of discrete probability distributions whose sample space is a subset of X and such that the probability of each element is not 0.

The Dirac distribution over an element x, denoted by $\mathcal{D}(x)$, is the probability space with a unique element x. The uniform distribution over a collection of elements $\{x_1, \ldots, x_n\}$, denoted by $\mathcal{U}(x_1, \ldots, x_n)$, is the probability space that assign probability $1/n$ to each x_i.

Throughout the paper we denote a probability space $(\Omega, \mathcal{F}, P)$ by $\mathcal{P}$. As a notational convention, if $\mathcal{P}$ is decorated with indices and primes, then the same indices and primes carry to its elements. Thus, $\mathcal{P}'_i$ denotes $(\Omega'_i, \mathcal{F}'_i, P'_i)$.

The *product* $\mathcal{P}_1 \otimes \mathcal{P}_2$ of two discrete probability spaces $\mathcal{P}_1, \mathcal{P}_2$ is the discrete probability space $(\Omega_1 \times \Omega_2, 2^{\Omega_1 \times \Omega_2}, P)$, where $P[(x_1, x_2)] = P_1[x_1]P_2[x_2]$ for each $(x_1, x_2) \in \Omega_1 \times \Omega_2$.

A function $f : \Omega \to \Omega'$ is said to be a *measurable* function from $(\Omega, \mathcal{F})$ to $(\Omega', \mathcal{F}')$ if for each set C of $\mathcal{F}'$ the inverse image of C, denoted by $f^{-1}(C)$, is an element of $\mathcal{F}$. Let P be a probability measure on $(\Omega, \mathcal{F})$, and let P' be defined on $\mathcal{F}'$ as follows: for each element C of $\mathcal{F}'$, $P'(C) = P(f^{-1}(C))$. Then P' is a probability measure on $(\Omega', \mathcal{F}')$. The measure P' is called the measure *induced* by f, and is denoted by $f(P)$. If $\mathcal{P}$ is a discrete probability space and f is a function defined on Ω, then f can be *extended* to $\mathcal{P}$ by defining $f(\mathcal{P})$ to be the discrete probability space $(f(\Omega), 2^{f(\Omega)}, f(P))$.

3 Probabilistic Automata

In this section we introduce the probabilistic automata of [19], which appear also in [20] with a slightly different terminology. We start with an informal overview of the model.

A labeled transition system, also called an *automaton*, is a state machine with labeled transitions. Each transition leaves from a state and leads to the occurrence of a label, also called an *action*, and to a state. A probabilistic automaton is like an ordinary automaton except that each transition leads to an action and to a probability distribution over states.

Resolving the nondeterminism in an automaton leads to a linear chain of states interleaved with actions, called an *execution* or a *computation*; resolving the nondeterminism in a probabilistic automaton leads to a Markov chain structure since each transition leads probabilistically to more than one state. Such a structure is called a *probabilistic execution*. A probabilistic execution can be visualized as a probabilistic automaton that enables at most one transition from each state (a *fully probabilistic automaton*). Due to the complex structure of a probabilistic execution, it is convenient to view it as a special case of a probabilistic automaton; in this way the analysis of a probabilistic execution is simplified.

However, nondeterminism could be resolved also using randomization: a scheduler for n processes running in parallel could choose the next process to schedule by rolling an n-side dice; similarly, if some actions model the input of an external environment, the environment could provide the input at random or could provide no input with some non-zero probability. Thus, in a probabilistic execution the transition that leaves from a state may lead to a probability distribution over both actions and states and also over deadlock (no input). This new kind of transition is not part of our informal definition of a probabilistic automaton; yet, it is still convenient to view a probabilistic execution as a probabilistic automaton.

Thus, our definition of a probabilistic automaton allows for a transition to lead to probability distributions over actions and states and over a symbol δ that models deadlock; however, except for the handling of probabilistic executions, we concentrate on *simple probabilistic automata*, which allow only probabilistic choices over states within a transition.

3.1 Probabilistic Automata

Definition 1. A *probabilistic automaton* M consists of four components:

1. a set $states(M)$ of states,
2. a nonempty set $start(M) \subseteq states(M)$ of start states,
3. an action signature $sig(M) = (ext(M), int(M))$ where $ext(M)$ and $int(M)$ are disjoint sets of *external* and *internal* actions, respectively,
4. a transition relation $trans(M) \subseteq states(M) \times Probs((acts(M) \times states(M)) \cup \{\delta\})$, where $acts(M)$ denotes the set $ext(M) \cup int(M)$ of actions.

A probabilistic automaton M is *simple* if for each transition $(s, \mathcal{P})$ of $trans(M)$ there is an action a such that $\Omega \subseteq \{a\} \times states(M)$. In such a case a transition can be represented alternatively as $(s, a, \mathcal{P}')$, where $\mathcal{P}' \in Probs(states(M))$, and is called a *simple transition*.

A probabilistic automaton is *fully probabilistic* if it has a unique start state and from each state there is at most one transition enabled. □

An ordinary automaton is a special case of a probabilistic automaton where each transition leads to a Dirac distribution; the generative model of probabilistic processes of [7] is a special case of a fully probabilistic automaton; simple probabilistic automata are partially captured by the reactive model of [7] in the sense that the reactive model assumes some form of nondeterminism between different actions. However, the reactive model does not allow nondeterministic choices between transitions involving the same action. By restricting simple probabilistic automata to have finitely many states, we obtain objects with a structure similar to that of the Concurrent Labeled Markov Chains of [8]; however, in our model we do not need to distinguish between nondeterministic and probabilistic states. In our model nondeterminism is obtained by means of the structure of the transition relation. This allows us to retain most of the traditional notation that is used for automata.

3.2 Executions and Probabilistic Executions

We now move to the notion of an execution, which is the result of resolving both the nondeterministic and the probabilistic choices in a probabilistic automaton; it corresponds to the notion of an execution for ordinary automata. We introduce also a notion of an extended execution, which we use later to study the probabilistic behavior of a probabilistic automaton.

Definition 2. An *execution fragment* α of a probabilistic automaton M is a (finite or infinite) sequence of alternating states and actions starting with a state and, if the execution fragment is finite, ending in a state, $\alpha = s_0 a_1 s_1 a_2 s_2 \cdots$, where for each i there exists a probability space $\mathcal{P}$ such that $(s_i, \mathcal{P}) \in trans(M)$ and $(a_{i+1}, s_{i+1}) \in \Omega$. Denote by $fstate(\alpha)$ the first state of α, and, if α is finite, denote by $lstate(\alpha)$ the last state of α. Denote by $frag^*(M)$ and $frag(M)$ the sets of finite and all execution fragments of M, respectively. An *execution* is an execution fragment whose first state is a start state. Denote by $exec^*(M)$ and $exec(M)$ the sets of finite and all executions of M, respectively.

An extended execution (fragment) of M is either an execution (fragment) of M, or a sequence $\alpha = s_0 a_1 s_1 \cdots a_n s_n \delta$ such that $s_0 a_1 s_1 \cdots a_n s_n$ is an execution (fragment) of M.

A finite execution fragment $\alpha_1 = s_0 a_1 s_1 \cdots a_n s_n$ of M and an extended execution fragment $\alpha_2 = s_n a_{n+1} s_{n+1} \cdots$ of M can be *concatenated*. In this case the concatenation, written $\alpha_1 \frown \alpha_2$, is the extended execution fragment $s_0 a_1 s_1 \cdots a_n s_n a_{n+1} s_{n+1} \cdots$. An extended execution fragment α_1 of M is a *prefix* of an extended execution fragment α_2 of M, written $\alpha_1 \leq \alpha_2$, if either $\alpha_1 = \alpha_2$ or α_1 is finite and there exists an extended execution fragment α_1' of M such that $\alpha_2 = \alpha_1 \frown \alpha_1'$. □

As we said already, an execution is the result of resolving both the nondeterministic and the probabilistic choices in a probabilistic automaton. The result of the resolution of nondeterministic choices only is a fully probabilistic automaton, called a *probabilistic execution*, which is the entity that replaces the executions of ordinary automata. Informally, since in ordinary automata there is no probability left once the nondeterminism is resolved, the executions and probabilistic executions of an ordinary automaton describe the same objects. Before giving the formal definition of a probabilistic execution, we introduce *combined transitions*, which allow us to express the ability to resolve the nondeterminism using probability. Informally, a combined transition leaving from a state s is obtained by choosing a transition that leaves from s probabilistically, and then behaving according to the transition chosen. Among the choices it is possible not to schedule any transition. This possibility is expressed by the term $(1 - \sum_i p_i)$ in the probability of δ in the definition below.

Definition 3. Given a probabilistic automaton M, a finite or countable set $\{\mathcal{P}_i\}_i$ of probability distributions of $Probs((acts(M) \times states(M)) \cup \{\delta\})$, and a weight $p_i > 0$ for each i such that $\sum_i p_i \leq 1$, the combination $\sum_i p_i \mathcal{P}_i$ of the distributions $\{\mathcal{P}_i\}_i$ is the probability space $\mathcal{P}$ such that

- $\Omega = \begin{cases} \cup_i \Omega_i & \text{if } \sum_i p_i = 1 \\ \cup_i \Omega_i \cup \{\delta\} & \text{if } \sum_i p_i < 1 \end{cases}$
- $\mathcal{F} = 2^{\Omega}$
- for each $(a, s) \in \Omega$, $P[(a, s)] = \sum_{i|(a,s)\in\Omega_i} p_i P_i[(a, s)]$
- if $\delta \in \Omega$, then $P[\delta] = (1 - \sum_i p_i) + \sum_{i|\delta\in\Omega_i} p_i P_i[\delta]$.

A pair $(s, \mathcal{P})$ is a *combined transition* of M if there exists a finite or countable family of transitions $\{(s, \mathcal{P}_i)\}_i$ and a set of positive weights $\{p_i\}_i$ with $\sum_i p_i \leq 1$, such that $\mathcal{P} = \sum_i p_i \mathcal{P}_i$. Denote $(s, \mathcal{P})$ by $\sum_i p_i(s, \mathcal{P}_i)$. □

We are now ready to define a probabilistic execution. A technical detail is that in order to name the states of a probabilistic execution, those states are represented by finite execution fragments of a probabilistic automaton. A probabilistic execution can be seen as the result of unfolding the transition relation of a probabilistic automaton and then choosing probabilistically a transition from each state.

Definition 4. Let α be a finite execution fragment of a probabilistic automaton M. Define a function $\alpha^\frown$ that applied to a pair (a, s) returns $(a, \alpha a s)$, and applied to δ returns δ. Recall from the last paragraph of Section 2 that the function $\alpha^\frown$ can be extended to discrete probability spaces.

A *probabilistic execution fragment* of a probabilistic automaton M, is a fully probabilistic automaton, denoted by H, such that

1. $states(H) \subseteq frag^*(M)$. Let q range over states of probabilistic executions.
2. for each transition $tr = (q, \mathcal{P})$ of H there is a combined transition $tr' = (lstate(q), \mathcal{P}')$ of M, called the *corresponding combined transition*, such that $\mathcal{P} = q^\frown \mathcal{P}'$.
3. each state of H is reachable and enables one transition, where a state q of H is reachable if there is an execution of H whose last state is q.

A *probabilistic execution* is a probabilistic execution fragment whose start state is a start state of M. Denote by $prfrag(M)$ the set of probabilistic execution fragments of M, and by $prexec(M)$ the set of probabilistic executions of M. Also, denote by q_0^H the start state of a generic probabilistic execution fragment H, and for each transition $(q, \mathcal{P})$ of H, denote the pair $(q, \mathcal{P})$ by tr_q^H, and denote $\mathcal{P}$ by $\mathcal{P}_q^H$. □

Example 1. Two examples of probabilistic executions appear in Figure 1. In particular, the probabilistic execution denoted by H is a probabilistic execution of the probabilistic automaton denoted by M. For notational convenience, in the representation of a probabilistic execution H we do not write explicitly the full names of the states of H since the full names are derivable from the position of each state in the diagram; moreover, whenever a state q enables the transition $(q, \mathcal{D}(\delta))$ we do not draw any arc leaving from the state of the diagram that represents q. □

There is a strong correspondence between the extended execution fragments of a probabilistic automaton and the extended executions of one of its probabilistic execution fragments. We express this correspondence by means of an operator $\alpha\downarrow$ that takes an extended execution of H and gives back the corresponding extended execution fragment of M, and an operator $\alpha \uparrow q_0^H$ that takes an extended execution fragment of M and gives back the corresponding extended execution of H if it exists.

3.3 Events

We now define a probability space $(\Omega_H, \mathcal{F}_H, P_H)$ for a probabilistic execution fragment H, so that it is possible to analyze the probabilistic behavior of a probabilistic automaton once the nondeterminism is resolved. The sample space Ω_H is the set of extended executions of M that represent complete extended execution fragments of H, where an extended execution α of H is complete iff it is either infinite or $\alpha = \alpha'\delta$ and $\delta \in \Omega^H_{lstate(\alpha')}$. For each finite extended execution fragment α of M, let C_α, the *cone* with prefix α, be the set $\{\alpha' \in \Omega_H \mid \alpha \leq \alpha'\}$, and let $\mathcal{C}_H$ be the class of cones for H. The probability $\mu_H(C_\alpha)$ of the cone C_α is the product of the probabilities associated with each edge that generates α in H. Formally, if $\alpha = q_0^H a_1 s_1 \cdots s_{n-1} a_n s_n$, then $\mu_H(C_\alpha) \triangleq P^H_{q_0}[(a_1, q_1)] \cdots P^H_{q_{n-1}}[(a_n, q_n)]$, where each q_i is defined to be $q_0^H a_1 s_1 \cdots a_i s_i$, and if $\alpha = q_0^H a_1 q_1 \cdots q_{n-1} a_n q_n \delta$, then $\mu_H(C_\alpha) \triangleq P^H_{q_0}[(a_1, q_1)] \cdots P^H_{q_{n-1}}[(a_n, q_n)] P^H_{q_n}[\delta]$, where each q_i is defined to be $q_0^H a_1 s_1 \cdots a_i s_i$. In [19] it is shown that there is a unique measure $\bar{\mu}_H$ that extends μ_H to the σ-field $\sigma(\mathcal{C}_H)$ generated by $\mathcal{C}_H$, i.e., the smallest σ-field that contains $\mathcal{C}_H$. Then, $\mathcal{F}_H$ is $\sigma(\mathcal{C}_H)$ and P_H is $\bar{\mu}_H$. With this definition it is possible to show that any union of cones is measurable.

3.4 Prefix

One of our objectives in the definition of the probabilistic model is that the standard notions defined on ordinary automata carry over to the probabilistic framework. One of this concepts is the notion of a prefix for ordinary executions. Here we just claim that it is possible to give a meaningful definition of a prefix for probabilistic executions.

Definition 5. A probabilistic execution fragment H is a prefix of a probabilistic execution fragment H', denoted by $H \leq H'$, iff H and H' have the same start state, and for each state q of H, $P_H[C_q] \leq P_{H'}[C_q]$. □

It is easy to verify that this definition of prefix coincides with the definition of prefix for ordinary executions when probability is absent. The reader is referred to [19] for a complete justification of Definition 5.

3.5 Parallel Composition

We now turn to the parallel composition operator, which is defined in the CSP style [9], i.e., by synchronizing two probabilistic automata on their common actions. As outlined in [8], it is not clear how to define a parallel composition operator for general probabilistic automata that extends the CSP synchronization style; thus, we define it only for simple probabilistic automata, and we concentrate on simple probabilistic automata for the rest of this paper. We use general probabilistic automata only for the analysis of probabilistic executions. The reader is referred to [19] for more details.

Definition 6. Two simple probabilistic automata M_1 and M_2 are said to be *compatible* if $int(M_1) \cap acts(M_2) = \emptyset$, and $int(M_2) \cap acts(M_1) = \emptyset$.

The *parallel composition* $M_1 \| M_2$ of two compatible simple probabilistic automata M_1 and M_2 is the simple probabilistic automaton M such that $states(M) = states(M_1) \times states(M_2)$, $start(M) = start(M_1) \times start(M_2)$, $ext(M) = ext(M_1) \cup ext(M_2)$, $int(M) = int(M_1) \cup int(M_2)$, and the transition relation satisfies the following: $((s_1, s_2), a, \mathcal{P}) \in trans(M)$ iff $\mathcal{P} = \mathcal{P}_1 \otimes \mathcal{P}_2$, such that

1. if $a \in acts(M_1)$ then $(s_1, a, \mathcal{P}_1) \in trans(M_1)$, else $\mathcal{P}_1 = \mathcal{D}(s_1)$, and
2. if $a \in acts(M_2)$ then $(s_2, a, \mathcal{P}_2) \in trans(M_2)$, else $\mathcal{P}_2 = \mathcal{D}(s_2)$. □

Remark. Another point in favor of these definitions is that it is possible to define the projection $H \lceil M_i$, $i = 1, 2$, of a probabilistic execution H of $M_1 \| M_2$ onto one of its components M_i. The definition is non-trivial and the interested reader is referred to [19]. □

3.6 Notation for Transitions

We conclude this section with some notation for transitions. We write $s \xrightarrow{a} \mathcal{P}$ whenever there is a simple transition $(s, a, \mathcal{P})$ in M, and we write $s \xrightarrow{a}_{\mathrm{C}} \mathcal{P}$ whenever there is a simple combined transition $(s, a, \mathcal{P})$ in M.

Similar to the non-probabilistic case, we extend the arrow notation to weak arrows ($\overset{a}{\Longrightarrow}_{\mathrm{C}}$) to state that $\mathcal{P}$ is reached through a sequence of combined transitions of M, some of which are internal. The main difference from the non-probabilistic case is that in our framework the transitions involved form a tree rather that a linear chain. Formally, $s \overset{a}{\Longrightarrow}_{\mathrm{C}} \mathcal{P}$, where a is either an external action or the empty sequence and $\mathcal{P}$ is a probability distribution over states, iff there is a probabilistic execution fragment H such that

1. the start state of H is s;
2. $P_H[\{\alpha\delta \mid \alpha\delta \in \Omega_H\}] = 1$, i.e., the probability of termination in H is 1;
3. for each $\alpha\delta \in \Omega_H$, $trace(\alpha) = a$, where $trace(\alpha)$ is the ordered sequence of external actions that occur in α;
4. $\mathcal{P} = lstate(\delta\text{-}strip(\mathcal{P}_H))$, where $\delta\text{-}strip(\mathcal{P}_H)$ is the probability space $\mathcal{P}'$ such that $\Omega' = \{\alpha \mid \alpha\delta \in \Omega_H\}$, and for each $\alpha \in \Omega'$, $P'[\alpha] = P_H[C_{\alpha\delta}]$;

Example 2. The left side of Figure 1 represents a weak transition with action a that leads to state s_1 with probability 5/12 and to state s_2 with probability 7/12. The action τ represents any internal action. From the formal definition of a weak transition, a tree that represents a weak transition may have an infinite branching structure, i.e., it may have transitions that lead to countably many states, and may have some infinite paths; however, each tree representing a weak transition has the property that infinite paths occur with probability 0.

The right side of Figure 1 represents a weak transition of a probabilistic automaton with cycles in its transition relation. Specifically, H represents the weak transition $s_0 \Longrightarrow \mathcal{P}$, where $P[s_0] = 1/8$ and $P[s_1] = 7/8$. If we extend H indefinitely on its right, then we obtain a new probabilistic execution fragment that represents the weak transition $s_0 \Longrightarrow \mathcal{D}(s_1)$. Observe that the new probabilistic execution fragment has an infinite path that occurs with probability 0. Furthermore, observe that there is no other way to reach state s_1 with probability 1. □

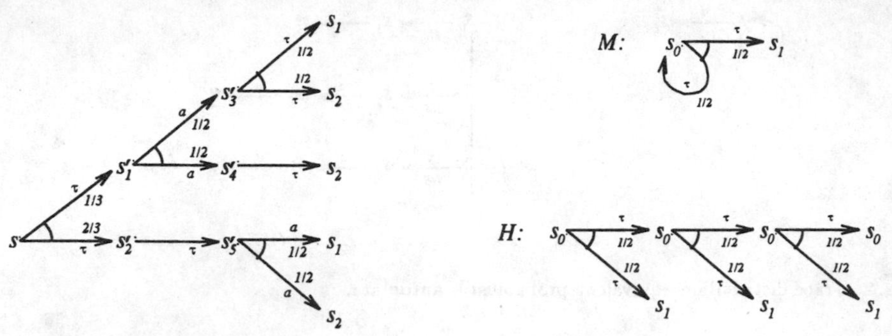

Fig. 1. Weak transitions (also probabilistic executions).

4 Trace Distribution Precongruence

The objective of this section is to extend the trace semantics to the probabilistic framework and to define a corresponding trace-based preorder. The problem is that a trace semantics is linear, i.e., it does not depend on the branching structure of a system, while in probabilistic automata the branching structure is important. Thus, the question is the following: under the condition that we want a trace semantics that describes the probabilistic behavior of a probabilistic automaton, how much of the branching structure of a probabilistic automaton do we have to know? We address the question above by defining a reasonable and natural trace semantics and by characterizing the minimum precongruence contained in it.

Definition 7. Let H be a probabilistic execution fragment of a probabilistic automaton M. For each extended execution fragment α of M, let *trace*(α) denote the ordered sequence of external actions of M that appear in α.

Let f be a function from Ω_H to $\Omega = ext(M)^* \cup ext(M)^\omega$ that assigns to each execution of Ω_H its trace. The *trace distribution* of H, denoted by *tdistr*(H), is the probability space $(\Omega, \mathcal{F}, P)$ where $\mathcal{F}$ is the σ-field generated by the cones C_β, where β is an element of $ext(M)^*$, and $P = f(P_H)$. The fact that f is measurable follows from standard arguments. Denote a generic trace distribution by $\mathcal{D}$. A trace distribution of a probabilistic automaton M is the trace distribution of one of the probabilistic executions of M. □

Given two probabilistic executions H_1 and H_2, it is possible to check whether $tdistr(H_1) = tdistr(H_2)$ just by verifying that $P_{tdistr(H_1)}[C_\beta] = P_{tdistr(H_2)}[C_\beta]$ for each finite sequence of actions β. This follows from standard measure theory arguments. In [12] Jou and Smolka study a probabilistic trace semantics for generative processes; our rule above to determine whether two probabilistic executions have the same trace distribution coincides with the trace equivalence of [12] (a probabilistic execution is essentially a generative process).

Example 3. The reader may wonder why we have not defined Ω to be *trace*(Ω_H). This is to avoid to distinguish two trace distribution just because they have different sample spaces. Figure 2 illustrates the idea. The two probabilistic automata of Figure 2 have the same trace distributions; however, the left probabilistic automaton has a probabilistic execution where the trace a^∞ occurs with probability 0, while the right probabilistic automaton does not. Thus, by defining the sample space of *tdistr*(H) to be *trace*(Ω_H), the two probabilistic automata of Figure 2 would be distinct. In Section 6 we define several simulation relations for

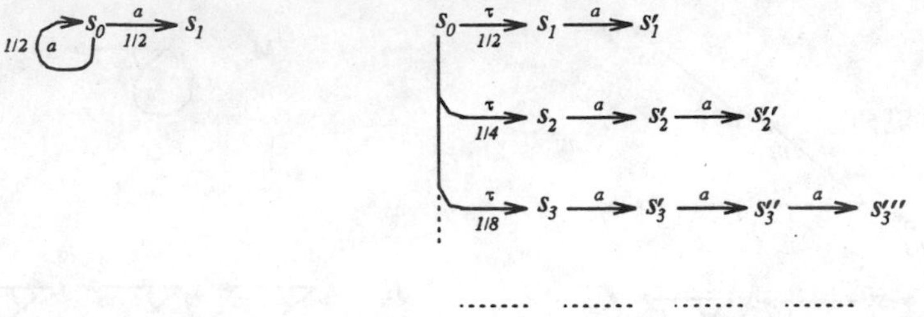

Fig. 2. Trace distribution equivalent probabilistic automata.

probabilistic automata and we show that they are sound for the trace distribution precongruence; such results would not be true with the alternative definition of Ω. □

It is easy to see that trace distributions extend the traces of ordinary automata: the trace distribution of a linear probabilistic execution fragment is a Dirac distribution. It is easy as well to see that prefix and action restriction extend to the probabilistic framework, thus enforcing our definition of a trace distribution. A trace distribution $\mathcal{D}$ is a *prefix* of a trace distribution $\mathcal{D}'$, denoted by $\mathcal{D} \leq \mathcal{D}'$, iff for each finite trace β, $P_{\mathcal{D}}[C_\beta] \leq P_{\mathcal{D}'}[C_\beta]$. Thus, two trace distributions are equal iff each one is a prefix of the other.

Lemma 8. *Let H_1 and H_2 be two probabilistic execution fragments of a probabilistic automaton M. If $H_1 \leq H_2$, then $tdistr(H_1) \leq tdistr(H_2)$.* □

Let β be a trace, and let V be a set of actions. Then $\beta \upharpoonright V$ denotes the ordered sequence of actions from V that appear in β. Let $\mathcal{D} = (\Omega, \mathcal{F}, P)$ be a trace distribution. The *restriction* of $\mathcal{D}$ to V, denoted by $\mathcal{D} \upharpoonright V$, is the probability space $(\Omega', \mathcal{F}', P')$ where $\Omega' = \{\beta \upharpoonright V \mid \beta \in \Omega\}$, $\mathcal{F}'$ is the σ-field generated by the sets of cones $C_{\beta'}$ such that $\beta' \leq \beta$ for some $\beta \in \Omega'$, and P' is the inverse image of P under the function that restricts traces to V.

Lemma 9. *Let $\mathcal{D}$ be a trace distribution of $M_1 \| M_2$. Then, $\mathcal{D} \upharpoonright ext(M_i)$, $i = 1, 2$, is a trace distribution of M_i.* □

Definition 10. Let M_1, M_2 be two probabilistic automata with the same external actions. The *trace distribution preorder* is defined as follows.

$$M_1 \sqsubseteq_D M_2 \text{ iff } tdistrs(M_1) \subseteq tdistrs(M_2). \qquad \square$$

The trace distribution preorder is a direct extension of the trace preorder of ordinary automata; however, it is not a precongruence. Consider the two probabilistic automata M_1 and M_2 of Figure 3. It is easy to see that M_1 and M_2 have the same trace distributions. Consider now the context C of Figure 3. Figure 4 shows a probabilistic execution of $M_2 \| C$ where there is a total correlation between the occurrence of actions d and f and of actions e and g. Such a correlation cannot be obtained from $M_1 \| C$, since the choice between f and g must be resolved before knowing what action among d and e is chosen probabilistically. Thus, $M_1 \| C$ and $M_2 \| C$ do not have the same trace distributions. This leads us to the following definition.

Definition 11. Let M_1, M_2 be two probabilistic automata with the same external actions. The *trace distribution precongruence*, denoted by $\sqsubseteq_{DC}$, is the coarsest precongruence that is contained in the trace distribution preorder. □

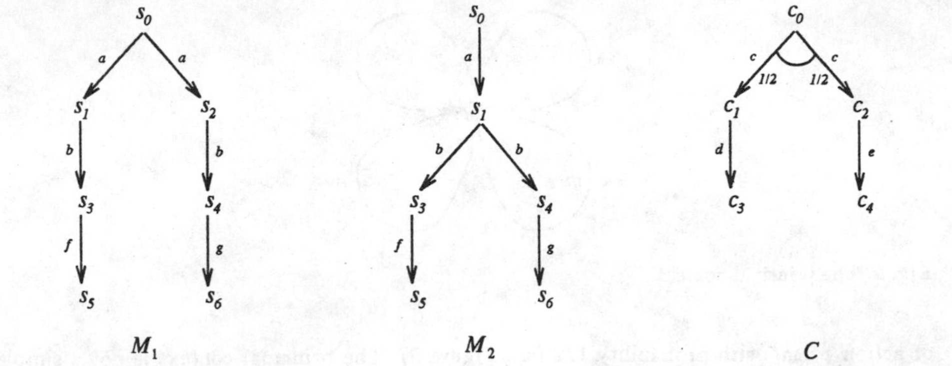

Fig. 3. The trace distribution preorder is not a precongruence.

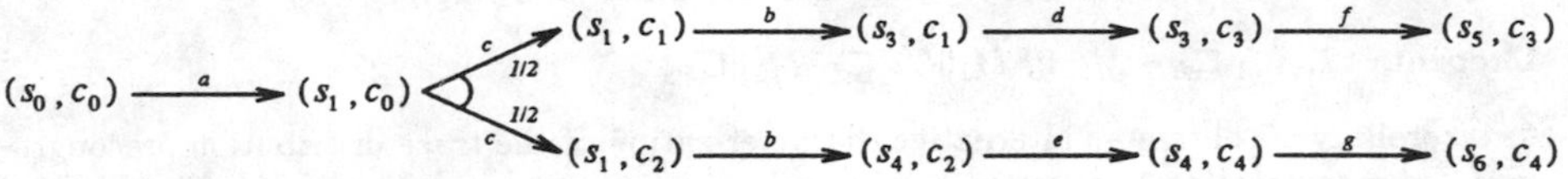

Fig. 4. A probabilistic execution of $M_2 \| C$.

The trace distribution precongruence preserves properties that resemble the safety properties of ordinary automata [1]. One example of such a property is the following.

> "*After some finite trace β has occurred, the probability that some action a occurs is not greater than p.*"

The property above means that in every trace distribution of a probabilistic automaton M the probability of the traces where action a occurs after β, conditional on the occurrence β, is not greater than p. Suppose that $M_1 \sqsubseteq_{DC} M_2$, and suppose by contradiction that M_2 satisfies the property above, while M_1 does not. Then there is a trace distribution of M_1 where the probability of a after β conditional to β is greater than p. Since $M_1 \sqsubseteq_{DC} M_2$, there is a trace distribution of M_2 where the probability of a after β conditional to β is greater than p. This contradicts the hypothesis that M_2 satisfies the property above.

5 The Principal Context

In this section we give an alternative characterization of the trace distribution precongruence that is easier to manipulate and that gives us an idea of the role of the branching structure of a probabilistic automaton. We define the *principal context*, denoted by C_P, and we show that there exists a context C that can distinguish two probabilistic automata M_1 and M_2 iff the principal context distinguishes M_1 and M_2.

The principal context is a probabilistic automaton with a unique state and three self-loop transitions labeled with actions that do not appear in any other probabilistic automaton. Two self-loop transitions are deterministic (Dirac) and are labeled with action *left* and *right*, respectively; the third self-loop transition is probabilistic, where one edge leads to the occurrence of action *pleft* with probability 1/2 and the other edge leads to the occurrence

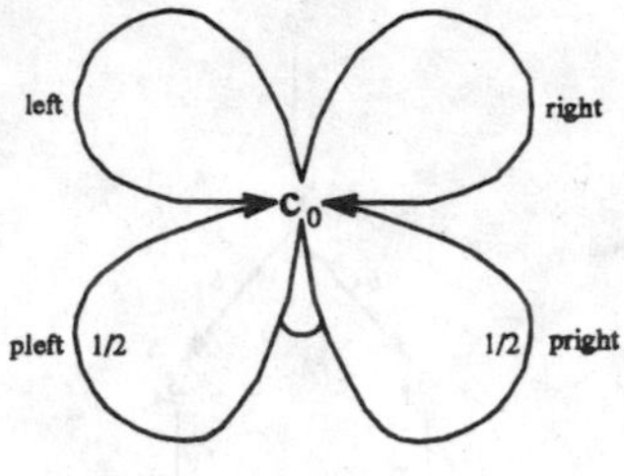

Fig. 5. The principal context.

of action *pright* with probability 1/2 (see Figure 5). The principal context is not a simple probabilistic automaton; however, since it does not have any action in common with any other probabilistic automaton, the parallel composition operator can be extended trivially: no synchronization is allowed. The main theorem is the following.

Theorem 12. *$M_1 \sqsubseteq_{DC} M_2$ iff $M_1 \| C_P \sqsubseteq_D M_2 \| C_P$.* □

As a corollary we obtain an alternative characterization of the trace distribution precongruence. Let a ***principal trace distribution*** of a probabilistic automaton M be a trace distribution of $M \| C_P$, and denote by *ptdistrs*(M) the set *tdistrs*$(M \| C_P)$.

Corollary 13. *$M_1 \sqsubseteq_{DC} M_2$ iff ext(M_1) = ext(M_2) and ptdistrs$(M_1) \subseteq$ ptdistrs(M_2).* □

We give a high level sketch of the proof of Theorem 12, which appears in [19]. The proof is structured in several steps where a generic distinguishing context C is transformed into a simpler distinguishing context C' till the point where the principal context is obtained. This shows the "if" part of the theorem. To show the "only if" part the principal context is transformed into a simple probabilistic automaton. The transformation steps are the following.

1. Ensure that C does not have any action in common with M_1 and M_2;
2. Ensure that C does not have any cycles in its transition relation;
3. Ensure that the branching structure of C is at most countable;
4. Ensure that the branching structure of C is at most binary;
5. Ensure that the probabilistic transitions of C lead to binary and uniform distributions;
6. Ensure that each action of C is external and appears exactly in one edge of the transition relation of C;
7. Ensure that each state of C enables two deterministic transitions and one probabilistic transition with a uniform binary distribution;
8. Rename all the actions of the context of 7 according to the action names of the principal context and then collapse all the states of the new context into a unique state, leading to the principal context.

We give an example of the first transformation. Let C be a distinguishing context for M_1 and M_2. Build C' as follows: for each each action a in common with M_1 and M_2, replace a with two new actions a_1, a_2, and replace each transition $(c, a, \mathcal{P})$ of C with two transitions (c, a_1, c') and $(c', a_2, \mathcal{P})$, where c' denotes a new state that is used only for the transition $(c, a, \mathcal{P})$. Denote c' by $c_{(c,a,\mathcal{P})}$.

Let $\mathcal{D}$ be a trace distribution of $M_1 \| C$ that is not a trace distribution of $M_2 \| C$. Consider a probabilistic execution H_1 of $M_1 \| C$ such that *tdistr*$(H_1) = \mathcal{D}$, and consider the scheduler that leads to H_1. Apply to $M_1 \| C'$ the same scheduler with the following modification: whenever a transition $((s_1, c), a, \mathcal{P}_1 \otimes \mathcal{P})$ is scheduled in $M_1 \| C$, schedule $((s_1, c), a_1, \mathcal{D}((s_1, c')))$, where c' is $c_{(c,a,\mathcal{P})}$, followed by $((s_1, c'), a, \mathcal{P}_1 \otimes \mathcal{D}(c'))$, and, for each $s'_1 \in \Omega_1$, followed by $((s'_1, c'), a_2, \mathcal{D}(s'_1) \otimes \mathcal{P})$. Denote the resulting probabilistic execution by H'_1 and the resulting trace distribution by $\mathcal{D}'$. Then, we prove that $\mathcal{D}' \upharpoonright acts(M_1 \| C) = \mathcal{D}$.

Suppose by contradiction that it is possible to obtain $\mathcal{D}'$ from $M_2 \| C'$, and let H'_2 be a probabilistic execution of $M_2 \| C'$ such that $tdistr(H'_2) = \mathcal{D}'$. Then, we show that it is possible to build a probabilistic execution H_2 of $M_2 \| C$ such that $tdistr(H_2) = \mathcal{D}$. The construction of H_2 is not simple since we need to handle all the internal actions of M_2 that occur in H'_2 between each pair of actions of the form a_1, a_2.

6 Probabilistic Forward Simulations

The second main result of this paper is that the simulation method of [15] extends to the probabilistic framework. Thus, the trace distribution precongruence relation can be verified by defining a relation between the states of two probabilistic automata and checking some simple local conditions. This is one of the major verification methods for ordinary automata.

We start with the coarsest simulation relation of [20], and we show that it distinguishes too much. Then, we introduce our probabilistic forward simulation relations and we show their soundness for the trace distribution precongruence.

A ***weak probabilistic simulation*** between two simple probabilistic automata M_1 and M_2 is a relation $\mathcal{R} \subseteq states(M_1) \times states(M_2)$ such that

1. each start state of M_1 is related to at least one start state of M_2;
2. for each pair of states $s_1 \, \mathcal{R} \, s_2$ and each transition $s_1 \xrightarrow{a} \mathcal{P}_1$ of M_1, there exists a weak combined transition $s_2 \overset{a \upharpoonright ext(M_2)}{\Longrightarrow}_C \mathcal{P}_2$ of M_2 such that $\mathcal{P}_1 \sqsubseteq_{\mathcal{R}} \mathcal{P}_2$,

where $\sqsubseteq_{\mathcal{R}}$ is the ***lifting*** of $\mathcal{R}$ to probability spaces [10, 20]. That is, $\mathcal{P}_1 \sqsubseteq_{\mathcal{R}} \mathcal{P}_2$ iff there exists a function $w : \Omega_1 \times \Omega_2 \to [0, 1]$ such that

1. for each $s_1 \in \Omega_1$, $\sum_{s_2 \in \Omega_2} w(s_1, s_2) = P_1[s_1]$,
2. for each $s_2 \in \Omega_2$, $\sum_{s_1 \in \Omega_1} w(s_1, s_2) = P_2[s_2]$,
3. for each $(s_1, s_2) \in \Omega_1 \times \Omega_2$, if $w(s_1, s_2) > 0$ then $s_1 \, \mathcal{R} \, s_2$.

The idea behind the definition of $\sqsubseteq_{\mathcal{R}}$ is that each state of Ω_1 must be represented by some states of Ω_2, and similarly, each state of Ω_2 must represent one or more states of Ω_1.

Example 4. Weak probabilistic simulations are sound for the trace distribution precongruence (cf. Theorem 16); however, they are too strong.

Consider the two probabilistic automata of Figure 6. The probabilistic automaton M_2, which chooses internally one element out of four with probability $1/4$ each, is implemented by the probabilistic automaton M_1, which flips two fair coins to make the same choice (by "implement" we mean $\sqsubseteq_D$). However, the first transition of M_1 cannot be simulated by M_2 since the probabilistic choice of M_2 is not resolved completely yet in M_1. This situation suggests a new preorder relation where a state of M_1 can be related to a probability distribution over states of M_2. The informal idea behind a relation $s_1 \, \mathcal{R} \, \mathcal{P}_2$ is that s_1 represents an intermediate stage of M_1 in reaching the distribution $\mathcal{P}_2$. For example, in Figure 6 state s_1 would be related to a uniform distribution $\mathcal{P}$ over states s'_3 and s'_4 ($\mathcal{P} = \mathcal{U}(s'_3, s'_4)$), meaning that s_1 is an intermediate stage of M_1 in reaching the distribution $\mathcal{P}$.

It is also possible to create examples where the relationship between s and $\mathcal{P}$ does not mean simply that s is an intermediate stage of M_1 in reaching the distribution $\mathcal{P}$, but rather

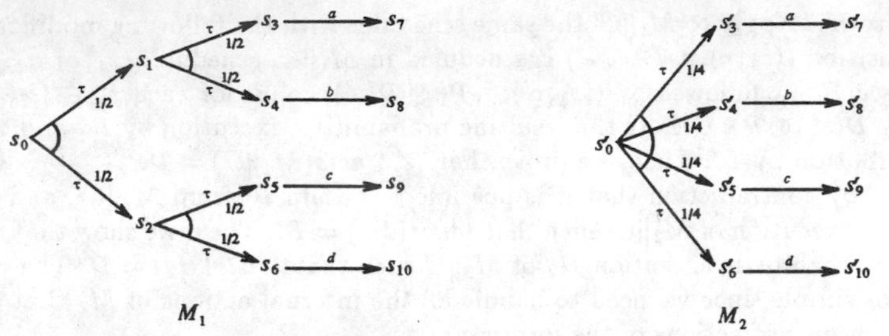

Fig. 6. Implementation of a probabilistic transition with several probabilistic transitions.

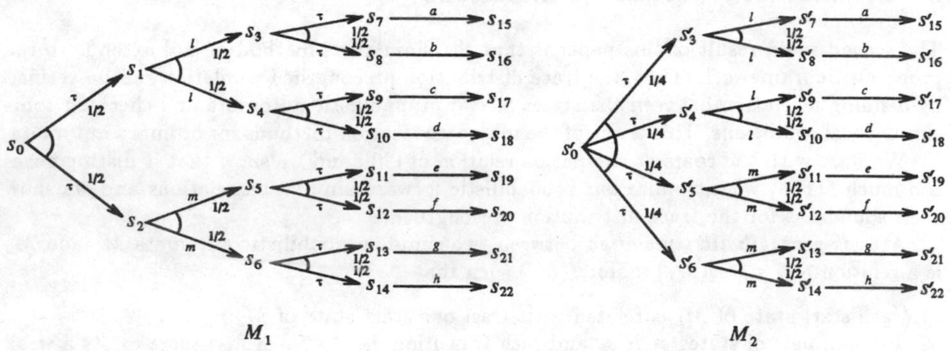

Fig. 7. A more sophisticated implementation.

that s is an intermediate stage in reaching a probability distribution that can be reached from $\mathcal{P}$. Consider the two probabilistic automata of Figure 7. Although not evident at the moment, M_1 and M_2 are in the trace distribution precongruence relation, i.e., $M_1 \sqsubseteq_{DC} M_2$. Following the same idea as for the example of Figure 6, state s_1 is related to $\mathcal{U}(s'_3, s'_4)$. However, s_1 is not an intermediate stage of M_1 in reaching $\mathcal{U}(s'_3, s'_4)$, since s_1 enables a transition labeled with an external action l, while in M_2 no external action occurs before reaching $\mathcal{U}(s'_3, s'_4)$. Rather, from s'_3 and s'_4 there are two transitions labeled with l, and thus the only way to simulate the transition $s_1 \xrightarrow{l} \mathcal{U}(s_3, s_4)$ from $\mathcal{U}(s'_3, s'_4)$ is to perform the two transitions labeled with l, which lead to the distribution $\mathcal{U}(s'_7, s'_8, s'_9, s'_{10})$. Now the question is the following: in what sense does $\mathcal{U}(s'_7, s'_8, s'_9, s'_{10})$ represent $\mathcal{U}(s_3, s_4)$? The first observation is that s_3 can be seen as an intermediate stage in reaching $\mathcal{U}(s'_7, s'_8)$, and that s_4 can be seen as an intermediate stage in reaching $\mathcal{U}(s'_9, s'_{10})$. Thus, s_3 is related to $\mathcal{U}(s'_7, s'_8)$ and s_4 is related to $\mathcal{U}(s'_9, s'_{10})$. The second observation is that $\mathcal{U}(s'_7, s'_8, s'_9, s'_{10})$ can be expressed as $1/2\mathcal{U}(s'_7, s'_8) + 1/2\mathcal{U}(s'_9, s'_{10})$. Thus, $\mathcal{U}(s'_7, s'_8, s'_9, s'_{10})$ can be seen as a combination of two probability spaces, each one representing an element of $\mathcal{U}(s_3, s_4)$. This recalls the lifting of a relation that we introduced at the beginning of this section. □

Definition 14. A *probabilistic forward simulation* between two simple probabilistic automata M_1 and M_2 is a relation $\mathcal{R} \subseteq$ *states*$(M_1) \times$ *Probs*(*states*(M_2)) such that

1. each start state of M_1 is related to at least one Dirac distribution over a start state of M_2;

2. for each $s \mathcal{R} \mathcal{P}'$, if $s \xrightarrow{a} \mathcal{P}_1$, then
   (a) for each $s' \in \Omega'$ there exists a probability space $\mathcal{P}_{s'}$ such that $s' \overset{a\lceil ext(M_2)}{\Longrightarrow}_C \mathcal{P}_{s'}$, and
   (b) there exists a probability space $\mathcal{P}'_2$ of $Probs(Probs(states(M_2)))$ satisfying $\mathcal{P}_1 \sqsubseteq_{\mathcal{R}} \mathcal{P}'_2$, such that $\sum_{s' \in \Omega'} P'[s']\mathcal{P}_{s'} = \sum_{\mathcal{P} \in \Omega'_2} P'_2[\mathcal{P}]\mathcal{P}$.

We write $M_1 \sqsubseteq_{FS} M_2$ whenever $ext(M_1) = ext(M_2)$ and there is a forward simulation from M_1 to M_2. □

Example 5. The probabilistic forward simulation for the probabilistic automata M_1 and M_2 of Figure 7 is the following: s_0 is related to $\mathcal{U}(s'_0)$; each state s_i, $i \geq 7$, is related to $\mathcal{D}(s'_i)$; each state s_i, $1 \leq i \leq 6$, is related to $\mathcal{U}(s'_{2i+1}, s'_{2i+2})$. It is an easy exercise to check that this relation is a probabilistic forward simulation. Observe also that there is no probabilistic forward simulation from M_2 to M_1. Informally, s'_3 cannot be simulated by M_1, since the only candidate state to be related to s'_1 is s_1, and s_1 does not contain all the information contained in s'_3. The formal way to see that there is no probabilistic forward simulation from M_2 to M_1 is to observe that M_2 and M_1 are not in the trace distribution precongruence relation and then use the fact that probabilistic forward simulations are sound for the trace distribution precongruence relation (cf. Theorem 16). In $M_2 \| C_P$ it is possible force action *left* to be scheduled exactly when M_2 is in s'_3, and thus it is possible to create a correlation between action *left* and actions a and b; in $M_1 \| C_P$ such a correlation cannot be created since action *left* must be scheduled before action l. □

Proposition 15. *$\sqsubseteq_{FS}$ is a preorder and is preserved by parallel composition.* □

The proof that $\sqsubseteq_{FS}$ is preserved by the parallel composition operator is standard. The proof that $\sqsubseteq_{FS}$ is transitive is much more complicated and is based on a probabilistic version of the execution correspondence lemma of [6]. The complete proofs can be found in [19].

Theorem 16. *Let $M_1 \sqsubseteq_{FS} M_2$. Then $M_1 \sqsubseteq_{DC} M_2$.* □

The proof of Theorem 16, which appears in [19], is carried out in two steps. Let $\mathcal{R}$ be a probabilistic forward simulation from M_1 to M_2. Given a probabilistic execution H_1 of M_1, we build a probabilistic execution H_2 of M_2 that *represents* H_1 via $\mathcal{R}$. The structure that describes how H_2 represents H_1 is called an *execution correspondence structure*. Then, we show that if H_2 represents H_1, then H_1 and H_2 have the same trace distribution. Thus, $M_1 \sqsubseteq_{FS} M_2$ implies $M_1 \sqsubseteq_D M_2$. Since from Proposition 15 $\sqsubseteq_{FS}$ is a precongruence, the proof of Theorem 16 is completed.

7 Concluding Remarks

We have defined a trace-based semantics for probabilistic automata that is preserved by the parallel composition operator, and we have extended the simulation method of [15] to the new framework. The main object of observation is a trace distribution, which is a probability distribution over traces. The compositionality result is obtained by studying the trace distributions of a system composed in parallel with an elementary context called the principal context. The new simulation relations have the interesting property that states are related to probability distributions over states.

In further work we plan to investigate on completeness results concerning probabilistic forward simulations and the trace distribution precongruence. We also plan to to apply the same methodology outlined in this paper to define a failure-based semantics for probabilistic automata. Finally, it is desirable to study further what can be done with general probabilistic automata and how to extend the work of this paper to models that include real-time or hybrid behavior. A trace-based semantics for probabilistic timed automata is studied in [19].

Acknowledgments. I would like to thank Nancy Lynch for useful discussion that lead to the definition of probabilistic forward simulations.

References

1. B. Alpern and F.B. Schneider. Defining liveness. *Information Processing Letters*, 21(4), 1985.
2. J. Aspnes and M.P. Herlihy. Fast randomized consensus using shared memory. *Journal of Algorithms*, 15(1):441–460, September 1990.
3. M. Ben-Or. Another advantage of free choice: completely asynchronous agreement protocols. In *Proceedings of the 2nd Annual ACM PODC*, 1983.
4. S.D. Brookes, C.A.R. Hoare, and A.W. Roscoe. A theory of communicating sequential processes. *Journal of the ACM*, 31(3):560–599, 1984.
5. I. Christoff. *Testing Equivalences for Probabilistic Processes*. PhD thesis, Department of Computer Science, Uppsala University, 1990.
6. R. Gawlick, R. Segala, J.F. Søgaard-Andersen, and N.A. Lynch. Liveness in timed and untimed systems. In *Proceedings 21th ICALP*, Jerusalem, LNCS 820, 1994. A full version appears as MIT Technical Report number MIT/LCS/TR-587.
7. R.J. van Glabbeek, S.A. Smolka, B. Steffen, and C.M.N. Tofts. Reactive, generative, and stratified models of probabilistic processes. In *Proceedings 5th Annual Symposium on Logic in Computer Science*, Philadelphia, USA, pages 130–141. IEEE Computer Society Press, 1990.
8. H. Hansson. *Time and Probability in Formal Design of Distributed Systems*, volume 1 of *Real-Time Safety Critical Systems*. Elsevier, 1994.
9. C.A.R. Hoare. *Communicating Sequential Processes*. Prentice-Hall International, 1985.
10. B. Jonsson and K.G. Larsen. Specification and refinement of probabilistic processes. In *Proceedings of the 6th IEEE Symposium on Logic in Computer Science*, pages 266–277, July 1991.
11. B. Jonsson and J. Parrow, editors. *Proceedings of CONCUR 94*, LNCS 836, 1994.
12. C.C. Jou and S.A. Smolka. Equivalences, congruences, and complete axiomatizations for probabilistic processes. In *Proceedings of CONCUR 90*, LNCS 458, pages 367–383, 1990.
13. K.G. Larsen and A. Skou. Compositional verification of probabilistic processes. In *Proceedings of CONCUR 92* LNCS 630, pages 456–471, 1992.
14. N.A. Lynch, I. Saias, and R. Segala. Proving time bounds for randomized distributed algorithms. In *Proceedings of the 13th Annual ACM PODC*, pages 314–323, 1994.
15. N.A. Lynch and F.W. Vaandrager. Forward and backward simulations for timing-based systems. In J.W. de Bakker, C. Huizing, W.P. de Roever, and G. Rozenberg, editors, *Proceedings of the REX Workshop "Real-Time: Theory in Practice"*, LNCS 600, pages 397–446, 1991.
16. G.D. Plotkin. A structural approach to operational semantics. Technical Report DAIMI FN-19, Computer science Department, Aarhus University, 1981.
17. A. Pogosyants and R. Segala. Formal verification of timed properties of randomized distributed algorithms. In *Proceedings of the 14th Annual ACM PODC*, 1995.
18. M.O. Rabin. Probabilistic automata. *Information and Control*, 6:230–245, 1963.
19. R. Segala. *Modeling and Verification of Randomized Distributed Real-Time Systems*. PhD thesis, MIT, Dept. of Electrical Engineering and Computer Science, 1995.
20. R. Segala and N.A. Lynch. Probabilistic simulations for probabilistic processes. In Jonsson and Parrow [11], pages 481–496.
21. K. Seidel. Probabilistic communicating processes. Technical Report PRG-102, Ph.D. Thesis, Programming Research Group, Oxford University Computing Laboratory, 1992.
22. M.Y. Vardi. Automatic verification of probabilistic concurrent finite-state programs. In *Proceedings of 26th IEEE Symposium on Foundations of Computer Science*, pages 327–338, 1985.
23. S.H. Wu, S. Smolka, and E.W. Stark. Composition and behaviors of probabilistic I/O automata. In Jonsson and Parrow [11].

Acceptance Trees for Probabilistic Processes*

Manuel Núñez, David de Frutos, and Luis Llana

Dept. de Informática y Automática
Facultad CC. Matemáticas
Universidad Complutense de Madrid, Spain
e-mail: {manuelnu,defrutos,llana}@eucmvx.sim.ucm.es

Abstract. In this paper we study the extension of classical testing theory to a probabilistic process algebra. We consider a *generative* interpretation of probabilities for a language with two choice operators (one internal and the other external), which are annotated with a probability $p \in (0, 1)$. We define a testing semantics for our language, and we write $P\ pass_p\ T$ to denote that the process P *passes* the test T with a probability p. We also give a set of *essential* tests which has the same *strength* as the full family of tests. Next we give an alternative characterization of the testing semantics, based on the idea of *acceptance sets*, and we prove that the new equivalence is equal to the testing equivalence. Finally, we present a fully abstract denotational semantics based on *acceptance trees*.

1 Introduction

During the last years there has been a great activity devoted to the study of time and probabilistic extensions of concurrent processes. These extensions are very adequate for the specification of *real* systems which strongly depend on stochastic behaviors or on time constraints, and have been proved useful for the specification of communication protocols, real-time systems, and fault-tolerant systems. Next we summarize some works on probabilistic processes which are related in some way with this paper.

[GJS90] presents a probabilistic version of SCCS called PCCS where the sum operator is extended with probabilities (i.e. $\sum_{i \in I}[p_i]E_i$, $p_i \in (0, 1]$ and $\sum p_i = 1$). [vGSST90] discusses the *reactive, generative*, and *stratified* models for PCCS. According to the interaction between the processes and the environment, the *reactive* model is defined as the model where the environment may only offer a single action at a time. In the *generative* model, the environment can offer several actions at the same time, and the process chooses between them according to some probability distribution. In the *stratified* model, the branching structure of the probabilistic choices is captured.

In [HJ90], a probabilistic and timed extension of CCS is studied. They have two choice operators: A probabilistic internal one and a (nonprobabilistic) external nondeterministic one. They define *alternating processes* which have a (strict) alternation between probabilistic and nondeterministic states. In [YL92], CCS is extended with a nondeterministic probabilistic choice operator. A new notion of

* Research partially supported by the CICYT project TIC 94-0851-C02-02

testing semantics is defined, where a process *can pass* a test with a set of probabilities. A process *must pass* a test if the minimum of the set of probabilities is equal to one, and *may pass* the test if the maximum is greater than zero. In [JY95] denotational characterizations of the induced testing preorders are given.

[Cua93] presents a probabilistic (reactive) version of CSP whose testing semantics is studied. He also gives a fully abstract denotational semantics. Also, [Sei92, Low95] develop probabilistic extensions of CSP, but their semantic frameworks are very far from our own.

In the framework of probabilistic labeled transition systems (*plts*), [Chr90] presents three equivalences based on testing. [CSZ92] presents a testing semantics for *plts*; as in the nonprobabilistic case, processes and tests are essentially the same, while in [Chr90] or in [Cua93] they were different. [YCDS94] presents an alternative characterization of the testing preorder given in [CSZ92], introducing a set of *essential* tests, called *probabilistic traces*, which are proved to have the same *strength* as the full family of tests.

Finally, [WSS94] studies probabilistic processes modeled by probabilistic I/O automata. Even though this syntactic framework is not too close to our approach, several of their results are rather thorough and it seems interesting to translate them to the field of probabilistic process algebras.

In this paper, we focus on the *generative* model, and we introduce a probabilistic extension of classical testing theory, as proposed in [Hen88]. In order to concentrate on the characteristics of the probabilistic extension, we restrict ourselves to the study of a subset of the language in [Hen88]. We consider the language built from *Nil*, Ω, prefix, choice (internal and external) and recursion, where the choice operators are extended with a probability. The main features of our work are:

1. In our language, as in [Hen88], we have two different choice operators that are extended with a probability.
2. We define a testing equivalence in the standard way, where tests are identical to processes but extended with a new action ω which denotes that the test has succeeded. Thus, we have in particular that several actions can be offered at the same time. This is why we have found natural to consider a *generative* interpretation of probabilities, although a *stratified* interpretation could be considered.
3. We present an alternative characterization of the testing equivalence based on acceptance sets [Hen88].
4. We develop a denotational semantics based on acceptance trees [Hen85], which is proved to be fully abstract with respect to the testing semantics.

The rest of this paper is structured as follows. Section 2 presents our language, its operational semantics, the associated testing semantics, and a set of *essential* tests. In Section 3, we describe the probabilistic extension of *acceptance sets.* In Section 4, we prove that the equivalences defined in the previous two sections are the same. Section 5 presents a denotational semantics which is fully abstract with respect to the testing semantics, while in Section 6 we give our conclusions and some outlines for future work.

2 A Testing Semantics

As we said in the Introduction, we will extend with probabilities the operators of a subset of the language presented in [Hen88] (this language first appeared in [dNH87]). In this paper we consider the simple language without parallel composition or restriction, and we call this language PPA (Probabilistic Process Algebra). We have two probabilistic choice operators: an internal choice operator, and an external one. Extremal values (0 and 1) of probabilities are not allowed in these two choice operators, because they cannot be simply treated in an adequate way within the generative model (see [SS90] where extremal values are used to capture priorities, but in a stratified model).

2.1 Syntax of PPA

Definition 1. Given a finite set of actions Act and a set of identifiers Id, the set of PPA processes is defined by the following BNF expression:

$$P ::= Nil \mid \Omega \mid X \mid a; P \mid P \oplus_p P \mid P +_p P \mid recX.P$$

where $p \in (0,1)$, $a \in Act$, and $X \in Id$. □

Now, we give an intuitive explanation of each operator:

- Nil is a process that cannot perform any action. Ω is a divergent process.
- $a; P$ is a process that first performs action a, and then behaves as P.
- $P \oplus_p Q$ is a process that behaves as P with probability equal to p, and as Q with probability equal to $1-p$. This choice is made internally nondeterministically, i.e. without interaction with the environment.
- $P +_p Q$ is a process that can behave either as P or as Q, but this choice depends on the environment. This means that if the environment offers actions that only one of the processes P or Q can perform, the corresponding process will be chosen. On the other hand, if both processes can perform actions from those offered by the environment, then the choice is made partially nondeterministically using the probability p.
- $recX.P$ is used to define recursive behaviors.

2.2 Operational Semantics

The set of rules that define the operational semantics is given in Fig. 1. There are two types of transitions. The intuitive meaning of a probabilistic transition $P \xrightarrow{a}_p Q$ is that if the environment offers all the actions in Act, then the probability with which P performs a and then behaves as Q is equal to p; the meaning of $P \succ\!\!\longrightarrow_p Q$ is that the process P evolves to Q with probability p, without interaction with the environment.

For the sake of simplicity, we have omitted indices in the definition of transitions. Usually (see [GJS90]) indices are used to distinguish among different occurrences of the same transition; instead we have supposed that if a transition can be derived in several ways, each derivation generates a different instance of this transition (this could be formalized using multisets of transitions).

$$(PRE)\frac{}{a;P \xrightarrow{a}_1 P} \qquad (INT1)\frac{}{P \oplus_p Q \succ\!\!\longrightarrow_p P} \qquad (INT2)\frac{}{P \oplus_p Q \succ\!\!\longrightarrow_{1-p} Q}$$

$$(EXT1)\frac{P \succ\!\!\longrightarrow_q P' \wedge Q_\oplus = 0}{P +_p Q \succ\!\!\longrightarrow_q P' +_p Q} \qquad (EXT2)\frac{Q \succ\!\!\longrightarrow_q Q' \wedge P_\oplus = 0}{P +_p Q \succ\!\!\longrightarrow_q P +_p Q'} \qquad (EXT3)\frac{P \succ\!\!\longrightarrow_{q_1} P' \wedge Q \succ\!\!\longrightarrow_{q_2} Q'}{P +_p Q \succ\!\!\longrightarrow_{q_1 \cdot q_2} P' +_p Q'}$$

$$(EXT4)\frac{P \xrightarrow{a}_q P' \wedge Q_\oplus = 0}{P +_p Q \xrightarrow{a}_{p \cdot \hat{q}} P'} \qquad (EXT5)\frac{Q \xrightarrow{a}_q Q' \wedge P_\oplus = 0}{P +_p Q \xrightarrow{a}_{(1-p) \cdot \hat{q}} Q'}$$

$$(REC)\frac{}{rec\, X.P \succ\!\!\longrightarrow_1 P\{rec\, X.P/X\}} \qquad (DIV)\frac{}{\Omega \succ\!\!\longrightarrow_1 \Omega}$$

$$R_\oplus = \sum_{R'} \{\!| \, s \mid R \succ\!\!\longrightarrow_s R' \, |\!\}, \; R_+ = \sum_{R'} \{\!| \, s \mid \exists a : R \xrightarrow{a}_s R' \, |\!\}, \; \hat{q} = \frac{q}{p \cdot P_+ + (1-p) \cdot Q_+}$$

Fig. 1. Operational Semantics of PPA.

Example 1. Let $P = a; Nil +_{\frac{1}{2}} a; Nil$. Then, this process has two times the transition $P \xrightarrow{a}_{\frac{1}{2}} Nil$. Also, $Q = Q' \oplus_{\frac{1}{2}} Q'$ has two times the transition $Q \succ\!\!\longrightarrow_{\frac{1}{2}} Q'$.

While the rules for prefix, internal choice, divergence and recursion do not need any explanation, we will briefly explain the rules for the external nondeterministic operator. The first three rules say that whenever any of the arguments of an external choice can evolve via an internal transition, this kind of transitions are performed until both arguments reach a stable state (i.e. no more internal transitions are possible). Let us remark that $+_p$ is not a static operator; these three rules simply indicate that internal choices do not *solve* external choices.

The other two rules are applied when none of the processes can perform more internal actions and (at least) one of the arguments may evolve by executing an external action. The value $\hat{q}$ is obtained from the probability q with which this external transition is executed, taking into account if both processes can perform external transitions. Whenever both of them can perform external actions, the value p (the value associated with the external choice) is considered.

Because of this definition of operational semantics, we have that internal and external transitions are not mixed, and then we have the following

Lemma 2. *Let P be a process.* $\exists p, P' : P \succ\!\!\longrightarrow_p P' \implies \nexists q, a, P'' : P \xrightarrow{a}_q P''$.

Note that we have not the converse; for example, *Nil* performs no transitions (neither internal nor external). Also note that the statement in the previous lemma is equivalent to $\exists q, a, P'' : P \xrightarrow{a}_q P'' \implies \nexists p, P' : P \succ\!\!\longrightarrow_p P'$.

Corollary 3. *Let P be a process. Then, the following holds*

$$(P_\oplus = 0 \vee P_\oplus = 1) \wedge (P_+ = 0 \vee P_+ = 1) \wedge (P_\oplus \neq 1 \vee P_+ \neq 1)$$

2.3 Probabilistic Tests

Once the operational semantics has been defined, in order to define a testing semantics we must define the concept of (*probabilistic*) *test*. As in the nonprobabilistic case, tests will be just processes where the alphabet *Act* is extended with a new action ω which indicates successful termination. The operational semantics of tests is the same as that of processes (considering ω as an ordinary

$$\frac{P \succ\!\!\longrightarrow_p P' \wedge T_\oplus = 0}{P \mid T \longmapsto_p P' \mid T} \qquad \frac{T \succ\!\!\longrightarrow_p T' \wedge P_\oplus = 0}{P \mid T \longmapsto_p P \mid T'} \qquad \frac{P \succ\!\!\longrightarrow_p P' \wedge T \succ\!\!\longrightarrow_q T'}{P \mid T \longmapsto_{p \cdot q} P' \mid T'}$$

$$\frac{P \xrightarrow{a}_p P' \wedge T \xrightarrow{a}_q T'}{P \mid T \longmapsto_{r_1} P' \mid T'} \qquad \frac{T \xrightarrow{\omega}_p T' \wedge P_\oplus = 0}{P \mid T \overset{\omega}{\longmapsto}_{r_2} Nil}$$

where $r_1 = \frac{p \cdot q}{\mu(P,T)}$ and $r_2 = \frac{p}{\mu(P,T)}$

Fig. 2. Rules for the parallel composition.

action). Now, we have to define how a process interacts with a test. As usual, this interaction is modeled by parallel composition of the process with the test. The rules which define this parallel composition are given in Fig. 2.

Let us briefly explain these rules. The first three rules deal with internal transitions and say that if one and only one of the processes can perform an internal transition, this transition is performed (first two rules). If both can perform an internal transition, then both perform their transitions at the *same time* (third rule). This does not imply that our calculus is synchronous. Since the two arguments of the parallel composition must solve their internal choices before evolving by an external transition, there is no problem in forcing the simultaneous resolution of the internal choices in both arguments.

If none of the processes can perform internal transitions, then the last two rules are applied. The first rule deals with *synchronization*. The second one deals with the special action ω. After this action is performed, no more actions can be performed by the composition (success of test). Note that in this rule, we also have a clause $P_\oplus = 0$, so that a divergent process (that is a process which has no finite maximal computation) would *not pass* any test.

In these last two rules, we use a *normalization factor* $\mu(P,T)$. This normalization factor is similar to that in [CSZ92] (considering that this factor is only used when just visible actions may be performed), and it is defined by

$$\mu(P,T) = \sum_a \{\!\!\{ p \cdot q \mid \exists P', T' : P \xrightarrow{a}_p P' \wedge T \xrightarrow{a}_q T' \}\!\!\} + \sum \{\!\!\{ p \mid \exists T' : T \xrightarrow{\omega}_p T' \}\!\!\}$$

Definition 4. Let P be a process and T a test. A *computation* is a *maximal* sequence of transitions $C = P \mid T \longmapsto_{p_1} P_1 \mid T_1 \longmapsto_{p_2} \cdots P_{n-1} \mid T_{n-1} \overset{*}{\longmapsto}_{p_n} R$, where $*$ denotes either an empty label or the special action ω. A sequence is said to be *maximal* when there do not exist $p > 0, R'$ such that $R \overset{*}{\longmapsto}_p R'$.

When the last transition is of the form $P_{n-1} \mid T_{n-1} \overset{\omega}{\longmapsto}_{p_n} Nil$, we say that the computation is *successful*. We denote by $\tilde{C}$ the *set* of *successful computations* from C. The probability of a successful computation S, $Pr(S)$, is inductively defined as

$$Pr(Nil) = 1 \text{ (i.e. } T \text{ has succeeded)}$$
$$Pr(P \mid T \overset{*}{\longmapsto}_p C) = p \cdot Pr(C)$$

We write $P\, pass_p\, T$ if $\sum_{S \in \tilde{C}} Pr(S) = p$. □

Now, given a family of tests we can define the corresponding notion of testing equivalence with respect to this family.

Definition 5. Given a set of probabilistic tests $\mathcal{T}$, and two processes P and Q, we say $P \approx_{\mathcal{T}} Q$ iff $\forall T \in \mathcal{T}: \; P \, pass_p \, T \wedge \; Q \, pass_q \, T \Longrightarrow p = q$. If the family of tests is the whole set of tests, we just write $P \approx Q$. □

2.4 A set of *essential* tests

In this section, we construct a family of tests $\mathcal{PB}$, which is equivalent to the whole family of tests, in the sense that $P \approx_{\mathcal{PB}} P' \Longleftrightarrow P \approx P'$. This family of tests will be close to the notion of *probabilistic traces* given in [YCDS94]. First, we need the following

Lemma 6. *Let P be a process, T, T' be tests, and $a \in Act$. Then,*

1. $P \, pass_q \, (T \oplus_p T') \Longleftrightarrow P \, pass_{q_1} \, T \wedge P \, pass_{q_2} \, T' \wedge p \cdot q_1 + (1-p) \cdot q_2 = q$
2. $P \, pass_q \, (a; T) +_p (a; T') \Longleftrightarrow P \, pass_q \, a; (T \oplus_p T')$

Now we will generalize the choice operators to n arguments. Note that in this definition we do not allow nondeterminism caused by prefixing two arguments of a generalized external choice by the same action.

Definition 7. Let $P_1, P_2, \ldots, P_n$ be processes, and $a_1, a_2, \ldots, a_n \in Act$ different actions. We inductively define the *generalized external choice* by

1. $\sum_{i=1}^{1} [1] a_1; P_1 = a_1; P_1$ 2. $\sum_{i=1}^{n} [p_i] a_i; P_i = (a_1; P_1) +_{p_1} (\sum_{i=1}^{n-1} [\frac{p_{i+1}}{1-p_1}] a_{i+1}; P_{i+1})$

where $p_1, p_2, \ldots, p_n > 0$ are such that $\sum p_i = 1$.
We inductively define the *generalized internal choice* by

1. $\bigoplus_{i=1}^{0} [p_i] \, P_i = \Omega$ 2. $\bigoplus_{i=1}^{1} [1] \, P_1 = P_1$

3. $\bigoplus_{i=1}^{n} [p_i] \, P_i = \bigoplus_{i=1}^{n} [\frac{p_i}{p}] \, P_i \oplus_p \Omega$ [if $p = \sum p_i < 1 \; \wedge n > 0$]

4. $\bigoplus_{i=1}^{n} [p_i] \, P_i = P_1 \oplus_{p_1} (\bigoplus_{i=1}^{n-1} [\frac{p_{i+1}}{1-p_1}] \, P_{i+1})$ [if $\sum p_i = 1 \; \wedge n > 1$]

where $p_1, p_2, \ldots, p_n > 0$ are such that $\sum p_i \leq 1$. □

Let us remark that in the generalized internal choice, the sum of probabilities may be less than 1. The difference between 1 and this value indicates the probability of divergence. For example, $\bigoplus_{i=1}^{2} ([\frac{1}{3}] \, P_1) \; ([\frac{1}{3}] \, P_2) = (P_1 \oplus_{\frac{1}{2}} P_2) \oplus_{\frac{2}{3}} \Omega$.

Taking into account that internal choices can be removed from tests and that only deterministic tests are needed (by Lemma 6), that infinite tests are redundant, and following [YCDS94], we obtain the following family of tests.

Definition 8. The set of *probabilistic barbed tests*, $\mathcal{PB}$, is defined by the BNF expression

$$T ::= \omega; Nil \mid \sum_{i=1}^{n} [p_i]\, a_i; R_i \qquad \text{where } R_i = \begin{cases} Nil & \text{if } 1 \leq i \leq n-1 \\ T & \text{if } i = n \end{cases}$$

$p_i > 0$, $\sum p_i = 1$, $a_i \in Act$, and $a_i \neq a_j$ for $i \neq j$ □

The following theorem is a simple adaptation of Theorem 2 in [YCDS94], although its proof requires more care, because now divergent processes are allowed.

Theorem 9. $P \approx_{\mathcal{PB}} Q \Longleftrightarrow P \approx Q$.

3 Probabilistic Acceptance Sets

In this section we present an alternative characterization of the testing equivalence defined in the previous section. We will use a version of *acceptance sets* [Hen88] introducing probabilities in order to capture the information given by probabilistic tests. The main changes in the definitions given in [Hen88], in order to adapt them to the probabilistic case, are the following:

- States are not sets of actions but sets of pairs (action, probability).
- In the nonprobabilistic case, acceptance sets are defined as the reachable states after a sequence of actions has been performed. In the probabilistic case, sequences of actions are not valid any more; instead we have to take sequences of pairs (state, action) where the action must belong to those contained in the state (see Example 2).
- The notion of equivalence must be modified taking into account the probabilistic information that appears in acceptance sets (see Example 3).

While the first change is clear, the other two need more explanation.

In the nonprobabilistic case, *states* (i.e. the different sets contained in the acceptance sets) can be just characterized by sequences of actions because the *continuations* of a process after an action is performed cannot be distinguished, and thus they must be joined into a common continuation. This is illustrated by the following

Example 2. Let P be the nonprobabilistic process $a; d \oplus ((a; b) + c)$, where *Nil*'s have been omitted. We have that P is equivalent to $P' = a; (d \oplus b) \oplus ((a; (d \oplus b)) + c)$ with respect to the equivalence induced by acceptance sets. That is, continuations after a has been performed are joined.

But this does not happen to the probabilistic case. Let us consider $P = a; d \oplus_{\frac{1}{2}} ((a; b) +_{\frac{1}{2}} c)$, and suppose that there exist R_1, R_2 such that P is (testing) equivalent to $P' = a; R_1 \oplus_{\frac{1}{2}} ((a; R_1) +_{\frac{1}{2}} c; R_2)$. If we consider $T = (a; b; \omega) +_{\frac{1}{3}} c$, we have $P \, pass_{\frac{1}{6}} \, T$. Since $P \approx P'$, we obtain $\frac{1}{6} = \frac{1}{2} \cdot q + \frac{1}{2} \cdot \frac{1}{3} \cdot q$, where $R_1 \, pass_q \, b; \omega$, and thus $q = \frac{1}{4}$ (i.e. $R_1 \, pass_{\frac{1}{4}} \, b; \omega$). But, if we consider $T' = a; b; \omega$, using a similar argument we obtain $R_1 \, pass_{\frac{1}{2}} \, b; \omega$, which is a contradiction.

In general we can distinguish two (or more) continuations of the same action if they correspond to different states, and so we must include states in the sequences defining probabilistic acceptance sets.

Example 3. Let P be the nonprobabilistic process $a \oplus b$, where *Nil*'s have been omitted. Then, $\mathcal{A}(P,\epsilon) = \{\{a\},\{b\}\}$, $\mathcal{A}(P,a) = \mathcal{A}(P,b) = \{\emptyset\}$ and if $s \neq \epsilon, a, b$ then $\mathcal{A}(P,s) = \emptyset$. This process is equivalent to $Q = (a \oplus b) \oplus (a + b)$.

But if we consider the probabilistic version of P, $P' = a \oplus_p b$, we have that P' has two reachable states: $\{a\}$ (with probability equal to p) and $\{b\}$ (with probability equal to $1-p$), while state $\{a,b\}$ is not reachable. But for any process $Q' = (a \oplus_p b) \oplus_q (a +_r b)$, the state $\{(a,r),(b,1-r)\}$ is reachable with probability equal to $(1-q) > 0$, and so there is no such Q' equivalent to P'.

Definition 10. Let $A \subseteq Act \times (0,1]$. We define the *multiset of actions* of A as $Act(A) = \{\!|\, a \mid \exists p : (a,p) \in A \,|\!\}$. We say that A is a *(probabilistic) state* if every $a \in Act$ appears at most one time in $Act(A)$ and either $\sum \{\!|\, p \mid (a,p) \in A \,|\!\}$ is equal to 0 (when $A = \emptyset$) or it is equal to 1. For each state A, we define the *probability* of a in A, denoted by $pro(a,A)$, as p if $(a,p) \in A$ and as 0 if $a \notin Act(A)$. □

Next we define the set of stable processes to which a process may evolve after performing a sequence of actions possibly interspersed with internal transitions.

Definition 11. Given a stable process P, we define its (immediately) *reachable state* as the set $S(P) = \{(a,p) \mid p = \sum_R \{\!|\, p_i \mid P \xrightarrow{a}_{p_i} R \,|\!\} \wedge p > 0\}$.

Given two processes P, P', where P' is stable, we say that P evolves to P' by a *generalized internal transition* with probability p if $P \succ\!\!\longrightarrow^*_p P'$ can be derived by applying the following rules:

$$P \succ\!\!\longrightarrow^*_1 P \text{ if } P \text{ is stable} \quad (\text{i.e. } \nexists q, Q : P \succ\!\!\longrightarrow_q Q)$$
$$P \succ\!\!\longrightarrow^*_p P' \text{ if } \exists q, q', Q : P \succ\!\!\longrightarrow_q Q \succ\!\!\longrightarrow^*_{q'} P' \wedge p = q \cdot q'$$

Finally, given $s = \langle A_1\, a_1, A_2\, a_2, \ldots, A_n\, a_n \rangle$, we define the relation $P \stackrel{s}{\Longrightarrow}_p P'$ by:

$P \stackrel{\epsilon}{\Longrightarrow}_p P'$ iff $P \succ\!\!\longrightarrow^*_p P'$

$P \stackrel{s}{\Longrightarrow}_p P'$ iff $\exists Q_1, P_1, p_1, q_1 : P \succ\!\!\longrightarrow^*_{p_1} Q_1 \xrightarrow{a_1}_{q_1} P_1 \stackrel{s'}{\Longrightarrow}_{p'} P' \wedge S(Q_1) = A_1 \wedge p = \frac{p' \cdot p_1 \cdot q_1}{r_1}$

where A_i is a state, $a_i \in Act(A_i)$, $s' = \langle A_2\, a_2, \ldots, A_n\, a_n \rangle$, $r_1 = pro(a_1, A_1)$. □

As in the case of $\succ\!\!\longrightarrow_p$ and $\xrightarrow{a}_p$ we must take care of repetitions when generating both $\succ\!\!\longrightarrow^*_p$ and $\stackrel{s}{\Longrightarrow}_q$. Note that $P \succ\!\!\longrightarrow^*_p P'$ iff P' is stable and P can evolve to P' by a finite sequence of internal transitions. Also note that $P \stackrel{s}{\Longrightarrow}_p P'$ iff P performs the sequence s, i.e. it performs the actions a_i from Q_i such that $S(Q_i) = A_i$, and then evolves to P' by a generalized internal transition. The value p is the *global* probability of the derived computation. It is obtained by multiplying the probabilities of the selected branches from all the nondeterministic choices solved along the computation. It is important to note that besides the syntactic internal choices which generate the generalized internal transitions, we must take care of the nondeterminism induced by the different observable transitions labeled by the same action leaving an stable state.

Definition 12. Let P be a (probabilistic) process and s be a sequence of pairs (state, action). We define the *(probabilistic) acceptance sets* of P *after* s as

$$\mathcal{A}(P,s) = \{(A, p_A/q_s) \mid p_A = \textstyle\sum_{P'} \{\!|\, p_i \mid P \stackrel{s}{\Longrightarrow}_{p_i} P' \wedge S(P') = A \,|\!\} \wedge p_A > 0\}$$

where $q_\epsilon = 1$ and $q_{s' \circ \langle B\, b \rangle} = \sum_{Q'} \{\!|\, q_i \mid P \stackrel{s'}{\Longrightarrow}_{q_i} Q' \wedge S(Q') = B \,|\!\}$ □

In order to calculate the probabilistic acceptance sets of P after a sequence s, first we calculate the reachable states by P after the sequence s, and then we sum the probabilities of reaching these states divided by the total probability of reaching the last state in s. Note that $\mathcal{A}(\Omega, s) = \emptyset$ for any s (even if $s = \epsilon$), since $\Omega \stackrel{s}{\Longrightarrow}_p P$ for no P, $p > 0$.

Definition 13. (Alternative Characterization)
Let P, P' be processes. We write $P \cong P'$ if for all $s = \langle A_1\, a_1, A_2\, a_2, \ldots, A_n\, a_n\rangle$ (n can be equal to zero) we have $(A,p) \in \mathcal{A}(P,s) \Longleftrightarrow (A,p) \in \mathcal{A}(P',s)$. □

Example 4. Let $P = (a +_{\frac{1}{3}} b) \oplus_{\frac{1}{4}} (b; (c \oplus_{\frac{1}{3}} d))$, where *Nil* 's have been omitted.

$\mathcal{A}(P,\epsilon) = \{\, (A, \frac{1}{4}), (B, \frac{3}{4}) \}$, where $A = \{(a, \frac{1}{3}), (b, \frac{2}{3})\}$ and $B = \{(b, 1)\}$
$\mathcal{A}(P, \langle A\, b\rangle) = \mathcal{A}(P, \langle A\, a\rangle) = \{\, (\emptyset, 1)\,\}$
$\mathcal{A}(P, \langle B\, b\rangle) = \{\, (\{(c,1)\}, \frac{1}{3}), (\{(d,1)\}, \frac{2}{3})\,\}$
...

Thus, for instance we have $P' = ((a +_{\frac{1}{3}} b) \oplus_{\frac{1}{2}} (b; c)) \oplus_{\frac{1}{2}} (b; d) \cong P$.

4 Characterization Theorem

Now, our main task is to prove that the two equivalence relations given by Defs. 5 and 13 are equivalent. In order to do it, we associate to each process its *computations tree* (not to be confused with *computations* in Definition 4). These trees are built by alternating *internal* and *external* states. Generalized internal transitions leave from internal states reaching external states, while observable transitions leave from external states reaching internal states. By associating the generalized internal choice to internal states, and the generalized external choice to external states, these trees can be seen as (possibly infinite) syntactic processes in normal form. By extending, in a trivial way, the operational semantics to this kind of processes, we can also define testing semantics for them.

Definition 14. Let P be a process. We define the *derived* (generalized) *process associated to* P, denoted by $\widehat{\mathcal{A}}(P)$, as $\widehat{\mathcal{A}}(P) = \widehat{\mathcal{A}}(P,\epsilon)$ where

$$\widehat{\mathcal{A}}(P,s) = \bigoplus_{i=1}^{n} [p_i] \sum_{j=1}^{r_i} [p_{i,j}]\, a_{i,j}\, ; \widehat{\mathcal{A}}(P, s \circ \langle A_i\, a_{i,j}\rangle)$$

where $\sum_{j=1}^{0} P_i$ just denotes *Nil*, $\mathcal{A}(P,s) = \{(A_1,p_1),(A_2,p_2),\ldots,(A_n,p_n)\}$ and $A_i = \{(a_{i,1},p_{i,1}),(a_{i,2},p_{i,2}),\ldots,(a_{i,r_i},p_{i,r_i})\}$. □

Lemma 15. $P \cong P' \Leftrightarrow \widehat{\mathcal{A}}(P) = \widehat{\mathcal{A}}(P')$.

Note the close relation between $\widehat{\mathcal{A}}(P)$ and the probabilistic acceptance sets of the form $\mathcal{A}(P,s)$. So, $\widehat{\mathcal{A}}(P)$ can be seen as the (*pseudo*) *normal form* of P.

Example 5. The process P in Example 4 is in normal form, that is $P = \widehat{\mathcal{A}}(P)$. The process P' in Example 4 is not in normal form, but $\widehat{\mathcal{A}}(P') = P$.

Theorem 16. *For each process P we have $P \approx \widehat{\mathcal{A}}(P)$.*

Proof. (Sketch) The proof is easy but cumbersome, noting that computations of $\widehat{\mathcal{A}}(P)$ are just computations of P where each sequence of internal transitions of P has become a generalized internal transition of P, and thus an internal transition of $\widehat{\mathcal{A}}(P)$. □

We have to prove that the notions of testing and acceptance sets equivalence are *equivalent*. By Lemma 15, it is enough to consider processes of the form $\widehat{\mathcal{A}}(P)$. By Theorem 9 we can restrict the whole set of tests to probabilistic barbed tests. First, we need the uniqueness result given in Lemma 17. This result is similar to that of Lemma 9 in [WSS94].

Lemma 17. *Suppose f and f' are two functions of $n \geq 0$ variables $x_1, x_2 \dots x_n$, defined as follows:*

$$f = \sum_{i \in I} \frac{c_i}{1 + \sum_{j=1}^{n} d_{j,i} \cdot x_j} \qquad f' = \sum_{i' \in I'} \frac{c'_{i'}}{1 + \sum_{j=1}^{n} d'_{j,i'} \cdot x_j}$$

where I, I' are finite sets of indices, $c_i, c'_{i'} > 0$, and for each $r, s \in I$, such that $r \neq s$, the tuples $(d_{1,r}; d_{2,r}, \dots, d_{r,r})$ and $(d_{1,s}, d_{2,s}, \dots, d_{r,s})$ are distinct. If $f = f'$, then there exists a bijection $h : I \longrightarrow I'$ such that $d_{j,i} = d'_{j,h(i)}$ and $c_i = c'_{h(i)}$ for all $i \in I$ and $1 \leq j \leq n$.

Theorem 18. $\widehat{\mathcal{A}}(P) \approx_{\mathcal{PB}} \widehat{\mathcal{A}}(P') \Longleftrightarrow \widehat{\mathcal{A}}(P) = \widehat{\mathcal{A}}(P')$.

Proof. (Sketch) The right to left implication is trivial. For the left to right implication, let $Act = \{a_1, \dots, a_n\}$ (note that Act is finite). Then

$$\widehat{\mathcal{A}}(P) = \bigoplus_{i=1}^{m} [p_i] \sum_{j=1}^{n} [p_{i,j}]\, a_j \,; C_{i,k} \quad \text{and} \quad \widehat{\mathcal{A}}(P') = \bigoplus_{i'=1}^{m'} [p'_{i'}] \sum_{j=1}^{n} [p'_{i',j}]\, a_j \,; C'_{i',k}$$

where to simplify the notation we take $p_{i,j} = 0$ if a_j did not appear in the i-th summand of $\widehat{\mathcal{A}}(P)$. For each probability distribution $\bar{q} = \langle q_1, q_2, \dots q_n \rangle$ ($q_i \geq 0$, $\sum q_i = 1$), and for each $1 \leq k \leq n$, such that $q_k \neq 0$, we consider the barbed tests

$$T_k^{\bar{q}} = \sum_{j=1}^{n} [q_j]\, a_j \,; T_{j,k} \qquad \text{where} \qquad T_{j,k} = \begin{cases} \omega \;, & \text{if } k = j \\ Nil \,, & \text{if } k \neq j \end{cases}$$

Composing the processes and the tests and using $\widehat{\mathcal{A}}(P) \approx_{\mathcal{PB}} \widehat{\mathcal{A}}(P')$, we have

$$p = \sum_{i=1}^{m} p_i \cdot \frac{p_{i,k} \cdot q_k}{\sum_{j=1}^{n} p_{i,j} \cdot q_j} = \sum_{i'=1}^{m'} p'_{i'} \cdot \frac{p'_{i',k} \cdot q_k}{\sum_{j=1}^{n} p'_{i',j} \cdot q_j}$$

where $\widehat{\mathcal{A}}(P)$ $pass_p$ $T_k^{\bar{q}}$ (and thus $\widehat{\mathcal{A}}(P')$ $pass_p$ $T_k^{\bar{q}}$). Whenever $p_{i,k} = 0$ we also take $(p_{i,k} \cdot q_k) / \sum p_{i,j} \cdot q_j = 0$. After some algebraic manipulations, we can apply Lemma 17 to conclude $\mathcal{A}(\widehat{\mathcal{A}}(P), \epsilon) = \mathcal{A}(\widehat{\mathcal{A}}(P'), \epsilon)$. Taking deeper barbed tests, and using a similar argument, we can also prove $\mathcal{A}(\widehat{\mathcal{A}}(P), s) = \mathcal{A}(\widehat{\mathcal{A}}(P'), s)$ for any arbitrary sequence s. □

Corollary 19. *Let P, P' be processes. Then $P \approx P' \Longleftrightarrow P \cong P'$.*

5 A Fully Abstract Denotational Semantics

In this section we present an interpretation which is fully abstract with respect to the testing equivalence $\approx$. This interpretation will be based on *acceptance trees* [Hen85], and as in the nonprobabilistic case, the key to this definition is the alternative characterization given by $\cong$.

The semantic domain (denoted by $\mathbf{PAT}_{\mathrm{Act}}$) of *probabilistic acceptance trees over Act* (*pat*) is the set of rooted trees with two kinds of nodes: internal nodes (labeled with $\oplus$) and external nodes (labeled with $+$) that satisfy:

- The root is an internal node.
- Arcs outgoing from internal nodes are labeled with different states (see Def. 10) together with a probability. The sum of these probabilities must be less than or equal to 1. These arcs go to external nodes.
- Arcs outgoing from external nodes are labeled with the actions in the state labeling the ingoing arc. For any action in that state there must be an (unique) arc labeled with this action. These arcs go to internal nodes.

We usually will denote by $R, R_1, \ldots$ the elements of $\mathbf{PAT}_{\mathrm{Act}}$. Let us remark that it is possible that several outgoing arcs from an internal node are labeled with states which have the same set of actions but with different probabilities associated with the actions in the state. For example, a process may have the states $\{(a, \frac{1}{2}), (b, \frac{1}{2})\}$ and $\{(a, \frac{1}{3}), (b, \frac{2}{3})\}$. In internal nodes, the sum of probabilities associated with outgoing arcs can be less than one. The difference between this sum and 1 denotes the probability of divergence. Some examples of probabilistic acceptance trees are given in Fig. 3. We will characterize the nodes of these trees as the reachable nodes after a sequence of pairs (action,state).

Definition 20. Let R be a *pat* and A a state. We define the *probability* with which R (immediately) *reaches* the state A, denoted by $p(R, A)$, as p_A if there is an outgoing arc labeled $[p_A]\ A$ from the root node of R. If there is no such arc, then $p(R, A) = 0$.

Let A be a state, such that $p_A = p(R, A) > 0$, and $a \in act(A)$. We define the *continuation after the execution of a in A*, denoted by $R/(A, a)$, as the tree whose root is the internal node reached by the arc labeled with a originating in the external node reached by the arc labeled with $[p_A]\ A$.

Let $s = \langle A_1 a_1, A_2 a_2, \ldots, A_n a_n \rangle$ be a sequence such that $a_i \in act(A_i)$ and A_i are states. We define the *probability* with which R *reaches the external node represented by the sequence s and A*, denoted by $p(R, s, A)$, as

$$\begin{aligned} p(R, \epsilon, A) &= p(R, A) \\ p(R, \langle A_1 a_1 \rangle \circ s, A) &= p(R, A_1) \cdot p(R/(A_1, a_1), s, A) \end{aligned}$$ □

It is easy to see that from the values of $p(R, s, A)$ we can rebuild the tree R. We will use this fact in the rest of the section, in order to (implicitely) define certain *pat*'s.

Definition 21. Let R_1 and R_2 be *pat*'s. We write $R_1 \sqsubseteq R_2$ iff for any sequence s we have $p(R_1, s, A) \leq p(R_2, s, A)$. We write $R_1 \doteq R_2$ if $R_1 \sqsubseteq R_2$ and $R_2 \sqsubseteq R_1$. □

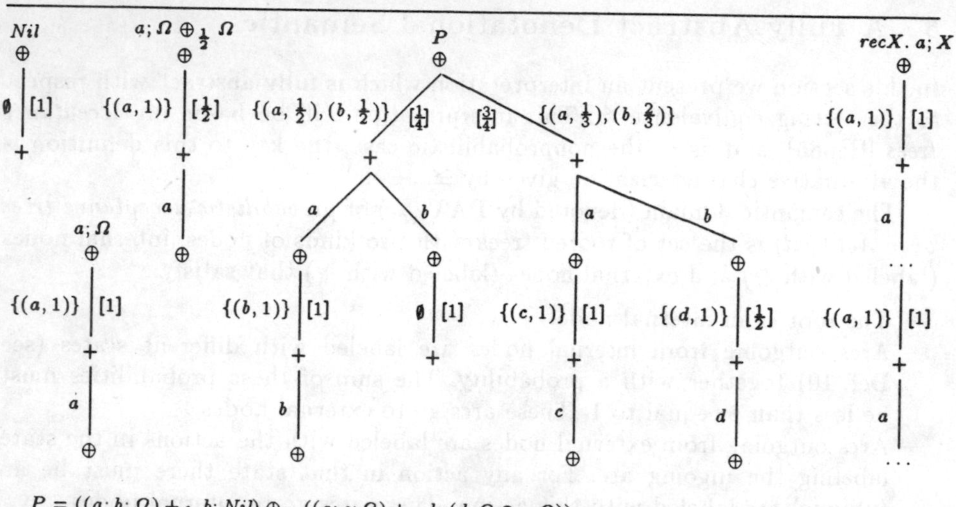

Fig. 3. Probabilistic acceptance trees.

Proposition 22. *The relation $\sqsubseteq$ is an order where the empty tree (the tree with no arcs) is the least element.*

Theorem 23. $(\mathbf{PAT}_{\mathrm{Act}}, \sqsubseteq)$ *is a complete partial order (cpo).*

Proof. (Sketch) Given a directed set $\{R_i\}$ of *pat*'s, it is not difficult to check, using basic notions of Real Analysis, that R defined by $p(R, s, A) = \sup p(R_i, s, A)$ is indeed a *pat* and that R is the *lub* of the set $\{R_i\}$. □

Once we have introduced the semantic domain for PPA processes, we define the semantic operators corresponding to the syntactic ones of the language. As usual, we denote by $[\![P]\!]$ the semantics of process P.

Nil and Ω

Nil has only an (immediately) reachable state: the state $\emptyset$ (reachable with probability equal to 1). Thus, $[\![Nil]\!]$ is a tree with an internal node, and under it, an external node.

$$p([\![Nil]\!], s, A) = \begin{cases} 1 & \text{if } s = \epsilon \ \wedge A = \emptyset \\ 0 & \text{otherwise} \end{cases}$$

Ω has no reachable states. Thus, $[\![\Omega]\!]$ is a tree with one internal node, with no node under it. That is, $p([\![\Omega]\!], s, A) = 0$ for any sequence s and any state A.

Prefix

For every $a \in Act$ we have a semantic function $a; \_ : \mathbf{PAT}_{\mathrm{Act}} \longrightarrow \mathbf{PAT}_{\mathrm{Act}}$. The *pat* $a; R$ is the tree R preceded by an internal and an external node which *corresponds* to a. Thus, the definition of $a; R$ is:

$$p(a; R, s, A) = \begin{cases} 1 & \text{if } s = \epsilon \wedge A = \{(a,1)\} \\ p(R, s', A) & \text{if } s = \langle(\{(a,1)\}, a)\rangle \circ s' \\ 0 & \text{otherwise} \end{cases}$$

Internal Choice

For a probability p, $\oplus_p$: $\mathbf{PAT}_{\mathrm{Act}} \times \mathbf{PAT}_{\mathrm{Act}} \longrightarrow \mathbf{PAT}_{\mathrm{Act}}$ is a function which returns a tree which is the *union* of the trees corresponding to its arguments considering the probability p:

$$p(R_1 \oplus_p R_2, s, A) = p \cdot p(R_1, s, A) + (1-p) \cdot p(R_2, s, A)$$

External Choice

Before defining the functions $+_p$, we will define an auxiliary operator to join states according to a probability.

Definition 24. Let X, Y be states and $p \in (0,1)$. We define the *union* of states X and Y with *associated probability* p as:

$$X \cup_p Y = \begin{cases} X & \text{if } Y = \emptyset \\ Y & \text{if } X = \emptyset \\ \{(a, p \cdot pro(a, X) + (1-p) \cdot pro(a, Y))\} & \text{otherwise} \end{cases}$$

□

As in the nonprobabilistic case, when we are defining the union of two trees, we must distinguish between defining *in the root* and *under the root*. In the root, we must consider the union of the (initial) states of the two trees composed with the external choice. Then,

$$p(R_1 +_p R_2, \epsilon, A) = \sum_{A = B \cup_p C} p(R_1, B) \cdot p(R_2, C)$$

That is, a state A is reachable (immediately) if there exist states B (reachable by R_1) and C (reachable by R_2) such that $A = B \cup_p C$. The probability with which A is reachable is equal to the sum of the product of the probabilities with which B's and C's are reached. As a consequence of this definition, we have that the function corresponding to the external choice is strict, because if an argument is equivalent to Ω, then the result will be Ω (Ω has not reachable states). That is, $[\![P +_p \Omega]\!] = [\![\Omega +_p P]\!] = [\![\Omega]\!]$ for any $0 < p < 1$.

Now we have to define the rest of the tree under the root.

$$\begin{aligned} p(R_1 +_p R_2, \langle A\, a\rangle \circ s', X) = & \sum_{A = B \cup_p C} \frac{p \cdot pro(a,B)}{p \cdot pro(a,B) + (1-p) \cdot pro(a,C)} \cdot p(R_1, s_B, X) \cdot p(R_2, C) \\ & + \sum_{A = B \cup_p C} \frac{(1-p) \cdot pro(a,C)}{p \cdot pro(a,B) + (1-p) \cdot pro(a,C)} \cdot p(R_2, s_C, X) \cdot p(R_1, B) \end{aligned}$$

where $s_B = \langle B\, a\rangle \circ s'$ and $s_C = \langle C\, a\rangle \circ s'$.

Intuitively, in order to calculate the reachable states after a sequence of the form $s = \langle A_1\, a_1, A_2\, a_2, \ldots, A_n\, a_n \rangle$, we must know if the first action a_1 could be executed by R_1 and/or R_2 and how the state A_1 can be reached by $R_1 +_p R_2$. Once we know which *pat performs* a_1, these states must be reachable by this *pat*.

Proposition 25. *For each* $a \in Act$, *the function* $a;\_ :: \mathbf{PAT}_{\mathrm{Act}} \longrightarrow \mathbf{PAT}_{\mathrm{Act}}$ *is continuous. The functions* $\oplus_p$, $+_p :: \mathbf{PAT}_{\mathrm{Act}} \times \mathbf{PAT}_{\mathrm{Act}} \longrightarrow \mathbf{PAT}_{\mathrm{Act}}$ *are continuous for each* $p \in (0,1)$.

Recursion

As usual when definiting a denotational semantics, the meaning of recursively processes defined by expressions of the form $recX.P(X)$ is obtained as the limit of the finite approximations $P_0 = \Omega, P_1 = P(\Omega), \ldots, P_n = P^n(\Omega)$. Because all the operators included in the term $P(X)$ are continuous, this limit is the least fixed point of the equation $X = P(X)$. That is, we define

$$[\![recX.\ P(X)]\!] = \bigsqcup_{n=0}^{\infty} [\![P_n]\!]$$

The close relation between the denotational semantics of a process and its operational behavior is underscored in the following

Theorem 26. *Let* P *be a process.* $\mathcal{A}(P,s) = \{(A_1,p_1),(A_2,p_2)\ldots(A_n,p_n)\}$ *iff* $\forall\, 1 \leq i \leq n:\ p_i = \frac{p([\![P]\!],s,A_i)}{p_s} \wedge p([\![P]\!],s,A) = 0$ if $A \neq A_i$, *where* $p_\epsilon = 1$ *and* $p_{s' \circ \langle B\, b \rangle} = p([\![P]\!], s', B)$

Proof. (Sketch) The proof is done by induction on the length of the sequence s. The only difficult case is that of external choice. □

Corollary 27. *Let* P, Q *be processes. Then,* $P \cong Q \Leftrightarrow [\![P]\!] \doteq [\![Q]\!]$.

Corollary 28. (Full Abstraction for $\mathbf{PAT}_{\mathrm{Act}}$)
Let P, Q *be processes. Then,* $P \approx Q \Leftrightarrow [\![P]\!] \doteq [\![Q]\!]$.

6 Conclusion and Future work

In this paper we have developed a probabilistic extension of classical testing semantics [Hen88]. We have presented an alternative characterization which is equivalent to the testing equivalence. We also have given a denotational semantics which has been proved to be fully abstract with respect to the testing equivalence.

As future work we plan to extend the studied language to a language where parallel and restriction operators are considered. We are working with two possibilities for the parallel operator: a parallel operator with one probability (as in [Cua93]) or the one with two probabilities described in [BBS92]. We are also very interested in the verification of properties for processes in our language, using HML extended with probabilities. A good starting point is the logic described in [LS92]. Finally, we will extend the complete axiomatization given in [Cua93] to our semantic model.

Acknowledgements

We would like to thank Scott A. Smolka for his very useful comments on a draft version of this paper and for his warm reception when the first author visited Stony Brook. We are also indebted to the anonymous referees for their valuable comments.

References

[BBS92] J.C.M. Baeten, J.A. Bergstra, and S.A. Smolka. Axiomatizing probabilistic processes: ACP with generative probabilities. In *CONCUR'92, LNCS 630*, pages 472–485, 1992.

[Chr90] I. Christoff. Testing equivalences and fully abstract models for probabilistic processes. In *CONCUR'90, LNCS 458*, pages 126–140, 1990.

[CSZ92] R. Cleaveland, S.A. Smolka, and A.E. Zwarico. Testing preorders for probabilistic processes. In *19 th ICALP, LNCS 623*, pages 708–719, 1992.

[Cua93] F. Cuartero. *CSP probabilístico (PCSP). Un modelo probabilístico de procesos concurrentes.* PhD thesis, Universidad Complutense de Madrid, 1993.

[dNH87] R. de Nicola and M. Hennessy. CCS without τ's. In *TAPSOFT'87, LNCS 249*, pages 138–152, 1987.

[GJS90] A. Giacalone, C.-C. Jou, and S.A. Smolka. Algebraic reasoning for probabilistic concurrent systems. In *Proceedings of Working Conference on Programming Concepts and Methods, IFIP TC 2*, 1990.

[Hen85] M. Hennessy. Acceptance trees. *Journal of the ACM*, 32(4):896–928, 1985.

[Hen88] M. Hennessy. *Algebraic Theory of Processes.* MIT Press, 1988.

[HJ90] H. Hansson and B. Jonsson. A calculus for communicating systems with time and probabilities. In *11th IEEE Real-Time Systems Symposium*, pages 278–287, 1990.

[JY95] B. Jonsson and W. Yi. Compositional testing preorders for probabilistic processes. In *10th IEEE Symposium on Logic In Computer Science*, 1995.

[Low95] G. Lowe. Probabilistic and prioritized models of timed CSP. *Theoretical Computer Science*, 138:315–352, 1995.

[LS92] K.G. Larsen and A. Skou. Compositional verification of probabilistic processes. In *CONCUR'92, LNCS 630*, pages 456–471, 1992.

[Sei92] K. Seidel. *Probabilistic Communicating Processes.* PhD thesis, Oxford University, 1992.

[SS90] S.A. Smolka and B. Steffen. Priority as extremal probability. In *CONCUR'90, LNCS 458*, pages 456–466, 1990.

[vGSST90] R. van Glabbeek, S.A. Smolka, B. Steffen, and C.M.N. Tofts. Reactive, generative, and stratified models of probabilistic processes. In *5th IEEE Symposium on Logic In Computer Science*, pages 130–141, 1990.

[WSS94] S.-H. Wu, S.A. Smolka, and E.W. Stark. Composition and behaviors of probabilistic I/O automata. In *CONCUR'94, LNCS 836*, pages 513–528, 1994.

[YCDS94] S. Yuen, R. Cleaveland, Z. Dayar, and S.A. Smolka. Fully abstract characterizations of testing preorders for probabilistic processes. In *CONCUR'94, LNCS 836*, pages 497–512, 1994.

[YL92] W. Yi and K.G. Larsen. Testing probabilistic and nondeterministic processes. In *PSTV XII*, pages 47–61, 1992.

Will I be Pretty, Will I be Rich? Some Thoughts on Theory vs. Practice in Systems Engineering

David Harel

The Weizmann Institute of Science, Rehovot, Israel

"The mathematician's patterns, like the painter's or the poets's, must be *beautiful*; ... there is no permanent place in the world for ugly mathematics."
(G. H. Hardy [H, p. 25])

(at a cocktail party) Person A: "I'm writing a best-seller."
Person B: "Short of money, eh?"
(Cartoon in the *New Yorker*)

1 Preamble

This is a very short summary of a talk presented at the 6th Int. Conf. on Concurrency Theory (CONCUR '95).[1] The talk attempted to put forward some thoughts on theoretical vs. applied research in the specification and design of reactive, highly concurrent systems. By its very nature, such a talk is bound to be disorganized, rambling, non-self-contained, and extremely subjective. It was; and the written summary you are reading is even worse, since it not only omits the details of the examples used in the talk, but also lacks the intonations, facial gestures and hand-waving that are part and parcel of talks that have little technical content.

Oh well. So be it.

2 A 3-way Classification

This is a conference on the theory of something very practical. Most of its participants do theory — that is, research whose methods and tools are mathematical — but theory geared towards particular kinds of real systems. In this case, it is concurrent systems. In other analogous conferences, such as those on Principles

[1] A similar talk, of the same title and with a very similar written summary, was given at the 13th ACM Symp. on Principles of Database Systems (PODS '94) in May, 1994.

of Programming Languages (POPL), Principles of Database Systems (PODS), or Principles of Distributed Computing (PODC), the setup is the same, but the kinds of systems differ.

What sort of theory do we do here, and why? Should the general theory community take notice of us? Should the applied crowd listen in? How about the converse questions: should we peddle our merchandise to other theoreticians? Are we doing enough to serve the needs of our own real-world practitioners?

At the heart of the talk was an attempt to clarify some of the issues behind these questions, by dividing the research carried out by theoreticians into three kinds, which will be referred to as Type 1, Type 2 and Type 3 theory.[2]

Type 1 theory concerns true foundations and principles. It should be robust, deep and of fundamental nature, and should explain, generalize and enlighten. Such are the basics of computability and complexity theory, for example, as they emerge from the work of Church, Turing, Rabin, Cook and many others.

Type 2 theory responds directly to the needs arising in applications. It should be pragmatic and specific, molding itself to fit the requirements posed by real-world difficulties, and it should result in things that work and can actually be used. Such is the Fast Fourier Transform, for example, or those parts of the theory of context-free languages that lead to efficient compilation techniques.

Type 3 is theory for the sake of theory (TST). It should be mathematically elegant, yet difficult and clever, and should be of interest to other theoreticians. Much of the work we do is of this type.

The borderlines between these are fuzzy, and as time goes by migration often take place: many Type 3 results and techniques eventually become Type 1, and sometimes — but more rarely — Type 3 work becomes applicable, converting it into Type 2.

TST is legitimate and desirable, and not only because it might get upgraded. It is absolutely essential to the well-being and substance of a scientific community. Even so, most theoreticians will never admit to doing Type 3 work.[3]

One difference between Types 1 and 2 on the one hand and Type 3 on the other is in the judges. While the quality of TST is inevitably determined by theoreticians, the ultimate test of both Type 1 and Type 2 is in the opinions of real-world people, such as systems engineers and programmers. A non-applicable piece of work can be considered by theoreticians to be Type 1, but it cannot fully

[2] While our interest here is mainly in theory carried out in conjunction with practical fields of computer science, such as concurrent systems and programming, many of the points made can be modified to apply to theory in general. Also, the 3-way classification proposed here is somewhat different from the one proposed by Raghavan [R] for general STOC/FOCS theory.

[3] Hardy, the great number theorist, was a notable exception, stating, in the famous passage from [H, p. 90]: "I have never done anything 'useful'. No discovery of mine has made, or is likely to make, directly or indirectly, for good or ill, the least difference to the amenity of the world. [...] I have just one chance of escaping a verdict of complete triviality, that I may be judged to have created something worth creating." He was wrong, of course, as any modern-day cryptographer will tell you.

deserve that label unless engineers and programmers can be made to appreciate its virtues too. Otherwise, there are exactly two possibilities: (i) the theory is bad, or (ii) it is TST (in which case it might be excellent, but the applied guys couldn't really have known).

3 Did Hoare and Milner do Theory?

This part of the talk, the main one, was dedicated to illustrating the points with examples. A sample question to ponder is this: were Hoare and Milner in their pioneering work on CSP [Ho] and CCS [M] doing theory, and, if so, was it Type 1, 2 or 3?

Some of the examples discussed in the talk included the following. Database topics, such Codd's work [C1, C2], Query-by-Example [Z], Datalog (cf. [U]), computable queries [CH] and Fagin's theorem [F]. State-based formalisms for specifying system behavior, such as Petri nets [Re] and statecharts [Ha1], including their practicality and results on their relative expressive power and succinctness [RS, MF, EZ, DH]. Theoretical and practical aspects of verifying finite-state systems by executable specifications (see, e.g., [Ha2]), or the recently proposed methods based on BDD's [B, B+]. Also mentioned was a research spinoff into drawing graphs nicely [DaH].

4 Post-Ramble

There was also a message in all this. Subjective, and perhaps trivial, but here it is anyway.

A typical theoretician wants his/her work to end up being Type 1. But setting out in advance with this in mind is usually pointless. We can try to *aim* in the direction of Type 1 by being collective and general. We should avoid overly specialized theories, ones that seem to apply only to a special case of some special language, model or approach. We should seek results that are as generic and as all-encompassing as possible. Robustness is the name of the game. And we should always keep in mind that the essence of true Type 1 must be appreciable by non-theoreticians too, and it is our responsibility to expose and elucidate it.

As to Type 2, while theory people are by no means obliged to produce applicable work, some of us really want to. If we are interested in *actively* carrying out Type 2 work, we should get out there and become involved. We should take a real interest, listen attentively to what the real-world people ask for, and study their thought-patterns and work-habits. Only then can we try to see if there are ways we can help. The problems arising out there are usually much harder than we tend to think. Riches don't come easy. Doing our work in isolation, and then trying to impose our ideas on the real world, is bound to fail. If engineers and programmers do not find it beneficial to use the result of an application-oriented

research effort — for whatever reasons — that piece of research is probably quite useless. We should be humble; they are the absolute judges.

So much for us theoreticians. What can be said here to the practitioners? Well, as far as Type 2 theory goes, simply don't give in. Be demanding; be pedantic, or even idiosyncratic. Explain and justify your problems and needs to the theoreticians. Let them in on your whims and fancies; you might just turn lucky. But be patient, since most theoreticians cannot muster the down-to-earth attitude an engineer needs in order to function well in the face of real-world problems. Some of us can't even program!

When it comes to Type 1 work, the practitioners should be the ones to show an interest. Theory can be more than just pretty mathematics. Some of it is deep, sweeping and fundamental. It will usually not be of direct help in your daily work, but it very often addresses truly basic issues, capturing phenomena that are at the heart of the field — that field in which your real-world work is done. Be open. Listen to it. It might not be quite as way-out as you think.

References

[B] R.E. Bryant, "Graph-Based Algorithms for Boolean Function Manipulation", *IEEE Trans. on Computers* C-**35**:8 (1986), 677–691.

[B+] J.R. Burch, E.M. Clarke, K.L. McMillan, D.L. Dill and J. Hwang, "Symbolic Model Checking: 10^{20} States and Beyond", *Inf. and Comput.* **98** (1992), 142–170.

[CH] A.K. Chandra and D. Harel, "Computable Queries for Relational Data Bases", *J. Comput. Syst. Sci.* **21** (1980), 156–178.

[C1] E.F. Codd, "A Relational Model of Data for Large Shared Data Banks", *Comm. Assoc. Comput. Mach.* **13**:6 (1970), 377–387.

[C2] E.F. Codd, "Relational Completeness of Data Base Sublanguages", In *Data Base Systems* (Rustin, ed.), Prentice-Hall, Englewood Cliffs, N.J., 1972.

[F] R. Fagin, "Generalized First-Order Spectra and Polynomial-Time Recognizable Sets", In *Complexity of Computations* (R. Karp, ed.), SIAM-AMS Proceedings, Vol. 7, 1974, pp. 43–73.

[DaH] R. Davidson and D. Harel, "Drawing Graphs Nicely Using Simulated Annealing", *Comm. Assoc. Comput. Mach.*, in press.

[DH] D. Drusinsky and D. Harel, "On the Power of Bounded Concurrency I: Finite Automata", *J. Assoc. Comput. Mach.* **41** (1994), 517–539. (Preliminary version appeared in *Proc. Concurrency '88*, LNCS 335, Springer-Verlag, New York, 1988, pp. 74–103.)

[EZ] A. Ehrenfeucht and P. Zeiger, "Complexity Measures for Regular Expressions", *J. Comput. Sys. Sci.* **12** (1976), 134–146.

[H] G.H. Hardy, *A Mathematician's Apology*, Cambridge Univ. Press, 1940.

[Ha1] D. Harel, "Statecharts: A Visual Formalism for Complex Systems", *Sci. Comput. Prog.* **8** (1987), 231–274.

[Ha2] D. Harel, "Biting the Silver Bullet: Toward a Brighter Future for System Development", *Computer* (Jan. 1992), 8–20.

[Ho] Hoare C.A.R, "Communicating Sequential Processes", *Comm. Assoc. Comput. Mach.* **21**, (1978), 666–677.

[MF] A.R. Meyer and M.J. Fischer, "Economy of Description by Automata, Grammars, and Formal Systems", *Proc. 12th IEEE Symp. on Switching and Automata Theory*, 1971, pp. 188–191.

[M] Milner, R., *A Calculus of Communicating Systems*, Lecture Notes in Computer Science, Vol. 94, Springer-Verlag, New York, 1980.

[RS] M.O. Rabin and D. Scott, "Finite Automata and Their Decision Problems", *IBM J. Res.* **3** (1959), 115–125.

[R] P. Raghavan, Electronic mail contribution to a debate on the future of theory, Feb. 17, 1994.

[Re] W. Reisig, *Petri Nets: An Introduction*, Springer-Verlag, Berlin, 1985.

[U] J.D. Ullman, *Principles of Database and Knowledge-Base Systems*, Vols. I and II, Computer Science Press, 1988.

[Z] M.M. Zloof, "Query-by-Example: A Data Base Language", *IBM Systems J.* **16** (1977), 324–343.

Towards a denotational semantics for ET-LOTOS

Jeremy Bryans[1], Jim Davies[2], and Steve Schneider[3]

Abstract

The formal specification language LOTOS is an international standard for use in Open Systems Interconnection. A timed extension called ET-LOTOS has been proposed. This paper presents a fully-abstract denotational semantics for the process algebraic component of this extension. The benefits of a denotational semantics are discussed, as are the applications.

1 Introduction

LOTOS is a language intended primarily for use in protocol specification. It is a synthesis of two process calculi—CCS [9] and CSP [4]—with the addition of data types. It is an international standard for use in Open Systems Interconnection [5], and has been used to specify a wide variety of information processing systems [12].

LOTOS is about to undergo its first major revision. It is to be extended to include an explicit treatment of time. In [7], the authors introduce a language called ET-LOTOS. They extend the standard language by giving a timed interpretation to existing operators and adding new operators to model delays and timeouts in process behaviour.

The language of ET-LOTOS is defined by means of an operational semantics: each construct is associated with a set of transition rules, describing the ways in which the resulting process may evolve. Although this provides a precise, unambiguous definition, a denotational semantics would be useful in system specification and refinement. This paper presents such a semantics.

2 The language of ET-LOTOS

ET-LOTOS is a language of *processes:* entities that are able to perform internal and external *actions*. The internal action, written `i`, occurs without the cooperation of other processes. An external action is an atomic synchronisation; it requires the cooperation of the environment.

The simplest process in the language, `stop`, can perform neither internal or external actions: it is used to represent the end of a pattern of communication. The other atomic process is `exit`, which can perform a single external action δ; this is used to indicate that the current process has terminated successfully.

[1]Dept. of Computer Science, University of Reading, Reading RG6 2AY.
[2]Programming Research Group, Wolfson Building, Parks Road, Oxford OX1 3QD.
[3]Dept. of Computer Science, Royal Holloway, University of London, Egham TW20 0EX.

If a is an action, and d_1 is a time value—a non-negative real number—then $a\{d_1\}$; P is a process that is able to perform a and then behave as P. If a is external, then the time value is a timeout: if the offer of a is not accepted by time d_1, then the offer is withdrawn, and the process behaves as `stop`. If a is internal, as in $\mathtt{i}\{d_1\}$; P, then the time value is an upper bound upon its time of occurrence: `i` will occur at some time between 0 and d_1.

The behaviour of a process may depend upon the delay between an action being offered and that offer being accepted. The process a @ t ; P is initially ready to perform a. If this action is performed after t_1 time units have elapsed, then the subsequent behaviour is described by $P[t_1/t]$: that is, P with actual delay value t_1 substituted for all free occurrences of variable t.

Alternative behaviour is modelled using a choice construct: P [] Q is a process that offers a choice between P and Q. This choice is resolved by the first action to occur. If the action involves P, then any subsequent behaviour is due to P, and similarly for Q.

The sequential composition P >> Q will behave as P until this component signals termination. This action is concealed within the composition, appearing to the environment as `i`. From this point onwards, P makes no contribution to the behaviour, and Q is said to be *enabled*.

It is possible to interrupt a process without its cooperation. The composition P [> Q behaves as P until the first action of Q. At this point, P is said to be *disabled*, and all subsequent behaviour is due to Q. It is important to note that the internal action `i` can be used to disable a process.

The parallel combinator describes the effect of two processes evolving concurrently. If A is a set of external actions then P |[A]| Q is a parallel composition in which components P and Q may evolve separately but must cooperate upon every action from set A; they must also cooperate upon termination.

The delay operator introduces an interval of waiting time into a process description. Δ^{t_1} P is a process that will delay for time t_1 before behaving as P. The end of the delay period is not marked by any action, internal or external.

The hiding operator provides a method of abstraction; we may conceal or internalise actions within a process description. If A is a set of actions, then **hide** A **in** P behaves according to the description of P, except that every action from the set A is replaced with the internal action `i`.

Processes are defined using an equational notation. If $\vec{X}$ is a vector of process names and $\vec{R}$ is a matching vector of processes, then the definition

$$P ::= Q \ \ \mathtt{where} \ \ \vec{X} := \vec{R}$$

introduces a process P whose behaviour is described by Q, where each name X_i is bound to the matching process R_i.

3 Operational Semantics

The language described above is defined in terms of an operational semantics. In [7], the authors present a set of transition rules, associating each process with a *labelled transition system*: a set of states linked by actions or time delays.

$$\frac{}{\texttt{stop} \overset{d}{\rightsquigarrow} \texttt{stop}}\ \texttt{s} \qquad \frac{}{\texttt{exit}\{d_1\} \overset{\delta}{\longrightarrow} \texttt{stop}}\ \texttt{x1}$$

$$\frac{d \leqslant d_1}{\texttt{exit}\{d_1\} \overset{d}{\rightsquigarrow} \texttt{exit}\{d_1 - d\}}\ \texttt{x2} \qquad \frac{d > d_1}{\texttt{exit}\{d_1\} \overset{d}{\rightsquigarrow} \texttt{stop}}\ \texttt{x3}$$

$$\frac{}{a \mathbin{@} t\{d_1\}\ ;\ P \overset{a}{\longrightarrow} P[0/t]}\ \texttt{a1} \qquad \frac{d \leqslant d_1}{a \mathbin{@} t\{d_1\}\ ;\ P \overset{d}{\rightsquigarrow} a \mathbin{@} t\{d_1 - d\}\ ;\ P[t+d/t]}\ \texttt{a2}$$

$$\frac{a \neq \texttt{i} \quad d > d_1}{a \mathbin{@} t\{d_1\}\ ;\ P \overset{d}{\rightsquigarrow} \texttt{stop}}\ \texttt{a3}$$

Table 1: Rules for action prefix and termination

There is an obvious relationship between states in the transition system of a process and other terms in the process language. Suppose that the current state of a process is described by a ; P: it is ready to perform a and behave as P. If a is performed, the new state of the process is described by P: we write

$$a\ ;\ P \quad \overset{a}{\longrightarrow} \quad P$$

to record this possibility.

The result of a delay transition may depend upon the delay value involved; the process $a\{d_1\}$; P may delay for any time $d \leqslant d_1$ and remain an action prefix process:

$$a\{d_1\}\ ;\ P \quad \overset{d}{\rightsquigarrow} \quad a\{d_1 - d\}\ ;\ P$$

If a is an external action, then this process may also delay for longer than d_1, but the result is a process that behaves exactly as `stop`: action a is no longer possible. The timeout value d_1 is optional: the default value is ∞.

If a is the internal action `i`, then it is impossible for the process to delay for longer than d_1 without performing an action; the process $\texttt{i}\{d_1\}$; P has no delay transitions with $d > d_1$. This reflects the fact that `i` occurs without the cooperation of the environment, and that the timeout value is a bound upon a nondeterministic delay preceding its occurrence. If no value is included, a value of 0 is assumed.

The transition rules in Table 1 refer to the most general forms of termination and action prefix: `exit` has an optional timeout; action prefix has a variable to record the time at which the action takes place. Notice that the instantiation of the timer variable changes with any delay transition.

The transitions of a compound process are determined by the transitions of its components: for example, if components P and Q are both capable of

$$\frac{P \xrightarrow{a} P' \quad a \neq \delta}{P >> Q \xrightarrow{a} P' >> Q} \text{ e1} \qquad \frac{P \xrightarrow{\delta} P'}{P >> Q \xrightarrow{\mathtt{i}} Q} \text{ e2}$$

$$\frac{P \overset{d}{\leadsto} P' \quad \neg(P \xrightarrow{\delta})}{P >> Q \overset{d}{\leadsto} P' >> Q} \text{ e3} \qquad \frac{P \xrightarrow{a} P' \quad a \neq \delta}{P \;[>\; Q \xrightarrow{a} P' \;[>\; Q} \text{ i1}$$

$$\frac{Q \xrightarrow{a} Q'}{P \;[>\; Q \xrightarrow{a} Q'} \text{ i2} \qquad \frac{P \xrightarrow{\delta} P'}{P \;[>\; Q \xrightarrow{\delta} P'} \text{ i3}$$

$$\frac{P \overset{d}{\leadsto} P' \quad Q \overset{d}{\leadsto} Q'}{P \;[>\; Q \overset{d}{\leadsto} P' \;[>\; Q'} \text{ i4} \qquad \frac{P \xrightarrow{a} P'}{P \;[]\; Q \xrightarrow{a} P'} \text{ c1}$$

$$\frac{Q \xrightarrow{a} Q'}{P \;[]\; Q \xrightarrow{a} Q'} \text{ c2} \qquad \frac{P \overset{d}{\leadsto} P' \quad Q \overset{d}{\leadsto} Q'}{P \;[]\; Q \overset{d}{\leadsto} P' \;[]\; Q'} \text{ c3}$$

Table 2: Rules for sequencing and alternation

delaying for time d without performing any action, then so too is the process $P \;[]\; Q$. We write

$$\frac{P \overset{d}{\leadsto} P' \quad Q \overset{d}{\leadsto} Q'}{P \;[]\; Q \overset{d}{\leadsto} P' \;[]\; Q'}$$

to indicate that this is the case. This is the only rule for delay transitions of a choice process.

Rule e2 of Table 2 tells us that termination of P is an internal action of the process $P >> Q$. Rule e3 reveals one of the assumptions of the computational model employed for ET-LOTOS: that internal actions are *urgent*: they occur as soon as all of components concerned are ready. The first component of a sequential composition cannot delay unless δ is impossible: this is indicated by the negative premise $\neg(P \xrightarrow{\delta})$.

The transition rules for the interrupt, or disabling, operator [> state that any action, internal or external, can disable a process. This is essential if this operator is to be used to model timed interrupts; the only action that can be scheduled at an interface is the internal action `i`.

The rules in Table 3 state that the agreement of both components is required before a parallel composition can terminate. They state also that no additional delays are introduced by concurrency. This reveals another assumption of the computational model: that there are no hidden delays due to shared resources. This is called the assumption of maximum parallelism.

$$\frac{P \xrightarrow{a} P' \quad a \notin A \cup \{\delta\}}{P \mid [A] \mid Q \xrightarrow{a} P' \mid [A] \mid Q} \text{ p1} \qquad \frac{Q \xrightarrow{a} Q' \quad a \notin A \cup \{\delta\}}{P \mid [A] \mid Q \xrightarrow{a} P \mid [A] \mid Q'} \text{ p2}$$

$$\frac{P \xrightarrow{a} P' \quad Q \xrightarrow{a} Q' \quad a \in A \cup \{\delta\}}{P \mid [A] \mid Q \xrightarrow{a} P' \mid [A] \mid Q'} \text{ p3} \qquad \frac{P \overset{d}{\rightsquigarrow} P' \quad Q \overset{d}{\rightsquigarrow} Q'}{P \mid [A] \mid Q \overset{d}{\rightsquigarrow} P' \mid [A] \mid Q'} \text{ p4}$$

$$\frac{P \xrightarrow{a} P'}{\Delta^0 \, P \xrightarrow{a} P'} \text{ d1} \qquad \frac{d_1 \geqslant d}{\Delta^{d_1} \, P \overset{d}{\rightsquigarrow} \Delta^{d_1 - d} \, P} \text{ d2}$$

$$\frac{P \overset{d}{\rightsquigarrow} P'}{\Delta^0 \, P \overset{d}{\rightsquigarrow} P'} \text{ d3} \qquad \frac{P \xrightarrow{a} P' \quad a \notin A}{\textbf{hide } A \textbf{ in } P \xrightarrow{a} \textbf{hide } A \textbf{ in } P'} \text{ h1}$$

$$\frac{P \xrightarrow{a} P' \quad a \in A}{\textbf{hide } A \textbf{ in } P \xrightarrow{\mathsf{i}} \textbf{hide } A \textbf{ in } P'} \text{ h2} \qquad \frac{P \overset{d}{\rightsquigarrow} P' \quad \neg \exists \, a \in A \bullet P \xrightarrow{a}}{\textbf{hide } A \textbf{ in } P \overset{d}{\rightsquigarrow} \textbf{hide } A \textbf{ in } P'} \text{ h3}$$

Table 3: Rules for delay, concurrency, and abstraction

A delayed process $\Delta^{d_1} P$ must wait for at least time d_1 before performing any actions; any delay transition will reduce the waiting time accordingly. Notice that the end of the delay period is not accompanied by an internal action; this is essential if the delay operator is to be used to introduce additional options in a choice construct: an internal action at this point would resolve the choice.

Finally, the rules for the hiding operator tell us that hidden actions appear as internal actions, and that internal actions are urgent. In the statement of Rule h3, we find that a process may delay only if none of the hidden actions are possible. This assumption, seen before in the semantics of sequential composition, is sometimes called the assumption of maximal progress.

4 Denotational Semantics

A denotational semantics associates each process in the language with a mathematical object, or denotation. In our semantics, the denotation of a process is the set of all observations that can be made of that process. This brings two immediate benefits: the semantic equations can be given an intuitive interpretation, and constraints upon observable behaviour can be written as predicates upon the semantics of a process.

The information content of an observation is determined by a number of considerations: we must be able to construct the semantics of a compound process from the semantics of its components; we must be able to distinguish between processes that are essentially different; we should not be able to distinguish between processes that are essentially the same. The first of these is a necessary condition for the definition of a semantic function; the others depend upon a notion of equivalence obtained from the operational semantics.

A standard component of observations is the *trace*: a finite linear record of external actions performed. This is a lower bound for information content in our observations. If there is some trace that is possible for one process but not for another, then we will regard these two processes as different. Trace information can be extracted in an obvious way from the transition rules given in Section 3: we record only those transitions that correspond to external actions.

We define an equivalence relation upon processes as follows: two processes are *trace equivalent* if they have precisely the same set of traces:

$$P \approx_t Q \Leftrightarrow \mathit{traces}(P) = \mathit{traces}(Q)$$

where '*traces*(P)' denotes the set of all traces of P, as extracted from the operational semantics.

In any timed language, this notion of equivalence is not preserved by composition. For example, the processes $\Delta^2\ a$; `stop` and a ; `stop` have the same traces, but the two parallel combinations below do not:

$$\Delta^2\ a\ ;\ \mathtt{stop}\ |[\ a\ ]|\ (a\{1\}\ ;\ \mathtt{stop}) \qquad a\ ;\ \mathtt{stop}\ |[\ a\ ]|\ (a\{1\}\ ;\ \mathtt{stop})$$

The process on the left cannot perform action a.

What we require is a congruence: an equivalence that is preserved by composition with each of the operators in our language. To give a formal definition of this relation, we introduce the notion of a *context*: a process term with a single free process variable. For example, $C[Y] = Y\ |[\ a\ ]|\ (a\{1\}\ ;\ \mathtt{stop})$ is the context used to distinguish between the two processes above.

We define *trace congruence* to be the weakest congruence stronger than trace equivalence: the weakest congruence such that

$$P \equiv_t Q \Rightarrow C[P] \approx_t C[Q]$$

for any context C. To obtain a notion of observation that reflects trace congruence, we must add more information: traces alone are not enough to make all the distinctions that we require.

It is not surprising that we are forced to include timing information in our traces, as contexts may include time-sensitive behaviour. However, we are forced also to include *refusal* information. Consider the processes i ; a ; `stop` and i ; a ; `stop` $\Box$ i ; `stop`. These processes have the same set of traces, even when timing information is included for each action; they differ in that the left-hand process cannot refuse to perform action a. In the context

$$C[Y] = \mathtt{hide}\ \{a\}\ \mathtt{in}\ Y\ |[\ a\ ]|\ (a\ ;\ \mathtt{stop}\ \Box\ \Delta^1\ b\ ;\ \mathtt{stop})$$

the left-hand process will perform the hidden action a before b becomes available; the trace $\langle b \rangle$ is possible for the right-hand process, but not for the left.

$$\mathcal{D}[\![\texttt{stop}]\!] = \{(\infty, \langle\rangle, X) \mid X \in TR\}$$

$$\begin{aligned}\mathcal{D}[\![\texttt{exit}\{d_1\}]\!] = {} & \{(\infty, \langle\rangle, X) \mid \delta \notin \alpha(X \uparrow [0, d_1])\} \\ & \cup \\ & \{(t_1, \langle(t_1, \delta)\rangle, X) \mid \delta \notin \alpha(X \uparrow [0, t_1)) \wedge t_1 \leqslant d_1\}\end{aligned}$$

$$\begin{aligned}\mathcal{D}[\![a \mathbin{@} t\{d_1\} \;;\; P]\!] = {} & \{(\infty, \langle\rangle, X) \mid a \notin \alpha(X \uparrow [0, d_1])\} \\ & \cup \\ & \{(t_1, s, X) \mid t_1 \leqslant d_1 \wedge \\ & \qquad \operatorname{head} s = (t_1, a) \wedge a \notin \alpha(X \uparrow [0, t_1)) \wedge \\ & \qquad \exists\, t_2 \bullet (t_2, \operatorname{tail} s, X \uparrow [t_1, \infty)) \in \mathcal{D}[\![\, P[t_1/t] \,]\!] + t_1\}\end{aligned}$$

$$\begin{aligned}\mathcal{D}[\![\texttt{i} \mathbin{@} t\{d_1\} \;;\; P]\!] = {} & \{(\infty, \langle\rangle, X) \mid \operatorname{end} X \leqslant d_1\} \\ & \cup \\ & \{(t_1, s, X) \mid t_1 \leqslant d_1 \wedge \exists\, t_2 \bullet (t_2, s, X) \in \mathcal{D}[\![P[t_1/t]]\!] + t_1\}\end{aligned}$$

Table 4: Equations for action prefix and termination

The processes `i ; a ; stop` and `a ; stop` have the same trace and refusal information, but they are essentially different. In the context below, the internal action of the left-hand process resolves the choice and ensures that b is never available.

$$C[Y] \;=\; Y \;\square\; \Delta^2\, b \;;\; \texttt{stop}$$

In the same context, the right-hand process is capable of performing b.

The same phenomenon arises with disabling, the other operator that is sensitive to internal actions. For this reason, we are forced to record the possibility of an internal action occurring before the beginning of the trace. As we shall see, this is all the information that we shall require.

A timed observation is a triple (t, s, X), where t is a time value, s is a timed trace, and X is a timed refusal set. The time value t marks the point at which the first internal or external action occurs; if no actions occur during the observation, then t takes the special value ∞.

A timed trace is a chronologically-ordered sequence of pairs: the first element of each is a timed value; the second is an action. A timed refusal set is a set of (time,action) pairs. The presence of a pair (t, a) in a timed trace indicates that action a is observed at time t. The presence of the same pair in a refusal set indicates that an offer of a at time t was seen to be refused.

In our semantics, each ET-LOTOS process will be associated with a set of timed observations. We define a semantic function $\mathcal{D}$ by recursion: for example,

$$\mathcal{D}[\![\texttt{stop}]\!] \;=\; \{(\infty, \langle\rangle, X) \mid X \in TR)\}$$

defines the semantics of `stop`. This process is associated with the set of all timed observations in which the time value is ∞ and the trace is empty; any timed refusal is possible.

$$\mathcal{D}[\![P \gg Q]\!] = \{(t_1, s, X) \mid \delta \notin \alpha(s) \wedge (t_1, s, X) \in \mathcal{D}[\![P]\!] \setminus \{\delta\}\}$$
$$\cup$$
$$\{(t_1, s, X) \mid \exists\, s_P, s_Q, t_2, t_3 \bullet \delta \notin \alpha(\text{front}\, s_P) \wedge (t_2, \delta) = \text{last}\, s_P \wedge (t_1, s_P, X \uparrow [0, t_2) \in \mathcal{D}[\![P]\!] \setminus \{\delta\} \wedge s = s_P \frown s_Q \wedge (t_3, s_Q, X \uparrow [t_2, \infty)) \in \mathcal{D}[\![Q]\!] + t_2\}$$

$$\mathcal{D}[\![P \;[\!> Q]\!] = \{(t_1, s, X) \mid (t_1, s, X) \in \mathcal{D}[\![P]\!] \wedge \exists\, t_2 \bullet t_2 \geqslant \max\{t_1, \text{end}\, s, \text{end}\, X\} \wedge (t_2, \langle\rangle, X) \in \mathcal{D}[\![Q]\!]\}$$
$$\cup$$
$$\{(t_1, s, X) \mid \exists\, s_P, s_Q, t_2, t_3 \bullet t_1 = \min\{t_2, t_3\} \wedge \text{end}\, s_P \leqslant t_3 \wedge s = s_P \frown s_Q \wedge (t_2, s_P, X \uparrow [0, t_3)) \in \mathcal{D}[\![P]\!] \wedge (t_3, s_Q, X) \in \mathcal{D}[\![Q]\!]\}$$

$$\mathcal{D}[\![P \;\Box\; Q]\!] = \{(t_1, s, X) \mid (t_1, s, X) \in \mathcal{D}[\![P]\!] \wedge \exists\, t_2 \bullet t_2 \geqslant t_1 \wedge (t_2, \langle\rangle, X \uparrow [0, t_1)) \in \mathcal{D}[\![Q]\!]\}$$
$$\cup$$
$$\{(t_1, s, X) \mid (t_1, s, X) \in \mathcal{D}[\![Q]\!] \wedge \exists\, t_2 \bullet t_2 \geqslant t_1 \wedge (t_2, \langle\rangle, X \uparrow [0, t_1)) \in \mathcal{D}[\![P]\!]\}$$

Table 5: Equations for sequencing and alternation

For convenience, we introduce notation for use in the other semantic equations. If s is a non-empty timed trace, then 'head s' and 'last s' are the first and last elements of s, while 'tail s' and 'front s' are traces containing everything but the first, and everything but the last element, respectively.

We write $s \upharpoonright A$ to denote the restriction of a trace to a set of actions A. This is the maximal subsequence of s containing only actions from A. Similarly, if X is a timed refusal, then $X \upharpoonright A$ denotes the restriction of X to A. We may also co-restrict, or hide, elements of a trace or refusal. We write $s \setminus A$ and $X \setminus A$ to denote the maximal subsequence of s, and the maximal subset of X, containing no actions from A.

If I is a set of time values, then $X \uparrow I$ is the set $\{(t, a) \in X \mid t \in I\}$. If s is a timed trace, and X is a timed refusal, then 'end s' and 'end X' denote the time of the last action in the trace and the supremum of time values in the refusal, respectively. Finally, if X is a timed refusal, then αX is the set of all actions mentioned in X.

The semantic equation for the termination process $\texttt{exit}\{d_1\}$ is given in Table 4. If the termination event δ does not occur during an observation, then the time value for that observation is ∞: no internal actions are possible for this process. Furthermore, the action δ could not be refused at any time before d_1.

If termination occurs during the observation, then the time at which δ is recorded must be between 0 and d_1. If this time is t_1, say, then δ could not have been refused at any time before t_1. This condition is captured by the requirement that $\delta \notin \alpha(X \uparrow [0, t_1))$: δ is not one of the actions mentioned in refusal set X during the interval $[0, d_1)$.

$$\mathcal{D}[\![\Delta^{d_1}\ P]\!] = \{(t_1, s, X) \mid (t_1, s, X \uparrow [d_1, \infty)) \in \mathcal{D}[\![P]\!] + d_1\}$$

$$\begin{aligned}\mathcal{D}[\![P \mid\![\ A\ ]\!\mid Q]\!] = \{(t_1, s, X) \mid \exists\, t_P, t_Q, s_P, s_Q, X_P, X_Q \bullet \\ t_1 = \min\{t_P, t_Q\} \wedge s_P \upharpoonright A = s_Q \upharpoonright A \wedge \\ s \in s_P \mid\![\ A\ ]\!\mid s_Q \wedge X = X_P \mid\![\ A\ ]\!\mid X_Q \wedge \\ (t_P, s_P, X_P) \in \mathcal{D}[\![P]\!] \wedge (u_Q, s_Q, X_Q) \in \mathcal{D}[\![Q]\!]\}\end{aligned}$$

$$\mathcal{D}[\![\mathbf{hide}\ A\ \mathbf{in}\ P]\!] = \{(t_1, s, X) \mid \exists\, s_P \bullet s = s_P \setminus A \wedge (t_1, s_P, X) \in \mathcal{D}[\![P]\!] \setminus A\}$$

Table 6: Equations for delay, concurrency, and abstraction

The semantic equation for action prefix employs a subsidiary function. If S is a set of observations, then $S + t$ is a translation of S by time value t. In every observation of S, we add t to the time of the first action, and to the times of actions in the trace and refusal. For example,

$$\{(t_0, \langle(t_1, a)\rangle, \{(t_2, a)\}\} + t \;=\; \{(t_0{+}t, \langle(t_1{+}t, a)\rangle, \{(t_2{+}t, a)\}\}$$

If S is the semantics of a process, then $S + t$ is the semantics of the same process starting at time t rather than at time 0.

If a process is prefixed with the internal action $\mathtt{i}$, then that action will occur at or before the timeout value. An observation of $\mathtt{i}\{d_1\}\ ;\ P$ in which no internal action occurs can extend no further than d_1. This is indicated by the requirement that $\operatorname{end} X \leqslant d_1$ when the time of the first action is ∞: that is, when no action has been performed.

If P is first component of a sequential composition, then termination of P is concealed. The assumption of maximal liveness means that any observation of P in this context must be consistent with δ occurring as soon as possible. We write $\mathcal{D}[\![P]\!] \setminus \{\delta\}$ to denote the set of all such observations of P; more generally, if S is a set of observations, then

$$S \setminus A \;=\; \{(t, s, X) \mid (t, s, X \cup [0, \max\{\operatorname{end} s, \operatorname{end} X\}) \times A) \in S\}$$

An observation (t, s, X) is consistent with every action from set A occurring as soon as possible if $(t, s, X \cup [0, \max\{\operatorname{end} s, \operatorname{end} X\}) \times A)$ is also an observation of S: that is, A could have been continuously refused.

The equation for parallel combination in Table 6 employs two subsidiary functions. If s_P and s_Q are two timed traces that agree upon all actions from set A, then $s_P \mid\![\ A\ ]\!\mid s_Q$ denotes the set of minimal sequences s such that s_P and s_Q are both subsequences of s. Notice that shared actions are not duplicated in an interleaving. If X_P and X_Q are timed refusals, then $X_P \mid\![\ A\ ]\!\mid X_Q$ denotes the unique refusal X such that $X \upharpoonright A = X_P \upharpoonright A \cup X_Q \upharpoonright A$ and $X \setminus A = X_P \setminus A \cap X_Q \setminus A$.

To give a denotational semantics to recursively-defined processes, we define a metric m upon a set $\mathcal{M}$: the set of all sets of observations S that satisfy the following properties: if (t, s, X) is an element of S, then the time of first action t is no greater than the beginning of trace s; if there is no upper bound upon the time at which the first internal event can occur, $\sup\{t \mid (t, \langle\rangle, X) \in S\} = \infty$, then it might never occur, $(\infty, \langle\rangle, X) \in S$.

If S is any observation set in $\mathcal{M}$, then the projection $S \upharpoonright t_1$ represents all information established before time t_1:

$$\begin{array}{l} S \upharpoonright t_1 = \{(t, s, X) \mid (t, s, X) \in S \wedge \max\{t, \mathrm{end}\, s, \mathrm{end}\, X\} < t_1\} \\ \qquad\quad \cup \\ \qquad\quad \{(\infty, \langle\rangle, X) \mid \exists\, t_2 \bullet (t_2, \langle\rangle, X) \in S, \mathrm{end}\, X < t_1 \wedge t_1 \leqslant t_2\} \end{array}$$

We may then define distance metric m as follows:

$$m(S_1, S_2) \;=\; \inf\{2^{-t} \mid S_1 \upharpoonright t = S_2 \upharpoonright t\}$$

The distance between two denotations S_1 and S_2 is 2^{-t_0}, where t_0 is the latest time at which all of the component observations agree; the longer that two processes have the same behaviour, the closer together they are. The result is a complete metric space over $\mathcal{M}$.

The range of our semantic function $\mathcal{D}$ is a subset of $\mathcal{M}$: the defining properties hold for every semantic set. The body of a recursive definition corresponds to a function upon $\mathcal{M}$: each recursive invocation of the process defined is an application of this function. The semantics of such a process is taken to be the fixed point of this function.

A sufficient condition for a unique fixed point to exist is that the function induced upon the semantic domain is a contraction mapping: this is the case precisely when each recursive invocation of the process name is guarded by some non-zero delay. We therefore impose a restriction upon the use of recursive definitions: in the definition

$$P \;\texttt{::=}\; Q \;\;\texttt{where}\;\; \vec{X} \;\texttt{:=}\; \vec{R}$$

we insist that each occurrence of an element of $\vec{X}$ in $\vec{R}$ is preceded by some non-zero time delay, and that there exists some lower bound upon these delays.

The semantics of P is obtained by evaluating Q in an environment where vector of processes $\vec{X}$ has the semantics 'fix $[\![\lambda \vec{X} \bullet \vec{R}]\!]$': that is, the fixed point of the contraction mapping on $\mathcal{M}$ corresponding to the syntactic function $\vec{R}$ of $\vec{X}$. A fully formal description requires a record of environments, or bindings, for process variables: a suitable example would be the treatment of recursion in [3].

5 Full abstraction

For the semantic function and model of Section 4 to be a suitable denotational semantics for language of ET-LOTOS, it should be *adequate* and *fully abstract* with respect to the operational semantics and trace congruence: two processes should have a different denotation exactly when there is a context which will distinguish between them.

To show that this is the case, we provide a way of extracting timed observations from the operational semantics of a process. We define a relation ex between processes and timed observations: 'P ex (t, s, X)' if and only if this statement is the last line of a proof constructed using the four inference rules described below.

The first rule states that the empty observation is exhibited by every process:

$$\frac{}{P \text{ ex } (\infty, \langle\rangle, \emptyset)} \text{ex1}$$

The second states that if P performs an external action a and P' ex (t, s, X), then we may conclude that P ex $(0, \langle(0, a)\rangle \frown s, X)$.

$$\frac{P \xrightarrow{a} P' \quad a \neq \mathtt{i} \quad P' \text{ ex } (t, s, X)}{P \text{ ex } (0, \langle(0, a)\rangle \frown s, X)} \text{ex2} \qquad \frac{P \xrightarrow{\mathtt{i}} P' \quad P' \text{ ex } (t, s, X)}{P \text{ ex } (0, s, X)} \text{ex3}$$

The third rule reflects the fact that an internal action makes no contribution to the trace or refusal information.

If a process P may delay for time d and then behave as P', a process that exhibits (t, s, X), then P exhibits $(t + d, s + d, X + d)$: the same observation with constant d added to every time value.

$$\frac{P \overset{d}{\leadsto} P' \quad P' \text{ ex } (t, s, X) \quad \text{end } Y \leqslant d \quad \forall\, a \in \alpha Y \bullet \neg(P \xrightarrow{a})}{P \text{ ex } (t + d, s + d, X + d \cup Y)} \text{ex4}$$

The operational semantics tell us that any action that is not an initial action of P may be refused throughout the delay interval; this property is called *reverse persistency* in [7]. As a result, we are justified in adding the set of timed actions Y to the refusal information.

Theorem 1 Let $\mathcal{E}[\![P]\!]$ be the set $\{ (t, s, X) \mid P \text{ ex } (t, s, X) \}$. Then $\mathcal{E}[\![P]\!] = \mathcal{D}[\![P]\!]$: that is, the ex relation matches the denotational semantics.

Proof 1 We proceed by structural induction upon the syntax of ET-LOTOS processes. As an illustration of the base case, consider **stop**: it is easy to see that $\mathcal{E}[\![\mathbf{stop}]\!] = \{ (\infty, \langle\rangle, X) \mid X \in TR \} = \mathcal{D}[\![\mathbf{stop}]\!]$.

The inductive step requires a case analysis. We present the case of parallel composition: if $\mathcal{E}[\![P_1]\!] = \mathcal{D}[\![P_1]\!]$ and $\mathcal{E}[\![P_2]\!] = \mathcal{D}[\![P_2]\!]$, then $\mathcal{E}[\![P_1 \mid[\, A \,]\mid P_2]\!] = \mathcal{D}[\![P_1 \mid[\, A \,]\mid P_2]\!]$ for any set of actions A. To prove this, we establish containment in both directions, and conclude that equality holds.

Assume that $(t, s, X) \in \mathcal{E}[\![P_1 \mid[\, A \,]\mid P_2]\!]$. From the definition of $\mathcal{E}$ we know that $(P_1 \mid[\, A \,]\mid P_2)$ ex (t, s, X) is the last line in a valid proof using the ex rules; we proceed by induction upon the length of this proof.

In the base case, the proof involves a single application of ex1, with consequent $(P_1 \mid[\, A \,]\mid P_2)$ ex $(\infty, \langle\rangle, \emptyset)$. From the denotational semantics, we know that the observation $(\infty, \langle\rangle, \emptyset)$ is an element of any denotation; in particular, it is an element of $\mathcal{D}[\![P_1 \mid\![A]\!\mid P_2]\!]$. Hence the result holds for proofs of unit length.

Our inductive hypothesis is that for any observation (t', s', X') and any processes R_1 and R_2, if (t', s', X') is an element of $\mathcal{E}[\![R_1 \mid\![A]\!\mid R_2]\!]$ and the length of the associated proof is k steps, then (t', s', X') is also an element of $\mathcal{D}[\![R_1 \mid\![A]\!\mid R_2]\!]$.

Suppose that $(t, s, X) \in \mathcal{E}[\![P_1 \mid\![A]\!\mid P_2]\!]$ and the length of the associated proof is $k + 1$. If k is greater than 0, then the last step in the proof must be an application of ex2, ex3, or ex4. This leads to a three-part case analysis: we will present only the case in which ex4 is the last rule to have been applied.

In this case, we may infer that there exist processes P_1' and P_2', an observation (t', s', X'), and a set Y such that

$$\frac{P \overset{d}{\leadsto} P' \quad P' \text{ ex } (t', s', X') \quad \text{end } Y \leqslant d \quad \forall\, a \in \alpha Y \bullet \neg(P \overset{a}{\longrightarrow})}{P \text{ ex } (t' + d, s' + d, X' + d \cup Y)}$$

is a valid instantiation of rule ex4, where P is the process $P_1 \mid\![A]\!\mid P_2$ and P' is the process $P_1' \mid\![A]\!\mid P_2'$.

From the definition of ex, there must be a proof of P' ex (t', s', X') that is k lines long. Our inductive hypothesis allows us to conclude that (t', s', X') is an element of $\mathcal{D}[\![P']\!]$, that is, $\mathcal{D}[\![P_1' \mid\![A]\!\mid P_2']\!]$. From the definition of $\mathcal{D}$, we know that there are observations $(t_1', s_1', X_1') \in \mathcal{D}[\![P_1']\!]$ and $(t_2', s_2', X_2') \in \mathcal{D}[\![P_2']\!]$ such that $t' = \min\{t_1', t_2'\}$, $s' \in s_1' \mid\![A]\!\mid s_2'$, and $X' = X_1' \mid\![A]\!\mid X_2'$.

From the rules in Table 3, we know that $P_1 \overset{d}{\leadsto} P_1'$ and $P_2 \overset{d}{\leadsto} P_2'$. Consider the case of component P_1: by rule ex4 we have that there exists Y_1 such that

$$\frac{P_1 \overset{d}{\leadsto} P_1' \quad P_1' \text{ ex } (t_1', s_1', X_1') \quad \text{end } Y_1 \leqslant d \quad \forall\, a \in \alpha Y_1 \bullet \neg(P \overset{a}{\longrightarrow})}{P_1 \text{ ex } (t_1' + d, s_1' + d, X_1' + d \cup Y_1)}$$

Processes P_1 and P_2 are both proper subcomponents of P, so our structural induction hypothesis allows us to conclude that $(t_1' + d, s_1' + d, X_1' + d \cup Y_1)$ is an element of $\mathcal{D}[\![P_1]\!]$ and that $(t_2' + d, s_2' + d, X_2' + d \cup Y_2)$ is an element of $\mathcal{D}[\![P_2]\!]$.

From the instantiation of ex4 with P and P', we know that the observation (t, s, X) matches $(t' + d, s' + d, X + d \cup Y)$. From the information above, we can show that $t' + d = \min\{t_1' + d, t_2' + d\}$, that $s' + d \in s_1' + d \mid\![A]\!\mid s_2' + d$, and that $X' + d \cup Y = X_1' + d \cup Y_1 \mid\![A]\!\mid X_2' + d \cup Y_2$, or $X' + d = X_1' + d \mid\![A]\!\mid X_2' + d \cup (Y_1 \mid\![A]\!\mid Y_2)$, where $Y = (Y_1 \mid\![A]\!\mid Y_2)$. Appealing to the definition of $\mathcal{D}$ once again allows us to conclude that $(t' + d, s' + d, X + d \cup Y) \in \mathcal{D}[\![P]\!]$, and hence that $(t, s, X) \in \mathcal{D}[\![P_1 \mid\![A]\!\mid P_2]\!]$.

Containment in other direction is established by a similar argument, except that this time the induction is based upon the combined length of the ex proofs for the structural subcomponents.

The remaining cases of our structural induction are entirely similar: in each case, the result is established by an inductive argument. In the case of recursion, we consider finite approximations to the semantics: every observation of the fixed point S must be an observation of $S \upharpoonright t$ for some finite time t. $\square$

The fact that $\mathcal{E}$ is equivalent to the denotational function $\mathcal{D}$, defined by structural recursion, tells us that $\mathcal{E}$ itself defines a congruence. The following theorem establishes that this congruence is in fact trace congruence.

Theorem 2 The congruence defined by $\mathcal{E}$ is trace congruence.

Proof 2 We begin by showing that the congruence defined by $\mathcal{E}$ is no stronger than trace congruence:

$$P_1 \equiv_t P_2 \Rightarrow \mathcal{E}[\![P_1]\!] = \mathcal{E}[\![P_2]\!]$$

Suppose for the contrapositive that there is an observation (t, s, X) in $\mathcal{E}[\![P_1]\!]$ that is not also in $\mathcal{E}[\![P_2]\!]$. We may then construct a context C such that $C[P_1]$ and $C[P_2]$ are not trace equivalent; it follows immediately that P_1 and P_2 are not trace congruent.

If there is no t' such that $\mathcal{E}[\![P_2]\!]$ contains (t', s, X), then the context

$$C[Y] = \texttt{hide}\ \Sigma\ \texttt{in}\ (Y\ |[\ \Sigma\ ]|\ (R_s\ |[\ \omega\ ]|\ T_X))$$

will distinguish between P_1 and P_2, where R is defined on the trace s by

$$R_{\langle\rangle} = \omega\ ;\ \texttt{stop}$$
$$R_{\langle(t,a)\rangle^\frown s} = \Delta^t\ a\{0\}\ ;\ R_{s-t}$$

and $T_X = T_1\ |[\ \omega\ ]|\ (T_2\ |[\ \omega\ ]|\ \ldots (T_{n-1}\ |[\ \omega\ ]|\ T_n)\ldots))$, where each T_i is a process complementing one of the finite collection of refusal tokens that go to make up X.

$$T_i = \Box_{a \in A_i}\ (\Delta^{t_i}\ a\{t_i' - t_i\}\ ;\ \texttt{stop})\ \Box\ (\Delta^{t_i'}\ \texttt{i}\ ;\ \omega\ ;\ \texttt{stop})$$

The indexed choice abbreviates a finite combination of binary choices.

If there is a finite time value t' such that $\mathcal{E}[\![P_2]\!]$ contains (t', s, X), then

$$\begin{aligned} C[Y] = \ & \texttt{hide}\ \Sigma\ \texttt{in}\ (v\ ;\ v\ ;\ \texttt{stop}\ [>\ Y) \\ & |[\ \Sigma\ ]| \\ & (R_{\langle(t,v)\rangle^\frown s}\ |[\ \omega\ ]|\ T_{X \cup [t,t+1) \times \{v\}}) \end{aligned}$$

will distinguish between the two processes. $C[P_1]$ is able to perform ω, provided that v is included in the set Σ.

If $\mathcal{E}[\![P_2]\!]$ contains (∞, s, X) then let $t_3 = \sup\{t \mid (t, s, X) \in \mathcal{E}[\![P_1]\!]\}$. The context

$$C[Y] = \texttt{hide}\ \Sigma\ \texttt{in}\ (T_X\ |[\ \Sigma \cup \{\omega\}\ ]|\ (Y\ \Box \Delta^{t_3+1}\ ;\omega\ ;\ \texttt{stop})$$

will distinguish between the two processes: $C[P_2]$ is able to perform ω.

To complete the proof, we must show that the congruence defined by $\mathcal{E}$ implies trace equivalence. This is easily established, as trace information is included in the observations extracted in the definition of $\mathcal{E}$. $\Box$

We are free to conclude that our denotational semantics of Section 4 defines the same language as the operational semantics of Section 3. It is both fully abstract and adequate with respect to our notion of trace congruence.

6 Discussion

This paper presents a denotational model for basic ET-LOTOS, a model that is adequate and fully abstract with respect to untimed trace congruence upon the operational semantics. As this congruence is the weakest useful congruence that may be defined—anything weaker will identify processes that can perform different events—this model associates a minimal amount of information with each process.

A denotational semantics is a valuable addition to the theory of real-time LOTOS. It complements the operational definition by considering the language at a higher level of abstraction, reinforcing the informal interpretation of the operational semantics, and encapsulating a particular notion of equivalence—in our case, trace congruence.

It permits an alternative approach to specification, in terms of properties of denotations. Constraints upon behaviour can be expressed as predicates upon timed observations, using a language such as temporal logic [8]. This can prove more convenient than the practice of choosing a representation for the constraint in the language of processes.

By its nature, a denotational semantics is compositional: the properties of a composite process are easily related to the properties of its components. This makes it possible to factor any proof obligations into smaller, more manageable objectives.

Our model supports an ordering based upon nondeterminism: we have thus a ready-made theory of process refinement. This theory can be extended to a notion of time-wise refinement, similar to the one defined in [11], making clear the relationship between ET-LOTOS and the existing untimed language.

The use of a metric space as our semantic domain makes for a simple, elegant fixed point theory. However, we are unable to provide a semantics to processes whose recursive definition is not time-guarded: such a definition need not correspond to a contraction mapping upon $\mathcal{M}$. Our model does not represent processes such as $P = a \; ; P$ which are capable of performing infinitely many actions at a single time instant.

Although seemingly unrealistic, such processes can be useful components of an abstract design. Furthermore, they are expressible in the syntax of basic ET-LOTOS. Thus a denotational semantics for the language should provide for their use. Initial investigations suggest that a metric space approach to fixed points will not succeed here; an alternative approach is required.

The syntax and semantics presented in this paper have since undergone a series of minor revisions: a more recent real-time extension is described in [6]. The difference between the two versions is one of fine tuning; the proof of full abstraction is entirely similar.

An alternative approach to timing information in LOTOS is presented in [1]. This is based on a different model of computation, in which internal actions may be delayed due to hidden resource constraints, and external actions may occur without the cooperation of the environment. Such a model would require a different denotational semantics; this is a subject for further research.

The language of real-time LOTOS is convergent with that of timed CSP. Since [2], the representation of sequential behaviour in CSP has been changed to match that of ET-LOTOS; delay and sequencing are now separate concerns. The operational semantics of real-time LOTOS embodies the same considerations as the operational semantics given in [10]. Most importantly, the computational model under each is the same.

The difference between LOTOS and CSP lies in the expression of internal activity and nondeterminism. The definition of each LOTOS operator must be consistent with the observability of `i`. Apart from the obvious difference in the interpretation of hiding, this means that the choice and disabling operators are more subtle than their CSP equivalents: they respond to internal activity.

As a result, a denotational semantics for timed LOTOS is more involved than a similar semantics for timed CSP. It is necessary to address the initial internal activity of a process. This paper shows that it is enough to record only the time at which the first action takes place. The proof of full abstraction shows that this is a natural semantics for the subset of the language examined here.

References

[1] T. Bolognesi, F. Lucidi, and S. Trigila. Converging towards a timed LOTOS standard. *Computer Standards and Interfaces*, 16(2), 1994.

[2] J. Davies. *Specification and proof in real time CSP*. Cambridge University Press, 1993.

[3] J. Davies and S. Schneider. Recursion induction for real-time processes. *Formal Aspects of Computing*, 5(6):530–553, 1993.

[4] C. A. R. Hoare. *Communicating Sequential Processes*. Prentice-Hall, 1985.

[5] ISO. *Information Processing Systems—Open Systems Interconnection—LOTOS, a Formal Description Technique based on the Temporal Ordering of Observational Behaviour*, February 1988. ISO/IEC-JTC1/SC21/WG1/FDT/C.

[6] JTC1/SC21/WG1/Q48.6. Revised draft on enhancements to LOTOS. obtainable from ftp.dit.upm.es, 1994.

[7] L. Léonard and G. Leduc. An enhanced version of timed LOTOS and its application to a case study. In *Formal Description Techniques VI*, 1994.

[8] Z. Manna and A. Pneuli. *The temporal logic of reactive and concurrent systems*. Springer-Verlag, 1992.

[9] R. Milner. *Communication and Concurrency*. Prentice-Hall, 1989.

[10] S. Schneider. An operational semantics for timed CSP. *Information and Computation*, 116(2), 1995.

[11] S. Schneider. Timewise refinement for communicating processes. *Science of Computer Programming*, 1995. to appear.

[12] Kenneth J. Turner, editor. *Using Formal Description Techniques — An Introduction to Estelle, LOTOS and SDL*. Wiley, New York, January 1993.

Reachability Analysis at Procedure Level through Timing Coincidence

Farn Wang*

Institute of Information Science, Academia Sinica, Taipei, Taiwan 115, Republic of China
+886-2-7883799 ext. 2420; FAX +886-2-7824814; farn@iis.sinica.edu.tw

Abstract. A procedure level model description language compatible with the concept of structured programming is devised for real-time concurrent systems with a global clock of discrete time domain. The complexities of its ID-vector reachability problems, both for recursive and nonrecursive systems, are investigated. A reachability analysis algorithm for nonrecursive systems is then introduced to take advantage of the synchrony among and the autonomy of multiple concurrent threads.

1 Introduction

With the theoretical development of real-time and hybrid automata[1, 11, 16, 20, 21, 23] and the successful engineering of automated verification tools[2, 5, 6], the research of computer-aided verification has received much attention. At this moment, various state-based [1, 6, 7, 8, 10, 11, 22] or event-based[14, 15] model description languages are available, to which the standard verification technique of global space reachability analysis is usually applied. We argue that such abstractions, although very elegant, may be at too low a level to make automatic verifiers efficiently uncover the behavior structures hidden in big system model descriptions. In this paper, we aim at devising a system model description language which not only compels the system designers, but also makes them feel easy, to describe high-level behavior structures of real-time concurrent systems.

A concurrent system may allow several *threads*[9] (basic autonomous sequential executions) running concurrently. In our description langauge, users are asked to present their system models as sets of ***single-source single-destination directed acyclic graphs*** (*DAG_1^1* in acronym) which represent procedures. Each node in a DAG_1^1 then represents a statement which is carried out by a procedure-call followed by a timed atomic operation. This concept provides a unified representation for procedure calls and do-loops in structured programming and should not make the users feel more difficult, or should even make software engineers feel easier, to encode their system models in our language than in the traditional state-based or event-based description techniques. *Rendezvous* is adopted as the basic synchronization primitive in our approach. Unlike the rendezvous in Ada which is binary and asymmetric[9], we take

* Supported by NSC, Taiwan, ROC under grant NSC 84-2213-E-001-012

it to its original meaning in a regular dictionary, *an appointment at which every participating party is expected to appear at the same moment.*

For the verification efficiency part of the paper, there are two things worth mentioning. First, the repetition patterns in reactive systems usually greatly influence their state space sizes. Since we require the systems to be described by DAG_1^1's, significant labor may be saved while, either explicitly or implicitly, constructing the state space. Secondly, the standard techniques in verifying concurrent systems involve calculating Cartesian products of the local state spaces of all autonomous threads. However, in concurrent systems, clocks are not only used to specify timing constraints but also used to coordinate behaviors of different threads. Prominent examples include the time-division multiplexion of telecommunication channels, machines talking to each other in synchronous mode, ..., etc. In between synchronizations, threads run independently and should generate verification subtasks which can be done separately. We have in this line developed a new technique called *timing-coincidibility analysis* which can successfully reduce the sizes of state spaces by an exponential factor in some cases.

In section 2, we define the syntax and operational semantics of our procedure-level real-time concurrent systems. In section 3, we define the reachability problem and discuss the complexities of the problems for recursive and nonrecursive systems. Section 4 presents our reachability analysis algorithm. Especially, the technique of timing coincidibility analysis is introduced in subsection 4.3. Section 5 reports our preliminary manual analysis on the railroad crossing benchmark[15]. Section 6 compares some previous work with ours and makes the conclusion.

We shall adopt the following notations. Given a set or sequence K, $|K|$ is the number of elements in K. We let $\mathcal{N}$ be the set of nonnegative integers, $\mathcal{Z}$ the set of integers, $\mathcal{N}^{\{\infty\}} = \mathcal{N} \cup \{\infty\}$, and $\mathcal{N}^{\{*\}} = \mathcal{N} \cup \{*\}$.

2 Real-time concurrent systems

2.1 Syntax

The underlying concept of our approach is DAG_1^1 *procedure* which is a single-source single-destination directed acyclic graph in which each node represents a compound statement of procedure-call and atomic operation. A statement is sequentially carried out in two phases, a *procedure-calling phase* and an *execution phase*. In the procedure-calling phase, a procedure specific to the statement, if any, is invoked for constantly or nondeterministically many times. In the execution phase, it waits to transit, either with a *rendezvous* or without, to another statement within a prespecified earliest starting time and deadline. We use the following example to give intuition to the readers before the formal definition.

Example 1. In Figure 1, we illustrate four procedures. Statements are represented by ovals with procedure-calls in their centers if any. P may loop nondeterministically many times (denoted by superscript "$*$" to Q) to invoke Q. V invokes P also as the body of a nondeterministic loop while W treats P as the body of a loop of three times (denoted by superscript "3" to P). Arcs among statements represent

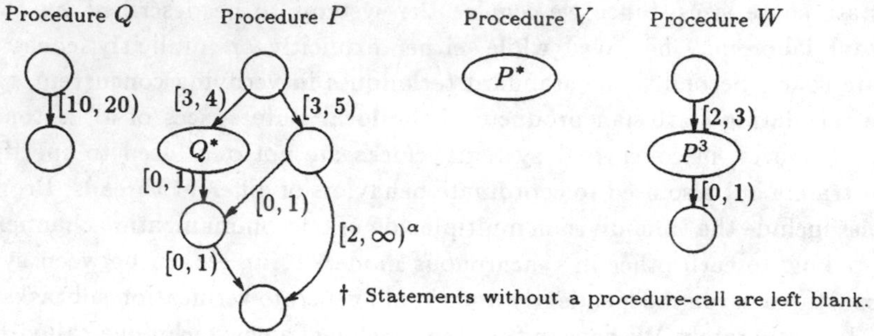

Fig. 1. Several simple procedures

transitions with the earliest starting times, and deadlines, and possibly rendezvous, by their sides. In P, while completing the transition labeled with $[2, \infty)^\alpha$, an instance of rendezvous α is expected. ||

Definition 1 : $\mathbf{DAG_1^1}$ procedure. A *procedure* P is a tuple $\langle S, \Theta, \chi, s_0, s_f, E, \Sigma, \pi\rangle$ satisfying the following restrictions.

- S is a set of statements.
- Θ is a set of procedure names.
- $\chi : S \mapsto \{\perp^0\} \cup (\Theta \times \mathcal{N}^{\{*\}})$. Given an $s \in S$, the following restrictions apply.
  - In case $\chi(s) = \perp^0$, at s no procedure is invoked.
  - In case $\chi(s) = Q^k$ (our special notation for elements in $\Theta \times \mathcal{N}^{\{*\}}$) for some procedure Q, procedure Q is invoked for k times consecutively at s. Specifically when $k = *$, it means a loop with nondeterministic count.
- $s_0, s_f \in S$ are called the *entry* and *exit* statements of P respectively.
- $E \subseteq S \times S$ is the set of transitions among statements.
- Σ is a set of rendezvous operations.
- $\pi : E \mapsto (\mathcal{N} \times \mathcal{N}^{\{\infty\}} \times \Sigma) \cup (\mathcal{N} \times \mathcal{N}^{\{\infty\}})$ such that for each $(s, s') \in E$,
  - in case $\pi(s, s') = [l, u)^\sigma$ (our special notation for elements in $\mathcal{N} \times \mathcal{N}^{\{\infty\}} \times \Sigma$), then $l < u$ and a thread, after fulfilling its obligation of calling procedure at s, may execute rendezvous σ within earliest starting time l and deadline $u - 1$ to go from s to s'.
  - in case $\pi(s, s') = [l, u)$, then $l < u$ and a thread, after fulfilling its obligation of calling procedure at s, can go from s to s' within earliest starting time l and deadline $u - 1$.

Given a procedure $P = \langle S, \Theta, \chi, s_0, s_f, E, \Sigma, \pi\rangle$, we shall let $S^P, \Theta^P, \chi^P, s_0^P, s_f^P, E^P, \Sigma^P, \pi^P$ be attribute $S, \Theta, \chi, s_0, s_f, E, \Sigma, \pi$ of P respectively. P is a DAG_1^1 *procedure* iff (S, E) is a single-source (s_0 can reach every node in S) single-destination (s_f is reachable from every node in S) directed acyclic graph. ||

Conceptually, a real-time concurrent system allows many threads running concurrently. By giving additional information on the starting statement of each thread and the participating parties of each rendezvous, a set of procedure definitions can be grouped to define a real-time concurrent system.

Definition 2 : Real-Time concurrent system. A *real-time concurrent system* is a tuple $\langle \Pi, \Omega, \tau \rangle$ satisfying the following properties.

- Π is a set of DAG_1^1 procedure definitions such that $\bigcup_{P \in \overline{\Pi}} \Theta^P \subseteq \overline{\Pi}$ where $\overline{\Pi} = \{P \mid \text{procedure } P \text{ is defined in } \Pi\}$.
- Ω is a sequence $\langle P_1, \ldots, P_m \rangle$ of procedure names in $\overline{\Pi}$ and declares the m threads in the system. For each $1 \leq i \leq m$, thread i starts by executing $s_0^{P_i}$.
- $\tau : (\bigcup_{P \in \overline{\Pi}} \Sigma^P) \mapsto 2^{\{1,\ldots,|\Omega|\}}$ defines the set of parties participating in each rendezvous. For each $i \in \tau(\sigma)$, thread i is expected to participate in each instance of rendezvous σ.

A real-time concurrent system is *unambiguous* iff the statement sets of each two procedures are disjoint. It is *recursive* iff its procedure-calls are recursive. ||

Ambiguous systems can be transformed to unambiguous ones by statement renaming. For simplicity, henceforth, we shall assume that all systems we shall discuss are unambiguous. Given an unambiguous real-time concurrent system R, we shall let $S^{\langle R \rangle}$ be the union of statement sets of procedures defined in R. Similarly, $\chi^{\langle R \rangle}$ and $\pi^{\langle R \rangle}$ are the unions of all χ and π mappings respectively defined in procedures in R.

Example 2. Assume we have the four procedure definitions in example 1. Then $R = \langle \{P, Q, V, W\}, \langle V, W \rangle, \{\alpha \rightarrow \{1, 2\}\} \rangle$ is a legitimate nonrecursive and unambiguous real-time concurrent system. ||

2.2 An operational semantics for systems with single discrete clock

The following constants for statements play a major role in presenting the finite characteristic of behavior structures of real-time concurrent systems. Given a statement s in a procedure P, we let C_s be the biggest finite constant used in $\pi^P(s, s')$ for all s', that is

$$C_s = \max\left\{c \,\middle|\, c \in \mathcal{N}; c \in \left\{l, u \,\middle|\, \exists s' \exists \sigma \left(\pi^P(s, s') = [l, u) \vee \pi^P(s, s') = [l, u)^\sigma\right)\right\}\right\}$$

The procedure-calling scheme in our real-time concurrent systems resembles the push-pop operation in stacks[13] which have often been used as theoretical abstraction of nested procedure-callings. The *ID (Instantaneous Description)*[13] of a thread can be conceptually recorded in a structure like the *control stack* (the name we shall adopt henceforth) in [3] and the *activation record* in [12, 24]. All possible executions from a moment can be deduced from the contents of the corresponding control stack. Given a thread ID (control stack) Γ represented as the following sequence

$$\begin{array}{ll} \text{bottom} & \qquad\qquad\qquad\qquad\qquad \text{top} \\ (s_0,t_0)\ (s_1,t_1)\ (s_2,t_2)\ \ldots\ldots & (s_{m-1},t_{m-1})\ \ (s_m,t_m) \end{array}$$

we let (s_0, t_0) and (s_m, t_m) be the *bottom* and *top* respectively of Γ. For each $0 \le i \le m$, $s_i \in S^{\langle R \rangle}$; and if $\chi(s_i) = Q^k$ for some Q and $k \in Z$, then $t_i \in \{-k, -k+1, \ldots, 0, 1, \ldots, C_{s_i}\} \cup \Sigma$; and if $\chi(s_i) = Q^*$ for some Q, then $t_i \in \{-*, 0, 1, \ldots, C_{s_i}\} \cup \Sigma$.

Given a control stack Γ, we let top(Γ) symbollically denote the top of Γ. $\Gamma\gamma$ is a new control stack obtained by pushing γ into Γ. pop(Γ) is a new control stack obtained by popping the top element from Γ. Given top(Γ) $= (s,t)$ with $t \in \mathcal{Z}$, we let tick(Γ) be an abbreviation of pop(Γ)$(s, t+1)$, i.e. the ID obtained by incrementing the top counter value by one.

Suppose we are given an ID $\Gamma = (s_0, t_0)(s_1, t_1)\ldots(s_m, t_m)$. For each $0 \le i \le m$, when $t_i < 0$ and $\chi^{\langle R \rangle}(s_i) = Q^k$ for some Q and k, it means the thread is now in the middle of executing procedure Q and is going to invoke Q consecutively for $|t_i|$ more times; when $t_i \ge 0$, it means the thread is now in the execution phase of statement s_i. It is obvious that for each $0 \le i < m$, $t_i < 0$. Also if $t_m < 0$, the ID is called a *nonexecution ID*; otherwise it is called an *execution ID*.

Similar to [13], we can define the succession of ID's which follows the intuition of control stack evolution during procedure-calling and strongly matches the relation among paths in activation trees as discussed in [3]. Nonetheless, for completeness, we shall put down our definition in the following.

Definition 3 : <u>Succession of thread ID's</u>. The succession relation, $\vdash$, between ID's are defined in the following way. Suppose we are given an ID Γ whose top is (s,t) with $\chi^{\langle R \rangle}(s) = Q^h$ and $\chi^{\langle R \rangle}(s_0^Q) = Q'^k$.

- **Fixed-loop procedure-call :** If $t < 0$, then $\Gamma \vdash \text{tick}(\Gamma)(s_0^Q, -k)$.
- ***-loop procedure-call :** If $t = -*$, then $\Gamma \vdash \Gamma(s_0^Q, -k)$ and $\Gamma \vdash \text{pop}(\Gamma)(s, 0)$.
- **Return from procedure-call :** If $t = 0$ and $s = s_f^P$, then $\Gamma \vdash \text{pop}(\Gamma)$.
- **Execution phase :** Suppose $t \ge 0$ and $s \ne s_f^P$.
  - If $t < C_s$, then $\Gamma \vdash \text{tick}(\Gamma)$.
  - If $t = C_s$ and $\pi^{\langle R \rangle}(s, s') = [l, \infty)$ (or $[l, \infty)^\sigma$) for some s', then $\Gamma \vdash \Gamma$.
  - If for some s' $\pi^{\langle R \rangle}(s, s') = [l, u)$, $l \le t < u$, and $\chi^{\langle R \rangle}(s') = \bar{Q}^k$, then $\Gamma \vdash \text{pop}(\Gamma)(s', -k)$
  - If for some s' $\pi^{\langle R \rangle}(s, s') = [l, u)^\sigma$, $l \le t < u$, and $\chi^{\langle R \rangle}(s') = \bar{Q}^k$, then $\Gamma \vdash \text{pop}(\Gamma)(s, \sigma)$ and $\text{pop}(\Gamma)(s, \sigma) \vdash \text{pop}(\Gamma)(s', -k)$

Also given two thread IDs Γ, Γ', we shall call Γ' an execution successor of Γ and write $\Gamma \to \Gamma'$ iff Γ' is an execution ID and there is a finite sequence $\Gamma_0\Gamma_1\ldots\Gamma_n$ such that $\Gamma = \Gamma_0$, $\Gamma_n = \Gamma'$, and for each $0 \le i < n$, Γ_{i+1} succeeds Γ_i. ||

Based on the concept of thread ID succession, we are now ready to define the computation in multi-thread real-time concurrent systems.

Definition 4 : <u>ID vectors and runs</u>. Suppose we are given a real-time concurrent system $R = \langle \Pi, \Omega, \tau \rangle$. An *ID vector* of R is a sequence of $|\Omega|$ ID's. A finite sequence $(\Delta_0, g_0)(\Delta_1, g_1)\ldots(\Delta_m, g_m)$ is called a Δ_0*-run* of R, where for each

$0 \leq k \leq m$, Δ_k is an ID vector and $g_k \in \{0,1\}$ indicates the presence of a global clock tick. Assume, for each $0 \leq k \leq m$, $\Delta_k = \langle \Gamma_k^{(1)}, \ldots, \Gamma_k^{(n)} \rangle$. The following requirements are imposed on a Δ_0-run.

- For each $0 \leq k < m$ and $1 \leq i \leq n$, either $\Gamma_k^{(i)} \rightarrow \Gamma_{k+1}^{(i)}$ or $\Gamma_k^{(i)} = \Gamma_{k+1}^{(i)}$.
- **Enforcement of synchrony to global clock** : For each $0 \leq k < m$, $g_k = 1$ iff every thread increments its time reading by 1, that is for each $1 \leq i \leq n$ such that $\text{top}(\Gamma_k^{(i)}) = (s,t)$ and $\text{top}(\Gamma_{k+1}^{(i)}) = (s',t')$, $s = s'$ and either $t \geq 0 \wedge t+1 = t'$ or $t = t' = C_s$.
- **Enforcement of rendezvous** : For each $\sigma \in \bigcup_{P \in \Pi} \Sigma^P$ and each $0 \leq k \leq m$, if $\text{top}(\Gamma_k^{(i)}) = (s,\sigma)$ for some s and $i \in \tau(\sigma)$, then for each $j \in \tau(\sigma)$, $\text{top}(\Gamma_k^{(j)}) = (s',\sigma)$ for some s'.

Given an ID vector Δ and a Δ-run $\Psi = (\Delta_0, g_0)(\Delta_1, g_1)\ldots(\Delta_m, g_m)$, for each $0 \leq k \leq m$, the time of the k-th ID vector in Ψ, in symbols $time_\Psi(k)$, is defined inductively by two cases : (1) $time_\Psi(0) = 0$. (2) For each $0 \leq k < m$, $time_\Psi(k+1) = time_\Psi(k) + g_k$. ||

One minor thing to notice in our semantics is that we treat each node in procedure definitions as a statement, instead of as a state. Thus a thread in the execution phase of a statement is obliged to finish executing the statement at sometime.

Example 3. Assume that we have the real-time concurrent system in example 2. It can be seen that while thread 1 may loop nondeterministically many times, thread 2 terminates after executing at most three instances of rendezvous α. Thus the whole system only has runs with at most three rendezvous instances. ||

3 ID-vector reachability problem and its complexities

We shall introduce a basic version of the reachability problem here. That is given two ID vectors Δ, Δ', if there is a *finite* run from Δ to Δ' ? Such a version is instrumental in constructing other interesting versions.

Definition 5 : ID-vector reachability. Given a real-time concurrent system $R = \langle \Pi, \Omega, \tau \rangle$, an ID vector Δ' is said *reachable from* another ID vector Δ in R iff there is a Δ-run $(\Delta_0, g_0)(\Delta_1, g_1)\ldots(\Delta_m, g_m)$ such that $\Delta' = \Delta_m$. ||

The reachability problem in our real-time concurrent systems can then be formulated in the following way. Given a real-time concurrent system R and two of its ID vectors Δ, Δ', the corresponding *ID-vector reachability problem* instance asks if Δ' is reachable from Δ in R. The following theorem shows that ID-vector reachability problem in recursive real-time concurrent systems is in general undecidable.

Theorem 6. *Two-counter machine halting problem[18] is reducible to the reachability problem of real-time concurrent systems.*

Proof. The heights of control stacks can emulate the counter contents. ||

Now we shall focus on nonrecursive real-time concurrent systems. Our first job is to determine how hard the problem is in the worst case. According to [17], it can be shown that the problem instance for a single-thread system is solvable without the cost of state explosion. The key observation is that after a thread has entered the execution phase of a statement for t time units, the only thing matters is not the actual value of t, but which intervals t falls into with respect to all the earliest starting time and deadline pairs of the statement. However when it comes to multi-thread systems, the intervals specified with different transitions along the executions of different threads can intersect each other and blow up the state space. The following two lemmas show the problem is PSPACE-complete

Lemma 7. *QBF[13] is reducible in PTIME to the ID-vector reachability problem for nonrecursive real-time concurrent systems.*

Proof. According to [13], a QBF (Quantified Boolean Formula with no free variable) is built form Boolean variables, $\vee$, $\wedge$, $\neg$, parentheses, and the quantifiers $\forall, \exists$ on Boolean variables. For convenience, we shall assume that no two variables use the same name and $\neg$ only appears right before atoms.

Suppose we are given a QBF B. We define a nonrecursive real-time concurrent system R in the following way. We shall use an interval to encode each possible valuation of the universally quantified variables in B. B is true iff there is a finite run from the beginning to a specific final ID vector at the end of the interval. First for each quantified variable x, we use five rendezvous symbols $\alpha_x, \alpha_{\neg x}, \beta_x, \beta_{\neg x}, \gamma_x$. α_x and $\alpha_{\neg x}$ assert the truth and falsity of x respectively. β_x and $\beta_{\neg x}$ are used to synchronize the beginning of the scopes of x with valuation of x set to TRUE and FALSE respectively. γ_x marks the end of the scopes. We need the four procedures defined in figure 2 for each literal x. P_x ($P_{\neg x}$) is used to request x to be TRUE

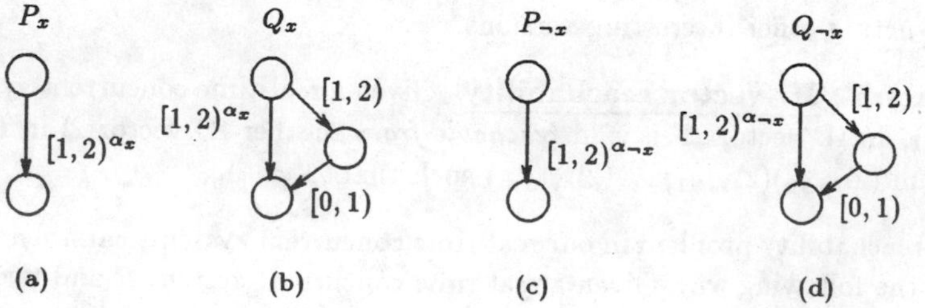

Fig. 2. Procedure definitions for universally quantified variables

(FALSE) while Q_x ($Q_{\neg x}$) enforces that x cannot be FALSE (TRUE) in certain scopes of x. The inductive definition of procedures for the six syntactic cases of QBF are then given in figure 3. Suppose the universally and existentially quantified

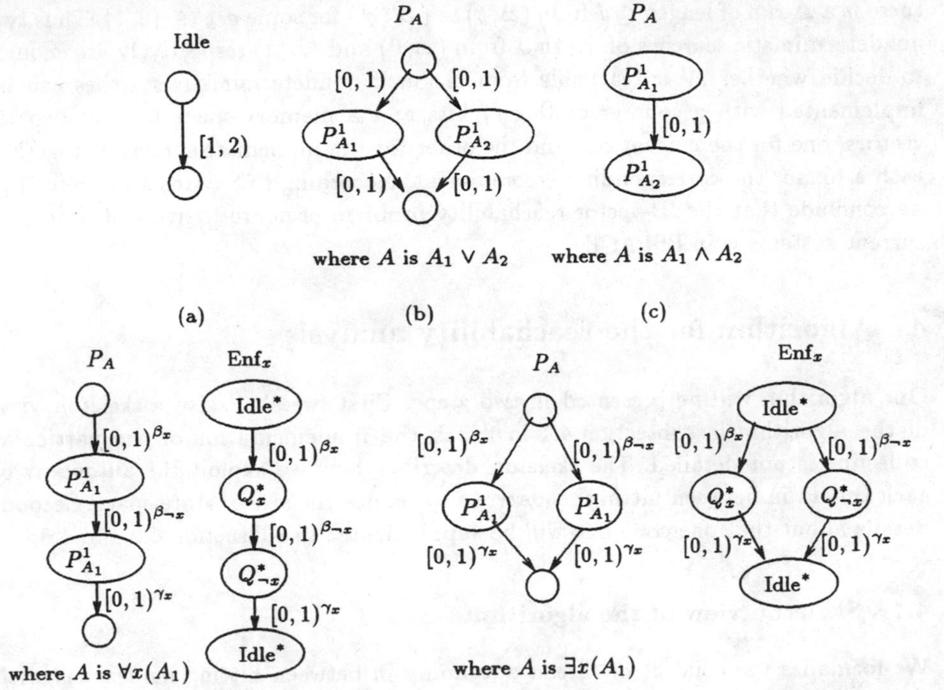

Fig. 3. Inductive procedure definition for QBF reduction

variables appear in B in sequence $x_1, \ldots, x_m$. Then there should be $m+1$ threads concurrently executing in the system, one for executing P_B and the rest for executing the enforcer of each variable scoping. That is $\Omega = \langle P_B, \mathrm{Enf}_{x_1}, \mathrm{Enf}_{x_2}, \ldots, \mathrm{Enf}_{x_m} \rangle$. For each variable x_i, $1 \le i \le m$, $\tau(\alpha_{x_i}) = \tau(\alpha_{\neg x_i}) = \tau(\beta_{x_i}) = \tau(\beta_{\neg x_i}) = \tau(\gamma_{x_i}) = \{1, i+1\}$. It is easy to check that such a reduction is in PTIME.

Now suppose $\chi^{(R)}(s_0^{P_B}) = Q_B^{k_B}$. We want to show that $\left(\langle (s_f^{P_B}, 0), (s_f^{\mathrm{Enf}_{x_1}}, 0), \ldots, (s_f^{\mathrm{Enf}_{x_m}}, 0) \rangle, 1\right)$ is reachable from $\left(\langle (s_0^{P_B}, -k_B), (s_0^{\mathrm{Enf}_{x_1}}, 0), \ldots, (s_0^{\mathrm{Enf}_{x_m}}, 0) \rangle, g\right)$ for some $g \in \{0, 1\}$. The proof of the lemma can be finished by a structure induction on the subformulas of B. ||

Lemma 8. *The ID-vector reachability problem of nonrecursive real-time concurrent systems is in PSPACE.*

Proof. It can be analyzed that the number of different (Δ, g) pairs of a nonrecursive real-time concurrent systems is exponential to its size (in bits). Suppose this number of a given system is J. Given two ID vectors Δ, Δ', Δ' is reachable from Δ in R iff there is a Δ-run of length $\leq J$ from (Δ, g) to (Δ', g') for some $g, g' \in \{0, 1\}$. Thus two nondeterministic searches of depth J from $(\Delta, 0)$ and $(\Delta, 1)$ respectively are enough to decide whether Δ' is reachable from Δ. Such nondeterministic searches can be implemented with a counter of $\lceil \log J \rceil$ bits and a memory space to hold two ID vectors, one for the current one and the other for the immediate successor, together with a bit for the corresponding g-component. According to Savitch's theorem [13], we conclude that the ID-vector reachability problem of nonrecursive real-time concurrent systems is in PSPACE. ||

4 Algorithm for the reachability analysis

Our algorithm will be presented in two steps. First, we shall give a skeleton view of the algorithm in subsection 4.1 in which the implementation of one particular code line is not detailed. The skeleton describes how we exploit the autonomy of each thread in between hitting rendezvous to reduce the size of state space. Second, details about that one code line will be supplemented in subsection 4.2 and 4.3.

4.1 Skeleton view of the algorithm

We formalize the concept of thread autonomy in between hitting rendezvous with the following definition.

Definition 9 : Successor through rendezvous-less run. Given a real-time concurrent system R, and two ID vector Δ and Δ', we say Δ' is a *successor through rendezvous-less run (or ¬r-successor)* of Δ iff there is a finite Δ-run $\Psi = (\Delta_0, g_0) \ldots (\Delta_m, g_m)$ of R such that

- Ψ ends at Δ', i.e. $\Delta' = \Delta_m$; and
- for each $0 < k < m$, Δ_k does not mark the completion of a rendezvous, that is, assuming $\Delta_k = \langle \Gamma_k^{(1)}, \ldots, \Gamma_k^{(n)} \rangle$, for each $1 \leq i \leq n$, there is no $\sigma \in \Sigma$ s.t. $\mathrm{top}(\Gamma_k^{(i)}) = (s, \sigma)$ for some s. ||

In between hitting rendezvous, each thread executes in an independent way. We say an ID vector $\langle \Gamma^{(1)}, \ldots, \Gamma^{(n)} \rangle$ is *at the stage of completion of rendezvous* σ iff for some $1 \leq i \leq n, s$, $\mathrm{top}(\Gamma^{(i)}) = (s, \sigma)$. A major source of efficiency of our algorithm comes from the fact that we only work with ID vectors which are at the completion stage of rendezvous. The algorithm in table 1 takes this characteristic of real-time concurrent systems into consideration to answer instances of ID-vector reachability problem. Succession relation among such ID vectors is figured out by manipulation of arithmetic set expressions as defined in subsection 4.2

Lemma 10. *Given two ID vectors Δ, Δ' of a nonrecursive real-time systems R, with the oracle for ¬r-successorship, Δ' is reachable from Δ in R iff Reachable(R, Δ, Δ') is TRUE.*

Reachable(R, Δ, Δ')
/* $R = \langle \Pi, \Omega, \tau \rangle$, is a nonrecursive real-time concurrent system. */ {
(1) Generate the set X of all ID vectors in which a rendezvous is at the stage of completion.
(2) Determine the pairwise $\neg r$-successor relation in $X \cup \{\Delta, \Delta'\}$ and call it Y.
(3) If Δ' is reachable from Δ in $(X \cup \{\Delta, \Delta'\}, Y)$, answer TRUE; else answer FALSE.
}

Table 1. Algorithm for ID-vector reachability problem

Proof. Δ' is reachable from Δ iff there is a finite Δ-run Ψ leading to Δ'. Ψ can be decomposed into finite runs which correspond to the edge relation Y used in procedure Reachable(). The lemma can be proven using this correspondence. ||

All but the second code line in table 1 are obvious. In subsection 4.2, we shall introduce arithmetic set expressions, as the abstraction tool used to construct a solution for the second code line. In subsection 4.3, we shall use the technique of timing coincidibility analysis to determine the $\neg r$-successor relation between two ID vectors.

4.2 Arithmetic set expressions and their operations

The transitions in our system models are carried out within intervals bounded by earliest starting times and deadlines. Since earliest starting times, and deadlines alike, of a sequence of consecutive transitions can be accumulated during the analysis of thread behavior, it is natural to define the addition and integer multiplication of integer intervals. And indeed our reachability analysis algorithm is presented based on this kind of arithmetic set operations.

Our arithmetic set expression is constructed by the following rules.

$$H ::= \{c\} \mid H_1 \cup H_2 \mid H_1 \cap H_2 \mid H_1 + H_2 \mid H_1^k \mid H_1^*$$

c, k are natural numbers. $\{c_1, \ldots, c_n\}$ is a shorthand for $\{c_1\} \cup \ldots \cup \{c_n\}$. Conceptually, we treat an integer interval $[a, b)$ as a shorthand for the set $\{a, a+1, \ldots, b-1\}$. Especially, $[a, \infty)$ is a shorthand for $\{a\} + \{1\}^*$. The meaning of these set expression is inductively given in the following.

- Case $H = \{c\}$, H is the set of integer c.
- Case $H = H_1 \cup H_2$ ($H = H_1 \cap H_2$), H is the union (intersection) of H_1 and H_2.
- Case $H = H_1 + H_2$, $H = \{a + b \mid a \in H_1; b \in H_2\}$.
- Case $H = H_1^k$, (1) when $k = 0$, then $H = \{0\}$; (2) otherwise $H = H_1^{k-1} + H_1$.
- Case $H = H_1^*$, $H = \bigcup_{k \geq 0} H_1^k$.

Note $\emptyset$ acts as a nullifier in arithmetic set addition, i.e. for all integer set expression H, $H + \emptyset = \emptyset$. Also, we allow distribution of addition against union and intersection.

An arithmetic set expression H is said to be in ***periodical normal form (PNF)*** iff $H = \bigcup_{1 \le i \le m}(\{a_i\} + \{c_i\}^*)$. In the following, we give a set of rewriting rules to transform arithmetic set expressions into PNF arithmetic set expressions.

1) $\left(\bigcup_{1 \le i \le m}(\{a_i\} + \{c_i\}^*)\right) \cap \left(\bigcup_{1 \le j \le n}(\{b_j\} + \{d_j\}^*)\right)$
$= \bigcup_{1 \le i \le m; 1 \le j \le n} K_\cap(\{a_i\} + \{c_i\}^*, \{b_j\} + \{d_j\}^*)$
where $K_\cap(\{a\} + \{c\}^*, \{b\} + \{d\}^*)$ is defined by the following two cases.
   - If there is no integer solution i, j to $a + ci = b + dj$, then $K_\cap(\{a\} + \{c\}^*, \{b\} + \{d\}) = \emptyset$
   - Otherwise, let $\bar{i}, \bar{j}$ be the minimum integer solution. $K_\cap(\{a\} + \{c\}^*, \{b\} + \{d\}^*) = \{a + c\bar{i}\} + \{\mathrm{lcm}(c, d)\}^*$

2) $\left(\bigcup_{1 \le i \le m}(\{a_i\} + \{c_i\}^*)\right) + \left(\bigcup_{1 \le j \le n}(\{b_j\} + \{d_j\}^*)\right)$
$$= \bigcup_{1 \le i \le m; 1 \le j \le n} \left(\begin{array}{l} \{a_i + b_j + \mathrm{lcm}(c_i, d_j)\} + \{\gcd(c_i, d_j)\}^* \\ \bigcup_k \{a_i + b_j + c_i h + d_j k \mid h, k \in \mathcal{N}; c_i h + d_j k < \mathrm{lcm}(c_i, d_j)\} \end{array} \right)$$

3) $\left(\bigcup_{1 \le i \le m}(\{a_i\} + \{c_i\}^*)\right)_k$
$$= \begin{cases} \{0\} & \text{if } k = 0 \\ \left(\bigcup_{1 \le i \le m}(\{a_i\} + \{c_i\}^*)\right)_{k-1} + \bigcup_{1 \le i \le m}(\{a_i\} + \{c_i\}^*) & \text{if } k > 0 \end{cases}$$
After application of the rule, rule 2 should be used immediately.

4) $\left(\bigcup_{1 \le i \le m}(\{a_i\} + \{c_i\}^*)\right)^* = \sum_{1 \le i \le m}(\{a_i\}^* + \{c_i\}^*)$
After application of the rule, rule 2 and distribution of addition against unions should be used iteratively to transform the formula to its PNF.

4.3 Timing coincidibility analysis

The technique of ***timing coincidibility analysis*** is based on the following observation. Given two concurrent threads starting their execution simultaneously, after running without interaction (rendezvous) for t time units according to the global clock, they may get to ID's Γ, Γ' respectively. Then due to the strong synchrony in global clock systems, we can conclude that Γ, Γ' may happen at the same time during the two thread's rendezvous-less executions respectively. This implies that we can separately work with the subtasks of searching in the local ID space of each thread while analyzing the reachability between ID vectors. By figuring out the general time patterns between pairs of ID's in the local ID spaces, we can tell the $\neg r$-successor relations by intersecting those time representations. In this approach, time representations are often very concise since it tends to ignore the difference among different ID sequences as long as they have the same time values.

Definition 11 : **Rendezvous-less procedure graph.** Given a DAG_1^1 procedure P in a nonrecursive real-time concurrent system R, the ***rendezvous-less procedure graph*** of $P = \langle S, \Theta, \chi, s_0, s_f, E, \Sigma, \pi \rangle$, denoted as $pgraph_{\neg r}(P) = (S, E_{\neg r})$, is a subgraph of (S, E) such that for every $s, s' \in S$, $(s, s') \in E_{\neg r}$ iff for some l, u, $\pi(s, s') = [l, u)$.
||

Definition 12 : Execution sequence. Given a real-time concurrent system $R = \langle \Pi, \Omega, \tau \rangle$, a finite ID sequence $\Phi = \Gamma_0 \Gamma_1 \ldots \Gamma_m$, with $\Gamma_k \rightarrow \Gamma_{k+1}$ for each $0 \leq k < m$, defines a legitimate thread execution in R from Γ_0 and is called a *Γ_0-sequence.* Φ is *rendezvous-less* iff for every $0 < k < m$, Γ_k is not at the completion stage of a rendezvous, i.e. there is no $\sigma \in \Sigma$ such that $\mathrm{top}(\Gamma_k) = (s, \sigma)$ for some s. ||

Definition 13 : Rendezvous-less time expressions. Given a DAG_1^1 procedure P with $pgraph_{\neg r}(P) = (S^P, E^P_{\neg r})$, the *rendezvous-less time expression* of P, $texp_{\neg r}(P)$, is defined inductively as follows.

- If $P = \perp$, then $texp_{\neg r}(\perp) = [0, 1)$, else $texp_{\neg r}(P) = texp_{\neg r}(s_0^P)$
- For each $s \in S^P$ with $\chi^P(s) = Q^k$ for some Q and k, then $texp_{\neg r}(s) = (texp_{\neg r}(Q))^k + \bigcup_{(s,s') \in E^P_{\neg r}} (\pi(s, s') + texp_{\neg r}(s'))$.

Suppose we are given a finite rendezvous-less execution sequence $\Phi = \Gamma_0 \ldots \Gamma_m$ with $\mathrm{top}(\Gamma_i) = (s_i, t_i)$ for each $0 \leq i \leq m$. We conveniently let $texp_{\neg r}(\Phi)$ equal to

$$\sum_{0 \leq i < m; t_i \geq 0; t_{i+1} \geq 0} (t_{i+1} - t_i) + \delta_\Phi^* + \sum_{0 \leq i < m; \chi^{(R)}(s_i) = Q^*} (texp_{\neg r}(Q))^*$$

be our notation for the time expression for rendezvous-less execution sequence Φ. Here δ_Φ is $\{1\}$ when $\exists 0 \leq i \leq m (t_i = C_{s_i})$; $\{0\}$ otherwise. Also we let

$$texp_{\neg r}(\Gamma, \Gamma') = \bigcup_{(\Phi \text{ is a finite simple rendezvous-less } \Gamma\text{-sequence of } R \text{ ends at } \Gamma')} texp_{\neg r}(\Phi)$$

where "simple" means no two ID's are the same. ||

We shall show that the execution times of all rendezvous-less execution sequences between two ID's can be figured out by doing some arithmetic on time expressions. The meaning of the time expression is proven by the following lemma.

Lemma 14. *Given two ID's Γ, Γ' of a nonrecursive real-time concurrent system, there is a rendezvous-less execution sequence of time t from Γ to Γ' iff $t \in \mathrm{texp}_{\neg r}(\Gamma, \Gamma')$ which is computable.*

Proof. The "if" direction is easy to understand. For the "only if" part, suppose there is such an execution sequence with total time t which corresponds to the finite path. By decomposing the path into a simple path and a set of execution sequences incurred by procedure invocations, we realize that t must be the execution time of the simple path plus the executions of those procedures. The rest of the proof goes like a case analysis and induction on the structure of the procedures.

The computability part is true because for a nonrecursive system, the number of valid ID's reachable from one of $(s_0^{P_i}, 0)$, $1 \leq i \leq n$, is finite, and hence the number of simple execution sequences is also finite. Given a finite simple rendezvous-less execution sequence, its $texp_{\neg r}()$ value can be proven to be computable by a structure induction according to the cases used in definition 13. ||

With definition 12, 13, and lemma 14, we have made the concept of autonomous execution of a single thread precise and proven our derivation of rendezvous-less thread execution time expression correct. Now all these can be readily combined to prove the correctness of the technique of timing coincidibility analysis.

Lemma 15. *Given $t \in \mathcal{N}$ and two ID vectors of a nonrecursive real-time concurrent system R,* $\Delta = \langle \Gamma^{(1)}, \ldots, \Gamma^{(n)} \rangle$ *and* $\Delta' = \langle \Gamma'^{(1)}, \ldots, \Gamma'^{(n)} \rangle$*,* Δ' *is a successor of* Δ *through rendezvous-less run of t time units in R iff* $t \in \bigcap_{1 \leq i \leq n} \text{texp}_{\neg r}(\Gamma^{(i)}, \Gamma'^{(i)})$.

Proof. According to definition 9, 12, 13, and lemma 14. ||

5 Railroad crossing example

We use a version of the familiar example of railroad crossing[15] to illustrate the usage of our description language and the potential of our timing-coincidibility analysis approach. There are two threads in the system : a monitor which watches the relative distances of approaching trains to the gate, and a gate-controller which controls the up and down of the gate to the crossing. The monitor and the gate-controller talk to each other through two rendezvous, *MD_rend* which asks the gate to be lowered down, and *MU_rend* which asks the gate to be lifted. Initially, the monitor is in mode *A* (trains *A*pproaching) and the gate-controller is in mode *Up* waiting for *MD_rend* to happen. When there is a train detected approaching at 1 miles, the monitor asks for a rendezvous *MD_rend* within time interval $[0, 6)$ to go to mode *BC* (*B*efore *C*rossing) in which the monitor should stay for 295 time units and then go to mode *C* (train *C*rossing). Upon completing a rendezvous *MD_rend*, the gate-controller goes from mode *Up* to *MD* (*M*ove *D*own) in which the gate-controller should stay 20 to 50 time units and go to mode *Down*.

Upon a train leaves the crossing, the monitor asks the gate to be lifted by requesting a rendezvous *MU_rend* within $[0, 6)$ time interval and go to mode *P* (train *P*assing) in which the monitor stays for 95 time units and goes to mode *A*. Upon completing a rendezvous *MU_rend*, the gate-controller goes from mode *Down* to *MU* (*M*ove *U*p) in which if a rendezvous *MD_rend* takes place, the gate-controller goes to mode *MD*, else it goes to mode *Up* within 20 to 50 time units.

Finally, we incorporate an auxiliary rendezvous *acc* and three auxiliary statements, *IDanger, CDanger, MDanger*, to signal the situation when the gate is not lowered down but a train is crossing. The real-time concurrent system,

$$R = \left\langle \Pi, \langle \mathit{Monitor}, \mathit{Controller} \rangle, \left\{ \begin{array}{l} \mathit{MD\_rend}, \\ \mathit{MU\_rend}, \\ \mathit{acc} \end{array} \right\}, \left\{ \begin{array}{l} \mathit{MD\_rend} \rightarrow \{1,2\}, \\ \mathit{MU\_rend} \rightarrow \{1,2\}, \\ \mathit{acc} \rightarrow \{1,2\} \end{array} \right\} \right\rangle$$

where Π contains procedure definitions shown in figure 4, specifies the railroad crossing example we introduced in the previous paragraphs. The system is unsafe iff one of the following four ID vectors

$$\langle ((\text{mloop}, -*)(\mathit{MD\_sync}, \mathit{MD\_rend}), \mathit{acc}), ((\mathit{init\_Up}, \mathit{MD\_rend}), \mathit{acc}) \rangle$$
$$\langle ((\text{mloop}, -*)(\mathit{MD\_sync}, \mathit{MD\_rend}), \mathit{acc}), ((\text{cloop}, -*)(\mathit{MU}, \mathit{MD\_rend}), \mathit{acc}) \rangle$$
$$\langle ((\text{mloop}, -*)(\mathit{MD\_sync}, \mathit{MD\_rend}), \mathit{acc}), ((\text{cloop}, -*)(\mathit{Up}, \mathit{MD\_rend}), \mathit{acc}) \rangle$$
$$\langle ((\text{mloop}, -*)(\mathit{MU\_sync}, \mathit{MU\_rend}), \mathit{acc}), ((\text{cloop}, -*)(\mathit{Down}, \mathit{MU\_rend}), \mathit{acc}) \rangle$$

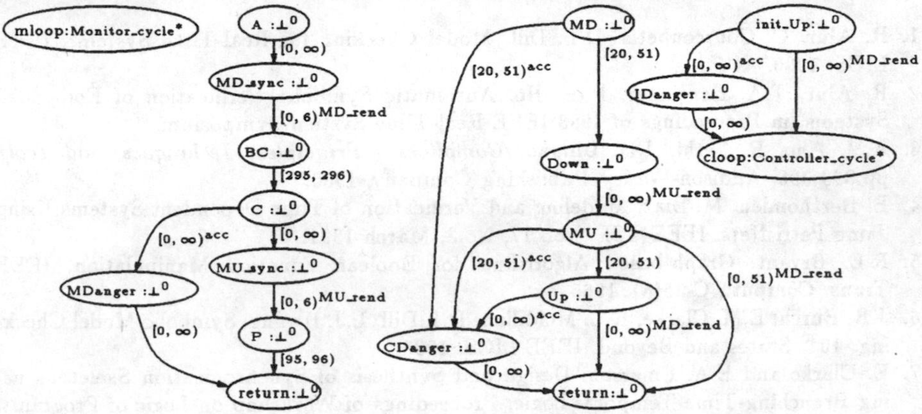

Fig. 4. Procedure definitions in the railroad crossing example

is reachable from $\langle(\text{mloop}, -*), (\textit{init\_Up}, 0)\rangle$ in R. A manual application of our technique of timing coincidibility analysis shows that the resulting state graph, $(X \cup \{\Delta, \Delta'\}, Y)$ as discussed in procedure Reachable() in table 1, can be constructed in time independent to the timing constants used in the model description, assuming that arithmetic integer binary operations can be done in unit time.

6 Conclusion

It is easy to see that given an arbitrarily connected real-time automaton, its timing behavior structure can be horribly difficult to analyze. But this kind of input assumption usually contradicts the common practice of structured programming in software engineerings, the high-level semantics of programming languages, and the design rules in real-time systems. We advocate procedure-level model descriptions and verifications for real-time concurrent systems for their potentially better average-case performance in automated verification. A model description language is devised and reachability analysis algorithm is proposed. At the current stage, an experimental verification system based on the theory proposed in this paper is under construction.

The concept of transitions labeled with earliest starting times and deadlines was also adopted in formal frameworks like [15, 19]. Special techniques for reachability analysis has also been reported under this kind of framework[15, 4]. However, we do not know if there is any previous formal framework for real-time concurrent systems aimed at taking advantage of local autonomy and program structures to improve the verification performance.

References

1. R. Alur, C. Courcoubetis, D.L. Dill. Model Checking for Real-Time Systems, IEEE LICS, 1990.
2. R. Alur, T.A. Henzinger, P.-H. Ho. Automatic Symbolic Verification of Embedded Systems. in Proceedings of 1993 IEEE Real-Time System Symposium.
3. A.V. Aho, R. Sethi, J.D. Ullman. *Compliers - Principles, Techniques, and Tools*, pp.393-396, Addison-Wesley Publishing Company, 1986.
4. B. Berthomieu, M. Diaz. Modeling and Verification of Time Dependent Systems Using Time Petri Nets. IEEE TSE, Vol. 17, No.3, March 1991.
5. R.E. Bryant. Graph-based Algorithms for Boolean Function Manipulation, IEEE Trans. Comput., C-35(8), 1986.
6. J.R. Burch, E.M. Clarke, K.L. McMillan, D.L.Dill, L.J. Hwang. Symbolic Model Checking: 10^{20} States and Beyond, IEEE LICS, 1990.
7. E. Clarke and E.A. Emerson. Design and Synthesis of Synchronization Skeletons using Branching-Time Temporal Logic, Proceedings of Workshop on Logic of Programs, Lecture Notes in Computer Science 131, Springer-Verlag, 1981.
8. E. Clarke, E.A. Emerson, and A.P. Sistla. Automatic Verification of Finite-State Concurrent Systems Using Temporal Logic Specifications, ACM Transactions on Programming Languages and Systems 8(2), 1986, pp. 244-263.
9. H.M. Deitel. An Introduction to Operating Systems, pp.110-115, Addison-Wesley, 1984.
10. E.A. Emerson, C.-L. Lei. Modalities for Model Checking: Branching Time Logic Strikes Back, Science of Computer Programming 8 (1987), pp.275-306, Elsevier Science Publishers B.V. (North-Holland).
11. T.A. Henzinger, X. Nicollin, J. Sifakis, S. Yovine. Symbolic Model Checking for Real-Time Systems, IEEE LICS 1992.
12. E. Horowitz. Fundamentals of Programming Languages, Computer Science Press, 1984.
13. J.E. Hopcroft, J.D. Ullman. Introduction to Automata Theory, Languages, and Computation, Addison-Wesley, 1979.
14. F. Jahanian and A.K. Mok. Safety analysis of timing properties in real-time systems, IEEE Transactions on Software Engineering, Vol.SE-12, No9, 1986, pp. 890-904.
15. F. Jahanian, D.A. Stuart. A Method for Verifying Properties of Modechart Specifications. IEEE RTSS 1988.
16. Y. Kesten, A. Pnueli, J. Sifakis, S. Yovine. Integration Graphs: a Class of Decidable Hybrid Systems. In Proc. Workshop on Theory of Hybrid Systems, LNCS 736, Springer-Verlag, 1993.
17. W.K.C. Lam, R.K Brayton. Alternating RQ Timed Automata. in proceedings of Conference on Computer-Aided Verification, 1993, LNCS 697, Springer-Verlag.
18. H.R. Lewis. Unsolvable Classes of Quantificational Formulus, 1979, Addison-Wesley Pub. Co.
19. P. Merlin, D.J. Faber. Recoverability of Communication Protocols. IEEE Trans. Commun, Vol. COM-24, no. 9, Sept. 1976.
20. O. Maler, Z. Manna, A. Pnueli. From Timed to Hybrid Systems. In Real Time : Theory in Practice, LNCS 600, pp. 447-484, Springer-Verlag, 1991.
21. Z. Manna, A. Pnueli. Verifying Hybrid Systems. In Proc. Workshop on Theory of Hybrid Systems, LNCS 736, Springer-Verlag, 1993.
22. F. Wang, A.K. Mok, E.A. Emerson. Real-Time Distributed System Specification and Verification in APTL. ACM TOSEM, Vol. 2, No. 4, Octobor 1993, pp. 346-378.
23. F. Wang. Timing Behavior Analysis for Real-Time Systems. IEEE LICS 1995.
24. W. Wulf, M. Shaw, P. Hilfinger, L. Flon. Fundamentals of Computer Science, Addison-Wesley, Reading, Mass., 1981.

Faster Asynchronous Systems

Walter Vogler *

Institut für Mathematik, Universität Augsburg
D-86135 Augsburg, Germany

Abstract

A testing scenario in the sense of De Nicola and Hennessy is developed to measure the worst-case efficiency of asynchronous systems. The resulting testing-preorder is characterized with a variant of refusal traces and shown to satisfy some properties that make it attractive as a faster-than relation. Finally, one implementation of a bounded buffer is shown to be strictly faster than two others – in contrast to a result obtained with a different approach by Arun-Kumar and Hennessy.

1 Introduction

In the testing approach of [DNH84], reactive systems are compared by embedding them – with a parallel composition operator $\|$ – in arbitrary test environments; if some system N_1 performs successfully in such an environment whenever a second system N_2 does, then N_1 is called an implementation of the specification N_2. There are two variants to evaluate the performance: N_1 *may* satisfy a test O, if some run of $N \| O$ reaches success, which is signalled by a special action; N_1 *must* satisfy O, if every run of $N \| O$ reaches success.

To take into account the efficiency of systems, we can add a time bound d to our tests and require that some or every run reaches success within time d, see [Vog93]. It is no problem to measure the duration of a run, if the parallel system $N \| O$ is synchronous, i.e. if all components perform their actions according to a common global time scale; this case is treated in [Vog93] as strict testing. In asynchronous systems, the components may idle unnecessarily or actions may take more time than necessary, which interferes with time measurements. Actually, may-testing is not problematic: if some run reaches success in time, then intuitively all components are well-behaved in this run, i.e. they only idle to wait for some favourable action and otherwise they comply with global time, see [Vog93]. But must-testing is concerned with the more interesting worst-case behaviour; this would be to idle until time d is up and, thus, no test at all must be satisfied.

*This work was partially supported by the DFG and the ESPRIT Basic Research Working Group 6067 CALIBAN (CAusal calcuLI BAsed on Nets). email-address: vogler@informatik.uni-augsburg.de

Nevertheless, we will develop a scenario of must-testing with time bounds for asynchronous systems and base a faster-than relation on it. The essential point about an asynchronous system is that its components work at indeterminate relative speeds. So we can change our point of view: we will assume that there is an upper time bound for an action to occur, i.e. we do not any more allow a component to idle or to take a lot of time with its current action; instead we let all others work very fast in comparison. This way we get a time bound for the performance of an asynchronous system; the idea goes back to at least [LF81].

In this paper, we use (labelled, safe) Petri nets to model concurrent systems. Synchronous systems correspond to nets with the maximum-step firing rule (i.e. the components of the system working in lockstep are the transitions of the net), whereas asynchronous systems usually correspond to nets with ordinary firing sequences. These Petri net notions together with parallel composition are defined in Section 2. The new firing rule for asynchronous systems with upper bound on action duration is introduced in Section 3. For simplicity, we use discrete time and assume that each action lasts at most 1; hence, the comparatively fast actions do not take any time at all. As a consequence, we do not have to perform complicated calculations of real time, and our asynchronous firing rule is a simple combination of the ordinary and the maximum-step firing rule.

It should be stressed that in asynchronous systems time cannot be used to guarantee correctness (e.g. by using time-outs); we only consider time to measure the efficiency of these systems. This is done in Section 4, where our testing scenario is defined; a system N satisfies a test (O, d) if every run of $N \parallel O$ reaches success within d units of time, assuming that each action takes at most one unit. If N_1 satisfies all tests (O, d) which N_2 satisfies, then N_1 is an implementation of N_2. In particular, it might satisfy some (O, d), where N_2 only satisfies $(O, d+1)$ but not (O, d); hence, we will call N_1 a *faster implementation*.

The main theorem is a characterization of the 'faster-implementation' relation with some variant of refusal traces; the relation turns out to be a precongruence for parallel composition. Using the characterization, some properties of the relation are shown in Section 5 which one might expect of a faster-than relation. In Section 6, we compare three implementations of a bounded buffer using a simulation technique; one implementation is the usual concatenation of 1-buffers, the other two use an array in a circular fashion to store the content of the queue. In contrast to the approach of [AKH92], it turns out that only one of the implementations is faster than the others, which are incomparable. Finally, related literature is discussed in the conclusion.

2 Petri Nets and Parallel Composition

In this section, a very brief introduction to Petri nets is given. We will deal with safe Petri nets (place/transition-nets) whose transitions are labelled with actions from some infinite alphabet Σ' or with the empty word λ. These actions are left uninterpreted; the labelling only indicates that two transitions with the same label from Σ' represent the same action occurring in different internal situations, while λ-labelled transitions represent internal, unobservable actions. Σ' contains a special action ω, which we will need in our tests to indicate success, and we put $\Sigma = \Sigma' - \{\omega\}$.

Thus, a *labelled Petri net* $N = (S, T, W, l, M_N)$ (or just a *net* for short) consists of finite disjoint sets S of *places* (local states) and T of *transitions* (possible activities), the *weight function* $W : S \times T \cup T \times S \to \{0,1\}$, the *labelling* $l : T \to \Sigma' \cup \{\lambda\}$, and the *initial marking* $M_N : S \to \{0,1\}$. When we introduce a net N, then we assume that implicitly this introduces its components S, T, W, ... If $W(x,y) = 1$, then (x,y) is called an *arc*; for each $x \in S \cup T$, the *preset* of x is ${}^\bullet x = \{y \mid W(y,x) = 1\}$ and the *postset* of x is $x^\bullet = \{y \mid W(x,y) = 1\}$.

- A *multiset* over a set X is a function $\mu : X \to I\!N_0$. We identify $x \in X$ with the multiset that is 1 for x and 0 everywhere else. A subset Y of X is identified with the multiset that is 1 for $y \in Y$ and 0 everywhere else. For multisets, comparison, multiplication with scalars from $I\!N_0$, and addition is defined elementwise.

- A *marking* (global state) is a multiset over S, a *step* is a nonempty multiset over T. A step μ is *enabled* under a marking M, denoted by $M[\mu\rangle$, if $\sum_{t \in \mu} \mu(t) \cdot {}^\bullet t \leq M$. The step is enabled under the *maximum* firing rule, if additionally: whenever $M[\mu'\rangle$ and $\mu \leq \mu'$, then $\mu = \mu'$.

  If $M[\mu\rangle$ and $M' = M + \sum_{t \in \mu} \mu(t) \cdot t^\bullet - \sum_{t \in \mu} \mu(t) \cdot {}^\bullet t$, then we denote this by $M[\mu\rangle M'$ and say that μ can *occur* or *fire* under M yielding the *follower marking* M'. We also say that the transitions of μ can fire *concurrently*. Since transitions are special steps, this also defines $M[t\rangle$ and $M[t\rangle M'$ for $t \in T$.

- This definition of enabling and occurrence can be extended to sequences as usual: a sequence w of steps is *enabled* under a marking M, denoted by $M[w\rangle$, and yields the follower marking M' when *occurring*, denoted by $M[w\rangle M'$, if $w = \lambda$ and $M = M'$ or $w = w'\mu$, $M[w'\rangle M''$ and $M''[\mu\rangle M'$ for some marking M''. If w is enabled under the initial marking, then it is called a *step sequence*, or – in case that $w \in T^*$ – a *firing sequence*. If all the steps are enabled under the maximum firing rule, then w is called a *maximum-step sequence*.

We can extend the labelling of a net to steps by $l(\mu) = \sum_{t \in T, l(t) \neq \lambda} \mu(t) \cdot l(t)$, where the empty sum equals the empty word. Then we can extend the labelling also to sequences of steps or transitions as usual, i.e. homomorphically; note that internal actions are automatically deleted in the labelling of a sequence. Next, we lift the enabledness and firing definitions to the level of actions:

- A sequence v of multisets over Σ' is *enabled* under a marking M, denoted by $M[v\rangle\rangle$, if there is some w with $M[w\rangle$ and $l(w) = v$. If $M = M_N$, then v is called a *step trace*; if additionally w is a maximum-step sequence, then v is called a *maximum-step trace*; if $w \in T^*$, then v is called a *trace*. We call two nets *(maximum-)step equivalent* if they have the same (maximum-)step traces. We call two nets *language equivalent* if they have the same traces.

- For a marking M the set $[M\rangle$ of markings *reachable* from M is defined as $\{M' \mid \exists w \in T^* : M[w\rangle M'\}$. A marking is called *reachable* if it is reachable from M_N. The net is *safe* if $M(s) \leq 1$ for all places s and reachable markings M.

General assumption All nets considered in this paper are safe and without isolated transitions.

For each set A of transitions or actions, A^+ denotes a disjoint copy of A whose elements are denoted a^+, $a \in A$; a^+ will stand for the start of the transition or action a, which only empties the corresponding preset. Note that we use A^* to denote – as usual – the set of all sequences over A.

Finally, we introduce parallel composition $\|_A$ with synchronization (in TCSP-style), an important operator for the modular construction of nets. If we combine nets N_1 and N_2 with $\|_A$, then they run in parallel and have to synchronize on actions from A. To construct the composed net, we have to combine each a-labelled transition t_1 of N_1 with each a-labelled transition t_2 from N_2 if $a \in A$.

In the definition of parallel composition, $*$ is used as a dummy element, which is formally combined e.g. with those transitions that do not have their label in the synchronization set A. (We assume that $*$ is not a transition or a place of any net.) This is the standard way to construct a disjoint union, which we denote by $\dot\cup$.

Let N_1, N_2 be nets, $A \subseteq \Sigma'$. Then the *parallel composition* $N = N_1 \|_A N_2$ *with synchronization* over A is defined by

$$\begin{aligned}
S &= S_1 \times \{*\} \cup \{*\} \times S_2 \\
T &= \{(t_1,t_2) \mid t_1 \in T_1, t_2 \in T_2, l_1(t_1) = l_2(t_2) \in A\} \\
&\quad \cup \{(t_1,*) \mid t_1 \in T_1, l_1(t_1) \notin A\} \\
&\quad \cup \{(*,t_2) \mid t_2 \in T_2, l_2(t_2) \notin A\} \\
W((s_1,s_2),(t_1,t_2)) &= \begin{cases} W_1(s_1,t_1) & \text{if } s_1 \in S_1,\ t_1 \in T_1 \\ W_2(s_2,t_2) & \text{if } s_2 \in S_2,\ t_2 \in T_2 \\ 0 & \text{otherwise} \end{cases} \\
W((t_1,t_2),(s_1,s_2)) &= \begin{cases} W_1(t_1,s_1) & \text{if } s_1 \in S_1,\ t_1 \in T_1 \\ W_2(t_2,s_2) & \text{if } s_2 \in S_2,\ t_2 \in T_2 \\ 0 & \text{otherwise} \end{cases} \\
l((t_1,t_2)) &= \begin{cases} l_1(t_1) & \text{if } t_1 \in T_1 \\ l_2(t_2) & \text{if } t_2 \in T_2 \end{cases} \\
M_N &= M_{N_1} \dot\cup M_{N_2}, \text{ i.e. } M_N((s_1,s_2)) = \begin{cases} M_{N_1}(s_1) & \text{if } s_1 \in S_1 \\ M_{N_2}(s_2) & \text{if } s_2 \in S_2 \end{cases}
\end{aligned}$$

3 Asynchronously Timed Behaviour

In this section, we define our new asynchronous behaviour and compare it shortly with existing firing rules. We start with the definition and explain it afterwards.

Definition 3.1 An *instantaneous description* (*ID*) of a net N is a pair (M,C) consisting of a marking M of N and a set $C \subseteq T$ of *current(ly firing) transitions*. The *initial ID* is $ID_N = (M_N, \emptyset)$. If we introduce an instantaneous description ID or ID' etc., this implicitly introduces its components M and C or M' and C' etc.

For *ID*'s (M,C) and (M',C') and $\varepsilon \in T \dot\cup T^+ \dot\cup \{\sigma\}$ we write $(M,C)[\varepsilon\rangle(M',C')$ if one of the following cases applies:

i) $\varepsilon = t \in T$, $M[t\rangle M'$ and $C = C' = \emptyset$

ii) $\varepsilon = t^+ \in T^+$, $M[t\rangle$, $M' = M - {}^\bullet t$ and $C' = C \cup \{t\}$

iii) $\varepsilon = \sigma$, $\neg M[t\rangle$ for all $t \in T$, $M' = M + \sum_{t \in C} t^\bullet$ and $C' = \emptyset$

This asynchronous firing rule is extended to sequences as usual. If $ID_N[w\rangle\, ID$, then w is an ***asynchronous(ly timed) firing sequence*** and ID is ***reachable***. The set of asynchronous firing sequences is denoted by $AFS(N)$.

These notions are lifted to the action level: if $ID[t\rangle\, ID'$, we write $ID[l_N(t)\rangle\rangle\, ID'$; if $ID[t^+\rangle\, ID'$, we write $ID[l_N(t)^+\rangle\rangle\, ID'$ for visible t and $ID[\rangle\rangle\, ID'$ otherwise; if $ID[\sigma\rangle\, ID'$, we write $ID[\sigma\rangle\rangle\, ID'$. Again, this action firing rule is extended to sequences; w is called an ***asynchronous(ly timed) trace*** of N, if $ID_N[w\rangle\rangle\, ID$. The ***asynchronous language*** $AL(N)$ consists of the asynchronous traces of N. Nets are ***asynchronously equivalent*** if they have the same asynchronous language.

We call $t^+ \in T^+$ or $a^+ \in \Sigma'^+$ the ***start*** of t or a, while t and a themselves are called ***complete***. The σ's subdivide an asynchronous firing sequence or trace w into ***rounds***, i.e. a round is the prefix of w up to the first σ or a substring of w reaching from one σ to the next; if w carries on after the last σ, then this suffix is the last round of w. □

The idea of the above asynchronous firing rule is that every enabled transition will fire within one unit of time; but it might also act faster, hence transitions can work with indeterminate relative speed. The former corresponds to the maximum-step firing rule, but due to the latter, we also consider behaviour that is impossible if transitions fire in lock-step, i.e. are synchronized via global time. The same idea, but with a different formalization, was advocated in the area of distributed algorithms in [LF81]. In our formalization one unit of time corresponds to one round; it starts with a sequence of 'fast' transitions, which does not take any time; then, one unit of time passes and, hence, all enabled transitions have to fire, i.e. a maximum-step occurs. For convenience, we list this step as a sequence of +-transitions or +-actions and close the list by a σ, indicating one tick of the clock; t^+ or a^+ corresponds to the start of t or a, and this occurrence of t or a ends with the next σ.

The following should be obvious: if $ID_N[w\rangle(M, C)$ and w' is obtained from w by deleting all +-signs and all σ's, then $M_N[w'\rangle(M + \sum_{t \in C} t^\bullet)$. Hence, since we are only interested in reachable ID's and our nets are safe, we can restrict attention to ID's (M, C) where M is actually a set, i.e. a function $S \to \{0, 1\}$. Furthermore, if (M, C) is a reachable ID and $(M, C)[t^+\rangle(M', C')$, then $t \notin C$, i.e. in Clause ii) above, t is really added to the set of current transitions when it starts firing.

If we use Clause i) only, we get the usual firing sequences as a special case of our asynchronous firing sequences. These sequences take no time at all; this is not very realistic, but does not pose a problem either: ultimately, we will only be interested in sequences that take a lot of time. If we never use Clause i), we essentially get the maximum-step sequences; in the absence of internal transitions, use of Clause i) is always indicated on the action level by the occurrence of a complete action. Hence:

Proposition 3.2 *Asynchronous equivalence implies language equivalence and, for nets without internal transitions, maximum-step equivalence.*

The following example in Figure 1 consists of two asynchronously equivalent nets, where only the net on the left can perform a under the maximum-step firing rule; hence, asynchronous equivalence does not imply maximum-step equivalence in general.

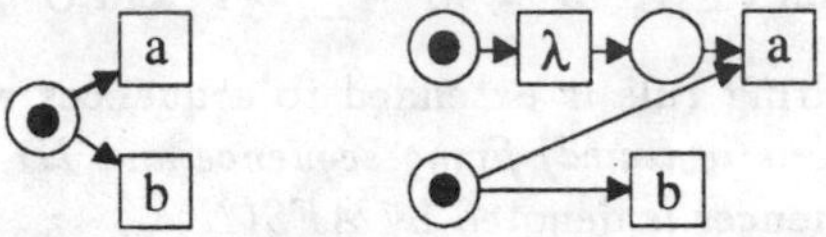

Figure 1

4 Asynchronously Timed Testing

When testing a net, we apply parallel composition to embed it into a testing environment and consider the behaviour of the composed system. Before defining our testing scenario in detail let us look at an example, showing how the asynchronous firing rule behaves in combination with parallel composition.

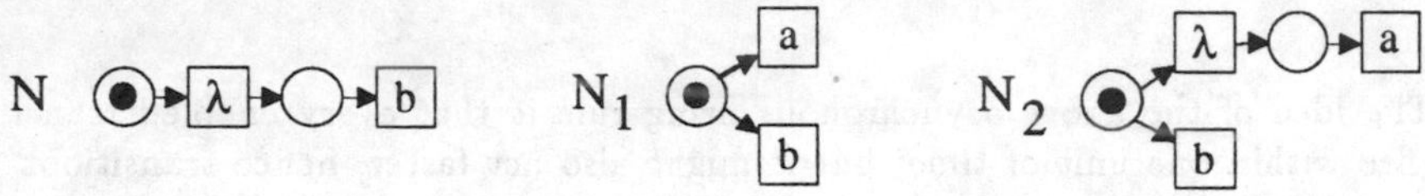

Figure 2

Consider the nets of Figure 2. $N \parallel_\Sigma N_1$ has the asynchronous trace σb; this shows that N_1 is willing to idle if the environment does not allow any of its activities. On the other hand, $\sigma b \notin AL(N \parallel_\Sigma N_2)$; if time passes and b is not possible, N_2 has to perform the internal action, thus deciding the choice to the disadvantage of b. The same holds if we use the maximum-step firing rule; the difference is that under this rule $N \parallel_\Sigma N_2$ will definitely not perform b, while $b \in AL(N \parallel_\Sigma N_2)$.

We now come to the definition of testing. Recall that $\Sigma' = \Sigma \dot{\cup} \{\omega\}$.

Definition 4.1 A net is *testable*, if none of its transitions is labelled with ω. An *(asynchronously) timed test* is a pair (O, d), where O is a net (the *test net*) and $d \in \mathbb{N}$ (the *time bound*). A testable net N *satisfies* a timed test (O, d), if each $w \in AL(N \parallel_\Sigma O)$ with d or more σ's contains some ω or ω^+. For testable nets N_1 and N_2, we call N_1 a *faster implementation* of N_2, $N_1 \sqsupseteq N_2$, if N_1 satisfies all timed tests that N_2 satisfies. □

This version of testing is a form of must-testing: *every* run that lasts at least d units of time must be successful, indicated by ω or ω^+. The corresponding may-testing is nothing new, since it disregards the time bound: if some asynchronous trace of $N \parallel_\Sigma O$ contains ω or ω^+, then there is also such a trace without any σ's, which meets any time bound. This trace corresponds to an ordinary trace; hence, may-testing in our setting coincides with ordinary may-testing.

It is usual to call N_1 an implementation of N_2, if N_1 satisfies all the tests N_2 satisfies – and possibly some more. Here, it might be the case that N_2 satisfies some $(O, d+1)$, but not (O, d), while N_1 satisfies (O, d) (– hence, obviously also $(O, d+1)$). Therefore, we call N_1 a *faster* implementation; we will see below that, indeed, $\sqsupseteq$ satisfies some properties one might expect of a 'faster-than' relation.

Our aim is now to characterize the faster-implementation relation. For this purpose we introduce the ART-semantics below. Its idea is to replace the maximum-steps in an asynchronous trace by steps that are maximal with respect to internal actions and to *some* visible actions; no further instances of these actions are possible at the respective time, i.e. by listing these actions as a set X we get something like a refusal trace. The sets X replace the σ's in an asynchronous trace.

Definition 4.2 For $\varepsilon \in T\dot{\cup}T^+\dot{\cup}\mathcal{P}(\Sigma')$ and instantaneous descriptions (M, C) and (M', C') we write $(M, C)[\varepsilon\rangle_r(M', C')$ if one of the following cases applies:

i) $\varepsilon = t \in T$, $M[t\rangle M'$ and $C = C' = \emptyset$

ii) $\varepsilon = t^+ \in T^+$, $M[t\rangle$, $M' = M - {}^\bullet t$ and $C' = C \cup \{t\}$

iii) $\varepsilon = X \subseteq \Sigma'$, $\neg M[t\rangle$ for all $t \in T$ with $l(t) \in X \cup \{\lambda\}$, $M' = M + \Sigma_{t \in C}\, t^\bullet$ and $C' = \emptyset$

The corresponding sequences are called ***asynchronous refusal firing sequences.*** We lift this to the action level as in Definition 3.1; in particular, we write $ID[X\rangle\rangle_r\, ID'$ if $ID[X\rangle_r\, ID'$ and call X a ***refusal set.*** The corresponding sequences are called ***asynchronous refusal traces*** with set $ART(N)$, and they induce ***ART-equivalence.*** □

Proposition 4.3 *For nets N_1 and N_2, $ART(N_1) \subseteq ART(N_2)$ implies $AL(N_1) \subseteq AL(N_2)$; ART-equivalence implies asynchronous equivalence.*

Proof: Consider only those traces in $ART(N_i)$ where all refusal sets equal Σ'. Replacing Σ' by σ gives $AL(N_i)$. □

Next we define the parallel composition of asynchronous traces in order to describe the behaviour of a composed net.

Definition 4.4 Let $u, v \in (\Sigma' \cup \Sigma'^+ \cup \mathcal{P}(\Sigma'))^*$, $A \subseteq \Sigma'$. Then $u \parallel_A v$ is the set of all $w \in (\Sigma'^* \Sigma'^{+*} \mathcal{P}(\Sigma'))^*$ such that for some n $u = u_1 \ldots u_n$, $v = v_1 \ldots v_n$, $w = w_1 \ldots w_n$ and for $i = 1, \ldots, n$ we have one of the following:

- $u_i = v_i = w_i \in A \cup A^+$
- $u_i = w_i \in (\Sigma' - A) \cup (\Sigma' - A)^+$ and $v_i = \lambda$
- $v_i = w_i \in (\Sigma' - A) \cup (\Sigma' - A)^+$ and $u_i = \lambda$
- $u_i, v_i, w_i \in \mathcal{P}(\Sigma')$ and $w_i \subseteq ((u_i \cup v_i) \cap A) \cup (u_i \cap v_i)$

□

This definition works as usual: when composing u and v, actions from A are merged, while others are interleaved; in w, actions from A can be refused if they are refused in u or v , while the others can only be refused if they are refused in both, u and v. Now the next theorem shows that composition of traces corresponds to composition of nets.

Theorem 4.5 *Let N_1, N_2 be nets and $A \subseteq \Sigma'$. Then*

$$ART(N_1 \|_A N_2) = \bigcup\{u \|_A v \mid u \in ART(N_1),\ v \in ART(N_2)\}$$

Now we are ready to state the characterization of the 'faster-implementation' relation, the main theorem of this paper.

Theorem 4.6 *For testable nets N_1 and N_2, $N_1 \sqsupseteq N_2$ if and only if $ART(N_1) \subseteq ART(N_2)$.*

Proof: 'if': Let (O, d) be a timed test. Then $ART(N_1) \subseteq ART(N_2)$ implies $AL(N_1 \|_\Sigma O) \subseteq AL(N_2 \|_\Sigma O)$ by Theorem 4.5 and Proposition 4.3. Thus, if N_1 fails the test due to some $w \in AL(N_1 \|_\Sigma O)$, then so does N_2.

'only if': somewhat complicated and omitted. □

With this characterization of our testing preorder, we get immediately that it is a precongruence; the corresponding ART-equivalence is fully abstract, i.e. it makes just the necessary distinctions if we want to distinguish nets with different asynchronous behaviour and want to work with parallel composition.

Corollary 4.7 *i) The relation $\sqsupseteq$ is a precongruence w.r.t. parallel composition.*

ii) ART-equivalence is fully abstract with respect to asynchronous equivalence and parallel composition, i.e. it is the coarsest congruence for parallel composition that respects asynchronous equivalence.

5 Further Properties of *ART*-Semantics

It is not always easy to check the faster-implementation relation, i.e. inclusion of ART-semantics, even for simple examples. Hence, one should compare nets in a structured way, e.g. by using forward simulations; see [LV93] for a survey on such techniques. Usually, in a forward simulation one system simulates the actions of another; here, it also simulates the action starts and refusal sets – observe that the occurrence of a refusal set corresponds to the end of a round and changes the state of the system.

Definition 5.1 For nets N_1 and N_2, a relation R between some ID's of N_1 and some of N_2 is a *(forward) simulation* from N_1 to N_2 if the following hold

i) $(ID_{N_1}, ID_{N_2}) \in R$

ii) If $(ID_1, ID_2) \in R$ and $ID_1[t\rangle_r ID_1'$ or $ID_1[X\rangle_r ID_1'$, then for some ID_2' with $(ID_1', ID_2') \in R$ we have $ID_2[l_1(t)\rangle\rangle_r ID_2'$ or $ID_2[X\rangle\rangle_r ID_2'$. Observe that these moves from ID_2 to ID_2' may involve several transitions. Similary, $ID_1[t^+\rangle_r ID_1'$ implies that for some ID_2' with $(ID_1', ID_2') \in R$ we have $ID_2[l_1(t)^+\rangle\rangle_r ID_2'$ for visible t and $ID_2[\rangle\rangle_r ID_2'$ for internal t.

□

Recall that a round consists of a sequence of transitions/actions followed by a step, which is 'maximal w.r.t. the following refusal set'. But instead of this monolithic step we write a sequence of action/transition starts; this way we get more reachable ID's (those with current transitions), but as a pay-off we only have to check single transitions or transition starts in the above definition.

It is not difficult to show the following theorem, which we will apply below and in Section 6; see [LV93] for a proof of a similar theorem.

Theorem 5.2 *If there exists a simulation from N_1 to N_2, then N_1 is a faster implementation of N_2.*

For the first applications of simulations we define three operations on nets:

Definition 5.3 The *τ-prefix* $\tau.N$ of a net N is obtained by removing all tokens and adding a marked place s and a λ-labelled transition t with ${}^\bullet t = \{s\}$ and $t^\bullet = M_N$.

N' is an *elongation* of N, if it is obtained from N by choosing a transition t, adding an unmarked place s and a λ-labelled transition t' with ${}^\bullet t' = \{s\}$ and $t'^\bullet = t^\bullet$ and, finally, redefining $t^\bullet$ by $t^\bullet := \{s\}$.

Call a transition t of N *conflict-free*, if no reachable marking M with $M[t\rangle$ enables a transition t' with ${}^\bullet t \cap {}^\bullet t' \neq \emptyset$. Now N' is an *internal sequentialisation* of N, if it is obtained from N by choosing two internal, conflict-free transitions t and t' and adding a marked place s to the pre- and postsets of t and t'. □

One might expect that N and $\tau.N$, but also N and an elongation N' or an internal sequentialisation N'' are essentially equivalent – with N being faster: $\tau.N$ and N' have an additional internal transition, which might take time. In N'', t and t' can only fire in sequence, which would take more time than a possible parallel execution in N. Internal sequentialisation can be applied e.g. if t and t' model the conflict-free transport of data; we will see a similar situation in Section 6. We have the following results, which recommend the asynchronous testing approach.

Proposition 5.4 *N is a faster implementation, but in general not an m-implementation, of $\tau.N$, of each elongation N' and of each internal sequentialisation N''.*

Proof: For exampe, the identity relation is a simulation from N to N'; if t and t' are the transitions involved in constructing N', then t in N is matched by tt' in N', t^+ in N is matched by t^+ in N', and some X-move that 'closes' t is matched by Xt'. □

It is interesting to note at this stage that the net N_1 in Figure 3 is not a faster implementation of the net N_2; these nets are in fact incomparable under $\sqsupseteq$ due to the asynchronous refusal traces a^+b^+ and $a^+\{b\}b^+$. This can be made plausible with

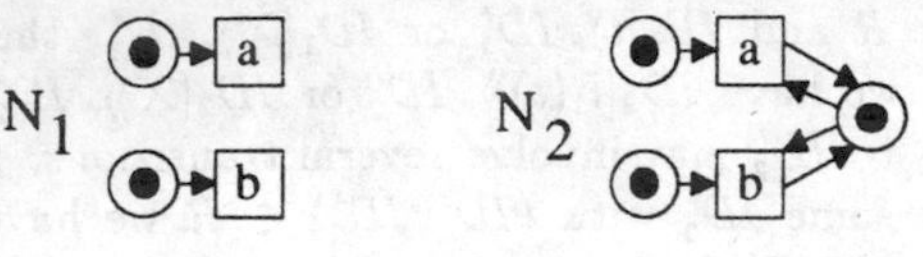

Figure 3

the test net O in Figure 4: N_2 satisfies the timed test $(O,2)$; N_1 can block the vital resources s and s' in the first round such that the time-critical activity, internal to O, takes place in the second and third round; hence, N_1 may fail $(O,2)$ with $a^+b^+\sigma\sigma$. Still, one might want to regard N_1 as being faster than N_2; in order to find a justification for this view, one could consider to modify our approach such that $N_1 \sqsupseteq N_2$ does hold, e.g. by restricting the test nets under consideration.

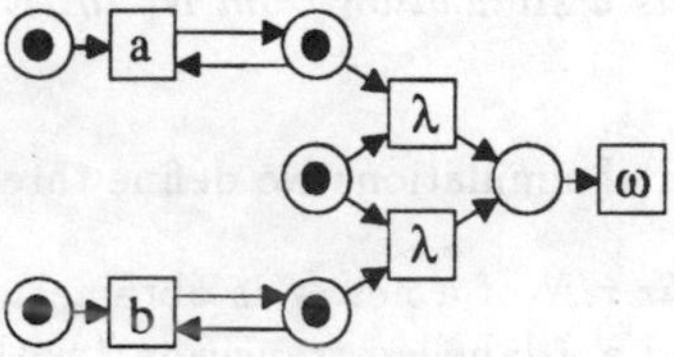

Figure 4

For the usual reason (i.e. problems with initial instability), *ART*-equivalence is not a congruence with respect to choice; but we have the following result (see e.g. [Vog92] for a definition of these operations on nets):

Theorem 5.5 $\sqsupseteq$ *is a precongruence with respect to hiding, relabelling and restriction.*

6 Three Implementations of a Bounded Buffer

In this section we will compare some implementations of a bounded buffer with respect to $\sqsupseteq$; this example has also been discussed in [AKH92]. The first implementation *PIPE* is the usual sequence of buffers of capacity 1; the other two, *BUFFC* and *BUFFD*, use a buffer controller and a circular queue to store the items. These two implementations differ only in a small detail making the buffer controller centralized in one case and distributed (between input and output) in the other. Both variants are mentioned in [AKH92], but only *BUFFC* is studied and shown to be faster than *PIPE*; and indeed, *BUFFC* and *BUFFD* are equivalent with respect to the efficiency preorder of [AKH92]. This is a consequence of the interleaving approach taken in [AKH92], which ingnores that actions can be performed in parallel. In our approach, it turns out that – surprisingly – *BUFFC* is not faster than *PIPE* (nor the other way round), but that *BUFFD* $\sqsupseteq$ *BUFFC* and *BUFFD* $\sqsupseteq$ *PIPE*.

For the rest of the section, we fix some $n \geq 4$ as capacity of the buffers. For simplicity, we assume that the items to be stored are from the set $\{0,1\}$. We formally define *PIPE*, *BUFFC* and *BUFFD* as safe P/T-nets, the type of nets we study in this paper throughout. But in the figures we draw them as some sort of high-level net and hope that the translation will be clear: places are annotated with the type of tokens they store, and V stands for $\{\bullet, 0, 1\}$; arcs without annotation refer to ordinary tokens ($\bullet$), while we always have $x \in \{0, 1\}$.

Figure 5

PIPE: The first implementation, *PIPE*, is shown in Figure 5 and defined as follows:

$S_{PIPE} \;=\; \{(s_i, v) \mid i = 1, \ldots, n,\; v \in V\}$
$T_{PIPE} \;=\; \{(t_i, x) \mid i = 0, \ldots, n,\; x \in \{0, 1\}\}$

We have arcs for the following pairs with $i = 1, \ldots, n,\; x \in \{0, 1\}$:

$$((s_i, \bullet), (t_{i-1}, x)),\; ((t_{i-1}, x), (s_i, x)),\; ((s_i, x), (t_i, x)),\; ((t_i, x), (s_i, \bullet))$$

Initially, the places $(s_i, \bullet)$, $i = 1, \ldots, n$, are marked. The transitions (t_0, x) are labelled inx, $x \in \{0, 1\}$, the transitions (t_n, x) are labelled $outx$, $x \in \{0, 1\}$, and all other transitions are internal. □

The other two implementations use one 'cell' for the recent input, one 'cell' for the next output and $n - 2$ 'cells' indexed from 0 to $n - 3$ for the other items in store. These 'cells' are used as a queue in a circular fashion; *first* gives the index of the next item to be moved to the 'output cell', *last* gives the index of the next free 'cell' in the circular queue. Alternatively, we can use *first* and a 'variable' *length*, which gives the length of the circular queue. For the following, we put $I = \{0, \ldots, n - 3\}$ and let $\oplus$ and $\ominus$ denote addition and subtraction modulo $n - 2$.

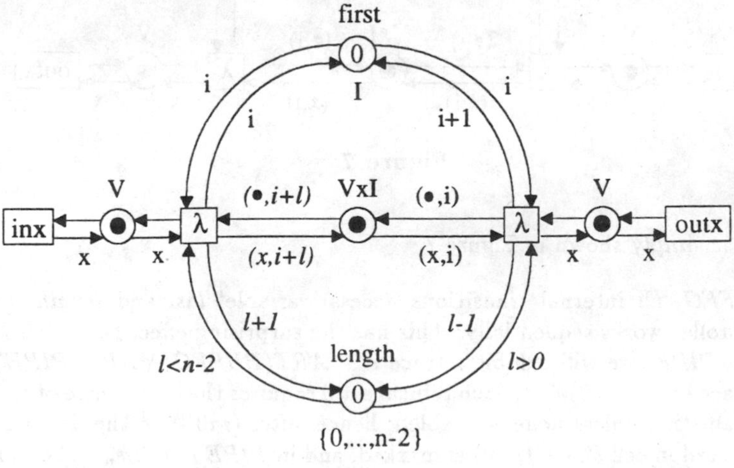

Figure 6

BUFFC: (see Figure 6)

$$\begin{aligned}
S_{BUFFC} &= \{(s,v),\ (s',v) \mid v \in V\} \\
&\cup\ \{(s_i,v) \mid i \in I,\ v \in V\} \\
&\cup\ \{\mathit{first}_i \mid i \in I\} \\
&\cup\ \{\mathit{length}_l \mid l = 0,\ldots,n-2\} \\
T_{BUFFC} &= \{(t,x),\ (t',x) \mid x = 0,1\} \\
&\cup\ \{(t_{i,l},x) \mid i \in I,\ l = 0,\ldots,n-3,\ x = 0,1\} \\
&\cup\ \{(t'_{i,l},x) \mid i \in I,\ l = 1,\ldots,n-2,\ x = 0,1\}
\end{aligned}$$

We have arcs for the following pairs with $x = 0,1$ and $i \in I$:

$$\begin{array}{rll}
((s,\bullet),(t,x)), & ((t,x),(s,x)) & \\
((s,x),(t_{i,l},x)), & ((t_{i,l},x),(s,\bullet)) & \text{with } l = 0,\ldots,n-3 \\
(\mathit{first}_i,(t_{i,l},x)), & ((t_{i,l},x),\mathit{first}_i) & \text{with } l = 0,\ldots,n-3 \\
(\mathit{length}_l,(t_{i,l},x)), & ((t_{i,l},x),\mathit{length}_{l+1}) & \text{with } l = 0,\ldots,n-3 \\
((s_{i\oplus l},\bullet),(t_{i,l},x)), & ((t_{i,l},x),(s_{i\oplus l},x)) & \text{with } l = 0,\ldots,n-3 \\
((s',\bullet),(t'_{i,l},x)), & ((t'_{i,l},x),(s',x)) & \text{with } l = 1,\ldots,n-2 \\
(\mathit{first}_i,(t'_{i,l},x)), & ((t'_{i,l},x),\mathit{first}_{i\oplus 1}) & \text{with } l = 1,\ldots,n-2 \\
(\mathit{length}_l,(t'_{i,l},x)), & ((t'_{i,l},x),\mathit{length}_{l-1}) & \text{with } l = 1,\ldots,n-2 \\
((s_i,x),(t'_{i,l},x)), & ((t'_{i,l},x),(s_i,\bullet)) & \text{with } l = 1,\ldots,n-2 \\
((s',x),(t',x)), & ((t',x),(s',\bullet)) &
\end{array}$$

Initially, the places $(s,\bullet)$, $(s',\bullet)$, first_0, length_0 and $(s_i,\bullet)$, $i \in I$, are marked. The transitions (t,x) are labelled inx, $x \in \{0,1\}$, the transitions (t',x) are labelled outx, $x \in \{0,1\}$, and all other transitions are internal. □

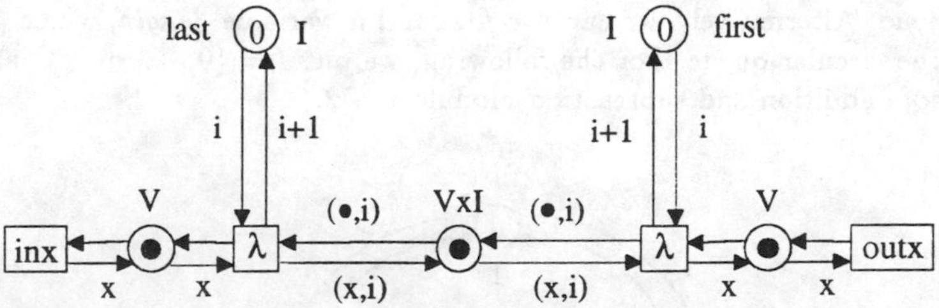

Figure 7

BUFFD: is simply shown in Figure 7 □

In *BUFFC*, all internal transitions access 'variable' *last* and *length*, hence the buffer controller works sequentially. This has the surprising effect that *BUFFC* is not faster than *PIPE*: we will exhibit a trace $w \in ART(BUFFC) \setminus ART(PIPE)$.

This trace starts $(in0)\emptyset^{n-1}$; each refusal set $\emptyset$ requires the occurrence of at least one internal transition unless none is enabled; hence, after $(in0)\emptyset^{n-1}$ the first item 0 is in *BUFFC* stored in cell s', i.e. $(s',0)$ is marked, and in *PIPE* in cell s_n. The next part is $(in1)\emptyset^{n-2}$, after which the second item 1 is in *BUFFC* in the queue in s_0 and in *PIPE* in s_{n-1}. The third part is $(out0)^+\emptyset$, i.e. 0 is removed from s', s_n resp. Now, in *PIPE* item 1 is moved to s_n in the next round and, henceforth, $out1$ is enabled – no matter what else happens. But in *BUFFC*, $in0$ might be performed very fast, followed by a transport of 0 to s_1 at the end of the round; consequently, 1 is not moved from s_0 to s' in this round and $out1$ may be refused in the next round. Hence, for *BUFFC* – but not for *PIPE* – we can continue with $(in0)\emptyset\{out1\}$. Actually, this sort of behaviour can be repeated as long as there is space in the circular queue, and $out1$ is blocked for several rounds. Hence, $w = (in0)\emptyset^{n-2}(in1)\emptyset^{n-1}(out0)^{+}\emptyset((in0)\{out1\})^{n-3}\{out1\}$ is a refusal trace as desired. In contrast, an m-refusal trace where $out1$ is blocked for several rounds is not possible; only in our asynchronous setting, the fast performance of input can block the output for an extended period.

Vice versa, $PIPE \sqsupseteq BUFFC$ is of course also wrong: we have $(in0)^{+}\emptyset\emptyset\emptyset\{in0\} \in ART(PIPE) \setminus ART(BUFFC)$.

In *BUFFD*, the buffer controller has an input and an output part, which communicate via the common store: the input part can store an item x in the circular queue only if the current cell s_{last} is marked as free with $\bullet$; the output part can remove an item from the circular queue only if the current cell s_{first} stores an item $x \in \{0, 1\}$. With this pattern of communication, the two parts can work in parallel and the input cannot block the output as above. In the full version it is shown that $BUFFD \sqsupseteq PIPE$ and $BUFFD \sqsupseteq BUFFC$ exhibiting two suitable simulations, which are defined more or less locally, mapping places and transitions of *BUFFD* to those of *PIPE* and *BUFFC*.

Theorem 6.1 *BUFFD is a faster implementation of PIPE and BUFFC, but no other $\sqsupseteq$-relations hold for the three variants of a bounded buffer.*

7 Conclusion

We have developed a testing scenario for the worst-case efficiency of asynchronous systems. The resulting testing preorder can be characterized with some kind of refusal traces and satisfies some properties which make it attractive as a faster-than relation. We have applied the approach to compare three implementations of a bounded buffer – *BUFFC*, *BUFFD* and *PIPE*.

In the approach of [AKH92], *BUFFC* and *BUFFD* are equivalent, and *BUFFC* is shown to be faster than *PIPE* in [AKH92]. This approach is based on some bisimulation-type preorder; visible actions are regarded as instantaneous and costs are measured as the number of internal actions; hence, [AKH92] presents an interleaving approach, which disregards the parallel execution of actions. This is taken into account in the present paper, and consequently *BUFFD* is strictly faster than *BUFFC* and *PIPE* while, quite surprisingly, the latter two are incomparable. In particular, this is an example where the present approach makes more distinctions than the one of [AKH92]. On the other hand, the latter approach applied to transition systems (which are sequential) without internal transitions gives ordinary bisimulation, while *ART*-equivalence can be shown to coincide with ordinary refusal trace equivalence. Hence, the approach of [AKH92] distinguishes some systems which are equivalent here.

Faster-than relations are also presented in [HR90, MT91, CZ91], where the behaviour of systems is influenced by timing considerations, i.e. the systems are not asynchronous. In [MT91], a bisimulation-type preorder is defined and actions are regarded as instantaneous; a unit-time-delay operator with a special treatment is introduced, which makes the comparison to our approach very difficult. Such an operator is also used in [HR90], where a testing scenario is developed based on the maximal progress assumption, which is suitable for synchronous systems. Finally, a testing approach with time-consuming actions is presented in [CZ91], where the systems and tests under consideration have to be restricted to arrive at a faster-than relation; transition systems are used as models and, hence, parallel execution is a priori excluded.

Neither of the two testing approaches above uses time bounds in the tests. These were introduced in [Vog93]; one could say that our approach fills a gap in that paper, namely it presents must-testing with time bounds for asynchronous systems – assuming a time bound for each action. In [Vog93], the duration of an action may vary depending on the circumstances, which are determined by the test environment O. This idea could be combined with our approach, but this is left for future efforts.

References

[AKH92] S. Arun-Kumar and M. Hennessy. An efficiency preorder for processes. *Acta Informatica*, 29:737–760, 1992.

[CZ91] R. Cleaveland and A. Zwarico. A theory of testing for real-time. In *Proc. 6th Symp. on Logic in Computer Science*, pages 110–119. IEEE Computer Society Press, 1991.

[DNH84] R. De Nicola and M.C.B. Hennessy. Testing equivalence for processes. *Theoret. Comput. Sci.*, 34:83–133, 1984.

[HR90] M. Hennessy and T. Regan. A temporal process algebra. Technical Report 2/90, Dept. Comp. Sci. Univ. of Sussex, Brighton, 1990.

[LF81] N. Lynch and M. Fischer. On describing the behaviour and implementation of distributed systems. *Theoret. Comput. Sci.*, 13:17–43, 1981.

[LV93] N. Lynch and F. Vaandrager. Forward and backward simulations – part i: Untimed systems. Technical Report Report CS-R9313, CWI, Amsterdam, 1993.

[MT91] F. Moller and C. Tofts. Relating processes with respect to speed. In J. Baeten and J. Groote, editors, *CONCUR '91*, Lect. Notes Comp. Sci. 527, 424–438. Springer, 1991.

[Vog92] W. Vogler. *Modular Construction and Partial Order Semantics of Petri Nets*. Lect. Notes Comp. Sci. 625. Springer, 1992.

[Vog93] W. Vogler. Timed testing of concurrent systems. In A. Lingas, R. Karlsson, and S. Carlsson, editors, *ICALP 93*, Lect. Notes Comp. Sci. 700, 532–543. Springer, 1993. full version to appear in Information and Computation.

Fair Testing

Ed Brinksma[1], Arend Rensink[2] and Walter Vogler[3]

[1] University of Twente; partially supported by the Esprit BRA 6021 'REACT'
[2] University of Hildesheim; partially supported by the HCM network 'EXPRESS'
[3] University of Augsburg

Abstract. We investigate the notion of *fair testing*, a formal testing theory in the style of De Nicola and Hennessy, where divergences are disregarded as long as there are visible outgoing transitions. The usual testing theories, such as the standard model of failure pre-order, do not allow such fair interpretations because of the way in which they ensure their compositionality with respect to *abstraction* from observable actions. This feature is usually present in the form of a hiding-operator (CSP, ACP, LOTOS) or part of parallel composition (CCS). Its application can introduce new divergences causing semantic complications. In this paper we present a testing scenario that captures the intended notion of fairness and induces a pre-congruence for abstraction. In the presence of a sufficiently strong synchronisation feature it is shown to be the *coarsest* pre-congruence contained in the (non-congruent) fair version of failure preorder. We also give a denotational characterisation.

1 Introduction

The usefulness of formalisms for the description and analysis of reactive and distributed systems is closely related to the underlying formal notions of behavioural equivalence. In a given application the formal equivalence should ideally both identify behaviours that are informally indistinguishable and distinguish between behaviours that are informally different. Of course, other criteria apply as well, such as for example the availability of a mathematically tractable and well-understood theory, so that in practice a compromise between the various requirements must be made.

In the past decade research in the field of transition systems has led to the discovery of a wealth of equivalences that can be used to formalise behavioural equivalence (the reader may consult [10] for an overview). Two important families of equivalences are those that employ the notion of *bisimulation* [18, 20], and those that are induced by a formalised notion of testing, the so-called *testing equivalences* [9, 14, 6]. Bisimulations provide the finer equivalences that keep track of the branching structure of behaviours, and have a rather elegant proof theory based of the construction of bisimulation relations. Abramsky has shown in [1] that bisimulation equivalences are also induced by a notion of testing, but only in the presence of a very strong notion of observability. Testing equivalences that can be characterised following the recipe of De Nicola and Hennessy [9] are generally coarser and distinguish mainly on the basis of difference in *deadlock* behaviour, which is in practical cases often sufficient. The higher resolution

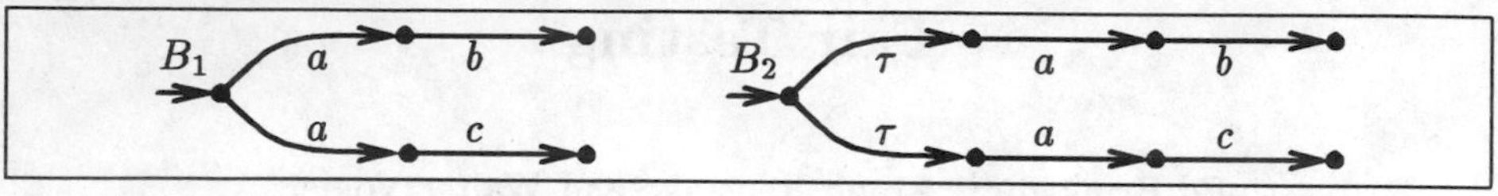

Fig. 1. Shifting nondeterminism

power of bisimulations that is based on the branching structure of processes is, in fact, often undesirable. The transition systems B_1 and B_2 in Fig. 1 are not weak bisimulation equivalent, but are testing equivalent.

In practice, we would sometimes like to implement behaviour B_1 by B_2, see for example [11], by resolving the choice between the two a-actions internally (hence the internal τ-actions in B_2), and not in the interaction with the environment. As the environment cannot influence the choice in either case, this should make no difference to the observable behaviour. A second advantage of testing equivalences is that they are generated by *pre-orders* that can be practically interpreted as *implementation relations*. They usually express that the implementation is some sort of deterministic reduction of the specified behaviour.

A feature of weak bisimulation equivalence is that it incorporates a particular notion of *fairness*. The two behaviours shown in Fig. 2 are weak bisimulation equivalent. Weak bisimulation works on the principle that the τ-loop of B_4 is executed an arbitrary but only finite number of times, in this case implying that eventually action b will be enabled. Such identification of behaviour can be very useful in practice, for example, when proving properties of systems that work with fair communication media. In such cases τ-loops, or *divergences*, represent the unbounded but finite number of message losses. Interesting proofs of protocol correctness that have been shown in this way can be found in [16, 5].

It is not difficult to define a testing pre-order that shares this fairness property with weak bisimulation, see for example [4]. The reason that this so-called fair failure pre-order is not very popular as a basis for developing an algebraic theory of behaviour is that it is not a pre-congruence with respect to the *abstraction* or hiding operation, which internalises observable actions and may thus produce new divergences. We give two examples showing that the fair failure preorder is not a pre-congruence with respect to abstraction.

Fig. 3 is taken from Bergstra et al. [3]; it shows two failure equivalent systems that differ when a is hidden. According to the standard testing scenario, the only observable fact is that after an arbitrary nonempty sequence of a's, either b is refused or c is refused; the difference between the two systems in Fig. 3 is that the left-hand system alternates between allowing b and allowing c, whereas the right-hand side keeps on offering the same action after the initial choice. After hiding a this difference becomes testable, at least if one takes a fair interpretation. Then the left-hand system cannot refuse to do b or c, whereas the right-hand system

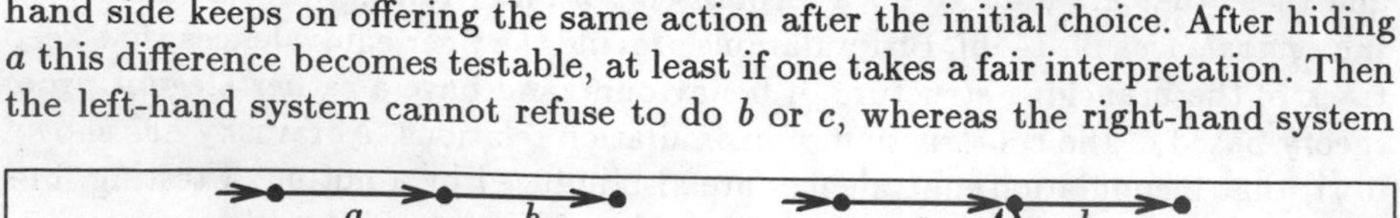

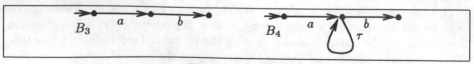

Fig. 2. Fair τ-loop

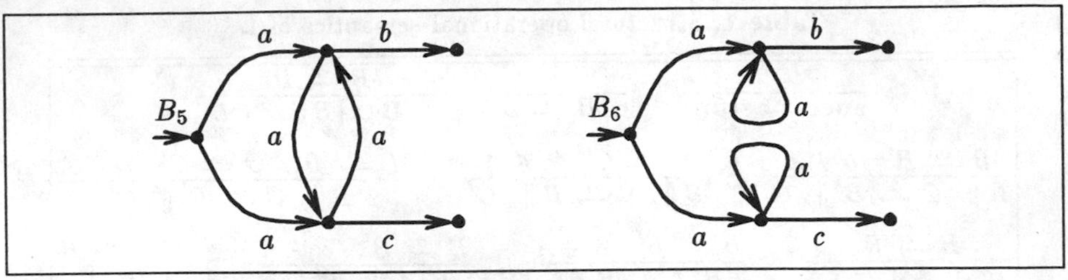

Fig. 3. Failure equivalent systems which are different after hiding *a*

will always refuse either *b* or *c*.

Note that this example is invalidated in some of the stronger notions of testing, such as *refusal testing* (cf. Phillips [21] or Langerak [15]) where testing may continue after a refusal has been observed. Consider, however, the behaviours in Fig. 4. The left hand system has strictly fewer failures than the right hand system, or in other words passes strictly more tests. After hiding *a* however, the failure inclusion no longer holds: in a fair testing scenario, B_6 will always succeed in performing a *b*-action whereas B_5 may refuse to do this.

It can be argued that this example shows that the removal of nondeterminism (taking away the *a*-*b* branch in Fig. 4) interferes with the congruence w.r.t. hiding we are after. In this paper we will show that this is true only if the nondeterministic option that is taken away is somehow the only remaining possibility for the system to terminate. Based on this insight we will develop a theory of fair testing that does possess the desired compositionality with respect to abstraction.

The rest of the paper is structured as follows. Sect. 2 contains the definitions of the basic concepts and notation that we use. In Sect. 3 we introduce a new notion of testing, viz. *should-testing*, and define the induced pre-order on behaviours. In Sect. 4 we study the congruence properties and in Sect. 5 the fairness properties of the should pre-order. In Sect. 6 we give an alternative characterisation of the should pre-order, based on a generalisation of the concept of failure pairs (cf. [6]). Finally, in Sect. 7 we draw our conclusions comparing our work to and draw our conclusions existing approaches.

2 Definitions

We assume a set **A** of actions, ranged over by a, b, c. Apart from **A** we use two special action symbols: the *invisible action* τ and the *success action* ω. The latter is used for the purpose of testing, to denote the successful conclusion of a test. In contrast, the actions in **A** are sometimes called *visible actions*. We use α to

Fig. 4. Failure included systems which are incomparable after hiding *a*

Table 1. Structural operational semantics of **L**

$$\frac{}{\mathbf{succ} \xrightarrow{\omega} \mathbf{stop}} \qquad \frac{}{\alpha; B \xrightarrow{\alpha} B} \qquad \frac{B \xrightarrow{\alpha} B'}{\Sigma(\mathbf{B} \cup \{B\}) \xrightarrow{\alpha} B'}$$

$$\frac{B \xrightarrow{\alpha} B' \quad \alpha \notin A}{B \parallel_A C \xrightarrow{\alpha} B' \parallel_A C} \qquad \frac{C \xrightarrow{\alpha} C' \quad \alpha \notin A}{B \parallel_A C \xrightarrow{\alpha} B \parallel_A C'} \qquad \frac{B \xrightarrow{\alpha} B' \quad C \xrightarrow{\alpha} C' \quad \alpha \in A}{B \parallel_A C \xrightarrow{\alpha} B' \parallel_A C'}$$

$$\frac{B \xrightarrow{\alpha} B'}{B[\phi] \xrightarrow{\phi(\alpha)} B'[\phi]} \qquad \frac{B \xrightarrow{\alpha} B' \quad \alpha \in A}{B/A \xrightarrow{\tau} B'/A} \qquad \frac{B \xrightarrow{\alpha} B' \quad \alpha \notin A}{B/A \xrightarrow{\alpha} B'/A} \qquad \frac{\theta(X) \xrightarrow{\alpha} B}{X \xrightarrow{\alpha} B}$$

range over $\mathbf{A} \cup \{\tau\}$. Furthermore we assume a set $\mathbf{X}$ of *process names*, ranged over by X. Process names are used in recursive process equations to specify infinite behaviour. We assume a *process environment* $\theta: \mathbf{X} \to \mathbf{L}$ containing the process definitions. We will use $X =_\theta B$ to denote $\theta(X) = B$. On this basis we define a language **L**, inspired by CCS (see Milner [18]) and CSP (see Brookes, Hoare and Roscoe [6]), with the following grammar:

$$B ::= \mathbf{succ} \mid \alpha; B \mid \Sigma \mathbf{setof}\, B \mid B \parallel_A B \mid B[\phi] \mid B/A \mid X \ .$$

Furthermore, we use abbreviated forms of summation and synchronisation:

$$\mathbf{stop} = \Sigma\varnothing$$
$$B_1 + B_2 = \Sigma\{B_1, B_2\}$$
$$B_1 \mid\mid\mid B_2 = B_1 \parallel_\varnothing B_2$$
$$B_1 \parallel B_2 = B_1 \parallel_{\mathbf{A}} B_2 \ .$$

The constant **succ** may only do an ω-action, after which it reduces to **stop**. In addition, the language features a family of action prefix operators ($\alpha \in \mathbf{A} \cup \{\tau\}$ arbitrary), a CCS-like infinitary summation operator Σ, a CSP-like parallel composition operator indexed by the set of synchronisation actions ($A \subseteq \mathbf{A}$ arbitrary), a renaming operator indexed by a function ($\phi: \mathbf{A} \to \mathbf{A}$ arbitrary, extended with $\tau \mapsto \tau$), a hiding operator indexed by the set of actions to be abstracted away from ($A \subseteq \mathbf{A}$ arbitrary) and process invocation. We take these operators to be sufficiently familiar to make an extensive discussion superfluous. Note that we have not included a restriction operator, on the grounds that the form of synchronisation we have chosen already allows restriction. As usual, we define a transition relation over terms, consisting of triples $B \xrightarrow{\alpha} C$ denoting that the term B evolves into the term C by doing the action α. This relation is defined inductively by way of the SOS rules in Table 1. The simple transition relation $\to$ gives rise to another, string-labelled relation defined as follows: for all $\sigma = a_1 \cdots a_n \in \mathbf{A}^*$

$$B \xRightarrow{\sigma} C :\Leftrightarrow B \xrightarrow{\tau}{}^* \xrightarrow{a_1} \xrightarrow{\tau}{}^* \cdots \xrightarrow{\tau}{}^* \xrightarrow{a_n} \xrightarrow{\tau}{}^* C$$

We also frequently use $B \xRightarrow{\sigma}$ to denote $\exists C. B \xRightarrow{\sigma} C$. We furthermore use the *label set* of a term, defined inductively in Table 2. We also briefly recall the standard notions of *observation equivalence* and *congruence* (cf. e.g. Milner [18]):

Table 2. Label set of a term

$L(\mathbf{succc})$	$:=$	$\emptyset$
$L(a; B)$	$:=$	$\{a\} \cup L(B)$
$L(\Sigma\mathbf{B})$	$:=$	$\bigcup\{L(B) \mid B \in \mathbf{B}\}$
$L(B_1 \parallel_A C)$	$:=$	$L(B_1) \cup L(C)$
$L(B[\phi])$	$:=$	$\phi(L(B))$
$L(B/A)$	$:=$	$L(B) - \{A\}$
$L(X)$	$:=$	$\bigcup\{L(X^i) \mid i \in \mathbb{N}\}$ where $X^0 := \mathbf{stop}$, $X^{i+1} := \theta(X)\{^{X^i}/_X\}$

Definition 1 observation congruence. *Observation equivalence* is the largest equivalence relation $\approx \subseteq \mathbf{L} \times \mathbf{L}$ such that $B_1 \approx C$ implies that for all $B_1 \xrightarrow{\sigma} B_1'$ there is a $C' \approx B_1'$ such that $C \overset{\sigma}{\Longrightarrow} C'$. *Observation congruence* is the largest relation $\approx^c \subseteq \approx$ that is a congruence for the operators of $\mathbf{L}$.

Now we recall the testing scenario presented by De Nicola and Hennessy in [9], and a variation studied by Brinksma in [4]. For this purpose we distinguish *system descriptions* and *tests* for those systems, all of which are represented formally as terms of $\mathbf{L}$. The constant **succ** is allowed only in tests. A test $t \in \mathbf{L}$ is *applied* to a system $B \in \mathbf{L}$ by letting the two synchronise, as in $B \parallel t$. This test application is then judged to be either successful or unsuccessful; the verdict relies on the presence of sufficiently many ω-transitions in strategic places. De Nicola and Hennessy consider two kinds of evaluation, called *may-testing* and *must-testing*, respectively. We define the latter through a binary relation between systems and tests. A *maximal run* is a sequence $B_0 \xrightarrow{\alpha_0} B_1 \xrightarrow{\alpha_1} \cdots \xrightarrow{\alpha_{n-1}} B_n \cdots$, which can be finite or infinite; in the former case, the final term should have no outgoing transitions.

$$B \,\mathbf{must}\, t \;:\Leftrightarrow\; \forall \text{ maximal runs } (B \parallel t) = B_0 \xrightarrow{\alpha_0} B_1 \xrightarrow{\alpha_1} \cdots .\, \exists i.\, B_i \xrightarrow{\omega} \;.$$

(May-testing may be defined in a like manner; however, we do not pursue this notion here.) A must-test, according to this definition, tests if every maximal run of B passes through a successful state. In particular, the presence of divergence in B (in the form of an infinite τ-path) may ruin a test. Brinksma has defined a "fair" variation on must-testing which concentrates on *finite, visible* runs; the effect is that divergence is ignored as long as there is a visible action available. The advantage of this notion is that it is compatible with observation congruence; an important disadvantage is that it is not a congruence for hiding. See [4] for a more extensive discussion. Recall that $\omega \notin \mathbf{A}$.

$$B \,\mathbf{fmust}\, t \;:\Leftrightarrow\; \forall \sigma \in \mathbf{A}^*, B' \in \mathbf{L}.\, B \parallel t \overset{\sigma}{\Longrightarrow} B' \text{ implies } (\exists a \in \mathbf{A} \cup \{\omega\}.\, B' \overset{a}{\Longrightarrow}) \;.$$

On the basis of binary relations $\rho \subseteq \mathbf{L} \times \mathbf{L}$ such as **must** and **fmust**, one may induce an *implementation relation* and a corresponding *equivalence*:

$$I \sqsubseteq_\rho S \;:\Leftrightarrow\; \forall t \in \mathbf{L}.\, (S \,\rho\, t) \Longrightarrow (I \,\rho\, t)$$
$$I \simeq_\rho S \;:\Leftrightarrow\; I \sqsubseteq_\rho S \wedge S \sqsubseteq_\rho I \;.$$

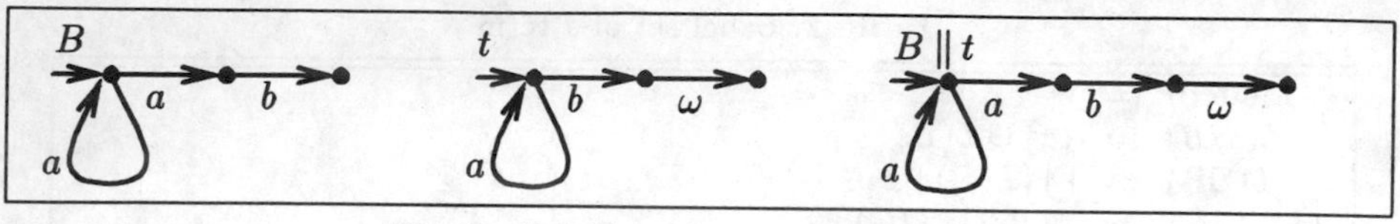

Fig. 5. Should-testing assumes fairness

Relations such as $\approx^c$ and $\sqsubseteq_{\mathbf{fmust}}$ are in a sense *fair* because of the nonchalant way they deal with divergences: essentially, since the only observations taken into account are visible transitions, τ-loops in a system are ignored. This kind of fairness can be expressed algebraically by the so-called *Koomen's Fair Abstraction Rule* (KFAR$_n$); see e.g. Baeten and Weijland [2]:

$$\frac{X_i = a_i; X_{i+1} + Y_i \quad a_i \in A}{X_i/A = \tau; \Sigma_{i \in \mathbb{N}_n}(Y_i/A)} \; (i \in \mathbb{N}_n) \tag{1}$$

where $X_i, Y_i \in \mathbf{L}$ are arbitrary and $\mathbb{N}_n$ denotes the natural numbers modulo n. It is a standard result that $\approx^c$ satisfies (1). For $\sqsubseteq_{\mathbf{fmust}}$ the situation is slightly more subtle, but since it is compatible with observation congruence ($\approx^c \subseteq \simeq_{\mathbf{fmust}}$) it is easily seen that $\simeq_{\mathbf{fmust}}$ satisfies the weaker property that if the X_i are *defined* as $a_i; X_{i+1} + Y_i$ in the binding environment θ, then certainly $X_i \approx^c a_i; X_{i+1} + Y_i$ and hence the conclusion of (1) holds. See also Sect. 5 below. Even this weaker property, however, does *not* hold for $\simeq_{\mathbf{must}}$; as remarked above, this was a major reason to investigate **fmust**. (Note that $\sqsubseteq_{\mathbf{must}}$ and $\sqsubseteq_{\mathbf{fmust}}$ are incomparable. See [4] for more details.)

3 Should-testing

To repair the non-congruence of fair must-testing for hiding, we introduce a new kind of test evaluation, which we call *should-testing*.

$$B \; \mathbf{should} \; t \; :\Leftrightarrow \forall \sigma \in \mathbf{A}^*, B' \in \mathbf{L}. \, (B \,\|\, t \stackrel{\sigma}{\Longrightarrow} B' \text{ implies } \exists \sigma' \in \mathbf{A}^*. \, B' \stackrel{\sigma'\omega}{\Longrightarrow}) \; .$$

The idea behind should-testing is that there is always a reachable successful state, and hence if choices are made fairly, a successful state should eventually indeed be reached. For instance, if B and t are as in Fig. 5, then $B \,\|\, t$ can in principle avoid ω forever by staying in the loop; nevertheless B **should** t because it is assumed that the other branch is not ignored forever.

The fairness properties of $\sqsubseteq_{\mathbf{should}}$ are studied in more detail in Sect. 5. Note the similarity of should-testing to fair must-testing. Fair must-testing states that a system may not deadlock unless a success action occurs first. Should-testing on the other hand requires something stronger: a success action must be reachable from every state in the system unless one has occurred already. For instance, the left hand system B in Fig. 4 passes the fair must-test $t = X$ where $X =_\theta a; X$ (there is no deadlock at all in $B \,\|\, t$), but it does not pass t as a *should*-test (there is no reachable ω-transition). In fact it is easy to verify that for all B and t

$$B \; \mathbf{should} \; t \Longrightarrow B \; \mathbf{fmust} \; t \; .$$

Furthermore it is easy to see that the difference between should- and fair must-testing only lies in the treatment of infinite behaviour. If there are no infinite visible paths in $B \parallel t$ then every failure to pass a should-test can be reduced to the failure of the corresponding fair must-test. To a certain degree we can control the occurrence of infinite paths of $B \parallel t$, by selecting t appropriately: it follows that for every B and every t with only finite visible runs

$$B\ \mathbf{should}\ t \iff B\ \mathbf{fmust}\ t\ .$$

This is in particular interesting because it is well known that $\sqsubseteq_{\mathbf{fmust}}$ can be decided on the basis of finite tests only; in fact, for deciding this relation the subclass of *failure tests* suffices.

Definition 2 failures and failure tests. A *failure* is a pair (σ, A), where $\sigma \in \mathbf{A}^*$ is a trace attempted by a system and $A \subseteq \mathbf{A}$ a set of actions that can subsequently be *refused*. To every failure there corresponds a *failure test*, denoted $t_{\sigma,A}$; these are defined inductively by

$$\begin{aligned} t_{\varepsilon,A} &:= \Sigma\{a; \mathbf{succ} \mid a \in A\} \\ t_{a\sigma,A} &:= \mathbf{succ} + a; t_{\sigma,A}\ . \end{aligned}$$

The characterisation result mentioned above is as follows: $I \sqsubseteq_{\mathbf{fmust}} S$ iff for all σ and A, $S\ \mathbf{fmust}\ t_{\sigma,A} \Rightarrow I\ \mathbf{fmust}\ t_{\sigma,A}$. We may conclude the following:

Corollary 3. $\sqsubseteq_{\mathbf{should}} \subseteq \sqsubseteq_{\mathbf{fmust}}$.

4 Congruence Properties of Should-Testing

We first prove that $\sqsubseteq_{\mathbf{should}}$ is a pre-congruence for hiding. This depends on an intermediate lemma. An auxiliary definition first: for all $A \subseteq \mathbf{A}$, let

$$R_A =_\theta \Sigma\{a; R_A \mid a \in A\}\ .$$

Theorem 4. $\sqsubseteq_{\mathbf{should}}$ *is a pre-congruence for hiding.*

Proof. First note that for all $B, t \in \mathbf{L}$ and $A \subseteq \mathbf{A}$ such that $A \cap L(t) = \varnothing$

$$B\ \mathbf{should}\ (t \mid\mid\mid R_A) \iff (B/A)\ \mathbf{should}\ t\ .$$

This follows by observing that for all such B and t the following holds:

$$(B/A) \parallel t \stackrel{\sigma}{\Longrightarrow} (B'/A) \parallel t' \quad \text{iff} \quad \exists \rho.\ \rho/A = \sigma \wedge B \parallel (t \mid\mid\mid R_A) \stackrel{\rho}{\Longrightarrow} B' \parallel (t' \mid\mid\mid R_A)$$

where ρ/A denotes the string obtained from ρ by removing all occurrences of actions from A. Using this fact, any failure of B w.r.t. $t \mid\mid\mid R_A$ can be converted to a failure of B/A w.r.t. t, and vice versa.

Now let $I \sqsubseteq_{\mathbf{should}} S$, and let $A \subseteq \mathbf{A}$ be arbitrary. If (S/A) **should** t for some arbitrary t then without loss of generality we may assume that t does not contain actions from A (because these are prevented from occurring anyway, due

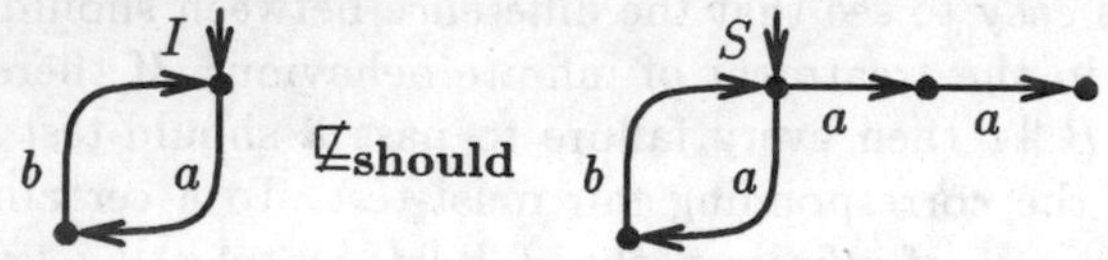

Fig. 6. $\sqsubseteq_{\mathbf{fmust}}$**-related systems after arbitrary abstraction, but not** $\sqsubseteq_{\mathbf{should}}$**-related**

to synchronisation); it follows that S **should** $(t \,|||\, R_A)$, hence I **should** $(t \,|||\, R_A)$, hence (I/A) **should** t. We may conclude $I/A \sqsubseteq_{\mathbf{should}} S/A$. □

For the other operators the situation is as for fair must-testing: we have congruence with respect to all operators except choice; to obtain congruence with respect to the latter, a straightforward side condition has to be added, stating that instability is preserved.

Theorem 5. $\sqsubseteq_{\mathbf{should}}$ *is a pre-congruence for prefixing, synchronisation and renaming.*

Proof sketch. By manipulating tests as in the proof of Theorem 4. The case of synchronisation is the most complex. Assume $I \sqsubseteq_{\mathbf{should}} S$; to be proved is $I \,\|_A\, B \sqsubseteq_{\mathbf{should}} S \,\|_A\, B$ for arbitrary $B \in \mathbf{L}$ and $A \subseteq \mathbf{A}$. We show the subcase that S is incapable of performing actions in $A' = L(B) - A$ (i.e., $S \stackrel{\sigma}{\Longrightarrow}$ implies $\sigma \in (\mathbf{A} - A')^*$); then it can be proved that in any interleaving semantics

$$(S \,\|_A\, B) \,\|\, t = S \,\|_{\mathbf{A}-A'}\, (B \,\|\, t) .$$

In turn, for the purpose of should-testing, the right hand term has the same failure capabilities as $S \,\|\, ((B \,\|\, t)/A')$, and hence we may conclude

$$(S \,\|_A\, B) \ \mathbf{should}\ t \iff S \ \mathbf{should}\ ((B \,\|\, t)/A') .$$

A similar property holds for $I \,\|_A\, B$; this essentially concludes the proof. □

Having established this, we return to the comparison of $\sqsubseteq_{\mathbf{should}}$ and $\sqsubseteq_{\mathbf{fmust}}$. We have that the former is a congruence for the majority of the operators in $\mathbf{L}$ and is contained in the latter. It is therefore natural to investigate the relation to the *coarsest congruence* in $\sqsubseteq_{\mathbf{fmust}}$. The initial observation is discouraging: $\sqsubseteq_{\mathbf{should}}$ is *not* the coarsest congruence for hiding within $\sqsubseteq_{\mathbf{fmust}}$. Consider the behaviour in Fig. 6. Here $I \not\sqsubseteq_{\mathbf{should}} S$; take for instance $t = X$ where $X =_\theta a; (b; X + a; \omega)$. On the other hand, it is easily seen that $I/A \sqsubseteq_{\mathbf{fmust}} S/A$ for arbitrary A.

As soon as we take more operators into consideration than just hiding, however, the situation suddenly changes for the better. It turns out that the coarsest congruence for hiding is *not* a congruence for parallel composition; and taking both operators into account at the same time *does* force the coarsest congruence down to $\sqsubseteq_{\mathbf{should}}$.

Theorem 6. $\sqsubseteq_{\mathbf{should}}$ *is the largest relation contained in* $\sqsubseteq_{\mathbf{fmust}}$ *that is a pre-congruence for both synchronisation and hiding.*

For the proof idea, consider once more Fig. 6. If we put both systems into the context $C[] = ([] \|_A Y)/A$ where $Y =_\theta a;(b;Y + a;c;\mathbf{stop})$ and $A = \{a,b\}$, then the right hand system satisfies the fair must-test $c;\mathbf{succ}$ whereas the left hand system does not. Note that the process Y in this context is very similar to the *should*-test t that was used to differentiate these systems in the first place: where t does the special success action ω, Y does an ordinary, but fresh action c; it then synchronises with the system on all actions except c and subsequently abstracts away from all actions except c. It is easy to see that B **should** t whenever $C[B]$ **fmust** $c;\mathbf{succ}$. The same pattern applies in general.

As mentioned above, the reason why $\sqsubseteq_{\mathbf{should}}$ fails to be a congruence with respect to choice is standard, as is the repair. We define

$$I \sqsubseteq^c_{\mathbf{should}} S :\Leftrightarrow I \sqsubseteq_{\mathbf{should}} S \wedge (I \xrightarrow{\tau} \text{ implies } S \xrightarrow{\tau})$$

This brings us to one of the main results of this paper. The proof is standard, combining the results achieved above.

Theorem 7. *$\sqsubseteq^c_{\mathbf{should}}$ is the largest relation contained in $\sqsubseteq_{\mathbf{fmust}}$ that is pre-congruent with respect to the operators of* $\mathbf{L}$.

5 Fairness Properties of Should-Testing

An important issue in introducing a new behavioural relation is to compare it to existing relations. Above we have done this for $\sqsubseteq^c_{\mathbf{should}}$ by showing it to be a coarsest congruence contained in a known relation; a further property is that its symmetric closure, $\simeq^c_{\mathbf{should}}$, contains observation congruence.

Theorem 8. $\approx^c \subseteq \simeq^c_{\mathbf{should}}$.

The proof has to be omitted for lack of space. However, this has an immediate consequence for the fairness properties of $\simeq^c_{\mathbf{should}}$, which "inherits" fairness from $\approx^c$ in the manner discussed in Sect. 2.

Corollary 9. *For all $X_i \in \mathbf{X}$ and $Y_i \in \mathbf{L}$ the following "weak KFAR" holds:*

$$\frac{X_i =_\theta a_i; X_{i+1} + Y_i \quad a_i \in A}{X_i/A \simeq^c_{\mathbf{should}} \tau;\Sigma(Y_i/A)} \, (i \in \mathbb{N}_n)$$

A natural question is if the full KFAR (Eq. 1) also holds. Unfortunately, this is not the case. Fig. 7 shows a counterexample with $n = 1$: $X \simeq_{\mathbf{should}} a;X + B$ but $X/a \not\simeq_{\mathbf{should}} B/a$ since (B/a) **should** $b;\mathbf{succ}$ but (X/a) ~~**should**~~ $b;\mathbf{succ}$.

The built-in fairness assumption of should-testing can also be expressed in another, more classical way. Loosely speaking, if a state is encountered infinitely often, then all its outgoing transitions will eventually be taken. To make this precise we define for $B_0 \in \mathbf{L}$: $B_0 \xrightarrow{\alpha_0} B_1 \xrightarrow{\alpha_1} \ldots \xrightarrow{\alpha_{n-1}} B_n \ldots$ is a *fair run* of B_0 if it is maximal and contains infinitely often each transition $B \xrightarrow{\alpha} B'$ for which B occurs infinitely often. Moreover, we call a process B *finite state* if there are only finitely many reachable B' (i.e., with $\exists \sigma \in \mathbf{A}^*.\, B \stackrel{\sigma}{\Longrightarrow} B'$).

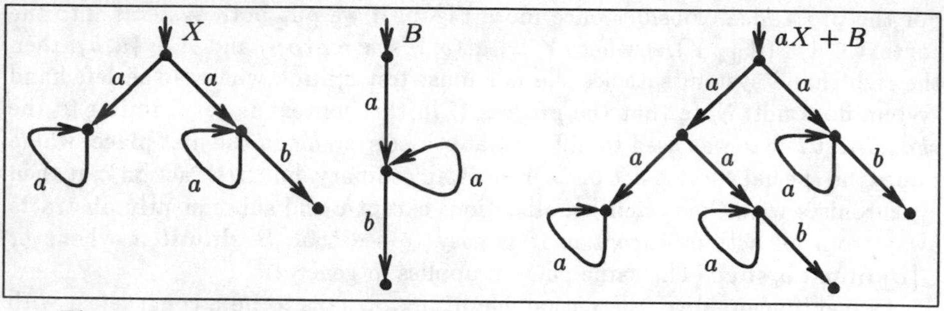

Fig. 7. A counterexample to Koomen's Fair Abstraction Rule for $\simeq^c_{\mathbf{should}}$

Lemma 10. *Let $B \in \mathbf{L}$ be a finite state process. If for every B' reachable from B there is some $\sigma \in \mathbf{A}^*$ with $B' \stackrel{\sigma\omega}{\Longrightarrow}$ then every fair run of B contains an ω-transition.*

The proof is straightforward and omitted here. The condition of the lemma is obviously connected to the **should**-relation. The following makes the connection explicit.

Corollary 11. *Let $B, t \in \mathbf{L}$ be finite state processes. B **should** t if and only if every fair run of $B \parallel t$ contains an ω-transition.*

6 An internal characterisation for should-testing

As all test-equivalences, $\sqsubseteq_{\mathbf{should}}$ is defined externally by referring to arbitrary test environments. We now present a failure-type semantics which allows to characterise $\sqsubseteq_{\mathbf{should}}$ internally; this semantics was first developed some time ago, and independently of the testing framework, in [23] to deal with liveness in the sense of Petri net theory.

Consider again the example of Fig. 4. In their initial states, both systems can only perform a as an immediate next action; they can refuse all other actions. This information is insufficient to determine the behaviour after hiding a; here it is important that the right-hand system can perform ab initially while the left-hand system cannot. Hence, one can get the idea to study refusals of sequences instead of single actions.

As a first step, we define a variant of failure semantics where the refusal sets lie in $\mathbf{A}^+$ instead of $\mathbf{A}$. For a term $B \in \mathbf{L}$, define $F^+(B)$ as the set of all (σ, A) with $\sigma \in \mathbf{A}^*$ and $A \subseteq \mathbf{A}^+$ such that

$$\exists B' \in \mathbf{L}.\, B \stackrel{\sigma}{\Longrightarrow} B' \wedge \forall \sigma' \in A.\, B' \stackrel{\sigma'}{\not\Longrightarrow} \quad .$$

The systems in Fig. 8 demonstrate that this easily defined semantics is too discriminating for our purpose. These systems have the same failure semantics, hence they are fmust-equivalent and —since their behaviour is finite— also should-equivalent. But the left-hand system can perform a and refuse $\{aa, b\}$,

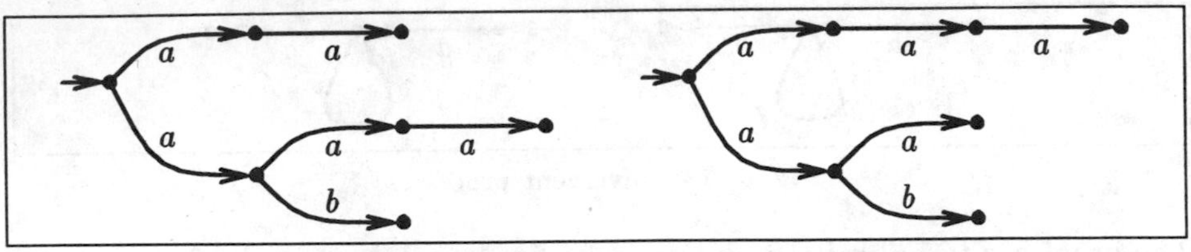

Fig. 8. F^+-semantics is too fine

while this is not possible for the right-hand system. It follows that we have to "saturate" the model somehow, so that this difference becomes unobservable.

Let us think back on the testing framework defined in Sect. 3. Just as the failure tests suffice to decide $\sqsubseteq_{\mathbf{fmust}}$, leading to the failure model, we might look for a minimal set of "essential tests" to decide $\sqsubseteq_{\mathbf{should}}$, and derive the denotational model from those. An immediate observation is that the deterministic tests suffice: for arbitrary t, the set T of deterministic tests obtained by resolving all nondeterministic choices in t arbitrarily, has the property that for arbitrary B, B **should** t iff $\forall t' \in T.\, B$ **should** t'. Indeed, the set of essential should-tests will be approximately *all deterministic, possibly infinite tests.*

Denotationally, rather than a pair of initial trace and refusal set, as in standard failures, every essential should-test can be represented by a pair of initial trace and *refusal tree*, which is a deterministic, possibly infinite tree whose maximal nodes correspond to success. A system refuses such a tree if it can do some initial prefix but then gets stuck, i.e., cannot reach a successful node any more. (From this point of view, a refusal set is a simple tree whose branches are single actions.) A refusal tree can be represented as the set of traces leading to successful nodes. The "tree failures" of a system B are those pairs (σ, T) with $T \subseteq \mathbf{A}^+$ such that $B \stackrel{\sigma\rho}{\Longrightarrow} B'$ where ρ is a prefix of some trace in T, and $\nexists \rho v \in T.\, B' \stackrel{v}{\Longrightarrow}$.

A set of nonempty traces T can be interpreted as a deterministic tree with nodes corresponding to prefixes of elements of T and "success nodes" corresponding to the elements of T. We denote

$$\begin{aligned} \downarrow T &:= \{\varepsilon\} \cup \{\rho \in \mathbf{A}^* \mid \exists v \in \mathbf{A}^*.\, \rho v \in T\} \\ \rho^{-1}T &:= \{v \mid \rho v \in T\}\ . \end{aligned}$$

for, respectively, the *node set* of T and the *remainder of T after ρ*. Note that even if T is empty, $\downarrow T$ contains the element ε, corresponding to the initial node of the tree. Now define

$$F^{++}(B) := \{(\sigma, T) \in \mathbf{A}^* \times \mathcal{P}(\mathbf{A}^+) \mid \exists \rho \in \downarrow T.\, (\sigma\rho, \rho^{-1}T) \in F^+(B)\}$$

Hence F^{++} is indeed a saturation of the model F^+ proposed and rejected earlier, since we can choose $\rho = \varepsilon$ in the above definition. The definition of F^{++} requires nothing for elements of T that do not have ρ as a prefix; e.g. $(a, \{aa, b\})$ is in the F^{++}-semantics of the right-hand system in Fig. 8, since $(aa, \{a\})$ is in its F^+-semantics. We now come to the fully abstract model for $\sqsubseteq_{\mathbf{should}}$.

Theorem 12. *For all $I, S \in \mathbf{L}$, $I \sqsubseteq_{\mathbf{should}} S$ if and only if $F^{++}(I) \subseteq F^{++}(S)$.*

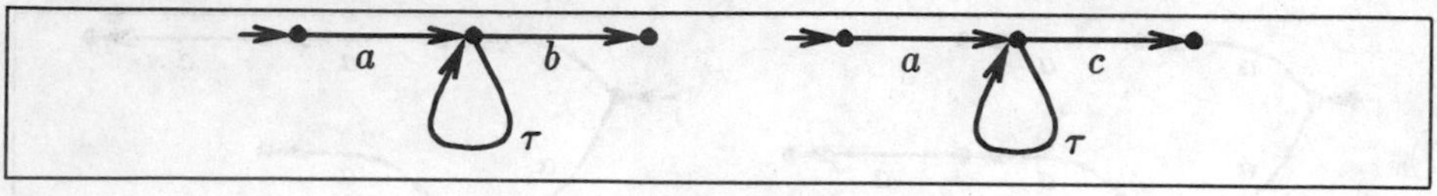

Fig. 9. Two divergent processes

The proof has to be omitted, due to lack of space. Note that the fact that the F^{++}-model is fully abstract does not imply that it is "optimal" in the sense of including no redundant test. This brings us back to the question of "essential tests" discussed above. For instance, the subset of (σ, T) where either $\sigma = \varepsilon$ or $T = \emptyset$ already suffices to establish full F^{++}-inclusion. The issue is an important one, because it concerns the question to what degree $\sqsubseteq_{\mathbf{should}}$ can be effectively proved. A detailed investigation, however, is outside the scope of this paper.

7 Concluding Remarks

To evaluate the contribution of this paper it is useful to summarize the main points of other existing work on testing pre-orders and divergences first.

Existing work. We start our comparison with the 'unfair' varieties. In the work on CSP, congruence with respect to hiding is obtained by a catastrophic interpretation of divergences. In the presence of a divergence all information is lost and a process may subsequently show any behaviour. This means that the behaviours of Fig. 9 are failure-equivalent, whereas the the transition systems even contain different actions. Technically, [6] achieves this by inserting the behaviour of the maximally nondeterministic process CHAOS whenever a divergence is encountered. To be able to decide in the semantic model whether maximal behaviour was specified explicitly or introduced by divergences, a refined model that explicitly keeps track of the divergences is presented in [7].

In the must-testing approach followed by De Nicola and Hennessy [9], divergences are also treated explicitly, represented by the constant Ω. Algebraically, Ω plays the role of the underspecified process that can be refined by arbitrary other behaviour, avoiding the drawback of [6]. The related model of (strong) acceptance trees [12, 14] is isomorphic to [7], and therefore also identifies the processes of Fig. 9. An overview of many other characterizations of unfair must-equivalence for transition systems can be found in [8]. Another approach to fairness is described in [13], where fairness is modelled as a structural property of the operator for parallel composition. This interpretation of fairness is compatible with the unfair interpretation of divergences of the underlying semantic model. In this framework a notion of testing is presented that can distinguish between fair and unfair forms of parallel composition.

The unfair interpretation of divergence is useful when one wants to distinguish between livelock and deadlock. This is the case if one, for example, wishes to analyse a specification for the presence of busy waiting-loops and other forms of improductive behaviour. As we have argued in the introduction, however,

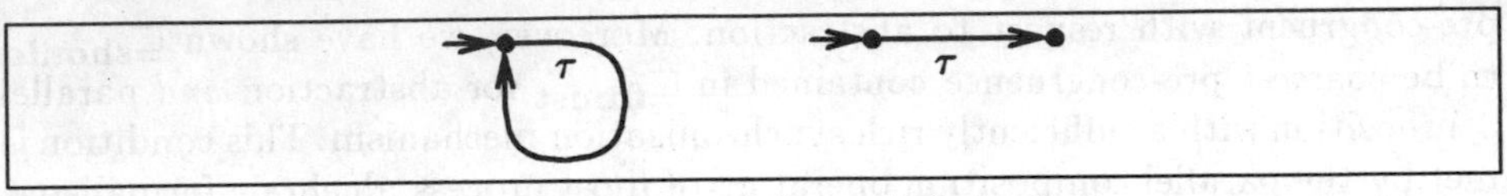

Fig. 10. livelock and (unstable) deadlock

there exist also a number of good reasons where a fair interpretation of divergence is useful. A first study of a fair interpretation of divergence was formulated by Bergstra, Klop, and Olderog in [3]. They make use of the concept of a *stable failure*. This is a failure that occurs in a stable state, i.e. a state without outgoing τ-transitions. The related equivalence *FS* is characterized equationally and a denotational model is constructed that consists of attributes of transition systems (traces, stable failures, and stability of the initial state). Syntactically, divergences are denoted by the constant Δ and the essential congruence is shown to be $\Delta.\tau = \tau$. This equation requires an outgoing τ-transition in order to abstract away from a divergence, and is therefore referred to as abstraction from *unstable* divergence. It is not sufficiently strong to conclude the equivalence of the behaviours in Fig. 10, which is sometimes paraphrased as *livelock* = (unstable) *deadlock*. These two processes are equated by $\sqsubseteq_{\mathbf{should}}$, as can be easily checked. The authors nevertheless show their equivalence to be fair in a reduced sense, viz. they show the following weaker version of KFAR to hold:

$$\frac{X = a; X + \tau; Y}{X/a = \tau; (Y/a)} \quad (\text{KFAR}^-)$$

In comparison to KFAR an extra τ appears as the guard of Y. ($\sqsubseteq_{\mathbf{should}}$ fails KFAR$^-$, for the same reason that it did KFAR; see however below.)

Valmari revisits in [22] the *FS*-equivalence of [3], and shows it to be the weakest deadlock-preserving congruence for the LOTOS operators $\|_G$ and [>. He also analyses two weaker equivalences that are congruences for other operator sets. Here deadlock is understood in the strong sense, viz. that a deadlock state has no outgoing transitions, including τ-transitions. A reformulation of the conformance testing theory of [4], which introduced $\sqsubseteq_{\mathbf{fmust}}$, using the pre-orders that generate the equivalences mentioned in [22] can be found in [17].

In the very recent [19], Natarajan and Cleaveland independently develop the **should**-testing scenario. They also present a denotational characterisation, and moreover give a topological argument that the difference with **must**-testing is small. Since they do not consider a language, they have no congruence results.

Contributions of this paper. We have introduced a testing pre-order $\sqsubseteq_{\mathbf{should}}$ that is fair in the sense that it ignores divergences that can always be exited. This was done by proposing a new evaluation criterion for tests in the style of De Nicola and Hennessy [9], leading to the definition of a **should**-test. We have shown that with respect to finite behaviours $\sqsubseteq_{\mathbf{should}}$ coincides with $\sqsubseteq_{\mathbf{fmust}}$, the fair version of the must-testing pre-order of De Nicola and Hennessy (and of the failure pre-order of Brookes et al. [6]). Whereas $\sqsubseteq_{\mathbf{fmust}}$, however, is not a pre-congruence with respect to operations that allow abstraction from observable behaviour, such as the hiding operation, we have shown $\sqsubseteq_{\mathbf{should}}$ to be pre-congruent with respect to abstraction. Moreover, we have shown $\sqsubseteq_{\mathbf{should}}$ to be coarsest pre-congruence contained in $\sqsubseteq_{\mathbf{fmust}}$ for abstraction *and* parallel composition with a sufficiently rich synchronisation mechanism. This condition is met by the parallel composition operators of most process algebraic formalisms, such as CCS, CSP, ACP, and LOTOS. Finally, to obtain congruence also with respect to the choice operator $+$ we have introduced the pre-congruence $\sqsubseteq^c_{\mathbf{should}}$, using the standard additional requirement that the instability of the left-hand argument implies that of the right-hand argument. This is also sufficient to obtain congruence with respect to the LOTOS disruption operator $[>$.

We have demonstrated the fairness properties of $\sqsubseteq^c_{\mathbf{should}}$ in two ways, viz. by showing its compatibility with observation (or weak bisimulation) congruence $\approx^c$, and, more directly, by proving that every fair run of a should-test of a behaviour terminates successfully. The former result is of great interest because $\approx^c$ satisfies KFAR, which represents a very strong notion of fairness. This means that the results of applications of KFAR (or indeed any other sound rule) for $\approx^c$, are inherited by $\sqsubseteq^c_{\mathbf{should}}$. Unfortunately, the combination of fairness with an abstraction-congruent testing pre-order comes at a price: we have also shown that $\sqsubseteq^c_{\mathbf{should}}$ itself does not satisfy KFAR. The premise of KFAR for $\sqsubseteq^c_{\mathbf{should}}$, $X \sqsubseteq^c_{\mathbf{should}} a; X + Y$, equates more behaviours than can be identified by applying fair abstraction when hiding a. This generosity of $\sqsubseteq^c_{\mathbf{should}}$ is also apparent in another way: it does not satisfy the *Recursive Specification Principle* (RSP), i.e. (observationally) guarded equations generally do not have unique solutions modulo $\sqsubseteq^c_{\mathbf{should}}$. (This in fact follows directly from the above results: if $X \sqsubseteq^c_{\mathbf{should}} a; X + Y$ had a unique solution, it would have to be identical (modulo $\sqsubseteq^c_{\mathbf{should}}$) to X in $X =_\theta a; X + Y$, which has been shown to be equivalent to Y/a after hiding a. In other words, RSP would imply KFAR.)

Summarising, $\sqsubseteq^c_{\mathbf{should}}$ answers the long standing question for a fair testing pre-order that is congruent with respect to a standard set of process algebraic operators. This combination, however, implies the loss of the unique solvability of guarded equations. The compatibility with observation congruence, on the other hand, makes this loss less acute. Proofs that require the application of KFAR or RSP should first be carried out in the context of the finer congruence $\approx^c$, only after which the coarser laws of $\sqsubseteq^c_{\mathbf{should}}$ or $\sqsubseteq^c_{\mathbf{should}}$ should be applied.

Future work. The denotational characterisation of $\sqsubseteq_{\mathbf{should}}$ that we have presented is still quite involved, and should be investigated for further possible simplification. This is of some importance as it affects the development of a proof theory for $\sqsubseteq_{\mathbf{should}}$. It also remains to find an axiomatic characterisation for sufficiently well-behaved cases, such as for example regular processes. On the practical side a larger application example should be elaborated that capitalises on the fairness features of $\sqsubseteq_{\mathbf{should}}$ and that cannot be carried out by using only finer equivalences with fair abstraction, such as observation congruence.

Acknowledgement. The first two authors gladly acknowledge fruitful discussions on the topic of this paper with Rom Langerak and Rob van Glabbeek (who put us on the right track towards the coarsest congruence property).

References

1. S. Abramsky. Observation equivalence as a testing equivalence. *Theoretical Comput. Sci.*, 53(3):225–241, 1987.
2. J.C.M. Baeten and W.P. Weijland. *Process Algebra.* Cambridge Univ. Press 1990.
3. J. A. Bergstra, J. W. Klop, and E.-R. Olderog. Failures without chaos: A new process semantics for fair abstraction. In M. Wirsing, ed., *Formal Description of Programming Concepts — III*, pp. 77–103. IFIP, Elsevier, 1987.
4. E. Brinksma. A theory for the derivation of tests. In Aggarwal and Sabnani, eds., *Protocol Specification, Testing, and Verification VIII*, pp. 63–74. Elsevier, 1988.
5. E. Brinksma. Cache consistency by design. In Vuong and Chanson [24], pp. 53–67.
6. S. D. Brookes, C. A. R. Hoare, and A. W. Roscoe. A theory of communicating sequential processes. *J. ACM*, 31(3):560–599, July 1984.
7. S. D. Brookes and A. W. Roscoe. An improved failures model for communicating processes. In Brookes, Roscoe and Winskel, eds., *Seminar on Concurrency*, vol. 197 of *LNCS*, pp. 281–305. Springer, 1985.
8. R. De Nicola. Extensional equivalences for transition systems. *Acta Inf.*, 24:211–237, 1987.
9. R. De Nicola and M. Hennessy. Testing equivalences for processes. *Theoretical Comput. Sci.*, 34:83–133, 1984.
10. R. J. van Glabbeek. The linear time – branching time spectrum II: The semantics of sequential systems with silent moves. In Best, ed., *Concur '93*, vol. 715 of *LNCS*, pp. 66–81. Springer, 1993. Extended abstract.
11. J. F. Groote. Implementation of events in LOTOS-specifications. Master's thesis, University of Twente, 1998. Technical Report, Philips CAM Centre C.F.T.
12. M. Hennessy. Acceptance trees. *J. ACM*, 32(4):896–928, Oct. 1985.
13. M. Hennessy. An algebraic theory of fair asynchronous communicating processes. *Theoretical Comput. Sci.*, 49:121–143, 1987.
14. M. Hennessy. *Algebraic Theory of Processes.* Foundations of Computing Series. MIT Press, Boston, 1988.
15. R. Langerak. A testing theory for LOTOS using deadlock detection. In Brinksma, Scollo and Vissers, eds., *Protocol Specification, Testing and Verification IX*, pp. 87–98. North-Holland 1989.
16. K. G. Larsen and R. Milner. Verifying a protocol using relativized bisimulation. In T. Ottman, ed., *Automata, Languages and Programming*, vol. 267 of *LNCS*, pp. 126–135. Springer, 1987.
17. G. Leduc. Failure-based congruences, unfair divergences, and new testing theory. In Vuong and Chanson [24].
18. R. Milner. *Communication and Concurrency.* Prentice-Hall, 1989.
19. V. Natarajan and R. Cleaveland. Divergence and fair testing. To be published in the proceedings of ICALP '95, 1995.
20. D. Park. Concurrency and automata on infinite sequences. In P. Deussen, ed., *Proc. 5th GI Conference*, vol. 104 of *LNCS*, pp. 167–183. Springer, 1981.
21. I. Phillips. Refusal testing. *Theoretical Comput. Sci.*, 50(2):241–284, 1987.
22. A. Valmari. The weakest deadlock-preserving congruence, 1995. To appear in *Information Processing Letters.*
23. W. Vogler. *Modular Construction and Partial Order Semantics of Petri Nets*, vol. 625 of *LNCS*. Springer, 1992.
24. S. Vuong and S. Chanson, eds. *Protocol Specification, Testing, and Verification, XIV*, IFIP Series. Chapman & Hall, 1995.

Formal Methods Technology Transfer: Impediments and Innovation (Abstract)

Dan Craigen

ORA Canada
267 Richmod Road, Suite 100
Ottawa Ontario K1Z 6X3
CANADA

Email: dan@ora.on.ca

1 Introduction

In my presentation, I shall discuss the state of formal methods with regards to technology transfer (diffusion and adoption) to industry. An *innovation diffusion* model [20, 10] is used to analyze data from a survey of industrial applications of formal methods [7]. The innovation diffusion model provides a framework with which to understand the forces advancing and/or retarding the diffusion of formal methods. With this understanding, we will be better placed to enhance the diffusion of formal methods to industry.

The results of applying the innovation diffusion model are reported in [8]. Susan Gerhart (University of Houston at Clear Lake), Ted Ralston (Odyssey Research Associates) and the author were the principal investigators of the survey and of the application of the innovation diffusion model to the survey data.

Interested readers are directed to the survey report [7] for a full presentation of the cases and our analyses. Five published papers [6, 13, 14, 19, 8] discuss various attributes of the survey. The first paper focuses on formal methods R&D issues arising from the survey. The second paper presents survey results in software engineering terms. The third paper focuses on the safety- and security-critical applications. The fourth paper discusses the role of education and training in the industrial application of formal methods. The final paper discusses the application of the innovation diffusion model to survey data.

2 International Survey

The international survey of industrial applications of formal methods had three primary objectives:

- To better inform deliberations within industry and government on standards and regulations.
- To provide an authoritative record on the practical experience of formal methods to date.

– To suggest areas where future research and technology development are needed.

The *methodology* of our survey was based on *common sense* and not based on a rigorous social scientific approach. Our use of an innovation diffusion model was an attempt to utilize a different analytic framework so as to elicit further insights into the survey data and technology transfer.

3 Cases

Summary descriptions of the survey case studies follow. For each case study, a citation to a published paper is provided. Further citations can be found in the survey report [7].

- Darlington Nuclear Reactor Shutdown Software. A certification effort requiring high assurance achieved using post-development mathematical analysis of requirements and code using the Software Cost Reduction method. (Reference: [1].)
- Inmos Transputer. Use of various formal methods to develop the components of three generations of transputers. (Reference: [2].)
- Hewlett-Packard Medical Instruments. A specification, using an HP variant of VDM, of a real-time database component of an HP patient monitoring system. (Reference: [3].)
- A CASE tool developed for the SSADM method by Praxis Systems Ltd. Z was used to produce a high-level design. (Reference: [4].)
- SACEM. A Train Control System requiring the certification of the new software control system for trains running on the Paris Metro. Hoare logic and B were used to express requirements and relate requirements to C code. (Reference: [5].)
- Multinet Gateway System. A development of a secure datagram network service using the Gypsy Verification Environment. (Reference: [9].)
- Tektronix Oscilloscope Software. A formal specification, using Z, of a software infrastructure for a new family of oscilloscopes. (Reference: [11].)
- Customer Information Control System (CICS). A re-engineering of transaction processing legacy code. Z was used to specify module interfaces. (Reference: [15].)
- TBACS. A smartcard authentication system for non-classified U.S. government systems. FDM was used to formally describe security properties. (Reference: [16].)
- Traffic Alert and Collision Avoidance System (TCAS). TCAS is a computer-controlled instrument system installed on commercial aircraft. A variant of the Statechart notation was used to reverse engineer two TCAS subsystems. (Reference: [17].)
- Cleanroom/COBOL SF. A full scale use of the Cleanroom methodology to implement a COBOL restructuring capability. (Reference: [18].)

– LaCoS. A European government technology transfer project seeking to transfer the RAISE formal method to industry. (Reference: [22].)

4 Innovation Diffusion

The analytic framework used in our analysis of the survey cases is based on the study of innovation. The framework [20] has come to be accepted by both academia and industry as a useful way to analyze strategies for innovation adoption and identify impediments.

In our version of the framework, our analysis uses the following criteria:

Relative advantage: An analysis of the technical and business superiority of the innovation over technology it might replace.

Compatibility: An analysis of how well the innovation meshes with existing practice.

Complexity: An analysis of how easy the innovation is to use and understand.

Trialability: An analysis of the type, scope and duration of feasibility experiments and pilot projects.

Observability: An analysis of how easily and widely the results and benefits of the innovation are communicated.

Transferability: An analysis of the economic, psychological and sociological factors influencing adoption and achieving critical mass [10]. Principal factors are *prior technology drag* (the presence of large and mature installed bases for prior technologies), *irreversible investments* (the cost of investing in the new technology), *sponsorship* (the presence of an individual or organization that promotes the new technology), and *expectations* (the benefits accruing from expectations that the technology will be extensively adopted).

Adoption of a superior innovation may still be negated by concerns, on the part of early adopters, arising from two early adoption risks: *transient incompatibility* and *risks of stranding* [10]. Transient incompatibility refers to risks accruing from delays in achieving a sufficiently large community interested in the new innovation. Stranding refers to the risks arising due to the failure to achieve critical mass.

5 Conclusions

Using the innovation diffusion model, summarized in the previous section, we concluded that formal methods is likely to have a low adoption trajectory due to the existence of significant impediments. Our findings for formal methods are similar to those of Fichman and Kemerer [10] regarding the low adoption trajectories of both structured methods and object orientation.

References

1. G. Archinoff, et al. "Verification of the Shutdown System Software at the Darlington Nuclear Generating Station." *International Conference on Control Instrumentation and Nuclear Installations*, Glasgow, Scotland, May 1990.
2. G. Barrett. "Formal Methods Applied to a Floating Point Number System." *IEEE Transactions on Software Engineering*, 1989.
3. S. Bear. "An Overview of HP-SL." *Proceedings of VDM'91: Formal Development Methods*, Volume 551, Lecture Notes in Computer Science, Springer-Verlag, 1991.
4. D. Brownbridge. "Using Z to Develop a CASE Toolset." *1989 Z User Meeting*, Workshops in Computing, Springer-Verlag 1989.
5. M. Carnot, C. DaSilva, B. Dehbonei and F. Meija. "Error-free Software Development for Critical Systems using the B methodology." *Third International Symposium on Software Reliability Engineering*, IEEE, 1992.
6. Dan Craigen, Susan Gerhart, Ted Ralston. "Formal Methods Reality Check: Industrial Usage." *IEEE Transactions on Software Engineering,* 21(2), February 1995.
7. Dan Craigen, Susan Gerhart, Ted Ralston. "An International Survey of Industrial Applications of Formal Methods." U.S. National Institute of Standards and Technology, March 1993, Technical Report NIST GCR 93/626 (Volumes 1 and 2). Also published by the U.S. Naval Research Laboratory (Formal Report 5546-93-9582, September 1993) and the Canadian Atomic Energy Control Board reports INFO-0474-1 (vol 1) and INFO-0474-2 (vol 2), January 1995. Also available at http://www.ora.on.ca/.
8. Dan Craigen, Susan Gerhart and Ted Ralston. "Formal Methods Technology Transfer: Impediments and Innovation." In *Applications of Formal Methods,* M.G. Hinchey and J.P. Bowen, Editors. Prentice-Hall International Series in Computer Science, 1995.
9. G. Dinolt, et al. "Multinet Gateway–Towards A1 Certification." *Symposium on Security and Privacy*, IEEE 1984.
10. Robert G. Fichman and Chris F. Kemerer. "Adoption of Software Engineering Process Innovations: The Case for Object Orientation." *Sloan Management Review*, Winter Issue, 1993.
11. D. Garlan and N. Delisle. "Formal Specifications as Reusable Frameworks." *Proceedings of VDM'90: VDM and Z!*, Vol. 428, Lecture Notes in Computer Science, Springer-Verlag 1990.
12. Susan Gerhart, Kevin Greene, Damir Jamsek, Mark Bouler, Ted Ralston, David Russinoff. "MCC Formal Methods Transition Study," MCC Technical Report FTP-FT-200-91, August 31, 1991.
13. Susan Gerhart, Dan Craigen and Ted Ralston. "Observations on Industrial Practice Using Formal Methods." In *Proceedings of the 15th International Conference on Software Engineering,* Baltimore, Maryland, May 1993.
14. Susan Gerhart, Dan Craigen and Ted Ralston. "Experiences with Formal Methods in Critical Systems." *IEEE Software*, January 1994.
15. I. Houston, S. King. "CICS Project Report: Experiences and Results from the use of Z." *Proceedings of VDM'91: Formal Development Methods*, Volume 551, Lecture Notes in Computer Science, Springer-Verlag, 1991.
16. D. Kuhn and J. Dray. "Formal Specification and Verification of Control Software for Cryptographic Equipment." *Sixth Computer Security Applications Conference*, 1990.

17. N. Leveson, et al. "Experiences using Statecharts for a System Requirements Specification." UC Irvine technical report, TR-92-106. Submitted for publication.
18. R. Linger and H. Mills. "A Case Study in Cleanroom Software Engineering: the IBM COBOL Structuring Facility." *COMPSAC*, IEEE 1988.
19. Ted Ralston, Susan Gerhart and Dan Craigen. "The Role of Education and Training in the Industrial Application of Formal Methods." *Proceedings of the Fourth International Conference on Algebraic Methodology and Software Technology (AMAST'95)*, Lecture Notes in Computer Science, Springer-Verlag, 1995.
20. Everett Rogers. "Diffusion of Innovations." Free Press, New York, 1983.
21. John Wordsworth. *Software Development with Z.* Addison-Wesley, 1992.
22. "Experiences from Applications of RAISE." LaCoS Project Reports, dated June 1991 and March 1992.

Decidability of Simulation and Bisimulation between Lossy Channel Systems and Finite State Systems*

(Extended Abstract)

Parosh Aziz Abdulla   Mats Kindahl

Dept. of Computer Systems, P.O. Box 325, 751 05 Uppsala, Sweden

E-mail: {parosh, matkin}@docs.uu.se

Abstract. We consider the verification of a class of infinite-state systems called *lossy channel systems*, which consist of finite-state processes communicating via unbounded but lossy FIFO channels. This class is able to model several interesting protocols, such as HDLC, the Alternating Bit Protocol, and other Sliding Window protocols. In earlier papers we have considered the decidability of various temporal properties for lossy channel systems. In this paper we study simulation and bisimulation relations between lossy channel systems and finite transition systems. More precisely, we show the decidability of (1) whether a state in a finite transition system *simulates* a state in a lossy channel system, and conversely, (2) whether a state in a finite transition system is *bisimilar* to a state in a lossy channel system, and (3) whether a state in a finite transition system *weakly simulates* a state in a lossy channel system. Furthermore, we show the undecidability of the following problems: (1) whether a state in a lossy channel system *weakly simulates* a state in a finite transition system, and (2) Whether a state in a finite transition system is *weakly bisimilar* to a state in a lossy channel system.

1 Introduction

Traditional approaches to automated verification model programs as finite-state systems. A program is described by an explicit representation of its state space. An obvious limitation of such models is that systems with infinitely many states, e.g. programs that operate on data from unbounded domains, fall beyond their capabilities.

We consider a class of infinite-state systems which consist of programs operating on unbounded FIFO channels. These programs have been used to model communicating finite-state processes, such as communication protocols [BZ83, Boc78]. The state space is infinite due to the unboundedness of the channels. It is well-known that such systems possess the same computational power as Turing Machines, and hence most verification problems are undecidable for them.

In this paper, we study a variant of this class where the FIFO channels are unreliable, in that they may nondeterministically lose messages. We call such systems *lossy channel systems*. In spite of the lossiness assumption, we can still model many interesting systems, e.g. link protocols such as the Alternating Bit Protocol [BSW69] and HDLC [ISO79]. These protocols and others are designed to operate correctly even in the case that the FIFO channels are faulty and may lose messages.

* Supported in part by ESPRIT BRA project No. 6021 (REACT), and by the Swedish Research Council for Engineering Sciences (TFR) under contract No. 92-814.

We have previously worked with verification of lossy channel systems. In [AJ93] we showed that several verification problems such as reachability, safety properties, and a simple class of eventuality properties are decidable. The decidability of the eventuality properties was also proven independently by Finkel [Fin94]. In [AJ94] we showed that most of the temporal properties that were not proven decidable in [AJ93] are in fact undecidable. More precisely, we showed that both model checking and verifying eventuality properties under the assumption that the channels are fair are undecidable.

In this work, we compare lossy channel systems with finite-state transition systems. We investigate the decidability of simulation and bisimulation relations between these two classes of systems. More precisely, we show the following problems to be decidable:

- whether a state in a finite transition system simulates a state in a lossy channel system, and conversely,
- whether a state in a finite transition system is bisimilar to a state in a lossy channel system, and
- whether a state in a finite transition system weakly simulates a state in a lossy channel system.

Furthermore, we show undecidability of the following problems:

- whether a state in a lossy channel system weakly simulates a state in a finite transition system, and
- whether a state in a finite transition system is weakly bisimilar to a state in a lossy channel system.

The idea of our verification algorithms is that we find ***finite representations*** for the simulation and bisimulation relations. Although these relations in general contain infinitely many pairs of states they can be decided by examining only a finite number of states, namely the states belonging to their finite representations. For example, given that a state of a finite transition system does not simulate a state of a lossy channel system, then it is also the case that it does not simulate any other "larger" state of the lossy channel system. A state is "larger" than another if the states differ only in that the content of each channel in the first state is a (not necessarily contiguous) superstring of the content of the same channel in the second state. This means that the "non-simulation" relation is "upward closed" with respect to the "larger than" ordering on states. To decide whether a state of a finite transition system simulates a state of a lossy channel system, we systematically generate all pairs of states of the two systems which belong to the non-simulation relation. Although non-simulation is *a priori* unbounded, two facts make it possible to represent it in a finite manner. The first fact is that (by the above reasoning) we do not have to analyze a state for which we have already analyzed a "smaller" state. The second fact is that by a result in language theory (Higman's theorem) only a finite number of states can be generated if we discard states that have smaller variants.

Related Work Algorithmic verification methods have recently been developed for several classes of infinite-state systems. Examples include certain types of real-time systems that operate on clocks [ACD90, Yi91, Čer92], data-independent systems [JP93, Wol86], systems with many identical processes [CG87, GS92, SG90], context-free processes ([BS92, CHS92, CHM93]), and Petri nets ([Jan90]).

Considerable attention has been paid to the problem of analyzing systems that communicate over perfect unbounded FIFO channels. All interesting verification problems for these systems are in general undecidable, since the channels may be used to simulate the tape of a Turing Machine [BZ83]. Decidability results have been obtained for limited subclasses. Most problems are decidable if the channel alphabets are of size one (in which case the system may be simulated by Petri Nets [KM69, RY86]), or if the language of each channel is bounded (in which case the system becomes finite-state [GGLR87, CF87]).

Algorithms for partial verification, which may or may not succeed in analyzing a given system, have been developed by Purushotaman and Peng [PP91] and by Brand and Joyner [BZ83]. These works do not characterize a class of systems for which their method works. Finkel [Fin88] presents a limited class of systems for which verification is decidable. This class does not cover e.g. the Alternating Bit protocol. Sistla and Zuck [SZ91] present a verification procedure for reasoning about a certain set of temporal properties over systems with FIFO channels. The method is not powerful enough to reason about arbitrary finite transition systems.

Outline In Section 2 we introduce lossy channel systems and finite transition systems. In Section 3 we define simulation and bisimulation between lossy channel systems and finite transition systems. In Section 4 and Section 5 we describe algorithms to decide simulation preorder. In Section 6 we show decidability of strong bisimulation. In Section 7 we consider the decidability of weak bisimulation and weak simulation.

2 Systems with Lossy Channels

In this section we present the basic definition of finite-state systems with unbounded but lossy FIFO channels. Intuitively such a system has two parts: a control part and a channel part. The channel part consists of a set of channels, each of which may contain a sequence of messages taken from a finite alphabet. The control part is a finite-state labeled transition system. Typically, the finite-state part models the total behavior of a number of processes that communicate over the channels. Each transition of the control part represents the performance of both an observable interaction with the environment of the system, and an operation on the channels. This operation may either be empty, remove a message from the head of a channel, or insert a message at the end of a channel. In addition, a channel can nondeterministically lose messages at any time. Message losses are not observed externally.

For a set M we use M^* to denote the set of finite strings of elements in M. For $x, y \in M^*$ we use $x \bullet y$ to denote the string resulting from the concatenation of the strings x and y. The empty string is denoted by ε. If $x \neq \varepsilon$, then ***first***(x) (***last***(x)) denotes the first (last) element of x. For sets C and M, a ***string vector*** w from C to M is a function $C \mapsto M^*$. For a string vector w from C to M we use $w\,[c := x]$ to denote a string vector w' such that $w'(c) = x$ and $w'(c') = w(c')$ for all $c' \neq c$. The string vector that maps all elements in C to the empty string is denoted by ε.

Definition 2.1. A *Lossy Channel System* $\mathcal{L}$ is a tuple $\langle S, \Lambda, C, M, \delta \rangle$, where

S is a finite set of *control states*,

Λ is a finite set of *labels*,

C is a finite set of *channels*,

M is a finite set of *messages*,

δ is a finite set of *transitions*. Each transition is a tuple of the form $\langle s_1, \alpha, \lambda, s_2 \rangle$, where s_1 and s_2 are control states, $\lambda \in \Lambda$ is a *label*, and α is an operation of one of the forms:

- $c!m$, where $c \in C$ and $m \in M$,
- $c?m$, where $c \in C$ and $m \in M$, or
- the empty operation e. □

Intuitively, the control part of the lossy channel system $\langle S, \Lambda, C, M, \delta \rangle$ is an ordinary labeled transition system with states S and transitions δ. The channel part is represented by the set C of channels, each of which may contain a string of messages in M. The set Λ denotes a set of observable interactions with the environment. A transition $\langle s_1, \alpha, \lambda, s_2 \rangle$ represents a change of control state from s_1 to s_2, while performing the observable interaction λ, and at the same time modifying the contents of the channels according to α, where

- $c!m$ appends the message m to the end of channel c,
- $c?m$ removes the message m from the head of channel c, and
- e does not change the contents of the channels.

The operational behavior of a lossy channel system is defined by formalizing the intuitive behavior of the system as a labeled transition system with infinitely many states. Let $\mathcal{L}$ be the lossy channel system $\langle S, \Lambda, C, M, \delta \rangle$. A *global state* γ of $\mathcal{L}$ is a pair $\langle s, w \rangle$, where $s \in S$ and w is a string vector from C to M. To model the fact that message losses are considered as unobservable events we introduce the silent event τ such that $\tau \notin \Lambda$, and define $\hat{\Lambda}$ to be the set $\Lambda \cup \{\tau\}$.

Definition 2.2. We shall define a relation $\longrightarrow$ as a set of tuples of the form $\langle \gamma, \lambda, \gamma' \rangle$ where γ and γ' are global states and $\lambda \in \hat{\Lambda}$. Let $\gamma \xrightarrow{\lambda} \gamma'$ denote $\langle \gamma, \lambda, \gamma' \rangle \in \longrightarrow$. We define $\longrightarrow$ to be the smallest set such that

1. if $\langle s, c!m, \lambda, s' \rangle \in \delta$, then $\langle s, w \rangle \xrightarrow{\lambda} \langle s', w\,[c := w(c) \bullet m] \rangle$, i.e. the control state changes from s to s', the observable action λ is performed, and m is appended to the end of channel c.
2. If $\langle s, c?m, \lambda, s' \rangle \in \delta$, then $\langle s, w\,[c := m \bullet w(c)] \rangle \xrightarrow{\lambda} \langle s', w \rangle$, i.e. the control state changes from s to s', the observable action λ is performed, and m is removed from the head of channel c. Notice that if $w(c) = \varepsilon$, or if $\mathit{first}(w(c)) \neq m$, then the transition $\langle s, c?m, \lambda, s' \rangle$ cannot be performed from the global state $\langle s, w \rangle$.
3. If $w(c) = x \bullet m \bullet y$, then $\langle s, w \rangle \xrightarrow{\tau} \langle s, w\,[c := x \bullet y] \rangle$, i.e. the message m in channel c is lost without changing the control state. The τ indicates that the event is not observable to the environment.
4. If $\langle s, e, \lambda, s' \rangle \in \delta$, then $\langle s, w \rangle \xrightarrow{\lambda} \langle s', w \rangle$, i.e. the control state changes from s to s' and the observable action λ is performed. The contents of the channels are not affected. □

For global states γ and γ', and sequence $\sigma \in \Lambda^*$, where $\sigma = \lambda_1 \lambda_2 \ldots \lambda_n$, we let $\gamma \overset{\sigma}{\Longrightarrow} \gamma'$ denote

$$\gamma \xrightarrow{\tau}{}^* \gamma_1 \xrightarrow{\lambda_1} \gamma_1' \xrightarrow{\tau}{}^* \gamma_2 \xrightarrow{\lambda_2} \gamma_2' \cdots \gamma_n \xrightarrow{\lambda_n} \gamma_n' \xrightarrow{\tau}{}^* \gamma'$$

for some global states $\gamma_1, \gamma_1', \gamma_2, \gamma_2', \ldots, \gamma_n, \gamma_n'$.

We say that a control state s_2 is *potentially reachable* from a control state s_1 through a label λ (written $s_1 \xrightarrow{\lambda}_P s_2$) if $\langle s_1, \alpha, \lambda, s_2 \rangle \in \delta$ for some α. We use $(s_1 \xrightarrow{\lambda}_P)$ to denote the set $\{ s_2 \mid s_1 \xrightarrow{\lambda}_P s_2 \}$.

In this paper we study simulation and bisimulation relations between lossy channel systems and finite labeled transition systems.

Definition 2.3 (Finite Labeled Transition Systems). A *finite labeled transition system* (or simply a finite transition system) $\mathcal{T}$ is a tuple $\langle Q, \Lambda, T \rangle$, where

Q is a finite set of *states*,

Λ is a finite set of *labels*, and

T is a finite set of *transitions* of the form $\langle q_1, \lambda, q_2 \rangle$, where $q_1, q_2 \in S$ and $\lambda \in \Lambda$. □

We use $q \xrightarrow{\lambda} q'$ to denote $\langle q_1, \lambda, q_2 \rangle \in T$. Notice that $\tau \notin \Lambda$. Let $(q \xrightarrow{\lambda})$ denote the set $\{ q' \mid q \xrightarrow{\lambda} q' \}$.

3 Simulation and Bisimulation

In this section we introduce the notions of simulation and bisimulation between lossy channel systems and finite transition systems. The simulation relation will be studied in both directions, i.e. whether a state of a finite transitions simulates a global state of a lossy channel system and conversely.

Definition 3.1 (Simulation Preorder). For a lossy channel system $\mathcal{L}$ and a finite transition system $\mathcal{T}$, a *simulation preorder* $\mathcal{S}$ between $\mathcal{L}$ and $\mathcal{T}$ is a set of pairs of the form $\langle \gamma, q \rangle$, where γ is a global state of $\mathcal{L}$ and q is a state of $\mathcal{T}$, such that if $\langle \gamma, q \rangle \in \mathcal{S}$ then, for all $\lambda \in \Lambda$:

- whenever $\gamma \stackrel{\lambda}{\Longrightarrow} \gamma'$, for some state γ', then there exists a q' such that $q \xrightarrow{\lambda} q'$ and $\langle \gamma', q' \rangle \in \mathcal{S}$. □

We say that γ *is simulated by* q, written $\gamma \sqsubseteq q$, if there exists a simulation $\mathcal{S}$ between $\mathcal{L}$ and $\mathcal{T}$ such that $\langle \gamma, q \rangle \in \mathcal{S}$.

In a similar manner we can define what it means for a state q of a finite transitions system to be *simulated by* a global state γ of a lossy channel system (written $q \sqsubseteq \gamma$), and what it means for γ to be *bisimilar* to q (written $\gamma \sim q$).

An alternative characterization of simulation preorder is given by the relation $\sqsubseteq_k$:

Definition 3.2. The relation $\sqsubseteq_k$ is defined for any natural number k as follows.

- $\gamma \sqsubseteq_0 q$, for all pairs γ and q.
- $\gamma \sqsubseteq_{k+1} q$, if for all $\lambda \in \Lambda$, whenever $\gamma \stackrel{\lambda}{\Longrightarrow} \gamma'$, for some state γ', then there exists a state q' such that $q \xrightarrow{\lambda} q'$ and $\gamma' \sqsubseteq_k q'$. □

In [Mil89] it is proved that for any finite-branching transition system $\sqsubseteq = \bigcap_k \sqsubseteq_k$. It is obvious that lossy channel systems and finite transition systems are finite-branching. This means that $\gamma \sqsubseteq q$ iff $\gamma \sqsubseteq_k q$ for each natural number k.

The relation $\sim_k$, for a natural number k, can be defined in a similar manner.

4 Deciding Simulation Preorder: LCS - FTS

In this section we describe and prove the correctness of an algorithm to decide whether a global state of a lossy channel system is simulated by a state of a finite transition system. The idea of the algorithm is that we compute the complement of $\sqsubseteq_k$, denoted $\not\sqsubseteq_k$, for $k = 1, 2, \ldots$, until we reach a point where $\not\sqsubseteq_k = \not\sqsubseteq_{k+1}$. As we will show later such a k always exists. We show that each $\not\sqsubseteq_k$ can be characterized by a finite set of pairs of states which we call the *finite representation* of $\not\sqsubseteq_k$. To check whether a pair of states belongs to $\not\sqsubseteq_k$, it suffices to inspect the finite representation of $\not\sqsubseteq_k$. We start by computing $\not\sqsubseteq_1$ and use Algorithm 1 to generate $\not\sqsubseteq_{k+1}$ from $\not\sqsubseteq_k$. When we reach the point where $\not\sqsubseteq_k = \not\sqsubseteq_{k+1}$, we know that $\not\sqsubseteq = \not\sqsubseteq_k$. To check $\gamma \sqsubseteq q$, we simply examine the finite representation of $\not\sqsubseteq$ which is identical to the finite representation of $\not\sqsubseteq_k$.

First we study some properties of strings and the $\sqsubseteq$ relation which will help us to construct our algorithms.

For a finite set M and $x_1, x_2 \in M^*$, let $x_1 \preceq x_2$ denote that x_1 is a (not necessarily contiguous) substring of x_2. If w_1 and w_2 are string vectors from C to M, then $w_1 \preceq w_2$ denotes that $w_1(c) \preceq w_2(c)$ for any $c \in C$. Let $\langle s_1, w_1 \rangle \preceq \langle s_2, w_2 \rangle$ denote that $s_1 = s_2$ and $w_1 \preceq w_2$.

We will use the following theorem to construct finite representations of relations and to prove termination of our algorithms.

Theorem 4.1 (Higman's theorem). *Let M be a finite set. There is no infinite sequence $w_1, w_2, \ldots$ of strings in M^* such that $w_i \not\preceq w_j$, for any $i < j$.*

It is straightforward to generalize Higman's theorem to sequences of string vectors and global states.

Let W be a set of string vectors. We say that $w \in W$ is a *minimal element* of W if for any $w' \in W$, we have $w' \not\preceq w$. We denote the set of minimal elements of W by $\min(W)$. By Higman's Theorem we know that $\min(W)$ is finite. Suppose that W is upward closed, i.e. if $w \in W$ and $w \preceq w'$ then $w' \in W$. We say that the set V is a *finite representation* of W if V is finite and $\min(W) \subseteq V$. Since $\min(W)$ is finite there exits a finite representation V for each upward closed set W. The set V is a representation of W in the sense that $w \in W$ if and only if there is a $w' \in V$ such that $w' \preceq w$, or equivalently W is exactly the set whose elements are larger than or equal to an element of V. This means that V characterizes a unique upward closed set, namely W. The notions of minimality and finite representation can easily be generalized to global states.

For string vectors $w_1, \ldots, w_n$ we define the set of *minimal upper bounds* to be the minimal elements of the set $\{ v \mid (w_1 \preceq v) \wedge \cdots \wedge (w_n \preceq v) \}$, and denote it $\sqcup\langle w_1, \ldots, w_n \rangle$. Observe that $\sqcup\langle w_1, \ldots, w_n \rangle$ is always finite and non-empty. It is easy to see that $\sqcup\langle w_1, \ldots, w_n \rangle$ is effectively computable for any $w_1, \ldots, w_n$. For sets of string vectors $W_1, \ldots, W_n$, let $\sqcup(W_1 \times \cdots \times W_n)$ denote the union of all $\sqcup\langle w_1, \ldots, w_n \rangle$ such that $\langle w_1, \ldots, w_n \rangle \in W_1 \times \cdots \times W_n$.

Proposition 4.2. *For any string vectors $w_1, \ldots, w_n, w$, and v*

$$(w_1 \preceq v) \wedge \cdots \wedge (w_n \preceq v) \supset \exists w \in \sqcup\langle w_1, \ldots, w_n \rangle . (w \preceq v)$$

In the following lemmas we show that $\sqsubseteq_k$ is downward closed, and consequently $\not\sqsubseteq_k$ is upward closed.

Lemma 4.3. *For any state q in a finite transition system and global states γ_1 and γ_2 in a lossy channel system we have* $(\gamma_1 \sqsubseteq_k q) \wedge (\gamma_2 \preceq \gamma_1) \supset (\gamma_2 \sqsubseteq_k q)$.

Corollary 4.4. $(\gamma_1 \not\sqsubseteq_k q) \wedge (\gamma_1 \preceq \gamma_2) \supset (\gamma_2 \not\sqsubseteq_k q)$.

In fact the above lemma and corollary can be shown for $\sqsubseteq$ and $\not\sqsubseteq$ in a similar manner.

From Corollary 4.4 we conclude that $\not\sqsubseteq$ and $\not\sqsubseteq_k$ are upward closed and consequently have finite representations.

When computing the finite representation of $\not\sqsubseteq_{k+1}$ from the finite representation of $\not\sqsubseteq_k$, we go backwards from pairs of states which belong to $\not\sqsubseteq_k$ to find pairs of states which belong to $\not\sqsubseteq_{k+1}$. We need to define a notion of "backward reachability" for global states of lossy channels systems. More precisely, we need to find a finite representation of the infinite set $\{ \gamma' \mid \gamma' \stackrel{\lambda}{\Longrightarrow} \gamma \}$. To achieve that we define a new transition relation $\leadsto$ on global states (Definition 4.5), such that (Lemma 4.6 and Lemma 4.7) the set $\{ \gamma' \mid \gamma \stackrel{\lambda}{\leadsto} \gamma' \}$ is a finite representation of $\{ \gamma' \mid \gamma' \stackrel{\lambda}{\Longrightarrow} \gamma \}$.

Definition 4.5. Let $\mathcal{L} = \langle S, \Lambda, C, M, \delta \rangle$ be a lossy channel system. Define $\leadsto$ to be the smallest relation on global states such that:

1. if $\langle s_2, c!m, \lambda, s_1 \rangle \in \delta$ then $\langle s_1, w\,[c := w(c) \bullet m] \rangle \stackrel{\lambda}{\leadsto} \langle s_2, w \rangle$,
2. if $\langle s_2, c!m, \lambda, s_1 \rangle \in \delta$, $w(c) \neq \varepsilon$, and $last(w(c)) \neq m$, then $\langle s_1, w \rangle \stackrel{\lambda}{\leadsto} \langle s_2, w \rangle$,
3. if $\langle s_2, c!m, \lambda, s_1 \rangle \in \delta$, and $w(c) = \varepsilon$, then $\langle s_1, w \rangle \stackrel{\lambda}{\leadsto} \langle s_2, w \rangle$,
4. if $\langle s_2, c?m, \lambda, s_1 \rangle \in \delta$ then $\langle s_1, w \rangle \stackrel{\lambda}{\leadsto} \langle s_2, w\,[c := m \bullet w(c)] \rangle$,
5. if $\langle s_2, e, \lambda, s_1 \rangle \in \delta$, then $\langle s_1, w \rangle \stackrel{\lambda}{\leadsto} \langle s_2, w \rangle$. □

We can capture the relation between $\leadsto$ and $\Longrightarrow$ in the following two lemmas:

Lemma 4.6. *For any global states γ_1, γ_2, and label λ,* $\gamma_1 \stackrel{\lambda}{\leadsto} \gamma_2 \supset \gamma_2 \stackrel{\lambda}{\Longrightarrow} \gamma_1$.

Lemma 4.7. *For any global states γ_1, γ_2, and γ_3, and label λ*

$$(\gamma_1 \stackrel{\lambda}{\Longrightarrow} \gamma_2) \wedge (\gamma_3 \preceq \gamma_2) \quad \supset \quad \exists \gamma_4 . (\gamma_4 \preceq \gamma_1) \wedge (\gamma_3 \stackrel{\lambda}{\leadsto} \gamma_4)$$

We now proceed by describing how to compute a finite representation of the initial set $\not\sqsubseteq_1$. From the definition of $\sqsubseteq_k$ we know that

$$\not\sqsubseteq_1 = \{ \langle \langle s, w \rangle, q \rangle \mid \exists \lambda . ((\langle s, w \rangle \stackrel{\lambda}{\Longrightarrow}) \neq \emptyset) \wedge ((q \stackrel{\lambda}{\longrightarrow}) = \emptyset) \}$$

It can easily be seen that minimal elements of this set have either all channels empty, or all but one channel is empty and the remaining channel contains exactly one message. This means that the effectively computable set

$$\{ \langle \langle s, w \rangle, q \rangle \mid \exists \lambda . ((\langle s, w \rangle \stackrel{\lambda}{\Longrightarrow}) \neq \emptyset) \wedge ((q \stackrel{\lambda}{\longrightarrow}) = \emptyset) \wedge (\textstyle\sum_{c \in C} |w(c)| \leq 1) \}$$

is a finite representation of $\not\sqsubseteq_1$.

To compute $\not\sqsubseteq_{k+1}$ given $\not\sqsubseteq_k$ we use Algorithm 1. It inputs a lossy channel system $\mathcal{L} = \langle S, \Lambda, C, M, \delta \rangle$, a finite transition system $\mathcal{T} = \langle Q, \Lambda, T \rangle$, and a finite representation W of $\not\sqsubseteq_k$, and produces a finite representation N of $\not\sqsubseteq_{k+1}$. To simplify the presentation of the algorithm, we assume that W is given as a collection of disjoint sets $W_{s,q}$, where $s \in S$ and $q \in Q$. A set $W_{s,q}$ contains a finite representation of the set of string vectors $\{ w \mid \langle s, w \rangle \not\sqsubseteq_k q \}$. The output set N is also given as a collection of disjoint sets $N_{s,q}$, where $N_{s,q}$ contains a finite representation of the set of string vectors $\{ w \mid \langle s, w \rangle \not\sqsubseteq_{k+1} q \}$.

Name: NEXTSIM$_1$
Input: An LCS $\mathcal{L} = \langle S, \Lambda, C, M, \delta \rangle$,
an FTS $\mathcal{T} = \langle Q, \Lambda, T \rangle$, and
a finite representation W of $\not\sqsubseteq_k$.
Output: A finite representation N of $\not\sqsubseteq_{k+1}$.
Algorithm:

```
for each s ∈ S and q ∈ Q do
    N_{s,q} ← W_{s,q}
    for each λ ∈ Λ and s' ∈ (s -λ->_P) do
        let {q_1, ..., q_n} denote the set (q -λ->)
        V ← ⊔(W_{s',q_1} × ··· × W_{s',q_n})
        for each v ∈ V do
            N_{s,q} ← N_{s,q} ∪ { w | ⟨s', v⟩ ~λ~> ⟨s, w⟩ }
        done
    done
done
```

Algorithm 1 Computing $\not\sqsubseteq_{k+1}$ from $\not\sqsubseteq_k$

The idea of the algorithm is that we start with pairs of states in $\not\sqsubseteq_k$, and go "backwards" to find pairs of states in $\not\sqsubseteq_{k+1}$. We know that $\langle s, w \rangle \not\sqsubseteq_{k+1} q$ if and only if there is a $\lambda \in \Lambda$ and w' such that

$$\langle s, w \rangle \stackrel{\lambda}{\Longrightarrow} \langle s', w' \rangle \tag{1}$$

$$\langle s', w' \rangle \not\sqsubseteq_k q_1, \ldots, \langle s', w' \rangle \not\sqsubseteq_k q_n \tag{2}$$

where $\{q_1, \ldots, q_n\}$ is the set $(q \stackrel{\lambda}{\longrightarrow})$. To find a string vector w' satisfying (2) we consider the sets W_{s',q_i} for $1 \leq i \leq n$. Suppose that $w_i \in W_{s',q_i}$. We know that $\langle s', w_i \rangle \not\sqsubseteq_k q_i$. Since $\not\sqsubseteq_k$ is upward closed, we know that for any $v \in \sqcup \langle w_1, \ldots, w_n \rangle$ we have $\langle s', v \rangle \not\sqsubseteq_k q_i$ and hence v satisfies (2). From the definition of $\rightsquigarrow$, it follows that (1) will be satisfied by any w such that $\langle s', v \rangle \stackrel{\lambda}{\rightsquigarrow} \langle s, w \rangle$.

The formal proof of correctness of the algorithm is given by the following lemmas.

Lemma 4.8. *If w is added to $N_{s,q}$, then $\langle s, w \rangle \not\sqsubseteq_{k+1} q$.*

Proof. Assume that w is added to $N_{s,q}$. If $w \in W_{s,q}$, we know that $\langle s, w \rangle \not\sqsubseteq_k q$ and hence $\langle s, w \rangle \not\sqsubseteq_{k+1} q$. Otherwise, there exists s' and v such that $\langle s', v \rangle \stackrel{\lambda}{\rightsquigarrow} \langle s, w \rangle$. Let $(q \stackrel{\lambda}{\longrightarrow})$ be of the form $\{q_1, \ldots, q_n\}$. From the algorithm we observe that there are $w_1, \ldots, w_n$ such that $v \in \sqcup\langle w_1, \ldots, w_n \rangle$, and $\langle s', w_1 \rangle \not\sqsubseteq_k q_1, \ldots, \langle s', w_n \rangle \not\sqsubseteq_k q_n$. From Corollary 4.4 it follows that $\langle s', v \rangle \not\sqsubseteq_k q_1, \ldots, \langle s', v \rangle \not\sqsubseteq_k q_n$. From Lemma 4.6 we know that $\langle s, w \rangle \stackrel{\lambda}{\Longrightarrow} \langle s', v \rangle$. It follows that $\langle s, w \rangle \not\sqsubseteq_{k+1} q$. □

Lemma 4.9. *If $k \geq 1$ and $\langle s, w \rangle \not\sqsubseteq_{k+1} q$, then some w' such that $w' \preceq w$ will be added to $N_{s,q}$.*

Proof. Assume that $\langle s, w \rangle \not\sqsubseteq_{k+1} q$. If $\langle s, w \rangle \not\sqsubseteq_1 q$ then $w \in W_{s,q}$ and some $w' \preceq w$ will be added to $N_{s,q}$. Otherwise, there exists λ, w', and a non-empty set $\{q_1, \ldots, q_n\}$, such that $(q \stackrel{\lambda}{\longrightarrow}) = \{q_1, \ldots, q_n\}$, $\langle s, w \rangle \stackrel{\lambda}{\Longrightarrow} \langle s', w' \rangle$, and $\langle s', w' \rangle \not\sqsubseteq_k q_1, \ldots, \langle s', w' \rangle \not\sqsubseteq_k q_n$. As W is a finite representation of $\not\sqsubseteq_k$, then there are $w_1, \ldots, w_n \preceq w'$, such that $w_1 \in W_{s',q_1}, \ldots, w_n \in W_{s',q_n}$. From Proposition 4.2 we know that there exists $v \in \sqcup\langle w_1, \ldots, w_n \rangle$ such that $v \preceq w'$. From Lemma 4.7 we know that there is a w'' such that $w'' \preceq w$ and $\langle s', v \rangle \stackrel{\lambda}{\leadsto} \langle s, w'' \rangle$. From the algorithm we observe that w'' will be added to $N_{s,q}$. □

Lemma 4.10. *If $k \geq 1$, then Algorithm 1 computes a finite representation N of $\not\sqsubseteq_{k+1}$.*

Proof. Follows from Lemma 4.8 and Lemma 4.9. □

Input: An LCS $\mathcal{L} = \langle S, \Lambda, C, M, \delta \rangle$ and
    an FTS $\mathcal{T} = \langle Q, \Lambda, T \rangle$.
Output: A finite representation W of $\not\sqsubseteq$
Algorithm:

```
W ← min(⋢_1)
repeat
    W_old ← W
    W ← min(NEXTSIM_1(W))
until W_old = W
```

Algorithm 2 Main procedure

Theorem 4.11. *Given a finite transition system $\mathcal{T}$ and a lossy channel system $\mathcal{L}$, Algorithm 2 computes a finite representation W of $\not\sqsubseteq$.*

Proof. We observe that in the k:th iteration of the algorithm (where $k > 0$), W_{old} and W are finite representations of $\not\sqsubseteq_k$ and $\not\sqsubseteq_{k+1}$ respectively (easily proved using Lemma 4.10). This means that when the algorithm terminates, we have $\not\sqsubseteq_k = \not\sqsubseteq_{k+1}$, and consequently $\not\sqsubseteq_k = \not\sqsubseteq$. To prove termination we observe that the set W is minimized at each iteration. This implies that if the loop is executed infinitely many times then infinitely many minimal elements will be added to the set W, which is a contradiction according to Higman's theorem. □

Theorem 4.12. *$\gamma \sqsubseteq q$ is decidable.*

Proof. We use Algorithm 2 to generate a finite representation W of $\not\sqsubseteq$. We know that $\gamma \sqsubseteq s$ if and only if there is no γ' such that $\gamma' \preceq \gamma$ and $\langle \gamma', s \rangle \in W$. □

5 Deciding Simulation Preorder: FTS - LCS

In this section we describe an algorithm to check whether a state of a finite transition system is simulated by a global state of a lossy channel system. The idea of the algorithm is similar to the one in Section 4. The difference is that we compute $\sqsubseteq_k$ instead of $\not\sqsubseteq_k$. In contrast to the simulation preorder in Section 4, where we decide simulation preorder in the direction $\gamma \sqsubseteq q$, we here decide simulation preorder in the opposite direction, i.e. if $q \sqsubseteq \gamma$. This results in that $\sqsubseteq_k$ is upward closed instead of, as in Section 4, downward closed. We make use of the upward closedness of $\sqsubseteq_k$ to provide a finite representation of $\sqsubseteq_k$ in the same manner as we did with $\not\sqsubseteq_k$ in Section 4. In Algorithm 3, given a lossy channel system $\mathcal{L} = \langle S, \Lambda, C, M, \delta \rangle$, a finite transition system $\mathcal{T} = \langle Q, \Lambda, T \rangle$, and a finite representation of $\sqsubseteq_k$, we provide a finite representation of $\sqsubseteq_{k+1}$ as follows. For $s \in S$ and $q \in Q$, we give a finite representation $W_{s,q}$ of the set of string vectors $\{ w \mid q \sqsubseteq_k \langle s, w \rangle \}$. We say that a string vector w is an *answer* to a transition $q \xrightarrow{\lambda} q'$ if there exists a string vector v such that $\langle s, w \rangle \overset{\lambda}{\Longrightarrow} \langle s', v \rangle$ and $q' \sqsubseteq_k \langle s', v \rangle$. In the algorithm, we compute a finite representation of the answers to each transition $q \xrightarrow{\lambda} q'$ and store it in $V_{\lambda,q'}$. The relation $q \sqsubseteq_{k+1} \langle s, w \rangle$ holds if and only if w is an answer to all transitions from q, or equivalently if w is a minimal upper bound to a set containing at least one element from each $V_{\lambda,q'}$.

Name: NEXTSIM$_2$
Input: An LCS $\mathcal{L} = \langle S, \Lambda, C, M, \delta \rangle$,
an FSM $\mathcal{T} = \langle Q, \Lambda, T \rangle$, and
a finite representation W of $\sqsubseteq_k$.
Output: A finite representation N of $\sqsubseteq_{k+1}$.

for each $s \in S$ **and** $q \in Q$ **do**
  $N_{s,q} \leftarrow \{\varepsilon\}$
  for each $\lambda \in \Lambda$ **and** $q' \in (q \xrightarrow{\lambda})$ **do**
    $V_{\lambda,q'} \leftarrow \{ w \mid \exists v, s'. v \in W_{s',q'} \wedge \langle s', v \rangle \overset{\lambda}{\leadsto} \langle s, w \rangle \}$
  for each $\lambda \in \Lambda$ **and** $q' \in (q \xrightarrow{\lambda})$ **do**
    $N_{s,q} \leftarrow \sqcup(N_{s,q} \times V_{\lambda,q'})$

Algorithm 3 Function to calculate $\sqsubseteq_{k+1}$ from $\sqsubseteq_k$

The formal proof of correctness of the algorithm can be carried out in a similar manner to that of Algorithm 1.

6 Bisimulation

In this section we show the decidability of bisimulation between a global state of a lossy channel system and a state of a finite transition system. It is easy to see that the relation $\sim_k$ between a finite transition system and a lossy channel system is downward closed and hence that the relation $\not\sim_k$ is upward closed.

To decide $\sim$ we could use an approach similar to the one in Section 4, i.e. to generate $\not\sim_1, \not\sim_2, \ldots$, until we get $\not\sim_k = \not\sim_{k+1}$. However, we introduce a different algorithm, where we generate $\sim_1, \sim_2, \ldots$, and in fact prove that there is an upper bound on the number of iterations we need to perform. As we shall see, it suffices to compute $\sim_1, \sim_2, \ldots, \sim_{m^2+1}$, where m is the size of the finite transition systems, and then use a reachability algorithm described in [AJ93].

For a lossy channel system $\mathcal{L}$, a finite transition system $\mathcal{T}$, a global state γ of $\mathcal{L}$, and a state q of $\mathcal{T}$, we show (Theorem 6.4) that the problem of checking $\gamma \sim q$ is equivalent to the following two problems: (1) that $\gamma \sim_{m^2+1} q$, where m is the number of states of $\mathcal{T}$, and (2) that it is not possible to reach "bad" global states from γ. A global state is "bad" if it is not bisimilar to any state of $\mathcal{T}$. We show (Theorem 6.5 and Theorem 6.6) that both these problems are decidable.

From the theory of bisimulation for finite state systems, we know that a finite transition system can be minimized with respect to bisimulation. We consider therefore (without loss of generality) only minimal finite transition systems. This means in particular that for any different states q_1 and q_2 of such a system, we have $q_1 \not\sim q_2$. We define the *size* of a finite transition system to be the number of states in it. We use the following result.

Lemma 6.1. *For a minimal finite transition system $\mathcal{T}$ with size m, and states s_1 and s_2 in $\mathcal{T}$, $q_1 \sim q_2 \equiv q_1 \sim_{m^2} q_2$.*

For a lossy channel system $\mathcal{L}$ we use $\gamma_1 \stackrel{*}{\Longrightarrow} \gamma_2$ to denote that there exits $\sigma \in \Lambda^*$ such that $\gamma \stackrel{\sigma}{\Longrightarrow} \gamma'$. By $(\gamma_1 \stackrel{*}{\Longrightarrow})$ we mean the set $\{\, \gamma_2 \mid \gamma_1 \stackrel{*}{\Longrightarrow} \gamma_2 \,\}$. For a lossy channel system $\mathcal{L}$ and a finite transition system $\mathcal{T} = \langle Q, \Lambda, T \rangle$ with size m, we define the set of *critical global states* (denoted $\mathcal{C}(\mathcal{L}, \mathcal{T})$) to be $\{\, \gamma \mid \exists q \in Q.\, \gamma \sim_{m^2+1} q \,\}$.

Lemma 6.2. *For a lossy channel system $\mathcal{L}$, a finite transition system $\mathcal{T}$ with size m, a global state γ of $\mathcal{L}$, and a state q of $\mathcal{T}$, we have $\gamma \sim q \supset (\gamma \stackrel{*}{\Longrightarrow}) \subseteq \mathcal{C}(\mathcal{L}, \mathcal{T})$.*

Lemma 6.3. *For a lossy channel system $\mathcal{L}$, a finite transition system $\mathcal{T}$ with size m, and a global state γ in $\mathcal{L}$, if $(\gamma \stackrel{*}{\Longrightarrow}) \subseteq \mathcal{C}(\mathcal{L}, \mathcal{T})$, then the set $\{\, \langle \gamma_1, q_1 \rangle \mid \gamma_1 \sim_{m^2+1} q_1 \wedge \gamma \stackrel{*}{\Longrightarrow} \gamma_1 \,\}$ is a bisimulation.*

Theorem 6.4. *For a lossy channel system $\mathcal{L}$, a finite transition system $\mathcal{T}$ with size m, a global state γ in $\mathcal{L}$, a state q in $\mathcal{T}$*

$$(\gamma \sim q) \equiv (\gamma \sim_{m^2+1} q) \wedge ((\gamma \stackrel{*}{\Longrightarrow}) \subseteq \mathcal{C}(\mathcal{L}, \mathcal{T}))$$

Proof. We prove both directions of the equivalence.

($\Longrightarrow$): Assume that $\gamma \sim q$. It is clear that $\gamma \sim_{m^2+1} q$. From Lemma 6.2 we get $(\gamma \stackrel{*}{\Longrightarrow}) \subseteq \mathcal{C}(\mathcal{L}, \mathcal{T})$.

($\Longleftarrow$): Assume that $\gamma \sim_{m^2+1} q$ and $(\gamma \stackrel{*}{\Longrightarrow}) \subseteq \mathcal{C}(\mathcal{L}, \mathcal{T})$. From Lemma 6.3 we know that the set $\{\, \langle \gamma_1, q_1 \rangle \mid \gamma_1 \sim_{m^2+1} q_1 \wedge \gamma \stackrel{*}{\Longrightarrow} \gamma_1 \,\}$ is a bisimulation. The result follows immediately from the fact that $\gamma \sim_{m^2+1} q$ and $\gamma \stackrel{*}{\Longrightarrow} \gamma$. □

Theorem 6.5. *For a lossy channel system $\mathcal{L}$ and a finite transition system $\mathcal{T}$, we can effectively compute a finite representation of $\sim_k$ for any natural number k.*

Proof. The idea of the algorithm is similar to Algorithm 1. □

Theorem 6.6. *For a lossy channel system $\mathcal{L}$, and a finite representation of a set Γ of global states of $\mathcal{L}$, we can effectively compute a finite representation of the set* $\{ \gamma' \mid (\gamma' \stackrel{*}{\Longrightarrow} \gamma) \wedge (\gamma \in \Gamma) \}$.

Proof. The proof can be found in [AJ93]. □

Theorem 6.7. *For a lossy channel system $\mathcal{L}$, a finite transition system $\mathcal{T}$, a global state γ of $\mathcal{L}$, and a state q of $\mathcal{T}$, it is decidable to check $\gamma \sim q$.*

Proof. The proof follows from Theorem 6.4, Theorem 6.5, and Theorem 6.6. □

7 Weak Simulation and Bisimulation

In this section we consider the decidability of a variant of the simulation and bisimulation problems which we call weak simulation/bisimulation.

We consider a more general form of lossy channel systems and finite transition systems. For a lossy channel system $\mathcal{L} = \langle S, \Lambda, C, M, \delta \rangle$, we allow the transitions in δ to have the form $\langle s_1, \alpha, \lambda, s_2 \rangle$ where $\lambda \in \hat{\Lambda}$. This means that the transitions may be labeled by the silent event τ. The same holds for finite transition systems.
For $\mathcal{T} = \langle Q, \Lambda, T \rangle$, $q_1, q_2 \in Q$, and sequence $\sigma \in \Lambda^*$, where $\sigma = \lambda_1 \lambda_2 \ldots \lambda_n$, we let $q \stackrel{\sigma}{\Longrightarrow} q'$ denote

$$q \stackrel{\tau}{\longrightarrow}^* q_1 \stackrel{\lambda_1}{\longrightarrow} q_1' \stackrel{\tau}{\longrightarrow}^* q_2 \stackrel{\lambda_2}{\longrightarrow} q_2' \cdots q_n \stackrel{\lambda_n}{\longrightarrow} q_n' \stackrel{\tau}{\longrightarrow}^* q'$$

for some states $q_1, q_1', q_2, q_2', \ldots, q_n, q_n' \in Q$.

Definition 7.1 (Weak Simulation). For a lossy channel system $\mathcal{L}$ and a finite transition system $\mathcal{T}$, a *weak simulation preorder* $\mathcal{S}$ between $\mathcal{L}$ and $\mathcal{T}$ is a set of pairs of the form $\langle \gamma, q \rangle$, where γ is a global state of $\mathcal{L}$ and q is a state of $\mathcal{T}$, such that if $\langle \gamma, q \rangle \in \mathcal{S}$ then, for all $\sigma \in \Lambda^*$:

- whenever $\gamma \stackrel{\sigma}{\Longrightarrow} \gamma'$, for some state γ', then there exists a q' such that $q \stackrel{\sigma}{\Longrightarrow} q'$ and $\langle \gamma', q' \rangle \in \mathcal{S}$. □

We say that γ *is weakly simulated by* q, written $\gamma \precsim q$, if there exists a weak simulation $\mathcal{S}$ between $\mathcal{L}$ and $\mathcal{T}$ such that $\langle \gamma, q \rangle \in \mathcal{S}$.

The relations $\precsim$ (in the reverse direction), $\precsim_k$ (in both directions), $\approx$, and $\approx_k$ are defined by making similar modifications to the definitions in Section 3.

To decide the relation $\precsim$ we generate $\precsim_k$, for $k = 0, 1, 2, \ldots$, until we obtain a k such that $\precsim_k = \precsim_{k+1}$. The idea of generating $\not\precsim_{k+1}$ from $\not\precsim_k$ is similar to that of generating $\not\sqsubseteq_{k+1}$ from $\not\sqsubseteq_k$ (Algorithm 1). We start from pairs of states which belong to $\not\precsim_k$ and go backwards to try to find pairs of states belonging to $\not\precsim_{k+1}$. The main difference between the two algorithms is that in the case of Algorithm 1, we need only to consider one step of the $\rightsquigarrow$ relation. However, to compute $\not\sqsubseteq_{\sim k+1}$, we need to take the silent transitions into consideration, and therefore have to replace the relation $\overset{\lambda}{\rightsquigarrow}$, for $\lambda \in \Lambda$, by the relation $\overset{\lambda}{\underset{*}{\rightsquigarrow}}$, where $\gamma \overset{\lambda}{\underset{*}{\rightsquigarrow}} \gamma'$ is defined by $\gamma \overset{\tau}{\rightsquigarrow}^* \gamma_1 \overset{\lambda}{\rightsquigarrow} \gamma'$. Although the $\underset{*}{\rightsquigarrow}$ is *a priori* unbounded, we get decidability through the following result which we have shown in [AJ93] for lossy channel systems.

Theorem 7.2. *For a lossy channel system $\mathcal{L} = \langle S, \Lambda, C, M, \delta \rangle$ and a global state γ of $\mathcal{L}$, we can effectively compute a finite representation of $(\gamma \overset{\lambda}{\underset{*}{\rightsquigarrow}})$.*

We prove the undecidability of the problem of checking whether a state of a finite transition system is weakly simulated by a global state of a lossy channel system. The result is shown through a reduction from the following problem which we have previously shown to be undecidable for lossy channel systems.

For a lossy channel system $\mathcal{L}$, we define a *computation* π *of* $\mathcal{L}$ as an infinite sequence $\gamma_1\gamma_2\ldots$ of global states in $\mathcal{L}$ such that for each $i = 1, 2, \ldots$ either (1) $\gamma_i \longrightarrow \gamma_{i+1}$ or (2) $\gamma_i = \gamma_{i+1}$, if there are no γ such that $\gamma_i \longrightarrow \gamma$.

Definition 7.3 (Recurrent State Problem). The *Recurrent State Problem* is defined as follows. Given a lossy channel system $\mathcal{L}$, a global state γ, and a control state s of $\mathcal{L}$, check whether $\mathcal{L}$ has a computation starting at γ and visiting s infinitely often. □

Theorem 7.4. *RSP is undecidable.*

The definition of RSP and the proof of its undecidability can be found in [AJ94].

Theorem 7.5. *For a lossy channel system $\mathcal{L}$, a finite transition system $\mathcal{T}$, a global state γ of $\mathcal{L}$, and a state q of $\mathcal{T}$, it is undecidable to check $q \sqsubseteq_{\approx} \gamma$.*

Proof. The proof is achieved through a reduction from RSP. □

We now proceed to prove undecidability of weak bisimulation between a lossy channel system and a finite transition system. The result is shown through a reduction from the following problem which we have previously shown to be undecidable for lossy channel systems.

Definition 7.6 (Global Reachability Problem). The *Global Reachability Problem (GRP)* is defined as follows. Given a lossy channel system $\mathcal{L}$, a global state γ, and a control state s of $\mathcal{L}$, check whether all computations of $\mathcal{L}$ starting at γ have the property that it is possible to reach s from any global state in the computation. □

Observe that the GRP property can be expressed as the temporal formula $\forall\Box\exists\Diamond\, s$. From [AJ94] we have the following theorem.

Theorem 7.7. *GRP is undecidable.*

Theorem 7.8. *For a lossy channel system $\mathcal{L}$, a finite transition system $\mathcal{T}$, a global state γ of $\mathcal{L}$, and a state q of $\mathcal{T}$, it is undecidable to check $\gamma \approx q$.*

Proof. The proof is achieved through a reduction from GRP in a similar manner to the proof of Theorem 7.5.

8 Conclusion and Future work

We have considered the decidability of simulation and bisimulation problems between lossy channel systems and finite transition systems. We intend to consider the corresponding problems for pairs of lossy channel systems. Early results indicate that simulation and bisimulation are decidable at least when one of the lossy channels systems is deterministic.

Although lossy channel systems are interesting in their own, we believe that many of the ideas presented here can be used to design verification algorithms for other classes of infinite-state systems such as Petri Nets, Relational Automata [Čer94], systems operating on unbounded graphs [JK95], etc. We hope this will lead us towards a general theory of verification for infinite-state systems.

Acknowledgements

We are grateful to Karlis Čerāns, Bengt Jonsson, and Yih-Kuen Tsay for comments and discussions.

References

[ACD90] R. Alur, C. Courcoubetis, and D. Dill. Model-checking for real-time systems. In *Proc. 5th IEEE Int. Symp. on Logic in Computer Science*, pages 414–425, Philadelphia, 1990.

[AJ93] Parosh Aziz Abdulla and Bengt Jonsson. Verifying programs with unreliable channels. In *Proc. 8th IEEE Int. Symp. on Logic in Computer Science*, 1993. Accepted for Publication in Information and Computation.

[AJ94] Parosh Aziz Abdulla and Bengt Jonsson. Undecidable verification problems for programs with unreliable channels. In Abiteboul and Shamir, editors, *Proc. ICALP '94*, volume 820 of *Lecture Notes in Computer Science*, pages 316–327. Springer Verlag, 1994.

[Boc78] G. V. Bochman. Finite state description of communicating protocols. *Computer Networks*, 2:361–371, 1978.

[BS92] O. Burkart and B. Steffen. Model checking for context-free processes. In Cleaveland, editor, *Proc. CONCUR '92, Theories of Concurrency: Unification and Extension*, number 630 in Lecture Notes in Computer Science, pages 123–137. Springer Verlag, 1992.

[BSW69] K. Bartlett, R. Scantlebury, and P. Wilkinson. A note on reliable full-duplex transmissions over half duplex lines. *Communications of the ACM*, 2(5):260–261, 1969.

[BZ83] D. Brand and P. Zafiropulo. On communicating finite-state machines. *Journal of the ACM*, 2(5):323–342, April 1983.

[Čer92] K. Čerāns. Decidability of bisimulation equivalence for parallel timer processes. In *Proc. Workshop on Computer Aided Verification*, volume 663 of *Lecture Notes in Computer Science*, pages 302–315, 1992.

[Čer94] K. Čerāns. Deciding properties of integral relational automata. In Abiteboul and Shamir, editors, *Proc. ICALP '94*, volume 820 of *Lecture Notes in Computer Science*, pages 35–46. Springer Verlag, 1994.

[CF87] A. Choquet and A. Finkel. Simulation of linear FIFO nets having a structured set of terminal markings. In *Proc. 8th European Workshop on Applications and Theory of Petri Nets*, 1987.

[CG87] E. M. Clarke and O. Grumberg. Avoiding the state explosion problem in temporal logic model checking algorithms. In *Proc. 6th ACM Symp. on Principles of Distributed Computing, Vancouver, Canada*, pages 294–303, 1987.

[CHM93] S. Christensen, Y. Hirshfeld, and F. Moller. Bisimulation equivalence is decidable for basic parallel processes. In *Proc. CONCUR '93, Theories of Concurrency: Unification and Extension*, pages 143–157, 1993.

[CHS92] S. Christensen, H. Hüttel, and C. Stirling. Bisimulation equivalence is decidable for all context-free processes. In W. R. Cleaveland, editor, *Proc. CONCUR '92, Theories of Concurrency: Unification and Extension*, pages 138–147, 1992.

[Fin88] A. Finkel. A new class of analyzable CFSMs with unbounded FIFO channels. In *Protocol Specification, Testing, and Verification VIII*, pages 1–12, Atlantic City, USA, 1988. IFIP WG 6.1, North-Holland.

[Fin94] A. Finkel. Decidability of the termination problem for completely specified protocols. *Distributed Computing*, 7(3), 1994.

[GGLR87] M.G. Gouda, E.M. Gurari, T.-H. Lai, and L.E. Rosier. On deadlock detection in systems of communicating finite state machines. *Computers and Artificial Intelligence*, 6(3):209–228, 1987.

[GS92] S. M. German and A. P. Sistla. Reasoning about systems with many processes. *Journal of the ACM*, 39(3):675–735, 1992.

[ISO79] ISO. Data communications – HDLC procedures – elements of procedures. Technical Report ISO 4335, International Standards Organization, Geneva, Switzerland, 1979.

[Jan90] P. Jančar. Decidability of a temporal logic problem for petri nets. *Theoretical Computer Science*, 74:71–93, 1990.

[JK95] Bengt Jonsson and Lars Kempe. Verifying safety properties of a class of infinite-state distributed algorithms, 1995. To appear in: Proc. CAV '95.

[JP93] B. Jonsson and J. Parrow. Deciding bisimulation equivalences for a class of non-finite-state programs. *Information and Computation*, 107(2):272–302, Dec. 1993.

[KM69] R.M. Karp and R.E. Miller. Parallel program schemata. *Journal of Computer and Systems Sciences*, 3(2):147–195, May 1969.

[Mil89] R. Milner. *Communication and Concurrency*. Prentice-Hall, 1989.

[PP91] W. Peng and S. Purushothaman. Data flow analysis of communicating finite state machines. *ACM Trans. on Programming Languages and Systems*, 13(3):399–442, July 1991.

[RY86] L.E. Rosier and H-C. Yen. Boundedness, empty channel detection and synchronization for communicating finite automata. *Theoretical Computer Science*, 44:69–105, 1986.

[SG90] Z. Shtadler and O. Grumberg. Network grammars, communication behaviours and automatic verification. In Sifakis, editor, *Proc. Workshop on Computer Aided Verification*, volume 407 of *Lecture Notes in Computer Science*, pages 151–165. Springer Verlag, 1990.

[SZ91] A.P. Sistla and L.D. Zuck. Automatic temporal verification of buffer systems. In Larsen and Skou, editors, *Proc. Workshop on Computer Aided Verification*, volume 575 of *Lecture Notes in Computer Science*. Springer Verlag, 1991.

[Wol86] Pierre Wolper. Expressing interesting properties of programs in propositional temporal logic (extended abstract). In *Proc. 13th ACM Symp. on Principles of Programming Languages*, pages 184–193, Jan. 1986.

[Yi91] Wang Yi. CCS + Time = an interleaving model for real time systems. In Leach Albert, Monien, and Rodriguez Artalejo, editors, *Proc. ICALP '91*, volume 510 of *Lecture Notes in Computer Science*. Springer Verlag, 1991.

Checking Regular Properties of Petri Nets

Petr Jančar*
Department of Computer Science
University of Ostrava
Dvořákova 7
701 00 Ostrava 1
Czech Republic
email: jancar@osu.cz

Faron Moller†
Swedish Institute
of Computer Science
Box 1263
164 28 Kista
Sweden
email: fm@sics.se

Abstract

In this paper we consider the problem of comparing an arbitrary Petri net against one whose places may contain only a bounded number of tokens (that is, against a regular behaviour), with respect to trace set inclusion and equivalence, as well as simulation and bisimulation. In contrast to the known result that language equivalence is undecidable, we find that all of the above are in fact decidable. We furthermore demonstrate that it is undecidable whether a given Petri net is either trace equivalent or simulation equivalent to any (unspecified) bounded net.

1 Introduction

This paper is concerned with narrowing the gap between decidable and undecidable classes of Petri nets with respect to the verification of various properties. For example, it is known that for bounded Petri nets, (that is, regular or finite-state automata), all standard behavioural properties (such as language equivalence) are decidable, whereas for Petri nets with at most two unbounded places, all of these are undecidable [10]; and for nets in which every transition has a single input place—the so-called Basic Parallel Processes BPP—bisimulation equivalence is decidable [2] whereas all other standard equivalences are undecidable [7, 9].

In this paper we consider the problem of comparing an arbitrary Petri net against one with bounded places. This problem may arise for example if the specification of a system is given as a regular behaviour yet the system itself is implemented by a

*The first author is supported by the Grant Agency of the Czech Republic, Grant No. 201/93/2123; and also received partial support from Esprit Network EXPRESS in order to visit the Swedish Institute of Computer Science, during which time the research reported here was carried out.

†The second author is supported by Esprit Basic Research Action No. 7166, "CONCUR2".

more general Petri net. The purpose for having a general Petri net implementation of a regular system could be to reduce the complexity of the system; a small Petri net with some number of unbounded places may exhibit a regular behaviour which can be represented only by very large bounded Petri nets.

Although we are considering regular properties, the class of problems considered here is nontrivial. Petri nets lack the universal computing power of Turing machines—for which the checking of such regular properties is clearly undecidable—but they may weakly simulate Turing machines [10], a state of affairs which provides for many undecidability results. As an example, it has long been known that language equivalence is undecidable in this case [20], even if we restrict attention to Petri nets with only one unbounded place.

Despite this initial negative result, our decidability results are generally positive. We first demonstrate that the simulation preorder is decidable in both directions, thus also providing the decidability of simulation equivalence. We then demonstrate the decidability of trace set inclusion in both directions, thus also providing the decidability of trace set equivalence. Finally we provide a proof of the decidability of bisimulation equivalence.

We then consider the problem of deciding if a given Petri net is either trace equivalent or simulation equivalent to any (unspecified) regular behaviour. At this point our results become negative. In contrast to the known result that the regularity of the set of traces of a net with an injective labelling (that is, where the transitions have unique labels) is decidable [20], we demonstrate the undecidability of both of these problems. However, we leave the corresponding question regarding bisimilarity open.

2 Preliminary Definitions

In this section we define the framework in which we shall work, in particular, the definitions and relevant results regarding finite labelled Petri nets (place/transition nets). We start by fixing some alphabet Σ, which is a set of observable actions which will label the transitions of our nets. We let $\mathcal{N}$ denote the set of nonnegative integers, and A^* the set of finite sequences of elements of the set A.

A *(finite, labelled, place/transition Petri) net* is a tuple $N = \langle P, T, F, M_N, \ell \rangle$ where

- P and T are finite disjoint sets of *places* and *transitions*, respectively;
- $F : (P \times T) \cup (T \times P) \to \mathcal{N}$ is a *flow function*: for $F(x, y) > 0$, there is an *arc* from x to y with *multiplicity* $F(x, y)$;
- $M_N : P \to \mathcal{N}$ is the *(initial) marking* or *state*, where a marking (state) associates a number of *tokens* with each place; and
- $\ell : T \to \Sigma$ is a *labelling*, which associates an action to each transition. ℓ will also be understood in a broader sense, denoting the homomorphic extension $\ell : T^* \to \Sigma^*$.

A transition t is *enabled* at a marking M, denoted by $M[t\rangle$, if $M(p) \geq F(p,t)$ for every $p \in P$. A transition t enabled at a marking M may *fire* yielding the marking M', denoted by $M[t\rangle M'$, where $M'(p) = M(p) - F(p,t) + F(t,p)$ for all $p \in P$. For any $a \in \Sigma$, by $M \xrightarrow{a}$ (and $M \xrightarrow{a} M'$) we mean that $M[t\rangle$ (and $M[t\rangle M'$) for some t with $\ell(t) = a$. These definitions can be extended homomorphically to finite sequences of transitions $\sigma \in T^*$ and finite sequences of actions $w \in \Sigma^*$.

The *reachability set* of a net N is defined as

$$\mathcal{R}(N) = \Big\{ M : M_N[\sigma\rangle M \text{ for some } \sigma \in T^* \Big\}.$$

We shall often refer to the states reachable from some marking M by $\mathcal{R}(M)$; in this case, the underlying net will be clear from the context. A place $p \in P$ is *unbounded* if for any $n \in \mathcal{N}$ there is $M \in \mathcal{R}(N)$ such that $M(p) > n$. Note that there exists an algorithm (based on that presented in [12]) which determines the unbounded places of a given net, and thus in particular whether or not a net is bounded, that is, represents a finite-state behaviour.

The *trace set* of a net N is defined as

$$\mathcal{T}(N) = \Big\{ w \in \Sigma^* : M_N \xrightarrow{w} \Big\}.$$

Note that by a trace here we mean simply a sequence of actions, as used for example by van Glabbeek [5], and not the partially ordered structures used by Mazurkiewicz [15]. As with reachability sets, we shall often refer to the trace set of a marking M of a net by $\mathcal{T}(M)$; again, in such a case the underlying net will be clear from the context. Two nets N_1, N_2 are *trace equivalent* if $\mathcal{T}(N_1) = \mathcal{T}(N_2)$.

The standard automata-theoretic notion of the *language* of a net N is defined with respect to a given finite set $\mathcal{F}$ of final states:

$$\mathcal{L}_{\mathcal{F}}(N) = \Big\{ w \in \Sigma^* : M_N \xrightarrow{w} M \text{ for some } M \in \mathcal{F} \Big\}.$$

In fact, using standard techniques [18] we can assume this set $\mathcal{F}$ to be the singleton set 0 consisting only of the zero marking; given any net defining a language based on a particular finite set of markings, we can effectively construct a net accepting the same language (minus the empty word) based on the singleton zero-marking set. We then have the following result from [20].

Theorem 2.1 (Valk and Vidal-Naquet) *It is undecidable whether $\mathcal{L}_0(N) = \mathcal{L}_0(R)$, where N is a net with only one unbounded place and R is a bounded net.*

We can actually show in this case that $\mathcal{L}_0(N) \subseteq \mathcal{L}_0(R)$ is decidable, using a reduction to the (decidable) problem of the inclusion of the language of a given push-down automaton within a given regular set [8]. Hence we can deduce from the above proposition that $\mathcal{L}_0(R) \subseteq \mathcal{L}_0(N)$ is undecidable.

We now present standard definitions of simulation preorder and bisimulation equivalence. Given two nets N_1 and N_2 a relation S between their markings is a *simulation* if for all $\langle M_1, M_2 \rangle \in S$ and for all $a \in \Sigma$:

- if $M_1 \xrightarrow{a} M_1'$ then $M_2 \xrightarrow{a} M_2'$ for some M_2' such that $\langle M_1', M_2' \rangle \in S$.

It is a *bisimulation* if for all $\langle M_1, M_2 \rangle \in S$ and for all $a \in \Sigma$:

- if $M_1 \xrightarrow{a} M_1'$ then $M_2 \xrightarrow{a} M_2'$ for some M_2' such that $\langle M_1', M_2' \rangle \in S$; and
- if $M_2 \xrightarrow{a} M_2'$ then $M_1 \xrightarrow{a} M_1'$ for some M_1' such that $\langle M_1', M_2' \rangle \in S$.

Given markings M_1 and M_2 from two nets N_1 and N_2, M_1 is *simulated* by M_2, written $M_1 \preceq M_2$, if they are related by some simulation, and they are *bisimilar*, written $M_1 \sim M_2$, if they are related by some bisimulation. We shall also refer to a net as being simulated by, or bisimilar to, another net if their initial markings are so related. It is easily confirmed that these two relations are respectively a preorder and an equivalence.

We shall occasionally rely on a stratified characterisation of these two relations as presented as follows. We first stipulate that $M_1 \preceq_0 M_2$ and $M_1 \sim_0 M_2$ for all pairs $\langle M_1, M_2 \rangle$. Then for every $n \in \mathcal{N}$ we let $M_1 \preceq_{n+1} M_2$ whenever

- if $M_1 \xrightarrow{a} M_1'$ then $M_2 \xrightarrow{a} M_2'$ with $M_1' \preceq_n M_2'$;

and we let $M_1 \sim_{n+1} M_2$ whenever

- if $M_1 \xrightarrow{a} M_1'$ then $M_2 \xrightarrow{a} M_2'$ with $M_1' \sim_n M_2'$; and
- if $M_2 \xrightarrow{a} M_2'$ then $M_1 \xrightarrow{a} M_1'$ with $M_1' \sim_n M_2'$.

Again we freely apply these relations to nets by considering their initial marking. The relations $\preceq_n$ are easily seen to form a nonincreasing (with respect to subset inclusion) sequence of preorders, and the relations $\sim_n$ are equally easily seen to form a nonincreasing sequence of equivalences. Furthermore, all of these relations are easily decidable. The following is then a standard result [16].

Lemma 2.2 *$M_1 \preceq M_2$ if and only if $M_1 \preceq_n M_2$ for all $n \in \mathcal{N}$; and $M_1 \sim M_2$ if and only if $M_1 \sim_n M_2$ for all $n \in \mathcal{N}$.*

It is often useful to think of these relations in terms of two-player games [19]. The rules of the *bisimulation* game, in which the two players alternate moves, are described as follows.

1. The playing board is given by a pair of nets N_1 and N_2.
2. Player 1 chooses one of the nets and fires an enabled transition, changing the marking appropriately.
3. Player 2 responds by firing a transition with the same label in the other net.
4. A player wins the game if ever the other player cannot make a move.

The rules for the *simulation* game are identical except that the first player must always choose the first net in rule 2.

Lemma 2.3

1. *Player 1 has a winning strategy in the simulation game if and only if $N_1 \not\preceq N_2$; in other words, Player 2 has a defending strategy if and only if $N_1 \preceq N_2$.*

   More precisely, Player 1 may force a win within k exchanges of moves if and only if $N_1 \not\preceq_k N_2$;

2. *Player 1 has a winning strategy in the bisimulation game if and only if $N_1 \not\sim N_2$; in other words, Player 2 has a defending strategy if and only if $N_1 \sim N_2$.*

   More precisely, Player 1 may force a win within k exchanges of moves if and only if $N_1 \not\sim_k N_2$;

Proof: If there is a simulation (bisimulation) S relating the initial markings of the nets, then Player 2 is always able to respond to moves by Player 1 in such a way that the resulting pair of markings is contained in the relation S; hence she has a defending strategy.

Conversely, if Player 2 has a defending strategy then the collection of all pairs of markings which appear after every exchange of moves during any and all games in which Player 2 uses this defending strategy defines a simulation (bisimulation).

The proofs for the stratified play are easily carried out by induction on k. □

We shall occasionally make use of the following result known as Higman's Theorem [6]. A partially-ordered set $\langle A, \leq \rangle$ has the *finite basis property (fbp)* if every infinite sequence of elements of A has an infinite (not necessarily strictly) ascending subsequence. For example, the integers $\langle \mathcal{N}, \leq \rangle$ equipped with the usual ordering has the finite basis property.

Theorem 2.4 *If $\langle A, \leq \rangle$ has the fbp then so does $\langle A^*, \widehat{\leq} \rangle$, where*

$$\widehat{\leq} \;=\; \Big\{ \langle\, a_1 a_2 \cdots a_n,\; v_0 b_1 v_1 b_2 \cdots v_{n-1} b_n v_n \,\rangle \;:\; a_i, b_i \in A,\; v_i \in A^*,\; a_i \leq b_i \Big\}.$$

A simple instance of Higman's Theorem, known as Dickson's Lemma [3], is presented as follows (and can be proven independently of Higman's Theorem using an obvious induction on k.)

Lemma 2.5 $\langle \mathcal{N}^k, \leq \rangle$ *has the finite basis property: given an infinite sequence of vectors $\vec{x}_1, \vec{x}_2, \vec{x}_3, \ldots \in \mathcal{N}^k$ we can always find i, j with $i < j$ such that $\vec{x}_i \leq \vec{x}_j$ (where $\leq$ is considered pointwise).*

We shall actually use this lemma as applied to markings of nets, where we view markings as vectors, and define the ordering between markings accordingly: $M \leq M'$ if and only if $M(p) \leq M'(p)$ for all places $p \in P$.

3 Simulation Preorder

In this section we suppose R to be a bounded (finite-state) net with states (markings) ranged over by s and s' and initial state s_R; and N to be an arbitrary net with markings ranged over by M and M' and initial marking M_N. We shall demonstrate that it is decidable both whether or not $R \preceq N$ and whether or not $N \preceq R$. First we provide a technical definition.

Definition 3.1 *Let S be a finite set of pairs of markings of nets N_1 and N_2. A set E is a* (one-step) simulation expansion *of S if*

- *for every pair $\langle \alpha, \beta \rangle$ in S and for every transition $\alpha \xrightarrow{a} \alpha'$ there is a transition $\beta \xrightarrow{a} \beta'$ such that $\langle \alpha', \beta' \rangle \in E$;*
- *E is minimal: no proper subset of E satisfies the above.*

Note that there are only finitely many simulation expansions of a given finite set of pairs, and that each of these is finite. Also, some simulation expansion of any (finite subset of a) simulation relation must be contained in that simulation relation. Finally note that there exists an expansion of a set S if and only if $\alpha \preceq_1 \beta$ for every $\langle \alpha, \beta \rangle \in S$, so there is no expansion exactly when there is some $\langle \alpha, \beta \rangle \in S$ such that $\alpha \not\preceq_1 \beta$; and if for every pair $\langle \alpha, \beta \rangle$ in S there are no transitions $\alpha \xrightarrow{a} \alpha'$, then the only simulation expansion of S is $\emptyset$.

Theorem 3.2 *$R \preceq N$ is decidable.*

Proof: Define a tree with root node $\{ \langle s_R, M_N \rangle \}$ and such that the children of a node are precisely the simulation expansions of the node with the following modification: we shall omit any pair $\langle s, M \rangle$ such that some ancestor node contains a pair $\langle s, M' \rangle$ with $M' \leq M$. (Note that when $M' \leq M$, we have $s \preceq M'$ implies $s \preceq M$, as $M' \preceq M$.) The node corresponding to the empty set is deemed to be a leaf of the tree. From Dickson's Lemma 2.5, along with König's Lemma (that every infinite finite-branching tree has an infinite path through it), it follows that the tree must be finite. (Note that a nonempty node is a leaf if it has no simulation expansion—that is, there is some (s, M) such that $s \not\preceq M$.)

If this tree has a branch terminating with a leaf labelled by the empty set, then it is straightforward to demonstrate that the set

$$\Big\{ \langle s, M \rangle \;:\; \langle s, M' \rangle \text{ appears in this branch for some } M' \leq M \Big\}$$

is a simulation, thus demonstrating $R \preceq N$.

Conversely, if $R \preceq N$ then there must be a branch terminating with the empty set, as some branch must contain only subsets of a simulation relation containing the root node. □

To demonstrate the decidability of $N \preceq R$, we use the following technical notion.

Definition 3.3 *Let* $\text{Rem}_p(N)$ *denote the net derived from* N *by deleting the place* p *along with all arcs leading into or out of it. For any marking* M *of* N*, we shall denote by* $\text{Rem}_p(M)$ *the marking of* $\text{Rem}_p(N)$ *which coincides with* M *on the non-*p *places.*

The net $\text{Rem}_p(N)$ thus behaves like N under the assumption that the place p always contains as many tokens as the maximum multiplicity of any of its outgoing arcs; that is, a transition can never be inhibited by the lack of sufficient tokens on the place p.

Lemma 3.4

1. *If* $\text{Rem}_p(M) \preceq s$ *then* $M \preceq s$.
2. *If* $\text{Rem}_p(M) \not\preceq s$ *then we may compute a value* v *such that* $M[p \mapsto v] \not\preceq s$*, and hence* $M'[p \mapsto v] \not\preceq s$ *for* $M' \geq M$*. (Here we use* $M[p \mapsto v]$ *to denote the mapping which coincides with* M *everywhere except on the place* p *where we have* $M[p \mapsto v](p) = v$*.)*

Proof:

1. This follows from the trivial observation that $M \preceq \text{Rem}_p(M)$, which follows from noting that the collection of all such pairs constitutes a simulation relation.
2. If $\text{Rem}_p(M) \not\preceq s$, then we may compute a value q such that $\text{Rem}_p(M) \not\preceq_q s$. (That is, Player 1 may force a win within q moves.) Taking $v = q{\cdot}w$, where w is the maximum multiplicity of any arc emanating from p, would then give us our desired result: $M[p \mapsto q{\cdot}w] \not\preceq s$. (Player 1 can simply use the same strategy for forcing a win within q moves.) We then get $M'[p \mapsto v] \not\preceq s$ for $M' \geq M$ from the fact that $M[p \mapsto q{\cdot}w] \preceq M'[p \mapsto q{\cdot}w]$. □

Theorem 3.5 $N \preceq R$ *is decidable.*

Proof: We proceed by induction on the number k of places of N. If N has no places ($k = 0$) then it clearly defines a finite-state (in fact, a one-state) behaviour, so the problem reduces to the (decidable) problem of comparing finite-state behaviours.

Suppose now that N has $k > 0$ places and that we can decide simulation preorder between a net with $k - 1$ places and a bounded net.

Define a tree with root node $\{ \langle M_N, s_R \rangle \}$ and such that the children of a node are precisely the collection of simulation expansions of the node with the following modifications: we shall omit any pair $\langle M, s \rangle$ such that either some ancestor node contains a pair $\langle M', s \rangle$ with $M' \geq M$ (in which case $M' \preceq s$ imples $M \preceq s$), or such that $\text{Rem}_p(M) \preceq s$ for some place p. (This latter condition can be decided due to the inductive hypothesis). A node is deemed to be a leaf of the tree if it corresponds to the empty set, or if it contains a pair $\langle M, s \rangle$ such that, for some place p, $\text{Rem}_p(M) \not\preceq s$ and $M(p) \geq v$, where v is as given by Lemma 3.4(2). Again from Dickson's Lemma 2.5 and König's Lemma it follows that this tree must be finite.

If this tree has a branch terminated with a leaf labelled by the empty set, then it is straightforward to demonstrate that the set

$$\Big\{ \langle M, s \rangle \;:\; \text{Rem}_p(M) \preceq s \text{ for some } p, \;\; or \\ \langle M', s \rangle \text{ appears in this branch for some } M' \geq M \Big\}$$

is a simulation, thus demonstrating $N \preceq R$.

Conversely, if $N \preceq R$ then there must be a branch terminated with the empty set, as some branch must contain only subsets of a simulation relation containing the root node. □

4 Trace Set Inclusion

In this section we again suppose R to be a bounded net with states (markings) ranged over by s and s' and initial state s_R; and N to be an arbitrary net with markings ranged over by M and M' and initial marking M_N. We shall demonstrate that it is decidable both whether or not $\mathcal{T}(R) \subseteq \mathcal{T}(N)$ and whether or not $\mathcal{T}(N) \subseteq \mathcal{T}(R)$. We can assume now though that R is a deterministic automaton: for each state s of R and each $a \in \Sigma$, there is at most one state s' of R such that $s \xrightarrow{a} s'$.

We begin with the easy direction.

Theorem 4.1 *$\mathcal{T}(N) \subseteq \mathcal{T}(R)$ is decidable.*

Proof: This follows from Theorem 3.5 (using the assumption that R is a deterministic automaton) once we note that the set

$$\big\{ \langle M, s \rangle \;:\; \mathcal{T}(M) \subseteq \mathcal{T}(s) \big\}$$

is a simulation; demonstrating this is straightforward. □

Theorem 4.2 *$\mathcal{T}(R) \subseteq \mathcal{T}(N)$ is decidable.*

Proof: Define a tree whose nodes are labelled by elements of $\mathcal{R}(R) \times 2^{\mathcal{R}(N)}$ with the root node labelled by $\langle s_R, \{M_N\} \rangle$, and whose edges are labelled by actions from Σ. For any transition $s \xrightarrow{a} s'$ the node $\langle s, A \rangle$ has a successor $\langle s', A' \rangle$ along an edge labelled by a, where A' contains the maximal (and hence pairwise incomparable) M' such that $M \xrightarrow{a} M'$ for some $M \in A$. The tree is thus constructed successively in such a way that for any node $\langle s, A \rangle$ reached from the root following a path labelled by w we have $s_R \xrightarrow{w} s$, and that A is the (finite) set of all maximal markings M such that $M_N \xrightarrow{w} M$; $A = \emptyset$ means that no marking M can be reached from M_N by performing the action sequence w.

The node $\langle s, \emptyset \rangle$ is deemed to be an unsuccessful leaf; and the node $\langle s, A \rangle$ (for $A \neq \emptyset$) is deemed to be a successful leaf if either there exists no transition from s, or if the node has an ancestor labelled by $\langle s, B \rangle$ such that for every $M \in B$ there is some $M' \in A$ such that $M \leq M'$. Due to Higman's Theorem 2.4 all branches must be finite, and therefore the constructed tree is finite. (For the application of Higman's Theorem, we view elements of $2^{\mathcal{R}(N)}$ as strings of markings with an arbitrarily-chosen ordering.)

If an unsuccessful node occurs then we can easily demonstrate that $\mathcal{T}(R) \not\subseteq \mathcal{T}(N)$; the label of the path to this unsuccessful node defines a trace of R which is not a trace of N. Conversely, if all nodes are successful, then we can easily demonstrate that $\mathcal{T}(R) \subseteq \mathcal{T}(N)$; the crucial fact is that $\mathcal{T}(M) \subseteq \mathcal{T}(M')$ when $M \leq M'$. □

5 Bisimulation Equivalence

In this section we again suppose R to be a bounded net with states (markings) ranged over by s and s' and initial state s_R; and N to be an arbitrary net with markings ranged over by M and M' and initial marking M_N. We shall demonstrate that it is decidable whether or not $R \sim N$. We can assume now that R is minimal with respect to bisimilarity: $s \not\sim s'$ whenever $s \neq s'$. In particular, this implies that $s \not\sim_{n-1} s'$ whenever $s \neq s'$, where R consists of n states. (This latter result is easily seen to be true by noting that the sequence of approximation equivalences $\sim_0, \sim_1, \ldots$ must stabilise within n steps.)

To establish our result, we use some known results concerning semilinear sets. A set $V \subseteq \mathcal{N}^k$ of vectors is *linear* if there are vectors $\vec{y}, \vec{x}_1, \vec{x}_2, \ldots, \vec{x}_p \in \mathcal{N}^k$ such that

$$V = \left\{ \vec{y} + c_1\vec{x}_1 + c_2\vec{x}_2 + \ldots + c_p\vec{x}_p \;:\; c_i \in \mathcal{N} \right\}.$$

V is *semilinear* if it is a finite union of linear sets.

Lemma 5.1 *It is decidable, given any net N and any semilinear set A, whether or not $\mathcal{R}(N) \subseteq A$.*

Proof: The complement $\overline{A}$ of the semilinear set A is an effectively computable semilinear set [4]. In a straightforward way, a net N' can be constructed such that $\mathcal{R}(N') \lceil P' = \overline{A}$ for some subset P' of places of N'. Using standard techniques we can then construct a net N'' from N and N' such that the zero marking is reachable in N'' if and only if there is some $M \in \mathcal{R}(N) \cap \overline{A}$. The result then follows from the decidability of the reachability problem [14]. □

Definition 5.2 *For our given nets R and N, let*

- $A_i = \left\{ \langle s, M \rangle \;:\; s \sim_i M \right\}$ *for each* $i \in \mathcal{N}$; *and*
- $B = \left\{ M \;:\; s \sim_n M \text{ for some } s \right\}$.

Note that for any M there is at most one s such that $s \sim_{n-1} M$. Hence for any $M \in B$, $s \sim_{n-1} M$ implies $s \sim_n M$.

Lemma 5.3 *A_i for each $i \in \mathcal{N}$, and B, are effectively computable semilinear sets.*

Proof: A_0 is clearly effectively semilinear. Suppose now that A_i is effectively semilinear. Note that $A_{i+1} = \{\langle s, M\rangle : \text{ any move } s \xrightarrow{a} s' \text{ is matched by a move } M \xrightarrow{a} M' \text{ such that } \langle s', M'\rangle \in A_i \text{ and vice versa}\}$. Since A_i is semilinear, we can easily characterise A_{i+1} by a formula in Presburger arithmetic (theory of addition); it is known [4] that any such formula can be effectively transformed into a semilinear set of its true values. Hence A_{i+1} is also effectively semilinear and we have completed the induction argument.

B is effectively semilinear as it is a restriction of the effectively semilinear set A_n.

□

Theorem 5.4 *$R \sim N$ is decidable.*

Proof: We shall show that $R \sim N$ if and only if $R \sim_n N$ and $\mathcal{R}(N) \subseteq B$, which can be checked due to Lemma 5.1.

If $R \sim N$, then $R \sim_n N$, and for any $M \in \mathcal{R}(N)$ there is $s \in \mathcal{R}(R)$ such that $s \sim M$. But then $s \sim_n M$, and hence $M \in B$.

Now suppose $R \sim_n N$ and $\mathcal{R}(N) \subseteq B$. Then

$$\Big\{\langle s, M\rangle : s \sim_n M \text{ and } M \in \mathcal{R}(N)\Big\}$$

can be easily seen to be a bisimulation containing the pair $\langle s_R, M_N\rangle$ thus demonstrating that $R \sim N$.

□

6 Undecidability of Regularity Testing

In this section we demonstrate that it is undecidable whether or not a given net is either trace equivalent, or simulation equivalent, to some (unspecified) bounded net. Our trace equivalence result is in contrast to the decidability result of [20] in the case of a net with an injective labelling, that is, where the transitions are all uniquely labelled. To do this, we rely on the undecidability of the halting problem for Minsky (counter) machines [17]. In particular, given an arbitrary Minsky machine C, we construct a net N_C (as in [10] with a modification inspired by [7]) for which we can demonstrate the following.

1. If the machine C halts, then the net N_C is simulation equivalent to some finite-state behaviour R. As a corollary, N_C and R are trace equivalent as well.
2. If the machine C does not halt, then the net N_C is not trace equivalent to any finite-state behaviour. Hence it cannot be simulation equivalent to any finite-state behaviour, either.

Formally, a *Minsky machine* is a sequence of labelled instructions

$$\begin{array}{ll} \mathtt{X}_1 & : \mathrm{comm}_1 \\ \mathtt{X}_2 & : \mathrm{comm}_2 \\ & \quad \cdots \\ \mathtt{X}_{n-1} & : \mathrm{comm}_{n-1} \\ \mathtt{X}_n & : \mathtt{halt} \end{array}$$

representing a simple program which uses counters $\mathtt{c}_1$, $\mathtt{c}_2$, ..., $\mathtt{c}_m$, where each of the first $n-1$ instructions is either of the form

X : $\mathtt{c}_j\mathtt{:=c}_j\mathtt{+1;}$ **goto** X'

or of the form

X : **if** $\mathtt{c}_j\mathtt{=0}$ **then goto** X'
else $\mathtt{c}_j\mathtt{:=c}_j\mathtt{-1;}$ **goto** X''

A Minsky machine C starts executing with the value 0 in each of the counters and the control at the label $\mathtt{X}_0$. When the control is at label $\mathtt{X}_k$ $(1 \leq k < n)$, the machine executes instruction comm_k, modifying the contents of the counters and transferring the control to the appropriate label mentioned in the instruction. The machine halts if and when the control reaches the **halt** instruction at label $\mathtt{X}_n$. We recall now the fact that the halting problem for Minsky Machines is undecidable: there is no algorithm which decides whether or not a given Minsky machine halts.

A Minsky machine C as described above gives rise to a particular net N_C with transitions labelled by $\Sigma = \{i, d, z\}$ as follows.

- The places of the net are given by $\{c_1, c_2, \ldots, c_m, , X_1, X_2, \ldots, X_n, U\}$. The initial marking consists of just one token, located on the place X_1.
- For every instruction X of the form

  X : $\mathtt{c}_j\mathtt{:=c}_j\mathtt{+1;}$ **goto** X'

  the net has a transition labelled by i (for "increment") with the single input place X and the two output places X' and c_j; see Figure 1(i). These arcs, as with all arcs in the net, have multiplicity 1.
- For every instruction X of the form

  X : **if** $\mathtt{c}_j\mathtt{=0}$ **then goto** X'
  else $\mathtt{c}_j\mathtt{:=c}_j\mathtt{-1;}$ **goto** X''

  the net has a transition labelled by d (for "decrement") with the two input places X and c_j, and the one output place X''; and two transitions labelled by z (for "zero"), the first with the single input place X and the single output place X', and the second with the two input places X and c_j, and the one output place U; see Figure 1(ii).

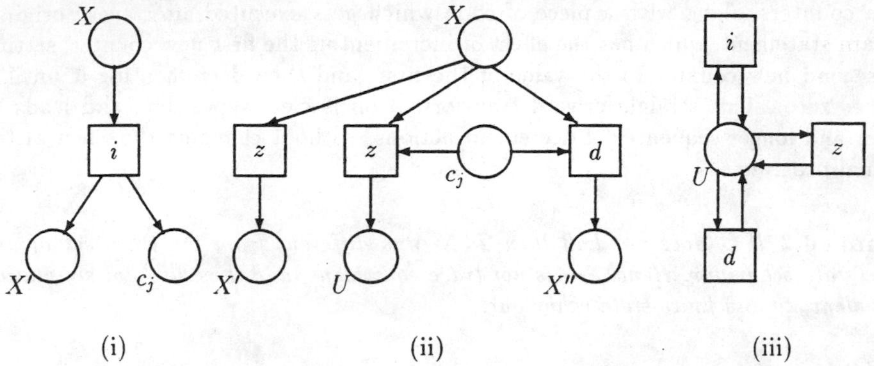

Figure 1: Constructions for N_C

- there are three further transitions associated with the place U (for "universal"). They each have U as both their single input place and their single output place, and they are labelled by i, d, and z, respectively; see Figure 1(iii).

The net N_C simulates the Minsky machine C in a weak sense: there is a unique computation of the net corresponding to the computation of the machine, and any incorrect ("dishonest") transition in the net can be made to lead to the universal state where any action is possible forevermore.

Lemma 6.1 *If C halts then N_C is simulation equivalent to a finite-state behaviour (i.e. a bounded net) R. Thus also $\mathcal{T}(N_C) = \mathcal{T}(R)$.*

Proof: The basis of the graph of R is the (finite) path corresponding to the (correct) computation of C (which halts by assumption). Outside of this path there is one further state which has three loops, labelled by i, d, and z respectively. From any state on the path which has an outgoing arc d, we add a further outgoing arc labelled by z and directed to this extra state. The finite-state behaviour can thus be pictured as follows.

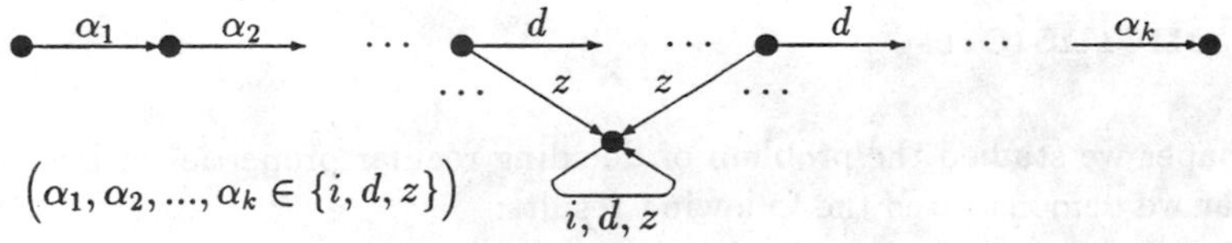

It can be easily verified that N_C both simulates, and is simulated by, this R. □

For the opposite direction, we shall assume without loss of generality that in any infinite computation of C we can find for any $q \in \mathcal{N}$ a subcomputation during which some counter is decreased q times in succession. This is possible by including two extra counters, along with a piece of code which gets executed after every original progam statement, which has the effect of incrementing the first new counter, setting the second new counter to the value of the first, and then decrementing it until it reaches zero. This straightforward transformation is clearly possible, and leads to longer and longer sequences of decrement actions, without changing the effect of the original program.

Lemma 6.2 *If C does not halt then $\mathcal{T}(N_C)$ is different from the trace set of any finite-state behaviour. Hence N_C is not trace equivalent, and thus also not simulation equivalent, to any finite-state behaviour.*

Proof: Suppose that $\mathcal{T}(N_C) = \mathcal{T}(R)$ for some finite-state behaviour R with, say, q states. Then R must accept the prefix of an honest computation sequence which includes a contiguous sequence of q decrement actions. Using the Pumping Lemma for finite-state behaviours [8], this means that R must be able to reach a state by following an honest computation sequence from which it can follow an arbitrary number of decrement actions, which clearly is not possible for N_C. Hence the trace sets of N_C and R cannot be equal. □

As described, these two results immediately yield our results, as summarized as follows.

Theorem 6.3

1. *It is undecidable whether or not a given net is simulation equivalent to some (unspecified) finite-state behaviour.*
2. *It is undecidable whether or not a given net is trace equivalent to some (unspecified) finite-state behaviour.*

As a final note, we leave the analogous question regarding bisimilarity open.

7 Conclusion

In this paper we studied the problem of deciding regular properties of Petri nets. In particular we demonstrated the following results:

- Given an arbitrary Petri net and a bounded Petri net,
  - it is decidable if the trace set of one is included in the trace set of the other, and thus it is decidable if they are trace equivalent;
  - it is decidable if one simulates the other, and thus it is decidable if they are simulation equivalent; and
  - it is decidable if they are bisimulation equivalent.

- Given an arbitrary Petri net,
  - it is undecidable if it is either simulation equivalent or trace equivalent to some (unspecified) bounded net.

In [20] Valk and Vidal-Naquet study similar questions, and arrive at results which contrast interestingly with ours. In particular, they demonstrate that language equivalence between a given net and a given bounded net is undecidable, while it is decidable if a given net with uniquely-labelled transitions is trace equivalent to some (unspecified) bounded net.

Mauw and Mulder [13] study a similar problem within the framework of context-free processes, so-called BPA-systems. Specifically, they demonstrate the decidability of the regularity of BPA-systems with respect to bisimulation equivalence. Within the framework of BPA, they are free to exploit the algebraic structure of terms allowed by the sequential composition operator of BPA. However in our instance we have no obvious such structure, and have left open the question of deciding if an arbitrary net is bisimilar to some (unspecified) bounded net.

In [11] the questions addressed here are extended to relations involving weak equivalences, that is, those which allow hidden internal events. In particular, the decidability results demonstrated here for trace set preorder and equivalence are extended in [11] to the weak versions of these relations; and the problem of deciding if a regular behaviour weakly simulates a net is decidable, whereas the opposite direction is only shown to be semidecidable. Finally it is shown that weak bisimulation equivalence is undecidable.

Our interest in the problems addressed in the paper was enhanced by inspiring discussions with Parosh Abdulla and Kārlis Čerāns on the problem of comparing two one-counter Petri nets, that is, nets with only one unbounded place. Partial results towards that study are described in [1] where we demonstrate the results presented in the present paper in the subcase of comparing one-counter nets vs bounded nets. The present paper thus extends all of the results presented in the earlier paper. However, both the decidability questions for one-counter nets, and the motivation given in the introduction of this paper—that is, that of implementing complex regular behaviours with simple general nets—are deserving of further exploration.

References

[1] Abdulla, P., K. Čerāns, P. Jančar, and F. Moller. One counter Petri nets vs bounded Petri nets. Research Report, 1995.

[2] Christensen, S., Y. Hirshfeld, and F. Moller. Bisimulation is decidable for basic parallel processes. In E. Best (editor), *Proceedings of CONCUR'93: Concurrency Theory, Lecture Notes in Computer Science* **715**, pp143–157, Springer-Verlag, 1993.

[3] Dickson, L.E. Finiteness of the odd perfect and primitive abundant numbers with distinct factors. *American Journal of Mathematics* **35**, pp413–422, 1913.

[4] Ginsburg, S., and E. Spanier. Semigroups, Presburger formulas, and languages. *Pacific Journal of Mathematics* **16**, pp285–296, 1966.

[5] van Glabbeek, R.J. The linear time – branching time spectrum. In J.C.M. Baeten, and J.W. Klop (editors), *Proceedings of CONCUR'90: Concurrency Theory, Lecture Notes in Computer Science* **458**, pp278–297, Springer-Verlag, 1990.

[6] Higman, H. Ordering by divisibility in abstract algebras. *Proceedings of the London Mathematical Society* **3**(2), pp326–336, 1952.

[7] Hirshfeld, Y. Petri nets and the equivalence problem. In E. Börger, Y. Gurevich, and K. Meinke (editors), *Proceedings of CSL'93: Computer Science Logic, Lecture Notes in Computer Science* **832**, pp165–174, Springer-Verlag, 1994.

[8] Hopcroft, J.E., and J.D. Ullman. **Introduction to Automata Theory, Languages, and Computation**. Addison Wesley, 1979.

[9] Hüttel, H. Undecidable equivalences for basic parallel processes. In R.K. Shyamasundar (editor), *Proceedings of FSTTCS'93: Foundations of Software Technology and Theoretical Computer Science, Lecture Notes in Computer Science* **761**, Springer-Verlag, 1993.

[10] Jančar, P. Undecidability of bisimilarity for Petri nets and some related problems. *Journal of Theoretical Computer Science* (to appear). (A preliminary version appears in P. Enjalbert, E.W. Mayr and K.W. Wagner (editors), *Proceedings of STACS'94: Symposium on Theoretical Aspects of Computer Science, Lecture Notes in Computer Science* **775**, pp581–592, Springer-Verlag, 1994.)

[11] Jančar, P. Decidability questions for equivalences on Petri nets. Czech Habilitation Thesis. Masaryk University, Brno. (Submitted April 1995.)

[12] Karp, R., and R. Miller. Parallel program schemata. *Journal of Computer and System Sciences* **3**, pp167–195, 1969.

[13] Mauw, S., and H. Mulder. Regularity of BPA-systems is decidable. In B. Jonsson and J. Parrow (editors), *Proceedings of CONCUR'94: Concurrency Theory, Lecture Notes in Computer Science* **836**, pp34–47, Springer-Verlag, 1993.

[14] Mayr, E. An algorithm for the general Petri net reachability problem. *SIAM Journal of Computing* **13**, pp441–460, 1984.

[15] Mazurkiewicz, A. Trace theory. In W. Brauer, W. Reisig, and G. Rozenberg (editors), *Petri Nets: Applications and Relationships to Other Models of Concurrency, Lecture Notes in Computer Science* **255**, pp279–324, Springer-Verlag, 1987.

[16] Milner, R. **Communication and Concurrency**. Prentice Hall, 1989.

[17] Minsky, M. **Computation: Finite and Infinite Machines**. Prentice Hall, 1967.

[18] Peterson, J.L. **Petri Net Theory and the Modeling of Systems**. Prentice Hall, 1981.

[19] Stirling, C. Local model checking games. Department of Computer Science Research Report, University of Edinburgh, 1995.

[20] Valk, R., and G. Vidal-Naquet. Petri nets and regular languages. *Journal of Computer and System Sciences* **23**(3), pp299–325, 1981.

Metric Predicate Transformers: Towards a Notion of Refinement for Concurrency

Marcello M. Bonsangue[1], Joost N. Kok[2] and Erik de Vink[1]

[1] Department of Computer Science, Vrije Universiteit Amsterdam
De Boelelaan 1081a, NL-1081 HV Amsterdam, the Netherlands
e-mail: marcello@cs.vu.nl, vink@cs.vu.nl

[2] Department of Computer Science, Leiden University
P.O. Box 9512, NL-2300 RA Leiden, the Netherlands
e-mail: joost@cs.ruu.nl

Abstract. A compositional weakest precondition semantics is given for a parallel language with recursion using a new metric resumption domain. By extending the classical duality of predicate vs. state transformers, the weakest precondition semantics for the parallel language is shown to be isomorphic to the standard metric state transformer semantics. Moreover, a notion of refinement for predicate transformers is proposed which corresponds to the familiar notion of simulation for state transformers.

1 Introduction

Starting from the seventies, a vast amount of research has been undertaken in which statements are seen as predicate transformers. One of the concerns is the development of refinement calculi for program derivation, where the soundness of the refinement rules is to be taken with respect to a weakest precondition semantics. Parallelism in the framework of program refinement is usually treated UNITY-style ([CM88]), i.e., as the fair interleaved execution of an action system consisting of a fixed number of processes with communication through shared variables.

Some results in the literature are established dealing with the superposition of action systems (e.g. [BS94]). In general, however, the underlying weakest precondition semantics is not tuned to a *compositional* treatment of concurrency. Several authors have proposed a predicate transformer semantics for concurrency. Recent references are, e.g., [Bes89, Lam90, SZ92]. Taking all together none of these combine compositionality and recursion for an explicit parallel operator. The main contribution of the present paper is the construction of a predicate transformer semantics which does combine all this, especially a treatment of 'dynamic' concurrency. A notion of refinement is proposed for the parallel setting which conservatively extends the familiar sequential/nondeterministic refinement relation. More importantly, by comparison with state transformers—extending the classical duality of predicate vs. state transformers—the refinement relation is characterized as the counterpart of simulation for transition systems.

Let us sketch the principal content of the paper. We will treat two languages, $\mathcal{L}_1$ and $\mathcal{L}_2$. These are introduced in Section 3. Both languages have assignment, test, sequential composition, binary choice and recursion. Additionally, $\mathcal{L}_2$ features a parallel operator and a simple form of atomization. The semantics for the parallel language $\mathcal{L}_2$ will be couched in a branching domain which caters for interleaving points, whereas for the sequential language $\mathcal{L}_1$ the traditional input/output setting suffices.

In Section 4, the domains Π_1 and Π_2 for $\mathcal{L}_1$ and $\mathcal{L}_2$, respectively, are introduced. The technical details of their definitions are suppressed here. (The interested reader though is referred to the technical report [BKV94].) Pivotal is the formulation of a so-called *backward* distance, which makes it possible to deal with predicate transformers in a metric framework.

The weakest precondition semantics for the languages are given in Section 5. In particular, the model wp_2 for the language $\mathcal{L}_2$ is illustrated with examples involving the parallel operator. It will become clear that the branching structure of the underlying domain Π_2 enforces a more descriptive form of postcondition as one might expect beforehand. However, it is pointed out how, by means of *'saturation'* of predicates, reasoning goes quite well using wp_2.

For the predicate transformer domain Π_1 the isomorphism with domain of state transformers is well known. In Section 6 we will extend this duality by showing that Π_2 is isomorphic to the metric resumption domain Σ_2. The main purpose of establishing such a relationship is to explain the correspondence of *refinement* in predicate transformer semantics and *simulation* in state transformer semantics. We close the paper with a section of concluding remarks and future work.

2 Preliminaries

Below in Section 4 a domain of metric predicate transformers is constructed on which, a weakest precondition semantics will be based. The domain is given by an equation of the form $X = F(X)$. The solution of the quation will be a complete metric space. In [AR89] the full theory is given; here, we will only sketch the main ideas. We will use operators $F(\cdot)$ of the form

$$F(\cdot) ::= \mathcal{S} \mid \tfrac{1}{2}(\cdot) \mid \mathit{op1}(F(\cdot)) \mid F(\cdot)\ \mathit{op2}\ F(\cdot),$$

where $\mathcal{S}$ is a set, $\mathit{op1} \in \{\mathcal{P}_{co}, \mathcal{S} \rightarrow\}$ and $\mathit{op2} \in \{\times, +\}$. An equation is formed by choosing a variable X, say. The left-hand side of the equation is then the variable X and the right-hand side is obtained by 'filling' the operator $F(\cdot)$ with this variable, yielding $F(X)$.

Since we want to obtain a complete metric space as solution, we have to interpret the symbols over the class of complete metric spaces as well. Before we give this interpretation, consider the equation

$$X = \mathcal{S} \rightarrow (\mathcal{P}_{co}(\mathcal{S} + (\mathcal{S} \times \tfrac{1}{2}(X))))$$

and assume that the complete metric space Σ is its solution. Intuitively, an element of Σ is a function which takes as input an element of S and yields a compact set of elements of $\mathcal{S}$ or pairs of elements of $\mathcal{S}$ with elements of Σ. The factor $\frac{1}{2}$ is added to guarantee solvability of the domain equation and will only affect the distance on the domain, but not the elements itself.

As articulation of the above example we give next the interpretation of the basic operators.

(i) The set $\mathcal{S}$ can be turned into a complete metric space using the discrete metric.

(ii) Given a complete metric space M, the complete metric space $\frac{1}{2}(M)$ is the same as M but with all distances divided by two.

(iii) The operators of arity 1 take either compact subsets ($\mathcal{P}_{co}$) or construct a function space ($\mathcal{S} \rightarrow$). The Hausdorff distance on (compact) sets is defined by

$$d_H(A, B) = \inf\{\epsilon \mid (\forall a \in A.\ \exists b \in B.\ d(a, b) \leq \epsilon) \ \&\ \text{symm.}\}$$

with the convention that $\inf(\emptyset) = 1$. The function space $\mathcal{S} \rightarrow M$ is endowed with the metric of pointwise convergence given by

$$d_F(f, g) = \sup\{d(f(s), g(s)) \mid s \in \mathcal{S}\},$$

for $f, g \in \mathcal{S} \rightarrow M$.

(iv) As to the operators with two arguments: '$\times$' is the Cartesian product of two complete metric spaces (taking the maximum of the two distances), and '+' is the disjoint union of two complete metric spaces (points have distance 1 if they come from different summands, and have the original distance otherwise).

Below in Section 4, we will define a new operator that can be used in domain equations. Indeed we will use it to define a domain of metric predicate transformers for the semantics of the language $\mathcal{L}_2$ presented in the next section.

3 Two languages with recursion

In this section we define the two languages $\mathcal{L}_1$ and $\mathcal{L}_2$. The language $\mathcal{L}_1$ is a variation of a language for which the weakest precondition semantics is well known (see [Dij76]). The compositional weakest precondition semantics for the language $\mathcal{L}_2$, which incorporates a parallel operator, constitutes the main contribution of the present paper.

The basic building blocks are elements of the sets $(v \in) IVar$ of individual variables, $(e \in) Exp$ of expressions, $(b \in) BExp$ of boolean expressions, and $(x \in) PVar$ of procedure variables. For a fixed set of values Val, the set of states $(s, t \in) \mathcal{S}$ is given by $\mathcal{S} = IVar \rightarrow Val$. Also, we postulate valuations

$$\mathcal{E}\colon Exp \rightarrow \mathcal{S} \rightarrow Val \text{ and } \mathcal{B}\colon BExp \rightarrow \mathcal{S} \rightarrow \{tt, f\!f\}.$$

First we introduce the sequential language $\mathcal{L}_1$. Below, the conditional $b\rightarrow$ deadlocks in a state in which the boolean expression b does not evaluate to true, and acts as a skip otherwise. The demonic choice executes one of its components.

(The adjective 'demonic' refers to the game-theoretic point of view of angels vs. demons, where the latter will always make those choices that —if possible— leads away from termination.) The intended meaning of the other constructs is as usual.

3.1. Definition. (i) The set $(S \in)$ $Stat_1$ of *statements* is given by

$$S ::= v := e \mid b\!\rightarrow \mid x \mid S;S \mid S \square S .$$

(ii) The set $(G \in)$ $GStat_1$ of *guarded statements* is given by

$$G ::= v := e \mid b\!\rightarrow \mid G;S \mid G \square G .$$

(iii) The set $(d \in)$ $Decl_1$ is defined by $Decl_1 = PVar \rightarrow GStat_1$.
(iv) The language $\mathcal{L}_1$ is given by $Decl_1 \times Stat_1$.

Dijkstra's guarded commands can be simulated in $\mathcal{L}_1$. Indeed, following [Hes88], the guarded command $b\!\rightarrow S$ is equivalent in $\mathcal{L}_1$—in the sense that they have the same meaning—to $b\!\rightarrow ;S$, the conditional command **if** $b\!\rightarrow S$ **fi** corresponds in $\mathcal{L}_1$ to the procedure variable x declared as $d(x) = (b\!\rightarrow ;S)\square(\neg b\!\rightarrow ;x)$, and the iteration command **do** $b \rightarrow S$ **od** is equivalent to the procedure variable x declared as $d(x) = (b \rightarrow ;(S;x))\square\neg b \rightarrow$. Other derived statements are $skip = \mathbf{true}\!\rightarrow$, $magic = \mathbf{false}\!\rightarrow$, and $div = x$ where $d(x) = \mathbf{false}\!\rightarrow ;x$, and $\{b\} = x$ where $d(x) = b\!\rightarrow \square(\neg b\!\rightarrow ;x)$.

Note that, though resembling in their name, the guarded *statements* in Definition 3.1 and elsewhere in the paper are different—both syntactically and as to their intended usage— from Dijkstra's guarded *commands*. The declarations $d \in Decl_1$ associate a procedure body to each procedure variable x. For technical reasons (obtaining contractivity of higher-order transformations) we restrict procedure bodies to guarded statements.

Next we add the parallel composition '$\|$' to the language $\mathcal{L}_1$ obtaining $\mathcal{L}_2$. A simple form of atomization is also present in order to facilitate synchronization. The parallel composition then is the interleaving of the *atomic* steps of its two components.

3.2. Definition. (i) The set $(A \in)$ $AStat_2$ of *atomic statements* is given by

$$A ::= v := e \mid b\!\rightarrow \mid A;A \mid A \square A .$$

(ii) The set $(S \in)$ $Stat_2$ of *statements* is given by

$$S ::= [A] \mid x \mid S;S \mid S \square S \mid S \| S .$$

(iii) The set $(G \in)$ $GStat_2$ of *guarded statements* is given by

$$G ::= [A] \mid G;S \mid G \square G \mid G \| G .$$

(iv) The set $(d \in)$ $Decl_2$ is defined by $Decl_2 = PVar \rightarrow GStat_2$.
(v) The language $\mathcal{L}_2$ is given by $Decl_2 \times Stat_2$.

Atomic statements are sequential nondeterministic statements which always terminate. Their execution may not be interrupted by any other process. In order to distinguish atomic sequential composition and atomic choice on the one hand, with the ordinary sequential composition and choice on the other we use brackets [,] around atomic statements.

Consider, for example, the statements $S_1 \equiv [v{:} = 1; v{:} = v + 1] \| [v{:} = 0]$ and $S_2 \equiv ([v{:} = 1];[v{:} = v + 1]) \| [v{:} = 0]$. They are not equivalent since for a given initial state s, after the execution of S_1 the value of the variable v is either 0 or 2 while after the execution of S_2 the value of v is one of 0, 1 or 2. Clearly, the language $\mathcal{L}_1$ can be considered a sublanguage of $\mathcal{L}_2$ (after an obvious renaming of the parentheses).

In $\mathcal{L}_2$, synchronization and communication by shared variables can be implemented using semaphores: Let $v \in \mathit{IVar}$ and $P_v, V_v \in \mathit{PVar}$ be declared as follows

$$d(P_v) = [v = 0 \rightarrow ; v{:} = 1] \Box ([v \neq 0 \rightarrow]; P_v)$$
$$d(V_v) = [v{:} = 0]$$

Now, assuming that v is an auxiliary program variable for S_1 and S_2, in the program

$$\langle d, ([v{:} = 1]; ((S_1; V_v) \| (P_v; S_2))) \rangle$$

the statement S_2 can be executed only after the execution of the statement S_1; in the program $\langle d, ([v{:} = 0]; ((P_v; S_1; V_v) \| (P_v; S_2; V_v))) \rangle$ the execution of S_1 and of S_2 are mutually exclusive.

The conditional delay **await** b can be expressed in $\mathcal{L}_2$ by a procedure variable x declared as $[b \rightarrow] \Box ([\neg b \rightarrow]; x)$: in a state where b is evaluated to false, the computation loops busy waiting for some other process which possibly will change the state. Note that this definition of **await** b coincides with the definition of $\{b\}$ for $\mathcal{L}_1$. However, the intended meaning of the two conditionals $\{b\}$ and **await** b is the same in a state where b evaluates to true, while if b evaluates to false then $\{b\}$ can evolve to any computation and **await** b will loop until b becomes satisfied. In the setting of $\mathcal{L}_1$ the two commands will be identified. In a more detailed process description they should obtain different meanings.

4 Domains for predicate transformers

In this section we introduce two domains of predicate transformers, Π_1 and Π_2, for the respective languages given in Section 3.

4.1. Definition. (i) Let S and M be two sets. A *predicate transformer* over M and S is a function $\pi \in \mathcal{P}(M) \rightarrow \mathcal{P}(S)$. It is called *conjunctive* if $\pi(\bigcap \mathcal{X}) = \bigcap\{\pi(Q) \mid Q \in \mathcal{X}\}$ for all non-empty $\mathcal{X} \subseteq \mathcal{P}(M)$. A predicate transformer π is called *continuous* if $\pi(\bigcup \mathcal{D}) = \bigcup\{\pi(Q) \mid Q \in \mathcal{D}\}$ for all $\subseteq$-directed $\mathcal{D} \subseteq \mathcal{P}(M)$.

(ii) For the set of states $\mathcal{S}$ introduced in the previous section, define Π_1 as the domain of all conjunctive and continuous predicate transformers in $\mathcal{P}(\mathcal{S}) \rightarrow \mathcal{P}(\mathcal{S})$, ordered by the pointwise extension of the subset order, that is, $\pi_1 \sqsubseteq \pi_2$ if and only if $\pi_1(Q) \subseteq \pi_2(Q)$ for all $Q \subseteq \mathcal{S}$.

Next we want to define the domain Π_2. This domain is obtained as the solution of a domain equation. Some preparatory steps are necessary.

We use the distance to identify specific predicates: open sets are the observable predicates of a metric space M. Their collection is denoted by $\mathcal{O}(M)$. The intuition of an open set $o \in \mathcal{O}(M)$ is that it represents a predicate in which we cannot distinguish with finite information a point $x \in o$ from all other points y closer to x than some distance ϵ.

4.2. Definition. Let S be a set and (M, d) be a metric space. An *observable predicate transformer* over M and S is a function $\pi \in \mathcal{P}(M) \to \mathcal{P}(S)$ such that

(i) it is *multiplicative*, that is, for all $\mathcal{X} \subseteq \mathcal{P}(M)$

$$\pi(\bigcap \mathcal{X}) = \bigcap\{\pi(Q) \mid Q \in \mathcal{X}\};$$

(ii) it is *open-continuous*, that is, for all directed $\mathcal{D} \subseteq \mathcal{O}(M)$

$$\pi(\bigcup \mathcal{D}) = \bigcup\{\pi(Q) \mid Q \in \mathcal{D}\}.$$

We denote the set of all observable predicate transformers over M and S by $OPT(M, S)$.

For a complete metric space (M, d) we obtain the complete metric space $OPT(M, S)$ using a *backward* distance: for $\pi_1, \pi_2 \in OPT(M, S)$ we put

$$d(\pi_1, \pi_2) = \sup\{d_H(\{P \mid s \in \pi_1(P)\}, \{P \mid s \in \pi_2(P)\}) \mid s \in S\},$$

where d_H on the right-hand side denotes the Hausdorff distance for $\mathcal{P}(\mathcal{P}(M))$.

The domain Π_2 of metric predicate transformers is given by an equation involving the operator $OPT(\cdot, \mathcal{S})$. (In [BKV94] it is shown that $OPT(\cdot, \mathcal{S})$ is a locally contractive functor in the category of complete metric spaces.)

4.3. Definition. The complete metric space $(\pi \in)\, \Pi_2$ is given by

$$\Pi_2 = OPT(\mathcal{S} + (\mathcal{S} \times \tfrac{1}{2}(\Pi_2)), \mathcal{S}),$$

for the set of states $\mathcal{S}$ introduced in the previous section.

Predicate transformers in Π_2 are multiplicative and open-continuous functions in $\mathcal{P}(\mathcal{S} + \mathcal{S} \times \frac{1}{2}(\Pi_2)) \to \mathcal{P}(\mathcal{S})$. The intuition behind an element $\pi \in \Pi_2$ is as follows. Given a set P it yields the set of all states such that when execution starts in one of these states, it either terminates in an $s \in P$, or it makes a first (atomic) step to a state s, with $\langle s, \pi' \rangle \in P$, passes an interleaving point, and executes further according to the predicate transformer π'.

Though we have not yet given a formal semantic mapping from syntax to the domain, the following example might help the reader. Consider, on the one hand, the statement $[x := 1];[y := 2]$. According to Definition 5.5 below, the corresponding metric predicate transformer π is

$$\pi(P) = \{s \mid \langle s[1/x], \pi' \rangle \in P\},$$

with the obvious meaning for $s[1/x]$, and π' (the semantics of $[y := 2]$) such that

$$\pi'(P) = \{s \mid s[2/y] \in P\}.$$

If we consider, on the other hand, the atomic version $[x := 1; y := 2]$ (in which the interleaving point is not present) then we have as corresponding predicate transformer

$$\rho(P) = \{s \mid s[1/x] \in \pi'(P)\} = \{s \mid s[1/x][2/y] \in P\}.$$

The domain Π_2 allows a refinement relation, generalizing the familiar notion of refinement in the setting of Π_1. It will turn out in Section 6, that this refinement is dual to simulation for state transformers.

4.4. Definition. A refinement relation R is a binary relation on Π_2 such that $(\pi, \rho) \in R$ implies

$$\forall P.\ \pi(P) \subseteq \rho(\{s \in \mathcal{S} \mid s \in P\} \cup \{\langle s, \rho' \rangle \mid \exists \langle s, \pi' \rangle \in P.\ (\pi', \rho') \in R\}).$$

We say 'π is refined by ρ', notation $\pi \trianglelefteq \rho$, if there exists a refinement relation R containing (π, ρ).

With abuse of language, we refer to '$\trianglelefteq$' as the refinement relation. The basic idea is that a refinement reduces the non-determinacy. In the case of standard predicate transformers, this implies that the number of initial states increases (for a given fixed postcondition, the weakest precondition becomes weaker): for standard predicate transformers in Π_1 we require

$$\pi \trianglelefteq \rho \iff \forall P \in \mathcal{P}(S).\ \pi(P) \subseteq \rho(P).$$

Could we have taken a similar definition for the domain Π_2? The answer is no, as is shown by the following example. Consider the statements

$$[x := 1];([y := 1]\Box[y := 2]) \text{ and } [x := 1];[y := 1].$$

We want to have that the first statement is refined by the second. Based on the definitions given in Section 5, we obtain as predicate transformer for $[y := 1]\Box[y := 2]$:

$$\pi'(P) = \{s \mid s[1/y] \in P \;\&\; s[2/y] \in P\}.$$

As predicate transformer for the statement $[x := 1];([y := 1]\Box[y := 2])$ we have $\pi(P) = \{s \mid \langle s[1/x], \pi' \rangle \in P\}$; for $[y := 1]$ we have $\rho'(P) = \{s \mid s[1/y] \in P\}$; and for $[x := 1];[y := 1]$ we have $\rho(P) = \{s \mid \langle s[1/x], \rho' \rangle \in P\}$. If we take (for a fixed s) $P = \{\langle s[1/x], \pi' \rangle\}$ then $\pi(P) = \{s[\alpha/x] \mid \alpha \in \mathit{Val}\}$ and $\rho(P) = \emptyset$. Hence $\pi(P)$ is not a subset of $\rho(P)$.

Now we can identify the problem: we have to add all pairs $\langle s[1/x], \pi'' \rangle$, with π'' a refinement of π', to the argument of ρ, such that ρ can pick $\langle s[1/x], \rho' \rangle$. This explains Definition 4.4 above.

5 Predicate Transformer Semantics

Preparatory to the semantics of the two languages, we introduce the predicates $P[e/v]$ and $b\!\rightarrow P$ obtained from a predicate P.

5.1. Definition. The operations '$(\cdot)[e/v]$' and '$b\!\rightarrow (\cdot)$' are given by

$$\begin{aligned} P[e/v] &= \{s \in \mathcal{S} \mid s[\alpha/v] \in P, \alpha = \mathcal{E}(e)(s)\} \\ b\!\rightarrow P &= \{s \in \mathcal{S} \mid \mathcal{B}(b)(s) \Rightarrow s \in P\}. \end{aligned}$$

In fact, the definition above is parametric, in that P will range over Π_1 and Π_2. The definitions, however, are conceptually the same, and therefore gathered here. Further, on Π_1, we have the usual operators ';' and '$\Box$'.

5.2. Definition. The operators ';' and '$\Box$' on Π_1 are given by

$$\begin{aligned} (\pi_1;\pi_2)(P) &= \pi_1(\pi_2(P)), \\ (\pi_1\Box\pi_2)(P) &= \pi_1(P) \cap \pi_2(P). \end{aligned}$$

Well-definedness of ';' and '$\Box$' is straightforward. The weakest precondition semantics wp_1 for $\mathcal{L}_1$ can now be given.

5.3. Definition. The weakest precondition semantics $wp_1[\![\cdot]\!]{:}\mathcal{L}_1 \rightarrow \Pi_1$ is given by

$$\begin{aligned} wp_1[\![\langle d, v := e\rangle]\!] &= \lambda P.\, P[e/v], \\ wp_1[\![\langle d, b\!\rightarrow\rangle]\!] &= \lambda P.\, b\!\rightarrow P, \\ wp_1[\![\langle d, x\rangle]\!] &= wp_1[\![\langle d, d(x)\rangle]\!], \\ wp_1[\![\langle d, [S_1;S_2]\rangle]\!] &= wp_1[\![\langle d, S_1\rangle]\!];wp_1[\![\langle d, S_2]\!]\rangle, \\ wp_1[\![\langle d, [S_1\Box S_2]\rangle]\!] &= wp_1[\![\langle d, S_1\rangle]\!]\Box wp_1[\![\langle d, S_2\rangle]\!]. \end{aligned}$$

The above semantics for $\mathcal{L}_1$ is well-known including the separate treatment of tests $b\!\rightarrow$. In [BKV94] the semantics is justified employing an higher-order transformation.

We next turn to the predicate transformer semantics for $\mathcal{L}_2$. As $\mathcal{L}_2$ can be considered an extension of $\mathcal{L}_1$ we will base our present semantics on wp_1. However, the presence of the parallel operator '$\|$' in $\mathcal{L}_2$ invokes, when insisting on a compositional treatment, the branching domain Π_2. In this domain interleaving points are explicitly represented. This complicates the definitions of the operators on predicate transformers in Π_2 which reflect the constructions available in $\mathcal{L}_2$.

5.4. Definition. The operators ';', '+' and '$\|$' on Π_2 are given by

$$\begin{aligned} (\pi_1;\pi_2)(P) &= \pi_1(\{s \mid \langle s,\pi_2\rangle \in P\} \cup \{\langle s,\rho\rangle \mid \langle s,\rho;\pi_2\rangle \in P\}), \\ (\pi_1\Box\pi_2)(P) &= \pi_1(P) \cap \pi_2(P), \\ (\pi_1\|\pi_2)(P) &= \pi_1(\{s \mid \langle s,\pi_2\rangle \in P\} \cup \{\langle s,\rho\rangle \mid \langle s,\rho\|\pi_2\rangle \in P\}) \cap \\ &\qquad \pi_2(\{s \mid \langle s,\pi_1\rangle \in P\} \cup \{\langle s,\rho\rangle \mid \langle s,\pi_1\|\rho\rangle \in P\}). \end{aligned}$$

Well-definedness of '$\Box$' is clear. Well-definedness of the other mappings can be supported by higher-order transformations. Based on the $\mathcal{L}_1$-semantics wp_1 and the operators just given we are now ready to present the semantics wp_2 for $\mathcal{L}_2$.

5.5. Definition. The weakest precondition semantics wp_2 is the unique function in $\mathcal{L}_2 \to \Pi_2$ satisfying

$$\begin{aligned}
wp_2[\![\langle d, [A]\rangle]\!] &= \lambda P.\, wp_1[\![\langle \hat{d}, A\rangle]\!](P \cap \mathcal{S}),\\
wp_2[\![\langle d, x\rangle]\!] &= wp_2[\![\langle d, d(x)\rangle]\!],\\
wp_2[\![\langle d, (S_1;S_2)\rangle]\!] &= wp_2[\![\langle d, S_1\rangle]\!];wp_2[\![\langle d, S_2\rangle]\!],\\
wp_2[\![\langle d, S_1 \Box S_2\rangle]\!] &= wp_2[\![\langle d, S_1\rangle]\!]\Box wp_2[\![\langle d, S_2\rangle]\!],\\
wp_2[\![\langle d, S_1 \,\|\, S_2\rangle]\!] &= wp_2[\![\langle d, S_1\rangle]\!] \,\|\, wp_2[\![\langle d, S_2\rangle]\!]
\end{aligned}$$

where $\hat{d}$ is some arbitrary declaration in $Decl_1$.

Some remarks are in order here. First, justification of the definition can be obtained by another application of the higher-order transformation technique. The construction makes essential use of the guardedness of procedure bodies.

Second, the invocation of wp_1 enforces the restriction of $P \in \mathcal{P}(\mathcal{S} + \mathcal{S} \times \Pi_2)$ to $(P \cap \mathcal{S}) \in \mathcal{P}(\mathcal{S})$. Also the declaration $d \in Decl_2$, needs to be adapted to a declaration $\hat{d} \in Decl_1$. However, since the atomic statements A do not contain procedure variables, any declaration in $Decl_1$ will do.

The usage of the input/output semantics wp_1 for atomic statements A is intuitively clear. No interleaving possibilities are provided during execution of such atomic command (whence their name). This explains the contrast between the two sequential compositions $[A_1;A_2]$ and $S_1;S_2$:

$$\begin{aligned}
wp_1[\![\langle d, [A_1;A_2]\rangle]\!] &: \mathcal{P}(\mathcal{S}) \to \mathcal{P}(\mathcal{S}),\\
wp_2[\![\langle d, S_1;S_2\rangle]\!] &: \mathcal{P}(\mathcal{S} + \mathcal{S} \times \Pi_2) \to \mathcal{P}(\mathcal{S}),
\end{aligned}$$

the former denying, the latter allowing interleaving with the environment.

Let us, for the moment consider some examples, especially involving the parallel operator, to illustrate the semantics wp_2. The sequential statement $[x := 1];[y := 2]$ will act as the first example. Maybe surprisingly we will obtain for the predicate

$$P = \{s \mid s(x) = 1 \;\&\; s(y) = 2\}$$

that $wp_2[\![x := 1;y := 2]\!](P) = \emptyset$ (for some fixed, but arbitrary and suppressed declaration d). Let us write π_1, π_2 for $wp_2[\![[x := 1]]\!]$, $wp_2[\![[y := 2]]\!]$, respectively. We then have

$$\begin{aligned}
&wp_2[\![[x := 1];[y := 2]]\!](P)\\
&= (\pi_1;\pi_2)(P)\\
&= \pi_1(\{s \mid \langle s, \pi_2\rangle \in P\} \cup \{\langle s, \rho\rangle \mid \langle s, \rho;\pi_2\rangle \in P\})\\
&= \{s \mid \langle s[1/x], \pi_2\rangle \in P\}\\
&= \emptyset.
\end{aligned}$$

The point is that P only allows *immediately* terminating computations, whereas the sequential composition also has one intermediate state as reflected in the pair $\langle s[1/x], \pi_2\rangle$. Since, in general at the specification level, one will be indifferent as to how a final state will be reached, we can incorporate such pairs as $\langle s[1/x], \pi_2\rangle$ in the predicate. So the predicate P has to be 'saturated'—enhanced with pairs representing the same input/output information—to accommodate for composite elements in $\mathcal{S} + \mathcal{S} \times \Pi_2$. We want the saturation P^* to satisfy

$$P^* = P \cup \{\langle s, \rho\rangle \mid s \in \rho(P^*)\}.$$

Hence P^* consists of elements of P and those pairs $\langle s, \rho\rangle$ for which s is appropriate in that it will lead to P^* following ρ. The predicate P^* can be given by

$$P_1 = P,\ P_{k+1} = P_k \cup \{\langle s, \rho\rangle \mid s \in \rho(P_k)\},\ P^* = \textstyle\bigcup_k P_k.$$

Turning back to the example for $[x := 1];[y := 2]$ we now calculate the semantics for P^*.

$$\begin{aligned}
&wp_2[\![[x := 1];[y := 2]]\!](P^*)\\
&= (\pi_1;\pi_2)(P^*)\\
&= \pi_1(\{s \mid \langle s, \pi_2\rangle \in P^*\} \cup \{\langle s, \rho\rangle \mid \langle s, \rho;\pi_2\rangle \in P^*\})\\
&= \dots\\
&= \mathcal{S},
\end{aligned}$$

which is the result to be expected.

Let us use, for the next example, $\pi_{1,..,k}$ to denote the left associated parallel composition of $\pi_1, \dots, \pi_k$, the shorthand $\pi^r_{1,..,k}$ (with $1 \leq r \leq k$) for $\pi_{1,..,k}$ but leaving out the operand π_r, and $\hat{\pi}^r_{1,..,k}$ for $\pi_{1,..,k}$ but now replacing the operand π_r by the predicate transformer ρ. We then have

$$\pi_{1,..,k}(P) = \bigcap_{r=1}^{k} \pi_r(\{s \mid \langle s, \pi^r_{1,..,k}\rangle \in P\} \cup \{\langle s, \rho\rangle \mid \langle s, \hat{\pi}^r_{1,..,k}\rangle \in P\}). \qquad (1)$$

Equation (1) can be verified by a straightforward inductive argument using the various definitions.

Now, as a more involved and likely more interesting application of the semantics wp_2, we treat the so-called accumulator example (cf. [US93])

$$[x := x + 2^0] \| [x := x + 2^1] \| \dots \| [x := x + 2^n].$$

We want to calculate the weakest precondition for $P = \{s \mid s(x) = 2^{n+1}\}$. As discussed already, we first have to saturate the predicate yielding

$$P^* = \{s \mid s(x) = 2^{n+1}\} \cup \{\langle s, \rho\rangle \mid s \in \rho(P^*)\}.$$

Let, for convenience, $\pi_i = wp_2[\![x := x + 2^i]\!]$. So, we are heading, under the notational conventions given above, for $\pi_{0,..,n}(P^*)$. First we establish, for $0 \leq i_1 < \ldots < i_k \leq n$, the equation

$$\pi_{i_1,..,i_k}(P^*) = \{s \mid s(x) + \sum_{r=1}^{k} 2^{i_r} = 2^{n+1}\}, \tag{2}$$

by induction on k. We leave the base case, $k = 1$, to the reader. For the induction step, $k + 1$ we will employ equation (1).

$$\begin{array}{ll} \pi_{i_1,..,i_{k+1}}(P^*) & \\ = \bigcap_{r=1}^{k+1} \pi_{i_r}(\{s \mid \langle s, \pi^{i_r}_{i_1,..,i_{k+1}}\rangle \in P^*\} \cup \{\langle s, \rho\rangle \mid \langle s, \hat{\pi}^{i_r}_{i_1,..,i_{k+1}}\rangle \in P^*\}) & \\ & \text{[equality (1)]} \\ = \bigcap_{r=1}^{k+1} \{s \mid \langle s\{\, s(x) + 2^{i_r}/x\,\}, \pi^{i_r}_{i_1,..,i_{k+1}}\rangle \in P^*\} & \text{[definition } \pi_{i_r}] \\ = \bigcap_{r=1}^{k+1} \{s \mid s\{\, s(x) + 2^{i_r}/x\,\} \in \pi^{i_r}_{i_1,..,i_{k+1}}(P^*)\} & \text{[definition } P^*] \\ = \bigcap_{r=1}^{k+1} \{s \mid (s(x) + 2^{i_r}) + (\sum_{q=1, q\neq r}^{k+1} 2^{i_q}) = 2^{n+1}\} & \text{[induction hypothesis]} \\ = \bigcap_{r=1}^{k+1} \{s \mid s(x) + (\sum_{q=1}^{k+1} 2^{i_q}) = 2^{n+1}\} & \text{[independence of } r] \\ = \{s \mid s(x) + (\sum_{q=1}^{k+1} 2^{i_q}) = 2^{n+1}\}. & \end{array}$$

From equation (2) we immediately derive

$$\pi_{1,..,n}(P^*) = \{s \mid s(x) + (\textstyle\sum_{i=1}^{n} 2^i) = 2^{n+1}\} = \{s \mid s(x) = 1\}.$$

This concludes the examples for the predicate transformer semantics wp_2.

6 Refinement, simulation and state transformers

The refinement relation given in Definition 4.4 is closely related to the notion of simulation for transition systems in a sense that we will explain below. The relationship will be based on two isomorphisms between the predicate transformer domains, Π_1 and Π_2, and the state transformers domains Σ_1 and Σ_2. The domain Σ_1 is based on the Smyth power domain, while the domain Σ_2 is a (variation of) the metric resumption domain of De Bakker and Zucker [BZ82]. We start with the definition of the Smyth power domain.

6.1. Definition. Let $\mathcal{S}$ be a set of states and let $\mathcal{S}_\perp$ be the set $\mathcal{S} \cup \{\perp\}$. The Smyth power domain of $\mathcal{S}_\perp$ is defined as the set

$$\mathcal{SP}_{co}(\mathcal{S}_\perp) = \{A \mid A \subseteq \mathcal{S} \,\&\, A \text{ finite }\} \cup \{\mathcal{S}_\perp\}$$

ordered by the superset order.

The state transformer domain Σ_1 is given by $\Sigma_1 = \mathcal{S} \to \mathcal{SP}_{co}(\mathcal{S}_\perp)$. It is ordered by pointwise extension of the superset ordering on the Smyth power domain. Now, statements are viewed as functions. Values in $\mathcal{P}(\mathcal{S})$ represent the results of terminating non-deterministic computations, while the divergent computations are mapped to $\mathcal{S}_\perp$. The empty set is interpreted as deadlock.

On Σ_1 we have the usual operations ';' and '□'.

6.2. Definition. Define the operators ';' and '□' on Σ_1 by

$$(\sigma_1;\sigma_2)(s) = \begin{cases} \bigcup\{\sigma_2(t) \mid t \in \sigma_1(s)\} & \text{if } \sigma_1(s) \neq \mathcal{S}_\perp \text{ and } \forall t \in \sigma_1(s).\ \sigma_2(t) \neq \mathcal{S}_\perp \\ \mathcal{S}_\perp & \text{otherwise.} \end{cases}$$

$$(\sigma_1 \Box \sigma_2)(s) = \sigma_1(s) \cup \sigma_2(s).$$

The relationship between predicate transformers in Π_1 and the state transformers in Σ_1 is well-known being a variation of the result in [Plo79]:

6.3. Theorem. *There is an order-isomorphism* $pt\colon \Sigma_1 \to \Pi_1$. *Moreover,*
(i) $pt(\sigma_1;\sigma_2) = pt(\sigma_1);pt(\sigma_2)$,
(ii) $pt(\sigma_1 \Box \sigma_2) = pt(\sigma_1)\Box pt(\sigma_2)$.

The refinement relation is defined in [Bac80] for the domain Π_1. It coincides with pointwise extension of the subset order in $\mathcal{P}(S)$. Since the isomorphism $pt\colon \Sigma_1 \to \Pi_1$ is an order isomorphism, the above theorem gives also a state transformer representation of Back's refinement relation: the pointwise extension of the order of the Smyth power domain. Turning back to the isomorphism between state and predicate transformers, we define Σ_2 as a variation of the domain introduced in [BZ82]. Let S be a set of states and consider the domain Σ_2 given as the unique (up to isometries) solution of the domain equation

$$X = \mathcal{S} \to (\mathcal{P}_{co}(\mathcal{S} + \mathcal{S} \times \tfrac{1}{2}(X))).$$

The intuition behind the above domain is as follows: statements are functions which deliver for each input state a set consisting of output states and/or pairs composed of the output after one atomic computation step together with a function representing the rest of the computation. The domain Σ_2 comes equipped with the following operations (cf. [BZ82]).

6.4. Definition. The operators ';', '□' and '‖' on Σ_2 are given by

$$\begin{aligned} \sigma_1;\sigma_2(s) &= \{\langle t, \sigma_2\rangle \mid t \in \sigma_1(s)\} \cup \{\langle t, \tau;\sigma_2\rangle \mid \langle t, \tau\rangle \in \sigma_1(s)\}, \\ \sigma_1 \Box \sigma_2(s) &= \sigma_1(s) \cup \sigma_2(s), \\ \sigma_1 \| \sigma_2(s) &= \{\langle t, \sigma_2\rangle \mid t \in \sigma_1(s)\} \cup \{\langle t, \tau \| \sigma_2\rangle \mid \langle t, \tau\rangle \in \sigma_1(s)\} \cup \\ &\quad\ \{\langle t, \sigma_1\rangle \mid t \in \sigma_2(s)\} \cup \{\langle t, \sigma_1 \| \tau\rangle \mid \langle t, \tau\rangle \in \sigma_2(s)\}, \end{aligned}$$

for $\sigma_1, \sigma_2 \in \Sigma_2$ and $s \in \mathcal{S}$.

On the basis of the duality results between state and predicate transformers in [BK94] we can formulate (see [BKV94] for a proof) the relationship between Σ_2 and Π_2: the two domains are isomorphic. However, the isomorphism is here not an order-isomorphism as for pt from the complete partial order Σ_1 to the complete partial order Π_1, but an isometry from the complete metric space Σ_2 to the complete metric space Π_2 .

6.5. Theorem. *There is a isometry* $pt\colon \Sigma_2 \to \Pi_2$ *such that*
(i) $pt(\sigma_1;\sigma_2) = pt(\sigma_1);pt(\sigma_2)$,

(ii) $pt(\sigma_1 \Box \sigma_2) = pt(\sigma_1) \Box pt(\sigma_2)$,
(iii) $pt(\sigma_1 \| \sigma_2) = pt(\sigma_1) \| pt(\sigma_2)$.

A few steps are still necessary for relating refinement with simulation. First of all notice that the domain Σ_2 can be seen as the transition system $\rightarrow \subseteq (\mathcal{S} \times \Sigma_2) \times ((\mathcal{S} \times \Sigma_2) \cup \mathcal{S})$ where $\langle s, \sigma \rangle \rightarrow \theta$ if $\theta \in \sigma(s)$. This is an instance of the so-called 'processes as terms' paradigm. For Σ_2, interpreted as a transition system, the notion of (backward) simulation is given in the following definition.

6.6. Definition. A relation $R \subseteq \Sigma_2 \times \Sigma_2$ is called a (backward) simulation if for all $(\sigma, \tau) \in R$ and for all $s \in \mathcal{S}$
(i) if $t \in \tau(s)$ then $t \in \sigma(s)$,
(ii) if $\langle t, \tau' \rangle \in \tau(s)$ then there exists $\langle t, \sigma' \rangle \in \sigma(s)$ such that $(\sigma', \tau') \in R$.
We say that a state transformer σ simulates τ—denoted by $\sigma \trianglelefteq \tau$—if there exists a simulation relation R with $(\sigma, \tau) \in R$.

We refer to the paper [LV93] for a survey on simulation for transition systems. Intuitively, a state transformer σ simulates τ if, for all input states s, every computation of $\tau(s)$ can be performed by $\sigma(s)$, preserving all the output states of the atomic steps of the computation. Notice that this not only implies that all the interleaving states are preserved, but also the branching structure. Of special interest for concurrency is the notion of bisimulation for transition systems. If we look at (backward) simulation as a recursively-defined superset order, then bisimulation is a recursively-defined equality.

6.7. Definition. A relation $R \subseteq \Sigma_2 \times \Sigma_2$ is called a (strong) bisimulation if for all $(\sigma, \tau) \in R$ and for all $s \in \mathcal{S}$
(i) $t \in \tau(s)$ if and only if $t \in \sigma(s)$;
(ii) if $\langle t, \tau' \rangle \in \tau(s)$ then there exists $\langle t, \sigma' \rangle \in \sigma(s)$ such that $(\sigma', \tau') \in R$;
(iii) if $\langle t, \sigma' \rangle \in \sigma(s)$ then there exists $\langle t, \tau' \rangle \in \tau(s)$ such that $(\sigma', \tau') \in R$.
Two state transformers σ and τ are strongly bisimilar —denoted by $\sigma \underline{\leftrightarrow} \tau$—if there exists a bisimulation relation R such that $(\sigma, \tau) \in R$.

Clearly, if $\sigma \underline{\leftrightarrow} \tau$ then $\sigma \trianglelefteq \tau$ and $\tau \trianglelefteq \sigma$. However the converse is not true (see [BKV94]).

We are now ready to state the relationships between simulation and refinement. Though expressed in two different domains, the two notions coincide. The following theorem additionally gives a representation of bisimulation as equality in the domain Σ_2. Since Π_2 is isomorphic to Σ_2 we have, as corollary, a representation of bisimulation for predicate transformers in Π_2. As far as we know, this is novel in the context of predicate transformers.

6.8. Theorem. *Let $\sigma, \tau \in \Sigma_2$. Then*
(i) $\sigma \trianglelefteq \tau$ *if and only if* $pt(\sigma) \trianglelefteq pt(\tau)$;
(ii) $\sigma \underline{\leftrightarrow} \tau$ *if and only if* $\sigma = \tau$;
(iii) $\sigma \underline{\leftrightarrow} \tau$ *if and only if* $pt(\sigma) = pt(\tau)$.

Employing the theory developed here, one could easily give some refinement axioms and rules for the language $\mathcal{L}_2$. For an example of a sound refinement calculus we again refer the reader to the complete paper [BKV94]. It is however an open problem how to establish a completeness result in a context with assignment and test.

7 Concluding Remarks

In this paper we have proposed a compositional weakest precondition semantics for a parallel language with recursion. The semantics is based on a new metric resumption domain obtained from a domain equation involving a functor for 'observable' predicates. For this domain a notion of refinement is defined, extending the familiar refinement relation for the sequential non-deterministic case. By establishing a duality between the semantic domain on the one hand and the De Bakker-Zucker domain on the other, a direct correspondence, not only between the introduced semantics, but, more interestingly, between the given refinement relation for predicate transformers and the notion of backward simulation for state transformers is obtained. As a corollary a definition of bisimulation for predicate transformers is derived. A few examples illustrate the proposed model.

A first question to address next, facing the two domains Π_1, Π_2 and semantics wp_1, wp_2, concerns their relative correctness. In work in progress we relate the domains via abstraction mappings. By tuning the abstraction to be applied in their treatment of divergence, we may either obtain a weakest precondition semantics or weakest liberal precondition semantics from the parallel models. Thus, both partial and total correctness are represented in wp_2.

It is to be expected that, with some minor modifications, strong fairness conditions can be embodied in $\mathcal{L}_2$ and, consequently, UNITY programs can be expressed in the language. The assertion guards $\{b\}$ have to be added to $\mathcal{L}_2$ as primitive and a subsequent extension of the models is necessary. However, an additional clause involving the operator $\{b\}(P) = \{s \mid \mathcal{B}(b)(s) \ \&\ s \in P\}$ is sufficient. The underlying domain then needs to be adapted as well. Conjunctivity will replace the multiplicativity condition for this. The dual domains of state transformers need to be extended with a special element to give a denotation for *abort*. Locality can be dealt with using techniques developed for the metric setting. It is an open problem, however, how to deal with *angelic* nondeterminacy here.

Acknowledgments We wish to thank Jaco de Bakker for suggesting us to apply the general framework of [BK94] to a concurrent language. Several discussions with Franck van Breugel, Jan Rutten and Daniele Turi have been very helpful. We appreciate the feedback of the members of the Amsterdam Concurrency Group and others on a preliminary version of the paper. We finally wish to thank Frits Vaandrager for his kind bibliographic assistance.

References

[AR89] P. America and J.J.M.M. Rutten. Solving Reflexive Domain Equations in a Category of Complete Metric Spaces. *Journal of Computer and System Sciences*, 39(3):343–375, 1989.

[Bac80] R.-J.R. Back. *Correctness Preserving Program Refinements: Proof Theory and Applications*, volume 131 of *Mathematical Centre Tracts*. CWI, Amsterdam, 1980.

[Bes89] E. Best. Towards Compositional Predicate Transformer Semantics for Concurrent Programs. In *J.W. de Bakker, 25 jaar Semantiek*, pages 111–117, CWI, Amsterdam, 1989.

[BK94] M.M. Bonsangue and J.N. Kok. Relating Multifunctions and Predicate Transformers through Closure Operators. pages 822–843. LNCS 789, 1994.

[BKV94] M.M. Bonsangue, J.N. Kok, and E.P. de Vink. Metric Predicate Transformers: Towards a Notion of Refinement for Concurrent Programs. Report IR-371, Vrije Universiteit Amsterdam, 1994. Available through anonymous ftp from ftp.cs.vu.nl as pub/papers/theory/IR-371.ps.Z.

[BS94] R.J.R. Back and K. Sere. Action Systems with Synchronous Communication. In E.-R. Olderog, editor, *Proc. Programming Concepts, Methods and Calculi*, pages 107–126. IFIP, North Holland, 1994.

[BZ82] J.W. de Bakker and J.I. Zucker. Processes and the Denotational Semantics of Concurrency. *Information and Control*, 54:70–120, 1982.

[CM88] K.M. Chandy and J. Misra. *Parallel Program Design: A Foundation*. Addison-Wesley, 1988.

[Dij76] E.W. Dijkstra. *A Discipline of Programming*. Prentice-Hall, 1976.

[Hes88] W.H. Hesselink. Deadlock and fairness in morphisms of transition systems. *Theoretical Computer Science*, 59:235–257, 1988.

[Lam90] L. Lamport. win and sin: Predicate Transformers for Concurrency. *ACM Transaction on Programming Languages and Systems*, 12(3):396–428, 1990.

[LV93] N.A. Lynch and F.W. Vaandrager. Forward and Backward Simulation — Part I: Untimed Systems. Report CS-R9313, CWI, Amsterdam, 1993. To appear in *Information and Computation*.

[Plo79] G.D. Plotkin. Dijkstra's Predicate Transformer and Smyth's Powerdomain. pages 527–553. LNCS 86, 1979.

[SZ92] D. Scholefield and H.S.M. Zedan. Weakest Precondition Semantics for Time and Concurrency. *Information Processing Letters*, 43(6):301–308, 1992.

[US93] A. Udaya Shankar. An Introduction to Assertional Reasoning for Concurrent Systems. *ACM Computing Surveys*, 25:225–262, 1993.

A Refinement Theory that Supports both 'Decrease of Nondeterminism' and 'Increase of Parallelism'

(extended abstract)

M. Siegel *

Christian-Albrechts-Universität zu Kiel
Institut für Informatik und Praktische Mathematik II
Preusserstrasse 1-9, 24105 Kiel, Germany
Email: mis@informatik.uni-kiel.d400.de

Abstract. The *decrease of nondeterminism* development paradigm that underlies most refinement approaches for concurrent systems is contrasted with the less studied *increase of parallelism* paradigm used by many protocol designers. We show that the widely used refinement notion of Abadi & Lamport exclusively supports the first paradigm and formulate a generalization that allows derivations of systems applying both paradigms alternatively. We develop the proof technique *delayed simulation* to prove Abadi & Lamport refinement and its generalization.

1 Introduction

The development of correct, concurrent systems from requirement specifications is notoriously complicated. A prominent development approach is stepwise refinement where an abstract system that satisfies the requirement specification is stepwise refined into a concrete, implementable system such that the specification is preserved by each refinement step. However, formal frameworks that support stepwise refinement [6] not only have to be based on sound mathematical concepts to allow correctness proofs for refinement steps but also have to support those practical development paradigms for concurrent systems that are used by actual system developers.

With this end in view we contrast the *decrease of nondeterminism* development paradigm with the less studied *increase of parallelism* paradigm. Based on the refinement theory in [1], which is a powerful tool for the first paradigm, we formulate a generalization that allows to develop concurrent systems by a *combination* of refinement steps according to the first paradigm and refinement steps according to the second paradigm.

The development paradigm that underlies most refinement relations, e.g. [1, 3, 7, 10, 14, 16, 23], is decrease of nondeterminism during system development. These relations define refinement as inclusion of observable behaviors. In

* Partially supported by the ESPRIT Project 6021 (REACT)

a setting in which properties of programs are described by means of linear time temporal logic (LTL for short) and in which the satisfaction relation is also defined as inclusion of observable behaviors, each refinement step preserves *all* temporal properties of previous systems in the development process [24, 27] and thus automatically also the original specification.

The less studied 'increase of parallelism' development paradigm for stepwise refinement has been advocated by [3, 4, 5, 9, 24] and is used by many protocol designers, e.g. [20]. This paradigm originates from the observation that the functionality of any large concurrent algorithm can be described by a *sequentialized* variant of the algorithm [5], called its *functional design*. The functional design is considerably easier to develop and verify (w.r.t. the specification) than the concurrent system, because logically independent tasks are clearly separated by the temporal precedence relation.

When starting from the envisaged functional design in order to develop a network protocol, stepwise refinement amounts to increasing the degree of parallelism until a completely distributed variant of the functional design is obtained. Due to concurrent execution of tasks, the distributed variant generates, in general, *more* observable behaviors than the functional design and is consequently no valid refinement according to the 'decrease of nondeterminism' paradigm.

A refinement setup for the 'increase of parallelism' paradigm must have the capability to preserve only a specific set of *desirable* properties, such as the original specification, while ignoring undesired properties such as the too strong temporal ordering of tasks in the functional design [24]. Our first main contribution is a refinement setup that allows a combination of refinement steps according to the 'decrease of nondeterminism' paradigm (preserving all temporal properties) and refinement steps according to the 'increase of parallelism' paradigm (preserving only specific properties) in order to develop concurrent systems.

As our second main contribution we formulate the proof technique *delayed simulation*, inspired by the work on transduction [12], for the refinement notion in [1] and its generalization.

Both the concept of generalized refinement and delayed simulation are illustrated by the derivation of a distributed coloring algorithm from its functional design. We prove that this derivation is neither possible within refinement setups exclusively supporting the decrease of nondeterminism paradigm nor within communication closed layers approaches as e.g. [9, 13, 26].

This paper is organized as follows: Section 2 introduces some notation. In Section 3 we recall the refinement relation in [1] and define its generalization. Section 4 introduces delayed simulation. The derivation of the coloring algorithm is given in Section 5. Section 6 contains conclusions and future work. Due to space limitations most proofs are omitted in this paper; see [21] for details.

2 Preliminaries

In this section we introduce the notion fair transition system (cf. [11, 15, 18]), our specification language, as well as some technical notions and conventions.

We assume a countable set *Var* of typed variables in which each variable is associated with a domain describing the possible values of that variable. A *state* is a type consistent interpretation of a subset $V \subseteq Var$ of variables. The set of all states interpreting variables in V is denoted by Σ_V.

Definition 1. A *fair transition system* $A = (\Sigma, I, T, WF, SF)$ consists of a set Σ of states, a set $I \subseteq \Sigma$ of ***initial states***, a finite set $T = \{t_1, \ldots, t_n\}$ of ***transitions*** with $t_i \subseteq \Sigma \times \Sigma$ including the idling transition $t_{idle} \stackrel{\text{def}}{=} id_\Sigma$, as well as *weak* and *strong fairness constraints* $WF \subseteq T$, $SF \subseteq T$. □

Fair transition systems are typically denoted by $A, B, C, \ldots$ and states of a system by the corresponding lower case letter. To refer to the components of system A we use A as index with the additional convention that V_A refers to the set of *variables* evaluated by states in Σ_A. A transition $t \in T$ is *enabled* in state $s \in \Sigma$ if there exists $s' \in \Sigma$ with $(s, s') \in t$. We also write $s \stackrel{t}{\longrightarrow} s'$ for $(s, s') \in t$.

Definition 2. A *computation* of a system $A = (\Sigma, I, T, WF, SF)$ is an infinite sequence $\sigma = \langle s_0, s_1, s_2, \ldots \rangle$ of states $s_i \in \Sigma$, s.t.

1. $s_0 \in I$,
2. for all $i \in \mathbb{N}$ there exists a transition $t \in T$ with $(s_i, s_{i+1}) \in t$,
3. for all $t \in WF$ that are continuously enabled from some point onwards in σ, there are infinitely many $i \in \mathbb{N}$ with $(s_i, s_{i+1}) \in t$ and $s_i \neq s_{i+1}$ (cf. [15]),
4. for all $t \in SF$ that are infinitely often enabled in σ, there are infinitely many $i \in \mathbb{N}$ with $(s_i, s_{i+1}) \in t$ and $s_i \neq s_{i+1}$ (cf. [15]). □

We use capital letters to stand for both fair transition systems and the set of computations generated by them.

As specification language we use a stutter-closed [15] fragment of linear time temporal logic [18], referred to as LTL$^-$. Formulas are constructed from first-order state predicates and temporal operators $\Box$ (always), $\Diamond$ (eventually), and U (strong until). Temporal formulas are denoted by φ, ψ and state formulas by p. We write $FV(p)$ for the set of free variables of predicate p. Temporal formulas are interpreted over infinite sequences of states [18]. A fair transition system A satisfies formula $\varphi \in$ LTL$^-$, denoted by $A \models \varphi$, if all its computations satisfy φ.

We specify sets of state pairs (s, s') by predicates over primed and unprimed variables; unprimed variables are evaluated according to s, primed variables according to s'. Variables not mentioned in the predicate have, by convention, the same value in s and s'.

For some set E of variables, Π_E denotes the restriction of states to domain E. We write $s_1 =_E s_2$ for $\Pi_E(s_1) = \Pi_E(s_2)$. Operator Π_E is extended pointwise to sequences of states with $\Pi_E(\langle\rangle) \stackrel{\text{def}}{=} \langle\rangle$ where $\langle\rangle$ stands for the empty sequence. For state predicate p, operator Π_p projects a computation σ to the sequence of states in σ which satisfy p.

If R is a binary relation we write $R[e]$ for the set of images of e under R. Operator $\circ$ denotes concatenation of sequences. For a sequence *seq*, $|seq|$ returns the number of elements in *seq* ($|seq| \stackrel{\text{def}}{=} \omega$ if *seq* is infinite), $last(seq)$ returns the last element of *seq* if $1 \leq |seq| < \omega$ (otherwise $last(seq) \stackrel{\text{def}}{=} \bot$), and $tail(seq)$ is defined by $seq = tail(seq) \circ last(seq)$ if $1 \leq |seq| < \omega$ (otherwise $tail(seq) \stackrel{\text{def}}{=} \bot$).

3 Observers and Refinement

In this section we give a recap of the refinement notion in [1] and define its generalization.

In [1] the set of variables of a system is partitioned into a set E of so-called *externally visible* variables and a set of *internal* variables. The observable behavior of a computation is defined relative to an observer that only observes set E in the states of the computation.

Definition 3. Let σ be a computation of some system A and $E \subseteq V_A$. The *observable behavior* of σ w.r.t. E is defined by $beh_E(\sigma) \stackrel{\text{def}}{=} \Pi_E(\sigma)$. □

Refinement in [1] is defined as inclusion of observable behaviors modulo stuttering. We say that a sequence of states $seq = \langle s_0 s_1 s_2 s_3 \ldots \rangle$ is *stutter free* if $s_{i-1} \neq s_i$ holds for all $0 < i < |seq|$. Operator $\natural$ assigns to each sequence *seq* its stutter free version, i.e. the stutter free sequence obtained by replacing every maximal subsequence $\langle s_i s_{i+1} \ldots \rangle$ of identical elements in *seq* by element s_i. Two sequences σ, τ are *stutter equivalent*, denoted by $\sigma \simeq \tau$, if $\natural(\sigma) = \natural(\tau)$. To obtain a simpler proof method, operator $\natural$ removes final stuttering in contrast to the stutter operator in [1]. No matter whether final stuttering is preserved or removed, the induced stutter equivalence $\simeq$ remains unchanged in the Abadi & Lamport setup. The *stutter closure* of a set A of sequences is defined as $\Gamma(A) \stackrel{\text{def}}{=} \{\tau \mid \exists \sigma \in A.\ \sigma \simeq \tau\}$. The refinement relation in [1] can now be defined as follows.

Definition 4. Given systems A, C and set $E \subseteq V_A \cap V_C$. C *refines* A w.r.t. E, denoted by $C \ \mathsf{ref}_E\ A$, if $\Gamma(beh_E(C)) \subseteq \Gamma(beh_E(A))$. □

Relation ref_E preserves all LTL^- properties over set E in refinement steps. As motivated in the introduction we generalize relation ref_E such that also only *particular* LTL^- properties can be preserved in refinement steps. The generalization is based on the following observation: The amount of information necessary to decide whether a computation σ satisfies a temporal formula is often *strictly less* than the complete behavior $beh_E(\sigma)$ of that computation. Consider for example the formula $\Diamond(x = 0)$. To decide whether a computation satisfies this formula the only relevant information is, whether there exists a state in the computation where the value of x equals 0; the values of x in states where x is different from 0 are *irrelevant*. The generalization of ref_E allows to exclusively preserve those parts of the abstract system's behavior in a refinement step that guarantee that also the concrete system satisfies the property to be preserved.

This is achieved by modifying the definition of observable behavior of a computation by generalizing the observer notion.

Definition 5. An *observer* $\mathcal{O}$ is characterized by a tuple $\mathcal{O} = (p, E)$ consisting of a state predicate p and a set E of externally visible variables. We define the set of free variables of $\mathcal{O}$ as $V_{\mathcal{O}} \stackrel{\text{def}}{=} FV(p) \cup E$. □

An observer observes set E of variables but only in those states of a computation that satisfy the so-called *filter predicate* p. Using state predicates as observation criterion for states of a computation is a powerful concept; by adding auxiliary variables to the state space of a program (cf. [1]), observability of states may be defined e.g. dependent on occurrences of actions or the computation history. This observer notion induces the following adapted definitions of observable behavior and refinement.

Definition 6.

a) Let σ be a computation of some system A. For an observer $\mathcal{O} = (p, E)$ with $V_{\mathcal{O}} \subseteq V_A$ the *observable behavior* of σ w.r.t. $\mathcal{O}$ is defined by $beh_{\mathcal{O}}(\sigma) \stackrel{\text{def}}{=} \Pi_E(\Pi_p(\sigma))$.
b) Given systems A, C and observer $\mathcal{O} = (p, E)$ with $V_{\mathcal{O}} \subseteq V_A \cap V_C$. C *refines* A w.r.t. $\mathcal{O}$, denoted by $C\ \mathsf{ref}_{\mathcal{O}}\ A$, iff $\Gamma(beh_{\mathcal{O}}(C)) \subseteq \Gamma(beh_{\mathcal{O}}(A))$. □

The refinement relation ref_E of Abadi & Lamport corresponds to $\mathsf{ref}_{\mathcal{O}}$ for $\mathcal{O} = (true, E)$. From reflexivity and transitivity of the subset relation we obtain the following:

Proposition 7. *For any observer* $\mathcal{O} = (p, E)$, $\mathsf{ref}_{\mathcal{O}}$ *is a preorder on the set of systems* A *with* $V_{\mathcal{O}} \subseteq V_A$. □

A new aspect in refinement relations that support the 'increase of parallelism' paradigm is the preservation of an increasing set of properties during program development [24]. In the following we identify predicates with the sets of states satisfying them and, similarly, properties with sets of computations.

Definition 8.

a) Relation ref *preserves property* $\varphi \in LTL^-$ if for all systems A, C we have that $A \subseteq \varphi$ and C ref A implies $C \subseteq \varphi$.
b) Given observers $\mathcal{O}_i = (p_i, E_i), i \in \{1, 2\}$. Observer $\mathcal{O}_2$ is *more discriminating* than $\mathcal{O}_1$, denoted by $\mathcal{O}_1 \preceq \mathcal{O}_2$, if $\mathsf{ref}_{\mathcal{O}_2}$ preserves all LTL^- properties that are preserved by $\mathsf{ref}_{\mathcal{O}_1}$. □

Relation $\preceq$ is a preorder on the set of observers; if the logic used to formulate properties of systems is sufficiently expressive, relation $\preceq$ is even a cpo.

Theorem 9. *Given observers* $\mathcal{O}_i = (p_i, E_i), i \in \{1, 2\}$. *If* $p_1 \subseteq p_2$ *and* $E_1 \subseteq E_2$ *and* $(=_{E_2} [p_1]) \cap p_2 \subseteq p_1$ *then* $\mathcal{O}_1 \preceq \mathcal{O}_2$. □

As immediate consequence from Theorem 9 and Proposition 7 we get the following generalized transitivity.

Composition: If $C \ \mathsf{ref}_{\mathcal{O}} \ B$ and $B \ \mathsf{ref}_{\mathcal{O}'} \ A$ with $\mathcal{O}' \preceq \mathcal{O}$ then $C \ \mathsf{ref}_{\mathcal{O}'} \ A$. □

This is a central property for refinement relations that allow to preserve specific properties during refinement. It states how to strengthen the refinement relation during the development of a system in order to preserve an increasing set of properties.

As demonstrated in the derivation of the distributed coloring algorithm in Section 5 it is convenient to lift $\mathsf{ref}_{\mathcal{O}}$ to *sets* of observers.

Definition 10. Given systems A, C and a set $\Omega = \{\mathcal{O}_1, .., \mathcal{O}_n\}$ of observers. We define that C *refines* A w.r.t. set Ω, denoted by $C \ \mathsf{ref}_{\Omega} \ A$, if for all $\mathcal{O} \in \Omega$ we have $C \ \mathsf{ref}_{\mathcal{O}} \ A$. □

In [22] we have proved that this lifting allows to capture the notion of partial order refinement, as used in communication closed layers approaches, but not vice versa. The previous results for $\mathsf{ref}_{\mathcal{O}}$ can be lifted to ref_{Ω}.

Theorem 11. *Given the sets* $\Omega = \{\mathcal{O}_1, .., \mathcal{O}_n\}$ *and* $\Omega' = \{\mathcal{O}'_1, .., \mathcal{O}'_m\}$ *of observers. If for all* $\mathcal{O} \in \Omega$ *there exists an* $\mathcal{O}' \in \Omega'$ *with* $\mathcal{O} \preceq \mathcal{O}'$ *then* $\mathsf{ref}_{\Omega'}$ *preserves all properties that are preserved by* ref_{Ω}. □

We get the corresponding corollary for ref_{Ω}.

Composition: If $C \ \mathsf{ref}_{\Omega'} \ B$ and $B \ \mathsf{ref}_{\Omega} \ A$ with $\forall \mathcal{O} \in \Omega . \exists \mathcal{O}' \in \Omega' . \ \mathcal{O} \preceq \mathcal{O}'$ then $C \ \mathsf{ref}_{\Omega} \ A$. □

Theorem 11 and composition of ref_{Ω} imply that it is valid to strengthen the sets of observers used in successive refinement steps by either choosing more discriminating observers or by adding new observers in order to preserve an increasing set of properties during the development of a system. In particular it is possible to switch at any stage to the standard refinement relation ref_E in order to preserve all temporal properties over E in the following refinement steps since for all observers $\mathcal{O}$ with $V_{\mathcal{O}} \subseteq E$ we have $\mathcal{O} \preceq \mathcal{O}_E = (true, E)$.

4 Delayed Simulation

In this section we elaborate the technique of *delayed simulation* to prove refinement according to relation ref_E and $\mathsf{ref}_{\mathcal{O}}$ in presence of fairness constraints.

Forward simulation is a commonly used technique for proving refinement defined as inclusion of observable behaviors. (See [17] for a comprehensive overview of simulation techniques.) The idea of forward simulation is to *immediately* match each non-stuttering state change, called an observation from now on, generated by the concrete system by a corresponding observation in the abstract system. Consequently a forward simulation can be viewed as a mechanism for *scheduling* abstract transitions depending on the current observation generated by the concrete system.

An extensively studied problem is the incompleteness of forward simulation in case the abstract system has to make a nondeterministic choice that the concrete system postpones. This incompleteness originates from the necessity to *immediately* schedule a matching abstract transition whenever an observation has been produced by the concrete system. This immediate scheduling has been relaxed in the work on transduction [12]. In that method a FIFO queue is placed between C and A which stores the *sequence of observations* generated by C that have not yet been matched by the abstract system. Now abstract transitions that display the same observations as those stored in the queue can be scheduled depending on the *whole contents* of the queue, rather than only on the first element as in forward simulation. In particular, abstract transitions can be *delayed* until a nondeterministic choice in C has been resolved.

We make use of this idea and adapt it to prove refinement according to relation ref_E in the presence of fairness constraints.

4.1 Delayed Simulation for ref_E

To illustrate the idea of delayed simulation we start with an example.

Example 1. Let the variables x, y range over the natural numbers. We consider the systems

$A \stackrel{\text{def}}{=} (\Sigma_A, I_A, T_A, WF_A, SF_A)$	$C \stackrel{\text{def}}{=} (\Sigma_C, I_C, T_C, WF_C, SF_C)$
$\Sigma_A = [\{x,y\} \longrightarrow \mathbb{N}]$	$\Sigma_C = [\{x\} \longrightarrow \mathbb{N}]$
$I_A = \{a \in \Sigma_A \mid a(x) = 0\}$	$I_C = \{c \in \Sigma_C \mid c(x) = 0\}$
$T_A = \{inc_A, reset_A\}$	$T_C = \{inc_C, reset_C\}$
$inc_A = (y > 0 \land x' = x+1 \land y' = y-1)$	$inc_C = (x' = x+1)$
$reset_A = (y = 0 \land x' = 0 \land y' \in \mathbb{N})$	$reset_C = (x' = 0)$
$WF_A = \{inc_A, reset_A\}$	$WF_C = \{inc_C, reset_C\}$
$SF_A = \emptyset$	$SF_C = \emptyset$

Then $C\,\mathsf{ref}_{\{x\}}\,A$ holds because both systems compute (up to finite stuttering) a sawtooth function in x, i.e infinite sequences of natural numbers of the form $\langle 0,1,2,\ldots,n_0,0,1,2,\ldots,n_1,0,1,2,\ldots\rangle$ for $n_i \in \mathbb{N}$.

In C the reset of variable x to 0 is forced by the fairness constraints on $reset_C$, while in A the internal state component determines the reset. $C\,\mathsf{ref}_{\{x\}}\,A$ cannot be proved by standard simulation techniques. Forward simulation fails due to the delayed nondeterminism in C, backward simulations necessarily violate the image finiteness condition [17]. Combinations of forward and backward simulations do not succeed either.

To prove that C refines A we use the idea of delayed simulation where transitions are scheduled according to the following policy: Until a reset occurs in C only concrete transitions are scheduled; these store a sequence of states with increasing values for x in the queue. As soon as a reset occurs in C the state $x \mapsto 0$ is added to the queue and abstract transitions are scheduled. First, the internal state component y of A is set to the maximal value of x in the queue;

afterwards successive execution of transition inc_A match and thus remove the stored elements from the queue. If the queue is emptied up to state $x \mapsto 0$ control moves back to C till the next reset occurs. □

We develop the technique of delayed simulation in three steps. First the idea that C generates observable state changes and stores them in the queue while A consumes, i.e. matches, these state changes in a FIFO order is formalized in system $C \rhd A$. Then a *delayed simulation* DS is imposed as a scheduling mechanism on $C \rhd A$ to prevent abstract transitions from removing elements from the queue too early and to disable concrete transitions from going on generating and storing new observations in the queue if abstract transition are scheduled. For the resulting scheduled system $C \rhd_{DS} A$ we formulate the correctness conditions that every element stored in the queue is eventually removed and that the fairness constraints of A are met.

There is a subtle point in the idea of delayed simulation concerning initial states. Commonly used simulation techniques [17] require that initial states of the concrete system must be related to initial states of the abstract system. The idea of delayed simulation requires also a delay in relating initial states. It is for example not possible to relate the initial state of system C in Example 1 to any initial state of A in order to set up a simulation. To handle this situation we add designated initial states i_A, i_C to A and C in the definition of $C \rhd A$.

Definition 12.

a) Given $A = (\Sigma, I, T, WF, SF)$ we define $A^+ \overset{\text{def}}{=} (\Sigma^+; I^+; T^+; WF^+; SF^+)$ by:

$$\Sigma^+ = \Sigma \cup \{i\} \qquad I^+ = \{i\} \qquad T^+ = \{t_{init}\} \cup T$$
$$c \xrightarrow{t_{init}} c' \text{ iff } c = i \wedge c' \in I \quad WF^+ = WF \cup t_{init} \quad SF^+ = SF$$

b) Given A, C and $E \subseteq V_A \cap V_C$. We define $C \rhd A = (\Sigma, I, T^C \cup T^A, WF, SF)$ by:

$$\Sigma = \Sigma_C \times \Sigma_{qu} \times \Sigma_A \quad I = \{(i_C, \langle\rangle, i_A)\} \quad T^C = \{t_i^C \mid t_i \in T_C^+\}$$
$$T^A = \{t_i^A \mid t_A \in T_A^+\} \quad WF = \emptyset \quad SF = \emptyset$$

In the following specification of the transitions we assume that $i_C \neq_E c$ for all $c \in \Sigma_C$ (accordingly for i_A) and $s = (c, qu, a)$:

$$s \xrightarrow{t_i^C} s' \text{ iff } c \xrightarrow{t_i} c' \wedge (c =_E c' \Rightarrow qu = qu') \wedge (c \neq_E c' \Rightarrow \Pi_E(c') \circ qu = qu')$$

$$s \xrightarrow{t_i^A} s' \text{ iff } a \xrightarrow{t_i} a' \wedge (a =_E a' \Rightarrow qu = qu') \wedge (a \neq_E a' \Rightarrow qu = qu' \circ \Pi_E(a'))$$

□

(We omit set E as index from $C \rhd A$ because E is always clear from the context.) In case of delayed nondeterminism in C, system $C \rhd A$ contains computations with observations stored in qu which will never be removed. We impose a delayed simulation as scheduling mechanism on $C \rhd A$ to control the occurrence of abstract and concrete transitions in order to remove such computations.

Definition 13. Given system $C \rhd A = (\Sigma, I, T^C \cup T^A, WF, SF)$. Set $DS \subseteq \Sigma$ is a *delayed simulation* for $C \rhd A$ if:

1. $(i_C, \langle\rangle, i_A) \in DS$ and
2. $s \in DS$ implies $\forall t \in T^C.\forall s' \in \Sigma.s \xrightarrow{t} s' \Rightarrow s' \in DS$
   or $(\exists t \in T^A.\exists s' \in \Sigma.s \xrightarrow{t} s' \wedge s' \in DS) \wedge \Pi_{qu}(s) \neq \langle\rangle$ □

We call a transition $t \in T^C \cup T^A$ *scheduled* in state $s \in DS$ if there exists $s' \in DS$ with $(s, s') \in t$. Clause 2) states that in all DS-states either all enabled concrete transitions are scheduled and/or there exists at least one enabled abstract transition that is scheduled by DS. If only abstract transitions are scheduled, condition $\Pi_{qu}(s) \neq \langle\rangle$ guarantees that the queue is not empty. Next we define system $C \rhd A$ scheduled by a delayed simulation DS.

Definition 14. Given systems A, C, and set $E \subseteq V_A \cap V_C$. For $C \rhd A = (\Sigma, I, T^C \cup T^A, WF, SF)$ and a delayed simulation DS for $C \rhd A$ we define $C \rhd_{DS} A = (\Sigma_\rhd, I_\rhd, T^c_\rhd \cup T^a_\rhd, WF_\rhd, SF_\rhd)$ by:

$$\Sigma_\rhd = DS \qquad\qquad I_\rhd = \{(i_C, \langle\rangle, i_A)\}$$
$$T^C_\rhd = \{t^C_{i,\rhd} \stackrel{\text{def}}{=} t^C_i \cap (DS \times DS) \mid t^C_i \in T^C\}$$
$$T^A_\rhd = \{t^A_{i,\rhd} \stackrel{\text{def}}{=} t^A_i \cap (DS \times DS) \mid t^A_i \in T^A\}$$
$$WF_\rhd = \{t^C_{i,\rhd} \mid t_i \in WF^+_C\} \cup \{t^A_{i,\rhd} \mid t_i \in T^+_A\} \qquad SF_\rhd = \{t^C_{i,\rhd} \mid t_i \in SF_C\}$$
□

The delayed simulation DS schedules $C \rhd A$ by just allowing transition between DS-states. The fairness assumptions on the concrete transitions guarantee progress in generating state changes in C. The fairness assumptions on the abstract transitions guarantee that scheduled abstract transitions are eventually taken.

Now we can formulate the technique of delayed simulation for proving refinement according to relation ref_E. Predicate $en(t)$ is true for an abstract transition t in a state s of the scheduled system if t is enabled in the state component of s corresponding to the abstract state; predicate $taken(t)$ is true in a state s_i of a computation if $(s_{i-1}, s_i) \in t$.

Theorem 15. *Given systems A, C and set $E \subseteq V_A \cap V_C$. If there exists a delayed simulation DS for $C \rhd A$ s.t.:*

$$C \rhd_{DS} A \models \Box(qu \neq \langle\rangle \Rightarrow \Diamond tail(qu) = qu')$$
$$C \rhd_{DS} A \models \Diamond\Box en(t_i) \Rightarrow \Box\Diamond taken(t^A_{i,\rhd}),\ \textit{for all}\ t_i \in WF_A$$
$$C \rhd_{DS} A \models \Box\Diamond en(t_i) \Rightarrow \Box\Diamond taken(t^A_{i,\rhd}),\ \textit{for all}\ t_i \in SF_A$$

then C ref_E A.

□

The proof obligations in this theorem correspond to those formulated for the transducer except that we have replaced the transducer by system $C \rhd_{DS} A$. A comparison of delayed simulation with transduction and refinement mappings can be found in [21].

Example 2. Recall systems A, C from Example 1. System C decides nondeterministically after each step whether to reset or increase variable x, whereas A predicts the reset in the internal variable y. In order to imitate C, system A has to wait for the occurrence of the next reset in C. For only then A can choose the appropriate value for y. The delayed simulation DS encodes this waiting for the next reset. To simplify the exposition we specify the possible values of the variables in $(x, qu, (x, y))$ instead of specifying sets of states. We define DS as the disjoint union of three sets of states DS^C, DS_1^A, DS_2^A specified below.

$$\begin{aligned} DS^C = \; & \{(i_C, \langle\rangle, i_A)\} \\ & \cup\{(n, \langle n, \ldots, 0\rangle, i_A) \mid n \in \mathbb{N}\} \\ & \cup\{(n, \langle n, \ldots, 0\rangle, (m, 0)) \mid n, m \in \mathbb{N}\} \end{aligned}$$

$$\begin{aligned} DS_1^A &= \{(0, \langle 0, n, \ldots, 0\rangle, (m, 0)) \mid n \in \mathbb{N}^+, m \in \mathbb{N}\} \\ DS_2^A &= \{(0, \langle 0, n, \ldots, m\rangle, (m-1, n-(m-1))) \mid 0 < m \leq n \in \mathbb{N}\} \end{aligned}$$

The proof obligations of Theorem 15 are satisfied (see [21] for details). This proves refinement between C and A w.r.t. observable variable x. □

Refinement in this example cannot be proven by transduction, because the transducer does not allow a delay in relating initial states.

4.2 Delayed Simulation for $\mathsf{ref}_{\mathcal{O}}$

The mechanism of delayed simulation is independent from any particular refinement notion. To obtain a proof method for refinement relation $\mathsf{ref}_{\mathcal{O}}$ we just have to adapt the mechanism how C generates observations for the queue and how A consumes these observations from the queue.

Given an observer $\mathcal{O} = (p, E)$. If a state c generated by C satisfies filter predicate p and if c is not a stutter state then the observable state component of c is appended to the queue. The mechanism how A removes elements from the queue is similar. We introduce two new state components in, out in the construction of $C \triangleright A$. Component in records the last state that C stored into the queue, while out records the last state that A removed from the queue.

Definition 16. Given the systems A, C and observer $\mathcal{O} = (p, E)$ with $V_{\mathcal{O}} \subseteq V_A \cap V_C$. We define $C \triangleright A = (\Sigma, I, T^C \cup T^A, WF, SF)$ by:

$$\begin{array}{lll} \Sigma = \Sigma_C \times \Sigma_{link} \times \Sigma_A & \Sigma_{link} = \Sigma_E \times \Sigma_{qu} \times \Sigma_E & I = \{(i_C, (\bot, \langle\rangle, \bot), i_A)\} \\ T^C = \{t_i^C \mid t_i \in T_C^+\} & T^A = \{t_i^A \mid t_i \in T_A^+\} & \\ WF = \emptyset & SF = \emptyset & \end{array}$$

We assume that $s = (c, (in, qu, out), a)$ and that in and out have $\bot$ as initial value, where $c \neq_E \bot$ for all concrete states c (accordingly for abstract states).

$$\begin{aligned} s \xrightarrow{t_i^C} s' \text{ if } c \xrightarrow{t_i} c' & \wedge [(c' \notin p \vee c' =_E in) \Rightarrow (in = in' \wedge qu = qu')] \\ & \wedge [(c' \in p \wedge c' \neq_E in) \Rightarrow (in' = c' \wedge \Pi_E(c') \circ qu = qu')] \\ s \xrightarrow{t_i^A} s' \text{ if } a \xrightarrow{t_i} a' & \wedge [(a' \notin p \vee a' =_E out) \Rightarrow (out = out' \wedge qu = qu')] \\ & \wedge [(a' \in p \wedge a' \neq_E out) \Rightarrow (out' = a' \wedge qu = qu' \circ \Pi_E(a'))] \end{aligned}$$

Now we can use the machinery of the previous section and obtain the following result.

Theorem 17. *Given systems* A, C *and observer* $\mathcal{O} = (p, E)$ *with* $V_{\mathcal{O}} \subseteq V_A \cap V_C$. *If there exists a delayed simulation* DS *for* $C \rhd A$ *such that:*

$$C \rhd_{DS} A \models \Box(qu \neq \langle\rangle \Rightarrow \Diamond tail(qu) = qu')$$
$$C \rhd_{DS} A \models \Diamond\Box en(t_i) \Rightarrow \Box\Diamond taken(t^a_{i,\rhd}),\ \textit{for all}\ t_i \in WF_A$$
$$C \rhd_{DS} A \models \Box\Diamond en(t_i) \Rightarrow \Box\Diamond taken(t^a_{i,\rhd}),\ \textit{for all}\ t_i \in SF_A$$

then C $\mathsf{ref}_{\mathcal{O}}$ A. □

An example of the advocated refinement notion and the application of delayed simulation is given in the next section.

5 A Substantial Example: Distributed Coloring

In this section we derive a distributed coloring algorithm [8] according to the 'increase of parallelism' paradigm from an abstract program that describes its functional design. We also recall results from [22, 25] that neither commonly used refinement relations such as [1, 3, 7, 10, 16] support this derivation nor communication closed layers approaches [9, 13, 26].

The input to the coloring program is an undirected, finite graph without self-loops in which every non-empty subgraph contains at least one node having less than six neighbors; such graphs are called *admissible*. The program has to color the nodes of the graph with at most six colors such that adjacent nodes get different colors.

Let $(\mathcal{V}, \mathcal{E})$ be an admissible graph with set $\mathcal{V}$ of nodes and set $\mathcal{E} \subseteq \mathcal{V} \times \mathcal{V}$ of edges. We identify each node with an element in set $\{1, 2, \ldots, m\}$, where m is the number of nodes in $\mathcal{V}$. Each node $i \in \mathcal{V}$ maintains a variable c_i to record the color $col \in \{col_1, \ldots, col_6\}$ assigned to node i. Let $Col \stackrel{\text{def}}{=} \{col_1, \ldots, col_6\}$ and $C \stackrel{\text{def}}{=} \{c_1, \ldots, c_m\}$. The initial specification of the program is that the following property eventually always holds:

$$\text{(properly colored) } pc \stackrel{\text{def}}{=} \forall i, j \in \mathcal{V}. j \in \mathcal{E}[i] \Rightarrow c_i \neq c_j.$$

The functional design of the algorithm which we set out to develop is described by a program working in two phases: In the *redirection phase*, directions are given to edges and these directions are changed until each node has at most five outgoing edges. We call such a graph properly directed. Then the *coloring phase* starts. Relying on the fact that the graph is now properly directed, it eventually establishes a properly colored graph.

In detail the algorithm works as follows. In order to give directions to edges each node i maintains an integer variable x_i whose initial value is arbitrary; let $X \stackrel{\text{def}}{=} \{x_1, \ldots, x_m\}$. Edge e is directed from i to neighbor j, denoted by $i \longmapsto j$, if $(x_i < x_j) \vee (x_i = x_j \wedge i < j)$ holds. In this case j is called a *successor* of i. We use the abbreviations $out_i \stackrel{\text{def}}{=} \{j \in \mathcal{E}[i] \mid i \longmapsto j\}$, (properly directed)

$pd \stackrel{\text{def}}{=} \forall i \in \mathcal{V}.|out_i| \leq 5$, and $outcol_i \stackrel{\text{def}}{=} \{col \in Col \mid \exists j \in out_i.c_j = col\}$. A fair transition system, denoted by $Ph_1; Ph_2$, that corresponds to the functional design is defined as the component wise union of the following two systems:

$Ph_1 \stackrel{\text{def}}{=} (\Sigma_1, I_1, T_{red}, WF_1, SF_1)$	$Ph_2 \stackrel{\text{def}}{=} (\Sigma_2, I_2, T_{col}, WF_2, SF_2)$
$\Sigma_1 = \Sigma_{X \cup C}$	$\Sigma_2 = \Sigma_{X \cup C}$
$I_1 = \Sigma_{X \cup C}$	$I_2 = \Sigma_{X \cup C}$
$T_{red} = \{t_{red_1}, \ldots, t_{red_m}\}$	$T_{col} = \{t_{col_1}, \ldots, t_{col_m}\}$
$WF_1 = \{t_{red_1}, \ldots, t_{red_m}\}$	$WF_2 = \{t_{col_1}, \ldots, t_{col_m}\}$
$SF_1 = \emptyset$	$SF_2 = \emptyset$

with:

$$s \xrightarrow{t_{red_i}} s' \text{ iff } \quad |out_i| > 5 \wedge x'_i = 1 + max\{x_j | j \in out_i\} \quad \text{and}$$

$$s \xrightarrow{t_{col_i}} s' \text{ iff } \quad pd \wedge \exists j \in out_i.(c_j = c_i \wedge |outcol_i| < 6) \Rightarrow c'_i \in Col \setminus outcol_i$$

The precondition that the algorithm works on an admissible graph is formalized as follows; here $gr(\mathcal{V}, \mathcal{E})$ expresses that $(\mathcal{V}, \mathcal{E})$ constitutes a graph without self-loops:

$$\text{(admissible graph)} \quad ag \stackrel{\text{def}}{=} gr(\mathcal{V}, \mathcal{E}) \wedge \forall \mathcal{V}', \mathcal{E}'.\emptyset \neq \mathcal{V}' \subseteq \mathcal{V} \wedge \mathcal{E}' \subseteq \mathcal{E} \Rightarrow \exists i \in \mathcal{V}'.|\mathcal{E}'[i] \cap \mathcal{V}'| \leq 5$$

In [8, 25] it is proved that system $Ph_1; Ph_2$ satisfies the initial specification $is \stackrel{\text{def}}{=} ag\ U\ pc \wedge stable(pc)$ where $stable(pc)$ abbreviates the formula $\Box(pc \rightarrow \Box pc)$.

A distributed implementation of $Ph_1; Ph_2$ which does not enforce global synchronization can be obtained by removing the conjunct pd from T_{col} transitions. The refined system $Ph_1 \parallel Ph_2$ performs the redirection of edges and coloring of nodes *in parallel*. System $Ph_1; Ph_2$ generates — due to the separation of its phases — strictly less observable behaviors than $Ph_1 \parallel Ph_2$ and thus satisfies more temporal properties, such as $\xi = \exists i \in \mathcal{V}.\exists col \in Col.\Box(c_i = col)$. Thus $Ph_1 \parallel Ph_2$ neither refines $Ph_1; Ph_2$ in the standard sense w.r.t. set $C = \{c_1, \ldots, c_m\}$ of externally visible variables nor in the communication closed layer approaches, because computations in $Ph_1 \parallel Ph_2$ where each nodes changes its color at least once are not permutation equivalent [19] to any computation in $Ph_1; Ph_2$ (see [22]).

But we are not at all interested in preserving all temporal properties of $Ph_1; Ph_2$ but only in the preservation of its initial specification. We prove that the specification is preserved by showing that the following stronger specification *sts* is preserved by this particular refinement step.

$$\text{(stronger specification)} \quad sts \stackrel{\text{def}}{=} (ag\ U\ pd) \wedge ((ag \wedge pd)\ U\ pc) \wedge stable(ag) \wedge stable(pd) \wedge stable(pc)$$

One can show by local reasoning about transitions in isolation that $(Ph_1 \parallel Ph_2$ satisfies the stable predicates. We use observer $\mathcal{O}_1 = (true, X)$ to prove preservation of $sts_1 = (ag U pd)$ and observer $\mathcal{O}_2 = (pd, C)$ to prove preservation of $sts_2 = ((ag \wedge pd)\ U\ pc)$. Observer $\mathcal{O}_1$ observes the redirection of edges while $\mathcal{O}_2$ observes the coloring of nodes as soon as a *pd*-graph has been established. These observers exactly capture the informal argument given in [8] why the overall functionality of $Ph_1; Ph_2$ is preserved by this refinement step according to the 'increase of parallelism' paradigm.

Lemma 18. $Ph_1 \parallel Ph_2 \ \mathsf{ref}_{\mathcal{O}_1}\ Ph_1; Ph_2$.

Proof. We give a delayed simulation $DS \stackrel{\text{def}}{=} DS^C \cup DS^A$ for $(Ph_1 \parallel Ph_2 \triangleright Ph_1; Ph_2)$ such that the premises of Theorem 15 are satisfied. Details can be found in [21]. We omit the *in*, *out* component of the link because they are always identical to state c, respectively a, in the following definition.

$$\begin{aligned} DS^C = \ & \{(i_C, \langle\rangle, i_A)\} \\ & \cup\{(c, \langle\rangle, a) \mid c =_{X\cup C} a\} \end{aligned}$$

$$\begin{aligned} DS^A = \ & \{(c, \langle \Pi_X(c)\rangle, i_A) \mid c \in \Sigma_{X\cup C}\} \\ & \cup\{(c, \langle \Pi_X(c)\rangle, a) \mid \exists i \in \mathcal{V}.(c \neq_{x_i} a) \wedge (c =_{X\setminus x_i} a) \wedge (c =_C a)\} \end{aligned}$$

□

Lemma 19. $Ph_1 \parallel Ph_2 \ \mathsf{ref}_{\mathcal{O}_2}\ Ph_1; Ph_2$.

Proof. Again we only give the deterministic delayed simulation $DS \stackrel{\text{def}}{=} DS^C \cup DS^A$. The same remark for *in*, *out* as in Lemma 18 applies here, too.

$$\begin{aligned} DS^C = \ & \{(i_C, \langle\rangle, i_A)\} \\ & \cup\{(c, \langle\rangle, i_a) \mid c \notin pd\} \\ & \cup\{(c, \langle\rangle, a) \mid c \in pd \wedge c = a\} \end{aligned}$$

$$\begin{aligned} DS^A = \ & \{(c, \langle \Pi_X(c)\rangle, i_A) \mid c \in pd\} \\ & \cup\{(c, \langle \Pi_X(c)\rangle, a) \mid \exists i \in \mathcal{V}.(c \neq_{c_i} a) \wedge (c =_{C\setminus c_i} a) \wedge (c =_X a)\} \end{aligned}$$

□

Theorem 20. $Ph_1 \parallel Ph_2 \ \mathsf{ref}_{\{\mathcal{O}_1,\mathcal{O}_2\}}\ Ph_1; Ph_2$. □

In [22] only a semantical argument for the correctness of this theorem is given. Here we applied the proof technique for $\mathsf{ref}_{\mathcal{O}}$, based on delayed simulation. In [22] we have shown that $\mathsf{ref}_{\{\mathcal{O}_1,\mathcal{O}_2\}}$ preserves specification *sts* for systems $Ph_1; Ph_2$ and $Ph_1 \parallel Ph_2$. So we conclude that $Ph_1 \parallel Ph_2$ is a correct refinement of $Ph_1; Ph_2$ according to the 'increase of parallelism' paradigm.

Implementing system $Ph_1 \parallel Ph_2$ under the assumption that we have only read/write atomicity on shared variables can be done by a locking mechanism where each process tries to lock the x_i variables of all its neighbors and itself. This refinement step would preserve all temporal properties w.r.t. set $X \cup C$ of externally visible variables. So we can use observer $\mathcal{O} = (true, X \cup C)$ which is more discriminating than $\mathcal{O}_1$ and $\mathcal{O}_2$ (cf. Definition 8b) and can choose between such proof techniques as refinement mappings [1] or delayed simulation in order to prove correctness of this refinement step.

6 Conclusion

We have stated the two main development paradigms for concurrent systems and have suggested a generalization of the refinement notion in [1] that supports both paradigms. The technique of delayed simulation has been elaborated to prove refinement in the sense of [1] and its generalized version.

When using a refinement theory that allows to preserve only specific properties rather than all properties during refinement, one is inevitably faced with the additional proof obligation that the chosen refinement relation preserves the properties of interest. To bridge the gap between properties and refinement relations preserving these properties we are currently addressing techniques to *synthesize* appropriate observers from the properties to be preserved. We have first results for self-stabilizing systems. For a general theory we consider a different treatment of stuttering in the definition of relation $\mathsf{ref}_{\mathcal{O}}$.

Concerning delayed simulation we are going to investigate completeness results and the combination of prophecy variables and delayed simulation.

Further examples, such as a distributed reset algorithm for networks with changing topology [2], will be elaborated to demonstrate the applicability of the advocated refinement approach.

Acknowledgment: I would like to thank W.P. de Roever, B. Jonsson, A. Pnueli, F. Stomp, C. Petersohn, E. Mikk, and in particular K. Engelhardt for constant inspiration, help, and encouragement when writing this paper.

References

1. M. Abadi and L. Lamport. The existence of refinement mappings. *Theoretical Computer Science*, 82(2), 1991.
2. A. Arora and M. Gouda. Distributed reset. *IEEE Transactions on Computers*, 43(9), 1994.
3. R. J. R. Back. Refinement calculus: Parallel and reactive systems. In J.W. de Bakker, W.P. de Roever, and G. Rozenberg, editors, *Stepwise Refinement of Distributed Systems*, volume 430 of *LNCS*, 1990.
4. K. M. Chandy and J. Misra. *Parallel Program Design: a Foundation.* Addison-Wesley, 1988.
5. Ching-Tsun Chou and Eli Gafni. Understanding and verifying distributed algorithms using stratified decomposition. In *7th ACM Symp. on Principles of Distributed Computing*, 1988.
6. J.W. de Bakker, W.P. de Roever, and G. Rozenberg, editors. *Stepwise Refinement of Distributed Systems: Models, Formalisms, Correctness*, volume 430 of *LNCS*. Springer Verlag, 1990.
7. R. Gerth. Foundations of compositional program refinement. In J.W. de Bakker, W.P. de Roever, and G. Rozenberg, editors, *Stepwise Refinement of Distributed Systems*, volume 430 of *LNCS*, 1990.
8. S. Ghosh and M.H. Karaata. A self stabilizing algorithm for graph coloring. In *Proceedings of the 29th Allerton Conference on Control, Communication, and Computing*, October 1991.

9. W. Janssen and J. Zwiers. Protocol design by layered decomposition, a compositional approach. In *Proceedings Formal Techniques in Real Time and Fault Tolerant Systems*, volume 571 of *LNCS*, 1992.
10. B. Jonsson. On decomposing and refining specifications of distributed systems. In J.W. de Bakker, W.P. de Roever, and G. Rozenberg, editors, *Stepwise Refinement of Distributed Systems*, volume 430 of *LNCS*, 1990.
11. B. Jonsson. Simulations between specifications of distributed systems. In J. C. M. Baeten and J. F. Groote, editors, *CONCUR '91*, volume 527 of *LNCS*, 1991.
12. B. Jonsson, A. Pnueli, and C. Rump. Proving refinement using transduction. In R. Gerth, editor, *Verifying sequentially consistent memory*. 1993. To be published as a special issue of Distributed Computing.
13. S. Katz and D. Peled. Verification of distributed programs using representative interleaving sequences. *Distributed Computing*, 6, 1992.
14. S. S. Lam and A. U. Shankar. Refinement and projection of relational specifications. In J.W. de Bakker, W.P. de Roever, and G. Rozenberg, editors, *Stepwise Refinement of Distributed Systems*, volume 430 of *LNCS*, 1990.
15. L. Lamport. The temporal logic of actions. Technical Report 79, DEC, Systems Research Center, December 1991. To appear in Transactions on programming Languages and Systems.
16. N. Lynch and M. Tuttle. Hierachical correctness proofs for distributed algorithms. Proc. of the 6th ACM Symposium on Distributed Computing, 1987.
17. N. Lynch and F. Vaandrager. Forward and backward simulations for timing based systems. In *Real-Time: Theory in Practice*, volume 600 of *LNCS*, 1991.
18. Z. Manna and A. Pnueli. *The Temporal Logic of Reactive and Concurrent Systems*. Springer Verlag, 1992.
19. A. Mazurkiewicz. Trace semantics, proceedings of an advanced course. volume 354 of *LNCS*, Bad Honnef, 1989.
20. M. Raynal and J.-P. Helary. *Synchronization and control of distributed systems and programs*. Wiley, 1990.
21. M. Siegel. Combining development paradigms in stepwise refinement. Technical report, University of Kiel, 1995. To appear.
22. M. Siegel and F. Stomp. Extending the limits of sequentially phased reasoning. In P. S. Thiagarajan, editor, *FST&TCS 14*, volume 880 of *LNCS*, 1994.
23. E. W. Stark. Proving entailment between conceptual state specifications. *Theoretical Computer Science*, 56, 1988.
24. F. Stomp. Preserving specific properties in program development. In Cleaveland, editor, *CONCUR '92*, volume 630 of *LNCS*,1992.
25. F. Stomp. Structured design of self-stabilizing programs. Proc. of the 2nd Isreal Symposium on Theory of Computing and Systems, 1993.
26. F. Stomp and W.P. de Roever. A principle for sequentially phased reasoning about distributed algorithms. *Formal Aspects of Computing*, 6(6), 1994.
27. Shengzong Zhou, R. Gerth, and R. Kuiper. Transformations preserving properties and properties preserved by transformations in fair transition systems. volume 715 of *LNCS*, 1993.

Model Checking
and
Efficient Automation of Temporal Reasoning*

E. Allen Emerson

University of Texas at Austin, Austin, Tx 78712, USA

emerson@cs.utexas.edu

Reactive programs such as operating systems, network protocols, computer hardware circuits, and other types of concurrent systems are of ever growing importance. It is widely recognized that some type of temporal logic is most appropriate for specifying and reasoning about the ongoing behavior of such systems [Pn77]. There is also a growing awareness of the need to cater for automated reasoning about reactive systems owing to the unmanageability of manual proof methods [Ku94].

Automation is feasible only when it is efficient. One useful approach to automation is through model checking, which provides an algorithmic method of verifying that a finite state reactive system meets a temporal logic specification [CE81]. Provided that the global state transition graph can be succinctly represented very efficient model checking algorithms can be given for useful temporal logics. Unfortunately, the state explosion problem can cause the state graph to be intractably large. We discuss methods for ameliorating state explosion such as factoring out the symmetry inherent in systems with many homogeneous subcomponents or subprocesses [ES93], [ES95] (cf. [CFJ93], [ID93], [Je94]). Another promising approach to efficient automation is through use of restricted temporal logics that admit efficient decision procedures (cf. [ESS92], [EES90]).

* This work was supported in part by NSF grant CCR-9415496 and by SRC contract 94-DP-388.

References

[CE81] Clarke, E. M., and Emerson, E. A., Design and Verification of Synchronization Skeletons using Branching Time Temporal Logic, Logics of Programs Workshop 1981, Springer LNCS no. 131.

[CFJ93] Clarke, E. M., Filkorn, T., Jha, S. Exploiting Symmetry in Temporal Logic Model Checking, 5th International Conference on Computer Aided Verification, Crete, Greece, June 1993; journal version to appear in *Formal Methods in System Design.*

[EES90] Emerson, E. A., Evangelist, M., and Srinivasan, J., On the Limits of Efficient Temporal Satisfiability, 5th IEEE Symp. on Logic in Computer Science (LICS), Philadelphia, pp. 464-475, 1990.

[ESS92] Emerson, E. A., Sadler, T. H., and Srinivasan, J., Efficient Temporal Satisfiability, *Journal of Logic and Computation*, vol. 2, no. 2, pp. 173-210, 1992.

[ES93] Emerson, E. A., and Sistla, A. P., Symmetry and Model Checking, 5th International Conference on Computer Aided Verification, Crete, Greece, June 1993; journal version to appear in *Formal Methods in System Design.*

[ES95] Emerson, E. A., and Sistla, A. P., Utilizing Symmetry when Model Checking under Fairness Assumptions: An Automata-theoretic Approach, to appear in 7th International Conference on Computer Aided Verification, Liege, Belgium, Springer LNCS, July 1995.

[ID93] Ip, C-W. N., Dill, D. L., Better Verification through Symmetry, Computer Hardware Description Language Conference, April 1993; journal version to appear in *Formal Methods in Systems Design.*

[Je94] Jensen, K., Colored Petri Nets: Basic Concepts, Analysis Methods, and Practical Use, vol. 2: Analysis Methods, EATCS Monographs, Springer-Verlag, 1994.

[Ku94] Kurshan, R. P., *Computer-Aided Verification of Coordinating Processes: The Automata-Theoretic Approach*, Princeton University Press, Princeton, New Jersey 1994.

[Pn77] Pnueli, A., The Temporal Logic of Programs, 17th IEEE Symp. on Foundations of Computer Science (FOCS), October, 1977.

Verifying Parameterized Networks using Abstraction and Regular Languages *

E. M. Clarke[1] and O. Grumberg[2] and S. Jha[1]

[1] Carnegie Mellon University, Pittsburgh, PA 15213
[2] Computer Science Dept, The Technion, Haifa 32000, Israel

Abstract. This paper describes a technique based on network grammars and abstraction to verify families of state-transition systems. The family of state-transition systems is represented by a context-free network grammar. Using the structure of the network grammar our technique constructs an invariant which *simulates* all the state-transition systems in the family. A novel idea used in this paper is to use *regular languages* to express state properties. We have implemented our techniques and verified two non-trivial examples.

1 Introduction

Automatic verification of state-transition systems using temporal logic model checking has been investigated by numerous authors [3, 4, 5, 12, 16]. The basic model checking problem is easy to state

Given a state-transition system P and a temporal formula f, determine whether P satisfies f.

Current model checkers can only verify a single state-transition system at a time. The ability to reason automatically about entire families of similar state-transition systems is an important research goal. Such families arise frequently in the design of reactive systems in both hardware and software. The infinite family of token rings is a simple example. More complicated examples are trees of processes consisting of one root, several internal and leaf nodes, and hierarchical buses with different numbers of processors and caches.

The verification problem for a family of similar state-transition systems can formulated as follows:

Given a family $F = \{P_i\}_{i=1}^{\infty}$ of systems P_i and a temporal formula f, verify that each state-transition system in the family F satisfies f.

In general the problem is undecidable [1]. However, for *specific* families the problem may be solvable. This possibility has been investigated by [2]. They consider the problem of verifying a family of token rings. In order to verify the entire family, they establish a *bisimulation* relation between a 2-process token ring and an n-process token ring for any $n \geq 2$. It follows that the 2-process token ring and the n-process token ring satisfy exactly the same temporal formulas. The drawback of their technique is that the bisimulation relation has to be constructed manually.

Induction at the process level has also been used to solve problems of this nature by two research groups [9, 10]. They prove that for rings composed of certain kinds of processes there exists a k such that the correctness of the ring with k processes implies the correctness of rings of arbitrary size. In [20] an alternative method for checking properties of parametrized systems is proposed. In this framework there are two types of processes: G_s (slave processes) and G_c (control processes). There can be many slave processes with type G_s, but only one control process with type G_c. The slave processes G_s can only communicate with the control process G_c.

Our technique is based on finding *network invariants* [11, 21]. Given an infinite family $F = \{P_i\}_{i=1}^{\infty}$ this technique involves constructing an invariant I such that $P_i \preceq I$ for all i. The preorder $\preceq$ preserves

* This research was sponsored in part by the Avionics Laboratory, Wright Research and Development Center, Aeronautical Systems Division (AFSC), U.S. Air Force, Wright-Patterson AFB, Ohio 45433-6543 under Contract F33615-90-C-1465, ARPA Order No. 7597 and in part by the National Science Foundation under Grant no. CCR-8722633 and in part by the Semiconductor Research Corporation under Contract 92-DJ-294. The second author was partially supported by grant no. 120-732 from The United States-Israel Binational Science Foundation (BSF), Jerusalem, Israel.

The views and conclusions contained in this document are those of the authors and should not be interpreted as representing the official policies, either expressed or implied, of the U.S. government.

the property f we are interested in, i.e. if I satisfies f, then P_i satisfies f. Once the invariant I is found, traditional model checking techniques can be used to check that I satisfies f. The original technique in [11, 21] can only handle networks with one repetitive component. Also, the invariant I has to be explicitly provided by the user.

In [17, 13] context-free network grammars are used to generate infinite families of processes with multiple repetitive components. Using the structure of the grammar they generate an invariant I and then check that I is *equivalent* to every process in the language of the grammar. If the method succeeds, then the property can be checked on the invariant I. The requirement for equivalence between all systems in F is too strong in practice and severely limits the usefulness of the method. Our goal is to replace *equivalence* with a suitable *preorder* while still using network grammars.

We first address the question of how to specify a property of a global state of a system consisting of many components. Such a state is a n-tuple, $(s_1, \ldots, s_n)$ for some n. Typical properties we may want to describe are "some component is in a state s_i", "at least (at most) k components are in state s_i", "if some component is in state s_i then some other component is in state s_j". These properties are conveniently expressed in terms of *regular languages*. Instead of n-tuple $(s_1, \ldots, s_n)$ we represent a global state by the word $s_1 \cdot \ldots \cdot s_n$ that can either belong to a given regular language $\mathcal{L}$, thus having the property $\mathcal{L}$, or not belong to $\mathcal{L}$, thus not having the property. As an example, consider a mutual exclusion algorithm for processes on a ring. Let nc be the state of a process outside of the critical section and let cs be the state inside the critical section. The regular language $nc^*\ cs\ nc^*$ specifies the global states of rings with any number of processes in which exactly one process is in its critical section.

After deciding the types of state properties we are interested in, we can partition the set of global states into equivalence classes according to the properties they possess. Using these classes as *abstract states* and defining an abstract transition relation appropriately, we get an *abstract state-transition system* that is greater in the simulation preorder $\preceq$ than any system in the family. Thus given a $\forall CTL^*$[6] formula, defined over this set of state properties, if it is true of the abstract system, then it is also true of the systems in the family.

Following [17] and [13] we restrict our attention to families of systems derived by *network grammars.* The advantage of such a grammar is that it is a finite (and usually small) representation of an infinite family of finite-state systems (referred to as the language of the grammar). While [17, 13] use the grammar in order to find a representative that is equivalent to any system derived by the grammar, we find a representative that is greater in the simulation preorder than all of the systems that can be derived using the grammar.

In order to simplify the presentation we first consider the case of an unspecified composition operator. The only required property of this operator is that it must be monotonic with respect to the simulation preorder. At a later stage we apply these ideas to synchronous models (Moore machines) that are particularly suitable for modeling hardware designs. We use a simple mutual exclusion algorithm as the running example to demonstrate our ideas. Two realistic examples are given in a separate section.

Our paper is organized as follows. In Section 2 we define the basic notions, including network grammars and regular languages used as state properties. In Section 3 we define abstract systems. Section 4 presents our verification method. In Section 5 we describe a synchronous model of computation and show that it is suitable for our technique. In Section 6 we apply our method to two non-trivial examples. Section 7 concludes with some directions for future research.

2 Definitions and Framework

Definition 1 (LTS). A *Labeled Transition System* or an *LTS* is a structure $M = (S, R, ACT, S_0)$ where S is the set of states, $S_0 \subseteq S$ is the set of initial states, ACT is the set of actions, and $R \subseteq S \times ACT \times S$ is the *total* transition relation, such that for every $s \in S$ there is some action a and some state s' for which $(s, a, s') \in R$. We use $s \xrightarrow{a} s'$ to denote that $(s, a, s') \in R$.

Let L_{ACT} be the class of LTSs whose set of actions is a subset of ACT. Let $L_{(S,ACT)}$ be the class of LTSs whose state set is a subset of S and the action set is the subset of ACT.

Definition 2 (Composition). A function $\|: L_{ACT} \times L_{ACT} \mapsto L_{ACT}$ is called a *composition function* iff given two LTSs $M_1 = (S_1, R_1, ACT, S_0^1)$ and $M_2 = (S_2, R_2, ACT, S_0^2)$ in the class L_{ACT}, $M_1 \| M_2$ has the form $(S_1 \times S_2, R', ACT, S_0^1 \times S_0^2)$. Notice that we write the composition function in infix notation.

Our verification method handles a set of LTSs referred to as a *network*. Intuitively, a network consists of LTSs is obtained by composing any number of LTSs from $L_{(S,ACT)}$. Thus, each LTS in a network is defined over the set of actions ACT, and over a set of states in S^i, for some i.

Definition 3 (Network). Given a state set S and a set of actions ACT, any subset of $\bigcup_{i=1}^{\infty} L_{(S^i,ACT)}$ is called a *network* on the tuple (S, ACT).

2.1 Network grammars

Following [17], [13], we use context-free network grammars as a formalism to describe networks. The set of all LTSs derived by a network grammar (as "words" in its language) constitutes a network. Let S be a state set and ACT be a set of actions. Then, $G = \langle T, N, \mathcal{P}, \mathcal{S} \rangle$ is a grammar where:

- T is a set of terminals, each of which is a LTS in $L_{(S,ACT)}$. These LTSs are sometimes referred to as *basic processes.*
- N is a set of non-terminals. Each non-terminal defines a network.
- $\mathcal{P}$ is a set of production rules of the form

$$A \rightarrow B \|_i C$$

  where $A \in N$, and $B, C \in T \cup N$, and $\|_i$ is a composition function. Notice that each rule may have a different composition function.
- $\mathcal{S} \in N$ is the start symbol that represents the network generated by the grammar.

Example 1. We clarify the definitions on a network consisting of LTSs that perform a simple mutual exclusion using a token ring algorithm. The production rules of a grammar that produces rings with one process Q and at least two processes P are given below. P and Q are terminals, and A and $\mathcal{S}$ are nonterminals where $\mathcal{S}$ is the start symbol.

$$\mathcal{S} \rightarrow Q \| A$$
$$A \rightarrow P \| A$$
$$A \rightarrow P \| P$$

P and Q are LTSs defined over the set of states $\{nc, cs\}$ and the set of actions $ACT = \{\tau,$ **get-token**, **send-token**$\}$. They are identical, except for their initial state, which is cs for Q and nc for P. Their transition relation is shown in Figure 1.

For this example we assume a synchronous model of computation in which each process takes a step at any moment. We will not give a formal definition of the model here. In Section 5 we suggest a suitable definition for a synchronous model. Informally, a process can always perform a τ action. However, it can perform a **get-token** action if and only if the process to its left is ready to perform a **send-token** action. We refer to the rightmost process P as being to the left of process Q. We can apply the following derivation $\mathcal{S} \Rightarrow Q\|A \Rightarrow Q\|P\|P$ to obtain the LTS $Q\|P\|P$. The reachable states with their transitions are shown in Figure 2. Here, as well, we leave the precise definition of the composition operator unspecified.

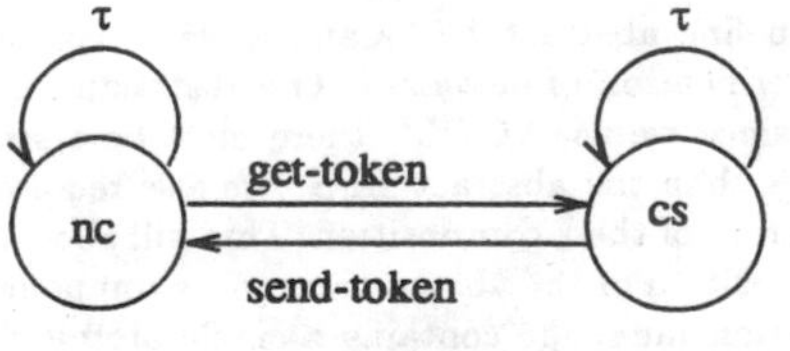

Fig. 1. Process Q, if $S_0 = \{cs\}$; process P if $S_0 = \{nc\}$

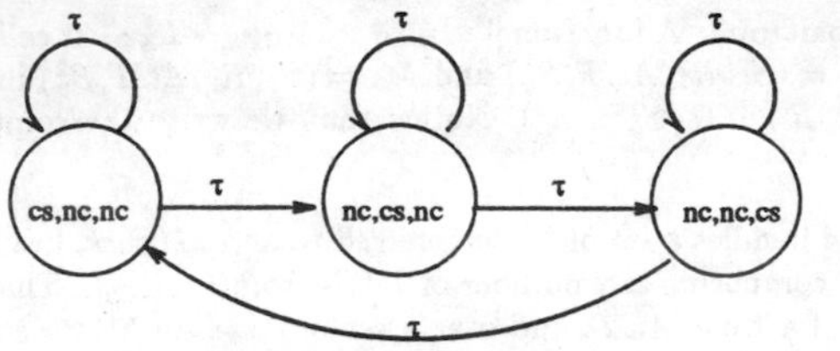

Fig. 2. Reachable states in $LTS\ Q\|P\|P$

2.2 Specification language

Let S be a set of states. From now on we assume that we have a network defined by a grammar G on the tuple (S, ACT). The automaton defined below has S as its alphabet. Thus, it accepts words which are sequences of state names.

Definition 4 Specification. $\mathcal{D} = (Q, q_0, \delta, F)$ is a *deterministic automaton* over S, where

1. Q is the set of states.
2. $q_0 \in Q$ is the initial state.
3. $\delta \subseteq Q \times S \times Q$ is the transition relation.
4. $F \subseteq Q$ is the set of accepting states.

$\mathcal{L}(\mathcal{D}) \subseteq S^*$ is the set of words accepted by $\mathcal{D}$.

Our goal is to specify a network of LTSs composed of any number of components (i.e., of basic processes). We will use finite automata over S in order to specify atomic state properties. Since a state of a LTS is a tuple from S^i, for some i, we can view such a state as a word in $S^\star$. Let $\mathcal{D}$ be an automaton over S. We say that $s \in S^\star$ satisfies $\mathcal{D}$, denoted $s \models \mathcal{D}$, iff $s \in \mathcal{L}(\mathcal{D})$. Our specification language is a *universal branching temporal logic* (e.g., $\forall CTL$, $\forall CTL^*$ [6]) with finite automata over S as the atomic formulas. The relation $\models$ for other formulas of the logic is defined in the standard way (with respect to the temporal logic under consideration) and is omitted here.

Example 2. Consider again the network of Example 1. Let $\mathcal{D}$ be the automaton of Figure 3, defined over $S = \{cs, nc\}$, with $\mathcal{L}(\mathcal{D}) = \{nc\}^* cs\{nc\}^*$. The formula $\mathbf{AG}\,\mathcal{D}$ specifies mutual exclusion, i.e. at any moment there is exactly one process in the critical section. Let $\mathcal{D}'$ be an automaton that accepts the language $cs\{nc\}^*$, then the formula $\mathbf{AG\,AF}\,\mathcal{D}'$ specifies non-starvation for process Q. Note that, for our simple example non-starvation is guaranteed only if some kind of fairness is assumed.

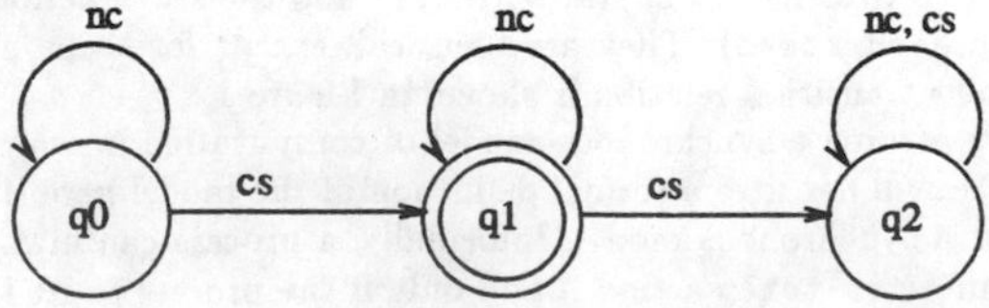

Fig. 3. Automaton $\mathcal{D}$ with $\mathcal{L}(\mathcal{D}) = \{nc\}^* cs\{nc\}^*$

3 Abstract LTSs

In the following sections we define abstract LTSs and abstract composition in order to reduce the state space required for the verification of networks. The abstraction should preserve the logic under consideration. In particular, since we use $\forall CTL^*$, there must be a *simulation preorder* $\preceq$ such that the given LTS is smaller by $\preceq$ than the abstract LTS. We also require that composing two abstract states will result in an abstraction of their composition. This will allow us to replace the abstraction of a composed LTS by the composition of the abstractions of its components. For the sake of simplicity, we assume that the specification language contains a single atomic formula $\mathcal{D}$. In Appendix A we extend the framework to a set of atomic formulas $\mathcal{D}_i$.

3.1 State equivalence

We start by defining an equivalence relation over the state set of an LTS. The equivalence classes will then be used as the abstract states of the abstract LTS. Given a LTS M, we define an equivalence relation on the states of M, such that if two states are equivalent then they both either satisfy or falsify the atomic formula. This means that the two states are either both accepted or both rejected by the automaton $\mathcal{D}$. We also require that our equivalence relation is preserved under composition. This means that if s_1 is equivalent to s'_1 and s_2 is equivalent to s'_2 then (s_1, s_2) is equivalent to (s'_1, s'_2).

We will use $h(M)$ to denote the abstract LTS of M. The straightforward definition that defines s and s' to be equivalent iff they belong to the language $\mathcal{L}(\mathcal{D})$ has the first property, but does not have the second one. To see this, consider the following example.

Example 3. Consider LTSs defined by the grammar of Example 1. Let $\mathcal{D}$ be the automaton in Figure 3, i.e., $\mathcal{L}(\mathcal{D})$ is the set of states that have exactly one component in the critical section. Let s_1, s'_1, s_2, s'_2 be states such that $s_1, s'_1 \in \mathcal{L}(\mathcal{D})$, and $s_2, s'_2 \notin \mathcal{L}(\mathcal{D})$. Further assume that, the number of components in the critical section are 0 in s_2 and 2 in s'_2. Clearly, $(s_1, s_2) \in \mathcal{L}(\mathcal{D})$ but $(s'_1, s'_2) \notin \mathcal{L}(\mathcal{D})$. Thus, the equivalence is not preserved under composition.

We therefore need a more refined equivalence relation. Our notion of equivalence is based on the idea that a word $w \in S^*$ can be viewed as a function on the set of states of an automaton. We define two states to be equivalent if and only if they induce the same function on the automaton $\mathcal{D}$.

Formally, given an automaton $\mathcal{D} = (Q, q_0, \delta, F)$ and a word $w \in S^*$, $f_w : Q \mapsto Q$, the *function induced* by w on Q is defined by

$$f_w(q) = q' \text{ iff } q \xrightarrow{w} q'.$$

Note that $w \in \mathcal{L}(\mathcal{D})$ if and only if $f_w(q_0) \in F$, i.e., w takes the initial state to a final state.

Let $\mathcal{D} = (Q, q_0, \delta, F)$ be a deterministic automaton. Let f_w be the function induced by a word w on Q. Then, two states s, s' in S^* are *equivalent*, denoted $s \equiv s'$, iff $f_s = f_{s'}$. It is easy to see that $\equiv$ is an equivalence relation. The function f_s corresponding to the state s is called the *abstraction* of s and is denoted by $h(s)$. Let $h(s) = f_1$ and $h(s') = f'_1$. Then, the abstraction of (s, s') is $h((s, s')) = f_1 \circ f'_1$ where $f_1 \circ f'_1$ denotes composition of functions.

Note that $s \equiv s'$ implies that $s \in \mathcal{L}(\mathcal{D}) \Leftrightarrow s' \in \mathcal{L}(\mathcal{D})$. Thus, we have $s \models \mathcal{D}$ iff $s' \models \mathcal{D}$. We also have,

Lemma 5. If $h(s_1) = h(s_2)$ and $h(s'_1) = h(s'_2)$ then $h((s_1, s'_1)) = h((s_2, s'_2))$.

In order to interpret specifications on the abstract LTSs, we extend $\models$ to abstract states so that $h(s) \models \mathcal{D}$ iff $f_s(q_0) \in F$. This guarantees that $s \models \mathcal{D}$ iff $h(s) \models \mathcal{D}$.

Example 4. Consider again the automaton $\mathcal{D}$ of Figure 3 over $S = \{cs, nc\}$. $\mathcal{D}$ induces functions $f_s : Q \mapsto Q$, for every $s \in S^*$. Actually, there are only three different functions, each identifying an equivalence class over S^*. $f_1 = \{(q_0, q_0), (q_1, q_1), (q_2, q_2)\}$ represents all $s \in nc^*$ (i.e., $f_s = f_1$ for all $s \in nc^*$). $f_2 = \{(q_0, q_1), (q_1, q_2), (q_2, q_2)\}$ represents all $s \in nc^*\ cs\ nc^*$, and $f_3 = \{(q_0, q_2), (q_1, q_2), (q_2, q_2)\}$ represents all $s \in nc^*\ cs\ nc^*\ cs\ \{cs, nc\}^*$.

3.2 Abstract Process and Abstract Composition

Let $\mathcal{F}_\mathcal{D}$ be the set of functions corresponding to the deterministic automaton $\mathcal{D}$. Let Q be the set of states in $\mathcal{D}$. In the worst case $|\mathcal{F}_\mathcal{D}| = |Q|^{|Q|}$, but in practice the size is much smaller. Note that $\mathcal{F}_\mathcal{D}$ is also the set of abstract states for $s \in S^*$ with respect to $\mathcal{D}$. Subsequently, we will apply abstraction both to states $s \in S^*$ and to abstract states f_s for $s \in S^*$. To unify notation we first extend the abstraction function h to $\mathcal{F}_\mathcal{D}$ by setting $h(f) = f$ for $f \in \mathcal{F}_\mathcal{D}$. We further extend the abstraction function h to $(S \cup \mathcal{F}_\mathcal{D})^*$ in the natural way, i.e. $h((a_1, a_2, \cdots, a_n)) = h(a_1) \circ \cdots \circ h(a_n)$. From now on we will consider LTSs in the network $\mathcal{N}$ on the tuple $(S \cup \mathcal{F}_\mathcal{D}, ACT)$.

Next we define abstract LTSs over abstract states. The abstract transition relation is defined as usual for an abstraction that should be greater by the simulation preorder than the original structure [7]. If there is a transition between one state and another in the original structure, then there is a transition between the abstract state of the one to the abstract state of the other in the abstract structure. Formally,

Definition 6. Given a LTS $M = (S, R, ACT, S_0)$ in the network $\mathcal{N}$, the corresponding *abstract LTS* is defined by $h(M) = (S^h, R^h, ACT, S^h_0)$, where

- $S^h = \{h(s) \mid s \in S\}$ is the set of abstract states.
- $S^h_0 = \{h(s) \mid s \in S_0\}$.
- The relation R^h is defined as follows. For any $h_1, h_2 \in S^h$, and $a \in ACT$

$$(h_1, a, h_2) \in R^h \Leftrightarrow \exists s_1, s_2[h_1 = h(s_1) \text{ and } h_2 = h(s_2) \text{and } (s_1, a, s_2) \in R].$$

We say that M *simulates* M' [14] (denoted $M \preceq M'$) if and only if there is a *simulation preorder* $\mathcal{E} \subseteq S \times S'$ that satisfies: for every $s_0 \in S_0$ there is $s'_0 \in S'_0$ such that $(s_0, s'_0) \in \mathcal{E}$. Moreover, for every s, s', if $(s, s') \in \mathcal{E}$ then

1. We have that $h(s) = h(s')$.
2. For every s_1 such that $s \xrightarrow{a} s_1$ there is s'_1 such that $s' \xrightarrow{a} s'_1$ and $(s_1, s'_1) \in \mathcal{E}$.

Lemma 7. $M \preceq h(M)$, i.e. M simulates $h(M)$.

Recall that the abstraction h guarantees that a state and its abstraction agree on the atomic property corresponding to the automaton $\mathcal{D}$. Based on that and on the previous lemma, the following theorem is obtained. A proof of a similar result appears in [6].

Theorem 8. Let ϕ be a formula in $\forall CTL^*$ over an atomic formula $\mathcal{D}$. Then, $h(M) \models \phi$ implies $M \models \phi$.

Let M and M' be two LTSs in the network $\mathcal{N}$, and let $\|$ be a composition function. The abstract composition function corresponding to $\|$ (denoted by $\|_h$) is defined as follows:

$$M \|_h M' = h(M \| M')$$

Definition 9. A composition $\|$ is called *monotonic* with respect to a simulation preorder $\preceq$ iff given LTSs such that $M_1 \preceq M_2$ and $M'_1 \preceq M'_2$ it should be true that $M_1 \| M'_1 \preceq M_2 \| M'_2$.

4 Verification method

Given a grammar G, we associate with each terminal and nonterminal A of the grammar an abstract structure *rep*(A) that *represents* all LTSs derived from A by the grammar. Thus for every LTS (a) derived from A we have that *rep*$(A) \succeq a$. This implies that for every network t, derived from the initial symbol $\mathcal{S}$, *rep*$(\mathcal{S}) \succeq t$ and therefore, any property of *rep*$(\mathcal{S})$, expressed in the logic $\forall CTL^*$ is also a property of t. We require that the composition functions used in the grammar G are monotonic with respect to $\preceq$ when applied to ordinary LTSs and to abstract LTSs.
Our verification method is as follows:

- 1. For every terminal A, choose *rep*$(A) = h(A)$ [3].
  2. Given a rule $A \rightarrow B \| C$ of the grammar, if *rep*(A) is not defined yet, and if *rep*(B) and *rep*(C) are defined, then define *rep*$(A) =$ *rep*$(B) \|_h$ *rep*(C).

  If every symbol of the grammar is reachable by some derivation from the initial symbol, and if each symbol derives at least one LTS then the algorithm will terminate and *rep*(A) will be defined for every symbol A. In particular, when rules of the form $A \rightarrow A \| C$ are encountered, *rep*(A) is already defined.
- For every rule $A \rightarrow B \| C$ in G show: *rep*$(A) \succeq$ *rep*$(B) \|_h$ *rep*(C).

Theorem 10. Assume that the verification method has been successfully applied to the grammar G. Let A be a symbol in G and let a be a LTS derived from A in G, then *rep*$(A) \succeq a$.

5 Synchronous model of computation

In this section we develop a synchronous framework that will have the properties required by our verification method. We define a synchronous model of computation and a family of composition operators. We show that the composition operators are monotonic with respect to $\preceq$.

Our models are a form of LTSs, $M = (S, R, I, O, S_0)$, that represent *Moore machines*. They have an explicit notion of inputs I and outputs O that must be disjoint. In addition, they have a special

---

[3] Actually, for a terminal A it is sufficient to choose any abstract LTS (defined over $\mathcal{F}_\mathcal{D}$) that satisfies *rep*$(A) \succeq A$

internal action denoted by τ (called silent action in the terminology of CCS [15]). The set of actions is $ACT = \{\tau\} \cup 2^{I \cup O}$, where each non-internal action is a set of inputs and outputs. In standard Moore machine the outputs are usually associated with the states while the inputs are associated with the transitions. Here, we associate both inputs and outputs with the transitions while maintaining the distinction between inputs and outputs. A transition $s \xrightarrow{\tau} s_1$ in a machine M can always be executed. It has not effect on other machines. It is used to hide wires once they are connected, in order to avoid the output signal from being connected to other input wires. Refer to the use of τ in the hiding function defined later.

The composition of two *LTS*s M and M' is defined to reflect the synchronous behavior of our model. It corresponds to standard composition of Moore machines. To understand how this composition works we can think of the inputs and outputs as "wires". If M has an output and M' has an input both named a, then in the composition the output wire a will be connected to the input a. Since an input can accept signal only from one output, $M \| M'$ will not have a as input. On the other hand, an output can be sent to several inputs, thus $M \| M'$ still has a as output. Consequently, the set of outputs of $M \| M'$ is $O \cup O'$ while the set of inputs is $(I \cup I') \setminus (O \cup O')$.

A transition $s \xrightarrow{a} t$ from s in a machine M with $a = i \cup o$ such that $i \subseteq I$ and $o \subseteq O$ occurs only if the environment supplies inputs i and the machine M produces the outputs o. Assume transitions $s \xrightarrow{a} t$ in M and $s' \xrightarrow{a'} t'$ in M'. There will be a joint transition from (s, s') to (t, t') iff the outputs provided by M agree with the inputs expected by M' and the outputs provided by M' agree with the inputs expected by M.

Formally, let $O \cap O' = \emptyset$. The *synchronous composition* of M and M', $M'' = M \parallel M'$ is defined by:

1. $S'' = S \times S'$.
2. $S_0'' = S_0 \times S_0'$.
3. $I'' = (I \cup I') \setminus (O \cup O')$.
4. $O'' = O \cup O'$.[4]
5. $(s, s') \xrightarrow{a''} (s_1, s_1')$ is a transition in R'' iff the following holds: $s \xrightarrow{a} s_1$ is a transition in R and $s' \xrightarrow{a'} s_1'$ is a transition in R' for some a, a' such that either $a = \tau$ and $a'' = a$ or $a' = \tau$ and $a'' = a$ or $a \cap (I' \cup O') = a' \cap (I \cup O)$ and $a'' = (a \cup a') \cap (I'' \cup O'')$.

Lemma 11. The composition $\|$ is monotonic with respect to $\preceq$.

5.1 Network grammars for synchronous models

Only a few additional definitions are required in order to adapt our general definition of network grammars to networks of synchronous models. Like before a network grammar is a tuple $G = \langle T, N, \mathcal{P}, \mathcal{S} \rangle$, but now, every terminal and nonterminal A in $T \cup N$ is associated with a set of inputs I_A and a set of outputs O_A.

In G we allow different composition operators $\|_i$ for the different production rules. In order to define the family of operators to be used in this framework we need the following definitions.

A *renaming function* $\mathcal{R}$ is an injection. When applied to A, it maps inputs to inputs and outputs to outputs such that $\mathcal{R}(I_A) \cap \mathcal{R}(O_A) = \emptyset$. Applying $\mathcal{R}$ to a *LTS* M results in an *LTS* $M' = \mathcal{R}(M)$ with $S = S'$, $S_0 = S_0'$, $I' = \mathcal{R}(I)$, $O' = \mathcal{R}(O)$, and $(s, a, s') \in R$ iff $(s, \mathcal{R}(a), s') \in R'$.

A *hiding function* $\mathcal{R}_{act}$ for $act \subseteq I \cup O$, is a function that maps each element in act to τ. Let $M' = \mathcal{R}_{act}(M)$ then $S' = S$, $S_0' = S_0$, $I' = I \setminus act$, and $O' = O \setminus act$. Moreover, $s \xrightarrow{a} s'$ is a transition in M iff $a \setminus act \neq \emptyset$ and $s \xrightarrow{a \setminus act} s'$ is a transition in M' or $a \setminus act = \emptyset$ and $s \xrightarrow{\tau} s'$ is a transition in M'.

A typical composition operator in this family is associated with two renaming functions, $\mathcal{R}_{\mathtt{left}}$, $\mathcal{R}_{\mathtt{right}}$ and a hiding function $\mathcal{R}_{act}$, in the following way.

$$M \|_i M' = \mathcal{R}_{act}(\mathcal{R}_{\mathtt{left}}(M) \| \mathcal{R}_{\mathtt{right}}(M')),$$

where $\|$ is the synchronous composition defined before.

[4] Note that, $ACT'' = 2^{I'' \cup O''}$ is not identical to ACT and ACT'. This is a technical issue that can be resolved by defining some superset of actions from which each LTS takes its actions.

To be used in our framework, we need to show that every such operator is monotonic, i.e., if $M_1 \preceq M_2$ and $M_1' \preceq M_2'$ then $M_1 \|_i M_1' \preceq M_2 \|_i M_2'$. The latter means that $\mathcal{R}_{act}(\mathcal{R}_{\texttt{left}}(M_1) \| \mathcal{R}_{\texttt{right}}(M_1')) \preceq \mathcal{R}_{act}(\mathcal{R}_{\texttt{left}}(M_2) \| \mathcal{R}_{\texttt{right}}(M_2'))$.

The following lemma, together with monotonicity of the synchronous composition $\|$ imply the required result.

Lemma 12. Let M, M' be synchronous *LTS*s and let $\mathcal{R}$ be a renaming function and let $\mathcal{R}_{act}$ be a hiding function. If $M \preceq M'$, then $\mathcal{R}(M) \preceq \mathcal{R}(M')$ and $\mathcal{R}_{act}(M) \preceq \mathcal{R}_{act}(M')$.

Corollary 13. The composition operators $\|_i$, defined as above are monotonic.

Example 5. We return to Example 1 and reformulate it within the synchronous framework. Doing so we can describe more precisely the processes and the network grammar that constructs rings with any number of processes. The processes P and Q will be identical to those described in Figure 1 except that now we also specify for both processes $I = \{\texttt{get-token}\}$ and $O = \{\texttt{send-token}\}$.

The derivation rules in the grammar apply two different composition operators:

$$\boxed{\begin{array}{l} S \rightarrow Q\|_1 A \\ A \rightarrow P\|_2 A \\ A \rightarrow P\|_2 P \end{array}}$$

$\|_1$ is defined as follows (see also Figure 7 in appendix B):

- $\mathcal{R}^1_{\texttt{left}}$ maps **send-token** to some new action **cr** (stands for **connect right**) and **get-token** to **cl** (stands for **connect left**).
- $\mathcal{R}^1_{\texttt{right}}$ maps **send-token** to **cl** and **get-token** to **cr**.
- The hiding function hides both **cr** and **cl** by mapping them to τ.

Thus, the application of this rule results in a network with one terminal Q and one nonterminal A, connected as a *ring*.
$\|_2$ is defined by (see Figure 7 in appendix B):

- $\mathcal{R}^2_{\texttt{left}}$ maps **send-token** to **cr** and leaves **get-token** unchanged.
- $\mathcal{R}^2_{\texttt{right}}$ maps **get-token** to **cr** and leaves **send-token** unchanged.
- The hiding function hides **cr**

The application of the third rule, for instance, results in a network in which the nonterminal A is replaced by a *LTS* consisting of two processes P, such that the **send-token** of the left one is connected to the **get-token** of the right one. The **get-token** of the left process and **send-token** of the right one will be connected according to the connections of A (see Figure 7 and Figure 8 in Appendix B). Note that, in the derivation of an *LTS* by the grammar, the derivation is completed before the renaming and the hiding functions are applied. These functions are applied to *LTS*s and not to the non-terminals representing them.

6 Examples

We implemented the algorithm for network verification for the synchronous model and applied it to two examples of substantial complexity. These examples were verified with the aid of our verification tool.

6.1 Dijkstra's Token Ring

The first is the famous Dijkstra's token ring algorithm [8]. This algorithm is significantly more complicated than the one used as a running example along the paper. There is a token t which passes in the clockwise direction. To avoid the token from passing unnecessarily, there is a signal s which passes in the counter-clockwise direction. Whenever a process wishes to have the token, it sends the signal s to its left neighbor. The states of the processes have the following three properties:

- It is either n (in the neutral state), d (the process is delayed waiting for the token) or c (the process is in the critical section)

- It is either b (black–an interest in the token exists to the right), w (white–no one is interested in the token)
- It is either t (with the token), or e (empty–without the token).

The name of a state is a combination of its properties. Thus *wne* is a neutral state with no request on the right and no token. Each process has **get-token** and **get-signal** as inputs and **send-token** and **send-signal** as outputs. The notation $x_1 \xrightarrow{\alpha/\beta} x_2$ means that on the input α a transition is made from the state x_1 to the state x_2 producing output β. If the input is missing, it means that on any input the transition is made. If the output is missing, it means that no output is produced on that transition. The list of transitions for a process that performs the token ring protocol is shown in the table below. The symbol s stands for either **get-signal** or **send-signal** and t stands for either **get-token** or **send-token**. Each state has also a self loop on the internal transition τ. These transitions are omitted from the table. Note that, when a process makes a τ transition it does not communicate with its neighbors. Thus, its neighbors have to be involved in some other transition–either internal or a communication with another process.

$wne \xrightarrow{s/s} bne$	$wne \xrightarrow{/s} wde$	$bne \rightarrow bde$
$bne \xrightarrow{t/t} wne$	$wde \xrightarrow{s/} bde$	$wde \xrightarrow{t/} wct$
$bde \xrightarrow{t/} bct$	$wnt \xrightarrow{s/t} wde$	$wnt \rightarrow wct$
$wct \xrightarrow{s/} bct$	$wct \rightarrow wnt$	$bct \xrightarrow{/t} wne$

Let Q be the process with *wnt* as the initial state and the transition relation shown above. Let P be the process with *wne* as the initial state and with the same transition relation as Q. The network grammar generating a token-ring of arbitrary size is similar to that of Example 5, where **get-signal** or **send-signal** are treated similarly to **get-token** or **send-token**. It turns out that *LTS*s consisting of less than three processes of type P have different behaviors than the *LTS*s composed of three or more P processes. We exclude such *LTS*s by replacing the last rule in the grammar by:

$$A \rightarrow P \| P \| P.$$

Let S be the set of states in a *basic* process of the token ring. Let `t` be the subset of states which has the token. Let `not-t` be the set $S \setminus t$. The automaton $\mathcal{D}$ is the same as the automaton in Figure 3 with `t` substituted for *cs* and `not-t` substituted for *nc*. The automaton accepts strings S^* such that the number of processes with the tokens is exactly one. Let h be the abstraction function induced by the automaton. We choose $rep(P) = h(P)$,and $rep(Q) = h(Q)$ and $rep(A) = h(P) \|_h h(P) \|_h h(P)$. Using the first rule of the grammar we have that $rep(\mathcal{S}) = h(Q) \|_h h(A)$. Using our verification tool we were automatically able to check that $rep(A) \succeq rep(A) \|_h rep(P)$. By Theorem 10 we conclude that $rep(\mathcal{S})$ simulates all the *LTS*s generated by the grammar G. Notice that if $rep(\mathcal{S})$ satisfies the property $\mathbf{AG}\,\mathcal{D}$, then Theorem 8 implies that every *LTS* generated by the grammar G satisfies $\mathbf{AG}\,\mathcal{D}$. Using our verification tool we established that $rep(\mathcal{S})$ is a model for $\mathbf{AG}\,\mathcal{D}$.

6.2 Parity tree

We consider a network of binary trees, in which each leaf has a bit value. We describe an algorithm that computes the parity of the leaves values. The algorithm is taken from [19]. A context-free grammar G generating a binary tree is given below, where **root**, **inter** and **leaf** are terminals (basic processes) and $\mathcal{S}$ and SUB are nonterminals.

$\mathcal{S} \rightarrow$ **root**‖SUB‖SUB
SUB $\rightarrow$ **inter**‖SUB‖SUB
SUB $\rightarrow$ **inter**‖**leaf**‖**leaf**

The algorithm works as follows. The **root** process initiates a wave by sending the *readydown* signal to its children. Every internal node that gets the signal sends it further to its children. When the signal *readydown* reaches a **leaf** process, the leaf sends the *readyup* signal and its *value* to its parent. An internal node that receives the *readyup* and *value* from both its children, sends the *readyup* signal and the $\oplus$ of the values received from the children to its parent. When the *readyup* signal reaches the **root**, one wave of the computation is terminated and the **root** can initiate another wave. This description is somewhat informal. Actually, at any step of the computation each process outputs its relevant state variables to its neighbors. It also gets inputs from its neighbors and updates its state variables accordingly. Thus saying that a process gets a signal actually means that at the current step, the value of this signal (received by the process as input) is 1. The semantics of the composition used in the grammar G should be clear from Figure 4. For example, the inputs *readyup_l* and *value_l* of an internal node are identified with the outputs *readyup* and *value* of its left child. Next, we describe the various signals in detail. First we describe the process **inter**. The process **inter** is the process

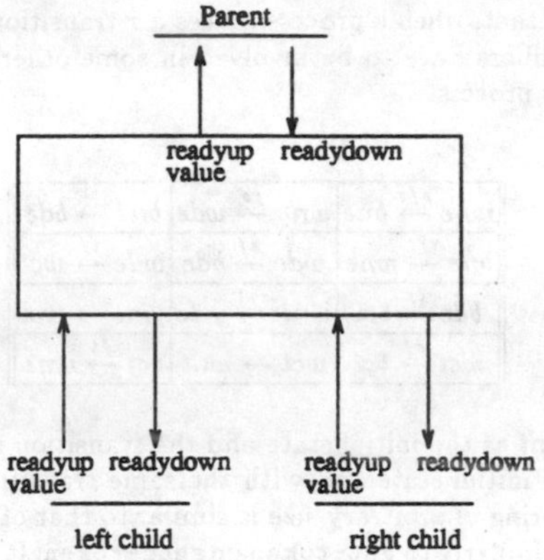

Fig. 4. Internal node of the tree

in the internal node of the tree. The various variables for the process are shown in the table:

state vars	output vars	input vars
root_or_leaf	*readydown*	*readydown*
readydown	*readyup*	*readyup_l*
readyup_l	*value*	*readyup_r*
readyup_r		*value_l*
value		*value_r*
readyup		

The following equations are invariants for the state variables:

$$root\_or\_leaf = 0$$
$$readyup = readyup\_l \wedge readyup\_r$$

The output variables have the same value in each state as the corresponding state variable, e.g. the output variable *readydown* has the same value as the state variable *readydown*. The equations given below show how the input variables affect the state variables. In the equations given below the primed variables on the left hand side refer to the next state variables and the right hand side refers to the input variables.

$$readydown' = readydown$$
$$readyup\_l' = readyup\_l$$
$$readyup\_r' = readyup\_r$$
$$value' = (readyup\_l \wedge value\_l) \oplus (readyup\_r \wedge value\_r)$$

Since the **root** process does not have a parent, it does not have the input variable *readydown*. The invariant $root\_or\_leaf = 1$ is maintained for the **root** and the **leaf** process. Since the **leaf** process does not have a child, the output variable *readydown* is absent. The **leaf** process has only one input variable *readydown* and the following equation between the next state variables and input variables is maintained:

$$readyup' = readydown$$

For each **leaf** process the assignment for the state variable *value* is decided non-deterministically in the initial state and then kept the same throughout.

A state in the basic processes (**root,leaf,inter**) is a specific assignment to the state variables. We call this state set S. Notice that the state set $S \cong \{0,1\}^6$ because there are 6 state variables. The automata we describe accept strings from S^*. Let $value_1, \cdots, value_n$ be the values in the n leaves. Let *value* be the value calculated at the root. Since at the end of the computation the root process should have the parity of the bits $value_i$ $(1 \leq i \leq n)$, the following equation should hold at the end of the computation:

$$value \oplus \bigoplus_{i=1}^{n} value_i = 0.$$

Let p be defined by the following equation:

$$p = \{s \in S | s \text{ satisfies } root\_or\_leaf \wedge value\}.$$

Let $not(p) = S - p$. The automaton $\mathcal{D}_{par}$ given in Figure 5 accepts the strings in S^* which satisfy the equation given above. Since $root\_or\_leaf = 0$ for internal nodes, the automaton essentially ignores the values at the internal nodes. We also want to assert that everybody is finished with their computation.

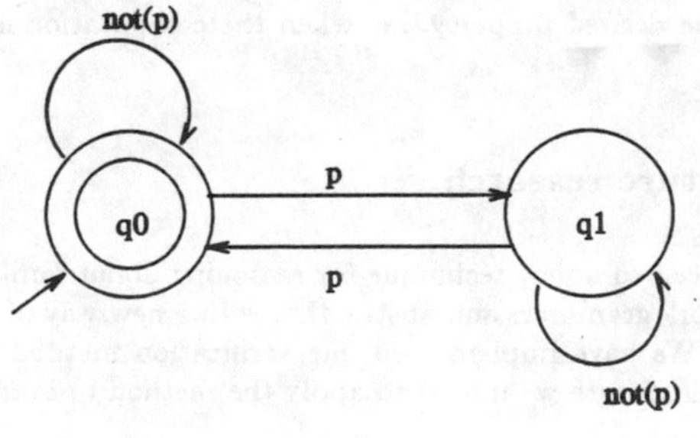

Fig. 5. Automaton (D_{par}) for parity

This is signaled by the fact that $readyup = 1$ for each process. The automaton $\mathcal{D}_{ter}$ given in Figure 6 accepts strings in S^* iff $readyup = 1$ in each state. i.e. all processes have finished their computation. The property $D_{ter} \Rightarrow D_{par}$ says that if the computation is finished in a state, then the parity is correct at the **root**. We want to check that every reachable state of an LTS in the network has the desired property, i.e. $\mathbf{AG}(D_{ter} \Rightarrow D_{par})$ is true. We use as our atomic formula the union of $\mathcal{D}_{par}$ and $\mathcal{D}_{\neg ter}$ (the complement of $\mathcal{D}_{ter}$). Let h be the abstraction function induced by this automaton (see Section 3 for the definition of h). Let $\|_h$ be the abstract composition operator and $\preceq$ the simulates relation. Let I_1, I_2 be abstract processes defined as follows:

$$I_1 = h(inter)\|_h h(leaf)\|_h h(leaf)$$
$$I_2 = h(inter)\|_h I_1 \|_h I_1$$

The following equations were verified automatically by our verification tool:

$$h(inter)\|_h I_1 \|_h I_1 \not\preceq I_1$$
$$I_1 \preceq I_2$$
$$h(inter)\|_h I_2 \|_h I_2 \preceq I_2$$

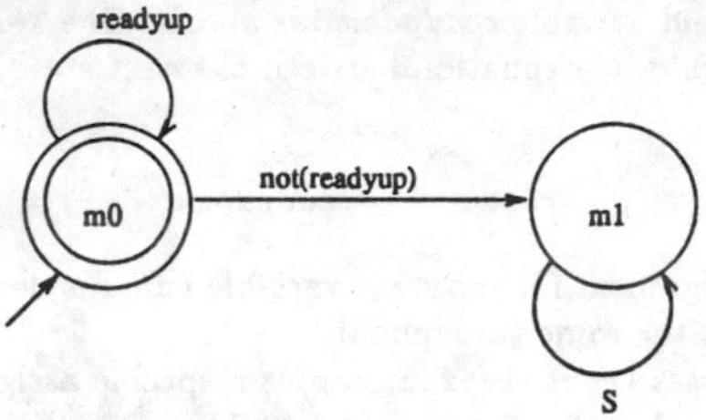

Fig. 6. Automaton (D_{ter}) for ready

From the first equation given above it is clear the I_1 cannot be used as a representative for the non-terminal SUB, i.e if we set *rep*(SUB) $= I_1$, the induction corresponding to the second rule of the grammar does not hold. Notice that I_2 was derived from the second rule of the grammar by substituting I_1 for SUB. Suppose we use *rep*(SUB) $= I_2$ and $rep(\mathcal{S}) = h(\text{root})\|_h I_2\|_h I_2$ as the representatives for the non terminals. From the equations given above the following inequalities can be derived:

$$rep(\text{SUB}) \succeq h(\text{inter})\|_h rep(\text{SUB})\|_h rep(\text{SUB})$$
$$rep(\text{SUB}) \succeq h(\text{inter})\|_h h(\text{leaf})\|_h h(\text{leaf})$$

Now using Theorem 10 we can conclude that $H = h(root)\|_h I_2\|_h I_2$ simulates all the networks generated by the context free grammar G. After we constructed H, we verified automatically, that all reachable states in H have the desired property. Now by Theorem 8 we have the result that every LTS derived by G has the desired property, i.e. when the computation is finished the root process has the correct parity.

7 Direction for future research

In this paper we have described a new technique for reasoning about families of finite-state systems. This work combines network grammars and abstraction with a new way of specifying state properties using regular languages. We have implemented our verification method and used it to check two non-trivial examples. In the future we intend to apply the method to even more complex families of state-transition systems.

There are several directions for future research. The context-free network grammars can be replaced by context-sensitive grammars. Context-sensitive grammars can generate networks like square grids and complete binary tree which cannot be generated by the context-free grammars. The specification language can be strengthened by replacing regular languages by more expressive formalisms. We might also consider adding fairness to our models (LTSs). Finally, we intend to extend the techniques described in this paper to asynchronous models of computation.

References

1. K. Apt and D. Kozen. Limits for automatic verification of finite-state systems. *IPL*, 15:307–309, 1986.
2. M. Browne, E. Clarke, and O. Grumberg. Reasoning about networks with many identical finite-state processes. *Inf. and Computation*, 81(1):13–31, Apr. 1989.
3. J. Burch, E. Clarke, K. McMillan, D. Dill, and L. Hwang. Symbolic model checking: 10^{20} states and beyond. *Inf. and Computation*, 98(2):142–170, June 1992.
4. E. M. Clarke and E. A. Emerson. Synthesis of synchronization skeletons for branching time temporal logic. In *Logic of Programs: Workshop, Yorktown Heights, NY, May 1981*, volume 131 of *LNCS*. Springer-Verlag, 1981.
5. E. M. Clarke, E. A. Emerson, and A. P. Sistla. Automatic verification of finite-state concurrent systems using temporal logic specifications. *ACM Trans. Prog. Lang. Syst.*, 8(2):244–263, 1986.
6. E. M. Clarke, O. Grumberg, and D. E. Long. Model checking and abstraction. In *Proc. 19th Ann. ACM Symp. on Principles of Prog. Lang.*, Jan. 1992.
7. D. Dams, O. Grumberg, and R. Gerth. Abstract interpretation of reactive systems: Abstractions preserving ACTL*,ECTL*, and CTL*. In *IFIP working conference and Programming Concepts, Methods and Calculi (PROCOMET'94)*, San Miniato, Italy, June 1994.

8. E. Dijkstra. Invariance and non-determinacy. In C. Hoare and J. Sheperdson, editors, *Mathematical Logic and Programming Languages.* 1985.
9. E. Emerson and K. S. Namjoshi. Reasoning about rings. In *Proc. 22nd Ann. ACM Symp. on Principles of Prog. Lang.*, Jan. 1995.
10. S. German and A. Sistla. Reasoning about systems with many processes. *J. ACM*, 39:675–735, 1992.
11. R. P. Kurshan and K. L. McMillan. A structural induction theorem for processes. In *Proc. 8th Ann. ACM Symp. on Principles of Distributed Computing.* ACM Press, Aug. 1989.
12. O. Lichtenstein and A. Pnueli. Checking that finite state concurrent programs satisfy their linear specification. In *Proc. 12th Ann. ACM Symp. on Principles of Prog. Lang.*, Jan. 1985.
13. R. Marelly and O. Grumberg. GORMEL—Grammar ORiented ModEL checker. Technical Report 697, The Technion, Oct. 1991.
14. R. Milner. An algebraic definition of simulation between programs. In *In proceedings of the 2nd International Joint Conference on Artificial Intelligence*, pages 481–489, 1971.
15. R. Milner. *A Calculus of Communicating Systems*, volume 92 of *LNCS.* Springer-Verlag, 1980.
16. J. Quielle and J. Sifakis. Specification and verification of concurrent systems in CESAR. In *Proc. Fifth Int. Symp. in Programming*, 1981.
17. Z. Shtadler and O. Grumberg. Network grammars, communication behaviors and automatic verification. In Sifakis [18].
18. J. Sifakis, editor. *Proc. 1989 Int. Workshop on Automatic Verification Methods for Finite State Systems*, volume 407 of *LNCS.* Springer-Verlag, June 1989.
19. J. D. Ullman. *Computational Aspects of VLSI.* Computer Science Press, 1984.
20. I. Vernier. Parameterized evaluation of CTL-X formulae. In *Workshop accompanying the Internation Conference on Temporal Logic (ICTL'94)*, 1994.
21. P. Wolper and V. Lovinfosse. Verifying properties of large sets of processes with network invariants. In Sifakis [18].

A Appendix: Extension to multiple atomic formulas

Our framework can easily be extended to any set of atomic formulas. The restriction to one atomic formula was done in order to simplify presentation. However, in practice we may want to have several such formulas, related by boolean and temporal operators.

The notion of equivalence can be extended to any set of atomic formulas. Let $\mathcal{AF} = \{\mathcal{D}_1, \ldots, \mathcal{D}_k\}$ be a set of atomic formulas, where $\mathcal{D}_i = (Q_i, q_0^i, \delta_i, F_i)$. Let f_s^i be the function induced by s on Q_i. Then, two states s, s' are *equivalent* if and only if for every i, $f_s^i = f_{s'}^i$.

The abstraction of s is now $h(s) = < f_s^1, \ldots, f_s^k >$, and we have that, if $s \equiv s'$ then for every i, $s \in \mathcal{L}(\mathcal{D}_i) \Leftrightarrow s' \in \mathcal{L}(\mathcal{D}_i)$. Abstract *LTS*s are defined as before.

The relation $\models$ is extended for abstract states by defining $h(s) \models \mathcal{D}_i$ iff $f_s^i(q_0^i) \in F_i$. Thus, we again have that for every $\mathcal{D}_i \in \mathcal{AF}$, $s \models \mathcal{D}_i$ iff $h(s) \models \mathcal{D}_i$.

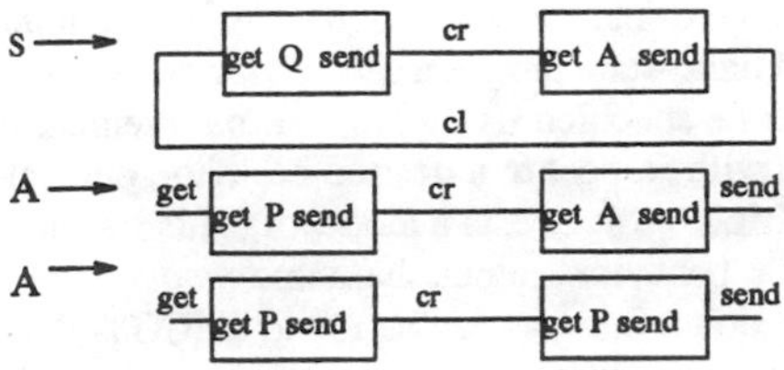

Fig. 7. Derivation rules with renaming

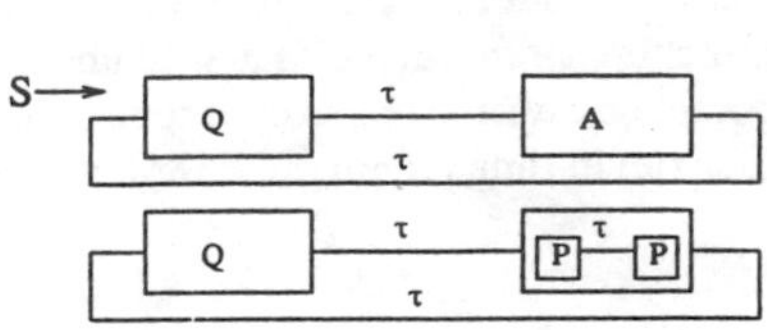

Fig. 8. Derivation of a ring of size 3

On the Complexity of Branching Modular Model Checking (Extended Abstract)

Orna Kupferman[1] and Moshe Y. Vardi[2]

[1] The Technion, Department of Computer Science, Haifa 32000, Israel.
Email: ornab@cs.technion.ac.il
[2] Rice University, Department of Computer Science, P.O. Box 1892, Houston, TX 77251-1892, U.S.A. Email: vardi@cs.rice.edu

Abstract. In *modular verification* the specification of a module consists of two parts. One part describes the guaranteed behavior of the module. The other part describes the assumed behavior of the system in which the module is interacting. This is called the *assume-guarantee* paradigm. In this paper we consider assume-guarantee specifications in which the assumptions and the guarantees are specified by universal branching temporal formulas (i.e., all path quantifiers are universal). Verifying modules with respect to such specifications is called the *branching modular model-checking problem*. We consider both ∀CTL and ∀CTL*, the universal fragments of CTL and CTL*. We develop two fundamental techniques: building maximal models for ∀CTL and ∀CTL* formulas and using alternating automata to obtain space-efficient algorithms for fair model checking. Using these techniques we classify the complexity of satisfiability, validity, implication, and modular model checking for both ∀CTL and ∀CTL*. In particular, branching modular model checking is PSPACE-complete for ∀CTL and EXPSPACE-complete for ∀CTL*.

1 Introduction

Temporal logics, which are modal logics geared towards the description of the temporal ordering of events, have been adopted as a powerful tool for specifying and verifying concurrent programs [Pnu77]. One of the most significant developments in this area is the discovery of algorithmic methods for verifying temporal logic properties of *finite-state* programs [CES86, LP85, QS81]. This derives its significance both from the fact that many synchronization and communication protocols can be modeled as finite-state programs, as well as from the great ease of use of fully algorithmic methods. Finite-state programs can be modeled by transition systems where each state has a bounded description, and hence can be characterized by a fixed number of Boolean atomic propositions. This means that a finite-state program can be viewed as a finite *propositional Kripke structure* and its properties can be specified using *propositional* temporal logic. Thus, to verify the correctness of the program with respect to a desired behavior, one only has to check that the program, modeled as a finite Kripke structure, is a model of (satisfies) the propositional temporal logic formula that specifies that behavior. Hence the name *model checking* for the verification methods derived from this viewpoint. Surveys can be found in [CG87, Wol89, CGL93].

We distinguish between two types of temporal logics: linear and branching [Lam80]. In linear temporal logics, each moment in time has a unique possible future, while in branching temporal logics, each moment in time may split into several possible futures. The complexity of model checking for both linear and branching temporal logics is well understood. Suppose we are given a program of size n and a temporal logic formula of size m; for a branching temporal logic such as CTL, model-checking algorithms run in time $O(nm)$ [CES86], while, for a linear temporal logic such as LTL, model-checking algorithms run in time $O(n2^m)$ [LP85]. Since model checking with respect to a linear temporal logic formula is PSPACE-complete [SC85], the latter bound probably cannot be improved. The difference in the complexity of linear and branching model checking has been viewed as an argument in favor of the branching paradigm.

Model checking suffers, however, from the so-called *state-explosion* problem. In a concurrent setting, the program under consideration is typically the parallel composition of many modules. As a result, the size of the state space of the program is the product of the sizes of the state spaces of the participating modules. This gives rise to state spaces of exceedingly large sizes, which makes even linear-time algorithms impractical. This issue is one of the most important ones in the area of computer-aided verification and is the subject of active research (cf. [BCM+90]).

Modular verification is one possible way to address the state-explosion problem, cf. [CLM89]. In modular verification, one uses proof rules of the following form:

$$\left.\begin{array}{l} M_1 \models \psi_1 \\ M_2 \models \psi_2 \\ C(\psi_1, \psi_2, \psi) \end{array}\right\} M_1 \| M_2 \models \psi$$

Here $M \models \theta$ means that the module M satisfies the formula θ, the symbol "$\|$" denotes parallel composition, and $C(\psi_1, \psi_2, \psi)$ is some logical condition relating ψ_1, ψ_2, and ψ. The advantage of using modular proof rules is that it enables one to apply model checking only to the underlying modules, which have much smaller state spaces.

The state-explosion problem is only one motivation for pursuing modular verification. Modular verification is advocated also for other methodological reasons; a robust verification methodology should provide rules for deducing properties of programs from the properties of their constituent modules. Indeed, efforts to develop modular verification frameworks were undertaken in the mid 1980s; [Pnu85] is a good survey.

A key observation, see [Jon83, Lam83], is that in modular verification the specification should include two parts. One part describes the desired behavior of the module. The other part describes the assumed behavior of the system within which the module is interacting. This is called the *assume-guarantee* paradigm, as the specification describes what behavior the module is *guaranteed* to exhibit, *assuming* that the system behaves in the promised way.

For the linear temporal paradigm, an assume-guarantee specification is a pair $\langle \varphi, \psi \rangle$, where both φ and ψ are linear temporal logic formulas. The meaning of such a pair is that all the computations of the module are guaranteed to satisfy ψ, assuming that all the computations of the environment satisfy φ. As observed in [Pnu85], in this case the assume-guarantee pair $\langle \varphi, \psi \rangle$ can be combined to a single linear temporal logic formula $\varphi \rightarrow \psi$. Thus, model checking a module with respect to assume-guarantee specifications in which both the assumed and the guaranteed behaviors are linear temporal logic formulas is essentially the same as model checking the module with respect to linear temporal logic formulas.

The situation is different for the branching temporal paradigm. Here the guarantee is a branching temporal formula, which describes the computation tree of the module. There are two approaches, however, to the assumptions in assume-guarantee pairs. The first approach, implicit in [CES86, EL85, EL87] and made explicit in [Jos87a, Jos87b, Jos89, DDGJ89], is that the assumption in the assume-guarantee pair concerns the interaction of the module with its environment along each computation, and is therefore more naturally expressed in linear temporal logic. Thus, in this approach an assume-guarantee pair should consist of a *linear* temporal assumption φ and a *branching* temporal guarantee ψ. The meaning of such a pair is that ψ holds in the computation tree that consists of all computations of the program that satisfy φ. The problem of verifying that a given module M satisfies such a pair $\langle \varphi, \psi \rangle$, which we call the *linear-branching modular model-checking problem*, is more general than either linear or branching model checking and is studied in depth in [Var95].

A second approach was considered in [GL94], where assumptions are taken to apply to the computation tree of the system within which the module is interacting. Accordingly, assumptions in [GL94] are also expressed in branching temporal logic. There, a module M satisfies an assume-guarantee pair $\langle \varphi, \psi \rangle$ iff whenever M is part of a system satisfying φ, the system also satisfies ψ. We call this *branching modular model checking*. Furthermore, it is argued there, as well as in [DDGJ89, Jos89, GL94, DGG93], that in the context of modular verification it is advantageous to use only *universal* branching temporal logic, i.e., branching temporal logic without existential path quantifiers. That is, in a universal branching temporal logic one can state properties of all computations of a program, but one cannot state that certain computations exist. Consequently, universal branching temporal logic formulas have the helpful property that once they are satisfied in a module, they are satisfied also in a system that contains this module. The focus in [GL94] is on using $\forall$CTL, the universal fragment of CTL, for both the assumption and the guarantee.

In this paper, we focus on the branching modular model-checking problem, which we show to be a proper extension of the linear-branching modular model-checking problem. We consider assumptions and guarantees in both $\forall$CTL and in the more expressive $\forall$CTL*. We start by examining the most fundamental questions about these logics: *satisfiability*, *validity*, and *implication* (since $\forall$CTL and $\forall$CTL* are not closed under negation, these problems are not inter-reducible as they are for CTL and CTL*).

We use two fundamental techniques to solve these questions. The first technique is the *maximal-model* technique introduced in [GL94]. It is shown there that with every $\forall$CTL formula φ one can associate a *maximal model* M_φ (called the *tableau* of φ in [GL94]) such that a module M satisfies φ precisely when M *simulates* M_φ (we define simulation later on). We use here automata-theoretic techniques for CTL* [VS85, EJ88] to construct maximal models for $\forall$CTL* formulas. While maximal models for $\forall$CTL involve an exponential blow-up, maximal models for $\forall$CTL* involve a doubly exponential blow-up.

The second technique is the automata-theoretic framework to branching-time model checking introduced in [BVW94]. It is shown there how to use *alternating* tree automata to obtain space-efficient model checking methods. Since the maximal models that we construct include fairness conditions, we extend the automata-theoretic method of [BVW94] to yield space-efficient *fair* model-checking algorithms. We then show how performing fair model checking over maximal models can solve the satisfiability, validity, and implication problems for $\forall$CTL and $\forall$CTL*. Our results show that these problems are computationally easier than the analogous problems for CTL and CTL*. For example, while all three problems are EXPTIME-complete for CTL, we have that satisfiability and implication are PSPACE-complete and validity is NP-complete for $\forall$CTL.

We turn on to the branching modular model-checking problem. It turns out that the same two fundamental techniques of maximal models and space-efficient fair model checking also yield a solution to the branching modular model-checking problem. We prove that the problem is PSPACE-complete for $\forall$CTL and EXPSPACE-complete for $\forall$CTL*. We show that the increase in complexity is solely to the assumption part of the specification. This suggests that modular model checking in the branching temporal framework can be practical only for very small assumptions.

2 Preliminaries

2.1 Universal Branching Temporal Logics

We assume that the reader is familiar with the syntax and the semantics of the linear temporal logic LTL, as well as with these of the branching temporal logics CTL* and CTL. The formal definition of these logics can be found in [Eme90]. We define here the universal fragments ∀CTL* and ∀CTL of CTL* and CTL.

The logic ∀*CTL** combines both branching-time and linear-time operators. A path quantifier A ("for all computations") can prefix an assertion composed of an arbitrary combination of the linear-time operators X ("next time") and U ("until"). There are two types of formulas in ∀CTL*: *state formulas*, whose satisfaction is related to a specific state, and *path formulas*, whose satisfaction is related to a specific computation. Formally, let AP be a set of atomic proposition names. A ∀CTL* state formula is either:

- $\varphi_1 \wedge \varphi_2$ or $\varphi_1 \vee \varphi_2$, where φ_1 and φ_2 are ∀CTL* state formulas.
- $A\psi_1$, where ψ_1 is an ∀CTL* path formula.

An ∀CTL* path formula is either:

- **true**, **false**, p, or $\neg p$, for all $p \in AP$.
- A CTL* state formula.
- $\psi_1 \wedge \psi_2$, $\psi_1 \vee \psi_2$, $X\psi_1$, $\psi_1 U \psi_2$, or $\psi_1 \tilde{U} \psi_2$, where ψ_1 and ψ_2 are ∀CTL* path formulas.

∀CTL* is the set of state formulas generated by the above rules.

Note that unlike the logic CTL*, the only path quantifier allowed in ∀CTL* is the universal one. As negation in ∀CTL* can be applies only to atomic propositions, assertions of the form $\neg A\psi$, which is equivalent to $E\neg\psi$, are not allowed either. Note also that ∀CTL* interprets atomic propositions, as well as the Boolean constants **true** and **false**, with respect to paths. Thus, propositional assertions are always in a scope of a universal path quantifier. The logic ∀CTL is a restricted subset of ∀CTL* in which the temporal operators must be immediately preceded by the universal path quantifier.

We define the semantics of ∀CTL* with respect to *fair modules* (*modules*, for short). A module $M = \langle AP, W, R, W^0, L, \alpha \rangle$ consists of a set AP of atomic propositions, a set W of states, a total transition relation $R \subseteq W \times W$ (i.e., for every $w \in W$ there exists $w' \in W$ such that $\langle w, w' \rangle \in R$), a set W^0 of initial states, a labeling function $L : W \to 2^{AP}$ that maps each state to a set of atomic propositions that hold in this state, and a Rabin fairness condition α (our choice of this type of fairness condition is technically motivated, as will be clarified in the sequel). We use $w \models \varphi$ to denote that the state w satisfies the formula φ. A computation of a module is a sequence of states, $\pi = w_0, w_1, \ldots$ such that for every $i \geq 0$, we have that $\langle w_i, w_{i+1} \rangle \in R$. A computation of M is *fair* iff it satisfies the fairness condition α. That is, if $\alpha = \{\langle G_1, B_1 \rangle, \ldots, \langle G_k, B_k \rangle\}$ then π is fair iff there exists $1 \leq i \leq k$ such that $w_j \in G_i$ for infinitely many j's and $w_j \in B_i$ for finitely many j's. When defining the semantics of CTL* over modules, path quantifiers range only over fair computations, cf. [CES86]. In particular, the formula Ap, for an atomic proposition p, means that p holds in the first state for all fair paths. Thus, for a state $w \in W$, we have that $w \models Ap$ iff $p \in L(w)$ or there exists no fair path starting at w. A module M satisfies a formula φ if φ holds in *all* initial states of M. We say that a module is *nonempty* iff there exists a fair computation that starts at an initial state.

2.2 Simulation Relation and Composition of Modules

In the context of modular verification, there is a need to define an order relation between modules [GL94]. Intuitively, we want to define what it means for a module M' to have "more behaviors" than a module M.

Let M and M' be two modules with sets $AP' \subseteq AP$ of atomic propositions, and let w and w' be states in W and W', respectively. A relation $H \subseteq W \times W'$ is a *simulation relation* from $\langle M, w \rangle$ to $\langle M', w' \rangle$ iff the following conditions hold:

(1) $H(w, w')$.
(2) For all s and s', we have that $H(s, s')$ implies the following:
   (2.1) $L(s) \cap AP' = L(s')$.
   (2.2) For every fair computation $\pi = s_0, s_1, \ldots$ in M, with $s_0 = s$, there exists a fair path $\pi' = s'_0, s'_1, \ldots$ in M', with $s'_0 = s'$, such that for all $i \geq 0$, we have $H(s_i, s'_i)$.

A simulation relation H is a *simulation from M to M'* iff for every $w \in W^0$ there exists $w' \in W^{0'}$ such that $H(w, w')$. If there exists a simulation from M to M', we say that M *simulates* M' and we write $M \leq M'$. Intuitively, it means that the module M' has more behaviors than the module M. In fact, every possible behavior of M is also a possible behavior of M'.

Let M and M' be two modules with sets AP and AP' of atomic propositions. The *composition* of M and M', denoted $M \| M'$, is a module that has exactly these behaviors which are joint to M and M' and are fair in both of them. In order to define $M \| M'$, we define first a structure $M'' = \langle AP'', W'', R'', W^{0''}, L'' \rangle$, which has no fairness condition and which has exactly the joint behaviors of M and M', ignoring their fairness conditions. Thus, $AP'' = AP \cup AP'$, $W'' = \{\langle w, w' \rangle : L(w) \cap AP' = L(w') \cap AP\}$, $W^{0''} = (W^0 \times W^{0'}) \cap W''$, $R'' = \{\langle \langle w, w' \rangle, \langle s, s' \rangle \rangle : \langle w, s \rangle \in R \text{ and } \langle w', s' \rangle \in R'\}$, and $L''(\langle w, w' \rangle) = L(w) \cup L'(w')$ for $\langle w, w' \rangle \in W''$. In order to get $M \| M'$, we have to constrain M'' so that its behaviors will be fair in both M and M'. Clearly, a computation π in M'' is fair iff there exist a pair $\langle G, B \rangle \in \alpha$ and a pair $\langle G', B' \rangle \in \alpha'$ such that π visits states from $G \times W'$ infinitly often, visits states from $W \times G'$ infinitly often, and visits states from $(B \times W') \cup (W \times B')$ only finitely often. Thus, checking the fairness of π with respect to such pair of pairs can be done, as in the product of two Büchi automata, by augmenting each state of M'' with a Boolean flag. For mm' such pairs of pairs (originating from m pairs in α and m' pairs in α'), checking the fairness of π can be done, by augmenting each state of M'' with a $2mm'$-valued flag, resulting in $M \| M'$ with $2mm'|W''|$ states.

Theorem 1. [GL94]

(1) *The simulation relation $\leq$ is a preorder.*
(2) *For every M and M', we have $M \| M' \leq M$.*
(3) *For every M, M', and M'', if $M \leq M'$ then $M \| M'' \leq M' \| M''$.*
(4) *For every M, we have $M \leq M \| M$.*
(5) *For every M and M' such that $M \leq M'$, and for every universal branching temporal logic formula φ, $M' \models \varphi$ implies $M \models \varphi$.*

A module M is a *maximal model* for an $\forall$CTL* formula φ if it allows all behaviors consistent with φ. Formally, M is a maximal model of φ if $M \models \varphi$ and for every module M' we have that $M' \leq M$ if $M' \models \varphi$. Note that by the preceding theorem, if $M' \leq M$, then $M' \models \varphi$. A construction of maximal models for $\forall$CTL formulas is described in [GL94]. We will describe later a construction of maximal models for $\forall$CTL* formulas.

2.3 Alternating Tree Automata

For an introduction to the theory of automata on infinite trees see [Tho90]. *Alternating automata* on infinite trees generalize nondeterministic tree automata and were first introduced in [MS87]. For simplicity, we refer first to automata over infinite binary trees. Consider a nondeterministic tree automaton $\mathcal{A} = \langle \Sigma, Q, \delta, Q^0, F \rangle$. The transition relation δ maps an automaton state $q \in Q$ and an input letter $\sigma \in \Sigma$ to a set of pairs of states. Each such pair suggests a nondeterministic choice for the automaton's next configuration. When the automaton is in a state q and is reading a node x labeled by a letter σ, it proceeds by first choosing a pair $\langle q_1, q_2 \rangle \in \delta(q, \sigma)$ and then splitting into two copies. One copy enters the state q_1 and proceeds to the node $x \cdot 0$ (the left successor of x), and the other copy enters the state q_2 and proceeds to the node $x \cdot 1$ (the right successor of x).

Let $\mathcal{B}^+(\{0,1\} \times Q)$ be the set of positive Boolean formulas over $\{0,1\} \times Q$ (i.e., Boolean formulas built from elements in $\{0,1\} \times Q$ using $\wedge$ and $\vee$), where we also allow the formulas **true** and **false** and, as usual, $\wedge$ has precedence over $\vee$. We can represent δ using $\mathcal{B}^+(\{0,1\} \times Q)$. For example, $\delta(q,\sigma) = \{\langle q_1, q_2\rangle, \langle q_3, q_1\rangle\}$ can be written as $\delta(q,\sigma) = (0,q_1) \wedge (1,q_2) \vee (0,q_3) \wedge (1,q_1)$.

In nondeterministic tree automata, each conjunction in δ has exactly one element associated with each direction. In alternating automata on binary trees, $\delta(q,\sigma)$ can be an arbitrary formula from $\mathcal{B}^+(\{0,1\} \times Q)$. We can have, for instance, a transition

$$\delta(q,\sigma) = (0,q_1) \wedge (0,q_2) \vee (0,q_2) \wedge (1,q_2) \wedge (1,q_3).$$

The above transition illustrates that several copies may go to the same direction and that the automaton is not required to send copies to all the directions. Formally, an *alternating tree automaton* is a tuple $\mathcal{A} = \langle \Sigma, Q, \delta, Q^0, F\rangle$, where Σ is the input alphabet, Q is a finite set of states, $Q^0 \subseteq Q$ is a set of initial states, F specifies the acceptance condition, and $\delta : Q \times \Sigma \rightarrow \mathcal{B}^+(\{0,1\} \times Q)$ is the transition function. If $|\Sigma| = 1$, then we call A a 1-letter automaton. A run r of an alternating automaton $\mathcal{A}$ on a binary tree T is a tree where the root is labeled by $q_0 \in Q^0$ and every other node is labeled by an element of $\{0,1\} \times Q$. Each node of r corresponds to a node of T. Suppose that the path to a node y in r is labeled by $q_0, (c_1, q_1), \ldots, (c_m, q_m)$, then y corresponds to the node $x = c_1 \cdots c_m$ of T. Intuitively, the node y of r describes the automaton reading the node x of T. Note that many nodes of r can correspond to the same node of T; in contrast, in a run of a nondeterministic automaton on T there is a one-to-one correspondence between the nodes of the run and the nodes of the tree. The labels of a node and its successors have to satisfy the transition function. The run is accepting if all its infinite paths satisfy the acceptance condition. We use $\mathcal{L}(\mathcal{A})$ to denote the language of $\mathcal{A}$; i.e., the set of trees that $\mathcal{A}$ accepts. An automaton is *nonempty* if it accepts some tree. For formal details see [MS87]. Generalizing the definition to trees with a fixed branching degree n, we define the transition function as $\delta : Q \times \Sigma \rightarrow \mathcal{B}^+(\{0,\ldots n-1\} \times Q)$.

3 An Automata-Theoretic Framework to Fair Model Checking

3.1 Libi Alternating Automata

In [BVW94], we introduced *hesitant alternating automata* (HAA). An HAA that run over trees of a fixed branching degree n is a tuple $\mathcal{A} = \langle \Sigma, Q, \delta, Q^0, \alpha\rangle$, where Σ is the input alphabet, Q is a finite set of states, $\delta : Q \times \Sigma \rightarrow \mathcal{B}^+(\{0,\ldots n-1\} \times Q)$ is a transition function, $Q^0 \subseteq Q$ is a set of initial states, and $\alpha = \langle G, B\rangle$, with $G \subseteq Q$ and $B \subseteq Q$, is the acceptance condition. As in *weak alternating automata* [MSS86], there exists a partition of Q into disjoint sets Q_i, $1 \leq i \leq m$, and a partial order $\leq$ on the collection of the Q_i's such that for every $q \in Q_i$ and $q' \in Q_j$ for which q' occurs in $\delta(q,\sigma)$ for some $\sigma \in \Sigma$, we have $Q_j \leq Q_i$. Thus, transitions from a state in Q_i lead to states in either the same Q_i or a lower one. In addition, each set Q_i is classified as either *transient*, *existential*, or *universal*, such that for each set Q_i and for all $q \in Q_i$, $\sigma \in \Sigma$, the following hold:

1. If Q_i is a transient set, then $\delta(q,\sigma)$ contains no elements of Q_i.
2. If Q_i is an existential set, then $\delta(q,\sigma)$ only contains *disjunctively related* elements of Q_i (i.e. if the transition is rewritten in disjunctive normal form, there is at most one element of Q_i in each disjunct).

3. If Q_i is a universal set, then $\delta(q,\sigma)$ only contains *conjunctively related* elements of Q_i (i.e. if the transition is rewritten in conjunctive normal form, there is at most one element of Q_i in each conjunct).

It follows that every infinite path of a run ultimately gets trapped within some either an existential or a universal set Q_i. For a path π, we denote by $inf(\pi)$ the set of states that π visits infinitely often. The path then satisfies an acceptance condition $\alpha = \langle G, B\rangle$ if and only if either Q_i is an existential set and $inf(\pi) \cap G \neq \emptyset$, or Q_i is an universal set and $inf(\pi) \cap B = \emptyset$. Note that the acceptance condition of HAA combines the Rabin and the Streett acceptance conditions: existential sets refer to a Rabin condition $\{\langle G, \emptyset\rangle\}$ and universal sets refer to a Streett condition $\{\langle B, \emptyset\rangle\}$. The number of sets in the partition of Q is defined as the *depth* of $\mathcal{A}$.

Theorem 2. [BVW94]

(1) *Given a CTL formula ψ and $n \in \mathbb{N}$, there exists an HAA $\mathcal{A}_\psi = \langle 2^{AP}, Q, \delta, Q^0, \alpha\rangle$ of size and depth $O(|\psi|)$ such that $\mathcal{L}(\mathcal{A}_\psi)$ is precisely the set of n-ary tree structures satisfying ψ.*
(2) *Given a CTL* formula ψ and $n \in \mathbb{N}$, there exists an HAA $\mathcal{A}_\psi = \langle 2^{AP}, Q, \delta, Q^0, \alpha\rangle$ of size $2^{O(|\psi|)}$ and depth $O(|\psi|)$ such that $\mathcal{L}(\mathcal{A}_\psi)$ is precisely the set of n-ary tree structures satisfying ψ.*

We briefly describe here the construction of HAA for ∀CTL(which is, essentially, a special case of the construction of HAA for CTL). Given ψ, the state set Q is the set of all the subformulas of ψ augmented with the state *Afalse*. The acceptance condition α is $\langle \emptyset, B\rangle$, where B consists of all the formulas of the form $A\varphi_1 U \varphi_2$ in Q and the state *Afalse*. The set of initial states in the singleton $\{\psi\}$. It remains to define the transition function δ. For all $\sigma \in 2^{AP}$, we define:

- $\delta(Ap, \sigma) = \textbf{true}$ if $p \in \sigma$. - $\delta(Ap, \sigma) = \textbf{Afalse}$ if $p \notin \sigma$.
- $\delta(A\neg p, \sigma) = \textbf{true}$ if $p \notin \sigma$. - $\delta(A\neg p, \sigma) = \textbf{Afalse}$ if $p \in \sigma$.
- $\delta(\textbf{Afalse}, \sigma) = \bigwedge_{c=0}^{n-1}(c, \textbf{Afalse})$.
- $\delta(\varphi_1 \wedge \varphi_2, \sigma) = \delta(\varphi_1, \sigma) \wedge \delta(\varphi_2, \sigma)$.
- $\delta(\varphi_1 \vee \varphi_2, \sigma) = \delta(\varphi_1, \sigma) \vee \delta(\varphi_2, \sigma)$.
- $\delta(AX\varphi_2, \sigma) = \bigwedge_{c=0}^{n-1}(c, \varphi_2)$.
- $\delta(A\varphi_1 U \varphi_2, \sigma) = \delta(\varphi_2, \sigma) \vee (\delta(\varphi_1, \sigma) \wedge \bigwedge_{c=0}^{n-1}(c, A\varphi_1 U \varphi_2))$.
- $\delta(A\varphi_1 \tilde{U} \varphi_2, \sigma) = \delta(\varphi_2, \sigma) \wedge (\delta(\varphi_1, \sigma) \vee \bigwedge_{c=0}^{n-1}(c, A\varphi_1 \tilde{U} \varphi_2))$.

It is easy to see that the state *Afalse* constitutes a universal set. The task of this state will get clearer later.

In order to perform fair model checking, we introduce here *Libi alternating automata* (LAA). An LAA is an HAA with an acceptance condition $\alpha \in 2^Q \times 2^Q$ extended with a Rabin acceptance condition $\beta \subseteq 2^Q \times 2^Q$. For a run of an LAA with $\beta = \{\langle G_1, B_1\rangle, \ldots, \langle G_k, B_k\rangle\}$, a path π which gets trapped within a set Q_i is accepted by the run iff either Q_i is an existential set, in which case π satisfies α and there exists $1 \leq j \leq k$ such that $inf(\pi) \cap G_j \neq \emptyset$ and $inf(\pi) \cap B_j = \emptyset$, or Q_i is a universal set, in which case π satisfies α or π satisfies, for all $1 \leq j \leq k$, either $inf(\pi) \cap G_j = \emptyset$ or $inf(\pi) \cap B_j = \emptyset$.

We now show that the space complexity result of [BVW94] for the 1-letter nonemptiness of HAA extends to LAA.

Theorem 3. *The 1-letter nonemptiness problem for LAA of size n and depth m can be solved in space polynomial in $m \log n$.*

Proof. Consider an LAA with $\alpha = \langle B, G\rangle$ and $\beta = \{\langle G_1, B_1\rangle, \ldots, \langle G_k, B_k\rangle\}$. The property of LAA we use is that, from a state in Q_i, it is possible to search for another reachable state in the same Q_i nondeterministically using space $O(\log n)$. For transient Q_i, there are no such states. For universal and existential Q_i, the exact notion of reachability we use is the transitive closure of the following notion of *immediate reachability*. Consider a set Q_i and assume that we have a Boolean value for all states in sets lower than Q_i. Then, a state $q' \in Q$ is immediately reachable from a state q, if it appears in the transition from q when this transition has been simplified using the known Boolean values for states in lower Q_i's. Note that the simplified transition is always a disjunction for a state of an existential Q_i, and a conjunction for a state of a universal Q_i. A key step in our algorithm is the evaluation of Boolean expressions. It is known that this can be done using space that is logarithmic in the size of the expression [Lyn77]. Here, we evaluate expressions over Q, using a recursion of depth at most m to trace their Boolean value.

We call a state q' of Q_i *provably true* if, when the evaluation procedure is applied to the successors of q' that are not in Q_i, and the Boolean expression for the transition from q' is simplified, it is identically true. States that are *provably false* are defined analogously. Also, for a set $S \subseteq Q$ and two states q and q', we say that q' is *S-reachable* from q, if q' is reachable from q using states from S only (in particular, q and q' are members of S).

The following recursive procedure labels the states of the automaton with 'T' (accepts) or 'F' (does not accept). The language of the LAA is nonempty iff an initial state is labeled 'T'.

(1) One starts at an initial state.
(2) At a transient state q, one evaluates the transition from q by recursively applying the procedure to the successor states of q. The state is labeled with the Boolean value that is obtained for the transition.
(3) At a state q of an existential Q_i, one proceeds as follows.
  (3.1) One searches for a reachable state q' of the same Q_i that is provably true (note that this requires applying the procedure recursively to all states from lower Q_i's that are touched by the search). If such a state q' is found, the state q is labeled 'T'.
  (3.2) If no such state exists, one guesses $1 \le j \le k$ and searches for states q' and q'' of Q_i such that the following hold:
    1. $q' \in G$.
    2. $q'' \in G_j$.
    3. q' is reachable from q.
    4. q'' is $Q_i \setminus B_j$-reachable from q'.
    5. q' is $Q_i \setminus B_j$-reachable from q''.
  If such q' and q'' are found (possibly $q' = q''$), then q is labeled 'T'.
  (3.3) if none of the first two cases apply, q is labeled 'F'.
(4) At a state q of a universal Q_i, one proceeds as follows.
  (4.1) One searches for a reachable state q' of the same Q_i that is provably false. If such a state q' is found, the state q is labeled 'F'.
  (4.2) If no such state exists, one guesses $1 \le j \le k$ and searches for states q' and q'' of Q_i such that the following hold:
    1. $q' \in B$.
    2. $q'' \in G_j$.
    3. q' is reachable from q.
    4. q'' is $Q_i \setminus B_j$-reachable from q'.
    5. q' is $Q_i \setminus B_j$-reachable from q''.
  If such q' and q'' are found, then q is labeled 'F'.
  (4.3) if none of the first two cases apply, q is labeled 'T'.

The procedure is recursive, but since each recursive call takes us to a lower Q_i, the depth of the recursion is bounded by m. Since each invocation of the procedure can be executed nondeterministically using space $O(\log n)$, the whole procedure can thus be executed using space $O(m \log n)$. The claim then follows by Savitch Theorem [Sav70].

3.2 Fair Model Checking

It is well known that for nondeterministic tree automata the nonemptiness problem can be reduced to the 1-letter nonemptiness problem [Rab69]. As discussed in [BVW94], this is not the case for alternating tree automata, where the 1-letter nonemptiness problem is easier than the general nonemptiness problem. The key idea underlying the automata-theoretic approach to branching temporal model checking is that by taking the product of an alternating automaton with a module we get an alternating automaton over a 1-letter alphabet.

Given a branching temporal logic formula ψ, let $\mathcal{A}_\psi = \langle \Sigma, Q_\psi, \delta_\psi, \psi, \alpha_\psi \rangle$ be an HAA that accepts precisely all the n-ary tree models of ψ. Consider a module $M = \langle \Sigma, W, R, W^0, L, \beta_M \rangle$. For $w \in W$, let $succ_R(w) = \langle w_0, \ldots, w_{n-1} \rangle$ be an ordered list of w's R-successors (it is technically convenient to assume that each state has n successors and that the states of W are ordered). The product automaton of $\mathcal{A}_\psi$ and M is the LAA $\mathcal{A}_{M,\psi} = \langle \{a\}, W \times Q_\psi, \delta, W^0 \times \{\psi\}, \alpha, \beta \rangle$, where δ, α, and β are defined as follows:

- Let $q \in Q_\psi, w \in W, succ_R(w) = \langle w_0, \ldots, w_{n-1} \rangle$, and $\delta_\psi(q, L(w)) = \theta$. Then $\delta(\langle w, q \rangle, a) = \theta'$, where θ' is obtained from θ by replacing each atom (c, η) in θ by the atom $(c, \langle w_c, \eta \rangle)$.
- For $\alpha_\psi = \langle G, B \rangle$, we have that $\alpha = \langle W \times G, W \times B \rangle$.
- For $\beta_M = \{\langle G_1, B_1 \rangle, \ldots, \langle G_k, B_k \rangle\}$, we have that $\beta = \{\langle G_1 \times Q_\psi, B_1 \times Q_\psi \rangle, \ldots, \langle G_k \times Q_\psi, B_k \times Q_\psi \rangle\}$.

Proposition 4.

(1) $|\mathcal{A}_{M,\psi}| = O(|M| * |\mathcal{A}_\psi|)$.
(2) *$\mathcal{L}(\mathcal{A}_{M,\psi})$ is nonempty if and only if $M \models \psi$.*

Let $Q_1 \leq \ldots \leq Q_m$ be the partition of the states of $\mathcal{A}_\psi$ into sets. Then, $W \times Q_1 \ldots W \times Q_m$ is a partition of the states of $\mathcal{A}_{M,\psi}$ into sets. Thus, $\mathcal{A}_{M,\psi}$ has the same depth as $\mathcal{A}_\psi$.

In conclusion, given an HAA $\mathcal{A}_\psi$ that accepts precisely all the n-ary tree models of the formula ψ, model checking of a module M with a fixed branching degree n with respect to ψ is reducible to checking the 1-letter nonemptiness of an LAA of size $O(|M| * |\mathcal{A}_\psi|)$ and of the same depth as $\mathcal{A}_\psi$. Thus, Theorem 3 implies the theorem below.

Theorem 5. *Given an HAA $\mathcal{A}_\psi$ of size n and depth m, and a module M of size l, model checking of M with respect to ψ can be done using space polynomial in $m \log(nl)$.*

Theorem 5, together with the HAA described in Theorem 2, imply that the fair model-checking problem for both CTL and CTL* is solvable in space polynomial in $|\psi| \log |M|$. In the following sections, we show how this result can be used to derive tight space complexity bounds also for the satisfiability, validity, and implication problems of universal branching temporal logics, as well as for the branching modular model-checking problem.

4 Satisfiability, Validity, and Implication

The basic decision problem for a specification language are *satisfiability*, i.e., whether the specification is not trivially false, *validity*, i.e., whether the specification is trivially true, and *implication*, i.e., whether one specification logically implies another specification. For a specification language that is closed under negation, these problems are inter-reducible. This is not the case, however, for universal branching temporal logics.

The satisfiability problem for a universal branching temporal logic is defined as follows: given a formula φ, is there a *nonempty* module M such that φ holds in M? As a module with no fair path trivially satisfies any $\forall$CTL* formula, the nonemptiness requirement is essential. The validity problem is defined as follows: given a formula φ, does φ hold in all modules? (It is easy to see that φ holds in all modules iff φ holds in all nonempty modules.) The implication problem is defined as follows: given two formulas φ and ψ, does ψ hold in every module in which φ holds? We now show that the satisfiability and the validity problems are special cases of the implication problem.

Lemma 6. *Let φ be a formula in $\forall$CTL*. Then,*

(1) *The formula φ is satisfiable if and only if φ does not imply* **A**false.
(2) *The formula φ is valid if and only if* **A**true *implies φ.*

4.1 Maximal Models and Implication

By definition, the implication $\varphi \rightarrow \psi$ is valid iff ψ holds in all modules M in which φ holds. Since the more behaviors M has the less likely it is to satisfy ψ, it makes sense to examine the implication by checking ψ in a maximal model of φ (we assume, without loss of generality, that φ and ψ are defined over the same set AP of atomic propositions). The following theorem is proved in [GL94] for $\forall$CTL, but the proof applies also to $\forall$CTL*.

Theorem 7. *Let φ and ψ be $\forall$CTL* formulas, and let M_φ be a maximal model of φ. Then φ implies ψ iff $M_\varphi \models \psi$.*

To complete the reduction of implication to fair model checking, we have to describe the construction of maximal models.

Theorem 8. *For every $\forall$CTL* formula φ, there exists a maximal model M_φ of size $2^{2^{O(|\varphi|)}}$.*

Proof. For a $\forall$CTL* formula φ, let $sf(\varphi)$ denote the set of state subformulas of φ. Given φ, let $\forall(\varphi) \subseteq sf(\varphi)$ denote the set of all the state subformulas of φ of the form $A\xi$. Let $\mathcal{A}_{\forall(\varphi)}$ be a Büchi ω-automaton over $\Sigma = 2^{sf(\varphi)}$ such that $\mathcal{A}_{\forall(\varphi)}$ accepts an infinite word $\pi = w_0, w_1, \ldots$ iff there exists a suffix $w_i, w_{i+1}, \ldots$ of π and a formula $A\xi \in \forall(\varphi)$ such that $A\xi \in w_i$ and $w_i, w_{i+1}, \ldots$ does not satisfy ξ. That is, $\mathcal{A}_{\forall(\varphi)}$ nondeterministically guesses a location i and a formula $A\xi$ and then proceeds as the Büchi ω-automaton of $\neg\xi$. By [VW94], such $\mathcal{A}_{\forall(\varphi)}$ of size $2^{O(|\varphi|)}$ exists. Note that though ξ is a path formula of a branching temporal logic, we interpret it here over linear sequences. Since these sequences are labeled with all the branching subformulas of ξ, this causes no difficulty, as we can regard the branching subformulas of ξ as atomic propositions and regard ξ as a linear temporal logic formula.

We now take $\mathcal{A}_{\forall(\varphi)}$ and co-determinize it. The resulted automaton, called $\tilde{\mathcal{A}}_{\forall(\varphi)}$, is a deterministic Rabin automaton which accepts exactly all the words $\pi = w_0, w_1, \ldots$ for which if a state w_i is labeled with some $A\xi \in \forall(\varphi)$, then ξ is satisfied in the suffix $w_i, w_{i+1}, \ldots$ of π. By [Saf89], the automaton $\tilde{\mathcal{A}}_{\forall(\varphi)}$ is of size $2^{2^{O(|\varphi|)}}$.

For a set $s \subseteq sf(\varphi)$, we say that s is *consistent* iff the following four conditions hold:

1. For every $p \in AP$, if $p \in s$, then $\neg p \notin s$.
2. For every $p \in AP$, if $\neg p \in s$, then $p \notin s$.
3. For every $\varphi_1 \wedge \varphi_2 \in s$, we have that $\varphi_1 \in s$ and $\varphi_2 \in s$.
4. For every $\varphi_1 \vee \varphi_2 \in s$, we have that $\varphi_1 \in s$ or $\varphi_2 \in s$.

Let $c(\varphi)$ denote the set of all consistent subsets of $sf(\varphi)$. Consider the module $M = \langle AP, c(\varphi), c(\varphi) \times c(\varphi), W^0, L, \{\langle c(\varphi), \emptyset \rangle\}\rangle$, where the initial set W^0 includes all states $w \in c(\varphi)$ for which $\varphi \in w$, and for every $w \in c(\varphi)$, we have that $L(w) = w \cap AP$. So far M is more general than any model of φ, but it is not necessarily a model of φ. To make it a maximal model, we take the product of M with $\bar{A}_{\forall(\varphi)}$ as follows. Let $\bar{A}_{\forall(\varphi)} = \langle \Sigma, Q, \delta, q^0, \beta \rangle$, where $\beta = \{\langle G_1, B_1 \rangle, \ldots, \langle G_k, B_k \rangle\}$. Then, $M_\varphi = \langle AP, c(\varphi) \times Q, R, W^0 \times \{q^0\}, L, \beta' \rangle$, where R and β' are defined as follows.

- $R = \{\langle \langle w, q \rangle, \langle w', q' \rangle \rangle : \delta(q, w) = q'\}$.
- $\beta' = \{\langle c(\varphi) \times G_1, c(\varphi) \times B_1 \rangle, \ldots, \langle c(\varphi) \times G_k, c(\varphi) \times B_k \rangle\}$.

Theorem 9. *For every $\forall$CTL formula φ, there exists M_φ of size $2^{O(|\varphi|)}$.*

Proof. Exactly as for $\forall$CTL*. Here, however, $\bar{A}_{\forall(\varphi)}$ is of size $2^{O(|\varphi|)}$.

4.2 Complexity

We are now ready to combine the maximal-model technique with the space-efficient fair-model-checking algorithm to solve the implication problem.

Theorem 10. *Given two universal branching temporal logic formulas φ and ψ, the implication problem $\varphi \rightarrow \psi$ can be solved in space polynomial in $m \log(nl)$ where m and n are the depth and the size, respectively, of an HAA corresponding to ψ, and l is the size of a maximal model for φ.*

Proof. By Theorem 7, the validity problem of $\varphi \rightarrow \psi$ is reducible to model checking of ψ in M_φ. The result follows from Theorem 5.

The complexity of our method with respect to two logics L_1 and L_2 depends on the ability to associate with formulas of L_2 HAA, in the size of these HAA, their depth, as well as in the size of the maximal models for formulas in the logic L_1. In Theorem 11 below, we apply the method to the logics CTL and CTL*. We also show that the upper bounds that follow are tight.

Theorem 11.

(1) *The implication problem for $\forall$CTL is PSPACE-complete.*
(2) *The implication problem for $\forall$CTL* is EXPSPACE-complete.*

Proof. Theorems 8 and 9 provide us with a doubly-exponential bound for maximal models of $\forall$CTL* and an exponential bound for maximal models of $\forall$CTL. Theorem 2 provides us with sizes and depths for HAA of CTL and CTL*. Together with Theorem 10, this yields the upper bounds. The PSPACE lower bound for the implication problem for $\forall$CTL, follows from the PSPACE lower bound for the satisfiability problem for $\forall$CTL. The later is proved by a reduction from LTL satisfiability, proved to be PSPACE-hard in [SC85], and the result then follows from Lemma 6. The EXPSPACE lower bound for the implication problem for $\forall$CTL* is proved similarly to the EXPSPACE lower bound proved in [Var95] for linear-branching modular model checking.

Note that the implication problem $\varphi \rightarrow \psi$ for φ in $\forall$CTL and ψ in $\forall$CTL* is still in PSPACE.

We now consider the satisfiability and validity problems, which, as observed earlier, are special cases of the implication problem.

Theorem 12.

(1) *The satisfiability problems for $\forall$CTL and $\forall$CTL* are PSPACE-complete.*
(2) *The validity problem for $\forall$CTL is NP-complete.*
(3) *The validity problem for $\forall$CTL* is PSPACE-complete.*

Proof. The results for the satisfiability follow from the PSPACE-completeness of the satisfiability problem for LTL. Since $\forall$CTL subsumes propositional logic, hardness in NP for the validity problem for $\forall$CTL is immediate. Membership in NP follows from a linear-size model property for $\exists$CTL. It remains to prove PSPACE-completeness for the validity problem for $\forall$CTL*. Since a $\forall$CTL* formula ψ is valid iff the implication A**true** $\rightarrow \psi$ is valid, and since the implication problem $\varphi \rightarrow \psi$ for φ in $\forall$CTL and ψ in $\forall$CTL* is still in PSPACE, membership in PSPACE is easy. To prove hardness, we use the PSPACE-hardness of the validity problem for LTL.

5 Modular Model Checking

5.1 Branching Modular Model Checking

In modular verification, one uses assertions of the form $\langle\varphi\rangle M\langle\psi\rangle$ to specify that whenever M is part of a system satisfying the universal branching temporal logic formula φ, the system satisfies the universal branching temporal logic formula ψ too. Formally, $\langle\varphi\rangle M\langle\psi\rangle$ holds if $M \| M' \models \psi$ for all M' such that $M \| M' \models \varphi$. Here φ is an assumption on the behavior of the system and ψ is the guarantee on the behavior of the module. Assume-guarantee assertions are used in modular proof rules of the following form:

$$\left.\begin{array}{l} \langle\varphi_1\rangle M_1\langle\psi_1\rangle \\ \langle\mathbf{true}\rangle M_1\langle\varphi_1\rangle \\ \langle\varphi_2\rangle M_2\langle\psi_2\rangle \\ \langle\mathbf{true}\rangle M_2\langle\varphi_2\rangle \end{array}\right\} \langle\mathbf{true}\rangle M_1 \| M_2\langle\psi_1 \wedge \psi_2\rangle$$

Thus, a key step in modular verification is checking that assume-guarantee assertions hold, which we called the *branching modular model-checking problem*. We now show that the techniques developed in the previous sections, i.e., maximal models and space-efficient fair model checking, yield also a solution to the branching modular model-checking problem.

Theorem 13. *For all $\forall$CTL* formulas φ and ψ, and for every module M, we have that $\langle\varphi\rangle M\langle\psi\rangle$ iff $M \| M_\varphi \models \psi$.*

Proof. Assume first that $\langle\varphi\rangle M\langle\psi\rangle$. Thus, whenever M is part of a system satisfying φ, the system satisfies ψ too. Since $M_\varphi \models \varphi$ and $M \| M_\varphi \leq M_\varphi$, we have that $M \| M_\varphi$ satisfies φ. Consequently, $M \| M_\varphi$ satisfies ψ.

Assume now that $M \| M_\varphi \models \psi$ and let $M \| M'$ be such that $M \| M' \models \varphi$. Then, $M \| M' \leq M_\varphi$, which implies that $M \| M \| M' \leq M \| M_\varphi$. Thus, $M \| M' \leq M \| M_\varphi$ and therefore $M \| M' \models \psi$. Hence, $\langle\varphi\rangle M\langle\psi\rangle$.

Theorem 14. *Given a module M and two universal branching temporal logic formulas φ and ψ, the problem of determining whether $\langle\varphi\rangle M\langle\psi\rangle$ is solvable in space polynomial in $m\log(nl * |M|)$ where m and n are the depth and the size, respectively, of an HAA corresponding to ψ, and l is the size of a maximal model for φ.*

Proof. By Theorem 13, the problem of determining whether $\langle\varphi\rangle M\langle\psi\rangle$ is reducible to model checking of ψ in $M\|M_\varphi$. The result then follows from Theorem 5.

In Theorem 15 below we apply the method to the logics CTL and CTL*. We also show that the upper bounds that follow are tight.

Theorem 15.

(1) *The branching modular model-checking problem for ∀CTL is PSPACE-complete.*
(2) *The branching modular model-checking problem for ∀CTL* is EXPSPACE-complete.*

Proof. The upper bounds follow from Theorem 14. The lower bound for ∀CTL* follows from [Var95] and the relation between the branching modular framework and the linear-branching modular framework (to be discussed in the next section). To get the lower bound for ∀CTL, we reduce the implication problem for ∀CTL to branching modular model-checking of a fixed-size module.

In the full paper we provide a more detailed analysis of the complexity of branching modular model checking. We show that the increase in complexity is solely to the assumption part of the specification. This suggests that modular model checking in the branching temporal framework can be practical only for very small assumptions. Indeed, in many examples the assumptions do tend to be of a very small size [Jos87b, Jos89, GL94]; see also [AL93].

5.2 The Linear-Branching Modular Model Checking Problem

The modular proof rule in the preceding section uses branching assumptions and guarantees. As mentioned in the introduction, there is another approach in which the assumption is a linear temporal formula, while the guarantee is a branching temporal formula. In this approach, the assumption in the assume-guarantee pair concerns the interaction of the module with its environment along each computation, and is therefore more naturally expressed in a linear temporal logic. We denote this kind of assertion by $[\varphi]M\langle\psi\rangle$. The meaning of such an assertion is that the branching temporal formula ψ holds in the computation tree that consists of all computations of the program that satisfy the linear temporal formula φ. Verifying such assertions is called the *linear-branching modular model-checking problem*. This problem is studied in [Var95]. We now show that the branching modular framework is more general than the linear-branching modular framework.

Theorem 16. *For every LTL formula φ, module M, and a ∀CTL* formula ψ, we have that $\langle A\varphi\rangle M\langle\psi\rangle$ iff $[\varphi]M\langle\psi\rangle$.*

Proof. To prove the claim, we need to generalize the notion of module. An *extended module* is a pair $\langle M, P\rangle$, where M is a module and P is a set of computations of M that start from some initial state. Formulas of ∀CTL* can be interpreted over an extended module $\langle M, P\rangle$ by letting path quantifiers range over suffixes of computations in P. The notion of simulation can be easily extended to extended modules. As detailed in [Var95], the truth of $[\varphi]M\langle\psi\rangle$ is determined by interpreting ψ over the extended module $\langle M_t, P_\varphi \rangle$, where M_t is the computation tree of M and P_φ is the set of computations of M_t that satisfy φ.

Given φ, M, and ψ, assume first that $[\varphi]M\langle\psi\rangle$ holds. Let M' be such that $M \| M' \models A\varphi$. Then, all fair computations in $M \| M'$ satisfy φ. Since $M \| M' \leq \langle M_t, P_\varphi \rangle$, it follows that $M \| M' \models \psi$. Thus, $\langle A\varphi \rangle M \langle \psi \rangle$.

Assume now that $\langle A\varphi \rangle M \langle \psi \rangle$ holds. Since $M_{A\varphi} \models A\varphi$, it follows that $M \| M_{A\varphi} \models \psi$. For every module M, we have that $\langle M_t, P_\varphi \rangle \leq M$ and $\langle M_t, P_\varphi \rangle \leq M_{A\varphi}$. This can be shown to imply that $\langle M_t, P_\varphi \rangle \leq M \| M_{A\varphi}$. It follows that $\langle M_t, P_\varphi \rangle \models \psi$, which means that $[\varphi]M\langle\psi\rangle$ holds.

It is known that the $\forall$CTL formula $AFAGp$ is not equivalent to any formula of the form $A\varphi$, where φ is an LTL formula [CD88]. Thus, the branching modular framework is strictly more expressive than the linear-branching modular framework, with no increase in worst-case computational complexity (it is shown in [Var95] that linear-branching modular model checking is EXPSPACE-complete). We note, however, that the algorithm in [Var95] for linear-branching modular model checking is simpler than the algorithm here, as it avoids the use of Safra's co-determinization construction.

Acknowledgment: We thank Libi for many helpful suggestions and discussions and Orna Grumberg for useful comments on an earlier draft of this paper.

References

[AL93] M. Abadi and L. Lamport. Composing specifications. *ACM Transactions on Programming Languages and Systems*, 15(1):73–132, 1993.

[BCM+90] J.R. Burch, E.M. Clarke, K.L. McMillan, D.L. Dill, and L.J. Hwang. Symbolic model checking: 10^{20} states and beyond. In *Proc. 5th LICS*, pp. 428–439, 1990.

[BVW94] O. Bernholtz, M.Y. Vardi, and P. Wolper. An automata-theoretic approach to branching-time model checking. In *Proc. 6th CAV*, LNCS 818, pp. 142–155, 1994. Full version available from authors.

[CD88] E.M. Clarke and I.A. Draghicescu. Expressibility results for linear-time and branching-time logics. In *Proc. Workshop on Linear Time, Branching Time, and Partial Order in Logics and Models for Concurrency*, pp. 428–437. LNCS, Springer-Verlag, 1988.

[CES86] E.M. Clarke, E.A. Emerson, and A.P. Sistla. Automatic verification of finite-state concurrent systems using temporal logic specifications. *ACM Transactions on Programming Languages and Systems*, 8(2):244–263, 1986.

[CG87] E.M. Clarke and O. Grumberg. Research on automatic verification of finite-state concurrent systems. In *Annual Review of Computer Science*, vol. 2, pp. 269–290, 1987.

[CGL93] E.M. Clarke, O. Grumberg, and D. Long. Verification tools for finite-state concurrent systems. In J.W. de Bakker, W.-P. de Roever, and G. Rozenberg, eds., *Decade of Concurrency – Reflections and Perspectives (Proc. of REX School)*, LNCS, pp. 124–175. Springer-Verlag, 1993. g.

[CLM89] E.M. Clarke, D.E. Long, and K.L. McMillan. Compositional model checking. In *Proc. 4th LICS*, pp. 353–362, 1989.

[DDGJ89] W. Damm, G. Döhmen, V. Gerstner, and B. Josko. Modular verification of Petri nets: the temporal logic approach. In *Proc. REX Workshop*, LNCS 430, pp. 180–207, 1989.

[DGG93] D. Dams, O. Grumberg, and R. Gerth. Generation of reduced models for checking fragments of CTL. In *Proc. 5th CAV*, LNCS 697, pp. 479–490, 1993.

[EJ88] E.A. Emerson and C. Jutla. The complexity of tree automata and logics of programs. In *Proc. of the 29th FOCS*, 1988.

[EL85] E.A. Emerson and C.-L. Lei. Temporal model checking under generalized fairness constraints. In *Proc. 18th Hawaii International Conference on System Sciences*, 1985.

[EL87] E.A. Emerson and C.-L. Lei. Modalities for model checking: Branching time logic strikes back. *Science of Computer Programming*, 8:275–306, 1987.

[Eme90] E.A. Emerson. Temporal and modal logic. *Handbook of theoretical computer science*, pp. 997–1072, 1990.

[GL94] O. Grumberg and D.E. Long. Model checking and modular verification. *ACM Trans. on Programming Languages and Systems*, 16(3):843–871, 1994.

[Jon83] C.B. Jones. Specification and design of (parallel) programs. In R.E.A. Mason, ed., *Information Processing 83: Proc. IFIP 9th World Congress*, pp. 321–332, North-Holland, 1983.

[Jos87a] B. Josko. MCTL – an extension of CTL for modular verification of concurrent systems. In *Temporal Logic in Specification*, LNCS 398, pp. 165–187, 1987.

[Jos87b] B. Josko. Model checking of CTL formulae under liveness assumptions. In *Proc. 14th ICALP*, LNCS 267, pp. 280–289, 1987.

[Jos89] B. Josko. Verifying the correctness of AADL modules using model chekcing. In *Proc. REX workshop*, LNCS 430, pp. 386–400, 1989.

[Lam80] L. Lamport. Sometimes is sometimes "not never" - on the temporal logic of programs. In *Proc. 7th POPL*, pp. 174–185, 1980.

[Lam83] L. Lamport. Specifying concurrent program modules. *ACM Trans. on Programming Languages and Systenms*, 5:190–222, 1983.

[LP85] O. Lichtenstein and A. Pnueli. Checking that finite state concurrent programs satisfy their linear specification. In *Proc. 20th POPL*, pp. 97–107, 1985.

[Lyn77] N. Lynch. Log space recognition and translation of parenthesis languages. *J. ACM*, 24:583–590, 1977.

[MS87] D.E. Muller and P.E. Schupp. Alternating automata on infinite trees. *Theoretical Computer Science*, 54:267–276, 1987.

[MSS86] D.E. Muller, A. Saoudi, and P.E. Schupp. Alternating automata, the weak monadic theory of the tree and its complexity. In *Proc. 13th ICALP*, 1986.

[Pnu77] A. Pnueli. The temporal logic of programs. In *Proc. 18th FOCS*, pp. 46–57, 1977.

[Pnu85] A. Pnueli. In transition from global to modular temporal reasoning about programs. In *Logics and Models of Concurrent Systems*, vol. F-13 of *NATO Advanced Summer Institutes*, pp. 123–144, 1985.

[QS81] J.P. Queille and J. Sifakis. Specification and verification of concurrent systems in Cesar. In *Proc. 5th Symp. on Programming*, LNCS 137, pp. 337–351, 1981.

[Rab69] M.O. Rabin. Decidability of second order theories and automata on infinite trees. *Transaction of the AMS*, 141:1–35, 1969.

[Saf89] S. Safra. *Complexity of automata on infinite objects*. PhD thesis, Weizmann Institute of Science, Rehovot, Israel, 1989.

[Sav70] W.J. Savitch. Relationship between nondeterministic and deterministic tape complexities. *J. on Computer and System Sciences*, 4:177–192, 1970.

[SC85] A.P. Sistla and E.M. Clarke. The complexity of propositional linear temporal logic. *J. ACM*, 32:733–749, 1985.

[Tho90] W. Thomas. Automata on infinite objects. *Handbook of theoretical computer science*, pp. 165–191, 1990.

[Var95] M.Y. Vardi. On the complexity of modular model checking. In *Proc. 10th LICS*, 1995.

[VS85] M.Y. Vardi and L. Stockmeyer. Improved upper and lower bounds for modal logics of programs. In *Proc 17th STOC*, pp. 240–251, 1985.

[VW94] M.Y. Vardi and P. Wolper. Reasoning about infinite computations. *Information and Computation*, 115(1):1–37, 1994.

[Wol89] P. Wolper. On the relation of programs and computations to models of temporal logic. In *Proc. Temporal Logic in Specification*, LNCS 398, pp. 75–123, 1989.

Axiomatising Linear Time Mu-calculus

Roope Kaivola*

Laboratory for Foundations of Computer Science
University of Edinburgh
The King's Buildings, Edinburgh EH9 3JZ, United Kingdom

Abstract. We present a sound and complete axiomatisation for the linear time mu-calculus νTL, a language extending standard linear time temporal logic with fixpoint operators. The completeness proof is based on a new bi-aconjunctive non-alternating normal form for νTL-formulae.

1 Introduction

This paper solves the problem of providing a complete natural axiomatisation for the linear time mu-calculus νTL. The logic νTL is an extension of standard linear time temporal logic TL by fixpoint operators [3], allowing the expression of all ω-regular properties (for surveys of the area, see [5, 13]). It is expressively equivalent to Wolper's extended temporal logic ETL [21, 22]. However, requiring only the single *nexttime* temporal operator, the fixpoint-based νTL is syntactically more elegant than ETL, which requires an infinite family of temporal operators.

Although νTL is syntactically concise and straightforward, the axiomatisation problem for it has turned out to be rather intricate. The main culprit for this is the minimal fixpoint operator μ, or more exactly, the prevention of infinite regeneration of minimal fixpoints when trying to build a model for a consistent formula.

Previously the axiomatisation of νTL has been addressed by at least Lichtenstein [8] and Dam [4]. A closely related question, axiomatising the modal mu-calculus, a fixpoint formalism similar to νTL but interpreted over branching structures, has been examined by Kozen [7] and Walukiewicz [19, 20].

Generalising, there have been two approaches to showing the satisfiability of a consistent formula, the essential problem of the completeness proof of an axiomatisation. First, one may try to devise a method of constructing a model directly from a given consistent formula. In this line, Kozen [7] introduced the concept of aconjunctivity, restricting the structure of minimal fixpoint formulae to make it easier to build a model of a consistent formula, and showed the completeness of an axiomatisation of the modal mu-calculus restricted to the aconjunctive fragment of the language. The same approach was pursued by Lichtenstein in [8] to show the completeness of an axiomatisation of νTL restricted to a class of aconjunctive formulae.

* e-mail: Roope.Kaivola@dcs.ed.ac.uk

Another approach, and the one adopted here, is defining some normal form for formulae, and showing that any formula can be provably transformed to this normal form. If we know how to build a model for a consistent formula in this form, the satisfiability of any consistent formula has been shown. Pushing formulae to the normal form can be done inductively, by providing for every operator of the language a corresponding transformation. In the context of a related calculus $S1S$, the monadic second order theory of one successor, this approach was already used early by Siefkes in [12]. In the context of νTL, Dam [4] used Büchi automata -like normal forms to show the completeness of an axiomatisation of νTL containing an 'impure' axiom stating that a formula and its normal form are equivalent.

The axiomatisation of νTL used here is essentially the same as in [7, 8]. The completeness proof is based on a new normal form, the *bi-aconjunctive non-alternating form* for νTL formulae. The crucial property of such formulae is that not only is it easy to construct a model of a consistent formula, but the same holds also of its negation. In our opinion, the remarkable thing about the normal form and the completeness proof here is that after the expressive equivalence of the full νTL and the fragment in the normal form has been established by a purely semantic argument (section 3), the semantic equivalence can be lifted to the level of provability rather elegantly on the basis of what is already known about aconjunctivity (section 4).

Very recently, Igor Walukiewicz has presented a completeness proof for an axiomatisation of the modal mu-calculus [20], based on *disjunctive* normal forms, resembling nondeterministic tree automata. This result naturally carries over from the modal mu-calculus to the the linear mu-calculus νTL, as well. However, the proof involves an extremely complex argument using games between tableaux and a priority technique to create a winning strategy in a game. In this respect the easy negatability of formulae in the bi-aconjunctive non-alternating normal form, a property the disjunctive normal form lacks, makes the approach here considerably more straightforward. Bar one observation that was used in passing in Walukiewicz's work and has been adopted here to give a more elegant solution (see proof of Lemma 36), the work presented in the current paper was carried out independently. It should be pointed out that the argument presented here for νTL does not appear to carry over to the modal case, so Walukiewicz's proof is more general in this sense.

2 Preliminaries

Let us recall definitions of linear mu-calculus syntax and semantics, and introduce some related notation. The language is built from propositions, standard boolean connectives, the minimal fixpoint operator μ, and a temporal operator, the *nexttime* $\odot$. The maximal fixpoint operator ν is introduced as a derived operator. To keep the presentation simple, we assume that all the models on which νTL-formulae are interpreted are infinite. This means that we do not need separate weak and strong nexttime operators.

Definition 1. Σ^* (Σ^ω) is the set of finite (infinite) strings of elements of Σ, $|s|$ is the length of s, and ϵ the empty string. If $s = a_1 \dots a_n \dots$, s_i is the element a_i. Ord is the class of ordinals, and $\preceq$ their standard ordering.

Definition 2. Fix a countable set $\mathcal{Z}$ of propositions. The formulae of νTL are defined by the abstract syntax:

$$\phi ::= z \mid \neg\phi \mid \phi_1 \wedge \phi_2 \mid \odot\phi \mid \mu z.\phi$$

where z varies over $\mathcal{Z}$. In $\mu z.\phi$, each occurrence of z in ϕ is required to be *positive*, i.e. in the scope of an even number of negations. The derived operators $\vee$, $\Rightarrow$, $\Leftrightarrow$, $\top$, $\bot$ are as usual, and νz stands for $\nu z.\phi = \neg\mu z.\neg\phi[\neg z/z]$. The symbol σ refers to both the μ and ν-operators. The notation $\phi \trianglelefteq \phi'$ means that ϕ' is a subformula of ϕ.

An occurrence of a variable z in a formula ϕ is *bound* iff it is within a subformula $\sigma z.\phi' \trianglerighteq \phi$ and *free* otherwise. If $\phi, \phi_1, \dots, \phi_n$ are formulae and $z_1, \dots, z_n$ variables, $\phi[\phi_1/z_1, \dots, \phi_n/z_n]$ is the result of simultaneously substituting each ϕ_i for all free occurrences of z_i in ϕ. If some free variable z' of ϕ_i would be captured by a fixpoint $\sigma z'$ of ϕ in the substitution, the bound variable z' in ϕ is systematically renamed.

An occurrence of a variable z in a formula ϕ is *guarded* iff it is in a subformula of the type $\odot\phi'$. A formula ϕ is guarded iff for every fixpoint subformula $\sigma z.\phi'$ of ϕ, every occurrence of z in ϕ' is guarded.

Definition 3. A *model* is an infinite sequence of sets of propositions, $M \in (2^{\mathcal{Z}})^\omega$.

The set of states of M satisfying a formula ϕ, denoted $\|\phi\|_M$, is defined by $\|z\|_M = \{i \in N \mid z \in M_i\}$, $\|\neg\phi\|_M = N \setminus \|\phi\|_M$, $\|\phi \wedge \phi'\|_M = \|\phi\|_M \cap \|\phi'\|_M$, $\|\odot\phi\|_M = \{i \in N \mid i+1 \in \|\phi\|_M\}$, $\|\mu z.\phi\|_M = \bigcap\{W \subseteq N \mid \|\phi\|_{M[W/z]} \subseteq W\}$, where $M[W/z]$ is defined by: $M[W/z]_i = M_i \cup \{z\}$ if $i \in W$, $M[W/z]_i = M_i \setminus \{z\}$ if $i \in N \setminus W$.

A formula ϕ is *true at state i of M*, denoted by $M, i \models \phi$, iff $i \in \|\phi\|_M$. A formula ϕ is *universally valid*, denoted by $\models \phi$, iff $M, m \models \phi$ for all models M and all states m of M. A formula ψ is *satisfiable* iff there exists a model M and a state m of M such that $M, m \models \phi$.

Definition 4. For all ordinals $\alpha \in$ Ord, the *fixpoint approximants* $\mu^\alpha z.\phi$ and $\nu^\alpha z.\phi$ are defined inductively by: $\mu^0 z.\phi = \bot$, $\nu^0 z.\phi = \top$, $\sigma^{\alpha+1} z.\phi = \phi[\sigma^\alpha z.\phi/z]$, $\mu^\lambda z.\phi = \bigvee_{\alpha \prec \lambda} \mu^\alpha z.\phi$ and $\nu^\lambda z.\phi = \bigwedge_{\alpha \prec \lambda} \nu^\alpha z.\phi$, where λ is a limit ordinal.

Proposition 5 (Knaster-Tarski). *$\mu z.\phi = \bigvee_\alpha \mu^\alpha z.\phi$ and $\nu z.\phi = \bigwedge_\alpha \nu^\alpha z.\phi$.*

Definition 6. The *closure* of a formula ϕ, denoted cl(ϕ), is the minimal set of formulae that contains ϕ and fulfils: if $\psi \wedge \psi' \in$ cl(ϕ) then $\psi, \psi' \in$ cl(ϕ), if $\neg\psi \in$ cl(ϕ) or $\odot\psi \in$ cl(ϕ) then $\psi \in$ cl(ϕ), and if $\mu z.\psi \in$ cl(ϕ) then $\psi[\mu z.\psi/z] \in$ cl(ϕ).

Using the derived operators, every formula can be expressed in a form where negations are applied only to atomic propositions, i.e. in the positive normal form as defined e.g. in [13].

name	application	name	application
$\vee L$	$\dfrac{i,\ \Gamma \cup \{\phi \vee \phi'\},\ d}{i,\ \Gamma \cup \{\phi\},\quad d}$	$\vee R$	$\dfrac{i,\ \Gamma \cup \{\phi \vee \phi'\},\ d}{i,\ \Gamma \cup \{\phi'\},\quad d}$
$\wedge$	$\dfrac{i,\ \Gamma \cup \{\phi \wedge \phi'\},\ d}{i,\ \Gamma \cup \{\phi, \phi'\},\ d}$		
σ	$\dfrac{i,\ \Gamma \cup \{\sigma z.\phi\},\ d}{i,\ \Gamma \cup \{u\},\quad d \cdot (u, \sigma z.\phi)}$ **1**	U	$\dfrac{i,\ \Gamma \cup \{u\},\quad d}{i,\ \Gamma \cup \{\phi[u/z]\},\ d}$ **2**
$\odot$	$\dfrac{i,\quad \Gamma \cup \{\odot\phi_1, \ldots, \odot\phi_k\},\ d}{i+1,\ \{\phi_1, \ldots, \phi_k\},\quad d}$ **3**		
Note:	**1:** u does not appear in d **3:** $\Gamma \subseteq \mathcal{Z} \cup \{\neg z \mid z \in \mathcal{Z}\}$. In each rule, Γ is disjoint from the other set		**2:** $d(u) = \sigma z.\phi$

Fig. 1. Tableau rules

Definition 7. A formula ϕ is in *positive normal form* (abbr. *pnf*) iff it only contains atomic propositions, their negations, and the $\vee, \wedge, \odot, \mu$ and ν-operators.

If ϕ is a formula, pnf(ϕ) is the unique formula in positive normal form obtained from ϕ by pushing negations inwards using DeMorgan's laws and the rules $\neg\odot\phi = \odot\neg\phi$, $\neg\mu z.\phi = \nu z.\neg\phi[\neg z/z]$ and $\neg\nu z.\phi = \mu z.\neg\phi[\neg z/z]$.

Next, we give a tableau-like account of truth in a model, related to [2, 8, 15, 17]. For this, the notation is extended with definition constants and lists [14].

Definition 8. Fix a set $\mathcal{U}$ of *definition constants.* The notion of an *extended formula* is as that of a formula, but allowing definition constants in place of free atomic propositions. A *definition list* is a finite sequence $d = (u_1, \phi_1) \ldots (u_n, \phi_n)$ where every $u_i \in \mathcal{U}$ and ϕ_i is an extended formula, all u_i are distinct, and if u occurs in ϕ_i, then $u = u_j$ for some $j < i$. For every u_i, define $d(u_i) = \phi_i$. We say that u_i is *active* in ϕ iff either u_i occurs in ϕ, or there is some u_j, $i < j$, such that u_j occurs in ϕ and u_i is active in $d(u_j)$. If ϕ is an extended formula and d a definition list, $\phi[d]$ is defined by $\phi[\epsilon] = \phi$ and $\phi[d \cdot (u, \psi)] = (\phi[\psi/u])[d]$. If Γ is a set of extended formulae, $\Gamma[d] = \{\phi[d] \mid \phi \in \Gamma\}$.

Definition 9. Let ϕ be a formula in pnf. A *tableau* T for ϕ is an infinite sequence $T = (i_1, \Gamma_1, d_1)(i_2, \Gamma_2, d_2) \ldots$ where

- every $i_j \in N$, Γ_j is a finite set of extended formulae in pnf, and d_j is a definition list containing all definition constants in Γ_j,
- every $(i_{j+1}, \Gamma_{j+1}, d_{j+1})$ is derived from (i_j, Γ_j, d_j) by applying one of the rules in figure 1, and
- $(i_1, \Gamma_1, d_1) = (1, \{\phi\}, \epsilon)$.

We say that $j \in N$ is a $\odot$-*point* of T iff the $\odot$-rule is applied at point j of T. For every $j \in N$, the rule applied at point j induces a *dependency relation* $\rightarrow \subseteq \Gamma_j \times \Gamma_{j+1}$ by:

- if the rule is not $\odot$, the formula in Γ_j to which the rule is applied depends on the resulting formulae (e.g. $\phi \vee \phi' \rightarrow \phi$ for $\vee L$) and $\psi \rightarrow \psi$ for every other $\psi \in \Gamma_j$
- if the rule is $\odot$, $\odot\phi \rightarrow \phi$ for every formula of the form $\odot\phi \in \Gamma_j$.

For any $n \in N$, a sequence $\phi_0, \phi_1, \ldots$ is a *dependency sequence* from point n iff every $\phi_i \in \Gamma_{n+i}$ and $\phi_i \rightarrow \phi_{i+1}$ relative to the rule applied at point $n+i$. A tableau is *proper* iff there is no $n \in N$, $u \in \mathcal{U}$ and infinite dependency sequence $\phi_0, \phi_1, \ldots$ from point n such that $d_n(u) = \mu z.\phi$ for some ϕ, and $\phi_i = u$ for infinitely many $i \in N$. A tableau *agrees* with a model M iff for every $\odot$-point j of T and every $z \in \mathcal{Z}$, if $z \in \Gamma_j$ then $z \in M_{i_j}$, and if $\neg z \in \Gamma_j$ then $z \notin M_{i_j}$.

Notice that as a special case, the $\odot$-rule allows deriving $(i+1, \emptyset, d)$ from $(i, \emptyset, d)$ for any i and d.

Proposition 10. *Let ϕ be a guarded formula in pnf and M a model. Then $M, 1 \models \phi$ iff there is a proper tableau T for ϕ agreeing with M.*

Proof. Standard, see e.g. [15, 17, 8, 14].

3 Normal forms

In this section we introduce a normal form for νTL-formulae, the bi-aconjunctive non-alternating form, and show that the fragment of νTL consisting of formulae in this normal form has the same expressive power as the whole νTL.

The concept of aconjunctivity was introduced by Kozen [7] as a technical restriction, stating intuitively that in a formula $\mu z.(\ldots \phi \wedge \phi' \ldots)$ the minimal fixpoint μz cannot be regenerated in both ϕ and ϕ'.

Definition 11. Let $\sigma z.\phi$ be a formula, and ϕ' a subformula of it. We say that z is *active in* ϕ' iff either

- there is a free occurrence of z in ϕ', or
- there is a free occurrence of some z' in ϕ' such that ϕ' is a subformula of $\sigma z'.\phi''$, $\sigma z'.\phi''$ is a subformula of $\sigma z.\phi$, and z is active in $\sigma z'.\phi''$.

Definition 12. Let $\sigma z.\phi$ be a formula in pnf. We say that $\sigma z.\phi$ is *aconjunctive with respect to* z iff there is no subformula $\phi_1 \wedge \phi_2$ of $\sigma z.\phi$ such that z is active in both ϕ_1 and ϕ_2. A formula ϕ in pnf is *aconjunctive* iff every subformula of type $\mu z.\phi'$ of ϕ is aconjunctive with respect to z. An arbitrary formula ϕ is aconjunctive iff pnf(ϕ) is.

The new concept of bi-aconjunctivity requires not only that a formula itself is aconjunctive, but also that its dual is, as well.

Definition 13. A formula ϕ is *bi-aconjunctive* iff ϕ and $\neg\phi$ are aconjunctive.

In the same way that the alternation of existential and universal quantification leads to arithmetical and analytical hierarchies in recursion theory, the alternation of minimal and maximal fixpoints in mu-calculi leads to a hierarchical classification of formulae [6, 11]. In the normal form we are working with formulae that are extremely low in this hierarchy, and do not have any essential alternation of fixpoints.

Definition 14. Let ϕ be a formula in pnf. We say that ϕ is *non-alternating* iff

- there are no formulae $\nu z.\phi'$ and $\mu z'.\phi''$ such that $\phi \trianglelefteq \nu z.\phi' \triangleleft \mu z'.\phi''$ and z occurs free in $\mu z'.\phi''$, and
- there are no formulae $\mu z.\phi'$ and $\nu z'.\phi''$ such that $\phi \trianglelefteq \mu z.\phi' \triangleleft \nu z'.\phi''$ and z occurs free in $\nu z'.\phi''$,

An arbitrary formula ϕ is non-alternating iff pnf(ϕ) is.

Let us now define the normal form that forms the basis of the completeness proof in next section.

Definition 15. We say that a formula ϕ is in the *bi-aconjunctive non-alternating normal form* (abbreviated *banan-form*) iff

- ϕ is guarded,
- ϕ is bi-aconjunctive, and
- ϕ is not alternating.

To understand the motivation behind this normal form, it may help to relate it to automata on infinite objects. The automata having an exact correspondence with νTL-formulae in banan-form are a restricted form of weak alternating automata [10] on strings.[1]

Notice some easy properties of formulae in the normal form.

Lemma 16. *Let ϕ, ϕ' be formulae in banan-form. Then $\neg\phi$, $\odot\phi$, $\phi \wedge \phi'$ and $\phi[\phi'/z]$ are in banan-form.*

Proof. Straightforward.

The rest of this section is dedicated to showing the expressive equivalence of the class of formulae in banan-form and the whole νTL, i.e. showing that for an arbitrary formula ϕ, there is a formula ϕ' in the banan-form such that $\models \phi \Leftrightarrow \phi'$. Let us see first that alternation is not essential.

Lemma 17. *For any formula ϕ, there exists a non-alternating formula ϕ' such that $\models \phi \Leftrightarrow \phi'$.*

---

[1] The restriction is: in accepting (rejecting) components, $\vee$ ($\wedge$) branching is allowed only when at least one of the successors belongs to a strictly lower component.

name	application	name	application
$\vee$	$\dfrac{\Gamma \cup \{\psi \vee \psi'\}}{\Gamma \cup \{\psi\} \qquad \Gamma \cup \{\psi'\}}$	$\wedge$	$\dfrac{\Gamma \cup \{\psi \wedge \psi'\}}{\Gamma \cup \{\psi, \psi'\}}$
μ	$\dfrac{\Gamma \cup \{\mu x.\psi\}}{\Gamma \cup \{\psi[\mu x.\psi/x]\}}$	$\odot$	$\dfrac{\Gamma \cup \{\odot\psi_1, \ldots, \odot\psi_k\}}{\{\psi_1, \ldots, \psi_k\}}$ **1**

Note: **1:** $\Gamma \subseteq \mathcal{Z} \cup \{\neg z \mid z \in \mathcal{Z}\}$.
In each rule, Γ is disjoint from the other set

Fig. 2. Tableau tree rules

Proof. Take any formula ϕ. By [8, Thm. 7.7] [21, Thm. 2.13] νTL and $S1S$, the monadic second-order theory of one successor, are expressively equivalent, i.e. there is an $S1S$-formula ϕ_S equivalent to ϕ.

As a consequence of the McNaughton's theorem [9], we know that $S1S$ and $WS1S$, the weak monadic second-order theory of one successor, are expressively equivalent (see e.g. [16, Thm. 4.6]), i.e. there is a $WS1S$-formula ϕ_{WS} equivalent to ϕ_S, hence equivalent to ϕ.

Moreover, from the results of [1] and [10] relating $WSnS$ and non-alternating fixpoint calculi, we can see as a special case that $WS1S$ and alternation-free νTL are expressively equivalent, i.e. there is a non-alternating νTL-formula ϕ' equivalent to ϕ_{WS}, therefore equivalent to ϕ.

An alternative argument establishing the claim is by mapping a νTL-formula directly to a Büchi-automaton [17, 4], mapping this to an ETL-formula [18], and mapping the ETL-formula back to a non-alternating νTL-formula [8, section 7.5.7].

Next we show that for any non-alternating formula ϕ there is an equivalent formula ϕ' in the banan-form. For this, let us first show the claim for formulae with only minimal fixpoints.

Definition 18. Let ϕ be a guarded formula in pnf without any subformulae of the form $\nu z.\psi$. A *tableau tree* Tr for ϕ is a finite tree labelled with sets of formulae, such that

- The root of Tr is labelled with $\{\phi\}$.
- The sons of each internal node of Tr are derived by applying one of the rules in figure 2. Depending on the rule applied at a node t, t is called a $\vee, \wedge, \mu$ or $\odot$-node, respectively.
- Each leaf t of Tr is labelled with a set $\Gamma \cup \{\odot\psi_1, \ldots, \odot\psi_k\}$, $k \geq 0$, where $\Gamma \subseteq \mathcal{Z} \cup \{\neg z \mid z \in \mathcal{Z}\}$, and the same set labels a $\odot$-node earlier on the path from the root to the current node. If a leaf t is labelled with $\emptyset$, it is a *proper* leaf, otherwise it is a *loop* leaf. The earlier $\odot$-node with the same label is called the *loop node corresponding to* t, and denoted by $l(t)$.

It is easy to see that for any guarded ϕ with only minimal fixpoints, we can produce a tableau tree Tr for ϕ by just applying the derivation rules in any order. Each branch of the tree must eventually reach a leaf, since there are only finitely many different sets of formulae that can be produced by the derivations.

Definition 19. Let ϕ be a guarded formula in pnf without any subformulae of the form $\nu z.\psi$, and Tr a tableau tree for ϕ. For any node t of Tr, define the formula Δ_t by $\Delta_t = \bigwedge(\Gamma \cap (\mathcal{Z} \cup \{\neg z \mid z \in \mathcal{Z}\}))$, where Γ is the label of t.

Fix a distinct fresh variable z_t for every $\odot$-node t of Tr. Define a formula ϕ_t for every node t of Tr inductively by:

- if t is a $\vee$-node, $\phi_t = \phi_{t_1} \vee \phi_{t_2}$, where t_1 and t_2 are the sons of t
- if t is a $\wedge$ or μ-node, $\phi_t = \phi_{t'}$, where t' is the son of t
- if t is a $\odot$-node and is not the loop node for any leaf, then $\phi_t = \Delta_t \wedge \odot\phi_{t'}$, where t' is the son of t
- if t is a $\odot$-node and it is a loop node for some leaf, then $\phi_t = \mu z_t.\Delta_t \wedge \odot\phi_{t'}$, where t' is the son of t
- if t is a proper leaf, $\phi_t = \top$
- if t is a loop leaf, $\phi_t = z_{l(t)}$

Finally, define the formula ϕ_{Tr} as ϕ_t, where t is the root of Tr.

Lemma 20. *Let ϕ be a guarded formula in pnf without any subformulae of the form $\nu z.\psi$. Then there is a formula ϕ' in banan-form such that $\models \phi \Leftrightarrow \phi'$.*

Proof. Let Tr be tableau tree for ϕ. It is easy to see that ϕ_{Tr} is in banan-form. Let us show that $\models \phi \Leftrightarrow \phi_{Tr}$. By Prop. 10, for any model M,

- $M, 1 \models \phi$ iff there is a proper tableau $T = (i_1, \Gamma_1, d_1)\ldots$ for ϕ agreeing with M, and
- $M, 1 \models \phi_{Tr}$ iff there is a proper tableau $T' = (i'_1, \Gamma'_1, d'_1)\ldots$ for ϕ_{Tr} agreeing with M

Since ϕ has no subformulae of the form $\nu z.\psi$, any tableau T for ϕ is proper iff there is some $n \in N$ such that $\Gamma_j = \emptyset$ for all $j \geq n$. The same holds for ϕ_{Tr} and any tableau T' for ϕ_{Tr}. As it is easy to read a tableau T' for ϕ_{Tr} agreeing with M, from a tableau T for ϕ agreeing with M, and vice versa, this means that we can read a proper tableau T' for ϕ_{Tr} agreeing with M from any proper tableau T for ϕ agreeing with M, and vice versa.

A formula with only minimal fixpoints can be viewed as an alternating finite automaton on finite strings. The tableau tree construction corresponds then to mapping such automata to normal non-deterministic finite automata on finite strings.

Generalising this result to all non-alternating formulae is done inductively on the syntactic alternation depth of formulae. Notice that even non-alternating formulae, i.e. formulae without any proper alternation, can still be syntactically alternating.

Definition 21. Define the *syntactic alternation classes* Π_n and Σ_n for all $n \in N$ as the minimal sets fulfilling:

- $\Pi_0 = \Gamma_0$ is the set of all formulae in pnf without any fixpoint operators
- if ϕ is in pnf and has no subformulae of the form $\nu z.\psi$, and $\phi_1, \ldots, \phi_m \in \Sigma_n \cup \Pi_n$, then $\phi[\phi_1/z_1, \ldots, \phi_m/z_m] \in \Sigma_{n+1}$
- if ϕ is in pnf and has no subformulae of the form $\mu z.\psi$, and $\phi_1, \ldots, \phi_m \in \Sigma_n \cup \Pi_n$, then $\phi[\phi_1/z_1, \ldots, \phi_m/z_m] \in \Pi_{n+1}$

Lemma 22. *For any non-alternating formula ϕ, there exists a formula ϕ' in banan-form such that $\models \phi \Leftrightarrow \phi'$*

Proof. Any non-alternating formula ϕ can be trivially transformed into pnf, and further, into an equivalent guarded non-alternating formula by the transformations of [2, subsection 2.4]. Therefore it is enough to show the claim for all guarded non-alternating formulae in pnf. This is done by induction on the syntactic alternation depth hierarchy.
Induction basis: If $\phi \in \Pi_0 = \Gamma_0$, choosing $\phi' = \phi$ fulfils the claim.
Induction step: Let $\phi_1, \ldots, \phi_m \in \Sigma_n \cup \Pi_n$. By induction assumption, there are formulae $\phi'_1, \ldots, \phi'_m$ in banan-form such that $\models \phi_i \Leftrightarrow \phi'_i$ for all $1 \leq i \leq m$.

Take any ϕ in pnf which has no subformulae of the form $\nu z.\psi$. By Lemma 20, there exists a formula ϕ' in banan-form such that $\models \phi \Leftrightarrow \phi'$. By Lemma 16, $\phi'[\phi'_1/z_1, \ldots, \phi'_m/z_m]$ is in banan-form. Since $\models \phi[\phi_1/z_1, \ldots, \phi_m/z_m] \Leftrightarrow \phi'[\phi'_1/z_1, \ldots, \phi'_m/z_m]$, the claim holds for $\phi[\phi_1/z_1, \ldots, \phi_m/z_m]$, and therefore for the class Σ_{n+1}.

Take then any $\phi \in \Pi_{n+1}$, and define $\phi' = \text{pnf}(\neg\phi)$. It is easy to see that $\phi' \in \Sigma_{n+1}$. By the above there is a ϕ'' in banan-form such that $\models \phi' \Leftrightarrow \phi''$, implying $\models \phi \Leftrightarrow \neg\phi' \Leftrightarrow \neg\phi''$. Furthermore, by Lemma 16, $\neg\phi''$ is in banan-form, so the claim holds for ϕ, and therefore for the class Π_{n+1}.

Now the expressive equivalence of the whole νTL and the fragment of formulae in banan-form is immediate.

Theorem 23. *For any formula ϕ, there exists a formula ϕ' in banan-form such that $\models \phi \Leftrightarrow \phi'$.*

Proof. Direct from Lemmas 17 and 22.

It needs to be pointed out that the previous theorem does not imply that for every ϕ there is a ϕ' in banan-form such that $\models \sigma z.\phi \Leftrightarrow \sigma z.\phi'$: although $\sigma z.\phi$ would be well-defined, i.e. although z would occur only positively in ϕ, this does not necessarily hold of ϕ'. In the mapping of Lemma 20, the positivity of free variables in the formula is preserved. However, in the mapping of Lemma 17 from an arbitrary formula to an equivalent non-alternating formula this does not appear to be possible.

4 Axiomatisation

This far we have operated purely on the semantic level. Let us define now the axiomatic system, essentially the same as in [7, 8], and show its completeness on the basis of the semantic expressive equivalence shown in the previous section.

Definition 24. We say that a formula ϕ is *provable* and write $\vdash \phi$, iff it is derivable in the following deductive system.

Axiom schemas:

ax1 All propositional tautologies

ax2 $\odot(\phi \Rightarrow \psi) \Rightarrow (\odot\phi \Rightarrow \odot\psi)$

ax3 $\odot\phi \Leftrightarrow \neg\odot\neg\phi$

ax4 $\phi[\mu z.\phi/z] \Rightarrow \mu z.\phi$

Rules of inference:

modus ponens:	from ϕ and $\phi \Rightarrow \psi$ infer ψ
necessitation:	from ϕ infer $\odot\phi$
fixpoint induction:	from $\phi[\psi/z] \Rightarrow \psi$ infer $\mu z.\phi \Rightarrow \psi$

We say that a formula ϕ is *consistent* iff not $\vdash \neg\phi$.

Showing the soundness of this axiom system is easy.

Theorem 25 (Soundness). *If* $\vdash \phi$ *then* $\models \phi$.

Proof. All instances of the axiom schemas are clearly universally valid, and the modus ponens and necessitation rules validity-preserving. To see that also the fixpoint induction rule preserves universal validity, assume that $\not\models \mu z.\phi \Rightarrow \psi$. As by Prop. 5, $\mu z.\phi = \bigvee_\alpha \mu^\alpha z.\phi$, there is an α such that $\not\models \mu^\alpha z.\phi \Rightarrow \psi$ but $\models \mu^{\alpha'} z.\phi \Rightarrow \psi$ for all $\alpha' \prec \alpha$. This α cannot be 0 or a limit ordinal. Consequently, there are M, m such that $M, m \models \mu^\alpha z.\phi \wedge \neg\psi$, and by definition of μ^α, $M, m \models \phi[\mu^{\alpha-1} z.\phi/z] \wedge \neg\psi$. But as $\models \mu^{\alpha-1} z.\phi \Rightarrow \psi$ and z occurs only positively in ϕ, $\models \phi[\mu^{\alpha-1} z.\phi/z] \Rightarrow \phi[\psi/z]$, implying $M, m \models \phi[\psi/z] \wedge \neg\psi$, i.e. $\not\models \phi[\psi/z] \Rightarrow \psi$.

For the completeness proof, we need some technical lemmas.

Lemma 26 (Substitution). *If* $\vdash \phi$, *then* $\vdash \phi[\phi'/z]$.

Proof. Induction on the length of the proof of $\vdash \phi$.

Let us show first that the axiomatisation is complete in the class of all aconjunctive formulae. This follows easily from Kozen's results for the modal mu-calculus [7]. However, as the result is extended slightly in Lemma 35, a proof of it is sketched down here, as well. The formulation of the proof presented here is due to Stirling.

Definition 27. A tableau $T = (i_1, \Gamma_1, d_1)(i_2, \Gamma_2, d_2)\ldots$ is *consistent* iff $\bigwedge \Gamma_j[d_j]$ is consistent for every $j \geq 1$.

Lemma 28. *Let ϕ be a guarded formula in pnf. If there is a proper consistent tableau T for ϕ, then ϕ is satisfiable.*

Proof. Given a proper consistent tableau $T = (i_1, \Gamma_1, d_1)(i_2, \Gamma_2, d_2)\ldots$ for ϕ, define a model M by: for every $k \in N$, $M_k = \Gamma_j[d_j] \cap \mathcal{Z}$, where j is the unique $\odot$-point of T such that $i_j = k$. Then $M, 1 \models \phi$ by Prop. 10.

name	application	name	application
σ'	$\dfrac{i,\ \Gamma \cup \{\sigma z.\phi\},\ d,\ d^s}{i,\ \Gamma \cup \{u\},\ d',\ d^{s\prime}}$ 1	$U\nu$	$\dfrac{i,\ \Gamma \cup \{u\},\ d,\ d^s}{i,\ \Gamma \cup \{\phi[u/z]\},\ d,\ d^s}$ 2
$U\mu$	$\dfrac{i,\ \Gamma \cup \{u\},\ d,\ d^s}{i,\ \Gamma \cup \{\phi[u/z]\},\ d,\ d^{s\prime}}$ 3		

Note: **1:** u does not appear in d, $d' = d \cdot (u, \sigma z.\phi)$, $d'_s = d_s \cdot (u, \sigma z.\phi)$.
2: $d(u) = \nu z.\phi$
3: if $d = (u_1, \sigma z_1.\phi_1) \ldots (u_n, \sigma z_n.\phi_n)$, $u = u_m$,
$d(u_m) = \mu z.\phi$ and $d^s(u_m) = \mu z.(\phi \wedge \alpha)$, then
$d^{s\prime}(u_i) = d^s(u_i)$ for $1 \leq i < m$, $d^{s\prime}(u_i) = d(u_i)$ for $m < i \leq n$, and
$d^{s\prime}(u_m) = \mu z.(\phi \wedge \alpha \wedge \neg \bigwedge \Gamma[d^x])$ where
$d^x(u_i) = d^s(u_i)$ for $1 \leq i \leq m$, $d^x(u_i) = d(u_i)$ for $m < i \leq n$

Fig. 3. Strong tableau rules

It is easy to see that for any tableau element (i, Γ, d), if $\bigwedge \Gamma[d]$ is consistent, then some tableau rule can be applied to (i, Γ, d) to yield an element (i', Γ', d') so that $\bigwedge \Gamma'[d']$ is consistent. Therefore, it is easy to construct a consistent tableau T for any consistent formula ϕ. However, there is nothing in this construction to guarantee that the resulting T would be proper as well as consistent. To this purpose we use a technique similar to Kozen's [7] for strengthening minimal fixpoints, based on the following lemma.

Lemma 29. *If $\psi \wedge \mu z.\phi$ is consistent and z does not occur free in ψ, then $\psi \wedge \phi[\mu z.(\phi \wedge \neg\psi)/z]$ is consistent.*

Proof. If $\phi[\mu z.(\phi \wedge \neg\psi)/z] \wedge \psi$ is inconsistent, $\vdash \phi[\mu z.(\phi \wedge \neg\psi)/z] \Rightarrow \neg\psi$, hence $\vdash \phi[\mu z.(\phi \wedge \neg\psi)/z] \Rightarrow \mu z.(\phi \wedge \neg\psi)$. By fixpoint induction rule then $\vdash \mu z.\phi \Rightarrow \mu z.(\phi \wedge \neg\psi)$, implying $\vdash \mu z.\phi \Rightarrow \neg\psi$, i.e. $\mu z.\phi \wedge \psi$ is inconsistent.

Definition 30. Let ϕ be a formula in pnf. A *strong tableau* T for ϕ is an infinite sequence $T = (i_1, \Gamma_1, d_1, d_1^s)(i_2, \Gamma_2, d_2, d_2^s) \ldots$ where

- every (i_j, Γ_j, d_j) is as in Def. 9, and d_j^s is a definition list such that if $d_j = (u_1, \sigma z_1.\phi_1) \ldots (u_n, \sigma z_n.\phi_n)$, $d_j^s = (u_1, \sigma z_1.\phi_1 \wedge \alpha_1) \ldots (u_n, \sigma z_n.\phi_n \wedge \alpha_n)$ for some formulae α_i (possibly $\top$),
- every $(i_{j+1}, \Gamma_{j+1}, d_{j+1}, d_{j+1}^s)$ is derived from $(i_j, \Gamma_j, d_j, d_j^s)$ by one of the rules $\vee L$, $\vee R$, $\wedge$ or $\odot$, which are as in figure 1 or by σ', $U\nu$ or $U\mu$ in figure 3, and
- $(i_1, \Gamma_1, d_1, d_1^s) = (1, \{\phi\}, \epsilon, \epsilon)$.

A strong tableau T being *proper* is defined as in Def. 9. T is *consistent* iff for every $j \in N$, $\bigwedge \Gamma_j[d_j^s]$ is consistent.

Lemma 31. *Let ϕ be an aconjunctive formula in pnf, and T a (strong) tableau for ϕ. For every $j \in N$ and $u \in \mathcal{U}$ such that $d_j(u) = \mu z.\phi'$ for some z and ϕ', the constant u is active in at most one formula $\psi \in \Gamma_j$.*

Proof. The claim holds trivially for the first element of T. All the (strong) tableau rules except $\wedge$ clearly preserve the validity of the claim, and $\wedge$ preserves it thanks to the aconjunctivity of ϕ.

Lemma 32. *Let ϕ be an aconjunctive formula in pnf. If ϕ is consistent, there is a consistent strong tableau T for ϕ.*

Proof. Let (i, Γ, d, d^s) be an element of a strong tableau such that $\bigwedge \Gamma[d_s]$ is consistent. It is easy to see that if any of rules $\wedge$, $\odot$, σ' or $U\nu$ can be applied to it, then for the resulting element $(i', \Gamma', d', d^{s\prime})$, $\bigwedge \Gamma'[d^{s\prime}]$ is consistent. By Lemmas 29 and 31 the same holds for the $U\mu$ rule. If $\vee L$ and $\vee R$ rules can be applied to (i, Γ, d, d^s), then at least one of them yields a $(i', \Gamma', d', d^{s\prime})$ such that $\bigwedge \Gamma'[d^{s\prime}]$ is consistent. As some rule is always applicable, this means that we can construct a consistent strong tableau T for ϕ, starting from the element $(1, \{\phi\}, \epsilon, \epsilon)$.

Lemma 33. *Let ϕ be a guarded formula in pnf, and T a strong tableau for ϕ. If T is consistent, then T is proper.*

Proof. Assume that $T = (i_1, \Gamma_1, d_1, d_1^s) \ldots$ is not proper, and take the smallest $m \in N$ such that for some $k \in N$ and $n \geq m$, $d_k = (u_1, \sigma z_1.\phi_1) \ldots (u_n, \sigma z_n.\phi_n)$, $d_k(u_m) = \mu z_m.\phi_m$, and $u_m \in \Gamma_j$ for infinitely many j. For every $j \in N$ define $\Gamma'_j = \{\psi \in \Gamma_j \mid u_m \text{ not active in } \psi\}$.

As ϕ is guarded, there is an infinite sequence of indices $j_1, j_2 \ldots$ such that the $U\mu$-rule is applied to u_m at point $j_h - 1$ of T for every $h \in N$. By Lemma 31 this means that for all $h \in N$, $\Gamma_{j_h-1} = \Gamma'_{j_h-1} \cup \{u_m\}$ and $\Gamma'_{j_h-1} = \Gamma'_{j_h}$, implying $\vdash \bigwedge \Gamma'_{j_h-1}[d^s_{j_h-1}] \Rightarrow \bigwedge \Gamma'_{j_h}[d^s_{j_h}]$ and $\vdash u_m[d^s_{j_h}] \Rightarrow \neg \bigwedge \Gamma'_{j_h}[d^s_{j_h}]$. By the choice of m we can assume without loss of generality that for every $m' < m$, if $d_k(u_{m'}) = \mu z_{m'}.\phi_{m'}$ then $u_{m'} \notin \Gamma_j$ for all $j \geq j_1$, meaning that the $U\mu$-rule is not applied to any of $u_1, \ldots, u_{m-1}$ at any point $j \geq j_1$. Remembering the above, this implies that $\vdash u_m[d^s_j] \Rightarrow \neg \bigwedge \Gamma'_{j_h}[d^s_{j_h}]$ for all $j \geq j_h$ and all $h \in N$. Furthermore, $\Gamma'_{j_h}[d^s_{j_h}] \subseteq \mathrm{cl}(\Gamma_{j_1}[d^s_{j_1}])$ for all $h \in N$.

Since $\mathrm{cl}(\Gamma_{j_1}[d^s_{j_1}])$ is finite, there are some $h < l$ such that $\Gamma'_{j_h}[d^s_{j_h}] = \Gamma'_{j_l}[d^s_{j_l}]$. But then $\vdash \bigwedge \Gamma_{j_l-1}[d^s_{j_l-1}] \Rightarrow (u_m[d^s_{j_l-1}] \wedge \bigwedge \Gamma'_{j_l-1}[d^s_{j_l-1}]) \Rightarrow (\neg \bigwedge \Gamma'_{j_h}[d^s_{j_h}] \wedge \bigwedge \Gamma'_{j_l}[d^s_{j_l}]) \Rightarrow \bot$, implying that T is not consistent.

Proposition 34. *Let ϕ be a guarded aconjunctive formula. If ϕ is consistent, then ϕ is satisfiable.*

Proof. As $\vdash \phi \Leftrightarrow \mathrm{pnf}(\phi)$, we can assume that ϕ is in pnf. If ϕ is consistent, by Lemmas 32 and 33, there is a proper consistent strong tableau and therefore a proper consistent tableau T for ϕ. By Lemma 28 this means that ϕ is satisfiable.

Lemma 35. *Let ψ and χ be formulae such that*
- *$\psi \wedge \nu x.\chi$ is well-formed and consistent,*
- *ψ is guarded, aconjunctive and in pnf, and*
- *there exists a guarded aconjunctive formula $\bar{\chi}$ in pnf such that $\vdash \chi \Leftrightarrow \bar{\chi}$.*

Then $\psi \wedge \nu x.\chi$ is satisfiable.

<table>
<tr><th>name</th><th>application</th></tr>
<tr><td>$U\nu\chi$</td><td>$\dfrac{i,\ \Gamma \cup \{u\}, \qquad d,\ d^s}{i,\ \Gamma \cup \{u, \bar{\chi}[u/x]\},\ d,\ d^s}$ 1</td></tr>
<tr><td>$\odot$</td><td>$\dfrac{i, \qquad \Gamma \cup \{\odot\phi_1, \ldots, \odot\phi_k\},\ d,\ d^s}{i+1,\ \{\phi_1, \ldots, \phi_k\}, \qquad d,\ d^s}$ 2</td></tr>
<tr><td colspan="2">Note: 1: $d(u) = \nu x.\chi$ and $U\nu\chi$ has not been applied after previous application of $\odot$
2: $\Gamma \subseteq \mathcal{Z} \cup \{\neg z \mid z \in \mathcal{Z}\} \cup U_\chi \cup \{\neg u \mid u \in U_\chi\}$ where
$U_\chi = \{u \in U \mid d(u) = \nu x.\chi\}$
and for every $u \in U_\chi \cap \Gamma$ the $U\nu\chi$-rule has been applied to u
after previous application of $\odot$.</td></tr>
</table>

Fig. 4. Modified strong tableau rules

Proof. Let us modify slightly the rules for a strong tableau by adding a new $U\nu\chi$-rule and modifying the $\odot$-rule as in figure 4, and by requiring that the $U\nu$-rule is not applied to a constant u such that $d(u) = \nu x.\chi$. Notice that as x does not necessarily occur only positively in $\bar{\chi}$, we can have negated occurrences of a constant u corresponding to $\nu x.\chi$ in a tableau.

Since $\vdash \chi \Leftrightarrow \bar{\chi}$ implies $\vdash \nu x.\chi \Leftrightarrow \chi[\nu x.\chi/x] \Leftrightarrow \bar{\chi}[\nu x.\chi/x]$ by Lemma 26, the $U\nu\chi$-rule preserves consistency. As in Lemma 32, the consistency of $\psi \wedge \nu x.\chi$ implies then the existence of a consistent strong tableau (with the modified rules) $T = (i_1, \Gamma_1, d_1, d_1^s) \ldots$ for $\psi \wedge \nu x.\chi$. As in Lemma 33 the consistency of T means that it is proper, as well.

Define a model M on the basis of T as in the proof of Lemma 28, and define a set $W \subseteq N$ by $W = \{k \in N \mid \exists j \in N, u \in \mathcal{U} : i_j = k, u \in \Gamma_j \text{ and } d_j(u) = \nu x.\chi\}$. For every $w \in W$, we can read from T a proper tableau witnessing $M[W/x], w \models \bar{\chi}$ by Lemma 10. Since $\vdash \chi \Leftrightarrow \bar{\chi}$, this implies by Theorem 25 that $M[W/x], w \models \chi$ for all $w \in W$. As $1 \in W$, this implies $M, 1 \models \nu x.\chi$. From T we can also read a proper tableau witnessing $M, 1 \models \psi$. Consequently, $M, 1 \models \psi \wedge \nu x.\chi$, as required.

The following lemma is the heart of the completeness proof. Essentially it shows that we can lift the expressive equivalence of the whole νTL and the fragment of formulae in banan-form from the level of semantics to the level of provability.

Lemma 36. *For any formula ϕ, there exists a formula ϕ' in banan-form such that $\vdash \phi \Leftrightarrow \phi'$.*

Proof. We show the claim by induction on the structure of the formula ϕ. As before, we assume that ϕ is written using just the $\wedge, \neg, \odot$ and μ-operators.
Induction basis: For an atomic ϕ, choosing $\phi' = \phi$ clearly fulfils the claim.

Induction step for $\wedge$, $\neg$, $\odot$: Suppose that for ϕ_1, ϕ_2 we have ϕ'_1, ϕ'_2 in banan-form such that $\vdash \phi_1 \Leftrightarrow \phi'_1$ and $\vdash \phi_2 \Leftrightarrow \phi'_2$. By Lemma 16 $\phi'_1 \wedge \phi'_2$, $\neg\phi'_1$ and $\odot\phi'_1$ are in banan-form and clearly $\vdash \phi_1 \wedge \phi_2 \Leftrightarrow \phi'_1 \wedge \phi'_2$, $\vdash \neg\phi_1 \Leftrightarrow \neg\phi'_1$ and $\vdash \odot\phi_1 \Leftrightarrow \odot\phi'_1$.

Induction step for μ: Suppose that for ϕ we have a ϕ' in banan-form such that $\vdash \phi \Leftrightarrow \phi'$. By Theorem 23, there exists a formula ψ in banan-form such that $\models \mu z.\phi \Leftrightarrow \psi$. If we have $\vdash \mu z.\phi \Leftrightarrow \psi$, the induction step is satisfied, as ψ is in banan-form. Suppose then that $\not\vdash \mu z.\phi \Leftrightarrow \psi$. This means that either

1 $\not\vdash \mu z.\phi \Rightarrow \psi$, or

2 $\not\vdash \psi \Rightarrow \mu z.\phi$

In case 1 we must have $\not\vdash \phi[\psi/z] \Rightarrow \psi$, as otherwise $\vdash \mu z.\phi \Rightarrow \psi$ could be derived by the fixpoint induction rule.[2] This means that $\phi[\psi/z] \wedge \neg\psi$ is consistent. As $\vdash \phi \Leftrightarrow \phi'$, by Lemma 26 $\vdash \phi[\psi/z] \Leftrightarrow \phi'[\psi/z]$, implying that $\phi'[\psi/z] \wedge \neg\psi$ is consistent. Since ϕ' and ψ are in banan-form, by Lemma 16 $\phi'[\psi/z] \wedge \neg\psi$ is in banan-form, hence guarded and aconjunctive. As it is consistent, by Prop. 34 it is satisfiable, i.e. there are M, m such that $M, m \models \phi'[\psi/z] \wedge \neg\psi$.

Since $\vdash \phi[\psi/z] \Leftrightarrow \phi'[\psi/z]$, by Theorem 25 $\models \phi[\psi/z] \Leftrightarrow \phi'[\psi/z]$, which implies $M, m \models \phi[\psi/z] \wedge \neg\psi$. By the choice of ψ, we know that $\models \psi \Leftrightarrow \mu z.\phi$, which implies $\models \phi[\psi/z] \Leftrightarrow \phi[\mu z.\phi/z]$, i.e. $\models \phi[\psi/z] \Leftrightarrow \mu z.\phi$. Consequently, $M, m \models \mu z.\phi \wedge \neg\psi$. But this contradicts $\models \mu z.\phi \Leftrightarrow \psi$, meaning that case 1 cannot hold.

In case 2, $\psi \wedge \neg\mu z.\phi = \psi \wedge \nu z.\neg\phi[\neg z/z]$ is consistent. As $\vdash \phi \Leftrightarrow \phi'$, by Lemma 26 $\vdash \neg\phi[\neg z/z] \Leftrightarrow \neg\phi'[\neg z/z]$. Since ϕ' is in banan-form, by Lemma 16 $\neg\phi'[\neg z/z]$ is in banan-form, hence guarded and aconjunctive. But then by Lemma 35 $\psi \wedge \nu z.\neg\phi[\neg z/z] = \psi \wedge \neg\mu z.\phi$ is satisfiable, contradicting $\models \mu z.\phi \Leftrightarrow \psi$, i.e. case 2 cannot hold either.

Consequently, $\vdash \mu z.\phi' \Leftrightarrow \psi$, which concludes the induction step.

Based on this lemma, the completeness of the axiomatisation follows easily.

Theorem 37. *If a formula ϕ is consistent, then ϕ is satisfiable.*

Proof. Direct from Lemma 36, Proposition 34, and Theorem 25.

Corollary 38 (Completeness). *If $\models \phi$ then $\vdash \phi$.*

Proof. If $\models \phi$, then $\neg\phi$ is not satisfiable, therefore not consistent, implying $\vdash \neg\neg\phi$, i.e. $\vdash \phi$.

Acknowledgements

I would like to thank Colin Stirling for many useful discussions. This work has been funded by the Academy of Finland, the British Council, the CVCP Overseas Research Students Awards Scheme and the Finnish Cultural Foundation.

[2] For the record, this in retrospect very natural observation had escaped us, leading to a more restricted and cumbersome solution, until we saw it used in passing in Igor Walukiewicz's work [20].

References

1. Arnold, A. & Niwiński, D.: Fixed Point Characterisation of Weak Monadic Logic Definable Sets of Trees, in Nivat, M. & Podelski, A. (eds.): *Tree Automata and Languages*, Elsevier, 1992, pp. 159-188
2. Banieqbal, B. & Barringer, H.: Temporal Logic with Fixed Points, in *Temporal Logic in Specification*, LNCS vol. 398, Springer-Verlag, 1989, pp. 62-74
3. Barringer, H. & Kuiper, R. & Pnueli, A.: A Really Abstract Concurrent Model and its Temporal Logic, in *Proc. of the 13th ACM POPL*, 1986
4. Dam, M.: Fixpoints of Büchi automata, in *Proceedings of the 12th FST & TCS*, LNCS vol. 652, Springer-Verlag, 1992, pp. 39-50
5. Emerson, E. A.: Temporal and Modal Logic, in van Leeuwen, J. (ed.): *Handbook of Theoretical Computer Science*, Elsevier/North-Holland, 1990, pp. 997-1072
6. Emerson, E. A. & Lei, C. L.: Efficient Model-Checking in Fragments of the Propositional Mu-calculus, in *Proc. of the First IEEE LICS*, 1986, pp. 267-278
7. Kozen, D.: Results on the Propositional μ-calculus, in *Theoretical Computer Science*, vol. 27, 1983, pp. 333-354
8. Lichtenstein, O.: *Decidability, Completeness, and Extensions of Linear Time Temporal Logic*, PhD thesis, The Weizmann Institute of Science, Rehovot, Israel, 1991
9. McNaughton, R.: Testing and Generating Infinite Sequences by a Finite Automaton, in *Information and Control*, vol. 9, 1966, pp. 521-530
10. Muller, D.E. & Saoudi, A. & Schupp, P.: Alternating Automata, the Weak Monadic Theory of the Tree, and its Complexity, in *Proc. of the 13th ICALP*, LNCS vol. 226, Springer-Verlag, 1986, pp. 275-283
11. Niwiński, D.: On Fixed Point Clones, in *Proc. of the 13th ICALP*, LNCS vol. 226, Springer-Verlag, 1986, pp. 402-409
12. Siefkes, D.: *Büchi's Monadic Second Order Successor Arithmetic, Decidable Theories I*, LNM vol. 120, Springer-Verlag, 1970
13. Stirling, C.: Modal and Temporal Logics, in Abramsky, S. & al. (eds.): *Handbook of Logic in Computer Science*, Oxford University Press, 1992, pp. 477-563
14. Stirling, C. & Walker, D.: Local Model Checking in the Modal Mu-calculus, in *Theoretical Computer Science*, vol. 89, 1991, pp. 161-177
15. Streett, R. S. & Emerson, E. A.: An Automata Theoretic Decision Procedure for the Propositional Mu-Calculus, in *Information and Computation*, vol. 81, 1989, pp. 249-264
16. Thomas, W.: Automata on Infinite Objects, in van Leeuwen, J. (ed.): *Handbook of Theoretical Computer Science*, vol. 2, North-Holland, 1989, pp. 133-191
17. Vardi, M. Y.: A Temporal Fixpoint Calculus, in *Proceedings of the 15th ACM Symposium on Priciples of Programming Languages*, 1988, pp. 250-259
18. Vardi, M. Y. & Wolper, P.: Reasoning about Infinite Computations, in *Information and Computation*, vol. 115, 1994, pp. 1-37
19. Walukiewicz, I.: On Completeness of the μ-calculus, in *Proc. of the 8th IEEE LICS*, 1993, pp. 136-146
20. Walukiewicz, I.: Completeness of Kozen's Axiomatisation of the Propositional μ-calculus, to appear in *Proc. of the 10th IEEE LICS*, 1995
21. Wolper, P.: *Synthesis of Communicating Processes from Temporal Logic Specifications*, PhD thesis, Stanford University, 1982
22. Wolper, P.: Temporal Logic can be More Expressive, in *Information and Control*, vol 56, 1983, pp. 72-99

A Trace Consistent Subset of PTL

P.S. Thiagarajan *
School of Mathematics
SPIC Science Foundation
92 G.N. Chetty Road
T. Nagar, Madras-600 017
India
E-mail: pst@ssf.ernet.in

Abstract. The Propositional Temporal logic of Linear time (PTL) is often interpreted over sequences (of states or actions) that can be grouped into equivalence classes under a natural partial order based semantics. It has been noticed in the literature that many PTL formulas are consistent with respect to such an equivalence relation. Either all members of an equivalence class satisfy the formula or none of them do. Such formulas can be often verified efficiently. One needs to test satisfiability of the concerned formula for just one member of each equivalence class.
Here we identify an interesting subset of such equivalence consistent PTL formulas - denoted $PTL^{\otimes}$ - by purely semantic means. We then use a partial order based linear time temporal logic denoted $TrPTL^{\otimes}$ to obtain a simple syntactic characterization of $PTL^{\otimes}$. We also provide solutions to the satisfiability problem and an associated model checking problem for $TrPTL^{\otimes}$ using networks of Büchi automata.

0 Introduction

The Propositional Temporal logic of Linear time (PTL) is often interpreted over sequences (of states or actions) capturing the behaviour of a distributed program. It is well known that such a collection of sequences can be grouped together into equivalence classes under a natural partial order based semantics; two sequences are equivalent just in case they are two interleavings of the same partially ordered stretch of behaviour. It has been noticed in the literature in different contexts (for instance in [V] and [KP]) that many of the dynamic properties of a distributed program that one would like to verify are consistent with respect to such a partial order based semantics. Either all the members of an equivalence class satisfy the property or none of them do. Such consistent properties can be often verified efficiently. One needs to verify the concerned property for just one member of each equivalence class of runs. This observation lies at the heart of so called partial order based verification methods reported for instance in [V], [KP], [P] and [GW].

With this as motivation, the question we address here is: When is a PTL formula amenable to partial order based verification techniques? In order to make

* This work has been partly supported by the IFCPAR Project 502-1.

the question precise, we choose the familiar setting consisting of a network of communicating automata that coordinate their behaviour by performing common actions together. In such a setting, there is a natural notion of causal independence of actions induced by the distribution of actions over the agents; two actions are independent if they are performed by disjoint sets of agents. This leads via standard notions in the theory of traces, to an equivalence relation, say $\approx$, over the runs of the network. The PTL formula ψ may then said to be trace consistent if for any two runs r_1 and r_2 that are $\approx$-equivalent, r_1 satisfies ψ if and only if r_2 satisfies ψ. The point is, trace consistent formulas are precisely those that are amenable to partial order based verification methods.

The general problem of characterizing the set of trace consistent PTL formulas appears to be hard. Hence as a partial solution we present here a characterization of an interesting subset of trace consistent formulas. We do so by semantically identifying a subset of PTL formulas denoted $\mathrm{PTL}^{\otimes}$. We then show that $\mathrm{PTL}^{\otimes}$ has the same expressive power as the linear time temporal logic called product TrPTL and denoted $\mathrm{TrPTL}^{\otimes}$. Unlike PTL which is interpreted over sequences, the logic $\mathrm{TrPTL}^{\otimes}$ is interpreted over Mazurkiewicz traces which may be viewed as restricted kinds of labelled partial orders. It has a very simple syntax. Moreover, our result showing that $\mathrm{PTL}^{\otimes}$ and $\mathrm{TrPTL}^{\otimes}$ are expressively equivalent yields the corollary that every formula of $\mathrm{PTL}^{\otimes}$ is semantically equivalent to a very easily constructed syntactic image of a $\mathrm{TrPTL}^{\otimes}$ formula. In this sense, we have also a syntactic characterization of $\mathrm{PTL}^{\otimes}$.

A second result that we establish is a strong relationship between $\mathrm{PTL}^{\otimes}$ and networks of communicating automata called product automata in this paper. This result consists of a decision procedure for $\mathrm{TrPTL}^{\otimes}$ in terms of product automata. This in turn leads to the solution of the model checking problem for $\mathrm{TrPTL}^{\otimes}$ when programs are modelled as product automata.

Our automata-theoretic solutions are an easy extension of the ones developed for PTL in terms of Büchi automata by Vardi and Wolper [VW]. Our decision procedure and the model checking procedure has the same time complexity as the corresponding procedures for PTL; the decision procedure runs in time $2^{O(n)}$ and the model checking procedure runs in time $O(m \cdot 2^{O(n)})$ where n is the size of the input formula and m is the size of the model of the input program. The logic is a strictly weaker subsystem of the logic TrPTL studied in [T]. TrPTL is also interpreted over Mazurkiewicz traces. However its decision procedure runs in time $2^{O(n^2 \log n)}$ and uses Büchi asynchronous automata which are strictly more expressive than product automata.

Our result concerning $\mathrm{PTL}^{\otimes}$ has been triggered by the work of Niebert and Penczek [NP]. They show that the set of trace consistent PTLformulas treated by Valamari [V1] and by Peled [P] can be easily translated into $\mathrm{TrPTL}^{\otimes}$. This subset of formulas is however identified by placing severe syntactic restrictions; for instance, the next state modality is not allowed. The work of Peled in [P] is very relevant because it defines the notion of trace consistent formulas (but called equivalence robust), points out their importance in the context of efficient model checking and proceeds to identify a subset of trace consistent formulas.

One can not directly compare the set of trace consistent formulas identified in [P] with $\mathrm{PTL}^{\otimes}$. However once the necessary adjustments have been made, it is easy to show $\mathrm{PTL}^{\otimes}$ properly subsumes the set of trace consistent formulas identified in [P]. Yet another paper by Peled [P1] is closely related thematically to the present paper. However [P1] is based on state sequences and our work is based on action sequences and hence it is not obvious at present how to relate the results of the two papers.

As for other linear time temporal logics based on traces we wish to mention here the μ-calculus version of Niebert [N] as well as the version containing branching time modalities (but interpreted over causal chains within a trace) by Alur, Peled and Penczek [APP]. Finally, an axiomatization of $\mathrm{TrPTL}^{\otimes}$ has been proposed in [MR].

Due to lack of space, we present most of our results without proofs. All the details appear in the full version of the paper [T1].

1 Distributed Alphabets and $\mathrm{PTL}^{\otimes}$

As mentioned in the introduction, the setting we will focus on in this paper will consist of a fixed set of communicating automata that synchronize by performing common actions together. Consequently, through the rest of the paper, we fix a distributed alphabet $\widetilde{\Sigma} = (\Sigma_1, \Sigma_2, \ldots, \Sigma_K)$ with $K \geq 1$ and each Σ_i, a finite non-empty alphabet of actions. We set $\Sigma = \bigcup_{i=1}^{K} \Sigma_i$ and let a, b range over Σ. We set $\mathrm{Loc} = \{1, 2, \ldots, K\}$ and let i, j, k to range over Loc. For $a \in \Sigma$ we define $\mathrm{loc}(a) = \{i \mid a \in \Sigma_i\}$. This distribution of action in Σ over Loc, induces the independence relation $I_{\widetilde{\Sigma}} \subseteq \Sigma \times \Sigma$ given by:
$I_{\widetilde{\Sigma}} = \{(a, b) \mid \mathrm{loc}(a) \cap \mathrm{loc}(b) = \emptyset\}$. Clearly $I_{\widetilde{\Sigma}}$ is irreflexive and symmetric and hence $(\Sigma, I_{\widetilde{\Sigma}})$ is a concurrent alphabet in the sense of Mazurkiewicz [M]. The associated dependence relation $(\Sigma \times \Sigma) - I_{\widetilde{\Sigma}}$ will be denoted as $D_{\widetilde{\Sigma}}$. From now on we will write $I(D)$ instead of $I_{\widetilde{\Sigma}}(D_{\widetilde{\Sigma}})$.

The theory of (Mazurkiewicz) traces is usually formulated in terms of a concurrent alphabet. A distributed alphabet may be thought of as a particular concrete realization of the associated concurrent alphabet. As a result, most of the work presented here can be easily extended to the framework of concurrent alphabets. We prefer to work with distributed alphabets because they are more flexible and allow for many kinds of redundancies. For instance, we could well have $\Sigma_i \subseteq \Sigma_j$ with $i \neq j$.

The syntax and semantics of PTL that we present is geared towards describing linear time behaviours over $\Sigma(= \bigcup_{i=1} \Sigma_i)$. For ease of presentation, we do not deal with atomic propositions - other than True and False - here. The means for doing so are explained in [T1]. The syntax we will work with is given by:

$$\mathrm{PTL}(\widetilde{\Sigma}) ::= \top \mid \sim \psi \mid \psi \vee \psi' \mid \langle a \rangle \psi \mid \psi \, \mathcal{U} \, \psi' \quad (a \in \Sigma).$$

From now on, we will often write PTL instead of $\mathrm{PTL}(\widetilde{\Sigma})$. The derived connectives of propositional calculus $\wedge$, $\supset$ and $\equiv$ as well as the derived modalities $\Diamond$ and $\Box$ are obtained in the usual way.

Before defining the models of PTL, we fix some notations concerning sequences. For the alphabet A, A^* is the set of finite words over A and A^ω is the set of infinite words over A. We set $A^\infty = A^* \cup A^\omega$. We shall treat finite and infinite behaviours uniformly throughout. For $A' \subseteq A$ and $\sigma \in A^\infty$, $\sigma|A'$ will denote the word obtained by erasing from σ all appearances of letters that are not in A'. If $\sigma \in \Sigma$ then we will write $\sigma|i$ instead $\sigma|\Sigma_i$. Finally, Prf(σ) is the set of finite prefixes of σ and $\preceq$ is the usual prefix ordering over sequences.

A model is any $\sigma \in \Sigma^\infty$. For $\tau \in \text{Prf}(\sigma)$ and a formula ψ we let $\sigma, \tau \models \psi$ stand for the fact that ψ is satisfied in the model σ at the stage τ and define it in the usual way.

- $\sigma, \tau \models \top$; $\sigma, \tau \models \sim \psi$ iff $\sigma, \tau \not\models \psi$ and $\sigma, \tau \models \psi \vee \psi'$ iff $\sigma, \tau \models \psi$ or $\sigma, \tau \models \psi'$.
- $\sigma, \tau \models \langle a \rangle \psi$ iff $\tau a \in \text{Prf}(\sigma)$ and $\sigma, \tau a \models \psi$.
- $\sigma, \tau \models \psi \, \mathcal{U} \, \psi'$ iff $\exists \, \tau' \in \text{Prf}(\sigma)$. $\tau \preceq \tau'$ and $\sigma, \tau' \models \psi'$ and for every $\tau'' \in \text{Prf}(\sigma)$ with $\tau \preceq \tau'' \prec \tau'$, it is the case that $\sigma, \tau'' \models \psi$.

Through the rest of the paper we let $\sigma, \sigma', \sigma''$ range over Σ^∞ and let τ, τ', τ'' range over Σ^*. Note that for every σ, the null word ε is always a member of Prf(σ). Abusing notation we shall write $\sigma \models \psi$ to mean $\sigma, \varepsilon \models \psi$. The formula ψ is said to be valid - denoted $\models \psi$ - iff $\sigma, \tau \models \psi$ for every σ and every $\tau \in \text{Prf}(\sigma)$. It is easy to check that ψ is valid iff $\sigma \models \psi$ for every σ. We also note that conventional PTL is PTL($\widetilde{\Sigma}$) when $\widetilde{\Sigma}$ consist of a 1-component 1-letter alphabet. More precisely, when $\widetilde{\Sigma} = (\Sigma_1, \ldots, \Sigma_K)$ with $K = 1$ and $\Sigma_1 = \{a\}$, we get exactly classical PTL with the convention that $\langle a \rangle \psi$ is to be written as $\bigcirc \psi$.

Each formula of PTL($\widetilde{\Sigma}$) now defines a language. Formally, $L_\psi \triangleq \{\sigma \mid \sigma \models \psi\}$. A central notion in partial order based verification methods can now be introduced. Before doing so, we adopt the terminology that if $L \subseteq \Sigma^\infty$ and $R \subseteq \Sigma^\infty \times \Sigma^\infty$ is an equivalence relation then L is R-consistent iff $\forall \, \sigma, \sigma' \in \Sigma^\infty$, if $\sigma \, R \, \sigma'$ and $\sigma \in L$ then $\sigma' \in L$. In other words, either *all* members of an R-equivalence class are in L or *none* of them are in L when L is R-consistent.

Definition 1.1.

(i) $\approx_i \subseteq \Sigma^\infty \times \Sigma^\infty$ is the equivalence relation given by: $\sigma \approx_i \sigma'$ iff $\sigma|i = \sigma'|i$.
(ii) ψ is i-consistent iff L_ψ is $\approx_i$-consistent. In other words, if $\sigma|i = \sigma'|i$, then $\sigma \models \psi$ iff $\sigma' \models \psi$.
(iii) $\approx_I$ is the equivalence relation given by $\sigma \approx_I \sigma'$ iff $\sigma \approx_i \sigma'$ for every i.
(iv) ψ is I-consistent (trace consistent) iff L_ψ is $\approx_I$-consistent. In other words, if $\sigma \approx_I \sigma'$ then $\sigma \models \psi$ iff $\sigma' \models \psi$.

From now on, we will often write $\approx$ instead of $\approx_I$. What are called I-consistent formulas here are the ones referred to as equivalence robust formulas in [P]. As mentioned earlier, these formulas can often be verified efficiently. For those familiar with trace theory, it should be clear that $\approx$ is the usual equivalence relation induced by I using which traces (i.e. $\approx$-equivalence classes) can be formed.

An example of an I-consistent formula is $\psi_0 = \Box \bigvee_{a\in\Sigma}\langle a\rangle\top$ which declares that the run under consideration does not end in a deadlock. It seems however hard to syntactically characterize the set of I-consistent formulas. One of the main results of this paper is to provide such a characterization for an interesting subset of PTL.

Note that the notion of a formula ψ being i-consistent is a purely semantic one (just like the notion of I-consistency). ψ could well mention actions that are not in Σ_i and still be i-consistent. We now define $\text{PTL}^{\otimes}$ to be least subset of PTL satisfying:

- If ψ is i-consistent for some i then $\psi \in \text{PTL}^{\otimes}$.
- If $\psi, \psi' \in \text{PTL}^{\otimes}$ then $\sim \psi$, $\psi \vee \psi' \in \text{PTL}^{\otimes}$.
- If $\models \psi \equiv \psi'$ and $\psi \in \text{PTL}^{\otimes}$ then $\psi' \in \text{PTL}^{\otimes}$.

An interesting fact is the formula $\psi_0 = \Box \bigvee_{a\in\Sigma}\langle a\rangle\top$ is in $\text{PTL}^{\otimes}$. This is so because $\models \psi_0 \equiv \bigvee_i \psi_i$ where $\psi_i = \Box\Diamond \bigvee_{a\in\Sigma_i}\langle a\rangle\top$ and ψ_i is an i-consistent formula for each i. We observe that $\text{PTL}^{\otimes}$ indeed is a collection of I-consistent formulas.

Proposition 1.2. *Let $\psi \in \text{PTL}^{\otimes}$. Then ψ is I-consistent.*

Proof Sketch. Suppose ψ is i-consistent and therefore a member of $\text{PTL}^{\otimes}$. Let $\sigma \approx \sigma'$ and $\sigma \models \psi$. But $\sigma \approx \sigma'$ implies $\sigma \approx_i \sigma'$ and since ψ is i-consistent and $\sigma \models \psi$ we must also have $\sigma' \models \psi$. The rest of the proof is routine. □

As might be expected, not every I-consistent formula is in $\text{PTL}^{\otimes}$. For instance, with $\widetilde{\Sigma} = (\{a, \overline{a}, d\}, \{d, b, \overline{b}\})$ one can construct an I-consistent formula ψ such that $L_\psi = (d(ab + ba + \overline{a}\overline{b} + \overline{b}\overline{a}))^\omega$. Using our later results one can also show that $\psi \notin \text{PTL}^{\otimes}$.

Now we wish to establish that $\text{PTL}^{\otimes}$ can be characterized by the trace based linear time temporal logic $\text{TrPTL}^{\otimes}$. As preparation, we will first introduce product automata and traces.

2 Product Automata

In the definition to follow and elsewhere, $x[i]$ is the ith component of the K-tuple $x = (x_1, x_2, \ldots, x_K)$; in other words, $x[i] = x_i$.

Definition 2.1. A product automaton over $\widetilde{\Sigma}$ is a structure $\mathcal{A} = (\{\mathcal{A}_i\}_{i=1}^K, Q_{in})$ where for each i, $\mathcal{A}_i = (Q_i, \longrightarrow_i, F_i, \widehat{F}_i)$ with,

- Q_i is a finite set of i-local states and $\longrightarrow_i \subseteq Q_i \times \Sigma_i \times Q_i$ is the transition relation of the ith component.
- $F_i \subseteq Q_i$ is the set of finitary accepting states.
- $\widehat{F}_i \subseteq Q_i$ is the set of infinitary accepting states.
- $Q_{in} \subseteq Q_1 \times Q_2 \times \cdots \times Q_K$ is the set of global initial states. □

We use two types of accepting states for the components because even if the global run is infinite, a component might quit after engaging in a finite number of actions. We use global initial states because the automaton will not always be able to branch off from a single initial state into different parts of the state space.

Let $\mathcal{A} = (\{\mathcal{A}_i\}_{i=1}^{K}, Q_{in})$ be a product automaton. We will often write $\{\mathcal{A}_i\}_{i=1}^{K}$ as $\{\mathcal{A}_i\}$. Let $\mathcal{A}_i = (Q_i, \longrightarrow_i, F_i, \widehat{F}_i)$. We set $Q_G^{\mathcal{A}} = Q_1 \times Q_2 \times \cdots \times Q_K$. When $\mathcal{A}$ is clear from the context we will write Q_G instead of $Q_G^{\mathcal{A}}$. The global transition relation of the automaton $\mathcal{A}$ is denoted as $\longrightarrow_{\mathcal{A}}$ and it is the subset of $Q_G \times \Sigma \times Q_G$ given by:

$$q \stackrel{a}{\longrightarrow}_{\mathcal{A}} q' \text{ iff } \forall\, i \in \mathrm{loc}(a).\ q[i] \stackrel{a}{\longrightarrow}_i q'[i] \text{ and } \forall\, i \notin \mathrm{loc}(a).\ q[i] = q'[i].$$

Let $\sigma \in \Sigma^{\infty}$. Then a run of $\mathcal{A}$ over σ is a map $\rho : \mathrm{Prf}(\sigma) \longrightarrow Q_G$ such that $\rho(\varepsilon) \in Q_{in}$ and $\rho(\tau) \stackrel{a}{\longrightarrow}_{\mathcal{A}} \rho(\tau a)$ for every $\tau a \in \mathrm{Prf}(\sigma)$. The run ρ is *accepting* iff for each i, ρ satisfies:

- If $\sigma|i$ is finite, then $\rho(\tau)[i] \in F_i$ where $\tau \in \mathrm{Prf}(\sigma)$ such that $\sigma|i = \tau|i$.
- If $\sigma|i$ is infinite then $\rho(\tau)[i] \in \widehat{F}_i$ for infinitely many $\tau \in \mathrm{Prf}(\sigma)$.

$\mathcal{L}(\mathcal{A}) \triangleq \{\sigma \mid \exists$ an accepting run of $\mathcal{A}$ over $\sigma\}$ is the language accepted by $\mathcal{A}$. We note that the language $\{ad, bd\}$ is accepted by a product automata over $(\{a, d\}, \{d, b\})$ but *no* product automaton with a single global initial state will accept this language. This example also shows why we can not choose the global initial states to be the cartesian product of i-local initial state sets.

Product automata will lead to transparent solutions to the decidability and the model checking problems associated with the logic TrPTL$^{\otimes}$ to be presented in Section 4. With this in mind, we put down two results which are easy to prove. Before stating these results, we define the size of the product automaton $\mathcal{A}$ to be $|Q_G|$.

Theorem 2.2.

(i) *Let $\mathcal{A}$ be a product automaton. Then the question $\mathcal{L}(\mathcal{A}) \stackrel{?}{=} \emptyset$ can be decided in time $O(2^{2K} \cdot n^2)$ where n is the size of $\mathcal{A}$.*

(ii) *Let $\mathcal{A}^1$ and $\mathcal{A}^2$ be two product automata over $\widetilde{\Sigma}$. Then one can effectively construct a product automaton $\mathcal{A}$ over $\widetilde{\Sigma}$ such that $\mathcal{L}(\mathcal{A}) = \mathcal{L}(\mathcal{A}^1) \cap \mathcal{L}(\mathcal{A}^2)$ and $n = O(2^K \cdot n_1 \cdot n_2)$ where n is the size of $\mathcal{A}$ and n_m is the size of $\mathcal{A}^m$ for $m = 1, 2$.* □

It is not difficult to observe that the language accepted by a product automaton is $\approx$-consistent. The class of languages accepted by product automata is precisely the boolean combinations of languages expressible as a synchronized product (not shuffle!) of regular subsets of Σ_i^{∞}. The details can be found in [T1].

3 Traces

A trace over $\widetilde{\Sigma}$ may be defined in many equivalent ways. Here we wish to use traces as temporal frames for a partial order based version of PTL. Hence we shall define a trace over $\widetilde{\Sigma}$ to be a certain kind of a Σ-labelled poset.

First some terminology concerning posets. If $(X, \leq)$ is a poset and $Y \subseteq X$ then $\downarrow Y \stackrel{\Delta}{=} \{x \mid \exists\, y \in Y.\ x \leq y\}$. In case $Y = \{y\}$ we shall write $\downarrow y$ instead of $\downarrow \{y\}$. The derived relation $\lessdot$ is defined as $\lessdot \stackrel{\Delta}{=} < - <^2$.

Definition 3.1. A trace over $\widetilde{\Sigma}$ is a triple $F = (E, \leq, \lambda)$ such that:

- E is a countable (finite or infinite) set of events.
- $\leq \subseteq E \times E$ is partial order called the causality relation such that $\downarrow e$ is a finite set for every $e \in E$.
- $\lambda : E \longrightarrow \Sigma$ is a labelling function which respects the dependency relation $D\ (= \Sigma \times \Sigma - I_{\widetilde{\Sigma}})$ in the following ways: If $e \lessdot e'$ then $(\lambda(e), \lambda(e')) \in D$; If $(\lambda(e), \lambda(e')) \in D$ then $e \leq e'$ or $e' \leq e$. □

The notion of a time point in a linear temporal frame generalizes to that of a configuration for a trace. Let $F = (E, \leq, \lambda)$ be a trace over $\widetilde{\Sigma}$. Then $c \subseteq E$ is a configuration iff c is finite and $c = \downarrow c$. We let C_F denote the set of configurations of F. We note that $\emptyset$, the empty set, is always a configuration and also $\downarrow e$ is a configuration for each $e \in E$.

The set of i-events of the trace $F = (E, \leq, \lambda)$ over $\widetilde{\Sigma}$ is denoted as E_i and is defined as: $E_i = \{e \mid e \in E \text{ and } \lambda(e) \in \Sigma_i\}$. Note that E_i is linearly ordered by $\leq$. In the run represented by F, the set of events that the ith agent participates in is precisely E_i. A related and important notion is that of the i-view of a configuration. For $c \in C_F$ where $F = (E, \leq, \lambda)$ is a trace over $\widetilde{\Sigma}$, we let $\downarrow^i (c)$ denote the i-view of c and define it to be:

$$\downarrow^i (c) \stackrel{\Delta}{=} \downarrow (c \cap E_i).$$

We note that $\downarrow^i (c)$ is also a configuration. It is the least configuration the agent i is aware of at the global configuration c.

Before proceeding one remark is in order. In this paper we will not distinguish between a trace F and its isomorphism class $\langle F \rangle$. Isomorphisms between traces (viewed as Σ-labelled posets) is defined in the obvious way. Thus when say $F = G$ for two traces F and G over $\widetilde{\Sigma}$, we will almost always mean $\langle F \rangle = \langle G \rangle$.

$TR(\widetilde{\Sigma})$ is the set of traces of $\widetilde{\Sigma}$. A trace language is simply a subset of $TR(\widetilde{\Sigma})$. A basic and very convenient fact is that $\approx$-consistent subsets of Σ^∞ and trace languages over $\widetilde{\Sigma}$ represent each other unambiguously. One can easily construct a map $wt : \Sigma^\infty \longrightarrow TR(\widetilde{\Sigma})$ which assigns a trace to each $\sigma \in \Sigma^\infty$. For $\sigma \in \Sigma^\infty$ we set $wt(\sigma) = (E_\sigma, \leq_\sigma, \lambda_\sigma)$ where $E_\sigma = \mathrm{Prf}(\sigma) - \{\varepsilon\}$ and $\leq_\sigma$ is the least partial ordering relation contained in $E_\sigma \times E_\sigma$ satisfying: if $\tau a \preceq \tau' b$ and $(a, b) \in D$ then $\tau a \leq_\sigma \tau' b$. Finally, $\lambda_\sigma(\tau a) = a$ for every $\tau a \in E_\sigma$.

We can also construct a map $tw : TR(\widetilde{\Sigma}) \longrightarrow \mathcal{P}(\Sigma^\infty)$ which assigns to each F a set of words in Σ^∞. We set $tw((E, \leq, \lambda))$ to be the words obtained by taking the linearizations of $(E, \leq)$ and reading off the underlying Σ-word using λ. The idea should be clear and we will not formalise it here. For $\widehat{L} \subseteq TR(\widetilde{\Sigma})$ we define $tw(\widehat{L}) = \bigcup\{tw(F) \mid F \in \widehat{L}\}$. For $L \subseteq \Sigma^{\infty}$, we define as usual $wt(L) = \{wt(\sigma) \mid \sigma \in L\}$. Using standard techniques from trace theory (see for instance, [WN]), one can show that the maps wt and tw fit together nicely in the following sense.

Proposition 3.2.

(i) *Suppose $\sigma, \sigma' \in \Sigma^{\infty}$. Then $\sigma \approx \sigma'$ if and only if $wt(\sigma) = wt(\sigma')$.*
(ii) *Suppose $F \in TR(\widetilde{\Sigma})$. Then $tw(F)$ is an $\approx$-equivalence class. In other words, there exists $\sigma \in \Sigma^{\infty}$ such that $tw(F) = \{\sigma' \mid \sigma \approx \sigma'\}$.*
(iii) *Let $\widehat{L} \subseteq TR(\widetilde{\Sigma})$. Then $tw(\widehat{L})$ is an $\approx$-consistent subset of Σ^{∞}.*
(iv) *Suppose $L \subseteq \Sigma^{\infty}$ is $\approx$-consistent. Then $tw(wt(L)) = L$.*
(v) *Suppose $\widehat{L} \subseteq TR(\widetilde{\Sigma})$. Then $wt(tw(\widehat{L})) = \widehat{L}$.* □

It is in the sense of parts (iii), (iv) and (v) of the above result that $\approx$-consistent subsets of Σ^{∞} and subsets of $TR(\widetilde{\Sigma})$ represent each other.

4 TrPTL$^{\otimes}$: Syntax and Semantics

In [T] we formulated a logic called - in light of the terminology introduced here - TrPTL($\widetilde{\Sigma}$). This logic is a conservative extension of PTL using infinite traces over $\widetilde{\Sigma}$ as its temporal frames. The satisfiability problem for TrPTL($\widetilde{\Sigma}$) was shown to be decidable in time $2^{O(n^3 \log n)}$ using a class of automata called Büchi asynchronous automata. (This time bound can be easily improved to $2^{O(n^2 \log n)}$). Based on this, an associated model checking problem was also solved by automata-theoretic means.

Here we present, in a self-contained fashion, a subsystem of TrPTL($\widetilde{\Sigma}$) denoted as TrPTL$^{\otimes}$($\widetilde{\Sigma}$) (called "product TrPTL"). As before, we will from now on write TrPTL$^{\otimes}$ instead of TrPTL$^{\otimes}$($\widetilde{\Sigma}$). We shall continue to ignore atomic propositions for the sake of convenience. They can be handled as in [T]. The formulas of TrPTL$^{\otimes}$ will built up along with the set of locations of each formula.

- $\top$ is a formula; $\text{loc}(\top) = \emptyset$. If α and β are formulas so are $\sim \alpha$ and $\alpha \vee \beta$; $\text{loc}(\sim \alpha) = \text{loc}(\alpha)$ and $\text{loc}(\alpha \vee \beta) = \text{loc}(\alpha) \cup \text{loc}(\beta)$.
- If $a \in \Sigma_i$ and α is a formula such that $\text{loc}(\alpha) \subseteq \{i\}$ then $\langle a \rangle_i \alpha$ is a formula; $\text{loc}(\langle a \rangle_i \alpha) = \{i\}$.
- If α and β are formulas such that $\text{loc}(\alpha), \text{loc}(\beta) \subseteq \{i\}$ then $\alpha\, \mathcal{U}_i\, \beta$ is also a formula; $\text{loc}(\alpha\, \mathcal{U}_i\, \beta) = \{i\}$.

For convenience we will, from now on, let $\Phi^{\otimes}$ denote the set of formulas of TrPTL$^{\otimes}$.

A model is a trace over $\widetilde{\Sigma}$. Let $F = (E, \leq, \lambda)$, $c \in C_F$ and α a formula. Then $F, c \models \alpha$ denotes that α is satisfied at c in F and is defined inductively:

- $F, c \models \top$; $F, c \models \sim \alpha$ if and only if $F, c \not\models \alpha$ and $F, c \models \alpha \vee \beta$ iff $F, c \models \alpha$ or $F, c \models \beta$.
- $F, c \models \langle a \rangle_i \alpha$ iff $\exists e \in E_i - c.\ \lambda(e) = a$ and $F, \downarrow e \models \alpha$ and $\forall e' \in E_i.\ e' < e$ iff $e' \in c$.
- $F, c \models \alpha\ \mathcal{U}_i\ \beta$ iff $\exists\ c' \supseteq c.\ F, c' \models \beta$ and $\forall c''.\ \downarrow^i (c) \subseteq \downarrow^i (c'') \subset \downarrow^i (c')$ implies $F, c'' \models \alpha$ (with $c', c'' \in C_F$).

The formula $\langle a \rangle_i \alpha$ asserts that the ith component will next engage in an a-labelled event, and at the resulting i-view, the property α will hold. Note that this promised event may not be immediately enabled at c. The formula $\alpha\ \mathcal{U}_i\ \beta$ asserts that along the linearly ordered sequence of i-views of configurations to be encountered from now on, α will hold until β eventually holds. TrPTL has exactly the same semantics but a more generous syntax; we remove the locational restrictions placed on formulas of the form $\langle a \rangle_i \alpha$ and $\alpha\ \mathcal{U}_i\ \beta$. This turns out to strictly add to the expressive power. As before, we will abuse notation and write $F \models \alpha$ to mean $F, \emptyset \models \alpha$. Each formula α defines a trace language. To be specific, $\widehat{L}_\alpha \triangleq \{F \mid F \in TR(\widetilde{\Sigma})$ and $F \models \alpha\}$.

Before proceeding, it will be convenient to rework the syntax of $\text{TrPTL}^{\otimes}$. Let $\Phi_i^{\otimes}$ denote the set of formulas contained in $\Phi^{\otimes}$ given by: $\alpha \in \Phi_i^{\otimes}$ iff $\text{loc}(\alpha) \subseteq \{i\}$. Then it is easy to see that every formula in $\Phi^{\otimes}$ can be expressed as a boolean combination of formulas taken from $\bigcup_i \Phi_i^{\otimes}$. In the sequel, this fact will be used in a number of places. This fact also makes it clear that one can make full use of conventional PTL to build up local assertions about the behaviour of a component while indexing the formulas suitably. A boolean combination of such indexed local assertions then yields a global assertion. The crucial point is, such assertions are interpreted over traces which force the components to combine in an orderly way. Hence the logic can indeed say non-trivial things about the global behaviour. As an extreme example, consider the two component alphabet $\widetilde{\Gamma} = (\{a\}, \{b\})$. Then $\Box_1 \langle a \rangle_1 \top \supset \Box_2 \langle b \rangle_2 \top$ is a formula in $\text{TrPTL}^{\otimes}(\widetilde{\Gamma})$. It asserts that if the first component executes infinitely often so does the second component. Notice that no communication is possible between the two components!

5 Solutions to the Satisfiability and Model Checking Problems

We now show that the satisfiability problem for $\text{TrPTL}^{\otimes}$ can be easily settled using product automata. This then leads to the solution of an associated model checking problem for programs modelled as product automata.

Our solution closely follows the one developed for PTL in terms of Büchi automata by Vardi and Wolper [VW]. We do not wish to directly use the automata theoretic techniques developed in [T] for TrPTL because that solution involves the use of Büchi asynchronous automata which are strictly more expressive than product automata.

To start with, we expand the syntax of $\text{TrPTL}^{\otimes}$. To the formation rules for the formulas we add: If α is a formula with $\text{loc}(\alpha) \subseteq \{i\}$, then $O_i \alpha$ is formula; $\text{loc}(O_i\alpha) = \{i\}$. To the semantic definitions, we add: $F, c \models O_i\alpha$ iff $F, c \models \langle a\rangle_i\alpha$ for some $a \in \Sigma_i$. Everything else remains the same including the definitions of the sets $\Phi_i^{\otimes}$ and $\Phi^{\otimes}$. Clearly O_i is expressible in terms of $\langle a\rangle_i$ but a more efficient decision procedure is obtained by making O_i a first class modality. For each formula α we will construct a product automaton $\mathcal{A}_\alpha$ such that α is satisfiable iff $\mathcal{L}(\mathcal{A}_\alpha) \neq \emptyset$. By the first part of Theorem 2.2, this will yield a decision procedure.

Fix a formula α_0. Let $CL(\alpha_0)$ be the least set of formulas which contains the subformulas of α_0 and satisfies:

- If $\beta \in CL(\alpha_0)$ then $\sim \beta \in CL(\alpha_0)$ (with the convention $\sim\sim \beta$ is identified with β).
- If $\alpha\, \mathcal{U}_i\, \beta \in CL(\alpha_0)$ then $O_i\alpha\, \mathcal{U}_i\, \beta \in CL(\alpha_0)$.

Set $CL_i(\alpha_0) = CL(\alpha_0) \cap \Phi_i^{\otimes}$ for each i. We declare $A \subseteq CL_i(\alpha_0)$ to be an i-type atom iff it is propositionally consistent and in addition, satisfies: $\forall \alpha\, \mathcal{U}_i\, \beta \in CL_i(\alpha_0)$. $\alpha\, \mathcal{U}_i\, \beta \in A$ iff $\beta \in A$ or ($\alpha \in A$ and $O_i\alpha\, \mathcal{U}_i\, \beta \in A$).

Let AT_i be the set of i-type atoms for each i. We set $U_i = \{\alpha\, \mathcal{U}_i\, \beta \mid \alpha\, \mathcal{U}_i \beta \in CL_i(\alpha_0)\}$ for each i. Finally for each $\alpha \in CL(\alpha_0)$ and each $(A_1, A_2, \ldots, A_K) \in AT_1 \times AT_2 \times \cdots \times AT_K$ the predicate $\text{M}(\alpha, (A_1, \ldots, A_K))$ denoted from now on as $\alpha \in (A_1, \ldots, A_K)$ is defined as follows.

- Suppose $\alpha \in \Phi_i^{\otimes}$. Then $\alpha \in (A_1, \ldots, A_K)$ iff $\alpha \in A_i$.
- $\sim \alpha \in (A_1, \ldots, A_K)$ iff $\alpha \notin (A_1, \ldots, A_K)$ and $\alpha \vee \beta \in (A_1, \ldots, A_K)$ iff $\alpha \in (A_1, \ldots, A_K)$ or $\beta \in (A_1, \ldots, A_K)$.

We now define the product automaton $\mathcal{A}_{\alpha_0}$ to be $\mathcal{A}_{\alpha_0} = (\{\mathcal{A}_i\}, Q_{in})$ where for each i, $\mathcal{A}_i = (Q_i, \longrightarrow_i, F_i, \widehat{F}_i)$ is specified as follows:

- $Q_i = AT_i \times \{0, 1\} \times \mathcal{P}(U_i)$
- $\longrightarrow_i \subseteq Q_i \times \Sigma_i \times Q_i$ is given by, $(A, x, u) \xrightarrow{a}_i (B, y, v)$ iff the following conditions are met.
  - (i) $x \neq 1$ and $\forall \langle a\rangle_i\alpha \in CL_i(\alpha_0)$, $\langle a\rangle_i\alpha \in A$ iff $\alpha \in B$ and $\forall O_i\alpha \in CL_i(\alpha_0)$, $O_i\alpha \in A$ iff $\alpha \in B$. Moreover, if $\langle b\rangle_i\beta \in A$, then $b = a$.
  - (ii) If $u \neq \emptyset$ then $v = \{\alpha\, \mathcal{U}_i\, \beta \mid \alpha\, \mathcal{U}_i\, \beta \in u \text{ and } \beta \notin B\}$. If $u = \emptyset$ then $v = \{\alpha\, \mathcal{U}_i\, \beta \mid \alpha\, \mathcal{U}_i\, \beta \in B \text{ and } \beta \notin B\}$.
- $F_i \subseteq Q_i$ is given by, $(A, x, u) \in F_i$ iff $x = 1$ and $\forall\, \langle a\rangle_i\alpha \in CL_i(\alpha_0)$, $\langle a\rangle_i\alpha \notin A$ and $\forall\, O_i\alpha \in CL_i(\alpha_0)$, $O_i\alpha \notin A$.
- $\widehat{F}_i \subseteq Q_i$ is given by, $(A, x, u) \in \widehat{F}_i$ iff $u = \emptyset$.
- $Q_{in} \subseteq Q_1 \times Q_2 \times \cdots \times Q_K$ is given by, $((A_1, x_1, u_1), \cdots, (A_K, x_K, u_K)) \in Q_{in}$ iff $\alpha_0 \in (A_1, \ldots, A_K)$ and $u_i = \emptyset$ for every i

It is easy to check that $\mathcal{A}_{\alpha_0}$ is indeed a product automaton.

Theorem 5.1.

(i) *α_0 is satisfiable iff $\mathcal{L}(\mathcal{A}_{\alpha_0}) \neq \emptyset$*
(ii) *The satisfiability problem for* TrPTL$^{\otimes}$ *is decidable in time $2^{O(n)}$ where n is the length of the input formula.* □

For proving the first part of the theorem as well as for formulating the model checking problem, it will be convenient to view a product automaton as an acceptor of traces. To bring this out, let $\mathcal{A} = (\{\mathcal{A}_i\}, Q_{in})$ be a product automaton and $F = (E, \leq, \lambda)$ be a trace. Then a trace run of $\mathcal{A}$ over F is a map $\rho : C_F \longrightarrow Q_G$ such that $\rho(\emptyset) \in Q_{in}$ and $\rho(c) \xrightarrow{\lambda(e)}_{\mathcal{A}} \rho(c')$ for every $c \overset{e}{\Longrightarrow}_F c'$. Here $\Longrightarrow_F \subseteq C_F \times E \times C_F$ is the obvious transition relation given by: $c \overset{e}{\Longrightarrow}_F c'$ iff $e \notin c$ and $c' = c \cup \{e\}$. The trace run ρ is accepting iff for every i the following condition is satisfied.

- If E_i is finite then $\rho(\downarrow E_i)[i] \in F_i$.
- If E_i is infinite then for infinitely many $e \in E_i$, $\rho(\downarrow e)[i] \in \widehat{F}_i$.

We define $\mathcal{L}_{Tr}(\mathcal{A}) = \{F \mid F \in TR(\widetilde{\Sigma})$ and $\exists$ an accepting run of $\mathcal{A}$ over $F\}$ as the trace language accepted by $\mathcal{A}$. It is easy to prove that $tw(\mathcal{L}_{Tr}(\mathcal{A})) = \mathcal{L}(\mathcal{A})$ for every product automata $\mathcal{A}$. (tw is the map from traces to words introduced in Section 3). Hence $\mathcal{L}_{Tr}(\mathcal{A}) \neq \emptyset$ iff $\mathcal{L}(\mathcal{A}) \neq \emptyset$.

To prove part (i) of the theorem it suffices to show that $\widehat{L}_{\alpha_0} = \mathcal{L}_{Tr}(\mathcal{A}_{\alpha_0})$. Suppose ρ is an accepting trace run of $\mathcal{A}_{\alpha_0}$ over $F = (E, \leq, \lambda)$. By structural induction, we can show that, for every $\beta \in CL(\alpha_0)$ and for every $c \in C_F$ that $F, c \models \beta$ iff $\beta \in (A_1, A_2, \ldots, A_K)$ where $\rho(c) = ((A_1, x_1, u_1), \ldots, (A_K, x_K, u_K))$. If $F, \emptyset \models \alpha_0$ then it is laborious but straightforward to construct an accepting trace run of $\mathcal{A}_{\alpha_0}$ over F.

To prove part (ii) of Theorem 5.1, we first observe that, by part (i) of Theorem 2.2, decidability at once follows. The required complexity bound is obtained from two observations. Firstly, it is easy to prove that with a suitably "reduced" representation of $CL(\alpha_0)$ it is the case that $|CL_1(\alpha_0)| + |CL_2(\alpha_0)| + \cdots + |CL_K(\alpha_0)| = O(n)$ where $n = |\alpha_0|$. Secondly, $|\text{loc}(\alpha_0)| \leq n$. As a result, the construction of $\mathcal{A}_{\alpha_0}$ can be tightened up. For each $i \in \text{loc}(\alpha_0)$, we construct the component $\mathcal{A}_i$ as specified above. But if $i \notin \text{loc}(\alpha_0)$ we set $Q_i = \{\top\} = F_i = \widehat{F}_i$ and $\longrightarrow_i = \{\top\} \times \Sigma_i \times \{\top\}$. Thus the factor 2^{2K} mentioned in Theorem 2.2 can be replaced by 2^{2n}. We now turn to a model checking problem.

A program Pr, in the present setting is simply a product automaton $\mathcal{A}_{Pr} = (\{\mathcal{A}_i\}, Q_{in})$ over $\widetilde{\Sigma}$ with $\mathcal{A}_i = (Q_i, \longrightarrow_i, F_i, \widehat{F}_i)$. We say that the specification α_0 is met by Pr - denoted $Pr \models \alpha_0$ - iff $\mathcal{L}_{Tr}(\mathcal{A}_{Pr}) \subseteq \widehat{L}_{\alpha_0}$ $(= \{F \mid F \models \alpha_0\})$.

Theorem 5.2. *The question* $Pr \overset{?}{\models} \alpha_0$ *can be settled in time* $O(m \cdot 2^{O(n)})$ *where* m *is the size of* $\mathcal{A}_{Pr}$ *and* n *is the size of* α_0. □

To prove Theorem 5.2 one checks, as usual, whether $\mathcal{L}_{Tr}(Pr) \cap \mathcal{L}_{Tr}(\mathcal{A}_{\sim\alpha_0}) = \emptyset$ using part (ii) of Theorem 2.2. One takes care again to introduce just one i-local state for each component i that is not mentioned in α_0.

6 An Expressiveness Result

We wish to show that PTL$^{\otimes}$ and TrPTL$^{\otimes}$ have the same expressive power. Recall that, $\Phi^{\otimes}$ is the boolean combination of formulas taken from $\bigcup_i \Phi_i$ where, for each i, $\Phi_i^{\otimes}$ consists of formulas α satisfying $\mathrm{loc}(\alpha) \subseteq \{i\}$.

We must have a common ground for comparing PTL$^{\otimes}$ and $\Phi^{\otimes}$. To this end, we say that $L \subseteq \Sigma^{\infty}$ is PTL$^{\otimes}$-definable iff there exists a PTL$^{\otimes}$ formula ψ such that $L = L_{\psi}$. We say that $L \subseteq \Sigma^{\infty}$ is TrPTL$^{\otimes}$-definable iff there exists a formula α in $\Phi^{\otimes}$ such that $tw(\widehat{L}_{\alpha}) = L$. Recall that $\widehat{L}_{\alpha} = \{F \mid F \models \alpha\}$ and tw is the map introduced in Section 3 which assigns, to each trace an $\approx$-equivalence class. The main result of this section is,

Theorem 6.1. *$L \subseteq \Sigma^{\infty}$ is* PTL$^{\otimes}$*-definable iff it is* TrPTL$^{\otimes}$*-definable.* □

To prove this result we will construct two maps $f : \mathrm{PTL}^{\otimes} \longrightarrow \Phi^{\otimes}$ and $g : \Phi^{\otimes} \longrightarrow \mathrm{PTL}^{\otimes}$. To define f, we first define the maps $f_i : \mathrm{PTL} \longrightarrow \Phi^{\otimes}$ for each i. The map $f_i : \mathrm{PTL} \longrightarrow \Phi^{\otimes}$ is given by:

- $f_i(\top) = \top$, $f_i(\sim \psi) = \sim f_i(\psi)$ and $f_i(\psi \vee \psi') = f_i(\psi) \vee f_i(\psi')$.
- $f_i(\langle a \rangle \psi) = \perp$ if $a \notin \Sigma_i$ ($\perp \overset{\Delta}{\Longleftrightarrow} \sim \top$); $f_i(\langle a \rangle \psi) = \langle a \rangle_i f_i(\psi)$, if $a \in \Sigma_i$.
- $f_i(\psi \,\mathcal{U}\, \psi') = f_i(\psi) \,\mathcal{U}_i\, f_i(\psi')$.

It is easy to check that $f_i(\psi) \in \Phi_i^{\otimes}$ for every ψ. It is important to notice that the domain of f_i is PTL and not just PTL$^{\otimes}$.

Now recall that wt is the map which assigns to each $\sigma \in \Sigma^{\infty}$, a trace in $TR(\widetilde{\Sigma})$. Here are two useful observations.

Lemma 6.2.

(i) *Let $\alpha \in \Phi_i^{\otimes}$, $F \in TR(\widetilde{\Sigma})$ and $c \in C_F$. Then $F, c \models \alpha$ iff $F, \downarrow^i (c) \models \alpha$.*

(ii) *Let $\alpha \in \Phi_i^{\otimes}$, $F \in TR(\widetilde{\Sigma})$ and $c, c' \in C_F$. If $c \cap E_i = c' \cap E_i$ then $F, c \models \alpha$ iff $F, c' \models \alpha$.* □

Lemma 6.3. *Let $\sigma \in \Sigma^{\infty}$ and ψ a formula of* PTL*. Then $\sigma | i \models \psi$ iff $wt(\sigma) \models f_i(\psi)$.* □

Let $wt(\sigma) = F = (E, \leq, \lambda)$. For each $\tau \in \mathrm{Prf}(\sigma)$ define $ev(\tau) = \{\tau' \mid \tau' \preceq \tau \text{ and } \tau' \neq \varepsilon\}$. We can show by structural induction on ψ that $\forall \tau \in \mathrm{Prf}(\sigma).\ \sigma|i, \tau|i \models \psi$ iff $F, ev(\tau) \models f_i(\psi)$. In doing so and elsewhere one ends up repeatedly appealing to Lemma 6.2 which is easy to prove.

Before constructing the map $f : \mathrm{PTL}^{\otimes} \longrightarrow \Phi^{\otimes}$ it will be convenient to refine the presentation of PTL$^{\otimes}$. For each i, set $\mathrm{PTL}_i^{\otimes}$ to be set of i-consistent PTL formulas. Define $\mathrm{PTL}_0^{\otimes}$ to the boolean combinations of the formulas in $\bigcup_{i=1}^{K} \mathrm{PTL}_i^{\otimes}$. It is easy to show that $\mathrm{PTL}^{\otimes} = \{\psi \mid \exists\, \psi' \in \mathrm{PTL}_0^{\otimes} \text{ such that } \models \psi \equiv \psi'\}$. Next fix an enumeration of PTL and define the map witness : $\mathrm{PTL}^{\otimes} \longrightarrow \mathrm{PTL}_0^{\otimes}$ via: $\mathrm{witness}(\psi) = \psi'$ iff ψ' is the member of $\mathrm{PTL}_0^{\otimes}$ with the least index (in the enumeration we have fixed for PTL) such that $\models \psi \equiv \psi'$.

Now define the map $f_0 : \mathrm{PTL}_0^{\otimes} \longrightarrow \Phi^{\otimes}$ via:

- If $\psi \in \mathrm{PTL}_i^{\otimes}$ then $f_0(\psi) = f_i(\psi)$

- If $\psi, \psi' \in \mathrm{PTL}_0^{\otimes}$ and $f_0(\psi)$ and $f_0(\psi')$ are defined then $f_0(\sim \psi) = \sim f_0(\psi)$ and $f_0(\psi \vee \psi') = f_0(\psi) \vee f_0(\psi')$.

Using the fact that $\mathrm{PTL}_0^{\otimes}$ can be expressed in a canonical form (say in the disjunctive normal form) one can show that f_0 is well defined. We now extend f_0 to the desired $f : \mathrm{PTL}^{\otimes} \longrightarrow \Phi^{\otimes}$ via:

- If $\psi \in \mathrm{PTL}_0^{\otimes}$ then $f(\psi) = f_0(\psi)$.
- If $\psi \in \mathrm{PTL}^{\otimes} - \mathrm{PTL}_0^{\otimes}$ then $f(\psi) = f(\psi')$ where $\mathrm{witness}(\psi) = \psi'$.

It is easy to check that f is well defined and for every ψ in $\mathrm{PTL}^{\otimes}$, $f(\psi)$ is in $\Phi^{\otimes}$.

Lemma 6.4.

(i) *Suppose* $\psi \in \mathrm{PTL}_0^{\otimes}$ *and* $\sigma \in \Sigma^{\infty}$. *Then* $\sigma \models \psi$ *iff* $wt(\sigma) \models f_0(\psi)$.
(ii) *Suppose* $\psi \in \mathrm{PTL}^{\otimes}$ *and* $\sigma \in \Sigma^{\infty}$. *Then* $\sigma \models \psi$ *iff* $wt(\sigma) \models f(\psi)$.
(iii) *Suppose* $L \subseteq \Sigma^{\infty}$ *is* $\mathrm{PTL}^{\otimes}$*-definable. Then* L *is* $\mathrm{TrPTL}^{\otimes}$*-definable.*

Proof Sketch. To prove (i) first consider $\psi \in \mathrm{PTL}_i^{\otimes}$. Then $f_0(\psi) = f_i(\psi)$. The crucial observation is that ψ being i-consistent. $\sigma \models \psi$ iff $\sigma|i \models \psi$. This is so because $(\sigma|i)|i = \sigma|i$. But by the previous lemma $\sigma|i \models \psi$ iff $wt(\sigma) \models f_i(\psi)$. Thus $\sigma \models \psi$ iff $wt(\sigma) \models f_0(\psi)$. This is now sufficient to easily settle part (i) of the result. The other two parts follow easily. □

We now wish to construct the map $g : \Phi^{\otimes} \longrightarrow \mathrm{PTL}^{\otimes}$ with the desired properties. g will be put together with the help of the maps $g_i : \Phi_i^{\otimes} \longrightarrow \mathrm{PTL}$. In what follows we let $\overline{\Sigma_i}$ denote the set $\Sigma - \Sigma_i$. For each i, the map $g_i : \Phi_i^{\otimes} \longrightarrow \mathrm{PTL}$ is given by:

- $g_i(\top) = \top$; $g_i(\sim \alpha) = \sim g_i(\alpha)$ and $g_i(\alpha \vee \beta) = g_i(\alpha) \vee g_i(\beta)$.
- $g_i(\langle a \rangle_i \alpha) = \psi_i \,\mathcal{U}\, \langle a \rangle g_i(\alpha)$ where $\psi_i = \bigvee_{b \in \overline{\Sigma}_i} \langle b \rangle \top$.
- $g_i(\alpha \,\mathcal{U}_i\, \beta) = g_i(\alpha) \,\mathcal{U}\, g_i(\beta)$.

The full map $g : \Phi^{\otimes} \longrightarrow \mathrm{PTL}$ is then given by:

- If $\alpha \in \Phi_i^{\otimes}$ then $g(\alpha) = g_i(\alpha)$.
- $g(\sim \alpha) = \sim g(\alpha)$ and $g(\alpha \vee \beta) = g(\alpha) \vee g(\beta)$.

Lemma 6.5.

(i) *Let* $\alpha \in \Phi_i^{\otimes}$. *Suppose* $\sigma \in \Sigma^{\infty}$ *and* $\tau \in \mathrm{Prf}(\sigma)$. *Then* $\sigma, \tau \models g_i(\alpha)$ *iff* $\sigma|i,\ \tau|i \models g_i(\alpha)$.
(ii) *Let* $\alpha \in \Phi_i^{\otimes}$. *Then* $g_i(\alpha)$ *is* i*-consistent.*
(iii) *Let* $\alpha \in \Phi^{\otimes}$. *Then* $g(\alpha) \in \mathrm{PTL}^{\otimes}$. □

The proof of part (i) proceeds by structural induction on α. The remaining parts of the lemma are then easy to establish.

Lemma 6.6.

(i) *Suppose* $\alpha \in \Phi_i^{\otimes}$, $\sigma \in \Sigma^{\infty}$ *and* $\tau \in \mathrm{Prf}(\sigma)$. *Let* $wt(\sigma) = F$ *and* $ev(\tau) = \{\tau' \mid \tau' \preceq \tau \text{ and } \tau' \neq \varepsilon\}$. *Then* $\sigma, \tau \models g_i(\alpha)$ *iff* $F, ev(\tau) \models \alpha$.

(ii) *Suppose* $\alpha \in \Phi^{\otimes}$ *and* $\sigma \in \Sigma^{\infty}$. *Then* $\sigma \models g(\alpha)$ *iff* $wt(\sigma) \models \alpha$.

(iii) *Suppose* $L \subseteq \Sigma^{\infty}$ *is* $\mathrm{TrPTL}^{\otimes}$*-definable. Then* L *is* $\mathrm{PTL}^{\otimes}$*-definable.* □

As usual, part (ii) and (iii) follows easily from part (i). To prove part (i) one proceeds again by structural induction on α. Detailed examinations of the definitions as well an appeal to some of the previous lemmas is required but there are no serious difficulties. This establishes Theorem 6.1.

Corollary 6.7. *Let* ψ *be a* PTL *formula. Then* $\psi \in \mathrm{PTL}^{\otimes}$ *iff there exists* $\alpha \in \Phi^{\otimes}$ *such that* $\psi \equiv g(\alpha)$ *is a valid formula of* PTL. □

The corollary says that $g(\Phi^{\otimes}) \subseteq \mathrm{PTL}^{\otimes}$ is as expressive as $\mathrm{PTL}^{\otimes}$. Since $\Phi^{\otimes}$ and g have a simple syntactic presentation, we now have a syntactic characterization (upto semantic equivalence) of $\mathrm{PTL}^{\otimes}$. Moreover, we can use $g(\Phi^{\otimes})$ instead of $\mathrm{PTL}^{\otimes}$ in specifications without any loss of expressive power.

At present we have not investigated which properties can and can not be expressed in $\mathrm{PTL}^{\otimes}$. We note however deadlock and liveness of actions *can* be expressed within $\mathrm{PTL}^{\otimes}$. Various fairness properties can also be expressed in $\mathrm{PTL}^{\otimes}$. In this context, we wish to stress again that, depending on the structure of $\tilde{\Sigma}$, formulas in $\mathrm{PTL}^{\otimes}$ can express global properties by forcing the agents to interact with each other in sophisticated ways.

The question of determining whether a PTL formula is trace consistent appears to be decidable due to a result in [DGP]. However, the question of deciding if a PTL formula is a member of $\mathrm{PTL}^{\otimes}$ is open.

Acknowledgements. I thank Peter Niebert for pointing out the role of multiple initial states in product automata. Discussions with Ilaria Castellani on product behaviours have been very helpful.

References

[APP] R. Alur, D. Peled and W. Penczek: Model Checking of Causality Properties. To Appear in the *Proceedings of the 10th IEEE Symposium on Logic in Computer Science* (1995).

[DGP] V. Diekert, P. Gastin and A. Petit: Rational and Recognizable Complex Trace Languages. *Report LITP 92.39*, Institut Blaise Pascal, University of Paris, Paris, France (1992).

[GW] P. Godefroid and P. Wolper: Using Partial Orders for the Efficient Verification of Deadlock Freedom and Safety Properties. *LNCS 575*, Springer-Verlag Berlin-Amsterdam-New York (1991) 332-343.

[KP] S. Katz and D. Peled: Interleaving Set Temporal Logic. *Theoretical Computer Science*, 73 (3), 21-43, 1992.

[M] A. Mazurkiewicz: Concurrent Program Schemes and their Interpretations. *Technical Report DAIMI PB-78*, Computer Science Department, Aarhus University, Denmark (1977).

[MP] Z. Manna and A. Pnueli: *The Temporal Logic of Reactive and Concurrent Systems (Specification)* Springer-verlag, Berlin (1991).

[MR] S. Mahalik and R. Ramanujam: An Axiomatization of Product PTL. *Manuscript*, The Institute of Mathematical Sciences, Madras (1995).

[N] P. Niebert: A μ-Calculus with Local Views for Systems of Sequential Agents. To Appear in *Proc. MFCS'95*.

[NP] P. Niebert and W. Penczek: On the Connection of Partial Order logics and Partial Order Reduction Methods. *Manuscript*, 1995.

[P] D. Peled: All from One, One for All: On Model Checking Using Representatives. Proceedings of CAV'93, *LNCS 697*, 1993.

[P1] D. Peled: On Projective and Seperable Properties. *Proc. CAAP'94, LNCS 787* (1994).

[T] P.S. Thiagarajan: A Trace based Extension of Linear Time Temporal Logic. *Proceedings of 9th IEEE Symposium on Logic in Computer Science*, (1994) pp. 438-447.

[T1] P.S. Thiagarajan: PTL over Product State Spaces. *Report TCS-95-4*, School of Mathematics, SPIC Science Foundation, Madras (1995).

[V] A. Valamari: Stubborn Sets for Reduced State Space Generation. *LNCS 483* (1990) 491-515.

[V1] A. Valamari: A Stubborn Attack on State Explosion. *Formal Methods in System Design*, 1, 285-313, 1992.

[VW] M.Y. Vardi and P. Wolper: An Automata Theoretic Approach to Automatic Program Verification. *Proceedings of 1st IEEE Symposium on Logic in Computer Science*, (1986) 332-345.

[WN] G. Winskel and M. Nielsen: Models for Concurrency. *Report DAIMI-PB-429*, Computer Science Department, Aarhus University, Aarhus, Denmark (1992). Also to Appear in: Handbook of Logic in Computer Science, Eds: S. Abramsky, D.M. Gabbay and T.S.E. Maibaum.

Tutorial:
Proving Properties of Concurrent Systems with SPIN

Gerard J. Holzmann
AT&T Bell Laboratories
Murray Hill, New Jersey 07974, USA
gerard@research.att.com

Extended Abstract

SPIN is an on-the-fly model checking system for finite state systems, that is optimized for the verification of linear time temporal logic (LTL) properties.[1] SPIN's input language, PROMELA, can be used to specify concurrent systems with dynamically changing numbers of interacting processes, where process interactions can be either synchronous (rendez-vous) or asynchronous (buffered).

In the tutorial we will examine some of the algorithms that determine SPIN's functionality and performance. After a brief summary of the automata theoretic foundation of SPIN, we consider the methodology for LTL model checking, the recognition of B chi acceptance conditions, cycle detection, and the handling of very large verification problems.

Automata Theoretic Framework

The semantics of PROMELA is defined in terms of a standard labeled transition system. The language is founded on the notion of *executability*. A first rule determines for each type of statement whether it is executable or blocked in a given system state. A second rule determines how the given statement modifies a given system state if and when it is executed. As one small example: a plain condition such as `(a > b)` is a self-contained type of primitive statement in PROMELA: it is executable when the condition holds, and it has no effect on the system state when executed (other than the changing of the control-state of the process executing the statement). To avoid the obvious, all PROMELA expressions are required to be *pure* (side-effect free).

The behavior of a concurrent system, that is a dynamically changing ensemble of disjoint or interacting processes, is defined with in terms of interleaving semantics. Processes can interact by manipulating shared data objects: variables, data structures, or message queues. Message passing through shared queues is either synchronous (i.e., executed in an atomically linked combination of a matching send and receive operation on a given rendezvous port), or asynchronous, through finite and typed message buffers.

SPIN can compute the interleaving product of a set of concurrent processes in several different ways. The default algorithm is a straight exhaustive reachability analysis [H91]. For problem sizes that preclude exhaustive verification because of their size, a high-coverage approximation of an exhaustive run can be performed in minimal amounts of memory [H88],[H95]. The user has also the option of applying a partial order reduction algorithm to the search (either exhaustive or bitstate) that provably preserves all safety and liveness properties [HP94]. Finally, a weak fairness constraint can be imposed on the search, based on a direct application of Choueka's flag construction method [C74],[CVWY92].

---

1. All source is available via anonymous `ftp` from the machine `netlib.att.com`, directory `/netlib/spin`.

LTL Properties and B chi Automata

In the currently distributed version of SPIN it is the user's responsibility to convert an LTL formula into a B chi automaton (in PROMELA: a `never claim`) for the purposes of verification. Two recent improvements have made it possible to allow the user to specify an LTL formula directly, and leave the translation into a B chi automaton to the software [BCG95],[GPVW95]. We have implemented the algorithm from [GPVW95], and plan to integrate it into the SPIN system in an upcoming release.

The B chi acceptance conditions require the verifier to reliably detect the presence or absence of acceptance cycles in the reachability graph. Since SPIN performs all verifications on-the-fly, in a minimum amount of memory, the cycle detection method must conform to those constraints.

Memory-Efficient Cycle Detection

SPIN uses a nested depth-first search algorithm to detect both acceptance- and non-progress cycles on-the-fly [H91],[CVWY92]. The algorithm is implemented with just two bits of overhead per reachable state, using the encoding method detailed in [GH93]. The use of Tarjan's classic algorithm [T72] would require 64 bits of overhead per state (for storing two 32 bit numbers: the *dfs*-number and *lowlink*-number).

By using a nested depth-first search algorithm for cycle detection, we give up the ability to detect all possible variations of a cycle, but preserve the ability to detect and reproduce at least one cycle of the type searched for, provided that at least one such cycle exists. Because both non-progress and acceptance cycles in SPIN always constitute a counter-example to a correctness requirement, establishing only the absence or presence of such cycles suffices for the purposes of verification. After all, it takes no more than a single counter-example to disprove any correctness property.

Bitstate Hashing

SPIN also incorporates a competitive implementation of the frugal bitstate hashing or *supertrace* technique [H88],[H95]. We will give an analytical argument for its expected performance and compare those estimates with empirical tests. With this algorithm, again just two bits of memory are needed to store any given reachable state. The two bit addresses are computed with two statistically independent hash functions.

Industrial Applications

The bitstate hashing technique has made it possible to apply formal verification to problem sizes that would ordinarily have remained well beyond the scope of automated verification tools. We will summarize one of the recent experiences with formal verification based on this technique in a two-year case study performed in cooperation with AT&T International Switching [C91],[H94].

In this study, named the `NewCoRe` project, a routine implementation of an ISDN protocol was pursued by a team of five people, with a methodology based on formal verification. A total of 10,000 mechanical verification runs were performed, 145 LTL properties were formalized and proven to be satisfied for the final design, and a total of 112 design errors were detected. Many of the design errors could be traced back to the original design requirements.

Design for Verifiability

The number of both academic and industrial applications of SPIN is steadily growing. At the start of 1995, we estimated there to be well over 1,000 installations of the tool. Though this is encouraging, a sobering thought is that the number of systems that is designed without any benefit from formal verification tools, of this type or any other, still completely dominates the industry. How long will it take for the wider availability of verification tools to have a more measurable impact?

When Charles Babbage proposed the use of his analytical engine in 1825 to improve the accuracy of printing astronomical and logarithmic tables, he noted:

> "The great importance of having accurate tables is admitted by all who understand their uses; but the multitude of errors really occurring is comparatively little known. . . ."
> ". . . [it] is really extraordinary that, when it was demonstrated that all tables are capable of being computed by machinery [. . .] the Astronomer Royal did not become the most enthusiastic supporter of an instrument which could render such invaluable service to his own science."

Which only goes to say: in the long run, things do tend to change...

References

[C91] J. Chaves, 'Formal methods at AT&T, an industrial usage report,' *Proc. 4th FORTE Conference*, Sydney, Australia, 1991, pp. 83–90.

[C74] Y. Choueka, 'Theories of automata on ω-tapes: a simplified approach,' *Journal of Computer and System Science*, Vol. 8, 1974, pp. 117–141.

[BCG95] G. Bhat, R. Cleaveland, and O. Grumberg, 'Efficient on-the-fly model checking for CTL*,' *Proc. 10th Symp. on Logic in Computer Science*, San Diego, CA, 1995.

[CVWY92] C. Courcoubetis, M. Vardi, P. Wolper, M. Yannakakis, 'Memory efficient algorithms for the verification of temporal properties,' *Formal Methods in Systems Design*, Vol I, 1992, pp. 275–288.

[GPVW95] R. Gerth, D. Peled, M. Y. Vardi, P. Wolper, 'Simple on-the-fly automatic verification of linear temporal logic,' *Proc. IFIP/WG6.1 Symp. on Protocol Specification, Testing, and Verification*, PSTV95, Warsaw, Poland, June 1995.

[H88] G. J. Holzmann, 'An improved protocol reachability analysis technique,' *Software, Practice and Experience*, 18(2):137-161, 1988.

[GH93] P. Godefroid and G. J. Holzmann, 'On the verification of temporal properties,' *Proc. IFIP/WG6.1 Symp. on Protocol Specification, Testing, and Verification*, PSTV93, Liege, Belgium, June 1993.

[H91] G. J. Holzmann, *Design and validation of computer protocols*. Prentice Hall, Englewood Cliffs, NJ, 1991.

[H94] G. J. Holzmann, 'The theory and practice of a formal method: NewCoRe,' *Proc. 13th IFIP World Computer Congress*, Hamburg, Germany, 1994, pp. 35–44.

[HP94] G. J. Holzmann and D. Peled, 'An improvement in formal verification,' *Proc. 7th FORTE Conference*, Bern, Switzerland, 1994.

[H95] G. J. Holzmann, 'An analysis of bitstate hashing,' *Proc. IFIP/WG6.1 Symp. on Protocol Specification, Testing, and Verification*, PSTV95, Warsaw, Poland, June 1995.

[T72] R. E. Tarjan, 'Depth first search and linear graph algorithms,' *SIAM J. Computing*, 1:2, pp. 146-160, 1972.

On Sharing and Determinacy in Concurrent Systems

Anna Philippou and David Walker

Department of Computer Science, University of Warwick
Coventry CV4 7AL, U.K.

Abstract. The relationship between sharing and determinacy in concurrent systems is studied. Syntactic conditions on programs of a concurrent object language are isolated and it is established, on the basis of two different semantic definitions of the language, that they guarantee determinacy, indeed confluence. The first semantic definition is an operational semantics in which a program is interpreted as a labelled transition system whose points represent configurations of systems of objects. The second definition is by translation to a general process-calculus model of systems with dynamically-evolving structure.

1 Introduction

Many concurrent systems are inherently indeterminate. Consequently, general models of concurrent systems, and in particular semantic accounts of concurrent programming languages, are more complex than those for sequential systems and languages. But it is often the case that an intention in constructing a concurrent system or program is to create an entity whose behaviour is determinate. In a very large number of cases indeterminacy arises from *sharing* where we understand this term in a broad sense as including the sharing by two computational entities of the ability to interact, perhaps in quite different ways, with a third entity. It is thus of interest to study the relationship between sharing and determinacy in concurrent systems. Among the benefits of this study may be deeper understanding of concurrent systems in general, simpler semantic accounts of determinate fragments of concurrent languages, and improved techniques for constructing reliable concurrent programs.

In this paper we focus on a particular concurrent object language and seek syntactic conditions on its programs which guarantee determinacy. The language is a variant of the language $\pi o\beta\lambda$ of [5] which in turn is derived from the POOL family [1]. Although we work with this specific language, results similar to those to be presented can be obtained for other languages. It is necessary to give a precise semantic account of the language and to explicate an appropriate notion of determinacy on the basis of it. We do this in two ways. Firstly, we give an operational semantics [16] in which a program is interpreted as a labelled transition system whose points represent configurations of systems of objects and whose labels classify transitions between configurations as being internal computation steps or interactions with the environment. Second, we give a semantics by translation to a general calculus of systems with dynamically-evolving structure, the π_v-calculus [15, 7] which is an amalgamation of the π-calculus [10, 9] and value-passing CCS [8]. In the case of the first semantic definition, theory developed in the setting of CCS [8, 13] provides an appropriate account of determinacy. For the translational semantics it is necessary to extend this theory to accommodate name passing, a task treated in detail in [12]. In this paper we simply record relevant definitions.

We seek syntactic conditions on programs which ensure that references to objects may not be shared. To achieve this without impoverishing the language too severely we augment it with a statement form which expresses a destructive read of a variable. This gives a means of expressing cleanly that when one object sends to a second object a reference to a third object, the first object relinquishes the reference to the third. It would be very awkward to express this effect without the additional statement form. A similar destructive read is considered, from a different stance, in the somewhat difficult paper [4] which is concerned with aliasing in sequential object-oriented languages. We believe that many programs can naturally be expressed under this restrictive regime and that further study of its efficacy is worthwhile.

2 Preliminaries

We begin by recalling some ideas and notation which we will use. A *labelled transition system* $(S, \{\xrightarrow{\ell} \mid \ell \in L\})$ consists of a set S of configurations and a family of relations on S indexed by labels in some set L. A configuration $Q \in S$ is a *derivative* of a configuration P if there are $n \geq 0$ and $\ell_1, \ldots, \ell_n$ such that $P \xrightarrow{\ell_1} \cdots \xrightarrow{\ell_n} Q$. *Bisimilarity* is the largest symmetric relation $\sim$ on S such that if $P \sim Q$, $\ell \in L$ and $P \xrightarrow{\ell} P'$ then there is Q' such that $Q \xrightarrow{\ell} Q'$ and $P' \sim Q'$. A configuration P is *determinate* if whenever Q is a derivative of P, $\ell \in L$, $Q \xrightarrow{\ell} Q'$ and $Q \xrightarrow{\ell} Q''$, then $Q' \sim Q''$. Thus P is determinate if up to $\sim$ it has at most one evolution under any sequence of labels. A configuration P is *confluent* if it is determinate and for any derivative Q of P and distinct labels ℓ, ℓ', if $Q \xrightarrow{\ell} Q_1$ and $Q \xrightarrow{\ell'} Q_2$ then there exist Q_1', Q_2' such that $Q_1 \xrightarrow{\ell'} Q_1'$, $Q_2 \xrightarrow{\ell} Q_2'$ and $Q_1' \sim Q_2'$. Thus confluence is a strong version of determinacy. The work [8] contains a development of the theory of confluence in the process calculus pure CCS and a demonstration of its importance in the context of concurrent and communicating systems.

Consider now a labelled transition system on whose set of labels a partition Π is given. Milner [13] introduced the following notion (which we define here in a slightly different way). A configuration P is *Π-confluent* if it is determinate and for any derivative Q of P and labels ℓ, ℓ' which lie in different blocks of Π, if $Q \xrightarrow{\ell} Q_1$ and $Q \xrightarrow{\ell'} Q_2$ then there exist Q_1', Q_2' such that $Q_1 \xrightarrow{\ell'} Q_1'$, $Q_2 \xrightarrow{\ell} Q_2'$ and $Q_1' \sim Q_2'$. This definition of confluence is appropriate for systems in which the passing of values via ports, such as in value-passing CCS, is central.

We will employ it in a case when the label set L is $\{\text{in}(v) \mid v \in V\} \cup \{\text{out}(v) \mid v \in V\} \cup \{\varepsilon\}$ with in(v), resp. out(v), representing an input, resp. output, of a value $v \in V$, and ε an internal transition. In this case L will be partitioned into singletons except that all in(v) labels are collected in one block. Thus Π will be $\{\{\text{in}(v) \mid v \in V\}\} \cup \{\{\text{out}(v)\} \mid v \in V\} \cup \{\{\varepsilon\}\}$. So it is not required of a Π-confluent configuration that the occurrence of one input transition may not preclude that of another. Note, however, that determinacy with respect to in(v)-transitions is required.

3 The programming language

The programming language is a variant of the $\pi o\beta\lambda$-language [5] which in turn is derived from the POOL family [1]. The language has types NAT (natural numbers), BOOL (Booleans), UNIT (à la Standard ML) and ref(A) for A a class name. A value of type ref(A) is a reference to an object of class A; class definitions are explained below. The language has constant symbols true, false, 0, 1,... and nil, the last of which is overloaded and is used to represent a reference to no object, the 'undefined' value of type NAT and the value of type UNIT. In the abstract syntax definitions below we use K to range over constants, M over method names, A over class names, T over types, X, Y over variables, and S over statements, and we write $\widetilde{Z}$ for a tuple $Z_1, \ldots, Z_n$ of syntactic entities. Statements are the well-typed phrases given as follows:

$$\begin{array}{rcl} S & ::= & K \mid X \mid X^{\dagger} \mid \mathsf{new}(A) \mid \mathsf{op}(\widetilde{S}) \\ & \mid & X := S \mid S_1; S_2 \mid \mathsf{if}\ S\ \mathsf{then}\ S_1\ \mathsf{else}\ S_2 \\ & \mid & S!M(\widetilde{S}) \mid \mathsf{return}\ S \mid \mathsf{commit}\ S!M(\widetilde{S}) \\ & \mid & \mathsf{output}(S) \mid \mathsf{input}\,. \end{array}$$

An informal account of the meanings of statements follows. The computation of X involves reading the value of variable X from the (local) store. That of $X^{\dagger}$ is similar except that the variable X is set to nil when the value is read. Computation of new(A) results in the creation of a new object of class A; the value of the expression is a reference to that object. op ranges over simple arithmetic and Boolean operations. The assignment, sequence and conditional statements are standard. The computation of $S!M(\widetilde{S})$ involves the evaluation of S and the statements in the tuple $\widetilde{S}$ followed by the invocation of method M with parameters the values of $\widetilde{S}$ in the object to which the value of S is a reference. The value of the statement $S!M(\widetilde{S})$ is the simple value or reference returned to the object as the result of the method invocation. The return statement, by which a result is returned, and the commit statement, by which responsibility for returning a result may be delegated, are explained below via an example class definition. Computation of output(S), in which S is of type NAT, involves computation of S and the output of its value to the environment. Computation of input consumes an integer from the environment, that being the value of the statement.

Declarations are given as follows. Firstly, variable declarations are given by

$$Vdec \ ::= \ \mathsf{var}\ X_1 : T_1, \ldots, X_p : T_p \,.$$

Then method declarations are given by

$$Mdec \ ::= \ \mathsf{method}\, M(\widetilde{Y} : \widetilde{T}) : T,\ Vdec,\ S$$

where $\widetilde{Y}$ of types $\widetilde{T}$ are the formal parameters, T is the result type, and S is the body of the method with *Vdec* declaring variables local to it. Sequences of method declarations are given by

$$Mdecs \ ::= \ Mdec_1, \ldots, Mdec_m$$

and class declarations by

$$Cdec \ ::= \ \mathsf{class}\ A,\ Vdec,\ Mdecs \ .$$

Interaction with the environment is the function of objects of the following, distinguished class whose definition is assumed, without explicit mention, to be present in every program declaration:

```
class IO
method In():NAT
    return input
method Out(X:NAT):UNIT
    return nil ; output(X)
```

Finally, program declarations are given by

$$Pdec \ ::= \ Cdec_1, \ldots, Cdec_r,\ \mathsf{trigger}\ S_0$$

where S_0 is of the form $\mathsf{new}(A)!M(\widetilde{K})$. The statement S_0 acts as a trigger to initiate the computation by creating and activating a *root object* of one of the classes A. Each parameter of the method invocation is a constant except that one may be the statement new(IO). We restrict attention to programs in which new(IO) does not occur except in the trigger so that at most one object of class IO exists at any point during computation. We assume also that input and output occur only in the definition of the class IO. Thus, as we will see from the semantic definition of the language, if new(IO) is not one of the parameters in the trigger, a program will be incapable of interacting with the environment.

There follows an example class definition. Its instances may be used to construct binary tree-structured symbol tables.

```
class T
var K:NAT, V:ref(A), L:ref(T), R:ref(T)
method Insert(X:NAT, W:ref(A)):UNIT
    return nil ;
    if K=nil then (K:=X ; V:=W† ; L:=new(T) ; R:=new(T))
    else if X=K then V:=W†
         else if X<K then L!Insert(X,W†)
              else R!Insert(X,W†)
```

```
method Search(X:NAT):ref(A)
    if K=nil then return nil
    else if X=K then return V
         else if X<K then commit L!Search(X)
              else commit R!Search(X)
```

An object of this class represents a node which stores in its variables `K`, `V`, `L`, `R` an integer key, a value (a reference to an object of some class `A`), and references to two instances of the class (its left and right children in the tree structure of which it is a component). It has two actions: the method `Insert` which allows a key-value pair to be inserted, and the method `Search` which returns the value associated with its key parameter (or `nil` if there is none). When an object is created all its variables have `nil` values and it assumes a quiescent state in which any of its methods may be invoked. When one object invokes a method in a second object, the activity of the first object is suspended until it is released from the rendezvous by computation of a `return` statement by the second object or by some other object to which the responsibility for returning a result has been delegated: see the explanation of commit below. On completing the computation of a method body an object returns to its quiescent state; another method may then be invoked. Thus only one method may be active in an object at any point during computation. When an object α executes a `commit` statement by invoking a method in an object β, it is implicit (i) that β should return its result not to α but to the object γ to which α should return a result, and (ii) that α is freed from the task of returning a result to γ. In particular, activity of α may proceed in parallel with that of β. Thus if the `Search` method is invoked in a node with a key smaller (resp. larger) than that stored there, the node will commit that search to its left (resp. right) child, and we may think of the node as passing to the child the return address to which the result of the search should be sent. This address will have been received by the node either directly from the initiator of the search, if the node is the root, or from its parent in the tree.

4 The operational semantics

In the operational semantics a program is interpreted as a labelled transition system whose points represent global configurations of systems of objects. The transition relations on configurations are defined from a family of labelled transition relations which describe the possible actions of their component objects. The semantics is a slight variation of a semantics given in [16] which took as its starting point an operational semantics for POOL in [2]. The following kinds of entity are used in it. We assume an infinite set of *object names* ranged over by α, β, γ. We refer to the object names together with the symbols nil, **true**, **false**, 0, 1, ... as *values* and use v to range over values. A *family of method definitions* is a finite partial function μ from method names to pairs $\langle \widetilde{Y} \cup \widetilde{Z}, S\rangle$, with $\widetilde{Y}$ the formal parameters, $\widetilde{Z}$ the local variables and S the body of the associated method. A *class definition* is a pair $\langle \widetilde{X}, \mu\rangle$, with $\widetilde{X}$ the instance variables and

μ the family of method definitions of the associated class. An *environment* is a pair $\Phi = \langle \Phi_1, \Phi_2 \rangle$ with Φ_1 a finite partial function from class names to class definitions, and Φ_2 a finite partial function from object names to class names. A *store* is a finite partial map σ from variables to values. A *state* is a finite set Γ of triples of the form $\langle \alpha, S, \sigma \rangle$. Finally, a *configuration* is a pair $\langle \Phi, \Gamma \rangle$ consisting of an environment and a state.

A configuration $\Omega = \langle \Phi, \Gamma \rangle$ provides a description of a point in a computation of a program as follows. Φ_1 records the definitions of the classes of the program and is unchanged throughout the computation. Φ_2 records the name and class of each existing object; it is augmented each time an object is created. Γ records the local store and unexecuted statement of each existing object.

To give the semantics we augment the class of statements as follows:

$$S \ ::= \ \ldots \ | \ v \ | \ \mathsf{wait} \ | \ \mathsf{return}_\beta \ S \ | \ \mathsf{commit}_\beta \ S!M(\widetilde{S}) \ | \ \mathsf{quiescent}\,.$$

We write $S \Rightarrow \beta$ for S with each substatement $\mathsf{return}\ S$ replaced by $\mathsf{return}_\beta\ S$ and each substatement $\mathsf{commit}\ S!M(\widetilde{S})$ replaced by $\mathsf{commit}_\beta\ S!M(\widetilde{S})$. The roles of these additional forms are explained below.

Let Ω be the set of all configurations. The labels λ of the transition relations $\{\xrightarrow{\lambda}\}_\lambda$ on Ω are the empty label and in(v) and out(v) where v is an integer, the latter two representing interaction with the environment. They are defined from a family of local transition relations

$$\langle \alpha, \mu \rangle \vdash \langle S, \sigma \rangle \overset{\ell}{\longmapsto} \langle S', \sigma' \rangle$$

where the label ℓ is either empty or of the form new(A, β), call($\beta, M, \widetilde{v}, \gamma$), respond($M, \widetilde{v}, \gamma$), result($v$), return($\beta, v$), out($v$) or in($v$). If the label is empty or of the form new(A, β), in(v) or out(v) the transition represents an autonomous action of α. In the other four cases the label carries information pertinent to the way α may interact with other objects. The local relations are defined by the following axioms and rules.

(VAR) $\quad \langle \alpha, \mu \rangle \vdash \langle X, \sigma \rangle \longmapsto \langle \sigma(X), \sigma \rangle$

(DAG) $\quad \langle \alpha, \mu \rangle \vdash \langle X^\dagger, \sigma \rangle \longmapsto \langle \sigma(X), \sigma[X := \mathsf{nil}] \rangle$

(NEW) $\quad \langle \alpha, \mu \rangle \vdash \langle \mathsf{new}(A), \sigma \rangle \overset{\mathbf{new}(A,\beta)}{\longmapsto} \langle \beta, \sigma \rangle$

(OP) $\quad \langle \alpha, \mu \rangle \vdash \langle \mathsf{op}(\widetilde{v}), \sigma \rangle \longmapsto \langle v, \sigma \rangle \quad$ if $v = \widehat{\mathsf{op}}(\widetilde{v})$

(CALL) $\quad \langle \alpha, \mu \rangle \vdash \langle \beta!M(\widetilde{v}), \sigma \rangle \overset{\mathbf{call}(\beta,M,\widetilde{v},\alpha)}{\longmapsto} \langle \mathsf{wait}, \sigma \rangle \quad$ if $\beta \neq \mathsf{nil}$

(WAIT) $\quad \langle \alpha, \mu \rangle \vdash \langle \mathsf{wait}, \sigma \rangle \overset{\mathbf{result}(v)}{\longmapsto} \langle v, \sigma \rangle$

$$\text{(ASSIGN)} \quad \langle \alpha, \mu \rangle \vdash \langle X := v, \sigma \rangle \longmapsto \langle \mathsf{nil}, \sigma[X := v] \rangle$$

$$\text{(SEQ)} \quad \langle \alpha, \mu \rangle \vdash \langle \mathsf{nil}; S, \sigma \rangle \longmapsto \langle S, \sigma \rangle$$

$$\text{(COND1)} \quad \langle \alpha, \mu \rangle \vdash \langle \textsf{if true then } S_1 \textsf{ else } S_2, \sigma \rangle \longmapsto \langle S_1, \sigma \rangle$$

$$\text{(COND2)} \quad \langle \alpha, \mu \rangle \vdash \langle \textsf{if false then } S_1 \textsf{ else } S_2, \sigma \rangle \longmapsto \langle S_2, \sigma \rangle$$

$$\text{(RETURN)} \quad \langle \alpha, \mu \rangle \vdash \langle \mathsf{return}_\beta \; v, \sigma \rangle \overset{\mathbf{return}(\beta, v)}{\longmapsto} \langle \mathsf{nil}, \sigma \rangle$$

$$\text{(COMMIT)} \quad \langle \alpha, \mu \rangle \vdash \langle \mathsf{commit}_\gamma \; \beta ! M(\widetilde{v}), \sigma \rangle \overset{\mathbf{call}(\beta, M, \widetilde{v}, \gamma)}{\longmapsto} \langle \mathsf{nil}, \sigma \rangle \quad \text{if } \beta \neq \mathsf{nil}$$

$$\text{(QUIESCENT)} \quad \langle \alpha, \mu \rangle \vdash \langle \mathsf{quiescent}, \sigma \rangle \overset{\mathbf{respond}(M, \widetilde{v}, \gamma)}{\longmapsto} \langle (S \Rightarrow \gamma); \mathsf{quiescent}, \sigma' \rangle$$

$$\text{(OUTPUT)} \quad \langle \alpha, \mu \rangle \vdash \langle \mathsf{output}(v), \sigma \rangle \overset{\mathbf{out}(v)}{\longmapsto} \langle \mathsf{nil}, \sigma \rangle$$

$$\text{(INPUT)} \quad \langle \alpha, \mu \rangle \vdash \langle \mathsf{input}, \sigma \rangle \overset{\mathbf{in}(v)}{\longmapsto} \langle v, \sigma \rangle$$

where in (QUIESCENT) if $\mu(M) = \langle \widetilde{Y} \cup \widetilde{Z}, S \rangle$ then $\sigma' = \sigma\lceil \widetilde{X} \cup \{\widetilde{Y} := \widetilde{v}\} \cup \{\widetilde{Z} := \mathsf{nil}\}$ where $\Phi_1(\Phi_2(\alpha))_1 = \widetilde{X}$.

The axioms (VAR) and (DAG) capture respectively a non-destructive read and a destructive read of the variable X. A side condition on one of the global transition rules will ensure that an object created by (NEW) receives a fresh name. In (OP) $\widehat{\mathsf{op}}$ is the function denoted by the symbol op. Via (CALL), α may invoke method M with parameters $\widetilde{v}$ in β with the stipulation that the result be returned to α. In the global transition system a 'call' action will synchronize with a 'respond' action emanating from the (QUIESCENT) axiom. On invoking a method, α evolves to wait. The axiom (WAIT) represents the reactivation of α on receipt of the result of a method call. In the global transition system a result(v) action of α may synchronize with a return(α, v) action (which emanates from the axiom (RETURN)) of another object β to represent the return of the result v from β to α. The axioms for assignment, sequence and conditional statements are straightforward. The axiom (RETURN) describes how a result is returned from one object to another. (COMMIT) describes how α may delegate to β the task of returning to γ. Note the occurrence of γ in the label on the arrow. In (QUIESCENT) a request from any object to execute any appropriate method M with parameters $\widetilde{v}$ may be accepted, with $S \Rightarrow \gamma$ capturing that the appropriate body should be executed and the return made to γ or the responsibility for doing so committed to another object. The store is updated accordingly and on completion of the call the object assumes its quiescent state. The axioms (OUTPUT) and (INPUT) capture interaction with the environment.

The rules are most succinctly expressed as

$$\frac{\langle \alpha, \mu \rangle \vdash \langle S, \sigma \rangle \stackrel{\ell}{\longmapsto} \langle S', \sigma' \rangle}{\langle \alpha, \mu \rangle \vdash \langle C[S], \sigma \rangle \stackrel{\ell}{\longmapsto} \langle C[S'], \sigma' \rangle}$$

where $C[\cdot]$ is any of the following contexts (with hole '$\cdot$'): $\mathsf{op}(\widetilde{v}, \cdot, \widetilde{S})$, $X := \cdot$, $\cdot; S''$, $\mathsf{if}\ \cdot\ \mathsf{then}\ S_1\ \mathsf{else}\ S_2$, $\cdot!M(\widetilde{S})$, $\beta!M(\widetilde{v}, \cdot, \widetilde{S})$, $\mathsf{return}_\beta\ \cdot$, $\mathsf{commit}_\beta\ \cdot$, $\mathsf{output}(\cdot)$,

The global transition relations on Ω are defined by the following six rules. They describe how the configuration may change as a result of the independent activity of one object (LOCAL), the creation of a new object (NEW), the initiation of a method call (COM1), the return of a result of a method call (COM2), and communication with the environment (OUTPUT and INPUT).

(LOCAL) $$\frac{\langle \alpha, \mu \rangle \vdash \langle S, \sigma \rangle \longmapsto \langle S', \sigma' \rangle}{\langle \Phi, \Gamma \cup \{\langle \alpha, S, \sigma \rangle\} \rangle \longrightarrow \langle \Phi, \Gamma \cup \{\langle \alpha, S', \sigma' \rangle\} \rangle}$$

(NEW) $$\frac{\langle \alpha, \mu \rangle \vdash \langle S, \sigma \rangle \stackrel{\mathbf{new}(A,\beta)}{\longmapsto} \langle S', \sigma' \rangle}{\langle \Phi, \Gamma \cup \{\langle \alpha, S, \sigma \rangle\} \rangle \longrightarrow \langle \Phi', \Gamma \cup \{\langle \alpha, S', \sigma' \rangle, \langle \beta, \mathsf{quiescent}, \sigma'' \rangle\} \rangle}$$

provided $\beta \notin \mathrm{names}(\Gamma) \cup \{\alpha\}$, $\Phi' = \langle \Phi_1, \Phi_2[\beta := A] \rangle$, $\Phi_1(A)_1 = \widetilde{X}$, and $\sigma'' = \{\widetilde{X} := \mathsf{nil}\}$

(COM1)

$$\frac{\langle \alpha, \mu_\alpha \rangle \vdash \langle S_\alpha, \sigma_\alpha \rangle \stackrel{\mathbf{call}(\beta, M, \widetilde{v}, \gamma)}{\longmapsto} \langle S'_\alpha, \sigma'_\alpha \rangle \qquad \langle \beta, \mu_\beta \rangle \vdash \langle S_\beta, \sigma_\beta \rangle \stackrel{\mathbf{respond}(M, \widetilde{v}, \gamma)}{\longmapsto} \langle S'_\beta, \sigma'_\beta \rangle}{\langle \Phi, \Gamma \cup \{\langle \alpha, S_\alpha, \sigma_\alpha \rangle, \langle \beta, S_\beta, \sigma_\beta \rangle\} \rangle \longrightarrow \langle \Phi, \Gamma \cup \{\langle \alpha, S'_\alpha, \sigma'_\alpha \rangle, \langle \beta, S'_\beta, \sigma'_\beta \rangle\} \rangle}$$

(COM2)

$$\frac{\langle \alpha, \mu_\alpha \rangle \vdash \langle S_\alpha, \sigma_\alpha \rangle \stackrel{\mathbf{result}(v)}{\longmapsto} \langle S'_\alpha, \sigma'_\alpha \rangle \qquad \langle \beta, \mu_\beta \rangle \vdash \langle S_\beta, \sigma_\beta \rangle \stackrel{\mathbf{return}(\alpha, v)}{\longmapsto} \langle S'_\beta, \sigma'_\beta \rangle}{\langle \Phi, \Gamma \cup \{\langle \alpha, S_\alpha, \sigma_\alpha \rangle, \langle \beta, S_\beta, \sigma_\beta \rangle\} \rangle \longrightarrow \langle \Phi, \Gamma \cup \{\langle \alpha, S'_\alpha, \sigma'_\alpha \rangle, \langle \beta, S'_\beta, \sigma'_\beta \rangle\} \rangle}$$

(OUTPUT) $$\frac{\langle \alpha, \mu \rangle \vdash \langle S, \sigma \rangle \stackrel{\mathbf{out}(v)}{\longmapsto} \langle S', \sigma' \rangle}{\langle \Phi, \Gamma \cup \{\langle \alpha, S, \sigma \rangle\} \rangle \stackrel{\mathbf{out}(v)}{\longrightarrow} \langle \Phi, \Gamma \cup \{\langle \alpha, S', \sigma' \rangle\} \rangle}$$

(INPUT) $$\frac{\langle \alpha, \mu \rangle \vdash \langle S, \sigma \rangle \stackrel{\mathbf{in}(v)}{\longmapsto} \langle S', \sigma' \rangle}{\langle \Phi, \Gamma \cup \{\langle \alpha, S, \sigma \rangle\} \rangle \stackrel{\mathbf{in}(v)}{\longrightarrow} \langle \Phi, \Gamma \cup \{\langle \alpha, S', \sigma' \rangle\} \rangle}$$

The side condition on β in (NEW) ensures that a new object receives a fresh name; names(Γ) is the set of first components of Γ. The synchronization between sender and receiver in the rules (COM1) and (COM2) is achieved via the labels on the arrows in the premises. The initial configuration associated with a program declaration

$$Pdec \quad ::= \quad Cdec_1, \ldots, Cdec_r, \, \mathsf{trigger}\, S_0$$

is $\langle \Phi, \Gamma \rangle$ where Φ_1 is given by the definitions of the classes and $\Phi_2 = \{\langle \alpha_0, - \rangle\}$ where '$-$' indicates that the trigger is considered to have no type and $\Gamma = \{\langle \alpha_0, S_0, \emptyset \rangle\}$.

5 Determinacy

We wish to isolate syntactic conditions on programs which guarantee determinacy. The behaviour of an object, being sequential, is determinate. Nondeterminism may arise if two objects α and β share a reference to a third object γ. For consider a state in a computation at which both α and β wish to invoke methods in γ. The subsequent behaviour of γ, and hence of the system, will in general not be independent of which invocation proceeds. We may expect, however, that if in no state reachable from the initial configuration of a program do two objects share a reference, then the behaviour of the program is determinate. Having given the operational semantics we can state this claim precisely: if Ω_0 is the initial configuration of such a program then the transition system with root Ω_0 is determinate (in the precise sense defined in the Preliminaries). The purpose of this section is to substantiate this claim. In fact we will show that the transition system is confluent where here 'confluent' means Π-confluent for the partition Π of the labels described in the Preliminaries.

We first state and explain the syntactic conditions.

Definition 1. A *D-program* is a program each of whose method bodies S satisfies the following:

1. S does not contain $X := Y$ where $X, Y : \mathsf{ref}(A)$,
2. S does not contain $S_0!M(\widetilde{S}, X, \widetilde{S'})$ or $\mathsf{return}\ X$ where $X : \mathsf{ref}(A)$,
3. if S contains $X!M(S_1, \ldots, S_n)$ then there is no $j \in [1..n]$ such that S_j has a substatement $Y := X^\dagger$, $\mathsf{return}\ X^\dagger$ or $T_0!M(T_1, \ldots, T_m)$ where $T_k = X^\dagger$ for some $k \in [1..m]$, and
4. S is *responsible* (see below).

The first three conditions are concerned with the sharing of references. Condition 1 prevents a reference from being copied by an object. Note that an assignment of the form $X := Y^\dagger$ may appear in a D-program. Communication of a reference from one object to another can take place in two ways: as an argument of a method call or as a result of a method invocation. Condition 2 ensures that if an object sends a reference then it relinquishes it. Note that a D-program may contain statements similar to those prohibited by condition 2 but which differ in that $X^\dagger$ appears in the place of X. Moreover, in a statement of the form $X!M(S_1, \ldots, S_n)$, where a method is to be invoked in the object to which the value of X is a reference, computation of $S_1, \ldots, S_n$ should not result in the reference to X being moved within the store or communicated to another object: this is the purpose of condition 3. The purpose of condition 4 is to prevent competition for access to an object through irresponsible activity related to the return of a method call. That is, if a method is invoked in an object, it should either return a result to the caller or delegate the responsibility for doing so to another object: it should not attempt to return a result more than once, nor should it attempt to return a result and delegate the responsibility for doing so to another object, nor should it delegate the responsibility to two or more objects. This is made precise as follows.

Definition 2. 1. A statement is *return/commit free*, *rcf*, if it contains no return statement or commit statement.

2. The set of *responsible* statements is given by the following inductive definition.
   (a) return S is responsible if S is *rcf*;
   (b) commit $S!M(\widetilde{S})$ is responsible if $S!M(\widetilde{S})$ is *rcf*;
   (c) op$(S_1, \ldots, S_n)$ is responsible if exactly one of $S_1, \ldots, S_n$ is responsible and each of the others is *rcf*,
   (d) $X := S$ is responsible if S is responsible;
   (e) S_1; S_2 is responsible if exactly one of S_1, S_2 is responsible and the other is *rcf*;
   (f) if S_0 then S_1 else S_2 is responsible if
      i. S_0 is responsible and S_1, S_2 are *rcf*, or
      ii. S_0 is *rcf* and S_1, S_2 are responsible;
   (g) $S_0!M(S_1, \ldots, S_n)$ is responsible if exactly one of $S_0, \ldots, S_n$ is responsible and each of the others is *rcf*;
   (h) output(S) is responsible if S is responsible.

We now have the main result of this section.

Theorem 3. *Let P be a D-program with initial configuration Ω_0. Then the fragment of the transition system reachable from Ω_0 is confluent.*

To prove the theorem it is necessary to undertake a detailed analysis of the behaviour of D-programs as defined by the operational semantics. The main point is to formulate invariants on configurations reachable from the initial configuration of a D-program which show that sharing does not occur. It is then straightforward to deduce that the system is confluent. To express these invariants it is necessary to describe the ways in which an object name may occur in a configuration. We do this as follows.

Definition 4. An object name γ occurs in S

1. *in subject position* if S has a substatement $\gamma!M(\widetilde{S})$;
2. *in argument position* if S has a substatement $\alpha!M(\widetilde{v}, \gamma, \widetilde{S})$;
3. *in result position* if S has a substatement return$_\beta$ γ;
4. *in assignment position* if S has a substatement $X := \gamma$;
5. *in index position* if S has a substatement return$_\gamma$ S' or commit$_\gamma$ S'.

The following shorthand is convenient. We will treat occurrences in index position separately.

Definition 5. An object name γ *occurs in* $\langle S, \sigma\rangle$, written $\gamma \in \langle S, \sigma\rangle$, if γ occurs in σ, written $\gamma \in \sigma$, or γ occurs in subject, argument, result or assignment position in S.

The following lemma expresses the first invariant.

Lemma 6. *Suppose $\Omega = \langle \Phi, \Gamma\rangle$ is reachable from the initial configuration Ω_0 of a D-progam and that $\Gamma = \{\langle \alpha_1, S_1, \sigma_1\rangle, \ldots, \langle \alpha_n, S_n, \sigma_n\rangle\}$. Suppose that $\alpha \in \{\alpha_1, \ldots, \alpha_n\}$. Then there is at most one j such that α occurs in $\langle S_j, \sigma_j\rangle$, and if $\alpha \in \langle S_j, \sigma_j\rangle$ then*

1. *α occurs at most once in σ_j,*
2. *if α occurs in assignment position in S_j then $\alpha \notin \sigma_j$ and α occurs exactly once in S_j,*
3. *if α occurs in return position in S_j then $\alpha \notin \sigma_j$ and α occurs exactly once in S_j,*
4. *if α occurs in argument position in S_j then $\alpha \notin \sigma_j$ and α may occur in addition only in the subject position corresponding to the occurrence in argument position, and*
5. *if $\alpha!M(\widetilde{S})$ is a substatement of S_j then either $\alpha \notin \sigma_j$, or if $\sigma_j X = \alpha$ then $\widetilde{S}$ has no substatement of the form $Y := X^\dagger$, $\mathsf{return}_\gamma\ X^\dagger$ or $T!M(\widetilde{T})$ with $X^\dagger \in \widetilde{T}$.*

PROOF: The proof is by induction on the length of the derivation of Ω from Ω_0. Although long it shows clearly the rôles of the conditions in the definition of 'D-program' in guaranteeing preservation of the invariant. □

The second lemma uses the responsible nature of D-programs to ensure that no sharing arises in returning results of method calls.

Lemma 7. *Suppose $\Omega = \langle \Phi, \Gamma\rangle$ is reachable from the initial configuration Ω_0 of a D-program and that $\Gamma = \{\langle \alpha_1, S_1, \sigma_1\rangle, \ldots, \langle \alpha_n, S_n, \sigma_n\rangle\}$. Suppose that $\alpha \in \{\alpha_1, \ldots, \alpha_n\}$. Then there is at most one j such that α occurs in index position in $\langle S_j, \sigma_j\rangle$, and if α occurs in index position in $\langle S_j, \sigma_j\rangle$ and $\langle S_j, \sigma_j\rangle \xrightarrow{\ell} \langle S'_j, \sigma'_j\rangle$ where ℓ is* $\mathrm{return}(\alpha, v)$ *or* $\mathrm{call}(\beta, M, \widetilde{v}, \alpha)$ *then α does not occur in index position in $\langle S'_j, \sigma'_j\rangle$.*

PROOF: The proof is again by induction and the role of 'responsibility' is clearly exhibited in it. □

The theorem follows from these lemmas as if Ω is reachable from the initial configuration Ω_0 of a D-program, it is quite straightforward to show from the definition of the global transition relations that the confluence conditions are satisfied.

6 Determinacy in the π_v-calculus

In [8] a semantics for a parallel imperative language with shared variables was given by translation to CCS. The use of CCS as a semantic basis for object languages was studied in [11]. The π-calculus was first used to provide semantics for parallel object languages in [14]. Semantics for POOL and (variants of) $\pi o\beta\lambda$ have been given using the π-calculus [16, 6], the Higher-Order π-calculus [17] and, in [15, 7], a calculus called the 'π_v-calculus' which is essentially an amalgamation of the π-calculus and value-passing CCS. Due to lack of space we must refer to the papers just cited for an outline of the semantics by translation to the π_v-calculus to which the following discussion pertains. The semantics used here however contains some improvements on those cited particularly in the use of sorts which plays an important rôle in proofs.

In it a program is interpreted as a labelled transition system within the general π_v-calculus framework for systems with dynamically-evolving structure. To undertake a general study of determinacy and confluence of π_v-agents it is necessary to modify the definitions of 'determinacy' and 'confluence' from the setting of CCS to take due account of name passing. Although this is quite straightforward, it is not essential for the present purpose. For as we are concerned with the behaviour of *programs* and the encoding of a program declaration is an agent whose transition system contains only labels of the forms τ, $\mathsf{in}\langle k\rangle$ and $\overline{\mathsf{out}}\langle k\rangle$, we can adopt essentially the same definitions of 'determinacy' and 'Π-confluence' as in the operational semantics, employing the analogous partition Π which divides the labels into singletons except that all $\mathsf{in}\langle k\rangle$-labels form a single block. Were we interested, as in e.g. [7], in confluence of *fragments* of programs, it would be necessary to work with the extended definitions. A detailed presentation of these, and some work on extending the theory to this richer setting, will appear in [12].

Thus let us now use the terms 'bisimilar', 'determinate' and '(Π-)confluent' in the context of encodings of programs in the π_v-calculus. The encoding of a program declaration

$$Pdec \;\equiv\; Cdec_1\,, \ldots,\; Cdec_r,\; \mathsf{trigger}\; S_0$$

is an agent of the form

$$[\![Pdec]\!] \stackrel{\mathrm{def}}{=} (\nu\widetilde{p})([\![Cdec_1]\!]\langle\ldots\rangle \mid \ldots \mid [\![Cdec_r]\!]\langle\ldots\rangle \mid [\![S_0]\!]\langle\ldots\rangle)$$

and each $[\![Cdec_i]\!]$ is of the form

$$(new)\,!\,(\nu a)\,\overline{new}\langle a\rangle.\,\mathrm{Obj}\langle a,\ldots\rangle$$

with Obj being the encoding of an object of the class in question in its quiescent state. By examining the encoding it may be seen that a derivative of $[\![Pdec]\!]$ has the form

$$S \equiv (\nu\widetilde{p})(P_1\langle\ldots\rangle \mid \ldots \mid P_n\langle\ldots\rangle \mid [\![Cdec_1]\!]\langle\ldots\rangle \mid \ldots \mid [\![Cdec_r]\!]\langle\ldots\rangle \mid J\langle \mathsf{in}, \mathsf{out}, \ldots\rangle)$$

where each P_i, representing an object, is a derivative of some $[\![Cdec_j]\!]$ and J (which is absent if the trigger S_0 does not contain new(IO)) represents the object (if it exists) of class IO via which the agent interacts with the environment. Note that the form of such a system is preserved under derivation, although the number of P-components (the number of objects in the represented system) may grow. These agents have a close affinity with the *friendly* systems considered in [9]. In speaking of derivatives of encodings of program declarations we employ the following definitions from that work.

Definition 8. An agent P *bears* (resp. *handles*) the name x if x occurs free in P in positive (resp. negative) subject position. Further, an agent S of the kind above *uniquely bears* (resp. *uniquely handles*) the name x (or the name x is *uniquely borne* (resp. *uniquely handled*) *in* S) if at most one component of any derivative of S bears (resp. handles) x.

The proof that the encoding of a D-program is a confluent agent proceeds in two steps. First we have a result about π_v-agents of the kind considered above. In fact it can be given a more general formulation though in the present context it seems clearer to give the more specific statement. In it we write a : OBJ to indicate that a has sort OBJ[A] for some class A, a : RES to indicate that a has sort $\mathsf{RES}_A^M[T]$ for some class A, method name M and type T (with T being the result type of method M of class A), and a : CLASS to indicate that a is of sort CLASS[A] for some class A. (See the papers cited earlier for information on sorting.)

Theorem 9. *Suppose* Pdec *is a program declaration such that for any derivative* $S \equiv (\nu\,\tilde{p})(\Pi P_i \mid \Pi!\,C_j \mid J)$ *of* $[\![\mathrm{Pdec}]\!]$ *the following hold:*

1. $\mathrm{fn}(S) = \{\mathsf{in}, \mathsf{out}\}$, in *is borne by* J *and* out *is handled by* J, *and neither occurs in any other component of* S,
2. *if names* a *and* b *occur free and unguarded in subject position in* P_i *then* $a = b$,
3. *each* P_i *is determinate and is a derivative of some* $!\,C_j$,
4. *if* a : CLASS *then* a *is uniquely handled in* S, *and*
5. *if* a : OBJ *or* a : RES *then* a *is uniquely borne and uniquely handled in* S.

Then $[\![\mathrm{Pdec}]\!]$ *is confluent.*

Note that the term 'determinate' in condition 3 qualifies a π_v-agent and that we have omitted the precise definition of this term. The first four conditions in the above theorem are satisfied by the encoding of any program $Pdec$. So too are the properties in clause 5 that if a : OBJ or a : RES then a is uniquely borne in $[\![Pdec]\!]$. These facts follow from a detailed analysis of the semantic definition. The following theorem asserts that the unique handling properties are enjoyed by encodings of D-programs.

Theorem 10. *Suppose* Pdec *is a D-program. If* a : OBJ *or* a : RES *then* a *is uniquely handled in* $[\![\mathrm{Pdec}]\!]$.

As a corollary of the two theorems we have:

Corollary 11. *If* Pdec *is a D-program then* ⟦Pdec⟧ *is confluent.*

In the space available we can only outline the proofs of the theorems. The first is proved by induction on the length of the derivation from ⟦*Pdec*⟧ to S. The unique handling of names of sorts OBJ and RES, the fact that names of sort CLASS are uniquely handled by agents of the form $!\, C_j$, and the fact that the P_i are determinate, ensure that no names are shared in such a way that pre-emption of one action by another is possible, whether that action is an internal action of a P_i, an interaction between a P_i and a $!\, C_j$, an interaction between a P_i and the environment, or an interaction between two P_i's.

A direct proof of the second theorem is not easy. This is due to the fact that it is necessary to perform a very detailed analysis of the movement of names in the evolution of the encoding of a program. However, despite the fact that the operational and translational semantics are defined by quite different means, there is a very close correspondence between the two transition systems which they yield as the interpretations of a particular program. The proof utilizes this fact.

7 Conclusion

It is not difficult to construct examples to show that if any of the restrictions in the definition of '*D*-program' were omitted, the resulting condition would not guarantee determinacy. But there are of course many programs which although not *D*-programs are nonetheless determinate. The nature of the kind of language considered is such that we can not hope in general to determine on the basis of a simple analysis of its syntax that a program is determinate. We believe that the definition of '*D*-program' may capture a useful programming discipline. It may, in particular, be of value in relation to work such as that of Jones [5] concerned with the formal development of concurrent object programs by transformation from sequential programs.

As mentioned in the Introduction we may hope to give a simpler denotational semantics for the determinate sublanguage than is possible for the full language. This possibility is currently being studied. It is significant as models of concurrent object languages are in general extremely complex and difficult to comprehend and utilize; see e.g. [3]. We intend also to continue to study determinacy and confluence of concurrent systems with dynamically-evolving structure. We hope that such study may contribute to the understanding of concurrent object languages in particular and concurrent programming languages in general and to the development of concepts and techniques useful in the construction of reliable concurrent programs.

References

1. P. America. Issues in the design of a parallel object-oriented language. *Formal Aspects of Computing*, 1:366–411, 1989.

2. P. America, J. de Bakker, J. Kok, and J. Rutten. Operational semantics of a parallel object-oriented language. In *Conference Record of the 13th Symposium on Principles of Programming Languages*, pages 194–208. ACM Press, 1986.
3. P. America, J. de Bakker, J. Kok, and J. Rutten. Denotational semantics of a parallel object-oriented language. *Information and Computation*, 83:152–205, 1989.
4. J. Hogg. Islands: aliasing protection in object-oriented languages. In *Proceedings of OOPSLA'91*, pages 271–285. ACM Press, 1991.
5. C. Jones. Constraining interference in an object-based design method. In *Proceedings of TAPSOFT'93*, pages 136–150, 1993.
6. C. Jones. A pi-calculus semantics for an object-based design notation. In *Proceedings of CONCUR'93*, pages 158–172, 1993.
7. X. Liu and D. Walker. Confluence of processes and systems of objects. In *Proceedings of CAAP'95*. Springer, to appear.
8. R. Milner. *Communication and Concurrency.* Prentice-Hall, 1989.
9. R. Milner. The polyadic π-calculus: a tutorial. In *Logic and Algebra of Specification.* Springer, 1992.
10. R. Milner, J. Parrow, and D. Walker. A calculus of mobile processes, parts 1 and 2. *Information and Computation*, 100:1–77, 1992.
11. M. Papathomas. *Language Design Rationale and Semantic Framework for Concurrent Object-Oriented Programming.* PhD thesis, University of Geneva, 1992.
12. A. Philippou. PhD thesis, University of Warwick, forthcoming.
13. C. Tofts. *Proof methods and pragmatics for parallel programming.* PhD thesis, University of Edinburgh, 1990.
14. D. Walker. π-calculus semantics for object-oriented programming languages. In *Proceedings of TACS'91*, pages 532–547. Springer, 1991.
15. D. Walker. Algebraic proofs of properties of objects. In *Proceedings of ESOP'94*, pages 501–516. Springer, 1994.
16. D. Walker. Objects in the π-calculus. *Information and Computation*, 116:253–271, 1995.
17. D. Walker. Process calculus and parallel object-oriented programming lanaguages. In T. Casavant, editor, *Parallel Computers: Theory and Practice.* Computer Society Press, to appear.

Process Semantics of Graph Reduction

Simon Brock and Gerald Ostheimer
Computer Science Division
University of St Andrews
North Haugh
St Andrews
Fife KY16 9SS
{shb,gerald}@dcs.st-and.ac.uk

Abstract

This paper introduces an encoding of λ-terms in a subset of the π-calculus which mimics the graph reduction of the λ-terms. The encoding is sufficiently general to incorporate multiple reduction strategies, cycles and constants. As such it provides a concurrent operational semantics required for the parallel implementation of a lazy functional language. Only a small subset of π-calculus is used which enjoys a number of properties which make it eligible as an implementable compiler target language. The encoding is presented in terms of pure λ-terms and a correspondence to an established model of graph reduction is formally proved.

1 Introduction

Milner [16] showed that it is possible to encode terms from various λ-calculi in π-calculus such that the reduction of the encodings 'mimicked' reduction of the original λ-terms. In his concluding remarks Milner asks whether other strategies can be encoded in this way and in particular whether it is possible to model a reduction strategy with sharing. The first aim of this paper is to introduce an encoding of λ-terms which mimics a variant of lazy λ-calculus with sharing. While this is interesting from a theoretical standpoint, our original motivation was practical.

Modern implementations of lazy functional programming languages rely on sharing to increase performance. Wadsworth [21] first showed that this use of sharing could decrease the number of β-reduction steps in a call-by-name reduction sequence. Wadsworth coined the phrase 'call-by-need' to describe this, the basic idea being that a β-redex is only reduced when it is *needed* and all occurrences of it are shared. Unfortunately, the call-by-need strategy is inherently sequential and therefore must be augmented to gain performance on parallel machines. This usually takes the form of strictness annotations which force the evaluation of certain sub-terms *before* they are needed. Our interest was the implementation of such languages on a parallel message passing architecture [18]. As such we want some way of analyzing a compilation strategy and Milner's π-calculus models provided a good starting point.

Milner presents encodings of Abramsky's lazy λ-calculus [1] and a weak parallel call-by-value λ-calculus. Both encodings mimic reduction to weak head normal form but they are mutually incompatible. That is to say, they use different encodings for common structures (*i.e.* λ-abstractions) and therefore cannot be combined to produce a single model. Further, lazy functional programming makes use of many constructs which are not in pure λ-calculus. For example, cycles are created in the graphs and constants are used. The encoding presented here can accommodate all these structures in a natural way.

Our encoding also has a number of interesting properties. Firstly, only a small subset of the original π-calculus is used and the encodings enjoy a number of syntactic properties which mean they are easy implement. Therefore our encoding is interesting as a compiler target language for a provably correct parallel implementation. Secondly, the encodings themselves are remarkably concise and are arguably as easy to understand as other models of graph reduction in the literature. Lastly, the encoding is modular in nature. New structures and evaluation strategies can be added without changing what is already there.

The rest of this paper is structured as follows. We introduce the call-by-need λ-calculus of Ariola *et al* [2] and we use this to describe what it means for a λ-calculus reduction strategy to implement acyclic graph reduction. We then give an encoding of λ-terms in an asynchronous subset of the π-calculus and prove that this encoding simulates the call-by-need λ-calculus. At the end of the paper we show some extensions to the encoding to handle cycles, strictnesss and constants.

2 Related work

The idea of encoding functions in process calculi is not a new one. Kennaway and Sleep [13] introduce one method of doing this, representing combinator graphs in a variant of CCS called LNET. This is interesting as it captures many of the aspects of a functional programming implementation. However, LNET views communication as message exchange (*i.e.* it has a request-reply protocol) when our model makes use of a restricted form of asynchronous communication. Also, LNET incorporates a notion of process name which can be communicated to other processes. Glauert [7, 8] describes compatible encodings of lazy and eager evaluation in an asynchronous process notation. It is shown the process notation used can be translated into a graph reduction language. In Ostheimer and Davie [19], an encoding for shared reduction strategies was given in the (synchronous) monadic π-calculus but the correspondence to λ-terms was not formalized. Boudol [4] encodes a version of λ-calculus with explicit substitutions which provides sharing in an asynchronous version of π-calculus. The encoding is more complex than that presented here and correctness with respect to an established model of graph reduction is not established. Jeffrey [11] gives an

Syntactic domains

Variables:	x, y, z
Terms:	$M, N ::= x \mid \lambda x.M \mid M\ N \mid \mathsf{let}\ x = N\ \mathsf{in}\ M$
Values:	$V ::= \lambda x.M$
Answers:	$A ::= V \mid \mathsf{let}\ x = M\ \mathsf{in}\ A$
Evaluation Contexts:	$E ::= [\,] \mid EM \mid \mathsf{let}\ x = M\ \mathsf{in}\ E \mid \mathsf{let}\ x = E\ \mathsf{in}\ E[x]$

Reduction rules:

(let $_S$-I)	$(\lambda x.M)N \rightarrow \mathsf{let}\ x = N\ \mathsf{in}\ M$
(let $_S$-V)	$\mathsf{let}\ x = V\ \mathsf{in}\ E[x] \rightarrow \mathsf{let}\ x = V\ \mathsf{in}\ E[V]$
(let $_S$-C)	$(\mathsf{let}\ x = M\ \mathsf{in}\ A)N \rightarrow \mathsf{let}\ x = M\ \mathsf{in}\ AN$
(let $_S$-A)	$\mathsf{let}\ x = (\ \mathsf{let}\ y = M\ \mathsf{in}\ A)\ \mathsf{in}\ E[x] \rightarrow \mathsf{let}\ y = M\ \mathsf{in}\ \mathsf{let}\ x = A\ \mathsf{in}\ E[x]$

Figure 1: The standard call-by-need reduction system λ_{let}

encoding of a graph calculus into a form of π-calculus. λ-terms can be translated into the graph calculus which includes cycles and a simple form of strictness annotation. The encoding is interesting but relies on a conditional construct based on link name equality. Further the graph calculus is based on a low-level model of graph reduction. Our encoding directly encodes λ-terms without the translation step into an intermediate language.

3 Operational Semantics of Graph Reduction

The distinguishing feature of graph reduction is that parts of an expression may be shared. A number of different models have been developed that capture this sharing (for example, Jeffrey [12], Launchbury [14]) but here we will use the system of Ariola *et al* [2]. This system extends the normal term structure of λ-calculus with a let construct and replaces the usual β-reduction step $(\lambda x.M)N \rightarrow M[x := N]$ with the let$_S$-I rule that $(\lambda x.M)N \rightarrow \mathsf{let}\ x = N\ \mathsf{in}\ M$. There are then three rules that manipulate let constructs in various ways. The rewrite rules are introduced in a conventional way but *evaluation contexts* [6] are used to define the context for a redex. The system evaluates terms through to *answers* which are of the form $\mathsf{let}\ x_1 = M_1\ \mathsf{in}\ \ldots\ \mathsf{let}\ x_n = M_n\ \mathsf{in}\ \lambda x.M$. The final part of an answer is a term in weak head normal form (a *value*), the let bindings being associated with the free variables in this value. As the system does not evaluate "under λ's" these answers can be expanded to *weak head normal forms* in the lazy λ-calculus. The standard reduction strategy in λ_{let}, shown in Figure 1, models call-by-need reduction. We assume the definitions of equivalence and substitution from Barendregt [3]. When referring to λ_{let} in this paper we will always mean this standard reduction system. We will refer to the set of terms of λ_{let} as $\mathcal{L}$.

Standard reduction is organized in such a way that in $\mathsf{let}\ x = N\ \mathsf{in}\ M$, the subterm N is only reduced when it is needed (*i.e.* when the value associated with x is needed in M). If N then converges to an answer the value part replaces the needing occurrence of x and all subsequent occurrences of x when they need it.

The reduction rules define a single step reduction relation $\rightarrow$. The reflexive, transitive closure of $\rightarrow$ will be written $\twoheadrightarrow$. We say that: M *converges to* M', written $M{\downarrow}M'$, if $M \twoheadrightarrow M' \not\rightarrow$; $M{\downarrow}$ means that M converges to some M'; and $M{\uparrow}$ means M *diverges*, *i.e.* there does not exist M' such that $M{\downarrow}M'$. This notation will be used with all the rewrite relations presented in this paper. Generally rewrite relations will be disambiguated by context but it is sometimes necessary to distinguish the use of a particular rule which will be denoted by subscripting arrow $\rightarrow$ with the name of the rule (*e.g.* $(\lambda x.M)N \rightarrow_I \mathsf{let}\ x = N \mathsf{\ in\ } M$). Closed terms are defined in the usual way and the set of closed terms will be denoted with a superscript '0', *i.e.* $\mathcal{L}^0$. Ariola *et al* show that the evaluators for call-by-need and call-by-name are equivalent. Their paper explains in more detail how the reduction system works and gives examples.

We will use the λ_{let}-calculus as the basis of the proof that our encoding implements the 'call-by-need' reduction strategy. What exactly is our proof obligation? Clearly, similar termination properties and correspondences between normal forms are not enough. The whole idea of call-by-need reduction is that it preserves the normalization properties of call-by-name but may require fewer reductions. We propose to capture this argument as follows: assume we have an encoding of terms in λ_{let}-calculus into another calculus and an operation in the target calculus that corresponds to the let_S-I rule then:

Definition 3.1 A reduction relation $\rightarrow$ on a set of terms implements call-by-need if in the reduction of the encoding of any λ_{let}-term:

A. there is a one-to-one correspondence between a certain reduction step in that relation and let_S-I steps in the original term, and
B. for any terminating reduction sequence of length n in λ_{let} we have a corresponding terminating reduction sequence in the target calculus of length directly proportional to n.

The idea is that a faithful encoding of call-by-need does not introduce any more steps which correspond to β-reductions. The system which is implementing call-by-need may include other reduction steps but the number of such steps must be bounded. In this paper we prove this property for both an extended λ_{let}-calculus and for a π-calculus encoding of terms of the pure λ-calculus. We are confident that such correspondences can be established between the various presentations of call-by-need in the literature.

4 A π-calculus Encoding

The π-calculus was first presented by Milner *et al* [17] and is designed to specify processes with dynamically evolving configuration. In order not to obscure the main contribution of the present paper, we adopt an existing presentation of the π-calculus, namely that of Milner [16]. We will make only disciplined use of this calculus, adopting the restrictions on allowable terms suggested by Honda's ν-calculus [10]. Space precludes a full presentation of the system but the syntax of terms is:

$$P, Q \in \mathcal{P} \quad ::= \quad \overline{x}y \mid x(y).P \mid \mathbf{0} \mid P|Q \mid !x(y).P \mid (\nu x)P$$

where:

- $\overline{x}y$ is the process which outputs the channel y on the channel x.
- $x(y).P$ is the process which inputs the channel y' on channel x and then behaves like $P[y'/y]$.
- $\mathbf{0}$ is the empty process.
- $P \mid Q$ places P and Q in parallel.
- $!x(y).P$ is a replication operator.
- $(\nu x)P$ creates a new channel x for use in P.

The restricted system is asynchronous as output actions are prohibited from guarding non-empty processes. We only permit the replication of processes guarded by input actions which Honda calls 'lazy replication'. The motivation for using a restricted version of the calculus is our desire to use π-calculus as a model for a practical compiler target language. We are only interested in those constructs which have simple translations to message-passing computer architectures. Closer analysis of the following encodings reveals that other more subtle restrictions were also adopted which simplify implementation. A discussion of these and an outline of an implementation can be found in Brock and Ostheimer [5].

We will occasionally require the atomic transmission of pairs which is easily encoded in the monadic π-calculus as shown in Milner *et al* [17]. We will often abbreviate $(\nu x)(\nu y)P$ to $(\nu xy)P$.

The core idea of the translation is this: given a closed λ-term M and a name o of the π-calculus the encoding $[\![M]\!]o$ will simulate the reduction of M in the following sense. If $M \downarrow M'$ in the call-by-need λ-calculus then $[\![M]\!]o$ converges in the π-calculus such that the resulting term delivers a channel to the representation of M' at the channel o. In the translation, names of λ-variables are mapped directly to names of π-calculus channels. In order to be able to represent a call-by-need reduction strategy, these names will not stand for values, rather they provide access to values upon request.

Remembering weak head normal forms are our only values, we start by considering the encoding of abstractions:

$$[\![\lambda x.M]\!]o \stackrel{\text{def}}{=} (\nu f)(\overline{o}f \mid !f(x,p).[\![M]\!]p)$$

We can see that the representation of the function value, f, is immediately available at o. The replicated term represents an 'activation server' which allows the function value to be applied to an argument; the replication is necessary as a given function may be applied more than once. A process needing to apply a function sends an 'activation' consisting of (access to) the argument x and the place p where the result is required.

To encode an application (MN) we must ensure that M converges (to a function) and then apply it, in the style suggested by the encoding of abstractions, to a suspended form of the argument N. When the body of M requires the value of its argument, it sends a request r to the suspended argument and only then is the evaluation of N initiated. Once the value of N is available, the original request is satisfied and the value of N is 'stored'. Subsequent requests are then satisfied by returning this 'stored' channel. This leads to the encoding:

$$[\![MN]\!]o \stackrel{\text{def}}{=} (\nu amn)([\![M]\!]m \mid m(f).(\overline{f}(a,o) \mid a(r).([\![N]\!]n \mid n(g).(\overline{r}g \mid !a(r).\overline{r}g))))$$

The solution outlined above, while perfectly workable in practice, complicates the correctness proofs. When the first request for the argument N is generated, it is consumed and 'lost' until the argument N converges. As we wish to show a correspondence between the encoding and the λ_{let}-calculus we would have problems encoding a term like $\mathsf{let}\ a = N\ \mathsf{in}\ a$ as the encoding of a would vary according to whether $a = N$ was evaluating.[1]

Fortunately there is a straightforward solution to the problem: after consuming the initial request we can re-generate it, in order to consume it again only when the argument value is available. Incorporating this change we get

$$[\![MN]\!]o \stackrel{\text{def}}{=} (\nu amn)([\![M]\!]m \mid m(f).(\overline{f}(a,o) \mid a(r).(\overline{a}r \mid [\![N]\!]n \mid n(g).(!a(r).\overline{r}g))))$$

Finally, to request the value of a variable x the output channel is sent to x.

$$[\![x]\!]o \stackrel{\text{def}}{=} \overline{x}o$$

Example 4.1 Consider the case of the term $(\lambda x.M)N$. ν-declarations are omitted to save space, as these can be moved to the outermost level by using the structural equivalences.

$$[\![(\lambda x.M)N]\!]o \stackrel{\text{def}}{=} \left(\begin{array}{l} [\![(\lambda x.M)]\!]m \mid \\ m(f).\left(\overline{f}(x,o) \mid x(r).\left(\begin{array}{l} \overline{x}r \mid \\ [\![N]\!]n \mid \\ n(g).!x(r).\overline{r}g \end{array} \right) \right) \end{array} \right)$$

$$\stackrel{\text{def}}{=} \left(\begin{array}{l} \overline{m}f \mid !f(x,p).[\![M]\!]p \mid \\ m(f).\left(\overline{f}(x,o) \mid x(r).\left(\begin{array}{l} \overline{x}r \mid \\ [\![N]\!]n \mid \\ n(g).!x(r).\overline{r}g \end{array} \right) \right) \end{array} \right)$$

[1] When considering terms with strictness annotations, this encoding is non-confluent on divergence. If two sub-terms can generate requests for the same argument then two possible reduction paths exist. If the argument diverges then confluence cannot be obtained as the 'diamond cannot be closed'.

$$\rightarrow \left(\begin{array}{l} !f(x,p).[\![M]\!]p \mid \\ \overline{f}(x,o) \mid x(r). \left(\begin{array}{l} \overline{x}r \mid \\ [\![N]\!]n \mid \\ n(g).!x(r).\overline{r}g \end{array} \right) \end{array} \right)$$

$$\rightarrow \left(\begin{array}{l} !f(x,p).[\![M]\!]p \mid \\ [\![M]\!]o \mid x(r). \left(\begin{array}{l} \overline{x}r \mid \\ [\![N]\!]n \mid \\ n(g).!x(r).\overline{r}g \end{array} \right) \end{array} \right) \quad (*)$$

Note that the encoding performs two reductions without making any assumptions about the shape of M. Note also that in the case of M being an abstraction, the above process is in normal form and ready to deliver the value of M on o, without performing a copy step. This conveys a strong flavour of 'answers' in the λ_{let}-calculus, which would reduce the above term to let $x = N$ in M. For the moment, let us observe the modelling of β-reduction by assuming in the above $M \equiv x$ and N a value, *i.e.* $[\![N]\!]n \equiv (\overline{n}h \mid Q)$ where Q is the body of the λ-expression N accessible through h (ν-declarations have again be omitted). Then $(*)$ reduces as

$$\left(\begin{array}{l} !f(x,p).[\![x]\!]p \mid \\ [\![x]\!]o \mid x(r). \left(\begin{array}{l} \overline{x}r \mid \\ [\![N]\!]n \mid \\ n(g).!x(r).\overline{r}g \end{array} \right) \end{array} \right) \stackrel{\text{def}}{=} \left(\begin{array}{l} !f(x,p).[\![x]\!]p \mid \\ \overline{x}o \mid x(r). \left(\begin{array}{l} \overline{x}r \mid \\ (\overline{n}h \mid Q) \mid \\ n(g).!x(r).\overline{r}g \end{array} \right) \end{array} \right)$$

$$\rightarrow \left(\begin{array}{l} !f(x,p).[\![x]\!]p \mid \\ \overline{x}o \mid (\overline{n}h \mid Q) \mid n(g).!x(r).\overline{r}g \end{array} \right)$$

$$\rightarrow \left(\begin{array}{l} !f(x,p).[\![x]\!]p \mid \\ \overline{x}o \mid Q \mid !x(r).\overline{r}h \end{array} \right)$$

$$\rightarrow \left(\begin{array}{l} !f(x,p).[\![x]\!]p \mid \\ \overline{o}h \mid Q \mid !x(r).\overline{r}h \end{array} \right)$$

The latter is in normal form and delivers the value of N at o as required.

As is clear from the example, an encoded term may traverse several more states before converging than the original. These intermediate states have natural analogues in the λ_{let}-calculus and we can interpret the term in $(*)$ as an encoding of the let-construct. As the term $!f(x,p).[\![M]\!]p$ cannot participate in further reductions and therefore does not interfere with the simulation we drop it from the encoding and retain

$$[\![\text{let } x = N \text{ in } M]\!]o \stackrel{\text{def}}{=} (\nu nx)(x(r).(\overline{x}r \mid [\![N]\!]n \mid n(g).!x(r).\overline{r}v) \mid [\![M]\!]o)$$

By reinterpreting the encoding of pure λ-terms as an encoding of the λ_{let}-calculus we gain access to the results of Ariola *et al* [2]. For the correctness proof we shall find it convenient to identify several further intermediate states and define their analogues in a λ-calculus setting by extending λ_{let}. It should be noted that is possible to encode a version of λ-calculus without sharing simply by changing the encoding of application, as below:

$$[\![MN]\!]o \stackrel{\text{def}}{=} (\nu m,n,a)([\![M]\!]m \mid m(f).(\overline{f}(a,o) \mid !a(r).[\![N]\!]r))$$

This produces an encoding of the lazy λ-calculus which is similar in style to the encoding of the call-by-value λ-calculus presented by Milner [16].

5 Correctness

To show that the encoding presented in Section 4 does implement call-by-need it will be necessary to relate the reduction of the encoding of a λ-term to reduction in λ_{let}. This is complicated as the encoding includes certain pragmatics details which are not included in λ_{let}. Therefore in the next sub-section, an annotated version of λ_{let} is introduced and shown to implement call-by-need. We show that the encodings of this extended system occur at points in the reduction of the encoding of a λ-term. Therefore when we show that the encoding of the extended system implements call-by-need, we are showing that the encoding of λ-terms also implements call-by-need.

5.1 A Pragmatic Extension to λ_{let}

In λ_{let}, given that $M \to N$ then $\mathsf{let}\ x = M\ \mathsf{in}\ E[x] \to \mathsf{let}\ x = N\ \mathsf{in}\ E[x]$. In a message passing implementation, such as our π-calculus encoding, it might be expected that the process encoding the bound x in the evaluation context E sends a message to the process encoding $x = N$ which would then cause N to reduce to an answer. The process encoding the bound x does not have to take any further part in the reduction of N until N has converged. It can therefore be seen that there are three distinct states to a $\mathsf{let}\ x = N\ \mathsf{in}\ M$ term: firstly when M is reducing but does not need x; secondly the reduction of M needs the value associated with x and N is being reduced; and thirdly, N has converged and the value part can be copied into M. These states will be represented by annotating the let with a subscript. The annotated system will be called $\lambda_{let\bullet}$ and its terms can be related back to the originals via a simple function that erases the annotations.

The initial creation of a let becomes $(\lambda x.M)N \to \mathsf{let}_S\ x = N\ \mathsf{in}\ M$ where the subscript implies the evaluation of N is suspended. Subsequently when M needs x then the reduction $\mathsf{let}_S\ x = N\ \mathsf{in}\ E[x] \to \mathsf{let}_E\ x = N\ \mathsf{in}\ E[x] \to \mathsf{let}_E\ x = N'\ \mathsf{in}\ E[x]$ occurs, the let_E implying the bound term is evaluating. Subsequently, if N converges then let_E can enter a third state in which it can make the value part of the answer available to needing bound occurrences of x.

At this point the role of values must be considered and in particular how they are copied across multiple let clauses. In λ_{let}:

$$\mathsf{let}\ y = V\ \mathsf{in}\ \mathsf{let}\ x = y\ \mathsf{in}\ xN \quad \to^2 \quad \mathsf{let}\ y = V\ \mathsf{in}\ \mathsf{let}\ x = V\ \mathsf{in}\ VN$$

It appears that the value V is duplicated twice when it is only required once at the point of the application, *i.e.* at VN. Here a distinction will be made between where copies are produced by evaluation and where they are used, so that values are only copied into the left hand side of applications.

Therefore, if a term bound in a let binding converges to a value, *i.e.* the result of a reduction sequence in λ_{let_*} produces a binding of the form ... $\mathsf{let}_E\ y = V\ \mathsf{in}$ ... then this becomes a binding of the form ... $\mathsf{let}_D\ y = V_f\ \mathsf{in}$ ... where the name f is fresh. The intuition behind this annotation is that the value V is at a location f. In the subsequent encoding a distinction can now be made between this *defining* occurrence of the value and a copy of the value. The idea is that a defining occurrence resides at some location and the value is only copied from that location when it is copied into the left hand side of an application. This leads to the reduction sequence:

$$\begin{array}{rll} \mathsf{let}_E\ y = V\ \mathsf{in}\ \mathsf{let}_E\ x = y\ \mathsf{in}\ xN & \to & \mathsf{let}_D\ y = V_f\ \mathsf{in}\ \mathsf{let}_E\ x = y\ \mathsf{in}\ xN \\ & \to & \mathsf{let}_D\ y = V_f\ \mathsf{in}\ \mathsf{let}_E\ x = V_f\ \mathsf{in}\ xN \\ & \to & \mathsf{let}_D\ y = V_f\ \mathsf{in}\ \mathsf{let}_E\ x = V_f\ \mathsf{in}\ V_f N \end{array}$$

The complete reduction system λ_{let_*} is defined in Figure 2. There are two new rules which handle the propagation of need for a value associated with a binding and the formation of a defining occurrence of a value. The rest of the definition parallels that of λ_{let}. For certain rules (such as the definition of evaluation environments and the let_P-A rule) more cases have been added. Note that we use let_* to stand for the three different forms of let.

It should be noted that the use of locations for values could have been represented by introducing an extra let binding. Therefore the expression $\mathsf{let}_D\ x = V_f\ \mathsf{in}\ M$ in λ_{let_*} could be represented in λ_{let} as $\mathsf{let}\ f = V\ \mathsf{in}\ \mathsf{let}\ x = f\ \mathsf{in}\ M$. From one point of view this is more pleasing as it is in keeping with the nature of the original system but it leads to a number of technical complications. For example, the let_S-I rule becomes

$$\mathsf{let}\ f = \lambda x.M\ \mathsf{in}\ E[fN] \quad \to \quad \mathsf{let}\ f = \lambda x.M\ \mathsf{in}\ E[\mathsf{let}\ x = N\ \mathsf{in}\ M]$$

The definition of evaluation environments must also be extended. Also it would no longer be possible to relate terms in $\mathcal{L}_*$ to $\mathcal{L}$ by erasing the annotations.

5.2 The Relation Between λ_{let_*} and λ_{let}

Clearly reduction in these two systems is closely related. However, a term $M \in \mathcal{L}$ may be represented by a set of terms in $\mathcal{L}_*$. For example, $\mathsf{let}\ x = V\ \mathsf{in}\ V$ could be represented any of the λ_{let_*} terms $\mathsf{let}_S\ x = V\ \mathsf{in}\ V$, $\mathsf{let}_D\ x = V_f\ \mathsf{in}\ V$, or $\mathsf{let}_D\ x = V_f\ \mathsf{in}\ V_f$. The different representations will arise according to the reduction sequences that generated the original λ_{let} term. Therefore when lifting a term from $\mathcal{L}$ to $\mathcal{L}_*$ we will have to take into account all possible markings of let's and all possible regimes for sharing values across the term. As a preliminary, the obvious mapping from $\mathcal{L}_*$ to $\mathcal{L}$ is defined as:

Syntactic Domains

Locations:	f, g
Variables:	x, y, z
Values:	$V ::= \lambda x.M$
Located values:	$F ::= V_f$
Answers:	$A ::= V \mid V_f \mid \text{let}_* \; x = M \text{ in } A$
Terms:	$M, N \in \mathcal{L}_* ::= x \mid \lambda x.M \mid M\,N \mid \text{let}_S \; x = N \text{ in } M \mid$ $\text{let}_E \; x = N \text{ in } M \mid \text{let}_D \; x = V_f \text{ in } M$
Evaluation Contexts:	$E ::= [\,] \mid EM \mid \text{let}_E \; x = E \text{ in } E[x] \mid$ $\text{let}_* \; x = M \text{ in } E$

Reduction rules

$$
\begin{array}{lrcl}
(\text{let}_P\text{-I}) & (\lambda x.M)N & \rightarrow & \text{let}_S \; x = N \text{ in } M \\
 & (\lambda x.M)_f N & \rightarrow & \text{let}_S \; x = N \text{ in } M \\
(\text{let}_P\text{-V}) & \text{let}_E \; x = F \text{ in } E[x] & \rightarrow & \text{let}_E \; x = F \text{ in } E[F] \\
 & \text{let}_D \; x = F \text{ in } E[x] & \rightarrow & \text{let}_D \; x = F \text{ in } E[F] \\
(\text{let}_P\text{-C}) & (\text{let}_* \; x = M \text{ in } A)N & \rightarrow & \text{let}_* \; x = M \text{ in } AN \\
(\text{let}_P\text{-A}) & \text{let}_E \; x = (\text{let}_S \; y = M \text{ in } A) \text{ in } E[x] & \rightarrow & \text{let}_S \; y = M \text{ in } \; \text{let}_E \; x = A \text{ in } E[x] \\
 & \text{let}_E \; x = (\text{let}_D \; y = M \text{ in } A) \text{ in } E[x] & \rightarrow & \text{let}_D \; y = M \text{ in } \; \text{let}_E \; x = A \text{ in } E[x] \\
(\text{let}_P\text{-E}) & \text{let}_S \; x = M \text{ in } E[x] & \rightarrow & \text{let}_E \; x = M \text{ in } E[x] \\
(\text{let}_P\text{-D}) & \text{let}_E \; x = V \text{ in } E[x] & \rightarrow & \text{let}_D \; x = V_f \text{ in } E[x] \quad f \text{ fresh}
\end{array}
$$

Figure 2: The annotated call-by-need reduction system λ_{let_*}

Definition 5.1 If $M' \in \mathcal{L}_*$ then $|M'| \in \mathcal{L}$ is obtained from M' by erasing all subscripts from let's and values.

The method of lifting terms in $\mathcal{L}$ to $\mathcal{L}_*$ is defined in three stages. The first stage is to map let statements in $\mathcal{L}$ to let_S statements in $\mathcal{L}_*$.

Definition 5.2 For all $M \in \mathcal{L}$ then $\sigma(M) \in \mathcal{L}_*$ obtained from M by replacing all let's with let_S's.

The second stage is to impose on a term some regime for the sharing of values. When considering a term lifted from $\mathcal{L}$ to $\mathcal{L}_*$ we cannot know what reductions have occurred to produce this term and how any values in that term were created and therefore any valid sharing of these values must be taken into account. We do know that a shared value (which can only arise from a reduction of a term) cannot appear under a λ and if a value is shared then there is a unique defining occurrence for it.

Definition 5.3 For all $M \in \mathcal{L}$ where $M' = \sigma(M)$ then N' imposes a *value sharing regime* on M' if when a value V occurs in some context in M' then

$$\llbracket V_f \rrbracket o \stackrel{\text{def}}{=} \overline{o}f$$
$$\llbracket \mathsf{let}_S\ x = M \text{ in } N \rrbracket o \stackrel{\text{def}}{=} (\nu x)(x(r).(\overline{x}r \mid \llbracket M \rrbracket n \mid n(g).!x(r).\overline{r}g) \mid \llbracket N \rrbracket o)$$
$$\llbracket \mathsf{let}_E\ x = M \text{ in } N \rrbracket o \stackrel{\text{def}}{=} (\nu x)(\llbracket M \rrbracket n \mid n(g).!x(r).\overline{r}g \mid \llbracket N \rrbracket o)$$
$$\llbracket \mathsf{let}_E\ x = V_f \text{ in } N \rrbracket o \stackrel{\text{def}}{=} (\nu x)(!x(r).\overline{r}f \mid \llbracket N \rrbracket o)$$
$$\llbracket \mathsf{let}_D\ x = (\lambda x.M)_f \text{ in } N \rrbracket o \stackrel{\text{def}}{=} (\nu x)(!x(r).\overline{r}f \mid !f(x,p).\llbracket M \rrbracket p \mid \llbracket N \rrbracket o)$$

Figure 3: Encoding the extensions

1. V occurs in the similar context in N', or
2. V_f occurs in the similar context in N' (but not under a λ) and either: it is a unique defining occurrence of V_f *i.e.* it occurs in a sub-term of the form $\mathsf{let}_D\ x = V_f$ in ...; or there is a unique defining occurrence of V_f whose scope covers this occurrence.

The third stage is to consider the role of the let_P-E rule which makes a term in a binding eligible for reduction. A single reduction in λ_{let} may require some number of these *propagation of demand* steps in λ_{let*} before the corresponding reduction can occur. However, for finite terms this propagation is clearly finite, leading to the definition below:

Definition 5.4 If $M' \in \mathcal{L}_*$ then N' is a *propagation* of M' if $M' \twoheadrightarrow_E N'$.

Using the above definitions, a method of lifting $M \in \mathcal{L}$ to a set of terms in $\mathcal{L}_*$ is defined as:

Definition 5.5 For all $M \in \mathcal{L}$, $M' \in \mathcal{L}_*$ we say M' is a member of the set lift M if either: $M' \equiv \sigma(M)$; M' imposes a value sharing regime on $\sigma(M)$; or M' is a propagation of M'' and M'' imposes a value sharing regime on $\sigma(M)$.

The first step to the required simulation lemma is then:

Lemma 5.6 *For all $M \in \mathcal{L}$ if $M \to N$ then there exists an N such that $M' \in$ lift M such that $M' \twoheadrightarrow N'$ we have $N' \in$ lift N.*

Proof: See Brock and Ostheimer [5]. □

The main lemma of this section can now be proved:

Lemma 5.7 *For all $M \in \mathcal{L}$ with $M \twoheadrightarrow N$ in λ_{let} there exists $N' \in \mathcal{L}_*$ such that $\sigma(M) \twoheadrightarrow N'$ in λ_{let*} and $N' \in$ lift N.*

Proof: By the definition of lift and successive applications of lemma 5.6. □

Corollary 5.8 *For all $M \in \mathcal{L}$, the reduction of $\sigma(M)$ in λ_{let*} implements call-by-need.*

The extensions used in λ_{let*} can be encoded in π-calculus as shown in Figure 3. Note that these encodings already occur as intermediate states during reduction of terms encoded via the method shown in section 4.

5.3 Correctness of the Encoding of λ_{let}.

Following Milner [16] we require the *r-determinacy* property of the encoding which is similar to the sequential nature of the reduction in λ_{let}.

Definition 5.9 $P \in \mathcal{P}$ is *r-determinate* if whenever $P \twoheadrightarrow Q$ and also $Q \rightarrow Q_1$ and $Q \rightarrow Q_2$, then $Q_1 \equiv Q_2$.

The correspondence between the *closed* terms $\mathcal{L}_*^0$ and π-terms is:

Definition 5.10 Let the relation $\mathcal{S} \subseteq (\mathcal{L}_*^0 \times \mathcal{P})$ contain all pairs $(M', [\![M']\!]o)$ for some channel o such that M' possesses a value sharing regime.

Lemma 5.11 *For all* $(M', P) \in \mathcal{S}$ *then* P *is r-determinate and either:*

A. M' *is an answer and* $P \downarrow P'$

B. For some $(N', Q) \in \mathcal{S}$, $M' \rightarrow N'$ *and* $P \twoheadrightarrow Q$.

Proof: See Brock and Ostheimer [5]. □

Theorem 5.12 *For all closed* $M' \in \mathcal{L}_*^0$, $[\![M']\!]o$ *is r-determinate and one of the following conditions holds:*

A. $M' \downarrow N'$ *and* $[\![M']\!]o \downarrow [\![N']\!]o$

B. $M' \uparrow$ *and* $[\![M']\!]o \uparrow$.

Proof: by iterating lemma 5.11 starting from $[\![M]\!]o$. □

Corollary 5.13 *The encoding of λ-terms in section 4 implements call-by-need.*

6 Extensions

The encoding of pure λ-calculus is interesting from a theoretical standpoint but functional languages include extensions such as combining evaluation strategies; cycles; and constants whose encoding will be considered.

6.1 Mixing evaluations strategies

As the π-calculus is designed to represent concurrency it seems reasonable to extend λ_{let} calculus to include some parallelism. The usual method of introducing parallelism to a lazy functional language is via strictness annotations, which are either inserted safely by the compiler performing strictness analysis or, potentially less safely, by the programmer. Hankin *et al* [9] show the need to annotate applications and λ's. To accommodate this in λ_{let} we add an explicit application symbol @ to represent the normal application. This application and λ are then annotated with a subscript V when they are to be strict. The the extra encodings for these structures are shown in Figure 4.

The extended version of λ_{let} implements parallel call-by-value such that a let_S-I step for an $@_V$ application only occurs when the right hand side has

$$[\![M @_V N]\!]o \stackrel{\text{def}}{=} (\nu a, m, n)([\![M]\!]m \mid [\![N]\!]n \mid m(f).n(g).(\overline{f}(a, o) \mid !a(r).\overline{r}g))$$
$$[\![\lambda_V x.M]\!]o \stackrel{\text{def}}{=} (\nu n, f)(\overline{o}f \mid !f(a, p).(\overline{a}n \mid n(g).(!x(r).r(g) \mid [\![M]\!]p)))$$

Figure 4: The extra encodings for strictness annotations

converged. It does this by allowing both sides of this application to be evaluated in parallel, which is reflected in the encoding. When both sides have converged, the body of the function is activated. The encoding of the call-by-value λ-term is slightly more involved: upon receiving an activation it requests the evaluation of the supplied argument before entering the body.

The problem with implementing strictness in the manner shown above is that an application cannot be reduced until both sides have converged to a value. An alternative to this is to use *eager* or *lenient* reduction [20]. Here, both sides of an application are evaluated in parallel (as in parallel call-by-value) but the application can be reduced before the right hand side has converged to a value (as in call-by-name/need). This is achieved by setting up the argument computation as a separate process and passing a handle to this process in place of the argument. Requests for the argument value via the process handle must block until the value is available. The value is then memoized to achieve sharing. We like to refer to the parameter-passing mechanism as *call-by-process*. Representing it as $@_P$ its encoding is:

$$[\![M @_P N]\!]o \stackrel{\text{def}}{=} (\nu a, m, n)([\![M]\!]m \mid [\![N]\!]n \mid m(f).(\overline{f}(a, o) \mid n(g).!a(r).\overline{r}g))$$

These strategies can be accommodated within λ_{let} by enriching the evaluation environments to allow evaluation in a **let** binding. It should be noted that this style of evaluation is easily incorporated into λ_{let_*} as $(\lambda x.M)@_P N$ could reduce to $\mathsf{let}_E\ x = N \mathsf{\ in\ } M$. The evaluation environment $\mathsf{let}_E\ x = N \mathsf{\ in\ } E[x]$ is then generalized to $\mathsf{let}_E\ x = N \mathsf{\ in\ } M$.

6.2 Recursion

Efficient implementation of recursion in functional programming languages requires cycles. Ariola *et al.* [2] incorporate recursion within their system and similar enhancements can be made here. The encoding of a mutually recursive **let** construct is shown below:

$$[\![\mathsf{letrec}\ x_1 = M_1, \ldots x_n = M_n \mathsf{\ in\ } N]\!]o$$
$$\stackrel{\text{def}}{=} (\nu \vec{m}\vec{x}) \left(\begin{array}{l} (x_1(r).(\overline{x_1}r \mid [\![M_1]\!]m_1 \mid m_1(f).!x_1(s).\overline{s}f)) \mid \\ \ldots \\ (x_n(r).(\overline{x_n}r \mid [\![M_n]\!]m_n \mid m_n(f).!x_n(s).\overline{s}f)) \\ \mid [\![N]\!]o \end{array} \right)$$

This encoding is nothing more than an n-ary version of the encoding for **let** shown previously. The incorporation of recursion into λ_{let} substantially complicates the evaluation environments but it should be possible to extend the proofs presented here to that system.

Many run-time systems include a mechanism to recognize and report a *black hole* which is a detectable self-dependent infinite loop. The encoding given above has a similar property such that the encoding of a black hole causes deadlock, *i.e.* it is bisimilar to the empty process **0**. To prove that the encoding does deadlock for all black holes would require their incorporation into λ_{let} and an extension to the existing correctness proof. We also need to prove that deadlock does not occur under any other circumstances.

6.3 Constants

An important part of a functional programming language is constants and data type constructors. These can incorporated into the encoding at a number of levels. It is possible to incorporate either direct encodings of the equivalent λ-terms or direct implementations in π-calculus, as in the data structures examples given by Milner [15]. Alternatively if constants are added to the π-calculus they can be used in a natural way, as shown in Ostheimer and Davie [19].

7 Conclusions

This paper has shown that an encoding of λ-terms in the π-calculus can implement a call-by-need. This encoding is sufficiently simple to be used as a model for code generation for a parallel machine. Further this encoding can be extended to capture many of the requirements of a full implementation of functional programming languages. There is a great deal more work to be carried out in this area. We are currently advancing the theoretical side to take more account of the theory of the π-calculus. On the practical side, we are developing an abstract machine to execute the encoding on existing parallel systems.

Acknowledgments This paper was much improved by the comments of Tony Davie, John Glauert, Davide Sangiorgi and the anonymous referees. Gerald Ostheimer was supported by SERC grant GR-H18739 'Compiler Technology for Scalable Distributed Multiprocessor Architectures'.

References

[1] S. Abramsky. The lazy λ-calculus. In D. Turner, editor, *Research Topics in Functional Programming*, pages 65–117. Addison-Wesley, 1990.

[2] Z. Ariola, M. Felleisen, J. Maraist, M. Odersky, and P. Wadler. A call-by-need λ-calculus. In *The Conference Record of Principles of Programming Languages*, ACM, 1995.

[3] H. Barendregt. *The λ-calculus: its syntax and semantics, Studies in logic and the foundations of mathematics*, volume 103. Elsevier Science Publishers, 1984.

[4] G. Boudol. Some chemical abstract machines. In *A Decade of Concurrency — Reflections and Perspectives, Proceedings of the REX School Symposium*, LNCS 803, pages 92–123. Springer-Verlag, June 1993.

[5] S. Brock and G. Ostheimer. Process semantics of graph reduction. Technical report, Computer Science Division, University of St. Andrews, 1995.

[6] M. Felleisen and D. Friedman. Control operators, the SECD-machine, and the λ-calculus. In *3rd Working Conference on the Formal Description of Programming Concepts*, Ebberup, Denmark, August 1986.

[7] J. Glauert. Asynchronous mobile processes. In *Proceedings of PARLE 92*, LNCS 605. Springer-Verlag, 1992.

[8] J. Glauert, L. Leth, and B. Thomsen. A new process model for functions. In M. Sleep, M. Plasmeijer, and M. van Eekelen, editors, *Term Graph Rewriting: Theory and Practice*, chapter 20, pages 269–282. Wiley, 1993.

[9] C. Hankin, G. Burn, and S. Peyton-Jones. A safe approach to parallel combinator reduction (extended abstract). In B. Robinet and R.Wilhelm, editors, *Proceedings of ESOP 86*, LNCS 213, pages 99–110. Springer-Verlag, 1986.

[10] K. Honda. Two bisimilarities in ν-calculus. Technical Report 92-002, Keio University, 1992.

[11] A. Jeffrey. A chemical abstract machine for graph reduction — extended abstract. In *Proceedings of Ninth International Conference on Mathematical Foundations of Programming Semantics*, LNCS 802, pages 293–303, 1993.

[12] A. Jeffrey. Fully abstract semantics for concurrent graph reduction. In *Proceedings, Ninth Annual IEEE Symposium on Logic in Computer Science*, pages 82–91. IEEE, 1994.

[13] J. Kennaway and M. Sleep. Expressions as processes. In *Proceedings of LISP and Functional Programming*, ACM, 1982.

[14] J. Launchbury. A natural semantics for lazy evaluation. In *Proceedings of the Conference on Principles of Programming Languages*, ACM, 1993.

[15] R. Milner. The polyadic π-calculus: a tutorial. Technical Report ECS-LFCS-91-180., LFCS, Computer Science Department, University of Edinburgh, 1991.

[16] R. Milner. Functions as processes. *Mathematical Structures in Computer Science*, 2:119–141, 1992.

[17] R. Milner, J. Parrow, and D. Walker. A calculus of mobile processes, parts I and II. Technical report, LFCS, Computer Science Department, University of Edinburgh, 1989.

[18] G. Ostheimer. Parallel functional computation on STAR:DUST. In *Proceedings of the Workshop on the Parallel Implementation of Functional Languages*, University of Southampton Technical Report, 1991.

[19] G. Ostheimer and A. Davie. Modelling parallel graph reduction in the π-calculus. In *Proceedings of the Fifth International Workshop on Implementation of Functional Languages*, University of Nijmegen Technical Report, 1993.

[20] K. R. Traub. *Implementation of Non-Strict Functional Programming Languages.* MIT Press, 1991.

[21] C. Wadsworth. *Semantics and pragmatics of the λ-calculus.* PhD thesis, University of Oxford, 1971.

Bisimulations for a Calculus of Broadcasting Systems

M. Hennessy, J. Rathke*

University of Sussex

Abstract. We develop a theory of bisimulation equivalence for the broadcast calculus *CBS*. Both the strong and weak versions of bisimulation congruence we study are justified in terms of a characterisation as the largest *CBS* congruences contained in an appropriate version of barbed bisimulation.
We then present sound and complete proof systems for both the strong and weak congruences over finite expressions. The first system we give contains an infinitary proof rule to accommodate input prefixes. We improve on this by presenting a finitary proof system where judgements are relative to properties of the data domain.

1 Introduction

The Broadcast Calculus, CBS, is a value-passing process calculus where process intercommunication is achieved by the broadcasting of values. The calculus has been developed in series of papers [8, 9, 12] and has been implemented as an extension to Lazy ML, [10].

Here we are concerned with the development of a semantic theory for the Broadcast Calculus, in particular the provision of an equational theory and proof system for establishing process identities. Work to this effect has been investigated by Prasad in [9] where he defines both strong and weak bisimulation equivalence and provides a complete axiomatisation of the strong case for a pure version of the calculus. The problem of finding a complete axiomatisation for weak bisimulation equivalence was left open. Prasad's definitions of these bisimulations are a direct application of computational intuition and standard definitions for other process calculi such as CCS. But a priori there is no obvious reason why such definitions should be considered natural for the rather different computational paradigm of CBS.

One concern of the present work then is a reappraisal of bisimulation equivalence for CBS by taking very basic notions of observability as our starting point. CBS has no natural notion of an internal action, often referred to as τ moves. However it does possess a distinguished action $\tau!$ which corresponds to the production of noise. We first look for a suitable notion of strong equivalence, where the production of noise is treated no differently than the production of any other value, and then a suitable notion of weak equivalence, where noise is abstracted away. In each case we derive our notions of equivalence using reasonable criteria based on barbed bisimulation,

* This work has been supported by the ESPRIT/BRA CONCUR2 project and the EPSRC grant GR/H16537. Authors' address: Dept. of Cognitive and Computing Science, University of Sussex, Brighton BN1 9QH, United Kingdom. Telephone: (+44) 1273 606755. Email: {julianr,matthewh}@cogs.susx.ac.uk

[11]: in each case they turn out to be the least *CBS* congruences contained in an appropriate version of barbed bisimulation.

We study these equivalences further by giving two proof theoretic characterisations of each. The first concentrates on closed process, i.e. processes with no free occurrences of value-variables; this determines an equational characterisation except that an infinitary rule is required in order to deduce equivalences of the form $x?T = x?U$. The second characterisation is finitary, relative to an adequate proof system for expressions over the data domain. Here judgements are of the form

$$b \rhd T = U$$

meaning that in all evaluations which satisfy the boolean constraint b the evaluation of T is semantically equivalent to that of U. The proof rules depend on deductions which can be made in an independent proof system for the data domain.

We now outline the rest of the paper. The syntax and operational semantics of the particular version of CBS that we study is presented in Section 2. The calculus is essentially the calculus CBS+ of [9], augmented with pattern-matching on inputs. The input prefix $x?T$ of CBS+ is replaced with $x \in S?T$ where S can be any subset of Val, a possibly infinite set of values. We then define ***strong barbed bisimulation equivalence*** for CBS and we characterise the largest congruence contained within it. This we call ***noisy bisimulation equivalence*** and it can be defined directly in terms of certain types of bisimulations.

In Section 3 we give an infinitary equational characterisation of this congruence over closed finite expressions. Weak equivalence is addressed similarly in Section 4 using the corresponding notion of weak barbed bisimulation; the resulting weak equivalence coincides with that suggested in [9]. In Section 5 we give an equational characterisation for this equivalence, an extension of that of Section 3. Finally, Section 6 is devoted to removing the infinitary proof rule. We follow the approach of [3] in developing a *finitary* proof system over open terms which relies upon auxiliary proof systems for reasoning in the data domains.

Many of the details and most of the proofs are omitted from this paper. They may be found in [5, 6].

2 The Broadcast Calculus

The calculus we consider is a minor variation on that of [9]. The syntax is described by the following grammar:

$$T ::= \mathbf{O} \mid e!T \mid x \in S?T \mid b \gg T \mid \sum_{i \in I} T_i \mid T|T \mid T_{(f,g)} \mid A(\tilde{e}).$$

It has many of the usual operators of *CCS*, [7] but communication is achieved by broadcasting values to all processes in the environment. The process $e!P$ broadcasts the value of the expression e while $x \in S?T$ is a process which, on hearing the value v proceeds to act like the process $T[v/x]$ provided $v \in S$; otherwise the value is ignored. Let Val represent the set of values which can be broadcast and τ a special value not in Val; τ represents *noise* in the system, i.e. broadcasts of values which can not be deciphered by any process. Note that the sets S guarding input prefixes never contain the value τ. In $T_{(f,g)}$ both f and g are functions from $Val \cup \{\tau\}$ to $Val \cup \{\tau\}$, strict in the sense that $f(\tau) = g(\tau) = \tau$.

They are used to implement restriction and renaming and allow messages to be made local to particular processes. The strictness condition enforces the constraint that noise cannot be translated into an interpretable value.

This syntax presupposes a set of data expressions $ValExp$, ranged over by e, and a set of boolean expressions $BoolExp$, ranged over by b. We do not give a precise syntax for these languages but simply assume they have a minimal set of properties. Thus we assume $ValExp$ contains the set of values $Val \cup \{\tau\}$ and a set of variables Var, ranged over by x. We also assume that *evaluations*, functions ρ from Var to Val, behave in a reasonable manner when extended to $ValExp$ and $BoolExp$; when e (or b) is closed, i.e. contains no occurrences of variables, then the value of the expression e is independent of ρ and we denote it by $[\![e]\!]$. Substitutions in data and boolean expressions are written as $e[e'/x], b[e'/x]$ respectively and we extend substitutions to process terms in the obvious way, noting that $x \in S?T$ binds x in T. We write v for an arbitrary value in Val and w for a value in $Val \cup \{\tau\}$. Finally we use $T, U, \ldots$ to range over arbitrary process terms whereas $P, Q, \ldots$ denote closed process terms or *agents*, i.e. terms with no free variables.

We now consider an operational semantics for this language, *CBS*, see Figure 1; again this more or less coincides with that presented in [9]. Throughout we assume that with each constant name A we have an associated definition: $A(\tilde{x}) \stackrel{def}{=} T_A$ where $\tilde{x}$ contains all of the free variables that appear in T_A, and A occurs guarded in T_A. The most notable difference between the operational semantics of *CCS*, [7], and *CBS* is the introduction of a new kind of transition called *discard*, written $T \xrightarrow{w:} T$. This is essentially a 'negation' of the transition $T \xrightarrow{w?} T'$ for some T' (see Lemma 1 below) and is used to facilitate the presentation of the semantics for the parallel operator.

Some simple properties of these relations are given in the following lemma:

Lemma 1. *For every agent P*

- *if* $P \xrightarrow{w:} Q$ *then* Q *is* P
- $P \xrightarrow{v:} P$ *if and only if there does not exist a* Q *such that* $P \xrightarrow{v?} Q$
- $P \xrightarrow{\tau:} P$ □

At the level of labelled transition systems *CBS* appears to be very similar to the value-passing process algebras of [3] and the operational semantics given above corresponds very much to the *early* operational semantics of that paper. However it is worth pointing out that at least one expected property is not true: $P \xrightarrow{v?} Q$ does NOT imply that for every value v' there is a process $Q_{v'}$ such that $P \xrightarrow{v'?} Q_{v'}$. One reason is the use of guarded inputs, $x \in S?T$; here a value can be input only if it is in S. However even if the only input construct allowed is $x \in Val?T$ the property still does not hold. For example the process $(x \in Val?T)_{(f,g)}$ can only receive the values from Val which g doesn't map to τ.

Based on this operational semantics we wish to develop a version of strong bisimulation, [7], appropriate for *CBS*. Rather than develop a range of different theories we take the approach advocated in [11] by defining a version of ***barbed bisimulation***

Discard	Input	Output
$\mathbf{O} \xrightarrow{w:} \mathbf{O}$		
$\dfrac{w \notin S}{x \in S?T \xrightarrow{w:} x \in S?T}$	$\dfrac{v \in S}{x \in S?T \xrightarrow{v?} T[v/x]}$	
$e!P \xrightarrow{w:} e!P$		$\dfrac{[\![e]\!] = w}{e!P \xrightarrow{w!} P}$
$\dfrac{\forall i \in I \cdot P_i \xrightarrow{w:} P_i}{\sum_I P_i \xrightarrow{w:} \sum_I P_i}$	$\dfrac{\exists i \in I \cdot P_i \xrightarrow{v?} P'}{\sum_I P_i \xrightarrow{v?} P'}$	$\dfrac{\exists i \in I \cdot P_i \xrightarrow{w!} P'}{\sum_I P_i \xrightarrow{w!} P'}$
$\dfrac{[\![b]\!] = \mathbf{false}}{b \gg P \xrightarrow{w:} b \gg P}$		
$\dfrac{P \xrightarrow{w:} P}{b \gg P \xrightarrow{w:} b \gg P}$	$\dfrac{P \xrightarrow{v?} P' \quad [\![b]\!] = \mathbf{true}}{b \gg P \xrightarrow{v?} P'}$	$\dfrac{P \xrightarrow{w!} P' \quad [\![b]\!] = \mathbf{true}}{b \gg P \xrightarrow{w!} P'}$
$\dfrac{T_A[\tilde{e}/\tilde{x}] \xrightarrow{w:} T_A[\tilde{e}/\tilde{x}]}{A(\tilde{e}) \xrightarrow{w:} A(\tilde{e})}$	$\dfrac{T_A[\tilde{e}/\tilde{x}] \xrightarrow{v?} P'}{A(\tilde{e}) \xrightarrow{v?} P'}$	$\dfrac{T_A[\tilde{e}/\tilde{x}] \xrightarrow{w!} P'}{A(\tilde{e}) \xrightarrow{w!} P'}$
$\dfrac{P \xrightarrow{gw:} P}{P_{(f,g)} \xrightarrow{w:} P_{(f,g)}}$	$\dfrac{P \xrightarrow{gv?} P'}{P_{(f,g)} \xrightarrow{v?} P'_{(f,g)}}$	$\dfrac{P \xrightarrow{w!} P'}{P_{(f,g)} \xrightarrow{fw!} P'_{(f,g)}}$
$\dfrac{P \xrightarrow{\alpha} P' \quad Q \xrightarrow{\beta} Q'}{P \mid Q \xrightarrow{\alpha \bullet \beta} P' \mid Q'} \quad \alpha \bullet \beta \neq \bot$		$\begin{array}{c\|ccc} \bullet & w! & w? & w: \\ \hline w! & \bot & w! & w! \\ w? & w! & w? & w? \\ w: & w! & w? & w: \end{array}$

Fig. 1. Operational semantics for closed agents.

for *CBS*. This is straightforward and uncontroversial since it relies only on a notion of reduction, which we have in $\xrightarrow{\tau!}$, and a notion of when agents have the ability to produce values, which we have in $\xrightarrow{v!}$. The "correct" version of strong bisimulation for *CBS* will then be that version, if it exists, which coincides with the *CBS* congruence generated by $\sim_{barb}$.

For any value v let $P \downarrow v$ mean that $P \xrightarrow{v!} P'$ for some P'. Then a symmetric relation $\mathcal{R}$ between agents is called a *barbed bisimulation* if whenever $(P, Q) \in \mathcal{R}$

then:

$$\begin{array}{ll}\text{if } P \xrightarrow{\tau!} P' & \text{then } \exists Q'.Q \xrightarrow{\tau!} Q' \text{ and } P'\mathcal{R}Q' \\ \text{if } P \downarrow v & \text{then } Q \downarrow v.\end{array}$$

We use $\sim_{barb}$ to denote the maximal such relation which is obviously an equivalence. However it is preserved by very few of the operators of *CBS* and is not very interesting as a semantic equivalence. Instead we concentrate on the associated congruence.

Definition 2. For agents P and Q let $P \sim_{barb}^{c} Q$ if $C[P] \sim_{barb} C[Q]$ for every *CBS* context $C[\_]$.

The remainder of this section is devoted to giving a bisimulation type characterisation of $\sim_{barb}^{c}$.

The characterisation is easiest to explain in terms of a new transition relation. In a broadcasting calculus an observer can not see whether a given process actually inputs a particular broadcasted value or simply discards it. This is captured by the following definition:

$$\text{let } P \xrightarrow{v??} Q \text{ if } P \xrightarrow{v?} Q \text{ or } P \xrightarrow{v:} Q.$$

With this new arrow we define a new kind of bisimulation relation. A symmetric relation $\mathcal{R}$ between agents is called a *noisy bisimulation* if whenever $(P,Q) \in \mathcal{R}$ then:

$$\begin{array}{ll}\text{if } P \xrightarrow{w!} P' & \text{then } \exists Q'.Q \xrightarrow{w!} Q' \text{ and } P'\mathcal{R}Q' \\ \text{if } P \xrightarrow{v??} P' & \text{then } \exists Q'.Q \xrightarrow{v??} Q' \text{ and } P'\mathcal{R}Q'.\end{array}$$

We let $P \sim_n Q$ if there exists some noisy bisimulation R such that $(P,Q) \in R$, i.e. $\sim_n$ is the largest noisy bisimulation.

Because of Lemma 1 noisy bisimulations can be simplified considerably:

Proposition 3. *Let R be a symmetric relation over agents. Then R is a noisy bisimulation if and only if when $(P,Q) \in R$ then*

$P \xrightarrow{w!} P'$ *implies there is some Q' such that $P'\mathcal{R}Q'$ and $Q \xrightarrow{w!} Q'$*
$P \xrightarrow{v?} P'$ *implies there is some Q' such that $P'\mathcal{R}Q'$ and $Q \xrightarrow{v??} Q'$* □

Proposition 4. *The relation $\sim_n$ is preserved by all of the CBS operators except choice.* □

We can also capture noisy bisimulation equivalence from $\sim_{barb}$ using static contexts, i.e. contexts in which the 'hole' does not appear as a summand in a choice.

Proposition 5. *If $C[P] \sim_{barb} C[Q]$ for every static context $C[\_]$ then $P \sim_n Q$.*

Proof. Given P, Q defined over a value set Val, we suppose that $C[P] \sim_{barb} C[Q]$ for every static context C and we assume the existence of a larger value set[2] $Val^{+} \stackrel{def}{=}$

2 Strictly speaking this need not be a larger set if we make the reasonable assumption that Val is a solution to an equation such as $Val = B + Val \times Val$.

$Val \cup Val' \cup \{a, b\}$, where Val' is a set of values such that for each $v \in Val$ there exists exactly one v' in Val' with $v' \notin Val$ and $a, b \notin Val \cup Val'$. Let $f : Val^+ \cup \{\tau\} \rightarrow Val^+ \cup \{\tau\}$ be defined $f(w) = \tau$ if $w \in Val$ and $f(w) = w$ otherwise. Let $+$ denote binary choice and let D be the constant with associated definition

$$D = x \in Val?(a!\mathbf{O} + x'!\mathbf{O} + \tau!D) + \sum_{v \in Val} v!(b!\mathbf{O} + v'!\mathbf{O} + \tau!D)$$

and let $C[\,\_\,]$ be the context $(\,\_\,|D)_{[f,Id]}$.

Let $\mathcal{S} = \{(R, S) \mid C[R] \sim_{barb} C[S], R, S : Val\}$, where $R : Val$ means that R is a closed term defined over the value set Val. We know that $(P, Q) \in \mathcal{S}$ by hypothesis and we leave it to the reader to show that $\mathcal{S}$ is a noisy bisimulation. □

The reader should note that this noisy bisimulation equivalence differs from the strong bisimulation equivalence proposed by Prasad in [9]. Unlike strong bisimulation it turns out that noisy bisimulation is not preserved by the choice operator. For example $x \in Val?\mathbf{O} \sim_n \mathbf{O}$ but $v!\mathbf{O} + x \in Val?\mathbf{O} \not\sim_n v!\mathbf{O} + \mathbf{O}$. However it can be easily modified to take choice contexts into account:

Definition 6. Let $P \simeq_n Q$ be given by

$$\begin{array}{l} \text{if } P \xrightarrow{w!} P' \text{ then } \exists Q'.Q \xrightarrow{w!} Q' \text{ and } P' \sim_n Q' \\ \text{if } P \xrightarrow{v?} P' \text{ then } \exists Q'.Q \xrightarrow{v?} Q' \text{ and } P' \sim_n Q'. \end{array}$$

We say that P and Q are *strong noisy congruent.*

Theorem 7. *$P \sim^c_{barb} Q$ if and only if $P \simeq_n Q$.* □

This theorem justifies our choice of $\simeq_n$ as the appropriate version of strong bisimulation equivalence for *CBS* and will be studied in the next section.

3 Characterising Strong Noisy Congruence over Simple Agents

In this section we give an algebraic characterisation of Strong Noisy Congruence over a simple class of finite agents. In fact we restrict our attention to closed terms of the simple language given by

$$T ::= \mathbf{O} \mid e!T \mid x \in S?T \mid b \gg T \mid T + T.$$

In order to obtain a finite language we have replaced the summation operator $\sum_I$ with the binary choice $+$. The extra *CBS* operators, parallel and the translation functions are dealt with via a translation into the simple language. This translation is an extension of that in [9]; details can be found in [5], Section 7. Let us use $\mathcal{SA}$ to denote the set of agents definable in this sub-language.

The axioms required to characterise strong bisimulation equivalence over *CCS* terms are simply the idempotency, symmetry and associativity of $+$ together with the fact that $\mathbf{O}$ is a zero for $+$; these we call $\mathcal{A}$. In the setting of *CBS* this is

EQUIV	$\dfrac{}{P=P}\quad \dfrac{P=Q}{Q=P}\quad \dfrac{P=Q\quad Q=R}{P=R}$
AXIOM	$\dfrac{P=Q\in\mathcal{AX}}{P\rho=Q\rho}$
CONG	$\dfrac{P_1=Q_1\quad P_2=Q_2}{P_1+P_2=Q_1+Q_2}$
α-CONV	$x\in S?T=y\in S?T[y/x]\quad y\notin fv(T)$
cl-INPUT	$\dfrac{\tau!T[v/x]+\tau!U[v/x]=\tau!U[v/x]\quad \text{for every } v\in S}{x\in S?T+x\in S?U=x\in S?U}$
OUTPUT	$\dfrac{P=Q,\ [\![e]\!]=[\![e']\!]}{[\![e]\!]!P=[\![e']\!]!Q}$
BOOL	$\dfrac{[\![b]\!]=\mathbf{tt}}{b\gg P=P}\quad \dfrac{[\![b]\!]=\mathbf{ff}}{b\gg P=\mathbf{O}}$

Fig. 2. Inference Rules

insufficient. For example if Q is any process which can discard all values in S then $Q+x\in S?Q\sim_n Q$ which in turn means that $v!(Q+x\in S?Q)\simeq_n v!Q$. This phenomenon can be captured by a new axiom scheme, *Noisy*:

$$\textit{Noisy:}\quad w!(P+x\in S?P)=w!P\quad \text{if } S\cap I(P)=\emptyset$$

where $I(P)$ is the set of values which P is ready to receive immediately. This set, $I(P)$ is defined inductively on terms.

- $I(\mathbf{O})=\emptyset$
- $I(e!P)=\emptyset$
- $I(x\in S?T)=S$
- $I(P+Q)=I(P)\cup I(Q)$
- $I(b\gg P)=\begin{cases} I(P) & \text{if } [\![b]\!]=\mathbf{tt}\\ \emptyset & \text{otherwise}\end{cases}$

Proposition 8. *For every agent P, $v\in I(P)$ if and only if $\exists Q\cdot P\xrightarrow{v?}Q$.* □

Two further axiom schema, which provide the capability to manipulate the pattern sets which guard inputs, are required for our characterisation. These are

Pattern: $x\in S?X+x\in S'?X=x\in S\cup S'?X$
Empty: $x\in\emptyset?X=\mathbf{O}$.

We use $\mathcal{A}_N$ to denote the set of equations $\mathcal{A}$ together with the axiom schemes *Noisy, Pattern* and *Empty.*

There is an added complication for *CBS* which also exists for standard value-passing process algebras, [3]. In a Σ-algebra the congruence generated by a set of equations is easily characterised in terms of substitution of equals for equals and the application of instances of the axioms. For agents in *CBS* more powerful rules are required. For although we can infer $v!P \simeq_n v!Q$ from $P \simeq_n Q$ it is not possible, in general, to infer $x \in S?T \simeq_n x \in S?U$ from any finite set of statements about agents; we can not require the establishment of $T \simeq_n U$ because these are open terms and the proof system only allows the manipulation of closed terms.

To overcome this problem, following [4], we introduce an infinitary proof rule: cl-INPUT, a form of absorption rule for inputs. In short, for agents in $\mathcal{SA}$, instead of considering the congruence generated by a set of axioms $\mathcal{AX}$ we consider the identities derivable in the proof system given in Figure 2.

For any agents P, Q let $\mathcal{A}_N \vdash P = Q$ mean that $P = Q$ can be derived in this proof system from the axioms $\mathcal{A}_N$.

Theorem 9. *(Soundness and Completeness)*

$$\mathcal{A}_N \vdash P = Q \textit{ if and only if } P \simeq_n Q.$$

4 Observational Congruence

In this section we follow the programme of the previous section but consider τ as an unobservable (inaudible) action. We define the familar notion of a *weak* move using the operational semantics of Figure 1. Weak moves, $\xrightarrow{\tau!}{}^{*}\xrightarrow{\alpha}\xrightarrow{\tau!}{}^{*}$, are written as $\stackrel{\alpha}{\Longrightarrow}$ where $\alpha \in \{\varepsilon, w!, v?, w:\}$. We will occasionally use the notation $P \stackrel{\tau!\alpha}{\Longrightarrow} Q$ to mean $P \stackrel{\tau!}{\Longrightarrow}\stackrel{\alpha}{\Longrightarrow} Q$, and we will define $\hat{\alpha}$ to be ε when $\alpha = \tau!$ and α otherwise.

Once again we use the technique of barbed bisimulations [11] to provide us with our notion of weak bisimulation. This method provided a novel version of strong bisimulation called noisy bisimulation and it transpires that the congruence associated with weak barbed bisimulation will be characterised by the corresponding weak version of noisy bisimulation.

Definition 10. A symmetric relation $\mathcal{R}$ between agents is called a *weak barbed bisimulation* if $(P, Q) \in \mathcal{R}$ implies

- If $P \xrightarrow{\tau!} P'$ then $\exists Q' \cdot Q \stackrel{\varepsilon}{\Longrightarrow} Q'$ and $(P'.Q') \in R$
- For each $v \in Val$, if $P \downarrow v$ then $\exists Q' \cdot Q \stackrel{\varepsilon}{\Longrightarrow} Q'$ with $Q \downarrow v$.

We write $P \approx_{barb} Q$ if there exists a weak barbed bisimulation containing (P, Q).

It is easy to see that $\approx_{barb}$ is preserved by few of the operators of CBS so we focus on the congruence generated by this relation:

Definition 11. For agents P and Q let $P \cong_{barb} Q$ if $C[P] \approx_{barb} C[Q]$ for every CBS context $C[\_]$.

We aim to characterise this relation as a weakened version of noisy bisimulation.

Definition 12. A symmetric relation $\mathcal{R}$ is called a weak bisimulation if $(P, Q) \in \mathcal{R}$ implies

- If $P \xrightarrow{w!} P'$ then $\exists Q' \cdot Q \stackrel{\hat{w}!}{\Longrightarrow} Q'$ and $(P', Q') \in \mathcal{R}$.
- If $P \xrightarrow{v??} P'$ then $\exists Q' \cdot Q \stackrel{v??}{\Longrightarrow} Q'$ and $(P', Q') \in \mathcal{R}$.

We write $P \approx Q$ if there exists a weak bisimulation $\mathcal{R}$ such that $(P, Q) \in \mathcal{R}$.

This is the definition of weak bisimulation proposed in [9] and the presentation here justifies this choice of definition. In Proposition 3 we proved that discard need not be taken into account when defining noisy bisimulation. Unfortunately the same is not true for weak bisimulation in CBS. To illustrate this suppose that $\approx'$ is the largest of the symmetric relations $\mathcal{R}$ such that $(P, Q) \in \mathcal{R}$ implies

- If $P \xrightarrow{w!} P'$ then $\exists Q' \cdot Q \stackrel{\hat{w}!}{\Longrightarrow} Q'$ and $(P', Q') \in \mathcal{R}$.
- If $P \xrightarrow{v?} P'$ then $\exists Q' \cdot Q \stackrel{v??}{\Longrightarrow} Q'$ and $(P', Q') \in \mathcal{R}$.

Then it is easy to see that $\tau!P \approx' P$ for any agent P although $\tau!P$ is not in general weakly bisimilar to P. A counter-example to illustrate this is

$$\tau!x \in Val?x!\mathbf{O} \not\approx x \in Val?x!\mathbf{O}.$$

This is because the agent $\tau!x \in Val?x!\mathbf{O} \xrightarrow{v:} \tau!x \in Val?x!\mathbf{O}$ for any value $v \in Val$. In order to match this move the agent $x \in Val?x!\mathbf{O}$ must perform a reception, i.e. $x \in Val?x!\mathbf{O} \xrightarrow{v?} v!\mathbf{O}$ and the resulting processes are not weakly bisimilar. The counter-example also serves to show that $\approx'$ is not preserved by parallel composition, by using the context $v!v'!\mathbf{O} \| [\,\_\,]$ for $v \neq v'$. In fact the relation obtained by closing $\approx'$ under parallel composition coincides with $\approx$.

Proposition 13. $\approx$ *is congruent with respect to all of the CBS operators except summation.* □

We now show that it is possible to obtain this definition of weak bisimulation by considering barbed bisimulations in static contexts, that is contexts in which the hole does not appear as a summand in a choice.

Proposition 14. *If* $C[P] \approx_{barb} C[Q]$ *for every static context* $C[\,\_\,]$ *then* $P \approx Q$. □

Proof. We use a similar technique to that for the strong case, that is using the translation functions to translate all strong broadcasts into τ-moves and using renaming to preserve the barbs. There are added complications with matching τ-moves which are dealt with in the same manner as [11]. □

As one might expect the relation $\approx$ is not a congruence for CBS owing to the fact that it is not preserved by the summation operator. This fact is ascribed to the so called *pre-emptive* power of τ to resolve choices [7]. In CCS we define observational congruence as the largest congruence relation strictly contained in weak bisimulation and a characterisation of this observational congruence tells us that for two agents P and Q to be related any τ move from P must be matched by *at least one* τ move from Q. That is, for every possible choice made by one agent, then at least one choice must be made by the other agent and vice-versa. This helps in understanding the following definition.

Definition 15. We define observational congruence $\cong$ to be the symmetric relation for which, $P \cong Q$ implies

- If $P \xrightarrow{w!} P'$ then $\exists Q'.Q \stackrel{w!}{\Longrightarrow} Q'$ and $P' \approx Q'$
- If $P \xrightarrow{v?} P'$ then $\exists Q'.Q \stackrel{v?}{\Longrightarrow} Q'$ and $P' \approx Q'$
  or $Q \stackrel{\tau!v:}{\Longrightarrow} Q'$ and $P' \approx Q'$
- If $P \xrightarrow{v:} P$ then $Q \xrightarrow{v:} Q$

Theorem 16. *$P \cong_{barb} Q$ if and only if $P \cong Q$.* □

5 Characterising Observational Congruence over Finite Agents

We present an algebraic characterisation of observational congruence over the class $\mathcal{SA}$. Because noisy congruence is strictly contained in observational congruence it is clear that we will require the axioms $\mathcal{A}_N$ for our present characterisation. In addition to these axioms we require analogies of the tau laws of CCS:

A1 $\alpha.\tau.P =_{ccs} \alpha.P$.
A2 $\alpha.(P + \tau.Q) + \alpha.Q =_{ccs} \alpha.(P + \tau.Q)$.
A3 $P + \tau.P =_{ccs} \tau.P$.

The natural versions of *A1* and *A3* for CBS are unsound; we have already seen, for example, that $\tau!P$ is not, in general, weakly bisimilar to P. For *A3* we run into difficulties when P is allowed to receive any value v, say. For then $\tau!P$ may discard v but $P + \tau!P$ is obliged to receive it. We adopt admissible versions of these axioms. *A1* simply becomes

$Tau1 : e!(\tau!X + X) = e!X$,

A2 is adapted to

$Tau2 : \alpha.(X + \tau!Y) + \alpha.Y = \alpha.(X + \tau!Y)$,

and *A3* splits into two axiom schemes[3]

$Tau3 : X + x \in S?Z + \tau!(Y + x \in S?Z) = X + \tau!(Y + x \in S?Z)$ if $S \subseteq I(X)$

and

$Tau4 : e!X + \tau!(Y + e!X) = \tau!(Y + e!X)$.

Note that a version of *Tau1* for input prefixes is also sound but is derivable using the rule cl-INPUT.

We denote the set of axioms $\mathcal{A}_N$ together with the *Tau* axioms listed above by $\mathcal{A}_{N\tau}$. It is a simple matter to check that each axiom in $\mathcal{A}_{N\tau}$ is indeed sound with respect to observational congruence. For agents P, Q let $\mathcal{A}_{N\tau} \vdash P = Q$ mean that $P = Q$ can be derived from the axioms $\mathcal{A}_{N\tau}$ using the rules in Figure 2.

3 It is possible, for present purposes, to give these two as a single axiom scheme though to be consistent with the sequel we use two.

Theorem 17. *(Soundness) For all agents P and Q,*

$$\mathcal{A}_{N\tau} \vdash P = Q \text{ implies } P \cong Q.$$

The remainder of this section deals with the proof of the converse of this, completeness. The exposition of this completeness proof will require,as usual, a notion of a standard form.

We say a closed term is in *standard form* if it has the form

$$\sum_{i \in I_!} e_i!T_i + \sum_{i \in I_?} x_i \in S_i?T_i$$

for some finite indexing sets $I_!$ and $I_?$ such that S_i is non-empty for each $i \in I_?$. Furthermore we call a standard form, P, a *saturated standard form* if

(i) $P \stackrel{w!}{\Longrightarrow} P'$ implies $P \stackrel{w!}{\longrightarrow} P'$.
(ii) $v \in I(P)$ and $P \stackrel{v?}{\Longrightarrow} P'$ implies $P \stackrel{v?}{\longrightarrow}\stackrel{\varepsilon}{\Longrightarrow} P'$.
(iii) $v \in I(P)$ and $P \stackrel{\tau!v;}{\Longrightarrow} P'$ implies $P \stackrel{v?}{\longrightarrow} P'$.

Lemma 18. *For any agent $P \in \mathcal{SA}$ there exists a standard form $sf(P)$ such that $\mathcal{A}_N \vdash P = sf(P)$.*

Lemma 19. *(Derivation Lemma) For any agent $P \in \mathcal{SA}$, $P \stackrel{w!}{\Longrightarrow} Q$ implies $\mathcal{A}_{N\tau} \vdash P = P + w!P$.*

Proof. By induction on the length of the derivation $P \stackrel{w!}{\Longrightarrow} Q$ using the axioms $Tau2$ and $Tau4$.

Proposition 20. *Given any agent $P \in \mathcal{SA}$, there exists a saturated standard form $\hat{P}$ such that $d(P) \leq d(\hat{P})$ and $\mathcal{A}_{N\tau} \vdash P = \hat{P}$, where $d(P)$ denotes the usual notion of depth of a term.* □

We now prove an analogue of the decomposition theorem of CCS, i.e.

$$P \approx_{ccs} Q \text{ iff } P \cong_{ccs} Q \text{ or } P \cong_{ccs} \tau.Q \text{ or } \tau.P \cong_{ccs} Q.$$

Recall that, in CBS, not only does $\tau!$ have pre-emptive power but so has reception of values. This property manifests itself in noisy bisimulation not being preserved by choice and in [5] we present an analogue of the decomposition theorem which relates noisy bisimulation and noisy congruence. What we require here then is a happy combination of the decomposition theorems of [7] and [5].

Theorem 21. *(Decomposition) Let $S = I(Q) - I(P)$ and $S' = I(P) - I(Q)$.*
$P \approx Q$ iff one of the following holds:

(i) $P + x \in S?P \cong Q + x \in S'?Q$
and when S and S' are both non-empty there exist P', Q' such that $d(P') < d(P)$, $d(Q) < d(Q')$ and $P' \approx P, Q' \approx Q$.
(ii) $P + x \in S?P + \tau!P \cong Q + x \in S'?Q$
and when S' is non-empty there exist P', Q' such that $d(P') < d(P)$, $d(Q') < d(Q)$ and $P' \approx P$, $Q' \approx Q$.

(iii) $P + x \in S?P \cong Q + x \in S'?Q + \tau!Q$
and when S *is non-empty there exist* P', Q' *such that* $d(P') < d(P)$, $d(Q') < d(Q)$ *and* $P' \approx P$, $Q' \approx Q$. □

Theorem 22. *(Completeness) For all agents* P, Q

$$P \cong Q \text{ implies } \mathcal{A}_{N\tau} \vdash P = Q.$$

Proof. The proof is by induction on the combined depth of P and Q.

Because of Lemma 20 we can assume that P and Q can be transformed to saturated standard forms

$$\sum_I e_i!P_i + \sum_J x \in S_j?T_j, \quad \sum_K e_k!Q_k + \sum_L x \in S_l?U_l$$

respectively. It is sufficient to prove that each summand of P can be absorbed by a summand of Q and vice-versa. As an example we consider an arbitrary $j \in J$ and show that

$$\mathcal{A}_{N\tau} \vdash x \in S_j?T_j + \sum_L x \in S_l?U_l = \sum_L x \in S_l?U_l.$$

For each $v \in S_j$ we know that $P \xrightarrow{v?} T_j[v/x]$. This means $v \in I(P)$ and, since $P \cong Q$, then $v \in I(Q)$. We know that $Q \xrightarrow{v?} U_l[v/x] \overset{\varepsilon}{\Longrightarrow} Q_l^v$ for some $l \in L$ such that $v \in S_l$ and $T_j[v/x] \approx Q_l^v$ because $P \cong Q$ and Q is saturated. Let $S_l^j = \{v \in S_j \cap S_l \mid U_l[v/x] \approx T_j[v/x]\}$. This gives a *finite* partition $\{S_l^j\}_{l \in L}$ of S_j such that $S_l^j \subseteq S_l$ for each $l \in L$. Then, by the idempotency of + and the new axiom *Pattern* it is sufficient to show for each $l \in L$ that

$$\mathcal{A}_{N\tau} \vdash x \in S_l^j?T_j + x \in S_l^j?U_l = x \in S_l^j?U_l.$$

This can be inferred from the rule cl-INPUT if we can prove for each $v \in S_l^j$

$$\mathcal{A}_{N\tau} \vdash \tau!T_j[v/x] + \tau!U_l[v/x] = \tau!U_l[v/x].$$

So let us fix a particular $v \in S_l^j$ and see how this can be inferred. We know that $T_j[v/x] \approx Q_l^v$ so from this we will show that

$$\mathcal{A}_{N\tau} \vdash \tau!T_j[v/x] = \tau!Q_l^v$$

and the result will follow by the Derivation Lemma and *Tau*2.

For convenience let P, Q denote $T_j[v/x]$, Q_l^v respectively. We now apply Theorem 21 to get one of three possibilities

(i) $P + x \in U?P \cong Q + x \in V?Q$
(ii) $P + x \in U?P + \tau!P \cong Q + x \in V?Q$
(iii) $P + x \in U?P \cong Q + x \in V?Q + \tau!Q$

where $U = I(Q) - I(P)$ and $V = I(P) - I(Q)$. We show how to deal with case (iii) and leave cases (i) and (ii) to the reader. We have two eventualities to consider.

1. $U = \emptyset$
   Here we have $P \cong Q + x \in V?Q + \tau!Q$ and we can use induction to obtain $\mathcal{A}_{N\tau} \vdash \tau!P = \tau!(Q + x \in V?Q + \tau!Q)$. Now we can apply the *Noisy* scheme to obtain
   $$\mathcal{A}_{N\tau} \vdash \tau!P = \tau!(Q + x \in V?Q + \tau!(Q + x \in V?Q))$$
   from which $\mathcal{A}_{N\tau} \vdash \tau!P = \tau!(Q+x \in V?Q)$ follows by *Tau1*. Another application of *Noisy* gives the required result.
2. $U \neq \emptyset$
   Here we have $P+x \in U?P \cong Q+x \in V?Q+\tau!Q$ and in this case we cannot apply induction immediately as the combined depth of the terms has not decreased. But Theorem 21 tells us that there exists P', Q' such that $d(P') < d(P)$ and $d(Q') < d(Q)$ such that $P' \approx P$ and $Q' \approx Q$. Suppose without loss of generality that $d(P) \leq d(Q)$. Then, since $\tau!P \cong \tau!P'$, we can use induction to obtain $\mathcal{A}_{N\tau} \vdash \tau!P = \tau!P'$. A simple application of the cl-INPUT rule gives $\mathcal{A}_{N\tau} \vdash x \in U?P = x \in U?P'$. This in turn implies that $P + x \in U?P' \cong Q + x \in V?Q + \tau!Q$ and here we can apply induction since the combined size has decreased. So we obtain
   $$\mathcal{A}_{N\tau} \vdash \tau!(P + x \in U?P') = \tau!(Q + x \in V?Q + \tau!Q).$$
   Using the fact that $\mathcal{A}_{N\tau} \vdash x \in U?P = x \in U?P'$ we get
   $$\mathcal{A}_{N\tau} \vdash \tau!(P + x \in U?P) = \tau!(Q + x \in V?Q + \tau!Q)$$
   from which the required $\mathcal{A}_{N\tau} \vdash \tau!P = \tau!Q$ follows by applications of the *Noisy* and *Tau1* axioms. □

6 A Finitary Proof System

We now show that the proof system of the previous section can be improved upon by removing infinitary inference rules. The proof system we develop is for observational congruence over open terms of the finite sub-language presented in Section 3. It follows closely the corresponding proof systems given in [3].

The judgements of the proof system are now decorated with boolean expressions:
$$b \rhd T = U$$
and intuitively this is meant to denote that $T\rho \cong U\rho$ for every evaluation ρ such that $\rho(b) = \mathbf{tt}$. The inference rules for the proof system, save for the INPUT rule, are those of [3] and are presented in Figure 3. We also borrow the notation $\rho \models b$ to mean $[\![b\rho]\!] = \mathbf{tt}$ and $b \models b'$ to mean that $\rho \models b$ implies $\rho \models b'$.

We use more or less the same equations as in the proof system for closed terms. There are two exceptions, *Noisy* and *Tau3*. These are in fact axiom schemes and are defined in terms of the sets $I(P)$ for closed expressions P. In order to generalise these axiom schemes to open terms we need to extend the function I to open terms. We follow the approach taken in [5] and relativise it to a boolean world, defining $I(b, T)$, the set of values which the term T may receive when T is instantiated as an agent by an evaluation ρ such that $\rho \models b$. Moreover we give a syntactic definition of $I(b, T)$ for a subclass of terms T.

EQUIV	$\dfrac{}{\mathbf{tt} \rhd T = T} \quad \dfrac{b \rhd T = U}{b \rhd U = T} \quad \dfrac{b \rhd T = U \quad b \rhd U = V}{b \rhd T = V}$
AXIOM	$\dfrac{T = U \in \mathcal{AX}}{\mathbf{tt} \rhd T\rho = U\rho}$
CONG	$\dfrac{b \rhd T_1 = U_1 \quad b \rhd T_2 = U_2}{b \rhd T_1 + T_2 = U_1 + U_2}$
α-CONV	$\mathbf{tt} \rhd x \in S?T = y \in S?T[y/x] \quad y \notin fv(T)$
INPUT	$\dfrac{b \wedge x \in S \rhd \tau!T + \tau!U = \tau!U}{b \rhd x \in S?T + x \in S?U = x \in S?U}$ if $x \notin fv(b)$
OUTPUT	$\dfrac{b \models e = e' \quad b \rhd T = U}{b \rhd e!T = e'!U}$
TAU	$\dfrac{b \rhd T = U}{b \rhd \tau!T = \tau!U}$
GUARD	$\dfrac{b \wedge b' \rhd T = U \quad b \wedge \neg b' \rhd \mathbf{O} = U}{b \rhd b' \gg T = U}$
CUT	$\dfrac{b \models b_1 \vee b_2 \quad b_1 \rhd T = U \quad b_2 \rhd T = U}{b \rhd T = U}$
ABSURD	$\mathbf{ff} \rhd T = U$

Fig. 3. Inference Rules

We call an open term T a standard form if

$$T \equiv \sum_{i \in I_!} b_i \gg e_i!T_i + \sum_{i \in I_?} b_i \gg x \in S_i?T_i$$

for some finite indexing sets $I_!, I_?$ such that each S_i is non-empty. Given a boolean expression b we say that b is *T-uniform* if there exists a set $K \subseteq I_?$ such that $b \models b_K$ where b_K is defined by

$$\bigwedge_{i \in K} b_i \wedge \bigwedge_{i' \in I_? - K} \neg b_{i'}.$$

The syntactic definition of $I(b, T)$ is

$$I(b, T) = \bigcup \{S_i \mid i \in I_?,\ b \models b_i\}.$$

The following Lemma shows that this is a reasonable definition:

Lemma 23. *If b is T-uniform then $\rho \models b$ implies $I(T\rho) = I(b, T)$.* □

Given this it is a simple matter to adapt axioms *Noisy* and *Tau3*,

Op-Noisy: $b \rhd e!(T + x \in S?T) = e!T$
if $x \notin fv(T)$, b is T-uniform and $S \cap I(b,T) = \emptyset$,

Op-Tau3: $b \rhd T + x \in S?Z + \tau!(Y + x \in S?Z) = T + \tau!(Y + x \in S?Z)$
if b is T-uniform and $S \subseteq I(b,T)$.

We let $\mathcal{A}_N^{op}$ denote the axioms $\mathcal{A}$ together with axiom *Op-Noisy, Pattern*, and *Empty* and we let $\mathcal{A}_{N\tau}^{op}$ denote $\mathcal{A}_N^{op}$ together with the axioms *Tau1, Tau2, Op-Tau3, Tau4*. Then $\mathcal{A}_N^{op} \vdash b \rhd T = U$ will mean that $b \rhd T = U$ can be derived using the inference rules in Figure 3 from axioms in $\mathcal{A}_N^{op}$ and likewise for $\mathcal{A}_{N\tau}^{op} \vdash b \rhd T = U$.

Theorem 24. *(Soundness and Completeness)*

(i) $(\forall \rho \cdot \rho \models b$ *implies* $T\rho \simeq_n U\rho)$ *iff* $\mathcal{A}_N^{op} \vdash b \rhd T = U$
(ii) $(\forall \rho \cdot \rho \models b$ *implies* $T\rho \cong U\rho)$ *iff* $\mathcal{A}_{N\tau}^{op} \vdash b \rhd T = U$ □

The proof of this theorem relies heavily upon the use of symbolic bisimulations [2]. Symbolic bisimulations appropriate to CBS have been developed in [5, 6] and detailed accounts of the proof of Theorem 24 may be found there.

References

1. E. Best, editor. *Proceedings CONCUR 93*, Hildesheim, volume 715 of *Lecture Notes in Computer Science*. Springer-Verlag, 1993.
2. M. Hennessy and H. Lin. Symbolic bisimulations. Technical Report 1/92, University of Sussex, 1992.
3. M. Hennessy and H. Lin. Proof systems for message-passing process algebras. In Best [1], pages 202–216.
4. M. Hennessy and G.D. Plotkin. A term model for CCS. In P. Dembiński, editor, 9th *Symposium on Mathematical Foundations of Computer Science*, volume 88 of *Lecture Notes in Computer Science*, pages 261–274. Springer-Verlag, 1980.
5. M. Hennessy and J. Rathke. Strong bisimulations for a calculus of broadcasting systems. Computer Science Report 1/95, University of Sussex, 1995.
6. M. Hennessy and J. Rathke. Weak bisimulations for a calculus of broadcasting systems. Computer Science Report 3/95, University of Sussex, 1995.
7. R. Milner. *Communication and Concurrency*. Prentice-Hall International, Englewood Cliffs, 1989.
8. K.V.S. Prasad. A calculus of broadcast systems. In *TAPSOFT 91 Volume 1: CAAP*. Springer Verlag, 1991.
9. K.V.S. Prasad. A calculus of value broadcasts. Technical report, Dept. of Computer Science, Chalmers, 1992.
10. K.V.S. Prasad. Programming with broadcasts. In Best [1].
11. D. Sangiorgi. *Expressing Mobility in Process Algebras: First-Order and Higher-Order Paradigms*. PhD thesis, University of Edinburgh, 1993.
12. Martin Weichert. Algebra of communicating systems. In *Wintermötet Tanum Strand, draft proceedings*, 1993.

Delayed choice for process algebra with abstraction

P. R. D'Argenio[1] and S. Mauw[2]

[1] Depto. de Informática, Fac. de Cs. Exactas, Universidad Nacional de La Plata. CC 11 (1900) La Plata. Buenos Aires. Argentina.
pedro@info.unlp.edu.ar

[2] Dept. of Mathematics and Computing Science, Eindhoven University of Technology, P.O. Box 513, 5600 MB Eindhoven, The Netherlands.
sjouke@win.tue.nl

Abstract. The delayed choice is an operator which serves to combine linear time and branching time within one process algebra. We study this operator in a theory with abstraction, more precisely, in a setting considering branching bisimulation. We show its use in scenario specifications and in verification to reduce irrelevant branching structure of a process.

1 Introduction

The delayed choice is an operator that allows one to express linear time aspects in a branching time process algebra. It was introduced in [3] for a basic process algebra without abstraction. The intuition behind this operator for alternative composition is the following. If two processes start with a common initial action, then the delayed choice between these alternatives consists of executing this common action before making the choice between the resulting processes. This property is best displayed in the following equation. The delayed choice is denoted by $\mp$ (for Trace-+) and the normal non-deterministic choice by $+$.

$$ab \mp ac = a(b + c)$$

If the two alternatives have no initial action in common, the delayed choice and the non-deterministic choice coincide ($a \neq c$):

$$ab \mp cd = ab + cd$$

In [3] soundness and completeness of the definition was proven and an application in the realm of Message Sequence Charts was given.

In this paper we study the delayed choice operator in a process algebra theory extended with abstraction. In this setting, the delayed choice operator should also remove non-determinism due to internal steps. This property can be expressed as follows:

$$\tau a \mp b = \tau(a + b)$$

The behaviour of the delayed choice operator with respect to internal steps compares well to the behaviour of the deterministic choice operator $\Box$ from

TCSP [8]. This operator was studied in a branching time setting in [9], where it was called τ-angelic choice.

The main purpose of this paper is to show that the definition of the delayed choice operator can be combined with the definition of the τ-angelic choice operator in order to obtain a delayed choice operator for process algebra with abstraction.

We use branching bisimulation [11] as the semantics for the silent step. We consider divergence free processes only. The case of weak bisimulation is treated in [10].

Applications of this new operator can be found in the areas of specification and verification. Using the delayed choice it is possible to make so-called *scenario specifications*. A scenario specification consists of a collection of possible behaviours of a system. If two scenarios share an initial action, it is in general not the intention to specify a non-deterministic choice between these scenarios. For example, a possible scenario for a vending machine could be the insertion of a coin followed by choosing coffee and another scenario could be the insertion of a coin followed by choosing tea. The intention is not to express that the choice between coffee and tea is made by inserting the coin, which is the interpretation when combining these scenarios with a non-deterministic choice. Rather it is to express that the selection is made after paying. This can be expressed with the delayed choice.

The second application of the delayed choice operator is in verification. A verification in process algebra in most cases consists of a proof that an abstraction of some implementation specification is equivalent to a given requirements specification. Often the structure of such a requirements specification is quite complex due to the presence of an excess of internal choices, some of which may not be relevant for the insight that the implementation is correct. These less interesting choices between internal actions can be filtered out using the delayed choice, without adopting linear time semantics for the complete system. We give an example in Sect. 4.

This paper is structured as follows. In Sect. 2 we introduce the basic theory $\mathrm{BPA}_{\delta\varepsilon}$ and extend it with the silent step τ. We consider strong bisimulation and branching bisimulation as semantics. Next, we define the delayed choice operator and give an operational semantics in Sect. 3. We prove soundness, completeness and several other properties. Finally, we give some examples in Sect. 4.

We thank Jos Baeten and Michel Reniers for their valuable comments on drafts of this paper and Rob van Glabbeek for answering some technical questions. Jan Joris Vereijken was very helpful in doing calculations on the examples.

2 Basic Process Algebra with Empty Process

The aim of this section is to introduce the algebra of sequential processes [5]. We deal with the basic process algebra with empty process for concrete processes ($\mathrm{BPA}_{\delta\varepsilon}$) [6, 15] and with abstraction in the framework of branching bisimulation ($\mathrm{BPA}^{\tau}_{\delta\varepsilon}$) [11].

2.1 The Equational Theories

The signature of the several theories is parameterized by a set of constants $A = \{a, b, \ldots\}$ called *atomic actions*. There are three distinguished constants not belonging to A. They are δ, called *deadlock* or inaction, that denotes the process that has stopped executing actions and cannot proceed; ε, the *empty process*, that denotes the process that does nothing but terminate successfully; and τ, the *silent action*, that is a special action having the meaning of internal activity. Besides, the signature has two binary operators: the *alternative composition* ($+$) which, in $x + y$, executes process x or y, but not both; and the *sequential composition* ($\cdot$) that, given $x \cdot y$, first executes x and, upon completion, starts with the execution of y. We generally omit this operator writing xy instead of $x \cdot y$. Besides, we assume that $\cdot$ binds stronger than all the other operators we will deal with, and $+$ binds weaker. Notice that the signature of $\mathrm{BPA}_{\delta\varepsilon}$ also includes the silent action τ. It is dealt with as any other action in $\mathrm{BPA}_{\delta\varepsilon}$. Equations A1–A9 from Table 1 define $\mathrm{BPA}_{\delta\varepsilon}$. Adding axiom BE, we obtain $\mathrm{BPA}^{\tau}_{\delta\varepsilon}$.

Table 1. Axioms for $\mathrm{BPA}_{\delta\varepsilon}$ and $\mathrm{BPA}^{\tau}_{\delta\varepsilon}$.

A1 $x + y = y + x$	A6 $x + \delta = x$
A2 $(x + y) + z = x + (y + z)$	A7 $\delta x = \delta$
A3 $x + x = x$	
A4 $(x + y)z = xz + yz$	A8 $x\varepsilon = x$
A5 $(xy)z = x(yz)$	A9 $\varepsilon x = x$
BE $a(\tau(x + y) + x) = a(x + y)$	

2.2 Structured Operational Semantics and Equivalences

Table 2 defines the operational semantics in a structured way following the style of [17]. In our system we consider two kinds of predicates, each one having its own meaning. Predicate $\downarrow$ expresses that a process may terminate successfully. For every action $a \in A \cup \{\tau\}$, predicate $\xrightarrow{a}$ expresses that the first argument can perform action a and become the second argument. In addition, we define $\Longrightarrow$ as the reflexive transitive closure of $\xrightarrow{\tau}$.

Table 2. Operational semantics for the basic operators ($a \in A \cup \{\tau\}$)

$$\varepsilon\downarrow \qquad \frac{x\downarrow}{x + y\downarrow \quad y + x\downarrow} \qquad \frac{x\downarrow \quad y\downarrow}{x \cdot y\downarrow}$$

$$a \xrightarrow{a} \varepsilon \qquad \frac{x \xrightarrow{a} x'}{x + y \xrightarrow{a} x' \quad y + x \xrightarrow{a} x'} \qquad \frac{x \xrightarrow{a} x'}{x \cdot y \xrightarrow{a} x' \cdot y} \qquad \frac{x\downarrow \quad y \xrightarrow{a} y'}{x \cdot y \xrightarrow{a} y'}$$

In this paper we will deal with divergence free processes only. This means that a process cannot perform an infinite sequence of τ-steps.

Let $\mathcal{T}$ be the set of all closed terms in the signature of $\mathrm{BPA}_{\delta\varepsilon}$. Next, we define two well known equivalences over $\mathcal{T}$.

Definition 1 (Bisimulation). [16] A *(strong) bisimulation* is a symmetric relation $S \subseteq \mathcal{T} \times \mathcal{T}$ satisfying, for all $a \in A \cup \{\tau\}$:

if pSq and $p \xrightarrow{a} p'$, then $\exists q' \in \mathcal{T} : q \xrightarrow{a} q'$ and $p'Sq'$; and
if pSq then $p\downarrow$ iff $q\downarrow$.

Two processes p and q are *bisimilar* (notation $p \underline{\leftrightarrow} q$), if there exists a bisimulation S with pSq.

Definition 2 (Branching bisimulation). [11] A *branching bisimulation* is a symmetric relation $S \subseteq \mathcal{T} \times \mathcal{T}$ satisfying, for all $a \in A \cup \{\tau\}$:

$$\text{if } pSq \text{ and } p \xrightarrow{a} p', \text{ then } \begin{cases} a = \tau \text{ and } p'Sq, \text{ or} \\ \exists q'', q' \in \mathcal{T} : q \Longrightarrow q'' \xrightarrow{a} q' \text{ and } pSq'' \wedge p'Sq'; \textit{and} \end{cases}$$

if pSq and $p\downarrow$, then $\exists q' \in \mathcal{T} : q \Longrightarrow q' \downarrow$ and pSq'.

Two processes p and q are *branching bisimilar* (notation $p \underline{\leftrightarrow}_b q$), if there exists a branching bisimulation S with pSq.

Two processes p and q are *rooted branching bisimilar*, (notation $p \underline{\leftrightarrow}_{rb} q$) if for all $a \in A \cup \{\tau\}$:

1. $p \xrightarrow{a} p'$ implies $\exists q' : q \xrightarrow{a} q'$ and $p' \underline{\leftrightarrow}_b q'$;
2. $q \xrightarrow{a} q'$ implies $\exists p' : p \xrightarrow{a} p'$ and $p' \underline{\leftrightarrow}_b q'$;
3. $p\downarrow$ iff $q\downarrow$.

The relations above are ordered by set inclusion: $\underline{\leftrightarrow} \subset \underline{\leftrightarrow}_{rb} \subset \underline{\leftrightarrow}_b$. We have:

Theorem 3 (The term models).

1. *$\mathcal{T}/\underline{\leftrightarrow}$ is a model for $\mathrm{BPA}_{\delta\varepsilon}$. $\mathrm{BPA}_{\delta\varepsilon}$ is a complete axiomatization for $\mathcal{T}/\underline{\leftrightarrow}$.*
2. *$\mathcal{T}/\underline{\leftrightarrow}_{rb}$ is a model for $\mathrm{BPA}^{\tau}_{\delta\varepsilon}$. $\mathrm{BPA}^{\tau}_{\delta\varepsilon}$ is a complete axiomatization for $\mathcal{T}/\underline{\leftrightarrow}_{rb}$.*

3 The Delayed Choice

3.1 Equational Theory

The delayed choice considered here is an extension of the operator introduced in [3]. The difference is that we also consider abstraction. The delayed choice ($\mp$) between processes x and y, is the process obtained by joining the observable common initial parts of x and y and continuing with a normal choice between the remaining parts. In case internal activity is performed, the choice is delayed in the same way the τ-angelic choice [9] does. Thus, after executing an internal step of x the alternatives from y are still enabled, and vice versa. However, the nondeterministic choices which are internal to x or y, are not removed. This is expressed in the definition of the delayed choice in Table 3.

The definition of the delayed choice has five cases. We use three auxiliary operators. The first one is the join operator ($\bowtie$). $x \bowtie y$ selects exactly those summands of x and y having a common initial action which is observable (i.e. different from τ). The unless operator ($\triangleleft$) works exactly in the opposite way. In $x \triangleleft y$, only those summands of x having an initial observable action are selected for which y does not have any summand with the same initial action or with an initial silent action. Note that summands of x having an initial silent step are not selected. The τ-selecting operator ($\sqsubset$) delays the choice in case of silent actions, i.e., $x \sqsubset y$ selects the summands of x having an initial silent action.

Thus, the axioms in Table 3 extend $BPA_{\delta\varepsilon}$ and $BPA^{\tau}_{\delta\varepsilon}$ with the delayed choice and the auxiliary operators. We denote these extensions by $BPA_{\delta\varepsilon} + DC$ and $BPA^{\tau}_{\delta\varepsilon} + DC$.

Table 3. Axioms for delayed choice ($a, b \in A$)

DC	$x \mp y = x \bowtie y + x \triangleleft y + y \triangleleft x + x \sqsubset y + y \sqsubset x$		
J1	$\varepsilon \bowtie x = \delta$	U1	$\varepsilon \triangleleft \varepsilon = \varepsilon$
J2	$x \bowtie \varepsilon = \delta$	U2	$\varepsilon \triangleleft ax = \varepsilon$
J3	$\delta \bowtie x = \delta$	U3	$ax \triangleleft \varepsilon = ax$
J4	$x \bowtie \delta = \delta$	U4	$\delta \triangleleft x = \delta$
J5	$ax \bowtie ay = a(x \mp y)$	U5	$\varepsilon \triangleleft \delta = \varepsilon$
J6	$a \neq b \Rightarrow ax \bowtie by = \delta$	U6	$ax \triangleleft \delta = ax$
J7	$(x + y) \bowtie z = x \bowtie z + y \bowtie z$	U7	$ax \triangleleft ay = \delta$
J8	$x \bowtie (y + z) = x \bowtie y + x \bowtie z$	U8	$a \neq b \Rightarrow ax \triangleleft by = ax$
		U9	$(x + y) \triangleleft z = x \triangleleft z + y \triangleleft z$
		U10	$x \triangleleft (y + z) = (x \triangleleft y) \triangleleft z$
TJ1	$\tau x \bowtie y = \delta$	TS1	$\varepsilon \sqsubset x = \delta$
TJ2	$x \bowtie \tau y = \delta$	TS2	$\delta \sqsubset x = \delta$
		TS3	$ax \sqsubset y = \delta$
TU1	$\tau x \triangleleft y = \delta$	TS4	$\tau x \sqsubset y = \tau(x \mp y)$
TU2	$x \triangleleft \tau y = \delta$	TS5	$(x + y) \sqsubset z = x \sqsubset z + y \sqsubset z$

Operators $\bowtie$, $\triangleleft$ and $\sqsubset$ are needed for a finite axiomatization. The unless operator $\triangleleft$ is quite similar to the one used in the axiomatization of the priority operator [2], but our version filters according to equality instead of an ordering on observable actions. The τ-selecting operator $\sqsubset$ works in a similar way as the left box of [9] when dealing with summands starting with τ, but instead, our operator does not select summands having an initially observable action.

Example 1. We give some simple examples in order to make clear the behaviour of the delayed choice. Suppose a, b, c, d, e and f are distinct actions in A, then:

$$\begin{array}{l}
\mathrm{BPA}_{\delta\varepsilon} + \mathrm{DC} \vdash ab \mp a(c+d) = a(b+c+d) \\
\mathrm{BPA}_{\delta\varepsilon} + \mathrm{DC} \vdash (ab+\tau ac) \mp de = ab + \tau(ac+de) \\
\mathrm{BPA}_{\delta\varepsilon} + \mathrm{DC} \vdash (ab+ac) \mp a(b+c) = a(b+c) \\
\mathrm{BPA}_{\delta\varepsilon} + \mathrm{DC} \vdash (ab+\tau ac) \mp a(d+e) = a(b+d+e) + \tau a(c+d+e) \\
\mathrm{BPA}_{\delta\varepsilon} + \mathrm{DC} \vdash (ab+ac) \mp (ad+\tau f) = a(b+d) + a(c+d) + \tau(ab+ac+f) \\
\mathrm{BPA}_{\delta\varepsilon} + \mathrm{DC} \vdash (ab+ac) \mp a(\tau(b+c)+b) = a(\tau(b+c)+b) \\
\mathrm{BPA}^{\tau}_{\delta\varepsilon} + \mathrm{DC} \vdash (ab+ac) \mp a(\tau(b+c)+b) = a(b+c)
\end{array}$$

3.2 Structured Operational Semantics

The rules in Table 4 define the operational semantics for the delayed choice. In some rules, we make use of negative premises (see [18]). Expression $y \stackrel{a}{\not\longrightarrow}$ means that process y cannot execute action a. Moreover, our system is in *panth format* [18], which introduces several good properties that are useful in proving completeness of equational theories.

Our choice was to formulate the equational theory and afterwards state the operational rules which we will prove sound and complete. However, as the rule system can be simply translated into one in GSOS format [7] by changing the predicate $\downarrow$ into the action relation $\stackrel{\surd}{\longrightarrow}$ as done in [12], we could follow the algorithm proposed by [1] in order to help us on finding a complete axiomatization starting from the rules.

Table 4. Operational semantics for delayed choice $(a, b \in A)$

$$\frac{x \stackrel{a}{\longrightarrow} x' \quad y \stackrel{a}{\longrightarrow} y'}{x \mp y \stackrel{a}{\longrightarrow} x' \mp y' \quad x \bowtie y \stackrel{a}{\longrightarrow} x' \mp y'} \qquad \frac{x \stackrel{a}{\longrightarrow} x' \quad y \stackrel{a}{\not\longrightarrow} \quad y \stackrel{\tau}{\not\longrightarrow}}{x \mp y \stackrel{a}{\longrightarrow} x' \quad y \mp x \stackrel{a}{\longrightarrow} x' \quad x \triangleleft y \stackrel{a}{\longrightarrow} x'}$$

$$\frac{x \downarrow \quad y \stackrel{\tau}{\not\longrightarrow}}{x \mp y \downarrow \quad y \mp x \downarrow \quad x \triangleleft y \downarrow} \qquad \frac{x \stackrel{\tau}{\longrightarrow} x'}{x \mp y \stackrel{\tau}{\longrightarrow} x' \mp y \quad y \mp x \stackrel{\tau}{\longrightarrow} y \mp x' \quad x \sqsubset y \stackrel{\tau}{\longrightarrow} x' \mp y}$$

3.3 Soundness and Completeness

In this section we prove soundness and completeness of the term models. In order to do that, we use term rewrite techniques. Axioms A3–A9 in Table 1 and all axioms in Table 3 can be observed as rewrite rules, if they are oriented from left to right, i.e. for each axiom $s = t$ we consider the rule $s \rightarrow t$. Nevertheless, this term rewriting system is not confluent, that is, a term may have two different normal forms. This is due to the fact that e.g. axiom A9 is sometimes needed in the opposite direction. So, we complete the term rewriting system by adding the rewrite rules in Table 5. Note that each new rewrite rule is derivable from the axioms for the delayed choice. Let TRS be the new term rewriting system.

Table 5. Additional rewrite rules ($a \neq b$)

AR1	$a \bowtie a \longrightarrow a$	AR8	$x \bowtie \tau \longrightarrow \delta$	AR15	$\varepsilon \triangleleft a \longrightarrow \varepsilon$
AR2	$a \bowtie ax \longrightarrow a(\varepsilon \mp x)$	AR9	$a \triangleleft a \longrightarrow \delta$	AR16	$a \triangleleft \varepsilon \longrightarrow a$
AR3	$ax \bowtie a \longrightarrow a(x \mp \varepsilon)$	AR10	$a \triangleleft ax \longrightarrow \delta$	AR17	$a \triangleleft \delta \longrightarrow a$
AR4	$a \bowtie b \longrightarrow \delta$	AR11	$ax \triangleleft a \longrightarrow \delta$	AR18	$\tau \triangleleft x \longrightarrow \delta$
AR5	$a \bowtie bx \longrightarrow \delta$	AR12	$a \triangleleft b \longrightarrow a$	AR19	$x \triangleleft \tau \longrightarrow \delta$
AR6	$ax \bowtie b \longrightarrow \delta$	AR13	$a \triangleleft bx \longrightarrow a$	AR20	$a \sqsubset x \longrightarrow \delta$
AR7	$\tau \bowtie x \longrightarrow \delta$	AR14	$ax \triangleleft b \longrightarrow ax$	AR21	$\tau \sqsubset x \longrightarrow \tau(\varepsilon \mp x)$

Theorem 4. TRS *is strongly normalizing.*

Proof. This can be proved by applying the method of the lexicographical path ordering [13, 14]. The details can be found in [10]. □

Definition 5 (Basic Terms). Let B be the class of *basic terms* over the theory $\mathrm{BPA}_{\delta\varepsilon} + \mathrm{DC}$ (or $\mathrm{BPA}^{\tau}_{\delta\varepsilon} + \mathrm{DC}$), defined as the smallest class satisfying:

1. $\tau, \varepsilon, \delta \in B, A \subset B$
2. $a \in A, t \in B \Rightarrow a \cdot t \in B$
3. $t \in B \Rightarrow \tau \cdot t \in B$
4. $s, t \in B \Rightarrow s + t \in B$

The next theorem states that for every closed $\mathrm{BPA}_{\delta\varepsilon} + \mathrm{DC}$ term there exists a basic term (not containing $\mp$, $\bowtie$, $\triangleleft$ and $\sqsubset$) such that they can be proved equal. That is why it is called the *elimination theorem.*

Theorem 6 (Elimination Theorem in $\mathrm{BPA}_{\delta\varepsilon} + \mathrm{DC}$). *Let t be a closed term over $\mathrm{BPA}_{\delta\varepsilon} + \mathrm{DC}$. Then, there is a basic term s such that $\mathrm{BPA}_{\delta\varepsilon} + \mathrm{DC} \vdash t = s$.*

Proof. Because of Theorem 4, t has a normal form s. We prove that such an s is a basic term. Firstly, take into account that it is well known that rules A3-A9 rewrite a closed $\mathrm{BPA}_{\delta\varepsilon}$-term into a basic one. Now, if s contains a $\mp$ then DC can be applied and so s is not in normal form which contradicts our assumption. If s contains $\bowtie$, $\triangleleft$ or $\sqsubset$, take a smallest sub-term containing one of them, say $s_1 \bowtie s_2$, now we can assume that both sub-terms s_1 and s_2 are already basic terms, so one of the rules J1–J8, TJ1–TJ2 or AR1–AR8 can be applied. If this sub-term is $s_1 \lhd s_2$, one of the rules of U1–U10, TU1–TU2 or AR8–AR19 can be applied. Finally, if this sub-term is $s_1 \sqsubset s_2$, then one of the rules TS1–TS5 or AR20–AR21 can be applied. This concludes the proof. □

Corollary 7 (Elimination Theorem in $\mathrm{BPA}^{\tau}_{\delta\varepsilon} + \mathrm{DC}$). *Let t be a closed term over $\mathrm{BPA}^{\tau}_{\delta\varepsilon} + \mathrm{DC}$. Then, there is a basic term s such that $\mathrm{BPA}^{\tau}_{\delta\varepsilon} + \mathrm{DC} \vdash t = s$.*

Let $\mathcal{T}^{\mp}$ be the set of all closed $\mathrm{BPA}_{\delta\varepsilon} + \mathrm{DC}$ terms. We can immediately extend the notion of the several bisimulation equivalences to $\mathcal{T}^{\mp}$. Now, we have the following results.

Theorem 8 (Congruence). *$\leftrightarrow$ and $\leftrightarrow_{rb}$ are congruences for the $\mp$, $\bowtie$, $\lhd$ and $\sqsubset$ operators.*

Proof.

($\leftrightarrow$) The set of operational rules for $\mathrm{BPA}_{\delta\varepsilon} + \mathrm{DC}$ satisfies the *panth* format of [18] and it is also well founded. It remains to prove that it is stratifiable. As in [3], define the function S that, to each step $t \xrightarrow{a} t'$ and termination option $t\downarrow$, assigns the number of $\mp$ symbols plus the number of $\lhd$ symbols in t. It is now easy to prove that S is a strict stratification.

For proving that $\leftrightarrow_{rb}$ is a congruence, we need the following four properties. Their proof is straightforward.

1. $x \Longrightarrow x' \wedge y \Longrightarrow y'$ if and only if $x \mp y \Longrightarrow x' \mp y'$.
2. $x \sqsubset y \stackrel{a}{\not\longrightarrow}$ for all $a \neq \tau$.
3. $x \bowtie y \stackrel{\tau}{\not\longrightarrow}$.
4. $x \lhd y \stackrel{\tau}{\not\longrightarrow}$.

Now, it is tedious but not difficult to prove the following.

($\leftrightarrow_{rb}$) Take any rooted branching bisimulation R between x and x'. Let Id be the identity relation. Then, the following relations are also rooted branching bisimulations:

$R_1 = \{(z \mp y, z' \mp y) | (z, z') \in R\} \cup R \cup Id$ $\quad R_5 = \{(x \lhd y, x' \lhd y)\} \cup R$
$R_2 = \{(y \mp z, y \mp z') | (z, z') \in R\} \cup R \cup Id$ $\quad R_6 = \{(y \lhd x, y \lhd x')\} \cup Id$
$R_3 = \{(x \bowtie y, x' \bowtie y)\} \cup R_1$ $\quad R_7 = \{(x \sqsubset y, x' \sqsubset y)\} \cup R_1$
$R_4 = \{(y \bowtie x, y \bowtie x')\} \cup R_2$ $\quad R_8 = \{(y \sqsubset x, y \sqsubset x')\} \cup R_2$ □

Notice that $\leftrightarrow_b$ is also a congruence for $\mp$. However, this is not the case for the other operators.

Theorem 9 (Soundness).

1. $\mathcal{T}^{\mp}/\!\leftrightarrow\; \models \mathrm{BPA}_{\delta\varepsilon} + \mathrm{DC}$
2. $\mathcal{T}^{\mp}/\!\leftrightarrow_{rb}\; \models \mathrm{BPA}^{\tau}_{\delta\varepsilon} + \mathrm{DC}$

Proof. As usual. For every axiom $s = t$ having free variables in X, we define the relation $R = \{(\sigma(s), \sigma(t)) | \sigma \text{ substitutes variables in } X \text{ to closed terms}\} \cup Id$. It is not difficult to prove that R is a bisimulation or rooted branching bisimulation according to the soundness property we are proving. □

Theorem 10 (Equational Conservative Extension).

1. $\mathrm{BPA}_{\delta\varepsilon} + \mathrm{DC}$ *is a conservative extension of* $\mathrm{BPA}_{\delta\varepsilon}$.
2. $\mathrm{BPA}^{\tau}_{\delta\varepsilon} + \mathrm{DC}$ *is a conservative extension of* $\mathrm{BPA}^{\tau}_{\delta\varepsilon}$.

Proof. The operational conservativity follows since our rules are in *panth* format, and they are pure and well-founded (see [19]). This implies operational conservativity up to $\leftrightarrow$ and up to $\leftrightarrow_{rb}$. Because the axiomatizations of $\mathrm{BPA}_{\delta\varepsilon}$ and $\mathrm{BPA}^{\tau}_{\delta\varepsilon}$ are sound and complete (Theorem 3), and the axiomatizations of $\mathrm{BPA}_{\delta\varepsilon} + \mathrm{DC}$ and $\mathrm{BPA}^{\tau}_{\delta\varepsilon} + \mathrm{DC}$ are sound (Theorem 9), equational conservativity follows from [19, 4]. □

Theorem 11 (Completeness).

1. $\mathrm{BPA}_{\delta\varepsilon} + \mathrm{DC}$ *is a complete axiomatization for* $\mathcal{T}^{\mp}/\leftrightarrow$.
2. $\mathrm{BPA}^{\tau}_{\delta\varepsilon} + \mathrm{DC}$ *is a complete axiomatization for* $\mathcal{T}^{\mp}/\leftrightarrow_{rb}$.

Proof. Again, following [19, 4] and considering Theorem 6 and Corollary 7, this theorem is a corollary of the previous one. □

3.4 Properties

In this section, we prove several properties that hold for the new operators. Mainly, we show that $\mp$ satisfies common properties of choice operators (commutativity and associativity) and that δ is the neutral element for $\mp$. Nevertheless, idempotency does not hold for $\mp$.

Lemma 12. *The following properties are derivable from* $\mathrm{BPA}_{\delta\varepsilon} + \mathrm{DC}$

1. $ax \mp ay = a(x \mp y)$
2. $a \neq b \Rightarrow ax \mp by = ax + by$

Proof.

1. $$\begin{aligned} ax \mp ay &= ax \bowtie ay + ax \lhd ay + ay \lhd ax + ax \sqsubset ay + ay \sqsubset ax \\ &= ax \bowtie ay + \delta + \delta + \delta + \delta \;=\; a(x \mp y) \end{aligned}$$
2. Let $a \neq b$. Then
$$\begin{aligned} ax \mp by &= ax \bowtie by + ax \lhd by + by \lhd ax + ax \sqsubset by + by \sqsubset ax \\ &= \delta + ax + by + \delta + \delta \;=\; ax + by \end{aligned}$$

□

Remark. From now on, we will assume

$$X = \sum_i a_i x_i + \sum_j \tau x_j + \sum_k \varepsilon \qquad\qquad Y = \sum_m b_m y_m + \sum_n \tau y_n + \sum_l \varepsilon$$

with $i \in I$, $j \in J$, $k \in K$, $m \in M$, $n \in N$ and $l \in L$; I, J, K, M, N and L are finite disjoint sets; and $a_i \neq \tau$, $b_m \neq \tau$. In particular, we consider $\sum_{h\in\emptyset} t_h = \delta$, or, by A6, we omit it.

The proof of the following lemma is by straightforward calculations.

Lemma 13. *Let X and Y be as before. Then*

1. $X \bowtie Y = \sum_{i,m(a_i=b_m)} a_i(x_i \mp y_m)$
2. $X \triangleleft Y = \sum_{i(\forall m.a_i\neq b_m \wedge N=\emptyset)} a_i x_i + \sum_{k(N=\emptyset)} \varepsilon$
3. $X \sqsubset Y = \sum_j \tau(x_j \mp Y)$

Theorem 14 (Neutral Element). *Let x be a closed term. Then*

$$x \mp \delta = \delta \mp x = x$$

Proof. We prove it by induction on the number of symbols of x, say k. The base case ($k = 1$) is left to the reader. Assume X as in the previous remark. For the inductive case we have:

$$\begin{aligned} X \mp \delta &\overset{\text{DC}}{=} X \bowtie \delta + X \triangleleft \delta + \delta \triangleleft X + X \sqsubset \delta + \delta \sqsubset X \\ &\overset{\text{J4, U4, TS2}}{=} \delta + X \triangleleft \delta + \delta + X \sqsubset \delta + \delta \\ &\overset{13}{=} \sum_i a_i x_i + \sum_k \varepsilon + \sum_j \tau(x_j \mp \delta) \\ &\overset{\text{IH}}{=} \sum_i a_i x_i + \sum_k \varepsilon + \sum_j \tau x_j \overset{\text{A1, A2}}{=} X \end{aligned}$$

The second part of the theorem goes analogously. □

Definition 15 (Initial Actions). Define the set of initial action of a given term x as follows:

$$I(\delta) = \emptyset \qquad I(ax) = \{a\} \qquad I(x+y) = I(x) \cup I(y)$$
$$I(\varepsilon) = \emptyset \qquad I(\tau x) = \{\tau\}$$

Lemma 16. *Let x and y be any closed terms. Then*

1. $I(x \bowtie y) = (I(x) \cap I(y)) \backslash \{\tau\}$
2. $I(x \triangleleft y) = \begin{cases} I(x)\backslash(I(y) \cup \{\tau\}) & \text{if } \tau \notin I(y) \\ \emptyset & \text{otherwise} \end{cases}$
3. $I(x \sqsubset y) = \{\tau\} \cap I(x)$
4. $I(x \mp y) = \begin{cases} I(x) \cup I(y) & \text{if } \tau \notin I(x) \cup I(y) \\ I(x) & \text{if } \tau \in I(x) \wedge \tau \notin I(y) \\ I(y) & \text{if } \tau \notin I(x) \wedge \tau \in I(y) \\ I(x) \cap I(y) & \text{if } \tau \in I(x) \cap I(y) \end{cases}$

Proof. It follows from Definition 15 and Lemma 13. □

Lemma 17. *Let x, y and z be any closed terms. Then:*

1. $I(y) = I(z) \Rightarrow x \lhd y = x \lhd z$
2. $x \lhd (y \mp z) = x \lhd (y + z) = (x \lhd y) \lhd z$

Proof. Suppose $\tau \in I(y) = I(z)$, then both y and z has a summand with τ as initial action. Hence

$$x \lhd y \stackrel{\text{A1, A2, A3}}{=} x \lhd (y + \tau y_j) \stackrel{\text{U9}}{=} (x \lhd y) \lhd \tau y_j \stackrel{\text{TU2}}{=} \delta$$

Analogously, $x \lhd z = \delta$. Now, suppose $\tau \notin I(y) = I(z)$. Hence, we can write $y = \sum_m b_m y_m + \sum_l \varepsilon$ and $z = \sum_h c_h z_h + \sum_f \varepsilon$. Suppose X as before. Then

$$X \lhd y \stackrel{13}{=} \sum_{i(\forall m.a_i \neq b_m)} a_i x_i + \sum_k \varepsilon \stackrel{\text{I(y)=I(z)}}{=} \sum_{i(\forall h.a_i \neq c_h)} a_i x_i + \sum_k \varepsilon \stackrel{13}{=} X \lhd z$$

Part (2) follows from Lemma 16, part (4) and the definition of initial actions taking into account whether τ is an initial action of y and z or not. □

Theorem 18 (Commutativity). *For all closed terms x and y, we have:*

1. $x \bowtie y = y \bowtie x$
2. $x \mp y = y \mp x$

Proof. By mutual induction on the sum of symbols of x and y, we can prove (1); (2) follows directly from (1) and DC. □

Theorem 19 (Associativity). *For all closed terms x, y and z, we have:*

1. $(x \bowtie y) \sqsubset z = x \bowtie (y \sqsubset z) = (x \sqsubset y) \bowtie z = (x \lhd y) \sqsubset z = (x \sqsubset y) \lhd z = \delta$
2. $x \bowtie (y \lhd z) = (x \bowtie y) \lhd z = (x \lhd z) \bowtie y$
3. $x \sqsubset (y \mp z) = (x \sqsubset y) \sqsubset z = (x \sqsubset z) \sqsubset y$
4. $x \bowtie (y \bowtie z) = (x \bowtie y) \bowtie z$
5. $x \mp (y \mp z) = (x \mp y) \mp z$

Proof. Identities of (1) can be deduced from Lemma 13

For (2) consider X and Y as before and $Z = \sum_h c_h z_h + \sum_g \tau z_g + \sum_f \varepsilon$. Now, we have:

$$(X \bowtie Y) \lhd Z \stackrel{13(1)}{=} \left(\sum_{i,m(a_i=b_m)} a_i(x_i \mp y_m) \right) \lhd Z \stackrel{13(2)}{=} \sum_{\substack{i,m(a_i=b_m \\ \wedge \forall h.a_i \neq c_h \\ \wedge G=\emptyset)}} a_i(x_i \mp y_m)$$

$$\stackrel{13(1)}{=} \left(\sum_{i(\forall h.a_i \neq c_h \wedge G=\emptyset)} a_i x_i + \sum_{k(G=\emptyset)} \varepsilon \right) \bowtie Y \stackrel{13(2)}{=} (X \lhd Z) \bowtie Y$$

The other equation follows similarly.

Properties (3), (4) and (5) are proved by mutual induction on the sum k of symbols of x, y and z. For details we refer to [10]. □

We have already stated that $\mp$ is commutative, associative and has δ as neutral element. However, the delayed choice presented here is not idempotent and it does not satisfy the several laws of distributivity, just as the delayed choice of [3] and the τ-angelic choice [9]. We will not repeat the counter examples for the following fact given in [3].

Fact 20 *The following equations are* **not** *generally valid in the initial algebra:*
$x \mp x = x$
$(x + y) \mp z = (x \mp z) + (y \mp z)$
$(x \mp y) + z = (x + z) \mp (y + z)$
$(x \mp y)z = xz \mp yz$
$z(x \mp y) = zx \mp zy$

4 Examples

In [3] the delayed choice operator was used for the composition of Message Sequence Charts. In this section, we will show two more examples of its application.

4.1 Scenario specification

In communication protocols it is often the case that one can distinguish one main scenario and several alternative behaviours. If, e.g., the main scenario is a correct transmission, an alternative scenario could be the occurrence of a channel error followed by a retransmission. If both scenarios start with the same initial behaviour, the two alternative scenarios should not be combined with the normal non-deterministic choice (+). By using the delayed choice instead, the moment of choice is put at the point where the scenarios start to differ. In this case the benefit of using the delayed choice is not that it gives a shorter specification, but that it helps in designing and presenting the specification in a more modular way.

Next, we will give an example in which the delayed choice allows for a considerably shorter specification than without this operator. Consider an *access control* consisting of a digital key pad and a (locked) door. A user can enter any sequence of digits. The door may only be opened if the sequence ends in a special four digit code (say, 2908). Let 0–9 denote detection of the indicated key stroke and let *grantaccess* stand for offering the user the option to access, then the following is a specification of the access control.

$$AC = (0+1+2+3+4+5+6+7+8+9) \cdot AC \mp 2 \cdot 9 \cdot 0 \cdot 8 \cdot \mathit{grantaccess} \cdot AC$$

Please notice that this process is executed in parallel with the user behaviour. After selecting 2908, the user is not forced to take access. He can also enter another digit and lose access permission for that moment.

4.2 Requirements reduction

A verification in process algebra in general consists of proving $\tau_I(S) = R$, where S is an implementation specification and R is a requirements specification. The τ_I operator ([5]) is the abstraction operator, which renames actions from the set I into τ. It removes all internal actions, but keeps the internal branching structure. It often happens that one has a very simple requirements specification R in mind, while after calculating $\tau_I(S)$ an expression with an excess of internal choices remains. These internal choices probably represent implementation decisions. Then, there are two obvious ways to proceed. The first is to simply forget about R and consider $\tau_I(S)$ as the requirements specification, having to accept a more implementation directed requirement. The second way is to discard the branching structure and proceed in a linear time semantics, where $\tau_I(S) = R$ holds. In this case we lose all information about the branching structure of the requirements.

We propose to use the delayed choice operator. Let D be the operator which replaces all occurrences of the non-deterministic choice by the delayed choice, as defined in Table 6.

Table 6. The operator D for removing non-deterministic choices ($a \in A \cup \{\tau\}$)

DE1	$D(\varepsilon) = \varepsilon$
DE2	$D(\delta) = \delta$
DE3	$D(x + y) = D(x) \mp D(y)$
DE4	$D(ay) = a \cdot D(y)$

Now, a mixed linear time/branching time verification consists of proving

$$\tau_{I_1} \circ D \circ \tau_{I_2}(S) = R$$

The set I_2 contains all atomic actions which induce only irrelevant choices, while the choices between actions from I_1 should remain after abstraction.

We will illustrate this with parts of the verification of a *leader election protocol.* We call this protocol the *Paint Ball protocol*, because it is a formalization of the popular Paint Ball game, in which people fight each other by shooting paint balls.

Suppose that entities E_i ($i \in ID$, ID is the set of identifications $|ID| > 1$) have to elect a leader amongst themselves non-deterministically. Every entity can communicate synchronously with every other entity. Initially all entities are equal. We have the following quite simple requirements specification.

$$R = \tau \cdot \sum_{i \in ID} \tau \cdot leader(i)$$

where $leader(i)$ denotes that entity i has become leader. Notice that we prepend a silent step τ to represent some initial internal activity.

The Paint Ball protocol is specified as the parallel composition ($\|$, [5]) of all entities. The encapsulation operator ∂_H is applied to enforce successful communications only. It renames all atoms from the set H into δ.

$$S = \partial_H \left(\|_{i \in ID} \; E_i^{ID-\{i\}} \right)$$

Each entity E_i^V is indexed with a set V. This set contains all other entities that have not yet been defeated by i. If this set is empty, it means that i has defeated all other participants and that i will become the leader (L_i). If the set is not empty, a choice is made between shooting a paint ball at one of the remaining participants (s_{ij}), or receiving a paint ball (r_{ji}) and entering the failed state (F_i). If all but one of the entities have yielded, the leader informs all failed entities that the elections are finished ($sready_{ij}$) and finally executes action $leader(i)$.

$$\begin{array}{ll} E_i^{\emptyset} &= L_i \\ E_i^V &= \sum_{j \in V} \left(s_{ij} \cdot E_i^{V-\{j\}} + r_{ji} \cdot F_i \right) \qquad (V \neq \emptyset) \\ L_i &= \left(\|_{j \in ID-\{i\}} \; sready_{ij} \right) \cdot leader(i) \\ F_i &= \sum_{j \in ID-\{i\}} \left(r_{ji} \cdot F_i + rready_{ji} \right) \end{array}$$

We have the obvious communication function ($r_{ij} | s_{ij} = c_{ij}$, $rready_{ij} | sready_{ij} = cready_{ij}$) and encapsulation set $H = \{r_{ij}, rready_{i,j}, s_{ij}, sready_{i,j} | i, j \in ID\}$. Now let $I = \{c_{ij}, cready_{i,j} | i, j \in ID\}$ and consider $\tau_I(S)$. After several calculations we obtain a reduced specification such that $\tau \cdot \tau_I(S) = P^{ID}$.

$$\begin{array}{ll} P^V &= \tau \cdot \sum_{i \in V} \tau \cdot P^{V-\{i\}} \qquad (|V| > 1) \\ P^{\{i\}} &= \tau \cdot leader(i) \end{array}$$

The specification of P shows that during the execution of the protocol some internal choices are made, which denote that some entity i is removed from the list of candidates. This continues until one candidate remains. According to our requirements specification we are not interested in these implementation details. Using our proposed strategy we calculate (for $I_2 = \{c_{ij} | i, j \in ID\}$)

$$D \circ \tau_{I_2}(S) = \tau \cdot \sum_{i \in ID} \left(\left(\|_{j \in ID-\{i\}} \; cready_{ij} \right) \cdot leader(i) \right)$$

And if we set $I_1 = \{cready_{ij} | i, j \in ID\}$ then we get the desired equality.

$$\tau_{I_1} \circ D \circ \tau_{I_2}(S) = \tau \cdot \sum_{i \in ID} \tau \cdot leader(i) = R$$

5 Conclusion

We have defined the delayed choice operator in process algebra with abstraction. Using this operator we can express linear time specifications in a branching time setting. We have shown two applications of this operator, namely scenario specification and requirements reduction. A sound and complete axiomatization with respect to branching bisimulation was obtained.

References

1. L. Aceto, B. Bloom, and F.W. Vaandrager. Turning SOS rules into equations. *Information and Computation*, 111(1):1–52, 1994.
2. J.C.M. Baeten, J.A. Bergstra, and J.W. Klop. Syntax and defining equations for an interrupt mechanism in process algebra. *Fund. Inf.*, IX(2):127–168, 1986.
3. J.C.M. Baeten and S. Mauw. Delayed choice: an operator for joining Message Sequence Charts. In D. Hogrefe and S. Leue, editors, *Formal Description Techniques, VII*, pages 340–354. Chapman & Hall, 1995.
4. J.C.M. Baeten and C. Verhoef. *Concrete process algebra*, pages 149–268. Handbook of logic in computer science (Vol 4, Semantic modelling), eds. S. Abramsky, Dov. M. Gabbay and T.S.E. Maibaum. Clarendon press, Oxford, 1995.
5. J.C.M. Baeten and W.P. Weijland. *Process Algebra.* Cambridge Tracts in Theoretical Computer Science 18. Cambridge University Press, 1990.
6. J.A. Bergstra and J.W. Klop. Process algebra for synchronous communication. *Information & Control*, 60:109–137, 1984.
7. B. Bloom, S. Istrail, and A.R. Meyer. Bisimulation can't be traced: preliminary report. In *Proc. 15th ACM symposium on Principles of Programming Languages*, pages 229–239. San Diego, California, 1988.
8. S.D. Brookes, C.A.R. Hoare, and A.W. Roscoe. A theory of communicating sequential processes. *Journal of the ACM*, 31(3):560–599, 1984.
9. P. D'Argenio. τ-angelic choice for process algebra. Technical report, LIFIA, Dpto. de Informàtica, Fac. Cs. Exactas, UNLP, 1994.
10. P. D'Argenio and S. Mauw. Delayed choice for process algebra with abstraction. Report, Department of Computer Science, Eindhoven University of Technology, 1995. To appear.
11. R.J. van Glabbeek and W.P. Weijland. Branching time and abstraction in bisimulation semantics (extended abstract). In G.X. Ritter, editor, *Information Processing 89*, pages 613–618. North-Holland, 1989.
12. J.F. Groote and F.W. Vaandrager. Structured operational semantics and bisimulation as a congruence. *Information and Computation*, 100:202–260, 1992.
13. S. Kamin and J.-J. Lévy. Two generalizations of the recursive path ordering. Unpublished manuscript, 1980.
14. J.W. Klop. Term rewriting systems. In S. Abramsky, D. Gabbay, and T. Maibaum, editors, *Handbook of Logic in Computer Science*, volume II, pages 1–116. Oxford University Press, 1992.
15. C.P.J. Koymans and J.L.M. Vrancken. Extending process algebra with the empty process. Report LGPS 1, Dept. of Philosophy, University of Utrecht, 1985.
16. D.M.R. Park. Concurrency and automata on infinite sequence. In P. Deussen, editor, *Proc. 5th. GI Conference*, pages 167–183. LNCS 104, Springer-Verlag, 1981.
17. G.D. Plotkin. A structural approach to operational semantics. Report DAIMI-FN-19, Computer Science Department, University of Århus, 1981.
18. C. Verhoef. A congruence theorem for structured operational semantics with predicates and negative premises. In B. Jonsson and J. Parrow, editors, *Proc. CONCUR '94*, pages 433–448. Uppsala, Springer Verlag, 1994. LNCS 836.
19. C. Verhoef. A general conservative extension theorem in process algebra. In E.-R. Olderog, editor, *Proc. PROCOMET'94, IFIP 2 Working Conference*, pages 149–168. San Miniato, North-Holland, 1994.

CTR: A Calculus of Timed Refinement

Kārlis Čerāns*
Institute of Mathematics and Computer Science,
University of Latvia

Abstract. This paper presents CTR - a process algebraic framework for loose specification of time quantity sensitive operational behaviour of reactive systems. CTR terms are provided both with operational and specification semantics (via the notion of specification refinement). Besides the intuitive justification of appropriateness of the refinement notion, a preservation theorem is proved for a timed variant of Hennessy-Milner logic. A comparison of CTR with the related formalism of Timed Modal Specifications, and with the timed process calculi TCCS due to Wang is given. Some pragmatics of the application of CTR is sketched on a critical resource access example.

1 Introduction

The necessity and role of quantitative time information in reactive (open) system descriptions is nowadays quite appreciated[2], and there are already quite many specification formalisms, which alongside with system structural and/or behaviour event ordering specification permit to specify quantitative time information characterizing the valid behaviours (see e.g. [MF76, CC89, AD90, Wan91a, GMMP89] as a few examples of such formalisms).

Quite naturally, many of the existing "timed" specification formalisms do allow in certain natural sense "loose" specifications of time information (it would be not that natural to determine at early system design stage exactly what are the time quantities between specific events going to be[3]), at least [MF76, AD90, Che92, Dan92, CGL93] to be mentioned.

The calculus CTR presented in this paper is also designed to follow this tradition. Specifically, its aim is to provide a timed specification framework with mathematically precise and semantically justified notion of specification refinement (when one specification can be termed to be "more precise" than the other), allowing at the same time for clear operational intuition behind the specifications. In various respects, including those of the motivation, the CTR framework is similar to Timed Modal Specifications (TMS) of [CGL93], however, here we manage to achieve pragmatically more natural properties of the specification refinement, as well as are able to provide a better operational intuition behind the execution of specifications, and have a slightly stronger expressive power of the language. A detailed comparison of CTR and TMS is in Section 5. If compared to other frameworks for timed system refinement, such as [AIK92, LV93] and others, it is to be noted that CTR specification refinement is based on operational and branching time semantics (this refinement is

* Address: Rainis blvd. 29, LV-1459, Riga, Latvia, Tel: +371-2213716, Fax: +371-7820153, email: karlis@mii.lu.lv. This work has been partially supported by Grant No. 93-596 from Latvian Council of Science.

[2] Even if the observer of a system is not directly concerned about the actual time quantities between externally observable events, it could be relevant for him/her to put some timing information in the specifications of the system components in order to ensure the correct *qualitative* ordering of the whole system output events.

[3] It may appear impossible even on the level of implementations due to various unpredictable execution environment fluctuations.

a generalization of (a slight modification of) timed bisimulation equivalence of [Wan90], it can not be characterized as any kind of (timed) trace inclusion).

In essence, CTR is obtained by adding to the Milner's CCS [Mil89] the contruct of time interval prefix $[a,b].P$, where a, b are nonnegative real numbers, $0 \leq a \leq b$, possibly $b = \infty$. Such a specification is intended to describe all processes which first delay for some quantity $d \in [a,b]$, and then behave accordingly to some behaviour prescribed by P. (CTR can be seen as a generalization of Timed CCS due to Wang Yi in its version of [Wan90], where only delay prefixes of the form $[d,d].P$ were considered and denoted by $\epsilon(d).P$).

We define an operational semantics for CTR specification terms as a labelled transition system (each transition label denotes either some control action (externally visible or invisible), or it specifies some amount of time passage). Based on this semantics the specification refinement relation $\trianglelefteq$ is defined in a "bisimulation - like" fashion[4].

The CTR specification refinement relation is shown to be a preorder and to satisfy certain substitutivity properties (for instance, wrt. parallel composition). On Timed CCS terms $\trianglelefteq$ induces a so-called divergence refinement relation, which is a slightly stronger property than the weak bisimulation $\approx$ of [Wan90]. $\trianglelefteq$ is also *decidable* for finite control specifications[5] (these include, for instance, networks of regular specifications). It is shown also that $\trianglelefteq$ preserves logical properties expressible in a certain natural "timed" variant of Hennesy - Milner logic [HM85].

Pragmatically, the CTR refinement relation $\trianglelefteq$ is based on the intuition of resolving underspecification of timing information. So, $[e,f].S \trianglelefteq [d,g].T$ whenever $d \leq e \leq f \leq g$ and $S \trianglelefteq T$ [6] (the tighter the delay interval is, the finer is the specification). On the extreme, the term $[0,\infty].S$ covers any specification of the form $[d,e].S$, together with the "empty" specification *nil* which never exhibits any observable behaviour but waiting. In fact, the term $[0,\infty].S$ would specify just the ***possibility*** of the system to exhibit the behaviour prescribed by S after some (possibly none) initial delay[7]. This is the only way of achieving in CTR looseness of "non-timed" transition behaviour of specifications.

On the other hand, the CTR refinement relation $\trianglelefteq$ admits abstraction from internal transitions of specifications and is focusing just on the *externally observable* behaviour. As an example,

$$(a.[d,e].\bar{b} \mid b.[f,g].\bar{c})\backslash b \trianglelefteq a.[d+f, e+g].\bar{c}.$$

Here on the right hand side we have a specification of all media which after recieving a message on the channel a wait for some time amount $\delta \in [d+f, e+g]$, after what a message on the channel c is delivered. On the left hand side we have decomposed such a general message transmission specification into more detailed one, where the transmission is done in two stages - first from the channel a to the internal channel b, then from b to c. For each stage the looseness of the delay specification is maintained. Observing the substitutivity property of $\trianglelefteq$, one can during further stages of the design make further refinements of the components responsible for both transmission stages[8] still ensuring that the resulting system[9] will be a refinement of the initial general specification $a.[d+f, e+g].\bar{c}$.

This example illustrates how CTR is conceptually suitable for formal top-down system development by stepwise refinement. One can start with a general and very loose specificaton

[4] As the largest relation satisfying certain local "closeness" properties.

[5] To be precise, the decidability result hold for specifications whose initial delay bounds are given by integers (or at least rational numbers). In practice this is not a real restriction.

[6] This includes the case when $S = T$, due to the reflexivity of $\trianglelefteq$.

[7] In the notation of TMS the term $[0,\infty].a.S$ (observe the action label a necessary here) is written as $a_{\diamond}.S$ and is read semantically as "a transition a leading to S *may* be enabled".

[8] As a trivial possibility, one could tighten the message delivery delay intervals.

[9] Any system $(S|T)\backslash b$, where $S \trianglelefteq a.[d,e].\bar{b}$ and $T \trianglelefteq b.[f,g].\bar{c}$.

which captures only a few essential features of the system being designed. The stepwise refinement process allows, in a formal manner, to incorporate into the specification additional design decisions, both of structural and timing nature, each refinement step possibly being done locally in some component of the system[10].

In the rest of the paper, after introducing the CTR model in Section 2, in Section 3 we consider the definition and properties of the refinement relation. Section 4 sketches a possibility to apply the developed theory to a critical resource access specification example. Section 5 relates CTR and TMS, and suggests a semantic reformulation of TMS to improve its pragmatical applicability.

An earlier discussion of the topics addressed in this paper has appeared as [Cer94]. Here, however, we give a more careful definition of the specification refinement, as well as consider the logical preservation theorem (Theorem 1) and a larger example for the first time.

2 CTR: Syntax and Semantics

We start with defining the syntax of CTR specification terms.

Let $\Lambda = \Delta \cup \overline{\Delta}$ with $\overline{\overline{\alpha}} = \alpha$ for all $\alpha \in \Lambda$ be a set of *external actions*, ranged over by α, β, and let $\tau \notin \Lambda$ be a distinct symbol representing the internal actions. $\mathcal{A}ct = \Lambda \cup \{\tau\}$ is a set of all actions, ranged over by a, b. Let $\mathcal{V}ar$ be a finite set of process variables, ranged over by X. Then the set of *regular* CTR expressions over $\mathcal{V}ar$ is defined by the following grammar:

$$E ::= nil \mid X \mid [c,e].E \mid a.E \mid E+E,$$

where $c \in \mathbf{R}^{\geq 0}, e \in \mathbf{R}^{\geq 0} \cup \{\infty\}, c \leq e$. Here besides the standard process algebraic constructs nil, action prefix $a.E$, choice $E+E$ and variable (see [Mil89]) we have introduced a (closed) delay interval prefix[11]. We let also $\epsilon(d).E$ to be another notation for $[d,d].E$.

We assume furthermore that for every $X \in \mathcal{V}ar$ we are given a regular CTR expression E_X (over $\mathcal{V}ar$) that contains variable occurrences only guarded either by action or some delay interval prefix[12]. We let $\mathcal{E} = \{X \stackrel{def}{=} E_X | X \in \mathcal{V}ar\}$ and call it a system of variable defining equations.

Given such a system $\mathcal{E}$ we call any regular CTR expresion over $\mathcal{V}ar$ a *regular CTR specification* over $\mathcal{V}ar$ and $\mathcal{E}$ (possibly not mentioning $\mathcal{V}ar$ and $\mathcal{E}$, if they are clear from the context).

Let $\mathcal{G}(\mathcal{V}ar, \mathcal{E})$ be a set of all regular CTR specifications over $\mathcal{V}ar$ and $\mathcal{E}$, ranged over by G. We define the set $\mathcal{S} = \mathcal{S}(\mathcal{V}ar, \mathcal{E})$ of CTR networks (CTR specifications), over $\mathcal{V}ar$ and $\mathcal{E}$, by the grammar:

$$S ::= G \mid S|S \mid S \backslash A \mid S[f],$$

where $A \subseteq \Delta$ and $f : \Delta \to \Delta$ is a bijection, extended to $\mathcal{A}ct \to \mathcal{A}ct$ by $f(\overline{\alpha})) = \overline{f(\alpha)}$ and $f(\tau) = \tau$. We let S and T to range over the set of CTR networks.

We define for CTR specifications an operational semantics. Following the design of a standard timed process calculi TCCS [Wan90], we base it on the transition relations $S \xrightarrow{a} T$, meaning that S can execute a control transition $a \in \mathcal{A}ct$ and afterwards exhibit a behaviour

[10] Notice that the decidability of the refinement relation provides with (at least principal) possibility for automatic formal verification of the validity of every performed refinement step.

[11] In [Cer94] give an operational semantics also to the left-open delay interval prefix construct $]d, e]$ for $d < e$. To simplify the treatment of logical property preservation in Section 3.1, we do not focus on this construct here.

[12] In other words, all variable occurrences in E_X are allowed only within subterms of the form $a.E$, $[c, e].E$. Moreover, a delay prefix counts as a valid guard, only if $c > 0$.

prescribed by T, and $S \xrightarrow{\epsilon(d)} T$ meaning that S can become T just by delaying for d time units ($d \in \mathbf{R}^{>0}$).

The execution of $[c, e].S$ in time is defined to begin with a deterministic and synchronous decreasing of both its higher and lower time bounds: $[c, e].S \xrightarrow{\epsilon(d)} [c-d, e-d].S$ for $d \leq c$. When $[0, e].S$ is reached, we still let $[0, e].S \xrightarrow{\epsilon(d)} [0, e-d].S$ for $d \leq e$. However, now we want the specification to be able to choose also to exhibit the behaviour prescribed by S immediately. The design decision taken in CTR is to introduce a special new kind of internal transition $\xrightarrow{\imath}$ whose effect is to "leave the delay prefix": $[0, e].S \xrightarrow{\imath} S$ [13].

There are other possible ways to define a reasonable operational semantics for $[c, e].S$ construct. One such possibility is discussed in Section 5, yet another version corresponding to asynchronous reducing of delay bounds (during the course of the time the highest bound can reduce "faster", and the lowest bound can reduce "slower") is outlined in [Cer94]. However, the refinement notions defined on the basis of these three rather different semantics can be shown to coincide (see e.g. Theorem 4, also some variant of Theorem 2 from [Cer94] can be established).

Formally, we require $\imath \notin Act$ and let $Act^+ = Act \cup \{\imath\}$ to be ranged over by a^+. The whole operational semantics of CTR is given in Table 1 (we assume $f(\imath) = \imath$ for any relabelling function f). $x \dot{-} y$ means $max\{x - y, 0\}$. In the delay rules for $\xrightarrow{\epsilon(d)}$ we require $d \in \mathbf{R}^{>0}$. ν stands for either a^+, or $\epsilon(d)$.

For parallel composition, the sorts $Sort(d, S) \subseteq \Lambda$ in the side condition of the delay rule are computed in a standard way, as follows:

- $Sort(d, \alpha.S) = \{\alpha\}$, $\quad Sort(d, \tau.S) = Sort(d, nil) = \emptyset$,
- $Sort(d, [c, e].S) = Sort(d \dot{-} e, S)$,
- $Sort(d, X) = Sort(d, S)$, where $[X \stackrel{def}{=} S] \in \mathcal{E}$
- $Sort(d, S + T) = Sort(d, S|T) = Sort(d, S) \cup Sort(d, T)$
- $Sort(d, S[f]) = f(Sort(d, S)$ and $Sort(d, S \backslash A) = Sort(d, A) \setminus (A \cup \overline{A})$.

Following the design of Timed CCS, we have incorporated in our framework the principle of *maximal progress*, saying that an enabled internal τ transition has to be executed before the time progresses further[14].

In the semantics one should observe that unlike the $\xrightarrow{\tau}$ transitions, $\xrightarrow{\imath}$ does not resolve the nondeterministic choice $S + T$ (as do not the delay transitions). It is to be observed also that a specification of the form $[0, 0].S$ does not need to have any $\xrightarrow{\imath}$ transitions in order to "leave" the delay prefix. Intuitively this reflects the idea that $\xrightarrow{\imath}$ corresponds to an active choice, but in the case of $[0, 0].S$ no (timed) choice has been left.

Using the notation $\epsilon(d).S$ for $[d, d].S$ we can interpret all Timed CCS (network) terms of [Wan90] as CTR terms. This embedding preserves also the TCCS operational semantics (modulo ignoring $\xrightarrow{\imath}$ transitions which for TCCS terms can be essentially only of the form $S \xrightarrow{\imath} S$).

[13] This construction materializes the principle of letting the specification itself to make all time nondeterministic choice without any influence from the environment.

[14] There are no delay transitions for the $\tau.S$ terms, also the above side condition with sorts in parallel composition delay rule is just for this reason - time can pass only until the point where a synchronization between componets is enabled. Note that the maximal progress property does not apply to $\xrightarrow{\imath}$.

$$\frac{--}{nil \xrightarrow{\epsilon(d)} nil} \quad \frac{--}{a.S \xrightarrow{a} S} \quad \frac{--}{\alpha.S \xrightarrow{\epsilon(d)} \alpha.S} \quad \frac{S \xrightarrow{\nu} S'}{X \xrightarrow{\nu} S'}[X \stackrel{def}{=} S] \in \mathcal{E}$$

$$\frac{S \xrightarrow{a} S'}{S+T \xrightarrow{a} S'} \quad \frac{T \xrightarrow{a} T'}{S+T \xrightarrow{a} T'} \quad \frac{S \xrightarrow{i} S'}{S+T \xrightarrow{i} S'+T} \quad \frac{T \xrightarrow{i} T'}{S+T \xrightarrow{i} S+T'} \quad \frac{S \xrightarrow{\epsilon(d)} S' \;\; T \xrightarrow{\epsilon(d)} T'}{S+T \xrightarrow{\epsilon(d)} S'+T'}$$

$$\frac{S \xrightarrow{a^+} S'}{S|T \xrightarrow{a^+} S'|T} \quad \frac{T \xrightarrow{a^+} T'}{S|T \xrightarrow{a^+} S|T'} \quad \frac{S \xrightarrow{\alpha} S' \;\; T \xrightarrow{\overline{\alpha}} T'}{S|T \xrightarrow{\tau} S'|T'} \quad \frac{S \xrightarrow{\epsilon(d)} S' \;\; T \xrightarrow{\epsilon(d)} T'}{S|T \xrightarrow{\epsilon(d)} S'|T'} \; [Sort(d,S) \cap Sort(d,T) = \emptyset]$$

$$\frac{S \xrightarrow{a^+} S'}{S \backslash A \xrightarrow{a^+} S' \backslash A}[a, \overline{a} \notin A] \quad \frac{S \xrightarrow{\epsilon(d)} S'}{S \backslash A \xrightarrow{\epsilon(d)} S' \backslash A} \quad \frac{S \xrightarrow{a^+} S'}{S[f] \xrightarrow{f(a^+)} S'[f]} \quad \frac{S \xrightarrow{\epsilon(d)} S'}{S[f] \xrightarrow{\epsilon(d)} S'[f]}$$

$$\frac{-- \quad [d \leq e]}{[c,e].S \xrightarrow{\epsilon(d)} [c \dot{-} d, e-d].S} \quad \frac{--}{[0,e].S \xrightarrow{i} S} \quad \frac{S \xrightarrow{a^+} S'}{[0,0].S \xrightarrow{a^+} S'} \quad \frac{S \xrightarrow{\epsilon(d)} S'}{[c,e].S \xrightarrow{\epsilon(d+e)} S'}$$

Table 1 CTR Operational Semantics

3 CTR Specification Refinement

We want the CTR specification refinement $\trianglelefteq$ to capture the intuition of concretizing the timing properties of the specifications. Therefore, for $S \trianglelefteq T$ we ask for any transition sequence (behaviour) of S to be matched appropriately by a corresponding transition sequence of T[15]. The resulting states of both transition sequences are to be again in the relation $\trianglelefteq$ [16]. In a sense, the more general specification needs to admit more behaviours.

As for the immediate communication abilities of the specifications, we do require them to be preserved by the refinement *exactly* - for $S \trianglelefteq T$ any behaviour of T which does not involve $\xrightarrow{i}$, and does not involve delays, is to be matched appropriately also by S.

As for the preservation of delay abilities during the refinement process, we require just that, if S is able to perform an infinite transition chain within a single moment, then this should be allowed also by T. It turns out that this requirement is sufficient to ensure the preservation of waiting abilities of T also for all its refinements (see Theorem 1).

Let $\xrightarrow{i}_i = (\xrightarrow{i})^*$ and let $S \xrightarrow{a}_i S'$ denote $S \xrightarrow{i}_i \xrightarrow{a} \xrightarrow{i}_i S'$. Let also $\xrightarrow{\tau}_\tau = (\xrightarrow{\tau})^*$ and $\xrightarrow{\alpha}_\tau = \xrightarrow{\tau}_\tau \xrightarrow{\alpha} \xrightarrow{\tau}_\tau$, as well as $\xrightarrow{\tau}_{i,\tau} = \xrightarrow{i}_{i,\tau} = (\xrightarrow{\tau} \cup \xrightarrow{i})^*$ and $\xrightarrow{\alpha}_{i,\tau} = \xrightarrow{\tau}_{i,\tau} \xrightarrow{\alpha} \xrightarrow{\tau}_{i,\tau}$.

In what follows, we prepare for defining the matching of delay transitions. Let $S \in \mathcal{S}$ and $d \in \mathbf{R}^{>0}$, and let $f_-, f_+ : [0,d] \to \mathcal{S}$ are such that

- $f_-(0) = S$,
- for all $d' \in [0,d]$, $f_-(d') \xrightarrow{\tau}_{i,\tau} f_+(d')$, and
- there exist $d_0, d_1, \ldots, d_k \in [0,d]$ such that $d_0 = 0$, $d_k = d$ and $\forall i.\ d_{i+1} > d_i$, as well as
  - for all $d' \in [0,d] \setminus \{d_0, d_1, \ldots, d_k\}$, $f_-(d') = f_+(d')$, and

[15] This matching is abstracting from the externally non-observable transitions $\xrightarrow{i}$ and $\xrightarrow{\tau}$.

[16] In the case of timed transitions we require also the "matching" of the states visited "during" these transitions. This requirement is essential to ensure the compositionality of the formalism.

- for any i, for all $d' \in]d_i, d_{i+1}]$ we have $f_+(d_i) \xrightarrow{\epsilon(d'-d_i)} f_-(d')$.

Under these conditions we say that the pair of functions $f = \langle f_-, f_+ \rangle$ is an $\langle S, d\rangle$-trace. We denote the set of all $\langle S, d\rangle$-traces by $S \xrightarrow{\epsilon(d)}_{i,\tau}$. We have $S \xrightarrow{\epsilon(d)}_{\tau} \subseteq S \xrightarrow{\epsilon(d)}_{i,\tau}$ and $S \xrightarrow{\epsilon(d)} \subseteq S \xrightarrow{\epsilon(d)}_{\tau}$ as the sets of $\langle S, d\rangle$-traces not involving $\xrightarrow{i}$, and not involving any internal transition, respectively.

For $f \in S \xrightarrow{\epsilon(d)}_{i,\tau}$ and $g \in T \xrightarrow{\epsilon(d)}_{i,\tau}$, and a relation $\mathcal{R} \subseteq \mathcal{S} \times \mathcal{S}$, we say that $\langle f, g\rangle \in \mathcal{R}^t$, if both $\langle f_+(d'), g_+(d')\rangle \in \mathcal{R}$ and $\langle f_-(d'), g_-(d')\rangle \in \mathcal{R}$ for every $d' \in [0, d]$. Also for $S \in \mathcal{S}$ we let $S \xrightarrow{\tau^\infty}_i$ to denote the fact of existence of infinite chain of $\xrightarrow{\tau}_i$ transitions starting at S: $S \xrightarrow{\tau}_i S_1 \xrightarrow{\tau}_i S_2 \xrightarrow{\tau}_i \cdots$.

Definition 3.1 *A relation $\mathcal{R} \subseteq \mathcal{S} \times \mathcal{S}$ is a refinement relation, if for any $\langle S, T\rangle \in \mathcal{R}$*

1. *$S \xrightarrow{a}_{i,\tau} S'$ implies $\exists T'. T \xrightarrow{a}_{i,\tau} T'$ so that $\langle S', T'\rangle \in \mathcal{R}$;*
2. *$T \xrightarrow{a}_{\tau} T'$ implies $\exists S'. S \xrightarrow{a}_{\tau} S'$ so that $\langle S', T'\rangle \in \mathcal{R}$;*
3. *$f \in S \xrightarrow{\epsilon(d)}_{i,\tau}$ implies existence of $g \in T \xrightarrow{\epsilon(d)}_{i,\tau}$ such that $\langle f, g\rangle \in \mathcal{R}^t$;*
4. *$S \xrightarrow{\tau^\infty}_i$ implies $T \xrightarrow{\tau^\infty}_i$.*

We say that S is a refinement of T, and write $S \trianglelefteq T$ whenever there exists a refinement relation $\mathcal{R}$ containing $\langle S, T\rangle$ (In other words, $\trianglelefteq$ is the largest refinement relation).

It can be shown that all examples of $\trianglelefteq$ mentioned in the introduction indeed are valid refinement instances. There are more examples of $\trianglelefteq$ throughout the paper. An important note here is that the refinement $\trianglelefteq$ here is slightly changed from [Cer94] in order to ensure better conservativity (wrt. Timed CCS of [Wan90]) properties[17] (see Theorem 3).

Fact 3.2 *The relation $\trianglelefteq$ is reflexive and transitive.*

Lemma 3.3 *If $T \xrightarrow{i} S$, then $S \trianglelefteq T$.*

Proof: We show that the relation $\{\langle S, T\rangle | S = T \text{ or } T \xrightarrow{i} S\}$ is a refinement. The proof is a matter of combining definitions, given the following fact.

Fact 3.4 *If $T \xrightarrow{i} S$ and $T \xrightarrow{a} T'$, then either $S \xrightarrow{a} T'$, or there exists an S' such that $S \xrightarrow{a} S'$ and $T' \xrightarrow{i} S'$.*

Proof: If $T \xrightarrow{i} S$ and $T \xrightarrow{a} T'$ are done in distinct regular components of T, we have the second option. If, however, $T \xrightarrow{i} S$ is in a component which is involved in $T \xrightarrow{a} T'$ (in other branch of some choice (+) operator), then $S \xrightarrow{a} T'$ (recall that $\xrightarrow{i}$ does not resolve the choice, while any $a \in Act$ does). □□

Lemma 3.5 *A relation $\mathcal{R} \subseteq \mathcal{S} \times \mathcal{S}$ is a refinement relation, if and only if for any $\langle S, T\rangle \in \mathcal{R}$*

1. *$S \xrightarrow{a^+} S'$ implies $T \xrightarrow{a^+}_{i,\tau} T'$ so that $\langle S', T'\rangle \in \mathcal{R}$;*
2. *$T \xrightarrow{a} T'$ implies $S \xrightarrow{a}_{\tau} S'$ so that $\langle S', T'\rangle \in \mathcal{R}$;*
3. *$f \in S \xrightarrow{\epsilon(d)}$ implies existence of $g \in T \xrightarrow{\epsilon(d)}_{i,\tau}$ such that $\langle f, g\rangle \in \mathcal{R}^t$;*
4. *$S \xrightarrow{\tau^\infty}_i$ implies $T \xrightarrow{\tau^\infty}_i$.*

---

[17] The same conservativity properties were wrongly claimed also in [Cer94] for the "old version" $\trianglelefteq_o$ of the refinement, where $\langle f, g\rangle \in \mathcal{R}^t$ was defined just as $\langle f_+(d'), g_+(d')\rangle \in \mathcal{R}$ for every $d' \in [0, d]$. The counterexample to the conservativity of $\trianglelefteq_o$ is $[1,1].a.nil \trianglelefteq_o [1,1].(\tau.a.nil + b.nil)$ (what may appear also semantically undesirable).

Proof: Routine. □

Lemma 3.6 $\trianglelefteq$ *is preserved by the CTR network construction operations (parallel composition, restriction and relabelling).*

Proof: We prove that for any refinement relation $\mathcal{R}$ refinement relations are also $\mathcal{R}^+ = \{\langle S|T, P|T\rangle | \langle S,P\rangle \in \mathcal{R}\}$, $\mathcal{R}^+_{rs} = \{\langle S\backslash A, P\backslash A\rangle | \langle S,P\rangle \in \mathcal{R}\}$ and $\mathcal{R}^+_{rl} = \{\langle S[f], P[f]\rangle | \langle S,P\rangle \in \mathcal{R}\}$. For this purpose we use the characterization of refinement relations, given by Lemma 3.5.

Take $\langle S|T, P|T\rangle \in \mathcal{R}^+$. For $S|T \xrightarrow{a^+} X$ we easily have $P|T \xrightarrow{a^+} Y$ with $\langle X,Y\rangle \in \mathcal{R}^+$, what implies the first and the fourth clause of Lemma 3.5. The second clause is as easy.

For $f \in S|T \xrightarrow{\epsilon(d)}$, we have $f = f^1|f^2$ with $f^1 \in S \xrightarrow{\epsilon(d)}$ and $f^2 \in T \xrightarrow{\epsilon(d)}$. Since $\langle S,P\rangle \in \mathcal{R}$ we have $g \in P \xrightarrow{\epsilon(d)}_{i,\tau}$ with $f^1\mathcal{R}^t g$, we show first $g|f^2 \in P|T \xrightarrow{\epsilon(d)}_{i,\tau}$. In essence, we need to show that P can exhibit the same waiting behaviour in the presence of the T environment, as it were able to perform without T. All control transitions of P do not require any participation from T, nor any of them is blocked. For (non-abstracted) delays of P, if at some point d' they could not be continued, that would mean $a \in Sort(0, g_+(d')) \cap \overline{Sort(0, f^2_+(d'))}$. Then due to $f^1\mathcal{R}^t g$ we would have $a \in Sort(0, f^1_+(d')) \cap \overline{Sort(0, f^2_+(d'))}$[18], a contradiction with $f^1|f^2 \in S|T \xrightarrow{\epsilon(d)}$. The property $\langle (f^1|f^2), (g|f^2)\rangle \in (\mathcal{R}^+)^t$ follows by definition of $(\mathcal{R}^+)^t$ observing that for any d and any traces u, v, $(u|v)_+(d) = u_+(d)|v_+(d)$ and $(u|v)_-(d) = u_-(d)|v_-(d)$. The cases of restriction and relabelling are straightforward. □

It is also straightforward to establish the preservation of $\trianglelefteq$ by the action prefix (where this is syntactically applicable), also some standard preservation theorem for recursion combinator (constant definition) can be formulated and proved. Note also that the substitution of a tighter delay interval for a looser one gives a refinement instance in arbitrary context.

3.1 Logical properties of refinement

When developing a detailed description of a timed system within the CTR framework, a natural possibility is to express its specifications also as CTR terms. However, on the user level it may be desirable to give some characterization of the properties obeyed by the system in some logical language. Here we present one possible logics $\mathcal{L}$ whose properties are preserved by $\trianglelefteq$. It is a variation of Hennessy - Milner logic [HM85, Lar89] for characterization of bisimulation equivalence.

We define the set $\mathcal{L}$ of logical formulae, ranged over by F, G, by the following abstract syntax (we have $d \in \mathbf{R}^{>0}$):

$$F ::= tt \mid ff \mid F \wedge F \mid F \vee F \mid \langle a\rangle F \mid [a]F \mid [\epsilon(d) : F]G \mid WT(d).$$

We shall abbreviate $[\epsilon(d) : tt]F$ as $[\epsilon(d)]F$.

For $S \in \mathcal{S}$ we call a sequence $(s_j, \delta_j)_{j\in\mathbf{N}}$ an S-step sequence, if $(s_0, \delta_0) = (S, 0)$, $s_0 \xrightarrow{\epsilon}_{i,\tau}\xrightarrow{\epsilon(\delta_1)} s_1$, and for all $j > 0$ $s_j \xrightarrow{\epsilon\ +}_{i,\tau}\xrightarrow{\epsilon(d_j)} s_{j+1}$ and $\delta_{j+1} = \delta_j + d_j$ [19] for some d_j. Notice that any S-step sequence is by definition infinite. The set of all S-step sequences is denoted by $Step(S)$. The semantics $[\![\cdot]\!]$ of the $\mathcal{L}$ formulae is inductively defined as the sets of their satisfying states:

$$[\![tt]\!] = \mathcal{S} \qquad [\![ff]\!] = \emptyset$$
$$[\![F \wedge F']\!] = [\![F]\!] \cap [\![F']\!]$$
$$[\![F \vee F']\!] = [\![F]\!] \cup [\![F']\!]$$
$$[\![\langle\alpha\rangle F]\!] = \{s \mid \exists s'.s \xrightarrow{\alpha}_\tau s' \text{ and } s' \in [\![F]\!]\}$$
$$[\![[\alpha]F]\!] = \{s \mid \forall s'.s \xrightarrow{\alpha}_{i,\tau} s' \text{ implies } s' \in [\![F]\!]\}$$

[18] $f^1\mathcal{R}^t g$ implies $f^1_+(d')\mathcal{R}g_+(d')$ what on its turn implies $Sort(0, g_+(d')) \subseteq Sort(0, f^1_+(d'))$.
[19] $\xrightarrow{\epsilon\ +}_{i,\tau} = (\xrightarrow{i} \cup \xrightarrow{\tau})^+$.

$[\![[\epsilon(d):F]G]\!] = \{ s \mid \forall f \in s \xrightarrow{\epsilon(d)}_{i,\tau} f_+(d) \in [\![G]\!] \text{ and } \forall d' < d.\, f_-(d'), f_+(d'), f_-(d) \in [\![F]\!] \}$
$[\![WT(d)]\!] = \{ s \mid \forall (s_j, \delta_j) \in Step(s). \exists k. \delta_k \geq d \}$
We shall write $s \models \phi$ for $s \in [\![\phi]\!]$.

Intuitively, $s \models WT(d)$ means that during the course of execution from s no more than a finite number of elementary internal steps are performed within the first d time units. Thus, due to the transition liveness of CTR specifications (for any $S \in \mathcal{S}$ either $\xrightarrow{\tau}$, $\xrightarrow{i}$, or $\xrightarrow{\epsilon(d)}$ for some $d' > 0$ is enabled), $s \models WT(d)$ really means the (necessary) ability of s to exhibit an externally observable delay of d time units, no matter how (daemonically) its internal transitions are chosen.

It can be observed that without the WT operation it would not be possible to give a distinguishing property for a rather critical non-refinement case $P \stackrel{def}{=} \tau.P + \alpha.nil \not\trianglelefteq \alpha.nil$ (in the full logic $\mathcal{L}$ we have $\alpha.nil \models WT(1)$ and $P \stackrel{def}{=} \tau.P + \alpha.nil \not\models WT(1)$).

Theorem 1 *If $S \trianglelefteq T$, then for any $\phi \in \mathcal{L}$ $T \models \phi$ implies $S \models \phi$.*

Proof: Let $S \in \mathcal{S} = \mathcal{S}(\mathcal{V}ar, \mathcal{E})$ and let $c = \delta(\mathcal{E})$ be the smallest finite nonzero bound of a delay interval syntactically found within $\mathcal{E}$ [20] [21] (if there is no such finite bound at all, define $\delta(\mathcal{E}) = 1$).

Since $WT(d) \equiv WT(d_1) \wedge [\epsilon(d_1)]WT(d - d_1)$, we can rewrite the formula ϕ into an equivalent form ϕ', which contains subformulas of the form $WT(d)$ only for $d \leq c$.

By induction on the structure of ϕ' we prove for all its subformulas ϕ'' that "for all $S', T' \in \mathcal{S}(\mathcal{V}ar, \mathcal{E})$, if $T' \models \phi''$, and $S' \trianglelefteq T'$, then $S' \models \phi''$". All cases, except that of $WT(d)$ preservation, follow from definitions in a straightforward manner.

Let us prove that for all $S, T \in \mathcal{S}$ for $d \leq c$, if $S \trianglelefteq T$ then $T \models WT(d)$ implies $S \models WT(d)$. We note that this proof relies on the network form of CTR specifications.

Let $S \in \mathcal{S}$ be *locally stable*, if $\neg S \xrightarrow{\tau^\infty}_i$. We call S d-stable, and write $S \models WT_*(d)$, if $\forall d' < d$ $S \xrightarrow{\epsilon(d')}_{i,\tau} S'$ implies that S' is locally stable.

Lemma 3.7 *For $d \leq c$, $S \models WT(d)$ if and only if $S \models WT_*(d)$.*

Assume that we have proved the lemma, let $S \trianglelefteq T$ and $T \models WT(d)$, $d \leq c$. Then $S \not\models WT_*(d)$ by definition would imply existence of S' and $d' < d$ such that $S \xrightarrow{\epsilon(d')}_{i,\tau} S' \xrightarrow{\tau^\infty}_i$. By definition of $\trianglelefteq$ this implies $T \xrightarrow{\epsilon(d')}_{i,\tau} T' \xrightarrow{\tau^\infty}_i$, so $T \not\models WT_*(d)$, clearly, $T \not\models WT(d)$, a contradiction.

Proof of Lemma 3.7: We prove $S \models WT_*(d) \Rightarrow S \models WT(d)$, the reverse is obvious.

For $S \in \mathcal{S}(\mathcal{V}ar, \mathcal{E})$ let $\delta(S)$ denote the smallest finite nonzero delay bound in the description of S (including the initial delays). We have $\delta(S) \leq \delta(\mathcal{E})$. There may be (and usually are) $S \in \mathcal{S}(\mathcal{V}ar, \mathcal{E})$ with arbitrarily small $\delta(S)$.

Let $\#(S, \sigma)$ for any $\sigma \geq 0$ be the number of non-zero delay bounds c_k in the description of S for which $c_k + \sigma < d$ [22] (since $d \leq c = \delta(\mathcal{E})$, only the bounds in "initial" delay prefixes may contribute to $\#$, bounds of prefixes behind some variable definition are at least $\delta(\mathcal{E})$).

Lemma 3.8 *Let $S \in \mathcal{S}$ and $\sigma \geq 0$. Let $\delta \leq \delta(S)$. Then $S \models WT_*(\delta)$ implies $S \models WT(\delta)$. Moreover, if $\delta = \delta(S)$, then $S \xrightarrow{\epsilon(\delta)}_{i,\tau} X$ implies $\#(X, \sigma + \delta) < \#(S, \sigma)$.*

---

[20] Observe that $\mathcal{E}$, the set of variable defining equations, is by definition finite.
[21] We take the smallest among both left and right ends of the delay interval prefixes.
[22] Since any $S \in \mathcal{S}$ is described by a finite term, $\#(S, \sigma)$ is always finite.

Assume that we have proved the lemma. To prove Lemma 3.7 assume that for some $d \leq \delta(\mathcal{E})$ both $S \models WT_*(d)$ and $S \not\models WT(d)$. We have that there exists $(S_j, \sigma_j)_{j\in\mathbf{N}} \in Step(S)$ such that $\sigma_j < d$ for all j.

For arbitrary (S_j, σ_j) in this sequence, if $\#(S_j, \sigma_j) > 0$, by definition of $\#$ we have $\delta(S_j) + \sigma_j < d$. Since $S \models WT_*(d)$ and $S \xrightarrow{\epsilon(\sigma_j)}_{i,\tau} S_j$, we have $S_j \models WT_*(d - \sigma_j)$, so $S_j \models WT_*(\delta(S_j))$. By Lemma 3.8, $S \models WT(\delta(S_j))$, therefore $\sigma_l \geq \sigma_j + \delta(S_j)$ for some $l > j$. For the least such l it can be proved (again relying on Lemma 3.8) that $\#(S_l, \sigma_l) < \#(S_j, \sigma_j)$.

Repeating this construction as necessary we come to a point where $\#(S_j, \sigma_j) = 0$, by definition of $\#$ we have $\delta(S_j) + \sigma_j \geq d$. As above, we infer $S_j \models WT_*(d - \sigma_j)$. By Lemma 3.8, $S_i \models WT(d - \sigma_j)$. Therefore $\sigma_l \geq \sigma_j + (d - \sigma_j) = d$ for some $l > j$, a contradiction with the "boundedness" assumption about the sequence. Thus we have reduced proving Lemma 3.7 and, therefore, Theorem 1 to proving Lemma 3.8.

Proof of Lemma 3.8: We say that a relation $\mathcal{R} \in \mathcal{S} \times \mathcal{S}$ is a *stutter step simulation* (SSS) if for all $\langle S, T\rangle \in \mathcal{R}$ and $u \in \{i, \tau\}$ $S \xrightarrow{u} S'$ implies $\exists T'.T \xrightarrow{u} T'$ and $\langle S', T'\rangle \in \mathcal{R}$. $\mathcal{R} \in \mathcal{S} \times \mathcal{S}$ is a SS-bisimulation (SSB), if both $\mathcal{R}$ and $\mathcal{R}^{-1}$ are SSS.

Let $\langle d_1, \ldots, d_k\rangle$ be the tuple of all finite nonzero delay bounds in S, let T be obtained from S by substituting $\langle d'_1, \ldots, d'_k\rangle$ for $\langle d_1, \ldots, d_k\rangle$, where also $\forall i. d'_i > 0$. In this case we say that S and T are *equipotent*, and write $S \sim_e T$. Clearly, the equipotence relation $\sim_e$ is SSB. By combining syntactic arguments with the SSB properties of $\sim_e$ we have:

Fact 3.9 *If* $S \xrightarrow{\epsilon(d)} S'$ *for* $d < \delta(S)$, *then* $S \sim_e S'$.

Fact 3.10 *If* $S \xrightarrow{\epsilon(d)}_{i,\tau} S'$ *for* $d < \delta(S)$, *then* $\exists S''.S \longrightarrow_{i,\tau} S''$ *and* $S'' \sim_e S'$.

Hence we easily get that the local stability of S implies $S \models WT(\delta)$, what gives $S \models WT_*(\delta) \Rightarrow S \models WT(\delta)$.

To prove $\#(X, \sigma + \delta) < \#(S, \sigma)$ observe first that $\#$ never increases, that is $S \xrightarrow{\epsilon(\delta')}_{i,\tau} S'$ implies $\#(S', \sigma + \delta') \leq \#(S, \sigma)$ (this can be proved by induction along the $S \xrightarrow{\epsilon(\delta')}_{i,\tau} S'$ derivation chain, one has to take into account $d \leq \delta(\mathcal{E})$).

To prove the strict inequality $\#(X, \sigma + \delta) < \#(S, \sigma)$ in case of $\delta = \delta(S)$, consider in S one particular delay prefix $[c_k, c'_k]$ or $[0, c_k]$ such that $c_k = \delta(S)$. Let A be the regular component of S, to which this prefix belongs. Consider an S-step sequence from S to X. Within this sequence look, whether a τ - step with the participation of A has been performed, or not. In case, if there is such a τ - step, $\#$ has been strictly decreased during that step; otherwise, a delayed form of this prefix will be present during all the chain up to X, where the decreasment of $\#$ is by virtue of a delay bound becoming 0 (within $\#$ only non-zero bounds are counted). This proves the lemma. □ □ □

Let us call a specification $S \in \mathcal{S}(\mathcal{V}ar, \mathcal{E})$ *rationally timed* if all delay bounds in $\mathcal{E}$ are given by rational numbers. It can be shown that for rationally timed specifications S and T the consider logic $\mathcal{L}$ gives a *complete* characterization of $\trianglelefteq$ in the sense that $S \not\trianglelefteq T$ implies $T \models \phi$ and $S \not\models \phi$ for some $\phi \in \mathcal{L}$ (ϕ is called a *distinguishing formula* for $S \not\trianglelefteq T$). For instance, $\phi = [\epsilon(2)]([a]ff \vee [\epsilon(1)]\langle a\rangle tt)$ distinguishes $[2,4].a.nil \not\trianglelefteq [1,2].\tau.[1,2].a.nil$ [23].

The technical presentation of the completeness proof, however, heavily relies on the region graph methods, as developed in [AD90, Cer92a, Cer92b, CGL94, God94], and is beyond the scope of this paper. We conjecture that for specifications which are not rationally timed the completeness result does not hold.

[23] We have $[1,2].\tau.[1,2].a.nil \models \phi$ and $[2,4].a.nil \not\models \phi$. For reverse, of course, $[1,2].\tau.[1,2].a.nil \trianglelefteq [2,4].a.nil$.

3.2 Decidability

Using the abovementioned region graph methods it is possible to prove the following result.

Theorem 2 *The refinement relation $\trianglelefteq$ is decidable for rationally timed CTR specifications.*

The proof of this theorem unfortunately is beyond the scope of this paper. It can be discussed in a future work also how to generate automatically the distinguishing formulae for the case when the algorithm finds that $S \not\trianglelefteq T$ (for the related formalism of TMS [CGL93] such an algorithm is developed in and its implementation is described in [God94]).

3.3 Some Conservativity Properties

In this section we show what relation the CTR refinemnet $\trianglelefteq$ induces on the set of ("fully specified", time deterministic) process algebraic terms of Timed CCS. Let $\mathcal{P}$ denote the set of all TCCS (network) processes ($\mathcal{P} \subseteq \mathcal{S}$).

Following [Wan90], a relation $\mathcal{R} \subseteq \mathcal{P} \times \mathcal{P}$ is a (weak) bisimulation, if for all $\nu \in Act \cup \{\epsilon(d) | d \in \mathbf{R}^{>0}\}$ and all $\langle P, Q\rangle \in \mathcal{R}$

- whenever $P \xrightarrow{\nu}_\tau P'$ then $\exists Q'.Q \xrightarrow{\nu}_\tau Q'$ so that $\langle P', Q'\rangle \in \mathcal{R}$ and
- whenever $Q \xrightarrow{\nu}_\tau Q'$ then $\exists P'.P \xrightarrow{\nu}_\tau P'$ so that $\langle P', Q'\rangle \in \mathcal{R}$.

Here $X \xrightarrow{\epsilon(d)}_\tau Y$ is defined to mean $X(\xrightarrow{\tau})^* \xrightarrow{\epsilon(d_1)} (\xrightarrow{\tau})^* \cdots \xrightarrow{\epsilon(d_k)} (\xrightarrow{\tau})^* Y$, where $d_1 + \cdots + d_k = d$. The largest TCCS weak bisimulation is denoted by $\approx$. We can have the following result, whose intuitive interpretation is that the CTR specification refinement does not relate any two "fully specified" processes, unless they are weakly (or, observationally) bisimilar.

Fact 3.11 *For P and Q being TCCS processes, $P \trianglelefteq Q$ implies $P \approx Q$.*

To characterize the relation induced by $\trianglelefteq$ on TCCS terms precisely, let a relation $\mathcal{R} \subseteq \mathcal{P} \times \mathcal{P}$ be called a *divergence refinement* iff

- $\mathcal{R}$ is a weak bisimulation, and
- for any $\langle P, Q\rangle \in \mathcal{R}$ whenever $P \xrightarrow{\tau^\infty}$, then also $Q \xrightarrow{\tau^\infty}$.

Let $\triangleleft_D$ be the largest divergence refinement for TCCS processes.

Theorem 3 *For P and Q being TCCS processes, $P \trianglelefteq Q$ if and only if $P \triangleleft_D Q$.*

Proof sketch: We show first that $\trianglelefteq \cap \mathcal{P}$ is a divergence refinement (this gives $\trianglelefteq \cap \mathcal{P} \subseteq \triangleleft_D$). Observing that for TCCS processes, $\longrightarrow_{i,\tau} = \longrightarrow_\tau$, the crucial point to show becomes that for $P \trianglelefteq Q$ and $Q \xrightarrow{\epsilon(d)} Q'$ there exists P' such that $P \xrightarrow{\epsilon(d)}_\tau P'$ and $P' \trianglelefteq Q'$.

We use Theorem 1. By the maximal progress property for TCCS processes the delay ability excludes ability of any internal transition (only $\xrightarrow{\tau}$ may be available), therefore $Q \xrightarrow{\epsilon(d)} Q'$ implies $Q \models WT(d)$, hence $P \models WT(d)$, hence $f \in P \xrightarrow{\epsilon(d)}_{i,\tau}$ for some f. By time determinacy of TCCS processes we have that any trace $g \in Q \xrightarrow{\epsilon(d)}_{i,\tau}$ has $g_-(d) = Q'$. Therefore $f_-(d) \trianglelefteq Q'$, what suffices to complete the proof in this case.

For $\triangleleft_D \subseteq \trianglelefteq$ we show that $\triangleleft_D$ is a CTR refinement. The crucial point again is to establish the timed clause, namely that for $P \triangleleft_D Q$ and $f \in P \xrightarrow{\epsilon(d)}$ there exists $g \in Q \xrightarrow{\epsilon(d)}_\tau$ such that $f(\triangleleft_D)^t g$.

We exploit the definition of $\triangleleft_D$. For $P \xrightarrow{\epsilon(d)} f_+(d)$ we have that $Q \xrightarrow{\epsilon(d)}_\tau Q'$ for some Q' such that $f_+(d) \triangleleft_D Q'$. Let $g \in Q \xrightarrow{\epsilon(d)}_\tau$ with $g_+(d) = Q'$. We prove $f(\triangleleft_D)^t g$.

Let $g_*(d')$ denote either $g_+(d')$ or $g_-(d')$. Since $Q \xrightarrow{\epsilon(d')}_\tau g_*(d)$, we have that $P \xrightarrow{\epsilon(d')}_\tau P^{d'}$ for some $P^{d'} \triangleleft_D g_*(d)$. For $d' < d$ by time determinacy and maximal progress of TCCS

$\texttt{Mutex} \stackrel{def}{=} [0,\infty].\texttt{cs1\_in!}\ \texttt{InC1} + [0,\infty].\texttt{cs2\_in!}\ \texttt{InC2}$

$\texttt{InC1} \stackrel{def}{=} [0,\infty].\texttt{cs1\_out!}\ \texttt{Mutex} \qquad \texttt{InC2} \stackrel{def}{=} [0,\infty].\texttt{cs2\_out!}\ \texttt{Mutex}$

$P1 \stackrel{def}{=} [0,\infty].\texttt{tk0}.[0,b].\overline{\texttt{k1}}.[c,\infty].P1c$

$P1c \stackrel{def}{=} \texttt{tk1.cs1\_in!}\ [0,\infty].\texttt{cs1\_out!}\ \overline{\texttt{k0}}.P1 + \texttt{tk0}.P1 + \texttt{tk2}.P1$

$P2 \stackrel{def}{=} [0,\infty].\texttt{tk0}.[0,e].\overline{\texttt{k2}}.[f,\infty].P2c$

$P2c \stackrel{def}{=} \texttt{tk2.cs2\_in!}\ [0,\infty].\texttt{cs2\_out!}\ \overline{\texttt{k0}}.P2 + \texttt{tk0}.P2 + \texttt{tk1}.P2$

$\texttt{K} = (\texttt{k0.K0} + \texttt{k1.K1} + \texttt{k2.K2})$ /* this is just a macro */

$\texttt{K0} \stackrel{def}{=} \texttt{K} + \overline{\texttt{tk0}}.\texttt{K0} \qquad \texttt{K1} \stackrel{def}{=} \texttt{K} + \overline{\texttt{tk1}}.\texttt{K1} \qquad \texttt{K2} \stackrel{def}{=} \texttt{K} + \overline{\texttt{tk2}}.\texttt{K2}$

$Ksort = \{\texttt{k0,k1,k2,tk0,tk1,tk2}\} \qquad S = (P1|P2|K0)\backslash Ksort$

Figure 1 A mutual exclusion specification and its "implementation"

processes we have $P^{d'} = f_-(d') = f_+(d')$, as required. $f_+(d) \lhd_D g_+(d)$ by definition, it remains to show $f_-(d) \lhd_D g_-(d)$.

By definition of $\lhd_D$, there exists P' such that $P \xrightarrow{\epsilon(d)}_\tau P'$ and $P' \lhd_D g_-(d)$. By time determinacy and maximal progress, $f_-(d) \xrightarrow{\tau}_\tau P'$. Similarly, $g_-(d) \xrightarrow{\tau}_\tau Q''$ for some Q'' such that $f_-(d) \lhd_D Q''$ [24]. We obtain $f_-(d) \lhd_D g_-(d)$ by definition of $\lhd_D$. □

4 A Critical Resource Access Example

In this section we illustrate the capabilities of the CTR framework on a toy example of timing based critical resource access protocol with non-exact clocks. The idea of the example (its initial part regarding mutual exclusion) is taken from [AHH93].

For the sake of convenience of notation we introduce an abbreviation $\alpha!P$ to stand for $Q \stackrel{def}{=} \alpha.P + \tau.Q$ (in essence, $\alpha!P$ differs from $\alpha.P$ just in that it requires the action α to be performed immediately, before the time progresses further).

We consider first the specification Mutex of the mutual exclusion property and a candidate for its "loose" implementation S which are presented in a self-explanatory notation in Figure 1. It can be shown that $S \trianglelefteq \texttt{Mutex}$ whenever $c < e$ and $f < b$. This proof allows us to establish the mutual exclusion fact for quite a variety of timed behaviours, represented by S (for instance, the interval $[0,b]$ in the S component $P1$ can at each particular moment when being executed take any amount b' of time in the range $b' \in [0,b]$. This is the way of modeling the behaviour of hybrid system "drifting clocks" within the CTR framework. Further refinements of S may somewhat constrain this timing flexibility of S, still, the mutual exclusion property will remain valid also for the "constrained" systems).

The specifications Mutex and S are actually quite restrictive since they allow only implementations whose sort (the set of all possible actions) is included in $LC = \{\texttt{cs1\_in}, \texttt{cs2\_in}, \texttt{cs1\_out}, \texttt{cs2\_out}\}$. A more general variant of the mutual exclusion specification is $\texttt{Mutex}(L) = \texttt{Mutex}|Uni(L)$, where for some label set L, $Uni(L) = \sum_{a \in L \cup \{\tau\}} [0,\infty].a.Uni(L)$. If $LC \cap L = \emptyset$, in addition to the discipline imposed on the events from LC this specification would allow the system to participate in arbitrary events of the sort L [25]. By substitutivity

[24] We rely on $g_+(d') \lhd_D f_+(d')$, where d' is either 0, or the largest point on $[0,d[$ such that $g_-(d') \neq g_+(d')$).

[25] $Uni(L)$ is called the *universal* specification of the sort L since it is refined by any specification whose

of $\trianglelefteq$ (Lemma 3.6) for $c < e$ and $f < b$, $S|Uni(L) \trianglelefteq \texttt{Mutex}(L)$.

Consider the case when $L = \{\texttt{try1}\}$. Let us define:

$$P1' \stackrel{def}{=} [0,\infty].\texttt{try1}!\ P1t \qquad P1t \stackrel{def}{=} \texttt{tk0}.[0,b].\overline{\texttt{k1}}.[c,d].P1c'$$
$$P1c' \stackrel{def}{=} \texttt{tk1.cs1\_in}!\ [0,\infty].\texttt{cs1\_out}!\ \overline{\texttt{k0}}.P1' + \texttt{tk0}.P1t + \texttt{tk2}.P1t$$
$$P2' \stackrel{def}{=} [0,\infty].\texttt{tk0}.[0,e].\overline{\texttt{k2}}.[f,g].P2c'$$
$$P2c' \stackrel{def}{=} \texttt{tk2.cs2\_in}!\ [0,h].\texttt{cs2\_out}!\ \overline{\texttt{k0}}.[x,\infty].P2' + \texttt{tk0}.P2' + \texttt{tk1}.P2'.$$

It is not difficult to find out that $P1' \trianglelefteq P1|Uni(\{\texttt{try1}\})$, as well as $P2' \trianglelefteq P2$, therefore[26]

$$S' = (P1'|P2'|K0)\backslash Ksort \trianglelefteq (P1|P2|K0|Uni(\{\texttt{try1}\}))\backslash Ksort \trianglelefteq$$
$$\trianglelefteq ((P1|P2|K0)\backslash Ksort)|Uni(\{\texttt{try1}\}) = S|Uni(\{\texttt{try1}\}).$$

Therefore by transitivity of $\trianglelefteq$ we have $S' \trianglelefteq \texttt{Mutex}(\{\texttt{try1}\})$.

For the specification S' it would also be possible to prove certain "bounded responsiveness" property $S' \trianglelefteq BR(y)$, where

$$BR1(y) \stackrel{def}{=} [0,\infty].\texttt{try1}!\ [0,y].\texttt{cs1\_in}!\ BR1(y) \text{ and } BR(y) = BR1(y)|Uni(LC \setminus \{\texttt{cs1\_in}\}),$$

provided $x > b + d$ and $y > b + d + h + g$.

This example outlines the principal possibility of the CTR framework to have one specification (S) during the design process refined (into S') to ensure that the resulting system is obeying more "useful" properties. Observe that the proof of S correctness is reused to demonstrate the correctness (mutual exclusion) of S'. Furthermore, the refinement fact $S' \trianglelefteq S|Uni(\{\texttt{try1}\})$ has been established in a modular fashion by refining the regular components $P1$ and $P2$ of S independently. Also the "refined" system $S1$ is still a loose specification comprising a variety of timed behaviours, and can be refined further to incorporate additional system design requirements, or to become a real executable "implementation".

5 On Timed Modal Specifications

The idea of modal specifications originally appears in [LT88], and consists in attaching "necessary" and "possible" modes to the transitions in the system operational semantics (every "necessary" transition must be also "possible"). The intuition of the specification refinement in the modal framework is very simple - the more possible and fewer necessary transitions a specification has, the more general it is. In [CGL93, CGL94] this idea has been applied also to a timed process algebra (Timed CCS of [Wan90]), resulting in so-called framework of Timed Modal Specifications (TMS).

One of the semantic features of TMS is that it has the modalities attached also to the delay transitions, for this reason some semantic properties of the framework appear to be a little bit strange. For instance, in TMS it is not the case that $[1,2].\tau.[1,2].a.nil$ is a refinement of $[2,4].a.nil$ [27] [28]. The modalities on delay transitions also sometimes make the operational behaviour of specifications quite difficult to understand.

sort is included in L. This notion appears already in [CGL93]. If $M \cap L = \emptyset$, S is a specification with the sort M, $\phi \in \mathcal{L}$ (see Section 3.1) refers only to actions from M, and ϕ does not contain WT, then $S \models \phi$ if and only if $S|Uni(L) \models \phi$.

[26] We rely on some intuitively clear refinement laws which in the full presentation of the theory should, of course, be explicitly mentioned.

[27] In CTR $[1,2].\tau.[1,2].a.nil \trianglelefteq [2,4].a.nil$ of course is the case.

[28] The reason for not having this refinement instance in TMS is the delay transition $\xrightarrow{\epsilon(2)}$ performed by $[2,4].a.nil$ in the "necessary" mode, what can not be matched appropriately on the left hand side (as a delay in the necessary mode). More discussion on this is in [Cer94].

$$\frac{--}{nil \xrightarrow{\epsilon(d)} nil} \qquad \frac{--}{a.S \xrightarrow{a}_{\Box} S} \qquad \frac{S \xrightarrow{a}_m S'}{X \xrightarrow{a}_m S'}[X \stackrel{def}{=} S] \in \mathcal{E} \qquad \frac{S \xrightarrow{\epsilon(d)} S'}{X \xrightarrow{\epsilon(d)} S'}[X \stackrel{def}{=} S] \in \mathcal{E}$$

$$\frac{--}{a_{[c,e]}.S \xrightarrow{\epsilon(d)} a_{[c \dot{-} d, e \dot{-} d]}.S} \qquad \frac{-- \quad [d \leq e]}{\tau_{[c,e]}.S \xrightarrow{\epsilon(d)} \tau_{[c \dot{-} d, e-d]}.S} \qquad \frac{--}{a_{[0,e]}.S \xrightarrow{a}_{\Diamond} S}$$

$$\frac{S \xrightarrow{a}_m S'}{S+T \xrightarrow{a}_m S'} \qquad \frac{T \xrightarrow{a}_m T'}{S+T \xrightarrow{a}_m T'} \qquad \frac{S \xrightarrow{\epsilon(d)} S' \;\; T \xrightarrow{\epsilon(d)} T'}{S+T \xrightarrow{\epsilon(d)} S'+T'}$$

$$\frac{S \xrightarrow{a}_m S'}{S|T \xrightarrow{a}_m S'|T} \quad \frac{T \xrightarrow{a}_m T'}{S|T \xrightarrow{a}_m S|T'} \quad \frac{S \xrightarrow{\alpha}_m S',\, T \xrightarrow{\overline{\alpha}}_m T'}{S|T \xrightarrow{\tau}_m S'|T'} \quad \frac{S \xrightarrow{\epsilon(d)} S' \;\; T \xrightarrow{\epsilon(d)} T'}{S|T \xrightarrow{\epsilon(d)} S'|T'} \begin{array}{l}[Sort(d,S) \cap \\ Sort(d,T) = \emptyset]\end{array}$$

Table 2 Transition rules for A-TMS, $m \in \{\Diamond, \Box\}$

In the view of the developed theory of CTR we are able here to provide also a slight semantic reformulation A-TMS[29] of the TMS framework, which fixes the above mentioned example, and hopefully fixes also some operational intuition behind the specifications.

Syntactically the A-TMS terms are those of CTR in which every nondeterministic delay prefix is followed by a control action (A-TMS terms have $a_{[c,e]}$ and $\epsilon(d)$ instead of separate $[c, e]$ and control action prefixes). We abbreviate $a_{[0,0]}.E$ as $a_{\Box}.E$ (or simply $a.E$) and $a_{[0,\infty]}.E$ as $a_{\Diamond}.E$ [30].

The operational semantics of A-TMS is based on the necessary control transitions $\xrightarrow{a}_{\Box}$, possible control transitions $\xrightarrow{a}_{\Diamond}$ and delays $\xrightarrow{\epsilon(d)}$ [31] [32]. For a fragment of the framework the semantics is summarized in Table 2 (this fragment does not include $\epsilon(d)$ prefix, neither restriction and relabelling are considered). The $Sort$ function[33] in the parallel composition delay rule side condition is computed, as for CTR terms, by the rules given in Section 2.

In order to define the A-TMS refinement relation let $\mathcal{M}$ be the set of all TMS specifications (over certain sets of specification variables and equations). Let for $m \in \{\Box, \Diamond\}$ the observational (τ-abstracting) modal transition relations $\stackrel{\mu}{\Longrightarrow}_m$ also be defined in the usual way. The trace set $S \stackrel{\epsilon(d)}{\Longrightarrow}_{\Diamond}$ consists of all traces starting at S and containing interleaving of $\xrightarrow{\epsilon(d_i)}$ and $\xrightarrow{\tau}_{\Diamond}$ transitions, with the total delay amount being d [34].

Definition 5.1 *A relation $\mathcal{R} \subseteq \mathcal{M} \times \mathcal{M}$ is a(n) (observational) modal refinement relation, if for any $\langle S, T\rangle \in \mathcal{R}$*

1. $S \stackrel{a}{\Longrightarrow}_{\Diamond} S'$ implies $\exists T'. T \stackrel{a}{\Longrightarrow}_{\Diamond} T'$ so that $\langle S', T'\rangle \in \mathcal{R}$;

---

[29] As in "Another" TMS.

[30] In the original definition of TMS in [CGL93] the modal prefixes $a_{\Box}.E$ and $a_{\Diamond}.E$ were taken as primitives, and $a_{[c,e]}.E$ was defined as $\epsilon(c).a_{\Diamond}.E + \epsilon(e).a_{\Box}.E$.

[31] The delays always are in a sense in the possible mode.

[32] A suggested physical interpretation of the possible and necessary transitions is that of transitions of a specification being enabled in the *weak* and the *strong* sense. For $a_{[c,e]}.S$ during the first c time units the a transition is not enabled. Afterwards, for the next $e-c$ units this transition is enabled in the weak sense, after what (if it has not been carried out already), it becomes enabled in the strong sense.

[33] This function characterizes the transition availability in the strong sense.

[34] A formal definition can be given following the style of the trace definition in Section 3. In the same fashion also the relation $\mathcal{R}^t$ for $\mathcal{R} \subseteq \mathcal{M} \times \mathcal{M}$ is defined.

2. $T \overset{a}{\Longrightarrow}_{\Box} T'$ *implies* $\exists S'. S \overset{a}{\Longrightarrow}_{\Box} S'$ *so that* $\langle S', T' \rangle \in \mathcal{R}$*;*

3. $f \in S \overset{\epsilon(d)}{\Longrightarrow}_{\Diamond}$ *implies existence of* $g \in T \overset{\epsilon(d)}{\Longrightarrow}_{\Diamond}$ *such that* $\langle f, g \rangle \in \mathcal{R}^t$*;*

4. $S \overset{\tau^\infty}{\longrightarrow}_{\Diamond}$ *implies* $T \overset{\tau^\infty}{\longrightarrow}_{\Diamond}$.

We say that S is a modal refinement of T, and write $S \lhd_M T$ whenever there exists a refinement relation $\mathcal{R}$ containing $\langle S, T \rangle$ ($\lhd_M$ is the largest modal refinement relation).

Let $n : \mathcal{M} \to \mathcal{S}$ be a function giving for any A-TMS term S the same term, viewed as a CTR term[35]. The principal theorem of this section says:

Theorem 4 *For modal specifications S and T, $S \lhd_M T$ if and only if $n(S) \trianglelefteq n(T)$.*

Lemma 5.2 *1. Whenever $S \overset{a}{\longrightarrow}_{\Diamond} S'$, then $n(S) \overset{a}{\longrightarrow}_{i} n(S')$.*

2. Whenever $T \overset{a}{\longrightarrow}_{\Box} T'$, then $n(T) \overset{a}{\longrightarrow} n(T')$.

3. Whenever $n(S)(\overset{i}{\longrightarrow})^* \overset{a}{\longrightarrow} (\overset{i}{\longrightarrow})^* Y$, then $\exists S'. S \overset{a}{\longrightarrow}_{\Diamond} S'$ and $Y \trianglelefteq n(S')$.

4. Whenever $n(T) \overset{a}{\longrightarrow} X$, then $\exists T'. T \overset{a}{\longrightarrow}_{\Box} T'$ and $n(T') = X$.

To prove $S \lhd_M T \Rightarrow n(S) \trianglelefteq n(T)$ we show that a CTR refinement is the relation $\{\langle X, n(T) \rangle | X \trianglelefteq n(S),\ S \lhd_M T\}$.

The other direction $n(S) \trianglelefteq n(T) \Rightarrow S \lhd_M T$ goes by showing that a modal refinement is the relation $\{\langle S, T \rangle | n(S) \trianglelefteq n(T)\}$. In both directions we rely on Lemma 5.2. □

6 Conclusions

In this paper a mathematically sound and rather general process algebraic framework for refinement of timed system specifications has been proposed. One direction of the future work on this framework is to provide a collection of algebraic refinement laws (a few of them already were needed in the example of Section 4).

An even more important perspective may be to look at the pragmatics of real system specification within the framework. Some suggestions of the work in this direction possibly can be found in [LSW94]. Also the (possible) role of the left-open delay interval prefixes in the framework needs a better understanding. It is also of clear importance for achieving the practical applicability of the formalism to introduce in it more powerful means of interprocess communication, possibly allowing both the broadcasting and synchronization communication disciplines. Some ideas for this work could possibly be taken from [LV92].

It should be noted that CTR allows the specification and refinement also for certain kinds of hybrid systems (those dependent on non-exact clocks). The obtained results of robustness of the refinement notion (invariance wrt. the actual operational semantics of specifications, see e.g. Theorem 4) give in practical situations an excellent chance for every system designer to understand/imagine the behaviour of the specifications in the way he/she likes it most, all reasonable choices (standard CTR semantics, its A-TMS variant considered here, as well as a version of the "inline choice" semantics of [Cer94]) leading to the same formal result.

Though the algorithm for deciding the refinement relation is in principle rather clear (taking into account the previous work, mentioned in Section 3.2), an important issue of the future work is to achieve its practical feasibility. A possible step into this direction could be a theory of combining of the local validity checking and partition refinement methods for work on deciding "bisimulation - like" properties.

---

[35] n is an injective mapping of $\mathcal{M}$ into $\mathcal{S}$, introduced for the sake of further convenience.

Acknowledgements. The author wants to thank Bengt Jonsson and Wang Yi from University of Uppsala, Sweden and Kim Larsen from Aalborg University, Denmark for stimulating discussions and ideas on timed specification formalisms. Thanks are also to the anonymous referees for the help in locating an essential misprint and for good inquiring criticism.

References

[AD90] R. Alur and D. Dill, *Automata for Modelling Real-Time Systems*, in Proceedings of ICALP'90, Lecture Notes in Computer Science No. 443, 1990.

[AIK92] R. Alur, A. Itai and R. Kurshan, *Timing Verification by Successive Approximation*, in Proceedings of CAV'92, Lecture Notes in Computer Science No. 663, 1992.

[AHH93] R. Alur, T.H. Henzinger, P.-H. Ho, *Automatic Symbolic Verification of Embedded Systems* in Proceedings of 14th IEEE RTSS, 1993.

[CC89] CCITT, *Functional Specification and Description Language (SDL)*, Recommendations Z.100, 1989.

[Cer92a] K. Čerāns, *Decidability of Bisimulation Equivalences for Parallel Timer Processes*, in Proceedings of CAV'92, Lecture Notes in Computer Science No. 663, 1992.

[Cer92b] K. Čerāns, *Algorithmic Problems in Analysis of Real Time System Specifications*, Dr.sc.comp. theses, University of Latvia, 1992.

[Cer94] K. Čerāns, *A Calculus of Timed Refinement*, in Proceedings of NWPT6, BRICS-NS-94-6, Aarhus, Denmark, 1994.

[CGL93] K. Čerāns, J.Chr. Godskesen and K.G. Larsen, *Timed Modal Specification - Theory and Tools*, in Proceedings of CAV'93, Lecture Notes in Computer Science No. 697, 1993.

[CGL94] K. Čerāns, J.Chr. Godskesen and K.G. Larsen, *Timed Modal Specification - Theory and Tools*, submitted to Formal Aspects of Computing, 1994.

[Che92] L. Chen, *An Interleaving Model for Real Time Systems*, in Proceedings of LFCS'92, Lecture Notes in Computer Science No. 620, 1992.

[Dan92] M. Daniels, *Modelling Real-Time Behaviour with an Interval Time Calculus*, in Proceedings of Conference on Formal Techniques in RT and FT Systems, Nijmegen, 1992

[GMMP89] C. Ghezzi, D. Mandrioli, S. Morasca and M. Pezze *A General Way To Put Time in Petri Nets*, in ACM SIGSOFT Eng. Notes, Vol. 14, No. 3, 1989.

[GLS94] J.Chr. Godskesen, K.G. Larsen and A. Skou, *Automatic Verification of Real-Timed Systems Using* EPSILON, BRICS-RS-94-19, 1994.

[God94] J.Chr. Godskesen, *Timed Modal Specifications - A Theory for Verification of Real-Time Concurrent Systems*, Ph.D thesis, Aalborg University, 1994.

[HM85] M. Hennessy and R. Milner, *Algebraic Laws for Nondeterminism and Concurrency*, Journal of the ACM, 1985.

[Lar89] K.G. Larsen, *Modal Specifications*, in Proceedings of CAV, Lecture Notes in Computer Science No. 407, 1989.

[LSW94] K.G. Larsen, B. Steffen and C. Weise, *A Constraint Oriented Proof Methodology based on Modal Transition Systems*, BRICS-RS-94-47, 1994.

[LT88] K.G. Larsen and B. Thomsen, *A Modal Process Logic*, in Proceedings of the fifth IEEE Symposium on Logic in Computer Science, 1988.

[LV92] N.A. Lynch and F.W. Vaandrager, *Action Transducers and Timed Automata*, , in Proceedings of CONCUR'92, Lecture Notes in Computer Science No. 630, 1992.

[LV93] N.A. Lynch and F.W. Vaandrager, *Forward and backward simulations*, Part I and II, Reports CS-R9313 and CS-R9314, CWI, Amsterdam, 1993.

[MF76] P. Merlin and D.J. Farber, *Recoverability of Communication Protocols*, IEEE Trans. on Communication Protocols, Vol. COM-24, No. 9, 1976.

[Mil89] R. Milner, *Communication and Concurrency*, Series in Computer Science, Prentice-Hall International, 1989.

[Wan90] Yi Wang, *Real Time Behaviour of Asynchronous Agents*, in Proceedings of CONCUR'90, Lecture Notes in Computer Science No. 458, 1990.

[Wan91a] Yi Wang, *CCS + Time = an Interleaving Model for Real Time Systems*, in Proceedings of ICALP'91, Lecture Notes in Computer Science No. 510, 1991.

[Wan91b] Yi Wang, *A Calculus of Real Time Systems*, Ph.D thesis, University of Göteborg and Chalmers University of Technology, 1991.

Temporal Logic + Timed Automata : Expressiveness and Decidability

Ahmed Bouajjani[1] Yassine Lakhnech[2⋆]

[1] VERIMAG, Miniparc-Zirst, Rue Lavoisier, 38330 Montbonnot St-Martin, France.
email: Ahmed.Bouajjani@imag.fr

[2] Institut für Informatik und Praktische Mathematik Christian-Albrechts-Universität zu Kiel, Preußerstr. 1-9, D-24105 Kiel, Germany.
email: yl@informatik.uni-kiel.d400.de

Abstract

We investigate the verification problem of timed automata w.r.t. linear-time dense time temporal logics. We propose a real-time logic TATL which extends the propositional temporal logic with constraints involving timed automata. These constraints allow to require that the computation segment since some designated point is accepted by a given timed automaton. We identify an expressively powerful fragment of this logic, called TATL$^+$ for which the verification problem is decidable. To establish this result, we define a fragment of TATL, called TATL$^\times$, such that the negation of any formula in TATL$^+$ is equivalent to a TATL$^\times$ formula, and then, we prove that every TATL$^\times$ formula can be characterized by a nondeterministic timed Büchi automaton.

1 Introduction

Real-time temporal logics are widely accepted as suitable specification formalisms for systems with hard timing constraints [5, 7, 12, 11, 2, 8, 4]. These logics are interpreted on either discrete or dense time models.

Several works investigate the verification problem (model-checking) of real-time temporal logics, i.e., whether all the computations (trajectories in the dense-time case) of a timed system satisfy some property expressed by a formula in these logics. The first decidability results have been obtained for discrete time logics like TPTL [5]. This logic is obtained by extending the linear-time propositional temporal logic PTL [13] with the so-called *reset* quantification allowing to introduce clocks that are used in timing constraints (comparisons with natural constants). For instance, the formula

$$\Box(P \Rightarrow x.\Diamond(Q \wedge x \leq 5)) \tag{1}$$

expresses the bounded response property saying that *whenever P holds, a state satisfying Q will be eventually reached within* 5 *time units.*

Unfortunately, the logic TPTL is undecidable for dense-time models. Actually, there are mainly two dense-time temporal logics for which the verification problem has been shown to be decidable. The first one is the branching-time logic

⋆ This work has been performed while this author was visiting VERIMAG.

TCTL [2, 1, 10] obtained by extending the logic CTL [6] using the reset quantification and timing constraints in a similar way as for TPTL. This decidability result is based on the fact that TCTL induces a time-abstract bisimulation on timed automata that allows to solve the verification problem by reasoning on a finite-state region graph. The second logic is the linear-time logic MITL [4] which can be seen as the fragment of dense-time TPTL obtained by imposing two restrictions: One of these restrictions is that, between the occurrence of each clock x in some constraint and its binding ("$x.$"), there is exactly one temporal operator, i.e., one until ($\mathcal{U}$) operator. The other restriction is that punctual constraints, i.e., equalities as $x = 5$, are forbidden. Recently, the logic MITL has been extended in [15] by using automata operators instead of the until operator; these automata operators are (untimed) finite-state automata on finite sequences. The obtained logic, called EMITL, is shown to be also decidable.

In this paper, we adopt a different approach to get a temporal logic with a decidable verification problem. We introduce a linear-time temporal logic which is an extension of dense-time TPTL by using timed automata instead of timing constraints. Then, we identify a fragment of this logic for which the verification problem is decidable and where general reset quantification as well as punctual constraints are allowed.

The logic we define, called Timed Automata Temporal Logic (TATL), is an extension of PTL by a *position quantification* allowing to relate *position variables* with points in trajectories. Then, *automata constraints* can be used to express the fact that the trajectory segment since the point associated with some position variable is accepted by some given timed automaton. For instance, the TPTL formula (1) can be written in TATL as $\Box(P \Rightarrow u.\Diamond(Q \wedge A^{u}_{\leq 5}))$ where $A_{\leq 5}$ recognizes the set of bounded trajectories of length less or equal than 5.

While constraints in TPTL are simple timing constraints on trajectory segments, automata constraints in TATL allow to express finer conditions combining constraints on the order of occurrence of state properties with timing constraints between these occurrences.

Clearly, the verification problem of TATL is undecidable since it is already undecidable for dense-time TPTL [5, 9]. Then, we define a syntactical fragment of TATL, called TATL$^+$, and show that its verification problem is decidable. This fragment covers a wide class of interesting real-time properties like bounded invariance and bounded response properties. We prove that it is strictly more expressive than deterministic timed Muller automata. Moreover, concerning untimed properties, we show that TATL$^+$ can express any stuttering-closed ω-regular property.

To prove the decidability of the verification problem of TATL$^+$, we introduce another fragment of TATL, called TATL$^\times$, such that the negation of each TATL$^+$ formula can be transformed into an equivalent formula in TATL$^\times$. Then, we prove that for every TATL$^\times$ formula φ, we can construct a nondeterministic timed Büchi automaton which recognizes the set of trajectories satisfying φ.

The remainder of this paper is organized as follows. In Section 2, we introduce some basic notations and definitions. In Section 3, we define timed automata on bounded or unbounded trajectories. In Section 4, we introduce the logic TATL and its fragments TATL^+ and $\text{TATL}^\times$. In Section 5, we study the expressiveness of TATL^+ and $\text{TATL}^\times$ and compare them with timed automata. Section 6 presents decidability results, and concluding remarks are given in Section 7.

2 Preliminaries

2.1 Timing Constraints

Let $\mathcal{V}$ be a set of variables, called *clocks*, ranging over positive reals ($\mathbb{R}_{\geq 0}$). A *timing constraint* over $\mathcal{V}$ is a boolean combination of constraints of the form $x \prec c$ where $x \in \mathcal{V}$, $\prec \in \{<, \leq\}$, and c is a natural constant ($c \in \mathbb{N}$). The symbols $<$ and $\leq$ represent the usual (strict and nonstrict) ordering relations over $\mathbb{R}_{\geq 0}$. Let $\mathcal{C}_\mathcal{V}$ be the set of timing constraints over $\mathcal{V}$.

A *valuation* over $\mathcal{V}$ is a function in $[\mathcal{V} \to \mathbb{R}_{\geq 0}]$. A satisfaction relation is defined as usual between valuations and constraints. Given a valuation ν and $f \in \mathcal{C}_\mathcal{V}$, we denote by $\nu \models f$ the fact that ν satisfies f.

We denote by $\mathbf{0}$ the valuation that associates with each clock the value 0. Given a valuation ν and a set of variables $X \subseteq \mathcal{V}$, we denote by $\nu[X \mapsto 0]$ the valuation which associates with each variable in X the value 0, and coincides with ν on all the other variables. For every $t \in \mathbb{R}_{\geq 0}$, we denote by $\nu + t$ the valuation ν' such that $\forall x \in \mathcal{V}$, $\nu'(x) = \nu(x) + t$.

2.2 States, Interval Sequences, and Trajectories

Let $\mathcal{P}$ be a finite set of atomic propositions. A *state* is a subset of $\mathcal{P}$. Let Σ be the set of all possible states, i.e., $\Sigma = 2^\mathcal{P}$.

Let I be a nonempty subinterval of $\mathbb{R}_{\geq 0}$. Then, we denote respectively by $lb(I)$ and $ub(I)$ the lower and upper bounds of I. We denote also by $\ell(I)$ the length of the interval I, i.e., $\ell(I) = ub(I) - lb(I)$. Two nonempty intervals I_1 and I_2 are adjacent if $I_1 \cap I_2 = \emptyset$ and $lb(I_2) = ub(I_1)$.

Let I be a left-closed nonempty subinterval of $\mathbb{R}_{\geq 0}$ such that $lb(I) = 0$. An *interval sequence* over I is a finite or infinite sequence of nonempty intervals $\vec{I} = I_0 I_1 \cdots I_i \cdots$ such that

- $\forall i < |\vec{I}|$, the two intervals I_i and I_{i+1} are adjacent,
- $\forall t \in I.\ \exists i < |\vec{I}|.\ t \in I_i$,
- If I is bounded (resp. unbounded), the sequence $\vec{I}$ is finite (resp. infinite).

Now, consider a mapping $\tau : I \to \Sigma$. We say that τ is *finite-variable* if in every finite subinterval of I, τ changes its value a finite number of times (τ has a finite number of discontinuity points). Then, we call *trajectory* over I any mapping $\tau : I \to \Sigma$ which is finite-variable. We say that a trajectory $\tau : I \to \Sigma$ is *bounded* (resp. *unbounded*) if the interval I is bounded (resp. unbounded).

It can be seen that for every trajectory τ, there exists an interval sequence $\vec{I} = I_0 I_1 \cdots I_i \cdots$ such that $\forall i < |\vec{I}|.\ \forall t, t' \in I_i.\ \tau(t) = \tau(t')$, which means that τ is piecewise constant. Given a trajectory τ over an interval I, we denote by $\mathcal{D}(\tau)$ the set of infinite sequences $\sigma = s_0 s_1 \cdots \in \Sigma^\omega$ such that there exists an interval sequence $\vec{I}$ over I satisfying $\forall i \in \omega.\ \forall t \in I_i.\ \tau(t) = s_i$. This notation is generalized in the obvious way to sets of trajectories.

Let $\tau : I \to \Sigma$ be a trajectory, and I' a bounded closed nonempty subinterval of I. Then, we denote by $\tau(I')$ the bounded trajectory $\tau' : [0, \ell(I')] \to \Sigma$ such that $\forall t \in [0, \ell(I')].\ \tau'(t) = \tau(t + lb(I'))$.

3 Timed Automata

We introduce timed automata on either bounded or unbounded trajectories. These automata are similar to those used in [4].

3.1 Timed Transition Tables

Definition Recall that $\Sigma = 2^{\mathcal{P}}$ where $\mathcal{P}$ is a finite set of atomic propositions. A *timed transition table* $\mathcal{T}$ over Σ consists of the following components:

- $\mathcal{X}$, a finite set of clocks,
- $\mathcal{Q}$, a finite set of control locations,
- $\mathcal{I}nit$, a set of initial control locations ($\mathcal{I}nit \subseteq \mathcal{Q}$),
- $\mathcal{E}$, a set of edges. Each edge is a triplet $E = (q, X, q')$ where $q, q' \in \mathcal{Q}$ are the source and target locations, and $X \subseteq \mathcal{X}$ is the set of reset variables,
- Π, a function in $[\mathcal{Q} \to \Sigma]$, associating a state with each control location,
- Γ, a function in $[\mathcal{Q} \to \mathcal{C}_{\mathcal{X}}]$, associating with each control location q a timing constraint under which the computation is allowed to stay in q.

Runs, Paths, and Generated Trajectories Let I be a left-closed subinterval of $\mathbb{R}_{\geq 0}$ such that $lb(I) = 0$. Then, a *run* of $\mathcal{T}$ over the interval I is a finite or infinite sequence $\rho = \langle q_0, \nu_0, I_0\rangle\langle q_1, \nu_1, I_1\rangle \cdots \langle q_i, \nu_i, I_i\rangle \cdots$ such that

- $q_0 \in \mathcal{I}nit$, $\nu_0 = \mathbf{0}$, and
- $I_0 I_1 \cdots I_i \cdots$ is an interval sequence over I, and
- $\forall i < |\rho|.\ \forall t \in I_i.\ \nu_i + (t - lb(I_i)) \models \Gamma(q_i)$, and
- $\forall i < |\rho|$.
  - either $q_i = q_{i+1}$ and $\nu_{i+1} = \nu_i + \ell(I_i)$,
  - or $\exists (q_i, X, q_{i+1}) \in \mathcal{E}.\ \nu_{i+1} = (\nu_i + \ell(I_i))[X \mapsto 0]$.

With every run $\rho = \langle q_0, \nu_0, I_0\rangle\langle q_1, \nu_1, I_1\rangle \cdots \langle q_i, \nu_i, I_i\rangle \cdots$ defined as above, we associate a *path* of $\mathcal{T}$ over I which is a mapping $\theta : I \to \mathcal{Q}$ such that $\forall i < |\rho|.\ \forall t \in I_i.\ \theta(t) = q_i$. Then, the *trajectory generated* by ρ is defined as the mapping $\tau = \Pi \circ \theta$.

Standard form We say that a timed transition table is in *standard form* if for every control location q, the condition $\Gamma(q)$ is of the form

$$\bigwedge_{x \in \mathcal{X}} (a_x \prec_1^x x \prec_2^x b_x)$$

where the $\prec_j^x$'s are in $\{<, \leq\}$, the a_x's in $\mathbb{N}$, and the b_x's in $\mathbb{N} \cup \{+\infty\}$.

It can be verified that every timed transition table can be transformed into another one which is in standard form and generates the same set of trajectories. From now on, we only consider timed transition tables in standard form.

Deterministic Timed Transition Tables Let $\mathcal{T}$ be a timed transition table. Given q a control location of $\mathcal{T}$ with $\Gamma(q) = \bigwedge_{x \in \mathcal{X}}(a_x \prec_1^x x \prec_2^x b_x)$, and $X \subseteq \mathcal{X}$, we denote by $\Gamma_X(q)$ the constraint $\bigwedge_{x \in X}(a_x \prec_1^x x \prec_2^x b_x)$. Then, we say that $\mathcal{T}$ is *deterministic* if

- $\forall q, q' \in \mathcal{I}nit$. $\Pi(q) = \Pi(q')$ implies that $\Gamma(q) \wedge \Gamma(q')$ is equivalent to *false*, and moreover, $\forall s \in \Sigma$, the union of the conditions $\Gamma(q)$, for all the control locations $q \in \mathcal{I}nit$ such that $\Pi(q) = s$, is equivalent to *true*,
- $\forall \langle q, X, q' \rangle \in \mathcal{E}$, if $\Pi(q) = \Pi(q')$ then either $\Gamma_{\mathcal{X} \setminus X}(q) \wedge \Gamma_{\mathcal{X} \setminus X}(q')$ is equivalent to *false*, or $\exists x \in X$ such that $\Gamma_{\{x\}}(q)$ is equivalent to $x = c$, for some constant $c \in \mathbb{N}$,
- $\forall \langle q, X_1, q_1 \rangle, \langle q, X_2, q_2 \rangle \in \mathcal{E}$, if $\Pi(q_1) = \Pi(q_2)$ then $\Gamma_{\mathcal{X} \setminus X_1}(q_1) \wedge \Gamma_{\mathcal{X} \setminus X_2}(q_2)$ is equivalent to *false*,
- $\forall q \in \mathcal{Q}$, $\forall X \subseteq \mathcal{X}$, $\forall s \in \Sigma$ such that $s \neq \Pi(q)$, the union of the conditions $\Gamma(q')$, for all the edges $\langle q, X, q' \rangle$ with $\Pi(q') = s$, is equivalent to *true*,
- $\forall q \in \mathcal{Q}$, $\forall X \subseteq \mathcal{X}$, the union of $\Gamma(q)$ with the conditions $\Gamma(q')$, for all the edges $\langle q, X, q' \rangle$ with $\Pi(q') = \Pi(q)$, is equivalent to *true*.

Notice that when $\mathcal{T}$ is deterministic, for every (bounded or unbounded) trajectory τ, there exists a unique path θ of $\mathcal{T}$ such that $\tau = \Pi \circ \theta$.

3.2 Timed Automata on Bounded Trajectories

Definition A bounded trajectories timed automaton over Σ is a pair $\mathcal{A} = (\mathcal{T}, \mathcal{F})$, where $\mathcal{T} = (\mathcal{X}, \mathcal{Q}, \mathcal{I}nit, \mathcal{E}, \Pi, \Gamma)$ is a timed transition table over Σ, and $\mathcal{F} \subseteq \mathcal{Q}$, is a set of *final* control locations. The automaton $\mathcal{A}$ is deterministic if its table $\mathcal{T}$ is deterministic.

Let $\rho = \langle q_0, \nu_0, I_0 \rangle \cdots \langle q_n, \nu_n, I_n \rangle$ be a finite run of $\mathcal{T}$. Then, we say that ρ is an *accepting run* of $\mathcal{A}$ if $q_n \in \mathcal{F}$. We denote by $L(\mathcal{A})$ the set of bounded trajectories generated by accepting runs of $\mathcal{A}$.

Closure Properties Let (D)TA be the class of the sets of trajectories that are definable by (deterministic) bounded trajectories timed automata. It can be shown straightforwardly that TA is closed under union and intersection. The class TA is, however, not closed under complementation (this can be proved as in [3]). On the other hand, it can be easily seen that DTA is closed under all the boolean operators.

3.3 Timed Automata on Unbounded Trajectories

Definition Let $\mathcal{T} = (\mathcal{X}, \mathcal{Q}, \mathcal{I}nit, \mathcal{E}, \Pi, \Gamma)$ be a timed transition table. A Büchi (resp. Muller) acceptance condition is a set $\mathcal{F} \subseteq \mathcal{Q}$ (resp. $\Delta \subseteq 2^{\mathcal{Q}}$).

A timed Büchi (resp. Muller) automaton over Σ, is a pair $\mathcal{A} = (\mathcal{T}, \mathcal{C})$ where $\mathcal{T}$ is a timed transition table over Σ, and $\mathcal{C}$ is a Büchi (resp. Muller) acceptance condition. As in the case of automata on bounded trajectories, an automaton $\mathcal{A}$ is deterministic if its table $\mathcal{T}$ is deterministic.

Let $\rho = \langle q_0, \nu_0, I_0 \rangle \cdots \langle q_i, \nu_i, I_i \rangle \cdots$ be an infinite run of $\mathcal{T}$. We denote by $Inf(\rho)$ the set of contol locations q such that $q = q_i$ for infinitely many i's. Then, let $\mathcal{C}$ be a Büchi (resp. Muller) acceptance condition. We say that ρ is an *accepting run* of the automaton $\mathcal{A} = (\mathcal{T}, \mathcal{C})$ if $Inf(\rho) \cap \mathcal{C} \neq \emptyset$ (resp. $Inf(\rho) \in \mathcal{C}$). We denote by $L(\mathcal{A})$ the set of unbounded trajectories generated by accepting runs of $\mathcal{A}$.

Expressiveness, Closure Properties, and Emptiness Problem We give hereafter some results on unbounded trajectories timed automata that are relevant for this paper. In [3], a theory is developed for a slightly different version of timed automata. However, the results of [3] can be transposed easily to the automata we consider here.

Let (D)TBA (resp. (D)TMA) denotes the class of sets of trajectories definable by (deterministic) timed Büchi automata (resp. (deterministic) timed Muller automata). First, we recall that these classes are related by the inclusion relations:

$$\text{DTBA} \subset \text{DTMA} \subset \text{TBA} = \text{TMA}$$

Moreover, the classes DTBA and TBA (and hence TMA) are closed under intersection and union but not under complementation, whereas the class DTMA is closed under all the boolean operations.

Finally, we recall that the emptiness problem for TBA is decidable [3, 4].

4 Timed Automata Temporal Logic

We introduce in this section the real-time logic TATL which is an extension of the propositional temporal logic PTL [13] with bounded trajectories timed automata.

4.1 The logic TATL

Let $\mathcal{P}$ be a finite set of atomic propositions, and let $\Sigma = 2^{\mathcal{P}}$. We use letters $P, Q, \ldots$ to range over elements of $\mathcal{P}$. Let us introduce a set $\mathcal{W}$ of *position variables*. We use letters $u, v, \ldots$ to range over $\mathcal{W}$. Finally, we use letters $A, B, \ldots$ to range over bounded trajectories automata over Σ. The set of formulas of TATL is defined by:

$$\varphi ::= P \mid \neg\varphi \mid \varphi \vee \varphi \mid u.\varphi \mid A^u \mid \varphi \mathcal{U} \varphi$$

We consider as abbreviations the usual boolean connectives as conjunction ($\wedge$) and implication ($\Rightarrow$), $\Diamond\varphi$ for $true\mathcal{U}\varphi$, and $\Box\varphi$ for $\neg\Diamond\neg\varphi$.

TATL formulas are interpreted on unbounded trajectories. The operators $\mathcal{U}$, $\Diamond$, and $\Box$, are the classical *until*, *eventually*, and *always* operators of PTL. In the formula $u.\varphi$, the current time is associated with the position variable u. Then, subformulas of φ of the form A^u are used to express the fact that the bounded trajectory since the time associated with u is accepted by the automaton A. We call formulas of the form A^u *automata constraints*. For example, let $A_{\leq 5}$ be the deterministic automaton represented by the following picture:

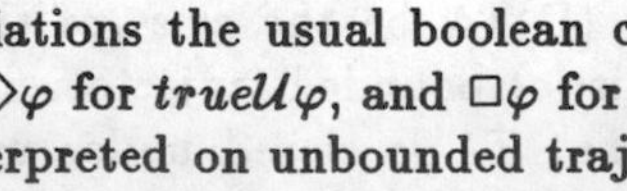

Then, the formula $u.\Diamond(P \wedge A^u_{\leq 5})$ expresses the fact that "*P will be eventually true within* 5 *time units*".

In the formula $u.\varphi$ (e.g., $u.\Diamond(P \wedge A^u_{\leq 5})$), the construction "$u.$", called *position quantification*, binds the position variable u in the subformula φ. We suppose without loss of generality that in every formula, each position variable is bound at most once. Then, every variable appearing in some formula is either *bound* or *free*. We denote by $\mathcal{F}ree(\varphi)$ the set of position variables occurring free in φ. A formula φ is *closed* if all the variables occurring in it are bound (i.e., $\mathcal{F}ree(\varphi) = \emptyset$), otherwise φ is *open*.

The formal semantics of TATL is defined using a satisfaction relation $\models$ between unbounded trajectories, time values, and formulas. Since formulas may be open, the satisfaction relation between a trajectory τ, a time value t, and a formula φ, is defined w.r.t. a *position association* E that associates with each position variable $u \in \mathcal{F}ree(\varphi)$ the time (which is less or equal than t) where u has been introduced. Then, the position association E is updated along the trajectory τ due to the introduction of new position variables. We denote by $E[u \mapsto t]$ the position association whose domain is the extension of the domain of E by u, and which associates with u the time value t and coincides with E on all the other position variables.

Now, let τ be an unbounded trajectory. For every $t \in \mathbb{R}_{\geq 0}$, every position association E (such that for every u in the domain of E, $0 \leq E(u) \leq t$), and every TATL formula φ, we define the meaning of $\langle \tau, t\rangle \models_E \varphi$ inductively on the structure of φ.

$$
\begin{array}{ll}
\langle \tau, t\rangle \models_E P & \text{iff } P \in \tau(t) \\
\langle \tau, t\rangle \models_E \neg\varphi & \text{iff } \langle \tau, t\rangle \not\models_E \varphi \\
\langle \tau, t\rangle \models_E \varphi_1 \vee \varphi_2 & \text{iff } \langle \tau, t\rangle \models_E \varphi_1 \text{ or } \langle \tau, t\rangle \models_E \varphi_2 \\
\langle \tau, t\rangle \models_E u.\varphi & \text{iff } \langle \tau, t\rangle \models_{E[u\mapsto t]} \varphi \\
\langle \tau, t\rangle \models_E A^u & \text{iff } \tau([E(u), t]) \in L(A) \\
\langle \tau, t\rangle \models_E \varphi_1 \mathcal{U} \varphi_2 & \text{iff } \exists t' \geq t.\ \langle \tau, t'\rangle \models_E \varphi_2, \text{ and } \forall t'' \in [t, t').\ \langle \tau, t''\rangle \models_E \varphi_1
\end{array}
$$

When φ is a closed formula, we omit the position association E, and write simply $\langle \tau, t\rangle \models \varphi$. Given a closed formula φ, we denote by $[\![\varphi]\!]$ the set of unbounded trajectories τ such that $\langle \tau, 0\rangle \models \varphi$. The formula φ is *satisfiable* iff $[\![\varphi]\!] \neq \emptyset$; it is *valid* iff $[\![\varphi]\!]$ is the set of all possible unbounded trajectories.

4.2 Dense-Time TPTL

Dense-time TPTL [5] is a real-time temporal logic allowing timing constraints to reason about the time elapsed between two states. For instance, the formula (1) given in the introduction is a typical TPTL formula expressing a bounded response property. In that formula, the variable x represents a clock which is reset when P holds, and which is tested when Q is encountered.

Actually, the logic TPTL can be defined as a fragment of the logic TATL. Indeed, for any natural constant c, let us consider the two deterministic automata $A_{<c}$ and $A_{\leq c}$ represented respectively by the following pictures:

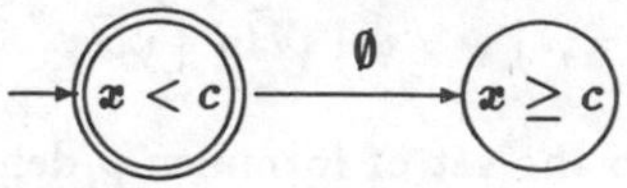

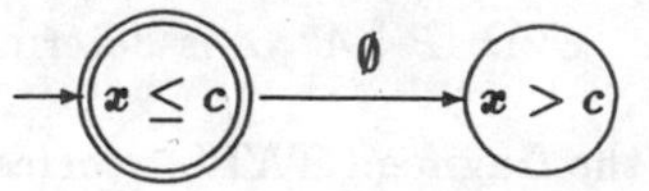

and let $u \prec c$ stand for $A^u_{\prec c}$ with $\prec \in \{<, \leq\}$. Then, the logic TPTL is the fragment of TATL corresponding to the set of formulas given by the following grammar:

$$\varphi ::= P \mid \neg\varphi \mid \varphi \vee \varphi \mid u.\varphi \mid u \prec c \mid \varphi \mathcal{U} \varphi$$

and augmented by all the abbreviations we have considered previously. Moreover, we consider that $\varphi_1 \mathcal{U}_{>0} \varphi_2$ abbreviates $u.\,(\varphi_1 \mathcal{U}\,(u > 0 \wedge \varphi_2))$ where u is a new position variable such that $u \notin \mathcal{F}ree(\varphi_1) \cup \mathcal{F}ree(\varphi_2)$.

4.3 On the semantics of the until operator

The semantics of the operator $\mathcal{U}$ says that a formula $\varphi_1 \mathcal{U} \varphi_2$ is true at some point t of a trajectory τ if and only if there exists some points t' where φ_2 is true, and φ_1 is true at every point in the right-open interval $[t, t')$. Now, let us consider a trajectory τ where, for some point t', $\varphi_1 \wedge \neg\varphi_2$ is true along $[t, t']$ and $\neg\varphi_1 \wedge \varphi_2$ is true along $(t', +\infty)$. Then, it is easy to see that $\varphi_1 \mathcal{U} \varphi_2$ is not true at the point t since, for every point $p > t'$, there exists a point $p' \in (t', p)$ where φ_1 is false. So, given two adjacent intervals where φ_1 and φ_2 are respectively true, the semantics of $\varphi_1 \mathcal{U} \varphi_2$ is in general sensitive to whether the second interval is left-closed or not. An alternative semantics of the until operator can be adopted which is not sensitive to this fact [10]. It corresponds to the definition of the operator $\widetilde{\mathcal{U}}$:

$$\varphi_1 \widetilde{\mathcal{U}} \varphi_2 = (\varphi_1 \vee \varphi_2) \mathcal{U} \varphi_2$$

A nice feature of the operator $\widetilde{\mathcal{U}}$ is that the negation of a formula $\varphi_1 \widetilde{\mathcal{U}} \varphi_2$ can be expressed in a similar way as in PTL using another until operator defined by:

$$\varphi_1 \overline{\mathcal{U}} \varphi_2 = \varphi_1 \mathcal{U} (\varphi_1 \wedge \varphi_2)$$

Indeed, the following equivalences can be proved from TATL semantics.

$$\neg(\varphi_1 \widetilde{\mathcal{U}} \varphi_2) = (\Box\neg\varphi_2) \vee (\neg\varphi_2 \overline{\mathcal{U}} \neg\varphi_1) \quad (2)$$

$$\neg(\varphi_1 \overline{\mathcal{U}} \varphi_2) = (\Box\neg\varphi_2) \vee (\neg\varphi_2 \widetilde{\mathcal{U}} \neg\varphi_1) \quad (3)$$

However, the expression of the negation of an $\mathcal{U}$ formula is more complicated:

$$\neg(\varphi_1 \mathcal{U} \varphi_2) = \neg(\varphi_1 \widetilde{\mathcal{U}} \varphi_2) \vee (\neg\varphi_2 \overline{\mathcal{U}}\, u.(u = 0 \widetilde{\mathcal{U}} (u > 0 \wedge \neg\varphi_1))) \quad (4)$$

Finally, notice that $\Diamond\varphi$ is equivalent to $true\,\widetilde{\mathcal{U}}\varphi$ as well as to $true\,\overline{\mathcal{U}}\varphi$.

4.4 The fragments TATL$^+$, TATL$^-$, and TATL$^\times$

We introduce hereafter the syntactical fragments of the logic TATL we consider for expressiveness and decidability issues in the next sections.

The fragment TATL$^+$ consists of the set of formulas φ defined by:

$$\varphi ::= \psi \mid u.\varphi \mid \varphi \vee \varphi \mid \varphi \wedge \varphi \mid \Box\varphi \mid \varphi \widetilde{\mathcal{U}} \psi \mid \varphi \overline{\mathcal{U}} \psi$$

$$\psi ::= P \mid A^u, A \text{ is deterministic } \mid \neg\psi \mid \psi \vee \psi \mid \psi \widetilde{\mathcal{U}} \psi \mid \psi \overline{\mathcal{U}} \psi$$

whereas the fragment TATL$^-$ corresponds to the set of formulas φ defined by:

$$\varphi ::= \psi \mid u.\varphi \mid \varphi \vee \varphi \mid \varphi \wedge \varphi \mid \psi\widetilde{\mathcal{U}}\varphi \mid \psi\overline{\mathcal{U}}\varphi$$
$$\psi ::= P \mid A^u, A \text{ is deterministic } \mid \neg\psi \mid \psi \vee \psi \mid \psi\widetilde{\mathcal{U}}\psi \mid \psi\overline{\mathcal{U}}\psi$$

and TATL$^\times$ corresponds to the set formulas φ defined by:

$$\varphi ::= \psi \mid u.\varphi \mid \varphi \vee \varphi \mid \varphi \wedge \varphi \mid \psi\mathcal{U}\varphi \mid \psi\widetilde{\mathcal{U}}\varphi$$
$$\psi ::= P \mid \neg P \mid A^u \mid \psi \vee \psi \mid \psi \wedge \psi \mid \Box\psi \mid \psi\widetilde{\mathcal{U}}\psi \mid \psi\overline{\mathcal{U}}\psi \qquad (5)$$

Notice that formulas of the form $\psi\overline{\mathcal{U}}\varphi$ are also in TATL$^\times$ since, by definition, they correspond to formulas of the form $\psi\mathcal{U}(\psi \wedge \varphi)$ that are clearly in TATL$^\times$.

Using (2) and (3) together with standard laws on boolean connectives, duality of $\Box$ and $\Diamond$, the fact that DTA is closed under complementation, and that $\neg u.\varphi$ is equivalent to $u.\neg\varphi$, we can prove by structural induction the following facts:

Proposition 4.1 *For every TATL$^-$ closed formula φ, there exists a TATL$^\times$ closed formula φ' such that $[\![\varphi]\!] = [\![\varphi']\!]$.*

Proposition 4.2 *For every TATL$^+$ closed formula φ, there exists a TATL$^-$ closed formula φ' such that $[\![\neg\varphi]\!] = [\![\varphi']\!]$, and conversely.*

Thus, TATL$^-$ charaterizes exactly the complements of the TATL$^+$ definable sets of trajectories, and conversely. While the negation of every TATL$^+$ formula is equivalent to a TATL$^\times$ formula, it can be seen that the converse, however, does not hold. The main reason is that the negations of $\mathcal{U}$ formulas are not TATL$^+$ definable in general (see (4)).

Finally, we introduce the fragments of TPTL, called TPTL$^+$, TPTL$^-$, and TPTL$^\times$, corresponding respectively to TATL$^+$, TATL$^-$, and TATL$^\times$ formulas where only constraints of the form $u \prec c$ are used. It is clear that Propositions 4.1 and 4.2 still hold when restricted to these fragments of TPTL.

Notice that, for instance, the bounded response formula (1) given in the introduction is in TPTL$^+$.

5 Expressiveness

In this section, we compare the expressive power of TATL$^+$, TATL$^-$, TATL$^\times$, and timed automata. First of all, we prove that TATL$^+$ as well as TATL$^-$ are strictly more expressive than deterministic timed Muller automata. Moreover, we prove that TATL$^+$ is not comparable with TATL$^-$, TATL$^\times$, and nondeterministic timed automata. On the other hand, we prove that TATL$^\times$ formulas can be characterized by nondeterministic timed automata; and this is our main result in this section.

Let us start by showing that DTMA is included in TATL$^+$ and TATL$^-$ (and hence, in TATL$^\times$). Let $\mathcal{A} = (\mathcal{T}, \Delta)$ be a deterministic timed Muller automaton over $\Sigma = 2^{\mathcal{P}}$, with $\Delta = \{\mathcal{F}_1, \cdots, \mathcal{F}_n\}$. For every control location q in $\mathcal{A}$, we denote by A_q the bounded trajectories timed automaton $(\mathcal{T}, \{q\})$, i.e., the automaton which accepts the set of bounded trajectories that reaches the location q. Then, it can easily be seen that the set of trajectories recognized by the automaton $\mathcal{A}$ is characterized by the formula

$$u.\bigvee_{i=1}^{n}((\bigwedge_{q\in\mathcal{F}_i}\Box\Diamond A_q^u)\wedge(\bigwedge_{q\notin\mathcal{F}_i}\neg\Box\Diamond A_q^u)) \qquad (6)$$

which is in both fragments TATL$^+$ and TATL$^-$. So, we have the following result.

Theorem 5.1 *For every deterministic timed Muller automaton $\mathcal{A}$ over Σ, there exists a closed formula φ in TATL$^+$ and TATL$^-$ such that $L(\mathcal{A}) = [\![\varphi]\!]$.*

By observing (6), we can deduce that every DTMA can be charaterized by a boolean combination of formulas of the form $u.\Box\Diamond A^u$, where A is a DTA. Actually, the converse also holds by the facts: (1) it can be shown that formulas of the form $u.\Box\Diamond A^u$, where A is deterministic, correspond exactly to DTBA, (2) every DTBA is a DTMA, and (3) DTMA is closed under all boolean operations.

Now, let us examine the expressiveness of TATL$^+$ and TATL$^-$ in terms of (untimed) ω-sequences of states. A set of sequences $S\subseteq\Sigma^\omega$ is *stuttering-closed* if whenever it contains a sequence $\sigma a\sigma'$, where $\sigma\in\Sigma^*$, $a\in\Sigma$, and $\sigma'\in\Sigma^\omega$, it contains also the sequence $\sigma aa\sigma'$, and vice versa. Then, it can be seen that every stuttering-closed ω-regular (deterministic Muller ω-automata definable) subset of Σ^ω can be charaterized by a DTMA, and hence, by TATL$^+$ and TATL$^-$ formulas.

Theorem 5.2 *For every stuttering-closed ω-regular set $S\subseteq\Sigma^\omega$, there exists a closed formula φ in TATL$^+$ and TATL$^-$ such that $S = \mathcal{D}([\![\varphi]\!])$.*

Actually, we can show that TATL$^+$ is strictly more expressive than DTMA. Inspired by [3], we exhibit a formula in TATL$^+$, actually in TPTL$^+$, that cannot be characterized by nondeterministic timed Muller automata. Let us consider the formula

$$\Phi = \Box(P \Rightarrow u.\Diamond(Q\wedge u = 1)) \qquad (7)$$

Then, an automaton recognizing the set of trajectories satisfying Φ must check that whenever P holds, Q will also hold after exactly 1 time unit. Since in any time interval the number of times the truth of P and Q can change is unbounded, it can be seen that such an automaton should dispose of infinitly many clocks, and hence, we have the following result.

Proposition 5.1 *There exists a TATL$^+$ closed formula Φ such that $[\![\Phi]\!]$ is not definable by (finite) nondeterministic timed Muller automata.*

Now, we show that also TATL$^-$ is strictly more expressive than DTMA. For that, let us consider the negation of the formula Φ of (7). By Proposition 4.2, the formula $\neg\Phi$ is equivalent to a TATL$^-$ formula. Suppose that there exists a deterministic timed Muller automaton which recognizes $[\![\neg\Phi]\!]$. Then, since the class DTMA is closed under complementation, $[\![\Phi]\!]$ should also be definable by some deterministic timed Muller automaton, which contradicts Proposition 5.1. Hence, we obtain the following result.

Proposition 5.2 *There exists a TATL$^-$ closed formula φ (equivalent to $\neg\Phi$) such that $[\![\varphi]\!]$ is not definable by deterministic timed Muller automata.*

We show hereafter our main result stating that TATL$^\times$ closed formulas can be characterized by nondeterministic timed Büchi automata, i.e., for every TATL$^\times$ closed formula φ, we can construct a nondeterministic Büchi automaton $\mathcal{A}_\varphi$ such that $L(\mathcal{A}_\varphi) = [\![\varphi]\!]$. We present here the intuition of this construction and leave the details to the full paper.

The essential reason why such a construction is possible is that TATL$^\times$ formulas allow to consider on trajectories only a finite number of points (positions) where automata constraints can be initialized. Indeed, we can show that each TATL$^\times$ formula can be transformed into an equivalent formula in *canonical form*, i.e., a disjunction of formulas of the form

$$\psi_0 \wedge u_1.\,(\psi_1\,\mathcal{W}_{>0}\,(\psi_1' \wedge \cdots u_n.\,(\psi_n\,\mathcal{W}_{>0}\,(\psi_n' \wedge u_{n+1}.\,\psi_{n+1}))\cdots)) \qquad (8)$$

where $\mathcal{W}$ stands for either $\mathcal{U}$ or $\widetilde{\mathcal{U}}$, and the ψ_i's are of the form given by (5). It is convenient to use in formulas in canonical form the constrained operator $\mathcal{W}_{>0}$ instead of $\mathcal{W}$. Notice that this is not a restriction by the fact that $\phi_1\mathcal{W}\phi_2$ is equivalent to $\phi_2 \vee (\phi_1\,\mathcal{W}_{>0}\,\phi_2)$, where $\mathcal{W}$ is either $\mathcal{U}$ or $\widetilde{\mathcal{U}}$.

Then, given a closed formula φ, the basic idea behind our construction is to consider separately the following problems:

1. checking that a trajectory τ is *propositionally consistent*, which means that, if we abstract from automata constraints and consider φ as a formula of the propositional temporal logic, then the sequences in $\mathcal{D}(\tau)$ satisfy φ,
2. checking that a trajectory is *dense-time semantics consistent*, which means essentially that it is consistent with the dense-time semantics of $\mathcal{U}$,
3. checking that a trajectory is *automata-constraints consistent*, which means that it respects the automata constraints involved in φ.

Let us illustrate on a small example the principle of this construction. Consider the formula in canonical form

$$\phi = u.\,(P_0\,\mathcal{U}_{>0}\,v.\,(P_1\,\widetilde{\mathcal{U}}_{>0}\,B^v))$$

First of all, we associate with each formula of the form $\phi_1\mathcal{U}_{>0}\phi_2$ a new atomic proposition which allows to distinguish the (right-open) interval where ϕ_1 holds and the point where ϕ_2 holds. Let Q be the atomic proposition associated with the $\mathcal{U}_{>0}$ operator of ϕ. Then, we consider the extended formula

$$\phi_{ext} = u.\,((P_0 \wedge Q)\,\mathcal{U}_{>0}\,(\neg Q \wedge v.\,(P_1\,\widetilde{\mathcal{U}}_{>0}\,B^v)))$$

It is easy to see that ϕ and ϕ_{ext} are equivalent modulo projection on the set of the (old) atomic propositions $\mathcal{P}$ (i.e., abstraction from Q).

Next, we reduce the problem (2) above to the problems (1) and (3). For that, we consider an equivalent formula to ϕ_{ext} defined by:

$$\phi_{ext}' = u.\,((P_0 \wedge Q)\,\widetilde{\mathcal{U}}_{>0}\,(A^u \wedge v.\,(P_1\,\widetilde{\mathcal{U}}_{>0}\,B^v)))$$

where A is the deterministic automaton represented by:

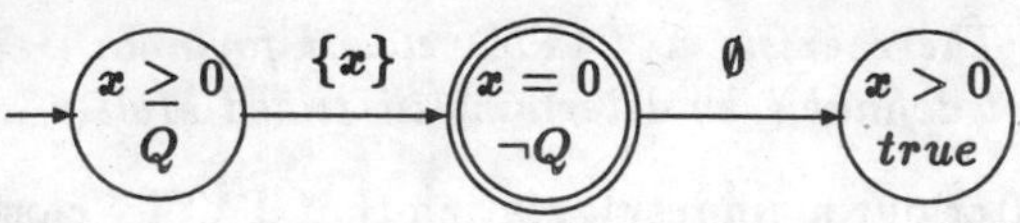

Thus, in the formula ϕ'_{ext} we replace each $\mathcal{U}_{>0}$ operator by the less restrictive one $\widetilde{\mathcal{U}}_{>0}$. However, the introduction of the constraint using the automaton A ensures that all the trajectories satisfying ϕ'_{ext} satisfy also ϕ_{ext}.

To check that a trajectory τ is *propositionally consistent*, we abstract from the actual meaning of the automata constraints and manipulate them as atomic propositions. So, let us associate with the formulas A^u and B^v the new atomic propositions $[A^u]$ and $[B^v]$. We also introduce two other propositions at-ℓ_0 and at-ℓ_1 and consider the formulas $\pi_0 =$ at-$\ell_0 \wedge \neg$at-ℓ_1, and $\pi_1 =$ at-$\ell_1 \wedge \neg$at-ℓ_0. These two formulas allow to mark the point p_v corresponding to the position variable v, that is, the point p_v where the automaton B should be initialized is marked by the end of the truth of π_0 and the beginning of the truth of π_1. Then, let us consider the new set of atomic propositions $\mathcal{P}' = \{[A^u], [B^v], Q, \text{at-}\ell_0, \text{at-}\ell_1\} \cup \mathcal{P}$, and let $\delta_0 = P_0 \wedge Q \wedge \pi_0$ and $\delta_1 = P_1 \wedge \pi_1$. Then, a trajectory is propositionally consistent if it satisfies the formula

$$\phi^* = u.\,(\delta_0\, \widetilde{\mathcal{U}}_{>0}\, ([A^u] \wedge v.\,(\delta_1\, \widetilde{\mathcal{U}}_{>0}\, [B^v])))$$

Now, to guaranty that a trajectory τ satisfies indeed ϕ'_{ext} (and hence, ϕ_{ext}), we must check that it is *automata-constraints consistent*, that is, for every $t \in \mathbb{R}_{\geq 0}$, if $[A^u] \in \tau(t)$ (resp. $[B^v] \in \tau(t)$), then $\tau[0, t] \in L(A)$ (resp. $\tau[p_v, t] \in L(B)$).

Then, the set of trajectories that satisfy ϕ_{ext} can be seen as the intersection of two sets of trajectories: the set of propositionally consistent trajectories and the set of automata-constraints consistent trajectories. Therefore, we construct two timed Büchi automata $\mathcal{B}_{\phi^*}$ and $\mathcal{B}_{\phi}^{const}$ over $\Sigma' = 2^{\mathcal{P}'}$ which recognize respectively these two sets of trajectories.

We present the construction of $\mathcal{B}_{\phi^*}$ as an adaptation of the construction of a Büchi automaton recognizing the set of infinite sequences in $(\Sigma')^\omega$ satisfying some appropriate PTL formula. Indeed, let us consider the PTL formula

$$\phi^*_{prop} = \delta_0\, \mathcal{U}\, (\delta_0 \wedge \bigcirc([A^u] \wedge (\delta_1\, \mathcal{U}\, (\delta_1 \wedge \bigcirc[B^v]))))$$

where $\bigcirc$ is the PTL next operator. This formula is obtained from ϕ^* by a syntactic transformation which consists of replacing recursively each subformula of the form $\phi_1\, \widetilde{\mathcal{U}}_{>0}\, \phi_2$ by the formula $\phi_1\, \mathcal{U}\, (\phi_1 \wedge \bigcirc\phi_2)$. It can be verified that the infinite sequences satisfying ϕ^*_{prop} and the trajectories satisfying ϕ^* are related as follows:

$$\forall \sigma.\, \forall \tau.\, \sigma \in \mathcal{D}(\tau) \text{ implies that } \sigma \in [\![\phi^*_{prop}]\!] \text{ iff } \tau \in [\![\phi^*]\!]$$

Then, following [14], we construct a nondeterministic Büchi automaton $\mathcal{B}_{\phi^*_{prop}}$ which recognizes the set of infinite sequences in $(\Sigma')^\omega$ satisfying (according to PTL semantics) the formula ϕ^*_{prop}. The obtained automaton can be transformed straightforwardly (by adding trivial timing constraints) to a timed automaton $\mathcal{B}_{\phi^*}$ which recognizes the set of trajectories satisfying ϕ^*. The automaton $\mathcal{B}_{\phi^*}$ can be represented by the following picture:

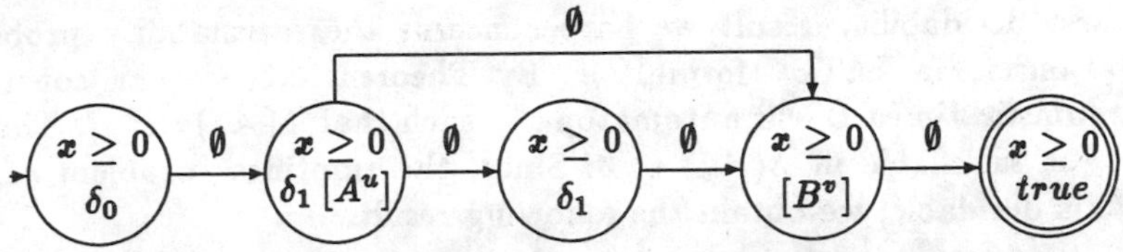

It remains to construct the automaton $\mathcal{B}_\phi^{const}$. This is done according to the following principle: The automaton has two layers; in the first one, it simulates the automaton A, and when it moves to the second one, it starts simulating the automaton B while continuing the simulation of A. The label of every control location of the first layer (resp. second layer) contains at-ℓ_0 but not at-ℓ_1 (resp. at-ℓ_1 but not at-ℓ_0). Moreover, the label of a control location contains the proposition $[A^u]$ (resp. $[B^v]$), if and only if this location corresponds to a final location of the automaton A (resp. B).

Finally, we consider an automaton $\mathcal{A}$ over Σ' contructed as a product of the automata $\mathcal{B}_{\phi^\bullet}$ and $\mathcal{B}_\phi^{const}$ so that it recognizes the set of trajectories $L(\mathcal{B}_{\phi^\bullet}) \cap L(\mathcal{B}_\phi^{const})$. The automaton $\mathcal{A}_\phi$ is obtained as the projection of $\mathcal{A}$ on Σ. The construction of $\mathcal{A}_\phi$ for all the TATL$^\times$ formulas is given in the full paper. Then, we have the following result.

Theorem 5.3 *For every TATL$^\times$ closed formula φ, we can construct a nondeterministic timed Büchi automaton $\mathcal{A}_\varphi$ such that $L(\mathcal{A}_\varphi) = [\![\varphi]\!]$.*

Then, by Proposition 5.1 and Theorem 5.3, we obtain the following fact.

Corollary 5.1 *There exists a TATL$^+$ closed formula Φ such that $[\![\Phi]\!]$ is not definable in TATL$^\times$.*

Now, we show the converse, i.e., TATL$^+$ cannot characterize all TATL$^\times$ formulas (actually, it cannot characterize even all TATL$^-$ formulas). Consider again the TATL$^+$ formula Φ (7). By Proposition 4.2, the formula $\neg\Phi$ is equivalent to a TATL$^-$ formula. Now, suppose that $\neg\Phi$ is definable in TATL$^+$. Then, again by Proposition 4.2, Φ is equivalent to a TATL$^-$ formula, and hence, by Theorem 5.3, that $[\![\Phi]\!]$ is in TMA; this contradicts Proposition 5.1. Thus, the formula $\neg\Phi$ is not definable in TATL$^+$, and we obtain the following result.

Proposition 5.3 *There exists a TATL$^-$ closed formula φ (equivalent to $\neg\Phi$) such that $[\![\varphi]\!]$ is not definable in TATL$^+$.*

Then, by Corollary 5.1 and Proposition 5.3, we obtain that the two fragments TATL$^\times$ and TATL$^-$ are not comparable with TATL$^+$. Moreover, as a consequence of Proposition 5.3, Theorem 5.3, and Proposition 5.1, we can deduce also that TMA and TATL$^+$ are not comparable.

6 Decidability

In this section, we present decidability results that are consequences of Theorem 5.3. Our main result is that the verification problem of timed automata w.r.t. TATL$^+$ formulas is decidable.

The first decidability result we have concerns the satisfiability problem of TATL$^\times$. Consider a TATL$^\times$ formula φ. By Theorem 5.3, we can construct a nondeterministic timed Büchi automaton $\mathcal{A}_\varphi$ such that $L(\mathcal{A}_\varphi) = [\![\varphi]\!]$. Then, the formula φ is satisfiable iff $L(\mathcal{A}_\varphi) \neq \emptyset$. Since, the emptiness problem of timed automata is decidable, we obtain the following result.

Theorem 6.1 *The satisfiability problem of TATL$^\times$ is decidable.*

Now, if we consider a TATL$^+$ formula φ, then, by Proposition 4.2, its negation $\neg\varphi$ can be transformed into an equivalent formula $\overline{\varphi}$ in TATL$^-$, and hence in TATL$^\times$ (by Proposition 4.1). Clearly, the formula φ is valid iff the formula $\overline{\varphi}$ is not satisfiable. Then, as a consequence of Theorem 6.1, we deduce that:

Corollary 6.1 *The validity problem of TATL$^+$ is decidable.*

Finally, let us consider the verification problem of timed automata w.r.t. TATL$^+$ formulas. The verification problem consists of, given a timed system modelled as a timed automaton $\mathcal{A}_{syst}$, and a property expressed as formula φ, checking whether all the behaviours (trajectories) of the system satisfy the property, i.e., that $L(\mathcal{A}_{syst}) \subseteq [\![\varphi]\!]$.

Given a TATL$^+$ formula φ, let $\mathcal{A}_{\overline{\varphi}}$ be the timed automaton which recognizes the set of trajectories satisfying a TATL$^\times$ formula $\overline{\varphi}$ which is equivalent to $\neg\varphi$. Then, verifying that $\mathcal{A}_{syst}$ satisfies φ reduces to checking whether $L(\mathcal{A}_{syst}) \cap L(\mathcal{A}_{\overline{\varphi}}) = \emptyset$. Since timed automata are closed under intersection, and their emptiness problem is decidable, we obtain the following decidability result:

Theorem 6.2 *The verification problem of timed automata w.r.t. TATL$^+$ formulas is decidable.*

7 Conclusion

We have investigated the verification problem of timed automata w.r.t. a linear-time dense time temporal logic. The logic we consider, TATL, is an extension of TPTL with timed automata constraints. In this logic, we can define positions on trajectories using the position quantification "$u.$", and use constraints saying that the trajectory segment since some position is accepted by a given timed automaton.

We have identified an expressively powerful fragment of the logic TATL, namely the fragment TATL$^+$, for which the verification problem is decidable. Consequently, we obtain a fragment of TPTL, i.e., the fragment TPTL$^+$, for which the verification problem is decidable.

The existing results in the literature concerning the verification problem of linear-time dense time temporal logics concern the logic MITL [4] and its extension EMITL [15]. Our decidability result concerns a class of timed properties which is not comparable with the properties definable in these logics. Indeed, in both MITL and EMITL, decidability is achieved by forbidding punctual timing constraints, whereas TATL$^+$ allows these kind of constraints (see for instance the formula (7) in Section 5). Moreover, each timing constraint in these logics is related to one temporal operator (which is $\mathcal{U}$ in MITL, or defined by some finite-state automaton on finite sequences in EMITL), whereas the constraints in TATL$^+$ are related to position variables, refering to particular points on a trajectory, following the more general style of TPTL. For instance, general position quantification is essential to the characterization of deterministic timed Muller automata in TATL$^+$ (see (6) in Section 5). Finally, notice that we use in TATL timed automata to express constraints on finite trajectories, whereas in EMITL untimed automata on finite sequences are used as logical operators.

Acknowledgment We thank S. Yovine for his valuable comments.

References

1. R. Alur. *Techniques of Automatic Verification of Real-Time Systems.* PhD thesis, Stanford Univ., 1991.
2. R. Alur, C. Courcoubetis, and D. Dill. Model-Checking for Real-Time Systems. In *LICS'90.* IEEE, 1990.
3. R. Alur and D. Dill. A Theory of Timed Automata. *TCS*, 126, 1994.
4. R. Alur, T. Feder, and T. Henzinger. The Benefits of Relaxing Punctuality. In *PODC'91*, 1991.
5. R. Alur and T. Henzinger. A Really Temporal Logic. In *FOCS'89.* IEEE, 1989.
6. E.M. Clarke, E.A. Emerson, and P. Sistla. Automatic Verification of Finite State Concurrent Systems using Temporal Logic Specifications: A Practical Approach. In *POPL'83.* ACM, 1983.
7. E.A. Emerson, A. Mok, A.P. Sistla, and J. Srinivasan. Quantitative Temporal Reasoning. In *1st Workshop on Computer Aided Verification.* 1989.
8. E. Harel, O. Lichtenstein, and A. Pnueli. Explicit-Clock Temporal Logic. In *LICS'90.* IEEE, 1990.
9. T. Henzinger. *Temporal Specification and Verification of Real-Time Systems.* PhD thesis, Stanford University, 1991.
10. T.A. Henzinger, X. Nicollin, J. Sifakis, and S. Yovine. Symbolic Model-Checking for Real-Time Systems. In *LICS'92.* IEEE, 1992.
11. R. Koymans. Specifying Real-Time Properties with Metric Temporal Logic. *Journal of Real-Time Systems*, 2, 1990.
12. J.S. Ostroff. *Temporal Logic for Real-Time Systems.* Research Stud. Press, 1989.
13. A. Pnueli. The Temporal Logic of Programs. In *FOCS'77.* IEEE, 1977.
14. M.Y. Vardi and P. Wolper. An Automata-Theoretic Approach to Automatic Program Verification. In *LICS'86.* IEEE, 1986.
15. Th. Wilke. Specifying Timed State Sequences in Powerful Decidable Logics and Timed Automata. In *FTRTFT'94.* LNCS 863, 1994.

Authors Index

Lecture Notes in Computer Science

For information about Vols. 1–886

please contact your bookseller or Springer-Verlag

Vol. 887: M. Toussaint (Ed.), Ada in Europe. Proceedings, 1994. XII, 521 pages. 1994.

Vol. 888: S. A. Andersson (Ed.), Analysis of Dynamical and Cognitive Systems. Proceedings, 1993. VII, 260 pages. 1995.

Vol. 889: H. P. Lubich, Towards a CSCW Framework for Scientific Cooperation in Europe. X, 268 pages. 1995.

Vol. 890: M. J. Wooldridge, N. R. Jennings (Eds.), Intelligent Agents. Proceedings, 1994. VIII, 407 pages. 1995. (Subseries LNAI).

Vol. 891: C. Lewerentz, T. Lindner (Eds.), Formal Development of Reactive Systems. XI, 394 pages. 1995.

Vol. 892: K. Pingali, U. Banerjee, D. Gelernter, A. Nicolau, D. Padua (Eds.), Languages and Compilers for Parallel Computing. Proceedings, 1994. XI, 496 pages. 1995.

Vol. 893: G. Gottlob, M. Y. Vardi (Eds.), Database Theory – ICDT '95. Proceedings, 1995. XI, 454 pages. 1995.

Vol. 894: R. Tamassia, I. G. Tollis (Eds.), Graph Drawing. Proceedings, 1994. X, 471 pages. 1995.

Vol. 895: R. L. Ibrahim (Ed.), Software Engineering Education. Proceedings, 1995. XII, 449 pages. 1995.

Vol. 896: R. N. Taylor, J. Coutaz (Eds.), Software Engineering and Human-Computer Interaction. Proceedings, 1994. X, 281 pages. 1995.

Vol. 897: M. Fisher, R. Owens (Eds.), Executable Modal and Temporal Logics. Proceedings, 1993. VII, 180 pages. 1995. (Subseries LNAI).

Vol. 898: P. Steffens (Ed.), Machine Translation and the Lexicon. Proceedings, 1993. X, 251 pages. 1995. (Subseries LNAI).

Vol. 899: W. Banzhaf, F. H. Eeckman (Eds.), Evolution and Biocomputation. VII, 277 pages. 1995.

Vol. 900: E. W. Mayr, C. Puech (Eds.), STACS 95. Proceedings, 1995. XIII, 654 pages. 1995.

Vol. 901: R. Kumar, T. Kropf (Eds.), Theorem Provers in Circuit Design. Proceedings, 1994. VIII, 303 pages. 1995.

Vol. 902: M. Dezani-Ciancaglini, G. Plotkin (Eds.), Typed Lambda Calculi and Applications. Proceedings, 1995. VIII, 443 pages. 1995.

Vol. 903: E. W. Mayr, G. Schmidt, G. Tinhofer (Eds.), Graph-Theoretic Concepts in Computer Science. Proceedings, 1994. IX, 414 pages. 1995.

Vol. 904: P. Vitányi (Ed.), Computational Learning Theory. EuroCOLT'95. Proceedings, 1995. XVII, 415 pages. 1995. (Subseries LNAI).

Vol. 905: N. Ayache (Ed.), Computer Vision, Virtual Reality and Robotics in Medicine. Proceedings, 1995. XIV,

Vol. 906: E. Astesiano, G. Reggio, A. Tarlecki (Eds.), Recent Trends in Data Type Specification. Proceedings, 1995. VIII, 523 pages. 1995.

Vol. 907: T. Ito, A. Yonezawa (Eds.), Theory and Practice of Parallel Programming. Proceedings, 1995. VIII, 485 pages. 1995.

Vol. 908: J. R. Rao Extensions of the UNITY Methodology: Compositionality, Fairness and Probability in Parallelism. XI, 178 pages. 1995.

Vol. 909: H. Comon, J.-P. Jouannaud (Eds.), Term Rewriting. Proceedings, 1993. VIII, 221 pages. 1995.

Vol. 910: A. Podelski (Ed.), Constraint Programming: Basics and Trends. Proceedings, 1995. XI, 315 pages. 1995.

Vol. 911: R. Baeza-Yates, E. Goles, P. V. Poblete (Eds.), LATIN '95: Theoretical Informatics. Proceedings, 1995. IX, 525 pages. 1995.

Vol. 912: N. Lavrac, S. Wrobel (Eds.), Machine Learning: ECML – 95. Proceedings, 1995. XI, 370 pages. 1995. (Subseries LNAI).

Vol. 913: W. Schäfer (Ed.), Software Process Technology. Proceedings, 1995. IX, 261 pages. 1995.

Vol. 914: J. Hsiang (Ed.), Rewriting Techniques and Applications. Proceedings, 1995. XII, 473 pages. 1995.

Vol. 915: P. D. Mosses, M. Nielsen, M. I. Schwartzbach (Eds.), TAPSOFT '95: Theory and Practice of Software Development. Proceedings, 1995. XV, 810 pages. 1995.

Vol. 916: N. R. Adam, B. K. Bhargava, Y. Yesha (Eds.), Digital Libraries. Proceedings, 1994. XIII, 321 pages. 1995.

Vol. 917: J. Pieprzyk, R. Safavi-Naini (Eds.), Advances in Cryptology - ASIACRYPT '94. Proceedings, 1994. XII, 431 pages. 1995.

Vol. 918: P. Baumgartner, R. Hähnle, J. Posegga (Eds.), Theorem Proving with Analytic Tableaux and Related Methods. Proceedings, 1995. X, 352 pages. 1995. (Subseries LNAI).

Vol. 919: B. Hertzberger, G. Serazzi (Eds.), High-Performance Computing and Networking. Proceedings, 1995. XXIV, 957 pages. 1995.

Vol. 920: E. Balas, J. Clausen (Eds.), Integer Programming and Combinatorial Optimization. Proceedings, 1995. IX, 436 pages. 1995.

Vol. 921: L. C. Guillou, J.-J. Quisquater (Eds.), Advances in Cryptology – EUROCRYPT '95. Proceedings, 1995. XIV, 417 pages. 1995.

Vol. 922: H. Dörr, Efficient Graph Rewriting and Its Implementation. IX, 266 pages. 1995.

Vol. 923: M. Meyer (Ed.), Constraint Processing. IV, 289 pages. 1995.

Vol. 924: P. Ciancarini, O. Nierstrasz, A. Yonezawa (Eds.), Object-Based Models and Languages for Concurrent Systems. Proceedings, 1994. VII, 193 pages. 1995.

Vol. 925: J. Jeuring, E. Meijer (Eds.), Advanced Functional Programming. Proceedings, 1995. VII, 331 pages. 1995.

Vol. 926: P. Nesi (Ed.), Objective Software Quality. Proceedings, 1995. VIII, 249 pages. 1995.

Vol. 927: J. Dix, L. Moniz Pereira, T. C. Przymusinski (Eds.), Non-Monotonic Extensions of Logic Programming. Proceedings, 1994. IX, 229 pages. 1995. (Subseries LNAI).

Vol. 928: V.W. Marek, A. Nerode, M. Truszczynski (Eds.), Logic Programming and Nonmonotonic Reasoning. Proceedings, 1995. VIII, 417 pages. 1995. (Subseries LNAI).

Vol. 929: F. Morán, A. Moreno, J.J. Merelo, P. Chacón (Eds.), Advances in Artificial Life. Proceedings, 1995. XIII, 960 pages. 1995 (Subseries LNAI).

Vol. 930: J. Mira, F. Sandoval (Eds.), From Natural to Artificial Neural Computation. Proceedings, 1995. XVIII, 1150 pages. 1995.

Vol. 931: P.J. Braspenning, F. Thuijsman, A.J.M.M. Weijters (Eds.), Artificial Neural Networks. IX, 295 pages. 1995.

Vol. 932: J. Iivari, K. Lyytinen, M. Rossi (Eds.), Advanced Information Systems Engineering. Proceedings, 1995. XI, 388 pages. 1995.

Vol. 933: L. Pacholski, J. Tiuryn (Eds.), Computer Science Logic. Proceedings, 1994. IX, 543 pages. 1995.

Vol. 934: P. Barahona, M. Stefanelli, J. Wyatt (Eds.), Artificial Intelligence in Medicine. Proceedings, 1995. XI, 449 pages. 1995. (Subseries LNAI).

Vol. 935: G. De Michelis, M. Diaz (Eds.), Application and Theory of Petri Nets 1995. Proceedings, 1995. VIII, 511 pages. 1995.

Vol. 936: V.S. Alagar, M. Nivat (Eds.), Algebraic Methodology and Software Technology. Proceedings, 1995. XIV, 591 pages. 1995.

Vol. 937: Z. Galil, E. Ukkonen (Eds.), Combinatorial Pattern Matching. Proceedings, 1995. VIII, 409 pages. 1995.

Vol. 938: K.P. Birman, F. Mattern, A. Schiper (Eds.), Theory and Practice in Distributed Systems. Proceedings,1994. X, 263 pages. 1995.

Vol. 939: P. Wolper (Ed.), Computer Aided Verification. Proceedings, 1995. X, 451 pages. 1995.

Vol. 940: C. Goble, J. Keane (Eds.), Advances in Databases. Proceedings, 1995. X, 277 pages. 1995.

Vol. 941: M. Cadoli, Tractable Reasoning in Artificial Intelligence. XVII, 247 pages. 1995. (Subseries LNAI).

Vol. 942: G. Böckle, Exploitation of Fine-Grain Parallelism. IX, 188 pages. 1995.

Vol. 943: W. Klas, M. Schrefl, Metaclasses and Their Application. IX, 201 pages. 1995.

Vol. 944: Z. Fülöp, F. Gécseg (Eds.), Automata, Languages and Programming. Proceedings, 1995. XIII, 686 pages. 1995.

Vol. 945: B. Bouchon-Meunier, R.R. Yager, L.A. Zadeh (Eds.), Advances in Intelligent Computing - IPMU '94. Proceedings, 1994. XII, 628 pages.1995.

Vol. 946: C. Froidevaux, J. Kohlas (Eds.), Symbolic and Quantitative Approaches to Reasoning and Uncertainty. Proceedings, 1995. X, 420 pages. 1995. (Subseries LNAI).

Vol. 947: B. Möller (Ed.), Mathematics of Program Construction. Proceedings, 1995. VIII, 472 pages. 1995.

Vol. 948: G. Cohen, M. Giusti, T. Mora (Eds.), Applied Algebra, Algebraic Algorithms and Error-Correcting Codes. Proceedings, 1995. XI, 485 pages. 1995.

Vol. 949: D.G. Feitelson, L. Rudolph (Eds.), Job Scheduling Strategies for Parallel Processing. Proceedings, 1995. VIII, 361 pages. 1995.

Vol. 950: A. De Santis (Ed.), Advances in Cryptology - EUROCRYPT '94. Proceedings, 1994. XIII, 473 pages. 1995.

Vol. 951: M.J. Egenhofer, J.R. Herring (Eds.), Advances in Spatial Databases. Proceedings, 1995. XI, 405 pages. 1995.

Vol. 952: W. Olthoff (Ed.), ECOOP '95 - Object-Oriented Programming. Proceedings, 1995. XI, 471 pages. 1995.

Vol. 953: D. Pitt, D.E. Rydeheard, P. Johnstone (Eds.), Category Theory and Computer Science. Proceedings, 1995. VII, 252 pages. 1995.

Vol. 954: G. Ellis, R. Levinson, W. Rich. J.F. Sowa (Eds.), Conceptual Structures: Applications, Implementation and Theory. Proceedings, 1995. IX, 353 pages. 1995. (Subseries LNAI).

VOL. 955: S.G. Akl, F. Dehne, J.-R. Sack, N. Santoro (Eds.), Algorithms and Data Structures. Proceedings, 1995. IX, 519 pages. 1995.

Vol. 956: X. Yao (Ed.), Progress in Evolutionary Computation. Proceedings, 1993, 1994. VIII, 314 pages. 1995. (Subseries LNAI).

Vol. 957: C. Castelfranchi, J.-P. Müller (Eds.), From Reaction to Cognition. Proceedings, 1993. VI, 252 pages. 1995. (Subseries LNAI).

Vol. 958: J. Calmet, J.A. Campbell (Eds.), Integrating Symbolic Mathematical Computation and Artificial Intelligence. Proceedings, 1994. X, 275 pages. 1995.

Vol. 959: D.-Z. Du, M. Li (Eds.), Computing and Combinatorics. Proceedings, 1995. XIII, 654 pages. 1995.

Vol. 960: D. Leivant (Ed.), Logic and Computational Complexity. Proceedings, 1994. VIII, 514 pages. 1995.

Vol. 961: K.P. Jantke, S. Lange (Eds.), Algorithmic Learning for Knowledge-Based Systems. X, 511 pages. 1995. (Subseries LNAI).

Vol. 962: I. Lee, S.A. Smolka (Eds.), CONCUR '95: Concurrency Theory. Proceedings, 1995. X, 547 pages. 1995.

Vol. 963: D. Coppersmith (Ed.), Advances in Cryptology —CRYPTO '95. Proceedings, 1995. XII, 467 pages. 1995.